PROPERTY

Aspen Treatise Series

PROPERTY

Seventh Edition

Joseph William Singer

Bussey Professor of Law
Harvard Law School

Nestor M. Davidson

Emma Bloomberg Professor of Real Estate
Harvard Graduate School of Design

ASPEN PUBLISHING

Cover image: Map provided courtesy of the Map Library at the University of Illinois at Urbana-Champaign.

To contact Customer Service, e-mail customer.service@aspenpublishing.com, call 1-800-950-5259, or mail correspondence to:

Aspen Publishing
Attn: Order Department
1 Wall Street
Burlington, MA 01803

1 2 3 4 5 6 7 8 9 0

ISBN 979-8-8941-0451-5

Library of Congress Cataloging-in-Publication Data

Names: Singer, Joseph William, 1954- author | Davidson, Nestor M. author
Title: Property / Joseph William Singer, Nestor M. Davidson.
Description: Seventh edition. | Burlington : Aspen Publishing, 2026. |
Includes index. | Summary: "Treatise on the subject of property law for law school students enrolled in property courses"— Provided by publisher.
Identifiers: LCCN 2025049793 (print) | LCCN 2025049794 (ebook) |
ISBN 9798894104515 Paperback | ISBN 9798894104539 epub
Classification: LCC KF560 .S55 2026 (print) | LCC KF560 (ebook) |
DDC 346.7304—dc23
LC record available at https://lccn.loc.gov/2025049793
LC ebook record available at https://lccn.loc.gov/2025049794

ABOUT ASPEN PUBLISHING

Aspen Publishing is a leading provider of legal education content and digital learning solutions in the United States and globally. Our innovative products and platforms—designed based on best practices in learning science—engage students and enhance outcomes. From textbooks and audiobooks authored by renowned experts to digital platforms and products like LEAF, Connected eBooks, Connected Quizzing, PracticePerfect, and JD-Next, we empower the next generation of legal professionals with innovative, trusted, and accessible resources.

The Aspen Casebook Series, affectionately known as the "red and black" casebooks among law faculty and students, includes hundreds of highly regarded textbooks across more than 80 disciplines. These range from foundational courses like Torts and Contracts to emerging electives such as Sustainability and the Law of Policing. Our study aids, including the popular *Examples & Explanations* series, help law students master complex topics with clarity and confidence.

Aspen's expertise extends to undergraduate education with our Paralegal, Criminal Justice, and Business Law series, offering the same hallmark quality to a broader audience. JD-Next, our groundbreaking online law school prep course and admissions test, provides a realistic preview of law school, equips students with essential skills for academic success, and evaluates their readiness for legal studies.

Aspen Publishing Is Proud to Be a UWorld Company

Since 2003, UWorld has been a global leader in developing high-quality learning tools for students preparing for high-stakes exams. With a commitment to excellence, UWorld has helped millions of students in undergraduate, graduate, and professional programs in fields such as medicine, nursing, finance, and law achieve their academic and career goals.

Founded by Chandra S. Pemmasani, M.D., during his medical residency, UWorld began focusing on medical education and has since expanded into various academic fields, including law. In 2020, UWorld launched its Legal vertical, starting with its comprehensive Multistate Bar Exam (MBE®) Question Bank, followed by the acquisition of Themis Bar Review, which integrated resources to provide a complete bar exam preparation experience. In 2024, UWorld expanded its offerings by acquiring Aspen Publishing, enhancing its suite of legal education products.

Today, UWorld offers an unparalleled range of study materials that blend active learning methods with expert content, ensuring students and educators can access the most effective resources. From bar preparation to law school success, UWorld is committed to supporting the next generation of legal professionals. Learn more at uworld.com.

For Justice Morris Pashman
Supreme Court of New Jersey
ז"ל
He will always be
the model of the good judge.

SUMMARY OF CONTENTS

Contents			*xi*
Preface			*xxiii*
	Chapter 1	Introduction	1
Part I	**The Right to Exclude and the Right of Access**		**21**
	Chapter 2	Trespass and Public Accommodations Law	23
Part II	**Relationships Among Neighbors**		**93**
	Chapter 3	Nuisance	95
	Chapter 4	Adverse Possession	139
	Chapter 5	Licenses and Easements	177
	Chapter 6	Covenants	225
Part III	**Common Ownership**		**299**
	Chapter 7	Present Estates and Future Interests	301
	Chapter 8	Concurrent Ownership	347
	Chapter 9	Family Property	391
Part IV	**Regulation of the Market for Real Estate**		**425**
	Chapter 10	Leaseholds	427
	Chapter 11	Real Estate Transactions	493
	Chapter 12	Fair Housing Law	575
Part V	**Public Land Use Planning**		**637**
	Chapter 13	Land Use Regulation	639
	Chapter 14	Eminent Domain and Regulatory Takings	679
Part VI	**Tribal Property**		**767**
	Chapter 15	American Indian Property	769
Part VII	**Personal and Intellectual Property**		**809**
	Chapter 16	Personal Property	811
	Chapter 17	Intellectual Property	835
Table of Cases			*859*
Table of Statutes and Regulations			*901*
Table of Restatements			*921*
Index			*923*

CONTENTS

Preface *xxiii*

Chapter 1 Introduction **1**

§1.1 What Is Property? 2
§1.1.1 Relations Among People Regarding Valued Resources 2
§1.1.2 Ownership v. Bundles of Rights 2
§1.1.3 Individual Entitlement v. Property as a System 3
§1.1.4 Regulation v. Construction of a Property System 4
§1.1.5 Legal Relations 5

§1.2 Core Tensions Within Property Law 6
§1.2.1 Right to Exclude v. Right of Access 6
§1.2.2 Privilege to Use v. Security from Harm 7
§1.2.3 Power to Transfer v. Limits on Disaggregation 7
§1.2.4 Immunity from Loss v. Power to Acquire 8

§1.3 Recurring Themes 8
§1.3.1 Rule Choices, Hard Cases, and Competing Arguments 8
§1.3.2 Social Context 10
§1.3.3 Formal v. Informal Sources of Rights 10
§1.3.4 The Alienability Dilemma 10
§1.3.5 Contractual Freedom and Minimum Standards 11
§1.3.6 Systemic Norms 12

§1.4 Theories of Property 13
§1.4.1 Normative Approaches 13
§1.4.1.1 Justice, Liberty, and Rights 13
§1.4.1.2 Consequentialism, Utilitarianism, and Efficiency 14
§1.4.1.3 Social Relations, Virtue, and Democracy 15
§1.4.1.4 Libertarian, Conservative, and Progressive Views 17
§1.4.2 Justificatory Norms 17
§1.4.2.1 Possession 17
§1.4.2.2 Labor (Desert) 18
§1.4.2.3 Personality and Human Flourishing 19
§1.4.2.4 Efficiency 19
§1.4.2.5 Justified Expectations 20
§1.4.2.6 Distributive Justice 20

PART I THE RIGHT TO EXCLUDE AND THE RIGHT OF ACCESS 21

Chapter 2 Trespass and Public Accommodations Law 23

§2.1 Introduction 24

§2.2 Excluding or Admitting People 27
§2.2.1 Private Property (Closed to the Public) 27
§2.2.2 Shared Use or Possession 29
§2.2.3 Public Accommodations (Open to the Public) 30

§2.3 Common Law Limits on the Right to Exclude 34
§2.3.1 Consent 34
§2.3.2 Estoppel 38
§2.3.3 Necessity 38
§2.3.4 Public Policy or Social Need 40
§2.3.5 Prescription 41

§2.4 Objects 41
§2.4.1 Encroaching Structures 41
§2.4.2 Vegetation and Trees 42
§2.4.3 Aviation 43
§2.4.4 Pollution 44

§2.5 Animals 46

§2.6 Public Accommodations Laws 46
§2.6.1 Title II of the *Civil Rights Act of 1964* 46
§2.6.2 *Civil Rights Act of 1866* 54
§2.6.3 *Americans with Disabilities Act of 1990* 62
§2.6.4 State Laws 71

§2.7 Free Speech Rights of Access to Private Property 75
§2.7.1 United States Constitution 75
§2.7.2 State Constitutions 80
§2.7.3 Labor Laws 84

§2.8 Public Trust Doctrine 85

§2.9 Trespass to Chattels 91

PART II RELATIONSHIPS AMONG NEIGHBORS 93

Chapter 3 Nuisance 95

§3.1 Introduction 96

§3.2 Private Nuisance 102
§3.2.1 Test 102
§3.2.2 Remedies 108
§3.2.3 Types of Nuisances 116

	§3.3	Public Nuisance	121
	§3.4	Water Rights	126
		§3.4.1 Diffuse Surface Water (Flooding)	126
		§3.4.2 Streams and Lakes	130
		§3.4.3 Groundwater	131
	§3.5	Support Rights	133
		§3.5.1 Lateral Support	133
		§3.5.2 Subjacent Support	135
	§3.6	Light and Air	136
Chapter 4	**Adverse Possession**		**139**
	§4.1	Introduction	140
	§4.2	Elements	143
		§4.2.1 Actual Possession	143
		§4.2.2 Open and Notorious	146
		§4.2.3 Exclusive	147
		§4.2.4 Continuous	148
		§4.2.5 Adverse or Hostile	149
		§4.2.6 For the Statutory Period	155
		§4.2.7 Under Color of Title	156
	§4.3	Justifications for Adverse Possession	156
	§4.4	Typical Cases	162
		§4.4.1 Color of Title	162
		§4.4.2 Border Disputes	163
		§4.4.3 Squatters	164
		§4.4.4 Co-tenants	165
	§4.5	Procedures and Effects of Adverse Possession	166
		§4.5.1 Level of Proof Required	166
		§4.5.2 Effect on Prior Encumbrances	166
	§4.6	Claims Against the Government	168
	§4.7	Informal Transfers of Title to Settle Boundary Disputes	169
		§4.7.1 Improving Trespasser	169
		§4.7.2 Dedication	170
		§4.7.3 Oral Agreement	170
		§4.7.4 Acquiescence	171
		§4.7.5 Estoppel	171
		§4.7.6 Riparian Owners	172
	§4.8	Adverse Possession of Personal Property	172
Chapter 5	**Licenses and Easements**		**177**
	§5.1	Introduction	178
	§5.2	Licenses	182

§5.3 Express Easements 184
§5.3.1 Formal Requirements to Create 184
§5.3.2 Substantive Limitations 185
§5.3.3 Running with the Land (Appurtenant v. In Gross) 187
§5.3.4 Scope, Location, and Extension of Appurtenant Easements 191
§5.3.5 Scope and Apportionment of Easements in Gross 197

§5.4 Implied Easements 199
§5.4.1 Easement by Estoppel 200
§5.4.2 Constructive Trust 204
§5.4.3 Implied from Prior Use 207
§5.4.4 Necessity 210

§5.5 Prescriptive Easements 213

§5.6 Terminating Easements 223

Chapter 6 Covenants 225

§6.1 Introduction 226

§6.2 Formal Requirements 234
§6.2.1 Writing 236
§6.2.2 Notice 239
§6.2.3 Intent to Run 242
§6.2.4 Privity of Estate 244

§6.3 Substantive Requirements 253
§6.3.1 Touch and Concern 253
§6.3.2 Enforcement in Gross 258

§6.4 Implied Reciprocal Negative Servitudes 261

§6.5 Remedies 266

§6.6 Interpretation of Ambiguous Covenants 270

§6.7 Public Policy Limitations 277
§6.7.1 Racial Restrictions 277
§6.7.2 Unreasonable Restraints on Alienation 280
§6.7.3 Unreasonable Restraints on Competition 285
§6.7.4 Public Policy 286
§6.7.5 Choice of Law 291

§6.8 Modifying or Terminating Covenants 291
§6.8.1 Changed Conditions 291
§6.8.2 Relative Hardship 294
§6.8.3 Conduct of the Parties 296
§6.8.4 Statutory Regulation 297

PART III COMMON OWNERSHIP 299

Chapter 7 Present Estates and Future Interests 301

§7.1 Introduction 302

§7.2 Fee Simple 305

§7.3 Defeasible Fees 306
§7.3.1 Fee Simple Determinable/Possibility of Reverter 307
§7.3.2 Fee Simple Subject to Condition Subsequent/Right of Entry 307
§7.3.3 Fee Simple Subject to Executory Limitation/Executory Interest 309

§7.4 Life Estates 310
§7.4.1 Remainders and Reversions 310
§7.4.2 Contingent and Vested Remainders 311
§7.4.3 Destructibility of Contingent Remainders 312
§7.4.4 Doctrine of Worthier Title 313
§7.4.5 Rule in *Shelley's Case* 314

§7.5 Trusts 314

§7.6 Interpretation of Ambiguous Conveyances 315
§7.6.1 Presumption Against Forfeitures 315
§7.6.2 Waste 320
§7.6.3 *Cy Pres* 321
§7.6.4 Changed Conditions 323

§7.7 Regulatory Rules 324
§7.7.1 Abolition of Fee Tail 325
§7.7.2 Restrictions on New Estates (*Numerus Clausus* Principle) 327
§7.7.3 Unreasonable Restraints on Alienation 328
§7.7.4 Rule Against Perpetuities 330
§7.7.5 Racial Restrictions 341
§7.7.6 Restraints on Marriage 342
§7.7.7 Public Policy 345
§7.7.8 Judicial Sale of Property Subject to Future Interests 346

Chapter 8 Concurrent Ownership 347

§8.1 Introduction 348

§8.2 Ownership in Common 349
§8.2.1 Tenancy in Common 349
§8.2.2 Joint Tenancy 350
§8.2.3 Tenancy by the Entirety 358

§8.3 Interpretation of Ambiguities 360

§8.4 Rights and Obligations of Co-tenants 360
§8.4.1 Partition 360
§8.4.2 Joint Management 363
§8.4.3 Contribution for Repairs and Maintenance 363
§8.4.4 Rental Benefits and Obligations 365
§8.4.5 Leasing 369
§8.4.6 Adverse Possession 370

§8.5 Common Interest Communities 370
§8.5.1 Condominiums and Homeowners' Associations 370
§8.5.2 Cooperatives 380
§8.5.3 Affordable Housing Arrangements 381
§8.5.4 Continuing Care Retirement Communities 382

§8.6 Business Property 382
§8.6.1 Partnerships 383
§8.6.2 Corporations 385
§8.6.3 Franchises 387

§8.7 Nonprofit Organizations 388

§8.8 Governmental Ownership 389

Chapter 9 Family Property 391

§9.1 Introduction 392

§9.2 Historical Background 394
§9.2.1 Dower and Curtesy 394
§9.2.2 *Married Women's Property Acts* 395

§9.3 Marital Property 397
§9.3.1 Separate Property 397
§9.3.2 Community Property 401
§9.3.3 Tenancy by the Entirety 407

§9.4 Same-Sex Marriage 407

§9.5 Unmarried Couples 411

§9.6 Parents and Children 417

§9.7 Inheritance 418
§9.7.1 Wills and Will Substitutes 418
§9.7.2 Intestate Succession 420
§9.7.2.1 Surviving Spouse But No Surviving Children or Parents 420
§9.7.2.2 Surviving Spouse and Surviving Parents But No Children 420
§9.7.2.3 Surviving Spouse and Children 420

PART IV REGULATION OF THE MARKET FOR REAL ESTATE 425

Chapter 10 Leaseholds 427

§10.1 Introduction 428

§10.2 Distinguishing Leaseholds from Other Interests 434

§10.3 Types of Tenancies (Leasehold Estates) 442
§10.3.1 Term of Years 442
§10.3.2 Periodic Tenancy 444
§10.3.3 Tenancy at Will 447
§10.3.4 Tenancy at Sufferance 448

§10.4 Tenant's Obligations and Landlord's Remedies 449
§10.4.1 Tenant's Duty to Pay Rent 449
§10.4.2 Tenant's Duty to Operate 453
§10.4.3 Illegality 455
§10.4.4 Landlord's Remedies 456
§10.4.4.1 Forfeiture (Landlord's Recovery of Possession) 456
§10.4.4.2 Holding the Tenant to a New Tenancy 457
§10.4.4.3 Self-Help v. Summary Process 458
§10.4.4.4 Surrender, Reletting, Damages, and the Duty to Mitigate Damages 461

§10.5 Landlord's Obligations and Tenant's Remedies 466
§10.5.1 Landlord's Duty to Deliver Possession 466
§10.5.2 Security Deposits 467
§10.5.3 Actual Eviction 467
§10.5.4 Anti-eviction Laws 468
§10.5.5 Rent Regulation 469

§10.6 Tenant's Right to Habitable Premises 469
§10.6.1 Constructive Eviction 469
§10.6.2 Housing Codes 473
§10.6.3 Implied Warranty of Habitability 473
§10.6.4 Retaliatory Eviction 481
§10.6.5 Landlord's Tort Liability 484
§10.6.6 Consumer Protection Laws 487
§10.6.7 Lead Paint Laws 489

§10.7 Transfers by Landlord or Tenant 490
§10.7.1 Landlord's Right to Transfer the Reversion 490
§10.7.2 Tenant's Rights to Assign or Sublet 490

Chapter 11 Real Estate Transactions 493

§11.1 Introduction 495

§11.2 Brokers 496

§11.3 Sales Contract (Purchase and Sale Agreement) 504
§11.3.1 The Attorney's Role 504
§11.3.2 Statute of Frauds 506
§11.3.3 What Constitutes Breach 509
§11.3.3.1 Fraud 509
§11.3.3.2 Warranty of Habitability for New Homes 514
§11.3.3.3 Marketable Title 515
§11.3.3.4 Good Faith Effort to Obtain Financing 521
§11.3.4 Remedies for Breach 521
§11.3.4.1 Buyer's Remedies 521
§11.3.4.2 Seller's Remedies 524
§11.3.5 Risk of Loss During Executory Period 527
§11.3.6 Death of a Contracting Party 527
§11.3.7 Mistake 528

§11.4 Deeds and Title Protection 528
§11.4.1 Formal Requirements 528
§11.4.1.1 Writing 528
§11.4.1.2 Delivery 530
§11.4.2 Substantive Requirements 533
§11.4.2.1 Forgery 533
§11.4.2.2 Fraud 534
§11.4.3 Title Covenants 534
§11.4.4 Marketable Title Acts 537
§11.4.5 Recording Acts 538
§11.4.5.1 How the System Works 538
§11.4.5.2 Types of Recording Acts 540
§11.4.5.3 Chain-of-Title Problems 544
§11.4.6 Title Insurance 553
§11.4.7 Title Registration 554

§11.5 Real Estate Finance 555
§11.5.1 Mortgages 555
§11.5.2 Installment Land Contracts, or Contracts for Deed 564
§11.5.3 Equitable Mortgages 566
§11.5.4 Subprime Mortgages 567
§11.5.5 Wrongful Foreclosure 573

Chapter 12 Fair Housing Law 575

§12.1 Introduction 576

§12.2 Intentional Racial or National-Origin Discrimination 578
§12.2.1 U.S. Constitution 578
§12.2.2 *Fair Housing Act of 1968* 582
§12.2.2.1 Prohibited Bases of Discrimination 582
§12.2.2.2 Covered Dwellings 583
§12.2.2.3 Exemptions 584
§12.2.2.4 Prohibited Conduct 587
§12.2.2.5 Standards of Proof 591
§12.2.2.6 Standing 596

§12.2.2.7 Advertising 598
§12.2.2.8 Remedies 598
§12.2.3 *Civil Rights Act of 1866* 600

§12.3 Sex Discrimination 602

§12.4 Sexual-Orientation and Gender Identity Discrimination 607

§12.5 Disability Discrimination 608

§12.6 Family Status Discrimination 611
§12.6.1 Families with Children 611
§12.6.2 Marital Status 612

§12.7 Religious Discrimination 614

§12.8 Disparate Impact Claims 615
§12.8.1 Race 615
§12.8.2 Sex 620
§12.8.3 Sexual Orientation and Gender Identity 621
§12.8.4 Disability 622
§12.8.5 Familial Status 625
§12.8.5.1 Families with Children 625
§12.8.5.2 Group Homes and Nontraditional Families 626
§12.8.6 Religion 628
§12.8.7 National Origin 629

§12.9 Economic Discrimination 630
§12.9.1 Intentional Wealth-Based Discrimination 630
§12.9.2 Exclusionary Zoning 631
§12.9.3 The Right to Be Somewhere: Homelessness and Public Loitering Laws 634

PART V PUBLIC LAND USE PLANNING 637

Chapter 13 Land Use Regulation 639

§13.1 Introduction 641

§13.2 Planning Process 641
§13.2.1 Federal, State, and Local Regulation 641
§13.2.2 Zoning Enabling Acts 642
§13.2.3 Comprehensive Plan 642
§13.2.4 Zoning Ordinances 643
§13.2.5 Board of Adjustment or Board of Zoning Appeals 644

§13.3 Zoning Laws 644
§13.3.1 Lot and Building Regulations 644
§13.3.2 Use Regulations 645
§13.3.3 Special Exceptions 646

§13.3.4 Contract or Conditional Zoning 647
§13.3.5 Floating Zones 650
§13.3.6 Overlay Zones 651

§13.4 Protection of Pre-Existing Property Rights 651
§13.4.1 Prior Nonconforming Uses 651
§13.4.2 Vested Rights 654
§13.4.3 Variances 655

§13.5 Rezoning: Limits on Preferential Zoning 657
§13.5.1 Conformity with Comprehensive Plan 657
§13.5.2 Spot Zoning 658

§13.6 Nonzoning Land Use Controls 658
§13.6.1 Building and Housing Codes 658
§13.6.2 Subdivision Regulations 659
§13.6.2.1 Subdivision Approval 659
§13.6.2.2 Planned Unit Developments 660
§13.6.2.3 Form-Based Codes 660
§13.6.3 Growth Management and Regional Planning 661
§13.6.4 Historic Landmarks 662
§13.6.5 Environmental Protection 662
§13.6.5.1 Wetlands Regulations 663
§13.6.5.2 Endangered Species Laws 663
§13.6.5.3 Hazardous Waste Laws 664
§13.6.6 Telecommunications Towers 665

§13.7 Constitutional Limits on Land Use Regulations 666
§13.7.1 Procedural Due Process 666
§13.7.2 Substantive Due Process 666
§13.7.2.1 Protection from Arbitrary Regulations 666
§13.7.2.2 Family Integrity and Freedom of Association 669
§13.7.3 Equal Protection 670
§13.7.4 First Amendment — Speech and Religion 671
§13.7.4.1 SLAPP Suits 671
§13.7.4.2 Free Speech 672
§13.7.4.3 Religious Uses 674

Chapter 14 Eminent Domain and Regulatory Takings 679

§14.1 Introduction 680

§14.2 Eminent Domain and the "Public Use" Requirement 682
§14.2.1 U.S. Constitution 682
§14.2.2 State Law 687
§14.2.2.1 State Constitutions 687
§14.2.2.2 State Statutes 689

§14.3 Just Compensation 689

§14.4 Regulatory Takings — Historical Background 694
§14.4.1 Before 1922 694
§14.4.2 1922 to 1978 696

§14.4.3 After 1978 702

§14.5 General Balancing Test for Regulatory Takings 707
§14.5.1 Character of Government Action 708
§14.5.2 Economic Impact (Diminution in Value) 713
§14.5.3 Interference with Reasonable Investment-Backed Expectations 715
§14.5.4 Fairness and Justice 715

§14.6 "Categorical" Regulatory Takings 718
§14.6.1 *Per Se* Takings 718
§14.6.1.1 Physical Invasions 718
§14.6.1.2 Deprivation of All Economically Viable Use 728
§14.6.2 Established Property Rights 743
§14.6.2.1 Core Property Rights 743
§14.6.2.2 Vested Rights 749

§14.7 Judicial Takings 752

§14.8 Exactions 757

§14.9 Takings Legislation 762

§14.10 Remedies and Procedures for Regulatory Takings 764
§14.10.1 Remedies for Regulatory Takings 764
§14.10.2 Procedures 765

§14.11 Tribal Property 766

PART VI TRIBAL PROPERTY 767

Chapter 15 American Indian Property 769

§15.1 Introduction 770

§15.2 Tribal Title 773
§15.2.1 Original Indian Title (Aboriginal Title) 773
§15.2.2 Recognized Title 777
§15.2.3 Executive Order Title 778

§15.3 Individual Title 779
§15.3.1 Restricted Trust Allotments 779
§15.3.2 Assignments 780

§15.4 Compensability 781
§15.4.1 Original Indian Title 781
§15.4.2 Recognized Title 784
§15.4.3 Executive Order Title 788
§15.4.4 Restricted Trust Allotments 790

§15.5 Protection of Tribal Possession 791
§15.5.1 Restraint on Alienation 791
§15.5.2 Extinguishment 792

§15.6 Reparations 794
§15.6.1 *Indian Claims Commission Act* 794
§15.6.2 Eastern Land Claims 795
§15.6.3 Land Claims Settlement Acts 801
§15.6.4 Breach of Trust Claims 802
§15.6.5 *Native American Graves Protection and Repatriation Act* 805

§15.7 Tribal Easements 806
§15.7.1 Hunting and Fishing Rights 806
§15.7.2 Water Rights 807

PART VII PERSONAL AND INTELLECTUAL PROPERTY 809

Chapter 16 Personal Property 811

§16.1 Introduction 812

§16.2 Animals 813

§16.3 Finders 816

§16.4 Gifts 821

§16.5 Bailments 824

§16.6 Good Faith Purchasers 825

§16.7 Adverse Possession 826

§16.8 Accession and Fixtures 826

§16.9 Human Bodies 827

Chapter 17 Intellectual Property 835

§17.1 Introduction 836

§17.2 Copyright 836

§17.3 Patents 841

§17.4 Trademarks 844

§17.5 Unfair Competition 847

§17.6 Publicity Rights 849

§17.7 Moral Rights of Artists 853

§17.8 Cultural Property 855

§17.9 Digital Property 856

Table of Cases *859*
Tables of Statutes and Regulations *901*
Table of Restatements *921*
Index *923*

PREFACE

This Seventh Edition is updated with references to recent changes in property law, including the Supreme Court's decision in *City of Grants Pass v. Johnson* (2024), rejecting the Ninth Circuit's interpretation of the Eighth Amendment limitation on criminalizing homelessness; the Supreme Court's important copyright fair use decision in *Andy Warhol Foundation for the Visual Arts, Inc. v. Goldsmith* (2023); recent developments in applying the First Amendment to land-use regulations such as billboards; and several important Supreme Court cases in the regulatory takings and exactions context, including *DeVillier v. Texas* (2024), *Tyler v. Hennepin County* (2023), and *Sheetz v. County of El Dorado* (2024). As with previous editions, it is striking that there have been remarkable and interesting developments in the last few years in the property area. Far from a staid, old-fashioned, formal, rule-bound system, property law is developing to meet evolving — and often contested — twenty-first century needs and values.

This treatise is designed with a mission in mind: to explain the law of property clearly, and to do so in a way that will show students, lawyers, and judges the internal tensions and competing policies and values that comprise the property system. We have sought to be accurate in the statement of current law; we have not, however, researched the law of every state on every issue. We have included recent citations that should provide an entry into the law on each issue, and we have cited secondary sources that have more comprehensive treatments. We have noted some (but obviously not all) statutes that alter common law property rules, and we have paid substantial attention to minority rules or disagreements among the states on what the rules of property law are or should be.

There is surprisingly more disagreement about property law than one might imagine. There is good reason for this disagreement. Property law is one of the ways we organize social life; it embodies some of the deepest and most cherished values we possess. Those values sometimes come into conflict with one another. When this happens, we are forced to accommodate these conflicting values. We do this by compromising, placing limits, drawing lines, and making distinctions. Yet, we do not all agree on the right way to go about drawing those lines. Even when we agree on how to think about the problem, the issues are often hard, requiring judgment, perspective, and the exercise of responsibility. For these reasons, the law of property is conflicted, controversial, and interesting. Accuracy in the description of the law requires attention to these controversies. It is especially instructive to pay attention to the disagreements among courts about the legal rules governing property and the competing values that give rise to these disagreements.

The complexity of the property system comes from the fact that we want conflicting things. On the one hand, we wish for owners to have full sets of rights over the things they own. We want this both to protect their autonomy and to promote social welfare. Ownership is a strong claim to be entitled to control things that human beings need. The legal system recognizes and protects those entitlements vigorously. On the other hand, owners do not live alone. Both ownership and use of property affect others — for good and for ill. The law of property recognizes the interests of those others who are affected by the exercise of property rights. It responds to those interests by limiting the entitlements that owners can legitimately claim. It does so to protect the legitimate interests and needs of both other owners and non-owners, as well as the community at large. Because others are entitled to limit what owners can do with their property, no property rights are absolute. Indeed, our property system confers not absolute ownership, but *shared* ownership—with legal rights in a particular valued resource divided among several, or even many, people.

We have sought to make the law both clear and muddy. We have tried to be clear in the presentation of legal rules and doctrine. We have also sought to present clearly the most important competing arguments and policies that animate different doctrinal fields. We have done so because these arguments are likely to shape both the application of existing law and future changes in that law. We have tried, however, to muddy the waters by emphasizing the disagreements among courts about the rules of property law and by explaining why hard cases are really hard. We state basic rules with their animating policies while also explaining the competing policies that might well lead to creation of exceptions or counter-rules that would limit the reach of existing rules to protect legitimate competing interests. We do this in two ways. First, at the beginning of each chapter, we explain the fundamental issues likely to arise in that doctrinal field.

Second, each chapter contains a series of "hard cases," which contain difficult issues that may cause judges to disagree about how the case should be resolved. We have explained such hard cases by giving short descriptions of the policy arguments that lawyers might present on both sides of the case. We have sought to highlight issues that arise—or should arise—in choices among alternative rules of property law. These discussions are meant to help students "spot issues." They also model for students what a good answer might look like on a final examination, explaining not why the case must come out a particular way, but why it might come out either way—in other words, why it is *hard*. We often explain to our students that if they are confused about how the rules apply to a complicated fact situation presented on an exam, they should be happy rather than worried. Law professors usually construct hard cases for exams and if students are confused about how the law applies to these hard cases, they got the point. A good answer will explain clearly the nature of their confusion; it will explain the reasons why the case could come out either way, ending with an educated guess about what an actual court might do with the hard case. Such equivocations are not evasions; nor are they refusals to answer the question. They accurately depict the state of the law, as they accurately describe the reality that a client would need to know in order to make informed decisions about how to conform her conduct to the dictates of the law, or to challenge existing rules.

Explaining both sides of a contested, hard case is also intended to be useful to judges and lawyers. Understanding the law requires knowledge, not only of legal doctrine and the policies that have been used to justify existing rules, but also the policies that might well justify limiting the application of those rules by creating exceptions or counter-rules that apply in distinguishable fact situations. When a case is genuinely hard, a lawyer will be able to explain the strongest arguments on both sides and respond to the strongest arguments on the other side. Seeing these arguments and counterarguments and being able to make them persuasive is a central task of lawyers and part of the way the legal system works to protect the interests of everyone affected by legal rules. Moreover, practicing attorneys also need to know about disagreements among the states because a minority rule elsewhere may be on the table in your jurisdiction—you may even put it there yourself.

In a book of this size and character, there will inevitably be mistakes. We would gratefully receive any comments or criticisms that point out such mistakes so that they can be corrected in future editions. Professor Singer can be reached at jsinger@law.harvard.edu and Professor Davidson can be reached at nestor_davidson@gsd.harvard.edu.

Many people helped us with this book over the years, whether or not they knew it. For their companionship—intellectual and otherwise—thanks and affection go to Martha Minow, Michelle Adams, Greg Alexander, Michelle Anderson, Keith Aoki, Bernadette Atuahene, David

Barron, Bethany Berger, Rashmi Dyal-Chand, Hanoch Dagan, Seth Davis, Eric Freyfogle, Phil Frickey, Jerry Frug, Kent Greenfield, Clare Huntington, Duncan Kennedy, Randy Kennedy, John Lovett, Marnie Mahoney, Frank Michelman, Jenny Nedelsky, Nell Newton, Jeremy Paul, Jed Purdy, Eduardo Peñalver, Peggy Radin, Judy Royster, Michael Schill, Avi Soifer, Debra Pogrund Stark, Laura Underkuffler, André van der Walt, Johan van der Walt, Kevin Washburn, and Rob Williams. We would also like to thank the numerous anonymous reviewers who made many suggestions, many of which we have incorporated into the text.

We also would like to acknowledge the authors of previous property treatises on whose research we build and to whom we are indebted for their originality, perspicuity, and wisdom. They include the late Roger Cunningham, William Stoebuck, Dale Whitman, and John Sprankling, as well as the authors of numerous specialized treatises cited throughout this book.

We would like to thank Mekonnen Ayano, Benjamin Beasley, Hillary Bendert, Ariane Buglione, Alice Feng, George Fibbe, Leigh Forsyth, David Foster, Melissa Friedman, Nicholas Gervasi, Jonathan Gingerich, Jordan Goodson, Joseph Harrington, Liviya James, Edward Kang, Jordan Kennedy, Vikas Khanna, Kylie Kim, Brian Korchin, Lerae Kroon, Jeeyoon Lim, Christina Lopez, Sara Madge, Matthew Peterson, Michael Qin, Luke Riley, Isaac Saidel-Goley, and Loren Washburn for outstanding research assistance on this and past editions. And, as always, Patricia Fazzone has facilitated this project with grace and humor.

Martha Minow has sustained Professor Singer with her encouragement, her example, her humor, and her insight. Mira Singer has inspired Professor Singer with her imagination, her sense of wonder, and her keen moral sense.

For Professor Davidson, Clare Huntington is ever the light to guide by, no matter the storms.

The late Justice Morris Pashman ז"ל served on the Supreme Court of New Jersey with distinction. Professor Singer's time clerking with him taught him much of what he believes he knows about making a good legal argument. He tried to see every case from the point of view of both sides. More fundamentally, he considered how the ruling of the court would affect those not in the courtroom — especially those who could not speak for themselves. He sought to explain his decisions to everyone who needed to understand them, including lower court judges, lawyers, the public at large, and, most importantly, the losing party.

Justice Pashman understood that hard cases often require lawmakers to protect one legitimate interest at the expense of another, equally legitimate interest. The doing of justice sometimes implied the doing of injustice. The ultimate constraint on judges, he believed, was not the stricture of rules, rigidly applied, but the obligation to explain to the losing side why they were losing. This required the judge to empathize with both sides and to try to understand — to really understand — the position being rejected.

It is not that he thought that judges could construct arguments that would induce the losing party to agree with an adverse outcome; he did not think formulas put an end to controversy. It is that he thought that the job of judging entailed the attempt to feel the pull of competing values at the moment of making a decision. The obligation to explain the legitimacy of a losing argument also entailed an inherent limit on what the winning side could legitimately claim. To Justice Pashman, judging was not a technical activity, but one that required practical wisdom, a trait he possessed in abundance. We are grateful that Justice Pashman was able to see the dedication to this book shortly before he died. He will always be the model of the good judge.

Joseph William Singer
Nestor M. Davidson
Cambridge, Massachusetts

5786 / 2026

PROPERTY

CHAPTER 1

Introduction

§1.1 What Is Property?
- §1.1.1 Relations Among People Regarding Valued Resources
- §1.1.2 Ownership v. Bundles of Rights
- §1.1.3 Individual Entitlement v. Property as a System
- §1.1.4 Regulation v. Construction of a Property System
- §1.1.5 Legal Relations

§1.2 Core Tensions Within Property Law
- §1.2.1 Right to Exclude v. Right of Access
- §1.2.2 Privilege to Use v. Security from Harm
- §1.2.3 Power to Transfer v. Limits on Disaggregation
- §1.2.4 Immunity from Loss v. Power to Acquire

§1.3 Recurring Themes
- §1.3.1 Rule Choices, Hard Cases, and Competing Arguments
- §1.3.2 Social Context
- §1.3.3 Formal v. Informal Sources of Rights
- §1.3.4 The Alienability Dilemma
- §1.3.5 Contractual Freedom and Minimum Standards
- §1.3.6 Systemic Norms

§1.4 Theories of Property
- §1.4.1 Normative Approaches
  - §1.4.1.1 Justice, Liberty, and Rights
  - §1.4.1.2 Consequentialism, Utilitarianism, and Efficiency
  - §1.4.1.3 Social Relations, Virtue, and Democracy
  - §1.4.1.4 Libertarian, Conservative, and Progressive Views
- §1.4.2 Justificatory Norms
  - §1.4.2.1 Possession
  - §1.4.2.2 Labor (Desert)
  - §1.4.2.3 Personality and Human Flourishing
  - §1.4.2.4 Efficiency
  - §1.4.2.5 Justified Expectations
  - §1.4.2.6 Distributive Justice

§1.1 What Is Property?

§1.1.1 Relations Among People Regarding Valued Resources

Control of things v. legal relations

Property concerns legal relations among people regarding control and disposition of valued resources.[1] Note well: Property concerns relations *among people*, not relations between people and things. It is sometimes thought that property concerns power over things. To some extent, that is true. But one problem with this definition is that many property rights do not concern "things" at all, but intangible resources, such as copyright or interests in an ongoing business. The more fundamental problem is that power over things is meaningless unless others have obligations to defer to an owner's power. If property means that one person, rather than another, has the legitimate power to say what happens to an object of value, then the law of property places obligations on non-owners to respect the claims of owners. Non-owners must refrain from invading or taking the property without the owner's consent, and they must live with the consequences of an owner's choices about how to use her own property. Thus, property is not about control of things; it is about relations among people regarding things, and because the things we value are not confined to tangible objects, it makes more sense to think of property in terms of valued resources.

§1.1.2 Ownership v. Bundles of Rights

Bundle of rights

When we think of property, we tend to think about ownership. Property, we may think, is the designation of some person as the "owner" of a resource or thing. An owner has the power to control the property she owns. Control may take various forms, including the right to exclude others, the privilege to use the property, the power to transfer it, and immunity from having it taken from the owner or harmed without the owner's consent. Nor is this list exhaustive. Because ownership concerns a package of distinct entitlements, we should understand it as comprising a bundle of rights.

Ownership rights are not absolute

We tend to assume that owners have the right to do what they want with their property. This is only partly true. When use of our property affects others, our legal rights may be limited to protect the legitimate interests of others. Indeed, the use of one person's property may harm the property of others. If an owner releases polluting chemicals into the air or the ground, she may harm neighboring owners, who have legal rights to be protected from such pollution. The free use of property must be limited to protect the security of neighboring owners. Similarly, although owners generally have the right to exclude non-owners from their property, public accommodations, such as restaurants, cannot refuse to serve customers because of race. Thus, property rights are limited to protect both the

[1] The *First Restatement of Property*, published between 1936 and 1944, defined property in a somewhat more restricted way: "The word 'property' is used in this Restatement to denote legal relations between persons with respect to a thing." 1 *Restatement of Property* Introductory Note, at 3 (1936). *Compare* Jeremy Waldron, *The Right to Private Property* 31 (1988) ("The concept of private property is the concept of a system of rules governing access to and control of material resources").

property and personal rights of others, as well as the interests of the community. Ownership does not mean the absolute right to control what one owns; rather, it is the fullest bundle of rights that the law will recognize.

Rights unbundled

Not only are property rights limited by the property and personal rights of others, but also the rights associated with ownership, which can be unbundled or disaggregated. If we think about ownership as a bundle of sticks, it becomes clear that it is possible to give one or more sticks away while keeping the rest. For example, an owner may rent her property to a tenant pursuant to a written lease to last for one year, granting the tenant the privilege to possess part of the landlord's land for that term. In this case, the owner has exercised her power to transfer a set of the sticks in the bundle to the tenant who has a privilege to enter and possess the property for the term of the lease. The owner no longer has the right to exclude the tenant from that portion of the property. The landlord reserves control of the rest of the property and retains the right to regain the tenant's apartment at the end of the lease term. The ability to unbundle the owner's rights and give some sticks to others while keeping the rest does not mean that there are no limits to the owner's ability to do this. Property law sometimes requires certain sticks to stay together, partly to ensure that owners have sufficient freedom to exercise and enjoy their property rights and partly to ensure that the property system functions efficiently and smoothly, avoiding both unfair surprise and overly complex or stunted bundles of rights.

Ownership of bundles of rights

Who is the owner of an apartment rented to a tenant? We conventionally think of the landlord as the owner. Lawyers, however, may think of the tenant as owning a bundle of rights that comprises a standard package of property entitlements — a leasehold called a "term of years." The landlord owns a different bundle of rights — a "reversion" (the right to recover possession at the end of the lease) and a set of contractual rights to receive the agreed-upon rent as it comes due. The individual rights that make up the ownership package have been disaggregated and divided up among the parties. It may sometimes serve our purposes to ask, "Who is the owner?" But often it may better serve our purposes to ask, "Owner of what?" A particular piece of property may have multiple owners of different sticks (or sets of sticks) in the bundle of rights that comprises full ownership. When we are asked to determine who owns a particular stick in the bundle, it may not help us to know who the "owner" of the land is because ownership of various sticks in the bundle may be spread among several people.

§1.1.3 Individual Entitlement v. Property as a System

Systemic norms

We tend to think of property as an individual entitlement. Property is about the things individuals own and their rights to stop others from using those things without their consent. But property is also a *system*, as well as an individual entitlement. Individuals do not live alone and the allocation and exercise of property rights affects others. Because this is so, property law rules have been developed to ensure that the system of property rights functions fairly and efficiently. A variety of norms has developed to ensure that the exercise of individual property rights is compatible with an environment that allows everyone to exercise his or her rights in appropriate ways.

Community norms

Efficiency

For example, antitrust laws limit the ability of individual businesses to dominate particular markets in ways that preclude others from entering those markets themselves. They also protect both efficiency and consumer welfare by ensuring adequate, healthy competition. Similarly, nuisance, zoning, and environmental laws prohibit owners from using their property in ways that injure other property owners, and common resources in air and water. Eviction laws allow landlords to get rid of tenants who do not pay rent, but grant such tenants procedural due process and prohibit eviction when the landlord has violated her own obligations to comply with the housing code. These laws not only protect individual entitlements, but they also regulate the rental housing market so that it adheres to minimum standards of decency, and the community is spared the negative effects of substandard housing.

Minimum standards

§1.1.4 Regulation v. Construction of a Property System

Property v. regulation

One way to look at property rights is to start with the concept of ownership and then ask when and whether an owner's right to control her property should be limited by government regulation either to protect similar rights of others or to prevent harm to the community. This way of posing the question suggests that property and regulation are opposites; regulations limit property rights and thus are inherently suspect.

Regulation as management of conflicting rights

Another way to look at the problem is to focus on the fact that the institution of a property system entails difficult judgments about the definition, allocation, and enforcement of legal rights, including both property rights and personal rights. For example, is a tenant in an apartment building entitled to play loud music at 3:00 A.M., or is the neighbor upstairs entitled to peace and quiet at nighttime so that he can sleep? We might think that one who wants to play music is claiming a right to use her property as she wishes (playing loud music) and the neighbor wants the state to regulate (limit) her property rights. But the problem here is that the neighbor *also* has property rights, including the right to quiet enjoyment of his own property. By asking the state to prevent loud music at 3:00 A.M., the neighbor is asking the state to protect his property rights and to limit the ability of the music lover from infringing on those property rights. If the state were to choose not to "regulate," it would in fact be protecting free use rights over security rights and denying property owners the right to quiet enjoyment of their property. When interests in free use of property clash with interests in security and quiet enjoyment, the state must draw a line between conflicting property claims. Similarly, when an owner wishes to disinherit his children, we must determine whether owners have the right to control the disposition of their property on death and, if so, do they have complete freedom in this regard, or should children and surviving spouses have fixed entitlements to some portion of the decedent's property owned at death?

Choices between conflicting property rights

Many issues concerning property are not really questions of whether the state should regulate property. Instead, they entail choices between competing property claims. If one is going to create a property system, then the government — through the legislatures and the courts — must adjudicate conflicts among property rights. When the property rights of one owner clash with either the property or the personal rights of others, the legal system must choose how to reconcile the incompatible entitlements. Such choices are regulatory choices and they are unavoidable if one wants to have the benefit of private property rights. Choosing to have a property system is choosing to have regulation. After all, "regulation" is just another word for "the rule of law."

§1.1.5 Legal Relations

Wesley Hohfeld

In classic articles, Wesley Hohfeld introduced the idea that legal rights (including property rights) describe relations among people, rather than relations between people and things.[2] He also identified four basic types of legal rights (rights, privileges, powers, and immunities). Each right has a correlative term that describes what the right means from the perspective of others who are obligated to respect the entitlement. This system of describing property rights is useful and was adopted by the *First Restatement of Property* in 1936.[3] This analysis was further developed by pragmatic legal scholars — called "legal realists" — from the 1920s through the 1930s. They interpreted property rights as delegations of sovereign power to individuals by the state; these rights should therefore be defined to accommodate the conflicting interests of social actors by reference to applicable social policies, norms, and values.[4]

Rights and duties

"Rights" are claims, enforceable by state power, that others act in a certain manner in relation to the right holder. The correlative of a right is a duty. A right holder is entitled to control the behavior of others, who are subject to duties not to interfere with the interests protected by the right. An example is the right to exclude; this right places duties on non-owners not to enter property without the owner's permission.

Privileges and "no-rights" or vulnerabilities

"Privileges" or "liberties" are permissions to act in a certain manner without being liable for damages to others and without others being able to summon state power to prevent those acts. An example is the freedom to use your property as you see fit. The correlative of a privilege is the vulnerability others face of suffering the consequences that exercise of the privilege might entail. For example, an owner who is privileged to build a three-story house may effectively block the neighbor's view of a wooded area and decrease the light available to the neighbor. If an owner is privileged to act in a certain way, others have no right to stop her. For this reason, Hohfeld called the correlative of a legal "privilege" a "no-right," an awkward but expressive term.

Powers and liabilities

"Powers" are state-enforced abilities to change legal entitlements held by oneself or others. The prime example of a power in the context of property

[2] Wesley Newcomb Hohfeld, *Some Fundamental Legal Conceptions as Applied in Judicial Reasoning*, 23 Yale L.J. 16 (1913), 26 Yale L.J. 710 (1917). *See also* Arthur Corbin, *Jural Relations and Their Classification*, 30 Yale L.J. 226 (1921); Arthur Corbin, *Legal Analysis and Terminology*, 29 Yale L.J. 136 (1919); Joseph William Singer, *The Legal Rights Debate in Analytical Jurisprudence from Bentham to Hohfeld*, 1982 Wis. L. Rev. 975.

[3] *See* 1 *Restatement of Property* §§1-4, at 3-9 (1936-1944).

[4] Walter Wheeler Cook, *Privileges of Labor Unions in the Struggle for Life*, 27 Yale L.J. 779 (1918); Robert Hale, *Bargaining, Duress, and Economic Liberty*, 43 Colum. L. Rev. 603 (1943); Morris Cohen, *Property and Sovereignty*, 13 Cornell L.Q. 8 (1927).

is the power to transfer title to another. The correlative of a power is the liability others face of having the power holder exercise the power. For example, a tenant at-will is vulnerable to the landlord's decision to terminate the tenancy at any time, ending the tenant's right to possess the apartment. The landlord has a power to grant possession to the tenant and the power to revoke such possessory rights. Similarly, the landlord may sell the property and the new landlord may choose to end the tenancy. If the landlord sells the property (which the landlord has a "power" to do), the buyer becomes the new owner and the tenant has no power to prevent the sale, remaining vulnerable to the possibility of being evicted by the new owner.

Immunities and disabilities

"Immunities" are security from having one's own entitlements changed by others. An example of an immunity is the entitlement to be free from the forced seizure of one's property by the state unless the state takes the property for a public purpose and pays just compensation. A tenant under a year-long lease (called a "term of years") is immune from being evicted or dispossessed by the landlord during the term unless the tenant breaches the terms of the lease. The term of years persists even if the landlord sells the property; the new owner is "disabled" (has no power) to evict a tenant granted a term of years until the term ends.

Utility of these concepts

Although the precise terms used by Hohfeld never caught on, the concepts he described are useful to understanding and analyzing property law. Ownership entails a host of rights, privileges, powers, and immunities. Moreover, because ownership is not absolute, non-owners have some legal entitlements in property owned by others, such as the privilege to enter a public accommodation such as a restaurant or retail store without regard to race. Because property rights are often shared or divided among more than one person, it is often crucial to look at the individual legal entitlements (the sticks in the bundle) to determine who owns which stick.

§1.2 Core Tensions Within Property Law

Conflicts among property rights

Both the concept of property and property law itself are beset by internal tensions that arise when the exercise of a property right by one person conflicts with the property and personal legal rights of others. One function of property law is to adjudicate such conflicts. It is helpful to catalog some of the core tensions we will see.

§1.2.1 Right to Exclude v. Right of Access

Homes v. public accommodations

Owners have the right to exclude non-owners from their property. However, owners of public accommodations such as hotels, common carriers (buses, airplanes, and the like), and recreational facilities, as well as retail establishments such as stores and physicians' offices, generally have the duty not to discriminate on the basis of race or other invidious grounds. Similarly, employers and landlords have obligations to deal with prospective employees and tenants without regard to such factors as race, sex, or disability. The law distinguishes between types of property where one is entitled to deny access and types of property where one is not entitled to deny access. You are free (legally) to engage in racial discrimination in determining whom to invite to your apartment for dinner, but you are not free to indulge such prejudices in choosing your tenants. The right to exclude is one of the central tenets of the property system. At the same time, the principle of racial equality—that access to property and the market should not depend on one's race—is also central to the property system. A free and democratic society treats each person with equal concern and respect; it does not assign people to unequal statuses (like lords and commoners) or into racial castes. Individuals may have the legal right to exclude others from their property, but they also have the legal right to be free from invidious discrimination in access to the marketplace. Sometimes the right of access will take precedence over the right to exclude.

§1.2.2 Privilege to Use v. Security from Harm

Freedom v. security

Owners are generally free to use their property as they wish, but they are not free to harm their neighbors' property substantially and unreasonably. A factory that emits pollutants into the air may be regulated to prevent the use of its property in ways that will destroy the individual property rights of others and common resources in air and water. Many uses of property impose "externalities" or spillover effects on other owners and on the community as a whole. Because owners are legally entitled to have their own property protected from pollutants dispatched to their property by others, owners' freedom to use their property is limited to ensure that their property use does not cause such externalities.

§1.2.3 Power to Transfer v. Limits on Disaggregation

Free disposition

Owners are generally free to transfer their property to whomever they wish, on whatever terms they want. They can sell it, give it away, or write a will identifying who gets it when they die. They are also free to transfer particular sticks, in the bundle of sticks comprising full ownership, to others while keeping the rest for themselves. Owners are also free to place conditions on the use of property when they sell it. They may, for example, limit the property to residential purposes by including a covenant in the deed stating that the property will be forever limited to such uses.

Limits on free disposition

However, the law will not allow owners to impose conditions that violate public policy by infringing unduly on the liberty interests of future owners too greatly. An owner could not impose an enforceable condition that all future owners agree to vote for the Democratic candidate for president; this condition infringes on the liberty of future owners and wrongfully attempts to tie ownership of the land to membership in a particular political party. Nor are owners allowed to limit the sale of the property to persons of a particular race. Racially restrictive covenants are invalid and unenforceable. Similarly, a covenant purporting to prevent sale of the property for a set period of time will also ordinarily not be enforced, both because it interferes with the liberty interests of owners to move and because it inefficiently prevents the transfer of property in the marketplace.

Freedom of contract v. ownership

The ability to burden property by restrictions must be, and is, limited by law, to ensure that property is available for transfer in the marketplace and that ownership is not tied to unwarranted restrictions on individual liberty. Although owners are free to disaggregate property rights in various ways, and to impose particular restrictions on the use and ownership of land, that freedom is limited by law. The freedom of the grantor (seller) to restrict the future use or ownership of property must be curtailed to protect the freedom of the grantee (the buyer or future possessor) to use her property as she wishes. The law limits freedom of contract and disposition to ensure that future owners have sufficient powers over their own property and so that the property system does not get clogged up with encumbered and unusable property.

§1.2.4 Immunity from Loss v. Power to Acquire

Limits to immunity rights

Your property cannot be taken from you by others without your consent. However, an owner's immunity from loss of her property rights is not unlimited. For example, cities may use their eminent domain powers to "take" private property for public purposes without the owner's consent if they pay just compensation. The need of the community to build roads and schools overrides the interest of the owner in resisting the taking of her land, even where compensation may appear inadequate. Immunity rights are also limited when they conflict with the immunity rights of others. For example, when a car is stolen and resold to a buyer who does not know (and has no way of knowing) it was stolen, the courts must determine whose immunity rights to protect: those of the first owner or those of the innocent buyer.

Formal v. informal sources of property rights

Immunity rights are also limited when owners allow others to possess their property for a sufficiently long time. An owner who mistakenly builds a fence two feet over and onto the neighbor's property, and possesses the strip for many years, may be granted ownership of the strip by the doctrine of adverse possession. Although owners are immune from losing their property without their consent, they are not immune from such loss if they allow a non-owner to occupy their property for a period long enough to run out the statute of limitations. In effect, the law places an obligation on owners to find out where their borders are or lose the right to object if they allow a neighbor to possess their property for a very long time. By failing to object to long-standing possession of her property, the owner has induced the neighbor to consider the property as her own. Although formal title will ordinarily prevail in a dispute against a trespasser, a non-owner's actual possession will prevail over formal title if the record title holder allows that possession to persist for a long enough period of time. Possession and title are alternative sources of property rights, and the immunity granted a title holder may be limited when the title holder fails to protect her own possession and allows an adverse possessor to establish control over her property and maintain that control for a long time.

§1.3 Recurring Themes

§1.3.1 Rule Choices, Hard Cases, and Competing Arguments

Evolving subject

Property law contains some rules that have been around for centuries and others that have just been created. It is an evolving subject. The subprime mortgage crisis created new challenges and led to significant changes in the law governing mortgages. Moreover, there is a fair amount of disagreement among the states on how to adjudicate property disputes. These differences in approach arise partly because property law protects multiple, conflicting goals and values and because we have differences of opinion on how to resolve those conflicts. They arise partly because some of the rules of property law are highly technical in nature, one might even say hypertechnical. Some of this technicality is a good thing; it has arisen out of case law that developed over time and it attempts to balance multiple, competing policy goals in a fine-tuned way. However, too much technicality can be a very bad thing; it may divert us from achieving sensible outcomes by creating artificial roadblocks to those same goals.

Technicalities

Disagreements among the courts

Our approach in this book will be to highlight the disagreements among courts on how to resolve particular issues, both because it is an accurate statement of the current law, and because such disagreements are quite instructive. They teach us about the competing values, norms, interests, and policies that are the underlying goals of the property system. We will therefore often describe the law in terms of choices among competing possible rules of law. We will also base our description of the law on recent case law. Because property is an evolving subject, it is important to test statements of the law by finding recent cases that express adherence to those rules. A doctrine that was in force in 1920 may not still be in effect today; a court adjudicating a similar case might well adopt a different rule. We have therefore sought to find recent citations for the principles of law we describe here.

Current citations

Law application

Not only do different states adopt different rules and standards about property rules, but each state also faces the task of interpreting, implementing, and applying the rules that they do adopt. At some point, the policy underlying the rule confronts a competing policy that may counsel limiting application of the rule. A particular fact, or set of facts, arguably distinguishes a case from others that had been resolved in the past. The interests of those protected by the rule clash with legitimate interests of others and a court may determine that a prior case should be distinguished — that the rule should not extend to this new fact pattern — either because the underlying policy has reached its limit or because a competing policy requires that an exception or competing rule takes hold. A rule that appears fair in one social context may appear unfair in another.

Distinguishing cases

Hard cases

We state, as clearly and accurately as we can, the rules in force and the disagreements among the courts on what those rules should be or how they should be interpreted. In each major section we present one or more "hard cases," explicitly identified as such. These may be cases on which the states disagree, with some courts adopting one rule and some another. Or they may be cases in which it is not clear whether the rule should be extended to a particular fact pattern. Our goal here is to present an accurate picture of the law, of legal practice, and of the experience of taking a law school examination. In all these situations, some cases are "easy"; they are clearly covered by existing rules and no disagreement arises as to what those rules should be or how to apply them. But many cases are hard, either because there is no precedent in your jurisdiction on point or because one or more facts makes your case arguably distinguishable from the core *fact situation* governed by the general rule or because there is a colorable argument to change existing law. A case may be hard because different states decide it differently and judges may confront the need to choose, on an ongoing basis, which rule is the best one.

Arguments and counterarguments

In such cases, what lawyers and judges do — and what good students do on exams — is to explore the strongest arguments on both sides. In discussing the hard cases, we do just that. We will sometimes give our opinion on how the case should be resolved, but most of the time we will not. We will not always provide an answer precisely because such cases are genuinely hard and because it is possible to see how reasonable judges could go either way. We will, rather, explain, as clearly as we can, *why* the case is hard. Understanding the arguments on both sides of hard cases, and being able to present them persuasively, is what enables decision makers to determine what the strongest claims are on both sides. It also provides a check on untested intuition by forcing the decision maker (and the litigating attorney) to consider the arguments on the other side. This enables judges to make better decisions, lawyers to better argue cases and to predict what judges will do, and students to write better exam answers.

§1.3.2 Social Context

Rules differ for property depending on social context

Property rules differ depending on the social context in which they operate. Landlord-tenant law operates differently, and with somewhat different rules, depending on whether we are dealing with residential or commercial property. Judges believe businesses are better able to protect themselves from unfair contract terms and are generally granted freer rein in agreeing to terms that would be looked upon with disfavor in the residential context. Property rights and institutions also differ in different areas of social life, such as family relationships, business, nonprofit organizations, and governmental ownership. Property that is open to the public, for example, such as a restaurant, is subject to different rules than property that is not open to the public, such as a private home. Contracts among family members may be treated very differently than contracts among strangers. The social setting in which a transaction or property use occurs is of paramount importance.

§1.3.3 Formal v. Informal Sources of Rights

Written v. unwritten transactions and norms

It is often presumed that property rights have their source in some formal grant or agreement. People obtain property by a deed, a will, a lease, a contract, or a government grant. However, property rights also arise informally, by an oral promise, a course of conduct, actual possession, a family relationship, long-standing reliance, and social customs and norms. Many of the basic rules of property law concern contests between formal and informal sources of property rights, and the law often chooses informally created rights over formally created ones.

§1.3.4 The Alienability Dilemma

The case for consolidation

It is a fundamental tenet of the property law system that property should be "alienable," meaning that it should be transferable from one person to another. This is partly because transferability allows a market to function and enables efficient transactions and property use to occur, but it is also partly because transferability promotes individual autonomy. Many rules of property law limit contractual freedom to ensure that particular bundles of property rights are consolidated in the same person, the "owner." If property has too many owners and no owner can use it without the consent of the others, unsolvable conflicts may arise among those owners, impeding their ability to use the property. Consolidating power in an "owner" ensures that resources can be used for current purposes and current needs.

The case for disaggregation

The alienability principle just described requires limiting freedom of contract. However, limiting free contract may *inhibit*, rather than promote, alienability. An owner who wants to sell only one of the sticks in the bundle, and who is not allowed to do so because of a rule requiring that stick be bundled with one or more other sticks, may be deterred from alienating the stick. The point of freedom of contract is to allow the parties to form the agreements that best promote their interests, and property rules that prevent parties from reaching mutually beneficial agreements may deter alienability. This suggests that alienability may sometimes be promoted by allowing owners to disaggregate their property rights as they wish.

The dilemma

The dilemma of alienability is that it may be promoted both by allowing owners to disaggregate property rights (the free contract principle) and by requiring owners to consolidate property rights in one or more owners of set bundles of rights (the ownership principle). To complicate things even further: Sometimes we *want* to prevent alienability. A donor who creates a charitable trust, for example, may want to ensure that the property remains used for charitable purposes, despite the temptation to sell the land for fair market value as that value rises. Allowing restraints on alienation may help preserve desirable charitable institutions. Determining when alienability is a good thing, and how to promote it when it is, is a central topic of property law.

§1.3.5 Contractual Freedom and Minimum Standards

Limits on free contract to protect basic norms of fair dealing

It is sometimes thought that property law should be generally governed by contractual norms, specifically, free contract. If regulatory rules are kept to a minimum, then individual choices about use and disposition may determine how property is divided up, who owns it, and what restrictions they have on their entitlements.[5] There should be substantial freedom for individuals to develop alternative forms of human relationships without having the government dictate the terms of their association. This, in turn, requires substantial freedom to rearrange property rights and enables various relationships to flourish. But there are also bounds to what is acceptable; this is why the law imposes certain minimum standards on contractual relationships. For example, although landlords are entitled to evict tenants who do not pay rent, the law in almost every state requires landlords to use court eviction proceedings to dispossess defaulting tenants. These proceedings

[5] *See, e.g.*, Richard A. Epstein, *Simple Rules for a Complex World* 53-70 (1995).

give tenants a chance to contest the landlord's possessory claim and to have time to find a new place to live, rather than having their belongings tossed on the street and being dispossessed overnight. These limitations on free contract protect basic norms of fair dealing and promote the justified expectations of individuals who enter market transactions.

§1.3.6 Systemic Norms

Rules designed to make the property system function well and fairly

As noted earlier, many existing rules of property law serve systemic goals or norms. By this we mean that they are geared not just to protecting "individual rights," but to creating a social and legal context in which human activities and relationships can flourish. We do not live alone, and exercise of our property rights affects others, both positively and negatively. As John Stuart Mill noted: "[A]ll that makes existence valuable to anyone depends on the enforcement of restraints upon the actions of other people."[6] Property rights must be limited to ensure that owners can enjoy their property. Property law creates an infrastructure to ensure that the environment in which property rights are exercised allows individuals to derive the fullest benefit possible without unduly interfering with the ability of others to exercise their own entitlements.

Rules promoting systemic norms are geared to creating a well-functioning property system. They are intended not only to protect the rights and autonomy of individuals but to also create a social context in which all individuals will have the opportunity to live with dignity. Some of these rules are intended to promote efficiency. For example, antitrust law was created partly to ensure the existence of a competitive market structure that can both discipline companies and better serve consumers. Other systemic rules aim at ensuring a fair distribution of property. Antidiscrimination laws, for example, ensure that individuals have access to the market without regard to race or other irrelevant factors, reflecting a long history in American society of deliberate public and private exclusion.[7]

Well-functioning property system

Similarly, antitrust law might be intended not just to ensure an efficient market, but to lower prices for consumers and to protect companies from being unfairly crowded out of the market by monopolistic practices. Still, other rules function to shape social relationships to create a context for human flourishing and dignity by setting minimum standards for human interaction. Such rules include, for example, requirements that landlords use judicial eviction proceedings that give defaulting tenants time to find a new place to live, rather than just throwing the tenant's belongings on the street and changing the locks on the door. And consumer protection laws prohibit businesses from engaging in unfair or deceptive practices to ensure that consumers get what they want when they enter the marketplace.

[6] John Stuart Mill, *On Liberty* 63-64 (Gertrude Himmelfarb ed. 1981) (original 1859).

[7] *See generally* Richard Rothstein, *The Color of Law: A Forgotten History of How Our Government Segregated America* (2017); *cf.* Cheryl I. Harris, *Whiteness as Property*, 106 Harv. L. Rev. 1707 (1993) (investigating the role of racial identity in the formation of property law and ways in which historical forms of white domination persist to reproduce subordination through property).

§1.4 Theories of Property

§1.4.1 Normative Approaches

Prescriptive approaches

Scholars, judges, and legislators have adopted a variety of normative approaches to debating what the rules of property law are and should be.[8] When existing laws or precedents are unclear, or a substantial argument is made to change the law, or a court must choose between competing possible rules of law (as when a court is asked to change from a majority to a minority approach or vice versa), judges and legislators must consider a variety of norms to determine how to construct property law.[9] These norms have their sources in a variety of philosophical traditions.[10] Each of these norms could be developed extensively and occupy an entire book by themselves. We only mention them here to flag them for your attention. Each of these sets of norms will be used in the course of talking about specific property law issues in the chapters that follow.

Rights, fairness, justice, autonomy, dignity

§1.4.1.1 Justice, Liberty, and Rights. The most fundamental consideration in choosing applicable law is the obligation to pursue justice and liberty.[11] Both scholars and judges seek to construct property rules that will be fair, and will be perceived to be fair, by those who are required to live with them. This is often based on the notion that law should protect individual rights.[12] Rights language, broadly conceived, includes any normative arguments that justify property regimes or rules because they are right—because they describe ways in which people *should* behave toward each other. Professor Jeremy Waldron defines rights theory as based on asking whether a particular interest is sufficiently important from a moral point of view that others have a duty to respect it.[13] If those interests are this important, they may serve as "trumps" that override more general considerations of public policy by which competing interests are balanced against each other. Such individual rights cannot legitimately be sacrificed for the

[8] For descriptions of various approaches, see Gregory S. Alexander & Eduardo M. Peñalver, *An Introduction to Property Theory* (2012); Alan Carter, *The Philosophical Foundations of Property Rights* (1989); Lawrence C. Becker, *Property Rights: Philosophic Foundations* (1977); Andrew Reeve, *Property* (1986); Alan Ryan, *Property* (1987); Alan Ryan, *Property and Political Theory* (1984).

[9] For collections of scholarly approaches to property, see *Perspectives on Property Law* (Robert C. Ellickson, Carol M. Rose & Henry E. Smith 5th ed. 2023); *Property Theory: Legal and Political Perspectives* (James Penner & Michael Otsuka eds. 2018); *A Property Anthology* (Richard H. Chused 2d ed. 2003).

[10] Some theorists are explicitly "pluralist" in their approach, using elements of more than one philosophical tradition. *See, e.g.*, Stephen R. Munzer, *A Theory of Property* (1990) (adopting a pluralist perspective including justice and equality, desert based on labor, and utility and efficiency); Carol M. Rose, *Property & Persuasion: Essays on the History, Theory, and Rhetoric of Ownership* (1994) (combining economic analysis, justice-based arguments, and feminist legal theory); Joseph William Singer, *Entitlement: The Paradoxes of Property* (2000) (using both justice and utilitarian considerations).

[11] J.W. Harris, *Property and Justice* (1996).

[12] Ronald Dworkin, *Law's Empire* (1986); Ronald Dworkin, *Taking Rights Seriously* (1978); Charles Fried, *Right and Wrong* (1978); Alan Gewirth, *The Community of Rights* (1996); John Stuart Mill, *On Liberty* (Gertrude Himmelfarb ed. 1981) (original 1859).

[13] Jeremy Waldron, *The Right to Private Property* 3 (1988).

good of the community.[14] At the same time, this does not mean that rights are necessarily absolute; they must be interpreted to define their appropriate meaning and scope of application and conflicts among rights must be adjudicated to determine how they fit together in appropriate ways. Defining what rights should be protected, and in what ways, and in what circumstances, and with what limits, involves complex analyses of justice, community values, and historical and legal traditions.

Variety of approaches

A wide variety of approaches to thinking about rights exists. Some natural rights scholars argue that rights have roots in the nature of human beings, or that they are natural in the sense that people who think about human relationships from a rational and moral point of view are bound to understand particular individual interests as fundamental or as objective goods or final ends.[15] Whether or not adopting a natural rights perspective, rights theorists focus on considerations such as autonomy, dignity, desert, human flourishing, distributive fairness, social justice, human needs, or a combination of these and similar norms.[16] Other theorists adopt social contract analysis to determine what basic rights individuals would agree upon if they were in a suitable initial choice situation.[17] Rights language therefore includes considerations of liberty, fairness, and justice, and other basic values embraced by a free and democratic society. In its broadest connotation, the language of rights can also encompass the considerations promoted by communitarians and environmentalists who emphasize the importance of community life as well as individual rights, and argue that individuals have obligations as well as rights.[18]

Cost-benefit analysis

§1.4.1.2 Consequentialism, Utilitarianism, and Efficiency. In contrast to rights or justice-based theories, consequentialist approaches focus on the consequences of adopting one rule or the other, rather than the inherent goodness or morality or fairness of the rules. Utilitarians compare the costs and benefits of different definitions and allocations of property entitlements. This approach asks how people will behave in response to competing alternative rules and then seeks to compare the good consequences of each rule with its bad consequences. Differences arise among utilitarians on how to measure the "goodness" or "badness" of those consequences, as well as whether to take distributive concerns into consideration. Some utilitarians, such as Jeremy Bentham, focus on pains and pleasures and treat them all as of equal importance, while others, such as John Stuart Mill, distinguish among interests based on their importance to

[14] Ronald Dworkin, *Taking Rights Seriously* (1978); Jeremy Waldron, *The Right to Private Property* (1988).

[15] *See* John Finnis, *Natural Law and Natural Rights* (1980); Robert Nozick, *Anarchy, State and Utopia* (1974); Judith Jarvis Thomson, *The Realm of Rights* (1990).

[16] *See, e.g.*, Richard A. Epstein, *Simple Rules for a Complex World* 53-70 (1995) (autonomy as a basic norm); Nancy Fraser, *Unruly Practices: Power, Discourse, and Gender in Contemporary Social Theory* (1989) (human needs); Frank Michelman, *Possession vs. Distribution in the Constitutional Idea of Property*, 72 Iowa L. Rev. 1319 (1987) (distributive justice); Robert Nozick, *Anarchy, State and Utopia* (1974) (liberty).

[17] John Rawls, *A Theory of Justice* (1971); Thomas M. Scanlon, *What We Owe to Each Other* (1998).

[18] Mary Ann Glendon, *Rights Talk: The Impoverishment of Political Discourse* (1991); Avishai Margalit, *The Decent Society* (1996); Jedediah Purdy, *For Common Things: Irony, Trust, and Commitment in America Today* (1999).

human flourishing.[19] Many utilitarians combine this approach with justice-oriented analysis; they engage in morally constrained utilitarianism by placing some preferences or interests off the table as incompatible with the basic values of individual freedom and equality while proceeding with cost-benefit analysis of consequences not ruled out by those basic moral constraints.[20]

Contemporary efficiency theorists focus on satisfying human preferences, whatever they happen to be, and then measuring those preferences by reference to market values (what people are willing and able to pay for entitlements).[21] Others note that preferences are partly determined by culture, history, and the legal rules themselves and are thus subject to revision when rules and practices change.[22] The goal of utilitarian approaches is to promote the general welfare or to maximize "social utility." Efficiency theorists sometimes talk about "wealth maximization" as the goal, with wealth as a stand-in for well-being; more broadly, they may speak about promoting "welfare" rather than fairness.[23] Again, some efficiency theorists combine their analyses with rights theory by acknowledging that some preferences should not be satisfied.

Contours of social relationships

§1.4.1.3 Social Relations, Virtue, and Democracy. While rights theorists focus on core individual entitlements and utilitarians focus on cost-benefit analysis and overall social welfare, social relations theorists emphasize the obligations that human beings have to create an environment that enables and promotes human flourishing or ensures individual autonomy.[24] Relational theorists argue that legal rules structure the contours of social relationships.[25] They examine the role property rights play in structuring social relations and the ways in which social relations shape access to property.[26] Antidiscrimination laws, for example, regulate market relationships by refusing to defer to the preferences of those who want to engage in invidious discrimination. These laws make access to the property system independent of such considerations.[27] Legal rules shape the contours of the social relationships that comprise the form of social life to which we are committed.[28] Those rules do not interfere with individual liberty; rather, they establish liberty by giving all persons a safe environment within which to live. Such rules do not

[19] Jeremy Bentham, *An Introduction to the Principles of Morals and Legislation* (J.H. Burns & H.L.A. Hart eds. 1996) (original 1789); John Stuart Mill, *Utilitarianism* (Roger Crisp ed. 1998) (original 1863).

[20] Mark Timmons, *Moral Theory* 144-145, 267-270 (2002).

[21] *Economic Foundations of Property Law* (Bruce A. Ackerman ed. 1975); Richard A. Posner, *Economic Analysis of Law* 35-111 (8th ed. 2011).

[22] Cass R. Sunstein, *Free Markets and Social Justice* (1997).

[23] Louis Kaplow & Steven Shavell, *Fairness versus Welfare* (2002).

[24] Hanoch Dagan, *A Liberal Theory of Property* (2021).

[25] Jennifer Nedelsky, *Law's Relations: A Relational Theory of Self, Autonomy, and Law* (2011).

[26] C. Edwin Baker, *Property and Its Relation to Constitutionally Protected Liberty*, 134 U. Pa. L. Rev. 741 (1986).

[27] Joseph William Singer, *The Anti-Apartheid Principle in American Property Law*, 1 Ala. C.R.-C.L. L. Rev. 83 (2011).

[28] Carol Gould, *Rethinking Democracy: Freedom and Social Cooperation in Politics, Economy, and Society* 179 (1988) (arguing that property should be understood "as the set of legal rights that specify the relations of social individuals to the conditions of their production or agency and to the products of this agency"); Joseph William Singer, *Entitlement: The Paradoxes of Property* (2000).

paternalistically deprive individuals of autonomy; rather, by requiring everyone to treat fellow citizens with common decency, they grant basic security to each person and assure each person the ability to exercise autonomy.[29]

Variety of approaches

Some relational theorists focus on the relation between alternative property law doctrines and conceptions of the proper social order.[30] Others apply a modern version of Aristotelian moral theory to argue for a legal infrastructure for property that promotes human flourishing or virtue.[31] Some focus on the values and norms of a free and democratic society that treats each person with equal concern and respect.[32] Others focus on the ways in which legal rules distribute power.[33] Still others focus on the ways in which property law distinguishes between "commodities" we buy and sell in the market and "personal" property that is, or should be, noncommodified or only partially commodified.[34] Law and society theorists investigate how the "law in practice" differs from the "law on the books" to determine which norms actually govern behavior in the real world with respect to property.[35] Critical legal studies theorists elaborate the competing norms internal to the property system and use suppressed or marginalized norms to criticize prevailing approaches and generate legal doctrines that protect justified expectations and promote both liberty and equality.[36] Critical race theorists focus on the ways in which the law helps construct, maintain, and combat racial hierarchy.[37] Feminist theorists focus on the ways in which property law constructs, maintains, and alters gender relations.[38] Feminists

[29] Jennifer Nedelsky, *Law, Boundaries, and the Bounded Self*, 30 Representations 162, 169 (1990); Jennifer Nedelsky, *Reconceiving Rights as Relationship*, 1 Rev. Const. Studies/Revue d'études constitutionelles 1 (1993).

[30] Gregory S. Alexander, *Commodity & Propriety: Competing Visions of Property in American Legal Thought, 1776-1970* (1997); Joseph William Singer, *Democratic Estates: Property Law in a Free and Democratic Society*, 9 Cornell L. Rev. 1009 (2009).

[31] Gregory S. Alexander, *Property and Human Flourishing* (2018); Eduardo M. Peñalver, *Land Virtues*, 94 Cornell L. Rev. 821 (2009).

[32] Joseph William Singer, *Subprime: Why a Free and Democratic Society Needs Law*, 47 Harv. C.R.-C.L. L. Rev. 141 (2012).

[33] Robert L. Hale, *Freedom Through Law: Public Control of Private Governing Power* (1952); *The Economy as a System of Power* (Marc R. Tool & Warren J. Samuels 2d ed. 1989).

[34] Michael J. Sandel, *What Money Can't Buy: The Moral Limits of Markets* (2012); Margaret Jane Radin, *Contested Commodities: The Trouble with Trade in Sex, Children, Body Parts, and Other Things* (1996); Margaret Jane Radin, *Reinterpreting Property* (1993).

[35] Robert C. Ellickson, *Order Without Law: How Neighbors Settle Disputes* (1991).

[36] Mark Kelman, *A Guide to Critical Legal Studies* (1987); Gary Minda, *Postmodern Legal Movements: Law and Jurisprudence at Century's End* (1995); Roberto Mangabeira Unger, *The Critical Legal Studies Movement* (1986); Roberto Mangabeira Unger, *Politics, A Work in Constructive Social Theory* (1987); Roberto Mangabeira Unger, *What Should Legal Analysis Become?* (1996); Joseph William Singer, *Entitlement: The Paradoxes of Property* (2000); Joseph William Singer, *The Reliance Interest in Property*, 40 Stan. L. Rev. 611 (1988).

[37] *Critical Race Theory: The Cutting Edge* (Richard Delgado & Jean Stefancic 2d ed. 2000); Patricia J. Williams, *The Alchemy of Race and Rights: A Diary of a Mad Law Professor* (1991); *see also* Reginald Leamon Robinson, *Human Agency, Negated Subjectivity, and White Structural Oppression: An Analysis of Critical Race Practice/Praxis*, 53 Am. U. L. Rev. 1361 (2005).

[38] Jeanne Lorraine Schroeder, *The Vestal and the Fasces: Hegel, Lacan, Property, and the Feminine* (1998); *Applications of Feminist Legal Theory to Women's Lives: Sex, Violence, Work, and Reproduction* (D. Kelly Weisberg ed. 1996); *see also* Lindsey H. Jemison, *Feminist Theory and Sex Work Regulation: Comparing Regulatory Models and Implementation of Theoretical Policy*, 21 J.L. Soc'y 163 (2021).

also have developed conceptions of autonomy that focus more on relations among people than individual sovereignty.[39] Critical race feminists focus on the overlap between racial and gender hierarchies.[40]

Liberty and equality

§1.4.1.4 **Libertarian, Conservative, and Progressive Views.** Property is not only an intensely interesting subject but it is also an intensely debated one. As much or more than any other subject typically covered in the first year of law school, property law is likely to elicit disagreement between libertarians who hope to minimize government regulation,[41] conservatives who seek to promote traditional values,[42] and progressives who hope to promote more equal opportunities to acquire property, emphasizing the inevitable role that law plays in structuring property systems.[43] These political/normative perspectives represent different conceptions of what liberty means.

§1.4.2 Justificatory Norms

Several different basic justificatory norms have been proposed by philosophers, and used by judges, to justify particular definitions and allocations of property rights. Here are some of the most important.

First possession as a source of property rights

§1.4.2.1 **Possession.** It is often accurately said that "possession is nine-tenths of the law." The rules in force protect peaceable possessors from dispossession by anyone but the title holder, and in some cases even the title holder will not be able to dispossess a possessor. The concept of "first possession" has deep historical and cultural roots; it may serve as a simple and workable rule to allocate ownership of unpossessed or abandoned objects.

Justifications for the first possession principle

It might seem that grabbing something would not be an attractive candidate for a moral premise for a property system. But the idea of first possession as a legitimate source of property rights may be justified, at least in some cases, by a variety of commonly held norms, including both rights and efficiency. Possessory

[39] Martha Minow, *Making All the Difference: Inclusion, Exclusion, and American Law* (1990); Jennifer Nedelsky, *Law, Boundaries, and the Bounded Self*, 30 Representations 162, 169 (1990); Jennifer Nedelsky, *Reconceiving Rights as Relationship*, 1 Rev. Const. Studies/Revue d'études constitutionelles 1 (1993).

[40] *Critical Race Feminism: A Reader* (Adrien Katherine Wing 2d ed. 2003); Elizabeth V. Spelman, *Inessential Woman: Problems of Exclusion in Feminist Thought* (1988).

[41] Richard Epstein, *Simple Rules for a Complex World* (1995); Richard Epstein, *Takings: Private Property and the Power of Eminent Domain* (1985). Although he is a natural rights theorist and eschews the libertarian label, Professor Eric Claeys has written extensively, and in a sophisticated manner, in a vein that seeks to limit government interference with the rights of owners. *See, e.g.*, Eric R. Claeys, *Virtue and Rights in American Property Law*, 94 Cornell L. Rev. 889 (2009); Eric R. Claeys, *Takings, Regulations, and Natural Property Rights*, 88 Cornell L. Rev. 1549, 1669-1671 (2003).

[42] Sherif Girgis, Robert P. George & Ryan T. Anderson, *What Is Marriage?*, 34 Harv. J.L. & Pub. Pol'y 245 (2010) (defending limiting civil marriage to male-female couples based on a normative conception of the purpose and reason for the institution of marriage).

[43] Symposium: *Property and Obligation*, 94 Cornell L. Rev. 743-1063 (2009), *including* Gregory S. Alexander, Eduardo M. Peñalver, Joseph William Singer & Laura S. Underkuffler, *A Statement of Progressive Property*, 94 Cornell L. Rev. 743 (2009); Gregory S. Alexander, *The Social-Obligation Norm in American Property Law*, 94 Cornell L. Rev. 745 (2009); Eduardo M. Peñalver, *Land Virtues*, 94 Cornell L. Rev. 821 (2009).

claims relate to labor in the sense that the work of enclosing or possessing is usually thought to be accompanied by some specific use of the land. Professor Carol Rose has noted that possession of property constitutes useful work even if nothing else is done on the land because it gives clear notice of who is the owner of the parcel. This is socially useful because "clear titles facilitate trade and minimize resource-wasting conflict."[44] Professor Richard Epstein has argued in favor of the rule that property goes to the first possessor on the ground that such a rule rewards the labor of using land. Further, the rule is long-standing and well understood and has been relied on for generations.[45] We use it in day-to-day life to take places in a line for the movie theater or at the checkout counter at the store.

Distributive implications

At the same time, possession as a justificatory norm is problematic. Jeremy Waldron has explained that the fact that someone grabs something is not a strong enough reason for others to recognize his rights to control it unless those others have similar opportunities to obtain property.[46]

Historical limitations to the first possession principle

Nor is the concept of first possession a completely accurate description of the process by which property rights originated in the United States. For the most part, settlers did not go off into the wilderness and settle on uninhabited land. That land was almost always possessed by Indian nations, and before individuals could claim rights in that land, it had to be transferred from the relevant Indian nation to the United States—generally by treaty.[47] Indian nations were the original first possessors of land in the United States. The rights of the first possessors of land were not fully respected; the United States often forced tribes to transfer land against their will to the United States. Moreover, the Supreme Court has ruled that tribal property may be taken by the United States without compensation unless Congress has expressly vested title in the relevant Indian tribe.[48] This unjust rule shows that the concept of first possession as a source of title has not always been respected in the courts of the United States. Once in the hands of the United States, the land was given or sold to non-Indian grantees. Most non-Indian titles in the United States therefore derive not from first possession, but from a grant from the federal government.

Conquest

Mixing one's labor

§1.4.2.2 **Labor (Desert).** John Locke argued that property rights have their origin in individual labor. "Whatsoever then [a person] removes out of the state that nature has provided and left it in, he has mixed his labor with, and joined to it something that is his own, and thereby makes it his property."[49] Labor theories sometimes focus on rewarding hard work; the person who does the work deserves or is entitled to its benefits.[50] Other theories focus on the utility of protecting the fruits of labor; people are

[44] Carol Rose, *Possession as the Origin of Property*, 52 U. Chi. L. Rev. 73, 81 (1985).

[45] Richard Epstein, *Possession as the Root of Title*, 13 Ga. L. Rev. 1221 (1979).

[46] Jeremy Waldron, *The Right to Private Property* (1988).

[47] Robert A. Williams, Jr., *The American Indian in Western Legal Thought: The Discourses of Conquest* (1990); Robert A. Williams, Jr., *Documents of Barbarism: The Contemporary Legacy of European Racism and Colonialism in the Narrative Traditions of Federal Indian Law*, 31 Ariz. L. Rev. (1989).

[48] *Tee-Hit-Ton Indians v. United States*, 348 U.S. 272 (1955).

[49] John Locke, *Second Treatise of Government* 17-18 (Bobbs-Merrill ed. 1952) (original 1690).

[50] This is Locke's approach.

unlikely to invest in long-term projects if they know the products of their labor can be seized at will by others.[51]

Drawbacks of the labor theory

In many ways, the legal system has not always lived up to the ideal of the labor theory. Feminists have long noted that the work women have historically done in the home, including managing the home and taking care of children, has been unpaid. If labor creates property rights, why is women's work uncompensated? As Charlotte Perkins Gilman noted, "the salient fact is that, whatever the economic value of the domestic industry of women is, they do not get it."[52] Karl Marx both adopted and criticized the labor theory of value by noting that goods workers produce belong not to the workers themselves but to their employer. "Political economy starts from labour as the real soul of production; yet to labour it gives nothing, and to private property everything."[53] And, of course, the institution of slavery failed to adhere to the labor theory, with unimaginable consequences.

Human flourishing

§1.4.2.3 Personality and Human Flourishing. Some theorists focus on the role that property rights play in both developing individual autonomy and satisfying human needs. Hegel believed that property was a way that human beings constituted themselves as people by extending their will to manipulate the objects of the external world.[54] Professor Margaret Jane Radin has argued that "to be a *person* an individual needs some control over resources in the external environment."[55] Property rights help individuals to live their lives on their own terms.

Wealth maximization

§1.4.2.4 Efficiency. As noted above, individual property rights are thought to increase efficiency by encouraging productive activity and by granting security to those who invest in economic projects. Clear property rights also facilitate both use and exchange by clarifying who owns what. They therefore create incentives to use resources efficiently and foster exchanges of property that tend to put resources in the hands of those who can put them to best use.[56] Other scholars note that the process of choosing efficient rules is a complex business,[57] and that efficiency determinations are dependent both on empirical information and on prior normative assumptions.[58]

[51] *See* Thomas Hobbes, *Leviathan* 186 (Penguin Books, 1968) (original 1651).

[52] Charlotte Perkins Gilman, *Women and Economics* 13-15 (Carl Degler ed. 1966) (original 1889).

[53] Karl Marx, *Economic and Philosophical Manuscripts*, in *The Marx-Engels Reader* 79 (Robert Tucker 2d ed. 1978).

[54] Georg Wilhelm Friedrich Hegel, *Philosophy of Right* 40-41 (T. Knox trans. 1942) (original 1821).

[55] Margaret Jane Radin, *Property and Personhood*, 34 Stan. L. Rev. 957 (1982).

[56] Richard Posner, *Economic Analysis of Law* 39-42 (8th ed. 2011). *See also* Garrett Hardin, *The Tragedy of the Commons*, reprinted in *Economic Foundations of Property Law* 4 (Bruce Ackerman ed. 1975); Harold Demsetz, *Toward a Theory of Property Rights*, 57 Am. Econ. Rev. 347 (1967); Jeremy Bentham, *Principles of the Civil Code*, chs. 3 & 19 (1802).

[57] Carol Rose, *Crystals and Mud in Property Law*, 40 Stan. L. Rev. 577 (1988); Carol Rose, *The Comedy of the Commons: Custom, Commerce, and Inherently Public Property*, 53 U. Chi. L. Rev. 711 (1986).

[58] Duncan Kennedy & Frank Michelman, *Are Property and Contract Efficient?*, 8 Hofstra L. Rev. 711 (1980); Frank Michelman, *Ethics, Economics, and the Law of Property*, 24 Nomos: Ethics, Economics, and the Law 3 (1982).

A basis of expectation

§1.4.2.5 Justified Expectations. In a famous phrase, Jeremy Bentham wrote that

> Property is nothing but a basis of expectation; the expectation of deriving certain advantages from a thing which we are said to possess, in consequence of the relation in which we stand towards it. Now this expectation, this persuasion, can only be the work of law. I cannot count upon the enjoyment of that which I regard as mine, except through the promise of the law which guarantees it to me.[59]

The idea that property law protects justified expectations is a recurring theme in the case law and the scholarly literature.[60]

Fair distribution

§1.4.2.6 Distributive Justice. Distributive considerations are central to property law.[61] "In a capitalist order," wrote Frank Michelman, "one person's proprietary value (or power) is obviously relative to other people's. A constitutional system of proprietary liberty is, therefore, incomplete without attending to the configurations of the values of various people's proprietary liberties." Thus, the "question of distribution is endemic in the very idea of a constitutional scheme of proprietary liberty."[62] In interpreting the takings clause of the Constitution, the Supreme Court has said that the key question is whether a regulation "forc[es] some people alone to bear public burdens which, in all fairness and justice, should be borne by the public as a whole."[63] This is, at base, a distributive question.[64]

[59] Jeremy Bentham, *The Theory of Legislation* 111-113 (C. K. Ogden ed. 1931).

[60] *See* Joseph William Singer, *Entitlement: The Paradoxes of Property* (2000).

[61] Gregory Alexander, *Commodity and Propriety: Competing Visions of Property in American Legal Thought, 1776-1970* (1997); Joseph William Singer, *Entitlement: The Paradoxes of Property* (2000); Jeremy Waldron, *The Right to Private Property* (1988); Jeremy Waldron, *Homelessness and the Issue of Freedom*, 39 UCLA L. Rev. 295 (1991); Duncan Kennedy, *Distributive and Paternalist Motives in Contract and Tort Law, with Special Reference to Compulsory Terms and Unequal Bargaining Power*, 41 Md. L. Rev. 563 (1982).

[62] Frank Michelman, *Liberties, Fair Values, and Constitutional Method*, 59 U. Chi. L. Rev. 91, 99 (1992).

[63] *Armstrong v. United States*, 364 U.S. 40, 49 (1960). *See also Agins v. Tiburon*, 447 U.S. 255, 260-261 (1980) (holding that the question under the takings clause is whether "the public at large, rather than a single owner, must bear the burden of an exercise of state power in the public interest").

[64] *See* Hanoch Dagan, *Takings and Distributive Justice*, 85 Va. L. Rev. 741 (1999).

PART I

THE RIGHT TO EXCLUDE AND THE RIGHT OF ACCESS

CHAPTER 2

Trespass and Public Accommodations Law

§2.1 Introduction
§2.2 Excluding or Admitting People
    §2.2.1 Private Property (Closed to the Public)
    §2.2.2 Shared Use or Possession
    §2.2.3 Public Accommodations (Open to the Public)
§2.3 Common Law Limits on the Right to Exclude
    §2.3.1 Consent
    §2.3.2 Estoppel
    §2.3.3 Necessity
    §2.3.4 Public Policy or Social Need
    §2.3.5 Prescription
§2.4 Objects
    §2.4.1 Encroaching Structures
    §2.4.2 Vegetation and Trees
    §2.4.3 Aviation
    §2.4.4 Pollution
§2.5 Animals
§2.6 Public Accommodations Laws
    §2.6.1 Title II of the *Civil Rights Act of 1964*
    §2.6.2 *Civil Rights Act of 1866*
    §2.6.3 *Americans with Disabilities Act of 1990*
    §2.6.4 State Laws
§2.7 Free Speech Rights of Access to Private Property
    §2.7.1 United States Constitution
    §2.7.2 State Constitutions
    §2.7.3 Labor Laws
§2.8 Public Trust Doctrine
§2.9 Trespass to Chattels

§2.1 Introduction

Right to exclude

Property law grants owners the power to control the resources they own. One of the main ways the law does this is by granting owners the right to exclude non-owners. Owners may also exclude physical objects that intrude on their property, such as encroaching structures, or objects sent onto their property by others, such as polluting smoke or chemicals. The converse, but close cousin, of the right to exclude is the right to include. The ability to exclude usually, but not always, goes along with the power to waive one's right to exclude by admitting non-owners to the property.

Not absolute

Although clearly a core property right, the right to exclude is not absolute, but is subject to a host of exceptions. Some exceptions apply in the case of necessity or other overriding public policies. Other exceptions allow rights of access to property possessed by another where the owner has opened her property to the public, transferred possession to a tenant, or permitted others to enter her property for specific purposes.

Extends to possessors

Because it is often expensive or difficult to prove ownership, the law presumes that the current possessor of the property has all the rights of the true owner. Possessors are those who exercise physical control over something with the intent to exercise such control (actual possession) or who, although not in actual possession, have the power and the intention to exercise control over the property, either directly or through another person (constructive possession).[1] One is in possession of land[2] if one occupies land with the intent to control it or has a legal right to immediate occupancy and no other person has occupied the land.[3] Possessors have the right to exclude everyone except the true owner (the record title holder). Possessors may even be entitled to exclude the record title holder if the title holder has transferred possessory rights to the possessor or someone else, through a lease agreement for example, or if the current possessor has occupied the property for a sufficiently long time without the owner's permission and has thereby acquired title by adverse possession.[4]

Treasured strand

The right to exclude has often been characterized as one of the central sticks in the bundle of rights comprising full ownership. The Supreme Court has noted that the "right to exclude is 'one of the most treasured' rights of property ownership."[5] It is so fundamental that courts sometimes strike down regulatory laws that force owners to accept involuntary intrusions on

[1] *People v. Ward*, 805 N.E.2d 645, 647 (Ill. App. Ct. 2004); *Popov v. Hayashi*, 2002 WL 31833731 (Cal. Super. 2002); *Prescott v. Philadelphia Housing Authority*, 555 A.2d 305, 307 n.3 (Pa. Commw. Ct. 1989); *Black's Law Dictionary* (12th ed. 2024).

[2] By "land" property lawyers mean "real property," which includes land and structures built on the land, such as buildings or fences and "fixtures" attached to the land structures. By contrast, "personal property" refers to movable items, such as cars, or intangible property, such as bank accounts, stocks, and intellectual property such as patents and copyrights.

[3] *Restatement (Second) of Torts* §157 (1965).

[4] *See* Chapter 4.

[5] *Cedar Point Nursery v. Hassid*, 594 U.S. 139, 149 (2021) (quoting *Loretto v. Teleprompter Manhattan CATV Corp.*, 458 U.S. 419, 435 (1982)). Morris Cohen wrote that "the essence of private property is always the right to exclude others." Morris Cohen, *Property and Sovereignty*, 13 Cornell L.Q. 8, 12 (1927).

their property by others as unconstitutional takings of property rights in violation of the Fifth or Fourteenth Amendment.[6]

Interests in possession and quiet enjoyment

The right to exclude protects a host of important interests, including interests in "exclusive possession" and "quiet enjoyment." The interest in "exclusive possession" refers to the ability to prevent others from using or invading the property without the owner's or possessor's consent. "Quiet enjoyment" may also refer to the interest in exclusive possession, but usually refers to other interests in enjoying the property without interference, such as protection from noise or pollution originating next door.

Human values

Protection of these interests promotes a host of human values, including privacy, autonomy, dignity, and religious and associational freedom. The ability to control property by excluding non-owners is essential to the ability to create a home, a business, a religious center, or a school. The ability to exclude or to grant access to others is a key component of the legal rights necessary to create a life for oneself and to develop relationships and to associate with others in common activities and enterprises. The right to exclude is normally, but not always, accompanied by one's own right of access to the property. It may seem obvious, but it bears noting that we know where we are going to sleep each night because we know that we not only have access to our own property, but that, when we return home at night, no one will be there before us, claiming dibs on the bed. The stability created by property rights is established, to a very large extent, by the right to exclude.

Efficiency

Protection of these vital human interests satisfies the preferences of owners and promotes their happiness and well-being. It may thereby promote social interests in improving economic efficiency or maximizing social welfare. If an owner has the power to exclude others from the property, she can use her property without interference and has incentives to do so. Allocating control powers to an owner enables individuals to develop property and to transfer it in the marketplace. The power to exclude grants non-owners incentives to contract with owners to obtain access to property that they need; conversely, the power to exclude grants owners the power to use their property for their own purposes, invest in its development, or exchange it for resources they need. Granting the "owner" the right to exclude thereby encourages both property development and exchange and helps to allocate property to those who value it.[7] On the other hand, a property rights system has costs as well as benefits. The grant of exclusive control of property to a particular owner may impede efficiency when transaction costs prevent reallocation of rights.[8]

[6] *Cedar Point Nursery v. Hassid*, 594 U.S. 139, 149 (2021); *Loretto v. Teleprompter Manhattan CATV Corp.*, 458 U.S. 419 (1982); *Kaiser Aetna v. United States*, 444 U.S. 164 (1979).

[7] Jonathan Klick & Gideon Parchomovsky, *The Value of the Right to Exclude: An Empirical Assessment*, 165 U. Pa. L. Rev. 917 (2017); Harold Demsetz, *Professor Michelman's Unnecessary and Futile Search for the Philosopher's Touchstone*, in *Nomos XXII: Ethics, Economics, and the Law*, 41, 43 (J. Roland Pennock & John W. Chapman eds. 1982); Richard A. Posner, *Economic Analysis of Law* §3.1, at 40-42 (8th ed. 2011). For an argument that the relation between property rights and economic efficiency is a complicated one, see Duncan Kennedy & Frank Michelman, *Are Property and Contract Efficient?*, 9 Hofstra L. Rev. 711 (1980).

[8] Richard A. Posner, *Economic Analysis of Law* §3.1 (9th ed. 2014).

Possession and power

The right to exclude grants the owner power over others. Often this power is legitimate and is exercised in legitimate ways. Sometimes, however, the power can be misused or can have negative social consequences. Exclusionary rights, by their nature, affect others by imposing duties on them not to enter property without the owner's permission. "[P]roperty is inescapably relational," explains Gregory Alexander. "When the state recognizes and enforces one person's property right, it simultaneously denies property rights in others. Thus, the owner's security as to particular assets comes at the expense of others being vulnerable to the owner's control over those assets. Ownership is power over persons, not merely things."[9] Exclusionary rights impose what economists call *externalities* or effects on others that may not be taken into account by the property owner in exercising her own rights. Exclusion based on race, sex, disability, age, sexual orientation, religion, or national origin may have systemic effects if they are widespread. If racial prejudice is common, for example, allowing owners to exclude on the basis of race could effectively establish a form of *apartheid* or racial caste. Avoiding such invidious systemic distortions is a prime goal of a property system dedicated to protecting human dignity and equality.

Rights of access

Because exclusion affects others, rights to exclude are not absolute. In a variety of instances, non-owners have rights to enter property possessed by others. The *Second Restatement of Torts* devotes an entire chapter to describing privileged (meaning lawful) nonpermissive entries onto property possessed by another.[10] Some of these privileges involve public interests in access, such as the power of police officers to trespass when in "hot pursuit" of suspects. Other exceptions involve the rights of neighbors who have mistakenly occupied or improved property belonging to another. Still, others involve consensual relationships in which the non-owner has exceeded the scope of the owner's permission, such as holdover tenants who stay beyond the end of the lease term. In a variety of cases, non-owners may have rights to enter or be present on property possessed by someone else in furtherance of their personal or property interests or in the service of overriding public interests in health, safety, or welfare.

Public accommodations laws

Perhaps the most significant limitation on the right to exclude concerns rights of access to property open to the public under public accommodations laws. These laws protect the rights of individuals to enter establishments open to the public without invidious discrimination. Such laws constitute substantial limits on the right to exclude. They limit exclusion rights both to protect individual rights to contract and to acquire property and to avoid the systemic effects of discrimination in the business and real estate markets. They also promote property itself by ensuring, in Justice Potter Stewart's words, "that a dollar in the hands of a Negro will

[9] Gregory S. Alexander, *Time and Property in the American Republican Legal Culture*, 66 N.Y.U. L. Rev. 273, 277 (1991). *See also* Joseph William Singer, *Entitlement: The Paradoxes of Property* (2000); C. Edward Baker, *Property and Its Relation to Constitutionally Protected Liberty*, 134 U. Pa. L. Rev. 741 (1986); Morris Cohen, *Property and Sovereignty*, 13 Cornell L.Q. 12 (1927); Laura Underkuffler-Freud, *Property: A Special Right*, 71 Notre Dame L. Rev. 1033 (1996); Frank Michelman, *Possession vs. Distribution in the Constitutional Idea of Property*, 72 Iowa L. Rev. 1319 (1987).

[10] *Restatement (Second) of Torts* ch. 8, §§167-215 (1965).

purchase the same thing as a dollar in the hands of a white man."[11] History teaches that protecting the ability to obtain access to property requires substantial limits on exclusionary rights. At the same time, hard cases may arise when interests in privacy, free association, and religion clash with interests in equal access.

§2.2 Excluding or Admitting People

Exclusionary rights differ depending on whether the property is (1) private (meaning not generally open to others); (2) shared (meaning permission has been granted to another to enter or to possess part or all of the property); or (3) open to the public (a "public accommodation").

§2.2.1 Private Property (Closed to the Public)

Right to exclude

Subject to exceptions, owners and possessors of real property that is not open to the public (such as homes) have the legal right to exclude others from their property. Conversely, owners and possessors have the power to waive their right to exclude by admitting others to their property. Permission to enter property possessed by another is called a *license* and is generally revocable at-will. A *trespass* is an unprivileged physical invasion of property possessed by another.[12] "The gist of an action of trespass is infringement on the right of possession."[13] The interest protected by trespass law is the interest in *exclusive possession* of the premises, meaning the right to occupy the property and to exclude others from entering or occupying the property. Because trespass law protects "possessors," only those with a present possessory right, such as owners or tenants, are protected by trespass law. Those with nonpossessory rights, such as holders of easements or future interests or beneficiaries of covenants, are not protected by trespass law, but by other legal rules.

License

Trespass

Standard of care

Trespass law protects possessors from physical invasion of their property. The standard of care imposed on non-owners is quite high. Any unprivileged entry constitutes a trespass even if the trespasser did not intend to commit a trespass. To show an intentional trespass, plaintiff need not prove the defendant intended to violate the plaintiff's property rights by a knowing, unlawful entry onto property possessed by another; all

No defense of mistake

[11] *Jones v. Alfred H. Mayer Co.*, 392 U.S. 409, 443 (1968).

[12] *Uthus v. Valley Mill Camp, Inc.*, 246 A.3d 1225, 1239 (Md. 2021) ("The longstanding common law tort of trespass is generally defined as an intentional or negligent intrusion upon or to the possessory interest in property of another."); *Kuntz v. Leiss*, 952 N.W.2d 35, 36 (N.D. 2020) ("This Court has defined trespass as an intentional harm, where a person intentionally and without a consensual or other privilege . . . enters land in possession of another or any part thereof or causes a thing or third person so to do."); *Exxon Mobil Corp. v. Albright*, 71 A.3d 30, 94 (Md. 2013) ("An action for trespass may lie when a defendant interferes with a plaintiff's interest in the exclusive possession of the land by entering or causing something to enter the land.").

[13] *Walker Drug Co., Inc. v. La Sal Oil Co.*, 972 P.2d 1238, 1243 (Utah 1998) (quoting *John Price Assocs. v. Utah State Conference, Bricklayers Locals*, 615 P.2d 1210 (Utah 1980)).

plaintiff need show is that defendant intended to enter the plaintiff's land.[14] It is irrelevant whether defendant knew she was entering land possessed by another. Courts have consistently ruled that mistake is not a defense to trespass; one who negligently wanders onto property possessed by another without knowing she has done so has nevertheless committed a trespass, although if no harm is done, damages may be denied or set at a nominal rate (such as one dollar).[15] If the defendant enters property accidentally (in a car crash for example), some courts will not hold the defendant liable for trespass unless she acted negligently, recklessly, or in the pursuit of an abnormally dangerous activity.[16]

Remedies

Possessors of property may sue the trespasser for damages or injunctive relief. *Nominal* damages are generally available for trespass without proof of harm to the property and *compensatory* damages are available to remedy actual harm to the property or persons on it resulting from the trespass.[17] If the property has been permanently damaged, the owner may wish to sue for *permanent damages*, which may be measured by the diminution in the fair market value of the land.[18] If the actions of the trespasser are "sufficiently malicious, oppressive, [or] rude," the court may award punitive damages.[19] In addition, because actual compensatory damages are often low to nominal, courts may award *punitive* damages as a means to deter trespasses from occurring.[20] The possessor may also be entitled to an *injunction* ordering the trespasser to cease the intrusion in the future or to remove intruding structures or agents of the trespasser.

[14] *G&D Enterprises v. Liebelt*, 949 N.W.2d 853, 858 (N.D. 2020) ("However, '[a] claim for trespass cannot exist where there is no intent or affirmative voluntary act by the alleged trespasser.' "); 9-64A *Powell on Real Property* §64A.02[1]; *see also Restatement (Second) of Torts* §158 (1965).

[15] *Johnson v. Paynesville Farmers Union Co-op. Oil Co.*, 817 N.W.2d 693, 701 (Minn. 2012) ("Actual damages are not an element of the tort of trespass. . . . In the absence of actual damages, the trespasser is liable for nominal damages."); *Smith v. Carbide & Chems. Corp.*, 226 S.W.3d 52, 55-56 (Ky. 2007) (whether trespass is intentional or negligent, owner is entitled to only nominal damages unless the land has been harmed); 9-64A *Powell on Real Property* §§64A.01[3] & 64A.05[2]; 8-68 *Thompson on Real Property, Third Thomas Edition* §68.02(b).

[16] 9-64A *Powell on Real Property* §64A.02[1]; 8-68 *Thompson on Real Property, Third Thomas Edition* §68.02(b).

[17] *Brown Jug, Inc. v. International Brotherhood of Teamsters, Chauffeurs, Warehousemen & Helpers of America, Local 959*, 688 P.2d 932, 938 (Alaska 1984) (trespass by boycott picketing); *Suggs v. Carroll*, 333 S.E.2d 510, 513-514 (N.C. Ct. App. 1985) (trespass by child who refused to move out of parent's home).

[18] *Glavin v. Eckman*, 881 N.E.2d 820, 824-825 (Mass. 2008) (discussing measures of damages for trespass).

[19] *Woodstone Townhouses, LLC v. S. Fiber Worx, LLC*, 855 S.E.2d 719, 730 (Ga. Ct. App. 2021).

[20] *See, e.g., Jacque v. Steenberg Homes, Inc.*, 563 N.W.2d 154 (Wis. 1997) ($1 in compensatory damages and $100,000 in punitive damages awarded when defendant seller of mobile home plowed path through owners' snow-covered property and used that path to deliver mobile home to third party without plaintiffs' permission). *But see Boring v. Google Inc.*, 362 Fed. Appx. 273 (3d Cir. 2010) (Google liable for $1 nominal damages and no punitive damages for entering a private road to photograph a house for Google Streetview); *Shiffman v. Empire Blue Cross & Blue Shield*, 681 N.Y.S.2d 511 (N.Y. App. Div. 1998) (no punitive damages available when reporters gain entrance to medical clinic fraudulently because the entry was not motivated by malice).

Ejectment

If a trespasser has physically occupied the property, the owner or rightful possessor may bring a suit for *ejectment* by which the court will order the wrongful possessor to leave the property.[21] In such a case, the owner may also want to sue for damages caused by the wrongful occupation and exclusion of the rightful possessor.[22] A series of individual acts of trespass may add up to a virtual dispossession of the owner but will not be held to do so if the owner has not been excluded from her property or if the trespasses appear to be the casual result of physical proximity rather than an indication of intent to control the property.[23] It is sometimes important to determine whether or not an owner is entitled to an ejectment remedy rather than merely a claim based on trespass. The statute of limitations (the time limit for bringing a lawsuit) may differ for trespass and ejectment.[24] More importantly, failure to bring a lawsuit for ejectment may result in a loss of ownership under adverse possession law if the nonpermissive occupation has lasted for a long enough period, as defined by the relevant statute of limitations.[25]

Criminal trespass

Trespass is a crime as well as a civil wrong. The common law meaning of trespass refers to the unprivileged entry onto land possessed by another. Most criminal statutes impose punishment only if one enters property knowing that one is not privileged to enter, or if one refuses to leave after being asked to do so.[26]

§2.2.2 Shared Use or Possession

Right to receive visitors

When an owner has agreed to allow others to enter her property or has agreed to transfer possession of her property to another, special rules may apply. For example, a farm owner who contracts with migrant farm workers, and grants them the right to live on her land while employed to harvest crops, may be held to have waived some of her rights to exclude non-owners from the property, such as social service workers, doctors, or lawyers.[27] Similarly, because tenants have the right to receive visitors, at least in the absence of any enforceable contractual limitations to that

[21] *MacMillan Bloedell, Inc. v. Ezell*, 475 So. 2d 493 (Alaska 1985) (action for ejectment appropriate but fails under circumstances of the case); *see also Tubwell v. FV-1, Inc.*, 387 So.3d 987 (Miss. 2024) (noting that ejectment actions allow counterclaims).

[22] *Wilson v. Diche*, 13 Cal. Rptr. 243, 244 (Dist. Ct. App. 1961) (plaintiff entitled to ejectment remedy only when the trespass is "of such a continuing nature as would establish an ouster" of the plaintiff).

[23] *Marder v. Realty Construction Co.*, 202 A.2d 175, 180 (N.J. Super. Ct. App. Div. 1964) (holding that defendant's separate acts of trespass, including parking vehicles and placing trash on plaintiff's premises, shoveling snow onto it, and trimming and landscaping the property, may add up to a virtual dispossession of the plaintiff, but that they did not in this case because defendant never prevented plaintiff from entering the disputed strip; the acts, taken together, did not indicate "to all the world that defendant was appropriating the property to its own use").

[24] *Blevins v. Mullan Contracting Co.*, 201 A.2d 348 (Md. 1964) (three-year statute of limitations for trespass claim versus twenty-year statute of limitations for ejectment remedy).

[25] *See* Chapter 4.

[26] *See, e.g.*, Ala. Code. §§13A-7-2 to 13A-7-4; Haw. Rev. Stat. §708-814; N.J. Stat. §2C:18-3; Mass. Gen. Laws ch. 266, §120.

[27] *State v. Shack*, 277 A.2d 369 (N.J. 1971).

right, the landlord may not be entitled to exclude such visitors from the property.[28] In general, the contractual relationship between the parties will determine whether the owner has retained a right to exclude non-owners or has effectively transferred the right to exclude to the tenant or possessor. However, public policy may well regulate such contracts, for example, by granting tenants the right to receive visitors no matter what the contract says.[29]

§2.2.3 *Public Accommodations (Open to the Public)*

Duty to serve

Public accommodations are facilities that are open to the public and hold themselves out as ready to serve members of the public for specific purposes. The common law has always imposed a duty to serve the public on owners or operators of public accommodations.[30] This means that they cannot refuse to serve a patron unless they have a good reason for doing so. Traditionally, public accommodations included innkeepers (motels, hotels) and common carriers (transportation facilities such as trains, ships, taxis, and bus lines) and, at least in eighteenth-century England, a host of other professions including blacksmiths, food sellers, veterinarians, surgeons, traders, and tailors.[31] In the second half of the nineteenth century in the United States, the categories of public accommodations with duties to serve the public narrowed to innkeepers and common carriers (and in some states, places of entertainment), and some current statements of the law still limit the common law duty to serve to such entities.[32] The Supreme Court of New Jersey, however, has held that the public has a right of reasonable access to

Innkeepers

Common carriers

[28] 277 A.2d at 374 (*citing Williams v. Lubbering*, 63 A. 90 (N.J. 1906)). *See also Odumn v. United States*, 227 A.3d 1099, 1105 (D.C. 2020) ("In the absence of the parties' agreement to the contrary, the tenant has the right to invite people onto the premises for any lawful purpose, and a landlord may not prevent such individuals from entering and exiting the property through its common area."); *State v. DeCoster*, 653 A.2d 891, 893 n.1 (Me. 1995) ("the right of a tenant to have visitors in their homes at reasonable times and for reasonable purposes is so fundamental it requires no statutory authority"). *But see State v. Blair*, 827 P.2d 356 (Wash. Ct. App. 1992) (holding that a public housing authority could restrict access to a public housing complex by excluding those engaging in illegal activities on the premises).

[29] *State v. Shack*, 277 A.2d 369 (N.J. 1971).

[30] *See* Joseph William Singer, *No Right to Exclude: Public Accommodations and Private Property*, 90 Nw. U. L. Rev. 1283 (1996).

[31] 3 William Blackstone, *Commentaries on the Laws of England* 165 (Professional Books Ltd., 1982 reprint) ("common taylors" and "other workmen" described as "common employments"); James Barr Ames, *The History of Assumpsit*, 2 Harv. L. Rev. 1, 4 (1888) (explaining the duties of "common callings" including surgeons); Joseph H. Beale, *The Carrier's Liability: Its History*, 11 Harv. L. Rev. 158, 163 (1897) (public accommodations included "innkeepers, victuallers, taverners, smiths, farriers, tailors, carriers, ferrymen, sherriffs, and gaolers"); Joseph William Singer, *No Right to Exclude: Public Accommodations and Private Property*, 90 Nw. U. L. Rev. 1283, 1309, 1327 (1996); Matthew O. Tobriner & Joseph R. Grodin, *The Individual and the Public Service Enterprise in the New Industrial State*, 55 Cal. L. Rev. 1247, 1249-1250 (1967) (blacksmiths, food sellers, veterinarians).

[32] *See, e.g.*, *Slade v. Caesars Entertainment Corp.*, 373 P.3d 74, 76-77 (Nev. 2016); *Brooks v. Chicago Downs Ass'n, Inc.*, 791 F.2d 512, 517-519 (7th Cir. 1986); *Uston v. Airport Casino, Inc.*, 564 F.2d 1216, 1217 (9th Cir. 1977); *Nation v. Apache Greyhound Park, Inc.*, 579 P.2d 580, 582 (Ariz. Ct. App. 1978); *see also Carrillo v. My Way Holdings, LLC*, 389 P.3d 1087 (N.M. Ct. App. 2016) (recognizing a racetrack owner's common law right to exclude but stating that the rule would be different if the owner had a de facto monopoly).

all businesses and facilities open to the public.[33] Moreover, modern public accommodation statutes, such as the 1990 *Americans with Disabilities Act*, define public accommodations broadly to include retail stores, doctor's and lawyer's offices, schools, and most commercial enterprises that sell goods and services to customers.[34]

History of the duty to serve the public

Before the Civil War, cases recognizing the duty to serve the public involved innkeepers and common carriers. Judges rested the duty to serve the public on the grounds that these establishments held themselves out as open to the public and were ready to serve anyone who sought their services.[35] Members of the public relied on this invitation and thus could not be turned away when they showed up and asked for service. This argument seemed to apply to other establishments as well, although no cases so held. The first case to hold that an establishment open to the public had the right to choose its customers in a discriminatory manner was an 1858 Massachusetts case, *McCrea v. Marsh*,[36] which adopted the rule that places of entertainment were not subject to the obligation to serve the public. In that case, a Black person had purchased a ticket to see a lecture at the Howard Athenæum but was excluded by the doorkeeper who refused to seat him. Increasingly after the Civil War, more courts limited the duty to serve the public to innkeepers and common carriers. It is often assumed that such remains the law today, although few courts have revisited the issue in recent years. One court that did revisit the issue is the Supreme Court of New Jersey, which noted the narrowing of the duty to serve in the context of cases that authorized racial discrimination and trenchantly observed that the modern rule limiting the duty to serve to innkeepers and common carriers "may have had less than dignified origins."[37]

Other facilities

Some common law precedents have extended the duty to serve to other facilities, such as hospitals,[38] while both state and federal statutes have extended the definition of a "public accommodation" to include virtually any facility that is open to, and offers goods or services to, the public.[39] Although the *Civil Rights Act of 1964* defines public accommodations to

[33] *Uston v. Resorts Int'l Hotel, Inc.*, 445 A.2d 370 (N.J. 1982). *But see Donovan v. Grand Victoria Casino & Resort, L.P.*, 934 N.E.2d 1111, 1118 (Ind. 2010) ("An owner of an Indiana business has long had the absolute right to exclude a visitor or customer, subject only to applicable civil rights laws").

[34] *See* §2.6.3.

[35] Joseph William Singer, *No Right to Exclude: Public Accommodations and Private Property*, 90 Nw. U. L. Rev. 1283, 1304-1321 (1996).

[36] 78 Mass. (12 Gray) 211 (1858). A Vermont case from 1829, *Watrous v. Steel*, 4 Vt. 629 (1829), noted that the "occupant of any house, store, or other building, has a legal right to control it, and to admit whom he pleases to enter and remain there." *Id.* at 631-632. Taken out of context, this might suggest an absolute right to exclude. Of course, taken literally, the reference to "any other building" would immunize innkeepers from the duty to serve the public, a proposition that was not accepted anywhere in the United States in the nineteenth century. Moreover, the plaintiff was thrown out of the bookstore in *Watrous* after he got into an argument with the proprietor and the ruling in *Watrous* affirms the right of a business owner to "expel any one from the room or building who abuses the privilege which has been given him." *Id.* This rule, of course, applies to public accommodations, which have the power to exclude rowdy or disruptive patrons.

[37] *Uston v. Resorts Int'l Hotel, Inc.*, 445 A.2d 370, 374 n.4 (N.J. 1982).

[38] *Doe v. Bridgeton Hosp. Ass'n, Inc.*, 366 A.2d 641 (N.J. 1976).

[39] *See, e.g.*, Minn. Stat. §363A.03(34).

include only restaurants, innkeepers, places of entertainment, and gas stations,[40] the *Americans with Disabilities Act of 1990*[41] defines the term "public accommodation" to include educational institutions, doctors' and lawyers' offices, restaurants, retail stores of all kinds, barber shops, and funeral parlors.[42] This expansion of the concept of public accommodation and changes in views about the rights of the public to obtain access to such facilities led the Supreme Court of New Jersey to rule in 1982 that "when property owners open their premises to the general public in the pursuit of their own property interests, they have no right to exclude people unreasonably. On the contrary, they have a duty not to act in an arbitrary or discriminatory manner toward persons who come on their premises."[43] This duty extends "to all property owners who open their premises to the public. Property owners have no legitimate interest in unreasonably excluding particular members of the public when they open their premises for public use."[44]

▶ HARD CASE

▷ DO RETAIL STORES HAVE A COMMON LAW DUTY TO SERVE THE PUBLIC?

Arguments for limiting the common law duty

Competition

Necessity

Profit motive

Cases that limit the duty to serve the public to innkeepers and common carriers argue that the policies upon which their duties historically rested do not extend to other businesses, such as retail stores.[45] It has been argued that innkeepers and common carriers have special duties because they are more likely to be monopolies and thus be insulated from competition; exclusion may leave individuals with no alternative place to go. In addition, access to transportation and overnight accommodation are necessities for the traveler who has no place else to stay.[46] It has been argued that the profit motive in competitive markets is likely to induce businesses to exclude individuals only if they have a good reason to do so, and that recognition of a right of reasonable access would impose unjustified costs on businesses, by making them prove in court that their reasons for exclusion were valid.[47] Businesses do not want to have to worry about being subject to a lawsuit anytime they exclude a patron. Fear of having to defend their decisions to a jury may inhibit them from excluding disruptive patrons even when they have good reasons to do so.

Arguments for extending the common law duty to serve to all places open to the public

The argument in favoring extending the duty to serve to all businesses open to the public is, first, there is no good reason to distinguish innkeepers and common carriers from other public accommodations, and, second,

[40] Common carriers are required to serve the public pursuant to the *Interstate Commerce Act*, 49 U.S.C. §10741(b) (rail carriers).
[41] 42 U.S.C. §§12101 to 12213.
[42] 42 U.S.C. §12181(7).
[43] *Uston v. Resorts Int'l Hotel, Inc.*, 445 A.2d 370, 375 (N.J. 1982).
[44] *Id.* at 375.
[45] *Uston v. Airport Casino, Inc.*, 564 F.2d 1216, 1217 (9th Cir. 1977).
[46] Bruce Wyman, *The Law of Public Callings as a Solution of the Trust Problem*, 17 Harv. L. Rev. 156 (1904). *See* Joseph William Singer, *No Right to Exclude: Public Accommodations and Private Property*, 90 Nw. U. L. Rev. 1283, 1404 (1996).
[47] *Brooks v. Chicago Downs Ass'n, Inc.*, 791 F.2d 512, 517-519 (7th Cir. 1986).

a right of reasonable access for all places of public accommodation both accords with common expectations today and is just. The traditional reasons for treating innkeepers and common carriers differently from other public accommodations are not persuasive today, if they ever were. There is no reason to think today that competition is more likely to be absent in the case of inns or common carriers than in the case of other businesses; indeed, competition in the hotel business and the airline business appears quite healthy. Although competition may sometimes be limited in the case of bus lines or subways or taxicabs, the existence of alternative means of transportation injects a fair amount of market pressure on such carriers. Moreover, businesses other than innkeepers and common carriers may be local monopolies (such as the only grocery store in a small town) and yet be exempt from the duty to serve the public. Nor do travel accommodations appear to be more of a necessity than other staples, such as food or medical care, which might obviously be needed by travelers as well as locals.

No valid distinction between inns and common carriers v. other places of public accommodation

The presence of extensive state and federal public accommodations legislation already requires businesses to serve the public without unjust discrimination on a number of grounds, such as race and religion. Such statutes make businesses vulnerable to claims of wrongful exclusion,[48] and it is probable that existing businesses act carefully before excluding particular customers because of fear of liability under such statutes.[49] Thus, requiring businesses to serve the public would not impose a new duty on them; it will simply grant a remedy for types of wrongful exclusions not covered by existing statutes. Such a remedy is arguably necessary, because the profit motive may actually induce businesses to exclude customers unreasonably. If most customers want certain types of people excluded, such as teenagers or people experiencing homelessness, then market pressures may induce property owners to exclude those individuals. Individuals may be wrongfully excluded or maltreated because of invidious prejudices on the part of business owners or their customers. Granting businesses the absolute right to exclude customers at-will may deny important interests in equality, including equal opportunity to acquire property and to participate in the market system. The right to exclude protects interests in privacy and autonomy, but businesses open to the public do not have strong privacy interests; moreover, their autonomy is arguably adequately protected by their retained rights to exclude customers when they have good, rather than invidious, reasons for excluding a customer. Public accommodations always had the right to exclude patrons who were rowdy or disruptive.[50] The common law duty to serve the public grants patrons only a right of

Balance of interests in favor of access

[48] Those laws include the *Civil Rights Act of 1866*, 42 U.S.C. §§1981 & 1982 (race) and the *Americans with Disabilities Act of 1990*, 42 U.S.C. §§12101 to 12213 (disability).

[49] Of course, this does not mean that exclusionary practices do not persist. For an account of repeated experiences with retail racism, see Nathalie Fanfan, *Shopping While Black: A Boston Stylist on Being Followed, Ignored, and Discredited*, Boston Globe, July 13, 2020. A sensational case of racial discrimination by a Denny's Restaurant resulted in a $54 million judgment. Stephen Labaton, *Denny's Restaurants to Pay $54 Million in Race Bias Suits*, N.Y. Times, May 25, 1994, at A1.

[50] *Uston v. Resorts Int'l Hotel, Inc.*, 445 A.2d 370, 375 (N.J. 1982).

reasonable access, not an absolute right to enter the property. It thus better protects the interests of *both* businesses and the public.

Relation to federal law

Although courts uniformly hold that the *Civil Rights Act of 1866*[51] mandates that public accommodations, such as retail stores, allow customers entrance without regard to race,[52] most courts have held that this statute does not require stores to refrain from discriminatory surveillance practices, such as following Black customers around the store as they shop.[53] If federal law does not provide a remedy for discriminatory surveillance, then state law is the only alternative source of a norm prohibiting stores from discriminating on the basis of race. However, a number of states do not have state public accommodations laws that regulate retail stores. It would be remarkable indeed if the courts in those jurisdictions would hold that retail stores have a common law right to exclude or maltreat customers on the basis of race.[54] Although it has traditionally been argued that the common law places duties to serve the public on innkeepers and common carriers but no other businesses (in the absence of a civil rights act), it is more likely that a court that faced the absence of an applicable civil rights act would require a public accommodation, such as a retail store, to refrain from wrongful discrimination, at least on the basis of race. ◀

Common law duty to refrain from unjust discrimination

§2.3 Common Law Limits on the Right to Exclude

§2.3.1 Consent

Explicit and implied consent

Entry onto property possessed by another is privileged if it is consensual or permissive.[55] One who enters property with the permission of the owner is a *licensee*. Consent may be explicit, as in the case of a lease or a dinner invitation, or it may be implicit, as in the case of a public accommodation that holds itself out as ready to serve the public. One who enters a store is not committing a trespass because the entry is presumptively privileged; the very act of opening a store conveys an implied invitation to the public to enter the premises. However, even if one enters property with permission

[51] 42 U.S.C. §§1981, 1982. *See* §2.6.2.

[52] *Hampton v. Dillard Dep't Stores, Inc.*, 247 F.3d 1091 (10th Cir. 2001); *Perry v. Command Performance*, 913 F.2d 99 (3d Cir. 1990); *Hall v. Pennsylvania State Police*, 570 F.2d 86 (3d Cir. 1978); *Henderson v. Jewel Food Stores, Inc.*, 1996 WL 617165 (N.D. Ill. 1996); *Shen v. A&P Food Stores*, 1995 WL 728416 (E.D.N.Y. 1995).

[53] *Gregory v. Dillard's Inc.*, 565 F.3d 464 (8th Cir. 2009); *Ackerman v. Food-4-Less*, 1998 WL 316084 (E.D. Pa. 1998) (§1981 claim stated when store patron was watched, followed, and detained by security guard if patron was prevented from purchasing items but no claim based merely on the surveillance and detention). For a critique of those cases, see Joseph William Singer, *The Anti-Apartheid Principle in American Property Law*, 1 Ala. C.R.-C.L. L. Rev. 83 (2011); *see also* Suja A. Thomas, *The Customer Caste: Lawful Discrimination by Public Businesses*, 109 Cal. L. Rev. 141 (2021).

[54] *Cf.* Shaun L. Gabbidon & George E. Higgins, *Shopping While Black: Consumer Racial Profiling in America* 63 (2020) ("A startling 75% of Black males believe they have been victims of consumer racial profiling," notably being closely watched and followed.).

[55] *Salisbury Livestock Co. v. Colorado Century Credit Union*, 793 P.2d 470, 475 (Wyo. 1990); 9-64A *Powell on Real Property* §64A.02[2].

as a licensee, refusal to leave after being asked to do so may constitute a trespass unless the property owner has violated her duty to serve the public by excluding the patron unreasonably.[56] A trespass may also occur if one exceeds the scope of the invitation by entering parts of the premises that were not intended to be open to the licensee.

▷ INVESTIGATIVE JOURNALISM **HARD CASE ◀**

Food Lion v. Capital Cities/ABC

When investigative journalists gain entrance to private property on false pretenses, have they committed a trespass? In the case of *Food Lion v. Capital Cities/ABC, Inc.*,[57] a producer of the television show *Primetime Live* used a false name and background for herself and several others to get jobs at plaintiff Food Lion's supermarket. They then used hidden cameras and tape recorders to record Food Lion employees without their consent. The false background included letters of recommendation written by persons who had never in fact hired the producer for the jobs described in the letters. These letters were read and relied upon by the plaintiff in hiring the producer. ABC aired part of the video, which appeared to show Food Lion employees involved in unsanitary food-handling procedures. Plaintiff Food Lion sued, claiming damages for trespass and fraud.

Consent fraudulently obtained

The district court found that a trespass had occurred for two distinct reasons. First, defendants obtained consent to enter the property by lying about who they were and what their purposes were. Because consent to enter the property had been fraudulently obtained, the court found that defendants had engaged in "wrongful conduct which could negate any consent to enter given by Food Lion."[58] Although Food Lion consented to the entry, that consent was not effective because it was induced by fraud.[59] It is possible that Food Lion would not have given consent had the fraud not occurred. Second, the court found that a trespass had occurred because the defendant's activity on the property exceeded the scope of the invitation. Food Lion had hired employees to work in the store, not to videotape the activities there for publication on national television. "Under North Carolina law," wrote Judge Tilley, "consent to enter upon real property can be negated by a subsequent wrongful act in excess or in abuse of the

Exceeded scope of permission

[56] *Commonwealth v. Lapon*, 554 N.E.2d 1225 (Mass. App. Ct. 1990) (patron convicted of criminal trespass when he refused to leave after store revoked its implied invitation to enter); *Alexis v. McDonald's Restaurants of Massachusetts, Inc.*, 67 F.3d 341, 350 (1st Cir. 1995) (implied license to enter restaurant can be revoked).

[57] 887 F. Supp. 811 (M.D.N.C. 1995), *aff'd in part and rev'd in part*, 194 F.3d 505 (4th Cir. 1999).

[58] 887 F. Supp. at 820.

[59] *Accord Med. Lab. Mgmt. Consultants v. ABC, Inc.*, 30 F. Supp. 2d 1182, 1201-1202 (D. Ariz. 1998) (quoting *Restatement (Second) of Torts* §892B(2) (1977)) ("if the plaintiff is induced to consent by a substantial mistake concerning the nature of the invasion of his interests or the extent of harm to be expected from it and the mistake is known to the other or is induced by the other's misrepresentation, the consent is not effective"); *Shiffman v. Empire Blue Cross & Blue Shield*, 681 N.Y.S.2d 511, 512 (App. Div. 1998) ("implied consent to enter the premises were legally insufficient since consent obtained by misrepresentation or fraud is invalid").

authority to enter."[60] The court awarded plaintiff $1,400 in compensatory damages and $5.5 million in punitive damages.[61]

Judgment reversed

On appeal, the Fourth Circuit reversed in part, agreeing to the second but not the first trespass holding. The court held that misrepresentations designed to induce consent did not render the consent invalid.[62] Defendant may have lied to gain entry, but plaintiff did voluntarily consent to the entry nevertheless. However, the court did find a trespass when defendant secretly videotaped activities inside the premises because this exceeded the scope of the permission to enter. However, the court determined that there were no actual damages resulting from the trespass and the act of fraud.[63] All the real harm to Food Lion came from the publication of Food Lion's practices on television, and the First Amendment's free speech guarantee protects the dissemination of truthful information, no matter how it is obtained. The court therefore overturned the punitive damages judgment entirely and awarded plaintiff only $1 in damages for the trespass and $1 for the fraud claim.

Desnick v. ABC

In contrast, in *Desnick v. ABC, Inc.*,[64] the Seventh Circuit, in an opinion by Judge Posner, denied a trespass claim entirely when *Primetime Live* sent seven testers to plaintiff's ophthalmic office to see surgeons who specialized in cataract surgery and were reputed to recommend unnecessary surgery. Testers used hidden cameras and tapes to record conversations. *Primetime Live* then sent reporters to interview the doctors and do a report on the center. The *Primetime Live* broadcast suggested that the clinic performed unnecessary surgery. When plaintiff sued for defamation and trespass, the court ruled for the defendants on the trespass claim, holding that the entry was consensual and thus not a trespass. Judge Posner conceded that consent is fictitious when it is "procured by a misrepresentation or a misleading omission."[65] However, he noted that fraudulently obtained consent may nonetheless be legally effective. People often conceal their true purposes when entering property possessed by others. Restaurant critics do not reveal their purposes when they order meals and people browse in shops when they have no intention of buying. Judge Posner explained,

May be no trespass despite fraudulently obtained consent

[60] 887 F. Supp. at 820. *Accord Med. Lab. Mgmt. Consultants v. ABC, Inc.*, 30 F. Supp. 2d 1182 (D. Ariz. 1998) (trespass occurred when individual pretending to be patient secretly videotaped inside medical office); *Special Force Ministries v. WCCO Television*, 584 N.W.2d 789 (Minn. Ct. App. 1998) (trespass exists when television station employee exceeded the scope of the owner's consent to enter by secretly videotaping activities at facility).

[61] Similar claims of trespass were upheld in *Federal Beef Processors, Inc. v. CBS Inc.*, 1994 WL 408366 (D.S.D. 1994); *Shiffman v. Empire Blue Cross & Blue Shield*, 681 N.Y.S.2d 511 (App. Div. 1998).

[62] *Food Lion, Inc. v. Capital Cities/ABC, Inc.*, 194 F.3d 505 (4th Cir. 1999); *cf.* Roseanna Sommers, *Commonsense Consent*, 129 Yale L.J. 2232 (2020) (noting that experimental data suggests most people perceive consent procured by fraud as valid).

[63] *Accord Med. Lab. Mgmt. Consultants v. ABC, Inc.*, 30 F. Supp. 2d 1182 (D. Ariz. 1998) (similarly finding a trespass but no causal connection between the videotaping and the damages complained of). *Compare Shiffman v. Empire Blue Cross & Blue Shield*, 681 N.Y.S.2d 511 (App. Div. 1998) (neither consent nor implied consent were viable defenses to trespass claim when reporters gained admission to an office by lying about who they were and what their purposes were there).

[64] 44 F.3d 1345 (7th Cir. 1995).

[65] *Id.* at 1351.

"The fact is that consent to an entry is often given legal effect even though the entrant has intentions that if known to the owner of the property would cause him for perfectly understandable and generally ethical or at least lawful reasons to revoke his consent."[66] On the other hand, some fraudulently obtained entries do constitute trespasses.

> If a homeowner opens his door to a purported meter reader who is in fact nothing of the sort—just a busybody curious about the interior of the home—the homeowner's consent to his entry is not a defense to a suit for trespass. And likewise, if a competitor gained entry to a business firm's premises posing as a customer but in fact hoping to steal the firm's trade secrets.[67]

The problem for Judge Posner is how to distinguish the two classes of cases. The real distinctions rest on the specific interest owners have in excluding others from their property. For example, "[t]he homeowner victimized by the phony meter reader does not want strangers in his house unless they have authorized service functions."[68]

Interests protected by trespass law

In ruling that no trespass claim was available in the *Desnick* case, Judge Posner argued that "[t]here was no invasion in the present case of any of the specific interests that the tort of trespass seeks to protect."[69] The office was "open to anyone expressing a desire for ophthalmic services."[70] Moreover, the physicians were videotaped while engaged in "professional, not personal communications." For both these reasons, he concluded that there was no invasion of privacy. Nor was there any disruption of the office activities. Moreover,

> [h]ad the testers been undercover FBI agents, there would have been no violation of the Fourth Amendment, because there would have been no invasion of a legally protected interest in property or privacy. "Testers" who pose as prospective home buyers in order to gather evidence of housing discrimination are not trespassers even if they are private persons not acting under color of law.[71]

Although the owner would not have allowed them in had it known their true purposes, it did consent to their entry. The entry was therefore "not invasive in the sense of infringing the kind of interest of the plaintiffs that the law of trespass protects; it was not an interference with the ownership or possession of land."[72] ◀

[66] *Id. Accord American Transmission, Inc. v. Channel 7 of Detroit, Inc.*, 609 N.W.2d 607 (Mich. Ct. App. 2000).
[67] 44 F.3d at 1351.
[68] *Id.*
[69] *Id.*
[70] *Id.*
[71] *Id.*
[72] *Id.* State statutes have sought to prohibit fraudulent entrance for investigations, but courts have found that such statutes violate First Amendment protections for speech. *See, e.g., People for the Ethical Treatment of Animals, Inc. v. North*, 60 F.4th 815 (4th Cir. 2023) (reviewing the North Carolina's Property Protection Act's punishment for "[a]ny person who intentionally gains access to the nonpublic areas of another's premises and engages in an act that exceeds the person's authority to enter").

§2.3.2 Estoppel

Permission or acquiescence and subsequent reliance

"A trespass plaintiff is estopped from pressing the charge if to grant relief would be inequitable under the circumstances."[73] For example, an owner who gives permission to enter her land and thereby induces the licensee to invest substantially in reasonable reliance on the license will not be allowed to revoke the license if revocation would be unjust under the circumstances. The doctrine of estoppel will convert the license — ordinarily revocable at-will — into a permanent, nonrevocable easement.[74] Similarly, if an owner fails to intervene to stop a non-owner from entering the owner's land, the owner may create the impression that the entry is permissive even if the owner intends not to grant permission. Once the owner acquiesces in such nonpermissive entries, the owner may be estopped from denying that permission was granted, and substantial reliance on that implied permission may render the license irrevocable.[75]

Easement by estoppel

§2.3.3 Necessity

Save lives or property

Within limits, non-owners are entitled to enter property possessed by another to save either lives or property or otherwise avert a serious harm. Defendants generally are required to show that "(1) they were faced with a choice of evils and chose the lesser evil; (2) they acted to prevent imminent harm; (3) they reasonably anticipated a direct causal relationship between their conduct and the harm to be averted; and (4) they had no legal alternatives to violating the law."[76] Entry may be privileged, for example, to stop the spread of a fire.[77] However, the privilege may be incomplete; an intruder who causes damage to the property may be responsible for paying to remedy the harm, although not be liable for damages for trespass.[78]

Defense to criminal trespass

Protesters sometimes claim necessity as a defense to criminal trespass charges when they believe the property owner is engaged in activity that may result in harm to individuals or the community at large. Examples include protesters at nuclear power facilities, military bases, abortion providers, railroads, and the Internal Revenue Service.[79] The defense is

[73] 8-68 *Thompson on Real Property, Third Thomas Edition* §68.06(b)(2)(iv).

[74] *Steel Creek Development Co. v. Smith*, 268 S.E.2d 205 (N.C. 1980). Easement by estoppel is covered more fully in §5.3.1.

[75] 8-68 *Thompson on Real Property, Third Thomas Edition* §68.06(b)(2)(iv).

[76] *United States v. Schoon*, 971 F.2d 193, 195 (9th Cir. 1991).

[77] *American Law of Property* §28.10 (A. James Casner ed. 1952); W. Page Keeton, Dan B. Dobbs, Robert E. Keeton & David G. Owen, *Prosser and Keeton on the Law of Torts* §24, at 147-148 (5th ed. 1984).

[78] *Vincent v. Lake Erie Transportation Co.*, 124 N.W. 221 (Minn. 1910); *United States v. Gardner*, 903 F. Supp. 1394 (D. Nev. 1995); 8-68 *Thompson on Real Property, Third Thomas Edition* §68.06(b)(2)(v); *Restatement (Second) of Torts* §197 (1965).

[79] *State v. Spokane County Dist. Ct.*, 491 P.3d 119, 124-127 (Wash. 2021) (climate activist protesting rail line used to transport oil entitled to jury determination of necessity defense); *United States v. Schoon*, 971 F.2d 193, 195 (9th Cir. 1991) (defense of necessity not available to trespassers at Internal Revenue Service offices engaged in protest of spending U.S. tax dollars to aid a repressive regime in El Salvador); *N.O.W. v. Operation Rescue*, 747 F. Supp. 760 (D.D.C. 1990), *aff'd in part and remanded in part on other grounds*, 37 F.3d 646 (D.C. Cir. 1997) (defense of necessity not available in this case because the U.S. Constitution protects the right to obtain an abortion).

ordinarily denied because the perceived harm is not imminent (such as the threat of nuclear war),[80] because the trespass is unlikely to prevent the harm even if the harm is likely to occur,[81] or because the threatened harm would result from statutorily authorized activity, as in the case of nuclear power,[82] or is itself the result of a constitutionally protected activity, as was the case, until recently, for access to abortion.[83]

▷ DO HOMELESS PERSONS HAVE A RIGHT TO TRESPASS IN WINTER? **HARD CASE ◀**

Homelessness

In *Commonwealth v. Magadini*,[84] the Supreme Judicial Court of Massachusetts ruled that a homeless man who repeatedly entered private property in wintertime to escape the cold was entitled to try to convince the jury that necessity justified the entries. David Magadini was homeless and was arrested and convicted seven times for sleeping in the lobby or hallway of commercial buildings that included retail establishments, offices, and apartments. Magadini was a lifelong resident of Great Barrington, Massachusetts, had no home, and had been barred in the past from staying at a homeless shelter in the town. The court held that necessity justifies trespass if (1) the trespasser faces a "clear and imminent danger"; (2) the trespasser has a reasonable expectation that the entry on property will abate the danger; (3) the trespasser has no "legal alternative which will be effective in abating the danger"; and (4) the "Legislature has not acted to preclude the defense by a clear and deliberate choice regarding the values at issue."[85] The court had little trouble determining that the wintry weather conditions on the dates of the offenses presented a clear and imminent danger. It found that Magadini's inability to find housing in Great Barrington that he could afford, along with his prior banishment from the local homeless shelter, were sufficient to find that he had no legally available alternatives on the nights in question.[86] ◀

[80] *Commonwealth v. Schuchardt*, 557 N.E.2d 1380, 1382 (Mass. 1990) (threat of nuclear war not imminent); *State v. Prince*, 595 N.E.2d 376, 380 (Ohio Ct. App. 1991) (threat of CIA violations of international law not imminent); *State v. Warshow*, 410 A.2d 1000 (Vt. 1979) (threat of nuclear accident at power plant not imminent).

[81] *State v. Cram*, 600 A.2d 733 (Vt. 1991) (trespasser could not reasonably believe his actions would result in delay of shipping of guns to El Salvador).

[82] *People v. Hubbard*, 320 N.W.2d 294 (Mich. Ct. App. 1982); *State v. Warshow*, 410 A.2d 1000 (Vt. 1979).

[83] *State v. Roeder*, 336 P.3d 831, 843-845 (Kan. 2014) (necessity defense precluded when the harm a protestor is trying to prevent is a legal abortion); *Hill v. State*, 688 So. 2d 901 (Fla. 1996); *City of Wichita v. Tilson*, 855 P.2d 911, 916 (Kan. 1993); *MacMillan v. City of Jackson*, 701 So. 2d 1105 (Miss. 1997) (no right to interfere with constitutionally protected rights of others).

[84] 52 N.E.3d 1041 (Mass. 2016).

[85] *Id.* at 1047.

[86] In *Martin v. City of Boise*, 920 F.3d 584 (9th Cir. 2019), the Ninth Circuit held that the Eighth Amendment's prohibition on cruel and unusual punishment barred a city from prosecuting someone for sleeping outside on public property when that person has no home or other available shelter. However, the Supreme Court reversed that decision in *City of Grants Pass v. Johnson*, 603 U.S. 520 (2024). For context, see Sara K. Rankin, *Hiding Homelessness: The Transcarceration of Homelessness*, 109 Cal. L. Rev. 559 (2021).

§2.3.4 *Public Policy or Social Need*

Residual category

This is a catch-all category for intrusions that are privileged because significant public policies override private interests in exclusive possession. "Many privileges to intrude upon private land exist as a balance between the rights of the occupant to freedom from intrusion and the needs of society to impose reasonable burdens upon such land for the general welfare."[87] First, intrusions onto property are privileged if they are necessary for the exercise of legitimate public authority.[88] Examples include lawful searches of property or entries by police officers in hot pursuit of fleeing suspects. Second, intrusions are privileged if the owner has transferred possession of the property to a tenant and the intrusions are a result of tenant's exercise of her own possessory rights. The tenant's right to receive visitors, regardless of what the written lease agreement may say, is an example.[89] Third, intrusions on or over property are privileged if they involve retained public rights that were never given over to private ownership, such as public rights of access to beaches, navigable waters or the airways, or retained native Hawaiian or American Indian fishing, hunting, or gathering rights under either customary law or reserved treaty rights.[90] Fourth, intrusions may be privileged in other cases of significant, justifiable social need.[91] An often-cited example is *State v. Shack*,[92] which authorized access to migrant farm workers by lawyers and doctors providing services funded by the federal government.

Public authority

Rights of occupants

Retained public rights

Social need

▶ HARD CASE ▷ FRAUDULENT CONSENT AND PUBLIC POLICY

The investigative journalism cases discussed above[93] raise the question of whether access to property should be privileged even if is obtained fraudulently.[94] In *Desnick v. ABC, Inc.*,[95] for example, television reporters for *Primetime Live* entered a medical office pretending to be patients and secretly videotaped conversations with the doctors for an episode, accusing the doctors of engaging in unnecessary cataract surgery. Understanding whether fraud rendered the invasion non-consensual or whether it exceeded the scope of the invitation is tied to the question of whether such trespasses should be privileged because of public policy interests in protecting the public through investigative journalism. Judge Posner analogized the reporters to discrimination testers who pretend to

[87] *American Law of Property* §28.10 (A. James Casner ed. 1952).
[88] *Restatement (Second) of Torts* §§202, 204-211 (1965).
[89] *State v. Shack*, 277 A.2d 369 (N.J. 1971).
[90] *See State v. Hanapi*, 970 P.2d 485 (Haw. 1998) (defendant failed in this case to demonstrate constitutionally protected native Hawaiian right to the subject property).
[91] Dale A. Whitman et al., *The Law of Property* §7.1, at 329 (4th ed. 2019); *American Law of Property* §28.10 (A. James Casner ed. 1952).
[92] 277 A.2d 369 (N.J. 1971).
[93] *See* §2.3.1.
[94] *Cf.* Roseanna Sommers, *Commonsense Consent*, 129 Yale L.J. 2232 (2020) (noting that experimental data suggests that most people perceive consent procured by fraud as valid).
[95] 44 F.3d 1345 (7th Cir. 1995).

be interested in renting an apartment or purchasing a home to determine whether the landlord or seller is engaging in racial discrimination. The courts have long found that testing is an appropriate way to prove intentional discrimination and even have held that testers themselves have a claim against a business that denied services for discriminatory reasons.[96] The question is whether the interests in preventing food poisoning[97] and unnecessary surgery are sufficiently important to override the businesses' interests in exclusive possession and privacy. By analogizing investigative reporters to housing discrimination testers, Judge Posner suggested that the answer might be yes. However, some other courts have disagreed with Posner's analysis, holding that a trespass occurs when a television network gains entry to a medical office by posing as a patient.[98] Their rulings suggest that property owners' interests in being free from snooping journalists outweigh the public interest in promoting such intrusions on private property. ◀

§2.3.5 *Prescription*

Adverse possession

Prescriptive easements

If a trespasser has possessed property openly, for a sufficiently long period without the owner's permission, she may not only have a defense to a trespass claim but may also be effectively granted title to the property through application of the doctrine of adverse possession. This topic is treated in Chapter 4. Use of another's property for a limited purpose, such as using a road, may similarly ripen into a permanent right called an easement, by application of the doctrine of easement by prescription. This topic is covered in Chapter 5.[99]

§2.4 Objects

§2.4.1 *Encroaching Structures*

Above, on, or below ground

Any structure that intrudes onto neighboring property constitutes a trespass whether it occurs beneath the ground, on the surface, or in the air. Thus, a foundation of a house or a well that slants under the ground to the neighbor's land, a septic system that intrudes onto adjacent property, a fence or building built over the line, an overhanging porch or bay window, or other objects such as wires that cross the air space over neighboring land, all constitute trespasses if built without permission.[100]

[96] *Havens Realty Corp. v. Coleman*, 455 U.S. 363, 376 (1982).

[97] *See Food Lion v. Capital Cities/ABC, Inc.*, 887 F. Supp. 811 (M.D.N.C. 1995), *aff'd in part and rev'd in part*, 194 F.3d 505 (4th Cir. 1999).

[98] *Shiffman v. Empire Blue Cross & Blue Shield*, 681 N.Y.S.2d 511 (App. Div. 1998). *See also Med. Lab. Mgmt. Consultants v. ABC, Inc.*, 30 F. Supp. 2d 1182 (D. Ariz. 1998) (holding that investigative journalists had committed trespass but imposing only nominal damages).

[99] *See* §5.5.

[100] *See Frisk v. Thomas*, 553 P.3d 350 (Mont. 2024) (fencing and a gate); *Goulding v. Cook*, 661 N.E.2d 1322 (Mass. 1996) (septic tank); *Newmark v. Vogelgesang*, 915 S.W.2d 337 (Mo. Ct. App. 1996) (gas station); 8-68 *Thompson on Real Property, Third Thomas Edition* §68.03.

▶ HARD CASE ▷ REMEDIES FOR ENCROACHING STRUCTURES

Removal

Relative hardship

When someone builds a structure that intrudes onto neighboring property, courts may order the removal of the structure. This is often done in the case of a fence or wall,[101] driveway,[102] or overhanging porch or fire escape,[103] but some courts go so far as to order the removal of an encroaching building.[104] Most courts, however, adopt the *relative hardship* doctrine and deny injunctive relief if the expenditure has been substantial and the invasion minimal, at least when the encroachment is innocent.[105]

Some courts will even deny relief when the invasion is substantial, instead ordering the parties to undergo a forced sale of the land on which the encroaching structure sits to the builder.[106] If the encroachment is innocent, one might conclude that the true owner of the land was negligent in allowing the construction to occur and thus partially the cause of the problem. In such cases, when the construction is substantial, removal of the structure may seem not only unfair but a waste of resources. On the other hand, one might argue that owners have no duty to police their own property to prevent such encroachments, and that the builder should bear the burden of determining whether she is building on her neighbor's land. When the encroachment is not innocent but intentional, however, the courts are much more likely to order removal, even if the investment was substantial and the encroachment minimal.[107]

Unjust enrichment v. forced sale

When the court refuses to order removal of the encroaching structure, it will either oversee a *forced sale* of the land from the record title holder to the builder of the encroaching structure or it will allow the owner of the land to keep the structure and use it herself.[108] In the latter case, the court may order a *forced purchase* of the structure by the owner of the land, ordering the landowner to compensate the builder for the value of the structure in order to avoid "unjust enrichment."[109] ◀

§2.4.2 Vegetation and Trees

Right to remove encroaching vegetation

Landowners have the legal right to engage in self-help to remove vegetation that intrudes onto their property, including overhanging tree branches,

[101] *Leffingwell v. Glendenning*, 238 S.W.2d 942 (Ark. 1951).
[102] *Storey v. Patterson*, 437 So. 2d 491 (Ala. 1983).
[103] *Geragosian v. Union Realty Co.*, 193 N.E. 726 (Mass. 1935).
[104] *Warsaw v. Chicago Metallic Ceilings, Inc.*, 676 P.2d 584 (Cal. 1984) (interference with easement); *Bishop v. Reinhold*, 311 S.E.2d 298 (N.C. Ct. App. 1984); *Rose Nulman Park Found. ex rel. Nulman v. Four Twenty Corp.*, 93 A.3d 25 (R.I. 2014).
[105] *Urban Site Venture II Limited Partnership v. Levering Assocs. Limited Partnership*, 665 A.2d 1062 (Md. 1995); *Williams v. South & South Rentals, Inc.*, 346 S.E.2d 665 (N.C. Ct. App. 1986); *Proctor v. Huntington*, 238 P.3d 1117 (Wash. 2010). The court would ordinarily order the title to the land be transferred to the trespasser who built the encroaching structure. However, if circumstances warrant it, the court could order the title to the encroaching structure be transferred to the owner of the land on which it sits.
[106] *Somerville v. Jacobs*, 170 S.E.2d 805 (W. Va. 1969).
[107] *Warsaw v. Chicago Metallic Ceilings, Inc.*, 676 P.2d 584 (Cal. 1984); *Goulding v. Cook*, 661 N.E.2d 1322 (Mass. 1996) (septic tank built when builder knew land ownership was in dispute).
[108] *See Banner v. United States*, 238 F.3d 1348 (Fed. Cir. 2001) (Seneca Nation owns houses built by lessees when their 99-year leases terminated).
[109] *Somerville v. Jacobs*, 170 S.E.2d 805 (W. Va. 1969).

invading shrubs or hedges, and even roots, especially if they threaten the foundation of one's house.[110] Owners have the right to trim encroaching branches or hedges to the boundary line even when the tree or plant is right on the boundary line.[111] However, they are not entitled to cut into the trunk of the tree or remove the tree or plant entirely if it is on the boundary, and may not injure it so severely that it dies, unless it is threatening structures on the land.[112] When a tree's branches or roots grow onto neighboring property, the owner of the tree will ordinarily not be held liable for trespass, while the owner of the land over which the branches hang has the right to use self-help to cut back the overhanging branches.[113] At the same time, the courts may hold that the owner of the tree also owns the branches cut from it or can remove a tree over the objection of a neighbor.[114] Perhaps surprisingly, older cases held that the owner of the tree not only owns the fruit on overhanging branches extending over neighboring land, but also owns fruit that falls onto the neighboring land. Those courts gave the owner of the tree the power to enter the neighboring land to harvest the fallen fruit.[115] Owners of encroaching trees that actually damage neighboring property may be liable for the damages under the law of nuisance if their failure to remedy the problem substantially and unreasonably damages neighboring property.[116] For perhaps understandable reasons, disputes over encroaching trees and plants generate strong emotions and a surprisingly high amount of litigation.

§2.4.3 Aviation

Public navigable air space

It used to be said that landowners own to the center of the earth and to the heavens above.[117] This rule changed with the advent of aviation. Legislation and court decisions recognized or created the idea that the public retained ownership of the airways and that navigable air rights were not subject to private ownership.[118] However, in *United States v. Causby*,[119] the Supreme Court held that regular military flights over plaintiff's land effectuated an unconstitutional taking of property rights when the noise of the planes

[110] *Haygood v. State*, 483 S.E.2d 302 (Ga. Ct. App. 1997); *Lemon v. Curington*, 306 P.2d 1091 (Idaho 1957); *Melnick v. C.S.X. Corp.*, 540 A.2d 1133 (Md. 1988); *Koresko v. Farley*, 844 A.2d 607 (Pa. Commw. Ct. 2004); *Lane v. W.J. Curry & Sons*, 92 S.W.3d 355, 357 (Tenn. 2002); 8-68 *Thompson on Real Property, Third Thomas Edition* §68.04.

[111] *Jones v. Wagner*, 624 A.2d 166 (Pa. Super. Ct. 1993).

[112] *Compare Young v. Ledford*, 37 So. 3d 832 (Ala. Ct. Civ. App. 2009) (owner cannot remove tree that straddles the boundary unless it is clearly dangerous); *Patterson v. Oye*, 333 N.W.2d 389 (Neb. 1983) (injunction against removing hedges on the boundary) *with Melnick v. C.S.X. Corp.*, 540 A.2d 1133 (Md. 1988) (right to remove plants threatening neighboring building).

[113] 8-68 *Thompson on Real Property, Third Thomas Edition* §68.04(b)(1).

[114] *Id.*; *Love v. Klosky*, 413 P.3d 1267 (Colo. 2018) (tree can be removed without consent of the neighbor when the tree was first planted on the owner's land and it encroached on the neighbor's land as it grew).

[115] 8-68 *Thompson on Real Property, Third Thomas Edition* §68.04(b)(2).

[116] *Lane v. W.J. Curry & Sons*, 92 S.W.3d 355, 357 (Tenn. 2002). *See* §3.2.

[117] The Latin phrase is "*cuius est solum eius est usque ad coelum*," meaning the owner of the soil owns upward to the heavens. 2-18A *Powell on Real Property* §18A.05[2].

[118] 9-64A *Powell on Real Property* §64A.01[5].

[119] 328 U.S. 256 (1946). *Accord*, *Griggs v. Allegheny Cnty.*, 369 U.S. 84, 87-90 (1962); *Andrews v. United States*, 108 Fed. Cl. 150 (2012); *see also* Stuart Banner, *Who Owns the Sky?* (2008).

was so loud and constant (and the planes so low) that it was impossible for the owner to use his property for normal living and farming purposes. Consider emerging issues with drones.[120] Amazon has been using drones to deliver some packages; surveyors use them for reviewing boundaries, and they have become a common law enforcement tool. While drones have much utility, using these low-flying objects may raise objections from property owners claiming they are intrusive, violate the privacy of property owners, and constitute trespassory invasions of real property. The Federal Aviation Agency (FAA) limits most drones to operating no higher than 400 feet above ground level and require operators to have an FAA-issued "Remote pilot certificate." FAA rules still leave room for more state and local regulation.[121]

§2.4.4 *Pollution*

Nuisance and trespass

Polluting land uses that inject smoke, sewage, chemicals, or other substances onto neighboring land are regulated by *nuisance* law, which provides relief for land uses that cause substantial and unreasonable harm. This topic is covered in Chapter 3.[122] However, because a trespass encompasses any physical invasion, courts have had to wrestle with the question of whether liability for trespass should be found in such cases. Some cases, especially older ones, held that trespass would not be found if the invading objects were microscopic or invisible to the eye, unless actual damage to the land could be shown.[123] Other cases characterize harms due to drifting chemicals or smoke as "indirect" harms and therefore not encompassed by trespass law.[124]

Invisible particles

Indirect harms

Significant physical damage required

Some recent decisions have extended trespass liability to invasion by invisible particles, although some have found such invasions not to constitute a trespass.[125] For example, a New York court held the manufacturer and distributor of an herbicide liable for trespass when it broke down

[120] Debra Cassens Weiss, *Does Property Owner Have the Right to Shoot Down Hobbyist's Hovering Drone?*, ABA J., Jan. 14, 2016.

[121] 14 CFR Pt. 107; *see generally* Henry H. Perritt, Jr., *Law Drones and Drone Laws*, 70 No. 3 Prac. Law 3 (2024); Troy A. Rule, *Drones, Airspace and the Sharing Economy*, 84 Ohio St. L.J. 157 (2023).

[122] *See* §3.2.

[123] *Bradley v. American Smelting and Refining Co.*, 635 F. Supp. 1154 (W.D. Wash. 1986); *Born v. Exxon Corp.*, 388 So. 2d 933 (Ala. 1980); *J.H. Borland v. Sanders Lead Co., Inc.*, 369 So. 2d 523 (Ala. 1979); *Martin v. Reynolds Metals Co.*, 342 P.2d 790 (Or. 1959); 9-64A *Powell on Real Property* §64A.04[1].

[124] *J.H. Borland v. Sanders Lead Co., Inc.*, 369 So. 2d 523 (Ala. 1979); *Chance v. BP Chemicals, Inc.*, 670 N.E.2d 985, 992 (Ohio 1996) (noting that the trespass complained of was an "indirect" one); 9-64 *Powell on Real Property* §64.01[2]; 9-64A *Powell on Real Property* §64A.04.

[125] *Compare Stevenson v. E.I. Dupont de Nemours*, 327 F.3d 400 (5th Cir. 2003) (applying Va. law) (trespass by invasion of airborne particulates and damages may be recoverable for diminution in property's fair market value caused by pollution of heavy metals) *and Hoery v. United States*, 64 P.3d 214, 222 (Colo. 2003) (migrating toxic chemicals constitute continuing trespass as well as nuisance) *with Adams v. Cleveland-Cliffs Iron Co.*, 602 N.W.2d 215 (Mich. Ct. App. 1999) (holding that physical invasion by dust, noise, and vibrations does not constitute a trespass and is cognizable only under nuisance law). *See Babb v. Lee Cnty. Landfill SC, LLC*, 747 S.E.2d 468 (S.C. 2013) (odors cannot constitute a trespass, only a nuisance).

in the soil after usage by customers and a chemical by-product leached through the soil and invaded the public water supply.[126] Courts allow trespass claims to be brought in the context of polluting substances only if the invasion causes significant harm to the land or persons on it.[127] This limitation has been imposed because otherwise, application of trespass law in this context would substantially increase the legal liability of those who engage in polluting activities. While nuisance liability applies only where the harm is both substantial and unreasonable, trespass liability is absolute. For example, an owner who installed an underground drainpipe that was inadequate in size was held liable for trespass without proof of negligence when it leaked water and sent water flooding into a neighbor's basement.[128] If trespass law is extended to invasion by microscopic particles or other substances, liability would be strict or even absolute. Most courts that have applied trespass doctrine to polluting smoke or chemicals have therefore created limiting doctrines, finding an unlawful trespass only if the invading particles actually seep into the ground (rather than dissipating into the air) and only if they could be shown to have caused significant physical damage.[129]

Vibrations caused by blasting

Some courts recognize that "a trespass is committed by a defendant's blasting operation when the vibrations and concussions to earth and air cause damage to the plaintiff's property."[130] Other courts impose liability when blasting harms neighboring property only when there is proof of negligence, unless rocks or debris actually invade neighboring land, in which case trespass claims will be allowed.[131] Despite their physical basis, it has repeatedly been held that harms arising from electric and magnetic fields emitted from electric power lines are intangible phenomena that cannot be the basis of a trespass claim.[132]

[126] *State of New York v. Fermenta ASC Corp.*, 630 N.Y.S.2d 884 (Sup. Ct. 1995).

[127] *Gill v. LDI*, 19 F. Supp. 2d 1188 (W.D. Wash. 1998); *J.H. Borland v. Sanders Lead Co., Inc.*, 369 So. 2d 523 (Ala. 1979); *Public Serv. Co. of Colo. v. Van Wyck*, 27 P.3d 377, 390 (Colo. 2001); *State of New York v. Fermenta ASC Corp.*, 630 N.Y.S.2d 884 (Sup. Ct. 1995); *Kitsap County v. Allstate Insurance Co.*, 964 P.2d 1173 (Wash. 1998); *Bradley v. American Smelting and Refining Co.*, 709 P.2d 782 (Wash. 1985).

[128] *Burt v. Beautiful Savior Lutheran Church of Broomfield*, 809 P.2d 1064 (Colo. Ct. App. 1990). The court also held that contributory negligence of the plaintiff was not available as a defense to the trespass claim. *Id.* at 1067. Other jurisdictions apply the defense of contributory or comparative negligence to the tort of negligent trespass. *See Smith v. McCullough Dredging Co.*, 152 So. 2d 194 (Fla. Dist. Ct. App. 1963).

[129] *Mercer v. Rockwell International Corp.*, 24 F. Supp. 2d 735 (W.D. Ky. 1998); *Satterfield v. J.M. Huber Corp.*, 888 F. Supp. 1567 (N.D. Ga. 1995); *Maddy v. Vulcan Materials Co.*, 737 F. Supp. 1528 (D. Kan. 1990); *Bradley v. American Smelting and Refining Co.*, 635 F. Supp. 1154 (W.D. Wash. 1986); *Williams v. Monsanto Co.*, 856 S.W.2d 338 (Mo. Ct. App. 1993); *Chance v. BP Chemicals, Inc.*, 670 N.E.2d 985 (Ohio 1996); *Martin v. Reynolds Metals Co.*, 342 P.2d 790 (Or. 1959); 9-64A *Powell on Real Property* §64A.04[1]. *But see Hoery v. United States*, 64 P.3d 214, 222 (Colo. 2003) ("The failure of the United States to remove the pollution from Hoery's property which it wrongfully placed there constitutes a continuing property invasion for the entire time the contamination remains").

[130] *Martin v. Reynolds Metals Co.*, 342 P.2d 790 (Or. 1959).

[131] *Coalite, Inc. v. Aldridge*, 229 So. 2d 539 (Ala. 1969).

[132] *San Diego Gas & Electric Co. v. Superior Court*, 920 P.2d 669 (Cal. 1996).

§2.5 Animals

Strict liability

Owners of animals are generally required to prevent them from entering property possessed by others. Most states impose an absolute duty on owners to prevent such trespasses; use of reasonable care is not a defense to a trespass claim in such cases.[133] However, distinctions are often made among pets, livestock, and wild animals. While trespass liability is generally absolute in the case of livestock and wild animals, many states allow household pets to roam and do not hold the owner liable for entry onto another's land, although they may be liable for any resulting damage.[134]

Household pets

Liability for harm

Although trespass liability is generally absolute,[135] some states impose liability for consequential damage caused by a trespassing animal, only if the owner voluntarily or negligently caused the trespass.[136] Other states impose strict liability on the owner for any damage resulting from such trespasses.[137]

Fencing-out v. fencing-in laws

Traditionally, the person keeping an animal was expected to prevent it from escaping and thus had a duty to fence in the animal. Some states, especially in the west and the south, had a custom of open range, allowing animals to wander and graze freely. They enacted statutes requiring landowners who wished to keep animals off their property to erect their own fences to keep the animals out. As populations became denser and customs changed, many states moved from the fencing-out laws to fencing-in laws.[138]

§2.6 Public Accommodations Laws

§2.6.1 *Title II of the* Civil Rights Act of 1964

"Full and equal enjoyment"

Title II of the *Civil Rights Act of 1964*,[139] often referred to as the federal public accommodations law, provides that "[a]ll persons shall be entitled to the full and equal enjoyment of the goods, services, facilities, privileges, advantages, and accommodations of any place of public accommodation, as defined in this section, without discrimination or segregation on the ground of race, color, religion, or national origin."[140] Note that the statute does not prohibit discrimination based on sex, sexual orientation, or gender identity. Places of public accommodation are defined to include "each of

Race, color, religion, or national origin

[133] *Monfee v. Seymore*, 392 So. 2d 1198 (Ala. Civ. App. 1980); 9-64A *Powell on Real Property* §64A.01[4].

[134] *Kiser v. Morris*, 274 S.E.2d 610 (Ga. Ct. App. 1980); 9-64A *Powell on Real Property* §64A.01[4].

[135] Absolute liability may entitle the possessor to nominal damages, at least, as well as injunctive relief.

[136] Ala. Code §3-5-2(a); *Fisel v. Wynns*, 667 So. 2d 761 (Fla. 1996).

[137] *Gunpowder Horse Stables, Inc. v. State Farm Automobile Insurance Co.*, 673 A.2d 721 (Md. 1996); *Nixon v. Harris*, 238 N.E.2d 785 (Ohio 1968).

[138] Alabama, for example, switched from a fencing-out rule to a fencing-in rule in 1951. *Compare* Ala. Code §3-4-6 (1975) *with* Ala. Code §3-5-2.

[139] 42 U.S.C. §§2000a to 2000a-6.

[140] 42 U.S.C. §2000a(a).

Hotels, restaurants, gas stations, or places of entertainment

the following establishments which serves the public":[141] (1) inns and hotels (unless they contain fewer than five rooms for rent and are occupied by the owner as his or her residence); (2) restaurants and gas stations; (3) places of entertainment, including sports facilities, theaters, and concert halls; and (4) any establishment "physically located within the premises" of those establishments or any establishment "within the premises of which is physically located any such covered establishment, and which holds itself out as serving patrons of such covered establishment."[142] Note that common carriers are regulated by the *Interstate Commerce Act*[143] and are prohibited from all forms of unreasonable discrimination, not just discrimination based on race, religion, and national origin.

Affect commerce

Supported by state action

These establishments are regulated only if they "affect commerce" or are "supported by state action."[144] These limitations were created in the statute because the public accommodations law passed by Congress in 1875 was struck down by the Supreme Court in 1883 in the *Civil Rights Cases*.[145] That 1883 decision held that the equal protection clause of the Fourteenth Amendment empowered Congress to prohibit discriminatory state action alone; it did not give Congress the power to outlaw discrimination by private parties.[146] Because of this narrow interpretation of congressional power under the Fourteenth Amendment, the 1964 public accommodations law was passed pursuant to the commerce clauses, which clearly authorizes Congress to regulate interstate commerce.[147] An alternative basis for the statute might have been the Thirteenth Amendment, whose prohibition on slavery was held by the Supreme Court in 1968 to be an appropriate basis for the *Civil Rights Act of 1866*.[148] In *Jones v. Alfred H.*

[141] 42 U.S.C. §2000a(b).

[142] *Id.*

[143] "A rail carrier providing transportation or service subject to the jurisdiction of the Board under this part may not subject a person, place, port, or type of traffic to unreasonable discrimination." 49 U.S.C. §10741(a)(1). "A rail carrier providing transportation or service subject to the jurisdiction of the Board under this part shall provide the transportation or service on reasonable request." 49 U.S.C. §11101(a). *See also Mitchell v. United States*, 313 U.S. 80 (1941) (interpreting 49 U.S.C. §3 (predecessor to 49 U.S.C. §10741) to prohibit racial discrimination by interstate common carriers in terms of service to passengers).

[144] 42 U.S.C. §2000a(b) defines "affects commerce" to include all inns, hotels and motels, restaurants, and gas stations that serve or "offer to serve" interstate travelers or have purchased in interstate commerce a substantial portion of the food or gasoline or other products it serves, as well as places of entertainment that present films, shows, etc., "which move in [interstate] commerce."

[145] 109 U.S. 3 (1883).

[146] The so-called state action doctrine is both well established and subject to numerous criticisms. *Compare* Lino Graglia, *State Action: Constitutional Phoenix*, 67 Wash. U. L.Q. 777 (1989) (supporting the state action doctrine) *with* Louis Henkin, Shelley v. Kraemer: *Notes for a Revised Opinion*, 110 U. Pa. L. Rev. 473 (1962); Erwin Chemerinsky, *Rethinking State Action*, 80 Nw. U. L. Rev. 503 (1985); Louis Michael Seidman, *Public Principle and Private Choice: The Uneasy Case for a Boundary Maintenance Theory of Constitutional Law*, 96 Yale L.J. 106 (1987); Mark Tushnet, Shelley v. Kraemer *and Theories of Equality*, 33 N.Y. L. Sch. L. Rev. 385 (1988); Isaac Saidel-Goley & Joseph William Singer, *Things Invisible to See: State Action & Private Property*, 5 Tex. A&M L. Rev. 439 (2018) (critiquing the doctrine).

[147] *See Heart of Atlanta Motel, Inc. v. United States*, 379 U.S. 241 (1964); *Katzenbach v. McClung*, 379 U.S. 294 (1964) (both upholding the Act as a valid exercise of Congress's power to regulate interstate commerce).

[148] 42 U.S.C. §§1981, 1982.

Mayer Co.,[149] the Supreme Court interpreted the Thirteenth Amendment to empower Congress to pass laws to abolish the "badges and the incidents of slavery"[150] as well as slavery itself, and upheld the constitutionality of the 1866 Act on that basis.

Injunctive relief only

Remedies

The 1964 public accommodations law provides for injunctive relief, but not for damages.[151] However, many courts have allowed claims to be brought under the *Civil Rights Act of 1866*[152] for exclusion from places of public accommodation on the basis of race and the courts have implied a damages remedy into §1981.[153]

▶ HARD CASE ▷ OTHER ESTABLISHMENTS

Does the 1964 public accommodations law regulate all establishments that serve the public, such as retail stores, or only those that are expressly listed in the Act (inns, restaurants, gas stations, and places of entertainment)?[154] The courts that have considered the issue have held the statutory list in §2000a(b) to be exclusive rather than illustrative, even though the statute nowhere expressly limits public accommodations to the list. Under this reasoning, other businesses, such as retail stores, are apparently not covered by the 1964 Act.[155]

Argument that the list is illustrative

One might argue against this established wisdom that the list is illustrative rather than exhaustive. Congress may have sought to emphasize that the listed places were clearly included because they were establishments where discrimination had previously been rampant. An appeal to the idea that "remedial statutes should be liberally construed to effectuate their purposes"[156] might counsel reading the list as illustrative, rather than exhaustive. A limited reading of the Act would mean that it is not a violation of the public accommodations law for a grocery store to refuse to serve a customer on the ground of race and it is hard to imagine why a rational Congress would require nondiscriminatory access to movie theaters and sports stadiums but not to grocery stores. Nor would such an expansive reading be without precedent. The New Jersey Supreme Court has interpreted a statutory list in a state antidiscrimination law to be illustrative rather than exhaustive when the statutory definition used the word

[149] 392 U.S. 409 (1968).

[150] *Jones v. Alfred H. Mayer Co.*, 392 U.S. 409, 440 (1968).

[151] 42 U.S.C. §2000a-3; *Bermudez Zenon v. Restaurant Compostela, Inc.*, 790 F. Supp. 41 (D.P.R. 1992).

[152] *Sanders v. Dobbs Houses, Inc.*, 431 F.2d 1097 (5th Cir. 1970).

[153] Section 1981 is discussed below in §2.6.2.

[154] *Clegg v. Cult Awareness Network*, 18 F.3d 752 (9th Cir. 1994).

[155] *Addison v. Signet Jewelers, Limited*, No. 1:23-cv-22956, 2025 WL 1766119, at *8 (D.N.J. Jun. 26, 2025) (reviewing caselaw excluding retail establishments from Title II); *Priddy v. Shopko Corp.*, 918 F. Supp. 358 (D. Utah 1995) (holding that retail establishments that do not sell food for consumption on the premises are not covered by the 1964 public accommodations law).

[156] *See United States v. Medical Society of South Carolina*, 298 F. Supp. 145 (D.S.C. 1969) (Title II is "to be accorded a liberal construction in order to carry out the purpose of Congress to eliminate the inconvenience, unfairness, and humiliation of racial discrimination").

"include" to preface a list of specific covered "places."[157] The court "reasoned that the Legislature's choice of the word 'include' indicated that the 'places' expressly mentioned were 'merely illustrative of the accommodations the Legislature intended to be within the scope of the statute.'"[158] The state legislature later vindicated the court's interpretation of the state law by amending the state statute less than a year after the court's decision to state explicitly that "a place of public accommodation shall include, but not be limited to" the listed places.[159] Similarly, as Judge Cummings noted in a dissenting opinion in *Welsh v. Boy Scouts of America*:[160]

> The impetus behind Title II was to aid the Black traveler in the South for whom "the road may be more like a desert and each inviting sign a mirage or, worse yet, a humiliating rebuff to him, his family or companions." But it is also clear that Congress targeted discrimination well beyond that suffered by African Americans moving in inhospitable territories. Lawmakers sought to eradicate discrimination in all things open and available to the general population. The meaning, if not the language, of Title II is simple and unambiguous enough: if it is open to the public, it must be open to all the public.[161]

Argument that the list is exhaustive

The courts have generally rejected these arguments, noting that the Act grants "full and equal enjoyment" to "any place of public accommodation, as defined in this section"[162] and this arguably means that the Act was to apply only to the listed entities, especially because the statute explains that "*each of the following* establishments is a place of public accommodation *within the meaning of this subchapter.*"[163] One might respond that "as defined in this section" merely means establishments that "affect commerce" or are "supported by state action" and that this caveat was intended to ensure that the statute not be struck down as a very similar one was in the *Civil Rights Cases*. However, the fact that only a short list of places is provided causes the courts to presume that the list is intended to define the scope of the statutory coverage not just to serve as an example of the types of businesses with such obligations.[164] ◀

Private clubs or establishments "not in fact open to the public"

The 1964 Act applies only to establishments that "serve the public."[165] However, it contains an additional exemption for any "private club or other establishment not in fact open to the public," unless its facilities are "made available to the customers or patrons" of establishments described

[157] *Dale v. Boy Scouts of America*, 734 A.2d 1196, 1208-1210 (N.J. 1999) (*citing Fraser v. Robin Dee Day Camp*, 210 A.2d 208 (N.J. 1965), *rev'd sub nom. Boy Scouts of America v. Dale*, 530 U.S. 640 (2000)).
[158] *Dale v. Boy Scouts of America*, 734 A.2d 1196, 1208 (N.J. 1999), *rev'd on other grounds sub nom. Boy Scouts of America v. Dale*, 530 U.S. 640 (2000).
[159] *Id.*
[160] 993 F.2d 1267 (7th Cir. 1993).
[161] *Welsh v. Boy Scouts of America*, 993 F.2d 1267, 1283 (7th Cir. 1993) (Cummings, J., dissenting).
[162] 42 U.S.C. §2000a(a).
[163] 42 U.S.C. §2000a(b).
[164] *Denny v. Elizabeth Arden Salons, Inc.*, 456 F.3d 427, 431 (4th Cir. 2006) (finding the list to be exhaustive).
[165] *Id.*

in §2000a(b).[166] On one hand, the private club exemption may seem redundant because §2000a(b) already provides that businesses are covered *only if* they "serve[] the public." Perhaps the private club example refers to establishments that keep membership lists. If that is the case, the sections are not duplicative since an establishment may not "serve the public," but also not keep a membership list and thus not qualify as a "private club." Although not falling in the private club exemption, such establishments would be excluded from coverage under the law.

▶ HARD CASE

▷ LOCKED STORES THAT ADMIT CUSTOMERS WITH A BUZZER

An additional example of an establishment that is not a private club but might not "serve the public" could be jewelry or clothing stores that keep their doors locked and allow customers in only after they press a buzzer.[167] Such stores arguably are not "private clubs" because they are not membership organizations. At the same time, one might argue that they do not "serve the public" because they are locked and admit customers one at a time, attempting to reserve the right to determine under what circumstances to allow people into the store. On the other hand, a store that serves people off the street and simply uses a visual examination to determine whether to admit customers seems like a regular store that is simply trying to choose its customers at-will. Its very existence as a store conveys an implied invitation to knock on the door. It holds itself out as ready to serve the public and thus may be open to the public in a functional sense. If its choices have a racial basis, then the store may be a public accommodation engaged in unlawful discrimination rather than private premises "not in fact open to the public."[168] The mere device of a lock and buzzer should not entitle the store to violate the statute, especially when no privacy or associational interests seem to be involved. ◀

▶ HARD CASE

▷ ARE MEMBERSHIP ORGANIZATIONS PUBLIC ACCOMMODATIONS?

Membership organizations as "places" of public accommodation

Courts have considered whether membership organizations like the Jaycees or the Boy Scouts of America are public accommodations required not to discriminate under either federal or state antidiscrimination laws.[169] The

[166] 42 U.S.C. §2000a(e). *See Donaldson v. Farrakhan*, 762 N.E.2d 835 (Mass. 2002) (theater rented by a mosque's men's class was a religious meeting and not a public accommodation and was thus entitled to exclude women from a lecture).

[167] *Compare* Patricia J. Williams, *Spirit-Murdering the Messenger: The Discourse of Fingerpointing as the Law's Response to Racism*, 42 U. Miami L. Rev. 127, 127-129 (1987) (criticizing such exclusion) *with* Walter E. Williams, *The Intelligent Bayesian*, The New Republic, Nov. 10, 1986, at 18 (reviewing arguments for approving such exclusion).

[168] *DeRosa v. Quang Loi Jewelry Co.*, No. 95-BPA-0068 (Mass. Comm'n Against Discrimination, June 17, 1998) (jewelry store that had an "open" sign in its window but had a locked door and excluded a customer based on race violated state public accommodations law).

[169] Cases involving the Jaycees include *United States Jaycees v. Richardet*, 666 P.2d 1008 (Alaska 1983); *United States Jaycees v. Bloomfield*, 434 A.2d 1379 (D.C. Ct. App. 1981); *United States*

issues include (1) whether membership organizations are a "place" of public accommodation; (2) whether they are open to the public or private clubs; (3) whether First Amendment rights of freedom of association exempt membership organizations from regulation by public accommodations statutes.

The first issue in such cases is whether membership organizations like the Jaycees and the Boy Scouts are "places" of public accommodation. In *Welsh v. Boy Scouts of America*,[170] the Seventh Circuit held that Boy Scouts are a "membership organization" and not a "place" of public accommodation within the meaning of Title II of the *Civil Rights Act of 1964*. The court concluded that Congress intended "to regulate facilities as opposed to gatherings of people."[171] Another federal court reached the same conclusion about Internet chat rooms,[172] and a number of state courts have interpreted their state public accommodations laws similarly.[173] Other state courts, however, have interpreted their state public accommodations laws to cover membership organizations, either because their laws do not contain the word "place"[174] or because they read the word "place" as a word of "convenience, not limitation."[175]

Jaycees v. Iowa Civil Rights Commission, 427 N.W.2d 450 (Iowa 1988); *United States Jaycees v. Massachusetts Comm'n Against Discrimination*, 463 N.E.2d 1151 (Mass. 1984); *United States Jaycees v. McClure*, 305 N.W.2d 764 (Minn. 1981), *aff'd sub nom. Roberts v. United States Jaycees*, 468 U.S. 609 (1984). Cases involving the Boy Scouts include *Randall v. Orange County Council, Boy Scouts of America*, 952 P.2d 261 (Cal. 1998) (entitled to exclude atheists); *Seabourn v. Coronado Area Council, Boy Scouts of America*, 891 P.2d 385 (Kan. 1995) (same); *Curran v. Mount Diablo Council of the Boy Scouts of America*, 952 P.2d 218 (Cal. 1998); *Dale v. Boy Scouts of America*, 734 A.2d 1196 (N.J. 1999), *rev'd sub nom. Boy Scouts of America v. Dale*, 530 U.S. 640 (2000); *Schwenk v. Boy Scouts of America*, 551 P.2d 465 (Or. 1976) (Boy Scouts may exclude girls); *Quinnipiac Council, Boy Scouts of America, Inc. v. Commission on Human Rights and Opportunities*, 528 A.2d 352 (Conn. 1987) (entitled to exclude female Scoutmaster).

170 993 F.2d 1267 (7th Cir. 1993).

171 *Welsh*, 993 F.2d at 1269. *Accord, Clegg v. Cult Awareness Network*, 18 F.3d 752 (9th Cir. 1994). *See* Tara E. Thompson, *Locating Discrimination: Interactive Web Sites as Public Accommodations Under Title II of the Civil Rights Act*, 2002 U. Chi. Legal F. 409.

172 *See also Noah v. AOL Time Warner Inc.*, 261 F. Supp. 2d 532, 541 (E.D. Va. 2003) (AOL chat rooms are not places of public accommodation under Title II of the *Civil Rights Act of 1964* because they are not "actual, physical places [or] structures").

173 *United States Jaycees v. Richardet*, 666 P.2d 1008, 1011 (Alaska 1983); *Seabourn v. Coronado Area Council, Boy Scouts of America*, 891 P.2d 385 (Kan. 1995); *United States Jaycees v. Massachusetts Comm'n Against Discrimination*, 463 N.E.2d 1151 (Mass. 1984). The California Supreme Court has interpreted its state public accommodations law, the *Unruh Civil Rights Act*, to regulate only "business establishments" and has thereby found the Boy Scouts outside the scope of the statute. *Curran v. Mount Diablo Council of the Boy Scouts of America*, 952 P.2d 218 (Cal. 1998); *Randall v. Orange County Council, Boy Scouts of America*, 952 P.2d 261 (Cal. 1998). For similar rulings under other state laws, see *Seabourn v. Coronado Area Council, Boy Scouts of America*, 891 P.2d 385 (Kan. 1995); *Schwenk v. Boy Scouts of America*, 551 P.2d 465 (Or. 1976).

174 *United States Jaycees v. McClure*, 305 N.W.2d 764 (Minn. 1981), *aff'd sub nom. Roberts v. United States Jaycees*, 468 U.S. 609 (1984).

175 *Dale v. Boy Scouts of America*, 734 A.2d 1196, 1209 (N.J. 1999), *rev'd on other grounds sub nom. Boy Scouts of America v. Dale*, 530 U.S. 640 (2000) (*citing National Organization for Women v. Little League Baseball*, 318 A.2d 33, 37 (N.J. Super. Ct. App. Div. 1974), *aff'd mem.*, 338 A.2d 198 (N.J. 1974)); *United States Power Squadrons v. State Human Rights Appeal Board*, 452 N.E.2d 1199, 1202-1204 (N.Y. 1983). *See also Quinnipiac Council, Boy Scouts of America, Inc. v. Commission on Human Rights and Opportunities*, 528 A.2d 352 (Conn. 1987); *United States Jaycees v. McClure*, 305 N.W.2d 764 (Minn. 1981), *aff'd sub nom. Roberts v. United States Jaycees*, 468 U.S. 609 (1984) (state statutory definition of "public accommodation" does not use the word "place").

Membership organizations as private clubs

A second issue is whether membership organizations are private clubs. "Private establishments" that are "not in fact open to the public" are exempted from the federal public accommodations statute.[176] Courts distinguish between "public accommodations" and private clubs or establishment, by reference to both size and selectivity. Establishments that solicit broad public participation and are unselective, large, and unlimited in size are likely to be held to be public accommodations while small, selective organizations are more likely to be considered to be private clubs.[177] Most courts have held that the Jaycees are a public accommodation because they are unselective in their membership, have no political or religious creed, solicit to increase their membership, and have no limits on their size and no selection criteria.[178] On the other hand, the Kiwanis Club has been held not to be a public accommodation because it limits how many members can join, requires that they be sponsored by current members and voted on by the board of directors, and requires that they be willing to pray, and recite the Pledge of Allegiance at meetings.[179] Some courts have held that the Boy Scouts of America are a public accommodation because they are generally unselective while discriminating on the basis of categories protected by statute such as religion, sex, and sexual orientation.[180] However, other courts have held that the Boy Scouts are selective on the basis of viewpoint and endeavor to inculcate particular values in their members, as evidenced in the Boy Scout Oath.[181]

Freedom of association

A third issue is whether membership organizations have constitutionally protected rights to freedom of association that exempt them from public accommodations laws. The First Amendment's protections for free speech and the free exercise of religion have been interpreted to encompass both the right to engage in intimate personal associations with others and expressive or political associations.[182] The ability to associate with like-minded individuals for religious or political purposes, and to exclude others from membership organizations, is one of the core freedoms in a free

[176] 42 U.S.C. §2000a(e).

[177] *United States Jaycees v. McClure*, 305 N.W.2d 764 (Minn. 1981), *aff'd sub nom. Roberts v. United States Jaycees*, 468 U.S. 609 (1984); *Dale v. Boy Scouts of America*, 734 A.2d 1196 (N.J. 1999), *rev'd sub nom. Boy Scouts of America v. Dale*, 530 U.S. 640 (2000). Not all kinds of selectivity will immunize an establishment from regulation as a public accommodation. For example, many state laws regulate educational institutions, such as universities, which are obviously selective in their admissions criteria. Restaurants may have a dress code and nonetheless be subject to regulation as public accommodations; gas stations may refuse to serve trucks because they do not sell diesel fuel; a theater may choose to exclude children by not showing G-rated movies. The kind of selectivity that seems to matter in turning a public accommodation into a private establishment involves criteria that suggest that legitimate associational interests are present. Private clubs are not exempt from public accommodations laws if they are unselective in their membership, accepting customers on a first-come, first-served basis, as, for example, some beach clubs do.

[178] *United States Jaycees v. McClure*, 305 N.W.2d 764 (Minn. 1981), *aff'd sub nom. Roberts v. United States Jaycees*, 468 U.S. 609 (1984).

[179] *Kiwanis Int'l v. Ridgewood Kiwanis Club*, 806 F.2d 468 (3d Cir. 1986).

[180] *Dale v. Boy Scouts of America*, 734 A.2d 1196, 1211 (N.J. 1999), *rev'd sub nom. Boy Scouts of America v. Dale*, 530 U.S. 640 (2000).

[181] *Welsh v. Boy Scouts of America*, 993 F.2d 1267, 1275-1276 (7th Cir. 1993).

[182] *Hurley v. Irish-American Gay, Lesbian, and Bisexual Group of Boston*, 515 U.S. 557 (1995).

and democratic society. The Supreme Court has rejected such claims in the context of the Jaycees but accepted them with regard to the Boy Scouts.[183] In *Roberts v. United States Jaycees*,[184] the Supreme Court upheld the application of Minnesota's public accommodations statute to require the Jaycees to admit women. It found that the Jaycees makes available to its members a range of products and services and that "acts of invidious discrimination in the distribution of publicly available goods, services, and other advantages cause unique evils that government has a compelling interest to prevent."[185] The Court noted that nothing in the state public accommodations law would prohibit the Jaycees from excluding individuals, whether men or women, based on their views.[186] In contrast, the Supreme Court held in *Boy Scouts of America v. Dale*[187] that New Jersey could not apply its public accommodations law to the Boy Scouts because it was a social rather than a commercial organization, and that it espoused particular beliefs, including opposition to homosexuality.[188] The First Amendment's protection of freedom of expression extended to freedom of association and overrode any state interest in prohibiting discrimination.[189] The Court distinguished the *Jaycees* case by noting that the Jaycees had not shown that admitting women would in any way affect any message it intended to communicate and thus the law had no discernable effect on its freedom of expressive association.[190] ◀

▷ DISPARAGING NAMES AND FREE SPEECH RIGHTS **HARD CASE ◀**

The 1964 public accommodations law guarantees "full and equal enjoyment" in places of entertainment. That necessarily leads to regulation of speech. A restaurant that put up a "whites only" sign would be in violation of the Act as would one that used racist language in serving customers.[191] On the other hand, the First Amendment does protect expressive speech, even if offensive.[192] When do First Amendment rights limit the reach of public accommodations laws? Imagine a football stadium called the Redskins Stadium — a name that has been adjudicated to be disparaging to

[183] *Compare Roberts v. United States Jaycees*, 468 U.S. 609 (1984) *with Boy Scouts of America v. Dale*, 530 U.S. 640 (2000).
[184] 468 U.S. 609 (1984).
[185] *Id.* at 628.
[186] *Id.* at 627.
[187] 530 U.S. 640 (2000).
[188] *Boy Scouts of America v. Dale*, 530 U.S. 640, 651 (2000).
[189] *Id.* at 648.
[190] *Id.* at 657-658.
[191] *Alexis v. McDonald's Restaurants of Massachusetts, Inc.*, 67 F.3d 341, 350 (1st Cir. 1995) (interpreting 42 U.S.C. §1981). *See also Pittsburgh Press Co. v. Human Relations Comm'n*, 413 U.S. 376 (1973) (no First Amendment violation to prohibit newspaper from listing jobs available only to persons of one sex); *Ragin v. New York Times Co.*, 923 F.2d 995 (2d Cir. 1991) (law can regulate discriminatory housing ads in newspaper); *United States v. Hunter*, 459 F.2d 205 (4th Cir. 1972) (no free speech right to advertise a "white home" for sale).
[192] *Cf. Matal v. Tam*, 137 S. Ct. 1744 (2017) (holding the clause of the Lanham Act that prohibited federal trademark registration for marks that might disparage any persons, 15 U.S.C. §1052(a), facially invalid under the First Amendment).

American Indians.[193] Does use of that name deny full and equal enjoyment to a public accommodation?[194] And if so, does the stadium owner have a First Amendment right to use the name?

The Rhode Island Human Rights Commission ruled that a restaurant violated the state public accommodations law by choosing a racially offensive term, "Sambo's," as its name.[195] The Commission made factual findings to the effect that the offensiveness of the name had a strong negative impact on Black people in Rhode Island and discouraged their patronage. The commission concluded that "the use of the name 'Sambo's' denie[d] black citizens full and equal accommodations" and therefore violated the state public accommodations law. The Sixth Circuit held, however, that the First Amendment protected the right to use the name "Sambo's" despite its offensive quality.[196] ◀

§2.6.2 Civil Rights Act of 1866

42 U.S.C. §§1981 and 1982

The *Civil Rights Act of 1866*, 42 U.S.C. §§1981 and 1982, provides, at §1981(a), that

> [a]ll persons within the jurisdiction of the United States shall have the same right in every State and Territory to make and enforce contracts, to sue, be parties, give evidence, and to the full and equal benefit of all laws and proceedings for the security of persons and property as is enjoyed by white citizens.

Section 1982 provides that "[a]ll citizens of the United States shall have the same right as is enjoyed by white citizens to inherit, purchase, lease, sell, hold, and convey real and personal property." For 100 years after passage of this statute in 1866, it was thought to apply only to discriminatory state laws, such as statutes that deprived Black people of the capacity to enter into binding contracts. However, in the 1968 case of *Jones v. Alfred Mayer Co.*,[197] the Supreme Court ruled that §1982, which grants equal rights to purchase property, applied to private discrimination by housing providers. This decision was followed in 1976 by the case of *Runyon v. McCrary*,[198] in

[193] *Pro-Football, Inc. v. Blackhorse*, 112 F. Supp. 3d 439 (E.D. Va. 2015), *vacated by* 709 Fed. Appx. 182 (4th Cir. 2018) (finding the name disparaging and denying the benefits of federal trademark registration).

[194] *See* Note (Aaron Colangelo), *A Public Accommodations Challenge to the Use of Indian Team Names and Mascots in Professional Sports*, 112 Harv. L. Rev. 904 (1999); Brooke A. Masters, *Team Names Go to Court: Redskins, Other Indian Logos Face Challenges*, Wash. Post, Apr. 7, 1999, at B01, 1999 WL 2209571; James F. McCarty, *Wahoo Foes Plan New Legal Strategy: Lawsuit Will Cite 1964 Rights Law*, Plain Dealer (Cleveland), Apr. 9, 1999, at 1B, 1999 WLNR 7370960.

[195] *Urban League of Rhode Island v. Sambo's of Rhode Island, Inc.*, File Nos. 79 PRA 074-06/06, 79 ERA 073-06/06, EEOC No. 011790461 (R.I. Comm'n for Human Rights 1981). *See* Note, *A Public Accommodations Challenge*, 112 Harv. L. Rev. at 914.

[196] *Sambo's Restaurants, Inc. v. City of Ann Arbor*, 663 F.2d 686 (6th Cir. 1981). *Accord*, *United States v. Hunter*, 459 F.2d 205 (4th Cir. 1972).

[197] 392 U.S. 409 (1968).

[198] 427 U.S. 160 (1976). This holding was reaffirmed in *Patterson v. McLean Credit Union*, 491 U.S. 164 (1989) and codified in the *Civil Rights Act of 1991* (42 U.S.C. §1981(c)).

which the Court held that §1981 prohibited a private school from excluding Black students. Congress amended §1981 in the *Civil Rights Act of 1991*[199] to overrule a restrictive interpretation of §1981 by the Supreme Court.[200] Because §1981 protected the right "to make and enforce contracts," but did not explicitly prohibit discrimination in the "terms and conditions" of contracts, the Supreme Court ruled in 1989 in *Patterson v. McLean Credit Union*[201] that an employee who had been subjected to discriminatory treatment on the job had no claim under §1981. In 1991, Congress overruled *Patterson* by amending §1981 to provide, in §1981(b), that "the term 'make and enforce contracts' includes the making, performance, modification, and termination of contracts, and the enjoyment of all benefits, privileges, terms, and conditions of the contractual relationship."[202] The *Civil Rights Act of 1991* also reaffirmed the Supreme Court's rulings that §1981 protects individuals against "impairment by nongovernmental discrimination" as well as discrimination "under color of State law."[203]

§1981 limited to racial discrimination

Section 1981 has been held to prohibit racial discrimination only.[204] It does not prohibit other forms of discrimination, such as discrimination based on sex, religion, or national origin. It has been held, however, that it covers discrimination against Jews and Arabs because they were viewed to be separate races in 1866.[205]

Remedies

The courts have implied a damages remedy into §1981.[206] This distinguishes the statute from the 1964 public accommodations law, which has been interpreted to allow only injunctive relief.[207]

Burdens of persuasion and production

Section 1981 claims are analyzed under the same burden-shifting standards utilized in Title VII employment discrimination cases.[208] Plaintiffs may establish a *prima facie* case by demonstrating "(1) that they are members of a racial minority; (2) that defendants intended to discriminate against them on that basis; (3) that defendants' racially discriminatory conduct abridged contract or other rights enumerated in §1981(a)."[209] If plaintiffs can establish a *prima facie* case, "defendants are required to assert some legitimate, nondiscriminatory basis for their conduct. Plaintiffs must then bear their ultimate burden of coming forward with evidence to prove that defendants' proffered reasons were really a pretext for discrimination."[210]

[199] Pub. L. No. 102-166, Title I, §101, Nov. 21, 1991, 105 Stat. 1071.
[200] *Patterson v. McLean Credit Union*, 491 U.S. 164 (1989).
[201] 491 U.S. 164 (1989).
[202] 42 U.S.C. §1981(b).
[203] 42 U.S.C. §1981(c).
[204] *But see Anderson v. Conboy*, 156 F.3d 167 (2d Cir. 1998), *cert. granted sub nom. United Brotherhood of Carpenters and Joiners of America v. Anderson*, 526 U.S. 1086 (1999), *cert. dismissed*, 527 U.S. 1030 (1999) (holding that §1981 protects noncitizens from discrimination on the basis of alienage).
[205] *St. Francis College v. Al-Khazraji*, 481 U.S. 604 (1987); *Shaare Tefila Congregation v. Cobb*, 481 U.S. 615 (1987).
[206] *Sanders v. Dobbs Houses, Inc.*, 431 F.2d 1097 (5th Cir. 1970).
[207] 42 U.S.C. §2000a-3; *Bermudez Zenon v. Restaurant Compostela, Inc.*, 790 F. Supp. 41 (D.P.R. 1992).
[208] *Lewis v. JC Penney, Co., Inc.*, 948 F. Supp. 367 (D. Del. 1996).
[209] *Ackaa v. Tommy Hilfiger Co.*, 1998 WL 136522, at *3 (E.D. Pa. 1998).
[210] *Id. See Jones v. R.R. Donnelley & Sons, Co.*, 541 U.S. 369 (2004) (general federal four-year statute of limitations, 28 U.S.C. §1658(a), applies for claims brought after 1990).

▶ HARD CASE ▷ IS §1981 A PUBLIC ACCOMMODATIONS LAW?

Does it regulate establishments not covered by the 1964 public accommodations law?

Following the ruling in *Runyon*, a number of courts have interpreted §1981 as akin to a public accommodations statute that grants individuals the right to enter property open to the public and to obtain access to the goods and services offered to the public without discrimination on the basis of race.[211] Courts have also held that §1981 covers establishments that are not regulated by the 1964 public accommodations law, such as hair salons and retail stores.[212] For example, in *Perry v. Command Performance*,[213] Judge Thompson ruled that the plaintiff had stated a claim under §1981 when she alleged that defendant refused to cut her hair because of her race. Although hair salons are not covered by Title II of the *1964 Civil Rights Act*, plaintiff was entitled to bring a civil rights claim under §1981.[214] In another case, *Watson v. Fraternal Order of Eagles*,[215] Judge Merritt noted that a "department store is not directly covered by Title II but would be amenable to suit under §1981."[216]

The argument that §1981 is not a public accommodations law

One might question the conclusion that §1981 was originally intended to protect the ability to enter a public accommodation to purchase goods and services without unjust discrimination. The statute was originally passed in 1866; when doubts arose about its constitutionality, it was repassed by Congress in 1870, after adoption of the Fourteenth Amendment (and its equal protection clause) in 1868. Only five years later, in 1875, Congress passed a public accommodations law similar to the 1964 statute. This statute was struck down as unconstitutional in 1883 in the *Civil Rights Cases* when the Supreme Court interpreted the Fourteenth Amendment to abolish discriminatory state action but not to empower Congress to abolish discriminatory private action.[217] If the 1866 Act created an obligation on places of

[211] *Alexis v. McDonald's Restaurants of Massachusetts, Inc.*, 67 F.3d 341 (1st Cir. 1995); *Christian v. Wal-Mart Stores, Inc.*, 252 F.3d 862 (6th Cir. 2001); *McCaleb v. Pizza Hut of America, Inc.*, 28 F. Supp. 2d 1043 (N.D. Ill. 1998); *Harrison v. Denny's Restaurant, Inc.*, 1997 WL 227963 (N.D. Cal. 1997); *Jackson v. Tyler's Dad's Place, Inc.*, 850 F. Supp. 53 (D.D.C. 1994), *aff'd by unpublished order*, 107 F.3d 923 (D.C. Cir. 1996); *Perry v. Burger King Corp.*, 924 F. Supp. 548 (S.D.N.Y. 1996); *Franceschi v. Hyatt Corp.*, 782 F. Supp. 712 (D.P.R. 1992); *Bermudez Zenon v. Restaurant Compostela, Inc.*, 790 F. Supp. 41 (D.P.R. 1992).

[212] *Christian v. Wal-Mart Stores, Inc.*, 252 F.3d 862 (6th Cir. 2001); *Hampton v. Dillard Dep't Stores, Inc.*, 247 F.3d 1091 (10th Cir. 2001). If neither the federal public accommodations law of 1964 nor the *Civil Rights Act of 1866* is interpreted to prohibit retail stores from discriminating on the basis of race, then the state laws will govern this question. While most states have public accommodations laws that prohibit discrimination in retail stores, six states do not. *See* Joseph William Singer, *No Right to Exclude: Public Accommodations and Private Property*, 90 Nw. U. L. Rev. 1283, 1290 (1996) (Alabama, Florida, Georgia, Mississippi, North Carolina, and Texas). South Carolina now prohibits discrimination in retail stores. S.C. Code §45-9-10(B)(4). Moreover, Mississippi has a statute on the books that affirmatively grants all businesses the power "to choose or select the person or persons [they] desire[] to do business with, [including the power] to refuse to sell to, wait upon or serve any person that the owner, manager, or employee of such public place of business does not desire to sell to, wait upon or serve." Miss. Code §97-23-17.

[213] 913 F.2d 99 (3d Cir. 1990).

[214] *Id. Accord, Denny v. Elizabeth Arden Salons, Inc.*, 456 F.3d 427 (4th Cir. 2006) (§1981 violated when salon refused service because it did not "do [B]lack people's hair").

[215] 915 F.2d 235, 243 (6th Cir. 1990).

[216] *Id.*

[217] 109 U.S. 3 (1883).

public accommodation, to serve the public without discrimination on the basis of race, the 1875 statute would have been entirely unnecessary.

The argument that §1981 is a public accommodations law

On the other hand, the Supreme Court has repeatedly held that the *Civil Rights Act of 1866* may cover activities that are also covered by later statutes. The courts have consistently held, for example, that plaintiffs are entitled to bring employment discrimination claims both on the basis of Title VII of the *Civil Rights Act of 1964*[218] and on the basis of §1981.[219] Similarly, housing discrimination claims are almost always based both on the *Fair Housing Act of 1968*[220] and §1982.[221] The plain terms of §§1981 and 1982 apply to retail stores, for example. If a store excludes customers on the basis of race, it is refusing to contract with them. The holdings in *Jones* and *Runyon* prohibit such discriminatory refusals to deal. ◀

▷ PRE- AND POST-CONTRACT DISCRIMINATION **HARD CASE ◀**

Assuming the *Civil Rights Act of 1866* requires retail stores to serve the public without discrimination on the basis of race, does it also prohibit discriminatory conduct that occurs before or after a contract is made? The courts seem to agree that the "right to make contracts" includes the right to enter a store.[222] This right is arguably also implied by §1982, which protects the right to "purchase personal property."[223]

A few courts also hold that it implies a right to browse and shop without being subject to discriminatory treatment or harassment of any kind.[224] Several courts have held that the "equal benefits" clause of §1981 entitles patrons of public accommodations to be free from discriminatory treatment.[225] However, most courts have narrowly interpreted the "right to make contracts," holding that this right is denied only when a patron is actually prevented from purchasing goods or services.[226] These courts have denied relief when a patron was treated disrespectfully or refused assistance,[227] subjected

[218] 42 U.S.C. §2000e.

[219] *See, e.g., Lytle v. Household Manufacturing, Inc.*, 494 U.S. 545 (1990).

[220] 42 U.S.C. §§3601 to 3619, 3631.

[221] *Asbury v. Brougham*, 866 F.2d 1276 (10th Cir. 1989).

[222] *Withers v. Dick's Sporting Goods, Inc.*, 636 F.3d 958 (8th Cir. 2011); *Causey v. Sewell Cadillac-Chevrolet, Inc.*, 394 F.3d 285 (5th Cir. 2004); *Christian v. Wal-Mart Stores, Inc.*, 252 F.3d 862 (6th Cir. 2001); *Clark v. Safeway, Inc.*, 478 F. Supp. 3d 1080 (D. Or. 2020).

[223] 42 U.S.C. §1982.

[224] *Chapman v. Higbee*, 319 F.3d 825 (6th Cir. 2003) (equal benefits clause in §1981 gives right to equal treatment in seeking contract); *McCaleb v. Pizza Hut of America, Inc.*, 28 F. Supp. 2d 1043 (N.D. Ill. 1998) (family denied "full benefits" of the contract when denied utensils and harassed and threatened while at restaurant); *Nwakpuda v. Falley's, Inc.*, 14 F. Supp. 2d 1213 (D. Kan. 1998) (§1981 claim for store patron who was wrongfully detained because he was thought to be individual who had previously robbed the store).

[225] *Chapman v. Higbee*, 319 F.3d 825 (6th Cir. 2003); *Phillip v. University of Rochester*, 316 F.3d 291 (2d Cir. 2003); *McCaleb v. Pizza Hut of America, Inc.*, 28 F. Supp. 2d 1043 (N.D. Ill. 1998).

[226] *See generally* Suja A. Thomas, *The Customer Caste: Lawful Discrimination by Public Businesses*, 109 Cal. L. Rev. 141 (2021).

[227] *Arguello v. Conoco, Inc.*, 330 F.3d 355 (5th Cir. 2003); *Wesley v. Don Stein Buick, Inc.*, 42 F. Supp. 2d 1192 (D. Kan. 1999). *See Bobbitt v. Rage Inc.*, 19 F. Supp. 2d 512 (W.D.N.C. 1998) (no §1981 claim for patrons who were treated disrespectfully but claim does exist for group asked to prepay for their meal).

to discriminatory surveillance, searches or detention,[228] or removed from a store for discriminatory reasons after making a purchase.[229]

Argument that §§1981 & 1982 do not apply to pre- and post-contract conduct

Courts that have denied relief have argued that the guarantee in §1981 that all persons shall have the same "right to make contracts as is enjoyed by white citizens" requires stores to sell their items or enter into service agreements, but that the right to contract does not protect customers from discriminatory treatment that does not actually prevent a customer from purchasing goods or services. For example, in *Ackerman v. Food-4-Less,*[230] a Black store patron was watched and followed by a security guard when she entered the store. She picked up a small container of Spanish spice powder, not concealing it, and was grabbed roughly by the security guard when she attempted to use the bathroom. She was detained for two hours and subjected to numerous racial slurs during the detention. She was not allowed to use the bathroom, causing her to defecate in her pants. The court held that she had no claim under §1981 for being followed, grabbed, or detained before purchasing an item but that she would have a claim if she had been actually prevented from purchasing the item.[231] According to the court, the plaintiff must show that she "was actually prevented, and not merely deterred, from making a purchase or receiv[ing] service after attempting to do so."[232] Some other courts have similarly held that "a §1981 claim for interference with the right to make and enforce a contract must involve the actual loss of a contract interest, not merely the possible loss of future contract opportunities."[233] Thus, *Wesley v. Don Stein Buick, Inc.*[234] held that a Black customer who was treated rudely, asked personal questions not asked of white customers, and denied assistance at a car dealership was held to have no claim under §1981. The court explained that "federal courts that have analyzed §1981 claims in the retail merchandise context have required plaintiffs to show that they were actually prevented from making a purchase."[235] Other courts have similarly held that post-contract conduct is not

[228] *Gregory v. Dillard's Inc.*, 565 F.3d 464 (8th Cir. 2009); *Garrett v. Tandy Corp.*, 295 F.3d 94 (1st Cir. 2002); *Morris v. Office Max, Inc.*, 89 F.3d 411 (7th Cir. 1996).

[229] *Flowers v. TJX Cos.*, 1994 WL 382515 (N.D.N.Y. 1994).

[230] 1998 WL 316084 (E.D. Pa. 1998).

[231] *Accord, Hampton v. Dillard Dep't Stores, Inc.*, 247 F.3d 1091 (10th Cir. 2001); *Morris v. Office Max, Inc.*, 89 F.3d 411 (7th Cir. 1996); *Wesley v. Don Stein Buick, Inc.*, 42 F. Supp. 2d 1192, 1200 (D. Kan. 1999); *Sterling v. Kazmierczak*, 983 F. Supp. 1186 (N.D. Ill. 1997); *Lewis v. JC Penney Co.*, 948 F. Supp. 367 (D. Del. 1996).

[232] 1998 WL 316084, at *2 (E.D. Pa. 1988) (quoting *Henderson v. Jewel Food Stores, Inc.*, 1996 WL 617165, at *1, *3 (N.D. Ill. Oct. 23, 1996)). *Cf.* Jon Burstein, *Shopper Wins Profiling Lawsuit, Customer Says Racial Bias Led to His Detention*, Sun-Sentinel Oct. 1, 2004, at 1B (customer awarded $2.6 million damages for tort of false imprisonment when suspected of stealing shoes based on his race).

[233] *Hampton v. Dillard Dep't Stores, Inc.*, 247 F.3d 1091 (10th Cir. 2001); *Wesley v. Don Stein Buick, Inc.*, 42 F. Supp. 2d 1192, 1200 (D. Kan. 1999) (*citing Phelps v. Wichita Eagle-Beacon*, 886 F.2d 1262, 1267 (10th Cir. 1989)). *Accord, Morris v. Office Max, Inc.*, 89 F.3d 411 (7th Cir. 1996); *Sterling v. Kazmierczak*, 983 F. Supp. 1186 (N.D. Ill. 1997); *Lewis v. JC Penney Co.*, 948 F. Supp. 367 (D. Del. 1996).

[234] 42 F. Supp. 2d 1192 (D. Kan. 1999).

[235] *Id.* at 1201; *see, e.g., Hampton v. Dillard Dep't Stores, Inc.*, 247 F.3d 1091 (10th Cir. 2001) (§1981 claim available to a woman who was prevented by store security guard from using free coupon to sample perfume that she had been given as a benefit for her purchase of children's clothing at the store but denied to her niece who had been given a free coupon

regulated by §1981, rejecting discrimination claims for conduct (such as detention or interrogation) that occurs after a patron has successfully purchased items in the store.[236]

Argument that §1981 and/or §1982 apply to pre- and post-contract conduct

In contrast, *Hall v. Pennsylvania State Police*[237] upheld a §1981 claim against a bank by a bank patron who was photographed upon entering the bank under a discriminatory bank policy of photographing "suspicious" Black customers. The court noted that §1981 "obligates commercial enterprises to extend the same treatment to contractual customers 'as is enjoyed by white citizens.'"[238] Similarly, in *Nwakpuda v. Falley's, Inc.*,[239] the court upheld a §1981 claim for a store patron who was wrongfully detained because he was thought to be an individual who had previously robbed the store and who alleged that he had been treated differently from white patrons because of his race. In *McCaleb v. Pizza Hut of America, Inc.*,[240] a §1981 claim was held to be available to a Black family that was denied "full benefits" of the contract when they were denied utensils and harassed and threatened while at the restaurant. These courts all assumed that the right to contract includes not only the right to buy but the right to enter the premises and receive nondiscriminatory treatment while there.

Effect of the *Civil Rights Act of 1991*

When the Supreme Court narrowly interpreted the right to contract in *Patterson v. McLean Credit Union*,[241] Congress promptly overturned the decision by amending §1981. *Patterson* held that §1981 prohibited employers from refusing to hire on the basis of race but that §1981 did not prohibit discriminatory racial harassment on the job. The *Civil Rights Act of 1991* amended §1981 to clarify that the "right to make and enforce contracts" included a right to nondiscriminatory terms and conditions in those contracts.[242] Given this legislative history, it would seem that courts interpreting §1981 in the context of retail stores should similarly broadly interpret the "right to make contracts" to include a right to obtain access to places of public accommodation and to obtain nondiscriminatory treatment while they are there.[243] ◀

---

but had not made a purchase); *Ackaa v. Tommy Hilfiger Co.*, 1998 WL 136522, at *5 (E.D. Pa. 1998) ("A §1981 claim must allege that the plaintiff was actually prevented, not merely deterred, from making a purchase or receiving service after attempting to do so."); *Sterling v. Kazmierczak*, 983 F. Supp. 1186, 1192 (N.D. Ill. 1997) (granting defendants' motion to dismiss plaintiff's §1981 claim where plaintiff failed to allege that he ever found the air rifle cartridges for which he was looking, failed to allege that he was prepared to buy such cartridges before he left the store, and failed to allege that he had the cartridges "in hand" when confronted by police officer).

[236] *See, e.g., Arguello v. Conoco, Inc.*, 330 F.3d 355 (5th Cir. 2003) (no §1981 claim when clerk shouted obscenities and made racially derogatory remarks at Latina customer after she completed her purchase); *Lewis v. JC Penney Company, Inc.*, 948 F. Supp. 367, 371 (D. Del. 1996) (no §1981 claim when patron alleged that she was wrongfully stopped and interrogated after purchasing items); *Flowers v. TJX Cos.*, 1994 WL 382515 (N.D.N.Y. 1994) (no §1981 claim when plaintiffs successfully completed their retail transactions).

[237] 570 F.2d 86 (3d Cir. 1978).

[238] *Id.* at 92.

[239] 14 F. Supp. 2d 1213 (D. Kan. 1998).

[240] 28 F. Supp. 2d 1043 (N.D. Ill. 1998).

[241] 491 U.S. 164 (1989).

[242] 42 U.S.C. §1981(b).

[243] Joseph William Singer, *The Anti-Apartheid Principle in American Property Law*, 1 Ala. C.R.-C.L. L. Rev. 83 (2011).

▶ **HARD CASE** ▷ DOES §1981 REGULATE PRIVATE CLUBS?

The argument that §1981 does regulate private clubs

It is a harder question whether §1981 regulates private clubs, which are exempt from the 1964 public accommodations law. Recall that the 1964 Act expressly exempts "private clubs" from its coverage.[244] Was this exemption intended to grant private clubs an entitlement to discriminate, or merely an exemption from the 1964 Act, leaving such clubs subject to regulation under other federal and state statutes, such as the *Civil Rights Act of 1866*? Some courts hold that the 1964 Act had no effect on the prior statute (§1981) and that private clubs are therefore required by §1981 not to discriminate when they offer their services to the public or when they seek members.[245] For example, in *Watson v. Fraternal Order of Eagles*,[246] the court held that the private club exemption to Title II's prohibition against discrimination in public accommodations, in 42 U.S.C. §2000a(e), did not preclude an independent civil rights action under §1981 against the private club. In *Watson*, Black guests at a private party were removed from a private club after they attempted to purchase soft drinks. Judge Merritt noted, first, that the Supreme Court had consistently held that the civil rights laws passed in the 1960s, like the 1964 public accommodations law, "do not impinge on actions that may be brought under earlier enactments"[247] and that the "later statutes did not repeal the earlier statutes."[248] Although, "[a]s a general rule, later, more specific statutes limit the interpretation of earlier, more general ones[, t]his principle does not apply if the legislature intended the general act to retain independent force."[249] The savings clause in §2000a-6(b)[250] continues the force of prior laws that are "not inconsistent" with the 1964 Act. Application of §1981 to a private club is "not inconsistent" with the private clubs exemption to §2000a(a) because that exemption in no way "give[s] the clubs carte blanche to violate all other antidiscrimination laws."[251] Second, Judge Merritt argued that "Congress has also indicated its intention to preserve both statutes, by not amending either one after the Supreme Court held [in 1976] that §1981 applies to private discrimination

[244] 42 U.S.C. §2000a(e).

[245] For cases suggesting that §1981 applies to employers who are exempt from Title VII of the *Civil Rights Act of 1964*, see *Rivers v. Roadway Express, Inc.*, 511 U.S. 298, 304 n.3 (1994) (noting that "in the employment context, §1981's coverage is broader than Title VII's, for Title VII applies only to employers with 15 or more employees, see 42 U.S.C. §2000e(b), whereas §1981 has no such limitation"); *Johnson v. Railway Express Agency*, 421 U.S. 454, 460 (1975) (noting but not holding that §1981, but not 42 U.S.C. §2000e(b), applies to employers with fewer than 15 employees). For cases holding that §1982 applies to landlords exempt from the *Fair Housing Act of 1968*, pursuant to 42 U.S.C. §3603, see *Morris v. Cizek*, 503 F.2d 1303 (7th Cir. 1974); *Johnson v. Zaremba*, 381 F. Supp. 165 (N.D. Ill. 1973) (both holding that §1982 applies to small landlords exempt from the *Fair Housing Act of 1968*, 42 U.S.C. §3603).

[246] 915 F.2d 235 (6th Cir. 1990).

[247] *Id.* at 239.

[248] *Id.* at 240.

[249] *Id.*

[250] "Nothing in this subchapter shall preclude any individual . . . from asserting any right based on any other Federal or State law not inconsistent with this subchapter . . . or from pursuing any remedy, civil or criminal, which may be available for the vindication or enforcement of such right." 42 U.S.C. §2000a-6(b).

[251] *Watson v. Fraternal Order of Eagles*, 915 F.2d 235 (6th Cir. 1990); *id.* at 241-242.

in *Runyon v. McCrary*."[252] This argument has even greater force today because §1981 was actually amended by Congress in 1991 and nothing in the amendment grants private clubs an exemption from its provisions. Third, the remedies in the two statutes are quite different. And fourth, their constitutional bases differ (§1981 is based on the Thirteenth Amendment and §2000a is based on the Commerce Clause). Congress's "determination to exclude private clubs from coverage reflects, therefore, a determination that such clubs did not have a sufficient impact on interstate commerce to warrant regulation under the Commerce Clause. That conclusion does not imply, however, that the regulation of contracts made by private clubs exceeds Congress's power from all provisions of the Constitution."[253]

The argument that §1981 does not regulate private clubs

Other courts, however, have concluded that the private clubs exemption in 42 U.S.C. §2000a(e) would be meaningless if identical claims could be brought under §1981 and that, even if §1981 could be read as a general public accommodations law, it was narrowed by §2000a(e), which had the effect of immunizing private clubs from antidiscrimination claims. For example, in *Cornelius v. Benevolent Protective Order of the Elks*,[254] Judge Blumenfeld held that an irrevocable conflict between a statute that authorizes conduct and one that prohibits it must be adjudicated by applying the later Act.[255] He argued first, that "courts may properly take into account [a] later Act when asked to extend the reach of [an] earlier Act's vague language to the limits which, read literally, the words might permit." Second, "the provisions of one statute which specifically focus on a particular problem will always, in the absence of express contrary legislative intent, be held to prevail over provisions of a different statute more general in its coverage." Third, the legislative history of the 1964 Act supports a harmonization of the statutes. When Congress passed the 1964 Act, it believed it was enacting the first federal legislation prohibiting private discrimination in public accommodations. "Prior to *Jones v. Mayer*,[256] sections 1981 and 1982 were thought to apply only to 'state action.' Thus, the absence of express language in the 1964 Act limiting the 1866 act is hardly evidence of an intention not to have that effect." Finally, the savings clause in the 1964 Act, 42 U.S.C. §2000a-6(b), provides for the possibility of a limitation of earlier legislation because it provides that "nothing in [§2000a] shall preclude any individual or any State or local agency from asserting any right based on any other Federal or State law *not inconsistent* with [§2000a]." If private clubs are exempt from regulation under §2000a(e), it would arguably be "inconsistent" with that provision to interpret §1981 to require such clubs to serve customers without regard to race. ◀

Right to exclude v. right to acquire property

If §1981 requires owners of public accommodations to serve the public, one might understand it as a limitation on property rights (specifically, the right to exclude) designed to promote equality norms. This view is too facile. For one thing, the right to exclude is limited by granting others

[252] *Id.*
[253] *Id.* at 241-242.
[254] 382 F. Supp. 1182 (D. Conn. 1974).
[255] *Id.* at 1201.
[256] *Jones v. Alfred H. Mayer Co.*, 392 U.S. 409 (1968).

a right of access to the property (a right to enter), as well as a power to purchase property. The right to enter public accommodations is a property claim as well as an equality claim. After all, in the modern world, if one can be denied access to businesses that sell goods and services, one's ability to acquire property is severely limited. This is why the Supreme Court has held that the right to contract and to purchase real and personal property enshrined in the *Civil Rights Act of 1866*[257] encompasses a power to force businesses to enter transactions without regard to race. The right to "purchase personal property" protected by §1982 is promoted by limiting the ability of owners of public accommodations to refuse to deal with prospective customers simply on the basis of race. There are property rights on both sides of the equation here. We are not limiting property rights to promote equality; we are accommodating competing property rights in ways that respond to a combination of concerns, which include equal access, associational freedoms, and autonomy. Public accommodations laws ensure the right to acquire property without regard to one's race.

§2.6.3 Americans with Disabilities Act of 1990

42 U.S.C. §§12101 to 12213

The *Americans with Disabilities Act of 1990* (the "*ADA*")[258] is one of the most important pieces of civil rights legislation approved by Congress since the *Civil Rights Act of 1964*.[259] After the *Fair Housing Act of 1968*[260] was amended in 1988 to prohibit discrimination on the basis of disability in housing,[261] the *ADA* added prohibitions against such discrimination in both employment and public accommodations. The public accommodations provisions of the *ADA* not only prohibit discrimination in access to the accommodations of existing facilities,[262] but require new buildings to provide access to persons with disabilities.[263] In addition, renovations of existing buildings trigger obligations to improve accessibility.[264] The U.S. Department of Justice has promulgated regulations implementing the statute and clarifying the scope of the obligations imposed on businesses.[265] Remedies under the statute are limited to injunctive relief; damages are not available.[266] However, the Attorney General is empowered to enforce the statute[267] and, in such cases, civil penalties can be imposed by a court.[268]

Disability

A disability is defined as (A) "a physical or mental impairment that substantially limits one or more of the major life activities"; (B) a "record of such impairment"; or (C) "being regarded as having such an impairment."[269]

[257] Section 1982 provides that "[a]ll citizens of the United States shall have the same right as is enjoyed by white citizens to purchase real and personal property." 42 U.S.C. §1982.
[258] 42 U.S.C. §§12101 to 12213.
[259] Pub. L. No. 101-336, July 26, 1990, 104 Stat. 327.
[260] 42 U.S.C. §§3601 to 3619, 3631.
[261] 42 U.S.C. §3604(f).
[262] 42 U.S.C. §12182.
[263] 42 U.S.C. §12183(a)(1).
[264] 42 U.S.C. §12183(a)(2).
[265] *See* 28 C.F.R. §§36.101 to 36.608.
[266] 42 U.S.C. §12188(a)(1). *A.R. v. Kogan*, 964 F. Supp. 269 (N.D. Ill. 1997).
[267] 42 U.S.C. §12188(b).
[268] 42 U.S.C. §12188(b)(2).
[269] 42 U.S.C. §12102(1).

Specifically excluded from the definition of "disability" are homosexuality and bisexuality,[270] as well as current use of illegal drugs.[271]

Definition of public accommodation

A public accommodation is broadly defined to include almost any "entity" that offers goods or services to the public, specifically including inns and hotels (unless the establishment contains not more than five rooms for rent and is actually occupied by the proprietor as his or her residence), restaurants, theaters, museums, auditoriums, convention centers, lecture halls, retail stores of all kinds (selling food, clothing, hardware, etc.), laundromats, dry cleaners, banks, barber shops, beauty shops, travel services, shoe repair services, funeral parlors, gas stations, accountants' or lawyers' offices, pharmacies, insurance offices, professional offices of health care providers, hospitals or other service establishments, transportation stations, libraries, parks, zoos, places of recreation, amusement parks, schools of all kinds from nursery schools and day care centers to postgraduate education, senior citizen centers, homeless shelters, food banks, adoption agencies or other social service centers, gymnasiums, health spas, bowling alleys, golf courses, or other places of exercise or recreation.[272]

Private club exemption

The Act does not apply to private clubs exempt from coverage under the public accommodations law of 1964, 42 U.S.C. §2000a(e), or to religious organizations, including places of worship.[273]

▷ "PLACE" OF PUBLIC ACCOMMODATION — HARD CASE ◀

In *Schultz v. Hemet Youth Pony League, Inc.*,[274] the court found that a youth baseball league was a public accommodation even though it did not operate at a particular facility. Judge Consuelo Bland Marshall ruled that "Title III's definition of 'place of public accommodation' is not limited to actual physical structures with definite physical boundaries."[275] In addition, a youth league does meet in a physical location, and the statute does not require a showing that a public accommodation owns or rents its property.[276] In addition, although the operative section, §12182, refers to a "*place* of public accommodation," the definition section, §12181, merely refers to "public accommodation" without using the word "place." On the other hand, all the listed places have physical facilities and courts interpreting Title II of the *Civil Rights Act of 1964* have generally interpreted it to apply only to "places" of public accommodation rather than membership organizations or "gatherings of people."[277] Although some state courts have held that the word "place" in their state public accommodations laws is a word of

[270] 42 U.S.C. §12211.
[271] 42 U.S.C. §12210.
[272] 42 U.S.C. §12181(7).
[273] 42 U.S.C. §12187.
[274] 943 F. Supp. 1222 (C.D. Cal. 1996).
[275] *Id.* at 1225.
[276] *See also Nathanson v. Spring Lake Park Panther Youth Football Ass'n*, 129 F. Supp. 3d 743, 747-748 (D. Minn. 2015) (youth football association found to be a place of public accommodation under Title III and state law).
[277] *Welsh v. Boy Scouts of America*, 993 F.2d 1267 (7th Cir. 1993).

"convenience, not limitation,"[278] others have refused to apply their public accommodations laws to organizations that do not have their own physical facilities.[279] ◀

▶ **HARD CASE**

▷ WEB SITES AS PLACES OF PUBLIC ACCOMMODATION

In 1999, the National Federation of the Blind sued America Online (AOL) claiming that AOL's Web services were a public accommodation regulated by the *ADA* and that AOL had an obligation to make its services available to blind persons.[280] Some courts have held that public accommodations under the *ADA* are limited to places with physical locations,[281] while others have held that the definition of a public accommodation might include businesses that do not offer their goods and services at a physical location, such as companies operated through websites or insurance plans.[282] Some courts have ruled that the *ADA* applies only to Web sites if they are connected to businesses that have physical locations, such as insurance companies and retail stores.[283]◀

[278] *Dale v. Boy Scouts of America*, 734 A.2d 1196, 1209 (N.J. 1999), *rev'd on other grounds sub nom. Boy Scouts of America v. Dale*, 530 U.S. 640 (2000).

[279] *United States Jaycees v. Richardet*, 666 P.2d 1008, 1011 (Alaska 1983); *Seabourn v. Coronado Area Council, Boy Scouts of America*, 891 P.2d 385 (Kan. 1995); *United States Jaycees v. Massachusetts Comm'n Against Discrimination*, 463 N.E.2d 1151 (Mass. 1984).

[280] *National Fed'n of the Blind v. America Online, Inc.*, No. 99CV12303EFH (D. Mass., filed Nov. 4, 1999) (complaint available at Americans With Disabilities: Practice and Compliance Manual 6:551 (1994 & Supp. 2000)). The lawsuit was settled with agreement that would make AOL's services accessible to the blind. *National Federation of the Blind and America Online Reach Agreement on Accessibility; AOL 6.0 to Work With Screen Reader Interface Enabling Easier Navigation for the Blind; NFB Withdraws Lawsuit Against America Online, Inc.*, PR Newswire (July 26, 2000).

[281] *Gil v. Winn-Dixie Stores, Inc.*, 993 F.3d 1266, 1277 (11th Cir. 2021); *MacNeil v. Time Ins. Co.*, 205 F.3d 179, 186 (5th Cir. 2000) (insurance company does not violate *ADA* when it caps benefits for patients with AIDS because the *ADA* does not "regulate the content of goods and services that are offered"); *Ford v. Schering-Plough Corp.*, 145 F.3d 601 (3d Cir. 1998) (no *ADA* violation when insurance company capped benefits for mental but not physical disabilities); *Parker v. Metropolitan Life Co.*, 121 F.3d 1006 (6th Cir. 1997) (disability benefits plan that distinguished between physical and mental disability was not a good offered by a place of public accommodation). *Cf. Noah v. AOL Time Warner Inc.*, 261 F. Supp. 2d 532, 541 (E.D. Va. 2003) (AOL chat rooms are not places of public accommodation under Title II of the *Civil Rights Act of 1964* because they are not "actual, physical places [or] structures").

[282] *Chalas v. Pork King Good*, 673 F. Supp. 3d 339, 342-44 (S.D.N.Y. 2023) (noting split and concluding that limiting "places of public accommodation to the brick-and-mortar standard would severely hamper Congress' effort to protect disabled persons who want and need access to the growing number of online-only providers"); *Robles v. Domino's Pizza, LLC*, 913 F.3d 898, 905 (9th Cir. 2019) (*ADA* applies to a business's Web site and smartphone app where they "facilitate access to the goods and services of a place of public accommodation"); *Carparts Distribution Center, Inc. v. Automotive Wholesalers Ass'n of New England*, 37 F.3d 12, 20 (1st Cir. 1994) (physical accommodations regulated by the *ADA* are not limited to physical places but include goods and services "sold over the telephone or by mail with customers never physically entering the premises of a commercial entity to purchase the goods or services"); *Nat'l Ass'n of the Deaf v. Netflix, Inc.*, 869 F. Supp. 2d 196 (D. Mass. 2012) (Netflix Web site is a place of public accommodation under the *ADA* and required to provide closed captioning for its content).

[283] *Cullin v. Netflix, Inc.*, 880 F. Supp. 2d 1017 (N.D. Cal. 2012); *Nat'l Fed'n of the Blind v. Target Corp.*, 452 F. Supp. 2d 946, 953 (N.D. Cal. 2006).

Prohibition against discrimination

The basic prohibition in the *ADA* provides that "[n]o individual shall be discriminated against on the basis of disability in the full and equal enjoyment of the goods, services, facilities, privileges, advantages, or accommodations of any place of public accommodation by any person who owns, leases (or leases to), or operates a place of public accommodation."[284] The statute specifically provides that individuals may not be denied the right to participate, may not be offered services that are not equal to those offered to others, may not be segregated or separated unless such separation is necessary to provide the services to individuals with disabilities, must be served in the most integrated setting possible, and, if separate services are offered, may not be denied the right to participate in activities that are not separate.[285]

Eligibility criteria

Public accommodations must also not impose "eligibility criteria" that "screen out or tend to screen out" individuals with a disability from "fully and equally enjoying" the goods or services of the establishment "unless such criteria can be shown to be necessary" for the provision of the accommodations being offered.[286] In *Coleman v. Zatechka*,[287] the court held that a university violated this provision when it refused to pair a student with a randomly assigned roommate. The school refused to modify its policy that each student takes up no more than half the room and not have frequent visitors. Because the student required use of a wheelchair and the services of a personal attendant, the school believed this would be too much of an imposition to place on a roommate and would only assign a roommate for plaintiff if one volunteered to live with her. The court held that these "eligibility requirements" for the roommate program tended to screen out persons with disabilities who needed a personal attendant from participating equally in the school's dormitory services. The court also found that these criteria were not "necessary" because the school did not police the amount of furniture students brought in to ensure that no student took up more than half the space; nor did it police visitation for students without disabilities. In effect, the school imposed an obligation on plaintiff that it did not in fact impose on students without disabilities. The defendant could not show that its requirements were even-handedly applied, and therefore it did not show that they were necessary.

Auxiliary aids and services

Public accommodations are required to "take such steps as may be necessary to ensure that no individual with a disability is excluded, denied services, segregated or otherwise treated differently than other individuals because of the absence of auxiliary aids and services, unless the entity can demonstrate that taking such steps would fundamentally alter the nature of the [accommodation] being offered or would result in an undue burden."[288] In *Bunjer v. Edwards*,[289] the court held that a McDonald's restaurant discriminated against a deaf patron when it failed to accommodate his inability to place his order verbally at the drive-through window. Judge Sporkin noted that defendant could easily post a sign instructing deaf patrons to

[284] 42 U.S.C. §12182(a).
[285] 42 U.S.C. §12182(b)(1).
[286] 42 U.S.C. §12182(b)(2)(A)(i); 28 C.F.R. §36.301.
[287] 824 F. Supp. 1360 (D. Neb. 1993).
[288] 42 U.S.C. §12182(b)(2)(A)(iii); 28 C.F.R. §36.303.
[289] 985 F. Supp. 165 (D.D.C. 1997).

proceed directly to the pick-up window to fill out the order in a written form. He also concluded that the workers were inadequately trained to deal with a deaf patron and treated him in an offensive and rude manner when he tried to submit a written order at the pick-up window. The failure to train employees adequately was particularly inappropriate given the restaurant's location near Gallaudet University, the foremost national university devoted entirely to the deaf and hard of hearing.

Architectural barriers

The *ADA* requires existing businesses to remove "architectural barriers, and communication barriers that are structural in nature," in existing facilities, where such removal is "readily achievable."[290] Removal is "readily achievable" if it is "easily accomplishable and able to be carried out without much difficulty or expense."[291] This suggests that a public accommodation has no obligation to install ramps or otherwise provide access to their existing facilities if this would be expensive. However, the statute also provides that in determining whether an action is "readily achievable," factors to be considered include "the nature and cost of the action" as well as the "overall financial resources of the facility," the number of persons employed, and the cost and resources of the facility and the impact of undertaking the corrective action on the facility.[292] This suggests that a business that is wealthy enough to afford installing ramps and other accessways may be obligated to do so. If removal is not readily achievable, the public accommodation must make the goods or services "available through alternative methods if such methods are readily achievable."[293]

Readily achievable

Reasonable modifications in policies and practices

Public accommodations are also required "to make reasonable modifications in policies, practices, or procedures, when such modifications are necessary" to provide goods or services to individuals with disabilities, "unless the entity can demonstrate that making such modifications would fundamentally alter the nature" of the goods or services provided.[294] In *Rodenberg-Roberts v. KinderCare Learning Centers, Inc.*,[295] the Eighth Circuit ruled that a day care center need not admit a child who needed one-on-one care when his personal care attendant could not be present, because this would place an unreasonable burden on the center. The court viewed the $95-per-week burden as significant given the center's monthly operating income of $9,600.

Reasonable modification ordered

On the other hand, in *Schultz v. Hemet Youth Pony League, Inc.*,[296] the court found that defendant baseball league violated the statute when it refused to allow a boy with cerebral palsy to play with boys in a younger age bracket. The court ruled that

> a baseball program must modify its traditional policies, rules and regulations to accommodate the needs of a child with a disability, in

[290] 42 U.S.C. §12182(b)(2)(A)(iv); 28 C.F.R. §36.304. *See Tennessee v. Lane*, 541 U.S. 509 (2004) (Congress has the constitutional power to require state governments to make courthouses accessible to persons who use wheelchairs).
[291] 42 U.S.C. §12181(9); 28 C.F.R. §36.304.
[292] For more detail, see 42 U.S.C. §12181(9).
[293] 42 U.S.C. §12182(b)(2)(A)(v); 28 C.F.R. §36.305.
[294] 42 U.S.C. §12182(b)(2)(A)(ii); 28 C.F.R. §36.302.
[295] 86 F.3d 844 (8th Cir. 1996).
[296] 943 F. Supp. 1222 (C.D. Cal. 1996).

> order to provide that child an opportunity to participate which is both appropriate for his needs as a person with a disability that substantially limits his mobility, and equivalent to opportunities provided to his non-disabled peers.[297]

The league excluded plaintiff "on the basis of assumed and unsubstantiated concerns of a possible risk of harm to Plaintiff and other players, and insurance ramifications."[298] The league did not investigate to determine whether the plaintiff was at risk; nor did it consider whether it could modify its policies or practices to enable him to participate. The defendant's

> failure to make necessary and reasonable attempts to ascertain what modifications, if any, were plausible in order to accommodate Plaintiff's disability, either by permitting him to "play down," or in the most integrated setting appropriate to plaintiff's individual needs, was discriminatory inaction against Plaintiff on the basis of Plaintiff's disability.[299]

Fundamentally alter the nature of the accommodations

Similarly, in a widely publicized case, professional golfer Casey Martin sued the Professional Golf Association (PGA) when it refused to let him use a cart to travel between holes in a professional golf tournament. The Sixth Circuit held, in *Martin v. PGA Tour, Inc.*,[300] that use of a golf cart was a reasonable modification for an individual who could do everything associated with golf except walk long distances. The harder question was whether the PGA was exempted from the duty to make this modification because it would "fundamentally alter the nature" of the game.[301] Although defendant claimed that the exertion associated with walking was part of the game, the court concluded that the modification would not fundamentally alter the nature of the game. The court distinguished *McPherson v. Michigan High School Athletic Association, Inc.*,[302] in which the Sixth Circuit held that a high school sports league could adhere to its rule excluding players who had been in high school more than eight semesters. Although plaintiff's learning disability prevented him from finishing high school in eight semesters, the Sixth Circuit concluded that it would "fundamentally alter the nature" of the activity to allow him to play because the eligibility requirements imposed were closely fitted with the purpose of high school athletics — to allow students of the same age group to compete against each other.[303] In contrast, in *Martin*, although the court found that it was legitimate to require walking to "inject the element of fatigue into the skill of shotmaking,"[304] it also found, as a factual matter, that "the fatigue factor injected into the game of golf by walking the course cannot be deemed significant

[297] *Id.* at 1224.

[298] *Id.* at 1225.

[299] *Id.* at 1225-1226.

[300] 984 F. Supp. 1320, 994 F. Supp. 1242 (D. Or. 1998), *aff'd*, 204 F.3d 994 (9th Cir. 2000), *aff'd*, 532 U.S. 661 (2001).

[301] 42 U.S.C. §12182(b)(2)(A)(ii).

[302] 119 F.3d 453 (6th Cir. 1997).

[303] *See Pottgen v. Missouri High School Activities Association*, 40 F.3d 926 (8th Cir. 1994) (similar result).

[304] 994 F. Supp. at 1250.

under normal circumstances"[305] and that modification of the requirement would therefore not fundamentally alter the nature of the game. However, the Seventh Circuit disagreed with this conclusion, holding in *Olinger v. United States Golf Association*[306] that it would "fundamentally alter the nature of the game" to allow a golfer to use a golf cart. The Supreme Court resolved the question when it affirmed the Sixth Circuit's conclusion that it would not "fundamentally alter the nature" of the game of golf if Casey Martin used a cart to travel between holes.[307] Justice Stevens noted that this accommodation neither gave Martin an advantage over other competitors nor affected an "essential aspect of the game of golf."[308] The essence of the game is "shotmaking" and this aspect remained over time despite changes such as the increase in the number and type of clubs, the use of golf bags, caddies, and carts pulled by hand.[309] Nor was the Court convinced that the fatigue caused by walking was at all significant.[310] Justices Scalia and Thomas dissented, arguing that the *ADA* does not regulate the content of the goods and services offered by places of public accommodation; it only requires equal access.[311] They further noted that it is impossible to answer a question of what is "essential" to golf and that it is therefore unreasonable to assume the Congress intended the Supreme Court to attempt to do so.[312]

HARD CASE ▶ ▷ SMOKING

The *ADA* provides that "[n]othing in this chapter shall be construed to preclude the prohibition of, or the imposition of restrictions on, smoking" in places of public accommodation.[313] This provision precludes a finding that smokers are persons with disabilities because of an addiction to nicotine. It does not answer other questions related to smoking, however. How much of an accommodation must a facility make to ensure that those who are adversely affected by smoking are not excluded from the establishment? In *Emery v. Caravan of Dreams, Inc.*,[314] the court ruled that a musical entertainment establishment had no obligation to exclude smokers even though failure to do so meant that plaintiffs suffering from cystic fibrosis, allergies, and asthma could not attend the concerts. Judge Sanders noted that the evidence showed that "banning smoking would have a major economic impact and would result in major national bands not coming to play at Caravan of Dreams. [The] requested modification would endanger Defendant's viability as a business, and such modifications are not

305 *Id.*
306 205 F.3d 1001 (7th Cir. 2000).
307 *PGA Tour, Inc. v. Martin*, 532 U.S. 661 (2001).
308 *Id.* at 682.
309 *Id.* at 683.
310 *Id.* at 687.
311 *Id.* at 699-700 (Scalia, J., dissenting).
312 *Id.* at 700-701 (Scalia, J., dissenting).
313 42 U.S.C. §12201(b).
314 879 F. Supp. 640 (N.D. Tex. 1995).

required."[315] However, in *Staron v. McDonald's Corp.*,[316] the Second Circuit ruled that it might well violate the *ADA* to refuse to ban smoking entirely in a restaurant if it would effectively exclude children with asthma and a woman with lupus. The court rejected the idea that a total smoking ban would necessarily constitute an "unreasonable" modification in business practices and remanded for a trial on the question of whether such a ban would impose an unreasonable financial burden on defendant. ◀

New construction

The *ADA* requires all new construction of facilities intended for first occupancy after January 26, 1993, to be designed to accommodate and provide access to persons with disabilities.[317] Such facilities must be "readily accessible to and usable by individuals with disabilities,"[318] except where "structurally impracticable" to do so. A Department of Justice implementing regulation (§4.33.3) requires: "[W]heelchair areas shall be an integral part of any fixed seating plan and shall be provided so as to provide people with physical disabilities a choice of admission prices and lines of sight comparable to those for members of the general public."[319] In *Caruso v. Blockbuster-SONY Music Entertainment Centre at the Waterfront*,[320] the court held that neither the *ADA* nor §4.33.3 required sightlines over standing spectators but merely dispersal of seating. In contrast, *Miller v. California Speedway Corp.*[321] held that a facility did violate the *ADA* and this regulation when it provided wheelchair seating that did not allow lines of sight to the racetrack over standing spectators.[322]

▷ WHEELCHAIR SEATS IN FRONT OF MOVIE THEATER **HARD CASE ◀**

If a new movie theater provides wheelchair seating at the front of the room but not farther back, does that comply with the *ADA* requirement that new facilities be "readily accessible to and usable by individuals with disabilities"?[323] A Justice Department regulation provides that theaters must supply "lines of sight comparable to those for members of the general public."[324] The Fifth Circuit held, in *Lara v. Cinemark USA, Inc.*,[325] that front-row wheelchair seating meets this criterion because wheelchair users are given

[315] *Id.* at 644.
[316] 51 F.3d 353 (2d Cir. 1995).
[317] 42 U.S.C. §12183, 28 C.F.R. §§36.301 to 36.406.
[318] 42 U.S.C. §12183(a)(1).
[319] *ADA Accessibility Guidelines* (*ADAAG*), §4.33.3, 28 C.F.R. pt. 36, App. A, §4.33.3.
[320] 193 F.3d 730 (3d Cir. 1999).
[321] 536 F.3d 1020 (9th Cir. 2008). While the *Miller* court does not explicitly state how much of the wheelchair accessible seating must have lines of sight over standing spectators, the case affirms *Paralyzed Veterans of America v. D.C. Arena L.P.*, 117 F.3d 579, 588 (D.C. Cir. 1997), which indicates that only 75-88 percent of the seating must have sightlines. Therefore, *Miller's* reliance on *Paralyzed Veterans* may indicate that most, but not all, seating is required to provide sightlines.
[322] *Accord, Paralyzed Veterans of America v. D.C. Arena L.P.*, 117 F.3d 579 (D.C. Cir. 1997). *See* 28 C.F.R. §36.308.
[323] *See* 42 U.S.C. §12183(a)(1).
[324] *ADA Accessibility Guidelines* (*ADAAG*), §4.33.3, 28 C.F.R. pt. 36, App. A, §4.33.3.
[325] 207 F.3d 783 (5th Cir. 2000). *Accord, United States v. Hoyts Cinemas Corp.*, 380 F.3d 558 (1st Cir. 2004) (front-row seating may comply with *ADA*).

places comparable to places reserved for other members of the public and the views are unobstructed. The Ninth and Sixth Circuits disagree, holding that front-row seating in a stadium-type movie theater does not provide lines of sight "comparable" to that provided to other patrons because most movie theater patrons normally choose to sit farther back than the front row, suggesting that front-row seats are generally viewed as the worst in the house and thus not comparable to those granted most other viewers who have a choice to avoid such seating.[326] ◀

Renovations

Facilities that are altered or renovated "in a manner that affects or could affect the usability" of the facility must make the alterations "in such a manner that, to the maximum extent feasible, the altered portions of the facility are readily accessible to and usable by individuals with disabilities, including individuals who use wheelchairs."[327] When an alteration affects usability of or access to an area of the facility "containing a primary function," the entity shall ensure, "to the maximum extent feasible," that "the path of travel to the altered area and the bathrooms, telephones, and drinking fountains serving the altered area are readily accessible to and usable by individuals with disabilities" as long as the alterations to the path of travel or to the bathrooms, telephones, and drinking fountains serving the altered area are not "disproportionate to the overall alterations in terms of cost and scope."[328]

Historic preservation laws and disability access law rights

The *ADA* exempts historic landmarks designated under federal or state law from some of the *ADA* requirements if alterations to improve accessibility would "threaten or destroy the historic significance" of the buildings or facilities.[329] Sites that are listed or "eligible for listing" as historical landmarks in the National Register of Historic Places under the *National Historic Preservation Act*[330] are subject to special regulations.[331] Facilities protected by state and local laws are subject to somewhat different requirements.[332] In addition, many state laws require access to public accommodations for persons with disabilities.[333] In practice, state and local boards often administer both historic preservation laws and disability access laws.[334] Sometimes an owner's desire to improve access to a historic building generates opposition by the historic landmark board, which may ask the owner to scale back alterations designed to improve accessibility. Sometimes the opposite occurs; the owner may wish to renovate

[326] *Oregon Paralyzed Veterans of America v. Regal Cinemas, Inc.*, 339 F.3d 1126 (9th Cir. 2003); *United States v. Cinemark USA, Inc.*, 348 F.3d 569 (6th Cir. 2003). *Accord, United States v. AMC Entertainment, Inc.*, 232 F. Supp. 2d 1092, 1112-1113 (C.D. Cal. 2002). *Cf. Fortyune v. American Multi-Cinema, Inc.*, 364 F.3d 1075 (9th Cir. 2004) (movie theater violates *ADA* by not reserving seats next to seats used by patrons in wheelchairs so that companions of such patrons may sit next to them).

[327] 42 U.S.C. §12183(a)(1).

[328] 42 U.S.C. §12183(a)(2).

[329] 42 U.S.C. §12204; 28 C.F.R. §36.405.

[330] 54 U.S.C. §300101 *et seq.*

[331] 42 U.S.C. §12204(c)(2). *See ADA Accessibility Guidelines for Buildings and Facilities*, 28 C.F.R. pt. 36, App. A, §4.1.7 (Accessible Buildings: Historic Preservation).

[332] 42 U.S.C. §12204(c)(3).

[333] *See, e.g.*, Mass. Gen. Laws ch. 272, §98A.

[334] *See, e.g.*, Mass. Gen. Laws ch. 9, §§26 to 27 (Massachusetts Historical Commission); Mass. Gen. Laws ch. 22, §13A (Massachusetts Architectural Access Board).

the building in a way that preserves its architectural character and that therefore provides only limited accessibility. The meaning of the "threaten or destroy" standard is subject to administrative discretion, and it is not clear how the balance will be struck in particular cases if a historic preservation board refuses to allow an alteration that a disability access board demands.[335]

§2.6.4 State Laws

Regulation of retail stores

Most states have public accommodations statutes.[336] Some of these track the 1964 federal law, prohibiting only racial, religious, national origin, and disability discrimination in inns, restaurants, and places of entertainment. Most states, however, have broader definitions of what constitutes a place of public accommodation. All but five states, for example, regulate retail stores and other providers of goods and services to the public.[337] Forty-five jurisdictions prohibit sex discrimination in places of public accommodations.[338] Other forms of discrimination prohibited by many states include marital status, age, familial status (generally referring to families with children), and discrimination against members of the military. At least 22 jurisdictions, as well as many cities, prohibit discrimination on the basis of sexual orientation in access to public accommodations.[339] Some have expressly included gender identity or expression as a protected category.[340]

Sex, marital status, age, familial status, military, sexual orientation

[335] Grant P. Fondo, *Access Reigns Supreme: Title III of the Americans with Disabilities Act and Historic Preservation*, 9 BYU J. Pub. L. 99 (1994).

[336] *See* Jeremy D. Bayless & Sophie F. Wang, *Racism on Aisle Two: A Survey of Federal and State Anti-Discrimination Public Accommodation Laws*, 2 Wm. & Mary Pol'y Rev. 288 (2011); Note, *Discrimination in Access to Public Places: A Survey of State and Federal Public Accommodations Laws*, 7 N.Y.U. Rev. L. Soc. Change 215, 217-218 (1978); Joseph William Singer, *No Right to Exclude: Public Accommodations and Private Property*, 90 Nw. U. L. Rev. 1283 (1996); *see also, e.g., McClure Mgmt., LLC v. Taylor*, 849 S.E.2d 604 (W. Va. 2020) (customers of hotel awarded $475,000 each for denial of equal services under West Virginia state public accommodation law).

[337] The five are Alabama, Georgia, Mississippi, North Carolina, and Texas.

[338] Elizabeth Sepper & Deborah Dinner, *Sex in Public*, 129 Yale L.J. 78, 146 (2019).

[339] Elizabeth Sepper & Deborah Dinner, *Sex in Public*, 179 Yale L.J. 78, 146 (2019). Statutes prohibiting discrimination on the basis of sexual orientation in public accommodations include Cal. Civ. Code §51 (as interpreted in *Hubert v. Williams*, 184 Cal. Rptr. 161 (App. Dep't Super. Ct. 1982)); Colo. Rev. Stat. §24-34-601; Conn. Gen. Stat. §46a-81d; Del. Code tit. 6, §4503; D.C. Code §2-1402.31; Haw. Stat. §489-3; 775 Ill. Comp. Stat. 5/1-101 to 5/1-103; Iowa Code §216.7; Me. Rev. Stat. tit. 5, §4592; Md. State Govt. Code §§20-101, 20-304; Mass. Gen. Laws ch. 272, §§92A, 98; Minn. Stat. §§363A.03(34), 363A.11; Nev. Rev. Stat. §233.010; N.H. Rev. Stat. §354-A:17; N.J. Stat. §§10:5-4, 10:5-5, 10:5-12; N.M. Stat. §§28-1-2, 28-1-7; N.Y. Exec. Law §296; Or. Rev. Stat. §659A.403; 43 Penn. Stat. §§ 951-963; R.I. Gen. Laws §11-24-2; §11-24-2.2; Va. Stat. §2.2-3904; Vt. Stat. tit. 9, §4502; Wash. Rev. Code §49.60.215; Wis. Stat. §106.52. City ordinances include Boston Code §12-9.7; Chicago Mun. Code §2-160-070; Philadelphia Fair Prac. Ordinance, ch. 9-1106; New York City, Admin. Code §8-107(4); and San Francisco Code, art. 33, §3305. *See also* Paul Vincent Courtney, *Prohibiting Sexual Orientation Discrimination in Public Accommodations: A Common Law Approach*, 163 U. Pa. L. Rev. 1497 (2015); Isaac Saidel-Goley, *The Right Side of History: Prohibiting Sexual Orientation Discrimination in Public Accommodations, Housing, and Employment*, 31 Wis. J.L., Gender & Soc'y 117 (2016).

[340] *See, e.g.,* Haw. Stat. §489-3; Mass. Gen. Laws ch. 272, §§92A, 98; N.J. Stat. §§10:5-4.

▶ HARD CASE ▷ SEX SEGREGATION IN HEALTH CLUBS

LivingWell (North) Inc. v. Pennsylvania Human Rights Comm'n

Can a health club be limited to women in a state that prohibits sex discrimination in public accommodations?[341] A Pennsylvania trial court held in *LivingWell (North) Inc. v. Pennsylvania Human Relations Commission*[342] that a health club did not violate the state public accommodations law when it excluded men. The court interpreted the state statute to include an implied exception based on the right of privacy. "[W]here there is a distinctly private activity involving exposure of intimate body parts, there exists an implied bona fide public accommodation qualification which may justify otherwise illegal sex discrimination," noted Judge Pellegrini. "Otherwise, . . . such sex segregated accommodations such as bathrooms, showers and locker rooms, would have to be open to the public."[343] Such a privacy exception would, for example, validate separate bathrooms for men and women where separate bathrooms for Black and white customers would plainly be unlawful. Segregation was lawful in this case because the evidence showed that many patrons were sensitive about their appearance and that, if men were admitted, many "women would suffer from extreme embarrassment, anxiety or stress and would not continue to exercise at LivingWell."[344] A privacy right may be "recognized where one has a reasonable basis to be protected against embarrassment or [would] suffer a loss of dignity because of the activity taking place."[345]

Foster v. Back Bay Spas, Inc. d/b/a Healthworks Fitness Center

In contrast, the Massachusetts Superior Court ruled in *Foster v. Back Bay Spas, Inc., d/b/a Healthworks Fitness Center*[346] that a health club that limited membership to women violated the state public accommodations law by discriminating on the basis of sex. Judge Burnes explained:

> While the Court recognizes the impact that the admission of men into the club may have on these women, intimidation and the assumption that all male Healthworks members will harass and leer at their exercise compatriots is still an insufficient ground on which to create a privacy exception. Absent the unclothed exposure of intimate body parts, or the touching of body parts by members of the opposite sex, this Court can find no basis for overriding the public accommodations statute's mandate.[347]

This opinion, however, was controversial, and was effectively overruled by the Massachusetts legislature in an amendment to the state public accommodations law in 1998.[348] ◀

[341] *See* Miriam A. Cherry, *Exercising the Right to Public Accommodations: The Debate over Single-Sex Health Clubs*, 52 Me. L. Rev. 97 (2000); *cf.* Shaun Ossei-Owusu, *Velvet Rope Discrimination*, 107 Va. L. Rev. 683 (2021) (discussing patterns of discriminatory dress codes and gender-based pricing in bars, restaurants, and night clubs).
[342] 606 A.2d 1287 (Pa. Commw. Ct. 1992).
[343] *Id.* at 1291.
[344] *Id.* at 1293.
[345] *Id.*
[346] 7 Mass. L. Rptr. 462, 1997 WL 634354 (Mass. Super. Ct. 1997).
[347] 1997 WL 634354, at *4.
[348] Mass. Gen. Laws ch. 272 §92A (as amended by 1998 Mass. Acts, ch. 19, §1), defining places of public accommodation now provides: [W]ith regard to the prohibition on sex

▷ RELIGIOUS LIBERTY, FREE SPEECH, AND SEXUAL ORIENTATION DISCRIMINATION **HARD CASE** ◀

After the Supreme Court upheld the constitutional right to marry for same-sex couples, some states started considering or passing laws designed to give owners of public accommodations the right to deny service to customers if that would be contrary to the owner's religious beliefs. One such law was passed and then repealed in Indiana. In its original version, the *Indiana Religious Freedom Restoration Act*[349] (IRFRA) prohibited any government entity, including a court adjudicating a private civil lawsuit, from substantially burdening a person's free exercise of religion unless the government act furthered a compelling government interest and was the least restrictive means of obtaining that interest. Because many people read that law as allowing public accommodations to refuse service to LGBT persons because of the owner's religious beliefs, there was a huge negative reaction to the law.

In response, the statute was amended to provide that it did grant any public accommodation the power to engage in discrimination on a statutorily prohibited basis because of the owner's religious beliefs.[350] The statutory scheme is confusing because Indiana does not prohibit discrimination based on sexual orientation. While the amendment to *IRFRA* states that the statute "does not authorize a provider to refuse to provide . . . use of public accommodations . . . on the basis of . . . sexual orientation," it also does not affirmatively prohibit such discrimination. If a state does not prohibit discrimination based on sexual orientation, then public accommodations are free to engage in such discrimination, since neither federal nor state law prohibits it. Passage of a religious liberty exemption statute would therefore seem to have no purpose other than try to ensure against any new state law that might prohibit such discrimination.

For states that prohibit discrimination based on sexual orientation, courts are increasingly confronting claims by owners that public accommodation laws do not apply because religious liberty or free speech rights provide reasons to engage in such discrimination.[351] The U.S. Supreme Court, in *Masterpiece Cakeshop, Inc. v. Colorado Civil Rights Commission*,[352] approved a Christian baker's claim that being required to provide a cake for a same-sex couple's wedding celebration would violate the First Amendment's right of religious freedom. The Court cited what it

---

discrimination, this section shall not apply to a place of exercise for the exclusive use of persons of the same sex which is a bona fide fitness facility established for the sole purpose of promoting and maintaining physical and mental health through physical exercise and instruction, if such facility does not receive funds from a government source, nor to any corporation or entity authorized, created or chartered by federal law for the express purpose of promoting the health, social, educational vocational, and character development of a single sex. . . .

[349] Ind. Code §§34-13-9-1 to 34-13-9-11.

[350] Ind. Code §34-13-9.0.7.

[351] *State v. Arlene's Flowers, Inc.*, 441 P.3d 1203 (Wash. 2019); *Gifford v. McCarthy*, 23 N.Y.S.3d 422 (App. Div. 2016).

[352] 584 U.S. 617 (2018).

thought were expressions of "clear and impermissible hostility towards [the baker's] sincere religious beliefs" on the part of the Colorado Civil Rights Commission that adjudicated the claim.[353] Owners have made similar claims based on free expression, and the U.S. Supreme Court agreed in *303 Creative L.L.C. v. Elenis*, finding First Amendment speech grounds to allow such owners to discriminate.[354]

Store owners may have sincere religious beliefs that selling a wedding cake constitutes participating in the religious ceremony of a same-sex couple, but same-sex couples also have religious freedom claims of their own. And expressive claims immunize owners from the reach of antidiscrimination law without recognizing the harm to those denied service. ◀

▶ HARD CASE

▷ IS SEXUAL ORIENTATION DISCRIMINATION A FORM OF SEX DISCRIMINATION?

While federal law prohibits sex discrimination in educational programs receiving federal funds (Title IX of the Education Amendments of 1972[355]), and in a variety of other civil rights statutes such as in employment under Title VII of the *Civil Rights Act of 1964*,[356] and in housing under the *Fair Housing Act of 1968*,[357] it does not explicitly prohibit sex discrimination in public accommodations. While 45 states that prohibit discrimination in public accommodations under their state laws include sex as a protected category, fewer than half prohibit sexual orientation discrimination.[358] Traditionally, courts have held that laws that prohibit sex discrimination do not prohibit sexual orientation discrimination, but recent developments have made it more likely that courts in the future may interpret statutes that prohibit sex discrimination to implicitly prohibit discrimination against LGBTQ persons. Most notably, the Supreme Court held in *Bostock v. Clayton County*[359] that the term "sex" in Title VII included sexual orientation and gender identity, and courts have begun similarly to clarify the meaning of the term "sex" under state public accommodations law.[360] For similar reasons that it would be gender stereotyping to assume that men should only have male sexual partners or attraction, and refusing to rent an apartment to a white woman because her boyfriend is Black is race discrimination experienced by the white woman, refusing to

[353] *Id.* at 1729.

[354] 600 U.S. 570 (2023) (finding that it would violate the First Amendment to require a website designer to convey messages inconsistent with her religious belief that marriage is reserved to unions between one man and one woman); *see also, e.g., Brush & Nib Studio, L.C. v. City of Phoenix*, 448 P.3d 890 (Ariz. 2019) (because custom wedding invitation designing is "pure speech," compelling production of invitations for same-sex weddings violates owner's First Amendment speech rights).

[355] 20 U.S.C. §§1681 *et seq.*; 34 C.F.R. §§106.1 *et seq.*

[356] 42 U.S.C. §2000e-2.

[357] 42 U.S.C. §3604 to 3606.

[358] *See* Elizabeth Sepper & Deborah Dinner, *Sex in Public*, 179 Yale L.J. 78, 146 (2019).

[359] 140 S. Ct. 1731 (2020).

[360] *See, e.g., R.M.A. ex rel. Appleberry v. Blue Springs R-IV Sch. Dist.*, 568 S.W.3d 420, 428-429 (Mo. 2019) (en banc) (finding the term "sex" to encompass claims based on gender identity).

allow access to a place of public accommodation because of sexual orientation would constitute discrimination on the basis of sex. ◀

▷ GENDER IDENTITY AND PUBLIC BATHROOMS **HARD CASE ◀**

In 2015, North Carolina passed a law referred to as HB2 that not only overturned local municipal ordinances that prohibited discrimination based on sexual orientation but required transgender persons to use public restrooms consistent with the sex listed on their birth certificates rather than their gender identity.[361] While that statute generated public support from its adherents, it also generated a huge backlash from advocates for transgender persons because the statute effectively denies their existence and requires persons who identify as female to use bathrooms set aside for men and vice versa, and North Carolina repealed the legislation in 2017,[362] similar bills have since proliferated across the country. While some may be uncomfortable having individuals who were born as biological males but have a female gender expression using a women's bathroom, the effect of the statute is that people who appear conventionally male would now be required to use the women's bathroom because their "biological sex" is female, something likely to generate as much or more discomfort than the discomfort the statute was intended to avoid. Proponents of the law worried that men would use gender identity antidiscrimination laws as an excuse to dress up as women and enter the women's bathroom giving them greater power to engage in sexual assault of women. Critics of the law find this scenario implausible; nor does a gender identity discrimination law protect a man whose gender identity is male but who "dresses up" as female in order to engage in unlawful assault.[363] ◀

§2.7 Free Speech Rights of Access to Private Property

§2.7.1 United States Constitution

First and Fourteenth Amendments

The First Amendment to the U.S. Constitution prohibits Congress from passing any laws "abridging freedom of speech."[364] These free speech guarantees have been "incorporated" into the Fourteenth Amendment's protection of "liberty" against deprivation by state governments.[365] One

[361] N.C. Sess. Laws 2016-3 (H.B. 2); N.C. Stat. §143-422.11(a).

[362] N.C. Sess. Laws 1017-4 (H.B. 142); *see also* Priya Krishnakumar, *This record-breaking year for anti-transgender legislation would affect minors the most*, CNN, Apr. 15, 2021 (noting the growing proliferation of anti-transgender legislation at the state level).

[363] One arena of litigation over these conflicts involves schools. *Compare A.C. v. Metro. Sch. Dist.*, 75 F.4th 760 (7th Cir 2023) (refusal to allow transgender male student to use boys' bathrooms violated Title IX, the federal statute prohibiting discrimination "because of sex" in education); *with Adams v. Sch. Bd. of St. Johns Cty.*, 57 F.4th 791 (11th Cir. 2022) (en banc) (similar refusal did not violate Title IX).

[364] U.S. Const. amend. I.

[365] *Gitlow v. New York*, 268 U.S. 652 (1921). "[N]or shall any State deprive any person of life, liberty, or property, without due process of law; nor deny to any person within its jurisdiction the equal protection of the laws." U.S. Const. amend. XIV.

of the core elements of freedom of speech is the right to speak in public places, such as in public parks, and the Supreme Court has also ruled that the First Amendment protects the right to hand out leaflets on public streets, sidewalks, and in public places, subject to reasonable time, place, and manner restrictions.[366] The fact that the government is the "owner" of a public area does not give it the right to exclude individuals engaged in protected speech.

Company town

In *Marsh v. Alabama*,[367] the Supreme Court faced the question of whether these rights extended to private property. The Court had previously ruled that the U.S. Constitution protects the right to engage in door-to-door distribution of literature, despite the fact that this often involves some entry onto private property to get to the front door.[368] In *Marsh*, a company prevented a Jehovah's Witness from distributing religious literature on the sidewalks of a company town. The Court ruled that, although owners generally have the right to exclude non-owners from their property, a private company that establishes a community with streets, homes, and businesses, and that is open to the public in general, cannot prevent individuals from distributing literature on the sidewalks of the town. The Court explained:

> We do not agree that the corporation's property interests settle the question. The State urges in effect that the corporation's right to control the inhabitants of Chickasaw is coextensive with the right of a homeowner to regulate the conduct of his guests. We can not accept that contention. Ownership does not always mean absolute dominion. The more an owner, for his advantage, opens up his property for use by the public in general, the more do his rights become circumscribed by the statutory and constitutional rights of those who use it.[369]

Because the town of Chickasaw "does not function differently from any other town,"[370] the inhabitants have the same rights as those of other municipalities. "When we balance the Constitutional rights of owners of property against those of the people to enjoy freedom of press and religion, as we must here, we remain mindful of the fact that the latter occupy a preferred position."[371]

State action doctrine

The tricky issue here is that the Supreme Court has interpreted the Fourteenth Amendment to protect freedom of speech from infringement

[366] *Marsh v. Alabama*, 326 U.S. 501, 504 (1946). *See also First Unitarian Church of Salt Lake City v. Salt Lake City Corp.*, 308 F.3d 1114 (10th Cir. 2002) (where city vacates public street and grants title to it to a church but retains a public pedestrian easement to access other public areas, the easement is a public forum and the city cannot authorize the church to limit free speech on the easement).

[367] 326 U.S. 501 (1946).

[368] *Id.* at 505 (*citing Martin v. Struthers*, 319 U.S. 141 (1943)).

[369] *Id.* at 505-506.

[370] *Id.* at 508.

[371] *Id. Accord, American Civil Liberties Union of Nevada v. City of Las Vegas*, 333 F.3d 1092 (9th Cir. 2003) (public pedestrian mall remains a public forum where First Amendment protects leafleting even when city contracts with private entity that invests substantially in renovating the area and seeks to compete with private malls that do have the right to exclude leafleteers).

by "state action," but not from infringement by private action.[372] A state that excludes an individual from public property is acting to limit speech; thus, it would almost certainly violate the Constitution for a public university to prevent students from distributing leaflets in areas of the campus open to the public. However, private universities are not "state actors" and thus are not limited by the strictures of the First Amendment. Under the *state action doctrine*, a private university could prevent students from distributing leaflets on the college campus without running afoul of First Amendment rights applicable to the state governments.

Trespass law and the state action doctrine

What role does trespass law play here? When a private owner excludes a non-owner, the state clearly becomes involved in the course of enforcing trespass law. However, the courts have been reluctant to identify every instance of enforcement of trespass law as a form of "state action" that triggers protection of constitutional rights under the Fourteenth Amendment. For example, owners have the right to choose their dinner guests as they please; if the Fourteenth Amendment applied to homeowners, they might be in violation of the equal protection clause if they discriminated in their invitations on the basis of race or sex. On the other hand, one might find that equal protection rights were outweighed by privacy rights or associational freedoms in the context of the private home. *Marsh* dealt with an arguably unique fact situation in which the state not only allowed normally public areas (streets and sidewalks) to be privatized, but it also allowed an entire town to be privatized, such that no public streets existed at all in the locality. Because the company town appeared to be the functional equivalent of an entire municipality, the court treated the private ways as if they were owned by the public.

▷ FREE SPEECH ACCESS TO SHOPPING CENTERS — **HARD CASE ◀**

Logan Valley Plaza

The question has arisen as to whether the rights recognized in *Marsh v. Alabama* extend to private property that is open to the public, such as a university or a shopping mall, and that today functions as the equivalent of what used to be the town square or the downtown business district of a municipality. In the 1968 case of *Amalgamated Food Employees Union Local 590 v. Logan Valley Plaza, Inc.*,[373] the Supreme Court held that a shopping center that was freely accessible and open to the public was the functional equivalent of a business block for First Amendment purposes and that the private owner could not exclude peaceful nonemployee picketing of a store in the center to protest its refusal to hire union labor. Although the state's rules against trespass to private property were "generally valid," Justice Thurgood Marshall explained that the shopping center premises here were "open to the public to the same extent as the commercial center of a normal town."[374] The Court held

[372] The Fourteenth Amendment provides: "Nor shall *any State* deprive any person of liberty without due process of law." U.S. Const. amend. XIV (emphasis supplied).

[373] 391 U.S. 308 (1968).

[374] *Id.* at 319.

> because the shopping center serves as the community business block "and is freely accessible and open to the people in the area and those passing through," the State may not delegate the power, through the use of its trespass laws, wholly to exclude those members of the public wishing to exercise their First Amendment rights on the premises in a manner and for a purpose generally consonant with the use to which the property is actually put.[375]

Of course, as with public property, the shopping center owner could regulate the distribution of literature to ensure that it does not interfere with the normal uses to which the property is put. A homeowner could, of course, exclude others from her home, because privacy interests are involved and because the property is devoted to purposes that are incompatible with free access by others. In contrast, no privacy interests are involved in the shopping center context. For that reason, the Court ruled that the owner's interests in exclusive possession, were outweighed by the constitutionally protected rights to distribute literature in a way likely to reach others.

Lloyd Corp. v. Tanner

In 1972, however, with four new Nixon appointees sitting on the Court,[376] the Supreme Court reversed course, and held in *Lloyd Corp., Ltd. v. Tanner*[377] that a shopping center was not the equivalent of a public square and that the First Amendment did not require shopping centers to allow leafleting on its premises. The Court first distinguished *Marsh* by noting that company towns were unique historical phenomena. "One must have seen such towns to understand that 'functionally' they were no different from municipalities of comparable size."[378] In the company town, "private interests were substituting for and performing the customary functions of government."[379] Because there were no publicly owned parks, streets, or sidewalks, protection of the right to exclude would effectively deny individuals the right to distribute literature entirely. The Court then distinguished *Logan Valley Plaza* by noting that the picketers there were protesting the non-union policy of a particular business at the center, and therefore "the First Amendment activity was related to the shopping center's operations,"[380] while the leafleteers in *Lloyd Corp.* were speaking on general matters of public concern. The Court also noted that the store being picketed in *Logan Valley* was located in the middle of the center and, if picketers were not allowed there, "no other reasonable opportunities for the pickets to convey their message to their intended audience [would be] available."[381] Contrary to the assertion in *Logan Valley Plaza* that shopping malls are the "functional equivalent of the business district of Chickasaw involved in *Marsh*,"[382] Justice Powell's opinion in *Lloyd Corp.* noted that leafleting

[375] *Id.* at 319-320.
[376] Chief Justice Burger and Justices Blackmun, Powell, and Rehnquist replaced Chief Justice Warren and Justices Black, Fortas, and Harlan.
[377] 407 U.S. 551 (1972).
[378] *Id.* at 561.
[379] *Id.* at 562.
[380] *Id.*
[381] *Id.* at 563.
[382] 391 U.S. at 318.

exceeded the scope of the owner's invitation to the public.[383] Although the mall was "open generally to the public,"[384] it had not allowed handbilling of any kind. Moreover, because the leaflets being distributed were unrelated to the shopping center's business, "[r]espondents could have distributed these handbills on any public street, on any public sidewalk, in any public park, or in any public building in the city of Portland."[385]

The argument that private property devoted to public use is subject to public obligations

Justice Marshall, writing for four dissenting Justices in *Lloyd Corp.*, quoted language from *Marsh* to the effect that "[t]he more an owner, for his advantage, opens up his property for use by the public in general, the more do his rights become circumscribed by the statutory and constitutional rights of those who use it."[386] Arguing that the result in *Lloyd* should be consistent with the ruling in *Logan Valley*, he focused on the function of the modern shopping mall and the fact that it has taken the place, to a large extent, of downtown shopping districts and public squares.[387] Privacy interests become attenuated as we go from a home to a store to a shopping center, while the fact that the public gathers in shopping centers rather than downtown shopping districts or public squares, means that the ability to communicate may depend on access to places where people congregate.[388] "We must remember that it is a balance that we are striking — a balance between the freedom to speak, a freedom that is given a preferred place in our hierarchy of values, and the freedom of a private property owner to control his property. When the competing interests are fairly weighed, the balance can only be struck in favor of speech."[389]

The argument that shopping centers have a "private character"

On the other hand, Justice Powell's majority opinion in *Lloyd Corp.* emphasized: "Nor does property lose its private character merely because the public is generally invited to use it for designated purposes."[390] Stores have an "essentially private character" that does not change "by virtue of being large or clustered with other stores in a modern shopping center."[391] The shopping center owner has created a shopping center, not a public auditorium; there has been no "dedication of Lloyd's privately owned and operated shopping center to public use as to entitle respondents to exercise therein the asserted First Amendment rights."[392] From this perspective, although a shopping center may be a "public accommodation" within the meaning of civil rights law because it holds itself out as ready to serve the public and invites the public in to browse and shop, it is not public property (meaning that it is not owned by the government) and, civil rights laws aside, the private owner retains the power to determine the scope of its invitation to the public.

[383] 407 U.S. at 564.
[384] *Id.* at 556.
[385] *Id.* at 565.
[386] *Id.* at 573 (Marshall, J., dissenting).
[387] *Id.* at 576 (Marshall, J., dissenting).
[388] *Id.* at 580 (Marshall, J., dissenting).
[389] *Id.*
[390] *Id.* at 569.
[391] *Id.*
[392] *Id.* at 570.

Hudgens v. NLRB

In *Hudgens v. National Labor Relations Board*,[393] the Supreme Court recognized that its reasoning in *Lloyd Corp.* was significantly at odds with its reasoning in *Logan Valley Plaza* and effectively overruled *Logan Valley Plaza* entirely.[394] Justice Stewart, who had voted with the dissent in *Lloyd*, now joined the majority to repudiate *Logan Valley*. He noted that the majority opinion in *Lloyd* quoted and relied on language in the dissenting opinion in *Logan Valley*, and found that the "constitutional guarantee of free speech is a guarantee only against abridgment by government, federal or state."[395] Although *Marsh v. Alabama* remains good law, it has been essentially ruled *sui generis* and confined to its facts. Only where a company is exercising "semi-official municipal functions" and "performing the full spectrum of municipal powers" will First Amendment protections kick in.[396] ◀

§2.7.2 State Constitutions

No free speech rights of access to shopping centers

Most state courts have interpreted their state constitutional free speech clauses consistently with *Lloyd Corp.*, holding that shopping center owners may exclude individuals handing out leaflets and asking for signatures for petitions, even if those petitions are for the purpose of getting someone's name on the ballot to run for public office or to get a referendum put on the ballot.[397] These courts have accepted the argument that free speech rights are constitutionally guaranteed against state action only and that enforcement of trespass laws does not constitute state action when it is the private owner that is choosing to exclude non-owners from its property.[398] In addition, they have argued that it is the job of the legislature, and not the courts, to balance free speech rights against property rights, and that, in the absence

[393] 424 U.S. 507 (1976).

[394] *Id.* at 521. The Court explained: "[T]he fact is that the reasoning of the Court's opinion in *Lloyd* cannot be squared with the reasoning of the Court's opinion in *Logan Valley*." *Id.* at 518.

[395] *Id.* at 513.

[396] 407 U.S. at 569.

[397] *See, e.g., Cologne v. Westfarms Assocs.*, 469 A.2d 476 (Conn. 1985); *Citizens for Ethical Government, Inc. v. Gwinnett Place Assocs.*, 392 S.E.2d 8 (Ga. 1990); *City of West Des Moines v. Engler*, 641 N.W.2d 803 (Iowa 2002); *Woodland v. Michigan Citizens Lobby*, 378 N.W.2d 337 (Mich. 1985); *Shad Alliance v. Smith Haven Mall*, 488 N.E.2d 1211 (N.Y. 1985); *State v. Felmet*, 273 S.E.2d 708 (N.C. 1981); *Eastwood Mall, Inc. v. Slanco*, 626 N.E.2d 59 (Ohio 1994); *Western Pennsylvania Socialist Workers 1982 Campaign v. Connecticut General Life Ins. Co.*, 515 A.2d 1331 (Pa. 1986); *Charleston Joint Venture v. McPherson*, 417 S.E.2d 544 (S.C. 1992); *Republican Party v. Dietz*, 940 S.W.2d 86 (Tex. 1997); *Waremart v. Progressive Campaigns*, 989 P.2d 524 (Wash. 1999) (no right to collect signatures in parking lot of "big box" store); *Southcenter Joint Venture v. National Democratic Policy Committee*, 780 P.2d 1282 (Wash. 1989); *Jacobs v. Major (Jacobs II)*, 407 N.W.2d 832 (Wis. 1987).

[398] *See, e.g., Cologne v. Westfarms Assocs.*, 469 A.2d 1201, 1209 (Conn. 1984); *Shad Alliance v. Smith Haven Mall*, 488 N.E.2d 1211, 1212 (N.Y. 1985); *Jacobs v. Major*, 407 N.W.2d 832, 839 (Wis. 1987). *See* Dahlia Lithwick, *Why Can Shopping Malls Limit Free Speech?*, Slate (Mar. 10, 2003) (shopping store patron arrested for refusing to remove a T-shirt with the words "Peace on Earth" and "Give Peace a Chance" at a shopping center in Albany, N.Y., shortly after the United States had invaded Iraq) (http://slate.msn.com/id/2079885); Winnie Hu, *A Message of Peace on 2 Shirts Touches Off Hostilities at a Mall*, N.Y. Times, Mar. 6, 2003, at B-1.

of legislation, owners possess the usual right to exclude non-owners from their property or to limit access to shopping purposes while excluding those whose entry to the property is for purposes unrelated to the owner's business.[399] "The State action requirement," wrote the New York Court of Appeals, "performs a vital function."[400] It limits state power and therefore provides a "crucial foundation for both private autonomy and separation of powers."[401] Extending constitutional obligations to private actors would deprive them of autonomy for the benefit of the autonomy of others to whom the constitutional rights were granted and, in this view, such conflicts of interests among private parties are best left to the legislature or the common law to resolve.

Rights of access to solicit signatures for ballot measures and potential candidates

Several state courts have interpreted their state constitutions to ensure rights to enter shopping centers for purposes specifically mentioned in the state constitution. For example, relying on a specific initiative provision in the state constitution[402] and state statutes implementing that provision,[403] the Washington Supreme Court found a state constitutional right for individuals to seek signatures on a petition to place a referendum question on the ballot.[404] Similarly, the Massachusetts Supreme Judicial Court relied on a state constitutional provision to find a right to enter a shopping center to solicit signatures to place a candidate's name on the ballot.[405]

State constitutional free speech rights of access to shopping centers and universities

The Supreme Courts of New Jersey[406] and California[407] have interpreted their state constitutions to guarantee general rights of access to shopping centers and possibly universities open to the public for various free speech purposes, especially handing out literature, subject to reasonable time, place, and manner restrictions imposed by the owner. Pennsylvania recognized a right to leaflet at a private university that had been opened to the public as a forum for public debate; the court held that the state constitution prohibited enforcement of trespass laws against individuals who sought to hand out leaflets protesting a speaker's views at an event that was open to the public.[408] However, the court limited that ruling in 1986, holding that "the Pennsylvania Constitution does not guarantee access to

[399] *Cologne*, 369 A.2d at 1209; *Jacobs*, 407 N.W.2d at 844.

[400] *Shad*, 488 N.E.2d at 1215.

[401] *Id.* at 1216; *see also Golden Gateway Ctr. v. Golden Gateway Tenants Ass'n*, 29 P.3d 797 (Cal. 2001).

[402] Wash. Const. art. 2 §1(a) (amend. 72).

[403] Wash. Rev. Code §§29A.72.010 to 29A.72.070.

[404] *Alderwood Assocs. v. Washington Envtl. Council*, 635 P.2d 108 (Wash. 1981). *But see Southcenter Joint Venture v. National Democratic Policy Committee*, 780 P.2d 1282 (Wash. 1989) (no general free speech right to hand out leaflets at privately owned shopping center).

[405] *Batchelder v. Allied Stores International, Inc.*, 445 N.E.2d 590 (Mass. 1983). *But see Commonwealth v. Hood*, 452 N.E.2d 188 (Mass. 1983) (no free speech rights to pass out leaflets on property that is not open to the public for such purposes).

[406] *Green Party of New Jersey v. Hartz Mountain Industries, Inc.*, 752 A.2d 315 (N.J. 2000) (community shopping mall); *New Jersey Coalition Against the War in the Middle East v. J.M.B. Realty Corp.*, 650 A.2d 757 (N.J. 1994) (regional shopping center); *State v. Schmid*, 423 A.2d 615 (N.J. 1980) (private university).

[407] *Robins v. PruneYard Shopping Center*, 592 P.2d 341 (Cal. 1979), *aff'd sub nom. PruneYard Shopping Center v. Robins*, 447 U.S. 74 (1980) (shopping center).

[408] *Commonwealth v. Tate*, 432 A.2d 1382 (Pa. 1981).

private property for the exercise of such rights where the owner uniformly and effectively prohibits all political activities and similarly precludes the use of its property as a forum for discussion of matters of public controversy."[409] Oregon recognized a right of access to gather signatures for initiative petitions under Oregon common law.[410] It later held that this right was protected by the Oregon state constitution[411] but overruled this constitutional finding in *Stranahan v. Fred Meyer, Inc.*[412]

N.J. Coalition Against the War in the Middle East v. J.M.B. Realty Corp.

The New Jersey Supreme Court has ruled that the New Jersey constitution "conferred on our citizens a right of free speech that was protected not only from governmental restraint—the extent of First Amendment protection—but from the restraint of private property owners as well."[413] In *State v. Schmid*,[414] the court ruled that a private university could not exclude handbillers from its property. It extended this ruling in 1994 to shopping centers in *New Jersey Coalition Against the War in the Middle East v. J.M.B. Realty Corp.*,[415] agreeing with the earlier ruling of the California Supreme Court in *Robins v. PruneYard Shopping Center.*[416] Justice Handler explained that the court had adopted a standard to determine when private property has been sufficiently devoted to public uses to trigger constitutional obligations not to abridge individual freedom of speech. "The standard takes into account the normal use of the property, the extent and nature of the public's invitation to use it, and the purpose of the expressional activity in relation to both its private and public use."[417] The court noted that the shopping center involved in the case effectively invited the public in, not only to shop, but to hang around, and that it functioned as a town square. The court concluded that the owner's business interests were harmed slightly, if at all, by the introduction of leafleting and that the ability to reach people in public to distribute leaflets would be significantly limited if individuals could not do so in the shopping centers where people now congregate. The court determined that the owner's

[409] *Western Pennsylvania Socialist Workers 1982 Campaign v. Connecticut General Life Ins. Co.*, 515 A.2d 1331 (Pa. 1986).

[410] *Lloyd Corp. v. Whiffen*, 773 P.2d 1294 (Or. 1989) (*Whiffen I*) (holding that the equitable determination whether an injunction should be issued to prevent a trespass required a balancing of the public interest implicated in the people's constitutionally protected power of initiative and referendum and the owner's interest in preventing injury to its commercial enterprise and that the balance came out on the side of free speech because the solicitation of signatures of patrons does not in and of itself constitute substantial interference with the owner's commercial enterprise).

[411] *Lloyd Corp. v. Whiffen*, 813 P.2d 573 (Or. 1991) (*Whiffen II*).

[412] *Stranahan v. Fred Meyer, Inc.*, 11 P.3d 228 (Or. 2000).

[413] *New Jersey Coalition Against the War in the Middle East v. J.M.B. Realty Corp.*, 650 A.2d 757, 760 (N.J. 1994).

[414] 423 A.2d 615 (N.J. 1980).

[415] 650 A.2d 757 (N.J. 1994). *Accord, Wood v. State*, 2003 WL 1955433 (Fla. Cir. Ct. 2003) (state constitution prohibits a private owner of a "quasi-public" place from using state trespass laws to exclude peaceful political activity); *but see Whole Foods Market Group, Inc. v. Sarasota Coalition for a Living Wage*, 2010 WL 2380390 (Fla. Cir. Ct. 2010) (limiting the *Wood* ruling to large multi-purpose shopping malls).

[416] *Robins v. PruneYard Shopping Center*, 592 P.2d 341 (Cal. 1979), *aff'd sub nom. PruneYard Shopping Center v. Robins*, 447 U.S. 74 (1980).

[417] 650 A.2d at 760.

interests in exclusion were outweighed by the plaintiff's "sufficiently compelling" free speech interests, thereby justifying a limitation on the owner's right to exclude.[418]

Free speech access v. right to exclude

When the California Supreme Court reached a similar result, the shopping center involved appealed to the U.S. Supreme Court on the grounds that the state law requiring it to allow non-owners onto its property constituted a taking of its property without just compensation in violation of the Fourteenth Amendment. Although the Supreme Court had ruled that the First Amendment did not grant a free speech right of access to shopping centers, it also ruled in *PruneYard Shopping Center v. Robins*[419] that a state could choose to require such access under its constitutional, statutory, or common law and that such a limitation on the right to exclude would not constitute an unconstitutional taking of property. The Constitution protects both free speech rights and property rights to a certain extent, and states are entitled to go further in protecting those rights than mandated by federal law, as long as those further protections do not violate another constitutional right. By holding that there is no First Amendment right to speak in a private shopping center and that the state can choose to create such a right, the Court has left it to the individual states to choose whether to privilege free speech rights or property rights in this context. The takings issue is treated in more depth in Chapter 14.

PruneYard Shopping Center v. Robins

▷ POLITICAL MESSAGES ON T-SHIRTS **HARD CASE ◀**

After the United States invaded Iraq (for the first time), a father and son were ousted from a mall in New York State for wearing T-shirts that protested the decision to go to war. The father's T-shirt read "Give Peace a Chance," while his son's shirt read "No War with Iraq" on one side and "Let Inspections Work" on the other.[420] As the father and son were eating lunch, security guards asked them to remove the shirts or to leave the premises. Although the son complied by removing his shirt, the father did not. It appears that he also refused to leave the premises. He was arrested and charged with criminal trespass. New York has not adopted the *PruneYard* rule, and no other New York law apparently limited the owner's decision to exclude under these circumstances. The director of operations of the mall explained that the father and son were "interfering with other shoppers" and that "[t]heir behavior, coupled with their clothing, to express to others their personal views on world affairs were disruptive of customers."[421] On the other hand, the legal director of the New York Civil Liberties Union asked whether the mall was going to start excluding customers who wore

[418] *Id.* at 761. *See also Green Party of New Jersey v. Hartz Mountain Industries, Inc.*, 752 A.2d 315 (N.J. 2000) (Green Party has state constitutional free speech right to enter community shopping mall to gather signatures on behalf of gubernatorial candidate).
[419] 447 U.S. 74 (1980).
[420] Winnie Hu, *A Message of Peace on 2 Shirts Touches Off Hostilities at a Mall*, N.Y. Times, Mar. 6, 2003, at B-1.
[421] *Id.*

political buttons. "The ultimate point is that we are a diverse society in which individuals hold diverse views."[422] ◀

§2.7.3 Labor Laws

National Labor Relations Act

Section 7 of the *National Labor Relations Act* (*NLRA*)[423] protects the rights of employees to form unions and engage in collective bargaining. Section 8 prohibits the employer from engaging in "unfair labor practices"[424] that interfere with Section 7 rights. In several cases, the Supreme Court has interpreted this statute to protect certain free speech rights of employees and nonemployees who seek to communicate with workers at the work site for the purpose of persuading employees to join a union, to go on strike, or to engage in other labor practices protected under the *NLRA*. For example, in *Hudgens v. National Labor Relations Board*,[425] although the Supreme Court effectively overruled *Logan Valley Plaza*,[426] it did conclude that the *NLRA* might statutorily limit an employer's right to exclude if the purpose of the intrusion was to exercise rights to organize workers into unions or engage in other collective actions protected by the federal labor laws. In *Lechmere v. National Labor Relations Board*,[427] the Court ruled that an employer did not commit an unfair labor practice when it barred union organizers from distributing handbills in the employer's parking lot at a shopping center. Justice Thomas noted that the Supreme Court had ruled, in *NLRB v. Babcock & Wilcox Co.*,[428] that although the *NLRA* imposed some limitations on an employer's right to exclude nonemployee union organizers from its property, it did not require employers to suffer picketing or handbilling on their property if the union had "reasonable alternative means" to communicate with the employees.[429] The Court concluded that the union could reach the employees by mailings, phone calls, home visits, advertising in local newspapers, and picketing on a public "grassy strip" adjoining the employer's parking lot.

Right to reach customers

In a case applying the rule in the *Lechmere* decision, *O'Neil's Markets v. United Food and Commercial Workers' Union, Meatcutters Local 88*,[430] the Eighth Circuit upheld the National Labor Relations Board's determination that an employer might have violated the *NLRA* by preventing union organizers from distributing handbills on the sidewalk and parking areas surrounding its grocery store. The court noted that the employer's property rights must be balanced against federally protected organizing and free speech rights if the union organizers do not have reasonable access to employees outside the employer's property. In this case, the union was

[422] *Id.*
[423] 29 U.S.C. §157.
[424] 29 U.S.C. §158.
[425] 424 U.S. 507 (1976).
[426] *Id.* at 521.
[427] 502 U.S. 527 (1992).
[428] 351 U.S. 105 (1956).
[429] 502 U.S. at 539.
[430] 95 F.3d 733 (8th Cir. 1996).

attempting to reach not the defendant's employees, but its customers, and they arguably could be reached only by distributing leaflets at the site itself. In addition, the court noted that the employer was a tenant at the shopping center and did not own the sidewalks or parking areas, but merely possessed an easement to use those areas in conjunction with its leasehold.

State constitutions

In addition, some state constitutions may protect free speech rights of workers. It was held that a union's right to picket trumps the owner's right to exclude under the California constitution.[431]

Takings law as a constraint on access for union organizing

In *Cedar Point Nursery v. Hassid*,[432] the Supreme Court held that a state regulation put out under the California Agricultural Labor Relations Act of 1975, which provided union organizers with the right to enter agricultural property for up to three hours per day 120 days per year (for limited windows before or after working hours or during a lunch break), constituted a "per se" regulatory taking of the farm owners' right to exclude — under the federal constitution.[433] In finding for the owners, the Court noted a variety of exceptions to its broad rule of takings liability for statutes that similarly require private access to achieve public goals, including public accommodations laws and traditional common law access rights as well as minor intrusions on the right to exclude (which should be evaluated under trespass law). *Cedar Point Nursery* is likely to generate litigation much outside the labor-organizing context, but its effects will be felt in that arena first.

§2.8 Public Trust Doctrine

Navigable waters

In *Illinois Central Railroad Co. v. State of Illinois*,[434] the Supreme Court affirmed that navigable waters are not subject to private ownership but are impressed with a "public trust" such that they must remain open to public rights of access for navigation purposes under regulations promulgated by Congress. These rights are owned by the public and cannot be alienated by the United States to a private owner. Thus, although owners of land on the shores of navigable waters like Lake Michigan have the right to construct piers to obtain access to the waters for themselves or others, they may not interfere with navigation or injure the rights of the public to enjoy the navigation of the waters. The title to the land underlying navigable waters is "a title held in trust for the people of the state, that they may enjoy the navigation of the waters, carry on commerce over them, and have liberty of fishing therein, freed from the obstruction or interference of private parties."[435]

Tidelands

The public trust doctrine has been extended to tidelands (the area between the high and low water marks over which the tide flows). As the Supreme Court of New Jersey later ruled, "land covered by tidal waters belonged to the sovereign, but for the common use of all the people."[436] If

[431] *National Labor Relations Board v. Calkins*, 187 F.3d 1080 (9th Cir. 1999).
[432] 594 U.S. 139 (2021).
[433] *Id.* at 152. Takings law is covered in more depth in Chapter 14.
[434] 146 U.S. 387 (1892).
[435] *Id.* at 452.
[436] *Borough of Neptune City v. Borough of Avon-By-The-Sea*, 294 A.2d 47, 51 (N.J. 1972).

such lands are sold to private owners, they remain subject to the public trust doctrine. Disagreements have arisen, however, over the extent of retained public rights of access to tidelands. In addition, some courts have held that the state may extinguish public rights of access under the public trust doctrine by conveying property to private owners free of such rights.[437]

▶ HARD CASE

▷ BEACH ACCESS

Courts have wrestled with the question of whether the public has rights of access to the wet or dry portions of beaches along the oceans. In *Borough of Neptune City v. Borough of Avon-By-The-Sea*,[438] the Supreme Court of New Jersey ruled that a municipality could not charge nonresidents higher fees than residents to use the public beach.[439] The court noted that "the tide-flowed land lying between the mean high and low water marks, as well as the ocean covered land seaward thereof to the state's boundary, is owned by the State in fee simple."[440] Plaintiffs claimed that the public trust doctrine created a common law "right of access to the ocean in all citizens of the state."[441] The court ruled that, although the "original purpose of the [public trust] doctrine was to preserve for the use of all the public natural water resources for navigation and commerce, waterways being the principal transportation arteries of early days, and for fishing, an important source of food,"[442] modern uses of the tidelands justified an extension of the public trust doctrine to encompass "recreational uses" as well, including "bathing, swimming, and other shore activities."[443] Thus, "at least where the upland sand area is owned by a municipality—a political subdivision and creature of the state—and dedicated to public beach purposes, a modern court must take the view that the public trust doctrine dictates that the beach and the ocean waters must be open to all on equal terms and without preference and that any contrary state or municipal action is impermissible."[444]

Extension to some dry-sand areas

The Supreme Court of New Jersey extended the public trust doctrine in *Matthews v. Bay Head Improvement Association*,[445] holding that the public had a right of access to privately owned dry-sand areas owned by a nonprofit corporation that had a virtual monopoly over public beach access in the town. Because the "ownership, dominion and sovereignty over land

[437] *See, e.g., Greater Providence Chamber of Commerce v. State of Rhode Island*, 657 A.2d 1038 (R.I. 1995).

[438] 294 A.2d 47 (N.J. 1972).

[439] *Leydon v. Town of Greenwich*, 750 A.2d 1122 (Conn. App. Ct. 2000), *aff'd on other grounds by* 777 A.2d 552 (Conn. 2001).

[440] 294 A.2d at 49. *Accord, Severance v. Patterson*, 370 S.W.3d 705, 717 (Tex. 2012) ("The wet beach is owned by the State as part of the public trust").

[441] 294 A.2d at 51.

[442] *Id.* at 52.

[443] *Id.* at 54, *citing State ex rel. Thornton v. Hay*, 462 P.2d 671 (Or. 1969); *Gion v. City of Santa Cruz*, 465 P.2d 50 (Cal. 1970) (*overruled by statute*, Cal. Civ. Code §1009); *Hixon v. Public Serv. Comm'n*, 146 N.W.2d 577, 582 (Wis. 1966). *See also White v. Hughes*, 190 So. 446, 449 (Fla. 1939).

[444] 294 A.2d at 54.

[445] 471 A.2d 355 (N.J. 1984).

flowed by tidal waters, which extend to the mean high water mark, is vested in the State in trust for the people,"[446] the court ruled that "ancillary to the public's right to enjoy the tidal lands, the public has a right to gain access through and to use the dry sand area not owned by a municipality but by a quasi-public body."[447] The public must have some way to get to the tidelands, argued Justice Schreiber, or the retained public recreational rights would be meaningless.[448] This ruling did not give the public the right to use dry-sand beaches adjacent to private property not held by nonprofit organizations and not generally open to the public. Thus, private beach clubs could apparently exclude nonmembers from the dry sand — less clear was whether they could exclude individuals from walking along the tidelands seaward of privately owned land.

Cases limiting uses of tidelands to navigation and fishing

The Massachusetts and Maine Supreme Judicial Courts have refused to extend the public trust doctrine to recreational uses, effectively limiting it to navigational and fishing purposes.[449] Thus, the Massachusetts Supreme Judicial Court held that a bill that would have created a public right of foot passage between the mean high water line and the extreme water line would unconstitutionally take the private property rights of beachfront owners.[450] The Maine Supreme Judicial Court struck down a similar statute for the same reasons.[451]

Dedication

Courts in other states have recognized public rights of access to some portion of oceanfront beaches under a variety of doctrines, including *dedication, prescription,* or *custom.* In *Gion v. City of Santa Cruz,*[452] the California Supreme Court upheld public rights of access to the beachfront, based on long-established public use. It found that the owner of the adjacent property had impliedly "dedicated" the property to public uses by acquiescing in public use. This doctrine focuses less on the fact of public use and more on the implied intent of the owner to donate the property to the public. The California legislature limited *Gion* by new legislation protecting the rights of private beachfront owners to exclude the public even if they previously allowed the public to use their property. Such uses will no longer ripen into public access rights; effectively, the owner can choose to revoke the invitation to the public, to enter the property without violating any public rights.[453]

[446] *Id.* at 358.
[447] *Id.*
[448] 471 A.2d at 364. *See also Raleigh Ave. Beach Ass'n v. Atlantis Beach Club, Inc.*, 851 A.2d 19 (N.J. Ct. App. 2004) (owner of beach property that had previously been open to the public had a duty to keep the dry-sand area open to the public and to provide private lifeguard services but could charge only a reasonable fee that is no greater than necessary to operate and maintain the facility to those who remained on the beach for an extended period of time).
[449] *Bell v. Town of Wells*, 557 A.2d 168 (Me. 1989); *Opinion of the Justices*, 313 N.E.2d 561 (Mass. 1974).
[450] *Opinion of the Justices*, 313 N.E.2d 561 (Mass. 1974).
[451] *Bell v. Town of Wells*, 557 A.2d 168 (Me. 1989). Maryland has taken a similar approach. *Department of Natural Resources v. Mayor and Council of Ocean City*, 332 A.2d 630 (Md. 1975).
[452] 465 P.2d 50 (Cal. 1970). *See also In re Banning*, 832 P.2d 724 (Haw. 1992); *Akau v. Olohana Corp.*, 652 P.2d 1130 (Haw. 1982) (discussing public rights of access to beaches in Hawai'i).
[453] Cal. Civ. Code §1009.

Prescription

The Florida and North Carolina Supreme Courts reached a similar result under the doctrine of *prescription*.[454] If the public has used the property for a particular purpose for a long time (measured by the relevant state statute of limitations), the public can acquire such rights permanently even if they never had them originally or if they had previously been reduced to private ownership. In effect, if the owner fails to exclude trespassers from her property, she may lose her right to sue them under the relevant statute of limitations.[455] This topic is covered in Chapter 5.[456] The Texas Supreme Court also recognizes that beach access rights can arise either from dedication or prescription.[457]

Custom

The Oregon Supreme Court used the doctrine of "custom" to justify its recognition of public rights of access to beaches. In *State ex rel. Thornton v. Hay*,[458] the court ruled that the state had the power to prevent beachfront landowners from putting up fences to enclose the dry-sand area of their property. The court first recognized public ownership of the tidelands (the "foreshore" or "wet-sand area"), which gave the public the right to use the tidelands for recreational purposes. The court then extended this right to the dry-sand area up to the vegetation line on the ground that long-standing use by the public of beaches along the coastline (both public and private) had established a custom that limited the rights of owners.[459] "The dry-sand area in Oregon," wrote Justice Goodwin, "has been enjoyed by the general public as a recreational adjunct of the wet-sand or foreshore area since the beginning of the state's political history." He continued:

> The first European settlers on these shores found the aboriginal inhabitants using the foreshore for clam-digging and the dry-sand area for their cooking fires. The newcomers continued these customs after statehood. Thus, from the time of the earliest settlement to the present day, the general public has assumed that the dry-sand area was a part of the public beach, and the public has used the dry-sand area for picnics, gathering wood, building warming fires, and generally as a headquarters from which to supervise children or to range out over the foreshore as the tides advance and recede. In the Cannon Beach vicinity, state and local officers have policed the dry sand, and municipal sanitary crews have attempted to keep the area reasonably free from man-made litter.[460]

These public rights were recognized by a statute that declared the state's "sovereignty" over the "ocean shore of the state from the Columbia River

[454] *City of Daytona Beach v. Tona-Rama, Inc.*, 294 So. 2d 73 (Fla. 1974); *Concerned Citizens of Brunswick County Taxpayers Association v. State ex rel. Rhodes*, 404 S.E.2d 677 (N.C. 1991).

[455] *But see Lay v. Inhabitants of Town of Merrimac*, 24 Mass. Lawyers Weekly 2460 (Aug. 8, 1996) (Mass. Land Ct. 1996) (public cannot obtain a prescriptive easement).

[456] *See* §5.5.

[457] *Severance v. Patterson*, 370 S.W.3d 705, 710-711 (Tex. 2012).

[458] 462 P.2d 671 (Or. 1969). *See also McDonald v. Halvorson*, 780 P.2d 714 (Or. 1989).

[459] *See also Matcha v. Mattox*, 711 S.W.2d 95 (Tex. Ct. App. 1986) (adopting the doctrine of custom).

[460] 462 P.2d at 673.

on the north to the Oregon-California line on the south so that the public may have the free and uninterrupted use thereof."[461]

Hawai'i public beach access

Hawai'i has a unique legal system recognizing public access to all beaches up to the "stable vegetation line" in accord with traditional Hawaiian custom.[462] ◀

▷ BEACH ACCESS AND THE TAKINGS CLAUSE

HARD CASE ◀

No taking found: ***Stevens v. City of Cannon Beach***

In subsequent cases, homeowners challenged the doctrine of custom, announced in *Thornton v. Hay* as an unconstitutional takings of property rights of oceanfront owners without just compensation.[463] The Oregon Supreme Court rejected this claim in *Stevens v. City of Cannon Beach*[464] on the grounds that no deprivation of private rights could occur if the rights in question were never subject to private ownership, and because the ruling in *Thornton* affirmed that under the doctrine of custom, public rights of access to the tidelands and to the dry-sand area were never given up to private ownership. While the beachfront property owners claimed that the doctrine of custom was a surprise to them, the court believed that the custom was well established. "This case deals solely with the dry-sand area along the Pacific shore, and this land has been used by the public as public recreational land according to an unbroken custom running back in time as long as the land has been inhabited."[465] For this reason, a ruling confirming the long-standing public uses "takes from no man anything which he has had a legitimate reason to regard as exclusively his."[466]

However, Justice Scalia, dissenting from a denial of *certiorari* in the *Stevens* case, noted that *Thornton v. Hay* had been narrowed by the ruling in *McDonald v. Halvorson*,[467] in which the Oregon Supreme Court held that the doctrine of custom did not apply to the entire coastline of Oregon, but only to those parcels of property that had in fact been used by the public for recreational purposes for a long time.[468] Justice Scalia further argued that the doctrine of custom had been newly announced in *Thornton*, and had not formed a part of Oregon law before the date of that decision. In his view, the doctrine granted a public easement to private property and thereby took the owner's right to exclude the public without compensation.[469]

[461] Or. Rev. Stat. §390.610.

[462] *See Diamond v. State Bd. of Land and Natural Resources*, 145 P.3d 704, 712 (Haw. 2006); *Application of Ashford*, 440 P.2d 76 (Haw. 1968). *Cf. Ka Pa'akai O Ka'aina v. Land Use Commission, State of Hawai'i*, 7 P.3d 1068 (Haw. 2000) and *Public Access Shoreline Hawai'i (PASH) v. Hawai'i County Planning Commission*, 903 P.2d 1246 (Haw. 1995) (recognizing customary gathering rights of native Hawaiians along the shoreline).

[463] *Stevens v. City of Cannon Beach*, 835 P.2d 940 (Or. Ct. App. 1992), *aff'd*, 854 P.2d 449 (Or. 1993), *cert. denied* 510 U.S. 1207 (1994) (with a dissenting opinion by Justice Scalia, joined by Justice O'Connor); *Hay v. Bruno*, 344 F. Supp. 286 (D. Or. 1972).

[464] *Stevens v. City of Cannon Beach*, 835 P.2d 940 (Or. Ct. App. 1992), *aff'd*, 854 P.2d 449 (Or. 1993), *cert. denied*, 510 U.S. 1207 (1994).

[465] 462 P.2d at 676-677.

[466] *Id.* at 678; *Hay v. Bruno*, 344 F. Supp. at 289.

[467] 780 P.2d 714 (Or. 1989).

[468] *Id.* at 724.

[469] *Stevens v. City of Cannon Beach*, 510 U.S. 1207 (1994) (Scalia, J., dissenting).

Taking found: ***Sotomura v. County of Hawai'i***

Justice Scalia's view echoed that of the federal District Court of Hawai'i in the 1978 case of *Sotomura v. County of Hawai'i*.[470] The Hawai'i Supreme Court had located the property owners' seaward boundary at the vegetation line, but the District Court found this to contradict the prior practice of drawing the line at the mean high-water line. Because the new line was inconsistent with accepted practice, common law, and relevant precedent, *Sotomura* ruled that the Hawai'i Supreme Court had taken property without just compensation when it stripped owners of the right to exclude the public from land between the mean high-water line and the vegetation line.

Robinson v. Ariyoshi

Similarly, the Ninth Circuit held, in *Robinson v. Ariyoshi*,[471] that a Hawai'i Supreme Court decision[472] recognizing native water rights constituted a taking of rights that have previously been vested in others by a prior judicial decision.[473]

Native rights

A number of cases have recognized pre-existing customary rights to hunt or fish or to gather naturally growing crops in areas in or alongside rivers or the shore. Some rights were retained by American Indian nations in treaties with the United States.[474] Other rights were retained by Native Hawaiians when property along the shore was conveyed to non-native owners. In *Public Access Shoreline Hawai'i (PASH) v. Hawai'i County Planning Commission*,[475] a developer sought a special permit to create a resort complex. The Supreme Court of Hawai'i noted that the Hawai'i constitution protects "all rights, customarily and traditionally exercised for subsistence, cultural and religious purposes and possessed by *ahupua'a* tenants who are descendants of native Hawaiians who inhabited the Hawaiian Islands prior to 1778, subject to the right of the State to regulate such rights."[476] Under this constitutional provision, as well as statutes, common law, and custom, ownership of undeveloped land in Hawai'i has been held to be subject to customary gathering rights as long as those customary rights do not harm the legitimate interests of the owner of the land.[477] Such reserved

[470] 460 F. Supp. 473 (D. Haw. 1978).

[471] 753 F.2d 1468 (9th Cir. 1985), *overruled*, 887 F.2d 215 (9th Cir. 1989).

[472] *McBryde Sugar Co. v. Robinson*, 504 P.2d 1330 (Haw. 1973).

[473] The judgment in *Robinson* was subsequently overturned on ripeness grounds. *Robinson v. Ariyoshi*, 887 F.2d 215 (9th Cir. 1989), *overruling* 753 F.2d 1468 (9th Cir. 1985).

[474] *United States v. State of Washington*, 135 F.3d 618 (9th Cir. 1998).

[475] 903 P.2d 1246 (Haw. 1995).

[476] Haw. Const. art. XII, §7. "*Ahupua'a*" refers to a kind of traditional land tenancy that existed in Hawai'i before its colonization by the United States.

[477] 903 P.2d at 1258. *See* Haw. Rev. Stat. §1-1 ("The common law of England, as ascertained by English and American decisions, is declared to be the common law of the State of [Hawai'i] in all cases, except as otherwise expressly provided by the Constitution or laws of the United States, or by the laws of the State, or fixed by Hawaiian judicial precedent, or established by Hawaiian usage") and Haw. Rev. Stat. §7-1 ("Where the landlords have obtained, or may hereafter obtain, allodial titles to their lands, the people on each of their lands shall not be deprived of the right to take firewood, house-timber, aho cord, thatch, or ki leaf, from the land on which they live, for their own private use, but they shall not have a right to take such articles to sell for profit. The people shall also have a right to drinking water, and running water, and the right of way. The springs of water, running water, and roads shall be free to all, on all lands granted in fee simple; provided that this shall not be applicable to wells and watercourses, which individuals have made for their own use"). *See also Ka Pa'akai O Ka'aina v. Land Use Commission, State of Hawai'i*, 7 P.3d 1068 (Haw. 2000); *Pele Defense Fund v. Puna Geothermal Venture*, 881 P.2d 1210 (Haw. 1994); *Kalipi v. Hawaiian Trust Co.*, 656 P.2d 745 (Haw. 1982). The court in

rights would not prevent land development entirely but would, of necessity, curtail it to some extent. Such rights limit the right of the owner to exclude those exercising them. ◀

§2.9 Trespass to Chattels

Interference with possession of personal property

Trespass is usually a doctrine that concerns intrusions to real property. A version of the doctrine, called *trespass to chattels*, applies to personal property. The tort of trespass to chattels allows owners of personal property to recover damages for intentional interferences with the possession of personal property.[478] The owner is entitled to injunctive relief stopping any such interference with the chattel. Mere touching of the object is not sufficient to constitute trespass; the plaintiff must either allege some injury to the property or show either dispossession or intentional "using or intermeddling" with it.[479]

▷ TRESPASS TO COMPUTER SYSTEMS **HARD CASE ◀**

In *Intel Corp. v. Hamidi*,[480] a former employee sent numerous e-mails to his former co-employees criticizing the employer. The e-mails breached no security barriers nor disrupted the employer's e-mail system. The trial court held and the appeals court affirmed that the former employee had committed trespass to chattels on the grounds that the former employee was "disrupting [the employer's] business by using its property."[481] However, the California Supreme Court reversed, holding that no trespass could be shown in the absence of dispossession unless the communication damaged the recipient's computer system or impaired its functioning. Similarly, *CompuServe v. Cyber Promotions, Inc.*[482] found a viable trespass claim when an advertising company sent unsolicited e-mail to an Internet service provider's customers after being asked not to do so if plaintiff could show harm to its personal property or "diminution of its quality, condition, or value."[483]

Public Access Shoreline Hawai'i noted that the "statutory exception [in Haw. Rev. Stat. §1-1 to the rights of landowners] is thus akin to the English doctrine of custom whereby practices and privileges unique to particular districts continued to apply to the residents of those districts even though in contravention of the common law." 903 P.2d at 1261.

[478] *Intel Corp. v. Hamidi*, 71 P.3d 296, 302 (Cal. 2003); *Restatement (Second) of Torts* §218 (1965).

[479] *Intel Corp. v. Hamidi*, 71 P.3d 296, 302 (Cal. 2003); *Restatement (Second) of Torts* §217 (1965).

[480] 71 P.3d 296, 302 (Cal. 2003).

[481] *Id.*

[482] 962 F. Supp. 1015 (S.D. Ohio 1997).

[483] *Id.* at 1022. *See also Kinslow v. State*, 860 S.E.2d 444 (Ga. 2021) (evidence insufficient to sustain conviction under statutory prohibition against computer trespass because employee who altered network settings to forward his employer's email to his own account did not block or impede any data).

In contrast, in *eBay, Inc. v. Bidder's Edge, Inc.*,[484] the court found both intentional interference with possession and "damage" when defendant Bidder's Edge's Internet-based auction aggregation site accessed plaintiff eBay's Internet-based auction trading site through an automated program that sent 80,000 to 100,000 information requests per day to plaintiff's site. Although plaintiff could show no loss of profits or interference with the operation of its computer system, the trial court in *eBay* found a likelihood that defendant's activities "diminished the quality or value of eBay's computer systems [by consuming] at least a portion of [eBay's] bandwidth and server capacity."[485] This was sufficient to show damage because defendant had "deprived eBay of the ability to use that portion of its personal property for its own purposes" as well as creating potential harm by encouraging other sites to use similar techniques. And in *In re Apple, Inc. Device Performance Litigation*,[486] a district court found that a class of Apple iPhone owners stated a valid claim for trespass to chattels when they alleged Apple installed software updates onto their devices to cause the phones to slow down to conceal a design defect that was harming battery life. Although users had consented to software updates, plaintiffs alleged that Apple exceeded the scope of that consent, having obtained it by misrepresenting its purpose as "bug fixes and improvements." The court found that users had only consented to software updates that would improve, not diminish, the performance of their devices. ◀

[484] 100 F. Supp. 2d 1058 (N.D. Cal. 2000).
[485] *Id.* at 1071.
[486] 347 F. Supp. 3d 434 (N.D. Cal. 2018).

PART II

RELATIONSHIPS AMONG NEIGHBORS

CHAPTER 3

Nuisance

§3.1 Introduction
§3.2 Private Nuisance
 §3.2.1 Test
 §3.2.2 Remedies
 §3.2.3 Types of Nuisances
§3.3 Public Nuisance
§3.4 Water Rights
 §3.4.1 Diffuse Surface Water (Flooding)
 §3.4.2 Streams and Lakes
 §3.4.3 Groundwater
§3.5 Support Rights
 §3.5.1 Lateral Support
 §3.5.2 Subjacent Support
§3.6 Light and Air

§3.1 Introduction

Land use conflicts

We don't live alone. It seems obvious, but this simple fact has profound consequences. Owners own property alongside other owners and disputes often arise among neighboring landowners over conflicting uses of property. A proposed building may be out of scale with other structures in the neighborhood, dwarfing surrounding buildings and blocking light and air. A factory may pollute the air or the water. A bar may be noisy, disturbing neighbors who wish to sleep at night. A neighbor's teenage child may be an incipient rock star, practicing at full volume all hours of the night. Herbicide used by a farmer may leach through the ground or waft through the air to neighboring land, harming vegetation there and even causing illness to inhabitants. A landlord may allow an apartment building to be overrun by drug dealers, decreasing the value of neighboring property and jeopardizing the security of the neighbors, as well as harming the quality of life in the entire neighborhood.

Conflicts among property rights

In each of these cases, we face a conflict between the interests of one owner in free use of her property and the interests of the neighbors in maintaining the secure enjoyment of their own property. Although owners are legally entitled to use their land as they wish, those rights are subject to significant limits designed to protect both other owners and the interests of the community as a whole. The extent of one's property rights is determined, significantly, by the effects that the exercise of one's rights have on others.

Freedom of action vs. security

Because use of land often affects other landowners, the privilege to use one's property is limited by the legal rights of other owners to be protected from uses that unreasonably harm their use or enjoyment of their own property. At the same time, the right to be secure from conduct that interferes with one's use or enjoyment of property is not absolute. Because interests in free use often clash with interests in security, we cannot provide absolute protection for either. As the *Restatement (Second) of Torts* notes, "[I]t is an obvious truth that each individual in a community must put up with a certain amount of annoyance, inconvenience and interference and must take a certain amount of risk in order that all may get on together."[1] However, free use rights must be limited when "the harm or risk to one is greater than he ought to be required to bear under the circumstances, at least without compensation."[2] Property rights exist on both sides in these cases and the law of property must determine how and where to draw the line between conflicting property claims to freedom of action (free use of one's own land) and security (the right to prevent other owners from using their property in ways that harm one's own property rights).

Property rights contingent on context in which exercised

The conflict between free use and security implies that one cannot define property rights *a priori* in a completely rigid sense. Rather, whether a property interest will be legally recognized is contingent on the effects of exercising that right on others. A factory that is not located near residential homes will not be

[1] *Restatement (Second) of Torts* §822, cmt. g (1977), *quoted in San Diego Gas & Electric Co. v. Superior Court*, 920 P.2d 669, 696 (Cal. 1996).
[2] *Id.*

causing an undue disturbance to other owners,[3] but if it is located near homes, a clash of interests will arise and one property interest or the other must yield. As Justice Sutherland noted, "A nuisance may be merely a right thing in the wrong place — like a pig in the parlor instead of the barnyard."[4] Whether a pig farm constitutes a lawful use of property depends not just on zoning law or compliance with applicable regulations, but on the effects the operation of the farm has on other owners. As Texas Supreme Court Justice Pope wrote, "What we do cannot be understood except in relation to those we touch."[5] Property rights cannot be defined rigidly, especially in the context of conflicting land uses, because the legitimacy of the exercise of a legal right is contingent on its compatibility with the legitimate interests and justified expectations of others.

Nontrespassory interferences with property rights

Trespass involves situations in which one person physically invades the land of another. Nuisance law provides remedies for *nontrespassory* invasions of property rights, *i.e.*, uses of *one's own property* that negatively affect the use or enjoyment of neighboring property. A nuisance is generally understood to be "something that is offensive, physically, to the senses and by such offensiveness makes life uncomfortable [such as] noise, odor, smoke, dust, or even flies."[6] Typical nuisance cases involve air or water pollution, excessive noise, or unpleasant odors. These cases involve physical invasion in the form of microscopic particles and sound waves, but they were not traditionally classified as trespasses.[7] The case of pollution was traditionally not thought to constitute a trespass because the particles could not be seen or because the physical invasion was considered "indirect" in the sense that the particles drifted onto the property rather than being propelled, as in the case of a gun firing a bullet onto neighboring land.

Trespass claims involving pollution

Increasingly, courts are allowing claims to be brought under both trespass and nuisance law in cases involving pollution. Most, but not all, courts have discarded the direct/indirect distinction and some have recently extended trespass law to pollution cases that used to be regulated only by nuisance law. However, the courts that have done so have generally denied liability unless the harm was substantial. In altering trespass law in this way, the courts have adopted important aspects of the framework underlying nuisance law.[8] Thus, the distinction between trespassory and nontrespassory invasions of property rights is less clear than it might appear.

Interference with use or enjoyment

What then is the difference between trespass and nuisance? They protect somewhat different interests. Trespass law is said to protect the interest

[3] However, if it pollutes the air, it harms a common resource — one owned by the entire community — and may therefore be liable for causing a "public nuisance" even if it does not directly hurt neighboring owners and is therefore not liable under "private nuisance" law.

[4] *Village of Euclid v. Ambler Realty Co.*, 272 U.S. 365, 388 (1926).

[5] *Friendswood Development Co. v. Smith-Southwest Industries, Inc.*, 576 S.W.2d 21, 33 (Tex. 1978) (Pope, J., dissenting).

[6] *In re Chicago Flood Litigation*, 680 N.E.2d 265, 278 (Ill. 1997). In contrast to complaints about pollution, which have been increasingly brought under trespass, as well as nuisance law, courts have allowed claims about noise only under nuisance law despite the physical effects produced on the ears by sound waves. *Wilson v. Interlake Steel Co.*, 649 P.2d 922 (Cal. 1982).

[7] *Johnson v. Paynesville Farmers Union Cooperative Oil Co.*, 817 N.W.2d 693, 704 (Minn. 2012) (reaffirming the nuisance/trespass distinction in the case of particulates); *Babb v. Lee County Landfill SC, LLC*, 747 S.E.2d 468, 476-480 (S.C. 2013).

[8] *See above* §2.4.4.

in exclusive possession, while nuisance law protects interests in use or enjoyment of one's own property.[9] Nuisance claims have sometimes been found in cases that involve no physical intrusion or effect of any kind. For example, some cases have applied nuisance law to landlords who allowed their properties to be used by drug dealers, thereby decreasing the value of neighboring land and undermining the safety and security of neighboring owners.[10]

Accommodating conflicting property rights

The paradigmatic nuisance case involves property rights on both sides, with one owner complaining that her property has been harmed by the way in which the other property owner has used her own property. Because property rights exist on both sides, the courts tend to "balance" or accommodate the conflicting interests of the parties. Liability will be found only if the harm is *substantial*; in addition, either the conduct creating the harm or the consequences of that conduct to the affected property must be deemed *unreasonable* for a nuisance claim to prevail. This framework contrasts sharply with the trespass paradigm, which assumes that any physical invasion constitutes a wrongful interference with the owner's interest in exclusive possession. Protection of property requires attention to the property interests of both parties when property claims clash.

Varieties of land use regulation

Land use conflicts are regulated in a variety of ways. First, the state may enact comprehensive governmental land use planning regulations on a regional or local level. The prime example is zoning law.[11] Second, a host

Statutory regulation

of federal and state statutes regulate land uses to protect the environment. Third, every state regulates construction through building codes designed to protect the safety of those who buy and use buildings. Other regulations promote access for persons with disabilities, protect historic landmarks, require de-leading or repainting to protect children from lead poisoning.

Land use agreements

Fourth, owners may regulate land use by contract. Developers of subdivisions and condominiums often impose "servitudes" on the owners limiting the uses to which the land can be put. These contractual arrangements may provide for enforcement by a homeowners' or condominium association and, subject to limitations, are enforceable in court against owners who bought with notice of them and who arguably impliedly agreed to the

Common law standards in the absence of contract

land use restrictions.[12] Fifth, common law and some statutory enactments accommodate conflicting interests in free use and security by defining the kinds of land uses that may be limited to protect the interests of owners in the use and enjoyment of their property. This chapter covers this area of the law.

Nuisance

Most land use conflicts are regulated by *nuisance* law. This catch-all category provides remedies for conduct that causes substantial and unreasonable harm to the use or enjoyment of property. Some land use conflicts

Water rights

are regulated by more specific rules. Water rights are a separate area of law

[9] *Willmschen v. Trinity Lakes Improvement Ass'n*, 840 N.E.2d 1275, 1281-1282 (Ill. App. Ct. 2005).

[10] *Lew v. Superior Court*, 25 Cal. Rptr. 2d 42 (Ct. App. 1993); *Kellner v. Cappellini*, 516 N.Y.S.2d 827 (Civ. Ct. 1986).

[11] These mechanisms are covered in Chapter 13.

[12] These devices are covered in Chapters 5 and 6.

involving conflicts over flooding, the use of streams or rivers by riparian owners and others,[13] and conflicts over use and harms caused by withdrawal of groundwater (percolating water diffused through the ground). Issues of support for land constitute another specialized area, including rules about lateral and subjacent support of land. Finally, interests in access to light and air have also been treated as a separate specialized topic subject to its own rules under common law.

Support

Light and air

In general, there was a fairly strong trend in the last quarter of the twentieth century to move away from rigid rules in this area to tests based on reasonableness. In one sense, this may be surprising. A great deal of literature on property emphasizes that property systems need clear rules about who owns property and what they are entitled to do with it to promote efficient land use and transfer.[14] However, rigid rules may be inefficient if they discourage developments whose benefits outweigh their costs or if they encourage land uses that have an overall negative impact on social welfare. The variety of land use conflicts that can arise defies easy categorization. Attention to the facts and contexts of particular cases may well be not only the fairest but the most efficient way to resolve these conflicts.

The trend toward reasonableness

Clear property rights might encourage bargaining, because we know who owns the entitlement, but they may also discourage it. Once one is assigned the entitlement, she may *feel* entitled and be resistant to giving up her rights. Transaction costs of reassigning rights may be high even in the case of two neighbors. Reasonableness tests, on the other hand, may encourage bargaining to an efficient result if both parties are trying to predict how a jury would react to the conflicting uses. They may agree that a fact finder is likely to determine that a particular use is unreasonable, or the uncertainty about the outcome may induce them to negotiate to a mutually acceptable resolution. This is why many cases settle just after the jury is picked. In addition, rigid rules do not discourage litigation if one litigant believes she can convince the court that application of the rigid rule will work an injustice in her case. When rules seem to generate bad results, courts have been very responsive to either creating exceptions or moving from rigid rules to more flexible reasonableness standards. In any event, the trend toward reasonableness as the baseline common law standard in land use conflicts is strong, although not complete.

Do clear rules or flexible reasonableness tests best promote bargaining?

Nuisance law mediates between conflicting interests of neighboring owners. When relief is denied, the law promotes interests in free use and development of land. The interest in using one's land as one wants is obviously a strong one and promotes a host of values, including autonomy, dignity, security, and comfort. The freedom to develop land allows the owner to create a home, business, or charitable entity. On the other hand, such uses and developments are not entirely self-regarding; they have effects both on other owners and on the community. Many of these effects are welcome and may be thought of as positive externalities. Some of the effects of particular land uses, however, may be negative, harming particular neighboring owners or the quality of life in the area. Limiting free use and

Interests protected by nuisance law

Free use and development

Secure use and enjoyment

Flexibility v. stability

[13] Riparian owners are landowners whose property borders a body of water, such as a stream, river, or ocean.

[14] Richard Posner, *Economic Analysis of Law* §§3.1-3.14 (9th ed. 2014).

development may be justified by the need to protect the ability of owners to derive benefit from their own property without undue interference by others. Investment in property can be rendered valueless if neighbors can use their own property in ways that make one's own property uncomfortable, unpleasant, dangerous to occupy, or otherwise substantially interfere with an owner's ability to derive benefit from her own land. The ability to develop property and use it for new purposes promotes desirable flexibility in property use, while limits on development to protect security promote the need for stability.

The paradox of regulation

Free use as a baseline

A common way of thinking about the relation between property and regulation assumes that owners are free to use their property as they see fit unless some rule of law limits their freedom. Limits on free use seem to be "regulations" of the owner because they limit the liberty of owners to do what they like. This way of looking at the problem assumes that the baseline is freedom of action (free use of property) and that the burden is on the state to justify limits to free use because such limits curtail liberty.

Security as a baseline

Land use regulation as a necessary component of property

This is not the only way to look at the relation between property and regulation. The institution of property presumes that the state will act to protect the rights of owners. Trespass law, for example, grants owners the right to call on the state to exclude non-owners from the property. If the state refused to enforce existing trespass law, it might well be liable for taking property without just compensation. Imagine if a stranger camped out on your front lawn, and the mayor of the city ordered the police not to evict her. Because, under current law, owners have the legal right to prevent others from sleeping on their property without their consent, the selective refusal to enforce trespass law might well be deemed an unconstitutional deprivation of property without just compensation.[15] Property rights are generally protected by state action. Although limits on free use arguably infringe on property rights by limiting owners' privileges, the state's failure to protect owners from harmful invasions of their property by others may similarly deprive owners of rights to which they are entitled under existing law and, in the extreme case, may constitute unconstitutional deprivations of property.

Nuisance immunity as a regulatory taking

For example, in *Bormann v. Board of Supervisors in and for Kossuth County*,[16] a state law authorized the creation of "agricultural areas" in which particular owners were entitled to immunity from certain nuisance claims by neighbors. Similar "right-to-farm" statutes have been enacted in many states. Neighbors challenged the statute because it deprived them of rights they had under prior law to be protected against nuisances committed on neighboring property. The Iowa Supreme Court held the statute unconstitutional on the ground that one of the rights associated with ownership is the right to be free from private nuisances caused by other owners, and that deprivation of this right constituted a *per se* taking of property without just

[15] *See Cedar Point Nursery v. Hassid*, 594 U.S. 139 (2021) (holding that an unconstitutional taking of property occurred when owners were forced to allow labor organizers on their property).

[16] 584 N.W.2d 309 (Iowa 1998).

compensation. Justice Lavarato argued that the power to commit a nuisance gives a person the right to harm the property rights of others and is therefore a kind of "easement," meaning a limited right to do something on someone else's land.[17] Although no physical invasion is involved, granting a farm the right to operate without liability for the harm it does to other property owners allows it to create odors and other environmental effects that may substantially harm neighboring homeowners and, in the extreme case, may make that land unsuitable for residential purposes. Because property law traditionally gave owners the right to be free from unreasonable and substantial interferences with their use or enjoyment of their property, the Iowa Supreme Court concluded that the statute authorizing farmers to commit nuisances effectuated an unconstitutional taking of the property rights of those affected by what would otherwise have constituted an actionable nuisance.[18] This right-to-farm statute at first looks "deregulatory" because it allows the farmer to operate freely without interference by the state; it lifts a "regulation" that had previously been imposed by nuisance law on the farmer. However, from the standpoint of the homeowners who have lost the right to prevent a nuisance next door, the statute appears to be a regulatory action that deprives them of pre-existing property rights, and, at least in this case, the court agreed that the failure to regulate the farmer's conduct effectuated a regulatory taking of the homeowners' property rights.

Freedom and coercion

The holding in *Bormann* is questionable, especially in the context of a facial challenge to the statute.[19] Taken to the extreme, it would mean that the legislature can never change the common law of property. But it recognizes a profound truth. Laws may be experienced as coercive when they constrain freedom of action, but they may also be experienced as coercive when they free individuals to act in ways that are harmful to others or that disappoint justified expectations based on prior law. Property occupies this middle position between freedom and security, and government protection of property both promotes freedom and constrains it.

[17] This is an unusual use of the "easement" concept. Traditionally, an "affirmative easement" was a right to do something physically on someone else's land, such as crossing it (a right of way), while a "negative easement" was a right to prevent someone else from doing something on her own land. The right to commit a nuisance fits in neither of these categories because it is a right to do something *on one's own land* that interferes with the use or enjoyment of other land. Conceptualizing the immunity from liability as an "easement" obviously increased the court's willingness to understand the statute as a deprivation of ownership rights. What is surprising about the case is that it arguably makes all changes in nuisance law unconstitutional takings of property. Taken to the extreme, it would prevent any modernization of land use law to accommodate changing values or conditions. The definition of what constitutes an "unreasonable" use has changed with time and nuisance immunities exist for various types of conduct, such as interferences with light and air and, in the absence of zoning laws to the contrary, placement of business uses next to residential uses. It would be unfortunate indeed if the legislature were deprived of the power to readjust conflicting land uses as social needs, values, and expectations change.

[18] *See also Richards v. Washington Terminal Co.*, 233 U.S. 546 (1914).

[19] *Compare, e.g., Ehlerbracht v. Crowned Ridge Wind II, LLC*, 972 N.W. 2d 477, 491-492 (S.D. 2022) (noting that *Bormann* is an outlier and declining to find the elimination of the right to maintain a nuisance to be a taking); *Himsel v. Himsel*, 122 N.E.3d 935 (Ind. Ct. App. 2019) (upholding and applying a right-to-farm statute).

§3.2 Private Nuisance

§3.2.1 Test

Definition

A nuisance is a substantial and unreasonable interference with the use or enjoyment of land.[20] This rule of law obviously leaves a little to the imagination. It is designed to apply flexibly to every conceivable type of conflict that might arise between neighbors over land use. This is a virtue. At the same time, application of the doctrine defies easy categorization or theorization, and it is not the most predictable rule to apply in practice. A leading torts scholar once opined that "[t]here is perhaps no more impenetrable jungle in the entire law than that which surrounds the word 'nuisance.'"[21] Because the kinds of conflicts that can arise over property use are infinite, the factors relevant to nuisance determinations cannot be contained in a closed list. And the activities that have been held to be nuisances have changed over time.[22]

Substantial harm

Nuisance law protects interests in the use or enjoyment of land, although liability extends to injuries to persons affected by the harmful conduct. Although trespass claims are generally available only to owners or current possessors of land (such as tenants), nuisance claims can be brought by anyone who has an interest in land, including mortgagees and owners of easements.[23]

Nuisance law protects not only ownership rights, but possessory rights and lesser property interests. One tenant in a building may bring a nuisance claim against another. Because nuisance cases usually involve conflicting land uses, the harm must be substantial; minor or insignificant harms are privileged and therefore lawful because they are understood to be the necessary consequences of owning property next door to another

[20] *Exxon Mobil Corp. v. Albright*, 71 A.3d 30, 94 (Md. 2013) ("To succeed on a nuisance claim, a plaintiff must establish an unreasonable and substantial interference with his or her use and enjoyment of his or her property, such that the injury is of such a character as to diminish materially the value of the property as a dwelling and seriously interfere with the ordinary comfort and enjoyment of it"). *Accord, San Diego Gas & Electric Co. v. Superior Court*, 920 P.2d 669 (Cal. 1996); *In re Chicago Flood Litigation*, 680 N.E.2d 265, 277 (Ill. 1997); *Nichols v. Mid-Continent Pipe Line Co.*, 933 P.2d 272 (Okla. 1996); *Lane v. W.J. Curry & Sons*, 92 S.W.3d 355, 364-365 (Tenn. 2002); *City of Tyler v. Likes*, 962 S.W.2d 489 (Tex. 1997); *Stevenson v. Goodson*, 924 P.2d 339 (Utah 1996); *Jones v. Hart*, 261 A.3d 1126, 1137 (Vt. 2021); *Tiegs v. Watts*, 954 P.2d 877 (Wash. 1998); *Vogel v. Grant-Lafayette Electric Cooperative*, 548 N.W.2d 829 (Wis. 1996).

[21] W. Page Keeton, Dan R. Dobbs, Robert E. Keeton & David G. Owen, *Prosser & Keeton on the Law of Torts* §86, at 616 (5th ed. 1984) (*quoting* Dean William Prosser); *see also* Dan B. Dobbs, Paul T. Hayden & Ellen M. Bublick, *Hornbook on Torts* §30.1, at 733 (2d ed. 2016).

[22] Louise Halper, *Untangling the Nuisance Knot*, 26 Envtl. Aff. 89 (1998); Louise Halper, *Why the Nuisance Knot Can't Undo the Takings Muddle*, 28 Ind. L. Rev. 329 (1995).

[23] Licensees and employees have not traditionally been entitled to bring nuisance claims, although one can imagine situations in which courts would be sympathetic to such claims. An employee who becomes ill because of pollution originating next door could bring a negligence claim against the actor who caused the harm while the owner is entitled to bring a nuisance claim. In cases where a nuisance is likely to be found while negligence is hard to prove, it is not clear why the employee should be denied recovery, especially if she must quit her job because she cannot work or cannot work comfortably on the site.

owner. Harm to use or enjoyment is substantial if it would be offensive or inconvenient to the ordinary or average person.[24] Relief will be denied if the plaintiff is "unusually sensitive."[25]

▷UNUSUALLY SENSITIVE PLAINTIFF **HARD CASE ◀**

Relief was denied in *Jenkins v. CSX Transportation, Inc.*[26] when plaintiff reacted to creosote fumes from railroad ties transported through defendant's neighboring rail yard because plaintiff suffered from an extremely rare allergic condition and was thus seen as an unusually sensitive plaintiff. This result might be justified on the ground that owners should not have to look out for unpredictable effects of their conduct and thus defendant could not reasonably foresee that a neighbor would have a rare condition and be harmed by an otherwise benign land use. In addition, restricting land use when anyone objects, might have the effect of curtailing free use of land too much, inhibiting development, and harming the whole community. On the other hand, "unusually sensitive" individuals still must live somewhere and if no one is under an obligation to consider the substantial harm otherwise benign land uses cause to such individuals, they will be denied the same rights as others to quiet enjoyment of their homes. Federal antidiscrimination laws require landlords to make reasonable accommodations for tenants with disabilities[27] and if it is possible to alter defendant's land use in ways that ameliorate or remove the hardship to a neighboring owner, without undue cost, it is arguably unreasonable not to require the defendant to do so. ◀

Unreasonable

In addition to the requirement that the harm be substantial, the interference with use or enjoyment of property must also be deemed "unreasonable." "Unreasonable" in nuisance "is not like 'unreasonable' in the law of negligence, for it does not refer to risk-creating conduct of the defendant, but to the reasonable expectations of a normal person occupying the plaintiff's land."[28] The courts have traditionally defined reasonableness in the nuisance context by comparing the interests of the parties. As the *Restatement (Second) of Torts* reports, interference with use or enjoyment of property is deemed unreasonable if "the gravity of the harm outweighs the utility of the actor's conduct."[29] This standard obviously leaves a vast area of discretion in application and room for argument. In addition, it is ambiguous as to whether even a substantial harm should be deemed reasonable provided that the social benefits to others outweigh the harm to the

[24] Dan B. Dobbs, Paul T. Hayden & Ellen M. Bublick, *Hornbook on Torts* §30.4, at 738 (2d ed. 2016).

[25] *Fitzgarrald v. City of Iowa City*, 492 N.W.2d 659, 664 (Iowa 1992); *Page County Appliance Center, Inc. v. Honeywell, Inc.*, 347 N.W.2d 171 (Iowa 1984); *O'Cain v. O'Cain*, 473 S.E.2d 460, 466 (S.C. 1996).

[26] 906 S.W.2d 460 (Tenn. Ct. App. 1995).

[27] *See* 42 U.S.C. §3604(k).

[28] Dan B. Dobbs, Paul T. Hayden & Ellen M. Bublick, *Hornbook on Torts* §30.4, at 738 (2d ed. 2016).

[29] *Restatement (Second) of Torts* §826(a) (1979).

victims of the conduct. Because this approach appears to grant insufficient protection for property rights, the *Restatement (Second) of Torts* has supplemented the balancing test with one that provides for damages, if not injunctive relief, to owners who have suffered substantial harm because of neighboring property uses, when "the harm caused by the conduct is serious and the financial burden of compensating for this and similar harm to others would not make the continuation of the conduct not feasible."[30]

Factors to be considered in determining whether the interference is "unreasonable"

In determining the gravity of the harm, courts consider

> (a) the extent of the harm involved; (b) the character of the harm involved; (c) the social value that the law attaches to the type of use or enjoyment invaded; (d) the suitability of the particular use or enjoyment invaded to the character of the locality; and (e) the burden on the person harmed of avoiding the harm.[31]

In determining the utility of the conduct, courts consider "(a) the social value that the law attaches to the primary purpose of the conduct; (b) the suitability of the conduct to the character of the locality; and (c) the impracticability of preventing or avoiding the invasion."[32]

Who is liable?

The defendant in a nuisance case is usually, but not always, another landowner or possessor. It is often stated that nuisance refers to a harmful use of land by the defendant, but courts have held defendants liable who were not themselves possessors of land but who substantially contributed to the offensive land use. For example, in *Page County Appliance Center, Inc. v. Honeywell, Inc.*,[33] a travel agency installed a computer that emitted radiation that harmed television reception at a television sales store two doors down. The court held that the manufacturer of the computer (which also had a contractual obligation to repair and maintain it) might be liable for nuisance if it "substantially contributed" to the state of affairs that led to the interference with plaintiff's television reception.[34] Similarly, a manufacturer and distributor of an herbicide were found potentially liable for nuisance when the chemical broke down in the soil and contaminated windblown soil spread to neighboring land.[35] In addition, courts have sometimes found prior owners to be liable for nuisance if their use of the land during the time they owned it caused the harm to occur, thereby interfering with the interests of later owners of the parcel.[36] Some cases have held owners to be liable when their customers have created disturbances in the neighborhood, and the owner did nothing to stop the ruckus, and it continued over time.[37] Courts will generally not allow tenants to sue

[30] *Restatement (Second) of Torts* §826(b) (1979).
[31] *Restatement (Second) of Torts* §827 (1979).
[32] *Restatement (Second) of Torts* §828 (1979).
[33] 347 N.W.2d 171 (Iowa 1984).
[34] *Id.*
[35] *Hall v. Phillips*, 436 N.W.2d 139 (Neb. 1989).
[36] *Wilshire Westwood Assocs. v. Atlantic Richfield Co.*, 24 Cal. Rptr. 2d 562 (Ct. App. 1993).
[37] *Packett v. Herbert*, 377 S.E.2d 438 (Va. 1989) (operator of self-service car wash might be liable for nuisance to neighboring owner if customers' objectionable conduct is related to the conduct of the business, even if the acts complained of occur off the premises). *Accord, Guillot v. Town of Lutcher*, 373 So. 2d 1385 (La. Ct. App. 1979).

landlords for nuisance,[38] but might do so if the conduct causing the disturbance takes place in common areas of the premises or in an apartment unit retained by the landlord.

Intentional nuisance

Nuisance is an intentional wrong. In the unusual case, the defendant may have acted with the intent to harm the plaintiff. Such cases of "malice" or "spite" are rare, but they exist.[39] However, a nuisance is deemed intentional even if the defendant is not motivated by the desire to harm the plaintiff. The harm is intentional if the defendant knows that his conduct interferes with the use or enjoyment of other property or knows that the conduct is substantially certain to do so.[40] The harm is intentional even if the defendant did not know, at the time she first acted, that her conduct would cause harm, if she continues to engage in the activity after knowing how it is harming the plaintiff.[41] This is the usual basis of a finding of intentionality in nuisance cases, but even this may not be required. Many courts hold that a defendant has acted intentionally if she knew or *should have known* that her conduct would cause harm.[42] Further still, many courts have often found liability for nuisance even when the defendant did not know, at the time she acted, that her conduct would cause harm. Many pollution cases, such as chemical contamination of the ground or water, result from the unintentional discharge of chemicals, as when petroleum leaks from pipes under the ground. Opinions in these cases often do not discuss the intentionality requirement, effectively discarding it as a requirement. At the same time, one might argue that intention is present merely because the defendant placed the pipes under the ground or currently owns and operates them and thus should have known they might leak or cause harm.

Distinguished from negligence

It is sometimes stated that the defendant's *conduct* must be deemed unreasonable.[43] This is somewhat misleading, however, because the test for nuisance is different from the test for negligence, which is also defined as unreasonable conduct. Negligence liability applies when a defendant acted in a way that caused an unreasonable risk of harm. "Ordinary negligence is defined as the doing of something that a reasonably careful person would not do under similar circumstances, or the failing to do something that a reasonably careful person would do under similar circumstances."[44] It is assumed that a reasonable person would have foreseen that the harm was possible and would have acted so as to avoid it. The focus is on the defendant's conduct, and a finding of negligence amounts to a conclusion that a reasonable person would not have done what the defendant did. In contrast, most courts hold that nuisance liability focuses not on the

[38] *Doe v. New Bedford Housing Authority*, 630 N.E.2d 248, 257 (Mass. 1994) (proper claim is breach of the leasehold agreement).

[39] *Tranfield v. Arcuni-English*, 215 A.3d 222 (Me. 2019).

[40] *Hall v. Phillips*, 436 N.W.2d 139, 142-144 (Neb. 1989); *Restatement (Second) of Torts* §825.

[41] *Thomsen v. Greve*, 550 N.W.2d 49 (Neb. Ct. App. 1996); *Bargmann v. Soll Oil Co.*, 574 N.W.2d 478, 486 (Neb. 1998); *Vogel v. Grant-Lafayette Electric Cooperative*, 548 N.W.2d 829 (Wis. 1996) (*citing Restatement (Second) of Torts* §825).

[42] *Crosstex North Texas Pipeline, L.P. v. Gardiner*, 505 S.W.3d 580, 605 (Tex. 2016); *Hendricks v. Stalnaker*, 380 S.E.2d 198, 202 (W. Va. 1989).

[43] 8-67 *Thompson on Real Property, Third Thomas Edition* §67.03(a).

[44] *Bargmann v. Soll Oil Co.*, 574 N.W.2d 478, 485 (Neb. 1998).

reasonableness of the defendant's conduct but the reasonableness of the *consequences* of that conduct. A nuisance is a "state of affairs."[45] If the harm is one that the plaintiff should not have to bear, then the conduct may be unreasonable, within the meaning of nuisance law, even if the defendant could not have foreseen that the conduct would cause the harm.[46]

Negligence v. nuisance claims

Plaintiffs often sue on the theory of negligence as well as nuisance.[47] In some cases, a nuisance can be proved even if the defendant's conduct was not negligent. For example, a chemical that is thought to be safe may later be found out to be harmful. Although the initial conduct in using the chemical may not have been negligent, the harm to the neighboring property (as understood at the time of trial) may be deemed both substantial and unreasonable. In other cases, an action may be negligent but not constitute a nuisance. For example, an action may be deemed to create an unreasonable risk of harm, but the resulting harm may not be "substantial" enough to qualify as a nuisance. In such cases, liability for negligence may nonetheless be available. Alternatively, a nuisance claim may be denied because the harm is not substantial or because plaintiff "came to the nuisance," moving in next door to a farm, for example, while a negligence claim might be upheld if the farm is managed in a way that does not accord with accepted safety standards.[48]

Negligence

Strict liability

When one owner commits a nuisance, such as pollution of a stream, the injured owner may sue on a variety of theories, including trespass, nuisance, negligence, and even strict liability. Property owners, like all others, are subject to a general requirement of acting reasonably to avoid conduct that poses an unreasonable risk of illegitimate harm to others. In addition, many courts have traditionally imposed strict liability for harms caused by "ultrahazardous" or "abnormally dangerous" activities such as blasting or storage of explosives. Such cases amount to determinations that harms caused by such land use are ones that owners should not have to bear, no matter what the relative costs and benefits of the opposing uses. It is sometimes stated that private nuisance may be either intentional or unintentional. The heart of nuisance law is the law of intentional nuisance and that is the focus of the discussion here.[49] Yet the courts sometimes talk about "unintentional nuisance"[50] when they impose liability for negligently inflicted harms. This term is confusing and is not used by most courts. The usual practice is to distinguish between claims based on nuisance from those based on negligence or recklessness or strict liability.

"Unintentional" nuisance

Rights, fairness, and distributive justice

One way to understand the traditional test for nuisance is that it combines consideration of fairness and efficiency.[51] Harm is substantial and

[45] Dale A. Whitman et al., *The Law of Property* §7.2, at 330 (4th ed. 2019).

[46] *Bargmann v. Soll Oil Co.*, 574 N.W.2d 478, 486 (Neb. 1998); *Vogel v. Grant-Lafayette Electric Cooperative*, 548 N.W.2d 829 (Wis. 1996) (*citing Restatement (Second) of Torts* §825).

[47] *Bargmann v. Soll Oil Co.*, 574 N.W.2d 478, 486 (Neb. 1998).

[48] On the difference between negligence and nuisance, see, for example, *Vagts v. N. Natural Gas Co.*, 8 N.W.3d 501, 508-513 (Iowa 2024); Robert E. Keeton, *Restating Strict Liability and Nuisance*, 48 Vand. L. Rev. 595 (1995).

[49] *In re Chicago Flood Litigation*, 680 N.E.2d 265, 280 (Ill. 1997); *New Jersey Dep't of Envtl. Prot. v. Alden Leeds, Inc.*, 708 A.2d 1161, 1167 (N.J. 1998).

[50] *Restatement (Second) of Torts* §822.

[51] A. Mitchel Polinsky, *Resolving Nuisance Disputes: The Simple Economics of Injunctive and Damage Remedies*, 32 Stan. L. Rev. 1075 (1980).

unreasonable if it is the kind of harm an owner should not have to suffer. Determining the appropriate limits to free use of land requires distinctions between favored and disfavored uses and judgments about the kinds of interferences with use or enjoyment of property that are the necessary price of living in a society with others, including other property owners like oneself. Nuisance law requires judgments about the fair parameters of property rights. Whether or not one is entitled to act as one does depends not just on the character of the action but the consequences of one's actions for other owners. Although some nuisances are said to be nuisances *per se*— usually illegal activities such as illegal gambling establishments or houses of prostitution — most nuisances are recognized only when plaintiff demonstrates their harmful effects (so-called nuisances in fact). Because nuisance law mediates between interests in liberty and interests in security, the distribution of the burdens and benefits of land ownership among owners is of paramount relevance.

Efficiency

On the other hand, the requirement that the harm be "unreasonable" is often analyzed in light of considerations of social welfare. Nuisance law requires a "weighing" or balancing or accommodating of the conflicting interests of the parties, as well as consideration of the effects of different rulings on others and on the community as a whole. The relative interests of the parties are relevant, but so are the overall social effects of imposing liability or leaving owners free to engage in that kind of conduct without liability. Similar considerations arise in determining whether to enjoin the offending activity. The relative costs and benefits of alternative rules are central concerns. Some scholars and a few judges have used the tools of economic analysis to determine, in particular classes of cases or lawsuits, which results promote economic efficiency. Most courts, however, do not reduce their consideration of costs and benefits to market values, but analyze both the magnitude and the character of harms and benefits associated with conflicting land uses in a broader conceptual framework. Protection of the environment, for example, may provide benefits that are not easily translated into market terms and especially not easily captured by specific dollar amounts.

Ambiguity in nuisance law

A crucial ambiguity pervades nuisance doctrine. Sometimes a land use is deemed unreasonable because the overall social harms it causes outweigh its social benefits. Such determinations take into account all the individuals and owners affected by the conflicting land uses. At other times, however, a land use is deemed unreasonable because the effect on the plaintiff is one that an owner should not have to bear even if the overall social benefits of the conduct outweigh its social costs. In such cases, a nuisance may nevertheless be found, despite the court's conclusion that the overall social benefits of the conduct outweigh its social costs. In effect, the court determines that it is unreasonable for the plaintiff to bear the costs associated with the defendant's activity and forces the defendant to internalize those costs by paying damages or perhaps even enjoining the defendant's conduct that causes the harm. For example, in *Boomer v. Atlantic Cement Co.*,[52]

[52] 257 N.E.2d 870 (N.Y. 1970).

the court refused to issue an injunction shutting down a cement factory worth $45 million with 300 employees despite the air pollution it was causing, amounting to damages of $185,000 to neighboring owners. The court refused to grant the injunction because of the public interest in the operation of the plant and because less injury would be caused by allowing the factory to operate while paying damages than by shutting down the factory with an injunction. On the other hand, the court did uphold a damages judgment against the defendant on the ground that it was unreasonable to allow the defendant to interfere with the plaintiffs' use and enjoyment of their property without compensation.

Individual and social conceptions of what is reasonable

This result in *Boomer* has been applauded and followed by many courts. But it is fundamentally inconsistent with the traditional "black-letter" nuisance law. Damages were awarded in *Boomer* because defendant committed a substantial and unreasonable interference with the use and enjoyment of plaintiffs' property. However, if the harm was both substantial and unreasonable (comparing the utility of the conduct with the gravity of the harm), why wasn't it enjoined? In fact, the court found the harm unreasonable *as between the parties* but reasonable *as a social matter.*

In other words, the overall benefits of operating the factory outweighed its costs, so the court allowed the operation to continue, denying injunctive relief shutting it down. However, although total social benefits outweighed total social costs, those costs were not fairly distributed but were concentrated on neighbors. The court determined that the costs associated with the unpleasantness of soot and smoke were not ones that owners should have to bear, at least not without compensation. Damages were awarded because the harm was both substantial and unreasonable for homeowners to bear without compensation; the injunction was denied because the conduct was reasonable from a social standpoint despite the harm to the plaintiffs. This standard has now been adopted by the *Restatement (Second) of Torts*, which provides that an "intentional invasion of another's interest in the use and enjoyment of land is unreasonable if (b) the harm caused by the conduct is serious and the financial burden of compensating for this and similar harm to others would not make the continuation of the conduct not feasible."[53]

§3.2.2 Remedies

Property rules and liability rules

Nuisance cases may result in four outcomes: (1) injunction, (2) no relief, (3) damages, and (4) a purchased injunction. The first two remedies create either an entitlement to be free from the harm or an entitlement to inflict it. In a famous article, Guido Calabresi and Douglas Melamed classified the first two remedies as "property rules" since they assign entitlements and allow the parties to choose whether or not they want to keep or sell their rights.[54] The last two remedies either allow the harm to be committed or

[53] *Restatement (Second) of Torts* §826(b).

[54] Guido Calabresi & A. Douglas Melamed, *Property Rules, Liability Rules, and Inalienability: One View of the Cathedral*, 85 Harv. L. Rev. 1089 (1972).

the harm to be prevented upon payment of compensation to the party who is being required either to suffer the harm or to cease causing it. Calabresi and Melamed classified these as "liability rules" because they involve court-imposed damages.

Veto rights and privileges

An injunctive remedy may order defendant to stop the offending activity. Alternatively, the court might order defendant to install pollution control devices or otherwise stop committing the harm. In addition, the court might order remediation of the harm that has already occurred. Injunctions grant plaintiffs rights to protection from the harm. They give plaintiffs the right to *veto* the defendant's decision to engage in the offending use. Conversely, if plaintiff is denied any remedy, defendant is entitled to commit the harm without liability to the plaintiff. In such cases, defendant is *privileged* to act without liability and owns the right to use her land in the desired way without needing to account to others for the externalities caused by her conduct.

Contractual renegotiation

In either the case of veto rights or privileges, the parties are free to negotiate with each other for a different outcome.[55] When the court grants plaintiff an injunction, defendant is free to offer enough in settlement to induce the plaintiff to agree to live with the nuisance. If such an agreement can be reached, plaintiff can agree to grant defendant the right to commit a nuisance. This might be done in the form of an easement by which plaintiff grants defendant the right to act without interference by the current or future owners of the affected property. Conversely, if the defendant is granted a privilege, the plaintiff may offer defendant a money settlement to induce defendant to agree to cease the offending activity. In such a case, plaintiff might purchase a negative easement from defendant by which defendant agrees not to use its property in the offending manner.

Property rules

The veto rights and privilege solutions share something in common. They grant an entitlement to a particular party and give them the right to sell it or keep it. As such, they resemble traditional property rights because they identify fixed rights and protect owners from being forced to sell against their will. They were thus classified as "property rules" by Calabresi and Melamed.[56]

Injunctions

Why might the courts apply property rules? An injunction should be granted when the activity both causes substantial harm and is unreasonable in the sense that the social costs of the activity outweigh its social benefits. This is the case of the traditional nuisance and it fits the nuisance doctrine well. Conversely, defendant may be judged privileged to engage in the offending activity either because the harm is not viewed as substantial or because it is a type of harm that is fair to impose on the plaintiff as a cost of living in a society with others. This result also fits traditional doctrine.[57]

[55] For an argument based on empirical evidence to the effect that this is extraordinarily unlikely, see Ward Farnsworth, *Do Parties to Nuisance Cases Bargain After Judgment? A Glimpse Inside the Cathedral*, 66 U. Chi. L. Rev. 373 (1999).

[56] Guido Calabresi & A. Douglas Melamed, *Property Rules, Liability Rules, and Inalienability: One View of the Cathedral*, 85 Harv. L. Rev. 1089 (1972).

[57] *Boomer v. Atlantic Cement Co.*, 257 N.E.2d 870, 872 (N.Y. 1970).

Damages

In contrast, an award of damages in lieu of an injunction gives the defendant the option to commit the harm, face a lawsuit, and either suffer a damages judgment or settle the case with a money payment. This third remedy amounts to a forced sale of the entitlement to be free from substantial, unreasonable interference with use and enjoyment of land. A plaintiff who wants to stop the use will not be allowed to do so; all she can do is go to court to get a court-determined measurement of the amount of damages. A defendant who is willing to make this money payment is legally privileged to commit the harm upon payment of damages. This is a forced sale of an entitlement because plaintiff cannot choose not to sell if defendant insists on causing the harm and is willing and able to pay the damages. Moreover, the amount of payment will be determined not by the plaintiff, but by a court (or a settlement with a view to what the court would have been likely to award). On the other hand, one might argue that conceptualizing the damages judgment as a forced sale assumes that plaintiff had a right to be free from the harm. One might conclude that the plaintiff never was entitled to be free of the harm; the only right the plaintiff owned was the right not to suffer financial loss because of the offending activity. In this case, assuming that damages are equal to the property value lost because of the nuisance, no forced sale is involved; rather, plaintiff is getting what she is entitled to, no more and no less.

Damages and traditional nuisance doctrine

Because traditional nuisance doctrine focused on a determination of whether interference with use or enjoyment existed, and how substantial and unreasonable it was, it led naturally to the idea that a nuisance was a *per se* violation of property rights.[58] A forced sale of property rights seems foreign to the notion of ownership. Although the damages remedy is the usual one in torts cases, it does not fit well with traditional property doctrine. Damages may be awarded when the court determines that a nuisance was committed. But if a nuisance is a substantial and unreasonable interference with property rights, why would a court not order the offending conduct to stop? Allowing the activity to continue, albeit after paying damages to plaintiff, lets defendant infringe on plaintiff's property rights. Alternatively, one might conclude that the harm is not unreasonable. But if so, why require damages to be paid?

Property and tort paradigms for nuisance law

The leading case of *Boomer v. Atlantic Cement Co.*[59] made it fashionable to award damages while denying injunctive relief. The traditional view, never fully adopted in all states, was that nuisance law was part of property law rather than tort law. The right to be protected from substantial, unreasonable interference with use or enjoyment of property was conceptualized as a property right that one owned. Property rights traditionally were understood as rights that one could sell or refuse to sell. Allowing someone to commit harm to property while paying damages, amounts to a forced sale of property rights. In the torts context, this always seemed natural because accidents were not always avoidable, and once the harm had

[58] Robert G. Bone, *Normative Theory and Legal Doctrine in American Nuisance Law: 1850 to 1920*, 59 S.C. L. Rev. 1101 (1986); Jeff L. Lewin, Boomer *and the American Law of Nuisance: Past, Present, and Future*, 54 Alb. L. Rev. 189 (1990).

[59] 257 N.E.2d 870 (N.Y. 1970).

occurred, compensation was the only way to restore the balance between the parties. Increasingly, however, the courts recognized that nuisance cases involve property rights on both sides and that enjoining an owner from committing harm to another owner might have the effect of harming both the defendant and the defendant's property rights, as well as the community as a whole. To order a factory to be shut down to protect the property rights of a few owners would allow those owners to impose harms on the factory owner, its employees, and shareholders by depriving them of the value of their property. It might also affect the entire community. For this reason, the courts began to consider when it was appropriate to protect interests in use and enjoyment of property by injunctive relief and when damages were preferable.

Efficiency and fairness reasons for imposing damages awards

Damages were awarded in *Boomer* because the harm from the soot and smoke was substantial and was not the kind of discomfort or inconvenience that a property owner should have to bear as a member of society without compensation. At the same time, the social benefits of operating the factory were so great that the community as a whole would have been worse off if it had been shut down. In effect, the court determined that the operation of the factory was reasonable from a social standpoint; it was economically efficient in the sense that those who benefited from its operation far outweighed those who were made worse off by it. For this reason, an injunction was denied. On the other hand, it was determined that it was unfair for the company to benefit from its activity without compensating the homeowners for the harm imposed on them. The court found it fair to impose the economic burden of the conflicting land uses on the factory rather than the homeowners.[60] As the *Restatement (Second) of Torts* explains: "It may sometimes be reasonable to operate an important activity if payment is made for the harm it is causing, but unreasonable to continue it without paying."[61] At the same time, courts may deny both damages and injunctive relief, despite substantial harm, if the utility of the conduct outweighs that harm.[62]

Damages and injunctions in the courts

The *Boomer* approach is almost universal today. Few, if any, courts will grant injunctions automatically in nuisance cases. Many courts have begun to use the general legal standard for issuing an injunction, commonly taught in civil procedure courses. Courts increasingly assume that damages are the ordinary remedy in nuisance cases and that injunctions are available only to avoid irreparable harm or if damages are inadequate.[63]

[60] *Restatement (Second) of Torts* §822 cmt. d explains:

> For the purpose of determining liability for damages for private nuisance, an invasion may be regarded as unreasonable even though the utility of the conduct is great and the amount of harm is relatively small. But for the purpose of determining whether the conduct producing the invasion should be enjoined, additional factors must be considered. It may be reasonable to continue an important activity if payment is made for the harm it is causing but unreasonable to initiate or continue it without paying.

[61] *Restatement (Second) of Torts* §826 cmt. f.

[62] *Loughhead v. 1717 Bissonnet, L.L.C.*, No. 2013-26155, 2014 WL 8774060 (Tex. Dist. May 1, 2014), *aff'd in part and rev'd in part*, 500 S.W.3d 488 (Tex. App. 2016); *Carpenter v. Double R Cattle Co.*, 701 P.2d 222, 228 (Idaho 1985); *cf.* Michael Lewyn, *Yes to Infill, No to Nuisance*, 42 Fordham Urb. L.J. 841, 842 (2015).

[63] *Tamalunis v. City of Georgetown*, 542 N.E.2d 402, 413 (Ill. App. Ct. 1989).

A review of recent case law suggests that injunctions are denied either when the court views compensation as adequate or it considers the social value of the defendant's activity to be great. Conversely, injunctions are most likely to be granted when the court views defendant's activity as unsuited to the neighborhood and the social cost of shutting down the nuisance is not seen as prohibitive or unfair to defendant.[64]

Purchased injunctions

In lieu of either damages or an injunction, a court might grant an injunction against defendant as long as plaintiff pays damages to compensate defendant either for the lost profits caused by shutting down the defendant's land use or the costs of relocation or the reduction in fair market value to defendant's property caused by the loss of the right to engage in the offending activity. Purchased injunctions are granted for fairness and efficiency reasons that are the opposite of those that support damages.[65] The injunction is awarded because, on balance, the overall social harms of the conduct outweigh its benefits. At the same time, those benefiting from the cessation of the activity are thought to be those who should fairly bear the costs associated with shutting down an otherwise profitable activity.

Spur Industries v. Webb

The leading case illustrating this remedy is *Spur Industries v. Webb.*[66] In that case, a developer created a residential subdivision near a cattle ranch. When the homeowners moved in, they discovered that the stench was unbearable. Because the plaintiff homeowners "came to the nuisance," it seemed unfair to allow them to insist that the cattle ranch be shut down. Before plaintiffs came, no nuisance was present because no clash of property interests existed. By coming to the nuisance, plaintiffs arguably created the nuisance. If they had bought homes elsewhere, in a neighborhood suited to residential uses, they would have suffered no harm. The court found it reasonable to require the ranch to shut down and relocate, perhaps because the market value of the property harmed by the ranch operation far exceeded the market value of the ranch itself. However, the court did not find it fair to place the burden of shutting down the ranch on the ranch owner. It therefore granted an injunction shutting down the ranch on the condition that the plaintiffs agree to compensate the ranch owner for the cost of relocation and/or lost profits.

Puts

An alternative remedy has been suggested by Professor Ian Ayres.[67] A purchased injunction is equivalent to a forced sale, otherwise known as

[64] Cases reflecting *Boomer* in which damages were awarded but injunctions were denied include *Tamalunis v. City of Georgetown*, 542 N.E.2d 402, 413 (Ill. App. Ct. 1989); *Weinhold v. Wolff*, 555 N.W.2d 454 (Iowa 1996); *Huynh v. Blanchard*, 694 S.W.3d 648 (Tex. 2024). Cases in which an injunction was granted include *Parker v. Ashford*, 661 So. 2d 213 (Ala. 1995); *Payne v. Skaar*, 900 P.2d 1352 (Idaho 1995); *Omega Chemical Co., Inc. v. United Seeds, Inc.*, 560 N.W.2d 820 (Neb. 1997); *Goeke v. National Farms, Inc.*, 512 N.W.2d 626 (Neb. 1994); *Harris v. Town of Lincoln*, 668 A.2d 321 (R.I. 1995); *Sunnyside Feed Co., Inc. v. City of Portage*, 588 N.W.2d 278 (Wis. Ct. App. 1998).

[65] Another possible remedy is a conditional injunction that will be dissolved if the defendant elects to pay damages in lieu of complying with the injunction. *See Baldwin v. McClendon*, 288 So. 2d 761 (Ala. 1974).

[66] 494 P.2d 700 (Ariz. 1972).

[67] Ian Ayres, *Protecting Property with Puts*, 32 Val. U. L. Rev. 793 (1998).

an "option." If plaintiffs own an option, they can force defendant to transfer (sell) to plaintiffs the defendant's entitlement to operate at a fixed price, which (under the purchased injunction scenario) will be set by the court.[68] This solution places the power in the hands of the plaintiffs. The opposite of a forced sale is a forced purchase, otherwise known as a "put." If defendant owns a put, defendant can force plaintiffs to buy the right to be free from the nuisance caused by defendant's activity at a court-determined price.[69] If one views the plaintiffs as having caused their own problem by coming to the nuisance, it might seem fair to give the defendant the power to determine whether to agree to give up his entitlement to operate at a price determined by a court. This is what Professor Ayres calls a put. On the other hand, if protecting the social value of plaintiff's investment is of the greatest importance (because it is of greater value than the value of defendant's business), one might want to give plaintiffs the power to force a sale over defendant's objections, again at a court-determined price.

Difference between property and liability rules

A major difference between property rules and liability rules is that exchanges of entitlements under property rules take place through bargains between the parties, while liability rules involve court-determined damages awards.[70] Damages are measured either by the decrease in the fair market value of the plaintiff's property caused by the nuisance or by a jury-determined amount designed to respond fairly to the type and magnitude of the harm suffered by the plaintiff. In contrast, if the plaintiff is entitled to an injunction, the price of any subsequent agreement will be determined by bargaining between plaintiff and defendant. In that bargain, plaintiff owns the entitlement and defendant is seeking to purchase it. The result will be affected by how much plaintiff demands to sell the entitlement (plaintiff's asking price) and how much defendant is willing to pay to commit the harm (defendant's offer price). The plaintiff's asking price is likely to be higher than the fair market value of the entitlement in question.[71]

Asking price v. fair market value

Why are asking prices (what one is willing to accept to sell an entitlement) likely to be higher than an offer price (what one is willing to pay to purchase an entitlement)? Consider that fair market value is an average value that considers what an average buyer would be willing to pay, and an average seller would be willing to accept. In economic terms, it is the point where the supply and demand curves cross. Many buyers would not be willing or able to pay the fair market value while some would

[68] Conversely, a damages remedy can be understood to be a forced sale of plaintiff's right to be free from the nuisance.

[69] Conversely, plaintiffs could own a put that gives them the right to force defendant to buy the right to pollute.

[70] Of course, parties may settle in the face of a damages judgment for either more or less than the judgment. A plaintiff may accept less than the court award to avoid the costs of an appeal or the possibility of defendant's bankruptcy. In rare cases, defendant may offer more than the court award, also to avoid an appeal by a plaintiff who thinks she could do even better under different legal rulings. These settlements, however, are substantially affected by the amount of the court judgment while settlement in the face of a property rule is more likely to be based on the relative values of the entitlements to the parties themselves, rather than the amount chosen by the court based on fair market value or other considerations.

[71] *See, e.g.*, Jeffrey J. Rachlinski & Forest Jourden, *Remedies and the Psychology of Ownership*, 51 Vand. L. Rev. 1541 (1998).

offer more than that; the same is true for sellers. At any point in time, most owners value their property more than the fair market value. If they did not, they would put the property up for sale. The fact that they choose to keep their property rather than sell it means that their asking price is likely to be higher (and sometimes much higher) than the amount they could obtain on the open market. This means that a plaintiff who has the right to an injunction against a nuisance is likely to insist on a higher price than would be awarded by a court in a damages judgment to that plaintiff. One purpose of choosing a damages remedy rather than an injunctive remedy, therefore, is to make it more likely that the defendant will be legally entitled to continue the activity causing the harm while providing compensation to those injured by the activity.

The ideological plaintiff

The difference can be dramatized by considering the ideological plaintiff. Imagine a company, like the factory in *Boomer*, that is willing and able to pay a $2 million damages judgment to continue operating the factory. Let us assume that this amount is equal to the decrease in the fair market value of the homes affected by the smoke from the factory, and no personal injuries, such as asthma or increased risk of cancer, are involved. If the plaintiffs are awarded damages of $2 million, it is likely the plant will continue to function, and the damages will be paid. It is unlikely the plaintiffs as a group, or any one of them alone, will offer defendant enough to induce it to close the factory. On the other hand, if the plaintiffs are granted an injunction, the company must negotiate with the plaintiffs to induce them to agree to allow the company to operate. A single environmental fanatic could refuse to sell at any price, effectively preventing the deal from going through. A court might grant the factory the right to operate while paying damages because it believes overall social welfare would be maximized by allowing the factory to operate. This conclusion rests on use of fair market value as the measure of the magnitude of the costs and benefits associated with the land use conflict and filters out the interests or desires of marginal or unusual parties. In contrast, if we identify the right to be free from substantial interference with use or enjoyment of property as a right owned by the ideological plaintiff, we might conclude that the factory is not willing or able to offer that plaintiff enough to induce him to give up his rights. In such a case, we might conclude that the costs of allowing the pollution outweighed the benefits, but that injunctive relief should be denied for *distributive* reasons to avoid imposing job losses on the entire community. In other words, depending on which measure we choose, we can say we are sacrificing efficiency for distributive fairness, or distributive fairness for efficiency. How we look at it depends on our baseline.

Alternative measures of efficiency

Many scholars have advocated using economic analysis in nuisance cases to determine whether an injunction should be granted to shut down the offending activity. The goal of increasing economic efficiency is a laudable one, but it contains an inherent ambiguity. The general goal of efficiency analysis is to maximize social welfare by satisfying human preferences. Those preferences are at least of two kinds: those that promote aggregate welfare by maximizing the size of the social pie (often referred to as "efficiency") and those that promote a fair distribution of the pie. In measuring the overall costs and benefits of an activity, economic analysts use market measures of value, including fair market value and either offer prices (how much someone is willing and able to pay for an entitlement) or asking prices (how much you would have to pay someone to induce them to sell an entitlement). Considering these different measures of market value, it is important to take into account the different measures of efficiency that could exist. Here is a short list of some of the possibilities.

Fair market value

(1) *Fair market value.* We might choose rules or results that maximize the joint fair market value of the affected parcels.

Auction

(2) *Auction.* We might assume the entitlement was not owned by anyone and ask which party or parties would pay the most to acquire it. This auction measure looks at the willingness and ability to pay of the parties and focuses on the amount they would *offer* to acquire the entitlement. In a case like *Boomer*, we would be likely to expect the profitable factory to outbid the homeowners, suggesting that denial of an injunction would promote efficiency.

Status quo baseline

(3) *Status quo.* We might assign the entitlement to the current owner, as determined by prior property law, and ask whether non-owners are willing and able to offer enough to induce the owner to sell. Under current law, owners can be said to own the right to be free from substantial and unreasonable interference with their use or enjoyment of their property. If this standard applies to injunctions, as well as damages claims,[72] then the homeowners own the right to stop the polluting activity. In this case, the factory must buy the right to commit the nuisance from the homeowners. Rather than comparing the offer price of the factory with the offer price of the homeowners (as done in the auction measure of efficiency), we compare the asking price of the homeowners with the offer price of the factory. Asking prices are likely to be higher than offer prices, and, in the case of the ideological plaintiff, may be infinite. In this kind of case, it is more likely the homeowners would refuse to sell their rights to be free from the nuisance and it would be efficient to grant the injunction.

Redistribution baseline

(4) *Redistribution.* We might, instead, conclude that existing allocations of the entitlement are unfair or presumptively inefficient and alter them. In such a case, we might change the law to grant the company a right to operate without fear of nuisance liability. In this case, we ask whether the homeowners (who now do not own an entitlement to shut down the factory) would offer the factory enough to induce it to give up its privilege to operate. The answer is probably no, and, if this measure of efficiency is adopted, the injunction should probably be denied.

Reverse auction baseline

(5) *Reverse auction.* We might ask which party would ask the most to give up the entitlement. If we grant the factory the right to operate, how much would the homeowners have to offer before it would agree to give up its rights? In other words, what is its asking price? Conversely, we could look at the asking price of the homeowners. We could then compare the asking prices of the factory versus the homeowners and assign the entitlement to the party who would be least likely to sell it. This measure is

[72] As noted above, it may not. Owners may be entitled to damages alone if the social benefits of the defendant's conduct outweigh its costs.

perhaps the hardest to apply. On the one hand, if the plant is profitable, the homeowners would have to offer an awful lot to induce it to shut down. On the other hand, one ideological plaintiff would make the homeowners' asking price exceed the factory's asking price.

Social welfare

(6) *Social welfare.* Finally, we could de-couple efficiency analysis from reliance on market measures. After all, it is hard to place a dollar figure on what the community loses because children can no longer freely play outside because of polluted air or adults can no longer swim in the river running through the city. This does not mean that we do not need to compare costs and benefits of alternative solutions to land use conflicts. It does mean that another way to do this is to rely less heavily on numbers and more on a combination of dollar amounts and subjective consideration of the magnitude, the character, and the distribution of the benefits and burdens of different resolutions of the problem.

Importance of the baseline

This review of different measures of efficiency shows that the baseline for our analysis matters a great deal. The use of fair market value as a measure of costs and benefits, leads to different answers than if one focuses on offer and asking prices. Similarly, if we compare offer prices, we give greater importance to the distribution of wealth between the parties than if we compare values based on an initial allocation of the entitlement to a property owner. Shifting the entitlement from one party to the other similarly may affect determinations of relative value because asking prices are likely to be higher than offer prices. Granting a property entitlement often creates a sense of entitlement and has a profound psychological effect on the "owner" who is reluctant to part with her property.[73] Moreover, as we have seen, considerations other than efficiency are central to nuisance law and substantially affect the assignment of entitlements and determinations about the reasonableness of particular interferences with use or enjoyment of land.

§3.2.3 *Types of Nuisances*

Odors, pollution, noise, and lights

The kinds of cases that might be covered by nuisance law are as various as the kinds of complaints neighbors might have about each other's land uses.[74] Cases that are frequently litigated include odors,[75] air pollution,[76]

[73] Jeffrey J. Rachlinski & Forest Jourden, *Remedies and the Psychology of Ownership*, 51 Vand. L. Rev. 1541 (1998).

[74] One court even found that planting trees and shrubs to attract birds, hanging multiple bird feeders, and seeding the ground constituted a nuisance when these activities attracted great numbers of birds that congregated over neighbor's land. *Simpkins v. Speck*, 443 P.3d 428 (Mont. 2019).

[75] *Riddle v. Lanser*, 421 P.3d 35, 45 (Alaska 2018) (odors from "septic lagoons"); *Payne v. Skaar*, 900 P.2d 1352 (Idaho 1995) (odors from cattle feed lot); *Weinhold v. Wolff*, 555 N.W.2d 454 (Iowa 1996) (odors from hog farm); *Goeke v. National Farms, Inc.*, 512 N.W.2d 626 (Neb. 1994) (swine raising facility); *Harris v. Town of Lincoln*, 668 A.2d 321 (R.I. 1995) (sewage treatment plant); *O'Cain v. O'Cain*, 473 S.E.2d 460, 466 (S.C. 1996) (hog farm); *Buchanan v. Simplot Feeders, Ltd. P'ship*, 952 P.2d 610 (Wash. 1998) (feedlot and meat processing plant).

[76] *Thomsen v. Greve*, 550 N.W.2d 49 (Neb. Ct. App. 1996) (wood stove).

leaking gas tanks,[77] water pollution,[78] chemical pollution,[79] sewage treatment facilities or landfills,[80] excessive light,[81] damage caused by encroaching trees,[82] and noise.[83] Recently, claims have alleged that electric power lines create magnetic fields that are harmful to human beings. However, nuisance claims based on such allegations have generally failed because plaintiffs have been unable to prove that such fields cause illness.[84] Several cases have involved homeowners who have created lavish displays of Christmas lights, attracting huge numbers of cars to quiet residential neighborhoods. In these cases, courts have found that a nuisance existed and enjoined the display.[85] One case recognized a nuisance in recreational use of a nude beach.[86] In general, however, nuisance claims based purely on differences in taste between neighbors about matters of aesthetics tend to fail.[87]

▷UNLAWFUL DRUG ACTIVITY **HARD CASE◀**

Several cases have involved claims by neighbors or cities against landlords, who have allowed their property to be used by drug dealers.[88]

[77] *Bargmann v. Soll Oil Co.*, 574 N.W.2d 478 (Neb. 1998) (petroleum contamination from leaking tanks at service station).
[78] *Scheufler v. General Host Corp.*, 126 F.3d 1261 (10th Cir. 1997); *Tiegs v. Watts*, 954 P.2d 877 (Wash. 1998).
[79] *Washington Suburban Sanitary Comm'n v. CAE-Link Corp.*, 622 A.2d 745 (Md. 1993); *Nichols v. Mid-Continent Pipe Line Co.*, 933 P.2d 272 (Okla. 1996) (leaking pipelines).
[80] *Southeast Arkansas Landfill, Inc. v. State*, 858 S.W.2d 665 (Ark. 1993); *T.K. Stanley, Inc. v. Cason*, 614 So. 2d 942 (Miss. 1992); *Harris v. Town of Lincoln*, 668 A.2d 321 (R.I. 1995).
[81] *Downey v. Jackson*, 65 So. 2d 825 (Ala. 1953); *Penn Cent. Transp. Co. v. Wilson*, 292 N.E.2d 827 (Ind. Ct. App. 1973).
[82] *Lane v. W.J. Curry & Sons*, 92 S.W.3d 355 (Tenn. 2002).
[83] *Howard Opera House Ass'n v. Urban Outfitters, Inc.*, 322 F.3d 125 (2d Cir. 2003) (noisy retail store); *Parker v. Ashford*, 661 So. 2d 213 (Ala. 1995) (racetrack); *Drummond Co., Inc. v. Boshell*, 641 So. 2d 1240 (Ala. 1994) (transformers); *Brewton v. Young*, 596 So. 2d 577 (Ala. 1991) (barking dogs); *Tomasso Bros., Inc. v. October Twenty-Four, Inc.*, 646 A.2d 133 (Conn. 1994) (quarry); *Taylor v. Tellez*, 610 A.2d 252 (D.C. 1992) (outdoor entertainment); *Rae v. Flynn*, 690 So. 2d 1341 (Fla. Dist. Ct. App. 1997) (barking dogs); *Stiglianese v. Vallone*, 637 N.Y.S.2d 284 (Civ. Ct. 1995) (neighbor's son practiced with heavy metal rock band and amplified home stereo and guitar music); *Harris v. Town of Lincoln*, 668 A.2d 321 (R.I. 1995) (generator noise); *Bowers v. Westvaco Corp.*, 419 S.E.2d 661 (Va. 1992) (truck loading and unloading); *Sramek v. Korth*, 559 N.W.2d 924 (Wis. Ct. App. 1996) (barking dogs); *see also Allen v. Dickerson*, 385 So.3d 1209 (Miss. 2024) (hunters repeatedly allowing hunting dogs to repeatedly invade property constituted a nuisance).
[84] *San Diego Gas & Electric Co. v. Superior Court*, 920 P.2d 669 (Cal. 1996); *Borenkind v. Consolidated Edison Co. of New York, Inc.*, 626 N.Y.S.2d 414 (Sup. Ct. 1995). *But see Public Serv. Co. of Colorado v. Van Wyck*, 27 P.3d 377 (Colo. 2001) (allowing claim to go forward).
[85] *Osborne v. Power*, 890 S.W.2d 570 (Ark. 1994) *(Osborne I)*; *Osborne v. Power*, 908 S.W.2d 340 (Ark. 1995) *(Osborne II)*; *Rodrigue v. Copeland*, 475 So. 2d 1071 (La. 1985).
[86] *Mark v. State Dep't of Fish & Wildlife*, 84 P.3d 155 (Or. App. 2004) (state agency liable in nuisance for failing to control a nude beach).
[87] *E.g., Myrick v. Peck Elec. Co.*, 164 A.3d 658, 661 (Va. 2017) ("An unattractive sight—without more—is not a substantial interference as a matter of law because the mere appearance of the property of another does not affect a citizen's ability to use and enjoy his or her neighboring land").
[88] *See, e.g., People v. Freetown Holdings Co.*, 320 Cal. Rptr. 3d 20 (Ct App. 2024); *see also* Wash. Rev. Code §7.43.010 (declaring every building used for manufacture, sale, or storage of illegal drugs to be a nuisance).

A couple of courts have upheld nuisance claims against the owner for affecting property values in the community and for causing mental distress to homeowners who did not feel safe in their homes.[89] In a New York case, owners of property located within 200 feet of defendant's property complained about rampant drug activity in defendant's building. In granting an injunction to shut down defendant's "crack house," Judge Tom explained:

> The use of real property for illegal purposes such as the sale and use of illegal drugs if unchecked will flourish and irreparably affect the entire neighborhood by disrupting its tranquility and increasing the crime rate in the area. If this condition is allowed to continue residents will abandon the neighborhood and the criminal elements will take over. This will lead to the degeneration of the neighborhood.[90]

This result is most understandable when there is evidence that the owner himself participated in the illegal activity,[91] but is more controversial when the landlord did not participate in the activity.[92] An innocent landlord might justifiably be afraid to attempt to evict his own tenants who are engaged in criminal activity. At the same time, the courts that have addressed the issue have required the landlord to take "reasonable measures" designed to prevent or decrease the likelihood of such activity.[93] ◀

▶ HARD CASE ▷ LANDSLIDES

Do owners have obligations to take reasonable steps to prevent natural conditions on their land from harming neighboring owners? Some courts have held that an owner who reasonably should know that her property is subject to landslides should take reasonable steps to protect property downhill from her.[94] However, other courts take the position that owners are not liable for harms caused by the natural condition of their land, although they may be liable for conditions caused by their development of their own land.[95] ◀

▶ HARD CASE ▷ STIGMA DAMAGES

Proximity to a contaminated site

There has been a great deal of litigation over the question of whether owners can obtain damages for loss of fair market value of their property, resulting from that property being located near property that is polluted

[89] *Lew v. Superior Court*, 25 Cal. Rptr. 2d 42 (Ct. App. 1993); *Kellner v. Cappellini*, 516 N.Y.S.2d 827 (Civ. Ct. 1986).
[90] *Kellner v. Cappellini*, 516 N.Y.S.2d 827, 830-831 (Civ. Ct. 1986).
[91] *Id.* at 829-830.
[92] *Lew v. Superior Court*, 25 Cal. Rptr. 2d 42 (Ct. App. 1993).
[93] 25 Cal. Rptr. at 46.
[94] *Sprecher v. Adamson*, 636 P.2d 1121 (Cal. 1981).
[95] *Price ex rel. Estate of Price v. City of Seattle*, 24 P.3d 1098 (Wash. Ct. App. 2001).

or that contains toxic waste, even though there has been no contamination (yet?) of the plaintiffs' property. Most courts deny damages associated with the stigma of being near polluted land,[96] although some will allow it on the ground that a substantial reduction in the market value of one's property is a harm one should not have to bear when it results from contamination of nearby land.[97] On the other hand, if plaintiff's land was in fact contaminated and its fair market value has been depressed because of the stigma attached to the prior contamination, most courts will allow such "stigma damages" to be counted in valuing the amount awarded as permanent damages.[98] In other cases, courts have enjoined construction of projects, such as landfills, located near residential neighborhoods on the ground that they were certain to result in nuisances and could thus be enjoined as "anticipatory nuisances."[99] ◀

▷ COMING TO THE NUISANCE **HARD CASE ◀**

It will be harder for a plaintiff to prevail in a nuisance case if she "came to the nuisance." However, this does not preclude a finding of nuisance; it only counts against it.[100] On the one hand, it would seem strange to allow a homeowner who moved next to a factory to shut it down or obtain damages because of the smoke. After all, there is the little problem of contributory negligence; the homeowner could have bought in a residential neighborhood rather than choosing to live next to a factory. In addition, the market value of the property would have been depressed precisely because it was located next to a factory. To allow a damages recovery would seem to compensate the plaintiff when he never lost anything; he would not only get the property at a lower price because it was near the factory, but he would

[96] *Adams v. Star Enterprise*, 51 F.3d 417 (4th Cir. 1995); *Berry v. Armstrong Rubber Co.*, 989 F.2d 822 (5th Cir. 1993); *Smith v. Kansas Gas Serv. Co.*, 169 P.3d 1052, 1062 (Kan. 2007) (no nuisance when natural gas escaped from a facility in the absence of physical injury to properties or interference with use and enjoyment "distinct from the claim that the property's value has diminished because of marketplace fear or stigma"); *Exxon Mobil Corp. v. Albright*, 70 A.3d 30 (Md. 2013) (owners near gas station where 26,000-gallon spill of gasoline from an underground tank occurred cannot sue for nuisance when their wells have not yet been contaminated); *Anglado v. Leaf River Forest Prods., Inc.*, 716 So. 2d 543 (Miss. 1998); *Ramirez v. Akzo Nobel Coatings, Inc.*, 791 N.E.2d 1031, 1034 (Ohio Ct. App. 2003). *See also Union Pacific Resources Co. v. Cooper*, 109 S.W.3d 557 (Tex. Ct. App. 2003) (denying nuisance claim for surface owners who were too fearful to live in their house after the mining lessee explained the evacuation plan that would be used in the event it encountered poisonous gases during the drilling process).

[97] *Scheg v. Agway, Inc.*, 645 N.Y.S.2d 687 (Sup. Ct. App. Div. 1996); *Toxic Dumpers to Pay Damages to Homeowners; Verdicts and Settlements*, 17 Nat'l L.J. 16 (Jan. 16, 1995) (referencing *DeSario v. Industrial Excess Land Fill Inc.*, No. 89-570 (Ohio Ct. Com. Pl. 1994), where, on December 6, 1994, the jury award of damages amounted to $6.7 million judgment).

[98] *Walker Drug Co. v. La Sal Oil Co.*, 972 P.2d 1238 (Utah 1998).

[99] *See, e.g., Acadian Heritage Realty, Inc. v. City of Lafayette*, 394 So. 2d 855 (La. Ct. App. 1981) (applying this doctrine although using other language).

[100] Dan B. Dobbs, Paul T. Hayden & Ellen M. Bublick, *Hornbook on Torts* §30.4, at 740 (2d ed. 2016).

also get damages from the factory. This seems like double dipping. On the other hand, the factory owner might be said to have a duty to conduct its business so as not to interfere with the use or enjoyment of neighboring property. Before others moved to the neighbor, the factory enjoyed a kind of subsidy; it did not need to account for the pollution it caused, because there were no neighbors to object. But this does not mean that, by locating there first, it obtained a right to condemn all other owners in the vicinity to suffer from air pollution. Later owners have the same rights as the first owner did to develop their land and to be protected from unreasonable infringements on their use or enjoyment of it. A change in the neighborhood may change the balance of equities. ◀

▶ **HARD CASE**

▷ CAN AN APARTMENT BUILDING BE A NUISANCE?

In 1926, the U.S. Supreme Court upheld the power of municipalities to enact zoning laws that limit land to residential use and even to single-family homes.[101] The *Euclid* decision suggested that apartment buildings might constitute nuisances and destroy the "residential character" of a neighborhood.[102] Is that a legitimate way to characterize apartment buildings and/or the people who live in them? In the 2014 case of *Loughhead v. 1717 Bissonnet, LLC,*[103] a Texas court actually found a proposed high-rise building in the city of Houston, Texas, to be a nuisance. Houston is unusual in the United States because it lacks a comprehensive zoning law. The proposed structure would have been 21 stories tall and contained 228 residential units along with commercial development. The judge upheld a jury verdict that the project would constitute a nuisance and granted the plaintiff neighbors damages for the decreased market value of their property, that would result from the construction. The judge did not order the project halted. Plaintiffs argued that the project would constitute a private nuisance not only because of lost property value but because of the confluence of various factors, including increased traffic, loss of privacy, foundation damages to neighboring property due to settlement, decreased light to adjacent landowners, construction annoyances, and the shadow cast by the high-rise. While agreeing that none of these factors alone would constitute a nuisance, the judge ruled that the jury acted reasonably and within the law to find that all together they constituted a nuisance. Damages were awarded to 20 neighbors in amounts ranging from $20,000 to $89,000. Many owners in the United States would find a high-rise of this sort to be out of place in a neighborhood of much lower buildings. On the other hand, most municipalities deal with issues like this by passing zoning laws that limit the height of buildings in different neighborhoods. Ruling that an apartment building is an unreasonable use of land is a somewhat startling

[101] *Village of Euclid v. Ambler Realty Co.*, 272 U.S. 365 (1926).
[102] *Id.* at 394-395.
[103] 2014 WL 8774060 (Tex. Dist. Ct. 2014), *final judgment at* 2014 WL 8774079 (Tex. Dist. Ct. 2014), *aff'd in part and rev'd in part by 1717 Bissonnet, LLC v. Loughhead*, 500 S.W.3d 488 (Tex. Ct. App. 2016) (no nuisance exists until market value actually declines).

interpretation of nuisance law. The Ninth Circuit, for example, rejected the idea that a high-rise hotel could constitute a nuisance.[104] ◀

▷ CAN AIRBNB BE A NUISANCE? **HARD CASE** ◀

Disputes have begun to flourish when someone's neighbor frequently opens her home to guests through Airbnb. An owner who does this may enjoy the extra income and the company she gets from inviting strangers to stay in her home on a short-term basis, but her neighbors may feel that suddenly, they are living next to a hotel or guest house. If such a use is held to be consistent with residential zoning, the neighbor may have an incentive to claim that frequent Airbnb use constitutes a nuisance because of added traffic, noise, or simple incompatibility with the neighborhood environment, because the property has been converted from residential to commercial use. ◀

§3.3 Public Nuisance

Harm to the public

A *public nuisance* is a violation of a legal right common to the public as a whole.[105] "A common or public nuisance is the doing of or the failure to do something that injuriously affects the safety, health or morals of the public, or works some substantial annoyance, inconvenience or injury to the public."[106] Some scholars emphasize the difference between public and private nuisance, suggesting that they have little or nothing in common,[107] while others suggest that "the difference between a public and private nuisance is chiefly a matter of degree."[108] What they have in common is that both public and private nuisances regulate the use of land (although public nuisance may also regulate what one does on publicly owned property). The difference is that "where a private nuisance affects one or a limited number of plaintiffs, a public nuisance is viewed as being so serious that it affects the public generally or at least a large number of the public."[109] Another difference is that the public nuisance doctrine traditionally applied only to certain kinds of criminal conduct, such as obstruction of a road, or operation of an illegal gambling or drinking

[104] *California Tahoe Regional Planning Agency v. Jenkins*, 594 F.2d 181 (9th Cir. 1979).

[105] *Restatement (Second) of Torts* §821B (1979); Dale A. Whitman et al., *The Law of Property* §7.2, at 333-334 (4th ed. 2019); Dan B. Dobbs, Paul T. Hayden & Ellen M. Bublick, *Hornbook on Torts* §30.6, at 744 (2d ed. 2016); 8-67 *Thompson on Real Property, Third Thomas Edition* §67.02(a); John C.P. Goldberg, *On Being a Nuisance*, 99 NYU L. 864, 898-900 (2024).

[106] *Commonwealth v. South Covington & Cincinnati Street Ry. Co.*, 205 S.W. 581, 583 (Ky. 1918).

[107] Dan B. Dobbs, Paul T. Hayden & Ellen M. Bublick, *Hornbook on Torts* §30.6, at 744 (2d ed. 2016) (public nuisance is "distinct from a private nuisance").

[108] Dale A. Whitman et al., *The Law of Property* §7.2, at 333 (4th ed. 2019).

[109] *Id.* Cal. Civ. Code §3480 defines a public nuisance as "one which affects at the same time an entire community or neighborhood, or any considerable number of persons, although the extent of the annoyance or damage inflicted upon individuals may be unequal."

facility or brothel, and claims were brought only by public officials, not private landowners or citizens.

Community interests

Although some actions may constitute both public and private nuisances (such as polluting the air), the public nuisance doctrine does differ from private nuisance in its focus on the community rather than individual rights. As Justice Brown wrote in *People ex rel. Gallo v. Acuna*,[110]

> Unlike the private nuisance tied to and designed to vindicate individual ownership interests in land the "common" or public nuisance emerged from distinctly different historical origins. The public nuisance doctrine is aimed at the protection and redress of community interests and, at least in theory, embodies a kind of collective ideal of civil life which the courts have vindicated by equitable remedies since the beginning of the 16th century.[111]

Public nuisance increasingly used today

Today, the public nuisance doctrine has been broadened to encompass any kind of improper land use that causes such extensive effects that it harms not just one plaintiff or a select group of plaintiffs, but the public generally. This means that many activities might cause both private and public nuisances.[112] A polluting factory, for example, might not only affect the use or enjoyment of neighboring property (and thus constitute a private nuisance), but affect air quality in the entire area (and thus constitute a public nuisance). In addition, public nuisance claims traditionally could only be brought by public officials, except that private owners could sue if their property was specially affected in a way not shared by the general public — a showing that is hard to make.[113] It is still the case that almost all public nuisance claims are brought by public officials, such as the state attorney general or the attorney for a city. Modern courts have increasingly relaxed the requirement that a private plaintiff in a public nuisance case demonstrate special injury when the plaintiff is seeking injunctive relief only. Special injury still seems to be required for a private landowner to obtain damages, however. This might be shown by contiguous owners or nearby owners whose property has been significantly depreciated in value or that cannot be sold.

Burgeoning case law

Although public nuisance was a little-used doctrine for much of the twentieth century, there was an explosion of interest in it in recent decades. It has not been generally used to combat pollution — environmental regulations and private nuisance suits have been most common in those kinds of cases. However, it has increasingly been used to combat illegal alcohol sales to minors by liquor stores or clubs,[114]

[110] 929 P.2d 596 (Cal. 1997).

[111] *Id.* at 603.

[112] 8-67 *Thompson on Real Property, Third Thomas Edition* §67.02(a).

[113] *Id. Compare, e.g., Palmer v. Amazon.com, Inc.*, 51 F.4th 491, 512 (2d Cir. 2022) (Amazon employees' injury from company failure to protect them from COVID-19 insufficiently distinctive) *with Severa v. Solvay Specialty Polymers USA, LLC*, 524 F. Supp. 3d 381 (D.N.J. 2021) (town water supply contamination gave town residents sufficient special injury).

[114] *Bosarge v. State ex rel. Price*, 666 So. 2d 485 (Miss. 1995) (club closed).

theaters or stores selling pornography,[115] property used for the sale of illegal drugs,[116] motels that served as sites for prostitution or lewd dancing,[117] and even harms from leaving property vacant and unmaintained.[118] Some cities sued gun shops for selling guns that wound up in the hands of criminals, but Congress preempted such rulings by a statute that immunizes gun stores and manufacturers from public nuisance claims.[119]

Constitutional issues

Many of these cases raise important constitutional issues. Closure of bookstores or theaters raises First Amendment free speech concerns, while closure of businesses or residential properties is sometimes challenged as unconstitutional takings of property without just compensation.[120] Prohibitions against gang members associating with each other implicates the constitutional right to freedom of association, especially when no evidence shows that the individuals being regulated have committed a crime.[121]

▷ DRUGS — HARD CASE ◀

As discussed earlier in the section on private nuisance, a number of courts have found that landlords who allowed their homes to be used for illegal drug sales, or participated in those sales, have committed a nuisance and may be subject to damages or injunctive relief ordering them to prevent the use from occurring.[122] Those cases did not distinguish between the law of public and private nuisances. They did not, for example, require plaintiffs

[115] *College Art Theatres, Inc. v. State*, 476 So. 2d 40 (Ala. 1985) (movie theater closed when used by customers for illegal sexual activity); *State ex rel. Bowers v. Elida Road Video & Books, Inc.*, 696 N.E.2d 668 (Ohio Ct. App. 1997) (closing adult bookstore because of masturbation taking place in video booths); *State ex rel. Rear Door Bookstore v. Tenth District Court of Appeals*, 588 N.E.2d 116 (Ohio 1992) (bookstore closed).

[116] *City of Miami v. Keshbro, Inc.*, 717 So. 2d 601 (Fla. Dist. Ct. App. 1998), *partially aff'd sub nom. Keshbro, Inc. v. City of Miami, and partially rev'd on other grounds*, 801 So. 2d 864 (Fla. 2001) (motel closed for prostitution and drug use); *Kellner v. Cappellini*, 516 N.Y.S.2d 827 (Civ. Ct. 1986).

[117] *City of Miami v. Keshbro, Inc.*, 717 So. 2d 601 (Fla. Dist. Ct. App. 1998), *partially aff'd sub nom. Keshbro, Inc. v. City of Miami, and partially rev'd on other grounds*, 801 So. 2d 864 (Fla. 2001) (motel closed for prostitution and drug use); *Michigan v. Dizzy Duck*, 535 N.W.2d 178 (Mich. 1995) (ordering defendant to cease "lap dancing" and other "lewd" activities that stop "just short of prostitution"); *Matthews v. Pernell*, 582 N.E.2d 1075 (Ohio Ct. App. 1990) (massage parlor closed).

[118] *D.A. Realestate Investment, LLC v. City of Norfolk*, 126 F.4th 309 (4th Cir. 2025).

[119] *Protection of Lawful Commerce in Arms Act of 2005*, 15 U.S.C. §§7901-7903. *St. Louis Joins Rush to Sue Gunmakers*, Chicago Tribune, May 2, 1999, at 9, 1999 WL 2869469.

[120] *Compare City of St. Petersburg v. Bowen*, 675 So. 2d 626 (Fla. Dist. Ct. App. 1996) (holding that municipal order closing an apartment complex for one year because of tenant drug use was an unconstitutional taking of landlord's property) *with City of Miami v. Keshbro, Inc.*, 717 So. 2d 601 (Fla. Dist. Ct. App. 1998), *partially aff'd sub nom. Keshbro, Inc. v. City of Miami, and partially rev'd on other grounds*, 801 So. 2d 864 (Fla. 2001) (no compensation required when motel was closed for prostitution and drug use). This issue will be treated in greater depth in Chapter 14.

[121] *People ex rel. Gallo v. Acuna*, 929 P.2d 596 (Cal. 1997).

[122] *Lew v. Superior Court*, 25 Cal. Rptr. 2d 42 (Ct. App. 1993); *Kellner v. Cappellini*, 516 N.Y.S.2d 827 (Civ. Ct. 1986).

to show that they were specially injured, perhaps because statutes identified the existence of criminal activity on the property as a nuisance that could be enjoined by a court action. Some commentators see this as a wonderful new weapon in the drug war. In one case, dealers operated in 30 of a building's 216 rooms. The building was seized and taken by the federal government pursuant to federal statutes that provide for the forfeiture of property used to facilitate criminal activity.[123] Although these statutes are not identical to public nuisance laws, they are based on a similar rationale. They aim to deter illegal activity and to protect the public by shutting down that activity. One commentator applauded the takeover of the building because of its deterrent effect on drug dealers and drug dealing.[124] However, another commentator criticized the use of a public nuisance law against a landlord in California on the ground that it was the job of the police, and not the landlord, to fight crime.[125] This commentator also worried that exposure to such suits would raise the price of housing, especially in poor neighborhoods, hurting those least able to afford rent increases.[126] ◀

▶ HARD CASE ▷ STREET GANGS

A number of cities have used public nuisance laws against gangs. For example, in *Iraheta v. Superior Court*,[127] the city of Los Angeles filed a civil lawsuit against certain alleged gang members for "wag[ing] a gang war, . . . engaging in drug dealing, shootings, robberies, drinking and urinating in public, threatening residents, vandalizing and defacing with graffiti public and private property, trespassing on property, and other injurious activities against the residents who live and work" in the affected areas.[128] In *In re Englebrecht*,[129] a district attorney obtained a preliminary injunction against gang members prohibiting them from associating with fellow gang members inside a specified two-square-mile area. In effect, these rulings limit access to public property to protect the security of residents in the area.

City of Chicago v. Morales

While these cases may promote safety and security for area residents, they pose significant dangers to civil liberties. By bypassing criminal prosecutions, they allow state control of individuals without proof of involvement in criminal activity beyond a reasonable doubt and may infringe on constitutionally protected freedom of intimate association. Such challenges were rejected by most courts[130] until the Supreme Court struck down Chicago's anti-gang ordinance in 1999 in *City of Chicago v. Morales*.[131] The Chicago ordinance

[123] Gideon Kanner, *California Makes Landlords Do the Police's Job*, Wall St. J., Jan. 27, 1993, at A19.
[124] David Anderson, *How to Rescue a Crack House*, N.Y. Times, Feb. 8, 1993, at A16.
[125] Gideon Kanner, *California Makes Landlords Do the Police's Job*, Wall St. J., Jan. 27, 1993, at A19.
[126] *Id.*
[127] 83 Cal. Rptr. 2d 471 (Ct. App. 1999).
[128] *Id.* at 473.
[129] 79 Cal. Rptr. 2d 89 (Ct. App. 1998).
[130] *See, e.g.*, *People ex rel. Gallo v. Acuna*, 929 P.2d 596 (Cal. 1997).
[131] 527 U.S. 41 (1999).

required a police officer, on observing a person whom she reasonably believed to be a criminal street gang member loitering in any public place with one or more other persons, to order all such persons to disperse, and made failure to obey such an order a crime. In a series of opinions with conflicting rationales, the Court held that the ordinance was impermissibly vague, that it failed to provide fair notice of what conduct was prohibited, and thereby infringed on constitutionally protected liberties of association and freedom of movement. Justices Stevens, Souter, and Ginsburg argued that the "freedom to loiter for innocent purposes" is part of the "liberty" guaranteed from arbitrary deprivation under the Fourteenth Amendment. The ordinance failed to give ordinary citizens adequate notice of what behavior was prohibited when it criminalized "remain[ing] in any one place with no apparent purpose." Justice O'Connor, in an opinion joined by Justice Breyer, emphasized that the law failed to give guidance to police officers to determine whether an individual has an "apparent purpose." She noted that a law that prohibited intimidation of residents by gang members would be constitutional. Justices Kennedy and Breyer, in separate opinions, emphasized the wide discretion given to police officers and the resulting risk that innocent, as well as legitimately criminalizable behavior, would be restricted.

Civil liberties issues

Justices Scalia and Thomas and Chief Justice Rehnquist dissented. Justice Scalia argued that it was legitimate for the city of Chicago to require a group to disperse when loitering in a public area with no apparent purpose in the company of a known gang member to restore liberty to those who were intimidated by gangs and would otherwise be afraid to venture into the public streets. Justice Scalia noted that it would be possible to argue in specific cases that the police acted in an unjustified manner but that the mere possibility that the statute would be applied unconstitutionally was not a justification for striking down the entire statute on its face, on the mere chance it would be applied in an impermissible manner. Justice Thomas emphasized the benefits of government regulation in promoting both liberty and security by explaining that, in striking down the ordinance, he "fear[ed] that the Court has unnecessarily sentenced law-abiding citizens to lives of terror and misery."[132] ◀

Dissenting opinions

▷ CLIMATE CHANGE AND PUBLIC NUISANCE **HARD CASE ◀**

In 2004, states and nonprofit land trusts sued a group of electric utilities, arguing that their greenhouse gas emissions — and resulting changes to the climate — constituted a public nuisance under state and federal law. The U.S. Supreme Court held that while federal environmental laws preempted any federal common law claims, the plaintiffs might be able to pursue public nuisance claims as a matter of state law.[133] In the intervening years,

[132] *Id.* at 98 (Thomas, J., dissenting).

[133] *American Electric Power Co. v. Connecticut*, 564 U.S. 410 (2011). One federal court later held that federal environmental laws also preempt state law nuisance claims. *See Comer v. Murphy Oil USA, Inc.*, 839 F. Supp. 2d 849 (S.D. Miss. 2012).

several states and local governments have sued oil and gas companies for the harms that those companies have caused, in terms of climate change under state public nuisance theories; the companies have repeatedly tried to remove the cases to federal court, but several federal courts have refused to allow removal.[134] The arguments in favor of allowing these suits echo earlier debates about private nuisance as a basis for remediating broad-scale environmental harms. On one hand, nuisance law is designed to provide a basis for courts to protect and compensate owners whose use and enjoyment of their land faces substantial interference. On the other hand, courts may be institutionally ill-suited to respond to harms that affect people literally all over the globe with chains of causation that may be difficult to untangle.[135] ◀

§3.4 Water Rights

§3.4.1 Diffuse Surface Water (Flooding)

Unwanted surface water

Diffuse surface water "occurs on the surface of the land in an unconfined state, such as 'water from rain, melting snow, springs or seepage, or detached from subsiding floods, that lies or flows on the surface of the earth but does not form a part of a watercourse or lake.'"[136] "Diffuse surface water" is distinguished from "groundwater" (or "percolating water") that does not rise to the surface without human assistance; it differs from lakes and streams because it is too dispersed or unstable to constitute a "confined water body."[137] It may coalesce in a pool or marsh, but the pool is not stable enough to constitute a pond. Owners often want to rid their land of diffuse surface water. They may want drier land for construction or recreational purposes. In developing land, they may install drainage systems that expel water onto neighboring property. In such cases, the neighbors may well object. Such disputes strongly resemble nuisance cases. Some owners want to use diffuse surface water, particularly for irrigation purposes.[138]

Wetlands regulations

The power to withdraw surface water is subject to substantial regulation even if no other owners are harmed through flooding or discharge of water onto their lands. Federal and state laws regulate drainage of "wetlands" and

[134] *See, e.g.*, *Rhode Island v. Shell Oil Products Co.*, 979 F.3d 50 (1st Cir. 2020); *City of Oakland v. BP plc*, 960 F.3d 570 (9th Cir. 2020); *Board of County Commissioners of Boulder County v. Suncor Energy (U.S.A.) Inc.*, 965 F.3d 792 (10th Cir. 2020); *Mayor and City Council of Baltimore v. BP plc*, 952 F.3d 452 (4th Cir. 2020); *Massachusetts v. Exxon Mobil Corp.*, 462 F. Supp. 3d 31 (D. Mass. 2020); *see also* Alanna Belmont, *Climate Accountability on the Brink*, Geo. Envt'l L. Rev. Online 1 (Dec. 5, 2024) (summarizing the cases decided through the end of 2024, and noting that Second Circuit is the only court to allow removal to federal court).

[135] For debates on this emerging litigation, *compare* Leslie Kendrick, *The Perils and Promise of Public Nuisance*, 132 Yale L.J. 702 (2023), *with* Thomas W. Merrill, *The New Public Nuisance: Illegitimate and Dysfunctional*, 142 Yale L.J. Forum 985 (2023).

[136] 6-50 *Thompson on Real Property, Third Thomas Edition* §50.20(a) (quoting *Restatement (Second) of Torts* §846).

[137] 6-50 *Thompson on Real Property, Third Thomas Edition* §50.20(b).

[138] 6-50 *Thompson on Real Property, Third Thomas Edition* §50.20(d).

the ability of owners to fill in such lands for development purposes.[139] The federal *Clean Water Act*[140] has been interpreted to place some limits on the ability of owners to fill in wetlands for development purposes and many states regulate such development to protect the environment.[141]

Three rules

When owners develop land and expel water onto neighboring property, the courts must determine whether this constitutes a valid exercise of the developer's right to use her own land or a violation of the rights of the neighbor to be free from flooding damage caused by neighboring development. Three common law rules have developed in different jurisdictions to deal with conflicts over expulsion of surface water: (1) *natural flow*; (2) *common enemy*; and (3) *reasonable use*. The states used to be fairly evenly divided between those that adhered to the common enemy rule and those that adhered to natural flow, with a small number adopting reasonable use. There is a strong trend these days toward the reasonable use test, and it is the current majority rule. Few states have the natural flow doctrine, but it is still in evidence in some states today.

Natural flow or "civil law rule"

The *natural flow* doctrine (also called the "civil law rule") prohibits owners from discharging water in any way other than through natural drainage paths. Liability will be imposed under this rule for "any interference with the natural surface drainage pattern that causes injury to another's land."[142] Each parcel of land is said to be subject to a "natural servitude" for the flow of surface water, so that the lower, servient, estate must accept water that would naturally drain into it, and the higher, dominant, estate cannot retain water that would naturally drain out of it.[143] Any changes to the natural flow of the water that result in increases in the force or flow of water, or that alter drainage directions from the natural path to a different direction and that thereby cause damage to neighboring land, are compensable and can be enjoined.[144] For example, liability was imposed under this rule in a Vermont case on a defendant who built a road and two culverts that resulted in concentrating the force of the flow of surface water onto plaintiffs' land in excess of natural drainage patterns.[145] This rule privileges interests in security and amounts to strict liability. Until recently, it had been the law in roughly half the states, but it persists today in only a few states.[146] Most states that have adopted this approach have modified it to permit changes in drainage patterns and even to increase the amount and force of the flow of water as long as the changes are "not substantial or do not unreasonably or negligently

[139] Sharon M. Mattox, *Regulatory Obstacles to Development and Redevelopment: Wetlands and Other Essential Issues*, SP033 ALI-ABA 2079 (2008).
[140] 33 U.S.C. §1344.
[141] *See Massachusetts Water Mgmt. Act*, Mass. Gen. Laws ch. 21G, §§1 to 19.
[142] *Heins Implement Co. v. Missouri Highway & Transp. Comm'n*, 859 S.W.2d 681, 688 (Mo. 1993). *Accord*, *Henrickson v. Wagners*, 598 N.W.2d 507 (S.D. 1999).
[143] *Id. See* 6-50 *Thompson on Real Property, Third Thomas Editions* §50.20(h).
[144] *Powers v. Judd*, 553 A.2d 139 (Vt. 1988). *See also Fisher v. Space of Pensacola, Inc.*, 483 So. 2d 392 (Ala. 1986); *Dougan v. Rossville Drainage Dist.*, 757 P.2d 272 (Kan. 1988); *Lee v. Schultz*, 425 N.W.2d 380 (S.D. 1988).
[145] *Id.*
[146] Dale A. Whitman et al., *The Law of Property* §7.4, at 337-338 (4th ed. 2019).

cause harm to the lower owner."[147] Despite this modification, the lower owner is "still considered to be burdened with a drainage easement in favor of the upper landowner and must receive the water."[148]

Common enemy

Many states adopt the opposite approach.[149] The *common enemy* rule grants each owner the privilege to expel unwanted water.[150] Under this rule, "each landowner has an unqualified right, by operations on his own land, to fend off surface waters as he sees fit, without being required to take into account the consequences to other landowners, who have the duty and right to protect themselves as best they can."[151] Granting owners freedom to expel the water obviously gives them the power to harm neighboring land by flooding it. This rule therefore privileges free use of land over interests in security. It effectively makes each owner responsible for installing drainage systems on her own land to protect her own property. Most courts have very substantially modified this rule. Some courts allowed claims to be based on negligence, effectively requiring owners to act reasonably, so as to avoid harm to their neighbors.[152] Most states with the common enemy rule prohibit landowners from damaging their neighbors' property by collecting water through artificial means and discharging it in one place if this results in an increased quantity of water being discharged or an increased force of the water being pushed onto neighboring land.[153] This qualification has been adopted in different forms in almost all states that have adopted the common enemy rule.[154] In some states, the modification merely requires the owner to refrain from negligent actions that create avoidable harm to neighbors and to adopt instead methods of drainage that avoid harm to others. In most states, however, the modification makes the common enemy rule look much like the natural flow doctrine, at least where the harm to plaintiff was caused by a drainage system installed by defendant and not merely by changes in the grading of land or construction on it.

Reasonable use

Nearly half of the states have adopted a middle position, allowing water to be discharged reasonably. This "*reasonable use*" test is similar to nuisance law generally, allowing reasonable discharge but not allowing

[147] 6-50 *Thompson on Real Property, Third Thomas Edition* §50.20(h).

[148] *Id.*

[149] *Id.* at §50.20(g).

[150] *Collett v. Cordovana*, 772 S.E.2d 584, 587 (Va. 2015); *Lucas v. Rawl Family Ltd. P'ship*, 598 S.E.2d 712 (S.C. 2004); *Halverson v. Skagit County*, 983 P.2d 643 (Wash. 1999).

[151] *Haith v. Atchison County*, 793 S.W.2d 151 (Mo. Ct. App. 1990). *But see Heins Implement Co. v. Missouri Highway & Transp. Comm'n*, 859 S.W.2d 681 (Mo. 1993) (effectively overruling *Haith* and adopting the reasonable use test). *See also Gillespie Land & Irrigation Co. v. Gonzalez*, 379 P.2d 135, 146 (Ariz. 1963); *Ballard v. Ace Wrecking Co.*, 289 A.2d 888, 890 (D.C. 1971); *Argyelan v. Haviland*, 435 N.E.2d 973, 976 (Ind. 1982); *State by and through Dep't of Highways v. Feenan*, 752 P.2d 182, 184 (Mont. 1988); *Nu-Dwarf Farms, Inc. v. Stratbucker Farms, Ltd.*, 470 N.W.2d 772 (Neb. 1991); *Romshek v. Osantowski*, 466 N.W.2d 482 (Neb. 1991); *Buffalo Sewer Auth. v. Town of Cheektowaga*, 228 N.E.2d 386 (N.Y. 1967); *Halverson v. Skagit County*, 983 P.2d 643 (Wash. 1999); *DiBlasi v. City of Seattle*, 969 P.2d 10 (Wash. 1998) (all adopting some version of the common enemy doctrine).

[152] 6-50 *Thompson on Real Property, Third Thomas Edition* §50.20(g).

[153] *Halverson v. Skagit County*, 983 P.2d 643, 653 (Wash. 1999) ("surface waters may not be artificially collected and discharged upon adjoining lands in quantities greater than or in a manner different from the natural flow thereof").

[154] 6-50 *Thompson on Real Property, Third Thomas Edition* §50.20(g).

substantial harm to be committed.[155] Explaining the rule, the California Supreme Court noted:

> This test requires consideration of the purpose for which the improvements were undertaken, the amount of surface water runoff added to the streamflow by the defendant's improvements in relation to that from development of other parts of the watershed, and the cost of mitigating measures available to both upper and downstream owners. Those costs must be balanced against the magnitude of the potential for downstream damage. If both plaintiff and defendant have acted reasonably, the natural watercourse rule imposes the burden of stream-caused damage on the downstream property.[156]

A difference between reasonable use and nuisance is that the reasonable use test does not necessarily envision weighing the utility of the conduct against the gravity of the harm; rather, substantial harm caused by discharge of water is likely to be held to be unlawful even if the utility of the defendant's land use far outweighs that of the plaintiff's land use. Some courts define reasonable use as akin to a negligence standard. As the Missouri Supreme Court defined it, the reasonable use test "impose[s] a duty upon any landowner in the use of his or her land not to needlessly or negligently injure by surface water adjoining lands owned by others, or in the breach thereof to pay for the resulting damages."[157] If the standard is interpreted in this way to cover substantial, foreseeable harm, it seems identical to negligence law. However, it may be applied by other courts in a manner closer to nuisance law, focusing not on foreseeability but on the fact of substantial unreasonable harm. If interpreted this way, the rule is closer to the natural flow rule as long as the costs of avoiding the harm are not unreasonable.[158] On the other hand, discharges are allowed if the harm is not substantial. As with the modifications to the common enemy rule, the reasonable use test seems closer to the natural flow doctrine (granting a remedy for substantial harm caused by discharge of water) than to the unmodified common enemy doctrine.

Trend in the law

The trend in the law is toward the reasonable use test with a number of jurisdictions adopting it in recent years.[159] It is safe to say that the reasonable

[155] *Whorton v. Malone*, 549 S.E.2d 57 61-62 (W. Va. 2001); *Armstrong v. Francis Corp.*, 120 A.2d 4 (N.J. 1956).

[156] *Locklin v. City of Lafayette*, 867 P.2d 724, 729 (Cal. 1994). *Accord, Page Motor Co., Inc. v. Baker*, 438 A.2d 739 (Conn. 1980); *Westland Skating Center, Inc. v. Gus Machado Buick*, 542 So. 2d 959 (Fla. 1989); *Klutey v. Commonwealth, Dep't of Highways*, 428 S.W.2d 766 (Ky. 1967); *Enderson v. Kelehan*, 32 N.W.2d 286 (Minn. 1948); *Hall v. Wood*, 443 So. 2d 834 (Miss. 1983); *Pendergrast v. Aiken*, 236 S.E.2d 787 (N.C. 1977).

[157] *Heins Implement Co. v. Missouri Highway & Transp. Comm'n*, 859 S.W.2d 681, 691 (Mo. 1993).

[158] *Locklin v. City of Lafayette*, 867 P.2d 724, 729 (Cal. 1994).

[159] *Id.* at 724; *Keys v. Romley*, 412 P.2d 529 (Cal. 1966); *Page Motor Co. v. Baker*, 438 A.2d 739 (Conn. 1980); *Westland Skating Center v. Gus Machado Buick, Inc.*, 542 So. 2d 959 (Fla. 1989); *Tucker v. Badoian*, 384 N.E.2d 1195 (Mass. 1978); *Heins Implement Co. v. Missouri Highway & Transp. Comm'n*, 859 S.W.2d 681 (Mo. 1993); *Morris Assocs., Inc. v. Priddy*, 383 S.E.2d 770 (W. Va. 1989). *See* Jennifer S. Graham, *The Reasonable Use Rule in Surface Water Law*, 57 Mo. L. Rev. 223 (1992).

use test is now the majority rule.[160] This trend recognizes that the common enemy rule was always subject to exceptions designed to prevent substantial harm caused by artificially induced discharges of water and that the natural flow rule allowed minor discharges to occur, especially when no substantial harm was caused thereby. At the same time, a significant number of states retain the modified common enemy rule and several retain the natural flow doctrine. Thus, the triumph of the reasonable use test is likely not to be complete.

§3.4.2 Streams and Lakes

Riparian owners

Unlike diffuse surface water, streams and lakes are beneficial to property owners, especially "riparian owners" whose land borders on those bodies of water. Most disputes about streams and lakes occur between competing claimants to the water or competing uses of it. Such water is used for irrigation, power, drinking water, and recreation. Lawsuits arise when one owner's use interferes with the ability of other riparian owners to use the stream.[161] Sometimes suits arise when an upstream owner builds a dam or appropriates water in a way that decreases the amount of water available for downstream owners. At other times, downstream owners may build dams that push back water onto upstream land, flooding it.

Riparian owners and the reasonable use doctrine

The majority of states resolve disputes of this kind by granting riparian owners rights to use water in streams or lakes bordering or passing through their property and denying such rights to non-riparian owners. Use rights by riparian owners are not absolute. Although many states traditionally applied the *natural flow* doctrine, prohibiting any interference with the force or flow of the stream,[162] the overwhelming majority of states today apply a *reasonable use* test, which requires consideration of the relative interests of the parties, the cost of preventing the harm, and the benefit of the activity that interferes with plaintiff's access to the water.[163] In this context, the reasonable use test is similar to nuisance law, prohibiting substantial harms to the interests of riparian owners when such harms are viewed as unreasonable. Most courts will interpret this rule to give each riparian owner some benefit from the water, requiring use rights to be apportioned so that all riparian owners have the right to some portion of the water.[164]

Prior appropriation

A substantial minority of states in the arid western part of the United States adopt the *prior appropriation* doctrine, which provides that the first user or developer prevails over a later user.[165] This doctrine does not

[160] *Heins Implement Co. v. Missouri Highway & Transp. Comm'n*, 859 S.W.2d 681, 690, 690 n.13 (Mo. 1993); *see* Janet Fairchild, *Modern Status of Rules Governing Interference with Drainage of Surface Waters*, Annot., 93 A.L.R.3d 1193 (originally published in 1979, updated through 2024) (listing 21 states that have adopted the reasonable use rule).

[161] *Evans v. Merriweather*, 4 Ill. 492 (1842).

[162] 6-50 *Thompson on Real Property, Third Thomas Edition* §50.08(j).

[163] *Lopardo v. Flemming Cos., Inc.*, 97 F.3d 921 (7th Cir. 1996); *Alburger v. Philadelphia Electric Co.*, 535 A.2d 729 (Pa. Commw. Ct. 1988); 6-50 *Thompson on Real Property, Third Thomas Editions* §50.08(k).

[164] Dale A. Whitman et al., *The Law of Property* §7.4, at 338 (4th ed. 2019).

[165] *San Carlos Apache Tribe v. Superior Court*, 972 P.2d 179 (Ariz. 1999); 6-50 *Thompson on Real Property, Third Thomas Edition* §50.09.

limit use rights to riparian owners. The rule allows prior users to prevail against later users. Those who establish a particular beneficial use of water may continue doing so, and later users are subordinate to earlier ones.[166] Moreover, use rights may lapse if the owner fails to use them for a significant period of time.[167] This is called the Colorado doctrine.[168] Some states combine the prior appropriation doctrine with riparian rights or the reasonable use doctrine, giving prior appropriators first priority but subject to reasonable use limitations and possibly subject also to rights of riparian owners to obtain benefit from the water.[169] This is called the California doctrine.[170]

Regulatory systems

States that have adopted the prior appropriation system have also established state water management systems. These regulatory programs include statutes requiring water users to obtain permits for use of water from the relevant administrative agency or official.[171] This is a specialized area of law with inherent complexities of both substance and procedure.

Reserved tribal water rights

Many treaties with American Indian nations reserved tribal rights to use water in streams and lakes that had been located inside or flowed through the tribe's traditional lands even after the lands surrounding the body of water were transferred to non-Indian ownership.[172] Throughout the Western part of the United States, substantial litigation has ensued in recent years to identify and protect reserved tribal water rights.[173]

§3.4.3 Groundwater

Percolating water in aquifers

Water permeates the ground and is contained in soil, gravel, sand, or rock formations beneath the earth.[174] This groundwater or "percolating water" collected in aquifers beneath the surface is useful for irrigation, drinking, and power.[175] Surface owners may use wells to extract this water, which is diffused through the soil beneath the surface. Because aquifers underlie the lands of many persons, the withdrawal by one owner may have the effect of drawing off water underlying a neighbor's property. To the extent the water in the aquifer is depleted, withdrawal by one owner may interfere with the ability of others to make like use of the water.

[166] Kan. Stat. §82a-707(c); 6-50 *Thompson on Real Property, Third Thomas Edition* §50.09(b).
[167] 6-50 *Thompson on Real Property, Third Thomas Edition* §50.09(b).
[168] Dale A. Whitman et al., *The Law of Property* §7.4, at 339 (4th ed. 2019) (noting that the doctrine exists in Arizona, Colorado, Idaho, Montana, Nevada, New Mexico, Utah, and Wyoming).
[169] *Id.*
[170] *Id.* (noting that the doctrine is said to exist in California, Kansas, Nebraska, North Dakota, Oklahoma, Oregon, South Dakota, Texas, and Washington).
[171] 6-50 *Thompson on Real Property, Third Thomas Edition* §50.09.
[172] Rebecca Tsosie et al., *American Indian Law: Native Nations and the Federal System* 1186-1238 (8th ed. 2025); 6-50 *Thompson on Real Property, Third Thomas Edition* §50.18.
[173] *Arizona v. San Carlos Apache Tribe of Arizona*, 463 U.S. 545 (1983); *Colorado River Water Conservation Dist. v. United States*, 424 U.S. 800 (1976); *Winters v. United States*, 207 U.S. 564 (1908); *San Carlos Apache Tribe v. Superior Court*, 972 P.2d 179 (Ariz. 1999); David H. Getches, et al., *Cases and Materials on Federal Indian Law* 819-891 (7th ed. 2017).
[174] 6-50 *Thompson on Real Property, Third Thomas Edition* §50.11.
[175] Dale A. Whitman et al., *The Law of Property* §7.5, at 342 (4th ed. 2019).

Free use or absolute ownership

Some courts have adopted a *free use*, or *absolute ownership*, doctrine.[176] Under this rule of law, each surface owner is free to withdraw as much water as he likes from beneath the surface of his property without liability, even if it has the effect of withdrawing water from underneath his neighbor's property.[177] It is therefore misleading to call the rule one of "absolute ownership"; rather than an absolute right to the water under one's land, the rule confers an absolute right to *withdraw* the water from one's land—even if this drains water from beneath neighboring land. Now a minority rule, a few states in the United States still follow this approach, effectively granting landowners the freedom to extract as much water as they can from their property, even if this means draining water from underneath neighboring property.[178] The rule also applies when excavation and withdrawal of sand or gravel on defendant's land has the effect of withdrawing groundwater from beneath plaintiff's land.[179] One exception is that owners are not permitted to withdraw the water in a way that wastes it. Nor may owners withdraw water merely out of spite.[180] This rule used to be the majority approach in the United States, but, as with recent rejection of the common enemy rule, it has been losing out in recent years to the reasonable use doctrine.[181]

Reasonable use

Most states now reject the free use approach. Instead, they adopt rules of law that require underground water to be shared by placing limits on the ability of surface owners to deprive their neighbors of access to groundwater. Under the *reasonable use* test, each owner is entitled to a reasonable amount.[182] Some states have historically used a *correlative rights* test, allowing each owner to withdraw a specified portion of the groundwater, based on dividing up rights to the "annual recharge" to the aquifer that comes from natural sources.[183]

Correlative rights

Regulatory systems

As with rivers, most states in the arid West have administrative regulatory systems to prevent waste and to allocate rights to withdraw groundwater in an orderly fashion.[184]

[176] *Sipriano v. Great Spring Waters of America, Inc.*, 1 S.W.3d 75 (Tex. 1999); *Maddocks v. Giles*, 728 A.2d 150 (Me. 1999); 6-50 *Thompson on Real Property, Third Thomas Edition* §50.11(e).

[177] *Wiggins v. Brazil Coal & Clay Corp.*, 452 N.E.2d 958, 964 (Ind. 1983); *Gamer v. Town of Milton*, 195 N.E.2d 65, 67 (Mass. 1964); *Maddocks v. Giles*, 728 A.2d 150 (Me. 1999); *City of Corpus Christi v. City of Pleasanton*, 276 S.W.2d 798 (Tex. 1955), *reaffirmed in Sipriano v. Great Spring Waters of America, Inc.*, 1 S.W.3d 75 (Tex. 1999); *White River Chair Co. v. Connecticut River Power Co. of N.H.*, 162 A. 859, 871 (Vt. 1932).

[178] *Maddocks v. Giles*, 728 A.2d 150 (Me. 1999).

[179] *Id.*

[180] *Sipriano v. Great Spring Waters of America, Inc.*, 1 S.W.3d 75 (Tex. 1999).

[181] Dale A. Whitman et al., *The Law of Property* §7.5, at 342-343 (4th ed. 2019); 6-50 *Thompson on Real Property, Third Thomas Edition* §50.11(f).

[182] *Martin v. City of Linden*, 667 So. 2d 732 (Ala. 1995); *Koch v. Wick*, 87 So. 2d 47 (Fla. 1956); *Farmer's Investment Co. v. Bettwy*, 558 P.2d 14 (Ariz. 1976); *Rothrauff v. Sinking Spring Water Co.*, 14 A.2d 87 (Pa. 1940); *Higday v. Nickolaus*, 469 S.W.2d 859 (Mo. Ct. App. 1971); *Volkmann v. City of Crosby*, 120 N.W.2d 18 (N.D. 1963); *City of Enid v. Crow*, 316 P.2d 834 (Okla. 1957); *Canada v. City of Shawnee*, 64 P.2d 694 (Okla. 1936).

[183] *City of Barstow v. Mojave Water Agency*, 99 Cal. Rptr. 2d 294 (Cal. 2000) (upholding the correlative rights test but modifying it by requiring consideration of overlying owners' legal water rights); 6-50 *Thompson on Real Property, Third Thomas Edition* §50.11(g).

[184] 6-50 *Thompson on Real Property, Third Thomas Edition* §50.11(i). The Texas Supreme Court has called for further legislative regulation of groundwater withdrawal. *Sipriano v. Great Spring Waters of America, Inc.*, 1 S.W.3d 75, 78-79 (Tex. 1999).

§3.5 Support Rights

§3.5.1 Lateral Support

Easement of lateral support for land

Owners have the legal right to have their land supported laterally by their neighbor's land.[185] An excavation near the border that removes support provided laterally (on the side) to neighboring land that makes the land fall in or fails to support plants or structures on it, is a violation of the property rights of the affected owner.[186] This obligation is absolute and does not rest on a showing that defendant acted negligently.[187] It is sometimes called a "natural right" because it inheres in land ownership; one does not have to purchase such a right from one's neighbor. Because this right gives owners the power to constrain how other owners use their own land, it resembles a "negative easement"[188] and is often conceptualized as an easement for lateral support of land.

No right to support of structures

In contrast, courts traditionally held that owners have no duty to support structures on neighboring land.[189] In the leading case of *Thurston v. Hancock*,[190] for example, defendants began to dig on their land near the boundary with plaintiff's land. As a result of the excavation, plaintiff's land began to slide away and fall into defendant's land. With the loss of the ground support, the foundation of the house became insecure and dangerous to occupy. The Massachusetts Supreme Judicial Court ruled in 1815 that owners have a duty to support their neighbor's land in its natural condition but have no duty to support structures on their neighbor's land. Thus, defendants were liable for the harm to the land but not liable for the harm to the structure.[191]

Negligence standard for harm to neighboring structures

Although there is no duty to support a structure on neighboring land (beyond the duty to support the land itself), there is a general duty on all owners of land and construction teams to act reasonably in excavating so as to avoid negligently withdrawing support for a neighboring structure. For example, an owner who is going to excavate may be obligated to provide temporary lateral support for neighboring land during construction and may be required to advise neighbors of any construction that might affect their properties or place their land or structures in danger so that the

[185] *Spall v. Janota*, 406 N.E.2d 378 (Ind. Ct. App. 1980); *Klebs v. Yim*, 772 P.2d 523 (Wash. Ct. App. 1989); *Noone v. Price*, 298 S.E.2d 218 (W. Va. 1982).

[186] "Lateral support is a landowner's right to have the soil in its natural condition supported by the soil of adjoining land in its natural condition." 8-69 *Thompson on Real Property, Third Thomas Edition* §69.01.

[187] *Powers v. Olsen*, 742 A.2d 799 (Conn. 2000); *Catalano v. Woodward*, 617 A.2d 1363 (R.I. 1992); *Creola v. Ruley*, 12 S.W.3d 848, 854 (Tex. Ct. App. 2000); 8-69 *Thompson on Real Property, Third Thomas Editions* §69.01.

[188] An easement is a limited right in land possessed by another. A negative easement is a right to prevent another owner from using her land in a particular way. An affirmative easement is a right to do certain acts on neighboring land; the most common such easement is a right of way—a right to cross land belonging to someone else. *See* Chapter 5.

[189] *Noone v. Price*, 298 S.E.2d 218 (W. Va. 1982).

[190] 12 Mass. 220 (1815). *See also Gilmore v. Driscoll*, 122 Mass. 199 (1877).

[191] 8-69 *Thompson on Real Property, Third Thomas Edition* §69.02(a) & (b).

neighbors have time to protect themselves if they need to do so.[192] Owners are also expected to avoid unnecessarily endangering neighboring structures and to use ordinary methods of excavating that would be used by a careful building contractor.[193]

▶ HARD CASE

▷ LIABILITY FOR CONSEQUENTIAL HARM TO STRUCTURES

Some courts retain the traditional rule that immunizes owners from liability for harm to neighboring buildings in the absence of negligence.[194] This rule protects owners from liability attendant upon development of their own land and creates incentives to build structures that will remain safe despite excavation on neighboring land. However, other courts today have modified this rule, holding that liability will be imposed for harm to a structure on neighboring land, if the harm to the structure was caused by withdrawal of lateral support for the land, on which the structure sits. If the land in its natural condition was sufficient to support the house and withdrawal of support for the land causes the house to subside, these courts will impose liability for the harm to the land and the building.[195] They reason that the harm to the building was caused by the withdrawal of support for the land; it is therefore consequential damages. However, if the house was built improperly, such that it would have subsided eventually even if defendant had not withdrawn lateral support for the land around it, there will be no liability for harm to the structure because in this case the fault lies with the builder rather than the neighboring excavator.[196] ◀

Building codes

Many states and municipalities have adopted building codes that regulate excavation. Such codes often alter the common law rule and require construction to be performed so as to preserve lateral support for neighboring land and structures if it is currently being provided.[197]

Duty to maintain retaining walls

In *Noone v. Price*,[198] an owner located downhill from plaintiff had a retaining wall at the back of the property that had been constructed by an earlier owner of the property. The owner failed to maintain the wall, which started to give way, and to undermine lateral support for the land farther up the hill. In addition, the foundation of the uphill house became unsound. The West Virginia Supreme Court held that the defendant had a duty to maintain the wall that was supporting the land on plaintiff's property up the hill. This duty "runs with the land" and is binding on all future owners of the parcel on which the retaining wall sits.[199] Retaining walls are

[192] *Spall v. Janota*, 406 N.E.2d 378, 382-383 (Ind. Ct. App. 1980); *Waters v. Biesecker*, 305 S.E.2d 539 (N.C. 1983); *Noone v. Price*, 298 S.E.2d 218, 223-224 (W. Va. 1982).
[193] 8-69 *Thompson on Real Property, Third Thomas Edition* §69.04(b)(2)(iii).
[194] 8-69 *Thompson on Real Property, Third Thomas Edition* §69.04(b)(2)(i).
[195] *Noone v. Price*, 298 S.E.2d 218 (W. Va. 1982); 8-69 *Thompson on Real Property, Third Thomas Edition* §69.02(b).
[196] *Id.*; 8-69 *Thompson on Real Property, Third Thomas Edition* §69.04(b)(2)(i).
[197] *See Mass. State Building Code*, 780 Mass. Code Regs. §3307.1.
[198] 298 S.E.2d 218 (W. Va. 1982).
[199] *Accord, Salmon v. Peterson*, 311 N.W.2d 205, 206-207 (S.D. 1981); *Klebs v. Yim*, 772 P.2d 523 (Wash. Ct. App. 1989).

generally constructed when land is excavated and not refilled (to flatten out the lot, for example) and the wall effectively substitutes for the natural lateral support that would have existed before the land was excavated. The owner has a duty to maintain the wall in a sufficiently strong condition to support the neighbor's land in its natural condition. If, however, the wall is stronger than necessary to do this, and it effectively holds up the neighbor's house as well as the neighbor's land, the owner of the wall has no duty to continue providing this level of support. At the same time, if the owner rebuilds the wall and makes it less strong, and thereby removes support that the wall had previously been providing a neighboring structure, the owner must provide sufficient notice to the neighbor to allow her to protect her own structure. Failure to do so is likely to result in liability for negligence.[200]

§3.5.2 *Subjacent Support*

Support for the surface

Surface owners have an absolute right to subjacent support for their land. This means that, in the absence of a contract to the contrary, owners of subsurface mineral rights have an obligation to maintain support for the surface.[201] Those who withdraw subjacent support for the surface are strictly liable for damage to the land in its natural condition.

Structures

Some courts extend this obligation to structures on the land, imposing strict liability for damage to surface structures caused by withdrawal of subjacent support.[202] Most courts, however, refuse to impose liability for withdrawal of subjacent support to structures in the absence of negligence.[203]

▷ GROUNDWATER RIGHTS v. SUBJACENT SUPPORT FOR LAND **HARD CASE ◀**

In *Friendswood Dev. Co. v. Smith-Southwest Industries, Inc.*,[204] defendant withdrew groundwater from underneath its land for sale to industrial users. As a result of this withdrawal, the land of the neighbors began to subside because their land depended on the presence of groundwater to help support the surface. Texas had adopted the free use or absolute ownership doctrine for withdrawal of groundwater and the common law rule of absolute right for lateral support of land. The question in the case was whether defendant was free to withdraw the groundwater without liability or whether, instead, its freedom to withdraw groundwater was limited by the rights of the neighbors to subjacent support for their land.

Free use rule

Traditionally, an owner who was free to withdraw groundwater under the absolute ownership rule would not be liable for any resulting harm to the land.[205] However, modern cases have modified or reversed this rule, and

[200] On the other hand, there is no duty to maintain a retaining wall to support a party's *own* land. *See Scott v. West*, 594 S.W.3d 397, 413 (Tex. 2019).
[201] 8-69 *Thompson on Real Property, Third Thomas Edition* §69.05.
[202] *Id.* at §69.05(d).
[203] *Id.*
[204] 576 S.W.2d 21 (Tex. 1978).
[205] *Restatement (First) of Torts* §818 (1939).

instead impose obligations on owners not to withdraw water or oil beneath the lands of others if this will result in a loss of support for the surface of neighboring land.[206] In *Friendswood*, the majority rejected the free use rule in this context and substituted a negligence test.[207] A vigorous dissent argued that nuisance law should apply,[208] while the *Restatement (Second) of Torts* has suggested that a strict liability standard might be appropriate, as is the case for lateral support.[209] Some other authorities similarly opine that groundwater may not be withdrawn from one's land if it undermines subjacent support for neighboring land.[210] ◀

Negligence test

§3.6 Light and Air

No easement for light and air

The rule is well established in the United States that, absent a zoning law to the contrary, owners are free to build in ways that interfere with their neighbors' interests in light and air. In the leading case of *Fontainebleau Hotel Corp. v. Forty-Five Twenty-Five, Inc.*,[211] one beach hotel owner began constructing a massive addition near its border with plaintiff (another hotel), which would cast a huge shadow across plaintiff's land, including over plaintiff's swimming pool. The court held that each owner is free to build in ways that cast shadows on neighboring property or that block the neighbor's view. In effect, owners have no easement for light and air; they have no legally protected interest in access to light and air that would allow them to prevent other owners from building on their own property in ways that interfere with those interests.

Spite fences

The sole exception to this rule is that many courts will issue an injunction preventing an owner from constructing or maintaining a "spite fence," which is constructed for the purpose of blocking the windows of a neighboring owner and which confers no discernable benefits on the owner who wishes to construct the fence other than enjoyment of the annoyance to the neighbor.[212] However, some courts have rejected this doctrine[213] and it is very difficult to get courts to apply it, even if they accept the doctrine, because most fences have a useful purpose and cannot be said to be in existence solely for the purpose of vexing the neighbors.

Zoning laws

Protection for access to light and air is granted by zoning laws that often include setback requirements and limit the height of structures.

[206] *Restatement (Second) of Torts* §818 (1979).
[207] 576 S.W.2d 21 (Tex. 1978). *See also Gamer v. Milton*, 195 N.E.2d 65 (Mass. 1964) (adopting a negligence test).
[208] 576 S.W.2d at 32 (Pope, J., dissenting).
[209] *Restatement (Second) of Torts* §818 illus. 2 (1979).
[210] 8-69 *Thompson on Real Property, Third Thomas Edition* §69.05(e).
[211] 114 So. 2d 357 (Fla. Dist. Ct. App. 1959); *accord Berger v. Sellers*, 996 N.W.2d 329 (N.D. 2023) (finding no "right to sunlight and open space on adjacent properties").
[212] Conn. Gen. Stat. §52-570; *DeCecco v. Beach*, 381 A.2d 543 (Conn. 1977). *See also Wilson v. Handley*, 119 Cal. Rptr. 2d 263 (Ct. App. 2002) (applying Cal. Civ. Code §841.4); *Gertz v. Estes*, 879 N.E.2d 617 (Ind. Ct. App. 2008) (applying Ind. Code §32-26-10-1 and -2); *Peters v. O'Leary*, 30 A.3d 825 (Me. 2011) (applying Maine Rev. Stat. tit. 17, §2801).
[213] *Maioriello v. Arlotta*, 73 A.2d 374 (Pa. 1950).

Nuisance law

Two states have rejected the *Fontainebleau* doctrine and apply ordinary nuisance law to disputes over access to light.[214] In *Prah v. Maretti*,[215] an owner of a home with solar roof panels sought a court order to make his neighbor relocate his proposed house several feet to ensure plaintiff's access to sunlight for his solar panels. Rather than dismiss the complaint, as would be proper under the *Fontainebleau* rule, the Wisconsin Supreme Court required application of nuisance law and remanded for a determination of whether defendant's construction caused substantial, unreasonable harm to plaintiff's property interests, in access to light for solar power, and whether it would be possible to alter the location or shape of defendant's home in reasonable ways to avoid unnecessary harm to plaintiff's property while allowing defendant to develop his property as he wishes.

[214] *Prah v. Maretti*, 321 N.W.2d 182 (Wis. 1982); *Tenn v. 889 Assocs.*, 500 A.2d 366 (N.H. 1985).
[215] 321 N.W.2d 182 (Wis. 1982).

CHAPTER 4

Adverse Possession

§4.1 Introduction
§4.2 Elements
  §4.2.1 Actual Possession
  §4.2.2 Open and Notorious
  §4.2.3 Exclusive
  §4.2.4 Continuous
  §4.2.5 Adverse or Hostile
  §4.2.6 For the Statutory Period
  §4.2.7 Under Color of Title
§4.3 Justifications for Adverse Possession
§4.4 Typical Cases
  §4.4.1 Color of Title
  §4.4.2 Border Disputes
  §4.4.3 Squatters
  §4.4.4 Co-tenants
§4.5 Procedures and Effects of Adverse Possession
  §4.5.1 Level of Proof Required
  §4.5.2 Effect on Prior Encumbrances
§4.6 Claims Against the Government
§4.7 Informal Transfers of Title to Settle Boundary Disputes
  §4.7.1 Improving Trespasser
  §4.7.2 Dedication
  §4.7.3 Oral Agreement
  §4.7.4 Acquiescence
  §4.7.5 Estoppel
  §4.7.6 Riparian Owners
§4.8 Adverse Possession of Personal Property

§4.1 Introduction

Immunity rights . . .

We have seen that the *right to exclude* is limited by public accommodations laws and other privileged rights of access to property possessed by others.[1] We have also seen that the *privilege to use* property is limited by nuisance law and other doctrines that protect the security of other owners and the community as a whole.[2] With all these limits to the legal rights of owners, one might think that owners at least must get to keep their ownership rights, circumscribed as they may be, until they choose to sell them or transfer them to others. Owners are immune from having their property taken from them by others. Or are they?

. . . and their limits

Owners generally have the *power to transfer* their property rights, and the obverse seems to be the right *not* to give up your property rights until you wish to do so. The right to keep your property until you want to part with it, is an example of what Wesley Hohfeld called an *immunity* right.[3] Such rights seem to be just as if not more important, than the right to exclude or the privilege to use property. But, as with rights of exclusion and use, limits have been imposed on the owner's immunity from forced transfer or loss of her property rights against her will. A prime example is the law of adverse possession.[4]

From trespasser to owner

This magical rule mutates a wrong into a right. A trespasser who not only intrudes onto property owned by another but also *occupies* it — treats the property as her own, effectively ousts the title holder, and who is brazen enough to do so for a long, long time — is rewarded by the legal system by being given ownership of the property she has wrongfully possessed. What a paradoxical rule! Only wrongdoers are rewarded and they are rewarded only if they can persist in their wrongdoing for a sufficiently long period of time. The law of adverse possession grants property rights to those who failed to respect the property rights of others. This is a mind-bending rule. No wonder law students are usually confused and startled by this doctrine. At the very least, the rule appears to reward negligence; at the most, it appears to reward theft. It is therefore surprising to law students to learn that the rule is a basic — one might even say foundational — principle of the law of private property, that it has existed in the United States since the beginning, and that it has existed in England in some form since the thirteenth century.

Statute of limitations

When a rule appears to be as perverse and surprising as this, we have either identified a great candidate for law reform or there must be a very

[1] *See* Chapter 2.

[2] *See* Chapter 3.

[3] Wesley Newcomb Hohfeld, *Some Fundamental Legal Conceptions as Applied in Judicial Reasoning*, 23 Yale L.J. 16 (1913), 26 Yale L.J. 710 (1917).

[4] Another is the possibility that one's property might be taken by the state through its eminent domain power and the owner given "just compensation" amounting to the fair market value of the land, an amount that is likely to be less than the owner's perceived value of the land. If the owner valued the land at fair market value, she would be happy to put it up for sale; owners who are not in the market to sell their property generally value it higher than the fair market value, meaning that a potential buyer would have to offer more than the fair market value to induce the owner to sell.

good reason why the rule exists. The traditional statement of the legal basis for adverse possession is the running of the statute of limitations. When a non-owner occupies property owned by another, the owner is entitled to bring an action in ejectment to recover possession.[5] As with almost all claims, the states have enacted statutes of limitation that limit how long one can wait to bring the lawsuit. If the owner waits too long, the statute will run, depriving the owner of the legal right to sue to recover the land from the wrongful possessor. Although the title holder normally has the right to eject the adverse possessor, the title holder will lose that right if she does not sue, to eject the adverse possessor before the statute of limitations runs out. The adverse possessor has the right to exclude everyone but the true owner. Once the statute of limitations runs out and the title holder has lost the right to eject the adverse possessor, no one has a superior right to possess the property than the adverse possessor. Because the adverse possessor has the right to exclude everyone but the title holder and the title holder has now lost the right to exclude the adverse possessor, the functional effect of the running of the statute of limitations is to convert the adverse possessor into a rightful title holder.

Adverse possessor

Holes in the theory

There are a number of holes in this argument. For example, even though the owner has lost the power to eject the possessor and recover possession, it is not clear why the owner has *also* lost the power to enter the property herself and possess it jointly with the adverse possessor. The remedy of ejectment allows the title holder to recover possession of the land by excluding (ejecting) the adverse possessor; the courts have interpreted statutes of limitation not only to bar ejectment but *also* to bar the title holder from seeking an injunction ordering the adverse possessor not to interfere with the title holder's privilege to enter the land. Although the adverse possessor has effectively excluded the title holder from the land, it is not necessarily the case that a statute that does nothing more than bar the particular remedy of ejectment should also bar the title holder from entering the land. Moreover, the owner loses not only the right to exclude the adverse possessor and the right to enter the land, but also all other rights as well, such as the power to transfer the property. A final oddity is that statutes of limitation normally function as *defenses to claims*; they ordinarily do not establish affirmative rights other than the right to be free from claims by others. Yet, adverse possession law not only immunizes adverse possessors from claims, but also transfers title to the property to the adverse possessor.[6]

Other remedies for trespass

Many states have statutes of limitation for bringing trespass claims for damages that are different from the statutes barring the remedy of ejectment. For example, in *Butler v. Lindsey*,[7] the court denied an adverse possession claim because the property had not been occupied for the requisite ten-year period. The court granted the title holder the right to obtain damages for trespass but applied the six-year statute of limitations applicable to trespass claims other than ejectment, thereby limiting the title

[5] 16-91 *Powell on Real Property* §91.01[2].

[6] John G. Sprankling, *Understanding Property Law* §27.04, at 481 (5th ed. 2023).

[7] 361 S.E.2d 621 (S.C. 1987).

holder to six years of damages. One might argue that even if the statute of limitations had passed to recover possession of the property, such that the possessor is entitled to retain possession, the title holder should be entitled to damages for whatever period of time is allowed, under tort or trespass statutes of limitation. In addition, although the title holder may have lost the right to sue for ejectment, other injunctive remedies could be fashioned for the continuing trespass other than recovery of possession. For example, the court could impose a variety of remedies, such as physical partition (splitting the property in two) or ordering it to be sold off if the parties cannot agree on who should possess it.

Long-standing possession transfers title

In fact, the courts unanimously reject the idea that remedies might be available, either in the form of injunctive relief or damages, when the statute of limitations for ejectment runs. Instead, they have assumed, for hundreds of years, that the running of the statute of limitations for ejectment has the extraordinary effect of transferring *all* property rights in the land from the prior owner to the adverse possessor. Moreover, the running of the statute retroactively changes these ownership rights in the sense that one who has possessed adversely for the statutory period is treated as if she had owned the property all along; thus, no damages for trespass are allowed even though the trespass was a wrong that continued up until recently.[8]

Formal v. informal sources of justified expectations

Clearly, the law of adverse possession rests on something more fundamental than the running of the statute of limitations. It is based on a policy conclusion that the property in question *should* belong to the long-standing possessor and that the record title holder should no longer be legally entitled to retain her ownership rights. The best explanation of the rule is that, like most rules of property law, it protects *justified expectations*. Most students are surprised by adverse possession law because they assume that the only legitimate source of property rights is formal title. They assume that the title holder is the "owner" and that it is a trespass, and therefore *prima facie* wrong, and unlawful for anyone other than the title holder to occupy the property without the owner's consent. What is missing in this understanding of property is the extent to which *informal* sources of property rights are as important in establishing our expectations as formal ones.

Possession as a source of property in addition to title

It turns out that title is not, in fact, the only basis for expectations of control over property; long-standing possession creates such expectations as well. Indeed, possession is a crucial component of property law; it is a common saying that "possession is nine-tenths of the law." In our day-to-day lives, we do not carry around written evidence of our ownership of all the things we possess. We would all be hard-pressed to prove even that we own the shirts we wear or the books we carry. What proof do we have of ownership other than possession? In most cases, the answer is none. It is true that for important property interests that are capable of conflicting claims, such as land or automobiles, we do have formal titles that can be produced if need be. At the same time, day-to-day expectations are not always based on reference to such formal documents, and the fact patterns covered by the law of adverse possession are prime examples of the

[8] 10-87 *Thompson on Real Property, Third Thomas Edition* §87.03.

importance of conduct, possession, acquiescence in established borders, and other informal indications of ownership in setting property expectations. We will explore the fact settings typical of adverse possession cases to better understand the kinds of settings in which expectations are formed on the basis of possession rather than title. In addition, we need to consider whether those informally based expectations are justified or whether, on the contrary, only expectations based on formalities of title are legitimate.

§4.2 Elements

Adverse possession

Adverse possession is established when someone (1) actually possesses property, in a manner that is (2) "open and notorious," (3) exclusive, (4) continuous, and (5) nonpermissive ("adverse" or "hostile") (6) for a period established by the statute of limitations for ejectment.[9] Some states have enacted different statutes of limitation depending on whether the possessor has acted under (7) "color of title" or has (8) paid property taxes on the land.[10] Some courts have formally required a showing that the occupation (9) was in "good faith" (meaning that the possessor did not know she was trespassing on land formally owned by another),[11] and some states suggest that the possessor must act (10) "under a claim of right"—an element susceptible to widely varying interpretations.[12] These last factors (good faith and claim of right) are really particular variations on the "adversity" requirement and embody significant substantive disagreements about the meaning of the requirement.

§4.2.1 Actual Possession

Physical occupation

The first requirement for adverse possession is that of "actual possession." This means that the possessor must physically occupy the premises in some manner.[13] What manner and how extensive the occupation must be is a heavily contested and often litigated issue. Some states specify what acts constitute actual possession by statute.[14] Others rely on common law. In general, the adverse possessor must treat the property as if she owns it. "Actual possession" means the "ordinary use to which the land is capable and such as an owner would make of it."[15] Which acts will be sufficient to constitute "actual" possession will vary depending on the "nature and

[9] *Snook v. Bowers*, 12 P.3d 771, 781 (Alaska 2000); *Nome 2000 v. Fagerstrom*, 799 P.2d 304 (Alaska 1990); *Fields v. Griffen*, 1999 WL 349872 (Ark. Ct. App. 1999); *Blaszkowski v. Schmitt*, 597 N.W.2d 773 (Wis. Ct. App. 1999).

[10] *See, e.g.*, Fla. Stat. §95.18.

[11] Colo. Rev. Stat. §38-41-101(3)(b)(II); Ga. Code §§44-5-161 to -162; N.M. Stat. §37-1-22; *Halpern v. Lacy Investment Corp.*, 379 S.E.2d 519 (Ga. 1989); *Carpenter v. Ruperto*, 315 N.W.2d 782, 785 (Iowa 1982).

[12] *Akin v. Castleberry*, 286 P.3d 638, 641 (Okla. 2012) ("claim of right" or "color of title" as necessary elements of an adverse possession claim).

[13] *Nome 2000 v. Fagerstrom*, 799 P.2d 304 (Alaska 1990); Dale A. Whitman et al., *The Law of Property* §11.7, at 749 (4th ed. 2019).

[14] Cal. Code Civ. Proc. §323; Fla. Stat. §95.16; N.Y. Real Prop. Acts. §522; John G. Sprankling, *Understanding Property Law* §27.03[B][2], at 473 (5th ed. 2023).

[15] *Peter H. & Barbara J. Steuck Living Trust v. Easley*, 325 Wis.2d 455, 471 (Wis. App. 2010).

location of the property, the uses to which it can be applied and all the facts and circumstances of a particular case."[16]

What constitutes "actual possession"

The easiest way to demonstrate "actual possession" is to build a fence around the land and use it (or some portion of it) in a visible manner.[17] It is not necessary to live on the land, but unless the adverse possessor builds a fence around the land and excludes the true owner, she must generally show evidence of significant activities conducted there.[18] In the absence of a fence, one might demonstrate adverse possession by building on the land and living there or conducting a business there. Other actions that are often sufficient to show actual possession are farming, clearing the land, and planting shrubs. In one case, an owner demonstrated "actual possession" of a residential front yard by planting grass on it and then mowing, as well as planting trees and cultivating lilac bushes there.[19] In general, the adverse possessor must treat the property as an owner would.[20] Many cases concern the question of whether the use of the land is sufficiently intense to constitute "actual possession."[21] In contrast to most states, New York has passed a statute that allows adverse possession in border cases only if the occupation involves construction more substantial than a shed or fence.[22]

Physical area of actual possession determines extent of rights acquired

In the absence of a fence (or other markings of physical use such as trees or hedges or other kinds of shrubbery), the extent of area acquired by adverse possession is determined by the extent of the occupation and use. In such cases, the extent of the claim may be harder to determine than when a fence exists. In addition, the actions required to show possession will differ for urban versus rural land and will also differ for property located in an area that is typically used seasonally.[23] The courts often state that adverse possession is established if an owner uses the property in a manner typical of property in the area and in ways for which the land is suited. In *Nome 2000 v. Fagerstrom*,[24] defendant possessors of rural land in Alaska established adverse possession of the northern portion of the disputed lot but

[16] *Smith v. Hayden*, 772 P.2d 47, 55 (Colo. 1989).

[17] *Boot Ranch, LLC v. Wagonhound Land & Livestock Co.*, 560 P.3d 887, 894 (Wyo. 2024). *See* Dale A. Whitman et al., *The Law of Property* §11.7, at 749 (4th ed. 2019). *But see Allen v. Moran*, 760 N.E.2d 198 (Ind. Ct. App. 2001) (landowner does not establish title by adverse possession to a portion of his neighbor's property between a fence and the record boundary line when the fence was built to contain cattle not to designate the border and the landowner did not make significant repairs or improvements that otherwise demonstrate possession of the disputed property).

[18] *But see Hovendick v. Ruby*, 10 P.3d 1119 (Wyo. 2000) ("fence of convenience" designed to contain or keep out animals gives rise to a presumption of permissive use while a boundary fence gives rise to a presumption of adverse possession).

[19] *Jutting v. Hendrix*, 606 N.W.2d 140, 142 (S.D. 2000); *see also Ballard v. Harman*, 737 N.E.2d 411 (Ind. Ct. App. 2000); (similar).

[20] 10-87 *Thompson on Real Property, Third Thomas Edition* §87.05.

[21] *Compare Krosmico v. Pettit*, 968 P.2d 345 (Okla. 1998) *and Blaszkowski v. Schmitt*, 597 N.W.2d 773 (Wis. Ct. App. 1999) (holding that actual possession was established) *with Nome 2000 v. Fagerstrom*, 799 P.2d 304 (Alaska 1990) (only part of the property was actually possessed).

[22] N.Y. Real Prop. Acts. §543.

[23] *Harris v. Lynch*, 940 S.W.2d 42 (Mo. Ct. App. 1997) (evidence to establish adverse possession differs for rural v. urban land).

[24] 799 P.2d 304 (Alaska 1990).

not the southern portion. On the northern portion, the adverse possessors placed a camper on the land for three months each year, built an outhouse, a fish rack, a large reindeer pen (which housed a reindeer for six months), a picnic area, and placed some building materials on the lot. Defendants visited the land and lived there periodically in the warm season. The court found these actions to be sufficient to establish "actual" possession. On the other hand, defendants did nothing on the southern portion of the disputed parcel except pass over it occasionally and place markers (not a fence) at the borders. These actions were held to be insufficient to constitute "actual possession."

When the adverse possessor has color of title

When the adverse possessor has "color of title," the rules are similar to the practice applicable to cases where the property is enclosed by a fence. When a fence is constructed around the property and some substantial portion inside is occupied, adverse possession will generally extend to all the enclosed property, rather than just the portion that is used. Similarly, an individual who buys property with a formal (but defective) deed that describes the disputed area can acquire it by adverse possession if she occupies any portion of the property described in the deed.[25] In effect, fences and deed descriptions are taken to be almost conclusive determinations of the physical land area acquired by adverse possession. It is in the absence of these indicators that the boundaries of the property acquired by adverse possession are more susceptible to the vagaries of the responses decision makers have to the facts.

Prescriptive easements

If the non-owner performs only specific actions on the land, rather than treating it generally as her own, she may be granted a *prescriptive easement* rather than adverse possession. Easements are limited rights to use the property of another. For example, the right to cross neighboring property—known as a "right of way"—is an *affirmative* easement, that is, a right to do something specific on the land of another. In contrast, *negative* easements are rights to limit or control the use of neighboring property. For example, to prevent a neighbor from adding an extra story onto its building, one can purchase from that neighbor the right to prevent any construction above the existing building. Affirmative easements, unlike negative easements, may be acquired by prescription. The elements for prescriptive easements are substantially the same as the elements for adverse possession, except that the "actual possession" element is replaced by "actual use," and most courts will drop the requirement that the use be "exclusive."[26]

Affirmative easement

Negative easement

▷ BOUNDARY DISPUTES: ADVERSE POSSESSION OR PRESCRIPTIVE EASEMENT — HARD CASE ◀

Cases involving mistaken boundaries may generate claims of either adverse possession or prescriptive easement. For example, if a property owner

[25] Dale A. Whitman et al., *The Law of Property* §11.7, at 750 (4th ed. 2019). Adverse possession may be needed to establish title if the deed has a technical defect (such as lack of signature) that makes the writing insufficient under the statute of frauds.
[26] *See* §5.5 for further information on prescriptive easements.

builds a driveway on what he believes is the edge of his property but that really extends onto his neighbor's side of the line, he may claim adverse possession of the overlap, or he may claim merely an easement to use the strip for driveway purposes. If granted only an easement, he cannot use the strip for any other purpose; if granted adverse possession of the strip, then he can change the use by, for example, taking out the driveway and putting in grass or shrubs or building a structure on it. The result will depend on the extent of his use of the strip and whether his actions could reasonably have been interpreted as asserting general powers over the strip of land. Deciding this issue requires difficult factual and interpretive judgments. It also requires a policy judgment about which an owner's interests are more deserving of legal protection. ◀

§4.2.2 *Open and Notorious*

Visible and obvious, placing title holder on notice

To establish adverse possession, possessory acts must be sufficiently visible and obvious to put a reasonable owner on notice that her property is being occupied by a non-owner with the intent of claiming possessory rights.[27] The adverse possessor does not need to prove that the title holder observed or knew about the adverse possessor's use of the property.[28] Nor must the adverse possessor show that the record owner knew or should have known that the adverse possessor was encroaching on property owned by the record owner.[29] The record owner is "charged with seeing what reasonable inspection would disclose."[30] A great deal of litigation has been generated over what acts are sufficient to put owners on notice and the cases construing what constitutes "actual possession" often blend the determination of which acts are sufficient to constitute "possession" with the determination of which acts are sufficiently "open and notorious" to conclude that a reasonable owner should have been aware of them. Enclosing land by a fence or a wall and occupying a house is generally recognized as sufficiently open and notorious.[31] Fences are particularly good indicators that someone is possessing the enclosed land. However, one court held that a fence was not

[27] *Smith v. Hayden*, 772 P.2d 47, 52 (Colo. 1989); *Carter v. Voncannon*, 327 A.3d 9, 24 (Me. 2024); *Glenn v. Shuey*, 595 A.2d 606 (Pa. Super. Ct. 1991); *Naab v. Nolan*, 327 S.E.2d 151, 154 (W. Va. 1985); 10-87 *Thompson on Real Property, Third Thomas Edition* §87.08. *But see Mannillo v. Gorski*, 255 A.2d 258 (N.J. 1969) (when "encroachment of an adjoining owner is of a small area and the fact of an intrusion is not clearly and self-evidently apparent to the naked eye but requires an on-site survey for certain disclosure" the occupation is not presumptively open and notorious although the possessor may be entitled to continue the possession upon payment of compensation to the owner whose property was thereby occupied for the statutory period).

[28] *See, e.g., Lawrence v. Town of Concord*, 788 N.E.2d 546 (Mass. 2003) (when town held future interest in property pursuant to a will that had been validly probated, town lost its rights to an adverse possessor who occupied the property for 30 years even though the town officials did not know about the future interest during the time of the possession).

[29] *Id.*

[30] Dale A. Whitman et al., *The Law of Property* §11.7, at 749 (4th ed. 2019).

[31] *See, e.g., Smith v. Tippett*, 569 A.2d 1186 (D.C. 1990) (enclosing a strip of property by a wall); *Brown v. Gobble*, 474 S.E.2d 489 (W. Va. 1996); *cf. Foster v. Wasson*, 483 S.W.3d 301 (Ark. Ct. App. 2016) (holding low, poorly maintained woodland fence was "fence of convenience" not sufficient to put title owner on notice).

sufficiently "open and notorious" when the fence was a wire mesh fence that was decrepit and had been overgrown by shrubbery so that most of it was not easily visible.[32] Other acts deemed sufficient include building a structure;[33] clearing the land; laying down a driveway; mowing grass; using the strip for parking, storage, garbage removal, and picnicking;[34] and planting and harvesting crops.[35]

▷ RURAL LAND **HARD CASE ◀**

Cases involving rural land create dilemmas for adverse possession law. On the one hand, the courts often state that land in urban areas may require more activity to establish "actual possession" than land in rural or seasonally used areas. This is because the uses made of the land need only be typical of the uses made by other owners of like land in the area.[36] On the other hand, property in rural areas, especially if it is extensive and wooded, may require more than minimal activity to place a reasonable record owner on actual notice that someone is possessing the property, especially when the land is not used for habitation but is being held for the potential use of its natural resources, such as timber or oil. In *Nome 2000 v. Fagerstrom*,[37] for example, a family occupied land in a remote area owned by a corporation. It might be argued that the title holder might well not be aware of campers living in a forested area in the middle of a large tract of isolated, rural land, and that, to place the absentee owner on reasonable notice that the land is being occupied, it might be sensible to acquire more extensive development in rural areas than would be required in a populous area. The requirement that land use be typical of what other owners would do with the land may suggest that lesser acts should be sufficient to establish "actual possession" in a rural area, while the requirement that the use be "open and notorious" may push in the direction of requiring more extensive development. ◀

§4.2.3 *Exclusive*

Effective exclusion of title holder

The exclusivity requirement does not mean that only the owner can use the property for the statutory period. Owners routinely allow others to

[32] *Stump v. Whibco*, 715 A.2d 1006 (N.J. Super. Ct. App. Div. 1998).
[33] *Smith v. Hayden*, 772 P.2d 47, 52 (Colo. 1989) (garage located on neighboring property); *Naab v. Nolan*, 327 S.E.2d 151, 154 (W. Va. 1985) (same).
[34] *Chaplin v. Sanders*, 676 P.2d 431 (Wash. 1984).
[35] *Cheek v. Wainwright*, 269 S.E.2d 443 (Ga. 1980) (timber). *Cf. Poullos v. Pine Crest Homes, LLC*, 876 N.W.2d 356 (Neb. 2016) (operation of a hidden sprinkler system and lawn maintenance were not sufficiently visible or "notorious" to put the record owner on notice of the adverse actions and thus could not ripen into adverse possession); *Rhodes v. Cahill*, 802 S.W.2d 643 (Tex. 1990) (holding that isolated and selective clearing of trees for timber or grazing purposes and grazing cattle and goats without enclosing the land are insufficient to show adverse possession over a ten-year period).
[36] *Peter H. & Barbara J. Steuck Living Trust v. Easley*, 325 Wis.2d 455, 471 (Wis. App. 2010); *Jarvis v. Gillespie*, 587 A.2d 981 (Vt. 1991) (evidence supported finding of adverse possession of rural, agricultural land).
[37] 799 P.2d 304 (Alaska 1990).

enter their property for various purposes. Exclusivity generally means that the use "is of a type that would be expected of a title holder of the land in question" and that "the adverse claimant's possession cannot be shared with the true holder."[38] Proving that possession was not shared with the title holder may require a showing that "the record owner has been effectively excluded," although occasional entry by the title holder may not defeat the claim.[39] Two adverse possessors who possess property jointly may acquire joint ownership rights as co-owners.[40]

§4.2.4 *Continuous*

No significant interruption

The adverse possessor's occupation must continue without significant interruption. This does not mean the adverse possessor cannot leave the land or even that the land must be occupied by someone at all times.[41] Depending on the type of property in question, even extended absences may not defeat the claim. In *Howard v. Kunto*,[42] for example, adverse possession was established over a parcel of land used seasonally as a summer cabin.[43] The court held the continuity requirement to mean that the adverse possessor must exercise control over the property in the ways customarily pursued by owners of that type of property. "[T]he requisite possession requires such possession and dominion 'as ordinarily marks the conduct of owners in general in holding, managing, and caring for property of like nature and condition.'"[44] Some courts may find seasonal use to be neither "continuous" nor "open and notorious."[45]

Seasonal use

Tacking

What happens if someone adversely possesses property for less than the time period required by the relevant statute of limitations and sells the property—or, more precisely, *purports* to sell it—to another owner? The general rule is that the succeeding periods of possession by different persons may be added together; this is called *tacking*.[46] Most states require, however, that successors can add the original adverse possessor's holding period only if they are in *privity* with one another, meaning that the original adverse possessor transferred title to the property to the successor

[38] *Smith v. Tippett*, 569 A.2d 1186, 1190 (D.C. 1990). *See also* 10-87 *Thompson on Real Property, Third Thomas Edition* §87.09.
[39] *Smith v. Hayden*, 772 P.2d 47, 52-53 (Colo. 1989).
[40] Dale A. Whitman et al., *The Law of Property* §11.7, at 754 (4th ed. 2019).
[41] *Glenn v. Shuey*, 595 A.2d 606 (Pa. Super. Ct. 1991).
[42] 477 P.2d 210 (Wash. Ct. App. 1970), *overruled on other grounds by Chaplin v. Sanders*, 676 P.2d 431 (Wash. 1984).
[43] *Accord, Nome 2000 v. Fagerstrom*, 799 P.2d 304 (Alaska 1990).
[44] 477 P.2d at 213-214.
[45] *See Weeks v. Krysa*, 955 A.2d 234, 239 (Me. 2008) ("Seasonal playing on and crossing over a lot, without more, does not demonstrate the necessary notoriety or hostility to put the true owner on notice or support an adverse possession finding."); *Hanson v. Summers* (Mich. Ct. App. Sept. 22, 2000) (Presque Isle Circuit Ct. No. 214536, LC No. 94-001989-CH) (unpublished opinion) (http://www.michbar.org/opinions/ home.html, then click on Opinions button and look under September 22, 2000 to find the case designated "opinions/appeals/2000/092200/8170.html") (holding that seasonal use is not sufficient to constitute "continuous" possession for purposes of establishing adverse possession).
[46] *Stump v. Whibco*, 715 A.2d 1006, 1010-1011 (N.J. Super. Ct. App. Div. 1998).

(again, purported to do so).[47] If, however, the successor dispossessed the prior adverse possessor, he will generally not be given the benefit of the tacking doctrine.[48]

§4.2.5 *Adverse or Hostile*

State of mind requirement

Of all the elements of adverse possession, the adversity requirement has given rise to the most confused and varied treatment. In general, the adverse possessor must treat the property as her own and the use must not result from the title holder's permission. There are two sides to this requirement: the state of mind of the adverse possessor and the state of mind of the record title holder. Most states focus on the state of mind of the record title holder and find adversity when the possession is without the title holder's permission. Other states require *both* that the use be nonpermissive *and* that the adverse possessor exhibit a particular attitude toward the property. The states that require some showing of the adverse possessor's state of mind differ wildly among themselves on what exactly the adverse possessor needs to show. The various tests include (1) an objective test based on use, and a number of subjective tests, including (2) a "claim of right," (3) intentional dispossession, and (4) good faith.

Tests

Title holder's state of mind

As to the record title holder's state of mind, all states require the adverse possessor to show that possession was not permissive. If the title holder has given permission to the possessor, then the possession, by definition, is not adverse and the basic premise of the adverse possession doctrine is absent. If a use is permissive, it is privileged; if it is privileged, no trespass or wrongful occupation exists, and in that case, the remedy of ejectment is not available and the statute of limitations for bringing such a claim does not start running.

Use must be nonpermissive

Presumption that occupation is nonpermissive

In some cases, the question of whether the use is permissive is decided by reference to evidence that the title holder either explicitly gave permission (through a written lease or an oral invitation or agreement) or that the title holder had clearly *not* given permission, perhaps by telling the possessor to get off the premises. In many cases, however, the title holder has said nothing at all about whether the use is permissive; she has simply allowed it to occur without interference. The courts uniformly hold that possession of another's property without either explicit objection or explicit permission is presumptively nonpermissive.[49] Thus, to defeat the presumption that the use is nonpermissive, the title holder must come up with evidence to show that she granted permission, in either written or oral form. In the ordinary case of mutual mistake, the courts overwhelmingly presume that possession is nonpermissive.[50] A few courts have adopted the

[47] *Shelton v. Strickland*, 21 P.3d 1179, 1184 (Wash. Ct. App. 2001).

[48] *Id.* at 1183-1184.

[49] Dale A. Whitman et al., *The Law of Property* §11.7, at 753-754 (4th ed. 2019). *But see* N.Y. Real Prop. Acts. §543 (2008 statute declares "de minimus non-structural encroachments" such as lawn mowing, plantings, fences, and sheds are deemed permissive uses).

[50] *Robarge v. Willett*, 636 N.Y.S.2d 938 (App. Div. 1996); *but see Hinman v. Cornett*, 900 S.E.2d 872, 875 (N.C. 2024); 10-87 *Thompson on Real Property, Third Thomas Edition* §87.10.

opposite presumption for rural or unenclosed and unoccupied land, treating possession as presumptively permissive rather than nonpermissive, in cases where social custom appears to justify this.[51] New York has passed a statute that presumes occupation of a neighbor's property is "permissive and non-adverse" if it involves only "non-structural components" such as lawn mowing, plantings, fences, and sheds.[52]

▶ **HARD CASE**

▷ SHOULD THE COURTS PRESUME THAT OCCUPATION IS PERMISSIVE WHEN THE OWNERS ARE FAMILY MEMBERS?

Should use be presumed to be permissive when the adverse possessor and record title holder are related to each other? In *Petsch v. Widger*,[53] the Nebraska Supreme Court held that possession is presumptively permissive when the possessor is a member of the record owner's family. This presumption applied in *Petch* because the record title holders were the cousin and step-grandmother of the possessor; because of the family relationship, possession was held to be presumptively permissive and the adverse possession claim failed. In contrast, the Massachusetts Supreme Judicial Court held in *Totman v. Malloy*[54] that no such exception existed to the general rule that possession of another's property is presumptively nonpermissive. One might argue that no special rules should be made for property possession by relatives because this will make adverse possession law less predictable. How close a relation is close enough to presume that the use is permissive? Where should we draw the line? Should possession be deemed permissive when the occupant is a friend rather than a family member? On the other hand, possession is more likely to be permissive rather than adverse in the family context. Moreover, it would seem inappropriate to reward kindness by a relative with loss of property rights. ◀

▶ **HARD CASE**

▷ A USE THAT STARTS OFF AS PERMISSIVE AND BECOMES NONPERMISSIVE

When a possession begins as permissive, it stays permissive until the permission is formally withdrawn. A wrongful occupation exists only when the owner revokes permission and asks the licensee to leave, and the licensee refuses to do so. Only then will the statute of limitations start running.[55] A use that starts off as permissive cannot become adverse without either an explicit revocation of permission by the title holder or an explicit

[51] *Warnack v. Coneen Family Trust*, 879 P.2d 715 (Mont. 1994); *Greenwalt Family Trust v. Kehler*, 885 P.2d 421 (Mont. 1994); Dale A. Whitman et al., *The Law of Property* §8.7, at 367-368 (4th ed. 2019).

[52] N.Y. Real Prop. Acts. §543.

[53] 335 N.W.2d 254 (Neb. 1983). *Cf. Androkites v. White*, 10 A.3d 677 (Me. 2010) (for purposes of prescriptive easement doctrine, use of another's property by a family member is presumed to be permissive).

[54] 725 N.E.2d 1045 (Mass. 2000).

[55] *See Brander v. Stoddard*, 164 A.3d 889, 901 (Conn. App. Ct. 2017).

statement by the adverse possessor to the title holder that he intends to oust the title holder from his property.[56] In the absence of a clear *revocation* of permission by the title holder or a clear *ouster* by the adverse possessor, the initial permission will constitute an absolute defense to an adverse possession claim notwithstanding the duration of the occupancy by the non-owner.[57] Some states, however, may allow the non-owner to acquire prescriptive rights despite initial permission by the title holder. They may do so by interpreting the title holder's conduct to imply a revocation of permission. Or they may declare the title holder *estopped* from asserting his ownership claims if he has acquiesced in long-standing use by a non-owner and the non-owner has reasonably relied on a continued right of access.[58] ◀

Implied revocation

Estoppel

Adverse possessor's state of mind

Four approaches (at least) exist to the adverse possessor's state of mind. The courts are sometimes less than clear about which test they have adopted. All are variations on the requirement of "adversity" or "hostility" and some courts are inconsistent about the requirements. It is useful to separate out four possible tests. They are: (1) an objective test based on *possession* (the rule in the vast majority of states); and subjective tests based on (2) a *claim of right*; (3) *intentional dispossession*; and (4) *good faith*. The first test makes the adverse possessor's state of mind irrelevant. The only thing that matters is the fact of *actual* possession, *i.e.*, that the adverse possessor *act* toward the land in a way that is characteristic of ownership. Her subjective attitude toward the land, her knowledge of whether she is using land technically owned by others, her statements about her ownership, if any, and her attitude about all this, are all irrelevant under this approach. Actual, exclusive, visible, continuous, nonpermissive possession of real property will give rise to adverse possession whether that occupation is knowing or mistaken.[59]

State of mind irrelevant

> [O]ne can take possession of land under a mistaken idea of the true boundary line and still acquire it by adverse possession. In other words, an adverse possessor can succeed in his claim even if he does not know he is occupying land not included in his deed or chain of title.[60]

This approach is the one adopted by the overwhelming majority of states.

Claim of right

Many courts state that the adverse possessor must allege a "claim of right" (not to be confused with "color of title").[61] A claim of right generally means that a possessor intends "to appropriate and use the land as his own

[56] *Williams v. Rogier*, 611 N.E.2d 189 (Ind. 1993), *disapproved of by Fraley v. Minger*, 829 N.E.2d 476 (Ind. 2005); 10-87 *Thompson on Real Property, Third Thomas Edition* §87.10.

[57] *See, e.g., Alford v. Alford*, 372 S.E.2d 389 (Va. 1988). However, other doctrines may be available to give the licensee rights to continued use or occupancy. Those doctrines include easement by estoppel and constructive trust, covered below in Chapter 5.

[58] Dale A. Whitman et al., *The Law of Property* §11.7, at 761-763 (4th ed. 2019).

[59] *Smith v. Tippett*, 569 A.2d 1186, 1190 (D.C. 1990); *Chaplin v. Sanders*, 676 P.2d 431 (Wash. 1984).

[60] *Petsch v. Widger*, 335 N.W.2d 254, 260 (Neb. 1983).

[61] *See* §4.2.7.

to the exclusion of all others."[62] In other words, the adverse possessor *acts* like an owner; this means that the possessor believes she is the owner and claims the land as her own. This claim of right need not be proven by statements of subjective intent. "That intention need not be expressed but may be implied by a claimant's conduct. Actual occupation, use, and improvement of the property by the claimant, as if he were in fact the owner, is conduct that can prove a claim of right."[63] In general, no evidence is needed about the adverse possessor's state of mind; actual possession raises the presumption that the adverse possessor is using the land as her own and, thus, claiming it as of right. In practice, the claim of right doctrine is usually the same as the objective test because the courts presume that a person who actually possesses property to the exclusion of the record owner believes the property to be her own and thus is acting under a claim of right.

Where "claim of right" may make a difference

On the other hand, in jurisdictions that require the adverse possessor to occupy under a "claim of right," adverse possession may not be established if there is evidence that the adverse possessor knew where the boundary was and, although possessing land beyond that border, never intended to claim it as her own. As one court noted, "the rule is well established that if the adverse claimant is under no misapprehension as to the location of the boundary line and does not occupy the land with the intent to own it, he will not be deemed to be an adverse possessor."[64] Similarly, if an adverse possessor testifies in court that she was not sure where the boundary was, and that she never had any intention of taking ownership over land that did not belong to her, the courts might similarly find a claim of right to be missing.[65] Although most courts equate the "claim of right" test with "actual possession," effectively making the adverse possessor's intent irrelevant, a small minority of jurisdictions will refuse to grant title by adverse possession if the evidence indicates that the adverse possessor expressed no interest in taking title to property that did not formally belong to her.[66]

Intentional dispossession

A third possible test would require evidence of *intentional dispossession.* Under this test, the adverse possessor must be aware that she is occupying property owned by someone else and must intend to oust or dispossess the title holder. This test differs from the claim of right test because it requires proof of intent to dispossess a rightful owner to obtain title by adverse possession (making this proof an element of the claim). In contrast, in the states that give the claim of right test independent force, they interpret the

[62] *Grappo v. Blanks*, 400 S.E.2d 168, 171 (Va. 1991).

[63] *Id.*

[64] *Petsch v. Widger*, 335 N.W.2d 254, 260 (Neb. 1983). *Accord, Mid-Valley Resources, Inc. v. Engelson*, 13 P.3d 118 (Or. Ct. App. 2000) (adversity presumed in cases of "pure mistake" but not present if the adverse possessor knows she is on another's property and does not show that she intended to take title away from the record owner).

[65] *See, e.g., Ellis v. Jansing*, 620 S.W.2d 569 (Tex. 1981) (holding that adverse possession could not be established where the adverse possessor "never claimed or intended to claim any property other than that described in his deed and he never intended to claim any property owned by the abutting property owner"). *Accord, Petsch v. Widger*, 335 N.W.2d 254 (Neb. 1983).

[66] *See Mannillo v. Gorski*, 241 A.2d 276 (N.J. Super. Ct. 1968), *rev'd*, 255 A.2d 258 (N.J. 1969) (mistaken encroachment cannot give rise to adverse possession); 10-87 *Thompson on Real Property, Third Thomas Edition* §87.10.

claim of right requirement to defeat the adverse possession if the rightful owner is able to prove that the adverse possessor never intended to claim what she did not already own. If the intentional dispossession test were adopted, a mistaken occupation of land would not give rise to an adverse possession. Some older cases adopted this approach, denying adverse possession when the encroachment was mistaken rather than intentional.[67] A few courts still may apply this rule in border cases, denying recovery if the adverse possessor testifies she never intended to take over property that did not rightly belong to her.[68] But the overwhelming majority of courts do not deny adverse possession merely because an owner testifies that her occupation of neighboring property was mistaken and not intended to appropriate property belonging to someone else.

Critique of intentional dispossession test

The intentional dispossession approach has been subjected to withering criticism because it protects the wrongdoer while failing to provide repose to the one who occupies land in good faith believing it belongs to her.[69] Although many states require a "claim of right," they tend to allow objective evidence of possession to satisfy the proof needed to show this, and they do not assume that adverse possessors win only if they know they are trespassing. To require a showing of knowing trespass seems perverse because it rewards wrongdoers while failing to protect innocent persons who have mistakenly occupied land belonging to another. This seems backward, from either the standpoint of morality or efficiency. "To limit the doctrine of adverse possession to the latter type places a premium on intentional wrongdoing, contrary to fundamental justice and policy."[70]

Good faith

On the other hand, a minority, but growing list, of states require the exact opposite of an intent to oust the title holder: They grant title by adverse possession only if the possession was in *good faith*. In these jurisdictions, only *innocent* possessors, those who *mistakenly* occupy property owned by someone else, can acquire ownership by adverse possession.[71]

[67] *McQueen v. Black*, 425 N.W.2d 203 (Mich. Ct. App. 1988); *Mannillo v. Gorski*, 241 A.2d 276 (N.J. Super. Ct. 1968), *rev'd*, 255 A.2d 258 (N.J. 1969); *Ellis v. Jansing*, 620 S.W.2d 569 (Tex. 1981). *But see Henson v. Boal*, 2009 WL 279336 (Mich. Ct. App. 2009) (an owner who occupies to a clear fence who believes in good faith it is the boundary has satisfied the adversity requirement); *Masonic Bldg. Ass'n of Houston v. McWhorter*, 177 S.W.3d 465 (Tex. Ct. App. 2005) (distinguishing *Ellis v. Jansing* and holding that construction of a fence that encroaches on neighboring property without permission is "adverse" even if the adverse possessor is not trying to appropriate land belonging to another).

[68] *Perry v. Heirs at Law and Distributees of Gadsden*, 449 S.E.2d 250 (S.C. 1994); *Brown v. Clemens*, 338 S.E.2d 338 (S.C. 1985). *See also Mid-Valley Resources, Inc. v. Engelson*, 13 P.3d 118 (Or. Ct. App. 2000) (adversity presumed in cases of "pure mistake" but not present if the adverse possessor knows she is on another's property and does not show that she intended to take title away from the record owner); *Wilcox v. Estate of Hines*, 849 N.W.2d 280 (Wis. 2014) (owners who thought a strip of land was not theirs but sought permission from someone who was not the true owner cannot establish adversity even though they occupied the property without permission of the actual owner).

[69] *Mannillo v. Gorski*, 255 A.2d 258 (N.J. 1969), *rev'g Mannillo v. Gorski*, 241 A.2d 276 (N.J. Super. Ct. 1968).

[70] *Smith v. Tippett*, 569 A.2d 1186, 1191 (D.C. 1990).

[71] *See, e.g.*, Alaska Stat. §09.45.052(a); Colo. Rev. Stat. §38-41-101(3)(b)(II); Fla. Stat. §95.18; Ga. Code §44-5-161; N.Y. Real Prop. Acts. §501; Or. Rev. Stat. §105.620(1)(b); N.M. Stat. §37-1-22; *see also Hurd v. Henley*, 478 P.3d 208, 219-221 (Alaska 2020) (interpreting Alaska's

Adopting this approach, the Iowa Supreme Court held that adverse possession doctrine "has no application to one who actually knows that he has no claim, or title, or right to a title."[72] One version of this test would place the burden of proof on the adverse possessor to demonstrate to the decision maker that she did not know she was possessing land belonging to another. An alternative version would allow the claim to be defeated if the title holder can come forward with evidence that the adverse possessor knew she was trespassing. And some states shorten the adverse possession period if possession is in good faith.[73]

▶ HARD CASE

▷ GOOD FAITH AS A COMPONENT OF LAW IN ACTION

Professor Richard Helmholz has argued that even though most states reject a good faith test, they *in fact* grant adverse possession only to good faith possessors. They do this, he claims, by manipulating the other elements of the test, such as the open and notorious, exclusivity, or continuity requirements.[74] Professor Roger Cunningham has rejected Helmholz's claim, arguing instead that the courts do not in fact require good faith to prevail.[75] Whoever is correct in this debate, it is clear that most courts have so far rejected the idea of adopting a good faith test as a formal element in adverse possession doctrine.[76] Should adverse possession be denied when there is evidence the adverse possessor knowingly trespassed?

Arguments for and against a good faith requirement

On the one hand, it seems both morally wrong and inefficient to reward wrongdoers with property rights; if possessors really value the property more than the title holder, they can offer the title holder enough money to induce her to sell. We naturally recoil from granting property rights to people who intentionally steal their neighbor's property by placing a fence in the wrong position to acquire ownership of some of the neighbor's property. On the other hand, an owner who does not object to such a fence may not even realize that she owns the land being occupied. If she does not object, she may even believe that is where the border is and setting the border at

requirement of good faith to mean subjective good faith); *Halpern v. Lacy Investment Corp.*, 379 S.E.2d 519 (Ga. 1989) (holding that those who knowingly occupy land of others are "trespassers" or "squatters" and cannot obtain title by adverse possession because they have not entered the land with a good faith claim of right); *Carpenter v. Ruperto*, 315 N.W.2d 782 (Iowa 1982) (no adverse possession because "claim of right" is essential element and it cannot be established if the adverse possessor knew she was possessing land she did not own).

[72] *Carpenter v. Ruperto*, 315 N.W.2d 782, 785 (Iowa 1982). *See also Halpern v. Lacy Investment Corp.*, 379 S.E.2d 519 (Ga. 1989).

[73] *Compare* La. Civ. Code arts. 3473 *and* 3475, *with* art. 3486 (ten-year period for prescription if possession in good faith and thirty-year period if not in good faith).

[74] Richard Helmholz, *Adverse Possession and Subjective Intent*, 61 Wash. U. L.Q. 331 (1983); Richard Helmholz, *More on Subjective Intent: A Response to Professor Cunningham*, 64 Wash. U. L.Q. 65 (1986).

[75] Roger Cunningham, *Adverse Possession and Subjective Intent: A Reply to Professor Helmholz*, 64 Wash. U. L.Q. 1 (1986); Roger A. Cunningham, *More on Adverse Possession: A Rejoinder to Professor Helmholz*, 64 Wash. U. L.Q. 1167 (1986).

[76] *See also Chaplin v. Sanders*, 676 P.2d 431 (Wash. 1984) (similarly rejecting a good faith requirement).

that location would seem to meet her expectations. Moreover, allowing good faith to become a crucial issue in adverse possession litigation would make the rule far less determinate and predictable than it is. Although much litigation exists about adverse possession claims, current law makes those cases more predictable by focusing on objective, observable evidence about long-standing use or possession. Making the case turn on what a party knew and when she knew it will make results depend more on the credibility of witnesses and do a great deal to undermine the purpose of adverse possession law, which is to give some stability to long-standing possessors of land.

Good faith and the statute of limitations

Although only a few states allow a showing of bad faith to defeat an adverse possession claim, a fair number have a shorter statute of limitations when the occupation is in good faith; these statutes generally also require payment of real estate taxes and/or color of title.[77] ◀

§4.2.6 For the Statutory Period

Statutory limitations on suits to recover possession of real property

The statutory period varies widely from state to state. The periods include five years (three states), seven years (four states), ten years (seventeen states), eleven years (one state), fifteen years (nine states), eighteen years (one state), twenty years (twelve states), twenty-one years (two states), thirty years (one state), and forty years (one state).[78] Some define different periods, depending on whether the adverse possessor has paid property taxes on the property in question or whether the adverse possessor has "color of title" or whether the occupation is in good faith.

Tolling due to disability

Many states will *toll* the statute of limitations if the title holder is under a *disability* such as infancy, insanity, or incompetence, either providing that

[77] *Compare* La. Civ. Code art. 3473 *with* art. 3475 (ten-year prescription period if in good faith and thirty-year period if occupation is in bad faith). *See also* 735 Ill. Comp. Stat. 5/13-101 (twenty years), 5/13-109 (seven years if good faith, payment of taxes and color of title); S.D. Codified Laws §15-3-1 (twenty years), §15-3-15 (ten years under color of title and made in good faith). Alaska (2003) and Colorado (2008) have joined the states requiring good faith. Alaska Stat. §09.45.052; Colo. Rev. Stat. §38-41-101(3)(b)(II).

[78] According to 10-87 *Thompson on Real Property, Third Thomas Edition* §87.01, the distribution of the general time limitation (not limitations applicable to special circumstances) is five years (two states—Cal. Civ. Proc. Code §§317-321; Mont. Code §§70-19-401 to -411), seven years (four states—Ark. Code §18-61-101; Fla. Stat. §§95.12, 14, 18; Tenn. Code §28-20-102; Utah Code §78B-2-214), ten years (seventeen states—Ala. Code §6-2-33; Alaska Stat. §09.01.030; Ariz. Rev. Stat. §12-526; Ind. Code §34-11-2-11; La. Civ. Code Ann. art. 3499; Miss. Code §§15-1-7, -13; Mo. Rev. Stat. §516.010; Neb. Rev. Stat. §25-202; N.M. Stat. §37-1-22; N.Y. Real Prop. Acts. §§501-551; Or. Rev. Stat. §12.050; R.I. Gen. Laws §34-7-1; S.C. Code §15-67-210, -220, -260; Tex. Code §16.026; Wash. Rev. Code §4.16.020; W. Va. Code §55-2-1; Wyo. Stat. §1-3-103); fifteen years (nine states—Conn. Gen. Stat. §52-575; Kan. Stat. §60-503; Ky. Rev. Stat. §413.010; Mich. Stat. §600.5801(4); Minn. Stat. §541.02; Nev. Rev. Stat. §40.090; Okla. Stat. tit. 12 §93; Vt. Code tit. 12 §501; Va. Code §8.01-236); eighteen years (one state—Colo. Rev. Stat. §38-41-101); twenty years (thirteen states—Del. Code tit. 10 §§7901, 7902; Ga. Stat. §44-5-163; Haw. Rev. Stat. §§675-31, -31.5; Idaho Code §5-203; Ill. Stat. ch., 5/13-101; Me. Rev. Stat. ch. 14 §801; Md. Cts. & Jud. Prac. Code §5-103; Mass. Gen. Laws ch. 260 §21; N.H. Rev. Stat. ch. 508 §2; N.C. Gen. Stat. §1-40; N.D. Cent. Code §28-01-08; S.D. Codified Laws §§15-3-1 to -10; Wis. Stat. §893.25); twenty-one years (two states—Ohio Rev. Code §2305.04; 42 Pa. Cons. Stat. §5530); thirty years (one state—N.J. Stat. §2A:14-30); forty years (one state—Iowa Code §614.31).

the statute begins running only after the disability ends[79] or shortening the limitations period once the disability is removed.[80] Some statutes provide a maximum period longer than the standard statute of limitations even if the disability has not terminated.[81]

§4.2.7 *Under Color of Title*

Defect in title

Color of title is "something usually in writing which, at face value, professes to pass title but which does not do it, either from want of title in the person making it or from the defective mode of conveyance that is used."[82] The defective title may lack a signature, contain mistaken "metes and bounds"[83] descriptions of the land, or have been procured by a faulty procedure, such as a sheriff's deed granted at a tax sale when the sheriff failed to follow statutorily mandated procedures. When color of title exists, courts may use the description in the title as conclusive evidence of the land area that is being adversely possessed. In such a case, color of title functions as fences do to help the court determine the boundaries of the land being claimed by adverse possession. In addition, a number of states apply a shorter statute of limitations to those who enter property under "color of title."[84]

§4.3 Justifications for Adverse Possession

Clarifying title

Judges and scholars have traditionally justified adverse possession by reference to two policies. They have suggested, first, that adverse possession law clarifies titles by eliminating stale claims, and second, that it encourages "active and efficient use of land."[85] The first justification is premised on the notion that possession may sometimes be a clearer, more determinate basis for resolving conflicting claims to land ownership than formal title.[86]

[79] Mont. Code §70-19-413.

[80] *Compare* N.D. Cent. Code §28-01-08 (twenty-year statute of limitations) *with* §28-01-14 (ten-year statute of limitations after the disability ceases).

[81] Or. Rev. Stat. §12.160 (statute suspended for up to five years during disability but the normal ten-year period cannot be extended longer than one year after disability ends).

[82] 10-87 *Thompson on Real Property, Third Thomas Edition* §87.12. *Accord Snook v. Bowers*, 12 P.3d 771, 780 (Alaska 2000) (good faith shown by "a written instrument which purports, but which may not be effective, to pass title" to the claimant).

[83] These are the "boundary lines of the land, with their terminal points and angles. A way of describing land by listing the compass directions and distances of the boundaries." *Black's Law Dictionary* 1012 (9th ed. 2009).

[84] *Compare* Tex. Code §16.026 (ten years if no color of title) *with* Tex. Code §16.025 (five years if cultivated, paid taxes, with registered deed) *and* Tex. Code §16.024 (three years if under color of title).

[85] *Stump v. Whibco*, 715 A.2d 1006 (N.J. Super. Ct. App. Div. 1998). *Accord*, 16-91 *Powell on Real Property* §91.01[4] (adverse possession "may help in the efficient allocation of our limited land resources by allowing the adverse possessor who has actually used the land to prevail over the record owner who did not assert ownership rights").

[86] Nadav Shoked, *Who Needs Adverse Possession?* 89 Fordham L. Rev. 2639 (2021) (arguing that adverse possession serves to remedy the unworkable aspects of our system of boundaries); Robert Cooter & Thomas Ulen, *Law and Economics* 154 (6th ed. 2012) (arguing that "a rule for acquiring title by adverse possession lowers the cost of establishing rightful

This might be true, for example, where two different deeds describe the same land. When a developer sells several parcels, the deeds will include physical metes and bounds descriptions of the land; if mistakes are made in surveying the land or writing the numbers, the deeds may describe parcels that overlap. Using the fact of physical possession to determine which deed is correct may be the easiest way to adjudicate disputes over title to the overlapping area.

Argument that adverse possession does not clarify title

On the other hand, a more determinate way to resolve such disputes may be to grant ownership to the title holder who recorded first. After all, the law of adverse possession generates huge amounts of litigation because the elements comprising the claim are not capable of exacting definition and require detailed attention to the facts of particular cases. Moreover, far more numerous cases involve border disputes where the adverse possessor does *not* have color of title to the disputed area, and in such cases, it is unconvincing to say that adverse possession law clarifies title. The truth is that it generates litigation. If one had to choose between title and possession, one would have to say that title is a clearer way to resolve such disputes than the law of adverse possession. Adverse possession settled boundary disputes before a working recording system was in place, but with both a recording system and the ability to use scientific surveying methods to fix the boundaries of property, it is almost always cheaper and more predictable to rely on the boundaries fixed in the record title than it is to conduct a lawsuit to determine whether the complicated and confusing elements of adverse possession have been met.

Title v. possession

Resolving disputes over ownership

Although adverse possession law is not the clearest way to resolve title disputes when title and possession diverge, it does promote clarity of a different kind. Although the adverse possessor does not have formal title, she may *feel* entitled to ownership if she has treated the land as hers for a long time and the title holder has effectively abandoned it. In such a case, even if there were a rigid rule granting ownership rights to the title holder, the possessor might have an incentive to litigate to try to challenge the title holder's claim. Whether or not their interpretation was correct, the courts have long based adverse possession law on statutes of limitation — statutes that the courts cannot simply ignore.

Protection of justified expectations

Moreover, the long-standing acceptance of adverse possession law, as well as numerous other equitable doctrines that affect title to land, suggests that formal title is often incompatible with established patterns of land use or with established expectations. It is simply a fact that long-standing possession gives rise to expectations and, given the title holder's failure to assert her rights, may be seen as creating justified expectations in the possessor. In such cases, even if the courts (or the legislature) announced that adverse possession would be henceforth abolished, it is certain that litigation about title will continue. Adverse possessors will invent new theories to justify recognizing their rights, and the courts are likely to be responsive to these

---

ownership claims by removing the risk that ownership will be disputed on the basis of the distant past"); Richard Epstein, *Past and Future: The Temporal Dimension in the Law of Property*, 64 Wash. U. L.Q. 667, 678 (1986) (adverse possession "spares the rightful owner the costs of litigation that might otherwise be needed to establish title").

demands. They will be responsive because it turns out that expectations are legitimately based not only on formal title, but on informal arrangements—possession being the foremost example. Titles are clarified not simply by developing a rule that cleanly and plainly answers the question of ownership when disputes arise but by granting rights to the person who all along thought she owned the land and who therefore is thought to be justifiably treated as the legal owner once the former title holder demonstrated a lack of interest in the land for such a long period of time that she effectively acquiesced in the occupation of her land by another.

Reliance and abandonment

All this suggests that adverse possession law is based less on a desire to clarify who owns the property than on a desire to grant ownership rights to the person who *thought* she was the owner and to strip those rights from the one who previously had formal title but did not act like an owner. Justice Oliver Wendell Holmes explained adverse possession by noting that a long-standing possessor has come to "shape[] his roots to his surroundings, and when the roots have grown to a certain size, cannot be displaced without cutting at his life."[87] This explanation rests on the desire to protect the settled expectations of the adverse possessor. Another way to put this is that adverse possession protects "the reliance interests that the possessor may have developed through long-standing possession of the property."[88] But how is adverse possession fair to the title holder? First, the title holder has acted in a way that gave the adverse possessor the impression that the land did not belong to the title holder. Adverse possession is established only if the title holder fails either to grant the adverse possessor permission or fails to oust the adverse possessor through a lawsuit claim for ejectment. The adverse possessor can win only if her possession was "in such tangible form that all those who are affected by it must be presumed to have acquiesced in it."[89]

Fungible and personal interests in property

Professor Margaret Jane Radin develops this argument by distinguishing between fungible and personal property: An object is "fungible" if "it is perfectly replaceable with money"; it is "personal" if it "has become bound up with the personhood of the holder and is no longer commensurate with money."[90] Radin argues that the adverse possessor's interest in the disputed strip, "initially fungible, becomes more and more personal as time passes."[91] On the other hand, "the titleholder's interest fades from personal to fungible and finally to nothingness."[92] When the title holder discovers that she owns a strip along the edge of her neighbor's land, she would regard recovery of the

[87] *Tioga Coal Co. v. Supermarkets General Corp.*, 546 A.2d 1, 5 (Pa. 1988) (quoting Holmes).

[88] Thomas Merrill, *Property Rules, Liability Rules, and Adverse Possession*, 79 Nw. U. L. Rev. 1122, 1131 (1984-1985). *See also* Richard A. Posner, *Savigny, Holmes, and the Law and Economics of Possession*, 86 Va. L. Rev. 535, 560 (2000) ("the adverse possessor may have relied on a reasonable belief that he is the true owner [and] made an investment that will be worthless if he loses the property to the original owner, to whom, however, the property may also be worthless, as indicated by his having 'slept' on his rights").

[89] 10-87 *Thompson on Real Property, Third Thomas Edition* §87.08.

[90] Margaret Jane Radin, *Time, Possession, and Alienation*, 64 Wash. U. L.Q. 739, 748 n.26 (1986).

[91] *Id.* at 739, 748-749.

[92] *Id.*

strip as an unexpected windfall like winning the lottery, while the adverse possessor would experience the loss as a deprivation of rights she thought she had. Radin explains that a "moral judgment" is required to determine when the "titleholder [is] detached enough and the adverse possessor attached enough to make the switch" in ownership rights.[93]

Promoting the efficient use of property

Granting title to the person who values it the most

The second traditional justification for adverse possession is that it promotes the socially beneficial use of land. Like Radin, Judge Richard Posner adds that the adverse possessor is likely to value the disputed strip more than the record title holder and that it would therefore increase the joint utility of the parties for title to be held by the one who values it the most, *i.e.*, the adverse possessor. Posner explains:

> Over time, a person becomes attached to property that he regards as his own, and the deprivation of the property would be wrenching. Over the same period of time, a person loses attachment to property that he regards as no longer his own, and so the restoration of the property would give him, therefore, only moderate pleasure. [94]

In other words, in terms of what economists describe as marginal utility of income, the benefits long-time adverse possessors might experience by keeping the property could outweigh the harm original owners might experience if not restored to land they have not occupied or been using. Stewart Sterk has similarly argued that the title holder has "demonstrated virtually no concern with the possessor's occupation"[95] and that the encroaching adverse possessor has shown by her actions that she values the strip more; it is therefore wealth-maximizing to transfer ownership to her.

Promoting efficient land use

Robert Cooter and Thomas Ulen adopt a different approach, arguing that adverse possession "prevents valuable resources from being left idle for long periods of time by specifying procedures for a productive user to take title from an unproductive user."[96] Those who do not use their property run the risk of losing that property to an adverse possessor.

Problems with the efficiency argument

These efficiency arguments seem either incomplete or wrong. If the adverse possessor really values the property more than the title holder, why not rely on private bargaining to correct the misallocation of resources? If the adverse possessor really values the strip more than the title holder, why shouldn't she *have* to offer the title holder enough money to induce the title holder to sell? After all, requiring a transaction will *test* the proposition that the adverse possessor is the most valued user. Sterk answers that the costs of strategic bargaining may discourage such a wealth-maximizing transaction. In a two-person bargaining situation, each party must guess what the other party's bottom line is — how much time she has to bargain and what price she is willing to pay or accept — and what bargaining strategy the

[93] *Id.*

[94] Richard Posner, *Economic Analysis of Law* §3.11, at 80-81 (9th ed. 2014). *See also* Robert C. Ellickson, *Adverse Possession and Perpetuities Law: Two Dents in the Libertarian Model of Property Rights*, 64 Wash. U. L.Q. 723 (1986).

[95] Stewart Sterk, *Neighbors in American Land Law*, 87 Colum. L. Rev. 55, 80 (1987).

[96] Robert Cooter & Thomas Ulen, *Law and Economics* 154 (6th ed. 2012).

other side will adopt. "If the costs of transmitting offers and counter-offers are high, the bargainer may find that his best strategy is to eschew bargaining altogether."[97] If the adverse possessor usually values the strip more, and the costs of bargaining may prevent a transfer from the title holder to the adverse possessor, then adverse possession doctrine promotes efficiency by vesting ownership in the adverse possessor.

Indeterminacy of efficiency analysis

As Sterk and others have noted, however, it is not a foregone conclusion that the adverse possessor places a higher value on the property than does the title holder. Determining who values the strip more may differ according to which side is required to buy the strip from the other.

> [T]he adverse possessor's offer price is likely to be lower, and may be much lower, than her asking price. The adverse possessor may not be able to come up with $10,000 in cash, or be willing to borrow $10,000 to buy the strip, but may be very willing to keep the strip rather than sell it to the title holder for the same price. Because of the difference between offer and asking prices, the result may differ depending on which party is declared the owner of the disputed strip.[98]

Under these circumstances, efficiency analysis is indeterminate. The most valued user varies depending on which baseline is chosen. In cases like this, other criteria are needed. Sterk, for example, argues that efficiency analysis must be supplemented by social norms about the proper relationships among neighbors.[99] The question then focuses on what social norms should be chosen.

Justified expectations

The best explanation for adverse possession is that it protects justified expectations. Protection of justified expectations, after all, is one of the core principles of any private property system.[100] The doctrine recognizes that expectations are, in fact, not based solely on formal documents of title, but on long-standing conduct, including possession. When actual conduct diverges from formal arrangements for a long enough period of time and everyone treats someone other than the title holder as the owner, then it would *upset* expectations — rather than *protect* them — to stick to formalities. The transfer of rights implemented by adverse possession law is justified both by the fact that expectations come from informal as well as formal arrangements and because the title holder has not acted toward the land as an owner would, effectively giving a signal to the adverse possessor that the title holder does not view it as her own. The failure to intervene, either to grant permission or eject the possessor, conveys a message to the adverse possessor that the formal title holder has abandoned the land. In the usual case of a border dispute, the title holder did not even know that she owned the land in question, so there is no sense of loss when she finds out that, lo and behold, she had title to land she did not even know about.

[97] Stewart Sterk, *Neighbors in American Land Law*, 87 Colum. L. Rev. 55, 72 (1987).

[98] Jack Beermann & Joseph William Singer, *Baseline Questions in Legal Reasoning: The Example of Property in Jobs*, 23 Ga. L. Rev. 911, 964-965 (1989).

[99] Stewart Sterk, *Neighbors in American Land Law*, 87 Colum. L. Rev. 55, 86-104 (1987).

[100] *See* Joseph William Singer, *Entitlement: The Paradoxes of Property* (2000).

The harder case to justify is the squatter. How can a system that protects property rights reward a knowing trespasser who intentionally trespasses and occupies neighboring land? Several reasons may justify granting title by adverse possession even if the adverse possessor knowingly occupied land belonging to another. First, the failure of the title holder to object might be understood as effective abandonment of the owner's rights, at least in relation to an adverse possessor.[101] An owner who cares so little about her property that she acquiesces in another, occupying it for many, many years conveys a message that she does not consider the property to be hers anymore. Finders generally become owners of abandoned goods. If an owner abandons her rights, it is not accurate to call the intentional trespasser a pirate or thief. After all, the doctrine requires the occupation to be open and notorious; a title holder who does not object to such an occupation may implicitly assent to it.[102]

The squatter

Abandonment

Second, one purpose of the adverse possession doctrine is to create security by encouraging owners to rely on existing practical arrangements that have persisted for a long time. Thus, the right of all owners generally to rely on actual use and occupation rather than formal title creates more security and predictability for all. Resting title on something as difficult to prove as good faith (how can we easily determine someone's state of mind?) will make property rights too unpredictable and generate even more litigation, making ownership less stable, certain, and predictable than it now is.

Security

Third, even if we view the land pirate as an immoral thief, one policy behind the statute of limitations is to give victims incentives to bring lawsuits within a reasonable time; when this is done, everyone has repose, knowing that she is not subject to lawsuits for actions undertaken long ago. The interest in repose is a strong one. Moreover, when the victim waits too long to vindicate her rights, this sends a message even to the intentional encroacher who will rely on the noninterference to develop expectations of continued access that may be morally justifiable. One can argue about the amount of time that is appropriate, but at some point, expectations become fixed. Consider that failing to allow time to create secure possessory rights in current possessors might have the result of authorizing ejectment actions by American Indian tribes ousting the current possessors of land that was illegally taken from them in the eighteenth and nineteenth centuries. There is a lot of land in the United States that was taken from Indian nations pursuant to procedures that would not pass current constitutional standards

Repose

American Indian land

[101] It is important to note that owners of real property are not generally entitled to "abandon" their property rights even by declaring that they wish to do so. They may "dedicate" their properties to public ownership but such dedication is not effective until it is accepted by public authorities. The reason for not allowing abandonment is that the property remains subject to regulatory laws, such as those designed to prevent toxic waste from being deposited on land, and tax laws, such that the property owner remains liable for property taxes.

[102] *See* Lawrence Berger, *Unification of the Doctrines of Adverse Possession and Practical Location in the Establishment of Boundaries*, 78 Neb. L. Rev. 1 (1998) (arguing that adverse possession law should be united with doctrines of estoppel, acquiescence, oral agreement, and other equitable doctrines that recognize informal means to set boundaries between two parcels); *cf.* Nadav Shoked, *Who Needs Adverse Possession?* 89 Fordham L. Rev. 2639 (2021) (highlighting the importance of adverse possession in boundary disputes).

and that did not conform to international law principles or established federal Indian law doctrines on the sanctity of tribal property. These tribal land claims are legitimate and have been recognized by the Supreme Court.[103] At the same time, long-standing occupation of land by non-Indians creates expectations in current possessors that have strong claims to protection, whatever their origin.[104]

Crystals and mud

It is often argued that property rights must be clearly delineated and ownership definitively established to protect the justified expectations of owners and to facilitate development and trade. If property rights are unclear, then we are not sure who the owner is, and thus not sure who has a right to do what with the land. We also cannot have trades if we do not know who is buying and who is selling. Professor Carol Rose has called property rules that fix rights *a priori* in a determinate fashion "crystals."[105] As she points out, however, many property rules take the form of "mud." Adverse possession, although workable in practice, does make ownership less easy to determine than a rule that would assign rights solely on the basis of formal title and priority of recording in the registry of deeds. Such standards may nonetheless be justified on the ground that rigid adherence to crystallized determinations of ownership may actually both upset settled expectations and increase the costs of land development by forcing multiple, costly surveys every time a new development occurs. Rules look good, Professor Rose argues, when we are in our planning mode, but when we adjudicate disputes, we see that legitimate interests can spring up despite the fact that individuals failed to follow those rules. We can rant and rave about formality, but it is often rational for human beings not to order their lives according to legal technicalities that may be both inefficient and harmful to neighborly relationships. Moreover, it is not the case that the formal title holder always looks completely innocent. Acquiescing in long-standing occupation of your land in which you have so little interest that you did not even know it belonged to you may legitimately constitute a form of abandonment, especially if you have stood by while someone else acted as the owner without objection from you for a period set by the legislature as sufficient to fix title in that person.

§4.4 Typical Cases

§4.4.1 *Color of Title*

Defect in the title

Cases involving color of title include situations in which the adverse possessor obtained ownership by way of a formal document (usually a

[103] *County of Oneida v. Oneida Indian Nation*, 470 U.S. 226 (1985).

[104] This does not mean that illegal possession of tribal land should leave the tribes without any current remedies. Indeed, the threat of eviction might be needed to induce the federal or state governments to settle cases involving such wrongful occupations. For an example of such litigation, consider the Oneida claim to land in New York state illegally seized from the Oneida Nation in the eighteenth century. *County of Oneida v. Oneida Indian Nation*, 470 U.S. 226 (1985). Fred Kaplan, *A High-Stakes Claim: Oneida Suit Seeks 250,000 Acres in Upstate New York*, Boston Globe, May 19, 1999, at A1.

[105] Carol Rose, *Crystals and Mud in Property Law*, 40 Stan. L. Rev. 577 (1988).

deed) believing that she was obtaining title to the land, but some defect in the deed itself or the process by which the deed was conferred makes the title technically defective and thus formally incapable of transferring title.[106] Examples include unsigned deeds, deeds with mistaken metes and bounds descriptions of boundaries, and sheriffs' deeds for land sold at public auction because of nonpayment of taxes that are defective because the sale did not comply with required procedures such as notice or timing.

The limits of formality

Title defects are serious. Both the statute of frauds and many other statutes, such as recording acts and wills statutes, regulate the transfer of property rights. They generally require formalities such as a writing of a particular kind and, in the case of wills, witnesses. The formalities are there for a reason: they help ensure that the document is not forged and they provide evidence of the grantor's intent to transfer her rights in the land. Compliance with formalities provides assurance to the buyer that she is getting what the seller purports to sell. The problem arises when, despite exhortations to follow the rules, and despite the widespread understanding that "ignorance of the law is no excuse," people do make mistakes. They fail to hire a lawyer to complete the transaction, or they make a mistake even if a lawyer is involved. When everyone ignores the mistake for many years, and everyone acts as if the transaction did what it seemed to do, it would upset expectations (rather than protect them) to insist on formalities.

The role of informality in establishing legitimate expectations

Suppose, for example, that a deed granted from a seller to the buyer is not signed by the seller and thus does not satisfy a basic formal requirement of the statute of frauds. When this is discovered 30 years later, expectations of everyone concerned will be upset if the courts were to hold that title belongs to the heirs of the original seller, rather than the buyer under that defective deed or a subsequent grantee of that buyer. The long-standing possession of the property and the acquiescence in that possession, form a basis for understanding property rights as having shifted rather than remained with the party that technically would otherwise retain title. The adverse possession doctrine recognizes that expectations are based not only on the formal documents and not only on compliance with technicalities, but on actual events. When everyone treats the property as having changed hands, it would upset expectations rather than protect them to stick to formalities. And because it is often stated that protection of justified expectations is a core value of property law, it may sometimes be appropriate to protect expectations based on the conduct of the parties and long-standing possession rather than to assume unrealistically that expectations are always based on formal expressions of title or contract.

§4.4.2 Border Disputes

Justified expectations

When a homeowner builds a fence, she may mistakenly place it several inches or even a foot or two onto neighboring property. She may do this because she failed to get a survey to determine the exact border line or because a survey was done incorrectly. She may have reached an oral

[106] *Anderson v. Jackson*, 338 So.3d 629, 642 (Miss. App. 2022).

agreement with her neighbor on where the border seemed to be. Or, even in the absence of agreement, the neighbor may not object to the placement of the fence on what is technically her own land because she also believes that this is where the boundary line is. If the fence is built and the owners act as if it is the border, and do so for many years, it would again upset expectations, rather than promote them, to allow a later owner to insist that the fence be moved when the mistake is discovered 30 years later.

Mutual mistake

Most disputes covered by the law of adverse possession are border disputes in which one owner places a fence, a driveway, or shrubbery a short distance over the line, thereby occupying the neighbor's property. These cases ordinarily are ones of mutual mistake. In such cases, the actual expectations of the parties are based on the arrangements on the ground rather than the different boundaries described in the deeds. The purpose of adverse possession in this context is to prevent upsetting expectations based on such possession.

§4.4.3 Squatters

Abandonment

Squatter cases involve knowing occupation of an entire parcel, or portion of a parcel, with the intent to use it as one's own. These are the hardest cases to justify from the standpoint of either morality or efficiency. Such occupants know they are trespassing and brazenly occupy land belonging to another. At the same time, such occupations are likely to occur only on land that is not being used by the title holder. This may be rural land,[107] or it may be urban land that has been effectively abandoned by the title holder. The law provides adequate remedies to the owner through ejectment, trespass suits, and even, in appropriate cases, self-help or calling the police. If the owner fails to intervene for many years, one might conclude that the "title holder" has abandoned his property rights. In this case, the adverse possession looks less like theft than first possession of unowned land. Even if the owner has not intended to abandon the land, she has sat by while others established homes or other possessory uses on her land. The title holder's failure to intervene, either by giving permission or ejecting the trespassers, conveys a silent message to them on which they come to rely more and more over the years. The title holder should not be surprised if the courts characterize the situation as effectuating an implicit transfer of rights.

▶ HARD CASE ▷ SQUATTERS IN PUBLICLY HELD PROPERTIES

In some large cities, groups of squatters have taken over buildings, improved them, and lived there for years. Often, such properties have been taken by the city for failure to pay property taxes, and, in such cases, the squatters generally do not obtain title by adverse possession under the doctrine that immunizes governmental bodies from loss of title through adverse possession. But should the city grant title to long-standing possessors of such

[107] *Nome 2000 v. Fagerstrom*, 799 P.2d 304 (Alaska 1990).

buildings? It might be argued that governments, especially, need to be protected from loss of title by adverse possession since the management of public lands is for the benefit of the whole community and not just individuals who are able to grab pieces of it. Moreover, the squatters may not be the neediest and the city might have different plans for development of the land that might be more in the interests of the community. On the other hand, once such squatters get settled and begin improvements, their reliance interests and desire for continued stability in their homes become relevant and the reasons for recognizing adverse possession come into play. The city's failure either to oust them or grant them rental agreements may fuel their belief that the city has effectively acquiesced in their occupation, tacitly recognizing their possession as lawful. One court has held that even if the time period for adverse possession has not passed (and even if adverse possession is not available because the land is government land), tenants who occupy property for a long period may be treated as tenants at-will entitled to statutory regulations requiring notice before termination of the tenancy and the use of court evictions proceedings rather than self-help.[108] ◀

§4.4.4 Co-tenants

Tenants in common and joint tenants

The last typical category of adverse possession cases involves co-owners. For example, a mother may leave the family house to her three daughters as joint tenants.[109] One of the daughters may choose to live in the house while the others live elsewhere. When one co-owner occupies a house jointly owned with others, it is not a rare event for the long-term occupant to claim that the owners out of possession have abandoned their rights and that the long-standing possessor should be entitled to sole ownership by adverse possession. The courts reject such claims. Because each daughter has the legal right to live in the house, acts of possession that otherwise might establish adverse possession will not do so. Occupation by one daughter is not wrongful; she is entitled to live there and thus does not need her sisters' permission to do so.

Ouster

The states seem to agree that no adverse possession can be established against a tenant in common or a joint tenant unless the tenant in possession "ousts" the tenants out of possession by both excluding them from the property and notifying them that the tenant in possession is asserting sole ownership rights. She will be entitled to claim 100 percent ownership (rather than a one-third divided interest in the property) only if she ousts her two sisters and effectively excludes them. This usually requires her to notify her sisters that they are being ousted. An explicit "ouster" is needed because occupation of the jointly owned property does not violate the property rights of the owners who are not living in or occupying the property. Each owner has the right to possess the whole and therefore no trespass is occurring and the remedy of ejectment is not available. Only when

[108] *City of New York v. Utsey*, 714 N.Y.S.2d 410 (App. Div. 2000).
[109] For an explanation of joint tenancy, see Chapter 8.

a co-owner entitled to possession is excluded from possession does the statute of limitations start running. Some courts recognize various forms of "constructive ouster," such as when the building is too small to house all the owners. This topic is covered below in §8.4.6.

§4.5 Procedures and Effects of Adverse Possession

§4.5.1 Level of Proof Required

Clear and convincing evidence

Preponderance of the evidence

Most courts hold that adverse possession must be proved by "clear and convincing evidence."[110] On the other hand, it is not uncommon to find courts applying the ordinary "preponderance of the evidence" standard.[111] In adopting the clear and convincing evidence standard, the West Virginia Supreme Court noted that the "function of a standard of proof is to instruct the factfinder concerning the degree of confidence our society thinks he [or she] should have in the correctness of a factual conclusion for a particular kind of adjudication."[112] The interest at stake in adverse possession cases is "not the mere loss of money as is the case in the normal civil proceedings. Rather, it often involves the loss of a homestead, a family farm or other property associated with traditional family and societal values."[113] One might respond to this argument by noting the interests gained by adverse possessors are equally likely to be family homesteads. Because the record title holder has effectively abandoned the disputed land and allowed it to be occupied by someone else, and that someone else is as likely as the record owner to have personal ties to the land, it is not clear why the interests of the title holder should be given greater protection than the interests of the actual possessor.

§4.5.2 Effect on Prior Encumbrances

Rights adverse possessors acquire

Some courts hold that adverse possessors generally obtain ownership rights subject to pre-existing liens, mortgages, easements, restrictive covenants, and mineral interests.[114] Unless the adverse possessor has acted in

[110] *Blankinship v. Payton*, 605 So. 2d 817 (Miss. 1992); *Dittmer v. Jacwin Farms, Inc.*, 637 N.Y.S.2d 785 (Sup. Ct. App. Div. 1996); *Locke v. O'Brien*, 610 A.2d 552 (R.I. 1992); *Brown v. Gobble*, 474 S.E.2d 489 (W. Va. 1996). *See also Harkins v. Fuller*, 652 A.2d 90 (Me. 1995); *Wanha v. Long*, 587 N.W.2d 531 (Neb. 1998); *Stump v. Whibco*, 715 A.2d 1006 (N.J. Super. Ct. App. Div. 1998) (all adopted a heightened burden of proof).

[111] *Moore v. Dudley*, 904 S.W.2d 496 (E.D. Mo. 1995); *Potlatch Corp. v. Hannegan*, 586 S.W.2d 256 (Ark. 1979); *Dugan v. Jensen*, 510 N.W.2d 313 (Neb. 1994); *Davis v. Konjicija*, 620 N.E.2d 1010 (Ohio 1993).

[112] *Brown v. Gobble*, 474 S.E.2d 489, 494 (W. Va. 1996).

[113] *Id.* at 494.

[114] *Stat-O-Matic Retirement Fund v. Assistance League of Yuma*, 941 P.2d 233 (Ariz. Ct. App. 1997) (statute of limitations for claim to recover property from an adverse possessor did not begin to run, as against deed of trust holders who acquired the property at a trustee's sale until the deed of trust holders gained a possessory right to the property by purchasing it at the sale); *Thornton v. Driscoll*, 2022 WL 4102263, at *5-*8 (Mass. Land Court, Sept. 8, 2022) (adverse possessor takes subject to mortgage); *Gustin v. Scheele*, 549 N.W.2d 135 (Neb. 1996).

a manner inconsistent with those interests, they have been held to persist. Some courts, however, hold that adverse possessors take the property free of some or all of these encumbrances.[115]

▷ MORTGAGES **HARD CASE ◀**

Consider the case of mortgages. When an adverse possessor occupies property for the statutory period, and thereby acquires title by adverse possession, is the new title subject to a prior mortgage on the land granted by the prior owner? Some courts hold that the mortgage is not destroyed by adverse possession. These states hold that a "stranger's adverse possession does not bar the mortgagee's rights to the property, with some cases limiting the application of this rule to situations where the adverse possession was initiated subsequent to the mortgage."[116] As the Nebraska Supreme Court noted, an adverse possessor does not acquire more than could have been acquired in conveyance from the original owner.[117] Moreover, adverse possession is not necessarily inconsistent with the mortgage owned by the bank. After all, only if the mortgage is not paid are the bank's legal rights violated and the bank entitled to bring legal action to foreclose on the property to satisfy the unpaid debt.

On the other hand, some courts hold that adverse possessors take property free of pre-existing mortgages. They hold that "a mortgagee takes no better title than the owner, and like the owner, is bound to take notice of any adverse possession claim being asserted at the time of the mortgage, with some cases making no distinction as to whether adverse possession preceded or followed the mortgage."[118] In *Fleming v. Watson*,[119] for example, the Alabama Supreme Court held that a purchaser of property at a foreclosure sale is on constructive notice of a competing claim if someone other than the mortgagor is in possession of the land. "Possession of the property to be sold at a foreclosure sale by one whose name does not appear on the mortgage document is an obvious fact which would lead an ordinarily prudent person to further inquiry, which inquiry would reveal the claimed interest of the possessor."[120] The court further argued that the "purchaser at a mortgage foreclosure sale should be in no better position than buyers in all situations who claim to be bona fide purchasers for value without notice of unascertainable defects or secret equities."[121] ◀

[115] 10-87 *Thompson on Real Property, Third Thomas Edition* §87.03.

[116] *Berryhill v. Moore*, 881 P.2d 1182, 1192 (Ariz. Ct. App. 1994).

[117] *Gustin v. Scheele*, 549 N.W.2d 135, 141 (Neb. 1996). Of course, even under this theory, if one has acted in a manner inconsistent with prior encumbrances so as to place the owner of those encumbrances on notice that an adverse claim is being made, they may be destroyed by adverse possession as well.

[118] 881 P.2d at 1192.

[119] 416 So. 2d 706 (Ala. 1982).

[120] *Id.* at 709.

[121] *Id.* at 710.

▶ HARD CASE ▷ FUTURE INTERESTS

Because adverse possession works only when the title holder has a right to claim possession of the property herself, it is generally held that adverse possession does not bar future interests in the property, at least in the majority of states that do not give holders of future interests the right to sue to eject trespassers.[122] However, it is a harder question whether future interest holders *should* be entitled to bring claims for trespass or ejectment against an adverse possessor before the statute of limitations has run even if they do not have current rights of possession. Although the adverse possession is not inconsistent with the rights of the future interest holder who has no current right to possession, the substitution of one present estate owner for another may affect the future interest holder's interests in the sense that any future disputes over whether the future interest is valid or has become possessory will conceivably involve a lawsuit with the adverse possessor rather than the original present estate owner. In addition, some states have statutes that grant adverse possessors a "full complete title," which might be interpreted as constituting fee simple title, free of future interests.[123] ◀

§4.6 Claims Against the Government

No adverse possession against the government

Courts generally hold that adverse possession claims cannot prevail against government property. Thus, those who possess or use public property can never acquire prescriptive rights in that property. The fact that the title holder is a government entity constitutes an absolute defense to an adverse possession claim in most states.[124] However, a significant number of states have limited or abolished governmental immunity from adverse possession.[125] Some states have abolished this rule by statute in whole or in part.[126] Some apply a longer statute of limitations to claims against state land.[127] Some exempt particular types of land, such as schools, from adverse possession claims.[128] Others have allowed adverse possession of state lands that are held for commercial rather than "governmental" or "public" uses. For example, in *American Trading Real Estate Properties, Inc. v. Town of Trumbull*,[129] the court held that a public entity is immune from adverse

[122] John G. Sprankling, *Understanding Property Law* §27.05[E], at 483 (5th ed. 2023); 10-87 *Thompson on Real Property, Third Thomas Edition* §87.18.

[123] Miss. Code §15-1-13 (granting the adverse possessor a "full and complete title"). *See also* N.D. Cent. Code §47-06-03 (granting the adverse possessor "title to real property").

[124] Dale A. Whitman et al., *The Law of Property* §11.7, at 748 (4th ed. 2019).

[125] Paula R. Latovick, *Adverse Possession Against the States: The Hornbooks Have It Wrong*, 29 U. Mich. J.L. Reform 939 (1996).

[126] *See* Ky. Rev. Stat. Ann. §413.150; N.C. Gen. Stat. §1-35; N.D. Cent. Code §28-01-01; Utah Code §78B-2-201; Wis. Stat. §893.29.

[127] N.D. Cent. Code §§28-01-01, 28-01-08; S.D. Codified Laws §§15-3-1 to -10, 15-3-4 (both requiring 40 years for state land and 20 years for private land).

[128] Paula R. Latovick, *Adverse Possession Against the States: The Hornbooks Have It Wrong*, 29 U. Mich. J.L. Reform 939, 952 (1996).

[129] 574 A.2d 796 (Conn. 1990).

possession only if the property is "held for public use."[130] If the property is not held for public use in a governmental capacity, for example, as a roadway, park, or government building, but is held in a proprietary capacity, then it may be lost through adverse possession.[131] Finally, in some states, estoppel can result in loss of state land.[132]

Federal lands

A 1986 federal statute allows adverse possession of federal lands in certain instances if a claimant has occupied the property for 20 years in good faith reliance on a claim or color of title and has either cultivated the land or constructed improvements.[133]

§4.7 Informal Transfers of Title to Settle Boundary Disputes

§4.7.1 Improving Trespasser

What happens when the statutory period for adverse possession has not yet run?

When an owner is mistaken about the location of a boundary, it may happen that she will construct a building, a fence or driveway, or a portion of a building, such as a porch or balcony, that intrudes on property belonging to another. If the intrusion lasts for the period defined in the statute of limitations, either adverse possession or a prescriptive easement may be acquired. But if the statute has not yet run, the courts face the task of determining whether to require the structure to be removed or, instead, to oversee a forced transfer of ownership rights in the land, with or without compensation by the party to whom the property is transferred.[134] Under the *relative hardship* doctrine, the court might allow the encroaching structure to remain, while forcing the owner of the land underneath it to sell that land for its fair market value to the builder who mistakenly encroached on the neighbor's land.[135] Some courts retain the older rule giving the owner of the land the power to order the structure removed.[136]

Removal

Forced sale or purchase

[130] *Id.* at 800. *Accord, Jarvis v. Gillespie*, 587 A.2d 981 (Vt. 1991).

[131] *City of Philadelphia v. Galdo*, 217 A.3d 811 (Pa. 2019) (adverse possession does not run against the state, but could run against a municipal government for land not dedicated to public use); *see also Devins v. Borough of Bogota*, 592 A.2d 199 (N.J. 1991); *Siejack v. City of Baltimore*, 313 A.2d 843 (N.J. 1974) (adverse possession applies to municipally owned property not dedicated to or used for a public purpose); *Eller Media Co. v. Bruckner Outdoor Signs, Inc.*, 753 N.Y.S.2d 28 (App. Div. 2002) (adverse possession granted against government property not held for a public purpose).

[132] *Daniell v. Sherrill*, 48 So. 2d 736 (Fla. 1950).

[133] 43 U.S.C. §1068.

[134] *Cf. Ward v. Ward*, 783 S.E.2d 873 (W. Va. 2016) (unjust enrichment for an owner to keep, without compensation, a cabin built on their land with permission).

[135] *See, e.g., Mannillo v. Gorski*, 255 A.2d 258, 264 (N.J. 1969) ("if the innocent trespasser of a small portion of land adjoining a boundary line cannot without great expense remove or eliminate the encroachment, or such removal or elimination is impractical or could be accomplished only with great hardship, the true owner may be forced to convey the land so occupied upon payment of the fair value thereof without regard to whether the true owner had notice of the encroachment at its inception"); *Hoffman v. Bob Law, Inc.*, 888 N.W.2d 569 (S.D. 2016); *Proctor v. Huntington*, 238 P.3d 1117 (Wash. 2010); *Somerville v. Jacobs*, 170 S.E.2d 805 (W. Va. 1969). *See* §2.4.1.

[136] *Rose Nulman Park Found. ex rel. Nulman v. Four Twenty Corp.*, 93 A.3d 25 (R.I. 2014).

§4.7.2 *Dedication*

Donation to the public

A dedication is a gratuitous transfer of real property from a private owner to a government entity such as a city. A valid dedication requires an *offer* by the owner of the property and an *acceptance* by the public. The offer consists of words or conduct on the part of the owner that demonstrate an intent to turn over the property to the public. The offer may be made by a written or oral statement from the owner. The courts may also find an implied offer by one who invites or merely permits the public to use her land for a long period of time. The acceptance may be made formally by passing a city council resolution or informally by taking over maintenance of the area or ceasing to collect property taxes on the parcel. Finally, just as an offer may be implied from the owner's long-standing acquiescence in public use, an acceptance may be implied from long and substantial public use, even absent governmental action.[137] Most courts take seriously the idea that the owner must express an intent to make a gift of the property to the public, whether this is expressed through an oral statement or by conduct evidencing an intent to make a gift; in addition, there must be clear evidence of acceptance by the municipality or state.[138] Some courts, however, have found dedication when the owner has objected to public use but has made no serious effort to stop that use. In *Gion v. City of Santa Cruz*,[139] for example, the California Supreme Court found that the owners of a private beach had "dedicated" their property to the public by acquiescing in long-standing public use; the owners' efforts to stop the use were "half-hearted and ineffectual." This opinion proved controversial, however, and was overturned by a subsequent California statute.[140]

§4.7.3 *Oral Agreement*

Informal understanding

Courts may uphold oral agreements between neighbors that set the boundary between their property if (1) both parties are uncertain where the true boundary lies, or a genuine dispute exists over the location of the boundary, (2) the parties can prove the existence of an agreement setting the boundary, and (3) the parties take (and/or relinquish) possession to the agreed line.[141] Many states also insist (4) that the parties live with the boundary for a substantial period of time, although generally less than required for adverse possession.[142] Such agreements appear to violate the statute of frauds that requires a writing to transfer interests in real property. The purpose of the statute of frauds is to avoid false claims by one owner that an

[137] Dale A. Whitman et al., *The Law of Property* §11.6, at 744-745 (4th ed. 2019).
[138] *General Auto Service Station v. Maniatis*, 765 N.E.2d 1176 (Ill. App. Ct. 2002).
[139] 465 P.2d 50 (Cal. 1970).
[140] *See* Cal. Civ. Code §§813, 1009.
[141] *Fogerty v. State*, 231 Cal. Rptr. 810 (Ct. App. 1986); *Shultz v. Johnson*, 654 So. 2d 567 (Fla. Dist. Ct. App. 1995); *Morrissey v. Haley*, 865 P.2d 961 (Idaho 1993); *Kendall v. Lowther*, 356 N.W.2d 181 (Iowa 1984); Lawrence Berger, *Unification of the Doctrines of Adverse Possession and Practical Location in the Establishment of Boundaries*, 78 Neb. L. Rev. 1, 7-11 (1999).
[142] *See, e.g.*, *Jones v. Rives*, 680 So. 2d 450 (Fla. Dist. Ct. App. 1996).

oral agreement occurred that, in fact, did not occur. On the other hand, owners violate the statute with great frequency. They fail to pay hundreds of dollars for a survey to ensure that they know where the border is and assume that oral agreement is sufficient. Insistence on strict compliance with the statute may both upset expectations and inefficiently induce owners to pay for wasteful surveys.

§4.7.4 *Acquiescence*

Long-standing acceptance

Even without an oral agreement, the courts may nonetheless recognize long-standing acquiescence by both neighbors in a common boundary.[143] "(1) [A]djoining owners (2) who occupy their respective tracts up to a clear and certain line (such as a fence), (3) which they mutually recognize and accept as the dividing line between their properties (4) for a long period of time, cannot thereafter claim that the boundary thus recognized is not the true boundary."[144] Acquiescence generally refers to tacit or passive acceptance rather than active agreement.[145] Silence in the face of another's use of one's land may constitute acquiescence;[146] however, some states require overt acts or words to demonstrate acquiescence.[147]

§4.7.5 *Estoppel*

Reasonable reliance on record title holder's representations or knowledge

A boundary may be established by estoppel when one owner "erroneously represents to the other that the boundary between them is located along a certain line [and] the second, in reliance on the representations, builds improvements which encroach on the true boundary or takes other detrimental actions."[148] The party who made the representations is then "estopped to deny them, and the boundary is in effect shifted accordingly."[149] Some states may find estoppel even when no explicit representation is made; they may infer a representation "from an owner's silence in the face of knowledge that his neighbor is building an encroaching structure."[150]

[143] *Tobin v. Stevens*, 251 Cal. Rptr. 587 (Ct. App. 1988); *James v. Griffin*, 626 N.W.2d 704 (N.D. 2001); *Mason v. Loveless*, 24 P.3d 997 (Utah Ct. App. 2001); Dale A. Whitman et al., *The Law of Property* §11.8, at 759 (4th ed. 2019).

[144] *Q-2 LLC v. Hughes*, 368 P.3d 86 (Utah 2016); *Tresemer v. Albuquerque Pub. Sch. Dist.*, 619 P.2d 819, 820 (N.M. 1980). *Accord*, *Huntington v. Riggs*, 862 N.E.2d 1263 (Ind. Ct. App. 2007); *Jedlicka v. Clemmer*, 677 A.2d 1232 (Pa. Super. Ct. 1996); *RHN Corp. v. Veibell*, 96 P.3d 935 (Utah 2004). *See also Sims v. Daker*, 303 P.3d 1231 (Idaho 2013) (boundary may be established by "agreement" even in the absence of a conversation when a fence has been constructed and both landowners treat it as the boundary between their properties).

[145] Lawrence Berger, *Unification of the Doctrines of Adverse Possession and Practical Location in the Establishment of Boundaries*, 78 Neb. L. Rev. 1, 11 (1999).

[146] *Ollinger v. Bennett*, 562 N.W.2d 167 (Iowa 1997).

[147] *Dobrinsky v. Waddell*, 599 N.E.2d 188 (Ill. App. Ct. 1992).

[148] Dale A. Whitman et al., *The Law of Property* §11.8, at 761-762 (4th ed. 2019).

[149] *Id.* at 762.

[150] *Id.*

§4.7.6 *Riparian Owners*

Accretion and avulsion

Special rules have developed to govern changes in borders of "riparian property" located on a river or other body of water. Slow changes in build-up of land caused by slow deposit of silt or sand on the border of the land (*accretion*) belong to the owner of the land whose borders are thus enlarged; gradual losses of land caused by *erosion* shrink the owner's land rights. However, very sudden changes caused by events such as earthquakes or floods (referred to as *avulsion*) are generally held not to change the borders of property.[151]

§4.8 Adverse Possession of Personal Property

Conversion, discovery, and demand rules

Like real property, personal property can be acquired by adverse possession. At least three different rules have developed in this context: (1) the *conversion* rule, (2) the *discovery* rule, and (3) the *demand* rule. The *conversion* rule starts the running of the statute of limitations when the property is wrongfully taken (converted) and the owner dispossessed of the property.[152] The leading case establishing the discovery rule is *O'Keeffe v. Snyder*.[153] In that case, the painter Georgia O'Keeffe sued a New York gallery owned by Barry Snyder to recover three paintings stolen from her and purchased for $35,000 by Snyder from a third party, Ulrich A. Frank, who had inherited them from his father. Snyder claimed that he had acquired title to the paintings by adverse possession under New Jersey's six-year statute of limitations. Snyder claimed that the six-year period started to run when the paintings were stolen. In contrast, O'Keeffe argued that she had not known where the paintings were after they were stolen and thus could not reasonably have made a demand to have the paintings returned. Because she had sued the possessor within six years of discovering where the paintings were, her claim should not be barred. The court agreed, noting that a thief can never acquire good title and that no one can acquire good title from a thief — even a bona fide purchaser who is unaware that the property was stolen will not ordinarily be able to retain ownership in a contest with the title holder.[154]

Stolen paintings

[151] John G. Sprankling, *Understanding Property Law* §31.05[B], at 542 (5th ed. 2023). *See Stop the Beach Renourishment, Inc. v. Fla. Dep't of Envtl. Prot.*, 560 U.S. 702 (2010); *Severance v. Patterson*, 370 S.W.3d 705 (Tex. 2012) (both applying the traditional rule that avulsion does not change property borders).

[152] *Songbyrd, Inc. v. Estate of Albert B. Grossman*, 23 F. Supp. 2d 219 (N.D.N.Y. 1998); *Vigilant Ins. Co. of America v. Housing Authority of the City of El Paso*, 660 N.E.2d 1121 (N.Y. 1995).

[153] 416 A.2d 862 (N.J. 1980). *See also Charash v. Oberlin College*, 14 F.3d 291 (6th Cir. 1994); *Autocephalous Greek-Orthodox Church of Cyprus v. Goldberg & Feldman Fine Arts, Inc.*, 717 F. Supp. 1374 (S.D. Ind. 1989) (all adopting the discovery rule). *See also* Tarquin Preziosi, *Applying a Strict Discovery Rule to Art Stolen in the Past*, 49 Hastings L.J. 225 (1997).

[154] An exception to this principle is contained in the Uniform Commercial Code, which provides that an owner who entrusts possession of goods to a merchant who deals in that kind of goods gives the merchant the power to transfer all the rights of the entruster to a buyer in

The court held that the statute of limitations for adverse possession would start to run only when the title holder discovers, or reasonably should have discovered, where the stolen personal property is located. This rule applies at least where the property has been subsequently purchased by a bona fide purchaser. Because the statute would start to run at the moment the owner *should* have discovered the location of the paintings, the court ruled that the owner must establish that she used *due diligence* to discover the location of the stolen works. California, for example, passed a statute that adopts the discovery rule, starting the running of the statute of limitations only when the location is discovered, although the courts seem to impose a requirement of reasonable diligence on the prior owner.[155]

Due diligence

Demand-and-refusal rule

In contrast to the discovery rule for adverse possession of personal property, the New York Court of Appeals has promulgated a "demand-and-refusal rule"—a rule that is rather more protective of the interests of the title holder.[156] In *Solomon R. Guggenheim Foundation v. Lubell*,[157] a Chagall gouache was stolen from the storeroom of the Guggenheim Museum in the late 1960s. However, the museum neither notified the police nor publicly announced the theft. The current possessor argued that the failure to attempt to recover the artwork meant that the museum's rights were barred by the three-year statute of limitations. The museum responded that this was a tactical decision "based upon its belief that to publicize the theft would succeed only in driving the gouache further underground and greatly diminishing the possibility that it would ever be recovered." The court rejected the discovery rule on the grounds that it was wrong to place a general obligation of due diligence on the title holder. Rather, the court held that "a cause of action for replevin"[158] against the good faith purchaser of a stolen chattel accrues when the title holder makes demand for return of the chattel and the person in possession of the chattel refuses to return it. Until demand is made and refused, possession of the stolen property by the good faith purchaser for value is "not considered wrongful."[159] The court explained that "our decision today is in part influenced by our recognition that New York enjoys a worldwide reputation as a preeminent cultural center. To place the burden of locating stolen artwork on the true owner and to foreclose the rights of that owner to recover its property if the burden is not met would, we believe, encourage illicit trafficking in stolen art."[160] This result would occur because "[t]hree years after the theft, any purchaser, good

---

the ordinary course of business, thereby vesting good title in the buyer as against the original owner. *See* U.C.C. §2-403(2).

[155] Cal. Civ. Proc. Code §338(c). *Jolly v. Eli Lilly & Co.*, 751 P.2d 923 (Cal. 1988) (a plaintiff is held to her actual knowledge as well as knowledge that could reasonably be discovered through investigation of sources open to her).

[156] Steven A. Bibas, *The Case Against Statutes of Limitations for Stolen Art*, 103 Yale L.J. 2437 (1994).

[157] 569 N.E.2d 426 (N.Y. 1991).

[158] Replevin is an action to recover possession of personal property, similar to an ejectment claim to recover possession of real property.

[159] 569 N.E.2d at 429.

[160] *Id.* at 431.

faith or not, would be able to hold onto stolen art work unless the true owner was able to establish that it had undertaken a reasonable search for the missing art. This shifting of the burden onto the wronged owner is inappropriate. In our opinion, the better rule gives the owner relatively greater protection and places the burden of investigating the provenance of a work of art on the potential purchaser."[161] The court qualified its ruling by noting that, after the demand is made and the refusal is communicated, the owner may not delay unreasonably in bringing suit to reclaim the property and that if the owner unreasonably delays, the suit might be barred by the equitable doctrine of *laches*.

▶ HARD CASE ▷ STOLEN ARTWORKS

Stolen artwork is a major problem. Recently, attention has focused on artworks confiscated by the Nazis from Jewish families during World War II.[162] Some of these works were subsequently sold and purchased by good faith buyers. Others were donated to museums. In either case, disputes have arisen between current possessors and the heirs of the original owners over ownership of the works. In most cases, these disputes are between two innocent victims of the criminal conduct of a third party.[163] Some states start the running of the statute of limitations when possession is acquired, whether or not it was acquired in good faith.[164] This approach might be justified because of the interest in repose for that possessor. In addition, display of the work in the museum should be sufficient to satisfy the "open and notorious" requirement. On the other side, is the argument that many works are not displayed, and that even if they are displayed, this may not be sufficiently "open and notorious" as to place the owner on reasonable notice of the location of the painting. The question is how much of an obligation should be placed on the heirs to locate the painting. Moreover, one can argue that theft cannot convey good title, and that, as between the original owner (or her heirs) and the defrauded buyer, the original owner should prevail, especially when the art was taken pursuant to racially motivated policies and the retention of ownership by the museum would allow it to benefit from those policies.

In 2016, Congress weighed into this debate when it passed the *Holocaust Expropriated Art Recovery Act (HEAR Act)*, seeking to address

[161] *Id.*

[162] Howard J. Trienens, *Landscape with Smokestacks: The Case of the Allegedly Plundered Degas* (2000); Ralph E. Lerner, *The Nazi Art Theft Problem and the Role of the Museum: A Proposed Solution to Disputes over Title*, 31 N.Y.U. J. Int'l L. & Pol. 15 (1998).

[163] Ashton Hawkins, Richard A. Rothman & David Goldstein, *A Tale of Two Innocents: Creating an Equitable Balance Between the Rights of Former Owners and Good Faith Purchasers of Stolen Art*, 64 Fordham L. Rev. 49 (1995); Alexandre A. Montagu, *Recent Cases on the Recovery of Stolen Art—The Tug of War Between Owners and Good Faith Purchasers Continues*, 18 Colum.-VLA J.L. & Arts 75 (1993).

[164] Lerner, *The Nazi Art Theft Problem*, 31 N.Y.U. J. Int'l L. & Pol. at 19-20.

what it saw as the challenge of legitimate claims to recover art looted by the Nazis not being heard substantively in court largely because of state statutes of limitations.[165] Congress sought to make it easier for claimants to overcome timeliness challenges, instituting a nationwide six-year limitations period that runs from the time a claimant has "actual knowledge" of the relevant facts,[166] allowing a claimant time to sue the current possessor of a work of looted art once the claimant becomes aware of the identity and location of a work lost during the Holocaust, and its claim to the work.[167] ◀

[165] Simon J. Frankel & Sari Sharoni, *Navigating the Ambiguities and Uncertainties of the Holocaust Expropriated Art Recovery Act of 2016*, 42 Colum. J.L. & Arts 157 (2019).

[166] In relevant part, the *HEAR Act* provides that: Notwithstanding any other provision of Federal or State law or any defense at law relating to the passage of time . . . a civil claim or cause of action against a defendant to recover any artwork or other property that was lost during the covered period because of Nazi persecution may be commenced not later than 6 years after the actual discovery by the claimant or the agent of the claimant of—(1) the identity and location of the artwork or other property; and (2) a possessory interest of the claimant in the artwork or other property. *Holocaust Expropriated Art Recovery Act of 2016*, Pub. L. No. 114-308, §5(a), 130 Stat. 1524 (codified at 22 U.S.C. §1621 Note).

[167] Simon J. Frankel & Sari Sharoni, *Navigating the Ambiguities and Uncertainties of the Holocaust Expropriated Art Recovery Act of 2016*, 42 Colum. J.L. & Arts 157, 167 (2019); *see, e.g., Cassirer v. Thyssen-Bornemisza Collection Foundation*, 862 F.3d 951, 960 (9th Cir. 2017) (family sued a collection for the return of a Camille Pissarro painting forcibly sold during World War II and allowed to file claim within five years of actual discovery).

CHAPTER 5

Licenses and Easements

§5.1 Introduction
§5.2 Licenses
§5.3 Express Easements
    §5.3.1 Formal Requirements to Create
    §5.3.2 Substantive Limitations
    §5.3.3 Running with the Land (Appurtenant v. In Gross)
    §5.3.4 Scope, Location, and Extension of Appurtenant Easements
    §5.3.5 Scope and Apportionment of Easements in Gross
§5.4 Implied Easements
    §5.4.1 Easement by Estoppel
    §5.4.2 Constructive Trust
    §5.4.3 Implied from Prior Use
    §5.4.4 Necessity
§5.5 Prescriptive Easements
§5.6 Terminating Easements

§5.1 Introduction

Licenses

Owners often let others come onto their property. When they do this, they waive their right to exclude the non-owners they have invited in and simultaneously exercise their privilege to admit others to the property. These permissive entries are of various types. The most common are temporary invitations called *licenses*. When you invite friends over for dinner, you grant them a license to enter your house or apartment. When you enter a store, you do so on the basis of an implied license. When you go to your job, your employer has waived the right to exclude you from the premises and granted you privileged access to the property. Consent is a defense to a trespass claim and thus a licensee who enters property held by another with the owner's permission does not commit a trespass unless she refuses to leave after permission is revoked.[1] Licenses, as permissible entries to land, are generally revocable by the owner. Consent can be given, and consent can be revoked. There are, of course, exceptions to this rule, as we shall see.

Generally revocable at will

Easements

Sometimes owners grant non-owners more permanent rights of access to the owner's property. An owner might, for example, grant to someone else the right to pass over the owner's land, perhaps by allowing her neighbor to use the owner's driveway to get to a public road. This kind of right is often called a *right-of-way*. Or an owner may grant a cable television company the right to string cables on poles across her land or in pipes under the earth. Rights to do specific acts on land owned by someone else are called *easements*. Easements differ from licenses because they are usually intended to be permanent, or at least to last for a specified period, and thus are not revocable at the will of the owner of the land over which the easement passes. They also fall short of granting full possession of the land, instead granting only the right to perform specific acts. When an owner grants *possession* of the land to another, by selling the property outright or leasing the property to a tenant, the new possessor generally is entitled to do whatever she wants with the property, unless the agreement provides to the contrary. In the case of a leasehold, the license is irrevocable during the course of the lease unless the lease agreement (contract) is breached by the tenant. In contrast, rights short of possession involve entitlements to perform specific acts; like sales or leases, however, they may be intended to be permanent or irrevocable for a specified period of time. Easements are usually created by a deed granted by the owner of the burdened land to the easement owner; such easements can be bought and sold. They are usually, but not always, granted to owners of neighboring or nearby land.

Distinguished from licenses

Distinguished from leases

Affirmative and negative easements

A right to do something on someone else's land is usually created in the form of an *affirmative easement* (also called a "positive" easement).

[1] A trespass may also sometimes be found when the licensee exceeds the scope of the permission and conducts activities on the property other than those for which she was given permission. *See, e.g., Food Lion v. Capital Cities/ABC, Inc.*, 194 F.3d 505 (4th Cir. 1999) (employee who was really an investigative reporter committed a trespass by engaging in activities on the property that went beyond the scope of the employer's invitation). *But see Desnick v. ABC, Inc.*, 44 F.3d 1345 (7th Cir. 1995) (holding that investigative reporters did not commit a trespass by exceeding the scope of the implied invitation).

In contrast, rather than allowing someone else to do something on your own land, you might agree not to do something on your own land. Such an arrangement is either a *negative easement* or a *restrictive covenant*. The law of easements developed historically before the law of covenants. Easements, whether positive or negative, were considered to be property rights and one could be said to "own" an easement. The courts limited the number and kind of easements that could be created to prevent land from being burdened with obsolete or intrusive impediments to use or development. In response, owners of estates in land began to make contractual agreements by which they agreed to restrict the use of their own land for the benefit of either their landlord or neighboring owners. These agreements were called "covenants," and the courts developed a set of rules for covenants that differed from the rules that applied to easements. Like easements, covenants can be affirmative or negative. Most covenants are negative or *restrictive*, limiting the uses to which land can be put. Some, however, are affirmative in the sense that they describe promises by an owner to perform certain actions on her own land for the benefit of her neighbors. A duty to do something on your own land to benefit other owners is usually created in the form of an *affirmative covenant*.

Affirmative and restrictive covenants

To recap: A right to do something on someone else's land is an affirmative easement. A right to prevent others from doing something on their own land is either a negative easement or a restrictive covenant. And a duty to do something on your own land for the benefit of others is usually an affirmative covenant.

Recap

We have come to use the general term "*servitudes*" to describe the various nonpossessory interests individuals can have in land belonging to someone else.[2] The main types of servitudes are easements and covenants.[3] Most servitudes are intended to "run with the land." This means that the rights in someone else's land are attached to ownership of another parcel; the servitude is "*appurtenant*" to ownership of a "*dominant estate*" whose owner benefits from the use of the servitude on the "*servient estate*" (the land burdened by the servitude). When a servitude "runs with the land," the rights encompassed by the servitude will continue to exist even if the parcels burdened and benefited by the easement are sold. Historically, the law of easements developed before the law of covenants. When the courts began to restrict the ability of owners to create new easements, landowners (or their lawyers) ingeniously invented the idea of contracting to limit or regulate land use, thus creating the law of *real covenants*. When technical and substantive rules limited the ability of owners to create or enforce such covenants, the equity courts extended enforcement of covenants by developing the law of *equitable servitudes*. Covenants and equitable servitudes

Servitudes

[2] *See Restatement (Third) of the Law (Servitudes)* §1.1 (2000). Servitudes are not the only kinds of nonpossessory interests one can own in land belonging to others. Mortgages, for example, and other kinds of security interests are an example of another class of interest one can possess in someone else's land.

[3] "Profits" or "*profits à prendre*" are easements that encompass the right to remove materials, such as lumber or minerals, from land belonging to another.

are the subject of the next chapter. This chapter will focus on licenses and easements.

Issues Several issues are prominent in the law of licenses and easements. The first question is whether a permitted use of land is intended to be *temporary* or *permanent.* **Revocable or permanent** Temporary permissions (licenses) are generally intended to be revocable at will by the owner who granted the permission. Easements, on the other hand, are generally not revocable at the will of the grantor and may be intended to be permanent, or at least to last for a specified period of time.

Creation Second, which acts or expressions of intent are sufficient to create easements in the first place? In general, as interests in land, the various state statutes of frauds require easements to be created by a formal writing. **Formality v. informality** However, a number of important rules allow easements to be enforced even in the absence of a writing, or in the face of a writing that does not include the terms of the easement. **Express v. implied** While most easements are formally created by *express agreement,* oral easements are enforceable in certain circumstances, and some easements are *implied* by conduct or informal circumstances.

Scope Third, conflicts arise over the *scope* of the permitted use. For example, when an owner grants a telephone company the right to erect telephone poles on her land to string telephone wires between them, does the telephone company also have the right to string cable television wires on those same poles? Conflicts over the scope of easements arise over both the *kind* of use allowed and the *intensity* of that use.

Relocation Fourth, does the owner of the easement have the right to determine its location or even relocate it? Conversely, can the owner of the "servient estate" (the land over which the easement passes) relocate the easement in another place over the objections of the easement owner?

Transferability Fifth, when are easements transferable? If the telephone company has the right to lay cable television wires as well as telephone wires over its poles, does it also have the right to sell to another company the right to place such lines on those poles?

Running with the land Sixth, can the easement be owned by anyone who wishes to buy it, or is the easement intended to benefit whoever happens to own the neighboring (or nearby) land? An easement to use a driveway, for example, might be intended to allow a particular individual to use the driveway to cross from one street to another. If that easement is transferable by itself, its ownership can move from person to person (an *easement in gross*) even if ownership of the underlying land does not change. On the other hand, if the easement is intended to allow the owner to get to the neighboring land, the owner who created the easement may have intended that it belong to whoever owns the land that was to benefit from the easement. In such cases, the easement is *appurtenant* to a particular parcel (or parcels) of land and ownership *runs with the land* belonging to whoever owns the *dominant estate* (the parcel benefited by the easement). Conversely, such an easement is likely to be intended to persist even if the property over which the easement passes (the *servient estate*) is sold; if so, the burden of the easement passes with ownership of the land over which it passes.

Termination Seventh, we need to know when, if ever, the easement will terminate. Do changed conditions in the neighborhood or in the surrounding property affect their viability? Can an easement be abandoned and, if so, which acts are sufficient to indicate an intent to abandon?

Interpretation and regulation

Finally, although many issues about easements concern the task of *interpreting* what rights the grantor intended to create when the easement was first granted, there is also a significant amount of *regulation* of easements, through both common law and legislation, which limits the kinds of easements that can be created. Both easements and covenants may benefit owners and the public by allowing the creation of specially tailored bundles of property rights attuned to the needs and interests of particular owners. Allowing owners to freely contract to create servitudes may therefore promote both autonomy and efficiency. On the other hand, the multiplication of servitudes may increase the costs of getting rid of burdens on the land that no longer serve their original purpose or that have come to be seen as obstacles to desirable redevelopment or changes in use of the land. If transaction costs block the reconsolidation of rights, the multiplication of easements may infringe on, rather than promote, both autonomy and efficiency.

Promoting alienability

Regulation of servitudes is necessary for a variety of reasons. First, it may be desirable to free land from obsolete or unduly restrictive limitations on land use or development. Without such regulatory rules, a few owners or even a single owner could effectively veto land use changes in the neighborhood. Such concentrations of power over neighboring owners may both interfere with the legitimate interests of owners in controlling their own land and prevent desirable development. Regulation of servitudes is therefore sometimes justified by both justice and utility, or both rights and efficiency considerations. Limitations on the ability to create or enforce servitudes may promote the alienability of the land, allowing it to transfer to other owners and to be used for new purposes. Promotion of alienability may serve autonomy because it allows owners to move and to change their activities on the land without undue interference. It may also promote efficiency by allocating resources to those who value them most. On the other hand, rules of law that destroy servitudes that seem either obsolete or unduly restrictive on land use or development do so over the objections of the owners of those servitudes. This may be justified where the interests of servient estate owners in free use of their land (or social interests in real estate development) are more important than the interests of servitude owners in continued secure enjoyment of their rights. But it may not be justified, precisely because termination of obsolete servitudes effectuates a forced transfer of property rights from those who benefit from the servitudes to those who are burdened by them. Servitudes therefore raise interesting and complex issues about the relations between change and stability in property law and between the goal of granting owners freedom to use their land as they like versus the goal of allowing owners to agree to complex land use restrictions and to multiple owners of interests in particular parcels.

Stability v. change

Disaggregation v. consolidation

By allowing interests short of full possession to be created, the law promotes the ability of owners to disaggregate the sticks in the bundle of ownership rights among different persons. The ability to do this may promote the alienability of property both because it allows the creation of

Alienability

rights short of possession or transfer of title and because owners may be more likely to part with ownership if they know they can affect the uses to which the land being sold is put. At the same time, the ability to freely agree (or contract) for specific allocations of property entitlements may have the effect of burdening property with numerous encumbrances; when this happens, transaction costs may prevent the owners from rebundling these entitlements together in ways that would maximize the value of the land and best satisfy human needs. To promote the ability to use land without undue interference and its relatively free ability to be exchanged in market transactions (its "alienability"), it may be appropriate to consolidate ownership rights in a particular person (the "owner"). To do this, the law sometimes limits the extent to which owners are allowed to disaggregate property rights among a number of persons. Consolidation of rights in owners may both promote the autonomy of the owner and social welfare. The law therefore adopts a balance between the goal of consolidating powers over property in owners entitled to use or develop them and the goal of allowing owners to divide property rights by contract among multiple owners.

§5.2 Licenses

Informal creation

Licenses are usually created informally. Some are created by oral statements, such as when you invite your friends for dinner. Others are implied; when you open a shop, you impliedly invite the public to enter the store to purchase the goods you have to sell.

Formal creation

Sometimes, however, licenses are created formally by written grant or agreement. In such cases, it is often necessary to determine whether the interest should be interpreted as license or as something else, such as an easement or a lease or a covenant.

Revocable

Licenses are generally revocable.[4] For example, in *Commonwealth v. Lapon*,[5] a customer at a grocery store tried but failed to convince the store manager that he was entitled to a free bottle of detergent. When he refused to leave, the manager called the police who removed the patron and charged him with criminal trespass. The court held that the store was entitled to revoke its implied license to enter the premises.[6] Licenses, however, are deemed irrevocable in certain circumstances. If the licensee invests substantially in reasonable reliance on the license, the courts may grant the licensee an easement by estoppel.[7] Licenses may be held irrevocable because they are interpreted to be leases or covenants rather than licenses. In addition, a public accommodation may have a common law or statutory duty not to revoke a license if its reasons are discriminatory.[8]

[4] *Astemborski v. Manetta*, 988 N.W.2d 857, 866 (Mich. App. 2022) (oral permission to store boat on lake shore was a license and terminated with sale of lakefront land).
[5] 554 N.E.2d 1225 (Mass. App. Ct. 1990).
[6] *See also Alexis v. McDonald's Restaurants of Massachusetts, Inc.*, 67 F.3d 341, 350 (1st Cir. 1995) (implied license to enter restaurant can be revoked).
[7] *See* §5.4.1.
[8] *See* §2.2.3.

▷ LICENSE v. EASEMENT **HARD CASE ◀**

In *Wilson v. Owen*,[9] a developer granted homeowners purchasing homes in the subdivision the "privilege" to use two lakes for swimming, boating, and fishing purposes. The deeds contained a variety of restrictive covenants limiting the use of the land and gave the homeowners' association, comprised of all the owners, the power to alter the covenants. When most of the owners voted to revoke the privilege of the owners to use the lakes for recreational purposes, some of the owners sued, claiming that they owned permanent easements of access to the lakes. The association argued that the "privilege" to use the lakes was a mere license revocable by the association. Alternatively, it argued that it was a "covenant" because it appeared as #8 in a list of "restrictions" on use of the conveyed land. Because the association had the power to amend the restrictions, it could revoke the access rights.

The argument for finding an easement

The court rejected the association's argument, holding that the association could amend "restrictions" on land use but that it could not revoke "privileges" conferred by the deeds. The court held that the privilege to use the lakes was not merely a revocable license but a permanent easement. In interpreting the word "privilege" to mean a permanent easement rather than a revocable privilege, Judge Conkling explained that "surrounding circumstances" might be considered to determine whether the parties intended to create an easement or a license where "the meaning is in doubt."[10] Because sales brochures and newspaper advertisements represented that owners in the subdivision would have exclusive rights to use the lakes, the buyers legitimately expected those rights to be permanent easements associated with ownership of the lots.

The argument for finding a license

A counterargument would be that easements are normally created by language that clearly expresses the fact that an irrevocable right is being created. This is normally done either by using the word "easement" or by otherwise making clear that the privilege is intended to be irrevocable. Neither of these was the case here. Easements constitute burdens on land that may impede their alienability, as well as their ability to be shifted to alternative uses. Owners retain whatever rights are not given away. It could be argued that unless the original conveyances clearly indicated that permanent easements were created, the owner of the burdened land, acting through the homeowners' association, should be presumed to have the power to revoke the privilege.[11] ◀

License v. lease

Many disputes concern the question of whether an arrangement constitutes a license or a lease. This issue arises in the context of department

[9] 261 S.W.2d 19 (Mo. 1953).

[10] *Id.* at 23.

[11] *See also, e.g., Dalliance Real Estate, Inc. v. Covert*, 1 N.E.3d 850 (Ct. App. Ohio 2013) ("license agreement" created a "perpetual right" to use a driveway and was thus an easement); *Markstein v. Countryside I, L.L.C.*, 77 P.3d 389, 399-400 (Wyo. 2003) (noting that in discerning a license from an easement, "the intent of the parties to the agreement is controlling," and finding that a "Fishing License Agreement" created an easement).

store concessions,[12] students living in college dormitories,[13] camp directors,[14] apartment complex managers[15] and migrant farm workers,[16] and rights to place signs on billboards or monuments.[17] These cases are generally decided by asking whether the owner has transferred exclusive "possession" of a defined space; if so, a lease will be found. If control of a particular space is not granted, or such possession is not exclusive, a license is likely to be found.[18]

§5.3 Express Easements

§5.3.1 *Formal Requirements to Create*

Writing

Easements are ordinarily created by agreement of the parties. Because easements are conceptualized as interests in land, the various state statutes of fraud require them to be in writing to be enforceable. An owner of land can grant an easement over her land to another by means of a deed. Easements are also created in the course of selling or transferring ownership or possession of the land itself. For example, a developer of a subdivision might convey a parcel to a buyer and include in the deed a grant of an easement over remaining land of the grantor. Similarly, a landlord may include in a lease agreement a clause granting the tenant both possession of the apartment and the right to use the backyard behind the apartment building for recreational purposes. Exceptions to the writing requirement, however, are significant. This chapter will address prescriptive easements, as well as easements by estoppel, implication, necessity, and constructive trusts below.[19]

Exceptions

Easements reserved in third parties

Many states hold that an owner may not transfer a parcel of property to one person while reserving an easement over the buyer's property in a third party.[20] For example, *O* may try to transfer a parcel of land to *A* while

[12] *Layton v. A.I. Namm & Sons*, 89 N.Y.S.2d 72 (App. Div. 1949), *aff'd*, 98 N.E.2d 590 (N.Y. 1951).

[13] *Compare Rhaney v. University of Maryland, Eastern Shores*, 880 A.2d 357, 367 (Md. 2005); *Burch v. University of Kansas*, 756 P.2d 431 (Kan. 1988); *Green v. Dormitory Authority of the State of New York*, 577 N.Y.S.2d 675 (App. Div. 1991) (all holding that students are "tenants"), *with Houle v. Adams State College*, 547 P.2d 926 (Colo. 1976); *Cook v. University Plaza*, 427 N.E.2d 405 (Ill. App. Ct. 1981) (holding that they are not).

[14] *Uthus v. Valley Mill Camp, Inc.*, 246 A.3d 1225 (Md. 2021) (camp director residing at the camp a licensee not a tenant).

[15] *Compare GENC Realty LLC v. Nezaj*, 860 N.Y.S.2d 106 (App. Div. Ct. 2008) *and Chan v. Antepenko*, 250 Cal. Rptr. 851 (Ct. App. 1988) (both holding that a building superintendent is not a tenant), *with Bigelow v. Bullard*, 901 P.2d 630 (Nev. 1995) (superintendent is a tenant).

[16] *Compare De Bruyn Produce Co. v. Romero*, 508 N.W.2d 150 (Mich. Ct. App. 1993) (migrant farm workers are licensees, not tenants) *with State v. DeCoster*, 653 A.2d 891 (Me. 1995) (migrant farm workers are "tenants").

[17] *Keller v. Southwood North Medical Pavilion, Inc.*, 959 P.2d 102 (Utah 1998).

[18] This topic is covered in more depth at §10.2.

[19] *See* §5.4.1 (estoppel); §5.4.2 (constructive trust); §5.4.3 (implied); §5.4.4 (necessity); §5.5 (prescription).

[20] *Jenkins v. Johnson*, 2006 WL 2506778, at *6 (Mass. Land Ct. 2006); *Tripp v. Huff*, 606 A.2d 792 (Me. 1992); *Estate of Thomson v. Wade*, 509 N.E.2d 309 (N.Y. 1987); *Beachside Bungalow Pres. Ass'n of Far Rockaway, Inc. v. Oceanview Assocs.*, 753 N.Y.S.2d 133 (App. Div. 2003); *Shirley v. Shirley*, 525 S.E.2d 274 (Va. 2000) (applying Va. Code §1-10); *Pitman v. Sweeney*,

reserving an easement over that land in *B*. This rule has its origins in medieval conceptions of *seisin* and has no current policy justification. In those states that retain it, one can draft around the rule. For example, the grantor can convey the property to the party who is intended to own the easement, after which that party then conveys the property to the ultimate grantee, reserving an easement over the property for herself. The easement owner becomes the grantor, rather than a third-party grantee, and the easement will be recognized because the grantor may reserve an easement in herself. Alternatively, the grantor can convey the easement to the third party and then transfer the parcel, subject to this new easement, to the grantee. Some courts have used the doctrine of estoppel to prevent the grantee from interfering in the easement reserved to the third party,[21] while other courts have changed the traditional rule, allowing reservation of an easement in a third party.[22] The *Restatement (Third) of Property (Servitudes)* has wisely suggested abandoning the rule.[23]

§5.3.2 *Substantive Limitations*

Limits on negative easements

Courts traditionally limited the kinds of negative easements that could be created. Four negative easements have traditionally been recognized: light, air, lateral support, and the flow of an artificial stream. Because owners are normally entitled to build on their property in ways that interfere with their neighbors' light and air,[24] owners sometimes enter agreements by which the servient owner agrees not to build in a certain spot or above a certain height to protect the interests of the neighbors in light, air, or a view. Because the common law generally requires owners to support their neighbors' land in its natural condition, but not to support the added weight of buildings on neighboring land, some owners agree that one will provide

---

661 P.2d 153 (Wash. Ct. App. 1983). Traditionally, courts made a distinction between "reservations" and "exceptions." Owners usually try to "reserve" an easement in the land that is being conveyed. The courts found this confusing because one could not create an easement in one's own land; they therefore interpreted this arrangement as a grant of land to the grantee and regrant back to the original grantor of an easement in what was now the grantee's land. However, when the grantor attempts to create an "exception," this generally refers to keeping ownership of a strip of land in fee simple; an "exception" that refers to an easement was therefore confusing to the courts because it appeared to create an easement in a retained strip of land. Jon W. Bruce, James W. Ely, Jr., & Edward T. Brading, *The Law of Easements and Licenses in Land* §3:9 (2025). Today, owners often use the words "exception" or "reservation" interchangeably, and the courts generally allow grantors to retain easement rights over land that is conveyed away. At the same time, many courts retain the technical, traditional rule, that an easement cannot be reserved in a third party, requiring instead that the grantor give an express easement to the third party through a separate deed.

[21] *Dalton v. Eller*, 284 S.W. 68 (Tenn. 1926).

[22] *Willard v. First Church of Christ, Scientist*, 498 P.2d 987 (Cal. 1972); *Townsend v. Cable*, 378 S.W.2d 806 (Ky. 1964).

[23] *Restatement (Third) of Property (Servitudes)* §2.6(b) (2000). In the states that retain the traditional rule, there is a division of authority over the remedy; some courts treat the easement as reserved by the grantor and thus owned by her, while others treat the easement as belonging to the land grantee, with the effect of merging the easement with the land ownership and creating a parcel unburdened by any easement. Jon W. Bruce, James W. Ely, Jr., & Edward T. Brading, *The Law of Easements and Licenses in Land* §3:9 (2025).

[24] *See above* §3.6.

(or continue to provide) support on her own land sufficient to help support structures on the neighboring land. If an artificial stream or flow of water crosses several parcels, the owners often are allocated by contract certain amounts of water that they are allowed to withdraw; an agreement that one owner would obtain more of the water could be created in the form of a negative easement limiting the ability of the servient owner to block the flow of the stream.

Reason for the limitation

Negative easements were limited by courts because, unlike affirmative easements, it is hard or impossible to observe their existence. Affirmative easements are visible because one can see a road with people passing over it, or utility lines, or timber cutting. Negative easements, however, are rights to prevent someone else from doing something, and buyers of the servient estate will not be on notice of them unless a working recording system provides buyers notice of encumbrances on land they are contemplating purchasing. England lacked a working recording system until 1925 and the English courts' reluctance to recognize new negative easements carried over into the United States, despite the existence of recording systems here.

Ancient lights

In addition, the English doctrine of "ancient lights" allowed an owner of land who had long enjoyed unobstructed light and air to prevent construction on neighboring land that harmed those interests. If the category of negative easements was not strictly limited, then *any* new use of property could result in a complaint by the neighbor that such use interfered with the neighbor's rights, and the long-standing failure to engage in such a use meant that the right to introduce the use now had been lost by prescription. Taken to the extreme, the prescriptive easement doctrine could have prevented any new uses of property to which neighbors objected.

New negative easements

In recent years, by statute or common law, the states have begun to recognize new negative easements. *Conservation* easements limit land development by restricting the use of land for environmental purposes.[25] *Historic preservation* easements prevent destruction or alteration of buildings that have historical or architectural importance, and *solar* easements protect access to sunlight for solar energy panels.

Negative easements and restrictive covenants

Because negative easements are nothing more than land use restrictions, it is possible to evade the rule limiting the creation of new easements by putting the restriction in the form of a covenant rather than an easement.[26] For this reason, there has been little pressure to change the rule limiting the creation of new negative easements. At the same time, retention of the rule against creation of new negative easements does have legal consequences. Because the law of easements and the law of covenants developed at different times and in different ways, the rules governing them have traditionally differed. For example, while there are limits on the kinds of negative easements that can be created, those that can be created are generally understood to be permanent. Covenants, in contrast, are governed by the changed conditions and undue hardship doctrines that may nullify

[25] *See, e.g.*, Alaska Stat. §§34.17.010 to .060; Idaho Code §§55-2101 to -2109; N.C. Gen. Stat. §§121-34 to -42; Unif. Conservation Easement Act §§1-6, 12 U.L.A. 170 (1981).

[26] For the law governing covenants, see Chapter 6.

them if conditions change.[27] These doctrines have not traditionally applied to easements. In addition, unlike covenants, easements could traditionally be owned *in gross*. For example, a conservation organization could own a conservation easement restricting the use of a parcel of land whether or not the organization owns any neighboring land. Traditionally, the courts have refused to recognize the right to enforce a covenant in gross, instead insisting that such restrictions benefit the owners of neighboring land.[28]

Restatement (Third) of Property (Servitudes)

The *Restatement (Third) of Property (Servitudes)* would abolish the distinction between negative easements and restrictive covenants, treating them both alike as "servitudes": land use restrictions intended to run with the land. The *Restatement (Third)* would further abolish some of the technical restraints on both easements and covenants (such as the rule limiting the number of negative easements that will be recognized) while applying the changed conditions and undue hardship doctrines to both negative easements and restrictive covenants. Instead of categorical rules about the types of easements that can be created, the *Restatement (Third)* would directly regulate land use restrictions by invalidating restrictions that serve no legitimate purpose or that contravene strong and articulable public policies.[29] It would also allow all servitudes (including easements and covenants) to be modified if changed conditions have made it "impossible as a practical matter to accomplish" the easement's purpose.[30] The *Restatement (Third)* would also allow easements (and covenants) to be terminated if modification is "not practicable."[31]

Easement v. covenant

Easements are different from covenants in another way as well. Most easements created by landowners are in fact affirmative, while most restrictions on land use take the form of covenants. Affirmative easements are rights to do something on someone else's land. The traditional law of easements did not allow creation of an affirmative duty to do something on someone's own land such as a duty to build a structure or pay a monthly fee to a condominium association. If the *Restatement (Third)*'s views are accepted, the distinctions between easements and covenants will blur or be eliminated. Instead, the *Restatement (Third)* would allow servitudes to be created unless there is a good public policy reason to prohibit their creation or limit their legal effect.

§5.3.3 *Running with the Land (Appurtenant v. In Gross)*

Appurtenant easements and easements in gross

Many easements are intended to benefit the owners of neighboring or nearby land. If an owner, for example, sells her backyard to a buyer who builds a house there, the back lot owner may also be given an easement to cross the driveway on the grantor's front lot to get to the public street. This

27 *See* §§6.8.1 & 6.8.2.

28 The *Restatement (Third) of Property* would change this to allow the benefit of a covenant to be held in gross if the beneficiary has a legitimate interest in enforcement. *Restatement (Third) of Property (Servitudes)* §2.6(d) (2000).

29 *See Restatement (Third) of Property (Servitudes)* §§3.1 to 3.7 (2000).

30 *Id.* at §7.10.

31 *Id.*

kind of easement is intended to benefit not just the immediate grantee, but any future owner of the back lot. Similarly, if the front lot is sold, the back lot owner wants assurance that she will still be able to use the easement. *Appurtenant* easements are easements that are intended to "run with the land," such that the benefit of the easement will pass to any future owner of the dominant estate (the parcel benefited by the easement) and the burden will be imposed on any future owner of the servient estate (the parcel over which the easement passes).[32] Easements *in gross*, in contrast, are not intended to be attached to the ownership of particular parcels of land. Prime examples include rights to place utility lines, such as electric or telephone lines, or sewer pipes over or under land belonging to someone else.

Requirements to run with the land

The intent of the parties creating the easement determines whether an easement is in gross or appurtenant. Easements intended to be appurtenant will in fact run with the land only if (1) they are in *writing*; (2) they were *intended* to run with the land; and (3) the owner of the servient estate purchased with *notice* of the easement. In analyzing whether an easement runs with the land, it is important to distinguish between the benefit and the burden. It is conceivable, for example, that an owner might create an easement that is intended to be binding on future owners of the servient estate but personal to the original grantee and thus not be available to future owners of the dominant estate. In that case, the burden might run and the benefit would not. Conversely, one might imagine creating a covenant intended to benefit any future owner of the dominant estate, but only as long as the servient estate remained in the hands of the original owner. In that case, the benefit would run but the burden would not. Such cases are unusual, however. Most appurtenant easements are intended *both* to benefit future owners of the dominant estate *and* to be binding on future owners of the servient estate.

Distinguishing between appurtenant and in gross easements

Courts determine whether an easement is appurtenant or in gross by reference to the intent of the parties.[33] "This intent is determined by considering the language and the relevant provisions of the deed in light of the then existing situation of the property and the current surrounding circumstances."[34] An easement will be appurtenant and run with the land only if the grantor who created the easement intended it to do so. Often the parties are clear about this. The deed creating the easement might state, for example, that it is an "appurtenant" easement and/or that it is "intended to run with the land" and be binding on future owners of the servient estate and enforceable by future owners of the dominant estate(s). Lawyers are well advised to use such clear language to avoid results that differ from what their clients intend.

Presumption in favor of appurtenant easements

When the deed is not clear, almost all courts voice a *constructional preference for appurtenant easements.*[35] Traditionally, this preference was

[32] *Block v. DEA Properties-2 LLC*, 501 P.3d 545, 550 (Or. Ct. App. 2021).

[33] *Stiefel v. Lindemann*, 638 A.2d 642, 647 (Conn. App. Ct. 1994).

[34] *Id.*

[35] *Smithson v. Lindzey*, 479 P.3d 759, 765 (Wyo. 2021); *French v. Estate of Selectmen of Amherst*, 646 N.E.2d 418, 423 (Mass. App. Ct. 1995); *French v. Estate of Gutzan*,128 A.3d 657, 660 (Me. 2015); *Green v. Lupo*, 647 P.2d 51 (Wash. Ct. App. 1982).

thought to maximize the value of land by limiting easements to neighboring landowners. This might be thought to limit the number of possible easements, thereby freeing the land from numerous burdensome encumbrances. In addition, it is easy to find the owner of a neighboring parcel to attempt to buy the easement back from her; on the other hand, it may be difficult to determine the identity and location of owners of easements held in gross, thereby impeding the reconsolidation of rights in a single owner if this is desired. If the owner of the servient estate cannot identify or find the owner of an easement held in gross, she cannot offer to induce the easement owner to give up the easement rights and it is costly for that owner (or a prospective buyer) to purchase full ownership rights in the lot free of the easement. Thus, it might be that appurtenant easements interfere with the alienability of the property less than do easements held in gross. For this reason, some courts will interpret ambiguous easements as appurtenant unless something in the language or circumstances strongly points the other way.

Easement in gross preferred

An exception is South Carolina, whose Supreme Court has held that an easement will be deemed appurtenant only if it is "essentially necessary" to the enjoyment of the dominant estate, on the ground that appurtenant easements are likely to last longer than easements in gross because they run with the land while easements in gross are personal and non-transferable under South Carolina law. Because they run with the land, appurtenant easements constitute greater encumbrances on the land and should not be enforced unless the parties clearly intended to so burden the land.[36]

Language

In deciding whether an easement is appurtenant or in gross, the courts attempt to ascertain the intent of the parties, both from the *language* of the easement and *surrounding circumstances.* If the language in the deed does not mention the "heirs or assigns" or "successors in interest" to the grantee, but simply conveys the easement to a named person, many courts will presume that it was intended to be in gross rather than appurtenant.[37] However, the absence of such language is not determinative if other factors suggest that the easement was intended to be appurtenant, such as its utility in obtaining access to a dominant estate.[38]

Commercial utility

If the easement is one that would be either useful or commercially marketable apart from ownership of nearby land (such as a utility easement), the presumption is likely to be that it was intended to be in gross.[39] If, in contrast, the easement has no value apart from ownership of the dominant estate (such as a right-of-way that provides access to the land), or if it is especially valuable to an owner of the dominant estate, it will

[36] *Tupper v. Dorchester County*, 487 S.E.2d 187, 191 (S.C. 1997).

[37] *Stiefel v. Lindemann*, 638 A.2d 642, 647 (Conn. App. Ct. 1994) ("It is well established that where the reservation creating an easement does not mention the heirs and assigns of the grantee, a presumption exists that the grantor and grantee intended the right-of-way to be in gross").

[38] *Green v. Lupo*, 647 P.2d 51 (Wash. Ct. App. 1982) (same).

[39] *Jones v. Cullen*, 1998 WL 811558 (Minn. Ct. App. 1998).

be presumed to be intended to be appurtenant.[40] In *Green v. Lupo*,[41] for example, an owner granted a neighbor a right to use his driveway to get to the neighbor's land. Although the deed did not state that the easement was appurtenant, the court found that it must have been intended to be appurtenant because the right would be useful to any future owner of the dominant estate.

Personal character

An easement will be found to be in gross if the character of the easement or the circumstances surrounding its creation suggest that it was intended to be a private accommodation to benefit a particular person for non-commercial purposes, rather than a permanent grant intended either to create a commercially valuable right (such as a utility line) or to create access to or service for a particular parcel of land. Thus, an owner who gives a neighbor the right to hunt on his land is likely to be granting a personal easement that is neither transferable to another person nor intended to pass with ownership of the neighbor's land.

Writing

An easement that is intended to be appurtenant will run with the land only if it is also in writing and the owner of the servient estate was on notice of the easement at the time she purchased her property. The writing requirement may be satisfied by a description of the easement in the deed granting the property, or, alternatively, the deed may refer to an earlier, recorded writing. The writing requirement is satisfied even if the easement is not included in subsequent deeds transferring possession of the servient estate; future buyers are on constructive notice of the writing in the earlier deed if it is in the "chain of title" and can be found by searching the deeds in the recording office. It is good legal practice, however, to include a specific reference to existing easements when either the dominant or servient estate is transferred.

Notice

Actual

Inquiry

Constructive

Easements are binding on subsequent owners of the servient estate only if they have notice of them. Three kinds of notice exist. First, if the subsequent owners in fact know about them, they have *actual* notice. Second, if there are visible signs of use by non-owners, such as telephone poles, above-ground utility lines, or a path across the property, the owner may be put on *inquiry* notice. This means that a reasonable buyer would do further investigation to discover whether an easement exists. Third, if the deed conveying the easement is recorded in the proper registry of deeds in the proper place, and if the deed is in the chain of title, meaning that a title search of prior owners of the property would lead to discovery of the deed, then subsequent owners are deemed to be on *constructive* notice. This means that, whether or not they actually knew about the easement at the time they purchased, they *should have known*. A reasonable buyer of property would conduct a title search and discover the existence of the easement. Owners are bound by easements they would have discovered had they performed the usual title search.

[40] *Stiefel v. Lindemann*, 638 A.2d 642, 648 (Conn. App. Ct. 1994); *Mays v. Hogue*, 260 S.E.2d 291, 293 (W. Va. 1979) stating that ("if an easement granted be in its nature an appropriate and useful adjunct of a dominant estate" it will be presumed to be appurtenant); *Restatement (Third) of Property (Servitudes)* §4.5 (2000).

[41] 647 P.2d 51 (Wash. Ct. App. 1982).

§5.3.4 *Scope, Location, and Extension of Appurtenant Easements*

Interpretation issues

Issues often arise about how to interpret the *scope* of easements. Because easements represent limited use rights, rather than full ownership or possession, the precise content of the rights encompassed by the easement is often at issue, especially when those uses interfere with interests sought to be retained by the owner of the servient estate. These questions are matters of interpretation of the scope of the rights given to the easement owner. The main issues of interpretation that arise are (1) the *scope* of allowable uses encompassed by the easement; (2) *divisibility* of the dominant estate; (3) whether the easement can be *extended* to obtain access to land other than the dominant estate; and (4) whether the easement can be *relocated* by either the easement owner or the servient owner.

Constructional presumption in favor of the grantee

Many courts resolve ambiguities in favor of the grantee. In cases of a grant of an easement, this constructional presumption is based on the idea that the "easement owner is entitled to full enjoyment of the easement"[42] and that doubts should be resolved in favor of broad use of the easement. In the case of easements reserved by the grantor over land conveyed to the servient owner, doubts tend to be resolved in favor of the servient owner. This is because it is thought that the burden should be on the grantor to explain clearly which rights are being reserved, with doubts resolved in favor of the grantee of the land.[43]

Scope determined by grantor's intent

The scope of an easement is determined by the intent of the grantor. This, in turn, is gleaned from the language in the deed and the circumstances surrounding its creation (especially if that language is ambiguous).[44] The behavior of the parties at the time of the creation of the easement and afterward may be accepted as evidence of the contemplated uses. This is true even when the uses change. When the servient owner acquiesces in certain uses of the easement for a sufficient time, the court may accept this as evidence that the uses were within the scope initially intended by the grantor.[45]

Kind of use

Issues may arise over the *kind of* use encompassed by the easement, as well as the *quantity* or *intensity* of that use. Issues of kind concern the

[42] *Carson v. Elliott*, 728 P.2d 778, 779 (Idaho Ct. App. 1986).

[43] *Columbia Gas Transmission Corp. v. Bishop*, 809 F. Supp. 220, 222 (W.D.N.Y. 1992); *Bergh and Mission Farms, Inc. v. Great Lakes Transmission Co.*, 565 N.W.2d 23, 26 (Minn. 1997) ("[A]n easement grant is to be strictly construed against the grantor"); Jon W. Bruce, James W. Ely, Jr., & Edward T. Brading, *The Law of Easements and Licenses in Land* §8:2 (2025).

[44] *Stiefel v. Lindemann*, 638 A.2d 642, 647 (Conn. Ct. App. 1994) ("Th[e] intent [of the parties] is determined by considering the language and the relevant provisions of the deed in light of the then existing situation of the property and the current surrounding circumstances"; *Leonard v. Pugh*, 356 S.E.2d 812, 814-815 (N.C. App. Ct. 1987); Jon W. Bruce, James W. Ely, Jr., & Edward T. Brading, *The Law of Easements and Licenses in Land* §8:2 (2025); 7-60 *Thompson on Real Property, Third Thomas Edition* §60.04(a)(1).

[45] *Anchors v. Manter*, 714 A.2d 134, 140 (Me. 1998) ("The parties' intent may be gleaned not only from the use of the land before the grant, but also the practical construction which the parties placed upon [the deed] by their conduct, by acts done by one party and acquiesced in by the other, especially when such conduct is proven to have continued for a long time . . ."); Jon W. Bruce, James W. Ely, Jr., & Edward T. Brading, *The Law of Easements and Licenses in Land* §8:1 (2025).

types of uses contemplated by the parties when the easement was created. For example, a right-of-way may be intended to be limited to passage by cars for access to the dominant estate or it may also include a right to string utility lines, such as cable television lines, over the road to provide service to the dominant estate. Courts demonstrate a wide range of approaches to interpreting the content of allowable uses. Many courts interpret expressly stated uses narrowly. Thus, it has been ruled that a parking easement did not include the right to store cars for sale on a used car lot,[46] and an easement for "agricultural related purposes" did not include the right to hunt.[47] On the other hand, other courts presume that the uses should be broadly construed, on the ground that easement owners have traditionally been entitled to "reasonable use" of the easement.[48] "When an easement is created, every right necessary for its enjoyment is included by implication."[49] So an easement granting the "right to use" waterfront property was interpreted to encompass recreational activities, such as swimming and fishing.[50] Similarly, an easement for "utility lines" was interpreted to encompass the installation of sewer lines.[51] Courts have disagreed, for example, over whether easements to lay electric lines entitle the easement owner to install cable television lines.[52]

▶ HARD CASE ▷ GENERAL RIGHTS OF WAY

Many cases address the question of how to interpret easements for a right-of-way that is granted in general terms.[53] While many courts rule that the easement can be used not only for passage but for the installation of utility lines,[54]

[46] *University Place-Lincoln Assocs. L.P. v. Nelson*, 530 N.W.2d 241, 243-244 (Neb. 1995).
[47] *Steil v. Smith*, 901 P.2d 395 (Wyo. 1995).
[48] *Loveridge v. United States*, 148 Fed. Cl. 279 (Fed. Cl. 2020); *Zissler v. Saville*, 240 Cal. Rptr. 3d 590, 599 (Ct. App. 2018); Jon W. Bruce, James W. Ely, Jr., & Edward T. Brading, *The Law of Easements and Licenses in Land* §8:3 (2025).
[49] *Commercial Wharf East Condominium Assoc. v. Waterfront Parking Corp.*, 552 N.E.2d 66, 76 (Mass. 1990).
[50] *Chase v. Eastman*, 563 A.2d 1099, 1102 (Me. 1989); *see also Dobie v. Morrison*, 575 N.W.2d 817, 819-820 (Mich. Ct. App. 1998) (easement for use of owners fronting on a lake interpreted to include a variety of recreational uses, including construction of a dock).
[51] *Kimlow, Inc. v. Seminole Landing Ass'n*, 586 So. 2d 1290, 1291 (Fla. Dist. Ct. App. 1991).
[52] *Compare West v. Louisville Gas & Electric Co.*, 951 F.3d 827 (7th Cir. 2020) (easement for "the transmission, distribution and delivery of electrical energy [and] for light, heat, power, telephone and/or other purposes" allowed fiber-optic cables), *with Marcus Cable Assocs. v. Krohn*, 90 S.W.3d 697 (Tex. 2002) (an easement for "an electric transmission or distribution line or system" did not allow the holder to install cable television lines).
[53] Jon W. Bruce, James W. Ely, Jr., & Edward T. Brading, *The Law of Easements and Licenses in Land* §8:4 (2025).
[54] *Fleming v. Napili Kai, Ltd.*, 430 P.2d 316, 319 (Haw. 1967) (easement for passage can be used for utility lines); *Cline v. Richardson*, 526 N.W.2d 166, 169 (Iowa Ct. App. 1994) (easement for ingress and egress can be used for utility lines); *Kelly v. Schmelz*, 439 S.W.2d 211 (Mo. Ct. App. 1969) (holding that a general right-of-way could be used for any reasonable purpose); *King v. Town of Lyme*, 490 A.2d 1369, 1373 (N.H. 1985) (easement can be used for utilities); *Hudson Valley Cablevision Corp. v. 202 Developers, Inc.*, 587 N.Y.S.2d 385, 387 (App. Div. 1992) (easement granting right-of-way "for all purposes of ingress and egress" allowed installation of cable television wires); *Harrington v. Bldg. Sys., Inc.*, 656 A.2d 624, 625 (R.I. 1995) (same).

other courts hold the opposite.[55] Some of these cases rest on an interpretation of language in the deed while most simply represent conflicting presumptions about the rights intended to be encompassed in a general easement of passage.[56] Still others rest their conclusions on circumstantial evidence of the parties' intent.[57] This difference of opinion rests on different interpretations of what it means to convey a "right-of-way" or a right of "ingress and egress." Some judges interpret these formulations to allow use for any reasonable purpose.[58] The original uses of the easement and the circumstances surrounding its creation, including parol evidence (oral statements), may be admitted to interpret ambiguities in its scope.[59] ◄

Overburdening the easement

Intensity of use

A different issue concerns the question of whether the easement owner has exceeded the scope of rights encompassed by the easement by *overburdening* it through a quantity or intensity of use that goes beyond what the grantor intended when the easement was created. Easement owners are entitled to *reasonable* use of the easement.[60] This issue sometimes overlaps with the question of the *divisibility* of the easement and the *width* of the easement. When the dominant estate is subdivided, the new owners of each parcel have a right to use the easement unless the terms of the easement provide otherwise or if the increase in intensity of use constitutes an unreasonable increase in the burden on the servient estate, which exceeds the use contemplated by the grantor.[61] In *Cox v. Glenbrook Co.*,[62] for example, the servient estate was a resort business that had granted an easement of access to a portion of its land it sold to the dominant owner. At the time the easement was established, it was a single-lane road and the dominant estate contained only one house. When the dominant owner sought to subdivide

[55] *Wendy's of Fort Wayne, Inc. v. Fagan*, 644 N.E.2d 159, 162-163 (Ind. Ct. App. 1994) (easement of ingress and egress does not include right to install utilities); *Ward v. McGlory*, 265 N.E.2d 78 (Mass. 1970) (a general right-of-way does not include the right to erect poles and maintain electric wires); *Guild v. Hinman*, 695 A.2d 1190, 1192-1193 (Me. 1997); *Thompson v. Pendleton*, 697 A.2d 56, 59 (Me. 1997); *Moore v. Leveris*, 495 S.E.2d 153, 156 (N.C. Ct. App. 1998) (road easement did not include right to lay down sewer lines); *Buhl v. U.S. Sprint Commc'ns Co.*, 840 S.W.2d 904, 912-913 (Tenn. 1992).

[56] *Compare Scruby v. Vintage Grapevine, Inc.*, 43 Cal. Rptr. 2d 810, 813-814 (Ct. App. 1995) ("A roadway easement does not include the right to use the easement for any other purpose") *with Fleming v. Napili Kai, Ltd.*, 430 P.2d 316, 318 (Haw. 1967) ("[A] grant or reservation of an easement of right-of-way in general terms should be construed as creating a general right-of-way for all reasonable purposes").

[57] *Fine Line, Inc. v. Blake*, 677 A.2d 1061, 1064 (Me. 1996) (right-of-way may or may not include right to lay utility lines; remand for evidence of parties' intent); *Mason v. Garrison*, 998 P.2d 531 (Mont. 2000) (scope of a broadly defined easement can be defined by custom and usage).

[58] *Lake Anne Homeowners Ass'n v. Lake Anne Realty Corp.*, 640 N.Y.S.2d 200, 202 (App. Div. 1996) (right-of-way could be used "in manner which is necessary and convenient"); *Shipp v. Stoker*, 923 S.W.2d 100, 103 (Tex. Ct. App. 1996) (roadway easement could be used "for any purpose connected to use of the property").

[59] *Meadows Country Club, Inc. v. Unnever*, 702 So. 2d 586, 588 (Fla. Dist. Ct. App. 1997) (holding that the court can "consider the circumstances surrounding the creation of the easement and the conduct of the parties"); *Cline v. Richardson*, 526 N.W.2d 166, 168 (Iowa Ct. App. 1994) (parol evidence admissible).

[60] Jon W. Bruce, James W. Ely, Jr., & Edward T. Brading, *The Law of Easements and Licenses in Land* §8:3 (2025).

[61] *Restatement (Third) of Property (Servitudes)* §5.7 (2000).

[62] 371 P.2d 647 (Nev. 1962).

and build between 40 and 60 homes, the servient owner argued that use of the easement by more than one owner would overburden the easement and exceed the scope of the rights given to the easement owner. The servient owner emphasized the character of the servient estate as a quiet resort and the disruption the increased traffic would cause. In contrast, *Cater v. Bednarek*[63] held that the court should interpret an easement whose width is not specified in a manner that "maximizes the aggregate utility of the dominant and servient estate" and that ensures that the easement can be used in a manner "that is reasonably necessary for the convenient enjoyment of the dominant estate."[64] To comply with local regulations on the width of roads, the court allowed the easement owner to widen the road.

Divisibility

Implicit in the servient owner's argument was the view that the dominant estate owner had no right to subdivide the dominant estate. The court held that it is an incident of land ownership that the owner has the right to subdivide the land (in accord with local zoning laws), that an easement of access to a dominant estate should be presumed to grant access to any part of the dominant estate, and that each new owner of the subdivided dominant estate therefore should have a similar right to use the easement.[65] At the same time, the court held that the right to subdivide did not answer the question of whether use by 40 to 60 homes would cause an "undue burden" to the servient estate, and the court remanded for factual findings on this issue, especially given the character of the servient estate.[66] These cases pose fundamental questions of the relation between change (development of the dominant estate) and stability (secure enjoyment of the servient estate) and the justified expectations of the parties, which may be very different for the grantee and the grantor. Cases holding that subdivision creates an undue burden are hard to find (although not nonexistent),[67] perhaps because the courts assume that the parties contemplated that the dominant estate would very likely be subdivided and judges have long favored land development.[68]

Prescription

When an easement owner exceeds the scope of the easement for a sufficiently long period of time, a right to continue the expanded use can be obtained by prescription.[69]

Width

The court in *Cox* ruled, however, that if the grant does not specify the width of the easement, it will be determined by its width at the time the easement was initially granted. The court held that the dominant estate

[63] 969 N.E.2d 705 (Mass. 2012).

[64] 969 N.E.2d at 714 (citing *Restatement (Third) of Property (Servitudes)* §4.10 cmt. b (2000)).

[65] *Cox v. Glenbrook Co.*, 371 P.2d 647 (Nev. 1962). *Accord*, *Krause v. Taylor*, 343 A.2d 767 (N.J. Super. Ct. App. Div. 1975); *Green v. Mann*, 655 N.Y.S.2d 627, 629 (App. Div. 1997); Jon W. Bruce, James W. Ely, Jr., & Edward T. Brading, *The Law of Easements and Licenses in Land* §8:15 (2025).

[66] *See Hayes v. Aquia Marina, Inc.*, 414 S.E.2d 820 (Va. 1992) (increase in road use resulting from expansion of marina from 84 slips to 280 did not constitute an unreasonable additional burden on the servient estate).

[67] *Boudreau v. Coleman*, 564 N.E.2d 1, 7 (Mass. App. Ct. 1990).

[68] Jon W. Bruce, James W. Ely, Jr., & Edward T. Brading, *The Law of Easements and Licenses in Land* §8:15 (2025).

[69] *Id.* at §8:12.

owner had no right to widen the road to make it a two-lane road.[70] Of course, without widening the road to two lanes, it might be impossible to subdivide the dominant estate because the homes might not be marketable if only a one-lane access road were available. Because an easement is a physical intrusion on land, most courts do interpret the width of the easement strictly based on historical uses and consider widening of the easement to be outside the scope of the original easement. On the other hand, failure to allow the road to be widened may effectively negate the right to subdivide. If an owner sells a large parcel, which can be subdivided, and which has no access to a public way other than through the easement that is simultaneously granted to the dominant owner, one might conclude that the dominant owner should have the right to widen the easement to afford access to the various lots that might be created when the land is subdivided. Otherwise, the right to subdivide is only theoretical. On the other hand, preventing the easement owner from widening the road simply places the burden on the dominant owner to compensate the servient owner for the increase while giving the servient owner the entitlement to reject the offer if it is more interested in peace and quiet than profit.

Extension to other land

Sometimes a dominant owner purchases or owns another parcel of land next to the dominant estate. Questions often arise as to whether the easement owner can use the easement not only to get to the dominant estate, but also to obtain access to neighboring land also owned by the dominant estate owner. An alternative version of this question is whether the dominant owner can grant to her neighbor the right to use the easement to get to the dominant owner's land and continue to the neighbor's land. It has long been held that appurtenant easements only benefit the dominant estate and cannot be used to obtain access to other land, unless the terms of the easement provide otherwise.[71] However, some courts have rejected the idea that use of an easement for non-dominant land is automatically an overburden of the easement, instead ruling that an extended easement is permissible if it does not result in material increase in the burden on the servient estate.[72] In *Brown v. Voss*,[73] when the dominant owner purchased another parcel, combined the two, and built only one home on the enlarged parcel, the court refused to enjoin the use and limited damages to one dollar, on the ground that the easement was still being used by only the dominant estate owner and the burden on the servient estate had not been increased.

Relocation

Sometimes the owner of the servient estate wishes to relocate the easement to facilitate construction on her land. Traditionally, courts have not allowed the servient owner to do this without the consent of the easement owner, on the ground that the easement has a fixed location

[70] 371 P.2d at 654. *But see Town of Bedford v. Cerasuolo*, 818 N.E.2d 561 (Mass. App. Ct. 2004) (easement can be widened to accommodate foreseeable development).

[71] *Hunt v. Pole Bridge Hunting Club, Inc.*, 631 N.Y.S.2d 711, 712 (App. Div. 1995); *Brown v. Voss*, 715 P.2d 514 (Wash. 1986); Jon W. Bruce, James W. Ely, Jr., & Edward T. Brading, *The Law of Easements and Licenses in Land* §8:14 (2025); *Restatement (Third) of Property (Servitudes)* §4.11 (2000).

[72] *Abington Ltd. P'ship v. Heublein*, 717 A.2d 1232, 1239-1240 (Conn. 1998); *Bateman v. Bd. of Appeals of Georgetown*, 775 N.E.2d 1276 (Mass. App. Ct. 2002).

[73] 715 P.2d 514 (Wash. 1986).

bargained for by the easement owner and that any changes that might reduce the value of the easement cannot be allowed without the agreement of the easement owner.[74] Some courts retain this view.[75] Recently, however, some courts have begun to allow servient owners to relocate the easement over the objections of the easement owner.[76] This position has been adopted by the *Restatement (Third)*, as long as the changes are "reasonable" and do not "(a) significantly lessen the utility of the easement, (b) increase the burden on the owner of the easement in its use and enjoyment, or frustrate the purpose for which the servitude was created."[77] And in 2020, the *Uniform Law Commission released a Uniform Easement Relocation Act* that would allow a burdened owner to obtain a court order, relocating the easement as long as doing so does not materially impair the utility of the easement to the easement holder, or the physical location, use, or value of the benefited property — although the owner of the servient estate bears the cost of relocation.[78] One court has allowed relocation by the servient owner as long as damages are paid to the easement owner.[79] The Colorado Supreme Court held in 2001 that a servient owner can relocate an easement but only after obtaining a declaration of a court that such alterations would cause no damage to the owner of the easement.[80] However, the court also ruled that if the servient owner has relocated the easement without a court order, the court may refuse to require restoration to the original location if there has been no diminution of benefit to the easement owner and the equities are appropriate. The Supreme Judicial Court of the Commonwealth of Massachusetts allowed a servient estate owner to narrow the width of an easement on the grounds that "an easement . . . may be modified by the servient land holder so long as the purposes for which the easement was created are not frustrated, and the utility of the easement is not lessened."[81]

Policy concerns

Allowing relocation by the servient estate owner might be sensible because it protects the rights of the dominant owner while allowing for

[74] *Town of Ellettsville v. DeSpirito*, 111 N.E.3d 987 (Ind. 2018); *Davis v. Bruk*, 411 A.2d 660 (Me. 1980).

[75] *Taylor v. Martha's Vineyard Land Bank Commission*, 60 N.E.3d 319 (Mass. 2016); *Herren v. Pettengill*, 538 S.E.2d 735 (Ga. 2000); *MacMeekin v. Low Income Hous. Instit., Inc.*, 45 P.3d 570 (Wash. Ct. App. 2002). *Cf. Koeppen v. Bolich*, 79 P.3d 1100 (Mont. 2003) (dominant estate owner has no right to relocate an easement against the wishes of the owner of the servient estate).

[76] *M.P.M. Builders v. Dwyer*, 809 N.E.2d 1053 (Mass. 2004) (adopting *Restatement (Third)* rule 4.8(3) allowing servient owner to relocate the easement); *Kline v. Bernardsville Assocs.*, 631 A.2d 1263 (N.J. Super. Ct. App. Div. 1993); *Lewis v. Young*, 705 N.E.2d 649 (N.Y. 1998). *See also Huggins v. Wright*, 774 So. 2d 408 (Miss. 2000) (servient owner has right to relocate easement by necessity); *Roy v. Woodstock Cmty. Trust, Inc.*, 94 A.3d 530 (Vt. 2014) (same). *See generally* John A. Lovett, *Easements and Change*, 74 Baylor L. Rev. 1 (2022).

[77] *Restatement (Third) of Property (Servitudes)* §4.8(3) (2000); *see Roaring Fork Club, L.P. v. St. Jude's Co.*, 36 P.3d 1229 (Colo. 2001); *Carrollsburg v. Anderson*, 791 A.2d 54, 63-64 (D.C. 2002); *Lewis v. Young*, 705 N.E.2d 649 (N.Y. 1998).

[78] Uniform Law Commission, *Uniform Easement Relocation Act* (2020). As of 2024, Nebraska, Utah, Arkansas, and Washington had adopted the UERA.

[79] *Umphres v. J.R. Mayer Enterprises*, 889 S.W.2d 86 (Mo. Ct. App. 1994).

[80] *Roaring Fork Club L.P. v. St. Jude's Co.*, 36 P.3d 1229 (Colo. 2001).

[81] *Martin v. Simmons Properties, LLC*, 2 N.E.3d 886 (Mass. 2014).

new development on the servient estate. This may therefore maximize the joint fair market value of the two parcels. On the other hand, this approach assumes that the easement owner is equally well-off if the easement is moved and, for reasons that may not be irrational, the easement owner may in fact not find the new location to be as beneficial or convenient as the old. If we understand the easement as an ownership interest, one might argue that it would be better to allow the servient estate owner to bargain with the easement owner to induce agreement to the relocation. If the easement owner does not agree, we have evidence that the change creates more harm to the easement owner than benefit to the servient owner. There is no easy answer to this rule choice partly because it turns on different ways to measure the value of the respective interests (fair market value versus offer and asking prices) and partly because it turns on competing conceptions of the entitlements or rights in question. If one thinks of the easement as a meddlesome intrusion on the rights of the servient owner, which intrusion should be minimized to promote the development and alienability of land, then one result may follow. If one thinks of the easement as property owned by the easement owner that she should not have to give up without her voluntary consent, another answer may follow.

Appurtenant easement cannot be converted to an easement in gross

The courts seem to agree that an owner of an appurtenant easement cannot convey it separate from ownership of the dominant land unless the original provisions of the easement made the benefit of the easement severable.[82] This means that an appurtenant easement cannot be converted to an easement in gross without the consent of the owner of the servient estate, and even with consent, it is conceptualized as a new easement.[83]

§5.3.5 *Scope and Apportionment of Easements in Gross*

Scope

As with appurtenant easements, the question often arises as to whether an owner of an easement in gross can extend the use to other purposes.[84] Courts split on the question of whether a general right-of-way encompasses the right to place utility lines, although most courts hold that a right of passage does not include the right to lay utility lines.[85] Courts are, however, likely to allow owners of utility easements to extend their uses to other utilities. A much-litigated example concerns easements for electric and telephone

[82] *Cook v. Nissimov*, 580 S.W.3d 745, 751 (Tex. App. 2019); *Rosen v. Keeler*, 986 A.2d 731 (N.J. Super. Ct. App. Div. 2010); *Restatement (Third) of Property (Servitudes)* §5.6 (2000).

[83] *Block v. DEA Properties-2 LLC*, 501 P.3d 545, 550 (Or. Ct. App. 2021); *Dorey v. Estate of Spicer*, 715 A.2d 182, 186 (Me. 1998); *Schwartzman v. Schoening*, 669 N.E.2d 228, 230 (Mass. App. Ct. 1996); Jon W. Bruce, James W. Ely, Jr., & Edward T. Brading, *The Law of Easements and Licenses in Land* §§9:1, 9:2 (2025).

[84] *Cf. Holmes v. Sprint United Telephone of Kansas*, 35 P.3d 928 (Kan. Ct. App. 2001) (digging a trench to bury telephone lines does not exceed scope of utility easement).

[85] *Compare Ward v. McGlory*, 265 N.E.2d 78 (Mass. 1970) (a general right-of-way does not include the right to erect poles and maintain electric wires) *with Kelly v. Schmelz*, 439 S.W.2d 211 (Mo. Ct. App. 1969) (holding that a general right-of-way could be used for any reasonable purpose).

lines; these have often been interpreted to allow the easement owner to string cable television lines.[86] One court has even allowed an easement for "electrical energy" to include the right to lay cable television lines.[87]

Transferability

Older cases, and some modern cases, hold that easements in gross are not transferable.[88] Almost all courts now hold that easements in gross are transferable when they are commercial in nature, such as easements for utility lines, but may well not allow them to be transferred if they serve a personal, or non-commercial, purpose, and appear to have been intended only to benefit the immediate recipient of the easement.[89] The *Restatement (Third)* provides that the benefits of in gross servitudes are freely transferable.[90] Profits are universally held to be transferable.[91] Recreational uses are the most common easements in gross that are viewed as personal and thus intended to be non-transferable. Some state statutes provide that commercial easements in gross are transferable by the owner[92] and others provide that all easements, including non-commercial easements in gross, are similarly transferable.[93]

Apportionment

Do easement owners have the power to license others to use the easement? Electric and/or telephone companies have granted cable television companies the right to string lines between the poles on the easement. Homeowners over whose property the lines pass have challenged these licenses on the ground that the servient owners, and not the easement owner, should have the right to determine whether to grant a new easement over the same path. This issue is generally described as the question of whether the easement is *apportionable* by the easement owner, *i.e.*, whether easement owner can grant others similar rights to use the easement. Most courts hold that easements in gross are apportionable if they are *exclusive* (meaning that the owner of the servient estate has no right to use the easement in the same way as the easement owner), but that they are not apportionable by the easement owner if they are non-exclusive (where the servient estate owner retains the right to conduct the same use as the easement owner over the same path). The *Restatement (Third)* provides, instead, that easements in gross can be divided unless this is contrary to the intent of the parties who created the easement or "unless the division unreasonably increases the burden on the servient estate."[94] This appears to

[86] *Salvaty v. Falcon Cable Television*, 212 Cal. Rptr. 31 (Ct. App. 1985); *Henley v. Cont'l Cablevision of St. Louis County, Inc.*, 692 S.W.2d 825 (Mo. Ct. App. 1985); *Hoffman v. Capitol Cablevision Sys., Inc.*, 383 N.Y.S.2d 674 (App. Div. 1976); *Jolliff v. Hardin Cable Television Co.*, 269 N.E.2d 588 (Ohio 1971).

[87] *Centel Cable Television Company of Ohio v. Cook*, 567 N.E.2d 1010 (Ohio 1991).

[88] *Gilder v. Mitchell*, 668 A.2d 879, 881 (Me. 1995); *Tupper v. Dorchester County*, 487 S.E.2d 187, 191 (S.C. 1997); *McDaniel v. Calvert*, 875 S.W.2d 482, 484 n.2 (Tex. Ct. App. 1994).

[89] *Estate of Thomson v. Wade*, 509 N.E.2d 309, 310 (N.Y. 1987); Jon W. Bruce, James W. Ely, Jr., & Edward T. Brading, *The Law of Easements and Licenses in Land* §9:5 (2025); *Restatement (Third) of Property (Servitudes)* §4.6 (2000).

[90] *Restatement (Third) of Property (Servitudes)* §5.8 (2000).

[91] Jon W. Bruce, James W. Ely, Jr., & Edward T. Brading, *The Law of Easements and Licenses in Land* §9:8 (2025).

[92] Ind. Code §32-23-2-2.

[93] Va. Code §55.1-105.

[94] *Restatement (Third) of Property (Servitudes)* §5.9 (2000).

be consistent with the trend in the law, which is to answer the question by reference to the intent of the grantor.[95]

Economic significance

These cases have substantial economic significance. If the company that owns the easement can license it to a cable television company, then it will make the money associated with the transaction rather than the various owners of the servient estates. In addition, the cable television company prefers this result because it has to bargain with only one owner (the easement owner) rather than the owners of each lot, any one of whom might hold out for a high price and effectively prevent the installation of the cable system unless the city intervenes by using its eminent domain powers to force individual owners to submit to the cable lines in exchange for constitutionally mandated just compensation.

Arguments for and against allowing apportionment

Obviously, allowing apportionment promotes the creation of a cable television system. It also is arguably implicit in the original grant of the easement. If an easement is an interest in land, it is not clear why it should not be alienable, especially if it has commercial value. On the other hand, although perhaps the easement owner should be able to *transfer* its right (if, for example, the electric company is sold to a different company), it is a different matter to allow the easement owner to *share* its rights, especially when the servient owner might not have intended to give up all control over future uses of the easement that are consistent with prior uses. Moreover, even if an easement is exclusive, in the sense that the grantor does not reserve the right to use the easement herself, this does not necessarily mean that the servient owner did not reserve the right to license another person to use the easement, especially if such use does not interfere in any way with the use of the easement by the existing easement owner.

§5.4 Implied Easements

Express v. implied easements

As we have just discussed, easements are normally created by express agreement. For example, an owner may expressly create an easement by giving a deed to his neighbor conferring on the neighbor (and perhaps any future owner of the neighbor's land) the right to use the owner's driveway to get to the neighbor's house. The deed will normally, explicitly state that the grantor conveys an "easement" to the grantee and will describe the nature and location of the easement. Implied easements, in contrast, are created by law when the express agreement between the parties is either silent or ambiguous on the question of whether the grantor intended to create an easement. In some cases, the issue is whether a clearly permitted use is a revocable license or a permanent easement. This issue is generally regulated by two rules of law: *easement by estoppel* and *constructive trust.* In other cases, an owner may transfer a portion of her land to someone else and, even though the deed is silent on the matter, the courts may find that the owner of one of the parcels has a right to pass over the land of the other to obtain reasonable access to her own land. Such an easement may

[95] Dale A. Whitman et al., *The Law of Property* §8.1110, at 465 (4th ed. 2019).

be *implied from prior use*[96] or it may be imposed because the transferred parcel is landlocked and access through the remaining land is imposed by *necessity*.[97]

§5.4.1 Easement by Estoppel

Permission plus reliance

Easements are created by estoppel when an owner gives someone else permission to use her property in a particular way and the licensee invests substantially in reasonable reliance on that permission, and revocation of the license would work an injustice.[98] The doctrine only applies if the reliance is reasonable and that is the case only if the licensor created the impression that the license would not be revoked, or a reasonable licensee would so construe the situation. When an owner conveys the impression that the licensee will have continued access, revocation of permission is the moral equivalent of fraud. It may actually be fraudulent, in the sense that the licensor made a false statement, which she knew was false at the time she made it, or the licensor deliberately failed to speak, knowing the licensee misunderstood the permission to be a grant of permanent rights, and the statement or silence was intended to induce reliance in the licensee.[99] But intention to mislead is not a requirement of the doctrine; it applies even if the licensor had no intention to mislead.[100] The doctrine protects the reliance interests of the licensee and applies even if the owner intended to create a revocable license when a reasonable licensee would have understood the arrangement to be a permanent one. The doctrine grants the licensee a permanent easement or an easement that will be irrevocable for whatever time is necessary to avoid injustice. The doctrine also applies when the grantor purports to grant an easement but does so orally or without a sufficient written memorandum that satisfies the requirements of the statute of frauds.

Revocation

Ambiguous deed references

Easements are created by estoppel in a variety of different situations.[101] First, an owner may grant an easement in writing but fail to satisfy the requirements of the statute of frauds. For example, in *Lawrence v. National*

[96] *See* §5.4.3.

[97] *See* §5.4.4.

[98] *Restatement (Third) of Property (Servitudes)* §2.10 (2000). The elements of an implied easement by estoppel are "a showing of inducement, reliance, user, and injury." *Jones v. Beavers*, 269 S.E.2d 775, 778 (Va. 1980). *See also Shearer v. Hodnette*, 674 So. 2d 548 (Ala. Civ. App. 1995); *Pinkston v. Hartley*, 511 So. 2d 168 (Ala. 1987); *Stoner v. Zucker*, 83 P. 808 (Cal. 1906); *Klobucar v. Stancik*, 485 N.E.2d 1334, 1336 (Neb. Ct. App. 1985); *Holbrook v. Taylor*, 532 S.W.2d 763 (Ky. 1976); *Kephart v. Portmann*, 855 P.2d 120 (Mont. 1993); *White v. Emmons*, 2012 WL 1595084 (Ohio Ct. App. 2012); *Shepard v. Purvine*, 248 P.2d 352 (Or. 1952); *Fast v. DeRaeve*, 714 P.2d 1077 (Or. Ct. App. 1986). *See also* Jon W. Bruce, James W. Ely, Jr., & Edward T. Brading, *The Law of Easements and Licenses in Land* §6:1, §§11:6 to 11:9 (2025).

[99] "One claiming an easement by estoppel must establish (1) misrepresentation or fraudulent failure to speak and (2) reasonable detrimental reliance." Jon W. Bruce, James W. Ely, Jr., & Edward T. Brading, *The Law of Easements and Licenses in Land* §6:1 (2025). *See Prospect Development Co., Inc. v. Bershader*, 515 S.E.2d 291 (Va. 1999) (fraudulent representations by seller that adjoining land would not be developed can entitle the buyer to an easement by estoppel preventing such development).

[100] Dale A. Whitman et al., *The Law of Property* §8.8, at 372-373 (4th ed. 2019).

[101] For still further permutations, see Jon W. Bruce, James W. Ely, Jr., & Edward T. Brading, *The Law of Easements and Licenses in Land* §6:1 (2025).

Fruit Co., Inc.,[102] a series of deeds referred to a road called "Strother's Lane" as the boundary line between several parcels of property. Although no deed explicitly created an easement to use the road, the court held that reference to the private road in a series of deeds implied that the road was available for use by the purchasers of contiguous land.[103] Although the court found that an express easement had been created, it also ruled that even if this were not the case, an easement would have been created by estoppel because the description of the road in the deeds suggested that the grantees could use the road, and, by purchasing the property, the grantees had relied on that implied representation. When this happens, the permission could no longer be revoked, even though none of the deeds explicitly described an "easement." The result was justified in two different ways. On the one hand, the court found that the grantor had intended to create an easement but had simply failed to use clear language in the deed stating so. On the other hand, the court implied that, even if the grantor had not intended to grant a permanent easement, the buyer had reasonably understood the reference to the road in the deed to constitute a grant of permission and when a buyer purchases property in reliance on such a representation, the licensor will not be allowed to revoke the permission.

Oral easements

Second, if an owner grants an easement orally, and the grantee invests in reliance on the ability to use the easement, the courts may find that an easement was created even though the grantor failed to put it in writing, as required by the statute of frauds. For example,

> if the vendor of land actually or constructively makes representations as to the existence of an easement appurtenant to the land sold to be enjoyed in land which the vendor has not sold [or] where a vendor describes the land sold as bounded on a street described as running through the vendor's unsold land, the vendor is, as against his vendee estopped from denying the existence of the easement.[104]

The doctrine also applies when a "grantor conveys an easement over land the grantor does not own and later the grantor acquires the property specified in the easement grant as the servient estate [the property over which the easement passes]."[105] Because easements have traditionally been

[102] 1997 WL 1070444 (Va. Cir. Ct. 1997).

[103] *See also Uliasz v. Gillette*, 256 N.E.2d 290, 295 (Mass. 1970) (holding that a grantor who conveys land by a description incorporating therein a recorded plan on which a street is shown, or by a description showing the land to be bounded on a street or way, is thereafter estopped, as are his successors in title, from denying the existence of an easement of travel over that street or way for the benefit of the grantee and his successors in title); *Bubis v. Kassin*, 733 A.2d 1232, 1236 (N.J. Super. Ct. App. Div. 1999).

[104] *Walters v. Smith*, 41 S.E.2d 617 (Va. 1947).

[105] When a grantor purports to create rights in land that the grantor does not own, and the grantor later comes to own that land, the courts will treat the rights as having been transferred to the grantee. This doctrine is called "estoppel by deed." 9-82 *Thompson on Real Property, Third Thomas Edition* §82.11. By analogy, the oral representation that a grantee will have an easement in the grantor's retained land may be enforced even though, because of mistake or inadvertence, no written memorandum of the easement is included in the deed transferred to the grantee.

conceptualized as "interests in land," every state requires them to be put in writing. The estoppel doctrine effects a judicially created exception to the state statute of frauds, which otherwise would treat the easement as a mere license, revocable at will.

Irrevocable licenses

The third and most controversial class of cases involves situations in which an owner intends to grant a revocable license, but the courts nevertheless convert it into a permanent (or semi-permanent) easement. If an owner gives someone else permission to perform certain acts on her land (such as passing over a road or driveway), and the licensee (the one given permission) invests substantially in reasonable reliance on that permission by expending money or labor or making improvements on her own land, the licensor who gave the permission may be *estopped* (prevented) from revoking that permission for whatever period is deemed necessary to protect the justified expectations of the licensee.[106] For example, in *Holbrook v. Taylor*,[107] defendant gave plaintiff neighboring landowners permission to use a road on defendants' property to get to plaintiffs' land. Plaintiffs built a home on their property in reliance on the ability to continue using that road to get to their property. No express easement was created in writing or otherwise. All defendants had done, was give plaintiffs permission to use the road to get to their property. After plaintiffs built their house, defendants tried to revoke permission and close off the road, but the court refused to let them do this. The licensor knew the licensees were building their house in reliance on the licensor's permission to use the road to get to their house. The court held that the licensor could not revoke under these circumstances and turned the revocable license into an "irrevocable license" — an oxymoron that effectively converts the license into an easement.

Promoting the intent of the grantor

Does the estoppel doctrine promote the intent of the grantor or protect the reliance interests of the grantee? Most of the reported cases involve situations in which the grantor has granted permission orally and has not used the technical word "easement" either orally or in writing. One interpretation of the doctrine is that the courts are presuming that grantors in these cases intend to grant easements but simply either fail to put this in writing or fail to use the correct technical language to do so. If this is true, granting the licensee an easement merely constitutes an exception to the statute of frauds; it does so by effectuating the intent of the grantor, preventing the grantor from revoking an express or implied promise to grant the easement.

Protecting the reliance interests of the grantee

However, an alternative interpretation is that the courts do not care whether the grantor intended to grant a license or an easement. Instead, they focus on the fact that the licensee reasonably relied on the permission, that the licensor knew or should have known that the licensee was so relying, that the licensee's expectations were justified, and that the licensee's justified expectations can be protected only by refusing to let the licensor

[106] *Holbrook v. Taylor*, 532 S.W.2d 763 (Ky. 1976); Dale A. Whitman et al., *The Law of Property* §8.8, at 372 (4th ed. 2019).

[107] 532 S.W.2d 763 (Ky. 1976).

revoke. Even if the grantor intended for the license to be revocable, the doctrine of easement by estoppel operates to make the license irrevocable.

Reliance and breach of trust

Most of the courts appear to adopt this second interpretation. They have adopted an interpretive rule that protects the reliance interests of the licensee over the interests of the licensor in revoking permission. They do so because a licensee who invests substantially in reliance on the permission obviously believes that the permission will not be revoked and, if this is not the case, the licensor should say something to the licensee. The failure to speak conveys a message to the licensee that the license will not be revoked; if the licensor intends to reserve the right to revoke, she must make this clear to the licensee. If the licensor does not clarify that the license is revocable at will and the licensee trusts the licensor's good will, the licensor will not be allowed to breach that trust by revoking permission after the investment has been made and the reliance has occurred.[108]

The argument against easement by estoppel

Some older cases (and a handful of recent cases) reject the doctrine entirely, arguing that those who want easements should bargain for them and put them in writing.[109] A number of courts insist that the crux of the doctrine is that the licensor misled the licensee by making a false representation or a representation that the licensor knew would be understood as granting more than the licensor intended to grant.[110] Those courts might not grant an easement by estoppel if they believed that the grantor intended to grant only a revocable license and that the licensor had no subjective intent to mislead the licensee. They might so limit the doctrine because they believe that any relaxation of the statute of frauds will increase uncertainty in land titles and encourage the very frauds that the statute of frauds was intended to prevent. Requiring easements to be described clearly in writing prevents owners from falsely claiming that others gave them oral permission to cross their property and that they relied on that oral statement in constructing their homes.[111] It therefore clarifies property rights, prevents fraud, and decreases needless litigation.

The counterargument for a more expansive interpretation of the doctrine, is that it is necessary to protect the justified expectations of the licensee, that it applies only in relatively clear and predictable circumstances, *i.e.*, when the licensee foreseeably invests substantially in reasonable reliance on the license, and that a reasonable licensor should have known that the licensee understood the permission as a permanent grant

[108] Dale A. Whitman et al., *The Law of Property* §8.8, at 372 (4th ed. 2019).

[109] *Girani v. Lovorn*, 270 So. 3d 1070 (Miss. Ct. App. 2018); *Kitchen v. Kitchen*, 641 N.W.2d 245 (Mich. 2002); *Nelson v. American Telephone & Telegraph Co.*, 170 N.E. 416 (Mass. 1930); *Henry v. Dalton*, 151 A.2d 362 (R.I. 1959).

[110] *Flaig v. Gramm*, 983 P.2d 396, 398-399 (Mont. 1999); *I.R.T. Property Co. v. Sheehan*, 581 So. 2d 591, 593 (Fla. Dist. Ct. App. 1991) ("A party may only prevail under the theory of equitable estoppel where there is proof of fraud, misrepresentation, or other affirmative deception"); *Jordan v. Rash*, 745 S.W.2d 549, 554 (Tex. Ct. App. 1988) ("Essential to the creation of an easement by estoppel is that a misrepresentation be communicated to, believed by, and relied upon by the innocent party").

[111] *Henry v. Dalton*, 151 A.2d 362 (R.I. 1959). *See also Nelson v. American Telephone & Telegraph Co.*, 170 N.E. 416 (Mass. 1930).

of an easement, and thus cannot reasonably complain she is losing rights that she did not intend to give away.

▶ **HARD CASE**

▷ HEARSAY

In *Van Schaack v. Torsoe*,[112] plaintiff who inherited property from her parents alleged that the neighbors had promised her parents that they would sell them a strip of land along the border for use as a driveway. The parents built their house in reliance on this permission, there being no other way to get to the parking spaces behind the house. For a while, they lived without the driveway, parking on the street. Plaintiff inherited the house from her parents, street parking was cut off, and she sued the neighbors, claiming an easement by estoppel. The court excluded plaintiff's proffered evidence on the ground that it was inadmissible "hearsay." The hearsay rules are grounded on worries about the reliability of evidence involving things said to people who cannot testify and the inability to cross-examine the one who spoke to determine whether they are credible. On the other hand, "[a]n easement by estoppel, once created, is binding upon successors in title if reliance upon the existence of the easement continues,"[113] and excluding the evidence might effectively allow the licensor to evade the result that would otherwise obtain under the doctrine of easement by estoppel and work an injustice against a party who reasonably relied on the representation to her detriment. ◀

Negative easements by estoppels

Although most easements by estoppel are affirmative, some cases involve representations that a grantor's reserved land will not be used for certain purposes. Such promises are usually regulated by the law of covenants, rather than the law of easements, and are called "equitable servitudes." They may arise, for example, if a developer sells some homes in a subdivision with restrictions that limit the land to residential use and orally promises the buyers that all the lots in the subdivision will be similarly restricted, but fails to include restrictions in some number of the properties that are later sold. Those "unrestricted" lots may be held subject to the restrictions by implying reciprocal "negative easements," otherwise known as "equitable servitudes." This topic is treated in depth in Chapter 6.

§5.4.2 Constructive Trust

Breach of trust

An alternative basis for imposing an easement by estoppel is the *constructive trust* doctrine. A trust is a property arrangement that empowers one person (the trustee) to manage property for the benefit of another person (the beneficiary). Trusts are usually created by a donor who wishes to give a gift but wants to ensure that the donee uses the property in a particular way. Constructive trusts are implied by law rather than created expressly by a

[112] 555 N.Y.S.2d 836 (App. Div. 1990).
[113] *Holden v. Weidenfeller*, 929 S.W.2d 124, 131 (Tex. Ct. App. 1996).

donor. They effectively require a property owner to use her property for the benefit of another, or to grant a non-owner access to the property, or to transfer possession or ownership to another. A constructive trust may be imposed when property has been acquired in such circumstances that the "holder of the legal title may not in good conscience retain the beneficial interest."[114] A constructive trust is "implied whenever the circumstances are such that the person holding legal title to property, either from fraud or otherwise, cannot enjoy the beneficial interest in the property without violating some established principle of equity."[115] When one person has been "wrongfully deprived" of some "right, benefit, or title" to property "either by mistake, fraud, or some other breach of faith or confidence," a court may deprive the holder of legal title of the right to control the property.[116] Instead, the legal holder may be "deemed to hold the property as a trustee for the beneficial use of that party which has been wrongfully deprived of its rights."[117]

▷ LICENSE TO BUILD A HOME ON LAND OWNED BY ANOTHER **HARD CASE ◀**

The doctrine generally is intended in equity to prevent "unjust enrichment" of the legal holder,[118] and may apply when a party is "induced to make valuable improvements on real property."[119] It therefore may apply in the same circumstances in which the doctrine of easement by estoppel is available. In *Rase v. Castle Mountain Ranch*,[120] for example, an owner of a large ranch allowed a number of his friends, neighbors, and employees to build cabins around a lake located on the ranch. The owner refused to sell or lease the land, instead merely granting revocable licenses. At first, the permission was oral, but later written license agreements were granted, which expressly provided that they were terminable by the licensor/landowner with 30 days' notice. The cabins remained for at least 50 years. When the property was sold, no written restrictions were placed in the deed that would have limited the ability of the buyer to terminate the licenses. When the new owner attempted to do so, the cabin owners sued, claiming that the licenses were irrevocable and should be interpreted as granting them permanent easements. The court applied the constructive trust doctrine, holding that the original landowner had "engaged in a course of conduct . . . that gave the cabin owners an implied assurance of a somewhat permanent tenure sufficient that they made substantial investments in erecting and maintaining

[114] *Sharper v. Harlem Teams for Self-Help, Inc.*, 696 N.Y.S.2d 109, 111 (App. Div. 1999).

[115] *Lathem v. Hestley*, 514 S.E.2d 440, 442 (Ga. 1999).

[116] Steven Gifis, *Law Dictionary* 213 (1975).

[117] *Id.; see also Snider v. Arnold*, 289 P.3d 43 (Idaho 2012) (finding constructive trust on cabin permitted in brother's name in favor of sister); *Simons v. Simons*, 978 N.W.2d 121 (Neb. 2022) (constructive trust imposed on business that ex-wife had helped to develop under her understanding of joint ownership but that ex-husband had titled only in in his name).

[118] Steven Gifis, *Law Dictionary* 213 (1975).

[119] *Lathem v. Hestley*, 514 S.E.2d 440, 442 (Ga. 1999).

[120] 631 P.2d 680 (Mont. 1981).

the cabins openly recognized by [the landowner]."[121] However, rather than granting permanent easements, the court gave the cabin owners the choice of staying for another 13 years (at which point they would be required to move their homes off the land if they wanted to keep them), or they could accept immediate payment from the new owner for the fair market value of their homes if the owner was willing and able to buy them out immediately. A concurring opinion would have granted the cabin owners 50 years to stay on the premises rather than 13.

Competing sources of property rights: formal arrangements v. informal expectations

These kinds of cases raise interesting conflicts between an approach to property rights that focuses on formal title and one that considers also informally created expectations. On the one hand, one might argue that the licensees knew that their licenses were revocable and that they had no legitimate expectation that they had a lease or easement or any more permanent right. They took a chance that the license would not be revoked, and it is arguably unfair to strip the owner of rights the owner had not given away. On the other hand, one can argue that the licensor should have known that no one would build a house on land belonging to another unless she had an expectation that the license was not revocable at will. The licensor who gives a revocable license to build a house on the licensor's land at least gives mixed messages. When the licensee is obviously trusting the licensor by building the home, it is unfair for the licensor to abuse that trust by treating the permission as a mere license. Of course, in the *Castle Mountain Ranch* case, the homes were allowed to exist for more than 50 years, and it might be argued that whatever expectations the licensees had had been more than fulfilled.

Fiduciary relationship

Some courts require a showing of a "confidential or fiduciary relationship" that would justify the reliance.[122] Other courts do not limit the constructive trust doctrine in this way.[123] The issue arises whether such a relationship should be required before the constructive trust doctrine can be applied, and, if so, what kinds of relationships satisfy the requirement? A narrow definition of a "fiduciary relationship" would look to relationships that are of a personal nature and have formal legal responsibilities, such as relations between spouses and between parents and children. A more expansive definition would focus on the fact of a relationship that suggests the parties are likely to repose trust in each other; this definition might include, for example, other family relationships outside the nuclear family (such as relations between an uncle and a nephew)[124] or unmarried couples.[125] A more expansive definition still would encompass any relationship where one party placed trust in the good will of the other; this might

[121] *Id.* at 685.

[122] *Sharper v. Harlem Teams for Self-Help, Inc.*, 696 N.Y.S.2d 109, 111 (App. Div. 1999).

[123] *Rase v. Castle Mountain Ranch*, 631 P.2d 680 (Mont. 1981).

[124] *Rudow v. Fogel*, 426 N.E.2d 155 (Mass. App. Ct. 1981).

[125] *Lathem v. Hestley*, 514 S.E.2d 440, 442 (Ga. 1999); *Sullivan v. Rooney*, 533 N.E.2d 1372 (Mass. 1989); *Watts v. Watts*, 405 N.W.2d 303 (Wis. 1987). *But see Collins v. Guggenheim*, 631 N.E.2d 1016 (Mass. 1994) (no constructive trust for unmarried couple in the absence of "fraud, breach of fiduciary duty or other misconduct").

include relations between employers and employees or among neighbors or friends, as existed in the *Castle Mountain Ranch* case.[126] The widest conception of the doctrine would not require a showing of a special relationship but would instead ask whether the reliance by the licensee was reasonable under the circumstances.[127] ◀

§5.4.3 Implied from Prior Use

Easement implied from prior use

When an owner of a large tract of land or two adjoining parcels sells one parcel and keeps the other, the owner of one of the parcels may sometimes claim an easement in the other, even though the deed fails to create an express easement. The courts will imply an easement from prior use if (1) the two parcels were at one time in common ownership;[128] (2) one of the parcels had derived a "benefit or advantage" from the other parcel prior to the sale; (3) this use was both apparent and continuous; and (4) continuation of the use is "reasonably necessary" or "convenient" to enjoyment of the dominant estate (the parcel seeking to use the easement on the other's land).[129] Easements implied from prior use are also called "quasi-easements."[130] Courts imply easements from prior use to enforce the presumed intent of the parties that was imperfectly expressed in the formal documents in cases where omission of the easement was clearly a mistake.[131] These cases present conflicts between the owner who claims a right to use her property free from any easements that were not reduced to writing, and the owner who claims that the prior use of the land strongly suggested that one of the parcels was subject to an easement for the benefit of the other.

Kinds of implied easements

Most implied easements concern rights of way for passage of people or vehicles,[132] but other common cases include continued access to sewer lines crossing under the grantor's remaining land,[133] rights to enter a neighbor's land to repair a common wall,[134] or rights to obtain water from a well.[135]

126 *Rase v. Castle Mountain Ranch*, 631 P.2d 680 (Mont. 1981).

127 This is the apparent holding of *Rase v. Castle Mountain Ranch*, 631 P.2d 680 (Mont. 1981).

128 *See Holden v. Weidenfeller*, 929 S.W.2d 124 (Tex. Ct. App. 1996) (no implied easement when the parcels had not previously been owned by a common grantor).

129 *Dubin v. Chesebrough Trust*, 116 Cal. Rptr. 2d 872 (Ct. App. 2002); *Harrington v. Lamarque*, 677 N.E.2d 258 (Mass. App. Ct. 1997); *Flaig v. Gramm*, 983 P.2d 396, 399 (Mont. 1999); *Graham v. Mack*, 699 P.2d 590 (Mont. 1984); *Bubis v. Kassin*, 733 A.2d 1232 (N.J. Super. Ct. App. Div. 1999); *Rogers v. Roach*, 2012 WL 2337616 (Tenn. Ct. App. 2012); *Houston Bellaire, Ltd. v. TCP LB Portfolio I*, 981 S.W.2d 916 (Tex. Ct. App. 1998).

130 7-60 *Thompson on Real Property, Third Thomas Edition* §60.03(b)(5)(i).

131 *Harrington v. Lamarque*, 677 N.E.2d 258 (Mass. App. Ct. 1997) ("Implied easements, whether by grant or by reservation, do not arise out of necessity alone. Their origin must be found in a presumed intention of the parties, to be gathered from the language of the instruments when read in the light of the circumstances attending their execution, the physical condition of the premises, and the knowledge which the parties had or with which they are chargeable"); *Restatement (Third) of Property (Servitudes)* §2.12 (2000).

132 *Granite Properties Limited Partnership v. Manns*, 512 N.E.2d 1230 (Ill. 1987); *Cheney v. Mueller*, 485 P.2d 1218 (Or. 1971).

133 *Bowers v. Andrews*, 557 A.2d 606 (Me. 1989).

134 *Pave v. Mills*, No. 97-5210B (slip opinion) (Mass. Super. Ct. 1999) (described in 27 Mass. Lawyers Weekly 2539 (7/19/99)).

135 *Storck v. Storck*, 1999 WL 326160 (Minn. Ct. App. 1999).

Other more controversial cases include access to recreational facilities (such as access to a lake or beach).[136] On the one hand, access to a lake cannot be said to be "necessary." On the other hand, such access may very well have induced the buyers to buy, and they may well have relied on the ability to use the lake in determining how much to offer for the property near it.

Easements by reservation and easements by grant

Courts are more likely to imply an easement to a grantee than to a grantor. A grantee (or buyer) who claims an easement over remaining land of the grantor seeks an *easement by grant*; the grantee claims that the land she bought includes an appurtenant easement to cross the grantor's remaining land. When the easement seems necessary to the reasonable enjoyment of the dominant estate, the courts are likely to view the omission of the easement as a mutual mistake and, in effect, reform the deed to comply with the presumed intent of the parties to grant the easement. Courts are far less likely, however, to recognize such easements in a grantor. When the grantor claims that she intended to *reserve* an easement over the land conveyed to the grantee, most courts want a higher level of certainty that the easement is necessary to the enjoyment of the grantor's retained land.[137] This is because the grantee is likely to assume that the grantor is parting with all her rights in the property being conveyed to the grantee. If the grantor intends to reserve some rights in the land being conveyed, she better do so explicitly, or the grantee will be unfairly surprised. A claim that the grantor did not intend to convey an unencumbered lot might even be fraudulent; it is, at least, misleading to the grantee. The courts, therefore, are loath to recognize easements by reservation, unless they are very confident that a reasonable grantee should have understood that the property being purchased would be subject to continuing rights by the grantor.

Easement implied from ambiguous deed language or map

Easements may also be implied from ambiguous deed references[138] or from roads drawn on a map to which the deed refers.[139]

It is firmly established that when land is sold with reference to a map on which lots and streets are delineated, the purchaser acquires an implied private right-of-way over the streets. The sale of lots with reference to a map on which streets are delineated also constitutes "a dedication of such streets to the public."[140]

In most circumstances, such implied easements give the landowners access "from or to some public highway."[141] "However, if the location of the lots or the circumstances surrounding the conveyance indicate that a more expansive right-of-way is necessary for the purchaser to obtain the full beneficial enjoyment of the lot, the courts will recognize whatever implied right of access is required to carry out the intent of the conveyance."[142] For

[136] *Bubis v. Kassin*, 733 A.2d 1232 (N.J. Super. Ct. App. Div. 1999); *Favart* v. *Ouellette*, 239 A.3d 994 (N.H. 2020).

[137] *Granite Properties Limited P'ship v. Manns*, 512 N.E.2d 1230, 1238 (Ill. 1987).

[138] *LeMay v. Anderson*, 397 A.2d 984 (Me. 1979); *Heim v. Conroy*, 621 N.Y.S.2d 210 (App. Div. 1995); 4-34 *Powell on Real Property* §34.06.

[139] 4-34 *Powell on Real Property* §34.06; *Restatement (Third) of Property (Servitudes)* §2.13 (2000).

[140] *Bubis v. Kassin*, 733 A.2d 1232, 1236 (N.J. Super. Ct. App. Div. 1999).

[141] *Id.* at 1237.

[142] *Id.*

example, in *Bubis v. Kassin*,[143] a developer of a seaside community prepared a map prior to selling the lots, which showed roads leading from the properties to the beach and included in the deeds a general easement of access to the beach. When one of those roads was later blocked off, the court held that, although ambiguous, "any person acquiring one of those lots would reasonably have assumed that one of the benefits of property ownership was convenient access to the beach and ocean by means of this street network."[144] Because the plaintiffs' lots were not contiguous to the beach, the only way they could obtain access to the beach "without passing over the lots of other property owners would have been by walking along the streets shown on the map."[145] Therefore, the court concluded that the use of the streets drawn on the map that provide access to the beach and ocean were "necessary or useful for the beneficial enjoyment of the lot[s] conveyed" and should be recognized as implied easements.

Reasonably necessary or highly convenient

A great deal of litigation concerns the question of "reasonable necessity."[146] When an owner sells an otherwise landlocked parcel, a right-of-way to a public road will be recognized under the doctrine of necessity if there is no other way for the grantee to get to a public way.[147] In such cases, no easement will be recognized unless the necessity is absolute, *i.e.*, no other exit to a public way is available. On the other hand, in the case of a non-landlocked parcel, an easement will be implied from prior use even if it is not absolutely necessary, as long as it is "reasonably necessary." Most courts interpret this to mean that the easement must be important to the enjoyment of the land. The requirement, thus, is sometimes said to be merely that the easement be "highly convenient"[148] rather than "necessary." The test is intended to prevent burdening neighboring land without a sufficiently strong reason while implementing the presumed intent of the parties. "The principle underlying the creation of an easement by implication is that it is so evidently necessary to the reasonable enjoyment of the granted premises, so continuous in its nature, so plain, visible, and open, so manifest from the situation and relation of the two tracts that the law will give effect to the grant according to the presumed intent of the parties."[149] Easements are likely to be implied if access to the land is extremely difficult by other routes,[150] and will be denied if the owner has easy access to public roads in another direction.[151]

143 *Id.* at 1232.

144 *Id.* at 1237.

145 *Id.*

146 *See, e.g.*, *Harkness v. Butterworth Hunting Club, Inc.*, 58 So. 3d 703 (Miss. Ct. App. 2011). *See* 7-60 *Thompson on Real Property, Third Thomas Edition* §60.03(b)(5)(ii).

147 *See* §5.3.4.

148 *Gemmell v. Lee*, 757 A.2d 1171 (Conn. App. Ct. 2000); *Granite Properties Limited Partnership v. Manns*, 512 N.E.2d 1230, 1235 (Ill. 1987).

149 *Il Giardino v. The Belle Haven Land Co.*, 1999 WL 436368, at *7 (Conn. Super. Ct. 1999), *rev'd on other grounds*, 757 A.2d 1103 (Conn. 2000).

150 *See, e.g.*, *Aizpitarte v. Minear*, 508 P.3d 1260 (Idaho 2022) (driveway was reasonably necessary despite alternative driveway because alternative was prone to flooding and too narrow to allow vehicles to turn around); *Granite Prop. Ltd P'ship v. Manns*, 512 N.E.2d 1230 (Ill. 1987) (no other reasonable access to apartment parking lot or to shopping center for delivery trucks).

151 *Clark v. Galaxy Apartments*, 427 N.W.2d 723 (Minn. Ct. App. 1988).

Cemetery rights

The descendants of persons who are buried in a cemetery may acquire an implied easement of access to the land where their ancestors are buried. They also may be entitled to an injunction preventing the owner of the land from defacing the graves or interfering with the "reverential character" of the graves.[152]

§5.4.4 *Necessity*

Landlocked parcels

Easements are implied by necessity when an owner sells a landlocked parcel. In such cases, the owner of the landlocked parcel has a right of access through the grantor's remaining land to get to a public road.[153] Unlike the rule that implies easements from prior use, no prior use is required to obtain an *easement by necessity.* At the same time, the necessity requirement is interpreted strictly; only landlocked parcels that have no other access to a public road can benefit from the doctrine.[154] It is important to remember as well that the doctrine only applies to *remaining land of the grantor*, not to neighboring land generally.[155]

▶ HARD CASE ▷ DEFAULT RULE OR MANDATORY RULE

Does the doctrine of easement by necessity promote the presumed intent of the parties or is it a mandatory rule? An owner might agree to buy the backyard of someone's house without an easement over the grantor's remaining land because the grantee intends to access the public street through a neighbor's driveway. If access to the neighbor's driveway is revoked, does an easement spring into being over the grantor's remaining land?

The argument for intent

Some courts hold that no easement will be recognized in this situation. They hold that easements are created by necessity to effectuate the presumed intent of the parties. "The public policy is implemented by

[152] *Bogner v. Villiger*, 796 N.E.2d 679 (Ill. App. Ct. 2003). *Accord, Mallock v. Southern Memorial Park, Inc.*, 561 So. 2d 330 (Fla. Dist. Ct. App. 1990) (discussing a Florida statute that creates such rights, Fla. Stat. §704.08); *Sanford v. Vinal*, 552 N.E.2d 579 (Mass. App. Ct. 1990) (discussing abandonment of such an easement).

[153] *Strollo v. Iannantuoni*, 734 A.2d 144 (Conn. App. Ct. 1999); *Hewitt v. Meaney*, 226 Cal. Rptr. 349 (Ct. App. 1986); *Machado v. Ryan*, 280 P.3d 715, 722 (Idaho 2012); *Finn v. Williams*, 33 N.E.2d 226 (Ill. 1941); *Taylor v. Hays*, 551 So. 2d 906, 908 (Miss. 1989); *Fike v. Shelton*, 860 So. 2d 1227 (Miss. Ct. App. 2003); *Pitts v. Foster*, 743 So. 2d 1066 (Miss. Ct. App. 1999); 4-34 *Powell on Real Property* §34.07.

[154] *Compare Morehouse v. Dux North LLC*, 226 N.E.3d 758 (Ind. 2024) (no necessity although rough terrain and wetlands meant there was no practical means of access), *with Mississippi Power Co. v. Fairchild*, 791 So. 2d 262 (Miss. Ct. App. 2001) (power company entitled to easement by necessity when its land was separated by river and cost of bridge construction was prohibitive) *and Bartkowski v. Ramondo*, 219 A.3d 1083 (Pa. 2019) (recognizing easement by necessity even though land contained a small strip connected to a public way, because lack of access would not allow ordinary uses of the property).

[155] One question that arises in easements implied by necessity is what uses are permitted on the easement. Courts, for example, have allowed easement by necessity for utilities over existing rights of way to support the continued use of property. *See Francini v. Goodspeed Airport, LLC*, 174 A.3d 779, 786-787 (Conn. 2018).

the law's presumption that a grantor implicitly conveys or reserves whatever is necessary to put property to beneficial use, despite the omission to make any such express provision. The law thus presumes the common owner intended the easement."[156] If the parties clearly intended *not* to create an easement, then one will not be recognized.[157] This is the view taken by the *Restatement (Third) of Property (Servitudes)*.[158] Indeed, the Supreme Court of California refused to recognize an easement by necessity for a landlocked parcel when there was insufficient evidence to demonstrate that the grantor (in this case, the federal government) had intended to reserve such an easement.[159]

This result might be justified if one thought that the prime goal of the law was to allow owners to divide up property rights in whatever way they see fit. The landlocked owner is free to try to purchase an easement from the grantor or any of the neighbors. If the landlocked owner really values the easement more than the grantor values keeping her property unencumbered by an easement, then the landlocked owner will offer enough to induce the grantor to agree to sell an easement. If the grantor nonetheless rejects the deal, it will arguably reduce social welfare to force a sale; this would grant the entitlement to the party who values it less. It might appear to be a waste of resources to have a landlocked parcel because the owner cannot get to her property and thus cannot use it. However, it is not the case that society would be better off if every single parcel were developed and used. Moreover, she is free to sell the property back to the grantor or one of the other neighbors. Third parties are always free to bargain with both owners to purchase the parcels, to reunite them.

The argument for public policy

On the other hand, some courts hold that easements are recognized by necessity regardless of the intent of the parties. In effect, they have created a mandatory rule that owners cannot create landlocked parcels, even if the owner of the landlocked parcel agrees. "A way of necessity is . . . supported by the rule of sound public policy that lands should not be rendered unfit for occupancy or successful cultivation."[160] As the Maine Supreme Court held, "Because of the strict necessity of having access to the landlocked parcel, an easement over the grantor's remaining land benefiting the landlocked lot is implied as a matter of law irrespective of the true intent of the common grantor."[161] These courts assume that owners have a right to get

[156] *Hewitt v. Meaney*, 226 Cal. Rptr. 349, 351 (Ct. App. 1986).

[157] *Kitras v. Town of Aquinnah*, 49 N.E.3d 198 (Mass. 2016).

[158] 226 Cal. Rptr. at 351 (holding that "an easement by necessity will not be imposed contrary to the actual intent of the parties"); *Shpak v. Oletsky*, 373 A.2d 1234 (Md. 1977) (holding that no law prohibits an owner from cutting herself off from all access to her land); *Vigeant v. Donel Realty Trust*, 540 A.2d 1243 (N.H. 1988) (no easement by necessity without implied intent); *Restatement (Third) of Property (Servitudes)* §2.15 (2000).

[159] *Murphy v. Burch*, 205 P.3d 289 (Cal. 2009).

[160] *Burley Brick and Sand Company v. Cofer*, 629 P.2d 1166, 1168 (Idaho 1981) (*quoting Martino v. Fleenor*, 365 P.2d 247, 249 (Colo. 1961)).

[161] *Frederick v. Consol. Waste Servs., Inc.*, 573 A.2d 387, 389 (Me. 1990). *Accord, Traders, Inc. v. Bartholomew*, 459 A.2d 974, 978 (Vt. 1983) ("[a] way of necessity rests on public policy often thwarting the intent of the original grantor or grantee, and arises to meet a special emergency in order that no land be left inaccessible for the purposes of cultivation").

to their own land; ownership is meaningless if one cannot get to the property one owns. These courts assume that allowing a parcel to be landlocked would "hold land in perpetual idleness."[162] Although the landlocked owner can try to buy an easement from the grantor or other neighbors, transaction costs may block a deal. The neighbors may be disinclined to bargain with each other.[163] The grantor may believe, for example, that she is *entitled* to be free of the intrusion and that sense of entitlement may either raise her asking price or may prevent her from even considering a deal. Similarly, the owner of the landlocked parcel may feel entitled to get to her own land and believe the grantor is acting unreasonably or unfairly; she may therefore refuse to offer enough to make a deal likely. Prohibiting owners from creating landlocked parcels will ensure that owners can get to their property; this, in turn, will ensure that each parcel is available for use or transfer in the marketplace. ◀

▶ HARD CASE

▷ SCOPE OF EASEMENT

In *Strollo v. Iannantuoni,*[164] the trial court recognized an easement by necessity but limited the road to 20 feet in width. The owner of the dominant estate appealed, arguing that, although 20 feet was adequate for the agricultural and recreational purposes to which the land had originally been used, it was inadequate if the owner wished to subdivide the land. The court of appeals refused to grant the request to widen the easement to 50 feet, as would be needed for a road adequate to a subdivision. The court held that it was not

> reasonably essential to the plaintiffs' use of their property to impose an easement of necessity that is fifty feet wide on the defendants' property simply to accommodate the plaintiffs' desire to profit from a potential subdivision. Moreover, the creation of such a right-of-way would work a serious inequity on the defendants.[165]

One might argue that an easement by necessity should be recognized, not just to provide access to the land, but to provide access to every part of the land. Because it was foreseeable that an owner might subdivide and develop the property, the owner of the landlocked parcel should be entitled to an accessway that is appropriate to such development.

Statutory remedies

Some states grant owners of landlocked parcels the power to obtain an easement over neighboring land for access to a public road by application to a public official with compensation paid to the landowner whose

[162] *Id.*
[163] Ward Farnsworth, *Do Parties to Nuisance Cases Bargain After Judgment? A Glimpse Inside the Cathedral*, 66 U. Chi. L. Rev. 373 (1999).
[164] 734 A.2d 144 (Conn. App. Ct. 1999).
[165] *Id.* at 145. *But see Town of Bedford v. Cerasuolo*, 814 N.E.2d 561 (Mass. App. Ct. 2004) (easement by necessity can be widened to accommodate foreseeable development).

property is burdened by the easement.[166] However, some courts have found such statutes unconstitutional takings of property under the state constitution because property may be taken by eminent domain only for a "public purpose" and transfer of property from one owner to another arguably does not constitute such a public purpose when its only goal is to protect the interests of an owner who could have avoided owning a landlocked parcel by bargaining originally for such an easement from the grantor.[167] This is not the view of the vast majority of courts, including the U.S. Supreme Court, which hold that public purposes are often served by transferring property from one private owner to another.[168] It would seem that preventing a scarce resource such as land from being rendered unusable or inalienable would constitute a legitimate public policy. ◀

§5.5 Prescriptive Easements

Prescription

Just as title to real property may be acquired by adverse possession, easements may be acquired by *prescription*.[169] If one uses someone else's property in a manner that is visible, continuous, and nonpermissive for a period established by the statute of limitations, one can acquire a prescriptive right to continue that use.[170] Nonpermissive use of another's land is a trespass, and just as the statute of limitations can run on a claim for possession or ejectment, so can the statute run on a trespassory but nonpossessive use, effectively precluding the owner of the land from interfering with that use in the future. Prescriptive easements run with the land and are binding on subsequent owners of the servient estate.[171]

Lost grant

Originally, statutes of limitation applied only to possessory claims, so English judges invented a common law doctrine analogous to the law of adverse possession to recognize prescriptive easements. They presumed that a use that had lasted for a long time had a lawful origin and that it was based on a "lost grant."[172] While American courts originally adopted this theory,

[166] Ala. Code §18-3-1; Ark. Stat. §27-66-401; Mass. Gen. Laws ch. 82, §24; Miss. Code §65-7-201; Or. Rev. Stat. §§376.150 - 200; Wash. Rev. Code §8.24.010.

[167] *See Tolksdorf v. Griffith*, 626 N.W.2d 163 (Mich. 2001); *In re Opening Private Road ex rel. O'Reilly*, 5 A.3d 246 (Pa. 2010). *See also State Highway Comm'n v. Batts*, 144 S.E.2d 126 (N.C. 1965) (use of eminent domain to construct road for access to one home does not serve a public purpose); *Jones v. Winckelmann*, 516 S.E.2d 876 (N.C. Ct. App. 1999) (Lewis, J., concurring).

[168] *See, e.g., Hawai'i Hous. Auth. v. Midkiff*, 467 U.S. 229 (1984).

[169] *See* John A. Lovett, *Restating the Law of Prescriptive Easements*, 104 Marq. L. Rev. 939 (2021).

[170] *McDonald v. Harris*, 978 P.2d 81 (Alaska 1999); *Wood v. Hoglund*, 963 P.2d 383, 386 (Idaho 1998); *Hoffman v. United Iron and Metal Co., Inc.*, 671 A.2d 55, 64 (Md. Ct. Spec. App. 1996); *White v. Hartigan*, 982 N.E.2d 1115, 1126 (Mass. 2013); *Burke-Tarr Co. v. Ferland Corp.*, 724 A.2d 1014, 1019 (R.I. 1999); *Edgell v. Canning*, 976 P.2d 1193, 1195 (Utah 1999); *Restatement (Third) of Property (Servitudes)* §§2.16, 2.17 (2000).

[171] *Cushman v. Davis*, 145 Cal. Rptr. 791 (Ct. App. 1978); *Logan v. McGee*, 320 So. 2d 792 (Miss. 1975).

[172] Jon W. Bruce, James W. Ely, Jr., & Edward T. Brading, *The Law of Easements and Licenses in Land* §5:1 (2025).

the modern approach bases the prescriptive easement doctrine on the idea that easements are interests in property and that such claims are lost if not brought within the time period for suing to protect property rights.[173]

Elements

There is a large amount of variation among courts in describing the elements necessary to establish a prescriptive easement. All courts require (1) that there be a *use* of property belonging to another; (2) that the use be "open and notorious" or visible;[174] (3) that it be "continuous" and/or "uninterrupted"; and (4) that it last for the statutory period.[175] A significant number of states require (5) that the owner of the land "acquiesce" in the adverse use. This is a confusing term. For some courts, it means that the owner did not assert her right to exclude by bringing a trespass action; this interpretation renders the requirement duplicative and unnecessary. For other courts, it means that the landowner must have *known* about the use.[176] Some states also require that the use be (6) "exclusive"[177] and a few require that the use be (7) under a "claim of right" or "ownership."[178] As with adverse possession, many courts require proof of adverse use by clear and convincing evidence,[179] while some require only that the claimant prove the elements by a preponderance of the evidence.[180]

Use

An easement is a nonpossessory right in someone else's property.[181] Possession is occupation of land with the intent to control it.[182] An easement is a use less than full possession or occupation. Generally, easements encompass only specific entitlements, such as a right to pass over the land, to remove minerals, lumber, or other physical aspects of the land,[183] or the right to use the property for specific purposes, such as recreational uses.

[173] *Id.*
[174] *Compare 143-145 Nahant Rd, LLC v. Mastoras*, 2014 WL 2548094 (Mass. Land Ct. 2014) (holding that no prescriptive easement can arise no matter how long a sewer pipe has traversed a neighbor's property because the nonpermissive use was not "open and notorious" and there were no other indications that the pipe was there) *with Dunning v. Larsen*, 2015 WL 5920263 (Mass. Land Ct. 2015) (utility easement is open and notorious when clues above land indicate its existence such as the existence of telephone and electricity service).
[175] Jon W. Bruce, James W. Ely, Jr., & Edward T. Brading, *The Law of Easements and Licenses in Land* §5:2 (2025).
[176] *Wood v. Hoglund*, 963 P.2d 383, 386 (Idaho 1998).
[177] *Albert v. Fort Worth & W. R.R. Co.*, 690 S.W.3d 92 (Tex. 2024).
[178] *Wood v. Hoglund*, 963 P.2d 383, 386-387 (Idaho 1998); *Rogers v. Marlin*, 754 So. 2d 1267, at 1272 (Miss. Ct. App. 1999).
[179] *McDonald v. Harris*, 978 P.2d 81 (Alaska 1999); *Wareing v. Schreckendgust*, 930 P.2d 37, 41-43 (Mont. 1996); *Daniello v. Wagner*, 200 N.Y.S.3d 423, 428 (App. Div. 2d Dep't 2023); *Cincotta v. Jerome*, 717 A.2d 639 (R.I. 1998) ("clear and satisfactory evidence"); Jon W. Bruce, James W. Ely, Jr., & Edward T. Brading, *The Law of Easements and Licenses in Land* §5:3 (2025).
[180] *Stiefel v. Lindemann*, 638 A.2d 642, 649 n.8 (Conn. App. Ct. 1994); *Vigeant v. Donel Realty Trust*, 540 A.2d 1243 (N.H. 1988) ("by the balance of probabilities"); Jon W. Bruce, James W. Ely, Jr., & Edward T. Brading, *The Law of Easements and Licenses in Land* §5:3 (2025).
[181] Jon W. Bruce, James W. Ely, Jr., & Edward T. Brading, *The Law of Easements and Licenses in Land* §1:1 (2025).
[182] *Sutherlin School District #130 v. Herrera*, 851 P.2d 1171, 1174 (Or. Ct. App. 1993); *Restatement (Second) of Torts* §157 (1965). Possession may also refer to the legal right to immediate occupancy when no other person has occupied the land. *Id.*
[183] A right to remove minerals or lumber or other physical parts of the land is called a "profit" or a *profit à prendre*.

When someone uses someone else's property without permission, the question often arises as to whether the adverse claimant has exercised sufficient control to obtain title by adverse possession or, on the contrary, has only engaged in specific acts that would result in a grant of an easement by prescription. In general, enclosing the land by a fence or building structures on it is sufficient to demonstrate an intent to possess the property. Use for passage or the laying of utility lines, on the other hand, normally does not constitute possession and, if done adversely, will usually result only in the grant of a prescriptive easement rather than title by adverse possession.

▷ DRIVEWAY **HARD CASE ◀**

The typical hard case in this area concerns driveways that encroach on neighboring land. If one owner uses the property for driveway purposes for a sufficiently long time, she may be held to have acquired a prescriptive easement to continue to use it for that purpose.[184] If, however, she can demonstrate that she treated the property as her own in a more general sense, she may be granted not just an easement, but title by adverse possession.[185] Most driveway cases result in prescriptive easements rather than adverse possession.[186] The courts usually require substantial acts other than driveway use to find adverse possession. For example, in one case, adverse possession to a driveway was awarded when defendant record owner had built a retaining wall on its property one foot from the border and had failed to stop plaintiff neighbor from paving the strip between the wall and the rest of plaintiff's driveway.[187] The result in these cases may turn on whether the record title owner has been effectively excluded from the property. If the record owner was not excluded, then the use of the driveway appears more like use of another's land; if, on the other hand, the record owner was excluded, the use appears more like an assertion of general control sufficient to constitute an ouster of the record owner and an establishment of possession by the non-owner.[188] ◀

Continuous

The continuity requirement means that the use must continue over the course of the statutory period without significant interruption. One is not required to be constantly driving or parking on a driveway to demonstrate a continuous "use." The use need not be constant; if you drive your car to work, you don't have to start the running of the statute all over again.

[184] *McDonald v. Harris*, 978 P.2d 81 (Alaska 1999); *Sutherlin School Dist. #130 v. Herrera*, 851 P.2d 1171 (Or. Ct. App. 1993); *Lingvall v. Bartmess*, 982 P.2d 690 (Wash. Ct. App. 1999).

[185] *Palazzolo v. Malba Estates, Inc.*, 500 N.Y.S.2d 327 (App. Div. 1986).

[186] *McDonald v. Harris*, 978 P.2d 81 (Alaska 1999); *Lingvall v. Bartmess*, 982 P.2d 690 (Wash. Ct. App. 1999).

[187] *Palazzolo v. Malba Estates, Inc.*, 500 N.Y.S.2d 327 (App. Div. 1986).

[188] This distinction is one reason the vast majority of courts do not count "exclusive" use as a requirement for a prescriptive easement. *McDonald v. Harris*, 978 P.2d 81, 84 (Alaska 1999). Because easements are limited rights, they are consistent with the landowner retaining the right to use the property for similar or other purposes. Only possession is inconsistent with joint use (unless the use by the record owner is with permission of the adverse possessor).

Seasonal use may satisfy the requirement if this is typical of similarly situated land or if it would be sufficient to place the owner on notice of a continued use.[189] Occasional or sporadic use is not likely to satisfy the requirement.[190] However, in *United States ex rel. Zuni Tribe of N.M. v. Platt*,[191] the court recognized a prescriptive easement of passage in the Zuni tribe, which had traversed a 110-mile path located on private lands every four years on a pilgrimage to a sacred site and probably had been doing so since 1540. Nor does use by other parties constitute an interruption in the use.[192] The requirement is only that there not be a significant interruption in the use.

Use is presumptively nonpermissive or under a "claim of right"

A majority of courts presume that use of another's property is nonpermissive, just as they do in the case of adverse possession.[193] Some courts say that such use is under a "claim of right," meaning that the easement claimant does not ask (or perhaps feels entitled not to have to ask) for permission from the landowner.[194] The landowner has the burden of showing that the use was permissive, to avoid being subject to a prescriptive easement or adverse possession. However, a fair minority of courts presume that use, unlike possession, is presumptively permissive rather than adverse.[195] They do so because owners often do allow their neighbors to cross over their land as a "neighborly gesture"[196] and there may therefore be more warrant for assuming that limited uses are permissive than there is for presuming that occupation is permissive.[197]

Minority presumption of permission

Particular presumptions

Some courts have created exceptions in specific contexts to the general principle that use of another's land is presumptively nonpermissive. First, some courts presume that use is permissive if the land is vacant, wild, unimproved, unenclosed, or remote.[198] "[W]here lands are open, undeveloped and unenclosed they are in a natural state and frequently in

Wild, unimproved land

[189] Jon W. Bruce, James W. Ely, Jr., & Edward T. Brading, *The Law of Easements and Licenses in Land* §5:15 (2025).

[190] *Barchowsky v. Silver Farms, Inc.*, 659 A.2d 347, 354 (Md. Ct. Spec. App. 1995).

[191] *United States ex rel. Zuni Tribe of N.M. v. Platt*, 730 F. Supp. 318 (D. Ariz. 1990).

[192] 978 P.2d 81 (Alaska 1999). In fact, use by several parties may result in prescriptive easements for all of them.

[193] John A. Lovett, *Restating the Law of Prescriptive Easements*, 104 Marq. L. Rev. 939, 984-990 (2021); Jon W. Bruce, James W. Ely, Jr., & Edward T. Brading, *The Law of Easements and Licenses in Land* §5:3 (2025).

[194] *United States on Behalf of Zuni Tribe of N.M. v. Platt*, 730 F. Supp. 318, 321 (D. Ariz. 1990); *Brooks, Gill & Co. v. Landmark Properties*, 503 N.E.2d 983, 985 (Mass. App. Ct. 1987); *Burke-Tarr Co. v. Ferland Corp.*, 724 A.2d 1014 (R.I. 1999). "Claim of right" does not mean that the easement claimant has permission or is not trespassing; rather, it means the opposite — that the easement claimant is using the neighbor's property without asking or receiving permission. *See Stiefel v. Lindemann*, 638 A.2d 642 (Conn. App. Ct. 1994) ("A claim of right exists only if the user does not recognize the right of the owner of the servient tenement to prevent the use. When the user has permission from the servient owner to use the property, the use is not prescriptive because the user has notice of the owner's right to terminate the use").

[195] *Riley v. Boles*, 394 So.3d 543, 548 (Ala. 2024); John A. Lovett, *Restating the Law of Prescriptive Easements*, 104 Marq. L. Rev. 939, 991 (2021) (citing decisions from Alabama, Alaska, Florida, North Carolina, Rhode Island, West Virginia, and Wyoming).

[196] *Jones v. Cullen*, 1998 WL 811558, at *5 (Minn. Ct. App. 1998).

[197] *Johnson v. Stanley*, 384 S.E.2d 577, 579 (N.C. Ct. App. 1989); *Shumway v. Tom Sanford, Inc.*, 637 P.2d 666, 670 (Wyo. 1981).

[198] Jon W. Bruce, James W. Ely, Jr., & Edward T. Brading, *The Law of Easements and Licenses in Land* §5:3 (2025).

large tracts, and owners may not know or care that others use their land casually."[199] Pennsylvania has passed a statute proscribing the acquisition of a prescriptive right over an unenclosed woodland.[200]

Use of road built by an owner

Second, other courts presume that use of a road constructed by an owner is presumptively permissive.[201] If the road was constructed by the easement claimant, rather than the landowner, this presumption would not apply.[202] For example, in *McDonald v. Harris*,[203] the Alaska Supreme Court adopted the minority view that use of a road on another's land is presumptively permissive, but held that the presumption did not apply where the road was not built by the landowner and had been used for many years as the only means of access to the land owned by the easement claimant.[204]

Family members, prior permitted users, and the public

Third, a few courts presume use is permissive if the parties are family members or otherwise have a relationship that suggests that it is reasonable to conclude that the use is not adverse.[205] Similarly, where a user once had permission, for example with a license agreement, some courts will not presume that continued use is adverse.[206] And some courts reject the presumption where the claimed prescriptive easement benefits the general public at large (usually for recreational purposes).[207]

▷ GOOD NEIGHBORS **HARD CASE ◀**

Should the law presume that use of another's property is permissive or non-permissive? In *Community Feed Store, Inc. v. Northeastern Culvert Corp.*,[208] two businesses were located next to each other, separated by a gravel area

[199] *Kruvant v. 12-22 Woodland Ave. Corp.*, 350 A.2d 102, 112 (N.J. Super. Ct. 1975), *aff'd*, 376 A.2d 188 (App. Div. 1997). *Accord, Chen v. Conway*, 829 P.2d 1355, 1359-1360 (Idaho Ct. App. 1991).

[200] Pa. Stat. tit. 68, §411. *See Sprankle v. Burns*, 675 A.2d 1287 (Pa. Super. Ct. 1996) (applying the statute).

[201] *Chen v. Conway*, 829 P.2d 1355, 1359 (Idaho Ct. App. 1991); *Mecimore v. Cothren*, 428 S.E.2d 470, 472-473 (N.C. Ct. App. 1993); Jon W. Bruce, James W. Ely, Jr., & Edward T. Brading, *The Law of Easements and Licenses in Land* §5:3 (2025).

[202] *McDonald v. Harris*, 978 P.2d 81 (Alaska 1999).

[203] *Id.*

[204] *Id.*

[205] *Lincoln v. Burbank*, 147 A.3d 1165, 1173 (Me. 2016) ("When the use at issue is by family members using one another's property . . . the familial relationship precludes application of" the presumption of adverseness); *Androkites v. White*, 10 A.3d 677, 684 (Me. 2010) ("Absent evidence to the contrary, the law will infer that comings and goings of family members, across property owned within the family, are by accommodation or permission and do not have the requisite adversity to support imposition of a prescriptive easement by one family member upon another."); *Turner v. Baisley*, 602 N.Y.S.2d 907, 909 (App. Div. 1993) (presuming the use was permissive because of the "blood relationship of one of the plaintiffs and one of the defendants").

[206] *Boyle v. City of Portsmouth*, 235 A.3d 985, 989 (N.H. 2020) ("When use of another's land begins with permission, it cannot become adverse in nature without an explicit repudiation of the earlier permission."); John A. Lovett, *Restating the Law of Prescriptive Easements*, 104 Marq. L. Rev. 939, 1005 (2021).

[207] *Jesurum v. WBTSCC Ltd. P'ship*, 151 A.3d 949, 953 (N.H. 2016); John A. Lovett, *Restating the Law of Prescriptive Easements*, 104 Marq. L. Rev. 939, 1006 (2021).

[208] 559 A.2d 1068 (Vt. 1989).

that was used by trucks serving one of the businesses to deliver bag feed to the facility. Neither owner appears to have been too worried about fixing the boundary and preventing encroachment. Although defendant bought the land in 1956, it did not discover until a survey was done in 1984 that trucks serving plaintiff's business were encroaching on defendant's land.

The argument for presuming use is nonpermissive

One might argue that the encroachment should be presumed to be nonpermissive because entry onto land owned by another is a trespass unless consent is given. The failure to speak does not mean that the owner has given consent. Alternatively, one can argue that acquiescing in long-standing use of one's property creates expectations that access will continue. The owner who wishes to preserve her right to exclude can easily do so by granting permission formally or by cutting off access.

The argument for presuming use is permissive

On the other hand, a landowner who does not object to the encroachment impliedly consents to it. Moreover, it seems wrong to punish an owner for being neighborly by forcing the owner to accept a permanent intrusion that was neither bargained for nor voluntarily accepted. Owners may well not know that if they acquiesce in a long-standing use of their property by another, they stand to lose their right to revoke access when it is in their interest to do so. ◀

Open and notorious

Visible

As with adverse possession, the use must be sufficiently visible or "open and notorious" that a reasonable owner would be on notice of the use.[209] When the claim is for use of a road, the visibility requirement may turn on how often the road was used and at what times of the day.[210] If it was used only at night, there is less reason to presume that a reasonable owner would know about the adverse use.[211] Similarly, if it was used only sporadically, not only the visibility requirement but the continuity requirement would be at issue.[212] The largest question here is whether use of rural, unoccupied land should be presumed to be noticeable by a reasonable owner or whether, on the contrary, a reasonable owner might well not know about uses of undeveloped, wooded, or remote land.[213]

[209] *Mavromoustakos v. Padussis*, 684 A.2d 51, 57 (Md. Ct. Spec. App. 1996) ("it is unfair to deprive a landowner of an interest in property unless he or she has had fair warning of the adverse use"); *Hahn v. J.C. Land, Inc.*, 1999 WL 378766, at *1 (Va. Cir. Ct. 1999) (use must be such as to "put a purchaser of the property on notice that it was burdened by an easement").

[210] *Compare Hasgo Power Equipment Sales, Inc. v. Lewis*, 624 N.Y.S.2d 713, 714 (App. Div. 1995) ("The annual plucking of flowers, however, is not the type of use that would provide notice of a hostile claim to the owner") *with Lemont Land Corp. v. Rogers*, 887 P.2d 724, 727 (Mont. 1994) (daily use of an access road by claimant and his guests satisfied the open and notorious requirement); *Willis v. Magette*, 491 S.E.2d 735, 737 (Va. 1997) (use of road by farm and logging equipment was open and visible).

[211] Jon W. Bruce, James W. Ely, Jr., & Edward T. Brading, *The Law of Easements and Licenses in Land* §5:13 (2025).

[212] *Alexy v. Salvador*, 630 N.Y.S.2d 133, 135 (App. Div. 1995) (no prescription when beach was used sporadically).

[213] Jon W. Bruce, James W. Ely, Jr., & Edward T. Brading, *The Law of Easements and Licenses in Land* §5:13 (2025).

Most courts do not require a showing that the landowner "acquiesced" in the adverse use.[214] Some courts do require this and those that do interpret it in a variety of ways. First, some courts interpret it simply as another way of saying that the landowner failed to do anything to protect her rights in the face of the adverse use. Second, some courts require proof that the landowner actually knew about the adverse use.[215] Third, still other courts state that a prescriptive easement will be found either where the landowner knows and acquiesces or where the use is so visible that acquiescence must be presumed.[216]

Acquiescence

Not ordinarily an element

Acquiescence as knowledge

An argument against a subjective knowledge requirement is that states of mind are notoriously hard to prove, thereby making application of the doctrine far more unpredictable. An objective test based on what a reasonable owner should have known is likely to be a more predictable rule and work to better clarify when an easement has been created by the prescription doctrine. On the other hand, it might be argued that an owner who did not know of the adverse use did not care enough to police the land and that, in such a case, it should be presumed that the use was with the implicit permission of the owner. Although possession by another seems quite inconsistent with intent by an owner to continue to assert ownership rights, limited use of one's land by others is not so incompatible with retained title as to suggest that a use is necessarily nonpermissive. The owner may simply be generous or neighborly. In any event, the majority of courts seem to have adopted the rule that subjective knowledge is not required to establish adversity or to fulfill the visibility requirement, perhaps on the ground that the doctrine protects the reliance interests of the easement claimant who has come to expect continued access and whose expectations have been fueled by the landowner's failure to intervene to stop the long-standing use.

Subjective v. objective test for acquiescence

One of the elements of an adverse possession claim is that the use be "exclusive," meaning that the adverse possessor must have effectively excluded the record owner.[217] Most courts do not include this element in the list required to establish a prescriptive easement because it is ordinarily possible for both the owner and the easement claimant to use the property.[218] They can share use of a driveway or road, for example, and using another's property for a limited purpose is not inconsistent with the owner using it for the same purpose at other times. However, some courts do require "exclusive" use by the easement claimant. "Exclusivity does not

Exclusive

[214] One court noted that a use is adverse "if the true owners merely acquiesce, and do not intend to permit a use," and that "a permissive use requires the acknowledgment by the possessor that he holds in subordination to the owner's title." *McDonald v. Harris*, 978 P.2d 81, 85 (Alaska 1999).

[215] *Sparling v. Fon Du Lac Twp.*, 745 N.E.2d 660 (Ill. App. Ct. 2001); *Daniello v. Wagner*, 200 N.Y.S.3d 423, 428 (App. Div. 2d Dep't 2023); *Bradley v. McLeod*, 984 S.W.2d 929, 935 (Tenn. Ct. App. 1998) (requiring a showing of "the owner's knowledge and acquiescence"); *Hahn v. J.C. Land, Inc.*, 1999 WL 378766, at *1 (Va. Cir. Ct. 1999) ("with the knowledge and acquiescence of the landowner").

[216] *Baptist Youth Camp v. Robinson*, 714 A.2d 809, 814 (Me. 1998); *Murphy v. Westberg*, 1998 WL 341965, at *4 (Wash. Ct. App. 1999).

[217] *See* §4.2.3.

[218] *Neyland v. Hunter*, 668 S.W.2d 530, 531 (Ark. 1984) ("[u]nlike adverse possession, prescriptive use need not be exclusive").

mean that the claimant must be the only person using the easement, to the exclusion of all others. It simply connotes that the claimant's use must be independent and not contingent upon the enjoyment of a similar right by others."[219] So a claimant may obtain a prescriptive easement even if the owner or a third party also uses it. Two non-owners may simultaneously obtain independent easements by prescription if they both use the land openly for the statutory period.[220] One state, Texas, has ruled, however, that a use is not exclusive (and hence not adverse) if the owner also uses the easement.[221]

No claims against the government

As with the majority rule applicable to adverse possession, no easements may be obtained by prescription against the federal or state governments in the absence of a statutory basis for prescription.[222]

Prescriptive easements acquired by the public

Many older cases held that the public could not acquire an easement by prescription.[223] However, the trend in the law is clearly to recognize that the public may acquire easements in this manner and this is the approach adopted by the *Restatement (Third) of Property (Servitudes).*[224] Some states have statutes providing that use by the public of a road for a certain amount of time creates a public highway.[225] A few states have used this doctrine to recognize prescriptive rights in the public to use beaches for recreational purposes.[226]

No negative prescriptive easements

Negative easements may not be acquired by prescription. A negative easement is a right to prevent another owner from doing something on her own land. Such easements can be created by contractual arrangements among neighbors. For example, one owner might agree not to build higher than two stories on her property to preserve light and air for her neighbor. Negative easements are not created by prescription because the failure to act on your own land violates no one else's rights; therefore, no statute of limitations starts to run. When a non-owner drives across your property, a visible trespass occurs that puts the owner on notice that her property

[219] Jon W. Bruce, James W. Ely, Jr., & Edward T. Brading, *The Law of Easements and Licenses in Land* §5:23 (2025).

[220] *Id.*

[221] *Vrazel v. Skrabanek*, 725 S.W.2d 709, 711 (Tex. 1987).

[222] *Kiowa Creek Land & Cattle Co., Inc. v. Nazarian*, 554 N.W.2d 175, 177 (Neb. Ct. App. 1996); Jon W. Bruce, James W. Ely, Jr., & Edward T. Brading, *The Law of Easements and Licenses in Land* §5:5 (2025).

[223] *Mihalczo v. Borough of Woodmont*, 400 A.2d 270, 272 (Conn. 1978); *Forest Hills Gardens Corp. v. Baroth*, 555 N.Y.S.2d 1000, 1002 (Sup. Ct. 1990); Jon W. Bruce, James W. Ely, Jr., & Edward T. Brading, *The Law of Easements and Licenses in Land* §5:25 (2025).

[224] *Bayberry Cove Childrens' Land Trust v. Town of Steuben*, 65 A.3d 1188, 1189-1190 (Me. 2013); *Public Land/Water Access Ass'n v. Robbins*, 483 P.3d 1102 (Mont. 2021); *Opinion of the Justices*, 649 A.2d 604, 610 (N.H. 1994); *Breiner v. Holt County*, 581 N.W.2d 89, 94 (Neb. 1998); *Concerned Citizens of Brunswick County Taxpayers Assoc. v. Rhodes*, 404 S.E.2d 677 (N.C. 1991); *Johnson v. Becker*, 903 P.2d 901, 902-903 (Or. Ct. App. 1995); Jon W. Bruce, James W. Ely, Jr., & Edward T. Brading, *The Law of Easements and Licenses in Land* §5:25 (2025); *Restatement (Third) of Property (Servitudes)* §2.18 (2000).

[225] Idaho Code §40-202; Jon W. Bruce, James W. Ely, Jr., & Edward T. Brading, *The Law of Easements and Licenses in Land* §5:26 (2025).

[226] *City of Daytona Beach v. Tona-Rama, Inc.*, 294 So. 2d 73, 75 (Fla. 1974); *Villa Nova Resort, Inc. v. State*, 711 S.W.2d 120, 127 (Tex. Ct. Civ. App. 1986); Jon W. Bruce, James W. Ely, Jr., & Edward T. Brading, *The Law of Easements and Licenses in Land* §5:27 (2025).

rights are being invaded. It is therefore reasonable to impose a duty on the owner to stop the adverse use or sanction it by granting permission. However, if a neighbor simply enjoys the fact that you have not built on your land, you have no way of knowing that they are relying on the fact (or hope) that you will not build in the future. You have no notice of any violation of your rights (because none is occurring).

Ancient lights doctrine rejected

Thus, the United States courts have all rejected the English doctrine of ancient lights by which a landowner who has enjoyed unobstructed access to sunlight for a building during the prescriptive period can acquire an easement of light and air across the property of an adjoining landowner [and] prevent the erection of any structure on the servient estate that would unreasonably block the flow of light.[227]

As one court noted, "If the first property owner on the block were given an enforceable right to unobstructed view over adjoining property, that person would fix the setback line for future neighbors, no matter what zoning ordinances provide."[228] This rule would tend to block development of land by allowing those who built first to prevent their neighbors from building as they did. "The practical implication of such a right would be the need of every 'servient' owner to obtain a waiver of the easement of view created in the 'dominant' landowner. Such obstacles to land ownership and development, for the sake of a clear view, hardly commend themselves."[229]

▷ NEGLIGENCE OR BAD FAITH **HARD CASE ◀**

In *Warsaw v. Chicago Metallic Ceilings, Inc.*,[230] plaintiffs negligently built a large commercial building on their property and left insufficient space to the side of the building to allow trucks to enter, unload their goods, turn around, and leave. The trucks encroached on the neighboring property to serve the plaintiffs' facility. Because they did so without permission for the statutory period, the court granted a prescriptive easement. Justice Reynoso dissented, arguing that it was wrong to reward a bad faith trespasser (one who knew he was trespassing) and that, if a prescriptive easement is awarded in such cases, the easement claimant should at least have to compensate the landowner for the easement. The counterargument is that a good faith requirement would require proof of the parties' state of mind and such proof of subjective intent or knowledge is hard to come by and would substantially increase the uncertainty involved in these cases.

Should compensation be awarded?

[227] *United States v. 0.08246 Acres of Land*, 888 F. Supp. 693, 710 n.22 (E.D. Pa. 1995); *Kucera v. Lizza*, 69 Cal. Rptr. 2d 582, 589 (Ct. App. 1997); *Fontainebleau Hotel Corp. v. Forty-Five Twenty-Five, Inc.*, 114 So. 2d 357 (Fla. Dist. Ct. App. 1959); *Mohr v. Midas Realty Corp.*, 431 N.W.2d 380, 381 (Iowa 1988); *Kruger v. Shramek*, 565 N.W.2d 742, 747 (Neb. Ct. App. 1997); Jon W. Bruce, James W. Ely, Jr., & Edward T. Brading, *The Law of Easements and Licenses in Land* §5:3 (2025). *But see Prah v. Maretti*, 321 N.W.2d 182 (Wis. 1982), *and Tenn v. 889 Assocs., Ltd.*, 500 A.2d 366 (N.H. 1985) (both holding that interference with a neighbor's light and air might constitute a nuisance).

[228] *Mohr v. Midas Realty Corp.*, 431 N.W.2d 380, 382-383 (Iowa 1988).

[229] *Id.*

[230] 676 P.2d 584 (Cal. 1984).

Similarly, a rule that would require compensation in the case of negligence would require not just proof of long-standing visible use, but a controversial determination about whether the easement claimant acted unreasonably. While some cases (such as *Warsaw*) strongly suggest negligence, many would not be so clear cut, again introducing a substantial element of uncertainty into prescription law. In addition, if the basis of the claim is a nonpermissive intrusion (a trespass), then the ordinary application of the statute of limitations should bar the claim if it is not brought within the prescriptive period. A compensation requirement, even if wise, should perhaps come from legislative amendment of the statute of limitations, rather than court law reform. ◀

▶ **HARD CASE** ▷ TREES

An exception to the prescriptive easement doctrine is that most courts will not grant tree owners prescriptive rights to have their tree branches hang over neighboring property, no matter how long their trees have been intruding.[231] Although some courts intimate that the doctrine should apply in this context, the policy of allowing owners to develop their property and to obtain sunlight by cutting overhanging branches seems to have prevailed in the courts over the idea that a long-standing invasion by a tree branch should be allowed to continue. ◀

▶ **HARD CASE** ▷ PRESCRIPTIVE RIGHT TO COMMIT A NUISANCE

In *Hoffman v. United Iron & Metal Co.*,[232] the court held that an automobile shredding facility that had been operating for more than 20 years acquired a prescriptive right to commit a nuisance by excessive noise, explosions, and air pollutants against persons who had owned or lived in the area for a continuous 20-year period. Judge Salmon reasoned that a nuisance was a violation of the neighbors' property rights and that their failure to sue to abate the nuisance within the applicable statute of limitations meant that those rights were lost. The failure to bring a nuisance lawsuit within the prescriptive period may constitute a legitimate waiver of rights or an admission that the harm is not substantial. Allowing owners to bring the claim after such a long time is unfair to the factory that has come to expect that its actions were lawful.

[231] *Pierce v. Casady*, 711 P.2d 766 (Kan. Ct. App. 1985) (holding that tree owners cannot acquire a prescriptive easement in a neighboring landowners' airspace); *Koresko v. Farley*, 844 A.2d 607 (Pa. Commw. Ct. 2004) (no easement by prescription can be acquired for right to have branches or roots of a tree extend onto neighboring property); *Cobb v. Western Union Tel. Co.*, 98 A. 758 (Vt. 1916) (owner can cut branches hanging over onto his property no matter how long they have been there); *Jones v. Wagner*, 624 A.2d 166 (Pa. Super. Ct. 1993) (no authority precludes this). *See also* §2.4.2.

[232] 671 A.2d 55 (Md. Ct. Spec. App. 1996).

A counterargument would be that nuisances substantially and unreasonably interfere with the rights of neighboring owners. By significantly reducing the usability and marketability of the affected properties, nuisances harm community interests, and not just the interests of neighboring owners. This interference with the interests of the servient estate owners may be more drastic than that suffered by those who are subject to rights of way or to utility lines or sewer lines passing over their property. Further, nuisances are likely to affect many owners rather than just a single servient estate over which a road runs, and transaction costs may well prevent all the affected owners from successfully bargaining with the polluting factory owner to abate the nuisance. In particular, freeloader problems may prevent suits from being brought as each owner hopes others will bear the expense and burden of bringing suit. ◀

Argument against allowing a prescriptive easement to commit a nuisance

§5.6 Terminating Easements

Easements last forever unless they are terminated, among other ways, (1) by agreement in writing (*release* of the easement by the holder); (2) by *their own terms*, for example, if the deed conveying the easement expressly states that it is to last for ten years; (3) by *merger*, when both servient estate and the dominant estate come to be owned by the same person; (4) by *abandonment*, if it can be shown that the owner of the easement, by her conduct, clearly indicated an intent to abandon the easement; or (5) by *adverse possession* or *prescription* by the owner of the servient estate or by a third party.[233]

Release

By their own terms

Merger

Abandonment

Adverse possession or prescription

Although owners of possessory estates in real property cannot abandon them, owners of easements can abandon them.[234] Mere nonuse of an easement, without more, does not constitute abandonment of an easement.[235] The easement owner must engage in affirmative action that clearly indicates an intent to abandon the easement.[236]

Abandonment of easement

Traditionally, unlike covenants,[237] easements were not subject to being modified or terminated by changed conditions. Sometimes, however, courts would terminate easements because of "frustration of purpose."[238]

Changed conditions

Frustration of purpose

[233] Jon W. Bruce, James W. Ely, Jr., & Edward T. Brading, *The Law of Easements and Licenses in Land* §§10:2 to 10:27 (2025); Dale A. Whitman et al., *The Law of Property* §8.12, at 382-387 (4th ed. 2019).

[234] Jon W. Bruce, James W. Ely, Jr., & Edward T. Brading, *The Law of Easements and Licenses in Land* §10:18 (2025).

[235] *Cater v. Bednarek*, 969 N.E.2d 705, 709 (Mass. 2012); *Hillary Corp. v. United States Cold Storage, Inc.*, 550 N.W.2d 889, 899-900 (Neb. 1996); *Consol. Rail Corp. v. MASP Equip. Corp.*, 490 N.E.2d 514 (N.Y. 1986); *Strahin v. Lantz*, 456 S.E.2d 12, 15 (W. Va. 1995); *Mueller v. Hoblyn*, 887 P.2d 500, 505-506 (Wyo. 1994) (nonuse for 27 years not abandonment); Jon W. Bruce, James W. Ely, Jr., & Edward T. Brading, *The Law of Easements and Licenses in Land* §10:19 (2025).

[236] *Stimson Lumber Company v. United States*, 82 F.4th 1346, 1353 (Fed. Cir. 2023); *Johnson-White v. Houston*, 229 N.E.3d 1259, 1264 (Ct. App. Ohio 2023).

[237] *See* §6.8.1.

[238] *Boissy v. Chevron*, 33 A.3d 1109, 1114 (N.H. 2011) (terminating easement to get water from well once well could no longer be located).

"Traditional doctrine terminates obsolete easements either by a liberal application of the abandonment principle, or by finding that the purpose of the easement has become impossible to accomplish, or that the easement no longer serves its intended purpose, rather than by the changed conditions doctrine."[239] However, the *Third Restatement* would extend the changed conditions doctrine to easements. That doctrine provides that a servitude (including an easement) can be modified if changed conditions have made it "impossible as a practical matter to accomplish" the easement's purpose.[240] An easement may be terminated if modification is "not practicable."[241]

Marketable title acts

Many states have enacted "marketable title acts," which may require that easements, along with other encumbrances on property interests, be re-recorded periodically (generally every 30 to 50 years) to be binding on future purchasers. The purpose of these statutes is to limit how far back a buyer must look in the chain of title to determine the validity of the seller's title and the existence of encumbrances on the land. However, they also have the effect of making unenforceable those interests that were put in place a long time ago and were of insufficient importance to anyone to be re-recorded in compliance with the statute. Failure to comply with the marketable title act by re-recording the easement may leave the easement owner unprotected from a subsequent purchaser of the servient estate who, depending on the language in the statute, may be entitled to buy the property free of the burden of the easement.[242]

[239] *Restatement (Third) of Property (Servitudes)* §7.10 Reporter's Note (2000).
[240] *Id.* at §7.10.
[241] *Id.*
[242] *See, e.g.*, *Walters v. Servidio*, 320 A.3d 1008 (Conn. App. Ct. 2024) (marketable title act extinguished easement where no road or other "physical facility" provided notice of the easement).

CHAPTER 6

Covenants

§6.1 Introduction
§6.2 Formal Requirements
    §6.2.1 Writing
    §6.2.2 Notice
    §6.2.3 Intent to Run
    §6.2.4 Privity of Estate
§6.3 Substantive Requirements
    §6.3.1 Touch and Concern
    §6.3.2 Enforcement in Gross
§6.4 Implied Reciprocal Negative Servitudes
§6.5 Remedies
§6.6 Interpretation of Ambiguous Covenants
§6.7 Public Policy Limitations
    §6.7.1 Racial Restrictions
    §6.7.2 Unreasonable Restraints on Alienation
    §6.7.3 Unreasonable Restraints on Competition
    §6.7.4 Public Policy
    §6.7.5 Choice of Law
§6.8 Modifying or Terminating Covenants
    §6.8.1 Changed Conditions
    §6.8.2 Relative Hardship
    §6.8.3 Conduct of the Parties
    §6.8.4 Statutory Regulation

§6.1 Introduction

Why owners may want to control the use of neighboring land

Real property owners often would like to ensure that neighboring property is restricted to uses that are compatible with their use of their own land. In a residential subdivision, owners may want to regulate the size, placement, or appearance of homes. They may want to separate single-family homes from apartment buildings or keep gas stations out of residential neighborhoods.[1] They may want to create a mix of residential and commercial uses to ensure that homeowners will be able to buy groceries in the neighborhood. They may want to impose architectural controls on the appearance of houses and form a homeowners' association to enforce these restrictions. Buyers of condominium units may also want to regulate the use of neighboring units, perhaps by preventing owners from leasing their apartments. Landlords often wish to restrict the uses to which their property is put by tenants; they may wish to exclude pets or prohibit subleasing. In addition, whether organized in the form of condominiums or leases, businesses in office complexes, industrial parks, or shopping centers may wish to promulgate mutually enforceable rights of access to common areas and restrictions on use of individual units or lots to ensure compatible and profitable development.

Contractual regulation of land uses

One way to impose legitimate land use restrictions is through zoning laws, which regulate the use of land in a municipality. But such laws generally only outline broad types of uses allowed in particular zones (industrial, commercial, residential, etc.) and tend to regulate general physical elements of buildings such as height and setback requirements. Developers may wish to create finely tailored property rights that contain highly specific packages of rights and obligations. These contractually based restrictions may go beyond the basic limitations imposed by general zoning laws. Developers accomplish this by placing restrictions on the use of their land when they sell or lease it to others. When such restrictions are placed in deeds or leases, buyers or tenants expressly or impliedly agree to them.

Running with the land

For these land use agreements to achieve their ends, it is not enough that they bind the original parties. They must also be binding on future owners of the parcels intended to be restricted in their uses, which are called the "servient estates." Similarly, because the restrictions are usually intended to benefit neighboring owners (or landlords), those owners of what are called "dominant estates" must be able to ensure that future owners of their land will similarly be entitled to enforce the restrictions. If future owners of the servient estate are bound by the restriction, we say that the burden of the restriction "runs with the land." Similarly, if future owners of the dominant estates are entitled to enforce the restriction against the servient owners,

[1] *Creegan v. State*, 391 P.3d 36, 39 (Kan. 2017) (property should be used for "single-family residence purposes only"); *Citizens for Covenant Compliance v. Anderson*, 906 P.2d 1314 (Cal. 1995) (owner cannot plant a vineyard, produce wine, or keep llamas on property restricted to residential use); *Grasso v. Thimons*, 559 A.2d 925 (Pa. Super. Ct. 1989) (covenant restricting property to "residential uses" precludes use of home for professional purposes).

then the benefit "runs with the land."[2] Land use restrictions intended to run with the land are called "covenants" or "servitudes."[3] When a dispute arises between the original covenanting parties, it is governed by general rules of contract.[4] When the issue is whether the covenant is enforceable by a later owner of the benefited parcel or enforceable against a later owner of the burdened parcel, or both, the rules in this chapter govern. Three sets of rules developed historically to govern this issue: the law of easements, the law of real covenants, and the law of equitable servitudes. Although efforts are now being made to unify these three lines of doctrine, many courts still treat them separately. Chapter 5 dealt with the law of easements and this chapter will focus on *real covenants* and *equitable servitudes.*

Homeowners' associations or community associations

Contractually created land use restrictions are normally enforced by owners of the dominant estates intended to benefit from the restrictions. When a servient owner breaches a covenant, a dominant owner can sue to compel compliance with the covenant. It is increasingly common, however, for a developer of a subdivision to create a homeowners' association (or "common interest community association"),[5] which is empowered to enforce the covenants or restrictions, usually by bringing lawsuits to compel compliance. Residential and commercial condominium complexes similarly create condominium associations, which usually have the power to enforce covenants and to promulgate by-laws or rules governing use of common areas and perhaps even individual units. In effect, these associations function somewhat like local governments, assessing fees to maintain common areas and passing rules to regulate both those areas and individual units as well.

Negative and affirmative covenants

Negative covenants prohibit certain land uses. They may provide, for example, that homes are restricted to "single-family use." Affirmative covenants obligate owners to perform certain acts for the benefit of their neighbors. They may, for example, require an owner to maintain a wall on her property that supports neighboring land.[6] Or an owner may be required to pay fees to the homeowners' association to help maintain commonly owned property, such as recreational facilities open to residents in the subdivision or condominium building.[7] Although most of the rules pertaining to negative and affirmative covenants are the same, some differences have

[2] In the landlord/tenant context, this means that future landlords and tenants will be bound and benefited. Thus, the landlord may wish to ensure that, when a tenant sublets or assigns an apartment, the subtenant or assignee will similarly be bound by restrictions in the original lease agreement. Conversely, the landlord may want to ensure that, if the property is sold, the new owner (who takes the place of the old landlord) is entitled to enforce the restrictions in the original lease.

[3] As explained in Chapter 5, some land use restrictions were traditionally created in the form of negative easements. The word "servitude" is used today to refer to all nonpossessory interests in land, including easements, profits, real covenants and equitable servitudes. *See Restatement (Third) of Property (Servitudes)* §1.1 (2000).

[4] As contracts concerning land, the statute of frauds writing requirements generally apply to covenants.

[5] *See Restatement (Third) of Property (Servitudes)* §6.2 (2000). *See* §8.5.

[6] For the law on owners' obligations to provide lateral support to land, see §3.5.1.

[7] *See, e.g., Timberstone Homeowner's Ass'n, Inc. v. Summerlin*, 467 S.E.2d 330 (Ga. 1996).

developed.[8] In general, courts are more wary of imposing affirmative than negative covenants on succeeding landowners.

Relation between easements and real covenants

Land use restrictions are created in a variety of ways. A developer may attempt to impose a land use restriction by creating a negative easement. However, the courts traditionally limited the number and type of negative easements that could be created.[9] For this reason, landowners began to use the covenant form to create new types of land use restrictions. While easements were traditionally characterized as nonpossessory interests in land, "real covenants" were originally conceptualized as contractual promises—but contracts of a special type because they created rights and obligations that were to "run with the land," binding and benefiting future owners of the affected parcels. The *Restatement (Third) of Property (Servitudes)* abolishes the distinction between negative easements and restrictive covenants. In effect, it uses the term "easement" to mean "affirmative easement" (such as a right-of-way, or any other right to do something on land possessed by another) and uses the term "negative covenant" to refer to both negative easements and restrictive covenants.[10] Covenants can be negative (restrictions on what one can do with one's own land) or affirmative (obligations to do something on one's land for the benefit of someone else).

How covenants are initially created

A developer of land may include covenants in the deeds to each of the parcels sold in a subdivision. Those deeds will state that the land being conveyed is restricted to particular uses or that the owner is obligated to act in certain ways. Similarly, a landlord may include restrictions, such as a "no pets" clause, in a written lease agreement. Alternatively, a developer may record a *declaration* of restrictions applicable to the subdivision as a whole and refer to the plan of restrictions in subsequent deeds to the parcels that are sold. Owners who purchase lots covered by the declaration who are on constructive notice of the recorded declaration are bound by the general plan, and restrictions in the declaration are not unenforceable merely because they are not additionally cited in the deed or other document at time of sale.[11] Finally, owners in an existing neighborhood may sign an agreement restricting the use of their land and record the agreement to put future owners on notice of the restrictions.[12]

Historical origin of real covenants and equitable servitudes

The law of real covenants was created to regulate the enforceability of contractually based land use restrictions. It was developed by the law courts in England at a time when they were reluctant to allow encumbrances on land, especially on fee simple ownership rights. The English judges were intent on promoting the alienability of land by limiting the ability of owners to restrict its use. They allowed covenants to run with the land only if the original covenanting parties had a special simultaneous relationship to

[8] *See Restatement (Third) of Property (Servitudes)* §§5.2 & 5.3 (2000).

[9] *See* §5.3.2. *See* 7-61 *Thompson on Real Property, Third Thomas Edition* §61.03(a).

[10] *Restatement (Third) of Property (Servitudes)* §1.2, §1.2 cmt. h (2000).

[11] *Citizens for Covenant Compliance v. Anderson*, 906 P.2d 1314 (Cal. 1995); *Timberstone Homeowner's Ass'n, Inc. v. Summerlin*, 467 S.E.2d 330 (Ga. 1996).

[12] This last method does not satisfy traditional requirements of "privity of estate," discussed below in §6.2.4, but the covenant may be enforceable as an implied reciprocal negative servitude, see §6.4, and would be enforceable despite the lack of privity of estate if the rules proposed by the *Restatement (Third) of Property (Servitudes)* are adopted by the courts.

land called "privity of estate." The effect of the technical privity rules was to allow covenants contained in leases to be binding on assignees but not to impose covenants contained in a deed of sale on subsequent landowners. The equity courts in England responded by loosening the rules and allowing enforcement of covenants in deeds against succeeding owners of land if they took possession with notice of the restrictions, whether privity (as the law courts defined it) existed between the original covenanting parties.

Developments in the United States

The U.S. courts adopted the law of real covenants, but extended the definition of privity to include sales as well as leasing arrangements. Nonetheless, they kept the privity requirements developed in the context of the relationship between the original covenanting parties (horizontal privity) and supplemented it with rules about the relationship required between the original covenanting parties and their successors in interest (vertical privity). However, the U.S. courts also adopted the law of equitable servitudes. They did so to avoid the technical rigors of the privity doctrine, which made it impossible to arrange for reciprocal enforcement of covenants among owners in a subdivision. In adopting rules that allowed enforcement of implied reciprocal negative servitudes, the courts supplemented, and did not repeal, either the law of real covenants or the law of easements. This leaves us today with a confused muddle.

Unification of the law of servitudes

The disjunction between the rules traditionally applicable to easements, real covenants, and equitable servitudes has not only sowed much confusion but has also long been the source of law reform proposals designed to unify the rules in this area to regulate enforcement of land use restrictions and obligations in a manner related to legitimate policy goals rather than historical and outdated conceptual distinctions. The *Restatement (Third) of Property (Servitudes)*, published by the American Law Institute in 2000, goes a long way in this direction, and if it is adopted by courts, it would change the law in this area substantially. The *Restatement (Third)* not only abolishes the distinction between negative easements and restrictive covenants (treating both as negative covenants), but it also abolishes the distinction between real covenants and equitable servitudes, treating both as covenants running with the land. The *Restatement (Third)* would abolish other technicalities as well, including the touch and concern test, and both horizontal and vertical privity. It also would make both damages and injunctive relief available as remedies for violation of any covenant.[13] In place of all these technicalities, the *Restatement (Third)* provides that covenants run with the land if they are intended to do so, the successors have notice of them at the time they purchase, and enforcement violates no statute or public policy.

Restatement (Third) of Property (Servitudes)

The argument that servitudes promote both contractual freedom and alienability

Servitudes pose a fundamental conflict between property and contract norms. Allowing owners to enter agreements to restrict the use of land furthers interests in contractual freedom; owners are free to make promises restricting land use for their mutual benefit and are secure in the knowledge that such restrictions will be enforceable. The ability to enforce

[13] *Restatement (Third) of Property (Servitudes)* §8.3(1) (2000) (servitudes can be enforced by "any appropriate remedy").

a covenant gives the owner of a dominant estate an added property right, *i.e.*, the right to restrict the use of neighboring land. This right gives the dominant owner security and, like all contract rights, creates a kind of property right in expectations; the promisee (the one to whom the promise was made) can rely on the promisor carrying out the promise or paying a penalty for breach. The security of knowing that neighboring land is restricted may increase the value and the marketability (or alienability) of the benefited land.

The argument that servitudes inhibit alienability and contractual freedom

On the other hand, enforcement of covenants restricts the freedom to use land. Restricted land, by definition, is less adaptable than unrestricted land. An owner wishing to change the use of restricted land cannot do so unless she obtains the consent of all the owners of the dominant estates or convinces most owners in the homeowners' association to amend the declaration. Moreover, those who wish to buy land for a purpose prohibited by a covenant will be deterred from buying the restricted land. Covenants may therefore inhibit the alienability of land. While it is possible to get rid of restrictions by obtaining the agreement of all owners affected by them, transaction costs may well prevent all such owners from agreeing to terminate the covenant. Thus, although restrictions may initially further interests in freedom of contract, they may also inhibit alienability, thus interfering with contractual freedom of owners of restricted land (and potential purchasers) in the future.

Disaggregation

We face a tension between the goals of disaggregation and consolidation of property rights. Ownership comprises a bundle of specific entitlements. Owners often wish to disaggregate these entitlements by granting some individuals rights in land belonging to another. Allowing owners to disaggregate property rights means that they have the contractual freedom to create specially tailored bundles of rights and obligations. The ability to disaggregate property rights is beneficial to owners. Covenants are often desirable because they grant owners the security of knowing that neighboring uses will be limited in predictable ways. This, in turn, gives owners the freedom to purchase property of a certain character. One is able, for example, to purchase a home coupled with the right to prevent neighbors from using their property for factory purposes. Of course, one's use of one's own property is usually similarly restricted, creating reciprocal rights and obligations on neighboring owners. If one knows that property in a subdivision is limited to residential use, then one can be sure that current and future owners of neighboring land will not operate a gas station or a funeral parlor or sell liquor, even if zoning laws change to allow this.

Facilitative and protective role

Covenants therefore play both a facilitative and a protective role in property law. Owners are free to contract for land use restrictions and they have the security of knowing that those restrictions will be enforceable against current and future owners of the restricted parcels. If the rights are reciprocal, the neighbors may similarly be able to restrict your use of your own land. These reciprocal rights and restrictions mean that the property rights on each parcel overlap; the owners have both rights to use their own land and obligations to their neighbors, and the particular set of rights and obligations is tailored by contractual arrangements designed to suit the buyers.

Consolidation, bundles of rights

On the other hand, the ability to disaggregate property rights into specialized bundles has a downside, as well. Useful as covenants may be, they limit the ability of owners to use their land as they see fit. Although covenants are a form of property right, they also limit the property rights of owners who wish to use their land in ways prohibited by those covenants. Because the freedom to use your land as you like is one of the core interests that owners have, covenants can seem burdensome rather than protective. Covenants are useful to buyers who like the packages of rights and land use restrictions available in the marketplace. However, if many subdivisions or condominiums have multiple restrictions on use, it may be difficult for someone looking for property in a particular area to find a bundle that suits her particular needs. Covenants are usually initiated by developers and they may or may not correctly judge which packages of rights and obligations are beneficial to purchasers. Buyers may also purchase property without reading all the covenants or understanding their significance. Rather than seeing covenants as voluntarily adopted packages of rights, buyers may see them as meddlesome interferences with the rights of owners to use their own property as they see fit. For these reasons, the law sometimes polices covenants for reasonableness, disregarding those that interfere too much in the freedom of owners to use their property as they like.

Hard to change

Covenants, once instituted, are hard to change. If they are enforceable by many dominant owners, then even a single owner can veto changes in the covenants unless the declaration creating the covenants provides otherwise. Even if the covenants can be changed by a majority vote of members of the homeowners' association, there are still significant transaction costs in getting the owners to agree to such a change. Moreover, it is almost impossible for a potential buyer to engineer such a change *before* purchasing property herself. The fact that covenants are hard to change means that these specially tailored bundles of property rights may be hard to unbundle. Rather than enjoying the security of knowing that neighboring property is restricted in its use, owners may feel oppressed by obsolete or intrusive restrictions that benefit fewer owners than they burden. For this reason, the courts and the legislatures have developed doctrines to change covenants so that property rights can be reconsolidated in owners who are then free to use their land for previously restricted purposes, or to create new bundles of restrictions better suited to their needs.

Reconsolidation

Governance issues

Residential associations can help build community and allow owners to combine with others to create a pleasant environment for their members. They may also allow varieties of housing types and communities. A developer, for example, could create a planned community that includes specially tailored services for families or for retired persons. However, because residential associations may exercise some powers traditionally associated with local government, their exercise of power may be problematic. They may, for example, have the power to consent to sales of property in the neighborhood and use this power in an exclusionary manner, preventing low- or moderate-income families from moving in. Or they may even use such rights to engage in prohibited racial discrimination. Some of these communities are fully privatized, with privately owned streets and common areas. These "gated communities" may seek to exclude outsiders and to exercise control over who enters the community to buy property or even to visit. As private entities, residential associations are not subject to constitutional limitations as are government actors. Regulations that might be struck down as unconstitutional deprivations of free speech or privacy if imposed by municipalities may be upheld if promulgated by residential associations because they are thought to be contractually based (and therefore private) and not governmentally imposed (and therefore subject to constitutional limitations on public actors). Some scholars have argued that residents should be protected against abuses of power by homeowners' associations that would constitute constitutional violations if promulgated by local governments.[14]

Free contract v. regulation

The law of servitudes has managed these tensions by compromising between the principle of allowing owners to create servitudes and impose them on future owners of the affected land and the principle of freeing landowners from restrictions not of their own choosing. The choices implicit in this area protect both interests in autonomy and efficiency and in the construction of a property system that grants due respect to individual owners and frees them from oppressive or archaic limitations on the use of their land while also protecting the reliance interests of neighbors who have legitimate claims to enforce land use restrictions. As the *Restatement (Third)* explains: "Numerous judicially created doctrines have limited the creation of servitudes to protect the social interest in preventing land from becoming unusable and unmarketable and to protect landowners from requirements akin to the feudal incidents of providing labor or other services to an overlord."[15]

Running with the land

As with easements, a number of basic issues emerge in the law governing covenants. First, the courts have developed a variety of doctrines to determine when land use restrictions "run with the land" to bind and benefit future owners and when such restrictions will be deemed to be personal contracts not intended to govern the legal rights of future owners.

Creation of servitudes: formality v. informality

Second, the law has developed a variety of doctrines designed to place owners on notice of existing land use restrictions by requiring covenants to be formalized in a writing that is recorded in the registry of deeds. At the same time, sometimes developers fail to adhere to the rules. They may explicitly or implicitly promise buyers that all land in a subdivision will be restricted but fail to adhere to the strict requirements of the statute of frauds. They may make such representations in sales literature, for example, but fail to place the restrictions in the deeds themselves. They may make oral representations that are relied on by buyers but fail to record a declaration of restrictions prior to the sale. To protect the interests of buyers

[14] *Compare* Michael C. Pollack, *Judicial Deference and Institutional Character: Homeowners Associations and the Puzzle of Private Governance*, 81 U. Cin. L. Rev. 839 (2013); Gregory Alexander, *Freedom, Coercion, and the Law of Servitudes*, 73 Cornell L. Rev. 883 (1988); Gerald Frug, *Cities and Homeowners Associations: A Reply*, 130 U. Pa. L. Rev. 1589 (1982); *and* Stewart Sterk, *Minority Protection in Residential Private Governments*, 77 B.U. L. Rev. 273 (1997) (citing the dangers of homeowners' associations) *with* Robert C. Ellickson, *New Institutions for Old Neighborhoods*, 48 Duke L.J. 75 (1998) *and* Robert C. Ellickson, *Cities and Homeowners Associations*, 130 U. Pa. L. Rev. 1519 (1982) (generally praising them).

[15] *Restatement (Third) of Property (Servitudes)* §3.1 cmt. e (2000).

who relied on such representations, the courts sometimes relax the strict requirements of the statute of frauds. In other cases, conflicts arise between the interests of owners who relied on formal or informal assurances that neighboring land would be restricted and the interests of their neighbors who purchased land that did not appear to be restricted and who thought that they were not bound by any limits on their land use. Sometimes the law protects the reliance interests of those to whom promises were made over the interests of those who assumed that their property was not restricted.

Interpretation of ambiguous servitudes

Third, covenants are often ambiguous as to what actions are prohibited or required. Courts often have to interpret the meaning of restrictions such as covenants restricting land to "single-family use." Does this mean, for example, that the land is restricted to a single-family home or does it mean that the property can only be occupied by a "single family"?

Covenants versus constitution

Fourth, covenants are sometimes created for illegitimate reasons. Until 1948, racial restrictions were not only common but were actively encouraged by the federal government. Covenants were commonly used to exclude Black people, Jews, Asian-Americans, and American Indians from particular neighborhoods. Other covenants or conditions imposed on land use may infringe on individual liberty or privacy. They may, for example, prohibit unmarried couples from occupying the property. Courts disagree about whether such restrictions legitimately protect the "family atmosphere" of the area or illegitimately impinge on personal freedoms. Because servitudes can be used for purposes that arguably violate constitutional, statutory, or public policy norms, the courts regulate their content to protect both existing and potential owners from onerous or improper provisions.[16]

Terminating servitudes

Finally, covenants may outlive their utility over time. Changes in the surrounding neighborhood, the value and character of land inside the restricted subdivision, or the desires of owners, may result in a situation where most of the owners wish to be free of the restrictions. If each owner is entitled to enforce the covenants forever, then a single owner could have effective veto power over changes in the neighborhood. This might be conceptualized as a legitimate exercise of that owner's property rights in the covenant or it could be conceptualized as an illegitimate interference with the freedom of all the other owners to be emancipated from outdated restrictions on their property rights. Sometimes, the interests of the owners who want to be free of the covenant seem to outweigh the interests of those who wish to continue to enforce it, and the courts are sometimes forced to choose between allowing change versus allowing existing owners to prevent change. Even if all the owners wish to be free of a covenant, the transaction costs of getting everyone to agree to waive or end the covenant may be prohibitive. For this reason, the courts have developed doctrines that allow covenants to be removed (or enforced only by damages rather than injunctive relief) if conditions change so as to limit substantially their utility or so as to impose an undue burden on the servient owners.

[16] *Id.* at §§3.1 to 3.7.

§6.2 Formal Requirements

Requirements to run with the land; real covenants

The law of servitudes is in flux now. Traditionally, *real covenants* were said to run with the land, binding the servient estate and benefiting the dominant estate if (1) the covenant was in *writing*; (2) the purchaser of the servient estate was on *notice* of the covenant at the time of purchase;[17] (3) the original covenanting parties *intended* both the burden and the benefit to run with the land;[18] (4) the original contracting parties were in *privity of estate* with each other (horizontal privity);[19] subsequent owners were in privity with the original contracting parties (vertical privity); and (5) the covenant "*touched and concerned*" the land. The traditional remedy for breach of a legal obligation associated with a real covenant was the assessment of damages.

Equitable servitudes

Also traditionally, covenants were said to be enforceable by injunctive relief as so-called *equitable servitudes* if (1) the purchaser of the servient estate was on *notice* of the covenant at the time of acquisition; (2) the original covenanting parties *intended* the covenant to run with the land; and (3) the covenant *touched and concerned* the land.[20] This test omits both the horizontal and vertical privity requirements and substitutes a notice requirement.[21] In addition, although equitable servitudes are usually created on the basis of a written agreement, they may also be recognized in certain cases even in the absence of a writing under the doctrine of *equitable estoppel*.[22]

Law is in flux

This statement of the law — although traditionally accurate — is problematic for several reasons. The distinction between real covenants and equitable servitudes may well be breaking down. Although many courts still accept the traditional elements and differences between the two approaches, scholars have long argued for a unification of these two strains of doctrine and there is a long-term trend in this direction. This unification not only encompasses real covenants and equitable servitudes, but the law of easements as well. Indeed, the *Restatement (Third) of Property (Servitudes)* has created a single framework of rules applicable to all nonpossessory interests in land.

Unification of the law of servitudes

[17] Some sources suggest that notice was a requirement for equitable servitudes but not for real covenants. *See* 7-61 *Thompson on Real Property, Third Thomas Edition* §61.04(f). Courts now generally require notice for both real covenants and equitable servitudes. *See* §6.2.2.

[18] Sometimes owners intend the benefit to run but not the burden or vice versa.

[19] Some courts hold that horizontal privity is required for the burden to run with the land but is not required for the benefit to run with the land. 7-61 *Thompson on Real Property, Third Thomas Edition* §61.04(a)(4), (5); *Restatement of Property* §548 (1944).

[20] *Selected Lands Corp. v. Speich*, 702 S.W.2d 197, 199 (Tex. Ct. App. 1985) ("A purchaser of a lot who takes with constructive notice of restrictions becomes bound thereby and becomes vested with the rights and benefits flowing therefrom"); *see also Baywood Ests. Prop. Owners Ass'n, Inc. v. Caolo*, 392 S.W.3d 776, 782 (Tex. Ct. App. 2012) ("A covenant runs with the land when it touches and concerns the land; relates to a thing in existence or specifically binds the parties and their assigns; is intended by the original parties to run with the land; and when the successor to the burden has notice").

[21] Notice was not originally an element of real covenants doctrine but is so today in most courts.

[22] *See* §6.2.2.

Two of the elements traditionally required for real covenants are especially problematic. The privity and "touch and concern" tests are both ambiguous and technical in nature and, at least in their traditional form, do not necessarily further legitimate policy goals. They have been the subject of withering criticism by scholars, and the *Restatement (Third) of Property (Servitudes)*, published in 2000 by the American Law Institute, proposed dropping both requirements[23] and replacing them with doctrines that more directly promote competing goals of balancing contractual freedom to disaggregate property rights with the promotion of alienability by consolidation of property rights in an owner who is entitled to full control over the property.

Problematic elements

Part of the reason for this unification movement is that privity of estate was never required to obtain injunctive relief. The law of covenants was developed by the law courts in England and the traditional legal remedy was damages. The law of equitable servitudes was developed by the chancery or equity courts and their characteristic enforcement mechanism was the injunction. The equity courts enforced covenants against buyers who had notice of them whether or not the strict technical requirements of the privity doctrine were present. Because most landowners who seek to enforce covenants seek injunctive relief, the traditional focus on the privity requirement has been replaced by the question of whether the servient owner was on adequate notice of the restriction at the time of purchase. At the same time, some version of the privity requirement retains substantial force because it expresses the idea that covenants are intended to connect two parcels of land in a system of rights and obligations and parcels outside the chain of title are usually not burdened by such obligations. Thus, although a strict privity test may be on the wane, a more relaxed version of the privity test still appears to play a substantial part in the law of covenants.

Privity of estate

Unlike the privity requirement, the touch and concern test always applied to both lines of doctrine. At the same time, the content of the test was never clear. Although covenants ordinarily satisfy the test by restricting the use of land, not all restrictions on use satisfy the test. Moreover, it is increasingly unclear what it means to "touch and concern" the land. Modern approaches turn our attention away from the question of whether a servitude is related to land and toward questions of reasonableness.[24] In general, covenants will be allowed to run with the land unless it is unreasonable for them to do so, either because they wrongly infringe on interests in individual liberty or because they inhibit the alienability or utility of land without compensating social or economic benefits.

Touch and concern

[23] *Restatement (Third) of Property (Servitudes)* §2.4 (2000) (no horizontal privity required); *Restatement (Third) of Property (Servitudes)* §3.2 (2000) (touch and concern doctrine superseded); *Restatement (Third) of Property (Servitudes)* §5.2 cmt. b (2000) (vertical privity doctrine rejected).

[24] *Davidson Bros., Inc. v. D. Katz & Sons, Inc.*, 579 A.2d 288, 295 (N.J. 1990) ("Reasonableness, not esoteric concepts of property law, should be the guiding inquiry into the validity of covenants at law"). *See also Restatement (Third) of Property (Servitudes)* §§3.1 to 3.2 (2000) (abolishing the touch and concern doctrine and providing that servitudes are enforceable unless they contravene public policy).

Formal requirements

The traditional elements are of two kinds. Formal elements require owners who wish to create enforceable covenants to do so in certain ways that are designed to place buyers on notice of the exact nature of the restrictions and to provide evidence to the courts that the parties really intended the restrictions to run with the land rather than just be personal to the contracting parties. Those formal elements include the writing, notice, intent, and privity requirements. These elements are formal in the sense that owners who wish to create enforceable covenants can do so by following the formal methods. They do not substantively limit the kinds of restrictions that can be created; they merely regulate the form in which they must be created.

Substantive requirements

The touch and concern test, on the other hand, is a substantive requirement. It is substantive because it limits the *types* of restrictions that the courts will allow to be binding on future landowners. A second traditional substantive requirement was that the benefit of the covenant be held by the owner of some dominant estate before it would be allowed to run with the land. This is one reason for the traditional privity requirement. The presence of vertical privity on the benefit side helps ensure that the covenant will be enforceable only by an owner of a lot intended to benefit from such enforcement. Unlike easements, which could always be owned in gross, the benefit of a covenant could not traditionally be held in gross. The *Restatement (Third)* would allow the benefit of a covenant to be held in gross if the beneficiary has a legitimate reason to enforce the covenant.[25]

§6.2.1 Writing

Original covenant must be in writing

The statute of frauds requires covenants to be in writing to be enforceable against subsequent owners.[26] At the same time, various exceptions to this principle have been created by the courts, the most important of which is the doctrine of *estoppel*. Covenants are ordinarily included either in a deed or lease that transfers property rights or in a recorded declaration that applies to an entire subdivision prior to sale of individual lots or to an entire condominium prior to sale of individual units.[27] A covenant is in writing if the original covenanting parties put it in writing. It need not be included

[25] *Compare Garland v. Rosenshein*, 649 N.E.2d 756, 758 (Mass. 1995) (benefit of covenant held in gross cannot be enforced) *with B.C.E. Dev., Inc. v. Smith*, 264 Cal. Rptr. 55 (Ct. App. 1989) (allowing enforcement by the developer's successor in interest when the covenant provided for such enforcement and the declaration gave the homeowners' association the power to amend the declaration and take control of the architectural commission by a two-thirds vote).

[26] *Ray v. Miller*, 916 S.W.2d 117, 119 (Ark. 1996).

[27] *See, e.g., Citizens for Covenant Compliance v. Anderson*, 906 P.2d 1314, 1325 (Cal. 1995) (restrictions in subdivision's declaration are enforceable against subsequent purchasers who have constructive notice of the restrictions even if the restrictions do not appear in their deeds). *Cf. Arnold v. Chandler*, 428 A.2d 1235 (N.H. 1981) (determining that an equitable servitude was created when developers wrote restrictions in a declaration recorded before the owners purchased their lots but holding that enforcement of the servitude was equitable in nature and subject to the sound discretion of the court).

in subsequent deeds (although it is good practice for sellers to do so).[28] For example, a developer *O* may convey a deed to buyer *A*, which recites that the parcel is "restricted to residential use." When *A* subsequently sells the property to a third party *B*, the writing requirement is still satisfied even if the deed *A* grants to *B* makes no mention of the restriction. *B* is on constructive notice of properly recorded restrictions in the chain of title and, under the law of covenants, impliedly agrees to be bound by such restrictions. This is part of what it means for the covenant to "run with the land." At the same time, it is good practice for real estate lawyers to include such restrictions in the deed to buyers such as *B* to make sure they actually know about the restriction and to resolve any ambiguities in the parties' mutual understanding of what their deal entails.

Map

Sometimes developers refer to restrictions in a plat or map of a proposed subdivision but fail to record a declaration that contains the restrictions and also fail to include any restrictions in the deeds themselves by which the lots are sold. Most courts would be hesitant to enforce such purported restrictions unless the plat clearly indicates the extent and nature of the restrictions. However, if the plat clearly refers to the covenants, they will be enforceable against owners who take with notice of them.[29] Moreover, if the grantor made oral statements to the effect that such restrictions were to exist, and buyers testify that they relied on such representations, then the court might enforce such restrictions under the doctrine of estoppel.

▷ ORAL REPRESENTATIONS AND SALES LITERATURE — HARD CASE ◀

Estoppel

Oral representations by developers are often accompanied by sales literature that indicates that a neighborhood will be restricted in particular ways. It not infrequently happens that developers make representations in sales literature that are not reflected in the deeds themselves or a recorded declaration. Such representations do not count as "writings" sufficient to satisfy the statute of frauds. Nonetheless, many courts will enforce such written representations if buyers rely on them by applying the equitable doctrine of estoppel.[30] Oral representations made to buyers, and relied upon by them in deciding to purchase, may be similarly enforced, although affirmative promises by developers to construct particular amenities are more likely to be enforced by damages than by injunctive relief.[31] The estoppel doctrine "hold[s] a person to a representation made or a position assumed where

28 *Restatement (Third) of Property (Servitudes)* §5.1 cmt. b (2000) (appurtenant benefits and burdens pass automatically).

29 *Cf. Bain v. Bain*, 360 S.E.2d 849 (Va. 1987) (ambiguity arising from conflict between plat and declaration resolved in favor of the deed because that imposed the least restriction on the lots). Gerald Korngold, *Private Land Use Arrangements: Easements, Real Covenants, and Equitable Servitudes* §9.03, at 341 (3d ed. 2016).

30 *Chesus v. Watts*, 967 S.W.2d 97 (Mo. Ct. App. 1998); *Restatement (Third) of Property (Servitudes)* §§2.9 & 2.10 (2000); *Restatement of Property* §524 (1944); 9-60 *Powell on Real Property* §60.02.

31 *PMZ Oil Co. v. Lucroy*, 449 So. 2d 201 (Miss. 1984) (specifically enforcing unrecorded representations).

otherwise inequitable consequences would result to another who, having the right to do so under all of the circumstances of the case, has in good faith relied thereon and been misled to his injury."[32]

Argument for enforcing oral representations

In *PMZ Oil Co. v. Lucroy*,[33] a developer told lot purchasers that all lots in the subdivision would be restricted to "one quality single-family dwelling per lot" and showed them an unrecorded plat noting the restrictions. Covenants restricting the lots to such uses were included in the deeds to all the lots sold. When the developer sought to build six town-house condominiums on one of the lots it retained, the court intervened. The court enforced the oral promise, explaining that a

> grantor, who induces purchasers, by use of a plat, to believe that streets, squares, courts, parks, or other open areas shown on the plat will be kept open for their use and benefit, and the purchasers have acted upon such inducement, is required by common honesty to do that which he represented he would do.[34]

This doctrine applies "[w]henever in equity and good conscience persons ought to behave ethically toward one another." It "has its roots in the morals and ethics of our society," as well as "[f]undamental notions of justice and fair dealings."[35]

Argument for strict enforcement of the statute of frauds

Some courts, however, refuse to enforce oral representations or sales promises not included in prior-recorded documents. In *Bennett v. Charles Corp.*,[36] the court allowed a developer to convert remaining unsold lots in a subdivided tract into a cemetery, in violation of the developer's oral promise to develop the tract as a residential subdivision. Noting that no restrictive covenants were contained in either the deeds or a recorded plat, and that the developer could not find a residential buyer for the lot, Justice Flowers concluded that it was reasonable for defendant to breach the promise because performance was impossible. Nor did the court find the developer's conduct to be "inequitable" or fraudulent because the developer had fully intended to develop the lots in accordance with its oral promises and breached those promises only when it could not sell the lots in question.[37] ◀

[32] *Id.* at 206.

[33] *Id.* at 201.

[34] *Id.* at 208. *See also Warren v. Detlefsen*, 663 S.W.2d 710, 712 (Ark. 1984) (oral representations that property would be restricted to single-family homes enforceable because a general plan or scheme "can be proven by express covenant, by implication from a field map, or by parol representation made in sales brochures, maps, advertising, or oral statements upon which the purchaser relied in making his decision to purchase"); *Haines v. Minnock Construction Co.*, 433 A.2d 30, 34 (Pa. Super. Ct. 1981) (applying estoppel doctrine to enforce representations in sales brochures that an area behind plaintiff's house would remain undeveloped "open space"); *Arthur v. Lake Tansi Village, Inc.*, 590 S.W.2d 923, 930 (Tenn. 1979) (denying enforcement of representations made in advertisements because there was insufficient evidence that the plaintiff acted in reliance on the representations).

[35] 449 So. 2d at 206.

[36] 226 S.E.2d 559 (W. Va. 1976).

[37] *Id.* at 564. *Accord, Kincheloe v. Milatzo*, 678 P.2d 855, 862 (Wyo. 1984) (oral representations enforceable only if developer engaged in intentional fraud, not if developer changed his mind because he could not sell the last lots or for some other reason).

▷ AMBIGUOUS MAP REFERENCES **HARD CASE ◀**

In *Reagan v. Brissey*,[38] a developer recorded a subdivision map in 1872 showing proposed lots and streets and parks in a subdivision with several irregularly shaped areas labeled as "Prospect Park" and "Plaza." Those "park" properties were never developed and remained wooded over the years. Years later, the court ruled that those lots could not be developed because their designation on the recorded map constituted a written representation that they would be open for park use by buyers of lots in the subdivision. The plaza owner had argued that the writing of the word "*Plaza*" on the map was not sufficient to constitute an express or an implied easement limiting the uses to which the property could be put. While the appeals court had agreed that the writing on the map was insufficient to impose an easement on the property, the Supreme Judicial Court disagreed. In contrast, in *Agua Fria Save the Open Space Ass'n v. Rowe*,[39] the court held that open space designated on a recorded plat is not sufficient to create an easement of access by owners of lots on the map in the absence of evidence the developer made representations to buyers inducing them to buy in reliance on promises those lots would remain open. The mere presence of open space on the map was insufficient to prevent the developer from selling that open space for development purposes. ◀

§6.2.2 Notice

Notice traditionally required for equitable servitudes but not for real covenants

Many authorities omit the notice requirement from the list of elements necessary for a real covenant to run with the land while including it as one of the requirements for an equitable servitude.[40] Some cases indeed suggest that privity is required for a real covenant to run with the land but that notice is not required.[41] Conversely, the law of equitable servitudes discarded the privity requirement and replaced it with a requirement that the buyer of the servient estate be on notice of the covenant at the time of purchase.[42] This is the approach taken by the Virginia Supreme Court.[43]

[38] 844 N.E.2d 672 (Mass. 2006).

[39] 255 P.3d 390 (N.M. Ct. App. 2011).

[40] 7-61 *Thompson on Real Property, Third Thomas Edition* §61.04(f)(1).

[41] *Dierberg v. Wills*, 700 S.W.2d 461, 464 n.1 (Mo. Ct. App. 1985) ("A real covenant 'runs with the land' and is binding on all successors in interest, regardless of whether they had any actual or constructive notice of such covenant when they acquired title"); *Sonoma Development, Inc. v. Miller*, 515 S.E.2d 577, 579-580 (Va. 1999) (distinguishing between real covenants and equitable servitudes).

[42] "[T]radition states that notice to successors is a requirement for creation of an equitable servitude, but treats notice as a matter of defense to enforcement of all other servitudes." *Restatement (Third) of Property (Servitudes)* xxii (Tentative Draft No. 1, Apr. 5, 1989); 7-61 *Thompson on Real Property, Third Thomas Edition* §61.04(f), 7-62 *Thompson on Real Property, Third Thomas Edition* §62.02 (elements for a covenant to run with the land are privity between the original covenanting parties, privity between original parties and their successors, intent for the covenant to run with the land, and touch and concern the land).

[43] *Sloan v. Johnson*, 491 S.E.2d 725, 727-728 (Va. 1997) (privity but not notice required for the running of real covenants; equitable servitudes enforced against subsequent owners of the burdened estate unless they did not have notice of the servitude). Traditionally, this

Notice is a requirement for a real covenant

This traditional statement of the law is problematic. Authority is scant for the proposition that a servient owner should be bound by a covenant even though, at the time she purchased the property, she did not know, and could not reasonably have known through a title search, of the existence of the covenant. The *Restatement (Third)* notes that servitudes may be extinguished by operation of recording statutes if they are not evident and discoverable by reasonable inspection or inquiry and are not recorded so that a buyer would be on constructive notice of them.[44] The cases that hold that notice is not a requisite for real covenants law almost all involve situations in which the purchasers would have been on constructive notice of the covenant. The law of real covenants and equitable servitudes is becoming unified and, although there are a few cases to the contrary,[45] American courts generally have imported the notice requirement to real covenants.[46]

Actual and constructive notice

Modern practice therefore requires notice before a covenant will be enforced against a landowner.[47] Notice can be proved by showing that the purchaser was actually aware of the covenant (*actual notice*). A buyer or lessee is said to be on *constructive notice* if the covenant was recorded in the registry of deeds as part of the deed or lease creating the covenant or if a declaration containing the restriction was recorded prior to the transfer of the property affected by the covenant. A reasonable purchaser is expected to search the title to find out whether the property is burdened by any land use restrictions, and the buyer is deemed to know what she would have discovered had she performed a search of her chain of title.

Inquiry notice

The buyer or lessee is on *inquiry* notice of a servitude if any condition of the premises indicates that the property is so encumbered. Inquiry notice is generally important only in the context of affirmative easements, such as rights of way, which a buyer can observe and which suggest that another party may have interests in the land. The observable condition of the land is unlikely to put a reasonable buyer or lessee on notice of a restrictive or negative covenant. The fact that land is not being used in a certain way does not, in any way, suggest that it could not be used in ways other than its current use. However, some courts have held that buyers are on inquiry notice when a property is located in a neighborhood that has a uniform pattern of

---

meant that damages could be obtained if the elements of real covenant were present but that injunctive relief could be obtained if the elements of an equitable servitude were shown. Today, however, injunctive relief is available when a real covenant is breached, as it is for an equitable servitude. *Sonoma Development, Inc. v. Miller*, 515 S.E.2d 577, 580-581 (Va. 1999) (issuing an injunction against violation of a real covenant).

[44] *Restatement (Third) of Property (Servitudes)* §7.14 (2000).

[45] *Dierberg v. Wills*, 700 S.W.2d 461, 464 n.1 (Mo. Ct. App. 1985) (holding that real covenants bind successors even if they did not have constructive notice; at the same time, the covenant was in the deeds to some lots in the subdivision, arguably placing all owners on constructive notice of them); *Sonoma Development, Inc. v. Miller*, 515 S.E.2d 577, 579-580 (Va. 1999) (distinguishing between real covenants and equitable servitudes).

[46] *See Inwood North Homeowners' Ass'n v. Harris*, 736 S.W.2d 632, 635 (Tex. 1987) (covenant is enforceable only when "the successor to the burden has notice"); 7-61 *Thompson on Real Property, Third Thomas Edition* §61.04(f). *But see Dierberg v. Wills*, 700 S.W.2d 461, 464 n.1 (Mo. Ct. App. 1985) (real covenant enforceable even if there is no actual or constructive notice).

[47] *Restatement (Third) of Property (Servitudes)* §7.14 cmt. b (2000) (actual or constructive notice by recording required for a servitude to run with the land).

use (all single-family homes, for example).[48] In such cases, the buyer may be obligated to search the deeds of surrounding lots to determine if they are restricted by covenants binding current owners. If enough of them are, some courts will hold that a "general plan" has been established that burdens all lots within the borders of the area covered by the general plan.[49] Nevertheless, courts generally find buyers to be on notice of the restrictions in the deeds to neighboring property, not because the uniform nature of land use in the area puts them on inquiry notice, but because they are obligated to research deeds to contiguous or neighboring parcels if they were once owned by a prior grantor of the parcel they are purchasing to see if a uniform plan of restrictions was intended to apply to the neighborhood. Courts usually find such buyers on notice of the general plan because they are on constructive notice of restrictions in the deeds to surrounding land, not because uniform development puts them on inquiry notice.

Grantor and grantee covenant notice problems

Courts are divided on the question of whether (or when) buyers are on constructive notice of covenants that are recorded in deeds relating to neighboring property. Two kinds of cases arise. The first type of case involves grantor covenants (promises by sellers to buyers). When a grantor promises a grantee that remaining land of the grantor will be restricted, is a buyer of that remaining land on notice of that covenant? The second type of case involves grantee covenants (promises from buyers to sellers). When many buyers in a neighborhood promise the seller that they will restrict the use of their own land, are buyers of unrestricted parcels in the neighborhood on constructive notice of those covenants?

▷ CONSTRUCTIVE NOTICE OF GRANTOR COVENANTS IN DEEDS TO NEIGHBORING LAND

HARD CASE ◀

In *Whitinsville Plaza v. Kotseas*,[50] a landowner (Kotseas) sold property to a buyer (Whitinsville Plaza) with a promise that the owner would not allow his retained property to be used to compete with the buyer's "discount store." The owner later leased his retained property to a business tenant (CVS) that arguably came within the prohibited category. Was CVS on constructive notice of the grantor covenant in the first deed?

Argument that buyers are not on constructive notice

Some courts hold that buyers or lessees of property only have an obligation to look up prior deeds or other transactions pertaining to the particular parcel of property they are purchasing or leasing. For example, suppose *O* owns Lots 1 and 2 and sells Lot 1 to *A* with an express covenant promising not to use *O*'s remaining Lot 2 for non-residential purposes. *O* then sells Lot 2 to *B* without placing a restriction on the grantee *B* in the deed from *O* to *B*. Is *B* on constructive notice of the restriction in the *O-A* deed? Some courts hold that *B* is not on constructive notice of the restriction because it is outside the chain of title. These courts hold that the buyer of Lot 2 has only to look at prior deeds to Lot 2 granted by *O* and *O*'s

[48] *See, e.g., Sanborn v. McLean*, 206 N.W. 496, 498 (Mich. 1925).
[49] For further discussion of this issue, see §6.4.
[50] 390 N.E.2d 243 (Mass. 1979).

predecessors in interest and need not look at all the deeds given out by *O* to all the property owned by *O* since *O* became the owner of Lot 2. Requiring the buyer of Lot 2 to examine deeds *O* has granted to land other than Lot 2 is a burden the buyer should not have to bear.[51]

Argument that buyers are on constructive notice

Courts are split on the question of whether *B* is on constructive notice of the restriction in the *O-A* deed.[52] They reason that the buyer is obligated to search all grants made by the seller during the time the seller owned the land being purchased (or at least all the deeds to contiguous or nearby land) to determine whether any of those written instruments includes reference to the land in question. If *O* has encumbered Lot 2 by a promise in a prior deed to Lot 1, then *O* has no power to transfer ownership of Lot 2 free of the restriction and *B* is on notice of the restriction because *B* can find out about the purchase by researching the deeds granted by the owner of the land during the time of ownership. At the same time, courts are much more likely to enforce the grantor's covenant made by *O* to benefit *B* if the grantor has established a common scheme or general plan of development for the subdivision. ◀

▶ HARD CASE ▷ GRANTEE COVENANTS ON NEIGHBORING PROPERTY

A different notice problem is created if a developer places grantee covenants in the deeds to most parcels in a subdivision by which each buyer agrees to restrict the use of her own land but then the developer fails to include the restrictions in some number of the remaining parcels. Are the buyers on constructive notice of the grantee covenants in the property of their neighbors? Although some courts hold buyers not to be on constructive notice of the covenants in deeds to neighboring property,[53] most courts find buyers to be on constructive notice of grantee covenants on nearby parcels if the land had all been previously owned by a single grantor and if that grantor effectively established a general plan.[54] This issue is discussed below in §6.4. ◀

§6.2.3 *Intent to Run*

Express or implied

A deed or lease that includes a restrictive covenant will be deemed to show the grantor's intent for the covenant to run to future possessors if it expressly recites that the covenant is made to, or is enforceable by, the "heirs or assigns" or "successors"[55] of the covenantee and/or if the covenant expressly states that it is "intended to run with the land" or "to bind (or benefit) future owners" of the affected property. When the document

[51] *Puchalski v. Wedemeyer*, 586 N.Y.S.2d 387 (App. Div. 1992); *Spring Lakes, Ltd. v. O.F.M. Co.*, 467 N.E.2d 537 (Ohio 1984).

[52] *Guillette v. Daly Dry Wall, Inc.*, 325 N.E.2d 572 (Mass. 1975); *Steagall v. Robinson*, 344 S.E.2d 803 (N.C. Ct. App. 1986); *Finley v. Glenn*, 154 A. 299 (Pa. 1931); Dale A. Whitman et al., *The Law of Property* §8.31, at 427 (4th ed. 2019); 9-60 *Powell on Real Property* §60.04[4].

[53] *See Riley v. Bear Creek Planning Committee*, 551 P.2d 1213 (Cal. 1976).

[54] *Sanborn v. McLean*, 206 N.W. 496 (Mich. 1925).

[55] *Bright v. Lake Linganore Ass'n, Inc.*, 656 A.2d 377, 390 (Md. Ct. Spec. App. 1995).

creating the covenants fails to state clearly that it is intended to run with the land, most courts will nevertheless hold that it does if it is the kind of covenant that was probably intended to run with the land.[56] Covenants are likely to be intended to run with the land if they satisfy the traditional "touch and concern" test, meaning that they restrict the use of the servient estate and that they are of use to owners of the dominant estates. For example, in *Stern v. Metropolitan Water District of Salt Lake & Sandy*,[57] the court held that a restrictive covenant limiting the use of two parcels of property to canal purposes was intended to run with the land despite the deed's lack of language to that effect or reference to "heirs and assigns." The restriction was integral to the burdened land and closely tied to the homeowners' use of their retained land, so it was unlikely that the water district and the homeowners would have intended this covenant "to be merely personal."[58] Because the covenant is of a type that the parties almost certainly intended to run with the land, it was so construed. This is the result one would expect in most courts.

Presumption rejected by some courts

Some courts, however, may require clear evidence a covenant is intended to run with the land. The South Carolina Supreme Court refused in *Charping v. J.P. Scurry & Co., Inc.*[59] to adopt a presumption that a land use restriction that touches and concerns the land is intended to run with the land. Rather, it insisted on clear evidence from the text of the conveyance or from surrounding circumstances that demonstrates such intent. This approach may be justified on the ground that covenants are an encumbrance on ownership and may inhibit alienability; thus, property rights should be construed in favor of free use unless the parties have clearly agreed to the contrary.[60]

Intent to run on one side only

In some cases, the original covenanting parties may intend the burden to run with the land but not the benefit, or vice versa. For example, it is possible that an owner would agree to give the benefit of a covenant to a particular owner but not intend that it pass to future owners. If the parties intend the burden but not the benefit to run, the covenantee (the owner of the benefited parcel) can enforce the covenant while it owns the land but the restriction will no longer apply once the dominant estate is sold.

[56] *See Stern v. Metropolitan Water District of Salt Lake & Sandy*, 274 P.3d 935, 947 (Utah 2012); *Bright v. Lake Linganore Ass'n, Inc.*, 656 A.2d 377, 390 (Md. Ct. Spec. App. 1995) (covenants intended to run with the land will do so if all requirements are met; express language stating that covenants are to run with the land to successors in interest are "advisable but not required"); *Mabee v. Nordic Aquafarms Inc.*, 290 A.3d 79, 95 (Me. 2023) (finding intent to run because a requirement "to remain residential" was "was more beneficial to [the owner's] successors in interest than to [the owner] personally"); *but see U & ME Homes, LLC v. Cnty. of Suffolk*, 148 N.Y.S.3d 682 (Sup. Ct. 2021) (failure to include express language specifying intent meant covenant did not run, despite circumstances suggesting such intent).

[57] 274 P.3d 935 (Utah 2012).

[58] *Id.* at 948.

[59] 372 S.E.2d 120 (S.C. Ct. App. 1988).

[60] *See, e.g., Yogman v. Parrott*, 937 P.2d 1019, 1023 (Or. 1997) (explaining that the traditional presumption in favor of free use avoids unfair surprise and promotes full and free use of property); *Collins v. City of El Campo*, 684 S.W.2d 756, 761 (Tex. Ct. App. 1984) (covenants construed strictly and freer use is preferred); *Foods First, Inc. v. Gables Associates*, 418 S.E.2d 888, 889 (Va. 1992) (covenants strictly construed against the party seeking enforcement).

The opposite may occur as well; the covenant may provide that the benefit runs with the land but that the burden will not — this would be highly unusual, however, because such a benefit would be extremely insecure, terminating once the servient estate was sold.

§6.2.4 *Privity of Estate*

Horizontal and vertical privity

Traditionally, a real covenant would run with the land, binding future owners of the servient estate and benefiting future owners of the dominant estate, only if something called *privity of estate* (or simply "privity") existed. This meant, roughly, that the original covenanting parties each had a simultaneous interest in land at the time the covenant was created and that the burdens and benefits of the covenant would pass to successors to those interests. Two kinds of privity were required for a covenant to run with the land: *horizontal privity* (comprising the relation between the original covenanting parties) and *vertical privity* (comprising the relation between the original covenanting parties and their successors in interest). Some courts have held that horizontal privity is not required for the benefit to run with the land, but that it is required for the burden to run.[61]

Ambiguous status of the privity requirement

The privity requirement has an ambiguous status today.[62] Many state courts continue to hold that privity, in some form, is a required element of the law of real covenants. Moreover, although never required to enforce a covenant as an equitable servitude, the idea behind the privity doctrine seems central to the law of both real covenants and equitable servitudes. After all, the purpose of servitudes law is to impose restrictions on some real property interests intended to benefit the owners of other property interests. Servitudes link together different lots or estates in a burden/benefit framework and pass on those burdens and benefits to succeeding owners. The idea of privity is that the law will attach such burdens and benefits to ownership of particular parcels only when the burden to the servient estate is justified by a compensating benefit to one or more dominant estates. The technical rules of horizontal privity helped to ensure that this was so, while the vertical privity rules allowed those benefits and burdens to pass to future owners. At the same time, when the technical requirements of the privity doctrine were not met, they sometimes served to free land from covenants that were obsolete or unduly burdensome.

Idea behind privity

Traditional version of privity has been rejected

Some courts continue to insist that privity, both horizontal and vertical, is required for the burden of a covenant to run with the land.[63] At the same time, the law of privity developed in a technical manner that imposed requirements that today seem unreasonable because they result in nonenforcement when no public policy reason for nonenforcement is present.

[61] 7-61 *Thompson on Real Property, Third Thomas Edition* §61.04(f); *Restatement of Property* §548 (1944).

[62] *See Beeren & Barry Investments, L.L.C. v. AHC, Inc.*, 671 S.E.2d 147 (Va. 2009); *BM-Clarence Cardwell, Inc. v. Cocca Development, Ltd.*, 65 N.E.3d 829, 835 (Ohio Ct. App. 2016); *Cunningham v. City of Greensboro*, 711 S.E.2d 477 (N.C. Ct. App. 2011).

[63] *Lake Arrowhead Community Club, Inc. v. Looney*, 770 P.2d 1046, 1050 (Wash. 1989); *Waynesboro Village v. BMC Properties*, 496 S.E.2d 64, 68 (Va. 1998).

Moreover, privity was never required for enforcement as an equitable servitude. Most disputes involving servitudes involve attempts to get servient owners to comply with covenants. Because privity was never required to obtain an injunction to enforce an equitable servitude, the strict traditional privity requirements seem beside the point. For this reason, various authorities assert that the horizontal privity requirement has been effectively abolished[64] and the *Restatement (Third) of Property (Servitudes)* wisely rejects the traditional strict doctrine of privity. However, the *Restatement (Third)* does retain the traditional idea behind the privity concept. Unless legitimate reasons exist for enforcement by an owner outside the chain of title, the *Restatement (Third)* does seem to require a *relaxed* form of both the horizontal and vertical privity requirements. It does so by basing the law of covenants on the idea that owners of property interests should be free to agree to contractually based restrictions on land use designed to burden one or more parcels for the benefit of other property owners in the vicinity (this is a relaxed form of horizontal privity) and that the benefits and burdens of such agreements should pass to owners who purchase those parcels with notice of the original agreement (this is a relaxed form of vertical privity).

Origins of the privity concept

The privity concept developed because, in the early nineteenth century, contract rights were generally not assignable to others. Promises were personal: A promise from *A* to *O* could not be enforced by anyone other than *O*; nor could *A* assign to another *A*'s contractual duties without the consent of *O*. However, the courts developed an exception to this principle of nonassignability in the context of real property; the benefits of contract rights were assignable if they were somehow conceived as being attached to an ownership interest in land created by two parties who had simultaneous rights in that land. This concept, called privity of estate, solved not only the problem of making the benefit run to future owners of the benefited interest (making the benefit assignable by the promisee), but also the problem of imposing the burden on future owners of the burdened interest (thus, making the burden "run with the land" and the obligation assignable). The concept was created in *Spencer's Case*,[65] the 1583 English case generally credited with beginning the modern law of covenants. That case held that an affirmative covenant (to build a brick wall) contained in a lease was enforceable against a party who had been assigned the leasehold by the original tenant because the covenant was intended to be binding on such future tenants, the covenant "touched and concerned" the land, and there was "privity of estate" between the original covenanting parties. The concept of privity of estate here was one of *mutual privity*: Landlords and tenants had simultaneous interests in the same parcel of land because ownership rights were divided between a present estate (the tenant's or lessee's term of years) and a future interest in the lessor or landlord (reversion).

Spencer's Case

After *Spencer's Case*, the question arose whether a covenant could be enforced if it were contained in a deed rather than a lease. In such a case, the

[64] 7-61 *Thompson on Real Property, Third Thomas Edition* §61.04(a)(4).

[65] 77 Eng. Rep. 72 (1583).

parties do not own simultaneous interests in the same piece of land; they are in privity only in the sense that the covenant is created at the fleeting moment a property interest is transferred from one to the other (so-called *instantaneous privity*). The law courts in England rejected the doctrine of instantaneous privity, holding that privity of estate did not apply to transfers of property from sellers to buyers; privity required simultaneous interests in the same parcel (mutual privity). The English courts thus limited covenants law to landlord/tenant relationships, enforcing covenants contained in leases against assignees of the lessee but not enforcing covenants contained in deeds to future owners of the land. If an owner wished to sell part of her land while ensuring that the property being sold would be restricted to a particular use, she could not do so under real covenants law.

Rejection of the instantaneous privity doctrine in England

Creation of the law of equitable servitudes

However, England had two court systems rather than one. Litigants who could not obtain relief in the law courts could approach the equity courts for relief from the harsh common law rule. The case of *Tulk v. Moxhay*,[66] which created the law of equitable servitudes, dropped the privity requirement and provided that covenants that touched and concerned the land and that were intended to be binding on future owners would be enforceable against buyers who took possession with notice of those covenants. Because the equity courts enforced personal obligations by use of the injunction, a distinction was born between the law of real covenants (enforced by damages in the law courts) and the law of equitable servitudes (enforced by injunctions in the equity courts).

Developments in the United States

Courts in the United States expanded the definition of privity from traditional tenurial relationships (involving simultaneous interests in the same parcel of land) to allow enforcement of covenants contained in deeds of sale. Some states did this by expanding the concept of simultaneous privity from the landlord-tenant relationship to situations in which one owner owns an easement in the property of the other and/or both owners have mutual easements in each other's property. This approach was long associated with Massachusetts.[67] Most courts expanded the privity concept by adopting the instantaneous privity doctrine; they found privity to exist if a covenant was created in the context of the sale of property transferring a property interest from a grantor to a grantee.[68] Thus, a covenant included in a deed of sale restricting use of the parcel might bind future owners of the property conveyed. At the moment the deed passes from seller to buyer (and the seller and buyer both have one hand on the deed), the parties have a fleeting, instantaneous, simultaneous interest in the property, and the covenant was thought to attach itself to the property interest conveyed from seller to buyer. At the same time, the U.S. courts accepted the equitable servitudes doctrine, which allowed enforcement of covenants by injunctive relief without regard to technical privity requirements if the owner of the servient estate purchased with notice of the covenant.

[66] 41 Eng. Rep. 1143 (1848).

[67] *Whitinsville Plaza, Inc. v. Kotseas*, 390 N.E.2d 243 (Mass. 1979).

[68] *See, e.g., Federated Retail Holdings, Inc. v. County of Ramsey*, 820 N.W.2d 553, 561 (Minn. 2012) (privity of estate includes grantor and grantee relationship).

Traditional privity law

Although the *Restatement (Third)* proposes abolishing the traditional privity requirements, many courts still appear to accept some aspects of the traditional privity requirements. It is therefore important to know the basic features of the traditional strict privity doctrines.

Diagram

The technical requirements of the traditional privity concepts will be easier to understand by reference to the following diagram:

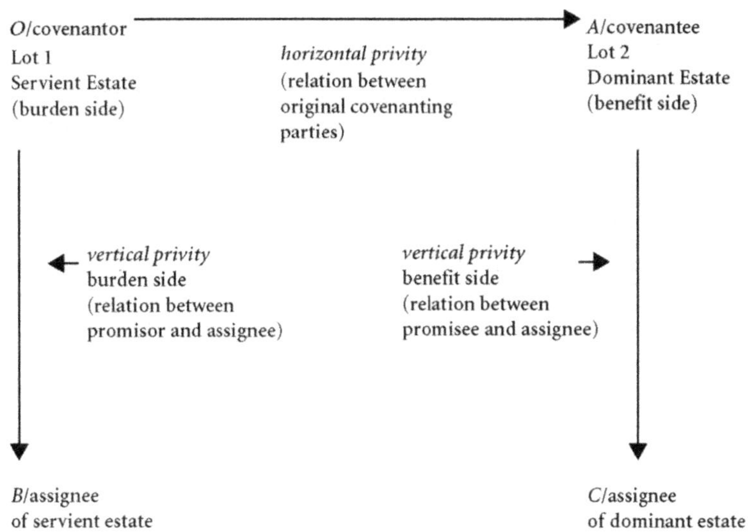

Strict horizontal privity

Horizontal privity can be satisfied by either mutual privity or instantaneous privity.[69] *Mutual privity* is established (1) if the covenant is contained in a lease transferring possession of land from landlord to tenant; (2) if the covenant is contained in a deed that divides property ownership between a present estate and a future interest (such as a life estate and a reversion in the grantor);[70] or (3) if the covenant is contained in a deed conveying ownership of land and one or both parties owns an easement burdening the property of the other (the so-called Massachusetts test).[71] *Instantaneous privity* is established by placing the covenant in a deed of sale that creates the restriction and impliedly or expressly states that the covenant is intended to benefit remaining land of the grantor. When a grantor covenant is involved, the grantor may sell part of her land with a promise by the grantor to restrict the use of the grantor's remaining land. Similarly, grantee covenants may be included in the deeds that comprise promises by grantees to restrict their own lots for the benefit of the remaining land belonging to the grantor in the vicinity.

Problems with strict horizontal privity

The strict horizontal privity requirements traditionally excluded three types of relationships that are, today, generally thought to be legitimate

[69] *Restatement of Property* §534 (1944).

[70] *Sonoma Development, Inc. v. Miller*, 515 S.E.2d 577, 580 (Va. 1999) ("to establish horizontal privity, the party seeking to enforce the real covenant must prove that the original covenanting parties made their covenant in connection with the conveyance of an estate in land from one of the parties to the other").

[71] *See also Moseley v. Bishop*, 470 N.E.2d 773, 777 (Ind. Ct. App. 1984) (applying the mutual privity test).

sources of covenants that should run with the land, especially because privity never was required to enforce a covenant as an equitable servitude.

Agreements among neighbors

First, the traditional strict test for horizontal privity excludes agreements among neighbors that are not part of a simultaneous conveyance of another property right. Thus, if all the neighboring owners in an area entered a contract by which they all agreed to restrict the use of their land to residential purposes and they recorded the document so as to place all future owners of property in the neighborhood on notice of the covenant, the contract would not have been enforceable as a real covenant against succeeding owners under traditional conceptions of horizontal privity because it was not created at the same moment another property interest was created or transferred. Neighbors are not in privity of estate with each other merely because of their physical location near each other. Only a covenant contained in a lease or deed (transferring possession, ownership, a present or future estate, or an easement in the affected land) could traditionally establish horizontal privity. Although such a covenant would be enforceable by injunctive relief as an equitable servitude (as long as future owners purchased with notice of the covenant), it would not be enforceable by a damages remedy under traditional real covenants law because horizontal privity is missing. The *Restatement (Third)* rejects this distinction and would allow such an agreement to run with the land and be enforceable by injunction or damages.[72]

Later agreements

Second, a covenant between a grantor and a grantee would not satisfy the traditional test if it were not entered into at the same moment the affected property interest was transferred. So, a contract between a grantor and a grantee to restrict the land use does not satisfy the strict horizontal privity test if it is entered into a few days after the sale of the land.

Obligations to earlier buyers

Third, because privity requires a simultaneous relation between buyer and seller regarding two parcels of land, it was traditionally thought that covenants by grantees to grantors were intended to benefit the grantor's remaining land. This creates a problem when a developer creates a residential subdivision and sells many parcels with deeds containing similar restrictions. In such a case, later grantees could sue earlier grantees for breach of the covenants contained in the earlier deed because the promises of the earlier buyer benefited the grantor's remaining land. However, it was not clear how earlier grantees could sue later grantees for breach of grantee covenants contained in the later deeds. At the moment the later grantees buy their land, there is no longer any relationship between the grantor and the earlier buyers. This problem had to be solved by implying a promise by such grantees to benefit earlier, as well as later, buyers and enforcing that promise despite the absence of a contract between the later buyer and the earlier buyer and despite the lack of privity of estate between the later buyer and the earlier buyer to support the promise of the later buyer to the earlier one. This problem led to the development of the law of implied reciprocal negative servitudes by which reciprocal promises by grantees to

[72] *Restatement (Third) of Property (Servitudes)* §2.4 (2000). For more background and a contemporary justification, see Norman P. Ho, *A Defense of Horizontal Privity in American Property Law*, 91 Miss. L.J. 109 (2022).

each other were implied if the grantor had intended to create a general plan of mutually enforceable restrictions.[73]

Relaxed horizontal privity

Although many courts still purport to adhere to the traditional strict horizontal privity requirements for the burden of a covenant to run with the land,[74] they should be abandoned. They are not required for enforcement as an equitable servitude, and they are formal in the sense that owners who wish to comply with the traditional requirements can do so by putting their transaction into a form that creates horizontal privity. For example, neighbors who wish to comply with the requirement can all transfer their property to a single person, such as a lawyer, who reconveys the properties back to them with the covenants in the new deeds. A similar approach can be taken to create a covenant between grantor and grantee at a time other than the original conveyance. For these reasons, the *Restatement (Third)* suggests that traditional strict horizontal privity is no longer part of the law.[75] However, the *Restatement (Third)* does not abandon the idea behind the horizontal privity requirement entirely. Covenants are thought to be beneficial because the limits on use of one parcel are offset by benefits to other land. When no other land is benefited, enforcement may be inappropriate unless the current owner of the servient estate has personally agreed to the restriction or if there is some legitimate basis for enforcement against the servient owner. The *Restatement (Third)* handles this problem by allowing enforcement of covenants whose benefit is held in gross if the beneficiary has a legitimate interest in enforcing the covenant.[76]

Strict vertical privity

Vertical privity refers to the relationship between the original covenanting parties and their successors in interest. As a general matter, vertical privity exists when an owner succeeds to the interest held by an original covenanting party.[77] The rules developed, however, to require that the succeeding owner to the servient estate must receive the entire estate of the prior owner; this meant, not that a succeeding owner had to own the entire area of land owned by the prior owner, but that the successor should own an estate that lasted as long as that of the prior owner.[78] Thus, successors in interest who had an estate of lesser duration than the prior owner were thought not to be in strict vertical "privity of estate" with the prior owner and thus not bound by the covenant. An owner of a fee simple interest (which can last forever) is not in vertical privity with a subsequent owner if that owner transfers a life estate (to last for the life of the grantee) and retains a reversion that will become possessory at the end of the life estate.

Estates of lesser duration

[73] *See* §6.4.

[74] *See, e.g., Equestrian Ridge Homeowners Ass'n v. Equestrian Ridge Estates II Homeowners Ass'n*, 953 N.W.2d 16, 33-34 (Neb. 2021); *Waynesboro Village v. BMC Properties*, 496 S.E.2d 64, 68 (Va. 1998). Although horizontal privity has traditionally been required for the burden of a covenant to run with the land, some courts have allowed the benefit to run to successor owners of the dominant estate even though horizontal privity is missing. *See Restatement of Property* §548 (1944) (adopting this approach).

[75] *Restatement (Third) of Property (Servitudes)* §2.4 (2000).

[76] *See id.* at §2.6 cmt. d (benefits generally enforceable in gross).

[77] *Runyon v. Paley*, 416 S.E.2d 177, 184 (N.C. 1992).

[78] *Restatement of Property* §535 (1944); 7-61 *Thompson on Real Property, Third Thomas Edition* §61.04(e).

Similarly, vertical privity is absent when an owner of a servient estate leases her property; the tenant is not bound by any covenants that would have bound her landlord.[79] In the landlord-tenant context, strict vertical privity exists when a tenant assigns the rest of her leasehold, but does not exist when a tenant sublets and retains a right to re-enter the property before the end of the leasehold. Many courts, however, never required strict vertical privity for the benefit to run with the land, allowing any succeeding owner or possessor of the dominant estate to enforce the covenant against a servient estate owner who was legally bound by the covenant.[80]

▶ HARD CASE

▷ THIRD-PARTY BENEFICIARIES

Argument against enforcement by third parties

The second category of owners excluded from the traditional strict definition of vertical privity are neighbors who are intended beneficiaries of the covenant but are not successor owners or possessors of the parcels owned by the covenanting parties. For example, in *Runyon v. Paley*,[81] Ruth Bragg Gaskins and her husband sold a parcel to Charles and Mary Robbins Runyon and then, the next day, sold the parcel next to the Runyon lot to Donald and Jacqueline Brugh with a covenant restricting the Brugh lot to two single-family homes. After Gaskins died and her remaining land passed to her daughter, Patsy Simpson Williams, the court allowed Williams to enforce the covenant against the Brughs' successor in interest, Warren Paley, because the promise made by the Brughs had been intended to benefit Gaskins' remaining land. However, the court refused to allow the Runyons to enforce the covenant because the promise made by the Brughs was made for the benefit of the grantor's retained land, not lots previously sold by Gaskins. No vertical privity — strict or otherwise — could be shown even though both the Brughs and the Runyons obtained interests from Gaskins and the promise from the Brughs was probably intended to benefit both the Gaskins property and the Runyon property.[82]

Argument for enforcement by third-party beneficiaries

The *Runyon* court did hold, however, that the Runyons could enforce the covenant as an equitable servitude and obtain injunctive relief if they could show that they were "intended beneficiaries" of the covenant.[83]

Most courts agree that "intended beneficiaries" of the restriction are entitled to enforce it, regardless of whether they are in strict vertical privity with the grantor who originally imposed the restriction.[84] This is also

[79] *Winn-Dixie Stores, Inc. v. Dolgencorp, LLC*, 746 F.3d 1008, 1031-1033 (11th Cir. 2014) (applying Mississippi law and refusing to enforce an anti-competitive covenant in a shopping center lease against a tenant occupying the servient estate).

[80] *Restatement of Property* §542 (1944).

[81] 416 S.E.2d 177 (N.C. 1992).

[82] *See also Brown v. Fuller*, 347 A.2d 127 (Me. 1975) (holding that public policy prevents creation of restrictions for the benefit of land not owned by the grantor except when there is a general plan or when landowners create mutual restrictions).

[83] 416 S.E.2d at 190.

[84] *See Auther v. Furst*, 2008 WL 4965347 ¶¶25-33 (Ariz. Ct. App. 2008); *Muldawer v. Stribling*, 256 S.E.2d 357 (Ga. 1979); *Roehrs v. Lees*, 429 A.2d 388 (N.J. Super. Ct. App. Div. 1981); *Nature Conservancy v. Congel*, 689 N.Y.S.2d 317, 320 (App. Div. 1999); *Allemong v. Frendzel*, 363 S.E.2d 487 (W. Va. 1987) (holding that adjacent owners who did not derive their title

the approach taken by *Restatement (Third) of Property (Servitudes)*.[85] How does one show that a neighbor is an intended beneficiary? The easiest way is to so state in the deed or contract creating the covenant.[86] An alternative way is to demonstrate a common scheme and show that the parcel is physically located within the boundaries of the common scheme.[87] The hardest, and most controversial, way is to try to show that a neighbor was an intended beneficiary despite the absence of a common scheme or an explicit mention of the neighboring property in the deed. Some courts will allow enforcement in such cases if the evidence suggests that the neighbor was an intended beneficiary.[88] *Runyon* held that physical proximity of property sold one day before the servient estate was sold was not sufficient to show that the property was intended to benefit from the covenant. Thus, the Runyons were denied the power to obtain either damages or injunctive relief. ◀

Relaxed vertical privity

Some courts traditionally have required vertical privity only for the burden to run with the land and have allowed a covenant to be enforced by a succeeding owner of the dominant estate despite the lack of strict vertical privity on the benefit side.[89] The owner seeking enforcement must be a subsequent owner or possessor of the estate owned by an original covenanting party, but states that adopt this approach allow the owner of an estate of lesser duration to enforce the covenant with a damages remedy or injunctive relief.[90] Under this approach, a subtenant could enforce a covenant in the original lease against the landlord.[91]

Effect of requiring strict vertical privity

The requirement of horizontal privity is a formality, but the requirement of vertical privity is not. One cannot structure a landlord-tenant relationship to establish vertical privity; by definition, to create vertical privity, the landlord must retain no future interest — but then she would not be a landlord. This fact has traditionally had crucial consequences. It means that a dominant owner could not obtain damages against a tenant who leased

---

from the grantor could enforce a covenant by injunction because, as owners of neighboring land, they were intended beneficiaries of the covenant); Dale A. Whitman et al., *The Law of Property* §8.28, at 425 (4th ed. 2019) (noting that some courts hold that owners outside the chain of title can enforce the restriction if they are intended beneficiaries of it and if the deed creating the covenant specifically mentions them as intended beneficiaries or if they own land within an area covered by a general plan).

85 *Restatement (Third) of Property (Servitudes)* §2.6 (2000).

86 *Muldawer v. Stribling*, 256 S.E.2d 357 (Ga. 1979). *Accord, Runyon v. Paley*, 416 S.E.2d 177, 190 (N.C. 1992).

87 *Allemong v. Frendzel*, 363 S.E.2d 487 (W. Va. 1987). *Accord, Runyon v. Paley*, 416 S.E.2d 177, 190 (N.C. 1992). *See* §6.4.

88 *Roehrs v. Lees*, 429 A.2d 388 (N.J. Super. Ct. 1981).

89 Dale A. Whitman et al., *The Law of Property* §§8.18 to 8.19, at 399-404 (4th ed. 2019); Gerald Korngold, *Private Land Use Arrangements: Easements, Real Covenants, and Equitable Servitudes* §9.14, at 408 (3d ed. 2016); 7-61 *Thompson on Real Property, Third Thomas Edition* §61.04(e)(1), (2).

90 *Restatement of Property* §§535, 542, 547 (1944).

91 This latter approach is adopted by the *Restatement of Property* §§535, 542, 547 (1944) and by the *Restatement (Third) of Property (Servitudes)* §2.6 (2000).

the servient estate and violated a covenant burdening the land.[92] Similarly, a landlord may not be able to sue a subtenant for unpaid rent.[93]

***Restatement (Third)* on negative covenants**

To avoid these results, the *Restatement (Third)* abolishes both the horizontal privity and the strict vertical privity requirement. Although the *Restatement (Third)* formally abolishes the vertical privity requirement, it effectively accepts a relaxed version of it by positing that those who succeed to interests in the servient estate are burdened by restrictive covenants of which they were on notice when they purchased the property.[94] This "relaxed" form of vertical privity might bind a succeeding possessor of the burdened parcel (such as a tenant) even if the grantor of the servient estate retains a future interest in the property. In addition, the *Restatement (Third)* provides that owners who do not derive their title from one of the covenanting parties can enforce the covenant if they are intended beneficiaries of it.[95] The burdens and benefits of covenants also run to adverse possessors.[96]

***Restatement (Third)* on affirmative covenants**

The *Restatement (Third)* adopts a different set of rules to govern when affirmative covenants run with the land. Affirmative covenants are those that require the covenantor (or her successor) to perform certain actions (rather than to refrain from particular acts on the land). The *Restatement (Third)* provides that the burdens of affirmative covenants are enforceable against lessees only if they can "more reasonably be performed by a person in possession than by the holder of a reversion in the burdened property."[97] Conversely, the benefits of affirmative covenants can be enforced by a lessee if they are covenants to repair the property, or if those benefits can be enjoyed by the lessee without "diminishing [their] value to the lessor and without materially increasing the burden of performance on the person obligated to perform the covenant."[98] Affirmative covenants are binding on life tenants but the life tenant's liability to perform such covenants is "limited to the value of the life estate."[99]

Homeowners' associations

A relaxing of the requirement of vertical privity on the benefit side has long been recognized in the context of homeowners' associations.[100]

[92] If the servient owner placed the covenant in a written lease agreement with the tenant, then the dominant owner might be able to sue the tenant as the intended third-party beneficiary of the promise made by the tenant to the landlord. But, of course, in this case, the covenant is not running with the land; the dominant owner is suing, not as the dominant owner, but as the beneficiary of the tenant's own contractual commitment to the landlord of the servient property.

[93] These issues are further discussed in §10.7.2.

[94] *BM-Clarence Cardwell, Inc. v. Cocca Development, Ltd.*, 65 N.E.3d 829, 837 (Ohio Ct. App. 2016) (applying relaxed vertical privity, and finding it would be inequitable to permit lessees to escape covenants by a strict vertical privity standard); *Restatement (Third) of Property (Servitudes)* §§5.2, 7.14 (2000). *See also id.* at §5.2 cmt. b, at 19 (distinguishing between "strict" and "relaxed" vertical privity). Those who are not successors are benefited by the covenant only if they can show that they were intended beneficiaries of it. *See Restatement (Third) of Property (Servitudes)* §2.6 (2000).

[95] *Restatement (Third) of Property (Servitudes)* §2.6 (2000).

[96] *Id.* at §5.2.

[97] *Id.* at §5.3(2).

[98] *Id.* at §5.3(1).

[99] *Id.* at §5.4.

[100] 7-61 *Thompson on Real Property, Third Thomas Edition* §61.04(e)(4).

Developers of subdivisions often provide for the creation of a homeowners' association and expressly grant it the power to administer and enforce the covenants imposed on the parcels in the subdivision. At one time it was unclear whether homeowners' associations had standing to sue to enforce restrictive or affirmative covenants. After all, the association itself owns no property and thus is not in privity of estate with anyone and is not obviously an "intended beneficiary" of the covenants because it owns no land. Only owners of land intended to benefit from a land use covenant traditionally had standing to enforce it. It is now well settled, however, that as agents of the property owners whose property is reciprocally benefited and burdened by servitudes, homeowners' associations have standing to enforce those servitudes if the declaration gives them this power.[101] The *Restatement (Third)* would grant homeowners' associations such standing unless the declaration expressly denies it.[102]

§6.3 Substantive Requirements

§6.3.1 *Touch and Concern*

Traditional meaning

Traditionally, a covenant will run with the land only if it "touches and concerns" the land. Restrictions on use of the land, such as a promise to use the land only for residential purposes or a promise not to sell liquor on the land, clearly satisfy the test. In *Mercantile-Safe Deposit and Trust Co. v. Mayor and City Council of Baltimore*,[103] the owner of a shopping center included a covenant in one of its leases requiring the lessee (the tenant) to restore the premises to certain conditions prior to the termination of the lease. In holding that the covenant to restore the condition of the premises ran with the land, the court found that it "touched and concerned" the land because "the thing required to be done affect[s] the quality, value, or mode of enjoying the [property interest] conveyed."[104] A covenant meets this test if it has something to do with the use of the land and/or is connected with enjoyment of the land.[105] The test may also require that the covenant affect the market value of the land by increasing the value of the benefited land.[106] In addition, some courts hold that a land use restriction touches and concerns the land if it affects the parties' interests "as landowners" such that the

[101] The leading case is *Neponsit Property Owners' Ass'n, Inc. v. Emigrant Industrial Savings Bank*, 15 N.E.2d 793 (N.Y. 1938). *See also Portola Hills Community Ass'n v. James*, 5 Cal. Rptr. 2d 580 (Ct. App. 1992); *Tuscarora MarketPlace Partners, LLC v. First National Bank*, 906 S.E.2d 171, 183 (Va. App. 2024) ("If the covenant is 'collateral to the land' and 'merely [a] personal covenant[ ]' the covenant cannot run with the land to bind successors in interest." (citations omitted)).

[102] *Restatement (Third) of Property (Servitudes)* §6.11 (2000).

[103] 521 A.2d 734 (Md. 1987).

[104] *Id.* at 736.

[105] *1515-1519 Lakeview Blvd. Condominium Ass'n v. Apartment Sales Corp.*, 43 P.3d 1233, 1238 (Wash. 2002) (touch and concern test requires the covenant to "concern the occupation or enjoyment of land").

[106] *Runyon v. Paley*, 416 S.E.2d 177, 183 (N.C. 1992); 7-61 *Thompson on Real Property, Third Thomas Edition* §61.04(d)(4).

benefits and burdens could not exist independently of the parties' ownership interests in real property.[107] "Where the burdens and benefits created by the covenant are of such a nature that they may exist independently from the parties' ownership interests in land, the covenant does not touch and concern the land and will not run with the land."[108]

Reasonableness

The dominant consideration in touch and concern cases seems to be the conclusion that the obligation and/or benefit is the kind that should run with the land, binding and benefiting future owners.[109] Traditionally, courts were loath to enforce anti-competitive covenants and covenants that involved payments of money (such as fees paid to homeowners' associations) for policy reasons. Rather than strike down such covenants directly as a matter of public policy, courts resorted to the touch and concern doctrine, holding that such covenants did not relate to the use of land but represented merely economic benefits. Today both anti-competitive covenants and covenants to pay dues to a homeowners' association are universally understood to touch and concern the land. Courts also traditionally used the touch and concern requirement to deny enforcement of covenants when the benefit of the covenant was held in gross; in such cases, the covenant did not touch or concern any dominant estate and thus the restriction was not balanced by any compensating benefit to other land. Modern law tends to address public policy concerns more directly. As Justice Marie Garibaldi noted in *Davidson Bros., Inc. v. D. Katz & Sons, Inc.*,[110] addressing the question whether anti-competitive covenants "touch and concern" the land, "[r]easonableness, not esoteric concepts of property law, should be the guiding inquiry into the validity of covenants at law."

Restatement (Third)

The *Restatement (Third) of Property (Servitudes)* would abolish the touch and concern requirement and provide instead that covenants will run with the land unless they are unconscionable, without rational justification, or otherwise violate public policy.[111] However, many courts still retain the touch and concern test.[112] Moreover, the *Restatement (Third)* seems to reintroduce the touch and concern element through the back door by providing that "appurtenant" benefits and burdens[113] should run with the land when they are "tied to ownership or occupancy" of land[114] in

[107] *Regency Homes Ass'n v. Egermayer*, 498 N.W.2d 783, 791 (Neb. 1993); *Runyon v. Paley*, 416 S.E.2d 177, 182-183 (N.C. 1992). *See also Restatement of Property* §537 (1944).

[108] *Runyon v. Paley*, 416 S.E.2d 177, 183 (N.C. 1992); *see also Tuscarora MarketPlace Partners, LLC v. First National Bank*, 906 S.E.2d 171, 183 (Va. App. 2024).

[109] As Susan French has noted, "When a court invalidates a covenant obligation on the ground that it does not touch and concern the land, it makes a substantive judgment that the obligation should not be permitted to run with the land. . . . The real reasons for the invalidation are seldom, if ever given." Susan French, *Servitudes Reform and the New Restatement of Property: Creation Doctrines and Structural Simplification*, 73 Cornell L. Rev. 928, 939-940 (1988).

[110] 579 A.2d 288, 295 (N.J. 1990).

[111] *See Restatement (Third) of Property (Servitudes)* §3.1 (2000).

[112] *See Equestrian Ridge Homeowners Association v. Equestrian Ridge Estates II Homeowners Association*, 953 N.W.2d 16, 32-33 (Neb. 2021) (enforcing fees to pay for access road because they touched and concerned the land).

[113] *Restatement (Third) of Property (Servitudes)* §5.2 (2000).

[114] *Id.* at §1.5(1).

the sense that they "obligate[] the owner or occupier of a particular unit or parcel in that person's capacity as owner or occupier" of land.[115] In addition, the *Restatement (Third)* notes that a servitude is appurtenant rather than in gross or personal only "if it serves a purpose that would be more useful to a successor to a property interest . . . than it would be to the original beneficiary."[116]

▷ AFFIRMATIVE COVENANTS

HARD CASE ◀

Held to touch and concern

Affirmative covenants today are generally enforceable to the same extent as are negative covenants.[117] However, some courts have had trouble with affirmative covenants that require owners to continue particular uses or to build on property, although many courts have enforced such covenants against later owners of servient estates.[118] For example, in *Nicholson v. 300 Broadway Realty Corp.*,[119] the court held that a covenant requiring the owner of one parcel to supply steam heat to the owner of the neighboring property "touched and concerned" the land because "it affected the legal relations of the parties to the covenant as owners of particular parcels of land."[120] It did so because it gave the covenantee a

> right, not possessed by other landowners, of having heat supplied to his building, as long as it stood, and it imposed upon the covenantor . . . so long as the heat-producing facilities remained on its land, the burden, not cast upon other landowners, of furnishing heat to premises adjoining its own.[121]

Held not to touch and concern

On the other hand, in *Eagle Enterprises v. Gross*,[122] the court held that a promise by a subdivision developer to supply water from a well on its retained land to its grantee buyers did not touch and concern the land because "it did not substantially affect the ownership interest of landowners in the Orchard Hill subdivision" because water was to be supplied for only six months out of the year and the homeowners had other available sources

[115] *Id.*

[116] *Id.* at §4.5(1)(a). *See* Dale A. Whitman et al., *The Law of Property* §8.16, at 397 (4th ed. 2019).

[117] *Restatement (Third) of Property (Servitudes)* §3.2 cmt. e (2000); 7-61 *Thompson on Real Property, Third Thomas Edition* §61.04(d)(5)(i).

[118] *Compare Lowenburg v. City of Saraland*, 489 So. 2d 562 (Ala. 1986) (requiring an owner to comply with a covenant to build a golf course within 5 years on at least 50 acres of the 220 acres conveyed); *Shalimar Ass'n v. D.O.C. Enterprises, Ltd.*, 688 P.2d 682 (Ariz. Ct. App. 1984) (requiring an owner to continue operating a golf course to comply with an affirmative covenant) *with Oceanside Community Associates v. Oceanside Land Co.*, 195 Cal. Rptr. 14 (Ct. App. 1983) (refusing to grant an injunction ordering an owner to renovate and operate a golf club but imposing a lien on the property for lost value to the dominant estates resulting from the failure to comply with the covenant).

[119] 164 N.E.2d 832, 835 (N.Y. 1959).

[120] *Id.* at 835.

[121] *Id.*

[122] 349 N.E.2d 816 (N.Y. 1976).

of water. The court further noted that affirmative covenants — promises to undertake affirmative acts for the benefit of the owners of other lots — are disfavored. The court distinguished *Neponsit Property Owners' Ass'n, Inc. v. Emigrant Industrial Savings Bank*,[123] a leading case holding that the obligation to pay dues to a homeowners' association to maintain common areas such as roads, paths, parks, beaches, and sewers does touch and concern the land, on the ground that such covenants "substantially affected the promisor's legal interest in his property since the latter received an easement in common and a right of enjoyment in the public improvements for which contribution was received by all the landowners in the subdivision."[124] Today the enforceability of affirmative covenants against subsequent owners is generally resolved, not by determining whether affirmative covenants "touch and concern" the land, but by asking whether conditions have changed such that there are good reasons not to enforce the covenant. These cases may also be approached by asking whether the servitude imposes an undue hardship on the servient owner or if changed conditions materially reduce its benefit.[125] ◀

Covenants to pay money

Covenants to pay money also traditionally raised problems for the courts.[126] The payment of money would arguably benefit the covenantee whether or not she was a landowner. At the same time, many payment obligations do have a strong relation to land use. The foremost example is dues payable to homeowners' associations. Although at one time problematic, they are now universally held to touch and concern the land when they involve fees to maintain common areas. This principle was established in the leading case of *Neponsit Property Owners' Ass'n v. Emigrant Industrial Savings Bank*.[127] Because only the owners of the affected parcels had the right to use the common facilities, payment of the fees benefited them as landowners and increased the value of their parcels. Today covenants to pay money, especially dues to homeowners' associations, are generally enforceable.[128]

▶ HARD CASE ▷ RECREATIONAL FACILITIES

Courts have reached divergent results, however, in cases involving recreational facilities. Most courts find that a covenant to pay dues to belong to a recreational facility does touch and concern the land.[129] For example, the

[123] 15 N.E.2d 793 (N.Y. 1938).
[124] 349 N.E.2d at 819.
[125] *See* §§6.8.1, 6.8.2.
[126] Gerald Korngold, *Private Land Use Arrangements: Easements, Real Covenants, and Equitable Servitudes* §9.12, at 397 (3d ed. 2016); 7-61 *Thompson on Real Property, Third Thomas Edition* §61.04(d)(5)(ii).
[127] 15 N.E.2d 793 (N.Y. 1938).
[128] *Restatement (Third) of Property (Servitudes)* §3.2 cmt. e (2000).
[129] *Streams Sports Club, Ltd. v. Richmond*, 457 N.E.2d 1226, 1231 (Ill. 1983); *Homsey v. University Gardens Racquet Club*, 730 S.W.2d 763 (Tex. Ct. App. 1987).

court in *Streams Sports Club, Ltd. v. Richmond*[130] held that such covenants touch and concern the land because the recreational facility was part of a common building plan and it was designed to be used by residents of the condominium. However, the court in *Chesapeake Ranch Club, Inc. v. C.R.C. United Members, Inc.*[131] held that a covenant to pay dues to belong to a recreational facility in a residential subdivision did not touch and concern the land. Judge Bell found that the obligation to pay the dues did not necessarily affect the value of the land and that the presence of a recreational facility in the community was not something that was necessarily tied to land ownership. It may be that the obligation seemed less appropriate in the context of a residential subdivision than in the context of a condominium building where the facilities are more integrated into a common structure. ◀

Problems with the touch and concern test

These cases demonstrate the problems with the traditional touch and concern test. After all, any obligation or benefit that applies to a landowner is likely to have some effect on the market value of the land, either making it more or less valuable. At the same time, the actual effect may be hard to quantify or predict. Similarly, the use of sports facilities could be separated from land ownership, but it is also the case that their availability could well increase the value of land. It is not clear that it should make a difference whether or not outsiders (non-owners) have the right to join the facility as members. The *Restatement (Third)* would make such covenants enforceable unless they violate public policy, and the strong trend in the law is to enforce such fee obligations for common athletic facilities.

▷ TENANT'S SECURITY DEPOSIT **HARD CASE ◀**

In *Castlebrook, Ltd. v. Dayton Properties Ltd. Partnership*,[132] the court held that a covenant to return a tenant's security deposit did not touch and concern the land and hence was not binding on a successor landlord. Judge Fain held that "[c]ovenants that will run with the land must be so connected with, attached to, and inherent in the land that the assignee of the reversion would have the right to take advantage of it or be obligated to perform it."[133] Security deposits are merely personal pledges separable from ownership of interests in the land.[134] Nor was there evidence that the parties intended the obligation to repay the security deposit to run with the land. Thus, a subsequent landlord would not have been on notice of the obligation.

Argument that it does not run with the land

Argument that it does run with the land

One could argue, in response, that the purpose of the security deposit is to protect the landlord from any financial obligations arising out of the

---

[130] 457 N.E.2d 1226, 1231-1232 (Ill. 1983). *Accord, Regency Homes Ass'n v. Egermayer*, 498 N.W.2d 783, 792-793 (Neb. 1993).

[131] 483 A.2d 1334 (Md. Ct. Spec. App. 1984). *Accord, Ebbe v. Senior Estates Golf and Country Club*, 657 P.2d 696 (Or. Ct. App. 1983).

[132] 604 N.E.2d 808 (Ohio Ct. App. 1992).

[133] *Id.* at 813.

[134] *Mullendore Theatres, Inc. v. Growth Realty Investors Co.*, 691 P.2d 970 (Wash. Ct. App. 1984).

need to repair the premises if the tenant damages them or fails to pay rent when due. The tenant has a contractual right to get her security deposit back at the end of the leasehold if the property has not been damaged and the rent has been paid. This entitlement should not be lost if the landlord sells the property in the middle of the leasehold. The tenant should not have to sue the original landlord or follow her to Florida to get back her security deposit. It is a simple matter for the owner of rental property to transfer the security deposit paid by existing tenants to the new landlord when the property is sold, giving the new owner the ability to return the moneys paid by the tenants and owed back to them at the end of the leasehold. There is no notice problem because the payment of security deposits is a common phenomenon and a buyer of rental property cannot claim unfair surprise that the tenant expects her money back at the end of the leasehold, as the contract provides. The obligation to pay back the security deposit at the end of the lease is an affirmative covenant in the lease and a buyer is on at least inquiry notice of it because a reasonable buyer of rental property would want to see the existing leases before buying the property. Moreover, it is less costly for a new owner to arrange for a transfer of the security deposits at the time of sale than for tenants to find and sue the old landlord. ◀

§6.3.2 *Enforcement in Gross*

Intent to allow original covenantee to enforce in gross after transfer

Once the original covenantee transfers the dominant estate, enforceability of the covenant shifts to the new owner. Once the dominant owner sells her the dominant estate, she is almost certain not to be an intended beneficiary of the promise. Covenants that touch and concern the use of land for the benefit of the owner of neighboring land are presumed enforceable only by the current owner of the benefited parcel. This rule constitutes a presumption about the probable intent of the parties to the original covenant. Although some courts say they will allow enforcement by the original covenantee if the parties to the original covenant intended to allow enforcement by the original covenantee after transfer of the dominant estate, they are extremely reluctant to find such an intent, absent explicit language to that effect.[135]

Covenants whose benefits are initially held in gross

Traditionally, the benefit of a covenant could not be held in gross even if the parties intended to create such an arrangement.[136] Some states prohibit

[135] *See Shaff v. Leyland*, 914 A.2d 1240, 1244 (N.H. 2006); *Caullett v. Stanley Stilwell & Sons, Inc.*, 170 A.2d 52 (N.J. Super. Ct. App. Div. 1961); Dale A. Whitman et al., *The Law of Property* §8.24, at 420 (4th ed. 2019) (covenant not enforceable by covenantee after covenantee's property is transferred). *See* Susan French, *Servitudes Reform and the New Restatement of Property: Creation Doctrines and Structural Simplification*, 73 Cornell L. Rev. 928, 943, 946 (1988) (covenant enforceable by developer in gross only if she can show "some damage from the violation or other legitimate interest in the enforcement"); *Restatement (Third) of Property (Servitudes)* §2.6 cmt. d (2000) (covenant whose benefit is held in gross can be enforced only if "the person seeking enforcement [can] demonstrate a legitimate interest in enforcing the servitude"); *Restatement (Third) of Property (Servitudes)* §3.1 (2000) (invalidating servitudes that have no rational justification or that violate articulable public policies).

[136] 7-61 *Thompson on Real Property, Third Thomas Edition* §61.04(d)(4).

enforcement of covenants in gross by statute.[137] This does not mean that a landowner cannot make an enforceable contract to restrict her own land use; it means that this obligation will not pass to future possessors of her land if the promise does not benefit the owner of another parcel. Covenants that restrict land use interfere with both the right of free use of property and the marketability of the property. This cost is thought to be justified if there is a sufficient compensating benefit; when neighboring land is benefited, there is a presumption that the burden to the servient estate is more than offset by the benefit to the dominant estate. But when the benefit is held by someone who has no interest in land benefited by the restriction, the presumption falls away. Even though the promisee wishes to enforce the promise against the owner of the servient estate, most courts will not allow the promisee to do so, in most circumstances, even if the original covenanting parties intended this result.[138]

Enforcement exceptions

Courts make an exception to the policy restricting enforcement of covenants whose benefit is held in gross when the covenant is held by a homeowners' association on behalf of owners in the neighborhood, by a government entity, or by a charity.[139]

***Restatement (Third)* allows enforcement in gross**

The *Restatement (Third) of Property (Servitudes)* would abolish the rule that disallows the benefit of a covenant to be held in gross.[140] It would substitute a requirement that the beneficiary of the covenant has a legitimate interest in enforcing the covenant.[141] For example, the benefits of conservation and historic preservation servitudes that limit the development of property are often held in gross by charitable entities and serve widely recognized interests in preserving the natural and historic environment.

▷ CAN THE DEVELOPER ENFORCE THE COVENANT IN GROSS AFTER ALL LOTS ARE SOLD?

HARD CASE ◀

When the developer of a subdivision attempts to continue to enforce the covenant after the last parcel is sold, the question arises whether the developer has a legitimate interest in continuing to exercise the power to enforce

[137] Cal. Civ. Code §§1460, 1462; Mont. Code Ann. §70-17-203.

[138] *Lacer v. Navajo County*, 687 P.2d 404, 411 (Ariz. Ct. App. 1983); *Garland v. Rosenshein*, 649 N.E.2d 756 (Mass. 1995); *Vulcan Materials Co. v. Miller*, 691 So. 2d 908, 913-915 (Miss. 1997); *Lakewood Racquet Club, Inc. v. Jensen*, 232 P.3d 1147 (Wash. Ct. App. 2010); Dale A. Whitman et al., *The Law of Property* §8.32, at 429 (4th ed. 2019) (some courts will not allow burden of covenant to run with the land if benefit is held in gross); Gerald Korngold, *Private Land Use Arrangements: Easements, Real Covenants, and Equitable Servitudes* §9.15, at 417-419 (3d ed. 2016) (most courts will not allow burden to run if benefit is held in gross, but some courts disagree); 7-61 *Thompson on Real Property, Third Thomas Edition* §61.04(d)(3).

[139] *Wetlands America Trust, Inc. v. White Cloud Nine Ventures, L.P.*, 782 S.E.2d 131, 137-138 (Va. 2016); *Inhabitants of Middlefield v. Church Mills Knitting Co.*, 35 N.E. 780 (Mass. 1894) (opinion by Justice Holmes). *See also* Mass. Gen. Laws ch. 184, §§31, 32 (providing that a covenant restricting the price at which land is sold and limiting its use to low- or moderate-income residents is not invalid merely because the benefit is held in gross if the holder is a government entity or charitable corporation or trust).

[140] *Restatement (Third) of Property (Servitudes)* §2.6(1) (2000).

[141] *Id.* at §2.6 cmt. d.

the covenant. The developer's legitimate interest in retaining control over development in the subdivision is to increase the marketability of the lots; assuring prospective buyers that the subdivision is restricted to residential use, or even single-family homes, may increase the market value of the property and attract buyers. Once the developer leaves, however, she is an outsider whose legitimate interests have already been satisfied; continued control by the developer is seen as meddling. In addition, control by an absentee grantor resembles the powers exercised by feudal lords and is incompatible with the devolution of control over property to current owners. Freeing current owners from the "dead hand" of the past — and the continuing control of prior grantors in particular — promotes both the liberty of current owners and efficient use of land. There is, therefore, a strong, although not universal, presumption against continued enforcement by absentee developers who no longer own property in the neighborhood.[142]

Current law

Although the *Restatement (Third)* makes covenants enforceable when the benefit is held in gross,[143] it still requires a legitimate interest in the party who seeks enforcement — an interest hard to show for the absentee developer.[144] Courts that have allowed developers to retain control of architectural control commissions after sale of the last unit have based their conclusions on promoting the intent of the parties (freedom of contract). They have suggested that this retained control by the developer benefits the homeowners by ensuring continued compliance with the servitudes for which they bargained. At the same time, courts have acknowledged limits to this principle. In *B.C.E. Development v. Smith*,[145] for example, the court noted that "this is not a case in which a developer is shown to have retained unreasonable or imperious control over artistic decisions of homeowners long after having completed the subdivision. Equity might well decline to enforce such asserted control, especially if it were shown to be contrary to the then desires of the homeowners."[146] ◀

[142] *Compare Garland v. Rosenshein*, 649 N.E.2d 756 (Mass. 1995) (benefit of covenant held in gross cannot be enforced); *Smith v. First Savings of Louisiana*, 575 So. 2d 1033 (Ala. 1991) (refusing to allow the developer to retain control of the architectural review commission empowered to approve building changes in the subdivision once the last parcel was sold); *Armstrong v. Roberts*, 325 S.E.2d 769 (Ga. 1985) (developer cannot waive a covenant after all parcels are sold and it has no economic interest in the subdivision) *with B.C.E. Development, Inc. v. Smith*, 264 Cal. Rptr. 55 (Ct. App. 1989) (allowing enforcement by the developer's successor in interest when the covenant provided for such enforcement and the declaration gave the homeowners' association the power to amend the declaration and take control of the architectural commission by a two-thirds vote); *Christiansen v. Casey*, 613 S.W.2d 906 (Mo. Ct. App. 1981) (holding that courts should effectuate intent of the parties by allowing a developer to enforce a covenant after all lots were sold when the developer owned another tract adjacent to the restricted subdivision but asserting that the intent of the parties to allow continued enforcement should prevail even if the developer owns no adjacent land).

[143] *Restatement (Third) of Property (Servitudes)* §2.6(1) (2000).

[144] *Id.* at §2.6 cmt. d ("[t]o the extent that the doctrine prohibiting benefits in gross has served a gatekeeper function in covenant-enforcement litigation, it has been replaced by the requirement in §8.1 that the person seeking enforcement demonstrate a legitimate interest in enforcing the servitude").

[145] 264 Cal. Rptr. 55 (Ct. App. 1989).

[146] *Id.* at 60.

§6.4 Implied Reciprocal Negative Servitudes

Subdivisions

In the United States, the law of equitable servitudes performed a crucial function in the context of subdivision developments. It provided the legal basis for reciprocal enforcement of negative servitudes among homeowners in subdivisions and, later on, in condominium arrangements. This doctrine, called the rule of *implied reciprocal negative servitudes*, solved problems associated both with privity of estate and notice in the context of subdivision developments.[147] First, the doctrine allowed reciprocal enforcement when the deeds in question formally restricted use of the land but the technical requirements of privity were nonetheless not met. Specifically, the doctrine allowed enforcement by early buyers against later buyers. Second, the doctrine imposed obligations on land purchasers to research the titles not only to the parcels they were buying, but to neighboring parcels that had previously been owned and conveyed by the seller of the land.

General plan

If the developer of land in a subdivision placed uniform restrictions on enough of the parcels, the courts might conclude that the developer had intended to create a general plan of restrictions, that the presence of these restrictions in the deeds to neighboring parcels should have put all buyers in the subdivision on notice of this intended general plan, and that such restrictions would therefore be enforceable against unrestricted lots in the area covered by the general plan.

Early v. later buyers

Privity of estate issues

Many of the technical problems in mutual enforcement of covenants in subdivisions arise from the problem of enforcement by early buyers against later buyers. Consider a development with ten lots owned by developer *O*. Lot 1 is sold to *A*, Lot 2 to *B*, Lot 3 to *C*, and so on, with Lot 10 sold to *J*. The developer *O* makes no grantor covenants by which *O* promises to restrict the use of its land; *O* makes only oral representations that all the lots in the development will be similarly restricted. The deeds contain only grantee covenants by which each owner agrees to restrict the use of her own land. When *A*, as buyer of Lot 1, covenants to restrict Lot 1 to residential purposes, the promise benefits grantor *O*'s remaining land. Later buyers can enforce the covenants in the deeds to earlier-sold property as successor owners of the dominant estate; the covenant was imposed in the *O-A* deed for the benefit of current and future owners of Lot 2 (as well as Lots 3-10) and both horizontal privity and vertical privity are present. However, earlier buyers cannot enforce the covenants contained in the deeds of later buyers under real covenants law because, at the time the later buyer, *B*, agrees to restrict the lot being purchased (Lot 2), no privity of estate exists between *A* (the earlier buyer) and *B* (the later buyer) or between *A* and *O* because *O* no longer owns *A*'s land. The problem is at its worst when enforcement is sought against the last buyer. The buyer of Lot 10 makes a promise — but to whom? Not to the grantor, who owns no other property to be benefited by the promise. Nor is the last buyer in privity of estate with the prior purchasers. In the absence of both privity of contract (a promise

[147] *Schovee v. Mikolasko*, 737 A.2d 578, 586-587 (Md. 1999); *Forster v. Hall*, 576 S.E.2d 746 (Va. 2003).

made to the purchasers of earlier lots) and privity of estate (conveyance of a property interest between the parties or simultaneous interests in the same parcel), how can anyone in the neighborhood enforce the promise made by the owner of Lot 10?

Grantor covenant as a solution to the problem

When the developer includes both a grantor covenant and a grantee covenant in each deed, the privity problem goes away.[148] The later buyer *B* can enforce the grantee covenant made by the earlier buyer *A* because *A*'s promise to *O* was intended to benefit *O*'s remaining land (part of which passed to *B*). On the other hand, the earlier buyer can enforce the grantor covenant made by *O* to *A* in the *O-A* deed against *O*'s successor, *B*, as long as the *O-A* deed was recorded and *B* is on constructive notice of the promise made by *O* to *A*. But note that under this theory, the later buyers are bound, not because of their own promises made in their deeds from their grantor, *O*, but because of *O*'s promise to earlier buyers to restrict *O*'s remaining land. When the later buyer *B* purchases Lot 2, the burden of the covenant made by *O* runs with the land; some of the sticks in the bundle of property rights have already been transferred to *A*. *O* can only convey what she owns, and that is all *B* can get when *B* buys Lot 2.

Third-party beneficiary doctrine

Is there any way to rest *B*'s obligation to the earlier buyer *A* on *B*'s own promise (as grantee) rather than on the promise made by *O* (as grantor) in the *O-A* deed? The answer is yes, if we use *third-party beneficiary doctrine*. This doctrine allows contractual promises to be enforced by someone for whose benefit a promise was made even though the promise was not made to that person. Thus, *A* might sue as the third-party beneficiary of *B*'s promise to *O*. In this scenario, *B*'s promise is intended to benefit not only *O* and *O*'s remaining land (Lots 3-10) but lots *previously* sold by *O* in the same subdivision (such as Lot 1). However, courts are generally quite reluctant to allow individuals who are not parties to a contract to enforce it as third-party beneficiaries; most contractual obligations are personal in nature and are not enforceable by everyone in the world, only by the parties themselves. Nor is privity of estate present to substitute for privity of contract. But in this case, the courts have felt satisfied that the developer intended to make the covenants mutually enforceable among all owners in the neighborhood. How do we know this? How do we know *A* was an intended beneficiary?

General plan makes servitudes reciprocal

Most courts answer this question again by reference to the idea of a *general plan* or *common scheme*.[149] If all of the lots in an area previously owned by a single grantor are similarly restricted, this provides evidence that the developer intended the restrictions to be mutually benefiting and thus reciprocally enforceable, such that each owner is both restricted and entitled to enforce the same restrictions against her neighbors. Under a general plan, each owner has the power to enforce the mutual servitudes against each other owner in the area covered by the plan; a homeowners' association established by the developer has the power to enforce the

[148] However, a notice problem remains. *See* §6.2.2.

[149] *Restatement (Third) of Property (Servitudes)* §2.14 (2000). *See Selected Lands Corp. v. Speich*, 702 S.W.2d 197, 199 (Tex. Ct. App. 1985) (finding a general plan).

covenants if the document creating the association gives it the power to do so. The general plan applies to each owner partly because this is the intent of the developer/grantor and partly because of reliance on the developer's oral representations by buyers.[150]

Factors showing existence of a general plan

A general plan can be shown by various factors, such as the presence of restrictions in all or most deeds to property in the area previously owned by a common grantor, a recorded plat (map) showing the restrictions, the presence of restrictions in the last deed,[151] observance by owners of similar development of their land and conformity to the written restrictions, language stating that the covenants are intended to run with the land, and the recording of a declaration stating that the covenants are intended to be mutually enforceable.[152] This proof may be supplemented by oral statements or sales literature that induced the buyers to believe all the lots would be similarly restricted and that the restrictions would be reciprocally enforceable. If an earlier buyer's property is located in the area covered by the common scheme the developer intended to create, that buyer is entitled to enforce the promise made by a later buyer to the developer, even though that promise was made after the developer had severed its connection with the earlier buyer and had no interest in the land owned by her. Evidence tending to show the absence of a general plan is that some deeds are unrestricted and that the restrictions are nonuniform.

Restatement (Third)

The *Restatement (Third)* abolishes the traditional horizontal privity requirement and provides that restrictions in deeds intended to benefit other property will be mutually enforceable if the purchasers have notice of them when they purchase.[153] The existence of a general plan provides express or implied evidence that the restrictions were intended to be reciprocal and mutually enforceable by each owner against the others. Although privity is no longer an issue under this approach, problems may still arise about the scope of a common scheme and the existence of adequate notice. This problem is best addressed by inducing or requiring developers to record a declaration that clarifies which properties are subject to the general plan and that puts subsequent purchasers on notice of applicable restrictions. In the absence of such a declaration, it is often unclear whether a general plan was intended to exist and, if so, which properties were intended to be included in it.

▷ SCOPE OF A GENERAL PLAN **HARD CASE ◀**

For example, in *Evans v. Pollock*,[154] a developer sold the seafront lots on a peninsula surrounding a hill with restrictions limiting the lots to

[150] Gerald Korngold, *Private Land Use Arrangements: Easements, Real Covenants, and Equitable Servitudes* §9.09, at 371-373 (3d ed. 2016).
[151] Because the grantor retains no land left to be benefited, the suggestion is that the intended beneficiaries of the promise are the other lots in the neighborhood.
[152] Gerald Korngold, *Private Land Use Arrangements: Easements, Real Covenants, and Equitable Servitudes* §9.09, at 377 (3d ed. 2016).
[153] *Restatement (Third) of Property (Servitudes)* §§2.14 & 7.14 (2000).
[154] 796 S.W.2d 465 (Tex. 1990).

residential use by single-family dwellings on each lot. The developers left unrestricted one lot at the tip of the peninsula and the large lot at the top of the hill. When the developers died, their devisees attempted to use the unrestricted lots to construct a marina, a private club, and a condominium development. The court had to determine whether a general plan had been created and whether the hilltop in the center of the peninsula and lone unrestricted seafront lot at the tip of the peninsula had been intended to be included in the general plan. The Texas Supreme Court held that the developer had created a general plan but that the hilltop property was outside the scope of the plan, and that no explicit or implicit promises had been made to limit that property, so the current owner was entitled to use it for non-residential purposes and to construct multifamily housing. The court held the seafront lot to be within the common plan. Given the proximity and centrality of the unrestricted lots, the case could easily have gone the other way to protect the expectations of the homeowners to a purely residential environment. ◀

▶ HARD CASE

▷ NOTICE ISSUES: UNRESTRICTED LOTS

Argument for enforcement against unrestricted lots

A hard question arises when the developer imposes restrictive grantee covenants in most, but not all, of the deeds to property in the subdivision, and the grantor makes no promise (oral or written) to restrict the remaining lots. Should the owners of lots restricted by grantee covenants be able to enforce them against buyers of the unrestricted lots? If the buyers of the remaining lots knew of the restrictions and orally promised to comply with them, one might apply equitable estoppel doctrine in conjunction with third-party beneficiary doctrine to allow enforcement by prior and later buyers. But what if no oral statements are made by the buyers of the unrestricted lots? Most courts hold that buyers of unrestricted lots are on constructive notice of covenants in recorded deeds to nearby property granted by a common grantor.[155] If this were not the case, the developer could lead buyers to believe that all lots will be similarly restricted and then opportunistically renege on that commitment by selling unrestricted lots. The developer might do this because she has trouble selling some of the lots or because they can fetch a higher price if they are sold without the restrictions. To protect the reliance interests of the early buyers, the courts have imposed reciprocal restrictions on subsequently sold lots and held that such buyers are on constructive notice of the restrictions in the deeds to the other lots sold by the common grantor.[156]

Argument against enforcement against unrestricted lots

However, the California Supreme Court refused in *Riley v. Bear Creek Planning Committee*[157] to apply the doctrine of implied reciprocal negative servitudes to restrict lots that were purchased with unrestricted deeds and that had no reference to the restrictions in their chain of title, holding instead that restrictions must be in writing or referred to in the deed of the

[155] *Petersen v. Beekmere, Inc.*, 283 A.2d 911 (N.J. Super. Ct. Ch. Div. 1971).

[156] *Restatement (Third) of Property (Servitudes)* §2.14 cmt. b (2000).

[157] 551 P.2d 1213 (Cal. 1976).

land sought to be restricted or appear in the chain of title to that parcel. In *Riley*, a declaration was filed nine months after the sale of property to the plaintiffs. Because no restrictions were contained in their deed and no declaration had previously been recorded restricting their property, the court found that it was unrestricted, even though the grantor had orally stated that the property would be restricted and the plaintiffs had notice of the grantor's intent to impose mutually enforceable negative servitudes on the entire development. The opinion by the court emphasized the importance of the policies underlying both the parol evidence rule and the statute of frauds. Both rules tend to protect individuals from fraudulent claims that oral promises were made by limiting enforcement to those promises that were reduced to writing. Although those who buy after recordation of a declaration are bound by the restrictions contained within it, the court refused to extend such restrictions to prior purchasers even if they purchased with notice that the grantor intended to impose such restrictions on them. This approach prevents the grantor from subsequently expanding the scope of the common scheme, ensures that buyers are on notice of restrictions on their land, and protects buyers (and sellers) from fraudulent claims of oral promises. Justice Tobriner dissented, noting that there was no dispute in the case that plaintiffs were on actual notice of the grantor's intent to impose the restrictions and that, in such a case, it is those buyers, rather than the later buyers or the developer, who are wrongfully attempting to escape their contractual obligations. ◀

▷ NEIGHBORING LAND OF THE GRANTOR **HARD CASE ◀**

Suppose all the covenants in the neighborhood contain grantee covenants restricting the property to single-family use. Moreover, the developer files a declaration to that effect describing all the property in the subdivision as restricted. The developer owns property across the street from this subdivision; the property is left undeveloped for several years after the subdivision is completed. The developer then seeks to build on this property in a manner inconsistent with the restrictions imposed on the subdivision. Can the developer do this? The question arises whether the neighboring tract should be treated as part of the general plan. If it was noted on the original plat, the courts are likely to hold that it was part of the general plan. But suppose it was never described on the plat or the declaration or orally as part of the development. May the developer sell to commercial users in a manner that does not constitute a common law nuisance but nonetheless interferes with the common residential scheme by substantially changing the environment? No promises of any kind were made to the buyers in the subdivision that the developer would not do this. Most courts hold that only parcels within the common scheme are restricted and that the grantor's intent to leave a tract or parcel out of the common scheme is determinative. This is the approach taken by the *Restatement (Third)* as well.[158]

[158] *Restatement (Third) of Property (Servitudes)* §2.14 cmt. g (2000).

Extent of the common plan

In *Duvall v. Ford Leasing Development Corp.*,[159] a developer subdivided and built homes on a large tract in stages over a 25-year period. Each of the subdivisions was restricted to residential use. The developer then sold its remaining land, expressly providing in the deed that a portion of it would remain free of restrictions of any kind. The buyer of that land sold the unrestricted parcel to an owner who sought to establish a car sales and service business. Relying on the piecemeal development and the fact that it occurred over a long period of time, the court held that the development consisted of separate subdivisions and that the entire property was not subject to a single general plan. In contrast, the court in *Snow v. Van Dam*[160] concluded that a lot across the street from the rest of a subdivision was intended to be in the same general plan, although it was sold more than 15 years after the first lot, because it was included in the description of the entire tract when it was registered and the delay in sale was caused by the inability to sell the property rather than an intent to exclude it from the restricted area. ◄

§6.5 Remedies

Damages and injunctions both available today

Although real covenants were traditionally enforced by damages and equitable servitudes by injunctions, it is fair to say that today land use restrictions, whether in the form of real covenants or equitable servitudes, may be enforced either by damages or injunctions, as the court deems appropriate.[161] This is the position taken by the *Restatement (Third)*[162] and it makes sense. For one thing, any covenant that is enforceable by damages is also almost certain to be enforceable by injunction.[163] This is because any covenant that satisfies the traditional criteria for enforcement as a real covenant will also satisfy the requirements for enforcement as an equitable servitude.[164] Although notice is not a traditional element for real covenants to run with the land, lack of notice is likely to constitute a defense to enforcement. At the same time, it is important to remember that the act of granting an injunction has always been discretionary; thus, an injunction may be denied if injunctive relief is overly burdensome or if the person seeking the injunction has acted unfairly.[165] "In determining whether to grant an injunction, the court must consider the relative convenience-inconvenience and the comparative injuries to the parties."[166]

[159] 255 S.E.2d 470 (Va. 1979).
[160] 197 N.E. 224 (Mass. 1935).
[161] *Restatement (Third) of Property (Servitudes)* §8.2 (2000); 7-61 *Thompson on Real Property, Third Thomas Edition* §61.05.
[162] *Restatement (Third) of Property (Servitudes)* §8.2 (2000).
[163] Dale A. Whitman et al., *The Law of Property* §8.24, at 420-422 (4th ed. 2019).
[164] *But see Sloan v. Johnson*, 491 S.E.2d 725, 727-728 (Va. 1997) (privity but not notice required for the running of real covenants, suggesting that a real covenant might be enforceable despite the lack of notice).
[165] 7-61 *Thompson on Real Property, Third Thomas Edition* §61.05.
[166] *Clark v. Asheville Contracting Co.*, 323 S.E.2d 765, 769 (N.C. Ct. App. 1984), *aff'd as modified*, 342 S.E.2d 832 (N.C. 1986).

There are situations in which courts might be inclined to grant damages while denying injunctive relief. In such cases, however, injunctive relief is denied not because it is unavailable as a general matter, but because the specific facts of the case suggest that it is inappropriate.

Situations where damages may be denied while injunctive relief is awarded

While all covenants in the United States today are generally enforceable by injunction, not all restrictions enforceable by injunction as equitable servitudes are necessarily enforceable by a damages remedy as real covenants. In states that retain the privity requirement for real covenants, some restrictions enforceable by injunction as equitable servitudes will not be enforceable as real covenants if privity is lacking, and thus damages may be unavailable in such cases. For example, an owner whose property is contiguous to property burdened by a covenant and whose property is intended to benefit by enforcement of the covenant may have a right to enforce the covenant as an equitable servitude even though the covenant nowhere appears in that owner's chain of title and is therefore unenforceable by damages as a real covenant. Similarly, in some states, an owner may be burdened by a restriction even though it is not in her "chain of title" if the original developer intended to create a common scheme in the neighborhood in which the parcel is located. In either or both cases, there may be good reasons of public policy to grant an injunction while denying a damages remedy. This remedy protects reliance interests of the covenantee by restricting use of the servient estate while limiting servient owners from unlimited financial exposure to owners outside the chain of title. At the same time, a court might be convinced in a particular case, or in general, that damages should be available to enforce an equitable servitude in the absence of privity.

Damages v. injunctions

Should covenants normally be enforced by damages or injunctive relief? Traditional contract law holds that damages are the usual remedy for breach of contract while injunctions are awarded only when damages are inadequate.[167] Property law, however, represents one of the most important areas in which damages are often thought inadequate because of the unique value attached to the location of land and the desire to use particular unique structures in particular ways.[168] Moreover, property rights have an aura of absoluteness (circumscribed as they may be by the legal rights of neighbors) and that sense of ownership may provide a justification for specific performance in that it protects the justified expectations of the owner of the covenant. The problem, of course, is that servitudes involve property rights on both sides; enforcement of a covenant protects the property rights of the covenantee but it also restricts the free use of the servient estate, thereby limiting ownership rights. The granting of an injunction, moreover, has always been discretionary. In addition, servitudes law developed in a way that seems contrary to the traditional idea that damages should be easier to obtain than injunctions (because injunctions are awarded only when damages are inadequate). Recall that enforcement as a real covenant requires a showing of privity while enforcement as an equitable servitude removed the privity requirement. This means that the list of elements

[167] E. Allan Farnsworth, *Contracts* §12.6, at 746-751 (4th ed. 2004).

[168] *Id.* at §12.6, at 747-748.

needed to enforce an equitable servitude by injunction was easier to prove than the list needed to enforce a real covenant through a damages remedy.

Argument for "efficient breach" through damages remedy

Judge Richard Posner has argued that injunctions should be the normal remedy for violation of a servitude. In *Walgreen Co. v. Sara Creek Property Co.*,[169] a shopping center landlord (Sara Creek) breached an anti-competitive covenant in a lease with a tenant pharmacy (Walgreen's) by arranging for a department store containing a pharmacy (Phar-Mor) to replace an anchor tenant whose business was doing badly. The issue was whether the covenant could be enforced by an injunction ordering the landlord not to allow a competitor to operate in the center or whether an injunction would be denied and the plaintiff relegated to damages. The Seventh Circuit upheld the trial court's decision to issue an injunction. Judge Posner noted that damages are normally the remedy in breach of contract cases because they are "efficient" in the sense that they adequately protect the reliance interests of the promisee while allowing the promisor the liberty to breach the promise. If the promisor is willing to pay damages to the promisee to compensate for the harm caused by breaking the promise, then the promisee will have the benefit of the bargain and be protected from financial harm while the promisor will be able to enter into a more valuable alternative use of the property. In such cases, breach may be efficient in the sense that it allows resources to be moved into a more valuable use while protecting the legitimate expectations of the promisee. Limiting the promisee to a damages remedy may also maximize the joint value of the landlord's and the tenant's respective property rights. In addition, enforcement by damages protects liberty interests by allowing promisors to change their minds; compelling performance seems an unjust constraint on freedom of action if damages are an adequate substitute for performance. If damages are adequate as a remedy, the reliance interests of the promisee may be protected without curtailing the liberty of the promisor.

Argument for injunctive relief

Judge Posner, however, rejected this argument on both fairness and efficiency grounds. First, he noted that the doctrine of efficient breach effectively transfers a property right from the promisee to the promisor against the will of the promisee. If the promisee owns the right to have the servient owner comply with the servitude, then forcing the promisee to accept damages in lieu of an injunction represents a forced sale of the entitlement from the owner (the promisee) to the non-owner (the promisor). Moreover, the sale will be at a price determined by the court; that price will approximate the fair market value of the servitude. This value, however, may well be less than the owner's asking price. In other words, if the court granted injunctive relief, the servient owner would have to offer the dominant owner enough to meet the dominant owner's asking price. The result would be determined, not by a court-determined fair market value, but by bargaining between the parties. Such bargaining may well result in a transfer that better protects the value of the covenant to the dominant owner as she sees it. When we are asking whether a transfer of a property right is "efficient," we usually want to know whether the redistribution will

[169] 966 F.2d 273 (7th Cir. 1992).

benefit the new owner more than it harms the old owner. We normally test this proposition by letting the parties bargain, and if they cannot come to agreement because the potential purchaser could not offer the existing owner enough to induce a sale, we may conclude that the value to the current owner is greater than the value to the potential owner. If we measure efficiency by asking whether the parties would voluntarily agree to a sale (rather than asking what result would maximize the fair market value of the property rights held by both parties), then we might well conclude that a forced transfer of property rights would not in fact be efficient because a refusal to sell the entitlement may indicate that its value to the dominant owner exceeded the value to the servient owner and that allowing breach (with payment of damages measured at fair market value) will actually decrease social welfare.

Criticism of the argument

Judge Posner's argument is not the last word on efficiency, however. It may well be the case that an award of an injunction will not be followed by bargaining between the parties. This may be because transaction costs (such as the costs of bargaining or strategic behavior) block an efficient transaction. Professor Ward Farnsworth has noted that in nuisance cases he studied, there never was any bargaining between the parties subsequent to a court judgment. This may be because the courts all adjudicated the cases correctly, or because transaction costs inhibit deals, but he argues that other factors explain this result. After judgment, parties may be unwilling to deal with each other because of hard feelings generated by the litigation. The winner may also feel entitled, as a result of the litigation confirming a right to enforce the servitude, and thus the judgment itself may increase the value of the entitlement to the dominant owner and solidify its unwillingness to sell.[170] Moreover, it is not clear whether efficiency is best measured by starting from the status quo allocation of property rights and comparing the offer price of the non-owner with the asking price of the owner, or whether we should focus on the fair market value of the respective property rights. The fair market value measure may be attractive because it is likely to be a more accurate assessment of the general value of the property interests in question than offer and asking prices since transaction costs may well inhibit a transfer of the entitlement from the covenantee to the covenantor. While the willingness of individuals to buy and sell may be a more accurate picture of who values the property the most, it also biases the efficiency determination in the direction of the status quo, given that asking prices are often likely to be higher than offer prices, and this measure of efficiency may give insufficient weight to social interests in removing old covenants that impede the reasonable development of land.

Relative hardship

In contrast to Judge Posner's argument for injunctive relief based on the idea that bargaining by the parties is more likely to be efficient than court-determined damages, Justice Stewart Pollock argued in a concurring opinion in *Davidson Bros., Inc. v. D. Katz & Sons, Inc.*[171] both that

[170] Ward Farnsworth, *Do Parties to Nuisance Cases Bargain After Judgment? A Glimpse Inside the Cathedral*, 66 U. Chi. L. Rev. 373 (1999).

[171] 579 A.2d 288, 305-307 (N.J. 1990).

transaction costs might prevent a mutually beneficial bargain and that the "economic efficiency of an injunction, although persuasive, is not dispositive. The right rule of law is not necessarily the one that is most efficient. In other cases, New Jersey courts have allowed cost considerations other than efficiency to affect the award of a remedy."[172] He notes that in *Gilpin v. Jacob Ellis Realties*,[173] the trial court denied an injunction but upheld an award of damages for breach of a covenant that disallowed all construction greater than 15 feet tall within 4 feet of the boundary between the parties' property. After the defendant breached the covenant, the trial court found that remodeling the structure would have cost defendant $11,500 while the plaintiff had only suffered $1,000 of harm. The trial court had found that the breach harmed plaintiff to the extent of $1,000 in damages. Emphasizing that the difference in these figures was "so grossly disproportionate in amount as to justify the denial of the mandatory injunction,"[174] the Appellate Division applied the "doctrine of relative hardship" and required the defendant to pay only $1,000 in damages. Justice Pollock thus concludes that the court opted for a damages remedy not based on efficiency considerations, but rather because of its sense of the equities in the situation.

§6.6 Interpretation of Ambiguous Covenants

Intent v. free use

Courts traditionally interpreted ambiguous covenants in the manner that would be the "least burdensome to the free use of land."[175] Some courts state that covenants should be construed against the drafter; this usually means the grantor or developer.[176] Today the touchstone for interpretation of covenants seems to be the *intent of the grantor*.[177] This intent must be shown by express language in the deed or a declaration but may be supplemented by extrinsic evidence where necessary to interpret an ambiguity.[178] When the dispute involves subsequent purchasers, the interests of those who seek to

[172] *Id.* at 306.

[173] 135 A.2d 204 (N.J. Super. Ct. App. Div. 1957).

[174] 579 A.2d at 306 (*quoting Gilpin v. Jacob Ellis Realties*, 135 A.2d 204 (N.J. Super. Ct. App. Div. 1957)).

[175] 7-61 *Thompson on Real Property, Third Thomas Edition* §61.04(b)(1). *See Wetlands America Trust, Inc. v. White Cloud Nine Ventures, L.P.*, 782 S.E.2d 121, 137-138 (Va. 2016); *Fleetwood Chateau Owners Corp. v. Fleetwood Garage Corp.*, 61 N.Y.S.3d 287 (App. Div. 2017); *Yogman v. Parrott*, 937 P.2d 1019, 1023 (Or. 1997) (explaining that the traditional presumption in favor of free use avoids unfair surprise and promotes full and free use of property); *Collins v. City of El Campo*, 684 S.W.2d 756, 761 (Tex. App. 1984) (covenants construed strictly and freer use is preferred); *Forster v. Hall*, 576 S.E.2d 746, 750 (Va. 2003).

[176] *Foods First, Inc. v. Gables Associates*, 418 S.E.2d 888, 889 (Va. 1992) (covenants strictly construed against the party seeking enforcement); *Country Club Dist. Homes Ass'n v. Country Club Christian Church*, 118 S.W.3d 185, 189 (Mo. Ct. App. 2003) ("restrictive covenants are regarded unfavorably and are strictly construed because the law favors the free and untrammeled use of real property") (internal quotations omitted).

[177] *Riss v. Angel*, 934 P.2d 669, 675 (Wash. 1997) ("The court's primary objective in interpreting restrictive covenants is to determine the intent of the parties").

[178] *Agua Fria Save the Open Space Ass'n v. Rowe*, 255 P.3d 390, 395 (N.M. Ct. App. 2011); *Restatement (Third) of Property (Servitudes)* §4.1 (2000).

use their property as they wish conflict with the reliance interests of those who believed that neighboring property would be restricted. Given the modern view that such reliance is reasonable and that reciprocal covenants often increase the value and attractiveness of property, the *Restatement (Third)* suggests that it is no longer generally acceptable that courts should err on the side of unburdening property from restrictions.[179] At the same time, some courts do retain the traditional presumption. In *Yogman v. Parrott*,[180] for example, the Oregon Supreme Court held that a covenant limiting property to "residential purposes" and prohibiting a "commercial enterprise" was ambiguous as to whether short-term rentals of beachfront property were permissible. Because the rental use was not clearly prohibited, the court applied the traditional presumption in favor of free use to allow the rentals.[181]

▷ GROUP HOMES **HARD CASE ◀**

A great deal of litigation has concerned the problem of group homes in neighborhoods that restrict property to "residential" use or to "single-family homes." These cases raise questions about (1) what constitutes "residential" as opposed to "commercial" or "business" use; (2) whether such covenants refer to the *structures* that can be built on the lots or to the *kinds of people* who can inhabit those structures ("single families"); (3) if they restrict ownership to single families, whether group homes constitute "families"; and (4) whether public policy or statutory regulations prohibit enforcement of a covenant that is intended to have the effect of excluding a group home.

Residential v. commercial use

In *Blevins v. Barry-Lawrence County Ass'n for Retarded Citizens*,[182] plaintiffs sought to enforce a covenant limiting property to "residential purposes only" and allowed only "single or double family dwellings." They argued that a group home for eight persons with mental retardation was a commercial and not a residential use. The court had little trouble concluding that the use was residential rather than commercial because the home was operated by a nonprofit organization and "the underlying theory behind establishing such a home is that it serves as a surrogate family arrangement."[183] Many other cases similarly hold that operation of a group

Argument that a group home is a residential use

[179] *Restatement (Third) of Property (Servitudes)* §4.1 cmt. a.

[180] 937 P.2d 1019 (Or. 1997).

[181] *Accord, City of Bowie v. MIE Properties, Inc.*, 922 A.2d 509, 522 (Md. 2007) ("If an ambiguity is present, and if that ambiguity is not clearly resolved by resort to extrinsic evidence, the general rule in favor of the unrestricted use of property will prevail and the ambiguity in a restriction will be resolved against the party seeking its enforcement."); *Terrien v. Zwit*, 648 N.W.2d 602 (Mich. 2002) (covenant precluding commercial enterprises and limiting use to residential purposes precludes operation of family day care center); *Country Club Dist. Homes Ass'n v. Country Club Christian Church*, 118 S.W.3d 185, 193 (Mo. Ct. App. 2003) (covenant restricting property to "private residential purposes" disallowed construction of church parking lot).

[182] 707 S.W.2d 407 (Mo. 1986).

[183] *Id.* at 408.

home is a "residential" use within the meaning of a restrictive covenant that restricts property to residential purposes.[184]

Argument that a group home is a commercial use

An appellate court in Washington state, however, found a group home for the elderly to be a commercial use. In *Hagemann v. Worth*,[185] the covenant restricted land to "residential and recreational use," limited buildings to "single-family residences," and prohibited "business, industry, or commercial enterprise of any kind or nature." The court rejected the owner's argument that the group home was not a business because it had a charitable purpose. Rather, the court focused on the fact that the couple that owned and managed the home charged between $900 and $1,250 for room, board, and personal care to each elderly resident, obtained a boarding house license from the state, and derived their primary income from operation of the facility. The court noted that "[t]he term business is the antonym of residential and to provide residence to paying customers is not synonymous with a residential purpose."[186] It is not clear whether the judge believed that property would be "commercial" rather than "residential" if an owner rented a single-family home to a single tenant rather than operating a group home, especially if rental income was the landlord's main source of livelihood.

Structure v. occupants

Most courts hold that a covenant that restricts property to a "single-family dwelling" may be intended to regulate architectural style rather than the relationship among the persons occupying the structure.[187] However, the court in *Shaver v. Hunter*[188] held that restriction of a lot for residential purposes that defined a residence as "a single-family dwelling" expressed the "clear intent and the plain and unambiguous purpose" of the grantor to regulate the use of the dwelling as well as its structure, thereby excluding a group home.[189]

Group home residents a "family"

In *Malcolm v. Shamie*,[190] the court held that "five mentally retarded women living with a foster parent in an environment therapeutically designed to emulate a more conventional family environment" constituted a

[184] *See, e.g., Knudtson v. Trainor*, 345 N.W.2d 4 (Neb. 1984); *Berger v. State*, 364 A.2d 993 (N.J. 1976); *Hill v. Community of Damien of Molokai*, 911 P.2d 861 (N.M. 1996).

[185] 782 P.2d 1072 (Wash. Ct. App. 1989). *Accord, Mains Farm Homeowners Ass'n v. Worthington*, 854 P.2d 1072 (Wash. 1993).

[186] 782 P.2d at 1075. *Accord, Mains Farm Homeowners Ass'n v. Worthington*, 824 P.2d 495 (Wash. Ct. App. 1992).

[187] *Blevins v. Barry-Lawrence County Ass'n for Retarded Citizens*, 707 S.W.2d 407 (Mo. 1986); *Knudtson v. Trainor*, 345 N.W.2d 4 (Neb. 1984); *Deep East Texas Regional Mental Health and Mental Retardation Servs. v. Kinnear*, 877 S.W.2d 550, 554-555 (Tex. App. 1994).

[188] 626 S.W.2d 574 (Tex. App. 1981). *But see Permian Basin Centers for Mental Health and Mental Retardation v. Alsobrook*, 723 S.W.2d 774, 777 (Tex. App. 1986) (limiting *Shaver* to the cases in which the covenant limits use to residential purposes and then defines a residence as a "single-family dwelling").

[189] *Accord, Crane Neck Ass'n, Inc. v. New York City/Long Island County Servs. Group*, 460 N.E.2d 1336 (N.Y. 1984) (holding that a covenant restricting property to "single-family dwellings" was imposed to preserve the area as "a neighborhood of single-family dwellings, not only architecturally but also functionally").

[190] 290 N.W.2d 101 (Mich. Ct. App. 1980).

"family" for purposes of a restrictive covenant precluding any building other than detached single-family dwellings.[191] The court explained:

> They do not have natural families on which to rely, and due to their unique circumstances, it is unlikely that these women will ever rejoin their parents or marry and form independent families. The substitute family provided by the group home allows the residents to lead more normal and meaningful lives within the community than would be feasible were they institutionalized.[192]

Similarly, a concurring opinion in *Shaver v. Hunter*[193] proposed the following definition of "family": "a stable housekeeping unit of two or more persons who are emotionally attached to each other and share a relationship that emulates traditional family values, promotes mutual protection, support, happiness, physical well-being and intellectual growth and is not in violation of the penal laws."

Not families

In contrast, the majority opinion in *Shaver v. Hunter*[194] held that the term "family" in the context of a covenant restricting occupancy to "single-family dwellings" meant "nuclear" or "extended" family. The court found that a group home consisting of five unrelated women did not constitute a "family" because they were unrelated by blood, marriage, or adoption.[195] A similar result was reached by the Supreme Court of Washington in the context of a for-profit group home for the elderly.[196] Justice Brachtenbach explained that, even if a family means "something more than only persons related by blood, marriage or adoption,"[197] a family requires a "sharing of responsibilities among the members, a mutual caring whether physical or emotional, (2) some commonality whether it be friendship, shared employment, mutual social or political interest, (3) some degree of existing or contemplated permanency to the relationship, and (4) a recognition of some common purpose, persons brought together by reasons other than a referral by a state agency."[198] A for-profit group home does not meet this definition because "total strangers would be brought together [with] no tie to the residence itself."[199]

Courts holding that covenants against group homes violate public policy

Several courts have held that although the operation of group homes violates covenants limiting property to "single-family dwellings," those

[191] *Id.* at 103. *Accord, Hill v. Community of Damien of Molokai*, 911 P.2d 861 (N.M. 1996).

[192] 290 N.W.2d at 103.

[193] 626 S.W.2d 574, 579 (Tex. App. 1981) (Countiss, J., concurring).

[194] 626 S.W.2d 574, 578 (Tex. App. 1981).

[195] *Accord, Crane Neck Ass'n, Inc. v. New York City/Long Island County Servs. Group*, 460 N.E.2d 1336, 1338-1339 (N.Y. 1984) (holding that a group home of eight unrelated individuals did not constitute a family because they were unrelated by blood, marriage, or adoption and because of the presence of a significant number of rotating nonresident professional attendants); *Omega Corp. of Chesterfield v. Malloy*, 319 S.E.2d 728 (Va. 1984) (holding that a group home was not a family because of the type of supervision by counselors who were government employees).

[196] *Mains Farm Homeowners Ass'n v. Worthington*, 854 P.2d 1072 (Wash. 1993).

[197] *Id.* at 1075.

[198] *Id.*

[199] *Id. But see* 854 P.2d at 1080 (Durham, J., dissenting).

covenants are unenforceable because they violate strong public policies prohibiting discrimination against persons with disabilities. In *Crane Neck Ass'n, Inc. v. New York City/Long Island County Servs. Group*,[200] Justice Judith Kaye wrote an opinion for the New York Court of Appeals holding that although a group home did not constitute a single-family dwelling under a restrictive covenant, the covenant could not be equitably enforced because to do so would contravene long-standing public policy favoring establishment of such residences for the mentally disabled. Similarly, in *Westwood Homeowners Ass'n v. Tenhoff*,[201] the court held that operation of a residential facility for six developmentally disabled children and young adults violated a covenant prohibiting use of property for the care of persons with disabilities but that the covenant was contrary to public policy and unenforceable. Quoting Justice Thurgood Marshall, the court noted that "[e]xcluding group homes deprives the retarded of much of what makes for human freedom and fulfillment — the ability to form bonds and take part in the life of a community."[202]

Courts holding such covenants do not violate public policy

In contrast, the court in *Shaver v. Hunter*[203] held that a restrictive covenant limiting property to single-family dwellings that was intended to exclude a group home of unrelated individuals was neither unreasonable nor against public policy. The court in *Hagemann v. Worth*[204] similarly held that a restrictive covenant excluding a group home for the elderly did not violate public policy because it "does not impede furtherance of the public's interest in developing alternate residential care for the elderly; it does prohibit the location of that care facility when it violates the contractual rights of the parties."[205]

Fair Housing Act

Restrictive covenants that discriminate against persons with disabilities may violate federal civil rights statutes, including the *Fair Housing Act of 1968*, as amended in 1988,[206] and the *Americans with Disabilities Act of 1990*.[207] An appeals court in Texas ruled that a covenant that excluded group homes for persons with mental disabilities had a discriminatory disparate impact on disabled persons in violation of the *Fair Housing Act*.[208] ◀

[200] 460 N.E.2d 1336 (N.Y. 1984).

[201] 745 P.2d 976 (Ariz. Ct. App. 1987).

[202] *Id.* at 983 (*quoting Cleburne v. Cleburne Living Center*, 473 U.S. 432, 461 (1985) (Marshall, J., *concurring in the judgment in part and dissenting in part*)). *Accord, Craig v. Bossenbery*, 351 N.W.2d 596 (Mich. Ct. App. 1984) (covenant not enforceable as a matter of public policy); *Deep East Texas Regional Mental Health and Mental Retardation Servs. v. Kinnear*, 877 S.W.2d 550, 556 (Tex. App. 1994).

[203] 626 S.W.2d 574, 579 (Tex. App. 1981).

[204] 782 P.2d 1072 (Wash. Ct. App. 1989).

[205] *Id.* at 1076. *Accord, Mains Farm Homeowners Ass'n v. Worthington*, 854 P.2d 1072, 1078 (Wash. 1993).

[206] *Hill v. Community of Damien of Molokai*, 911 P.2d 861 (N.M. 1996).

[207] 42 U.S.C. §§12101 to 12213.

[208] *Deep East Texas Regional Mental Health and Mental Retardation Servs. v. Kinnear*, 877 S.W.2d 550, 556 (Tex. App. 1994). *Accord, Hill v. Community of Damien of Molokai*, 911 P.2d 861 (N.M. 1996); *see also Gittleman v. Woodhaven Condo. Ass'n, Inc.*, 972 F. Supp. 894 (D.N.J. 1997) (amendments to covenants to allow accessible parking required as a reasonable accommodation).

▷ ARCHITECTURAL REVIEW COMMITTEES **HARD CASE ◀**

Some developers impose covenants requiring owners to obtain approval of an architectural review committee chosen by the homeowners' association when they seek to make structural changes to their homes or even when they paint their shutters. In such cases, a recurrent issue is whether the architectural review committee, as an agent of the homeowners' association, has a duty to act reasonably in administering the aesthetic controls imposed by the covenants, as well as whether the controls are reasonable in themselves.

Review of decisions for reasonableness

Most courts hold such committees to a standard of reasonableness.[209] For example, in *Westfield Homes, Inc. v. Herrick*,[210] the court held that an architectural review committee acted unreasonably when it refused to allow an owner to build an above-ground swimming pool. The restrictive covenants explicitly prohibited certain types of construction, such as television antennas and clotheslines, but did not specifically prohibit swimming pools. The covenants required owners to obtain the approval of the architectural review committee before making any addition or change to existing structures; the covenants provided that the committee "shall, in its sole discretion, have the right to refuse to approve any such construction plans."[211] The court noted that covenants should be "construed to give effect to the actual intention of the parties."[212] Despite the seemingly absolute grant of power to the committee, the court held that the "exercise of the power of review in a particular case must be reasonable and not arbitrary."[213] The committee could impose reasonable restrictions on the design and construction of the pool to minimize the auditory and visual impact on the neighboring properties, but it could not absolutely prohibit construction of the pool.[214]

No review for reasonableness

On the other hand, the Supreme Court of Oregon held that an architectural committee's decisions were unreviewable when the covenants gave it "discretion" to make such decisions and specifically provided that it be the "sole judge of the suitability" of the height of improvements.[215] Justice Van Hoomissen noted that the plaintiffs had purchased property knowing that the committee had plenary discretion to make such decisions and that they therefore "approved the covenants."[216] ◀

[209] *Oakbrook Civic Ass'n, Inc. v. Sonnier*, 481 So. 2d 1008 (La. 1986); *Smith v. Butler Mountain Estates Property Owners' Ass'n, Inc.*, 367 S.E.2d 401 (N.C. Ct. App. 1988); *Riss v. Angel*, 934 P.2d 669, 677-679 (Wash. 1997) (holding an architectural committee's decision to be unreasonable and unenforceable).

[210] 593 N.E.2d 97 (Ill. App. Ct. 1992).

[211] *Id.* at 100.

[212] *Id.* at 101.

[213] *Id.*

[214] *See also Portola Hills Community Ass'n v. James*, 5 Cal. Rptr. 2d 580 (Ct. App. 1992) (holding that it would be unreasonable for a homeowners' association to ban a satellite dish when the dish would be located in the backyard and would not be visible to the neighbors).

[215] *Valenti v. Hopkins*, 926 P.2d 813 (Or. 1996).

[216] *Id.* at 817.

▶ HARD CASE ▷ DISCRETIONARY POWERS

If the developer reserves the right to amend the covenants before all the units are sold, are there any limits on the developer's discretion? The *Restatement (Third) of Property (Servitudes)* §6.21 provides: "A developer may not exercise a power to amend or modify the declaration in a way that would materially change the character of the development or the burdens on the existing community members unless the declaration fairly apprises purchasers that the power could be used for the kind of change proposed." In *North Country Villas Homeowners Ass'n v. Kokenge*,[217] the court adopted this rule, holding that a developer's power to "amend" the covenants limiting land to single-family or duplex homes did not include the power to "revoke" them entirely by building four-unit housing. ◀

Developer's enforcement in gross

Sometimes the developer attempts to retain control of the architectural review commission after all the lots are sold. Most courts will not allow the developer to do this, applying the rule against holding the benefit of a covenant in gross or the modern doctrine that such covenants are enforceable only if the beneficiary has a legitimate interest or rational justification for continued control.[218] But some courts find such continued control legitimate, at least when the homeowners' association can change this by majority or supermajority vote.[219] The owners may, for example, rationally wish to delegate enforcement to the developer as their agent because this relieves them of the burden of enforcement.

▶ HARD CASE ▷ HOME DAY CARE

A covenant restricts land to "residential purposes." An owner of a single-family home in the restricted area begins a home day care center, taking care of six children from 8:30 A.M. to 5:30 P.M. The center is licensed by the state. Some courts find such uses to be consistent with the residential purpose covenant, while others find them to be non-residential or commercial uses.[220] ◀

[217] 163 P.3d 1247 (Kan. Ct. App. 2007).

[218] *Smith v. First Savings of Louisiana*, 575 So. 2d 1033 (Ala. 1991). *See Restatement (Third) of Property (Servitudes)* §2.6 cmt. d (2000) (legitimate interest required to enforce covenant).

[219] *See B.C.E. Development, Inc. v. Smith*, 264 Cal. Rptr. 55 (Ct. App. 1989) (allowing enforcement by the developer's successor in interest when the declaration gave the homeowners' association the power to amend the declaration and take control of the architectural commission by a two-thirds vote); *Christiansen v. Casey*, 613 S.W.2d 906 (Mo. Ct. App. 1981) (allowing developer to enforce covenant after all lots were sold when developer owned another tract adjacent to the restricted subdivision but asserting that the intent of the parties to allow continued enforcement should prevail even if the developer owns no adjacent land to effectuate the intent of the parties).

[220] *Compare Metzner v. Wojdyla*, 886 P.2d 154 (Wash. 1994) (holding that it is not a "residential" use) *and Lewis-Levett v. Day*, 875 N.E.2d 293 (Ind. Ct. App. 2008) (home day care is a prohibited "commercial" use) *with Berger v. State*, 364 A.2d 993 (N.J. 1976) (group home for preschool children with disabilities did not violate restrictive covenant limiting property to residential purposes).

§6.7 Public Policy Limitations

Covenants void if they violate public policy

Servitudes are not enforceable if they violate public policy.[221] Some specific public policies that have been used to invalidate particular servitudes include the policy against racially restrictive covenants and the policy against unreasonable restraints on alienation. However, many other public policies come into play in the servitudes area. Examples include policies "favoring privacy and liberty in choice of lifestyle, freedom of religion, freedom of speech and expression, access to the legal system, discouraging bad faith and unfair dealing, encouraging free competition, and socially productive uses of land."[222] In addition, courts have supported public policies "protecting family relationships from coercive attempts to disrupt them, and protecting weaker groups in society that exclude them from opportunities enjoyed by more fortunate groups to acquire desirable property for housing or access to necessary services."[223]

§6.7.1 Racial Restrictions

Equal protection

Before 1948, racial restrictions in deeds were not only common but were actively encouraged by the federal government.[224] Such deeds often prohibited the sale or occupancy of property by Black people, Jews, American Indians, and Latinos. In 1948, the Supreme Court declared in *Shelley v. Kraemer*[225] that court enforcement of racially restrictive covenants is an unconstitutional denial of equal protection of the laws.[226] Today, enforcement would not only violate the Constitution but would be unlawful under the federal *Fair Housing Act of 1968*,[227] the *Civil Rights Act of 1866*,[228] and state fair housing laws.[229] Moreover, racially restrictive covenants violate public policy and thus are invalid under the common law of real property.[230]

Controversy over *Shelley v. Kraemer*

Shelley has proved to be a controversial decision because it characterizes state enforcement of all contracts as "state action" potentially subject to the strictures of the equal protection clause. Moreover, *Shelley* found a violation of the equal protection clause even though the state was neutrally enforcing private agreements and the discriminatory impetus came not from the

[221] *Restatement (Third) of Property (Servitudes)* §3.1 (2000).
[222] *Id.* at §3.1 cmt. i.
[223] *Id.*
[224] Martha Mahoney, *Law and Racial Geography: Public Housing and the Economy in New Orleans*, 42 Stan. L. Rev. 1251 (1990).
[225] 334 U.S. 1 (1948).
[226] *See also Barrows v. Jackson*, 346 U.S. 249 (1953) (enforcement by a damages remedy similarly violates the equal protection clause).
[227] 42 U.S.C. §§3601 to 3619, 3631.
[228] *Id.* at §§1981, 1982.
[229] *See, e.g.*, Cal. Gov't Code §12955.
[230] *Restatement (Third) of Property (Servitudes)* §3.1 cmt. d (2000). *See also* Cal. Civ. Code §1352.5 (authorizing the board of directors of a homeowners' association to amend any declaration that contains a restriction on sale or occupancy based on race, color, religion, sex, familial status, marital status, disability, national origin, or ancestry); Cal. Civ. Code §12596.1 (creating an administrative process to remove such restrictive covenants from deeds).

state, but from the private parties to the contract.[231] Taken to the extreme, the *Shelley* doctrine would invalidate enforcement of a will leaving money to the United Negro College Fund because state action is needed to probate and validate the will. For this reason, "the reach of *Shelley v. Kraemer* is subject to some doubt."[232] The *Restatement (Third)* opines that *Shelley* is neither so narrow as to apply only to racial covenants nor so broad as to apply to state enforcement of all covenants; rather, *Shelley* prohibits court enforcement of covenants that burden fundamental constitutional rights.[233]

Defense of *Shelley*

Yet it would be remarkable if *Shelley* had gone the other way.[234] At the time the Supreme Court heard the case, the house in question had been sold by its owner in violation of a restrictive covenant and the Shelley family was living in it. If the Supreme Court had held that enforcement of real covenants does not constitute state action, and the Shelleys had refused voluntarily to leave their home, the plaintiffs would have been able to enforce the covenant by injunctive relief ordering them to move, and this order would have been carried out by use of the police. It is hard to see how one could find such an exercise of state power not to constitute "state action." Such enforcement would have allowed restrictive covenants to retain their legal force and, given that they were very common, the effect of such a rule would have been to provide state support for racial segregation, keeping Black people out of many neighborhoods. In addition, the effect of enforcement of such exclusionary covenants effectively would prevent excluded groups from purchasing property from sellers who wished to sell to them.[235]

Discriminatory charitable trusts

When an owner creates a charitable trust that provides scholarships to students of a particular race, is this enforceable in court or is court enforcement of it a violation of the equal protection clause? The Constitution prohibits state governments (including state universities) from administering racially discriminatory trusts.[236] Although some state courts historically allowed probate courts to substitute private trustees for public trustees and continue operating the trust in a discriminatory manner,[237] the Supreme Court has held that it violates the equal protection clause for a government entity to continue to operate and maintain a public facility by substituting private for public trustees while continuing to operate the facility with public funds.[238] Courts have differed, however, on whether to enforce racially

[231] *See* Lino Graglia, *State Action: Constitutional Phoenix*, 67 Wash. U. L.Q. 777 (1989).

[232] *Restatement (Third) of Property (Servitudes)* §3.1 cmt. d (2000).

[233] *Id.* at §3.1 Reporter's Note.

[234] For a recent argument supporting the result in *Shelley*, see Alfred L. Brophy & Shubha Ghosh, *Whistling Dixie: The Invalidity and Unconstitutionality of Covenants Against Yankees*, 10 Villanova Envtl. L.J. 57 (1999).

[235] For more on *Shelley v. Kraemer*, see §§7.7.5 & 12.2.1.

[236] *Pennsylvania v. Board of Directors of City Trusts of Philadelphia*, 353 U.S. 230 (1957). *See also Pennsylvania v. Brown*, 392 F.2d 120 (3d Cir. 1968) (holding that the lower court could not continue enforcement of the trust simply by replacing the public trustees with private ones).

[237] *See In re Girard College Trusteeship*, 138 A.2d 844 (Pa. 1958).

[238] *Evans v. Newton*, 382 U.S. 296 (1966). However, if the trust fails entirely, and the property reverts to the grantor or his heirs, the Supreme Court has held that the equal protection clause is not violated. *Evans v. Abney*, 396 U.S. 435 (1970).

limited trusts administered by private schools or trustees.[239] It has been held that such trusts do not violate the equal protection clause if administered by private trustees or private institutions.[240] However, many courts apply the *cy pres* doctrine to rewrite charitable trusts that have racial, gender, or religious restrictions to eliminate those restrictions on the grounds that they violate public policy and that the trustor, if he or she were alive today, would wish them to be removed and the charitable purposes of the trust to continue without the discriminatory provision.[241]

▷ PUBLIC POLICY **HARD CASE ◀**

Should a court excise a racial restriction in a private trust even if this contravenes the intent of the grantor? Most courts will allow racial restrictions to be enforced in private charitable trusts on the ground that individuals have the power to make gifts to limited classes of persons. As long as those discriminatory gifts are not administered by state officials, the freedom to choose an object of one's charitable intent should be respected. On the other hand, it can be argued that charitable trusts are administered partly by the state; state common law rules and state courts provide instructions to administrators of charitable trusts under such rules as the *cy pres* doctrine, which allows trusts to be changed to achieve the grantor's general charitable intent if the specific object or means of that intent cannot be realized.[242] As Professor Clark argued, "A charitable trust serves two masters—the property owner who created it and society which is its

[239] *See Matter of Estate of Wilson*, 452 N.E.2d 1228 (N.Y. 1983). *See also* Thomas P. Gallanis, *Family Property Law: Cases and Materials on Wills, Trusts, and Interests* 674-681 (9th ed. 2024).

[240] *Lockwood v. Killian*, 375 A.2d 998 (Conn. 1977) (no state action involved in enforcing a private trust). *See also Estate of Wilson*, 452 N.E.2d 1228 (N.Y. 1983) (no state action in administering private trust that was gender limited); Kathryn Voyer, *Continuing the Trend Toward Equality: The Eradication of Racially and Sexually Discriminatory Provisions in Private Trusts*, 7 Wm. & Mary Bill Rts. J. 943 (1999).

[241] *Dunbar v. Board of Trustees of Clayton College*, 461 P.2d 28 (Colo. 1969) (applying *cy pres* and excising a provision limiting the trust to "white orphans"); *Tinnin v. First United Bank of Mississippi*, 502 So. 2d 659 (Miss. 1987), *after remand*, 570 So. 2d 1193 (Miss. 1990); *Coffee v. William Marsh Rice University*, 408 S.W.2d 269, 271 (Tex. Civ. App. 1966) (using *cy pres* to excise racial restriction in endowment fund). *Cf. United States v. Hughes Memorial Home*, 396 F. Supp. 544 (W.D. Va. 1975) (*cy pres* doctrine applied to excise racial restriction on trust benefiting orphanage because racial exclusion from the orphanage would violate the *Fair Housing Act*, 42 U.S.C. §§3601 *et seq.*); *In re Long's Estate*, 5 Pa. D. & C.3d 602 (1978) (reforming will through *cy pres* doctrine to excise racial and gender restrictions on beneficiaries of trust for an asylum). *Compare Restatement (Second) of Property (Donative Transfers)* §4.2 cmt. t (1983) (forfeiture restraints on occupation or ownership of real property based on race, color, religion, or sex are unreasonable). *See* Roy Adams, *Racial and Religious Discrimination in Charitable Trusts: A Current Analysis of Constitutional and Trust Law Solutions*, 25 Clev. St. L. Rev. 1 (1976); Stephen J. Leacock, *Racial Preferences in Educational Trusts: An Overview of the United States Experience*, 28 How. L.J. 715 (1985).

[242] Courts have also sometimes applied the *cy pres* doctrine to excise gender conditions in charitable trusts. *See, e.g., In re Certain Scholarship Funds*, 575 A.2d 1325 (N.H. 1990); *Matter of Crichfield Trust*, 426 A.2d 88 (N.J. Super. Ct. Ch. Div. 1980).

beneficiary."[243] This suggests that public policy may intervene to invalidate racially restrictive trusts that provide unequal access to public accommodations. The Mississippi Supreme Court has noted that, although the "right of testation, the power by will to control from the grave what becomes of one's property [is] in theory almost sacred,"[244] it is also true that the "testator's right to make his will as he pleases is not unentailed."[245] "Whatever may once have been the attitudes of many, it is much too late to doubt that a major social policy of our society is that entitlement one is eligible to enjoy on one's merits shall not be denied by reason of one's race, color or creed."[246] This may suggest that a court should not grant legal support to a discriminatory trust, at least where the income from the trust benefits patrons of a public accommodation. Several states have passed statutes prohibiting racial discrimination in donative transfers.[247] ◀

§6.7.2 Unreasonable Restraints on Alienation

Categories of restraints

Property law has long been suspicious of restraints on alienation and has subjected such restraints to strict regulation. A restraint on alienation is a provision that prevents the transfer of a property interest from the current owner to others. Three types of restraints have been identified and been subject to varying levels of regulation. First, *disabling* restraints forbid the owner from transferring her interest in the property at all. For example, a deed may recite that the grantor conveys the property to the grantee "but any transfer of the property shall be null and void." Second, *promissory* restraints are covenants by which the grantee promises not to transfer her interest in the property. Third, *forfeiture* restraints provide that ownership of the property will shift to a specified person if the current (present estate) owner attempts to transfer ownership. For example, a deed may state that "*O* conveys the property to *A*, but if *A* attempts to transfer the property, then to *B*." This conveyance purports to establish a present estate in *A* (a fee simple subject to an executory limitation) and a future interest (an executory interest) in *B*.[248]

[243] Elias Clark, *Charitable Trusts, the Fourteenth Amendment and the Will of Stephen Girard*, 66 Yale L.J. 979 (1957). *See also* Florence Wagman Roisman, *The Impact of the Civil Rights Act of 1866 on Racially Discriminatory Donative Transfers*, 53 Ala. L. Rev. 463 (2002) (arguing that racially discriminatory donative transfers generally violate the *Civil Rights Act of 1866*, 42 U.S.C. §1981).

[244] *Tinnin v. First United Bank of Mississippi*, 502 So. 2d 659 (Miss. 1987), *and after remand*, 570 So. 2d 1193 (Miss. 1990) (affirming trial court's application of *cy pres* doctrine to excise racial restriction in charitable trust administered by public entity).

[245] 502 So. 2d at 664.

[246] *Id.*

[247] Cal. Civ. Code §§51(b), 53(a) (invalidating any provision in a "written instrument relating to real property" that purports to forbid or restrict the use by or the conveyance to any person because of "sex, race, color, religion, ancestry, national origin, disability, medical condition, genetic information, marital status, or sexual orientation"); N.J. Stat. §46:3-23 (invalidating all conditions and restrictions in *inter vivos* transactions limiting transfer to or use by "any person because of race, creed, color, national origin, ancestry, marital status or sex").

[248] This executory interest in *B* would be void under the traditional rule against perpetuities unless it were subject to an appropriate time limit. *See* §7.7.4.

Unreasonable restraints invalid

The law traditionally was hostile to almost all restraints on alienation, invalidating them categorically in particular classes of cases. However, the current approach emerging in the courts is to refuse to enforce restraints on alienation if they are unreasonable.[249] Reasonableness is determined by "weighing the utility of the restraint against the injurious consequences of enforcing the restraint."[250] Under this reasonableness test, a restraint will be enforced if there is a good reason for it and the benefits of enforcement are sufficient to outweigh the harm caused by limiting alienability.

Total restraints on alienation of fee interests

Total restraints on alienation of fee simple interests, whether in the form of disabling, promissory, or forfeiture restraints, are uniformly held void and unenforceable unless some specific, strong public policy justifies the restraint.[251] The policies underlying the rule against total restraints on alienation of fee simple interests include: (1) promoting dispersal of ownership of property and preventing concentration of land in passive family dynasties, (2) encouraging individual autonomy by vesting control of resources in current owners and giving them to freedom to move to live or set up a business elsewhere, and (3) promoting social utility and efficiency by allowing property to be transferred to its most valued use. Disabling restraints are especially problematic; because they cannot be waived by anyone, they are uniformly held to be void.[252] Forfeiture and promissory restraints, however, do not necessarily take property out of the market; the owner burdened by the condition or covenant has the power to bargain with the future interest holder or the owner of the dominant estate to induce her to give up her right to prevent alienation of the property. The rule invalidating such restraints is therefore more strongly supported by considerations of justice and autonomy. Allowing the current owner to sell or transfer ownership of the property grants that owner both the liberty to move and the power to obtain the economic benefits of the property by selling it and using those assets for other endeavors.

Partial restraints on alienation

Courts sometimes uphold partial restraints on alienation.[253] For example, if a conveyance prohibits transfer to a named individual or a small group of individuals, the courts may conclude that the interest is still

[249] *Rubin v. Moys*, 97 Wash. App. 1020 (Ct. App. 1999); *Restatement (Third) of Property (Servitudes)* §3.4 (2000).

[250] *Id.*

[251] *Estate of Cawiezell v. Coronelli*, 958 N.W.2d 842, 845 (Iowa 2021); *Robbins v. HNG Oil Co.*, 878 S.W.2d 351 (Tex. App. 1994) (restraints on alienation are against public policy); Sheldon F. Kurtz et al., *The Law of Property: An Introductory Survey* §5.5, at 141-143 (7th ed. 2018); Dale A. Whitman et al., *The Law of Property* §2.2, at 23 (4th ed. 2019).

[252] *See Restatement (Third) of Property (Servitudes)* §3.4 (2000) (servitudes that impose restraints on alienation are enforceable if they are reasonable, determined by weighing the utility of the restraint against the injurious consequences of enforcing the restraint); *Restatement (Second) of Property (Donative Transfers)* §4.1 (1983) (disabling restraints on alienation in donative transfers are enforceable if "the legal policy favoring freedom of alienation does not reasonably apply" unless the restraint, "if effective, would make it impossible for any period of time from the date of the donative transfer to transfer such interest").

[253] *Mardis v. Brantley*, 717 So. 2d 702, 709 (La. Ct. App. 1998) ("A contract purporting to remove property from the stream of commerce totally and perpetually is against public policy, but one placing partial and temporary restraints or conditions on alienation is not").

alienable because it may be conveyed to anyone else in the world.[254] On the other hand, one court held that a will prohibiting property left to the decedent's son ever to come into the possession of the daughter to be invalid as an unreasonable restraint on alienation because the restraint did not serve any legitimate purpose related to land use and was merely capricious or motivated by spite or malice.[255] Other courts allow partial restraints on alienation if they are created in the form of forfeitures if the forfeiture has the effect of transferring ownership to someone who is free to alienate the property to anyone she wishes.[256] Although some courts enforce restraints that are limited as to time, most courts find restraints on alienation of fee simple interests to be void no matter how short the time period unless there is a strong reason for upholding the restraint.[257]

Life estates

Most courts uphold total restraints on alienation of life estates when they are in the form of forfeiture or promissory restraints.[258] Disabling restraints on life estates, however, are generally not enforced, again because a disabling restraint inflexibly refuses to identify anyone who has the power to waive enforcement of the restraint.[259] One reason courts sometimes uphold restraints on alienation of life estates is that life estates are not very alienable anyway. Anyone who purchases a life estate has obtained a precarious interest that will terminate automatically the moment the grantor dies. In addition, most life estates are given to the grantor's children, with the remainder to go to some other members of the family — often the grandchildren. This arrangement ensures that property will be available for two generations; because the property will be alienable by the grandchildren, it has not been taken out of the market permanently. Some courts, however, treat life estates as they do fee simple interests, holding that total restraints on alienation of life estates are void under all circumstances.[260]

Condominiums and cooperatives

Condominiums and cooperatives are property arrangements in which individual owners of units in multi-unit projects have a certain amount of financial interdependence. Individual apartments or houses in the complex are owned by individuals, while common areas such as stairways and grounds are owned in common and maintained by members of the association. Because of financial interdependence, these associations sometimes impose restraints on alienation that require the association's approval of sales or leases by its members or that give the association a right of first refusal or "preemptive right" (the right to purchase the unit in preference to

[254] 3-29 *Thompson on Real Property, Third Thomas Edition* §29.02.

[255] *Casey v. Casey*, 700 S.W.2d 46 (Ark. 1985).

[256] *See Pritchett v. Turner*, 437 So. 2d 104 (Ala. 1983) (upholding a restriction against allowing children to give their mother any interest in the property when imposed as a forfeiture restraint); 10-77 *Powell on Real Property* §77.05; 3-29 *Thompson on Real Property, Third Thomas Edition* §29.02.

[257] 3-29 *Thompson on Real Property, Third Thomas Edition* §29.02

[258] *Id.*

[259] *Deviney v. Nationsbank*, 993 S.W.2d 443 (Tex. App. 1999) (invalidating a disabling restraint that prevented joint life estate owners from selling their ownership interests without the consent of their co-owners); *Restatement (Second) of Property (Donative Transfers)* §§4.1 to 4.2 (1983).

[260] *Rowley v. American Trust Co.*, 132 S.E. 347 (Va. 1926); 2-19 *Thompson on Real Property, Third Thomas Edition* §19.05.

other purchasers). These restraints are usually upheld if they are exercised reasonably.[261] Courts usually require such consent to sale provisions and preemptive rights to be exercised within a reasonable period of time and may invalidate them if they do not provide for payment of the fair market value of the property.[262] Many condominiums and coops regulate or prohibit owners from leasing their units to tenants and the courts normally uphold such restrictions on the ground that owners are on notice of them when they purchase or are subject to the imposition of such restrictions retroactively if the association adopts them in conformity with governing documents.[263]

Low-income housing cooperatives

It has become common for nonprofit organizations to create housing for low-income persons in the form of limited equity cooperatives. Such cooperatives allow individuals or families to own units in multifamily housing but prohibit owners from selling those units at market value, thereby preserving their availability for use by other low-income families in the future. Restraints on alienation of such units designed to preserve low-income housing are likely to be enforceable.[264]

Equitable interests

Courts generally uphold restraints on alienation of beneficial or equitable interests in property. The settlor or trustor may direct, for example, that the beneficiary has no right to alienate her beneficial interest; this arrangement is sometimes called a *spendthrift trust* because it protects the beneficiary's right to a continuing stream of income from the trust by limiting the beneficiary's power to alienate the right to receive that income.[265] A settlor may also direct the trustee not to sell the trust assets, and such limitations will ordinarily be enforced. If those assets become unproductive, the trustee may go to court for approval of a sale of the assets to generate income for the beneficiary in line with the settlor's intent; such approval may be granted under the *cy pres* doctrine.

Leaseholds

Courts ordinarily uphold limitations on the transfer of leaseholds. A lease stating that the tenant may not sublet or assign the leasehold, for example, is likely to be enforced.[266] Complications arise, however, when the lease simply requires the consent of the landlord before the tenant sublets or assigns the leasehold. In such cases, the issue arises whether consent may be arbitrarily withheld.[267]

Consent clauses

Prohibitions on transfer of property without the consent of another are unreasonable restraints on alienation "unless there is a strong justification for the prohibition, and, unless the consent can be withheld only for reasons

[261] *See* §8.5.1.
[262] *See Aquarian Foundation, Inc. v. Sholom House, Inc.*, 448 So. 2d 1166 (Fla. Dist. Ct. App. 1984); *Wolinsky v. Kadison*, 449 N.E.2d 151 (Ill. App. Ct. 1983).
[263] *See* §8.5.1.
[264] *See* Judith Bernstein-Baker, *Cooperative Conversion: Is It Only for the Wealthy? Proposals that Promote Affordable Cooperative Housing in Philadelphia*, 61 Temp. L. Rev. 394 (1988).
[265] Thomas Gallanis, *Family Property Law: Cases and Materials on Wills, Trusts, and Future Interests* 588-600 (9th ed. 2024).
[266] *Pacific First Bank v. New Morgan Park Corp.*, 857 P.2d 895 (Or. Ct. App. 1993) (restraint on alienation without landlord's consent is valid).
[267] *See* §10.7.2.

directly related to the justification for the restraint."[268] Restraints are usually upheld in the context of residential cooperative arrangements and affordable housing projects, but provisions that require the consent of the developer or grantor before properties are sold in the future are almost certain to be held void.[269] Provisions that require future purchasers to pay a fee to the original grantor also may well be struck down as unreasonable restraints on alienation.

Transfer fee on future sales

For example, in *LaFond v. Rumler*,[270] the court struck down a deed provision that would have required the consent of the grantor before a future sale and required the grantee to share the proceeds of any future sale of the property within 15 years with the grantor. The court noted that the sale took the form of an installment land contract[271] and that, in such cases, reasonable provisions would be enforceable to protect the grantor's interest in repayment of the debt, but that a right to a portion of future sales was not a necessary or appropriate way to accomplish this end. Many states have passed statutes prohibiting transfer fees.[272]

Indirect restraints on alienation

Some private controls on land use are so severe that they make the property very difficult to sell. Such restraints have sometimes been struck down as "indirect" restraints on alienation, on the theory that the grantor should not be able to do indirectly what he could not do directly. If limitations on use of property are so extensive that the property cannot be used for any legitimate purposes, the property is not alienable because no one would want to purchase it. In such cases, courts may find such limitations on use void as indirect restraints on alienation. Such claims, however, are difficult to win, and the *Restatement (Third)* would provide that servitudes are not invalid as indirect restraints on alienation unless they have "no rational justification."[273] Obsolete restrictions are generally handled by the doctrines of changed conditions and relative hardship.[274]

Charities

Restraints on alienation are generally allowed when the holder of the property interest is a charity.[275] The policy underlying this rule is to protect the property from being drawn back into the marketplace and to further the donor's interests in preserving the property for charitable purposes.

Options to purchase and rights of first refusal

An option to purchase is a right to buy property at an agreed price whenever the option holder wishes, while a right of first refusal is a right to buy property at an agreed price (or a right to match a third-party offer)

[268] *Restatement (Third) of Property (Servitudes)* §3.4 cmt. d (2000); 3-29 *Thompson on Real Property, Third Thomas Edition* §29.02.

[269] *Northwest Real Estate Co. v. Serio*, 144 A. 245 (Md. 1929); *Riste v. Eastern Washington Bible Camp, Inc.*, 605 P.2d 1294 (Wash. Ct. App. 1980).

[270] 574 N.W.2d 40 (Mich. Ct. App. 1998).

[271] *See also* §11.5.2.

[272] *See, e.g.*, N.J. Stat. §§46:3-28 to 46:3-33; 68 Pa. Cons. Stat. §§8101 to 8107; S.D. Codified Laws §§43-4-47 to 43-4-57; Va. Code §55-70.2; Wash. Rev. Code §§64.60.005 to 64.60.901. *Accord, DePeyster v. Michael*, 6 N.Y. 467 (1852).

[273] *Victorville West Limited Partnership v. Inverrary Association, Inc.*, 226 So. 3d 888 (Fla. Dist. Ct. App. 2017) (holding covenant prohibiting golf course owner from offering memberships to nonresidents of development was not invalid; although the golf course had become unprofitable, exclusivity created significant benefits for unit owners); *Restatement (Third) of Property (Servitudes)* §3.5(2) (2000).

[274] *See* §§6.8.1 & 6.8.2.

[275] *See In re Coe College*, 935 N.W.2d 581, 586 (Iowa 2019); *Horse Pond Fish & Game Club, Inc. v. Cormier*, 581 A.2d 478 (N.H. 1990).

whenever the current owner chooses to sell. Options and rights of first refusal were traditionally governed by the rule against perpetuities,[276] but are more commonly regulated today by the rule against unreasonable restraints on alienation.[277] If an option allows purchase at fair market value at the time the option is exercised, a long duration for the option may be justified, although an option with no time limit is quite likely to be struck down as an unreasonable restraint on alienation. When an option is for a set price, it is likely to be held to be an unreasonable restraint on alienation unless it lasts for only a short time.[278] Rights of first refusal (also called preemptive rights) are likely to be upheld if they allow the holder of the right to match a third-party offer within a reasonably short period of time, unless the purpose for which the right is being exercised is illegitimate.[279] If the price of the right of first refusal is fixed and it has a long duration, it is more likely to be held to be unreasonable unless there is a strong justification for it, such as the ability to preserve the property for use by low- or moderate-income families.[280] It might be argued that the courts could or should interpret options or preemptive rights to last for only a reasonable period of time to validate them as reasonable restraints on alienation.[281]

§6.7.3 *Unreasonable Restraints on Competition*

Antitrust law

Both common law and state and federal antitrust laws prohibit unreasonable restraints on competition.[282] It is common for owners or developers of shopping centers to include anti-competitive covenants in leases. For example, in *Dunafon v. Delaware McDonald's Corp.*,[283] an owner promised lessee McDonald's that it would not grant a lease "to any persons to engage in a

[276] *See* §7.7.4.

[277] *Restatement (Third) of Property (Servitudes)* §3.4 cmts. e & f (2000).

[278] *Id.* at §3.4 cmt. e. *See Shaffer v. Bellows*, 260 P.3d 1064, 1072 (Alaska 2011); *Sander v. Ball*, 781 So. 2d 527 (Fla. Dist. Ct. App. 2001).

[279] *Restatement (Third) of Property (Servitudes)* §3.4 cmt. f. *See Old Port Cove Condominium Ass'n One, Inc. v. Old Port Cove Holdings, Inc.*, 954 So. 2d 742 (Fla. Dist. Ct. App. 2007). *Cf. Hare v. McClellan*, 662 A.2d 1242 (Conn. 1995) (reviewing a preemptive right to see if it was reasonable). *Cf. Gilbert v. Beaver Dam Ass'n of Stratford, Inc.*, 2002 Conn. Super. LEXIS 2765 (Super. Ct. 2002), *rev'd on other grounds*, 858 A.2d 860 (Conn. App. 2004) (right of first refusal invalid when it could be exercised either by homeowners' association or by any individual homeowner when there was no mechanism to determine who could exercise the right if more than one person sought to buy the property).

[280] *City of Oceanside v. McKenna*, 264 Cal. Rptr. 275 (Ct. App. 1989). *Compare Gray v. Vandver*, 623 S.W.2d 172 (Tex. App. 1981) (invalidating a right of first refusal that allowed the grantor to repurchase the property for $175) *with Puckett v. St. Andrews Place Ret. Cmty., Inc.*, 2012 WL 1072418 (Ky. Ct. App. 2012) (fixed-price option valid when it was consistent with the nursing home's charitable mission). *See Restatement (Third) of Property (Servitudes)* §3.4 cmt. f (2000).

[281] *Cf. Kobrine, L.L.C. v. Metzger*, 824 A.2d 1031 (Md. Ct. Spec. App. 2003) (interpreting a future interest to last for only a reasonable period to avoid violating the rule against perpetuities); *Willson v. Strattan*, 2006 WL 287591 (Mich. Ct. App. 2006) (fixed-price option held to be an unreasonable restraint on alienation because too much time had passed since it was created).

[282] *Restatement (Third) of Property (Servitudes)* §3.6 (2000). *George S. May International Co. v. International Profit Ass'n*, 628 N.E.2d 647 (Ill. App. Ct. 1993).

[283] 691 F. Supp. 1232 (W.D. Mo. 1988).

carry-out fast-food restaurant in which food and beverages are dispensed that is in direct competition with lessee within the mall shopping center." An owner of a Taco Bell restaurant sued both the lessor and lessee for a declaratory judgment that the covenant violated the federal antitrust law, known as the *Sherman Act*.[284] The court held that such covenants were not *per se* unlawful under the *Sherman Act* but would constitute unreasonable restraints on trade only if they violate the "rule of reason."

The rule of reason

The rule of reason requires the court to examine the circumstances to determine whether the operation of the covenant actually effectuates an unreasonable restraint on competition.[285] The court will first define the relevant product (or service) market and the effective geographic area in which competition is likely to be present. It will then compare the anti-competitive effect of the covenant with its procompetitive effect. An anti-competitive covenant may increase competition because it provides security that induces a new competitor to enter the market, thereby generating new business and new competition. In *Dunafon*, the court determined that the covenant induced McDonald's to invest in creating a new restaurant and that the presence of this restaurant helped generate business for the shopping center. Because the area had previously had little commercial property and few fast-service restaurants, the covenant may have had the effect of inducing new competition to emerge, rather than stifling it. Given the availability of nearby sites where competing fast food restaurants could locate, the court found that the procompetitive effects of the covenant outweighed its anti-competitive effects and that it was therefore lawful and enforceable.

Common law

Anti-competitive covenants are also unenforceable under the common law if they constitute unreasonable restraints on trade.[286] They are enforceable only if they are "reasonably limited in time and space and consonant with the public interest" but unenforceable if they last for an unreasonable length of time, cover too large an area, or cover too wide a range of products or services.[287] Perhaps influenced by the developments in antitrust law described above, judges usually enforce anti-competitive covenants in shopping center leases and hold that they run with the land.[288]

§6.7.4 *Public Policy*

No review for reasonableness

It is sometimes argued that covenants should be reviewed for reasonableness. Indeed, a California statute prohibits enforcement of unreasonable covenants.[289] However, courts, including those in California, will generally invalidate land use restrictions only if they contravene specific, strong public

[284] 15 U.S.C. §1.

[285] *See also Optivision, Inc. v. Syracuse Shopping Center Associates*, 472 F. Supp. 665 (N.D.N.Y. 1979).

[286] *See BP Products North America, Inc. v. Stanley*, 669 F.3d 184, 188-189 (4th Cir. 2012); *Whitinsville Plaza v. Kotseas*, 390 N.E.2d 243 (Mass. 1979).

[287] *Id.*

[288] *Winn-Dixie Stores, Inc. v. Dolgencorp, LLC*, 746 F.3d 1008 (11th Cir. 2014).

[289] Cal. Civ. Code §5975.

policies.[290] A leading case is *Nahrstedt v. Lakeside Village Condominium Ass'n, Inc.*[291] In that case, a homeowner sued to enjoin enforcement of a "no pets" covenant in a 530-unit condominium complex. The California Supreme Court rejected the idea that courts should routinely review covenants contained in deeds or recorded declarations for reasonableness. "Use restrictions are an inherent part of any common interest development," Justice Kennard explained, "and are crucial to the stable, planned environment of any shared ownership arrangement."[292]

Free contract limited by public policy

The *Restatement (Third)* agrees, finding covenants enforceable unless they are illegal, unconstitutional, or "violate public policy."[293] Covenants were traditionally viewed as encumbrances on land that posed risks to the value and alienability of land.[294] The more modern approach "applies the modern principle of freedom of contract to creation of servitudes,"[295] regulating only those servitudes that contravene articulable public policies. After such policies are articulated, one must compare the negative impact of the servitude on the public policy and assess "predictable harm against the interests in enforcing the servitude."[296]

Review for reasonableness

On the other hand, some courts that have abolished the touch and concern requirement have substituted a general reasonableness standard for determining when a covenant will be allowed to run with the land.[297] After the Supreme Court of New Jersey abolished the touch and concern test in favor of an approach based on reasonableness, the court on remand held that a covenant that prohibited use of downtown property as a supermarket was unreasonable and contrary to public policy.[298] Judge D'Annunzio's opinion noted that "New Jersey courts have refused to enforce contracts that violate public policy."[299] The property had previously been used as a grocery store and the court found that the lack of a supermarket in the affected low-income city neighborhood made life especially difficult for residents who lacked easy transportation to other markets. The court noted

[290] *See, e.g., Terrien v. Zwit*, 648 N.W.2d 602 (Mich. 2002) (covenant precluding operation of family day care center does not violate public policy); *Restatement (Third) of Property (Servitudes)* §3.1 (2000); 7-61 *Thompson on Real Property, Third Thomas Edition* §61.07(e).

[291] 878 P.2d 1275 (Cal. 1994). *Accord, Hidden Harbour Estates v. Basso*, 393 So. 2d 637 (Fla. Dist. Ct. App. 1981).

[292] 878 P.2d at 1281. *See also Villa de las Palmas Homeowners Ass'n v. Terifaj*, 90 P.3d 1223 (Cal. 2004) (amendment to condominium declaration adopting a no-pet rule is reasonable; Cal. Civ. Code §4715 (prohibiting enforcement of a covenant that denies owners the right to keep at least one pet applies only to initial declaration and not to amendments adopted by association after initial recording of the declaration).

[293] *Restatement (Third) of Property (Servitudes)* §3.1 (2000).

[294] *Id.* at §3.1 cmt. a.

[295] *Id.*

[296] *Id.* at §3.1 cmt. i.

[297] *Id.* at §3.1 cmt. j (courts disagree about whether "unreasonable" covenants are enforceable).

[298] *Davidson Bros., Inc. v. D. Katz & Sons, Inc.*, 643 A.2d 642 (N.J. Super. Ct. App. Div. 1994), *on remand from* 579 A.2d 288 (N.J. 1990). *Compare Mulligan v. Panther Valley Property Owners Ass'n*, 766 A.2d 1186 (N.J. Super. Ct. App. Div. 2001) (remanding to determine reasonableness of covenant amendment precluding residency by a sex offender).

[299] 643 A.2d at 647.

> the personal hardship caused by the withdrawal of a supermarket as well as the damage to the ongoing efforts of government and private enterprise to revitalize the city. We are persuaded, therefore, that, in the absence of any equivalent reciprocal benefit to the city, Davidson's scorched earth policy is so contrary to the public interest in these circumstances that the covenant is unreasonable and unenforceable.[300]

Restrictions on use

In *Thayer v. Thompson*,[301] the court held that a covenant that prohibited construction on a particular lot without first obtaining the consent of the grantor (the neighboring landowner) did not violate public policy. In *Thayer*, the dominant owner claimed that the servient lot had only been sold to provide access to the back lots behind it and that the provision restricting development had been intended to allow the grantor to keep the servient estate vacant. Judge Ringold held that covenants restricting construction are invalid if they are unreasonable and a covenant that entirely prohibits the use of land is unreasonable and void. Because this covenant allowed use of the vacant lot for purposes other than construction, such as recreation, it was therefore held not to be invalid.

Condominium rules are reviewed for reasonableness

Courts do review rules and by-laws promulgated by a homeowners' association or condominium association for reasonableness.[302] Although most courts enforce restrictions contained in a deed or recorded declaration without regard to reasonableness (invalidating them only if they violate public policy), rules promulgated by governing boards or associations are subject to a reasonableness standard.[303]

Public policy and unconscionability

Covenants are not enforceable if they infringe on constitutionally protected rights, contravene a statute or administrative regulation, or violate public policy.[304] According to the *Restatement (Third)*, "public policy" is "made up of the many policies that guide judges in shaping and applying law," recognizing that those "policies change to meet changing conditions of society."[305] Some of the most important public policy concerns are as follows:

> Policies favoring privacy and liberty in choice of lifestyle, freedom of religion, freedom of speech and expression, access to the legal system, discouraging bad faith and unfair dealing, encouraging free competition, and socially productive uses of land have been implicated by servitudes. Other policies that become involved may include those protecting family

[300] *Id.* at 648.

[301] 677 P.2d 787 (Wash. Ct. App. 1984).

[302] *Ridgely Condominium Ass'n v. Smyrnioudis*, 660 A.2d 942 (Md. Ct. Spec. App. 1995) (invalidating as unreasonable a by-law that prohibited clients of commercial owners on the ground floor of a condominium from entering those businesses through the lobby).

[303] *Nahrstedt v. Lakeside Village Condominium Ass'n*, 878 P.2d 1275, 1283 (Cal. 1994). *See also O'Buck v. Cottonwood Village Condominium Ass'n, Inc.*, 750 P.2d 813 (Alaska 1988).

[304] *Restatement (Third) of Property (Servitudes)* §3.1 (2000). *See also* Cal. Civ. Code §1353.6(a) (homeowners' associations cannot prohibit the display of flags unless need to protect public health or safety or the flag would violate local, state or federal law); 765 Ill. Comp. Stat. 605/18.6, 805 Ill. Comp. Stat. 105/103.30 (prohibiting enforcement of a covenant that denies a homeowner the right to fly the American flag).

[305] *Restatement (Third) of Property (Servitudes)* §3.1 cmt. f (2000).

> relationships from coercive attempts to disrupt them, and protecting weaker groups in society from servitudes that exclude them from opportunities enjoyed by more fortunate groups to acquire desirable property for housing or access to necessary services.[306]

Void if unconscionable or "unreasonably burden fundamental constitutional rights"

The *Restatement (Third)* also provides that covenants are invalid if they are "unconscionable."[307] It also provides that covenants are unenforceable if they "unreasonably burden [fundamental constitutional rights],"[308] such as rights of free speech or free exercise of religion, privacy, or security from unreasonable searches. The *Restatement (Third)* effectively brings into the common law the most important interests protected by the Constitution and limits the ability of community associations to burden individual owners in ways that are reminiscent of constitutional violations, even if they would not in fact constitute constitutional violations, given that community associations are not classified as state actors subject to the strictures of the Bill of Rights.[309]

▷ FREE SPEECH **HARD CASE ◀**

American flag

After 9/11, Justice Clarence Thomas's father-in-law, Donald Lamp, hung an American flag outside the balcony of his condominium unit. The condominium association had passed a rule prohibiting any banners or flags outside units, including the American flag. It did so, it seems, for aesthetic reasons and to preserve a uniform appearance of the units. Lamp was asked to abide by the rule, but he refused. After nationwide publicity, the association amended its policy to make an exception for the American flag.[310] In 2006, Congress passed the *Freedom to Display the American Flag Act*,[311] which guarantees the right to fly the American flag on one's property, regardless of any condominium or homeowners' association rule or covenant to the contrary. Suppose a condo owner sought to engage in other forms of expressive activity, like putting a "Donald Trump for President" sign on the front lawn?

Political signs

In *Dublirer v. 2000 Linwood Avenue Owners, Inc.*,[312] the New Jersey Supreme Court applied state constitutional free speech guarantees to private covenants in a high-rise cooperative. The court struck down a coop rule that prevented a coop owner from distributing written materials in the building connected with his efforts to run for a seat on the board of directors. Similarly, in *Committee for a Better Twin Rivers v. Twin Rivers*

306 *Id.* at §3.1 cmt. i.

307 *Id.* at §3.7.

308 *Id.* at §3.1(2).

309 *See Midlake on Big Boulder Lake, Condominium Ass'n v. Cappuccio*, 673 A.2d 340 (Pa. Super. Ct. 1996) (no state action involved in enforcing private covenant prohibiting unit owners from erecting signs on their property visible from outdoors).

310 Tony Mauro, *An Unwelcome Mat for Free Speech*, USA Today, Aug. 18, 2004, at 13A.

311 *Freedom to Display the American Flag Act*, 4 U.S.C. §5 note (Pub. L. No. 109-243, 120 Stat. 572 (July 24, 2006)).

312 103 A.3d 249 (N.J. 2014).

Homeowners Ass'n,[313] dissident members of a homeowners' association sought to engage in various kinds of speech activity to change the policies of the association. They were stymied and sued for relief from a rule that prohibited the placement of more than one sign in a window and one sign in the front yard no more than three feet from the home. The court held that the rule might violate the common law prohibition on covenants that violate public policy or interfere with the public interest.[314]

Suppose the association banned all signs, including political ones, on aesthetic grounds or because of a desire to create a peaceful environment. Should such a rule be enforceable?

On one hand, it seems reasonable to allow groups of homeowners to adopt covenants and rules that create a mutually agreeable environment in which to live and raise a family. Owners may well have legitimate and even strong interests in the appearance of the properties they inhabit. At the same time, alternative means of participating in politics and expressing one's views exist other than placing a sign on one's front lawn. On the other hand, the placing of signs in front of properties during an election is an American tradition, and one of the main ways that voters communicate their support for candidates and thus seek to influence the votes of others. Preventing this from occurring may not only infringe on important interests in political expression but curtail the vigor of the democratic process.

Compelled government speech

In *Taylor v. Northam*,[315] the Virginia Supreme Court reviewed a challenge to the governor of Virginia's removal of a statue of Confederate General Robert E. Lee in the city of Richmond. An 1887 deed transferring the ground on which the statue sat required the grantee to use the site for a monument to Lee and required the grantee to hold the parcel "only for the said use."[316] After building the monument, the grantee transferred the site and the monument to Virginia with a deed, referencing a resolution of the state assembly, noting that the state would "guarantee that she will hold [the Lee Monument and the site] perpetually sacred to the Monumental purpose to which they have been devoted and that she will faithfully guard it and affectionately protect it."[317] In 2020, with new understanding of the racial harm of a monument to Lee in the state's capital, the governor of Virginia announced his intention to remove the statue, drawing a lawsuit that argued, among other things, that the 1890 deed created a restrictive covenant binding the state from removing the statue. The Virginia Supreme Court rejected this argument, holding that permanent monuments on public property constitute government speech and that as a matter of public policy, the state of Virginia could not be compelled by a deed covenant to preserve "a symbol of defiance to Reconstruction," communicating "an

[313] 929 A.2d 1060 (N.J. 2007).

[314] *Id.* at 1075. *See also Mazdabrook Commons Homeowners' Ass'n v. Khan*, 46 A.3d 507 (N.J. 2012) (association's prohibition on all political signs violated unit owner's right to free speech under the state constitution).

[315] 862 S.E.2d 458 (2021).

[316] *Id.* at 460.

[317] *Id.*

unapologetic statement regarding the continued belief in the virtue of the 'Lost Cause' and in the Confederacy's pre-Civil War way of life, including the subjugation of people of African descent."[318] ◄

§6.7.5 *Choice of Law*

Usually, real property is governed by the law of the "situs" — the state in which the property is located. Sometimes, however, an agreement may specify that the law of another jurisdiction is intended to control the interpretation and/or validity of the agreement. A national company that has stores in many states may ask for anti-competitive covenants in its leases when it rents property in a shopping center. If the agreements do not include a choice of law clause, the courts will assume that the law of the place where the store is located applies rather than the law of the place where the company has its corporate headquarters.[319] If the agreement states that another state's law applies, the courts will generally enforce that unless the law of the chosen state violates a strong public policy of the situs. If situs law would find the covenant invalid as an unreasonable restraint on competition, then situs law normally would apply since the situs has the strongest interest in determining the shape of real estate markets within its borders.

§6.8 Modifying or Terminating Covenants

§6.8.1 *Changed Conditions*

Changed circumstances

Covenants will not be enforced if conditions have changed so drastically inside the neighborhood restricted by the covenants that enforcement will no longer be of substantial benefit to the dominant estates.[320] It is important to note that the changed conditions doctrine applies only where "there has been such a radical change in conditions since creation of the servitude[] that perpetuation of the servitude would be of no substantial benefit to the dominant estate."[321] The change "must be so radical as to defeat the essential purpose of the covenant or render the covenant valueless to the parties."[322] The *Restatement (Third) of Property (Servitudes)* explains that very

318 *Id.* at 470.

319 *Winn-Dixie Stores, Inc. v. Dolgencorp, LLC*, 746 F.3d 1008, 1020-1021, 1026-1027 (11th Cir. 2014).

320 *EWB-I, LLC v. PlazAmericas Mall Texas, LLC*, 527 S.W.3d 447, 458 (Tex. App. 2017); *El Di, Inc. v. Town of Bethany Beach*, 477 A.2d 1066 (Del. 1984); *LoBianco v. Clark*, 596 N.E.2d 56 (Ill. App. Ct. 1992); *City of Bowie v. MIE Properties, Inc.*, 922 A.2d 509, 526, 527 (Md. 2007); *Fink v. Miller*, 896 P.2d 649 (Utah Ct. App. 1995); *Restatement of Property* §564 (1944); 9-60 *Powell on Real Property* §60.10[2]; 7-61 *Thompson on Real Property, Third Thomas Edition* §61.07(f)(1).

321 *Restatement (Third) of Property (Servitudes)* §7.10 cmt. c (2000). *Accord, Wilcox v. Timberon Protective Ass'n*, 806 P.2d 1068, 1076 (N.M. 1990).

322 *Dierberg v. Wills*, 700 S.W.2d 461, 467 (Mo. Ct. App. 1985). "Courts may extinguish covenants if, due to changes in the character and environment of the property, the purpose for which they were established can no longer be accomplished. . . ."; 7-61 *Thompson on Real Property, Third Thomas Edition* §61.07(f)(1).

few cases result in application of the doctrine: "The test is stringent: relief is granted only if the purpose of the servitude can no longer be accomplished."[323] Some state statutes also require covenants to be of "actual and substantial benefit" to be enforceable.[324]

Fringe lots

The changed conditions doctrine is applied especially strictly when changes have occurred outside the restricted subdivision that affect lots located on the fringe of the restricted area. If lots on the border of the restricted area could easily free themselves from the covenant, it would quickly lose its effect over time as succeeding blocks of fringe lots succumbed to external changes. The changed conditions doctrine applies to changes outside the restricted subdivision only when those changes have so adversely affected every lot in the subdivision that enforcement is pointless.[325]

Conservation or preservation servitudes

The changed conditions doctrine is not likely to apply in the context of servitudes that are intended to immunize the property from change. The *Restatement (Third)* provides, for example, that the doctrine does not apply to conservation or preservation servitudes that are designed to last forever.[326]

***Restatement (Third)*: modification or termination?**

The *Restatement (Third)* alters traditional law in two ways. First, it uses termination rules to substitute for controls that had traditionally been applied through the touch and concern test.[327] Second, it suggests modification of the covenant in lieu of termination if modification will allow the covenant to serve its original purpose. Under this test, only if modification is not feasible is termination allowed.

> When a change has taken place since the creation of a servitude that makes it impossible as a practical matter to accomplish the purpose for which the servitude was created, a court may modify the servitude to permit the purpose to be accomplished. If modification is not practicable, or would not be effective, a court may terminate the servitude.[328]

However, the *Restatement (Third)* cautions that a court should rarely intervene if a mechanism exists for terminating the covenant in a manner that does not require the unanimous consent of the beneficiaries, such as a supermajority vote of the members of a homeowners' association.[329]

The implied intent argument

The changed conditions doctrine has been justified both by the idea that it implements the implied intent of the parties and because it promotes the alienability of land. The *Restatement (Third)* explains that

323 *Restatement (Third) of Property (Servitudes)* §7.10 cmt. a (2000).
324 Mass. Gen. Laws ch. 184 §30; N.Y. Real Prop. Acts. §1951.
325 *Allemong v. Frendzel,* 363 S.E.2d 487 (W. Va. 1987).
326 *Restatement (Third) of Property (Servitudes)* §7.10 & 7.10 cmt. d (2000).
327 *Id.* at §7.11 cmt. a.
328 *Id.* at §7.10. Also, if the purpose of the servitude can be accomplished but "because of changed conditions the servient estate is no longer suitable for uses permitted by the servitude, a court may modify the servitude to permit other uses under conditions designed to preserve the benefits of the original servitude." *Id.*
329 *Id. at* §7.10 cmt. a (2000).

> [i]f the parties who created the servitude considered the matter at all, they probably understood that circumstances might change in such a way that the servitude would lose its utility. Rather than try to anticipate changes that might take place and incur the expense of providing alternative servitudes or establishing a mechanism to deal with future changes, they left the matter open, anticipating that the law would extricate their successors from intractable problems that might arise in the future.[330]

The counterargument, of course, is that the parties did not provide that the covenant would terminate without the unanimous consent of those subject to it. If all the parties affected by the servitude want to end it, they can do so by contract by agreeing to release the servitude. The changed conditions doctrine is always invoked when one or more owners wish to be free of the servitude and at least one other owner insists on enforcing it. It is not at all obvious that the original covenanting parties would have intended the covenant to terminate when at least one of the beneficiaries still saw benefit in it.

Public policy argument

The alternative basis for the doctrine is public policy: "[P]ermitting the enforcement of servitudes after they have lost their utility reduces land values and turns the law into an instrument of extortion."[331] This argument suggests that the servitude not only has no objective value (so that enforcement would be viewed as pointless by a reasonable objective observer) but that it also has no subjective value to the beneficiary. This assumes that the only reason the beneficiary insists on enforcing the servitude is to "exact an unreasonably high price for release of an encumbrance that otherwise has no value and interferes with the ability of the servient owner to use his or her property."[332]

Argument against the changed conditions doctrine

The counterargument is that the servitude is a property right owned by the servitude beneficiary. The notion of an "unreasonably high price" suggests that the beneficiary has an obligation to sell the entitlement when an objective third party would say that it was no longer of utility. An owner of a covenant can choose to sell or not at a price she chooses. If she holds out for a high price, that is her business. A holdout is an impediment to a transaction only if the holdout is hoping to get a higher price than the other party is going to be willing to offer, and the holdout has imperfect information about how much the other party is willing to offer.[333] If, in contrast, the holdout really does not want to sell for the price being offered, then the value of the entitlement to the beneficiary may be higher than the value to the servient owner(s) of being free of it. The question of whether enforcement of the covenant would be efficient will therefore differ depending on whether one measures efficiency by reference to a voluntary sale (beneficiary's asking price versus servient owner's offer price) or by reference to the fair market value of the servitude (which is likely to be very low given the objective lack of utility of the servitude).

[330] *Id.*
[331] *Id.*
[332] *Id.*
[333] *Id.*

Affirmative covenants

The *Restatement (Third)* treats affirmative covenants differently from negative ones. Such covenants were often struck down by courts on the ground that they did not touch and concern the land.[334] The modern view is that the real concern was with the appropriateness of enforcing the covenants against later owners of the servient estate. The *Restatement (Third)* approach would enforce such covenants unless they violate public policy. At the same time, the *Restatement (Third)* recognizes that continued enforcement of such affirmative obligations may become oppressive over time.

> Covenants to pay for services or facilities are troublesome if there is no incentive for the service provider to control costs and there are no competitive pressures to keep prices reasonable. Covenants that require property owners to pay for services provided by the developer or another third party may present such problems, particularly where the obligation to pay is indefinite in duration or for a long term.[335]

Therefore the *Restatement (Third)* provides that affirmative covenants to pay money or provide services should terminate after a reasonable time if the document creating them has no definite termination point.[336] In addition, "if the obligation becomes excessive in relation to the cost of providing the services or facilities or to the value received by the burdened estate,"[337] the changed conditions doctrine will apply.

Servitudes in gross

Traditionally, covenants could not be enforced against successors if the benefit was held in gross.[338] Many courts will now enforce such covenants and the *Restatement (Third)* affirms their validity as long as the beneficiary has a "legitimate interest" in enforcing them.[339] At the same time, a traditional worry surfaces: it may be difficult to find servitude beneficiaries when the benefit is held in gross. Such beneficiaries may move and are not required by recording acts to record their current address (a reform that might be considered). The *Restatement (Third)* handles this problem by providing that servitudes held in gross can be terminated by agreement with the beneficiaries who can be located if the servient owner cannot locate all the beneficiaries.[340]

§6.8.2 Relative Hardship

Relative hardship

Unlike the changed conditions doctrine, which focuses on whether the covenant remains of substantial benefit to the dominant estate, the relative hardship doctrine focuses on the servient estate. A covenant will not be enforced if the harm caused by enforcement, that is, the hardship to the owner of the servient estate, will be greater by a "gross or of considerable

334 *See* §6.3.1.
335 *Restatement (Third) of Property (Servitudes)* §7.12 cmt. a (2000).
336 *Id.* at §7.12(1).
337 *Id.* at §7.12(2).
338 *See* §6.3.2.
339 *Restatement (Third) of Property (Servitudes)* §8.1 (2000).
340 *Id.* at §7.13.

magnitude" than the benefit to the owner of the dominant estate.[341] If the hardship is great and the benefit small, the courts may refuse to enforce the covenant.[342] If, however, the benefit of the covenant is substantial, the courts are unlikely to apply the doctrine even if the hardship to the servient estate is substantial. In *Lange v. Scofield*,[343] the court refused to enforce a covenant requiring that all owners of property adjoining or across the street from a parcel consent to the construction of a house on the parcel. One of the adjacent owners refused to give her consent, arguing that another house in the neighborhood would increase density and lower property values. The court found that construction would have no effect on property values and that any benefit received by the neighbor through enforcing the covenant would be negligible and far outweighed by the hardship that enforcement would cause the landowner who wished to construct the house.

Restatement (Third)

The *Restatement (Third)* treats the relative hardship doctrine not as a basis for terminating or modifying servitudes, but, rather, as a factor to consider in determining the availability and selection of appropriate remedies.[344] If compliance with a covenant is unreasonable because the burden is great and the benefit small, the *Restatement (Third)* concludes that nonenforcement may be appropriate but some amount of damages is probably appropriate to compensate the servitude beneficiary for the loss of the benefit of the covenant, small as it may be.[345]

▷ AFFIRMATIVE COVENANTS AND ECONOMIC FRUSTRATION **HARD CASE ◀**

In *Shalimar Ass'n v. D.O.C. Enterprises, Inc.*,[346] the court enforced an equitable servitude requiring an owner to continue operating a golf course against a complaint by the current owner that such a use was not profitable. "A mere change in economic conditions rendering it unprofitable to continue the restrictive use is not alone sufficient to justify abrogating the restrictive covenant."[347] If the current owner is unable to comply with the covenants, it is free to sell to someone who can. It is true that the owner may suffer a financial loss because property subject to such an obligation is likely to be less valuable than unrestricted property. However, such a sale would protect the reliance interests of the owners who relied on enforcement of the servitude. In contrast, the court in *Bennett v. Charles Corp.*[348] allowed changes in economic circumstances to relieve a developer of prior promises regarding land use. In *Bennett*, the court allowed a developer to convert remaining unsold lots in a subdivided tract into a cemetery, in

341 *Lange v. Scofield*, 567 So. 2d 1299 (Ala. 1990); *Gilpin v. Jacob Ellis Realties, Inc.*, 135 A.2d 204 (N.J. Super. Ct. App. Div. 1957); *Restatement of Property* §563 (1944); 9-60 *Powell on Real Property* §60.10[3]; 7-61 *Thompson on Real Property, Third Thomas Edition* §61.07(f)(4).
342 *Lacer v. Navajo County*, 687 P.2d 404, 411 (Ariz. Ct. App. 1983).
343 567 So. 2d 1299 (Ala. 1990).
344 *Restatement (Third) of Property (Servitudes)* §8.3 (2000).
345 *Id.* at §8.3 cmts. a & h.
346 688 P.2d 682 (Ariz. Ct. App. 1984).
347 *Id.* at 691.
348 226 S.E.2d 559 (W. Va. 1976).

violation of the developer's oral promise to develop the tract as a residential subdivision. Judge Flowers concluded that it was reasonable for defendant to breach the promise when the lots could not be sold because performance was impossible.[349] ◀

§6.8.3 *Conduct of the Parties*

By their own terms

Many subdivisions or condominium associations are subject to covenants that terminate within a stated number of years unless they are periodically renewed by the homeowners' association or condominium owners' association. Many declarations provide that covenants can be changed with a majority or two-thirds vote of the owners. As with easements, if the burdened and benefited estates come under the ownership of the same person, the covenants will terminate under the doctrine of merger.[350] Moreover, all parties affected by the covenant may agree in writing to terminate the covenant or release the property from it.[351]

Merger

Release

Equitable limitations on enforcement

Unclean hands

Acquiescence or waiver

A variety of equitable doctrines may be invoked to prevent enforcement of servitudes, including unclean hands, acquiescence, abandonment, laches, waiver, merger, and prescription.[352] First, enforcement may be denied if the complaining party has violated the covenant herself — she is said to have "*unclean hands.*" Second, *waiver* or *acquiescence* occurs when the servient owner violates the covenant and the servitude beneficiary fails to object. In such cases, the beneficiaries may have conveyed the message to the servient owner that the covenant would no longer be enforced. Because acquiescence may induce reliance on behalf of the servient owner, in some such cases, enforcement seems unfair. However, if the servitude is part of a common plan, the courts are unlikely to find waiver unless many owners have violated the covenant without objection.[353] Third, the acquiescence doctrine is related to the *laches* doctrine, under which an owner who has waited too long to enforce her rights may be barred from doing so, if the other party has changed her position in reliance on such a failure.

Laches

Abandonment

Fourth, widespread violation of the covenant may also be held to constitute *abandonment* of the covenant, not only by the plaintiff, but by the entire neighborhood.[354] The doctrine of abandonment rests on a conclusion that beneficiary "relinquishes the rights created by a servitude."[355] Failure to take advantage of the benefits of a servitude is rarely enough to establish abandonment; the beneficiary ordinarily must act in a manner

[349] *Id.* at 564. *Accord, Kincheloe v. Milatzo*, 678 P.2d 855, 860 (Wyo. 1984) (oral representations enforceable only if developer engaged in intentional fraud, not if developer changed his mind because he could not sell the last lots or for some other reason).

[350] *Restatement (Third) of Property (Servitudes)* §7.5 (2000).

[351] *Id.* at §7.3.

[352] *See Morris v. Nease*, 238 S.E.2d 844 (W. Va. 1977); 9-60 *Powell on Real Property* §60.10[1]; 7-61 *Thompson on Real Property, Third Thomas Edition* §61.07(c).

[353] *Restatement (Third) of Property (Servitudes)* §7.4 cmt. b (2000).

[354] *Dierberg v. Wills*, 700 S.W.2d 461, 467 (Mo. Ct. App. 1985); 9-60 *Powell on Real Property* §60.10[1].

[355] *Restatement (Third) of Property (Servitudes)* §7.4 (2000).

inconsistent with the continuation of the servitude.[356] However, failure to take advantage of the servitude for a very long time may constitute abandonment.[357] Both waiver and abandonment will usually be recognized only in the context of "multiple or repeated violations" by many owners.[358]

> If restrictions apply to an entire area and redound to the benefit of all property owners in the restricted area, then waiver or abandonment occurs only when violations of the restrictions are so general as to indicate an intention or purpose to abandon the plan or scheme intended to be maintained by the restrictions.[359]

Trivial or minor violations, even if widespread, are not sufficient.[360] One court found that a covenant requiring owners to have wood shingle roofs had been abandoned when 23 of 81 homes did not comply with it.[361]

Estoppel

Fifth, if a servitude beneficiary represents to the owner of a servient estate "by conduct, words, or silence, an intention to modify or terminate the servitude," she may be *estopped* from enforcing the covenant if the servient owner changes her position in reasonable reliance on the representation, if such reliance is "reasonable to foresee."[362] Sixth, open and notorious violation of the covenant without permission for the statutory period may terminate the covenant by *prescription*.[363]

Prescription

§6.8.4 Statutory Regulation

Marketable title acts

As with easements, many states have marketable title statutes that terminate restrictive covenants if they are not re-recorded after a specified period of time.[364] Other states place rigid time limits on the enforceability of covenants and do not let them be continued simply by re-recording them.[365] In those states, owners who wish to continue the covenants would have to enter a new agreement.

Statutory time limits

[356] *Id.* at §7.4 cmt. c.
[357] *Id.*
[358] *Kalenka v. Taylor*, 896 P.2d 222 (Alaska 1995); *Restatement (Third) of Property (Servitudes)* §7.4 cmt. b (2000).
[359] *Dierberg v. Wills*, 700 S.W.2d 461, 466 (Mo. Ct. App. 1985). *Accord, Simms v. Lakewood Village Property Owners Ass'n, Inc.*, 895 S.W.2d 779 (Tex. App. 1995); *Swenson v. Erickson*, 998 P.2d 807 (Utah 2000).
[360] *Cook v. Hoover*, 428 So. 2d 836 (La. Ct. App. 1983).
[361] *Fink v. Miller*, 896 P.2d 649 (Utah Ct. App. 1995).
[362] *Restatement (Third) of Property (Servitudes)* §7.6 (2000).
[363] *See* §5.5. *Landgray Associates v. 450 Lexington Venture, L.P.*, 788 F. Supp. 776 (S.D.N.Y. 1992); *Restatement (Third) of Property (Servitudes)* §7.7 (2000).
[364] *See, e.g.*, Mass. Gen. Laws ch. 184, §27; N.C. Gen. Stat. §§47B-2, 47B-4; Wis. Stat. §893.33(6); 7-61 *Thompson on Real Property, Third Thomas Edition* §§61.07(b), 61.07(d).
[365] Minn. Stat. §500.20; 9-60 *Powell on Real Property* §60.09; *see also* Ga. Code Ann. §44-5-60(b) (limiting the effectiveness of covenants running with the land to 20 years in municipalities that have adopted zoning laws); *but see Sweeney v. Landings Ass'n, Inc.*, 595 S.E.2d 74 (Ga. 2004) (covenant that provided that it would renew automatically every 10 years as long as two-thirds of the residents of the affected subdivision did not object was valid under the statute).

Statutory changed conditions provisions

Some states have adopted statutes that expressly adopt versions of the changed conditions doctrine and/or equitable limitations on enforcement of servitudes. Massachusetts, for example, has a comprehensive statute that provides for nonenforcement of servitudes unless they are "of actual and substantial benefit" to the beneficiary.[366] In addition, the statute provides that servitudes will not be enforceable "except in appropriate cases by award of money damages" in a variety of circumstances, including, for example, if enforcement is "inequitable," or if it "would impede reasonable use of land for purposes for which it is most suitable, and would tend to impair the growth of the neighborhood or municipality in a manner inconsistent with the public interest."[367] The statute ends by prohibiting "enforcement, except by award of money damages, [if enforcement] is for any other reason inequitable or not in the public interest."[368]

[366] Mass. Gen. Laws. ch. 184, §30.

[367] *Id.*

[368] *Id. See Blakely v. Gorin*, 313 N.E.2d 903 (Mass. 1974) *and Atwood v. Walter*, 714 N.E.2d 365 (Mass. App. Ct. 1999) (applying the statute).

PART III

COMMON OWNERSHIP

CHAPTER 7

Present Estates and Future Interests

§7.1 Introduction
§7.2 Fee Simple
§7.3 Defeasible Fees
  §7.3.1 Fee Simple Determinable/Possibility of Reverter
  §7.3.2 Fee Simple Subject to Condition Subsequent/Right of Entry
  §7.3.3 Fee Simple Subject to Executory Limitation/Executory Interest
§7.4 Life Estates
  §7.4.1 Remainders and Reversions
  §7.4.2 Contingent and Vested Remainders
  §7.4.3 Destructibility of Contingent Remainders
  §7.4.4 Doctrine of Worthier Title
  §7.4.5 Rule in *Shelley's Case*
§7.5 Trusts
§7.6 Interpretation of Ambiguous Conveyances
  §7.6.1 Presumption Against Forfeitures
  §7.6.2 Waste
  §7.6.3 *Cy Pres*
  §7.6.4 Changed Conditions
§7.7 Regulatory Rules
  §7.7.1 Abolition of Fee Tail
  §7.7.2 Restrictions on New Estates (*Numerus Clausus* Principle)
  §7.7.3 Unreasonable Restraints on Alienation
  §7.7.4 Rule Against Perpetuities
  §7.7.5 Racial Restrictions
  §7.7.6 Restraints on Marriage
  §7.7.7 Public Policy
  §7.7.8 Judicial Sale of Property Subject to Future Interests

§7.1 Introduction

Present estates and future interests

Property ownership can be divided over time, with one person having the right to current possession and another having the right to obtain possession in the future. Perhaps the best-known example is the leasehold; the tenant has the right to present possession and the landlord has the right to regain possession at the end of the lease.[1] The leasehold is an example of a broader set of *present estates* and *future interests* that at one time formed the core of real property law.

Complexity

Although the concept of present and future ownership is simple, the execution of the concept in legal principles has been maddeningly complex. One might imagine a system that left owners completely free to divide property rights as they please without regulation by the state. That is not our system. Although the rules in force do give owners substantial powers to create future interests of their choosing, they also place significant limitations on those powers. Traditionally, property law did this by defining a limited set of allowable packages of ownership interests called *estates*. All property interests had to fit into one of the established categories. Each category had its characteristic rights and obligations, some of which could be avoided by careful drafting but many of which could not be avoided by owners, although they often tried. The rules that arose around the estates system were arcane and technical. Some of those old rules survived until today and can be explained only through their historical origins. At the same time, some of the old rules have good policy justifications, although the reasons why the rules are good today may be quite different from the reasons that justified them at their birth.

Feudalism

Allodialism or freehold property

The estates system originated in the feudal era in England. This fact is significant because many of the regulatory rules that arose around the system reflect the historical change from feudal to "freehold" or "allodial" ownership. The feudal system involved a vast hierarchy in which the king allocated land to a group of lords in return for services to the king. Those lords, in turn, gave access to the land to vassals in return for those or other services. The result was to tie almost everyone to land in a system of hierarchical rights and obligations. Under this system, land use was far from free because it was always intimately connected with services owed to some lord, who owed services to a higher lord, all the way up to the monarch. Over time, both policy and law in England shifted power downward from the lords to those at the bottom of the hierarchy who actually possessed the land, freeing them from the obligations owed to the lords above them. The feudal system gave way to the freehold system where owners did not hold land from some lord but possessed it free of feudal services and incidents to a lord.[2]

Regulatory rules

Many legal rules developed in this historical transformation and, bizarre as some of them seem today, were intended to create a system that

[1] Of course, this arrangement is almost always supplemented by contractually based rental obligations on the part of the tenant and duties of maintenance and repair on the part of the landlord.

[2] Freehold, *Black's Law Dictionary* (12th ed. 2024).

consolidates ownership rights in individuals who are relatively free to use their land as they please. The rules governing property developed to prevent the re-emergence of feudalism. Although the chance that feudalism may re-emerge seems farfetched, the tensions that led to some of those rules are still very much with us today. Moreover, the policies of promoting widespread ownership of property and protecting the autonomy of owners to use their land as they please and to transfer it if they wish are still of crucial importance.

Disaggregation v. consolidation

As is the case with the law of covenants, we face a tension between the policy of allowing owners to disaggregate property rights into specially tailored bundles and the policy of encouraging or mandating consolidation of rights in a single owner. On one hand, owners would like the freedom to divide property rights among several owners, either simultaneously or over time, to protect their interests or maximize the value of the land. On the other hand, certain forms of fragmentation may be intended to (or have the effect of) preventing the reconsolidation of rights in the future. In some cases, this may be a good thing, helping preserve land for environmental or charitable purposes. However, in other cases, everyone involved may wish to change the land use or ownership and yet may be unable to do so, either because previously created limitations on ownership prohibit this from occurring or because transaction costs block deals that could reconsolidate the interests.

Alienability

The first major policy tension that future interests generate is the conflict between allowing disaggregation and promoting consolidation of property rights. The estates system created rules that limited the ways in which property interests could be divided over time to prevent excessive fragmentation of rights initially and to allow rights to be appropriately reconsolidated over time. Consolidation of rights in a single owner arguably promotes the free use and transfer of land because others who wish to buy the land need negotiate only with that owner, rather than with multiple owners. Consolidation of rights may increase the alienability of land because it reduces the costs of transfer; this, in turn, gives owners the freedom to change the use of the land. These freedoms promote a host of interests, including the autonomy of the owner and potential buyers and the creation of a market for real estate.

Consolidation of rights may promote alienability

Consolidation of property rights may inhibit alienability

The legal rules that require or promote the consolidation of interests do so by limiting the power of owners to disaggregate those interests in inappropriate ways. They paradoxically promote alienability by prohibiting the creation of certain types of future interests. This is paradoxical because the ability to create future interests may have the opposite effect; it may promote, rather than discourage, alienability. An owner may be willing to part with her property only because she will get it back in the future. For example, an owner might be willing to lease her property for a year to a tenant because she will recover possession after a year. If the law prohibited leaseholds and allowed only sales, the owner who wants to keep the property will be deterred from transferring possession. Thus, allowing owners to create future interests, on terms chosen by them, may increase, rather than inhibit the alienability of land. The policy of promoting alienability requires property rules to be structured to allow desirable forms of disaggregation while prohibiting undesirable ones.

Reasons to limit alienability

In addition, the promotion of alienability is not the only goal of property law. It is sometimes desirable to promote stability of ownership by inhibiting alienability. For example, restrictions on the alienability of charitable property may ensure that it continues to be devoted to desirable — but non-profit-maximizing — charitable purposes.

Generational conflicts

A second major policy tension underlying the estates system is the problem of conflicts among generations. In families, parents often leave property to children with conditions on its ownership or use. This creates tensions between members of the older generation who may wish the law gave them the power to control their property after they die and members of the younger generation who wish to be free from such controls. In addition, problems arise when owners seek to control the property, not just for the next generation or two, but for longer; some owners try to control the use of the property forever. Our parents may be wise, but they are unlikely to be wise enough to know the best use of property 500 years into the future. For this reason, rules have developed that limit (but do not abolish) the ability of individuals to control the use or ownership of property after their death. The most important of these are the rules invalidating unreasonable restraints on alienation and the rule against perpetuities that abolishes future interests that are likely to vest too far into the future.

Estates

The estates system is complicated and technical. It has a particular vocabulary for different interests that you simply must learn. However, the basic features of the system are far less complicated than the terminology might suggest. In fact, there are only four major categories of interests: (1) the *fee simple*; (2) *defeasible fees*; (3) *life estates*; and (4) *leaseholds*.[3] The first three are traditionally classified as *freehold estates* that were created by "livery of seisin" and protected by the royal courts in England. Leaseholds are *nonfreehold estates* that were not created through the process of livery of seisin and were not granted common law protection until much later and were thus regulated by different rules.[4]

Freehold estates

Freehold Estates

(1) *Fee simple* ownership potentially lasts forever; the owner can leave it to her heirs or write a will determining who will get it when the owner dies.

(2) *Defeasible fees* could also last forever, but will terminate upon the happening of some event named in the original conveyance (an event that may or may not happen), at which time ownership passes to the owner of the future interest. For example, an owner might give property to a city for use as a school but provide in the deed that if the property ever ceases to be used for school purposes that ownership will revert to the grantor or her descendants. Defeasible fees are of three types: (1) *fee simple determinable* (future interest vests in grantor automatically when the condition occurs); (2) *fee simple subject to condition subsequent* (future interest vests in grantor

[3] Another traditional estate, the *fee tail*, has been substantially (although not completely) abolished. *See* §7.7.1.

[4] Dale A. Whitman et al., *The Law of Property* §2.1, at 20 (4th ed. 2019).

if she asserts it after the condition occurs); (3) *fee simple subject to executory limitation* (future interest vests in a third party other than the grantor after the condition occurs).

(3) *Life estates* last for the life of the owner and then pass either to the grantor or her heirs (as a *reversion*) or to a third party chosen by the grantor at the time the life estate was created (as a *remainder*).

Nonfreehold Estates

Nonfreehold estates

Leaseholds transfer possession for a fixed period of time (a *term of years*) or a renewable period (*periodic tenancy*) or exist at the will of the owner (*tenancy at will*).

Trusts

All the estates may be held in their *legal* form or in an *equitable* form as *trusts*. A trust splits ownership between a trustee (the legal owner) and a beneficiary (the equitable owner). The trustee is obligated to follow the instructions of the grantor to use or manage the property in particular ways for the benefit of the beneficiary. Many trusts involve family property, as when a parent dies leaving property to a sibling to manage for the benefit of the deceased's children. Some trusts are held for business purposes, while many trusts are created for charitable purposes with a board of trustees managing the property as a hospital, university, museum, religious organization, or foundation.

Issues

The law of estates determines, first, what estates can be created and, second, how to resolve ambiguities in conveyances when it is not clear which estate was created. The main regulatory rules that govern the creation of future interests are (1) the prohibition against creation of "new estates"; (2) the rule against perpetuities; (3) the prohibition of unreasonable restraints on alienation; and (4) the abolition of the fee tail. Other significant regulatory rules include (5) the prohibition of racial conditions on land ownership and (6) the prohibition of unreasonable restraints on marriage. Finally, some specific rules regulate life estates, including the doctrine of worthier title, the rule in *Shelley's Case*, and the destructibility of contingent remainders. These rules have been abolished in many jurisdictions but retain force in some others. Although the original justifications for some of these rules have no modern force, they may serve to promote alienability and thus present the question of whether they should be retained in some form.

§7.2 Fee Simple

Lasts forever

The *fee simple*, also known as the *fee simple absolute*, is the "largest possible aggregate of rights, privileges, powers and immunities with respect to the land in which it exists, and thus comprises full ownership of that land."[5] Ownership in *fee simple* could last forever. Of course, people don't live

[5] *In re Eastwood*, 192 B.R. 96, 99 (Bankr. D.N.J. 1996) (*quoting* Robert Cunningham, William Stoebuck & Dale Whitman, *The Law of Property* (2d ed. 1993)). *See* 2-17 *Thompson on Real Property, Third Thomas Edition* §17.02 (fee simple is of potentially infinite duration, inheritable, and transferable).

Inheritable

forever, but the key feature of the fee simple is that it can be inherited. The owner may write a will identifying who will get the property when she dies; she may *devise* real property to *devisees* and *bequeath* her personal property to *legatees*. If the owner does not leave a will, her property passes to the decedent's *heirs* identified in the state *intestacy* statute. In addition to being *inheritable*, the fee simple is also *alienable*. This means that the owner has the power to transfer ownership during her lifetime. Restrictions on the alienability of a fee simple interest are almost always void.[6]

Alienable

Language to create

Today, a conveyance is assumed to transfer all the rights that the owner possesses to the grantee unless the conveyance suggests otherwise. This means that a conveyance of property from "*O* to *A*" conveys a fee simple to *A* if that is what *O* owned. The law used to require the use of magic words to create a fee simple. The traditional formulation for creating a fee simple was a conveyance to "A *and her heirs*"; failure to use the words "and her (or his) heirs" traditionally meant that the conveyance would not be a fee simple but merely a life estate to last for the life of *A*.[7] This rule has been abolished almost everywhere.[8] Today, a transfer is assumed to convey the largest estate the grantor had unless language in the conveyance expresses a contrary intent.[9]

The phrase "and her heirs" does not in fact give the heirs any interests. They will inherit the property only if *A* does not transfer it in her lifetime or devise it to someone else in her will. All those words mean is that the interest given to *A* is a fee simple absolute. The words "to *A*" are called "words of purchase" because they identify who is purchasing (or receiving) the property, while the words "and her heirs" are called "words of limitation" because they describe the kind of property interest given to *A*. In this case, that interest is an inheritable interest, or a fee simple.

Words of purchase and limitation

§7.3 Defeasible Fees

A *defeasible fee* is inheritable and alienable, like all fee interests, but unlike the fee simple absolute, will terminate upon the happening of some event named in the original conveyance, transferring ownership to another person. Three types of defeasible fees exist: (1) the *fee simple determinable*; (2) the *fee simple subject to condition subsequent*; and (3) the *fee simple subject to executory limitation*. These estates distinguish between future interests held by the grantor (*possibility of reverter* or *right of entry*) versus those held by third parties (*executory interests*) and between interests in the

Categories of defeasible fees

[6] *See* §7.7.3.

[7] 2-17 *Thompson on Real Property, Third Thomas Edition* §17.01.

[8] Use of the magic words "and his heirs" *may* still be required in Connecticut, Hawai'i, and South Carolina. 2-17 *Thompson on Real Property, Third Thomas Edition* §17.06(d). *See Cole v. Steinlauf*, 136 A.2d 744 (Conn. 1957); *De Freitas v. Coke*, 380 P.2d 762 (Haw. 1963); *McLaurin v. McLaurin*, 217 S.E.2d 41 (S.C. 1975).

[9] "Where language is ambiguous, it will be construed to confer on [the] grantee the highest estate permissible under the instrument." 2-17 *Thompson on Real Property, Third Thomas Edition* §17.02 (*citing Seifert v. Sanders*, 358 S.E.2d 775 (W. Va. 1987)).

grantor that vest automatically (*possibility of reverter*) and those that vest only if the grantor asserts them (*right of entry*).[10]

§7.3.1 Fee Simple Determinable/Possibility of Reverter

Automatic forfeiture

A *fee simple determinable* ends automatically upon the happening of a stated event and transfers possession back to the grantor or her heirs or devisees.[11] For example, a conveyance from "*O* to *A* as long as used for school purposes" gives a fee simple determinable to *A* and reserves a *possibility of reverter* in *O*.[12]

Words needed to create

The fee simple determinable is created by words indicating that the ownership is to last only for a certain time period. The conveyance either requires a certain condition to exist for the present estate to continue or requires the present estate to terminate upon the happening of a particular event. The words traditionally used to create a fee simple determinable are "as long as," "during," "while," or "unless."

Statute of limitations and adverse possession

When the condition occurs, ownership automatically shifts back to the grantor or her heirs or devisees. If the grantor does nothing to assert her rights, such as demanding that the present estate owner leave or bringing an action in ejectment, and the present estate owner retains possession for the period set by the statute of limitations, she will regain ownership back by adverse possession. This assumes, of course, that violation of the condition is sufficiently obvious to satisfy the "open and notorious" requirement, placing *O* on reasonable notice of the violation.[13]

Transferability

At one time, future interests like possibilities of reverter were not transferable.[14] A few states may retain this traditional rule in whole or in part.[15] However, most states now hold that future interests are alienable as well as devisable and inheritable.[16]

§7.3.2 Fee Simple Subject to Condition Subsequent/ Right of Entry

Not automatic

Unlike the fee simple determinable, the *fee simple subject to condition subsequent* allows the grantor to reclaim the property upon occurrence of the

[10] California and New York have simplified terminology by merging the executory interest with the remainder and calling both a "remainder." Cal. Civ. Code §769; N.Y. Est. Powers & Trusts §6-3.2.

[11] 2-20 *Thompson on Real Property, Third Thomas Edition* §20.02; *but see* Cal. Civ. Code §885.020 (abolishing the fee simple determinable and converting such estates into fee simple subject to condition subsequent).

[12] *Canova Land & Inv. Co. v. Lynn*, 856 S.E.2d 581 (Va. 2021) (enforcing a possibility of reverter).

[13] *See* §4.2.2.

[14] *Denver & San Francisco Railway v. School District No. 22*, 23 P. 978, 979-980 (Colo. 1890); 3-24 *Thompson on Real Property, Third Thomas Edition* §24.04.

[15] *See* T.P. Gallanis, *The Future of Future Interests*, 60 Wash. & Lee L. Rev. 513, 516-520 (2003).

[16] *City of Carthage v. United Missouri Bank of Kansas City, N.A.*, 873 S.W.2d 610 (Mo. Ct. App. 1994); *Nichols v. Haehn*, 187 N.Y.S.2d 773 (App. Div. 1959); *Concord Oil Co. v. Pennzoil Exploration & Production Co.*, 966 S.W.2d 451 (Tex. 1998); 3-24 *Thompson on Real Property, Third Thomas Edition* §24.07(b).

condition but does not make a transfer of ownership automatic. Instead, the grantor (or her heirs) must claim a *right of entry* or a *power of termination.*[17] It is created by language of condition that is usually accompanied by an explicit "right of entry." For example, *O* may convey property to *A*, "*but if* the property is ever used for anything other than school purposes, *O* shall have a *right of entry* for condition broken." Other language traditionally associated with the fee simple subject to condition subsequent are the phrases "on condition that" and "provided that" combined with a right of entry.

Statute of limitations for adverse possession

When an owner of a fee simple determinable violates the condition, and title automatically shifts to the holder of the possibility of reverter, the present estate owner is immediately a trespasser on property owned by another.[18] The statute of limitations for adverse possession begins running, as long as the violation is "open and notorious." However, an owner of a right of entry, in contrast, does not get title automatically upon the happening (or violation) of the condition, and such an owner may never assert her rights. Under these circumstances, ownership stays with the present estate owner, despite violation of the condition. Traditionally, this meant that the statute of limitations would not start running until the owner of the right of entry asserted her rights and asked the present estate owner to leave or brought an action for ejectment. Only when there is a demand to leave does the owner of the right of entry have the right to possession, and only when the present estate owner refuses to leave does she become a trespasser, starting the running of the statute of limitations.[19] Under this construction of the law, the grantor could wait as long as she liked before asserting her interest.

Laches

Some courts have limited the amount of time the owner of the right of entry can wait before asserting her rights by applying the doctrine of *laches*, an equitable doctrine that prevents someone from delaying unreasonably in asserting a legal right if this works to the detriment of someone else.[20]

Waiver

Others may find the right has been *waived* if it is not exercised within a reasonable time.[21]

▶ HARD CASE

▷ STARTING THE RUNNING OF THE STATUTE OF LIMITATIONS WHEN THE CONDITION IS VIOLATED

Many courts now reject the idea that the owner of the right of entry can wait as long as she likes to assert her interest. Instead, they start the running of the statute of limitations at the moment the condition is violated,

[17] 2-20 *Thompson on Real Property, Third Thomas Edition* §20.05.

[18] *1000 Brickell, Ltd.* v. *City of Mia.*, 339 So. 3d 1091 (Fla. D. Ct. App. 2022).

[19] Lewis M. Simes, *Handbook on the Law of Future Interests* §50, at 105-110 (1966).

[20] *Martin v. City of Seattle*, 765 P.2d 257 (Wash. 1988); Lewis M. Simes, *Handbook on the Law of Future Interests* §50, at 109 (1966).

[21] *Sligh v. Plair*, 569 S.W.2d 58 (Ark. 1978); John G. Sprankling, *Understanding Property Law* §9.06[C][6], at 129 (5th ed. 2023); 2-20 *Thompson on Real Property, Third Thomas Edition* §20.18.

thereby treating rights of entry the same as possibilities of reverter.[22] Some states have statutes mandating this result.[23] As a policy matter, it is arguably inappropriate to allow the owner of a right of entry to delay as long as she likes in asserting her rights. Adverse possession law protects the interests of those who have possessed property for so long that they have legitimate expectations of continued access. A rule that gives the future interest owner all the time in the world to demand possession flies in the face of the policies underlying the statute of limitations. On the other hand, one can argue that the interests of the owner of a right of entry are better protected if the right can be exercised at any time. The present estate owner is, after all, not entitled to breach the condition and arguably does so at her own risk. ◀

Transferability

As with possibilities of reverter, rights of entry were traditionally not alienable and some states may retain this rule.[24] A few states held that rights of entry were destroyed if the owner attempted to transfer them.[25] However, there is a strong trend now to allow rights of entry to be transferred[26] and most states now allow all future interests to be conveyed as well as devised.[27]

§7.3.3 Fee Simple Subject to Executory Limitation/ Executory Interest

Executory interest in third party

The *fee simple subject to executory limitation* is the same as a fee simple determinable except that the future interest belongs to a third party rather than the grantor. For example, "*O* conveys to *A*, but if the property is not used for school purposes, then to *B*." The present estate in *A* is called a *fee simple subject to executory limitation* while the future interest in *B* is called an *executory interest.*

Automatic

These estates are ordinarily created in a manner that effectuates an automatic shift of ownership when the condition is violated. Most authorities suggest that this is the only form of executory interest that can be created.[28] However, it is not clear what the courts would do if a grantor attempted to create an executory interest that had the form of the right of entry in a third party and was intended to vest only if the third party asserted her rights. So, for example, an owner might convey "to *A*, but if the property is ever used for purposes other than as a school, *B* shall have a

[22] *Concord & Bay Point Land Co. v. City of Concord*, 280 Cal. Rptr. 623 (Ct. App. 1991); *Johnson v. City of Wheat Ridge*, 532 P.2d 985 (Colo. 1975); John G. Sprankling, *Understanding Property Law* §9.06[C][6], at 129 (5th ed. 2023); 3-25 *Thompson on Real Property, Third Thomas Edition* §25.03.

[23] Cal. Civ. Code §885.070; Md. Code Real Prop. §6-103.

[24] *Restatement of Property* §160 (1944); 3-21 *Powell on Real Property* §§21.02[3][a], [b]. *See* T.P. Gallanis, *The Future of Future Interests*, 60 Wash. & Lee L. Rev. 513, 516-520 (2003).

[25] Sheldon F. Kurtz, *Moynihan's Introduction to the Law of Real Property* 151 (8th ed. 2022); 3-25 *Thompson on Real Property, Third Thomas Edition* §25.02.

[26] 3-21 *Powell on Real Property* §21.02[3][a].

[27] 3-30 *Thompson on Real Property, Third Thomas Edition* §30.03(b).

[28] 3-20 *Powell on Real Property* §20.05[2] ("Generally, executory interests vest an estate in the holder of the interest upon the happening of a condition or event."); 2-17 *Thompson on Real Property, Third Thomas Edition* §17.01(c)(3) (stating that an executory interest "cut[s] short" the present estate).

right to retake possession." Because executory interests traditionally vest automatically, a court might interpret this language as showing the grantor's intent to create an automatic transfer of title to *B* upon violation of the condition. On the other hand, this language may be interpreted as suggesting that the grantor intended the present estate to be forfeited only if the owner of the executory interest took action to assert her rights.

Rule against perpetuities

The most important difference between executory interests and future interests in the grantor is that executory interests have traditionally been subject to the *rule against perpetuities*. This rule invalidates future interests that could vest too far into the future. Interests in the grantor are treated as already vested (although they will not become possessory unless the condition is violated) because the grantor already owns the property and is transferring a limited estate. In contrast, executory interests are new rights in third parties that are not vested at their creation and may never vest. If an executory interest has no time limit on it sufficient to bring it within the period allowed by the rule against perpetuities, it is void under the traditional rule. This rule is addressed in depth below at §7.7.4.

Other types of executory interests

Several common property arrangements have traditionally been classified as executory interests. First, conveyances that are to become possessory at some point in the future are traditionally understood as executory interests. An example is a conveyance from "*O* to *A* one year from today." This creates a fee simple subject to executory limitation in *O* and an executory interest in *A*. Second, *options to purchase* are generally viewed as executory interests. An option is a right to buy property for a contractually set price. Third, *rights of first refusal* or *preemptive rights* have similarly been classified as executory interests. These are rights to purchase property when and if the current owner decides to sell, usually by matching any offers made by third parties or paying the fair market value of the property.

Alienability

Like other contingent future interests, executory interests were traditionally held to be inalienable; however, only a few states appear to retain this rule.[29]

§7.4 Life Estates

§7.4.1 *Remainders and Reversions*

Held for life

A *life estate* lasts for the life of the present holder and is followed either by a *reversion* in the grantor (or her heirs) or a *remainder* in a third party. Unlike the owner of a fee simple, the owner of a life estate has no right to pass on the property when she dies; rather, it will go to the reversioner(s) or remainderperson(s) identified by the grantor. A transfer from "*O* to *A* for life" gives a life estate to *A* and a reversion to *O* or her heirs, while a conveyance from "*O* to *A* for life, then to *B*" gives a life estate to *A* and a remainder to *B*. Life estates are transferable (unless the conveyance provides otherwise),[30] but the transferee obtains what the transferor owned,

[29] *See* T.P. Gallanis, *The Future of Future Interests*, 60 Wash. & Lee L. Rev. 513, 516-520 (2003).

[30] Restraints on alienation of life estates are usually enforced by the courts.

i.e., an estate for the life of the transferor, or a life estate *pur autre vie* (for the life of another).

§7.4.2 Contingent and Vested Remainders

Vested remainders

Remainders are either *vested* or *contingent*. Vested remainders belong to an ascertainable person and there are no conditions precedent that must be satisfied before the remainder is certain to become possessory. An example is "*O* to *A* for life then to *B*." Because *B* is a named person and no conditions must be satisfied before *B's* interest will take effect (other than the death of *A*), *B*'s interest is a *vested remainder*. If *B* dies before *A*, the remainder interest passes to *B*'s heirs or devisees, who will obtain possession when *A* dies.

Contingent remainders; condition precedent

A remainder is contingent, rather than vested, if it belongs to an unascertained person or there is a condition precedent that must be fulfilled before it can become possessory. For example, a conveyance from "*O* to *A* for life, then to *B* if she has graduated from law school" creates a contingent remainder because *B* will never get the interest unless she graduates from law school. Graduation from law school is a condition that must occur before the remainder will become certain to become possessory (and thus be "vested").[31]

Unascertained persons

Similarly, a conveyance from "*O* to *A* for life, then to the first child of *B*" is a contingent remainder if *B* has no children at the time of the conveyance from *O* to *A*. The remainder is not vested because we do not know who the first child of *B* is; moreover, the remainder may never vest because *B* may never have children. A remainder in the "heirs of *B*" is also contingent because the heirs of *B* can only be identified when *B* dies. The "heirs of *B*" refers to those who inherit the property under the state intestacy law and those laws confer property rights only on living persons; we cannot tell who is alive at the time *B* dies until *B* dies.

Alienability

Like other contingent future interests, contingent remainders were traditionally held to be inalienable; however, only a few states appear to retain this rule.[32]

Further classification of vested remainders

Vested remainders are further classified as (1) *absolutely vested*; (2) *vested remainders subject to open*; or (3) *vested remainders subject to divestment*. An absolutely vested remainder is one that will not change, as in "*O* to *A* for life, then to *B*." The remainder in *B* is absolutely vested; if *B* dies prior to *A*, the remainder will pass to *B*'s heirs or devisees. If a remainder is to a class that can increase, it is a *vested remainder subject to open*. If *B* is alive and has children at the time of the conveyance from *O* to *A*, then a conveyance from "*O* to *A* for life, then to the children of *B*" creates a vested remainder in the children of *B* (because the living children are ascertainable persons), but the remainder is "subject to open" because more children can be born and join the class as co-owners of the remainder.[33] Finally,

[31] A contingent remainder vests when the condition that makes it contingent disappears; it will become possessory when the property shifts to the remainderperson (which will happen when the life estate owner dies if the condition is fulfilled before the life estate owner dies).

[32] *See* T.P. Gallanis, *The Future of Future Interests*, 60 Wash. & Lee L. Rev. 513, 516-520 (2003).

[33] The "rule of convenience" will close the class when the remainder becomes possessory, *i.e.*, when *A* dies.

a vested remainder can be divested by the happening of a later event. Thus, a conveyance from "*O* to *A* for life, then to *B*, but if *B* drops out of law school, then to *C*," gives *B* a *vested remainder subject to divestment*, with an executory interest in *C*.

Class gifts

Rule of convenience

When a remainder is given to a class that can increase in size, the courts will close the class when any member becomes entitled to distribution or possession. This "rule of convenience" allows the property to be distributed without waiting for new members to emerge and without requiring those members to give up some of their rights and share their property if new members are born.[34] For example, a transfer from "*O* to *A* for life, then to the children of *B*" creates a contingent remainder if no children are alive at the creation of the interest or a vested remainder subject to open if at least one child is alive at the creation of the interest. In either case, the gift to the class of children of *B* can increase as more children are born. If *B* has two children before *A* dies and *B* is still alive at the time of *A*'s death, the class will close, and the remainder go to the two children even though *B* could have more children in the future. The class closes so that the two children can take possession at *A*'s death and will not have to share the property with any after-born children.

Relation between contingent remainders and vested remainders subject to divestment

It is sometimes hard to tell the difference between a contingent remainder and a vested remainder subject to divestment. In general, if the remainder is given to a person and then lost because of the happening of a later event (a condition subsequent) it is vested subject to divestment, while if a condition must be fulfilled before the remainder is good (a condition precedent), it is a contingent remainder. In practice, a remainder may have the same functional effect, but be written in two different ways. For example, *B*'s contingent remainder in the conveyance "*O* to *A* for life, then to *B if she survives A, otherwise to C*" is the functional equivalent of *B*'s vested remainder subject to divestment in the conveyance "*O* to *A* for life, then to *B*, but if *B* does not survive *A*, then to *C*." Nonetheless, equivalent though they may be, the difference is legally significant because the rule against perpetuities traditionally applied to contingent remainders but not to vested remainders subject to divestment.[35]

§7.4.3 Destructibility of Contingent Remainders

Modern rule is that contingent remainders are not destroyed

Almost all states now hold that contingent remainders hang around after the life estate terminates even if the contingency has not yet been fulfilled.[36] Thus, in a conveyance from "*O* to *A* for life, then to *B* if she has graduated from law school," the property will revert to *O* if *B* has not yet graduated from law school when *A* dies; however, if *B* later graduates from law school, the property will spring from *O* to *B*. This means that *O*'s reversion is effectively a fee simple subject to executory limitation.

[34] 3-30 *Thompson on Real Property, Third Thomas Edition* §30.09(b).

[35] The rule against perpetuities did traditionally apply to vested remainders subject to open, as well.

[36] T.P. Gallanis, *The Future of Future Interests*, 60 Wash. & Lee L. Rev. 513, 530-534 (2003); John G. Sprankling, *Understanding Property Law* §14.14, at 223 (5th ed. 2023).

The traditional rule (which may still be in effect in some states) was that contingent remainders were destroyed if they did not vest before termination of the preceding life estate.[37] Thus, in the conveyance described above, if *B* has not graduated from law school before the death of *A*, the remainder is destroyed and *O* has a fee simple absolute. The traditional rule also provided that contingent remainders were destroyed if the life estate and remainder "merged" or came into the hands of the same owner. The modern approach may allow the contingent remainder to survive even in this case.[38]

Traditional rule of destructibility

§7.4.4 *Doctrine of Worthier Title*

Remainder in the grantor's heirs

When an owner *O* gives property "to *A* for life, remainder to the heirs of *O*," many states will interpret the remainder as a remainder in *O*, not in *O*'s heirs.[39] Originally, this type of conveyance was intended to avoid inheritance taxes; if *A* died after *O*, then *O*'s heirs would take the property, not as "heirs" of *O* but through the prior *inter vivos*[40] conveyance from *O* to *A*, which also created the remainder in *O*'s heirs. Because there was no inheritance, no inheritance taxes would be due.

Modern justification

A plausible modern justification for the rule is that it is impossible to tell who *O*'s heirs will be until *O* dies. It is possible for a life estate owner to sell a fee simple absolute if she can get the reversioner or remainderperson to agree to sell her interest as well to the same person. Thus, a third party who wanted to buy a fee simple interest in the property could negotiate both with the holder of the life estate and the holder(s) of the future interest(s); if the estates both come to be owned by the same person, then, under the doctrine of merger, that buyer will own a fee simple absolute. However, because the remainder here is owned by *O*'s heirs, no one can contract with them until *O* dies. This is because we will only know who they are when *O* dies. The result is that there is no way to create a fee simple absolute during *O*'s lifetime, even if everyone alive (including the potential heirs of *O*) wants this to happen. The doctrine of worthier title, by transforming a remainder in *O*'s heirs into a reversion in *O*, makes it possible for the interests to be merged in a third party and a fee simple is created. The inability to do this during *O*'s lifetime substantially limits the alienability of the property during *O*'s lifetime. On the other hand, life estates are never very alienable and preventing alienation during *O*'s life may be precisely what *O* intended.

[37] However, the traditional destructibility rule never applied to equitable interests, so a contingent remainder in a trust would not have been destroyed if it did not vest before termination of the preceding life estate.

[38] *Abo Petroleum Corp. v. Amstutz*, 600 P.2d 278 (N.M. 1979).

[39] *In re Estate of Grulke*, 546 N.W.2d 626 (Iowa Ct. App. 1996) (abrogating the doctrine but applying it to a will written before the rule was abrogated); 3-30 *Thompson on Real Property, Third Thomas Edition* §30.03(j). The rule, to the extent it exists today, is a rule of construction, not a mandatory rule. Dale A. Whitman et al., *The Law of Property* §3.15, at 90 (4th ed. 2019).

[40] A conveyance made during the grantor's lifetime, as contrasted with a testamentary transfer that occurs on death.

Statutes

The doctrine appears to have been abolished almost everywhere as applied to testamentary transfers.[41] Many states have abolished the doctrine of worthier title by statute.[42] A few states still retain the rule with regard to *inter vivos* conveyances as a rule of interpretation rather than a rigid regulatory rule, but the law is moving in the direction of abolition of the rule.[43]

§7.4.5 *Rule in* Shelley's Case

Remainder in the heirs of the life estate owner

Like the doctrine of worthier title, the rule in *Shelley's Case* transforms a contingent remainder into a vested one. If a conveyance is made from "*O* to *A* for life, then to the heirs of *A*," the rule in *Shelley's Case* transformed the contingent remainder in *A*'s heirs into a vested remainder in *A*. Because *A* now had both a life estate and a vested remainder, the estates merged and *A* owned a fee simple absolute. This rule has been abolished by statute in most states and appears to persist in only a few states.[44] The rule had origins similar to the doctrine of worthier title and was designed to prevent owners from avoiding inheritance taxes. It also may be similarly justified by the modern idea that prohibiting owners from creating a contingent remainder in heirs serves to promote the alienability of the property because it ensures that a fee simple can be created by agreement of the parties without waiting until someone dies to determine who can sell the remainder. And as with the doctrine of worthier title, abolition of the rule has been defended on grounds of freedom of contract or freedom of disposition.

§7.5 Trusts

Separation of legal and equitable title

A trust grants power to one person (the *trustee*) with instructions (and enforceable obligations) to manage the property for the benefit of another (the *beneficiary*). The trustee is said to possess "legal title" to the property, while the beneficiary possesses "equitable" or "beneficial" title. The creator of the trust is called the "settlor" or "trustor." Trusts can be created in real or personal property and can be in any of the estates that apply to real property, including defeasible fees and life estates. Some trusts are personal; they may be created by a parent who dies leaving property to her brother to manage for the benefit of her children. Other trusts are *charitable*; an owner

[41] *See* Mass. Gen. Laws ch. 190B, §2-710; T.P. Gallanis, *The Future of Future Interests*, 60 Wash. & Lee L. Rev. 513, 543-548 (2003).

[42] Dale A. Whitman et al., *The Law of Property* §3.15, at 90 (4th ed. 2019).

[43] John G. Sprankling, *Understanding Property Law* §14.12, at 220-221 (5th ed. 2023).

[44] *See Lusk v. Broyles*, 694 So. 2d 4 (Ala. Civ. App. 1997) (refusing to apply rule in *Shelley's Case*); 3-30 *Thompson on Real Property, Third Thomas Edition* §30.03(i). *See* T.P. Gallanis, *The Future of Future Interests*, 60 Wash. & Lee L. Rev. 513, 534-542 (2003) (clearly abolished in 43 states); Dale A. Whitman et al., *The Law of Property* §3.16, at 94 (4th ed. 2019) (abolished by statute in at least 36 states and the District of Columbia). According to Whitman, the rule retains its validity as to both wills and deed in only Arkansas, Colorado, Delaware, and Indiana. *Id.* Sprankling states that it has been abolished "in virtually all jurisdictions." John G. Sprankling, *Understanding Property Law* §14.13, at 222 (5th ed. 2023).

may transfer land or monetary assets to a law school with instructions to use the property in certain ways, such as providing scholarships for students, building a library, or endowing a professorship. Many educational, cultural, religious, and social service institutions are held in the trust form, including universities, museums, private schools, wildlife or park areas, churches and synagogues, and hospitals.

Fiduciary obligations

Trustees have fiduciary obligations to manage the trust funds in the interests of the beneficiary. Beneficiaries may bring lawsuits for an accounting or to challenge the trustee's management of the trust. Charitable trusts are generally supervised by the state attorney general, who is usually the only person entitled to bring a suit to challenge the trustee's management or use of the trust assets.

§7.6 Interpretation of Ambiguous Conveyances

§7.6.1 Presumption Against Forfeitures

Grantor's intent controls but ambiguities are resolved against forfeiture

When it is not clear which estate a grantor intended to create, most states express a strong constructional preference for an interpretation that protects the holder of the present estate and avoids forfeiture to the future interest holder. This is often called the *presumption against forfeitures*.[45] Thus, if the choice is between a construction that creates a future interest—and that would result in a forfeiture of the present estate to the future interest holder—or a present estate that would remain possessory in the present estate owner without the possibility of forfeiture, the courts prefer the present estate unless it is clear the grantor wished to create a future interest. For example, a conveyance from "*O* to *A* for school purposes only" might be interpreted either as a fee simple absolute (perhaps with a restriction on use that is either an enforceable covenant or unenforceable *precatory* language[46]) or as a fee simple determinable (with ownership contingent on use as a school and a possibility of reverter in *O* if the property is ever not so used).

Presumptions

The presumption against forfeitures would read this ambiguity as a fee simple rather than a fee simple determinable because this avoids a "forfeiture." The presumption against forfeitures means that (1) a fee simple is preferred to a defeasible fee or a life estate; (2) a defeasible fee is preferred to a life estate; (3) a fee simple subject to condition subsequent is preferred to a fee simple determinable (because forfeiture is not automatic with a right of entry); (4) a fee subject to a covenant is preferred to a defeasible fee; and (5) a fee with unenforceable precatory language is preferred to a fee subject to a real covenant.

[45] *Roberts v. Rhodes*, 643 P.2d 116 (Kan. 1982); *Oldfield v. Stoeco Homes, Inc.*, 139 A.2d 291 (N.J. 1958); 2-17 *Thompson on Real Property, Third Thomas Edition* §17.01(d).

[46] "Precatory" language in a contract or deed does not confer any legal rights; it is merely descriptive.

▶ HARD CASE ▷ MAGIC WORDS

When a conveyance fails to use the magic words traditionally associated with a particular estate, some courts will interpret the conveyance as a lesser estate, which avoids (or is likely to avoid) a forfeiture even if this clearly violates the intent of the grantor. For example, courts have traditionally required "time" words to create a fee simple determinable. Examples include the words "until," "unless," "while," or "during." For example, in *Howson v. Crombie Street Congregational Church*,[47] Gertrude Farnham conveyed a parcel to a church with a deed, stating that if the property "should ever cease" to be used as a parsonage or parish house or if the adjoining property should ever cease to be used for church purposes, that the property "shall revert" to her or her heirs. Although the language seems clearly to suggest that the property would revert automatically, the court held that the conveyance created a fee simple subject to condition subsequent, not a fee simple determinable.[48]

The argument for formality

One might interpret this approach as suggesting that, unless magic words are used, the conveyance is necessarily ambiguous and that ambiguities are resolved against forfeiture in order to consolidate interests in the present estate owner and promote the alienability of the property. On the other hand, this approach seems to suggest that the grantor's intent is irrelevant and that, even if the grantor intended an automatic forfeiture, the court will find a condition subsequent unless the correct magic words were used to create a fee simple determinable. This approach might be justified on the ground that formalities matter; if individuals are required to use particular words to create particular estates, on penalty of having a court declare those estates *not* to have been created, this provides an incentive to owners to learn the rules and use the appropriate words. If individuals respond in this way, the result will be to clarify the interests created by wills or deeds and it will be more likely that the courts can effectuate the intent of the parties. Refusing to stick to formalities encourages lax drafting and makes the courts' job of interpretation harder, making it more likely they will interpret conveyances in ways that grantors do not intend.

Encourage precision and promote clarity

The argument against formality

Promote the grantor's intent

The counterargument is that an approach that requires "magic words" often has the effect of enforcing a result that the grantor probably did not want. Because the law allows owners to create an estate such as the fee simple determinable, interpretation of the estate as something different violates the intent of the grantor and transfers property rights to someone other than the person who should rightfully own that property. The promotion of alienability is a legitimate public policy and it is promoted sometimes by consolidating interests in the present estate owner, freeing that owner from dead-hand control of the past. However, alienability is also promoted by allowing owners to create conditional estates; the ability to create such estates may well induce owners to part with their property. In addition, it is unlikely that owners will all learn the rules and use the

[47] 590 N.E.2d 687 (Mass. 1992).

[48] *Id.* at 689.

correct magic words. Often future interests are created in donative transfers to charitable organizations or family members; lawyers are often not involved in such conveyances or in the drafting of such wills. It is therefore unlikely that the requirement of special language will induce individuals to use those magic words.

Trend to focus on grantor's intent

While many courts still do require particular language to create particular estates, there is a long-term trend to focus on the grantor's intent and to apply the presumption against forfeitures only when that intent can be reasonably understood as ambiguous. While the promotion of alienability by consolidating interests is a legitimate social policy, it coexists with the social policy that delegates power to owners to disaggregate property rights by creating conditional estates. As long as the estate the grantor tried to create is a legitimate one that does not violate any public policy, there is little reason to ignore the grantor's intent just because an archaic verbal formulation was not used.[49] ◀

▷ CONFLICTS BETWEEN LANGUAGE IN THE GRANTING CLAUSE AND LATER LANGUAGE IN THE DEED

HARD CASE ◀

Many cases deal with conveyances that include internally contradictory language. Sometimes the initial grant appears to be an unencumbered fee simple while later language in the deed suggests an intent to create a lesser estate, such as a fee simple determinable. In some of these cases, the grantor intended to create a lesser estate but worded the deed in a way that appeared to create a greater estate and then limited the estate by later language in the deed. The older approach to this problem interpreted the initial language as creating a fee simple and then struck the later language as "repugnant" to the fee.[50] For example, in *Fox v. Snow*,[51] a testatrix[52] bequeathed to her husband "all of the money which I have on deposit at the [bank], however, any money which is in the said account at the time of my said husband's death, the said sum shall be held by my niece, Catherine King Fox, absolutely and forever." Although the grantor almost certainly intended to give her husband a life estate in the money, with the residue (if any) belonging to the niece at his death, the court interpreted the earlier language to convey a fee simple interest, which left nothing to give to the niece. This meant that the husband had the right to write a will bequeathing any leftover money to someone other than the niece.[53] The more modern approach, argued for by the dissenting judge in *Fox v. Snow*, looks at the document as a whole and attempts to determine the overall intent of the grantor. If the intent is

[49] *See, e.g.*, *Cain v. Finnie*, 785 N.E.2d 1039 (Ill. App. Ct. 2003) (grantor intended to create a life estate conditional on his grantee not remarrying by devising property to "Blanche Spurlock so long as she remains my widow" rather than finding a fee simple determinable).

[50] 2-17 *Thompson on Real Property, Third Thomas Edition* §17.01(a), (d).

[51] 76 A.2d 877 (N.J. 1950).

[52] The legal term referring to a woman who died leaving a valid will. The male term is testator, although this term is increasingly used for men and women.

[53] *Accord*, *Coble v. Patterson*, 442 S.E.2d 119 (N.C. Ct. App. 1994).

not ambiguous, then the intent will be followed.[54] However, if the intent is ambiguous, all the language considered together, most courts will apply the presumption against forfeitures and choose the formulation that is most likely to avoid a forfeiture of the present estate. ◀

▶ **HARD CASE**

▷ CONFLICTING MAGIC WORDS WITHIN THE GRANTING CLAUSE

In another class of cases, courts have to interpret ambiguities that arise when the conveyance includes traditional magic words that apply to two or more different estates. For example, in *Prieskorn v. Maloof*,[55] a conveyance "provided that" the property not be used for immoral purposes or the manufacture or sale of liquor and that if this occurred, the conveyance would be "null, void, and of no effect" and the property would "revert" to the grantors. The court noted that the phrase "provided that" is characteristic of the fee simple subject to condition subsequent while the statement that, on breach of the condition, the deed would immediately be "null, void and of no effect" and that the property would "revert" to the grantors are both characteristic of the fee simple determinable. Without reaching a final determination, Judge Bustamante noted that the presumption against forfeitures suggested interpreting such ambiguous language as a fee simple subject to condition subsequent. This result might be justified by the notion that, if an ambiguity is present, social policy is furthered by freeing the property from automatic forfeiture, consolidating power over the property in the present owner. The counterargument, of course, is that the ordinary meaning of the words (rather than their traditional technical legal meaning) strongly suggests an intent to create an automatic reverter. Holding the condition *not* to trigger a possibility of reverter does violence to the grantor's intent without protecting the reasonable expectations of the grantee. ◀

▶ **HARD CASE**

▷ PURPOSES

Precatory language

Many cases concern conveyances that include language stating the purpose for which the conveyance is being made. For example, in *Wood v. Board of County Commissioners of Fremont County*,[56] property was donated to a county "for the purpose of constructing and maintaining thereon a County Hospital in memorial to the gallant men of the Armed Forces of the United States of America from Fremont County, Wyoming." The county sold the hospital to a private owner that closed it one year later. The grantors sued, claiming that ownership was contingent on use as a hospital and that the cessation of use automatically terminated the present estate with

[54] *Accord, Farkas v. Calamia*, 373 S.W.2d 1 (Mo. 1963).

[55] 991 P.2d 511 (N.M. Ct. App. 1999).

[56] 759 P.2d 1250 (Wyo. 1988). *Accord, In re Estate of Campbell*, 942 P.2d 1008 (Wash. Ct. App. 1997).

ownership reverting to the grantors. The court applied the presumption against forfeitures, holding that the language of purpose did not specifically state that ownership would terminate on cessation of the contemplated use and that a recitation of the "purpose" for which the conveyance was made is merely *precatory language* that has no legal effect. The vast majority of courts agree with this approach.[57]

Other interpretations

However, some courts grant substantial legal effect to such language and may interpret it to create a future interest.[58] Such language has also been interpreted (1) as an enforceable covenant;[59] (2) as a fee simple subject to condition subsequent;[60] (3) as a constructive trust;[61] and (4) in the case of transfers to railroads, as an easement.[62] These interpretations might be justified because they promote the will of the grantor to restrict the use of the property and, when such restrictions serve charitable purposes there is a public policy in favor of limiting the alienability of property to preserve those charitable purposes. ◀

▷ REPURCHASE RIGHTS **HARD CASE ◀**

When a conveyance gives the grantor (or reserves to the grantor) a "right to repurchase" the property under certain circumstances, the right can be interpreted either as an *option to purchase* or as a *right of entry*. For example, in *Central Delaware County Authority v. Greyhound Corp.*,[63] a grantor gave property to a governmental entity, providing that if it ever ceased to be used for "public purposes" that the grantor would have the "right to repurchase, retake and reacquire" the property for $5,500. The trial court interpreted the conveyance as a fee simple subject to condition subsequent. The appeals court and the Supreme Court of Pennsylvania held that the conveyance was a fee simple absolute with a separate option to purchase. The interpretive choice mattered because, under Pennsylvania law, if it was a right of entry, it was valid and enforceable (triggering the repurchase right), while if it was an option, it would violate the rule against perpetuities and would be void, vesting the property in the present estate holder. The Pennsylvania Supreme Court held that the conveyance was ambiguous, applied the presumption against forfeitures, interpreted the right as an option, and invalidated it under the rule against perpetuities. In contrast, a

[57] *Clark v. City of Williamsburg*, 541 P.3d 764 (Kan. App. 2024) (Table); *Roberts v. Rhodes*, 643 P.2d 116 (Kan. 1982); *Lord v. Society for Preservation of New England Antiquities, Inc.*, 639 A.2d 623 (Me. 1994); Dale A. Whitman et al., *The Law of Property* §2.5, at 32-33 (4th ed. 2019).

[58] *See* Dale A. Whitman et al., *The Law of Property* §2.5, at 33 (4th ed. 2019).

[59] *Davis v. St. Joe School District*, 284 S.W.2d 635 (Ark. 1955); *Gordon v. Whittle*, 57 S.E.2d 169 (Ga. 1950). Note that the benefit of a covenant could not traditionally be held in gross. *See* §6.3.2.

[60] *Board of Trustees of Columbia Road Methodist Episcopal Church of Bogalusa v. Richardson*, 44 So. 2d 321 (La. 1949); *Cathedral of the Incarnation in the Diocese of Long Island, Inc. v. Garden City Co.*, 697 N.Y.S.2d 56 (App. Div. 1999).

[61] *United States v. Certain Land in Cape Girardeau*, 79 F. Supp. 558 (E.D. Mo. 1947).

[62] *Blakely v. Chicago, K.&N. R. Co.*, 64 N.W. 972 (Neb. 1895).

[63] 588 A.2d 485 (Pa. 1991).

Kentucky court in *Dennis v. Bird*[64] interpreted a similar repurchase option as a right of entry and validated it.

Disaggregation v. consolidation

The *Greyhound* approach can be justified on the ground that construction of ambiguities to avoid forfeiture has the effect of consolidating ownership in the current owner, freeing the land from archaic restrictions (the "dead hand" of the past) and promoting both its transfer and its free use for current purposes. This approach protects the autonomy of the current owner, limits the power of owners to control property illegitimately too far into the future, and promotes efficiency by allowing property to transfer to a more valued use. On the other hand, the *Dennis* approach can be justified on the grounds that it promotes the grantor's intent and that the forced consolidation of rights, against the wishes of the grantor, may well decrease both autonomy and efficiency by depriving owners of the power to donate land on a conditional basis and by forcing a redistribution of rights from a more- to a less-valued use, with transaction costs blocking a correction of the mistaken (inefficient) allocation of resources.

Trend in the law

The more modern approach is to focus on the grantor's intent and to find a future interest to have been created if that is what the grantor probably wanted, as long as no regulatory rule reflects a public policy that would prohibit creation of such an interest. This approach reflects the realization that both autonomy and efficiency may be promoted by allowing property rights to be disaggregated and that violation of the grantor's intent is appropriate only if sufficiently strong public policies suggest that it should be overridden. The traditional approach, which is still quite strong in the courts, ignores the grantor's intent where the conveyance can be reasonably seen as ambiguous, and relentlessly applies the presumption against forfeiture of the present estate, on the ground that consolidation of rights in the current owner promotes the alienability of the property and hence both autonomy and efficiency. ◀

§7.6.2 Waste

No major changes permitted to life tenant

A life tenant is permitted to use the land for present purposes as a reasonable owner would but is not permitted to commit "*waste.*" Traditionally, this meant (1) that the life tenant had a duty to repair the premises, to pay property taxes,[65] and maintain insurance on the property;[66] and (2) that the life tenant had no power to harm the property or to make major alterations of any kind.[67] Life tenants are generally immune from claims that they committed waste if the instrument creating the life estate provides that they shall be so immune.[68] Traditionally, any substantial change in the property, whether it benefited the property or harmed it, was impermissible waste

[64] *Dennis v. Bird*, 941 S.W.2d 486 (Ky. Ct. App. 1997).

[65] *McIntyre v. Scarbrough*, 471 S.E.2d 199 (Ga. 1996); *Younggren v. Younggren*, 556 N.W.2d 228, 232 (Minn. Ct. App. 1996).

[66] *In re Felker*, 211 B.R. 165 (Bankr. M.D. Pa. 1997); *Matter of Estate of Fisher*, 645 N.Y.S.2d 1020 (Sup. Ct. 1996); 2-19 *Thompson on Real Property, Third Thomas Edition* §19.09.

[67] 2-19 *Thompson on Real Property, Third Thomas Edition* §19.08.

[68] *See, e.g., Wolfe v. Estate of Wolfe*, 756 So. 2d 788 (Miss. Ct. App. 1999).

because the reversioner or remainderperson had a right to receive the property in substantially the same condition (normal wear and tear excepted) as when the life tenant received it.[69] This also meant that it would be waste to tear down a building even if this would increase the market value of the land and even if the life tenant intended to replace the building with a better structure.[70] The modern approach is more forgiving, and the current understanding is that conduct constitutes waste if it damages the inheritance. Thus, in a leading case, *Melms v. Pabst Brewing Co.*,[71] a house came to be surrounded by industrial property and the life tenant's decision to tear it down and convert it to nonresidential use was held not to constitute waste.

▷ IN KIND v. MARKET VALUE **HARD CASE ◀**

Destruction or alteration of a building may increase its market value and improve it in the eyes of most people, and yet the remainderperson may object to the change on the ground that she prefers to receive the property in its original condition, for sentimental or other reasons. In such cases, it may or may not constitute waste to allow the change. On the one hand, the remainderperson may have legitimate interests in receiving the property in its original form. On the other hand, the life tenant is the owner during her lifetime and should be entitled to derive benefit from the property as its present owner. Such cases present conflicts between the interests of the present estate owner in free use of the property and the security interests of the remainderperson in receiving the property in its original condition. ◀

§7.6.3 Cy Pres

Impracticability

It sometimes becomes impossible to administer a trust in the way it was intended by the donor. If property is given in trust to a particular charitable purpose and "it is or becomes unlawful, impossible, or impracticable to carry out that purpose," and the settlor (the creator of the trust) demonstrated a general intent to devote the property to charitable purposes, "the court will direct application of the property or appropriate portion thereof to a charitable purpose that reasonably approximates the designated purpose."[72] If the settlor did not have a general charitable intent, but sought only to aid the specific charity stated in the trust, then the trust will fail and the trust corpus will return to the donor or her heirs or to such third parties as are designated in the trust instrument. When the trust has an executory interest identifying who should get the property if it fails, the courts

[69] 2-19 *Thompson on Real Property, Third Thomas Edition* §19.08.
[70] *Id.*
[71] 79 N.W. 738 (Wis. 1899).
[72] *Restatement (Third) of Trusts* §67 (2012). *See also* N.H. Rev. Stat. §498:4-a; *Estate of Buck* (Cal. Super. Ct. 1986) (opinion reprinted in 21 U.S.F. L. Rev. 691 (1987)); Lawrence W. Waggoner et al., *Family Property Law: Cases and Materials on Wills, Trusts, and Future Interests* 15-9 to 15-22 (4th ed. 2006); *In re Crichfield Trust*, 426 A.2d 88, 89 (N.J. Super. Ct. Ch. Div. 1980).

generally interpret the settlor to have intended the trust to end if the particular charitable purpose became impossible to fulfill.[73] This interpretation follows from the fact that the creation of an executory interest shows that the settlor knew the trust might fail and intended that it not last forever if the original purpose could not be fulfilled. When no future interest is stated and there is no other express evidence that the settlor intended to benefit only the specific charity identified in the original trust, the courts are likely to substitute a similar charity for the original beneficiary if the trustee brings a lawsuit seeking instructions on what to do with the trust property when it becomes impossible to serve the original beneficiary, and courts increasingly presume general charitable intent unless the trust indicates otherwise.[74]

▶ HARD CASE

▷ DISCRIMINATORY TRUSTS

The *cy pres* doctrine has often been used in the context of discriminatory trusts.[75] For example, in *Trammell v. Elliott*,[76] a trust created a scholarship for "deserving and qualified poor white boys and girls" at a state university in Georgia. The court invalidated the racial limitation on the ground that administration of it by a governmental body violated the equal protection clause in the Constitution. Instead of finding that the trust had therefore failed, the court determined that, as between letting the trust fail and transferring the property back to the trustor's heirs versus striking the discriminatory provision and allowing the trust to continue, the trustor would probably have wanted the trust to continue. It therefore applied the *cy pres* doctrine to rewrite the trust, allowing the income to be used for students of any race.[77] The court noted that there was no evidence to support the notion that the trustor was so committed to the racial discrimination that she would have preferred the trust to fail. Because there is a general public policy to promote charitable trusts, as well as a policy against racial discrimination, this militated in favor of continuing the trust without the discriminatory provision. However, in other cases, courts have found the intent to benefit only one race (or gender) to be crucial to the donor's intent and have allowed the trust to fail entirely when the discriminatory provision could not be legally enforced.[78] ◀

[73] *In re Certain Scholarship Funds*, 575 A.2d 1325, 1329 (N.H. 1990).

[74] *See In re Robert T. Keeler Maint. Fund for Hanover Country Club*, 306 A.3d 795 (N.H. 2023) (discussing how courts generally have approached this question).

[75] *In re Certain Scholarship Funds*, 575 A.2d 1325, 1329 (N.H. 1990) (privately endowed college scholarship for "some poor and worthy Keene boy" reformed under the *cy pres* doctrine to delete the gender limitation); 10-75A *Powell on Real Property* §75A.03.

[76] 199 S.E.2d 194 (Ga. 1973).

[77] *Accord, United States v. Hughes Memorial Home*, 396 F. Supp. 544 (W.D. Va. 1975); *Home for Incurables of Baltimore City v. University of Md. Med. Sys. Corp.*, 797 A.2d 746 (Md. 2002); *Tinnin v. First United Bank of Mississippi*, 502 So. 2d 659 (Miss. 1987), *after remand*, 570 So. 2d 1193 (Miss. 1990); *In re Long's Estate*, 5 Pa. D. & C.3d 602 (1978); *Coffee v. William Marsh Rice University*, 408 S.W.2d 269, 271 (Tex. App. 1966).

[78] *See Evans v. Newton*, 148 S.E.2d 329, 330 (Ga. 1966), *upheld as constitutional by Evans v. Abney*, 396 U.S. 435 (1970). *See also Hermitage Methodist Homes of Virginia, Inc. v. Dominion Trust Co.*, 387 S.E.2d 740 (Va. 1990).

Public policy

It is a separate question whether discriminatory trusts are enforceable. Although government entities cannot administer discriminatory trusts,[79] private discriminatory trusts may be enforceable under the common law of trusts because the law of gifts allows individuals to give gifts to particular individuals or classes of individuals. At the same time, the administration of discriminatory trusts by private universities or charitable institutions may implicate or even violate public accommodations laws.[80]

§7.6.4 *Changed Conditions*

Traditionally applies only to covenants

Traditionally, covenants have been subject to the changed conditions doctrine while future interests have not.[81] The changed conditions doctrine renders a covenant unenforceable, or enforceable by damages alone rather than injunctive relief, if conditions have changed so much that enforcement of the covenant will provide no real benefit to the owner of the dominant estate.[82] Future interests are not subject to this rule. In the covenants context, the rule is justified by the need to free the land from archaic restrictions, especially if a lone owner could block changes in covenants applying to a whole neighborhood. In the context of future interests, the same policies do not apply. If a condition is triggered, then the future interest vests and can become possessory, transferring ownership to the future interest holder and (in the usual case) freeing the property from the restriction. Thus, even if the condition is obsolete, the change in ownership usually gets rid of the restriction on use, and no interference with alienability is involved.

Extending the doctrine to future interests

However, a few courts have applied the changed conditions doctrine to future interests.[83] For example, the trial court in the case of *Prieskorn v. Maloof*[84] applied the changed conditions doctrine to property subject to a reverter clause, which provided that if the land were used for "immoral purposes" or the manufacture or sale of "intoxicating liquors" that the property should revert to the grantor or his successors and assigns.[85] This ruling was overturned on appeal, on the ground that both possibilities of reverter and rights of entry are "estates," which cannot be destroyed by equitable doctrines such as the changed conditions doctrine.[86] This argument distinguishes between future interests and covenants by viewing future interests as property rights and covenants as mere contractual rights. This conceptual distinction is formalistic and unconvincing; the traditional refusal to apply the changed conditions doctrine is better justified on the grounds stated above, *i.e.*, that the existence of the future interest is unlikely to affect alienability because the transfer of ownership usually gets rid of the condition.

[79] *Evans v. Newton*, 382 U.S. 296 (1966).

[80] For more on this topic, see §§6.7.1 & 7.7.5.

[81] *Williamson v. Grizzard*, 387 S.W.2d 807, 809-810 (Tenn. 1965).

[82] *See* §6.8.1.

[83] *Cole v. Colorado Springs Co.*, 381 P.2d 13, 16 (Colo. 1963).

[84] 991 P.2d 511 (N.M. Ct. App. 1999).

[85] *See also El Di, Inc. v. Town of Bethany Beach*, 477 A.2d 1066 (Del. 1984) (applying the changed conditions doctrine to a "covenant" that contained a reverter clause).

[86] 991 P.2d at 516.

Viewing the reverter clause as a remedy

A counterargument, however, is that the reverter clause is intended to affect the behavior of the present estate owner, just as a real covenant does. The reverter is simply a stronger penalty for noncompliance than damages or injunctive relief. If we view the reverter clause as a contractually agreed-upon remedy for violation of a land use restriction, the issue arises whether the remedy is disproportionate to the wrong and whether private parties should be wholly free to determine the appropriate remedies for violation of their agreements. In the ordinary contracts case, specific performance is awarded only if damages are inadequate and only if specific performance does not violate public policy (as it does in the case of service contracts where specific performance smacks of compelled servitude). In addition, liquidated damages provisions in contracts are enforceable only if they are a reasonable estimate of the damages and do not amount to a "penalty" or "forfeiture." If conditions have changed in the neighborhood such that enforcement of a condition is of no substantial benefit to the holder of the future interest, then forfeiture of ownership may seem an unreasonable penalty on the present estate owner.

§7.7 Regulatory Rules

Purposes of regulation

Future interests have long been subject to regulation by common law rules and statutory enactments. These regulations are designed to achieve a variety of purposes. First, many rules are designed to promote the *alienability* of property by destroying or narrowly construing future interests, thereby consolidating power over property in the hands of the holder of the present estate. Promotion of alienability, in turn, both protects the autonomy of the present estate owner (lessening the so-called dead hand of the past) and promotes social welfare by allowing the use and ownership of property to shift over time. These rules attempt to achieve these ends by invalidating certain kinds of future interests that are likely to last too long or that inhibit transfer of the property. Rules designed to promote alienability include (1) the rule against creation of new estates; (2) the rule against unreasonable restraints on alienation; (3) the rule against perpetuities; and (4) the rule abolishing the fee tail.

Alienability

Liberty and equality

Second, future interests have been regulated to promote both *personal freedoms* and *equality*. Racial, religious, and other similar restrictions have often been struck down because they violate equality norms or because they interfere with personal liberties both of property owners and potential owners who wish to purchase property. In addition, restraints on marriage have often been struck down on the ground that they wrongfully inhibit a core individual liberty.

Tensions between fragmentation and consolidation of property rights

These regulatory rules evoke a tension between the policy of allowing owners to transfer property rights on conditions chosen by them and the policy of ensuring that grantees have sufficient powers over their property so that they can use it for their own purposes or transfer it to someone who values it more. Alienability may be promoted by allowing future interests to be created (because the ability to control the property after transfer of ownership may induce the original grantor to part with the property), but it may also be promoted by restricting the ability to create future interests (because this allows freer use and transfer by the grantee).

§7.7.1 *Abolition of Fee Tail*

Abolition The fee tail was an estate that kept property within the family. The fee tail was traditionally created by a conveyance "*to* A *and the heirs of his body.*" This would give a life estate in the property to *A*, with the remainder going to his children for life, then to their children for life, etc., until the line ran out and the property would revert to the grantor or her heirs. It has been abolished everywhere in the United States. If an owner tries to create a fee tail, most states will convert it to a fee simple.[87] The few states that still retain it either interpret it to create a life estate and remainder[88] or grant the current owner the power to turn it into a fee simple by transferring the property in fee simple to another.[89]

Fee simple conditional Before the fee tail was the *fee simple conditional*, an estate that is still recognized in a few jurisdictions.[90] Like the fee tail, the fee simple conditional was created by the words "to *A* and the heirs of his body." It gave a life estate to *A* and a remainder to *A*'s children (who could take as heirs) for life, remainder to their children, etc. However, either *A* or a later owner could convert the estate to a fee simple by transferring it after the birth of children who would be heirs to the owner.[91] If the owner dies survived by such children before making an *inter vivos* transfer of the property, those children would hold the property by fee simple conditional and similarly be able to convey a fee simple after the birth of issue.[92] The English Statute *De Donis Conditionalibus* of 1285 validated the intent of the creator of the fee simple conditional by preventing later owners from converting it to a fee simple. Thus was the fee tail born.

Fee tail The fee tail was different from a life estate because it was impossible to consolidate the future interests and the current estate to create a fee simple. With a life estate, one could buy both the life estate and the remainder and be left with merged interests creating a fee simple. However, with a fee tail, as soon as the current owner died and the property shifted to his heirs, a

[87] Cal. Civ. Code §763; Dale A. Whitman et al., *The Law of Property* §2.10, at 44 (4th ed. 2019). If the conveyance contains a "remainder," about half the states convert that remainder into an executory interest, which is to vest if the first taker dies without lineal descendants. *Id.* In the other states, the first taker would receive a fee simple absolute.

[88] Dale A. Whitman et al., *The Law of Property* §2.10, at 44 (4th ed. 2019).

[89] Colo. Rev. Stat. §38-30-106; Del. Code tit. 25, §302; Me. Rev. Stat. tit. 33, §156; Mass. Gen. Laws ch. 183, §§45 to 47; R.I. Gen. Laws §§34-4-15 to -17; Dale A. Whitman et al., *The Law of Property* §2.10, at 45 (4th ed. 2019).

[90] The fee simple conditional is still recognized in three states (Iowa, Oregon, and South Carolina) and appears to be in substantial use only in South Carolina. *See Prichard v. Department of Revenue*, 164 N.W.2d 113 (Iowa 1969); *Lytle v. Harden*, 275 P. 45 (Or. 1929); *Scarborough v. Scarborough*, 142 S.E.2d 706 (S.C. 1965); Dale A. Whitman et al., *The Law of Property* §2.10, at 45 (4th ed. 2019).

[91] Iowa allows an owner of a fee simple conditional to convert it to a fee simple by devising it to someone other than her children. *Prichard v. Department of Revenue*, 164 N.W.2d 113 (Iowa 1969).

[92] Dale A. Whitman et al., *The Law of Property* §2.10, at 46 (4th ed. 2019).

new remainder would be created in the new owner's heirs. Because a person's heirs cannot be determined until she dies, and because, at her death, a new remainder in the new owner's heirs would be created, there was no way to create a fee simple absolute. This was, of course, the intent of the original donor, who wished to keep the estate in the family and to prevent its profligate transfer outside. The fee tail could be transferred, but the recipient received only a life estate that would shift back to the heirs when the grantor died. This made it difficult to transfer the fee tail or find a willing buyer. If enforced, the fee tail could ensure the perpetuation of a landed estate and protect the family somewhat against a child who might squander the family fortune.

Common recovery

Because the owners of fees tail often wished to transfer the property, they created a bizarre lawsuit, called the "common recovery," to defeat the interests of the future heirs and assemble a fee simple. A.W.B. Simpson describes the common recovery in the following way:

> Suppose Smith to be tenant in tail in possession of Blackacre, which he wishes to sell for a fee simple to Jones. A collusive real action is brought by Jones against Smith on a feigned title, Jones having already paid or agreed to pay Smith for the land. Smith appears in court and vouches one Brown to warranty. Brown does not dispute his obligation to warrant Smith's title, and the action then proceeds between Jones and Brown. Instead of putting up a defense Brown asks for "leave to imparl" — that is, he asks the court for an adjournment whilst he talks the matter over with Jones in the hope of reaching a settlement, and he and Jones leave court to have their imparlance. Brown promptly disappears. This is a contempt of court, and when Jones arrives back before the Justices and tells them that Brown has absconded, they at once give judgment in favor of Jones. The judgment is that Jones recovers the land, and that Brown is to convey to Smith lands of equal value to those recovered. Unfortunately, Brown, who has been carefully selected for this reason (and paid for his trouble), has no land, so that the judgment can never [be] satisfied. If it ever was satisfied, then the land conveyed would be held on the same terms as that lost to Jones; it would be subject to the entail and to any interest in remainder or reversion after Smith's estate. Thus *if the judgment had been satisfied* neither the issue in tail nor the remaindermen or reversioner would suffer any loss, and although everybody knows that it never will be satisfied, the court's view is that it has done its best, and cannot be blamed if Brown is a man of straw. A blind eye is turned to the fact that the whole procedure is an obvious fraud, and neither the issue nor the remaindermen are allowed to do anything about it.[93]

Policies behind the abolition of the fee tail

The fee tail is a form of property ownership, suited to a static society with families who stay at the family home for generations. It is intended to prevent the current owner from selling the property and, if enforceable, would make it impossible *ever* to assemble all the present interests and future interests to consolidate ownership in fee simple. Because the fee tail is owned only for life, the property is not marketable because few

[93] A.W.B. Simpson, *A History of the Land Law* 130 (2d ed. 1986).

developers will want to buy or develop property if ownership will be lost at the death of the seller. The fee tail thus not only inhibits the autonomy of current and potential owners of the property, but substantially harms efficiency by preventing the property from being transferred to a use and a user that value the property more than the current user or use. The fee tail can be understood as efficient only if a society characterized by static family estates redounds to everyone's benefit; this is unlikely now to be the case, if it ever was. The fee tail also shackles the current generation with the wishes of the ancestor who created the family estate. Landed estates are associated with a way of life that is hierarchical, static, and stifling. This is not to say that life estates are necessarily similarly illegitimate; it is the permanency of the fee tail that distinguishes it from the life estate. Nor is this to say that certain forms of property, such as charitable uses, are not legitimately protected by relatively permanent restraints on alienation.[94]

§7.7.2 *Restrictions on New Estates (*Numerus Clausus *Principle)*

No new estates

There is a general rule against the creation of new estates.[95] Scholars may describe this as the *numerus clausus* principle.[96] The leading case is *Johnson v. Whiton*,[97] in which a conveyance "to Sarah A. Whiton and her heirs on her father's side" was construed as a fee simple absolute on the ground that it violated public policy to create an estate that would descend only to the grantee's heirs on one side. The meaning of the estate was not even clear. Was this an attempt to create a kind of fee tail, or was it merely an attempt to limit the class of persons to whom Sarah Whiton could leave the property by will? If it was the former, then it contained all the weaknesses associated with the fee tail. If it was the latter, however, it is not at all clear that it violated public policy. It would probably have been lawful, for example, to grant Whiton a life estate, with a remainder in "such beneficiaries on her father's side as she should appoint by will." At the same time, this conveyance is not necessarily the same as that which the grantor attempted to create in *Johnson v. Whiton*. After all, a life estate is not a fee simple, and it appears that the grantor was attempting to create some form of fee simple.

Promotion of alienability

Aside from the ambiguity in the conveyance, the policy against creating new estates is based on the notion that complicated estates both impede the alienability of property and may constitute illegitimate dead-hand control from the past. Without a general rule prohibiting the creation of new estates, it would be possible to create extraordinarily complicated property arrangements, which may hamper the ability to use the property. A prime example can be seen in fractionated Indian allotments; these are property rights created in the late nineteenth and early twentieth centuries that

[94] In the case of trusts, the trustee can go to court for instructions to change the use of the trust if the original instructions become burdensome or impracticable.
[95] John G. Sprankling, *Understanding Property Law* §9.04, at 113 (5th ed. 2023).
[96] Thomas W. Merrill & Henry E. Smith, *Optimal Standardization in the Law of Property: The* Numerus Clausus *Principle*, 110 Yale L.J. 1 (2000).
[97] 34 N.E. 542 (Mass. 1893).

granted individual tribal members ownership rights over land that were not alienable. Because rights could be inherited but not transferred during life, some allotments came to have thousands of owners, and the management of those properties became extremely cumbersome and expensive, destroying their value to their owners, the tribe, and society as a whole.[98] Structuring property rights in a relatively small set of standard packages arguably reduces information costs by letting buyers know what rights they will acquire when they purchase those packages. It is undeniably useful to categorize property rights as fee simple, defeasible fees, life estates, covenants, easements, mortgages, leases, trusts, marriages, corporations, and partnerships. Standard packages are useful as communication devices because they let grantees know what rights they will acquire unless the governing document states otherwise.

Policy favoring disaggregation

On the other hand, the rule against "new estates" does not clearly achieve the objectives on which it is based. It is partly formal in nature because it is often possible to achieve a particular complex arrangement of current and future interests by manipulating the existing categories. The standard packages do not prevent intricate customization; after all, one can create all kinds of future interests and covenants, and we can alter the terms of mortgages and leases through contract drafting as long as we do not violate statutory or other restrictions. We do not in fact limit ourselves to a small number of packages of property rights; the freedom of contract principle allows covenants, leases, and mortgages to be tailored to the grantor's wishes, and future interests can be defined at will unless a regulatory rule prohibits the arrangement. If it is possible to achieve a result by careful drafting, this means that the law allows the particular arrangement to be created as long as it is done in the right way. The real basis of the rule against creation of new estates is the prohibition of property arrangements that violate articulable public policies, such as the prevention of the re-emergence of feudalism (with individuals tied to land), the promotion of alienability, consumer protection, the prohibition of racial restrictions, and the protection of the autonomy of current generations from the illegitimate dead hand of the past. For this reason, the modern approach focuses on whether a particular arrangement violates substantive public policies rather than whether it violates a standard form. If the package of property rights could be created using available estates, then there is no reason to disallow it, but if the package of rights is not recognized by the legal system for policy reasons, then it should not be allowed no matter what wording or form is used.

§7.7.3 Unreasonable Restraints on Alienation

Forfeiture restraints

Restraints on alienation are limitations on the transfer or sale of property rights.[99] When they trigger future interests, they are called *forfeiture restraints*. For example, a conveyance might grant property from "*O* to *A*

[98] *Babbitt v. Youpee*, 519 U.S. 234 (1997); *Hodel v. Irving*, 481 U.S. 704 (1987).

[99] This topic is covered in more depth at §6.7.2.

and his heirs, but if *A* ever attempts to alienate the property, it shall revert to *O*." Forfeiture restraints on alienation that completely prohibit transfer are almost certainly void when attached to fee simple interests but are likely to be upheld if attached to life estates or leaseholds.[100]

Fee simple interests and life estates compared

Restraints on alienation of fee interests have traditionally been viewed as "repugnant to the fee"[101] because "unlimited power of alienation is one of the essential incidents of a fee-simple estate."[102] This conceptual, circular argument rests on a policy conclusion that, for reasons of both autonomy and social utility, owners should be able to transfer the property freely. This policy allows a market to function and prevents property from being forcibly kept within the family for generations against the wishes of the current owners. Life estates, in contrast, are not very marketable in any event, and forfeiture and promissory restraints on alienation of life estates are usually upheld.[103] They are usually intended to reserve the property for use by a spouse or children, with the remainder going to the next generation. Courts generally find this type of restraint to be valid while more permanent restraints illegitimately tie up the property for a longer period.[104] However, disabling restraints of life estates are likely to be held void because they deprive anyone of the power to waive the restraint.[105]

Partial restraints on alienation

Some courts uphold partial restraints on alienation of fee interests.[106] Restraints are partial if they limit the time period during which the restraint exists or identify a limited class of people to whom the property cannot be transferred. However, other courts find all restraints on alienation of a fee simple to be void if they do not serve a legitimate purpose.[107]

Charitable purposes exception

Restraints on alienation are generally upheld, even as to fee simple interests, if both the present estate and the future interest are held by charities.[108] In such cases, the restraint protects the continued use of the property for charitable purposes. This use is threatened if the property is

[100] *Poppleton v. Village Realty Co., Inc.*, 535 N.W.2d 400 (Neb. 1995); 3-29 *Thompson on Real Property, Third Thomas Edition* §29.04.

[101] *Hankins v. Mathews*, 425 S.W.2d 608, 610 (Tenn. 1968); 3-29 *Thompson on Real Property, Third Thomas Edition* §29.03 ("repugnant to the fee").

[102] 3-29 *Thompson on Real Property, Third Thomas Edition* §29.03(b); *see, e.g., Estate of Cawiezell v. Coronelli*, 958 N.W.2d 842, 845 (Iowa 2021).

[103] Dale A. Whitman et al., *The Law of Property* §2.15, at 58 (4th ed. 2019).

[104] 3-29 *Thompson on Real Property, Third Thomas Edition* §29.03.

[105] *Wise v. Poston*, 316 S.E.2d 412 (S.C. 1984); Dale A. Whitman et al., *The Law of Property* §2.15, at 58 (4th ed. 2019). *But see* §§7.4.4 & 7.4.5 (explaining that remainders in "heirs" are valid in most states despite the fact that such remainders cannot be merged with the life estate to create a fee simple).

[106] *Mardis v. Brantley*, 717 So. 2d 702, 709 (La. Ct. App. 1998) ("A contract purporting to remove property from the stream of commerce totally and perpetually is against public policy, but one placing partial and temporary restraints or conditions on alienation is not"); *Lamar Advertising v. Larry & Vicki Nicholls, LLC*, 213 P.3d 641 (Wyo. 2009); Dale A. Whitman et al., *The Law of Property* §2.2, at 24-25 (4th ed. 2019); 3-29 *Thompson on Real Property, Third Thomas Edition* §29.04.

[107] *See Casey v. Casey*, 700 S.W.2d 46 (Ark. 1985).

[108] *In re Coe College*, 935 N.W.2d 581, 586 (Iowa 2019); *Horse Pond Fish & Game Club, Inc. v. Cormier*, 581 A.2d 478 (N.H. 1990); *see also Canova Land & Inv. Co. v. Lynn*, 856 S.E.2d 581 (Va. 2021) (citing charitable purpose as one reason to uphold a possibility of reverter against a claim that the restriction was an unreasonable restraint on alienation).

freely alienable because the market value of the property can generally be substantially increased if devoted to for-profit, rather than nonprofit, purposes, giving the owner the incentive to abandon the charitable purpose and sell the land for fair market value.

§7.7.4 Rule Against Perpetuities

A complicated rule

In *Lucas v. Hamm*,[109] a lawyer wrote a will that misapplied the rule against perpetuities. If he had written the will correctly, plaintiffs would have gotten the property; because he violated the rule, they did not and were forced to enter settlement negotiations that netted them $75,000 less than they would have received had the will been properly drafted. The disappointed beneficiaries sued the lawyer for negligence. The California Supreme Court dismissed the complaint on the ground the rule against perpetuities is so complicated that many lawyers make mistakes in applying it and "it would not be proper to hold that defendant failed to use such skill, prudence, and diligence as lawyers of ordinary skill and capacity commonly exercise."[110] The decision that a lawyer of ordinary competence cannot be expected to understand and apply the rule against perpetuities correctly has not been followed in other jurisdictions, and is probably no longer the law in California, but it suggests the reason that many law students, lawyers, and judges face the rule with some trepidation. That being said, I should reassure you that the basic application of the rule against perpetuities is easily comprehensible, although its application to complex arrangements does present difficulties.

Traditional rule

The rule against perpetuities invalidates future interests unless they are certain to "vest" or fail to vest within the lifetime of someone who is alive ("in being") at the creation of the interest or no later than 21 years after her death. In John Chipman Gray's famous formulation, "[n]o interest is good unless it must vest, if at all, not later than twenty-one years after the death of some life in being at the creation of the interest."[111] The rule is "designed to prevent remoteness of vesting and thereby leave control of the wealth of the world more in the hands of the living than in the hands of the dead."[112]

Traditional and modern approaches

Every state has reformed the rule in important respects by statute. Half the states have now substantially changed the rule by adopting some form of the *Uniform Statutory Rule Against Perpetuities* and a growing number have abolished the rule in whole or in part.[113] These modern modifications can only be understood against the backdrop of the traditional rule, so that is where we should start.

Interests subject to the rule

The rule against perpetuities regulates *nonvested* interests. The only interests included in this category are (1) executory interests and (2) contingent

[109] 364 P.2d 685 (Cal. 1961).

[110] *Id.* at 690.

[111] John Chipman Gray, *The Rule Against Perpetuities* 191 (4th ed. 1942) (*quoted in* 3-28 *Thompson on Real Property, Third Thomas Edition* §28.02).

[112] 3-28 *Thompson on Real Property, Third Thomas Edition* §28.02.

[113] Lynn Foster, *Fifty-One Flowers: Post-Perpetuities War Law and Arkansas's Adoption of USRAP*, 29 U. Ark. Little Rock L. Rev. 411 (2007).

remainders. A special case traditionally regulated by the rule is (3) vested remainders subject to open because some of the remainders in this category are contingent and some are vested. Interests that have usually been classified as executory interests (and thus subject to regulation by the rule) are (4) options to purchase property[114] and (5) rights of first refusal or preemptive rights.[115] When an interest is "subject to" the rule against perpetuities, this means it must be tested to see if it complies with, or violates, the rule; it does not mean that the interest is necessarily void.

Interests immune from the rule

All interests in the grantor, such as reversions, possibilities of reverter, and rights of entry, are exempt from the rule.[116] Although these interests are immune from the rule against perpetuities, many states have subjected them to special statutory limitations, discussed below.

Definition of terms in the rule

The rule against perpetuities invalidates interests that are not certain to "vest" within 21 years of the death of some "life in being" at the "creation of the interest." The goal is to determine whether there is *any possibility at all* that the executory interest or contingent remainder will vest more than 21 years after the death of everyone alive at the creation of the interest. Let's define these terms.

Creation of the interest

Creation of the Interest. A future interest created by conveyance or *inter vivos* transfer is created at the moment of the sale, delivery of the gift, or when the trust document is signed if the trust is irrevocable, and if it is revocable, at the moment it becomes irrevocable. A future interest created by will is created at the moment the testator dies.

Vest

Vest. Vesting occurs when the condition that made the future interest contingent or uncertain to come into being occurs. An executory interest vests at the moment the contingency occurs. At exactly that same moment, the future interest becomes possessory because the executory interest automatically takes effect when the contingency happens. Thus, in the conveyance "*O* to *A* so long as used for residential purposes, then to *B*," the executory interest in *B* will vest, if ever, at the moment the property is used for nonresidential purposes; at that moment *B* will also gain the right to possess the property. The moment of vesting for a *contingent remainder* is similarly when the condition that makes it a contingent remainder disappears, regardless of whether the remainder becomes possessory at that moment. If, for example, the remainder is contingent because of a condition precedent, the remainder vests when the condition is fulfilled.

[114] *Central Delaware County Authority v. Greyhound Corp.*, 588 A.2d 485 (Pa. 1991). *But see Atlantic Richfield Co. v. Whiting Oil & Gas Corp.*, 320 P.3d 1179 (Colo. 2014) (an option that can be canceled any time before its exercise is not subject to the rule against perpetuities).

[115] *Morrison v. Piper*, 566 N.E.2d 643 (N.Y. 1990), *appeal after remand*, 567 N.Y.S.2d 903 (App. Div. 1991); Dale A. Whitman et al., *The Law of Property* §3.18, at 100-102 (4th ed. 2019).

[116] *Collins v. Church of God Prophecy*, 800 S.W.2d 418 (Ark. 1990) (rule against perpetuities does not apply to possibilities of reverter). *But see Central Delaware County Authority v. Greyhound Corp.*, 588 A.2d 485 (Pa. 1991) (classifying a grantor's repurchase right as an executory interest rather than a right of entry and invalidating it under the rule against perpetuities). Interests in the grantor may be subject to special statutory rules that cut off the interest if it does not vest within a specified period. *E.g.*, Mass. Gen. Laws ch. 184A, §5; N.C. Gen. Stat. §41-29.

In the conveyance "*O* to *A* for life, then to *B* if *B* graduates from law school," the contingent remainder in *B* becomes vested when *B* graduates from law school, even if *A* is still alive; it will not become possessory in *B* until *A*'s death. In the conveyance "*O* to *A* for life, then to the first child of *B*," the contingent remainder in *B* becomes vested the moment *B* has a child; however, *B*'s child will gain possession only after *A* dies.

Lives in being

Lives in Being. The rule requires us to determine whether there is any chance the interest could vest more than 21 years after the deaths of everyone alive at the creation of the interest. The easiest way to apply the rule is to look for a "validating life." A validating life is someone within whose lifetime (or 21 years afterward) the future interest is certain to vest *if it ever vests*. If you cannot identify a validating life, the future interest is void. Corporations are not counted as "lives in being." In a conveyance "from *O* to *X* Hospital so long as used for hospital purposes, then to *B*," the only possible validating lives are those of *O* and *B*. The hospital is not counted as a life in being.

Perpetuities period

The "perpetuities period" is the time within which the interest must vest if it is to be upheld as good under the rule. That period begins at the creation of the interest and ends 21 years after the death of every person alive at the creation of the interest.

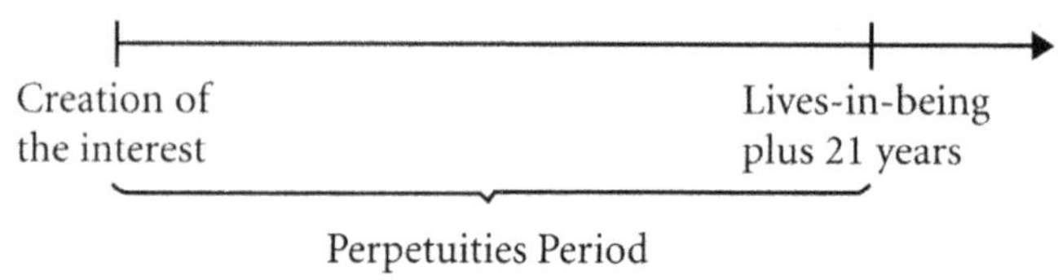

The question is whether there is any chance the interest will vest outside the perpetuities period.

Applying the rule

The rule can be best understood by applying it.

Interests in the grantor

Interests in the Grantor. Future interests in the grantor or her heirs are exempt from the rule against perpetuities. For example:

> 1. O *to* A *as long as used for residential purposes.* The possibility of reverter in *O* is exempt from the rule against perpetuities and the interest is good.
>
> 2. O *to* A *for life.* The reversion in *O* is exempt from the rule against perpetuities and the interest is good.

Executory interests

Executory Interests. Executory interests are subject to the rule against perpetuities. The main exception is that the rule does not apply if both the present estate owner and the future interest owner are charities. Because executory interests are subject to the rule, they are void unless they are certain to vest within 21 years of the death of some person alive at the creation of the interest. This means that executory interests are invalid unless they are limited in time. Moreover, the time limit must ensure that vesting, if it will ever occur, will happen within "lives in being plus 21 years." For example:

3. O *to* A *as long as used for residential purposes, then to* B. Because *A* owns a fee simple subject to executory limitation, the estate is inheritable and devisable and could last forever. It could also be used for residential purposes for 1,000 years, long after *O*, *A*, *B*, and everyone else alive at the creation of the interest has died and 21 years have passed. Because there is a possibility the executory interest in *B* may vest too far into the future, it is void. The traditional remedy is to strike out the words "then to *B*," leaving the words "O *to* A *as long as used for residential purposes.*" This is a recognizable estate (a fee simple determinable) and the possibility of reverter in *O* is immune from the rule and thus is good. Some courts, however, may strike out the whole condition, leaving *A* with a fee simple absolute.

4. O *to* A, *but if the property is ever used for nonresidential purposes, then to* B. *B*'s executory interest is invalid for the same reasons it was invalid in example #3, above. However, the remedy traditionally has been different. One cannot strike out only the words "then to *B*" because what is left is not a recognizable estate; it contains a "but if" clause, but then does not say what happens if the condition is fulfilled. The wording of example #3 implied that the present estate would automatically terminate and revert to *O* as a possibility of reverter. Because this wording in example #4 cannot support that result, the courts traditionally struck out all the language after "*O* to *A*" and *A* would be left with a fee simple absolute rather than a fee simple determinable as in example #3. The difference is a formal one and does not have any real policy justification because the two conveyances are otherwise functionally identical. For this reason, some scholars and courts have suggested that the two cases should be treated alike, one way or the other.[117] If the policy behind the rule is to cut off future interests that may come into being too far into the future, it would seem sensible to treat possibilities of reverter like executory interests. If the executory interest is problematic because it may vest and become possessory 1,000 years into the future, the same can be said of the possibility of reverter in *O*, even if it was traditionally considered already "vested." In that case, the appropriate remedy for both example #3 and #4 would be to strike the interest in *B* and leave *A* with a fee simple absolute.

5. O *to* A, *but if the property is used for nonresidential purposes within 21 years of this conveyance, then to* B. The executory interest in *B* is subject to the rule against perpetuities, but it does not violate it because it will vest, if ever, within 21 years of the conveyance and thus within 21 years of all lives in being at the creation of the interest. If vesting ever occurs, it will be within the perpetuities period even if everyone in the world died the day after the conveyance; the time limit prevents vesting later than 21 years after creation of the interest.

Contingent remainders

Contingent Remainders. Contingent remainders are harder to analyze than executory interests. The trick is to search for a validating life. If the interest is certain to vest within the lifetime of one of the named individuals (or no later than 21 years after they have died), then it does not violate the rule and it will be good. For example:

117 *See* T.P. Gallanis, *The Future of Future Interests*, 60 Wash. & Lee L. Rev. 513, 520-523 (2003).

> 6. O *to* A *for life, then to* B *if* B *marries* C. *B*'s interest is a contingent remainder because there is a condition precedent that must take place before the interest could vest. The contingent remainder in *B* is good whether or not the jurisdiction has abrogated the rule of destructibility of contingent remainders.[118] In a state that allows contingent remainders to be destroyed, *B*'s interest will be lost forever if *B* does not marry before *A* dies. Thus, it will vest, if at all, within *A*'s lifetime and thus is good. If contingent remainders are not destructible, and *B* has not married before *A* dies, then the property reverts to *O* as a fee simple subject to executory limitation, and the property will spring to *B if B* marries *C*. The interest in *B* will vest, if ever, when *B* marries *C*; because this must happen during the lifetime of both *B* and *C*, both of whom were lives in being at the creation of the interest, then there is no chance the interest will vest more than 21 years after the death of some life in being at the creation of the interest.
>
> 7. O *to* A *for life, then to the children of* B. If *B* is alive at the time of the conveyance from *O* to *A* and *B* has children at that time, those children have a vested remainder subject to open. Their interest is subject to the rule against perpetuities but does not violate it because their interest will vest when *A* dies, the class will close and there is no possibility the interest will vest more than 21 years after the death of *A*, a life in being at the creation of the interest.

If *B* has no children at the time of the conveyance, they have a contingent remainder because they are not ascertainable at that time. The remainder will vest when *B* has a child and *B* must have a child within *B*'s lifetime (or nine months after *B*'s death if *B* is a man).[119] Of course, new reproductive technologies render this traditional assumption — that people can only have children during their lifetimes or shortly thereafter — more than problematic!

If *B* has a child before *A* dies, the remainder will vest and be "subject to open" because *B* could have more children.[120] If *A* dies before *B*, the class of children will close at that point and title will shift to the children of *B*. Their interest is good because it vests right after *A*'s death. If *A* dies before *B* has had a child, and contingent remainders are destructible, the children's interest will fail and *O* (or *O*'s heirs or devisees) will have a fee simple. If contingent remainders are indestructible, as they are in almost all states, the property will revert to *O* (or *O*'s heirs or devisees) as a reversion subject to the interest in the children of *B*. If *B* has a child, title will spring from *O* to *B's* child. The interest in the "children of *B*" will vest, if at all, either right after *A* dies (if a child has been born before *A* died) or within the lifetime of *B* (if *A* dies before *B* and the property reverts to *O* and *B* then has a child and the property springs to that child). If *B* dies childless before *A* dies, the

[118] This rule provides that contingent remainders are "destroyed" if they do not vest immediately after the natural termination of the prior estate. This rule has been abolished almost everywhere. *See* §7.4.3.

[119] The traditional rule actually should read "lives-in-being-plus-21-years *and nine months*" because the courts allowed for the time associated with gestation.

[120] Under the *rule of convenience*, the class of children will close when *A* dies and the children of *B* at that point will get the remainder even if *B* is still alive and could have more children.

property goes to *O* as a reversion at *A*'s death; if *B* dies childless after *A* dies, *O*'s reversion becomes a fee simple absolute.

> 8. O *to* A *for life, then to the first child of* B *to be elected President of the United States*. Whether or not *B* has children at the time of the conveyance, *B* could have a daughter who would be born after the conveyance, so she is not a life in being at the creation of the interest; she could become president more than 21 years after the death of *O*, *A*, *B*, and any children of *B* (and anyone else in the world) alive at the creation of the interest, so the contingent remainder in *B*'s child violates the rule against perpetuities. There is no validating life here; there is no one alive at the creation of the interest within whose life (or 21 years later) it is certain that the interest will vest. Because the remainder is void, it is struck out, leaving "*O* to *A* for life"; *O* has a reversion that is not subject to the rule.

Well-known traps

There are some well-known, and rather humorous, traps that have been studied by generations of law students.

Unborn widow

Unborn Widow. The first is the "unborn widow." A conveyance from "*O* to *A* for life, remainder to *A*'s widow for life, remainder to *A*'s surviving children" creates a contingent remainder in *A*'s surviving children that violates the traditional rule against perpetuities because *A* could marry someone who was born after the conveyance from *O* to *A*; such a person is not a life in being at the creation of the interest and cannot serve as a measuring life who could validate the interest in her children. Even though she may not be a life in being at the creation of the interest, her remainder is good because it will vest, if at all, when *A* dies. However, she may live longer than 21 years after the deaths of *A* and *O* (and everyone else alive at the creation of the interest) and thus her children's interests may vest outside the perpetuities period. This assumes that "*A*'s surviving children" means "the children of *A* and *A*'s widow living at the time of *A*'s widow's death." The requirement that they "survive" means that there is a condition precedent to their interest vesting; they must survive the death of *A*'s widow. If the conveyance did not require them to survive *A*'s widow, their interests would vest when *A* died (even though they would not become possessory until the death of *A*'s widow). The requirement that they survive *A*'s widow delays their vesting because it creates a condition precedent to their being entitled to the interest; this requirement means that their interest may vest more than 21 years after the death of *A*.

Fertile octogenarian

Fertile Octogenarian. If *O* grants property to "*A* for life, remainder to *A*'s grandchildren," the assumption has always been that *A* could have more children until she dies, even if she is 80 years old. This assumption used to be humorous, but new reproductive technologies make it perfectly plausible today; imagine a frozen embryo of hers implanted in another woman who bears her child. The contingent remainder in the grandchildren (or vested remainder subject to open if there are grandchildren at the conveyance from *O* to *A*) violates the rule because *A* could have a child after the creation of the interest and that child could have a child more than 21 years after the death of *A* (and everyone else alive at the creation of the interest). *A*'s children alive at the time of the creation of the interest could all predecease *A*, with the property going back to *O* as a reversion. If the after-born child has a child more than 21 years later, the interest will have vested too remotely. Thus, the remainder violates the rule and is invalid.

The endless will contest

The Endless Will Contest. "*O* to *A* for life, then to *B* after *A*'s will is probated." The will contest could last for years—certainly more than 21 years after everyone alive at the creation of the interest has died—and the contingent remainder in *B* is void.

Drafting around the rule

Because interests retained by grantors are immune from the rule against perpetuities, a clever drafter can often avoid the rule in two ways. First, rather than convey an executory interest, the grantor should convey a fee simple determinable to the intended present estate holder and then transfer (in a separate transaction) the grantor's retained possibility of reverter to the third party to whom the grantor had wished to create an executory interest. So, instead of "*O* to *A* as long as used for residential purposes, then to *B*," *O* should convey "to *A* as long as used for residential purposes" and in a separate transaction, *O* should convey her retained possibility of reverter to *B*. Alternatively, *O* could convey a fee simple absolute to *B*; *B* could then convey a fee simple determinable to *A*, keeping a possibility of reverter for herself.

Wait-and-see

Some states modernized the traditional rule against perpetuities by waiting to determine whether an interest is valid until it either vests or the perpetuities period ends.[121] Under the traditional rule, a future interest is void if any possibility exists that it will vest outside the perpetuities period even if it in fact vests within the perpetuities period. This can be determined at the moment the interest is created. In contrast, under the "wait-and-see" test, the courts will not hold that a future interest violates the rule until the perpetuities period has passed and they are certain that the future interest has not vested within that period. For example, if *O* grants *A* property "so long as used for residential purposes, then to *B*," the executory interest in *B* is void under the traditional rule because it may vest too far into the future. In contrast, under the wait-and-see test, the courts identify a set of measuring lives (usually limited to persons named in the conveyance and intervening generations) and then determine whether the perpetuities period has run (in which case the interest is destroyed) or if the interest has vested within the perpetuities period. If *O*, *A*, and *B* die, and 21 years pass and the restriction on use has never been violated, then the perpetuities period has passed and the interest is void. If, however, the restraint on use is violated within the lifetime of *O*, *A*, or *B* (or within 21 years after their death(s)), then the interest is good, and it will both vest and become possessory.

Cy pres or equitable reformation

A conveyance may violate the rule against perpetuities because it contains an age limit greater than 21. For example, "*O* to *A* for life, then to the first child of *B* to attain 25 years of age," creates a contingent remainder in the first child of *B* to reach 25 (assuming *B* has no children at the time of the initial conveyance who have reached age 25). This remainder violates the rule because a child could be born after the conveyance and reach age 25 more than 21 years after the deaths of *O*, *A*, and *B*. Under the *cy pres*

[121] Iowa Code §558.68; Mo. Stat. §442.555; Ohio Rev. Code §2131.08.

doctrine (also called the doctrine of *equitable reformation*), a court may reduce the age contingency of 25 to 21 if this will validate the future interest.[122] In this case it will because, if any child of *B* is ever going to reach 21 years old, it will have to happen within 21 years of the death of *B*,[123] who is a life in being at the creation of the interest. Because the reduction in age in the conveyance from 25 to 21 saves the future interest, this test will reduce the age contingency to 21 and validate the future interest.

Implying a time limit on options to purchase

Options to purchase that contain no time limits are likely to violate the rule against perpetuities.[124] However, a court eager to preserve the option may interpret it to last for only a "reasonable" period that is sufficiently short to validate the option under the rule against perpetuities and thus better comply with the intent of the parties.[125] This is an application of the *cy pres* doctrine used in trust law to interpret a trust to achieve a purpose similar to that intended by the donor when the specified purpose is no longer achievable.[126]

Exceptions to the rule

Several exceptions to the rule against perpetuities have long existed and some new ones have recently arisen. First, recall that all interests in the grantor are immune from the rule. This is less an exception than a reminder that the rule does not even apply to them. Second, future interests are immune from the rule if both the present estate and the future interest are held by charities.[127] Third, some courts have recently held that *options to purchase* are immune from the rule (as are options to renew leases) if they are contained within a lease, giving the tenant the right to buy the reversion.[128] They have so held on the ground that such options do not "hinder alienability of the land" and "promotes tenant land improvements."[129] However, the rule will apply if the option is exercisable after the lease ends or if it partially applies to property that is not subject to a lease.[130] Fourth,

[122] 3-28 *Thompson on Real Property, Third Thomas Edition* §28.08.
[123] What do new reproductive technologies do to this argument? They rob it of its logic. Because both sperm and eggs can be preserved after death (not to mention frozen embryos), and implanted in someone else, it is possible for both men and women to "have a child" after they have died.
[124] *See Caruso v. Young*, 582 S.W.3d 634 (Tex. App. 2019) (invalidating option to purchase in lease); *Heritage Homes of De La Warr, Inc. v. Alexander*, 2005 WL 2173992 (Del. Ch. Sept. 1, 2005), *aff'd*, 900 A.2d 100 (Del. 2006) (option to purchase with no time limit void under traditional rule against perpetuities).
[125] *See, e.g., Broach v. City of Hampton*, 677 S.W.2d 851 (Ark. 1984) (interpreting an option to purchase to last only as long as the life of the grantee to validate it under the rule against perpetuities); *Reynolds v. Gagen*, 739 N.Y.S.2d 704 (App. Div. 2002) (interpreting an option to last for the lives of the parties and thus not to violate the rule against perpetuities).
[126] *See* §7.6.3 above.
[127] *United States on Behalf of U.S. Coast Guard v. Cerio*, 831 F. Supp. 530 (E.D. Va. 1993); *Smith v. Renne*, 46 N.E.2d 587 (Ill. 1943); 3-28 *Thompson on Real Property, Third Thomas Edition* §28.05.
[128] *Texaco Refining and Marketing, Inc. v. Samowitz*, 570 A.2d 170 (Conn. 1990); *Murphy Exploration & Production Co. v. Sun Operating Limited Partnership*, 747 So. 2d 260 (Miss. 1999). *Cf. Bleecker St. Tenants Corp. v. Bleeker Jones LLC*, 945 N.E.2d 484 (N.Y. 2001) (rule against perpetuities does not apply to options to renew a lease).
[129] Dale A. Whitman et al., *The Law of Property* §3.18, at 101 (4th ed. 2019).
[130] *Symphony Space, Inc. v. Pergola Properties, Inc.*, 669 N.E.2d 799 (N.Y. 1996) (rule against perpetuities does not apply to options in leases but does where the option also applies to property that is not subject to the lease).

many courts have held that rights of first refusal held by condominium associations or by other condominium unit owners are exempt from the rule against perpetuities.[131] Some courts have gone further and held that all preemptive rights are exempt from the rule.[132]

Statutory cut-offs for possibilities of reverter and rights of entry

The rule against perpetuities does not apply to rights of entry or possibilities of reverter. The common law courts in England treated these interests as vested from the very beginning because they defined interests in the grantor that were reserved when the present estate was created. Yet as a matter of public policy, it makes no sense to worry about executory interests because of the problem of dead-hand control while deferring to future interests in the heirs of the grantor that could similarly vest 300 years in the future. This is especially true considering the ability often to evade the rule against perpetuities by careful drafting. For these reasons, some states have passed statutes that cut off interests in the grantor following defeasible fees if the condition does not occur within a stated time period after the initial conveyance. In a typical statute, Massachusetts provides that possibilities of reverter and rights of entry are destroyed if they do not vest within 30 years of their creation.[133]

Marketable title acts

Some states have marketable title statutes requiring that future interests be re-recorded periodically in the local registry of deeds (typically every 30 or 40 years) to remain valid and enforceable.[134] Statutes that effectively nullify future interests have often been challenged on the ground that they constitute a taking of property without just compensation. Such statutes are ordinarily upheld if they give owners sufficient time (and notice) to re-record.[135]

Uniform Statutory Rule Against Perpetuities (USRAP)

A uniform law has substantially changed the rule against perpetuities in half the states. The *Uniform Statutory Rule Against Perpetuities* (*USRAP*), adopted in about half the states,[136] does two important things. First, it exempts all future interests in commercial transactions from the rule. The effect of this provision is to limit application of the rule against perpetuities to donative transfers.[137] These transfers could be either charitable or familial, *inter vivos* or testamentary (at death).[138] The statute also exempts any transfers in which the present and future interests are both held by

[131] *Cambridge Co. v. East Slope Investment Co.*, 700 P.2d 537 (Colo. 1985).

[132] *Bortolotti v. Hayden*, 866 N.E.2d 882 (Mass. 2007). *See Restatement (Third) Property (Servitudes)* §3.3 (adopting this position).

[133] Mass. Gen. Laws Ann. ch. 184A, §7. *See also* 765 Ill. Comp. Stat. 330/4 (40 years); Neb. Rev. Stat. §76-107 (30 years); N.C. Gen. Stat. §41-32 (60 years).

[134] *See, e.g.*, Cal. Civ. Code §§880.020 to 887.090; Iowa Code §614.24.

[135] *Compare Severns v. Union Pac. R.R. Co.*, 125 Cal. Rptr. 2d 100 (Ct. App. 2002) (upholding the validity of the California statute) *and Trustees of Schools of Township No. 1 v. Batdorf*, 130 N.E.2d 111 (Ill. 1955) (upholding the validity of the Illinois statute) *and Presbytery of Southeast Iowa v. Harris*, 226 N.W.2d 232 (Iowa 1975) *with Board of Education v. Miles*, 207 N.E.2d 181 (N.Y. 1965) (holding invalid the New York statute).

[136] *See, e.g.*, Ga. Code §§44-6-200 to 44-6-206; Mass. Gen. Laws ch. 190B, §§2-901 to 2-906; Mich. Comp. Laws §§554.71 to 554.78; Or. Rev. Stat. §§105.950 to 105.975.

[137] Some states did not adopt this provision, continuing to apply the rule against perpetuities to commercial options. *See Buck v. Banks*, 668 N.E.2d 1259 (Ind. Ct. App. 1996); *Bel-Aire, Inc. v. RB Trexlertown, LLC*, 2005 WL 2335372 (Va. Cir. Ct. 2005).

[138] U.P.C. §2-904.

charities.[139] Second, the statute creates a wait-and-see period of 90 years for all interests that would otherwise be void under the traditional rule. Such interests are good, even though they violate the traditional rule, as long as they vest within 90 years of the date of the creation of the interest. The 90-year wait-and-see provision applies only to interests that would have been invalid under the traditional rule. If an interest violates the 90-year wait-and-see period, the statute authorizes the courts to reform the deed, will, or trust in the manner that most closely approximates the transferor's manifested plan of distribution and is within the allowable 90-year period.

Statutory cut-offs for options to purchase and preemptive rights

Because the *USRAP* exempts commercial transactions from the rule against perpetuities, some states have passed statutes limiting the time period during which future interests in such transactions will be valid. North Carolina and Massachusetts, for example, have passed statutory wait-and-see periods of 30 years for options and preemptive rights.[140]

Abolition of the rule

At least a dozen states have abolished or substantially altered the rule against perpetuities. They have done so to allow the creation of so-called dynasty trusts of either real or personal property; such trusts generate income for the beneficiaries in perpetuity (or at any rate for a very long time) and take advantage of federal tax code provisions that make the gift tax-free.[141] Some states have abolished the rule against perpetuities either directly, as in states like Idaho, Rhode Island, New Jersey, and South Dakota,[142] or indirectly by adopting a very long perpetuities period.[143] Others have abolished the rule for personal property but kept it for real property.[144] Still other states have reformed the rule by allowing trusts with unvested future interests to last forever but have limited the time period during which the power of alienation of the trust corpus (the property giving rise to the income) can be suspended; this ensures that the property can become alienable after the perpetuities period.[145] Some states have kept the rule unless the grantor expressly opts out of it, in which case they limit the time during which the power of alienation can be suspended.[146] Some states have abolished the rule as long as the trustee retains the power to alienate

[139] *Id.* at §2-904(5). *Accord, Uniform Statutory Rule Against Perpetuities* §4(5).

[140] Mass. Gen. Laws ch. 184A, §5; N.C. Stat. §41-29. *Cf.* 765 Ill. Comp. Stat. 305/4(a)(7) (40-year limit). *See* Ronald C. Link & Kimberly A. Licata, *Perpetuities Reform in North Carolina: The Uniform Statutory Rule Against Perpetuities, Nondonative Transfers, and Honorary Trusts*, 74 N.C. L. Rev. 1783 (1996).

[141] T.P. Gallanis, *The Future of Future Interests*, 60 Wash. & Lee L. Rev. 513, 516-520, 554-560 (2003); Garrett Moritz, *Dynasty Trusts and the Rule Against Perpetuities*, 116 Harv. L. Rev. 2588 (2003).

[142] Idaho Code §55-111; R.I. Gen. Laws §34-11-38; N.J. Stat. §46:2F-9; S.D. Codified Laws §43-5-8.

[143] Colo. Rev. Stat. §15-11-1102.5 (1,000 years); Wash. Rev. Code §11.98.130 (150 years).

[144] Del. Code tit. 25, §503 (requires distribution of the corpus of a trust of real property after 110 years); *Cornell Glasgow, LLC v. LaGrange Properties, LLC*, 2012 WL 3157124 (Del. Super. Ct. 2012) (applying the traditional rule to real property).

[145] *See, e.g.*, Alaska Stat. §34.27.100(a); Ariz. Rev. Stat. §14-2901(A)(3); N.J. Stat. §46:2F-10; S.D. Codified Laws §43-5-1, -2.

[146] *E.g.*, Md. Code Est. & Trusts §11-102(b)(5); Ohio Rev. Code §2131.09(B).

the trust corpus.[147] Finally, some states have abolished the rule but required the trust corpus to be distributed within a set time period.[148]

Rule against unreasonable restraints on alienation

It is important to recall that the states that have abolished or substantially altered the rule against perpetuities have not abolished the common law rule against unreasonable restraints on alienation. It is therefore possible for an interest to be valid under the rule against perpetuities but invalid as an unreasonable restraint on alienation.[149]

▶ HARD CASE ▷ RIGHTS OF FIRST REFUSAL

As noted above, courts have routinely exempted *preemptive rights* or *rights of first refusal* from the rule against perpetuities in the context of condominiums. Note that half the states do so under the *USRAP* through exempting *all* non-donative transfers from the rule. Other courts have done so as a matter of common law. In *Cambridge Co. v. East Slope Investment Corp.*,[150] for example, the Supreme Court of Colorado upheld a right of first refusal that provided that any condominium unit owner who desired to sell and received a *bona fide* third-party offer should offer the unit to the remaining owners, who would have the opportunity to match the offer and buy the unit in place of the third party. Justice Dubofsky argued that the rule against perpetuities was intended to promote the alienability of property and that units subject to a right of first refusal were marketable at fair market value because the owner is entitled to whatever price she can get on the market. The counterargument is that the very existence of the preemptive right is likely to deter bids on the property and therefore depress the price.[151] A response to this counterargument is that owners of units are benefited, as well as harmed, by such rights because they own such rights with respect to neighboring condominium units. For this reason, and because the existence of the right will not completely prevent third-party bids, the property is likely to be transferable in the marketplace even if the price is depressed to some extent by the existence of the right. It is important to recall that the buyers of the condominium knew about the right when they purchased and, if it reduced the value of the property, probably paid less for it initially and thus lose nothing by its existence when they want to sell.[152] ◀

[147] *E.g.*, Wis. Stat. §700.16(5).

[148] *E.g.*, Del. Code tit. 25, §503(b).

[149] *See, e.g., Gray v. Vandver*, 623 S.W.2d 172 (Tex. App. 1981) (invalidating a time-unlimited right of first refusal in the grantors for $175 as an unreasonable restraint on alienation when the interest may have been valid under the rule against perpetuities); *Restatement (Third) of Property (Servitudes)* §3.4 cmts. e & f (2000) (noting that options to purchase are subject to the rule against unreasonable restraints on alienation).

[150] 700 P.2d 537 (Colo. 1985).

[151] It is also the case that the purpose of the rule is not just to promote alienability but to limit dead-hand control of the past. This control is not so significant in the context of preemptive rights because it is neighbors, rather than the grantor, who exercise control over the rights in question.

[152] *Cf. Martin v. Seeley*, 142 N.Y.S.3d 252 (App. Div. 2021) (right of first refusal valid under the rule against perpetuities because it could be exercised only by the original holder).

§7.7.5 *Racial Restrictions*

▷ DO AUTOMATIC FORFEITURES INVOLVE STATE ACTION? **HARD CASE** ◀

When the Supreme Court struck down racially restrictive covenants in 1948 in the case of *Shelley v. Kraemer*,[153] it did so because enforcement of covenants constitutes "state action" that deprives individuals of equal protection of the law by preventing them, because of their race, from purchasing property. When "state action" is not involved, as when an owner refuses to sell her own property to someone because of that person's race, the equal protection clause has been found not to be implicated.[154] Because reverter clauses are said to operate "automatically," a number of courts have held that no state action is involved when a racially restrictive condition is violated and an automatic possibility of reverter or executory interest is triggered, even if a lawsuit is brought to compel the present estate owner to honor the forfeiture.[155] But at least one court has held that enforcement of a racially discriminatory automatic forfeiture provision violates the equal protection clause.[156] ◀

▷ ARE FORFEITURES DISCRIMINATORY IF THEY RESULT IN FREEING THE PROPERTY FROM THE RESTRICTION? **HARD CASE** ◀

In *Evans v. Abney*,[157] property was donated in trust to a city for use as a public park, but its use was restricted to white persons. When it was held that it was unconstitutional for the city to operate a racially restricted park,[158] the Georgia Supreme Court held that the *cy pres* doctrine did not apply to the

[153] 334 U.S. 1 (1948). *See* §6.7.1.

[154] 334 U.S. at 13 ("the restrictive agreements standing alone cannot be regarded as a violation of any rights guaranteed to petitioners by the Fourteenth Amendment. So long as the purposes of those agreements are effectuated by voluntary adherence to their terms, it would appear clear that there has been no action by the State and the provisions of the Amendment have not been violated").

[155] *Charlotte Park and Recreation Commission v. Barringer*, 88 S.E.2d 114 (N.C. 1955) (no state action when possibility of reverter is triggered by violation of a racial condition). *But see Capitol Federal Savings and Loan Ass'n v. Smith*, 316 P.2d 252 (Colo. 1957) (holding that enforcement of an automatic executory interest would constitute state action in contravention of the equal protection clause).

[156] *Capitol Federal Savings and Loan Ass'n v. Smith*, 316 P.2d 252 (Colo. 1957). *See* Isaac Saidel-Goley & Joseph William Singer, *Things Invisible to See: State Action and Private Property*, 5 Tex. A&M L. Rev. 439 (2018) (reviewing state action doctrine and arguing that from a property perspective the critical constitutional question should be whether a state's laws provide for equal treatment in a free and democratic society's spheres of social life).

[157] 396 U.S. 435 (1970).

[158] *See also Pennsylvania v. Board of Directors of City Trusts of Philadelphia*, 353 U.S. 230 (1957) (holding that the administration of a discriminatory trust by an agency of the Commonwealth of Pennsylvania, benefiting poor, male, white orphans, was constitutionally impermissible); *In re Crichfield Trust*, 426 A.2d 88, 89 (N.J. Super. Ct. Ch. Div. 1980) (holding that state officials may not administer discriminatory trusts; gender limitation removed through use of *cy pres* doctrine).

trust, because the donor had clearly intended to engage in racial discrimination and the court believed the donor would have preferred the entire trust to fail rather than allow the park to be integrated. The U.S. Supreme Court upheld the constitutionality of the reversionary interests in the heirs after failure of the trust on the ground that reversion of the property to the grantor's heirs did not constitute discriminatory state action because, once the property reverted to the heirs, the discrimination would cease.[159]

Dissenting opinion

Justice Brennan argued, in dissent, that a judicial ruling that a public park should be closed and ownership transferred to a donor's heirs because of that donor's objections to racial integration constituted state action that deprived Black citizens of equal protection of the law. There was no dispute that a city could not constitutionally own or operate a segregated park and, in his view, "a State may not close down a public facility solely to avoid its duty to desegregate that facility"[160] because the closing of a public facility that "would remain open but for the constitutional command that it be operated on a non-segregated basis, the closing of that facility conveys an unambiguous message of community involvement in racial discrimination,"[161] even though the intent to discriminate originates in the mind of the private donor rather than public authorities. The Supreme Court rejected Justice Brennan's argument, however, and held the next year in *Palmer v. Thompson*[162] that a city could constitutionally close a public pool to avoid operating it in a nonsegregated manner. ◀

§7.7.6 *Restraints on Marriage*

Traditionally void

Restraints on marriage were traditionally held to be void. Thus, in a conveyance or devise from "*O* to *A*, but if *A* marries, then to *B*," the restraint on marriage would be struck down, leaving *A* with a fee simple absolute.[163] This rule was based on the notion that "marriage is society's method of initiating a family relationship" and that "the social consequences that would follow a successful endeavor to restrain the entering into that relationship justify strict regulation of such attempts."[164] Some states retain this rule as a matter of common law.[165] Some states have statutes that render void any restraints that are intended to prevent the donee from marrying at all.[166]

Void unless designed to provide support

However, the *Restatement (Second) of Property (Donative Transfers)*, published in 1983, provides that restraints on first marriages are "normally

[159] A similar approach was taken in *Hermitage Methodist Homes of Virginia, Inc. v. Dominion Trust Co.*, 387 S.E.2d 740 (Va. 1990).
[160] 396 U.S. at 453 (Brennan, J., dissenting).
[161] *Id.* at 453-454 (Brennan, J., dissenting).
[162] 403 U.S. 217 (1971).
[163] 10-78 *Powell on Real Property* §78.02; *see also Restatement (Second) of Property (Donative Transfers)* §6.1 (1983).
[164] 10-78 *Powell on Real Property* §78.02[1].
[165] *Beechler v. Beechler*, 641 N.E.2d 1189 (Ohio Ct. App. 1994).
[166] Ga. Code §19-3-6 ("Marriage is encouraged by the law. Every effort to restrain or discourage marriage by contract, condition, limitation, or otherwise shall be invalid and void, provided that prohibitions against marriage to a particular person or persons or before a certain reasonable age or other prudential provisions looking only to the interest of the person to be benefited and not in general restraint of marriage will be allowed and held valid").

valid" if "the dominant motive of the transferor is to provide support until marriage."[167] This new formulation invalidates restraints on marriage if the purpose (or "motive") of the donor is to prevent the donee from getting married but validates them if the donor intends to provide support until marriage.[168] This approach is problematic because it focuses on the intent of the grantor and that intent is often not ascertainable from the document itself; moreover, extrinsic evidence will be hard to find or assess, especially if the grantor has died. This means that the *Restatement (Second)* approach will only work if a presumption is adopted to adjudicate uncertain cases. Because most donors are not likely to want the donee not to get married, the courts are likely to interpret the *Restatement (Second)* principle to validate restraints on marriage unless evidence to the contrary exists. The result is that the *Restatement (Second)* approach is more likely to validate such restraints than the traditional rule. At the same time, the traditional approach is in tension with an even older approach that would allow owners to place substantial restrictions on whom the transferee can marry.[169]

The argument for validity

The argument in favor of validity is that restraints on marriage, unlike restraints on alienation, are legitimate for several reasons. First, if the restraint was made in an *inter vivos* conveyance, then the grantee expressly or impliedly agreed to it. Second, if it was made in a will, then the donee has no claim to greater rights than the deceased gave her. In general, individuals are allowed to determine to whom to leave their property. The major exception to this principle is that most states have laws that protect surviving spouses by ensuring their continued occupancy of the family house (*homestead laws*) and some portion of the property owned by the spouse at the time of death (*statutory forced share statutes*).[170] If none of those laws is at issue, then the decedent could have chosen to dispossess the donee entirely; receiving property that is limited by a restraint gives the donee more than she would have received if she had not been mentioned in the will at all. The greater power to leave the donee nothing arguably includes the lesser power to condition ownership in certain respects. For that reason, the Illinois Supreme Court enforced a will provision denying any inheritance to a grandchild if he married someone who was not Jewish.[171]

Surviving spouse

Power to condition

Restraints

Third, restraints on marriage do not actually prevent marriage; they simply result in forfeiture of property *if* the owner chooses to get married. Although this may place pressure on some individuals not to marry, the choice is still theirs and they have received the benefit of the property between the time of the donee's death and their marriage date (a benefit that the decedent could have chosen to withhold entirely).

The argument for invalidity

The argument for the traditional rule invalidating such restraints is, first, that such restraints violate public policy whether or not the recipient

[167] *Restatement (Second) of Property (Donative Transfers)* §6.1(2) (1983).

[168] *Lewis v. Searles*, 452 S.W.2d 153 (Mo. 1970) (enforcing a restraint on marriage on the ground that it was intended to serve the legitimate purpose of providing support until marriage and was not intended to prevent the donee from marrying).

[169] 10-78 *Powell on Real Property* §78.02[2].

[170] *See* §9.3.1.

[171] *In re Estate of Feinberg*, 919 N.E.2d 888 (Ill. 2009).

agrees to them. Allowing property ownership to be conditioned on the recipient complying with detailed standards of behavior set by the grantor ties ownership of land to status in the sense that ownership is linked to a certain lifestyle—and one usually chosen by someone in an earlier generation. This dead-hand control of the past infringes on personal liberties.

Personal liberties

Moreover, the personal liberty involved—the right to marry—is of such fundamental importance that it is a basic constitutional right.[172] In addition, tying land ownership to conduct smacks of feudalism; land ownership is embedded in a system of personal rights and obligations owed to the lord. Second, it is reasonable to expect that restraints on marriage will affect behavior. This is especially so because social norms have changed; one

Changing social norms

might well choose to "cohabit" with a life partner without getting married to avoid loss of property. Because the stigma that used to be attached to such arrangements has substantially lessened, restraints on marriage may well deter marriage without otherwise affecting behavior regarding property. Third, the idea that support is needed until marriage suggests a discriminatory assumption. Restraints on first marriage are usually imposed on conveyances to women (daughters); if designed to provide support until marriage, they suggest that women need support when single and that, once married, will no longer require it.[173] This wrongfully suggests that women cannot earn property on their own, that they will be supported by their husbands after marriage, and that they should not be entitled to control their own property after marriage.

Restraints on some first marriages

Valid only if they do not unreasonably limit the right to marry

The *Restatement (Second)* also provides that partial restraints on marriage that are designed to prevent "some, but not all, first marriages" are valid "only if, under the circumstances, the restraint does not unreasonably limit the transferee's opportunity to marry."[174] Sometimes donors attempt to prevent the donee from marrying a specific individual or marrying before a certain age.[175] More common are attempts to induce the donee to marry within the donor's religion. In *Shapira v. Union National Bank*,[176] for example, a bequest was left to the deceased's son only if he were married to a "Jewish girl." If he were not already married to a Jew, then he would get the bequest only if he married a Jew within seven years of his father's death. The court upheld the restraint on the ground that it did not unreasonably restrict his ability to marry.[177] Moreover, unlike the law in some European countries, his father was not obligated to leave him anything. If the greater power includes the lesser, the father had the power to condition his gift on terms the father chose.

172 *Loving v. Virginia*, 388 U.S. 1 (1967) (invalidating a state statute that prohibited any "white person" to "intermarry with a colored person" and vice versa).

173 *Matter of Estate of Donner*, 623 A.2d 307, 308 (N.J. Super. Ct. App. Div. 1993) ("Counsel for the widow necessarily admits that a gift of income to testator's widow may be limited to the period during which she will probably most need it, namely, while she remains a widow").

174 *Restatement (Second) of Property (Donative Transfers)* §6.2 (1983).

175 10-78 *Powell on Real Property* §§78.02[3], [4].

176 315 N.E.2d 825 (Ohio Ct. Com. Pl. 1974).

177 *Accord, In re Estate of Feinberg*, 919 N.E.2d 888 (Ill. 2009); *Gordon v. Gordon*, 124 N.E.2d 228, 230 (Mass. 1955).

Argument for invalidity

The argument on the other side is that such restraints are intended to, and often have the effect of, substantially altering behavior. Most restrictions on the ownership of land, whether in the form of covenants or future interests, relate to land use, not the personal conduct of the possessor. Tying ownership of land to personal conduct smacks of feudalism. Rather than freeing land for use by its current owner, enforcement of such provisions ties land ownership to a kind of servitude to the whims of the grantor. This privileges the "dead hand" of the past and arguably inhibits both autonomy of the present generation and efficiency. The *Restatement (Third) of Trusts* provides that conditions in trusts that purport to terminate benefits if a beneficiary marries someone who is not of a particular religion violate public policy and are unenforceable as invalid restraints on marriage; the trust is given effect as if the clause had been omitted from the terms of the trust.[178]

Restraints on remarriage

Restraints on remarriage are treated differently by the *Restatement (Second)*. They are invalid unless they relate to the spouse of the donor or are "reasonable under all the circumstances."[179] This provision is subject to the same criticisms as the rules about first marriages. The rule assumes that the spouse will need support until remarriage and then will not need it because the new spouse will provide support. Again, because such restraints are most often included in transfers to women, they suggest that women do not have the right to own property once married and that they will be supported by their husbands after marriage. The counterargument again is that the greater power includes the lesser; if the donor can choose not to give the property at all, why shouldn't he be able to give it on conditions chosen by him? The spouse, unlike the children, is protected by either a community property system or a statutory forced share, which ensures that she will inherit a substantial portion of the decedent's property on death, so we are talking about property over and above this minimum.[180]

Provisions designed to encourage divorce

Provisions designed to encourage separation or divorce have long been held to be void. This is the modern position as well.[181] The only exception is where the arrangement is designed to provide support if the donee gets divorced or separated.[182]

§7.7.7 *Public Policy*

Violation of public policy

Future interests may also be invalidated in other circumstances where the courts conclude that the condition violates public policy. For example, in *Matter of Estate of Romero*,[183] the court held that a condition in a will permitting a decedent's sons to live in his house as long as they did not live with their mother would be void as against public policy if the decedent's intent was to separate his sons from their mother. On the other hand, the

[178] *Restatement (Third) of Trusts* §29(c) cmt. j, illus. 3 (2003).

[179] *Restatement (Second) of Property (Donative Transfers)* §6.3 (1983).

[180] *See* §§9.3.1 & 9.3.2.

[181] *In re Estate of Owen*, 855 N.E.2d 603 (Ind. 2006); *Restatement (Second) of Property (Donative Transfers)* §7.1 (1983); 10-78 *Powell on Real Property* §78.02[5].

[182] 10- 78 *Powell on Real Property* §78.02[5].

[183] 847 P.2d 319 (N.M. Ct. App. 1993).

court upheld a condition permitting the decedent's fiancée to live in a house as long as she did not live with another man if the decedent's intent was to benefit the fiancée and not to impose a penalty on her for living with another man. The court noted that the public policy issue was based on a determination of whether the testator's purpose was legitimate.

§7.7.8 *Judicial Sale of Property Subject to Future Interests*

Sale can be ordered in cases of hardship

Nonfreehold estates

Property whose ownership is divided between present and future estates may create financial hardships for the parties. For example, an owner of a life estate may wish to move but be unable to rent or sell the property because life estates are so uncertain and the remainder persons are unwilling to agree to the sale. In such cases, courts may, upon petition of the life estate owner, order the property sold and the proceeds held in a trust for the benefit of all the owners.[184] Statutes in many states confirm this power, while in other states courts may simply exercise their equitable powers to protect the legitimate interests of the owners of property when the division of rights has caused unnecessary hardship.

[184] Dale A. Whitman et al., *The Law of Property* §4.10, at 137 (4th ed. 2019).

CHAPTER 8

Concurrent Ownership

§8.1 Introduction
§8.2 Ownership in Common
§8.2.1 Tenancy in Common
§8.2.2 Joint Tenancy
§8.2.3 Tenancy by the Entirety
§8.3 Interpretation of Ambiguities
§8.4 Rights and Obligations of Co-tenants
§8.4.1 Partition
§8.4.2 Joint Management
§8.4.3 Contribution for Repairs and Maintenance
§8.4.4 Rental Benefits and Obligations
§8.4.5 Leasing
§8.4.6 Adverse Possession
§8.5 Common Interest Communities
§8.5.1 Condominiums and Homeowners' Associations
§8.5.2 Cooperatives
§8.5.3 Affordable Housing Arrangements
§8.5.4 Continuing Care Retirement Communities
§8.6 Business Property
§8.6.1 Partnerships
§8.6.2 Corporations
§8.6.3 Franchises
§8.7 Nonprofit Organizations
§8.8 Governmental Ownership

§8.1 Introduction

Concurrent ownership

More often than not, property is owned by more than one person at a time. Residential property is often owned by married couples. Roommates often sign a lease and rent an apartment together. Increasingly, people live in neighborhoods with homeowners' associations that have the power to regulate the use or appearance of their property and to manage commonly owned areas. Condominium associations similarly manage common areas, such as stairways, rooftops, and backyards. Although many businesses are sole proprietorships, most are held in the form of partnerships or corporations, and thus have several or even thousands of owners. Nonprofit entities are often managed by a board of trustees that is both empowered and obligated to manage the institution to further its charitable, cultural, educational, or community goals. Governments own substantial amounts of property used for everything from public parks to office buildings, to streets, transportation facilities, schools, recreational facilities, military installations, and research facilities.

Categories of common ownership

These various types of common ownership are structured in particular ways by both law and contract. Different forms of ownership are characteristic of residential property, business property, family property, nonprofit property, and governmental property. Some of these categories overlap, of course; families often own residential property together and they may manage a family business or nonprofit foundation. Within each category, a fundamental distinction exists between types of property that are jointly owned with management informally shared among owners, and those that formally separate management from ownership. In the context of residential property, jointly owned and managed forms include (1) *tenancy in common*, (2) *joint tenancy*, and (3) *tenancy by the entirety.* A separate set of rules regulates the property rights of husbands and wives (marital property).[1] Forms that separate ownership and management in the residential (and the business) context include (4) *condominiums* and *homeowners' associations*, and (5) *cooperatives.*

Business and nonprofit organizations

In the business context, property can be held as a *sole proprietorship*, a *partnership*, or a *corporation*, among other forms. Partnerships are any collaborations designed to derive profit. Many partnerships have informal management arrangements and thus are somewhat similar to the tenancy in common or the joint tenancy. Other partnerships are closer to corporations in their management form, delegating power to a management committee similar to the board of directors elected by shareholders to run a corporation. *Nonprofit entities* usually have a board of directors or a board of trustees with powers and obligations to manage the organization in light of the goals established by its founding charter or in the trust that created it, as changed from time to time by the governing board. The rules about business and nonprofit property and the law of public lands are generally taught in upper-level courses in partnership, corporations, business planning, and nonprofit organizations. This chapter will only introduce these

[1] This topic (*marital property*) is covered in Chapter 9.

subjects to place the rules addressed here in a wider context. We will focus here on the forms of property most likely to be used for residential purposes.

Issues

A variety of issues arises in the context of commonly owned residential property. First, what rights and obligations do co-owners have? Are they each entitled to use the property as they wish or are their rights limited by the interests of their co-owners? Do they have any affirmative obligations to cooperate or to use their property in ways that benefit all the owners? Second, what happens when the parties cannot get along or agree on what to do with the property? How are disputes resolved? Third, can individual owners lease or sell their fractional interests in the property, and if so, do they need the consent of their co-owners? If they sell their interests, what relationship is created between the new owners and the old owners? Fourth, are jointly owned property interests inheritable or devisable? Fifth, in forms of common ownership that separate ownership and management (such as condominiums or cooperatives), what rules regulate the relationship between the condominium association and the individual unit members? Does the association have the power to regulate the use of individual units as well as common property? To what extent does the association have the power to choose who will move into or buy the units?

§8.2 Ownership in Common

§8.2.1 Tenancy in Common

Undivided fractional interests

A *tenancy in common* is a form of concurrent ownership in which two or more persons own the same property at the same time. Each tenant in common owns the right to possess the entire property. This means that the usage of the property must be worked out between the co-owners.[2] Although each owner has the right to possess 100 percent of the property, their ownership interests are fractional shares. If there are two owners, and they have been given equal interests by the grantor, they each own a 50 percent fractional interest in the property. This interest is called an "undivided" interest because each has the right to possess the whole. The grantor may choose to grant unequal interests to the grantees. For example, an owner may convey "to *A* and *B* as tenants in common, with a 75 percent undivided fractional interest in *A* and a 25 percent undivided fractional interest in *B*." Although each has the right to possess the whole, *A* is entitled to 75 percent of the proceeds from a sale of the property and *B* is entitled to only 25 percent; their share of any rental proceeds is similarly unevenly divided.

Characteristics of the tenancy in common

Alienable

Inheritable

Each tenant in common has the right to possess the whole property, although they may agree among themselves that only one will do so, or that they will use different parts of the property. Each tenant's interest is alienable, inheritable, and devisable. If a tenant in common transfers her

[2] If the parties cannot agree, their remedy is to partition the property. *See* §8.4.1.

interest, the grantee receives exactly what the grantor owned, unless the tenant in common sells less than her full interest. For example, if *A* owns a 75 percent undivided fractional share in the property, *A* can transfer this share to *C*, who will then be a tenant in common with *B*.

§8.2.2 *Joint Tenancy*

Right of survivorship

A *joint tenancy* differs from a tenancy in common because it is characterized by a *right of survivorship.* Unlike the tenancy in common, a joint tenancy interest is not inheritable or devisable. If *A* and *B* own property as joint tenants, and *A* dies before *B*, *A*'s interest immediately passes to *B*, who will own a 100 percent interest in fee simple. Conversely, if *B* dies first, *B*'s interest will pass to *A* giving *A* full ownership rights in the property. Similarly, if three people own property as joint tenants, each with a one-third undivided share, when one dies, her interest passes in equal shares to the other two joint tenants so that each will then own a 50 percent interest as a joint tenant with the other. If joint tenants die simultaneously, courts treat their interests as if they own as tenants in common, with each owner deemed to own her proportional share that will be inherited by her heirs or devisees.[3]

Equal interests

Unlike the tenancy in common, the joint tenancy traditionally had to be held in equal shares. If an owner wants to give *A* a 50 percent undivided interest and a 25 percent interest to each of *B* and *C*, she must do so in the form of a tenancy in common. If she wants *A*, *B*, and *C* to own as joint tenants, they must each own an undivided one-third interest. The courts generally do still require interests to be equal, although they might recognize unequal rights and obligations through contract or constructive trust doctrine if owners make such arrangements among themselves. Some states have statutorily abolished the rule that requires joint tenancy interests to be in equal undivided fractional shares.[4]

Formal requirements to create: "four unities"

In addition to requiring interests to be equal and to granting possessory rights to the whole property to each joint tenant, courts traditionally required joint tenancies to be created by a common title and at the same time. The courts have referred to this as the "four unities" of time, title, interest, and possession.[5] This meant that co-owners who obtained their titles at different times or through different conveyances were traditionally not allowed to have joint tenancy interests. The most common situation is a conveyance by an owner to herself and another "as joint tenants." In that case, because the owner already had title, she and the new owner did not initially obtain title at the same time and through the same instrument, and the courts would override the intent to create a joint tenancy and convert it to a tenancy in common. The way to get around this is to

[3] Uniform Probate Code §2-803(c); *Duncan v. Vassaur*, 550 P.2d 929 (Okla. 1976); *Lakatos v. Estate of Billotti*, 509 S.E.2d 594 (W. Va. 1998); John G. Sprankling, *Understanding Property Law* §10.02[B][1], at 140 (5th ed. 2023) (citing the Uniform Simultaneous Death Act §4).

[4] Conn. Gen. Stat. §47-14a.

[5] *Furnas v. Cirone*, 221 N.E.3d 772, 776 (Mass. 2023); *General Credit Co. v. Cleck*, 609 A.2d 553, 556 (Pa. 1992); 4-31 *Thompson on Real Property, Third Thomas Edition* §31.06(b) & (c).

use a straw person. If *A* transfers property to *C* and then *C* transfers property to "*A* and *B* as joint tenants, with right of survivorship," the problem is solved.

Abolition of four unities

Most states have begun to reject such formalistic and expensive procedures and will recognize a joint tenancy if this is the grantor's intent, whether or not a straw is used.[6] Some do this generally by stating that a joint tenancy will be found if this is the grantor's intent.[7] Others more specifically validate a joint tenancy created by a grantor to himself and another as joint tenants.[8] As noted above, some states have also abolished the requirement that each joint tenant possess an equal fractional share.

Severance

A joint tenancy is *severed* if one of the joint owners transfers her interest during her lifetime. This means that transfer of a joint tenancy interest destroys the right of survivorship as to the share that is transferred. Thus, if *A* and *B* own property as joint tenants and *A* conveys her 50 percent undivided interest to *C*, *B* and *C* will own the property as tenants in common. If *A*, *B*, and *C* own the property as joint tenants, and *A* transfers her interest to *D*, then *D* will own a one-third interest as a tenant in common, while *B* and *C* will still own their one-third interests as joint tenants with each other. When *D* dies, her property will go to her heirs or devisees (if she has not transferred it first). However, when *B* dies, her one-third interest will go to *C* (and vice versa if *C* predeceases *B*). Thus, if *B* dies, her one-third joint tenancy interest will pass to *C*, who will own a two-thirds interest as a tenant in common with *D* or her heirs or assigns.

Distinguished from joint life estates with alternative contingent remainders

The joint tenancy must be distinguished from a similar, but not identical, estate: joint life estates with alternative contingent remainders. A grantor may convey property "to *A* and *B* for life, remainder to go to whomever of them survives the other." The remainders in *A* and *B* are contingent (because they will take effect only if the other dies first) and alternative (because only one of the remainders will take effect). This arrangement is similar to a joint tenancy; however, a major difference is that one of the remainders is certain to take effect because a transfer of a present life estate does not destroy the remainder. In other words, severance is not possible; the remainder(s) are not affected by a present transfer of one or both of the life estates.[9]

Self-conveyance

A joint tenant can sever by transferring her interest to a friend who then conveys it back to her. Can she avoid this procedure and sever the joint tenancy by conveying her own interest to herself? Traditionally, this could not be done,[10] but most states, by statute or common law, are starting to allow this because the straw procedure is an expensive and unnecessary

[6] *Ratinska v. Estate of Denesuk*, 447 So. 2d 241, 243 (Fla. Dist. Ct. App. 1983); *Switzer v. Pratt*, 23 N.W.2d 837, 839 (Iowa 1946); R.H. Helmholz, *Realism and Formalism in the Severance of Joint Tenancies*, 77 Neb. L. Rev. 1, 5 (1998).

[7] Minn. Stat. §500.19(3) (abolishing the requirement for the unities); *Switzer v. Pratt*, 23 N.W.2d 837, 838-839 (Iowa 1946) ("the intention of the parties should prevail over the technical common law rules as to the creation of joint tenancies").

[8] Cal. Civ. Code §683(a); Haw. Rev. Stat. §509-2; Mass. Gen. Laws ch. 184 §8; N.J. Stat. §46:3-17.1; Me. Rev. Stat. tit. 33, §159.

[9] A court could interpret a partition statute (see §8.4.1) to apply to this arrangement, but this is not what courts have done. *Albro v. Allen*, 454 N.W.2d 85 (Mich. 1990).

[10] *Clark v. Carter*, 70 Cal. Rptr. 923 (Ct. App. 1968).

formality.[11] However, although many states have abolished the need for a straw to create a joint tenancy, most states still require the straw procedure to sever a joint tenancy.[12]

▶ HARD CASE

▷ SECRET CONVEYANCES

The problem that arises with the ability to convey one's interest to oneself is the possibility of doing so secretly. Consider a husband and wife (*A* and *B*) who own property as joint tenants. Husband *A* conveys his own 50 percent interest to himself, destroying *B*'s right of survivorship. Even if *A* records the deed he granted to himself, *B* may not become aware of the transaction.[13] If *A* can do this, he could leave the deed in a place in which it will be discovered by *B* after his death (or *A* could collude with a third party who will keep the deed secretly and produce it if *A* dies before *B*). Such secret conveyances could unfairly surprise *B*, who had thought that she would receive *A*'s 50 percent interest when he died. Conversely, if *B* dies first, the one who executed the self-conveyance (*A*) could tear up the deed and treat the joint tenancy as effective and claim the deceased's 50 percent interest. The unfairness of such secret conveyances suggests that they should not be effective unless the joint tenant is made aware of the conveyance so that she can plan based on the knowledge that the right of survivorship no longer exists. Some states prohibit conveyances from severing joint tenancies unless they are recorded.[14] While this would not completely solve the problem of secret conveyances, it would prevent a co-owner from benefiting from the right of survivorship after conveying the interest to himself. ◀

Homestead laws

Many states have homestead laws that protect a married person's continued ability to occupy the family home. Such laws limit a spouse's ability to leave the family home to someone other than the surviving spouse and often also protect the family home from creditors of one or both of the parties.[15] In *Pratt v. Langston*,[16] the Alabama Supreme Court interpreted Alabama homestead law to prohibit a spouse from transferring his joint tenancy interest without his wife's consent.[17] In addition, courts may interpret homestead laws

[11] *Stewart v. AmSouth Mortgage Co.*, 679 So. 2d 247 (Ala. Ct. App. 1995), *rev'd on other grounds*, 679 So. 2d 251 (Ala. 1996); *Taylor v. Canterbury*, 92 P.3d 961 (Colo. 2004); *Riddle v. Harmon*, 162 Cal. Rptr. 530 (Ct. App. 1980); *Countrywide Funding Corp. v. Palmer*, 589 So. 2d 994, 996 (Fla. Dist. Ct. App. 1991); *Sathoff v. Sutterer*, 869 N.E.2d 354 (Ill. App. Ct. 2007) (applying 765 Ill. Comp. Stat. 1005/1b); *Hendrickson v. Minneapolis Federal Savings & Loan Ass'n*, 161 N.W.2d 688, 690-691 (Minn. 1968); *Knickerbocker v. Cannon (In re Estate of Knickerbocker)*, 912 P.2d 969, 974-976 (Utah 1996).

[12] R.H. Helmholz, *Realism and Formalism in the Severance of Joint Tenancies*, 77 Neb. L. Rev. 1, 5 (1998).

[13] *See General Credit Co. v. Cleck*, 609 A.2d 553 (Pa. 1992) (mortgage by one joint tenant made secretly).

[14] Cal. Civ. Code §683.2(c); Colo. Rev. Stat. §38-31-101(5)(a); *see* John V. Orth, *The Perils of Joint Tenancies*, 44 Real Prop. Tr. & Est. L.J. 427 (2009).

[15] *See* N.C. Const. art. 10, §2.

[16] 669 So. 2d 967 (Ala. 1995).

[17] *Accord, Besnilian v. Wilkinson*, 25 P.3d 187 (Nev. 2001).

to preclude creditors from reaching joint tenancy interests unless both spouses had joined in the debt.[18] In North Carolina, for example, the state constitution provides that the family home cannot be reached by creditors (other than those who lent money to facilitate the purchase of the home).[19] Further:

> If the owner of a homestead dies, leaving a surviving spouse but no minor children, the homestead shall be exempt from the debts of the owner, and the rents and profits thereof shall inure to the benefit of the surviving spouse until he or she remarries, unless the surviving spouse is the owner of a separate homestead.[20]

▷ DO MORTGAGES SEVER THE JOINT TENANCY? **HARD CASE** ◀

Does a mortgage sever a joint tenancy? The states differ on this question.[21] A mortgage is a security interest in real estate designed to protect the lender who loaned money to the owner of the house (often to help purchase the property).[22] The lender loans money to the borrower, who signs a note promising repayment. The parties also agree to a mortgage contract, which allows the lender to foreclose on the property and have the house sold, with the proceeds used to pay off the unpaid debt. In most states that characterize the mortgage as a *lien*, the arrangement places title in the hands of the homeowner/purchaser and merely gives the bank a "security interest" in the house. A few states have the older *title theory* of mortgages. In title theory states, the lender takes the deed to the house and possesses the legal title, while the "owner" has an equitable interest called the *equity of redemption*. In states with the title theory, courts may consider a mortgage to be a transfer of ownership that has the effect of severing the joint tenancy,[23] although some hold that deeds of trust designed to secure loans do not sever joint tenancies.[24] States with the lien theory are likely to hold that mortgages do not sever joint tenancies,[25] but some do provide that mortgages do sever joint tenancies.[26] ◀

[18] *O'Hagan v. United States*, 86 F.3d 776 (8th Cir. 1996) (applying Minnesota law).
[19] Every homestead and the dwellings and buildings used therewith, to a value fixed by the General Assembly but not less than $1,000, to be selected by the owner thereof, or in lieu thereof, at the option of the owner, any lot in a city or town with the dwellings and buildings used thereon, and to the same value, owned and occupied by a resident of the State, shall be exempt from sale under execution or other final process obtained on any debt. But no property shall be exempt from sale for taxes, or for payment of obligations contracted for its purchase. N.C. Const. art. 10, §2(1).
[20] N.C. Const. art. 10, §2(3).
[21] 4-31 *Thompson on Real Property, Third Thomas Edition* §31.08(b).
[22] For more on mortgages, see §11.5.1.
[23] *Stewart v. AmSouth Mortgage Co.*, 679 So. 2d 247 (Ala. Ct. App.), *rev'd on other grounds*, 679 So. 2d 251 (Ala. 1996); *Schaefer v. Peoples Heritage Savings Bank*, 669 A.2d 185 (Me. 1996).
[24] *Biggers v. Crook*, 656 S.E.2d 835 (Ga. 2008).
[25] *Brant v. Hargrove*, 632 P.2d 978 (Ariz. Ct. App. 1981); *Smith v. Bank of America*, 957 N.Y.S.2d 705 (App. Div. 2012).
[26] *CitiMortgage, Inc. v. Brown*, 45 N.E.3d 258 (Ohio Ct. App. 2015); *General Credit Co. v. Cleck*, 609 A.2d 553 (Pa. Super. Ct. 1992) (mortgage severs joint tenancy in lien theory state).

▶ **HARD CASE**

▷ DO MORTGAGES SURVIVE THE DEATH OF A JOINT TENANT?

If a mortgage severs a joint tenancy, converting it to a tenancy in common, and the tenant who granted the mortgage dies, the mortgage interest will survive and the property interest inherited by the decedent's heirs or devisees will be owned subject to the mortgage. In states where the mortgage does not sever the joint tenancy, the courts are split. Some states conclude that the interest subject to the mortgage ends with the death of the joint tenant; it is like a life estate and the interest goes to the surviving joint tenant free of the mortgage.[27] You can only encumber what you own, and if you only own a right that exists during your lifetime, then any conveyance or encumbrance on that interest will be lost once you die. However, most states provide that, even though the mortgage does not sever the joint tenancy, it survives the death of the joint tenant who granted the mortgage and continues to burden that fractional interest that is now owned by the surviving joint tenant.[28] ◀

▶ **HARD CASE**

▷ DO LEASES SEVER THE JOINT TENANCY?

Similar conflicts of authority arise over leases. Some states hold that a lease severs a joint tenancy, turning it into a tenancy in common.[29] Others hold that it does not sever the joint tenancy.[30] Still others take a middle position, holding that a lease by one joint tenant severs the joint tenancy only if the lessor/joint tenant dies before the end of the lease, but that if the lease terminates before the lessor/joint tenant dies, then the right of survivorship remains intact.[31] In *Tenhet v. Boswell*,[32] a joint tenant, Raymond Johnson, leased his 50 percent interest to defendant Boswell without informing his co-owner, Hazel Tenhet. Johnson misled Boswell by including a right of first refusal in the lease, leading Boswell to believe that Johnson owned the property by himself. The lease was for ten years at a rental of $150 per year. Johnson died three months after execution of the lease. The court held that the lease did not sever the joint tenancy. Because Johnson could only convey what he owned, the lease automatically terminated when Johnson's property rights terminated — which they did upon his death. At that point, Tenhet owned 100 percent of the rights in the property. The court further held that the lease did not survive the death of Johnson and that she owned the property free of the lease.

[27] *Harms v. Sprague*, 456 N.E.2d 976 (Ill. App. Ct. 1983).

[28] Wis. Stat. §700.24 (mortgage does not sever joint tenancy but survives death of joint tenant); *Brant v. Hargrove*, 632 P.2d 978 (Ariz. Ct. App. 1981).

[29] *Estate of Gulledge*, 673 A.2d 1278 (D.C. 1996); *Alexander v. Boyer*, 253 A.2d 359 (Md. 1969); 2 *American Law of Property* 10 n.10 (A. James Casner ed. 1952); 4-31 *Thompson on Real Property, Third Thomas Edition* §31.08(c).

[30] *Tenhet v. Boswell*, 554 P.2d 330 (Cal. 1976). This appears to be the trend in the law. 7-51 *Powell on Real Property* §51.04[1][c].

[31] *See Tenhet v. Boswell*, 554 P.2d 330, 335 (Cal. 1976) (noting this possibility).

[32] 554 P.2d 330 (Cal. 1976).

The argument for severance

The argument for severance is that it promotes the alienability of the property. Each joint tenant has the right to lease his undivided interest in the property without obtaining his co-owner's consent.[33] If the lease does not sever the joint tenancy, the courts are likely to hold that the lessor's interest will terminate completely at death, thereby ending the leasehold as well.[34] Few will be willing to lease property knowing that the lease will end when the lessor dies. Holding that the lease does not sever the joint tenancy therefore inhibits the ability of the joint tenant to lease his interest because prospective lessees are likely to insist on having all the owners join the lease. This restricts the joint tenant's ability to transfer his undivided share. Nor is severance unfair to the other joint tenants. Because each joint tenant has the power to sever the joint tenancy by transferring her interest, joint tenants have no strong expectation of benefiting from their right of survivorship; it is a mere possibility.

The argument against severance

The argument against severance is that joint tenants *do* expect to benefit from the right of survivorship and that this right will better promote alienability of property. Joint tenants often are family members and generally make decisions together. When they choose to obtain property as joint tenants, they generally do so because of the advantages of the right of survivorship. When they receive the property by testamentary transfer, the testator intended that the survivor obtain the rights of deceased joint tenants. It is true that each owner may destroy the right of survivorship by transferring his interest. This is because a sale severs the ongoing relationship between co-owners and therefore entitles the buyer to an independent interest in the property. In contrast, a lease arguably *preserves* rather than severs the relationship between the co-owners. Nor is this unfair to potential tenants such as Boswell, who are on constructive notice of the existence of multiple owners if the deed is recorded or the will probated, as it is likely to be.[35] Moreover, the right of survivorship decreases, rather than increases, the number of owners. If Johnson's lease preserves the right of survivorship, Johnson's interest goes to Tenhet when Johnson dies. If the lease does not sever, Johnson's interest is inherited by his heirs (or obtained by his devisees), and if more than one person obtains the interest, the number of owners will increase. A potential buyer would rather negotiate with only one owner than several, any one of whom may hold out for a high price and block a sale. ◀

▷ DOES THE LEASE SURVIVE THE DEATH OF A JOINT TENANT? ◀ HARD CASE

If the lease severs the joint tenancy, it will survive the death of the joint tenant/lessor. Thus, if Johnson's ten-year lease to Boswell severs the joint

[33] *See* §8.4.5.

[34] Note that not all courts agree. Some hold that leases do not sever the joint tenancy but nonetheless survive the death of a joint tenant. 4-31 *Thompson on Real Property, Third Thomas Edition* §31.08(c). *See also Swartzbaugh v. Sampson*, 54 P.2d 73 (Cal. 1936).

[35] Of course, potential tenants may not do a title search and thus not be on actual notice of the existence of a co-owner.

Argument that the lease does not survive if the lease does not sever the joint tenancy

tenancy, destroying Tenhet's right of survivorship, and Johnson dies before the term of the lease expires, Johnson's heirs or devisees receive his fifty percent interest subject to the lease. What happens if the lease does not sever the joint tenancy? The California Supreme Court assumed in *Tenhet* that the lease would automatically terminate on the ground that Johnson's interest ended as soon as he died, and thus the lease must have ended also. You can only convey what you own, and Johnson had no power to transfer an interest that would last after his death. This assumes that the joint tenancy interest is akin to a life estate.

Argument that the lease survives even if the lease does not sever the joint tenancy

However, the joint tenancy is not like a life estate. Consider that a life estate owner has no power to destroy the right of survivorship. A transfer of a life estate gives the grantee an estate for the life of the grantor; when the grantor dies, the remainder or reversion becomes possessory. In contrast, a joint tenant has the power to destroy the right of survivorship completely by transferring his interest. Johnson could even have transferred his interest to a lawyer who would transfer it back to him. In that case, Tenhet would receive nothing when Johnson died. If the lease does not sever the joint tenancy and survives the death of the lessor, Tenhet would receive Johnson's 50 percent interest when he dies, subject to the benefits and burdens of the lease. Tenhet would receive the rental income for the rest of the term and possess the reversion, *i.e.*, the right to recover possession after the lease ends. She would, in other words, be better off than if Johnson had conveyed his interest. It can be argued that the greater right includes the lesser. If Johnson could destroy Tenhet's right to receive his interest entirely, why couldn't he encumber that interest with a lease? Tenhet would be better off with his 50 percent interest (although subject to the lease) than she would be with nothing. As noted above, this result obtains in some states when one joint tenant mortgages his interest and it was once the law in the United States for several decades.[36] Today, however, courts that hold that a lease does not sever the joint tenancy also hold that it does not survive the death of the joint tenant.[37] ◀

Murder of one joint tenant by another

What happens when one joint tenant murders the other? One court canvassed the possibilities this way:

> The question before us has been the subject for determination by a number of states with a number of different and contrary views, such as: (1) Some jurisdictions hold that the murderer is deprived of the entire interest except for a life interest in one-half. (2) The murderer is entitled to keep all the property. (3) The murderer holds upon a constructive trust to the extent of the computed value of one-half of the property as of the date of the victim's death for the period of the victim's expectancy. (4) The murderer is chargeable as constructive trustee of the entire property for the benefit of his victim's estate. (5) The murderer is chargeable as constructive trustee of one-half of the property for the benefit of the

[36] 4-31 *Thompson on Real Property, Third Thomas Edition* §31.08(c).

[37] This is the holding of *Tenhet v. Boswell*, 554 P.2d 330, 335 (Cal. 1976).

...is estate. (6) By the murder, the joint tenancy has separated and terminated and one-half of the property should go to the heirs of the deceased (murdered person) and the other one-half to the murderer, or to his heirs, when deceased.[38]

Murderers are not entitled to the right of survivorship

The law today is that murderers are not entitled to the right of survivorship.[39] Some states accomplish this result by providing that murder severs the joint tenancy, converting it to a tenancy in common with the fractional interest belonging to the victim devolving to her heirs or devisees. Many states have statutes to this effect.[40] Others reach this result by common law.[41] Still others reach a similar but not identical result by imposing a constructive trust on the property, obliging the murderer to hold it for the benefit of the heirs or devisees of the deceased or to transfer the property to them.[42] One Massachusetts court did this, for example, even in the face of a statute that provided no exception to the right of survivorship when one joint tenant murdered another.[43] Some states require the murderer to transfer the 50 percent interest belonging to the deceased to her heirs (or to give them 50 percent of the earnings of the property), on the ground that the murderer should not profit from his wrong but that the murder does not result in a forfeiture of his own 50 percent interest.[44] The *Restatement (First) of Restitution*, however, suggests that the murderer is only entitled to 50 percent of the profits of the property for his lifetime and that, on his death, the entire 100 percent of the estate should go to the heirs of the murdered spouse, the murderer having sacrificed his right to control the disposition of his interest after his own death.[45]

Abolition

A number of states have abolished the joint tenancy entirely.[46] As far back as 1836, a Connecticut court characterized the right of survivorship as "odious and unjust."[47] (Nonetheless, joint tenancies can now be created in Connecticut.[48]) In the states that have abolished the doctrine, one can create joint life estates with alternative contingent remainders, an estate that is

[38] *Duncan v. Vassaur*, 550 P.2d 929, 930-931 (Okla. 1976).

[39] John G. Sprankling, *Understanding Property Law* §10.02[B][1], at 140 (5th ed. 2023).

[40] *Ponke v. Ponke*, 564 N.W.2d 101 (Mich. Ct. App. 1997); 4-31 *Thompson on Real Property, Third Thomas Edition* §31.08(d).

[41] *Gallimore v. Washington*, 666 A.2d 1200 (D.C. 1995) (joint tenancy severed by murder under both common law and statute).

[42] *Ford v. Long*, 713 S.W.2d 798 (Tex. Ct. App. 1986); *Restatement (First) of Restitution* §188 (1937) ("Where two persons have an interest in property and the interest of one of them is enlarged by his murder of the other, to the extent to which it is enlarged he holds it upon a constructive trust for the estate of the other").

[43] *Lee v. Snell*, 25 Mass. Lawyers Weekly 1210 (Mass. Probate Ct., Feb. 10, 1997) (No. 95E-0019-GC1).

[44] *Gallimore v. Washington*, 666 A.2d 1200, 1208-1209 (D.C. 1995).

[45] *Restatement (First) of Restitution* §188 cmt. b (1937) ("if one [joint tenant] murders the other, the murderer takes by survivorship the whole legal interest in the property, but he can be compelled to hold the entire interest upon a constructive trust for the estate of his co-tenant, except that he is entitled to one-half of the income for life").

[46] *See, e.g.*, Alaska Stat. §34.15.130; Or. Rev. Stat. §93.180.

[47] *Whittlesey v. Fuller*, 11 Conn. 337, 340 (1836).

[48] Conn. Stat. §47-14a; *Household Realty Corp. v. Pelzar*, 1995 WL 371189 (Conn. Super. Ct. 1995).

not identical to the joint tenancy because the remainders can[...] destroyed by severance.[49]

§8.2.3 Tenancy by the Entirety

Available to married couples only

About half the states retain the *tenancy by the entirety*, a form of joint tenancy available only to married couples.[50] Like the joint tenancy, the four unities were traditionally required to create a tenancy by the entirety, plus one more — that of marriage.[51] As with the joint tenancy, many states have abolished the requirements that the parties obtain their title at the same time and by the same instrument, allowing a wife to transfer property to herself and her husband as tenants by the entirety.[52] The tenancy by the entirety differs from the joint tenancy because, in a substantial majority of states that recognize it, (1) the individual undivided interests cannot be transferred without the consent of both spouses;[53] (2) the individual interests cannot be reached by creditors of one spouse; and (3) partition[54] is unavailable as a remedy for owners who cannot agree about what to do with the property; instead, the owners can sever their relationship only by divorce. In a few states, each tenant by the entirety has the power to convey or encumber his or her interest without the consent of the spouse, but such a conveyance cannot deprive the spouse of her right to possession or her right of survivorship.[55]

Originally gave husband management powers

The tenancy by the entirety originated as a form of common ownership that did not give the owners equal management powers over the property. Rather, it gave the husband, and not the wife, the sole power to manage and control the disposition of the property.[56] Husbands traditionally could transfer both their present interest and the present interest of the wife, but could not thereby defeat her right of survivorship, because severance of a tenancy by the entirety could occur only through divorce. This construction of the tenancy by the entirety — giving the husband the power to manage

[49] Or. Rev. Stat. §93.180. *See Geib v. McKinney*, 617 A.2d 1377 (Conn. 1992).

[50] *See Trapasso v. Lewis*, 239 A.3d 703, 707 (Md. 2020); 4-33 *Thompson on Real Property, Third Thomas Edition* §33.06(f), n.120 (25 states recognize the tenancy by the entirety). Another form of joint marital property — community property — is available in a number of states. *See* §9.3.2.

[51] 4-33 *Thompson on Real Property, Third Thomas Edition* §33.06(a).

[52] Del. Code tit. 25, §309; Mass. Gen. Laws ch. 184, §8; N.C. Gen. Stat. §41-56(b); Or. Rev. Stat. §108.090.

[53] *E.g., Morrison v. Potter*, 764 A.2d 234, 236-237 (D.C. 2000). Some states have even constitutionalized this principle. *See, e.g.*, N.C. Const. art. 10, §2(4) ("no deed made by a married owner of a homestead shall be valid without the signature and acknowledgement of his or her spouse").

[54] *See* §8.4.1.

[55] *E.g., Pilip v. United States*, 186 F. Supp. 397, 401-402 (D. Alaska 1960); *Morris v. Solesbee*, 892 S.W.2d 281, 282 (Ark. Ct. App. 1995); *Freda v. Commercial Trust Co.*, 570 A.2d 409, 414 (N.J. 2000); *In re LaBorde*, 231 B.R. 162, 166 (Bankr. W.D.N.Y. 1999); *Oregon Account Systems v. Greer*, 996 P.2d 1025, 1030 (Or. Ct. App. 2000); Dale A. Whitman et al., *The Law of Property* §5.5, at 157 (4th ed. 2019).

[56] *King v. Greene*, 153 A.2d 49, 52 (N.J. 1959) ("in an estate by the entirety the husband had absolute dominion and control over the property during the joint lives"); 4-33 *Thompson on Real Property, Third Thomas Edition* §33.05.

and dispose of the wife's present interest — is no longer the law anywhere.[57] In the 1981 case of *Kirchberg v. Feenstra*,[58] the Supreme Court held that enforcement of unequal management rights by courts constituted state action in violation of the equal protection clause. In the nineteenth century, the various states passed *Married Women's Property Acts*, which granted married women the capacity to own, manage, and transfer real and personal property that had previously been under the lawful control of their husbands. A number of states interpreted these statutes to abolish the estate of tenancy by the entirety, leaving only the joint tenancy as an option.[59]

▷ REACH BY CREDITORS **HARD CASE ◀**

The states have been split on the question of whether creditors of one spouse may reach property held by an individual tenant by the entirety. As noted above, most states do not allow this property to be transferred or encumbered unless both spouses agree.[60] This approach treats the property as truly jointly owned and limits the ability of one owner to effectuate substantial changes in ownership unless that owner obtains the agreement of the other or ends the relationship entirely through divorce. This rule limits the freedom of the spouses to transfer their interests, while protecting each from unilateral actions of the other spouse. It protects the interests of each spouse in retaining her interest in the property without fear of having to share it with another person (other than the spouse) or by losing her possessory rights through a foreclosure sale. On the other hand, the inability to transfer or encumber the property without the consent of the spouse inhibits the freedom of each spouse by rendering them subject to the control of the other. Each needs the consent of the other to complete any transaction affecting the property. Some states, therefore, have allowed transfer or mortgage of a tenant's undivided fractional interest in a tenancy by the entirety without a need for spousal consent, as well as allowing creditors to attach the undivided present estate.[61] One leading case in New Jersey held in 1959 that the nineteenth-century *Married Women's Property Acts*, which gave married women the legal capacity to own property, destroyed the disabilities that had characterized married women previously. Because husbands could manage joint tenancy property, and convey or encumber their present estates without spousal consent, so now could married women, while neither could convey the fractional share of the other without his or her consent.[62] The majority of states appear to have rejected this approach,

[57] *See* Mass. Gen. Laws ch. 209, §1.

[58] 450 U.S. 455 (1981).

[59] *King v. Greene*, 153 A.2d 49, 59 (N.J. 1959) (at least nine states took this view).

[60] *Evans v. Evans*, 772 S.E.2d 576, 580 (Va. 2015); Bunker v. Peyton, 312 F.3d 145 (4th Cir. 2002) (applying Va. law); *Sawada v. Endo*, 561 P.2d 1291 (Haw. 1977); 4-33 *Thompson on Real Property, Third Thomas Edition* §33.07(f).

[61] *King v. Greene*, 153 A.2d 49, 60 (N.J. 1959). *But see* N.J. Stat. §46:3-17.4 (providing that tenancy by the entirety interests cannot be alienated or affected without the consent of both tenants).

[62] *King v. Greene*, 153 A.2d 49, 60 (N.J. 1959).

instead prohibiting transfer of fractional ownership interests in tenancy by the entirety property unless both spouses consent. ◀

§8.3 Interpretation of Ambiguities

Constructional preference for tenancies in common

There is a general constructional preference for tenancies in common over joint tenancies when conveyances are ambiguous.[63] This reverses the presumption that was in effect in the nineteenth century when joint tenancies were preferred over tenancies in common. However, some courts hold that the ultimate touchstone is the intent of the grantor and may imply a right of survivorship if it appears from the deed or will, or even from extrinsic evidence, that the grantor would have wanted this.[64] In states that have the tenancy by the entirety, some states interpret ambiguous conveyances to married couples as a tenancy by the entirety[65] while others apply the usual presumption in favor of tenancies in common.[66]

Tenancy by the entirety preferred in some states for married couples

Exceptions: class gifts, marriage

Joint tenancies are more commonly held by married couples than by anyone else. If property is transferred to a married couple, there is therefore a plausible argument for reversing the usual presumption. Joint tenancy is useful to married persons because the property passes immediately to the surviving spouse when one dies and the property interest does not have to go through the probate process, where the validity of a will could be contested and creditors may claim an interest in property to pay off unpaid debts. In those states that have abolished the tenancy by the entirety, a conveyance to a husband and wife as tenants by the entirety may be construed as a joint tenancy.[67] In addition, one state has held that when a gift is given to a class in a will, the presumption is that the joint ownership interests are held as a joint tenancy rather than a tenancy in common.[68]

§8.4 Rights and Obligations of Co-tenants

§8.4.1 *Partition*

Forced division or sale

Co-tenants have to work out among themselves how the property will be used. If they cannot agree on how the property is to be used, the main legal remedy is *partition*.[69] The owners may voluntarily partition the property by

[63] *Kipp v. Chips Estate*, 732 A.2d 127 (Vt. 1999); *Choman v. Epperley*, 592 P.2d 714 (Wyo. 1979); 4-31 *Thompson on Real Property, Third Thomas Edition* §31.03.
[64] *In re Estate of Vadney*, 634 N.E.2d 976 (N.Y. 1994) (implying a right of survivorship based on grantor's intent when it was omitted because of "scrivener's error").
[65] *Underwood v. Bunger*, 70 N.E.3d 338, 343 (Ind. 2017) (reciting presumption but holding it was rebutted when transfer was to a married couple and a third person "all as Tenants-in-Common"); N.Y. Est. Powers & Trusts §6-2.2(b); *Kinghorn v. Hughes*, 761 S.W.2d 930 (Ark. 1988); *Greeson v. Ace Pipe Cleaning, Inc.*, 830 S.W.2d 444 (Mo. 1992); 7-52 *Powell on Real Property* §52.02[2].
[66] 7-52 *Powell on Real Property* §52.02[2].
[67] *Id.* at §52.01[3].
[68] *Dewire v. Haveles*, 534 N.E.2d 782 (Mass. 1989).
[69] 7-50 *Powell on Real Property* §50.07[1]; 4-38 *Thompson on Real Property, Third Thomas Edition* §38.03(a). The remedy for tenants by the entirety is divorce.

dividing it physically or selling it and sharing the proceeds (*voluntary partition*), but they are also entitled to force the other owners to a partition by bringing a lawsuit for partition against the other co-tenants (*involuntary* or *judicial partition*). A tenant in common or joint tenant may go to court for an order that will result either in the physical division of the property (*physical partition*) or a forced sale of the property and division of the proceeds among the owners (*partition by sale*).

Physical partition generally preferred

In most jurisdictions, physical partition is preferred to partition by sale.[70] The property may be sold if physical partition will result in "great prejudice" to one of the owners.[71] Some states grant judges greater discretion to choose the appropriate form of partition, and some courts prefer partition by sale when the overall value to the co-owners will be greater, even over objections by some owners because of sentimental attachment to the property.[72]

Partition by sale

Tenancy by the entirety preferred in some states for married couples

When property is sold pursuant to a partition sale, the proceeds are generally divided according to the fractional shares of the parties. However, courts also often divide proceeds based on the relative contributions of the parties to the purchase price for the property, even though the deed of purchase does not formally grant them unequal fractional shares, on the presumption that they "intend[] to share in proportion to the amount contributed by each to the purchase price."[73] The court will also conduct a final accounting to determine whether any of the parties received more than her fair share of rents earned by third parties or is entitled to receive a greater share of the proceeds because of her expenditures to make necessary repairs or major improvements that significantly increased the value of the property. If the property is subject to a lease granted by all the co-owners, that leasehold will normally continue to exist after partition.[74] If only one of the co-owners has granted a lease, that interest will persist unless the sale proceeds are used to compensate the lessee for loss of the leasehold.[75]

Effect on existing leases

Partition not available for condominiums

In condominiums and in residential communities, some property is often owned in common. In condominiums, for example, the owners of individual units own the stairways and hallways, roof and yard as tenants in common. Partition is not available as a remedy for disputes over use of common areas in such cases. Any disputes are managed by the homeowners' association.[76]

Restraints on partition valid only if reasonable

Co-owners often agree not to partition jointly owned property. Many courts uphold these agreements.[77] However, because such agreements are

[70] 7-50 *Powell on Real Property* §50.07[4][a]; 4-38 *Thompson on Real Property, Third Thomas Edition* §38.04.

[71] *Ashley v. Baker*, 867 P.2d 792, 796 (Alaska 1994); *Eli v. Eli*, 557 N.W.2d 405 (S.D. 1997).

[72] Cal. Civ. Proc. Code §872.820; *FTR Farms, Inc. v. Rist Farms, Inc.*, 942 N.W.2d 204 (Neb. 2020); *Delfino v. Vealencis*, 436 A.2d 27 (Conn. 1980).

[73] *Sack v. Tomlin*, 871 P.2d 298, 303 (Nev. 1994).

[74] 7-50 *Powell on Real Property* §50.07[5].

[75] *Id.*

[76] *Restatement (Third) of Property (Servitudes)* §6.4 (2000).

[77] *Carter v. Carter*, 516 A.2d 917 (D.C. 1986); *Gore v. Beren*, 867 P.2d 330 (Kan. 1994); *Marchetti v. Karpowich*, 667 A.2d 724 (Pa. Super. Ct. 1995); 4-38 *Thompson on Real Property, Third Thomas Edition* §38.03(a)(2)(i)(A).

effectively restraints on alienation, courts enforce them only if they are "reasonable"[78] and only for a reasonable time or if limited to a reasonable duration, such as the time permitted by the rule against perpetuities.[79]

▶ HARD CASE ▷ LIENS ON ONE CO-TENANT'S INTEREST

Each co-tenant has the power to alienate or encumber her undivided fractional interest without the consent of her co-tenants. If a co-tenant fails to pay a debt, the courts may attach the cotenancy interest (or foreclose on the mortgage if the debt is secured by a mortgage that attaches to a fractional interest in the property) to pay off the debt. When a creditor buys the property at a foreclosure sale, and it is the residence of the nondebtor, partition may not be available. If the dwelling cannot be physically partitioned, and it is the residence of a nondebtor co-tenant, such as a spouse or relative of the debtor, courts have held that no automatic right to partition exists in such a setting.[80] Similarly, the right to partition may be limited in property subject to future interests.[81] ◀

Future interests

Heirs' property

When someone dies without a will, their property is distributed according to what are called intestacy statutes, which typically divide up the property among spouses and children, if there are any, then more distant relatives. A majority of Americans die without a will, with the highest proportions to be found in Black and Latino communities. This process often results in heirs owning property as tenants in common; if those heirs also die without a will, the property is further divided, and over generations such "heirs' property" may be held by a large number of co-owners.

Loss of land through partition

Partition sales pose particular problems for heirs' property. Because every co-owner has the right to sell, companies may purchase small shares, force a partition by sale, and buy the whole property. Such forced sales have hit particularly hard in Appalachian, Southern Black, and Hispanic land grant communities. Heirs' property, for example, is estimated to make up one-quarter to 40 percent of Black-owned rural property, and landownership in that community has dropped by more than 90 percent over the past century, in part because of partition sales.[82]

Reforming partition for heirs' property

A model statute called the *Uniform Partition of Heirs Property Act* (*UPHPA*) seeks to protect heirs in this situation, by helping them retain the

[78] *LEG Investments v. Boxler*, 107 Cal. Rptr. 3d 519 (2010); *Thompson on Real Property, Third Thomas Edition* §38.03(a)(2)(i)(B). *Accord*, John G. Sprankling, *Understanding Property Law* §10.04[B], at 154 (5th ed. 2023); Dale A. Whitman et al., *The Law of Property* §5.10, at 170-171 (4th ed. 2019).

[79] *Spratt v. Spratt*, 456 N.W.2d 181 (Iowa 1990); 10-77 *Powell on Real Property* §77.08; 4-38 *Thompson on Real Property, Third Thomas Edition* §38.03(a)(2)(i)(B).

[80] *Bauer v. Migliaccio*, 561 A.2d 674 (N.J. Super. Ct. Ch. Div. 1989); *Newman v. Chase*, 359 A.2d 474 (N.J. 1976).

[81] 7-50 *Powell on Real Property* §50.07[3][d].

[82] Thomas W. Mitchell, *From Reconstruction to Deconstruction: Undermining Black Landownership, Political Independence, and Community Through Partition Sales of Tenancies in Common*, 95 Nw. U. L. Rev. 505 (2001).

property if possible, or otherwise get a fair return.[83] Under the statute, court-ordered partition sales of heirs' property must be accompanied by an appraisal of its fair market value by a neutral appraiser, and non-petitioning co-owners may purchase the petitioning owner's fractional share at that appraised value. *UPHPA* §§6, 7. The Act then requires an evaluation of partition in kind, allowing consideration of factors such as "sentimental attachment to the property," including "ancestral or unique or other special value," "collective duration of ownership," the impact of a forced sale on a co-owner's use of the property, and the contribution of different co-owners to the maintenance and improvement of the property. *Id.* at §§8-9. And the Act regulates partition sales to try to replicate market conditions, rather than a judicial auction. *Id.* at §10. As of 2025, the Act has been adopted in 25 states, the District of Columbia, and the Virgin Islands,[84] and has been used to protect co-tenants.[85]

§8.4.2 Joint Management

Equal power

Commonly owned property is managed jointly by the co-tenants. This does not mean that each one must participate in management, but only that each tenant has an equal right to manage or control how the property is used. Any disputes must be worked out among the owners. They are free to agree that one (or more) of them will manage the property for the others. If the co-tenants cannot agree on management, the remedy is partition in the cases of tenancy in common and joint tenancy, and divorce in the case of tenancy by the entirety. In a partition proceeding, the court will either physically divide the property among the co-tenants or order it to be sold, and the proceeds distributed among them.[86]

§8.4.3 Contribution for Repairs and Maintenance

Co-owners may be liable to share costs of "necessary" repairs

Both the cases and the authorities are divided on the question of whether co-tenants (tenants in common, joint tenants, and tenants by the entirety) have a duty to contribute to the expenses for maintenance of commonly owned property.[87] Some courts hold that co-owners have no enforceable obligation to pay for repairs to the property, absent an agreement between them to do so.[88] Perhaps the courts do not want to get involved in disputes

[83] Thomas W. Mitchell, *Reforming Property Law to Address Devastating Land Loss*, 66 Ala. L. Rev. 1, 31-34 (2014).

[84] Alabama, Arizona, Arkansas, California, Connecticut, the District of Columbia, Florida, Georgia, Hawai'i, Illinois, Iowa, Maryland (substantially similar), Michigan, Mississippi, Missouri, Montana, Nevada, New Jersey, New Mexico, New York, South Carolina, Texas, U.S. Virgin Islands, Utah, Virginia (substantially similar), and Washington.

[85] *See, e.g.*, *Muhr v. Willenborg*, 6 N.W.3d 752 (Iowa Ct. App. 2024); *Gelinas LLC v. Hayes*, 221 N.Y.S.3d 877 (Sup. Ct. 2024).

[86] *See* §8.4.1.

[87] 7-50 *Powell on Real Property* §50.04[2]; Dale A. Whitman et al., *The Law of Property* §5.8, at 163-164 (4th ed. 2019).

[88] 7-50 *Powell on Real Property* §50.04[2]; John G. Sprankling, *Understanding Property Law* §10.03[E], at 150 (5th ed. 2023).

over the question of whether the repairs were necessary or frivolous. Other courts, however, hold that co-owners are obligated to share the costs of "necessary" repairs.[89] If such an obligation exists, a co-tenant who has paid more than her fair share of such expenses may sue the other tenants for an accounting to obtain contribution for their fair share of those expenses.

Accounting

No duty to share costs of major improvements

The courts all agree that co-owners have no obligation to contribute to the cost of major improvements unless the parties have previously agreed to share those costs.[90]

Credit on partition

Even though owners have no duty to share the cost of major improvements, an owner who contributed more than her share to substantial improvements is likely to be awarded a greater proportion of the proceeds if the property is sold pursuant to a partition.[91] This may also occur in the case of necessary repairs. Even if a jurisdiction would not allow an action for contribution to such costs, an owner who pays more than her proportional share of such necessary repairs may be awarded a greater portion of the proceeds if the property is sold at a partition.[92]

▶ HARD CASE

▷ CONTRIBUTION FOR REPAIRS FROM TENANT OUT OF POSSESSION

Argument that tenant in possession has no right to contribution

Some authorities state that a tenant who is occupying the property cannot obtain contribution from tenants who are not living in or occupying the premises for necessary repairs.[93] Alternatively, they assert that when a co-tenant in possession sues the non-occupying co-tenants for contribution to expenses of repair or maintenance, the claim should be offset by "the value of his or her use of the property which has exceeded his or her proportionate share of ownership."[94] This is so "even though he would not otherwise be liable; and similar adjustments are commonly made in partition suits generally."[95] Presumably, this approach is based on the notion that the tenant occupying the premises is obtaining greater benefit from the property than those out of possession and thus should be responsible for

[89] *Baran v. Juskulski*, 689 A.2d 1283, 1287 (Md. Ct. Spec. App. 1997); *Bednar v. Bednar*, 688 A.2d 1200, 1205 (Pa. Super. Ct. 1997); Dale A. Whitman et al., *The Law of Property* §5.8, at 164 (4th ed. 2019); 4-31 *Thompson on Real Property, Third Thomas Edition* §§31.07(b), 32.07(b), 33.07(b).

[90] *Hernandez v. Hernandez*, 645 So. 2d 171, 174 (Fla. Dist. Ct. App. 1994) (liability for necessary repairs); *Bednar v. Bednar*, 688 A.2d 1200, 1205 (Pa. Super. Ct. 1997) (no liability for contribution for improvements unless necessary to preserve the premises); 4-31 *Thompson on Real Property, Third Thomas Edition* §§31.07(a) & (b), 32.07(b), 33.07(b).

[91] 7-50 *Powell on Real Property* §50.04[2].

[92] John G. Sprankling, *Understanding Property Law* §10.03[E], at 150 (5th ed. 2023).

[93] 2 *American Law of Property* 78 n.2 (A. James Casner ed. 1952); 7-50 *Powell on Real Property* §50.04[2]; 4-31 *Thompson on Real Property, Third Thomas Edition* §31.07(b).

[94] *Barrow v. Barrow*, 527 So. 2d 1373, 1376 (Fla. 1988). *Accord, Esteves v. Esteves*, 775 A.2d 163 (N.J. Super. Ct. App. Div. 2001) (in accounting after house was sold, parents who occupied the house were entitled to be reimbursed by son for one-half of expenses of mortgage and update but son was allowed a credit against that moment equal to the value of his parents' sole possession of the property).

[95] 527 So. 2d at 1377.

ordinary repairs to the extent that the value of occupying the property exceeds her proportional share of ownership.

Argument that tenant in possession has a right to contribution from tenants out of possession

However, other authorities strongly criticize this approach, noting that each owner has "an equal right to possession" and that each owner should therefore have the obligation to contribute to necessary expenses to protect the property from waste.[96] The fact that one owner has chosen not to occupy the property does not change the fact that both owners have equal legal rights and thus should have equal obligations. If the tenant out of possession feels she is not deriving sufficient benefit from the property, the proper remedy is partition. ◀

Liability for mortgage and tax payments

Co-owners do have a duty to share the costs of charges necessary to preserve the property, and that could result in a lien against the property if not paid, including property taxes[97] and mortgage payments they have jointly assumed.[98] If property is inherited subject to a mortgage, the co-tenants are also likely to be found jointly responsible for those payments. However, co-tenants are not liable to share the cost of mortgages incurred by a fellow co-tenant on only her undivided fractional interest.[99] Similarly, no right of contribution exists if the taxes are assessed only against one owner's interest.[100] However, most authorities hold that a tenant in possession cannot obtain contribution from tenants out of possession for mortgage and tax payments if those payments are less than the fair rental value of the premises.[101]

§8.4.4 *Rental Benefits and Obligations*

Rental benefits

If the property is rented out, co-owners have the right to share the rental income in proportion to their respective fractional ownership interests. Thus, if property is rented to a third party, an owner of a one-quarter undivided fractional share is entitled to one-fourth of the rents, unless the parties agree otherwise.[102] However, if one owner rents her interests without first obtaining the consent of the others, they are free not to join in the lease and retain their possessory rights, including their right to lease their fractional interests.

[96] *Id. See also* 4-31 *Thompson on Real Property, Third Thomas Edition* §§31.07(b), 32.07(b) (criticizing the idea that tenants in possession have no right to contribution for necessary repairs).

[97] John G. Sprankling, *Understanding Property Law* §10.03[D], at 149 (5th ed. 2023); 4-31 *Thompson on Real Property, Third Thomas Edition* §§31.07(c), 32.07(c).

[98] *Martinez-Noda v. Pascual*, 305 So. 3d 321, 323 (Fla. Dist. Ct. App. 2020); John G. Sprankling, *Understanding Property Law* §10.03[D], at 150 (5th ed. 2023).

[99] 4-31 *Thompson on Real Property, Third Thomas Edition* §§31.07(c), 32.07(c).

[100] *In re Proceedings for Clallam County for Foreclosure of Liens*, 922 P.2d 73 (Wash. 1996); 4-32 *Thompson on Real Property, Third Thomas Edition* §32.07(c).

[101] 7-50 *Powell on Real Property* §50.04[2]; John G. Sprankling, *Understanding Property Law* §10.03[D], at 150-151 (5th ed. 2023); Dale A. Whitman et al., *The Law of Property* §5.8, at 165 (4th ed. 2019).

[102] Ala. Code §6-7-40; D.C. Code §16-101; N.Y. Real Prop. Acts. §1201.

▶ HARD CASE ▷ NO DUTY TO PAY RENT

Should co-tenants in possession pay rent to those who are not exercising their right to possess the property? All states agree that rent is due if the tenant in possession has *ousted* the other tenants by preventing them from occupying commonly owned property.[103] In the absence of ouster, the overwhelming majority of states hold that owners who chose to occupy commonly owned property have no obligation to pay rent to their co-owners who chose not to occupy the premises.[104] Each co-owner has the right to possess the whole, and each can choose whether to take advantage of this right. No owner loses anything if the other occupies the whole. However, a few states hold that occupying tenants do have a duty to pay rent to non-occupying tenants.[105]

Argument that there should be a duty to pay rent

Some scholars have argued that occupying tenants should pay rent to tenants who are not occupying the property.[106] One might argue, for example, that the tenant out of possession would receive a fractional share of rent if the property were rented out to a third party, and the co-owner's decision to occupy the property thereby deprives the non-occupying tenant of potential revenue from the property. To ensure that each owner receives benefit from the property, it is only fair for the tenant in possession to compensate the tenant out of possession for the fractional share of the rents she would receive if the property had been rented to a third party. The idea that the tenant in possession should pay rent is usually accompanied by the notion that the tenant out of possession has no duty to contribute to the expenses of undertaking ordinary repairs.

Criticism of the argument that co-tenants should pay rent

Although the notion that the tenant out of possession should derive some benefit from the property is appealing, it suggests that the tenant who chooses to occupy the property is exceeding her rights and depriving the others of something to which they are entitled. It is true that the property might generate rents if it were rented out to a third party, but this does not mean that each owner has a reasonable expectation that such rents will be earned. After all, each has the right to possess the whole. Thus, the tenant who chooses to occupy has done nothing wrong and is depriving the tenant out of possession of no rights to which she should be entitled. In addition, if the tenant out of possession is unhappy with the situation, the remedy of partition is available. ◀

Ouster

Rent is due to the non-occupying tenant(s) if the occupying tenant has ousted the non-occupying tenant(s) and effectively excluded them from the

[103] *Cohen v. Cohen*, 746 N.Y.S.2d 22, 23 (App. Div. 2002).

[104] 4-31 *Thompson on Real Property, Third Thomas Edition* §31.07(d). *See Hammonds v. Hammonds*, 522 So. 2d 305 (Ala. Civ. App. 1988); *H & Y Realty Co. v. Baron*, 554 N.Y.S.2d 111 (App. Div. 1990).

[105] *Lerman v. Levine*, 541 A.2d 523 (Conn. App. Ct.), *appeal denied*, 546 A.2d 281 (Conn. 1988); *Byse v. Lewis*, 400 S.E.2d 618 (Ga. 1990); *Sciotto v. Sciotto*, 288 A.2d 822 (Pa. 1972); *Albanese v. Condit*, 450 A.2d 1141 (Vt. 1982); *Blevins v. Shelton*, 383 S.E.2d 509 (W. Va. 1989).

[106] Evelyn Alicia Lewis, *Struggling with Quicksand: The Ins and Outs of Cotenant Possession Value Liability and a Call for Default Rule Reform*, 1994 Wis. L. Rev. 331.

property. An ouster can be accomplished only by such conduct as is sufficient both to exclude the non-occupying tenant(s) and to communicate to them an intent to do so.[107] Mere occupation of property by one of several owners is not sufficient to communicate an intent to oust the others.[108]

Constructive ouster

Some cases hold that constructive ouster may be shown where it is impracticable for the co-owners to occupy the property either because it is too small (physical impracticability) or because the parties cannot be reasonably expected to get along sufficiently well to live together (emotional impracticability).

▷ PHYSICAL IMPRACTICABILITY **HARD CASE ◀**

Argument in favor of constructive ouster

Some courts hold that constructive ouster is present if it is physically impracticable for all owners to occupy the property because it is too small.[109] A Georgia statute provides, for example, that a co-tenant is not liable for rent to other co-tenants only "[a]s long as a tenant in common occupies no greater portion of the joint property than his own share would be on partition."[110] Liability for rent attaches if a co-tenant "[d]eprives his co-tenant of the use of his fair proportion of the joint property; (4) [a]ppropriates the joint property to his exclusive use; or (5) [u]ses the joint property in a manner which must necessarily be exclusive."[111] If occupation by one tenant effectively excludes the others from the ability to use the property, then the excluded tenants are being deprived of their equal rights to possess the whole; this deprivation arguably should entitle the other tenants to receive rent.

Argument against finding constructive ouster

The counterargument is that the occupation of the property by one co-tenant does not, by itself, result in the exclusion of the other tenants. Each has the right to occupy, but not all may choose to exercise that right. The mere fact of occupation does not deny rights to a co-owner who did not intend or want to occupy the property. Only if the tenant out of possession wanted to move in and the tenant in possession refused would such a conflict arise. In that case, what is important is not the fact of occupation but the expressed intent of the tenant in possession to exclude the other(s). Under this reasoning, the mere fact of occupation should not be enough to constitute constructive ouster; rather, ouster arguably occurs only when the tenants out of possession demand a right to occupy and the tenant in possession refuses to accommodate them. This rule would then refuse to find exclusive possession to be constructive ouster, requiring the tenant seeking rent to show that there was a demand to share the possession and a

[107] *See Nelson v. Nelson*, 917 N.W.2d 479 (N.D. 2018) (finding ouster and ordering payment of rent when brother changed the locks on the door and refused to give his brother a key).
[108] 4-32 *Thompson on Real Property, Third Thomas Edition* §32.07(e).
[109] *Nott v. Gundick*, 180 N.W. 376, 378 (Mich. 1920); *Olivas v. Olivas*, 780 P.2d 640, 642 (N.M. Ct. App. 1989); *Oechsner v. Courcier*, 155 S.W.2d 963 (Tex. Ct. App. 1941).
[110] Ga. Code §44-6-121(a).
[111] Ga. Code §44-6-121(b)(3), (4), (5).

refusal; this, of course, is actual, not constructive ouster, and there is therefore no need for a rule of constructive ouster.[112] ◀

▶ **HARD CASE**

▷ EMOTIONAL OUSTER IN CONTEXT OF SEPARATION OR DIVORCE

In another class of cases, co-owners argue that they are entitled to rent under the constructive ouster doctrine because they could not get along with their co-owners and thus have been effectively excluded from jointly owned property. The usual case deals with a divorce or separation.[113] For example, in *Olivas v. Olivas*,[114] after a husband and wife separated, the husband moved out of the house. Although the wife filed for divorce two months later and the divorce was granted soon afterward, the property division was not finalized until three years later. The husband claimed that the separation meant that he and his wife could not live together, that he had been constructively ousted either when he moved out or she filed for divorce, and that he was therefore entitled to three years' rent from the wife (equal to one-half the fair rental value of the house). The court adopted the constructive ouster doctrine and held that "when the emotions of a divorce make it impossible for spouses to continue to share the marital residence pending a property division, the spouse who—often through mutual agreement—therefore departs the residence may be entitled to rent from the remaining spouse."[115] The court held, however, that the test for determining whether ouster was present was whether the tenant in possession had excluded the one who left. In this case, the husband had a girlfriend, and, in the words of Judge Hartz, "he was not pushed but pulled."[116] One court has created a rebuttable presumption of ouster of the spouse who moved out.[117]

Rejection of constructive ouster doctrine by some courts

However, other courts have refused to adopt the doctrine of constructive ouster.[118] They hold instead that a tenant has not been ousted unless the tenant in possession has physically excluded the other tenant and provided the ousted tenant with express notice of the occupying tenant's intent to assert ownership over the excluded tenant's fractional interest in the property.[119] ◀

[112] *See Newman v. Chase*, 359 A.2d 474, 481 (N.J. 1976) ("where one cotenant, with her family, remains in possession of a one-family house which is not susceptible of joint occupancy, and refuses to accede to plaintiff's demands for access to the property, such conduct clearly constitutes an ouster").

[113] *Hertz v. Hertz*, 657 P.2d 1169 (N.M. 1983); *Cummings v. Anderson*, 614 P.2d 1283, 1289 (Wash. 1980). *See also Cohen v. Cohen*, 746 N.Y.S.2d 22, 23 (App. Div. 2002) (no rent due despite ouster when tenant in possession had obtained a court protective order prohibiting co-tenant from occupying the property because of co-tenant's assaultive conduct).

[114] 780 P.2d 640 (N.M. Ct. App. 1989).

[115] *Id.* at 643. *Accord, In re Marriage of Watts*, 217 Cal. Rptr. 301 (Ct. App. 1985); *Palmer v. Protrka*, 476 P.2d 185, 190 (Or. 1970).

[116] 780 P.2d at 644.

[117] *Stylianopoulos v. Stylianopoulos*, 455 N.E.2d 477 (Mass. App. Ct. 1983).

[118] *Hughes v. Krueger*, 67 So. 2d 279 (Fla. 2011); *Curtis v. Dorn*, 234 P.3d 682 (Haw. 2010); *Newman v. Chase*, 359 A.2d 474 (N.J. 1976).

[119] *Barrow v. Barrow*, 527 So. 2d 1373 (Fla. 1988); *Newman v. Chase*, 359 A.2d 474 (N.J. 1976); *Kahnovsky v. Kahnovsky*, 21 A.2d 569 (R.I. 1941).

§8.4.5 *Leasing*

Right to lease without consent of other owners

Disputes often arise when one co-tenant leases her undivided fractional interest without consulting the other owners. It is sometimes argued that tenants in common and joint tenants should not be allowed to lease property without the consent of all the owners.[120] This is the majority approach with regard to tenancies by the entirety.[121] However, the courts uniformly reject this approach with regard to tenancies in common and joint tenancies.[122] Each owner has the power to alienate her interest without consent of the other owners, and this power to alienate includes the power to sell, mortgage, or lease the undivided fractional interest.[123] The remedy for co-owners who cannot agree on the disposition of the property is partition.[124]

Argument for freedom to lease

Each owner has the power to possess the whole property and thus must work together to determine how the property will be used. At the same time, no owner is forced to continue in a relationship with other owners if he or she wishes to end the relationship. The ability to transfer one's fractional ownership interest is therefore crucial, not only to making the property interest freely alienable in the marketplace, but also to protecting the autonomy of the owner who wants to obtain the market value of her property interest and be free from the duty to determine how to manage commonly owned property.

Argument for requiring agreement of all owners

The counterargument is that individually negotiated leases by individual owners can often harm the legitimate interests of their co-tenants. For example, in *Kresha v. Kresha*,[125] without consulting his wife, a husband leased his fractional share of the property to the son for a period of six years. Six days after the wife learned of the lease, she filed a lawsuit for separate maintenance, which the husband then converted into a divorce action. When the divorce was granted, the issue arose as to whether the lease would survive the divorce. Applying the majority rule, the court held that the husband was within his rights to lease his interest without the consent of his co-owner, and it made no difference that they were married. In addition, the court held that the lease survived the divorce, relegating the mother to partition as the only remedy. Allowing the husband to lease his interest without the consent of the wife protected his freedom to alienate his property, but it also substantially limited the wife's ability to control the property by forcing her to share it with a new co-possessor not of her own choosing.

Problematic application of partition when one co-tenant leased his interest

Although partition is available to the wife in this situation, it is not a wholly satisfactory remedy. If physical partition is viable, the property can be divided between the parties. The lessee would continue leasing one portion and the wife would own the other. The wife would then be free to sell

[120] *Carr v. Deking*, 765 P.2d 40 (Wash. Ct. App. 1988).

[121] See §8.2.3.

[122] *See* 20 Am. Jur. 2d *Cotenancy & Joint Ownership* §100 (2025); *James Vault & Precast Co. v. B&B Hot Oil Serv., Inc.*, 927 N.W.2d 452 (N.D. 2019); *Carr v. Deking*, 765 P.2d 40 (Wash. Ct. App. 1988).

[123] 7-50 *Powell on Real Property* §50.06[4].

[124] 4-38 *Thompson on Real Property, Third Thomas Edition* §38.03.

[125] 371 N.W.2d 280 (Neb. 1985).

the portion leased by the son to a buyer who would take it subject to the lease. She could sell her parcel as well. However, if physical partition is unavailable, partition by sale is far more problematic in this kind of situation. The property could be sold at a partition sale, but the buyer might get the property subject to the lease and the lessee would retain the right to possess the whole property, as he did beforehand, concurrently with the new buyer. If the lessee is restricted to part of the property and that part is sold, the new buyer would be buying subject to the lease and the market value of that parcel would reflect the benefit (in rental income) or burden (in terms of forgone opportunity for the new buyer to use the property herself) of the lease. However, an arrangement that will result in shared possessory rights between the lessee and a potential buyer may be much harder to manage and it may be even harder to find a potential purchaser in this situation. One solution would be to allow sale free of the burden of the lease, giving the lessee an appropriate portion of the partition proceeds.

§8.4.6 *Adverse Possession*

Ouster

Notice required before statute of limitations begins to run

Because co-owners have the right to possess the whole, no adverse possession claim can exist unless one of the owners effectively excludes the other(s). Such exclusion is called *ouster*. This almost always requires notice to the tenant being ousted that the tenant in possession intends to exclude the tenant out of possession.[126] Without such notice, the tenant living in the premises has violated no rights of the others and an intent to exclude the others must be communicated for the adversity of the occupation to be "open and notorious."

§8.5 Common Interest Communities

§8.5.1 *Condominiums and Homeowners' Associations*

Individual ownership of units and common ownership of common areas

Condominiums are, in the history of property law, a relatively recent innovation, unheard of before the 1960s.[127] Individuals own their units or apartments in fee simple and own common areas, such as stairways, the rooftop, and the exterior of the building, as tenants in common. Each owner is a member of the condominium association, with votes usually divided according to the size of the units. The association elects a governing board, which has powers to manage the common areas, to assess fees to maintain or improve common areas, and to pass rules regulating behavior in common areas and even in individual units when necessary to protect the interests of all owners. Although the common areas are owned by the individual

[126] *Pitson v. Sellers*, 613 N.Y.S.2d 1005 (App. Div. 1994). *Compare Parker v. Shecut*, 562 S.E.2d 620 (S.C. 2002) (ouster shown when brother made home his primary residence, changed the locks on the door, and refused to give his sister a key) *with Scott v. Yarbro*, 2008 WL 4613979 (Tenn. Ct. App. 2008) (no ouster even with more than fourty years of sole possession in the absence of any explicit acts to oust the other owners).

[127] Wayne S. Hyatt & Susan F. French, *Community Association Law: Cases and Materials on Common Interest Communities* 12 (2d ed. 2008).

owners jointly as tenants in common, the common property in a condominium is not subject to partition; ownership of it goes along with ownership of the individual units and partition is not available to an owner who wishes to opt out of such shared ownership of the common areas.

Relation to homeowners' associations

Condominium associations are similar (and in some cases identical) to homeowners' associations that may exist in residential subdivisions. One difference is that, in the case of homeowners' associations, it is often the association itself (a separate nonprofit corporation) that owns the common areas, rather than the homeowners as tenants in common.[128]

Declaration

A condominium or homeowners' association may be established in a new building or subdivision by filing a *declaration* in the registry of deeds. The declaration functions like a constitution for the association. It includes servitudes (including restrictive and affirmative covenants and mutual easements) applicable to the units, describes the powers of the association and the way in which the governing board is elected and its powers, and outlines the ways in which the declaration can be amended.

Condominium conversion

An existing building can also be converted to a condominium. For example, a landlord of a building with ten apartments can convert the building to a condominium by filing a declaration with the registry of deeds and then selling the individual units. The tenants may buy the units themselves, or others may buy them. Those new owners may choose to rent to the tenants already in place or evict them and either move in themselves or rent the units to other tenants. This process of conversion sometimes has the effect of displacing existing tenants because they cannot afford to buy their units. Some states and municipalities have attempted to protect the interests of existing tenants in remaining in their homes by passing legislation that places a moratorium on condominium conversion, or grants existing tenants a right of first refusal giving them the right to buy the unit for its fair market value in preference to any other buyer, or prohibits eviction of those tenants and imposes rent controls designed to protect existing tenants from rent increases that might cause them to move out.[129]

Relation to homeowners' associations

The popularity of the condominium form spilled over into residential subdivisions, resulting in homeowners' associations being created both to manage common property, such as recreational areas or private streets, and to enforce servitudes in the subdivision. These two developments have now merged and the law of condominiums and homeowners' associations has evolved into a common legal structure. The *Restatement (Third) of Property (Servitudes)* calls them "common interest communities" and refers to both homeowners' associations and condominium associations as "associations."[130] The regulatory rules in the *Restatement (Third)* are limited to residential communities on the ground that residential purchasers are less likely to "appreciate the significance of the details or be able to negotiate

[128] *Id.* at 21.

[129] *See, e.g.*, Mass. Acts 1983, ch. 527, §§1-5D, 7 (regulating condominium conversions); *Dumont Oaks Community Ass'n, Inc. v. Montgomery County*, 634 A.2d 459 (Md. 1993) (describing local condominium conversion ordinance granting tenants a right of first refusal); 4-36 *Thompson on Real Property, Third Thomas Edition* §36.12.

[130] *Restatement (Third) of Property (Servitudes)* §6.2 (2000).

changes in the documents governing association powers" than are commercial purchasers or lessees.[131]

Restatement (Third) of Property (Servitudes)

A "common interest community" is "a real-estate development or neighborhood in which individually owned lots or units are burdened by a servitude that imposes an obligation that cannot be avoided by nonuse or withdrawal" to support the maintenance of common property or to pay dues to an association that provides services to the owners, manages common property, and enforces other servitudes burdening the property in the development.[132]

Common interest communities

What is essential to the definition of a common interest community is the presence of an association. The *Restatement (Third)* seems also to limit the definition to associations that are empowered to assess fees or collect dues from members to assist in managing common property or in enforcing reciprocal covenants.[133] Condominiums, by definition, include such associations and such monetary obligations because individual ownership extends only to the interior of the individuals' units and the common property must be managed and maintained collectively.

New estate

When condominiums were first invented, their legal status was unclear. Although they combine traditional estates, they do so in such a new way that they appeared to create a new estate. Recall that there is a general bias in the legal system against the creation of new estates on the grounds that complicated new estates inhibit the alienability of property and may interfere both with the autonomy of owners and with efficient or socially beneficial land use.[134] For this reason, the states passed statutes that authorized the creation of condominiums and regulated their creation.[135] These statutes generally require condominium developers to write a declaration establishing the condominium; defining the ownership shares of the unit owners in the association, the way the governing board is elected and both its powers and the powers of the association; and describing enforceable covenants and easements, and the ways in which the declaration can be amended.

Condominium statutes

Relations with developer

Problems have often developed in the relationship between the developer and the condominium association. When the developer first establishes the condominium, she owns all the units. She therefore has a majority control of the votes and can control the association. Two problems have arisen in this situation.

Developer duty to relinquish control

First, depending on the real estate market, the developer may not be able to sell all the units. It may happen that a majority of the units remain in the hands of the developer for some time, allowing the developer to

[131] *Id.* at §6.1.

[132] *Id.* at §6.2.

[133] It is ordinarily the case that the association will be empowered to collect dues; this is universally the case where there is common property to be managed or maintained. However, it may not be so in the context of a residential subdivision; if no common property exists, an association may be empowered to enforce reciprocal negative servitudes but not empowered to collect dues or make assessments. It is not clear if the *Restatement* rules are intended to not apply in such a case.

[134] *See* §7.7.2.

[135] *See, e.g.*, Mass. Gen. Laws ch. 183A, §§1 to 22.

continue controlling the association and therefore making policy for the community. Some states have passed statutes that require the developer to turn over control of the association to the other owners after a reasonable time.[136] The *Restatement (Third)* itself now provides that developers have a duty to create an association and to turn over control to the association or the members of the association other than the developer "[a]fter the time reasonably necessary to protect its interests in completing and marketing the project."[137]

Power to avoid management contracts with developer

Second, many developers have signed long-term management contracts with the association, which give the developer the power and the right to manage the common areas. Because these contracts are signed at a time that the developer has a majority interest in the association, they amount to "self-dealing." Because the contracts are generally long term, they lock the association into the arrangement, often at relatively high prices, protecting the developer from facing competitive bids by other potential managers. Many state statutes, and the *Restatement (Third)*, provide that the association can repudiate any contracts entered into when the developer was in control of the association. The *Restatement (Third)* allows the association to repudiate three types of contracts entered into before the developer relinquishes control of the association, including (1) contracts for the provision of management or maintenance services; (2) any contract between the association and the developer; and (3) any contract that is "unconscionable."[138] Because the *Restatement (Third)* also requires the developer to relinquish control of the association after a reasonable marketing period, this provision would entitle a minority of owners to terminate any management contracts with the developer, even if the developer retains a majority of the votes, as long as the reasonable marketing period has ended.

Statutory regulation

Some state statutes allow associations to invalidate such contracts by a supermajority vote, such as two-thirds.[139] The federal government has passed a regulatory statute, the *Condominium and Cooperative Conversion Protection and Abuse Relief Act*,[140] giving condominium associations the power to terminate management contracts of more than three years entered into between the developer and the association, while the developer had a majority control of the association.[141] However, the association must exercise this right within two years of the developer's relinquishing control of the association or after the developer ceases to own twenty-five percent or less of the units — whichever happens first.[142]

[136] Tex. Prop. Code §209.00591(c); *Barclay v. DeVeau*, 429 N.E.2d 323 (Mass. 1981) (interpreting the state statute to obligate the developer to turn over control of the association to the other members after a reasonable marketing period).
[137] *Restatement (Third) of Property (Servitudes)* §6.19(1) & (2) (2000).
[138] *Id.* at §6.19.
[139] *Comcast of Florida v. L'Ambiance Beach Condominium Association, Inc.*, 17 So. 3d 839 (Fla. Dist. Ct. App. 2009) (Florida statute allowed 75 percent or more of unit ownership to repudiate contract permitting company to provide and manage cable service).
[140] 15 U.S.C. §§3601 to 3616.
[141] 15 U.S.C. §3607(a). *See Tudor City Place Ass'n v. 2 Tudor City Tenants Corp.*, 924 F.2d 1247 (2d Cir. 1991) (applying the statute).
[142] 15 U.S.C. §3607(b).

Restraints on alienation

Many condominiums have restraints on alienation of individual units. The most common types are (1) requirements that the governing board (or the association) consent to the sale of a unit;[143] (2) rights of first refusal held by the association itself (exercised through the board) or by other members of the association;[144] and (3) restrictions on leasing.[145] Restraints on alienation of condominium units are generally held to be enforceable but may be struck down as unreasonable restraints on alienation if they do not adequately protect the right of existing owners to transfer their interests for fair value. Restrictions on leasing are almost always upheld, although courts may not allow such restrictions to be placed retroactively on buyers who purchased before those restrictions were in place.[146] Requirements that the board consent to the sale of units are likely to be struck down if the declaration does not require consent to be granted or withheld within a reasonable period.[147] Moreover, denial of consent is likely to be held to be an unreasonable restraint on alienation unless the board has a good reason for the denial or has an obligation to purchase the unit itself for its fair market value.[148]

▶ HARD CASE ▷ RIGHTS OF FIRST REFUSAL

Argument that they may be exercised for any reason

The courts are divided on the question of whether rights of first refusal must be exercised reasonably. In *Wolinsky v. Kadison*,[149] a condominium board exercised a right of first refusal to prevent one of the unit owners from purchasing a unit that had just gone on the market. Some courts hold that rights of first refusal can be exercised for any nondiscriminatory reason[150] as long as the unit owner is guaranteed fair market value of her property. After all, the owners impliedly agreed to such restrictions when they purchased their units. Moreover, the ability to control the transfer of neighboring units may increase the market value of the units by giving the

[143] *See, e.g., Aquarian Foundation, Inc. v. Sholom House, Inc.*, 448 So. 2d 1166 (Fla. Dist. Ct. App. 1984).

[144] *Cambridge Co. v. East Slope Investment Corp.*, 700 P.2d 537 (Colo. 1985); *Wolinsky v. Kadison*, 449 N.E.2d 151 (Ill. App. Ct. 1983).

[145] *Breene v. Plaza Towers Ass'n*, 310 N.W.2d 730 (N.D. 1981).

[146] *Compare Breene v. Plaza Towers Ass'n*, 310 N.W.2d 730 (N.D. 1981) (leasing prohibition cannot be imposed retroactively) *with McElveen-Hunter v. Fountain Manor Ass'n, Inc.*, 386 S.E.2d 435 (N.C. Ct. App. 1989) (leasing prohibition may be enforced retroactively) *and Worthinglen Condo. Unit Owners' Ass'n v. Brown*, 566 N.E.2d 1275 (Ohio Ct. App. 1989) (retroactive enforcement does not nullify statutory right of notice of restrictions where the declaration sets out all restrictions at time of purchase).

[147] *Aquarian Foundation, Inc. v. Sholom House, Inc.*, 448 So. 2d 1166 (Fla. Dist. Ct. App. 1984). *See* Andrea J. Boyack, *American Dream in Flux: The Endangered Right to Lease a Home*, 49 Real Prop. Trust & Est. L.J. 203 (Fall 2014) (criticizing leasing restraints in condominiums).

[148] *Aquarian Foundation, Inc. v. Sholom House, Inc.*, 448 So. 2d 1166 (Fla. Dist. Ct. App. 1984).

[149] 449 N.E.2d 151 (Ill. App. Ct. 1983).

[150] Fair housing laws prohibit the exercise of a right of first refusal to prevent property from being occupied because of the purchaser's race, for example. *Wolinsky v. Kadison*, 449 N.E.2d 151 (Ill. App. Ct. 1983).

owners the power to control who moves into the community. The value associated with this power may increase the alienability of the units.

Argument that they must be exercised reasonably

However, the court in *Wolinsky* held that the law imposed an additional obligation that the exercise of the right of first refusal be reasonable. "A board must exercise a right of first refusal reasonably upon consideration of the prospective purchaser's qualifications in light of the economic and social reasons which justify the restraint itself."[151] The exercise of a right of first refusal can be used in an exclusionary, and even a discriminatory, manner, and can substantially harm the interests of individual owners who want to determine to whom to sell or lease their property and who feel that the power is exercised in an unreasonable or discriminatory manner by the association. ◀

Declaration enforceable unless contrary to public policy

The covenants in common interest community declarations are subject to the same rules as other servitudes. They are presumptively enforceable, but may be declared void and unenforceable if they infringe on constitutionally protected rights, contravene a statute or administrative regulation, violate public policy, or are "unconscionable."[152]

Free contract versus protection from onerous provisions

The declaration is akin to a constitution. It establishes the basic structure of the association, its powers, and the procedures for amending it. Because it is required to be recorded before the owners purchase their units, those purchasers are on actual or constructive notice of its contents and are deemed to have impliedly agreed to its terms.[153] This suggests that the terms of the declaration should be given great deference because the buyers have agreed to them and presumably could have searched elsewhere for housing if they did not like the terms of the declaration. On the other hand, many residential buyers do not read the declaration carefully (or at all) and may not actually be aware of its contents. It is therefore arguable whether its terms represent the "will of the parties." In addition, because the terms come packaged (or "tied") together, transaction costs are certain to prevent buyers who dislike some terms to bargain to have them removed before purchasing the property. If the market is working perfectly, one might hope that purchasers could find appropriate housing where they want to live that contains the terms they want to find, but, in reality, the terms created by developers may not magically line up with the demands of all consumers. It is therefore arguable that this market failure may justify a skeptical attitude toward declaration terms that seem onerous or go too far in limiting the legal rights of unit owners to control their own units, or to be free from control by the community.

[151] *Id.* at 155.

[152] *See* §6.7.4.

[153] "Because the declaration is ordinarily recorded before common interest community members purchase their properties, greater weight is often given the terms of the declaration than the terms of other governing documents that are not recorded," such as rules or by-laws. *Restatement (Third) of Property (Servitudes)* §6.2 cmt. e (2000).

▶ HARD CASE

▷ IMPLIED RIGHT TO CREATE COMMUNITY ASSOCIATION WITH ASSESSMENT (TAXING) POWERS

Developers sometimes sell lots with appurtenant rights to use one or more commonly owned lots. These common rights may be appurtenant easements or the lots may be owned in common by each of the appurtenant owners as tenants in common. If the developer has not made any provision for the management of the commonly owned property, some courts have held that there is an implied right in the owners to create a community association with the power to tax individual owners to maintain the common property. In *Weatherby Lake Improvement Co. v. Sherman*,[154] for example, the lot owners who owned a lake in common were required to pay dues to a homeowners' association established to maintain the lake even though the developer failed to create a homeowners' association or make provision for dues to such an association in the declaration. The court held that management of the common property was necessary and that an association was the best way to accomplish this end.[155] In contrast, in *Wendover Road Property Owners Ass'n v. Kornicks*,[156] the court refused to order a lot owner to contribute to the cost of sewers, water lines, and pavement installed on an easement road owned in common with other owners along the road; nor were the other appurtenant owners entitled to a share of the sales proceeds when that lot owner sold his house, even though its value had been substantially increased by the improvements to his easements to which he had not contributed. Judge Pryatel explained that "there is no precedent for compelling participation in the cost of street improvements by an unwilling landowner in the absence of a contract or legislative authority, nor are we aware of any."[157] "One who officiously confers a benefit upon another is not entitled to restitution therefor."[158]

Restatement (Third)

The *Restatement (Third)* provides that owners of a majority of lots "may create an association for the purpose of managing the common property."[159] The *Restatement (Third)* goes so far as to authorize a court to create an association — even if the declaration forbids it — if this is necessary to manage

[154] 611 S.W.2d 326 (Mo. Ct. App. 1980). *Cf. Evergreen Highlands Ass'n v. West*, 73 P.3d 1 (Colo. 2003) (association has power to add new declaration provisions including provisions authorizing, for the first time, mandatory assessments to maintain common areas).

[155] 611 S.W.2d at 331. *See also Evergreen Highlands Ass'n v. West*, 73 P.3d 1 (Colo. 2003) (homeowners' association could be created retroactively when common interest community was effectively implied in the covenants); *Wisniewski v. Kelly*, 437 N.W.2d 25 (Mich. Ct. App. 1989) (lot owners had power to manage common property even though developer had retained the power to manage that property and had never transferred that power to the association); *Windemere Homeowner's Ass'n v. McCue*, 990 P.2d 769 (Mont. 1999) (amending restrictive covenants to create a homeowners' association); *Sunday Canyon Property Owners Ass'n v. Annett*, 978 S.W.2d 654 (Tex. Ct. App. 1998) (covenant allowing 51 percent of owners to amend the covenants granted those owners the power to create a homeowners' association with assessment powers).

[156] 502 N.E.2d 226 (Ohio Ct. App. 1985).

[157] *Id.* at 229.

[158] *Id.*

[159] *Restatement (Third) of Property (Servitudes)* §6.3 (2000). *See Evergreen Highlands Ass'n v. West*, 73 P.3d 1 (Colo. 2003) (adopting this rule).

common property.[160] The idea that there is an implied power to create an association can be justified on the ground that it provides the best mechanism for managing common property. When more than a few individuals own property in common, transaction costs may well block creation of an association, and partition is generally not available as a remedy for tenants in common of property that is appurtenant to ownership of other lots.[161] Moreover, one could argue that, upon becoming a co-tenant of common property, the individual lot or unit owners should have known that they might have some obligations to share the cost of maintenance of that property; this suggests an implied promise to participate in any reasonable management scheme. On the other hand, implying a duty to pay assessments to an association created by one's neighbors (even though they are also co-tenants of common property) subjects individual owners to the taxing power of their neighbors in the absence of express agreement. This is an extraordinary obligation to impose on individual owners against their will. ◀

Power to amend declaration

The declaration normally defines the way it can be amended. Amendments often require a supermajority vote (such as two-thirds). The *Restatement (Third)* allows the declaration to be amended by majority vote only in the case of decisions to extend the term of the declaration or to make reasonably necessary administrative changes.[162] In other situations, unless the declaration or a statute provides otherwise, the *Restatement (Third)* requires a two-thirds vote to amend the declaration. However, a unanimous vote is required for changes that "prohibit or materially restrict the use or occupancy of, or behavior within, individually owned property" or that change the "basis for allocating voting rights or assessments among community members."[163] In one case, for example, a court struck down an amendment to a declaration that prohibited the clients of the seven first-floor commercial condominiums from using the lobby on the ground that it was unreasonable to deny them access to this commonly owned area and that it was discriminatory against seven of the two hundred and thirty-two owners.[164]

▷ RETROACTIVE LIMITS ON LEASING **HARD CASE ◀**

Can the declaration be amended retroactively to prohibit leasing of individual units? Most courts have answered in the affirmative on the ground that condominium owners expressly agreed to allow amendment of the declaration by a vote of the members of the association and thus impliedly agreed

[160] "The judicial power to authorize creation of an association is that of a court of equity with its attendant flexibility and discretion to fashion remedies to correct mistakes and oversights and to protect the public interest." *Restatement (Third) of Property (Servitudes)* §6.3 & cmt. a (2000).

[161] Partition is not available as a remedy for disputes about common property in the condominium context or in residential subdivisions.

[162] *Restatement (Third) of Property (Servitudes)* §6.10 (2000).

[163] *Id.*

[164] *The Ridgely Condominium Ass'n, Inc. v. Smyrnioudis*, 660 A.2d 942 (Md. Ct. Spec. App. 1995).

to whatever changes they would make.[165] However, other courts have held that restraints on alienation are disfavored and that they cannot be imposed retroactively on buyers who purchased before the leasing restrictions were imposed unless they voluntarily agree to the restrictions.[166] The *Restatement (Third)* requires unanimous consent for declaration amendments that "prohibit or materially restrict the use or occupancy of units"[167] or "that deprive owners of significant property or civil rights."[168] However, it makes this rule disclaimable; if the declaration provides otherwise, it is enforceable unless a statute prohibits retroactive enforcement. At least one state has passed a statute prohibiting retroactive leasing restrictions.[169] ◀

Power to make rules limited by reasonableness requirement

Condominium and homeowners' associations have the power to promulgate rules regulating use of common areas and even conduct inside individual units that affects other owners.[170] These powers are ordinarily included in the declaration. Sometimes these rules are challenged by individual owners who believe they cut too deeply into the rights of the unit owners to use their property as they like. Most courts review such rules and by-laws for *reasonableness* and strike them down if they unreasonably interfere with the ability of the unit owners to use their own property. Although provisions in the declaration are ordinarily enforced unless they violate public policy, rules adopted by the association that are not included in the declaration are subject to a higher degree of scrutiny. Because owners are on constructive notice of restrictions in the declaration, they arguably impliedly agree to be bound by them; however, rules adopted subsequently do not necessarily have the same imprimatur (although it is often argued that the owners purchased the property knowing they would be subject to rules promulgated by the association and thus impliedly agreed to be bound by whatever the majority agreed upon).[171]

Test for reasonableness

Some courts suggest that rules should be struck down as unreasonable if they are overly intrusive or not related to protecting legitimate interests of the neighbors.[172] The *Restatement (Third)*, for example, provides that, unless the declaration grants greater powers, the association's power to regulate

[165] *See, e.g., Ritchey v. Villa Nueva Condominium Ass'n, Inc.*, 146 Cal. Rptr. 695 (Ct. App. 1978); *Burgess v. Pelkey*, 738 A.2d 783 (D.C. 1999); *Hill v. Fontaine Condominium Ass'n, Inc.*, 334 S.E.2d 690 (Ga. 1985); *Adams v. Kimberley One Townhouse Owner's Ass'n*, 352 P.3d 492 (Idaho 2015); *McElveen-Hunter v. Fountain Manor Ass'n, Inc.*, 386 S.E.2d 435 (N.C. Ct. App. 1989); *Shorewood West Condominium Ass'n v. Sadri*, 992 P.2d 1008 (Wash. 2000). *See also Franklin v. Spadafora*, 447 N.E.2d 1244 (Mass. 1983) (by-law limiting ownership by any one person to two units held to be reasonable); Patrick A. Randolph, Jr., *Changing the Rules: Should Courts Limit the Power of Common Interest Communities to Alter Unit Owners' Privileges in the Face of Vested Expectations?*, 38 Santa Clara L. Rev. 1081 (1998).

[166] *Rancho Santa Paula Mobilehome Park, Ltd. v. Evans*, 32 Cal. Rptr. 2d 464 (Ct. App. 1994); *Breene v. Plaza Towers Ass'n*, 310 N.W.2d 730 (N.D. 1981); *Wilkinson v. Chiwawa Communities Ass'n*, 327 P.3d 614 (Wash. 2014).

[167] *Restatement (Third) of Property (Servitudes)* §6.10(2) (2000).

[168] *Id.* at §6.10 cmt. g.

[169] Fla. Stat. §718.110(13).

[170] *Restatement (Third) of Property (Servitudes)* §6.7(2) (2000).

[171] *Id.* at §6.7 cmt. b.

[172] *Pines of Boca Barwood Condominium Ass'n, Inc. v. Cavouti*, 605 So. 2d 984 (Fla. Dist. Ct. App. 1992); *Noble v. Murphy*, 612 N.E.2d 266 (Mass. App. Ct. 1993); *Restatement (Third) of Property (Servitudes)* §6.7, §6.7 cmt. e (2000).

conduct inside the units or lots is limited to regulating "nuisance-like activities" that interfere with the use or enjoyment of neighboring units.[173] This limitation is based on "the traditional expectations of property owners that they are free to use their property for uses that are not prohibited and do not unreasonably interfere with their neighbors' use and enjoyment of their property."[174] This standard suggests a fairly robust judicial review of such rules. However, other courts hold that condominium rules should ordinarily be upheld unless there is evidence of misconduct or self-dealing as long as the action was taken in good faith in the furtherance of the legitimate interests of the association.[175] This standard — often called the "business judgment rule" — does not allow the court to "second-guess" the reasonableness of the rule.[176] Some courts adopt a deferential stance but allow a rule to be struck down if it was adopted without a sufficient factual basis — a situation that might suggest it was not adopted in good faith.[177]

Business judgment rule

Both the association and its governing board have fiduciary obligations to the members to act fairly and reasonably in the management of the community.[178] For example, in *Wolinsky v. Kadison*,[179] the governing board of a condominium that exercised a right of first refusal to prevent a current owner from purchasing another unit in the building was held to have acted unreasonably when it failed to first obtain the requisite vote of the association, as required by the declaration. The court found that all condominium association board members and officers have fiduciary obligations to members of the association and must "act in a manner reasonably related to the exercise of that duty."[180] Violation of this duty may subject the individual board members to damages.

Fiduciary obligations of association and governing board to the members

---

▷ PETS **HARD CASE ◀**

Many associations have passed rules limiting or prohibiting pets in the units. Such rules are almost always upheld.[181] At the same time, a huge amount of litigation has ensued on this question, with many pet-lovers incensed that they could be restricted in their ability to keep pets in their apartments, especially in the absence of evidence that those pets affect the use or enjoyment either of neighboring property or common areas. And a court decision allowing such prohibitions was so unpopular in California

173 *Restatement (Third) of Property (Servitudes)* §6.7 cmt. b (2000).

174 *Id.*

175 *Gilman v. Pebble Cove Home Owners Ass'n, Inc.*, 546 N.Y.S.2d 134 (App. Div. 1989).

176 *In Matter of Levandusky v. One Fifth Avenue Apartment Corp.*, 553 N.E.2d 1317 (N.Y. 1990) (announcing the business judgment rule).

177 *See, e.g., Riss v. Angel*, 934 P.2d 669 (Wash. 1997) (decision of architectural board was unreasonable because it did not have an adequate factual basis).

178 *Restatement (Third) of Property (Servitudes)* §§6.13, 6.14 (2000).

179 449 N.E.2d 151 (Ill. App. Ct. 1983).

180 *Id.* at 157.

181 *Dulaney Towers Maintenance Corp. v. O'Brey*, 418 A.2d 1233 (Md. Ct. Spec. App. 1980) (board rule limiting units to one pet per unit reasonable because of potential for noise, odors, and soiling of common areas); *Noble v. Murphy*, 612 N.E.2d 266 (Mass. App. Ct. 1993) (ban on pets in condominium is reasonable).

that the legislature enacted a statute guaranteeing owners the right to keep at least one pet regardless of covenants to the contrary.[182] A hard question is whether such controls can be imposed retroactively, forcing existing owners to give up their pets. Pet limitations are normally imposed prospectively only to protect the relationships that have already been established between owners and their pets. ◀

▶ HARD CASE ▷ ARCHITECTURAL CONTROLS

Many condominiums have servitudes granting power to an architectural board (or to the governing board) to approve any changes to the external appearance of units. The courts unanimously hold that "discretionary design controls must be reasonably exercised."[183] At the same time, because aesthetic judgments differ, controls by architectural design commissions are ordinarily upheld if they are intended to promote uniformity or are otherwise thought to have a reasonable basis.[184] ◀

§8.5.2 Cooperatives

Collective ownership by nonprofit corporation

In a cooperative, the entire building is owned by a single nonprofit corporation. Individual owners buy shares in the corporation and then lease their individual units from the corporation. They do not own their own units individually; nor do they own the building except as shareholders of the corporation. Because ownership is vested in the corporation, the entire cooperative will be financed by a single "blanket" mortgage loan obtained by the corporation itself. The monthly payment by each owner (in the form of rent) covers that owner's share of the mortgage payment, as well as fees for upkeep and management. If an individual owner fails to make her monthly payment to the corporation, other owners must make up the difference to prevent foreclosure. Defaulting tenants can be evicted by the corporation and lose their stock.

Power to veto new members

The greater financial interdependence of cooperative owners makes this a more fragile structure than the condominium structure; it is therefore much less common. Because of the financial interdependence of cooperative owners, cooperatives often assume the power to approve or veto sales of particular units to protect other cooperative members' collective financial stake in the building. Cooperatives often do this by reserving the right to approve any transfer of any leasehold and the associated shares.

Danger of discrimination or arbitrary treatment

Often, cooperatives refuse to allow individuals to purchase shares and move into the facility for reasons that have nothing to do with financial

[182] Cal. Civ. Code §4715 (invalidating covenants that deny owners the right to keep at least one pet). *But see Villa de las Palmas Homeowners Ass'n v. Terifaj*, 90 P.3d 1223 (Cal. 2004) (declaration can be amended to exclude pets).

[183] *Appel v. Presley Cos.*, 806 P.2d 1054 (N.M. 1991); *Restatement (Third) of Property (Servitudes)* §6.9 cmt. d (2000).

[184] *Sprunk v. Creekwood Condominium Unit Owners' Ass'n*, 573 N.E.2d 197 (Ohio Ct. App. 1989) (rejection of owner's request to install a screen door was reasonable).

integrity. There is therefore a significant danger that this power can be used in a discriminatory fashion. For example, in *170 West 85 Street HDFC v. Jones*,[185] a gay man lived for sixteen years in a cooperative apartment with his life partner. When he died, the life partner tried to stay in the apartment, but the cooperative refused to allow him to stay. A clause in the lease agreement provided that neither the directors nor the shareholders may "unreasonably withhold consent to assignment of the lease and a transfer of the Shares to a financially responsible member of the Shareholder's family (other than the Shareholder's spouse, as to whom no consent is required) who shall have accepted all the terms and conditions of this lease."[186] The life partner sued, claiming that the exclusion was based on his sexual orientation, a form of housing discrimination illegal in New York. Civil rights laws prohibit cooperatives from denying access if their reasons are discriminatory.

§8.5.3 *Affordable Housing Arrangements*

Limited equity cooperatives

The cooperative form has been used as a vehicle for creating affordable housing and keeping it affordable. In a limited equity cooperative, both the lease and the share agreements allow sale of the owner's shares at a fixed price, thus preventing the owner from benefiting from increases in the market value of the unit. Sometimes the owner is allowed to sell the shares to a third party at the fixed price; often the arrangement gives the cooperative a right of first refusal to purchase the shares, with their accompanying possessory rights, at the prearranged price.[187]

Community land trust

A community land trust is a nonprofit corporation that generally has an elected board of directors (or board of trustees) and an open membership. The trust buys and holds title to property, ordinarily by acquiring inexpensive land located in a depressed area or land whose purchase is subsidized by government loans, loan guarantees, or subsidies. While retaining title to the land, the trust sells the building located on the land to a low-income purchaser or group of purchasers. Separating ownership of the land and the building requires a lease by the trust, as owner of the land, granting possessory rights to the owner of the building; this arrangement, called a "ground lease," is common in commercial transactions involving large office buildings. The ground lease ordinarily lasts for a long time and may be renewable. Because the trust retains title to the land and because, as a nonprofit organization, its purpose is to finance affordable housing for low-income persons, the trust sells the building and provides terms in the ground lease at rates that low-income persons can afford.

Limits on resale price to keep housing affordable

A crucial aspect of the ground lease arrangement is the agreement between the owner and the lessee-purchaser that the building will be sold only to the community land trust, or to another low-income owner, at a price well below market value (not on the open market for its fair market

[185] 673 N.Y.S.2d 830 (Civ. Ct. 1998).

[186] *Id.* at 834.

[187] Judith Bernstein-Baker, *Cooperative Conversion: Is It Only for the Wealthy? Proposals That Promote Affordable Cooperative Housing in Philadelphia*, 61 Temp. L. Rev. 393 (1988).

value). This price ordinarily is fixed at an amount equal to the owner's initial investment (the purchase price), future investment (mortgage principal payments plus costs of improvements made by the owner), with an adjustment for inflation.[188] Generally, the ground lease gives the community land trust a right of first refusal to purchase the building for the fixed price. This arrangement ensures that the property will remain, in the future, low-cost and therefore available to other low-income families and persons.

§8.5.4 *Continuing Care Retirement Communities*

CCRCs

A rapidly expanding form of common ownership is the continuing care retirement community (CCRC). Residents are normally senior citizens who purchase access to housing combined with access to complete medical care, including nursing home facilities. The communities differ from nursing homes because they contain separate living units and many residents do not yet need nursing care services. Ordinarily, a buyer will pay a substantial price for an apartment and then pay monthly fees. In return, the buyer gets a place to live plus the ability to move to different portions of the facility if the need for medical or nursing care changes. Some facilities have special areas for Alzheimer's patients that restrict exit to ensure that people are kept safe.

These facilities have a variety of legal structures. Some are structured as leases with contracts for care. Some resemble a condominium or cooperative structure while giving managing powers to a for-profit or nonprofit managing company. Others purport to deny any property rights at all to residents, structuring the arrangement as a license with contract rights and obligations similar to the way most college dormitories are structured.

Disputes may arise in these facilities when either the management itself or family members want to move a resident from one apartment to another (usually with more care or supervision) or bans a member from certain services such as a particular dining area. Residents may resist such changes. Conversely, residents may seek higher services that the management does not think they need. And residents may be expelled from the facility for nonpayment of fees or violation of rules.[189] State law is developing in this area and may prohibit eviction from such facilities in the absence of just cause. New Jersey, for example, has a *Continuing Care Retirement Community Regulation and Financial Disclosure Act* that regulates such facilities in this manner.[190] The agreements themselves normally provide this as well.

§8.6 Business Property

Partnerships; corporations; nonprofit organizations

The ownership forms associated with business are generally taught in upper-level courses in corporations, partnership, and nonprofit

[188] David Abramowitz, *Nuts and Bolts on Land Trusts, Housing Matters* 4-5 (Massachusetts Law Reform Inst., Jan./Feb. 1989).

[189] *Seabrook Village v. Murphy*, 853 A.2d 280 (N.J. Super. Ct. App. Div. 2004) (resident can be removed for nonpayment of fees).

[190] N.J. Stat. §52:27D-344(d); *see generally* N.J. Stat. §§52:27D-330 to -360.

organizations. It is helpful, however, to have a basic understanding of them because the models of ownership associated with business enterprises differ from those associated with concurrent ownership, family property, or residential common interest communities. The following is only the briefest introduction to the subject.

§8.6.1 Partnerships

Association of two or more persons for profit

A partnership is "an association of two or more persons to carry on as co-owners a business for profit."[191] Many partnerships are informal, begun by oral arrangements. Many partners, however, sign partnership agreements that describe in detail their respective powers and obligations. Partnerships can provide goods or services and often own or lease real estate where the business is conducted.

Aggregate theory

The partnership has long been the subject of two competing property models. The older model is the *aggregate theory*. This approach views the partnership as similar in certain respects to a tenancy in common and refers to the ownership structure as *tenancy in partnership*. This approach treats a partnership as "an aggregate of individuals that [hold] title to partnership property in trust for the partnership."[192] Under this view, each of the owners has an individual property right in the property owned by the partnership and has an equal right with the other partners to manage jointly owned property. The partnership does not own property in its own name.

Tenancy in partnership

Older common law approach

The common law before 1916 treated the partnership as a kind of tenancy in common, although individual partners stood in a trust relationship with the others. This meant that property "was acquired in trust for the partnership [and] the property was held by the partners as tenants in common."[193] The partners each had an equitable right (the "partner's equity") to have partnership property "applied first to the payment of firm debts and liabilities, including amounts owed to the partners themselves."[194]

Entity theory

The opposing, more modern, view treats the partnership as an independent *entity* that owns the property in its own right, with the partners having ownership rights in the partnership but not in the real or personal property owned by the partnership entity.

Revised Uniform Partnership Act

The *Uniform Partnership Act* (*UPA*), promulgated in 1916, compromised between the aggregate theory and the entity theory, allowing the partnership to acquire property in its own name while giving individual partners specified property interests in the partnership property.[195] The *Revised Uniform Partnership Act* (*RUPA*), promulgated in 1994 and amended in 1997, firmly rejects the aggregate theory and places ownership of all partnership property in the partnership itself, eliminating entirely the

[191] *Unif. Partnership Act* §101(6) (1997); Robert Charles Clark, *Corporate Law* §1.2, at 5 (1986).
[192] 4-34 *Thompson on Real Property, Third Thomas Edition* §34.01.
[193] *Id.* at §34.02(b)(1).
[194] *Id.* at §34.02(b)(2).
[195] *Unif. Partnership Act* §§8(3), 24-26 (1916).

notion of a "tenancy in partnership." Property acquired by the partnership "is property of the partnership and not of the partners individually."[196] Partners are agents of the partnership entitled to act on its behalf unless the partnership agreement allocates decision making authority differently.[197] Partners owe a duty of loyalty to the partnership and duties of due care and good faith and fair dealing.[198] Partners are liable for the debts of the partnership.[199] About 40 states have adopted the 1997 version of *RUPA*.[200]

Limited liability partnerships

Limited liability partnerships differ significantly from partnerships because some or all partners are immune from the debts of the partnership just as shareholders of corporations are not liable for debts of the corporation.[201]

▶ HARD CASE ▷ FIDUCIARY OBLIGATIONS

Partnerships are created by contract among the partners. At the same time, the law has long imposed fiduciary obligations on partners to act and to manage partnership property in the best interests of the partnership. The scope of those obligations is often difficult to define. In a famous case, *Meinhard v. Salmon*,[202] two partners leased property for use as shops and offices for a term of twenty years. One of the partners, Walter J. Salmon, managed the business, while the other, Morton H. Meinhard, provided the necessary funds. Toward the end of the lease, the landlord, Elbridge T. Gerry, had begun to make plans to combine the property with other property he owned and redevelop the whole site. Gerry approached Salmon and offered to lease this larger site to him for the purpose of undertaking this larger development. When Meinhard found out about the arrangement, he sued, arguing that, as Salmon's partner, he should have shared in the opportunity to develop the larger site. The New York Court of Appeals agreed. In a famous discussion, Justice Benjamin Cardozo explained:

> Joint adventurers, like copartners, owe to one another, while the enterprise continues, the duty of the finest loyalty. Many forms of conduct permissible in a workaday world for those acting at arm's length, are forbidden to those bound by fiduciary ties. A trustee is held to something stricter than the morals of the market place. Not honesty alone, but the punctilio of an honor the most sensitive, is then the standard of behavior. As to this there has developed a tradition that is unbending and inveterate. Uncompromising rigidity has been the attitude of courts of equity when petitioned to undermine the rule of undivided loyalty by the "disintegrating erosion" of particular exceptions. Only thus has the level of

[196] *Unif. Partnership Act* §203 (1997).
[197] *Unif. Partnership Act* §301 (1997).
[198] *Unif. Partnership Act* §103(b) (1997).
[199] *Unif. Partnership Act* §306 (1997).
[200] *See* https://www.uniformlaws.org/committees/community-home?CommunityKey=52456941-7883-47a5-91b6-d2f086d0bb44.
[201] *Unif. Ltd. Partnership Act* §303 (2001).
[202] 164 N.E. 545 (N.Y. 1928).

> conduct for fiduciaries been kept at a level higher than that trodden by the crowd. It will not consciously be lowered by any judgment of this court.[203]

Justice Cardozo noted that, if Gerry had known that Salmon had a silent partner, he would have approached them both, and Salmon's failure to tell Meinhard about the opportunity was unfair because it had arisen out of their joint venture together. The case has been criticized on the ground that a joint venture is a partnership for the purpose of carrying out a specific project[204] and, once the twenty-year lease reached its end, the partnership was over. Teaming up with a business partner for twenty years in a specific project does not mean one is married to him for life. ◀

§8.6.2 *Corporations*

Corporate structure

Separation of ownership and management

A corporation is a business enterprise that separates ownership and management, limits the liability of the owners, provides for perpetual existence of the business as a separate legal entity, allows easy transferability of individual ownership interests, and provides mechanisms by which one corporation can acquire or merge with another.[205] Corporations separate ownership and management by requiring the owners (shareholders) to adopt a corporate charter (akin to a constitution) establishing the corporate structure and by requiring the shareholders to elect a board of directors with the power to manage the day-to-day affairs of the corporation. The board of directors, in turn, hires the management, which in turn hires employees, obtains credit, and produces the firm's goods or services for sale to the public. Corporate law limits the liability of the owner/shareholders to the value of their shares. This feature encourages investment in the corporate enterprise because investors know that their liability for corporate debts is limited to the possibility of losing the value of their shares and no more. On the downside, limited liability may also decrease corporate incentives to avoid negligence. Perpetual existence of the corporation as a legal entity allows it easily to contract, to purchase real or personal property, and to maintain the business regardless of changes in the identity of the shareholders, who are free to trade their shares.

Conflicts within the corporation

The various actors within the corporate enterprise have conflicting interests that are partially managed by legal rules that regulate their relationships.[206] Conflicts also arise between corporate insiders and the public at large, including potential investors, as well as business collaborators other than shareholders or employees, such as creditors, other corporations who might be potential takeover targets, and, finally, the communities within which corporations operate.

[203] *Id.* at 546.
[204] Joint Venture, *Black's Law Dictionary* (11th ed. 2019).
[205] John C. Coffee, Jr., Ronald J. Gilson & Brian JM Quinn, *Cases and Materials on Corporations* 1-3, 849-850, 853-854 (9th ed. 2021).
[206] *See* Robert Charles Clark, *Corporate Law* (1986).

Conflicts among shareholders

Corporate law manages conflicts that arise among shareholders, especially between majority and minority shareholders, when the majority acts in a manner inimical to the interests of the minority and limitations have been placed on the power of shareholders to protect the interests of minority shareholders. Conflicts also arise between shareholders and management. The law imposes a *duty of loyalty* on management so that they act to maximize the value of the firm to the shareholders and not to feather their own nests. Conflict of interest and self-dealing rules seek to prevent managers from using their positions to act in their own interests and contrary to the interests of the shareholders and the corporation as an entity. The law also imposes a *duty of care* on corporate managers to prevent negligence or misfeasance in the management of the corporation. At the same time, the *business judgment rule* insulates directors from liability except in extraordinary situations by creating a strong presumption that their actions were taken in good faith to further the interests of the corporation.[207] Securities laws protect the interests of actual and potential investors by requiring corporations to disclose material information to the public. Takeover and antitrust laws regulate the ways in which corporations merge and acquire each other.

Conflicts between shareholders and managers

Securities laws

Who owns the corporation?

The traditional view of the corporation is that it is owned by the shareholders. Under this view, the unique problems of the corporation arise because of the separation of ownership and management, especially the problem of inducing managers to operate the corporation in the interests of the shareholders. A more recent view characterizes the corporation as a nexus of contracts. Under this view, the dominant issues are defining default terms that should govern the relations among shareholders and between shareholders and management to lower the costs of transacting and the identification of mandatory rules to govern situations where transaction costs prevent mutually beneficial contracts from being made. This newer view, however, coheres with the older view in the sense that it assumes that the primary duty of the corporation is to maximize shareholder value. Either view, in other words, deems shareholders the primary group to whom management owes a duty of both care and loyalty.

Stakeholder laws

More than half the states have passed laws that authorize corporate directors to consider the interests of "stakeholders" other than the shareholders in making corporate policy.[208] Those stakeholders include the employees, creditors, suppliers, and the communities in which the corporation operate. Because these statutes do not grant standing to those stakeholders to challenge corporate actions inimical to their interests, they arguably do nothing but give directors and managers a new set of excuses for ignoring the interests of the shareholders.[209] As a practical matter, they may increase manager discretion rather than induce managers to protect the interests of non-shareholder constituencies. On the other hand, these stakeholder laws arguably change property rights in the corporation in a

[207] *Id.* at §3.4, at 123-125.

[208] *See* Conn. Gen. Stat. §33-756; N.J. Stat. §14A:6-1(2); N.Y. Bus. Corp. §717(b); Kent Greenfield, *The Place of Workers in Corporate Law*, 39 B.C. L. Rev. 283 (1998).

[209] Robert A.G. Monks & Nell Minow, *Power and Accountability* 117-121 (1991).

fundamental way. Traditionally, corporate directors had a duty only to the shareholders to maximize corporate profits and the value of shares. Stakeholder laws treat corporations as entities with obligations to constituencies other than the shareholders. Profits can be pursued, and even maximized, in various ways. Although most stakeholder laws do not *require* managers to consider the interests of corporate constituencies other than shareholders, the fact that they authorize consideration of these interests suggests that legislatures believe those interests are legitimate. If they are legitimate, perhaps managers *should* consider the interests of stakeholders even if they are not legally required to do so. In effect, these laws modify ownership rights in the corporation by redefining the default rules underlying the contracts between the corporation and all the constituencies with whom it forms relationships.

§8.6.3 Franchises

Promotion of uniformity in provision of goods or services

Franchises are business arrangements in which a company that has a unique product or service contracts with others who are obligated to provide the same product or service under the same name and under conditions designed to promote uniformity.

License to use trademark

> In its simplest terms, a franchise is a license from [an] owner of a trademark or trade name permitting another to sell a product or service under that name or mark. More broadly stated, a "franchise" has evolved into an elaborate agreement under which the franchisee undertakes to conduct a business or sell a product or service in accordance with methods and procedures prescribed by the franchiser, and the franchiser undertakes to assist the franchisee through advertising, promotion and other advisory services.[210]

Franchisee protections

Many states have passed statutes protecting franchisees from wrongful termination of their franchise agreements.[211] The federal government has passed such a law regulating gas stations, the *Petroleum Marketing Practices Act (PMPA)*.[212] These statutes require written notice stating the reason for termination and prohibit termination before the notice period has passed (a period that varies from only ten days to as long as one hundred and eighty days).[213] Exceptions to the notice requirement exist for "emergency" situations.[214] Most statutes also prohibit termination except for "good cause" or "just cause;" others allow termination unless the termination is "in bad faith" or "unfair."[215]

[210] *H&R Block, Inc. v. Lovelace*, 493 P.2d 205, 211-212 (Kan. 1972).

[211] ABA Antitrust Section, *Franchise Protection: Laws Against Termination and the Establishment of Additional Franchises* (1990).

[212] 15 U.S.C. §§2801 to 2806.

[213] ABA Antitrust Section, *Franchise Protection: Laws Against Termination and the Establishment of Additional Franchises* 17 (1990).

[214] *Id.* at 17-18.

[215] *Id.* at 18.

▶ HARD CASE ▷ GOOD CAUSE FOR TERMINATION

The meaning of the good cause standard varies widely. Some states only require a good business reason for the termination; in effect, if the termination is in the economic interest of the franchiser, then it is lawful. For example, in *Ziegler Co., Inc. v. Rexnord, Inc.*,[216] the Wisconsin Supreme Court interpreted a statute that allowed termination for good cause, which was defined as "failure by a dealer [franchisee] to comply substantially with essential and reasonable requirements imposed upon him or sought to be imposed by the grantor [franchiser]."[217] The court held that "the grantor's economic circumstances" might constitute good cause to alter its method of doing business with its dealers, but such changes must be "essential, reasonable and nondiscriminatory."[218] Other states, however, interpret their laws to prohibit termination during the term of the agreement unless the franchisee has violated the agreement or otherwise acted in a way that justified termination. Interpreting a somewhat differently worded statute, which prohibited termination unless the franchisee failed to comply with "requirements imposed upon him by the franchise," the Supreme Court of New Jersey ruled, in *Westfield Centre Serv. Inc. v. Cities Serv. Oil Co.*,[219] that the state law prohibited termination unless the franchisee had breached the terms of the agreement.[220] ◀

§8.7 Nonprofit Organizations

Crucial function

Nonprofit organizations own a huge amount of property and serve crucial functions in economic and social life.[221] They include institutions such as hospitals, universities and private schools, museums, recreational facilities, religious institutions, charitable organizations, social clubs, and political organizations. Many legal issues arise in the management of such organizations. One major set of issues concerns the obligations of the managing board, because it may fail to pursue the purposes for which the organization was first established. In general, the states do not give the beneficiaries (or potential beneficiaries) of charities standing to sue to force the trustee to execute the duties set out in the trust document establishing the organization; rather, enforcement is relegated to the charitable trust division of the state attorney general's office. Second, many charitable organizations are exempt from federal income tax and the tax code itself has strict requirements to establish and maintain eligibility for this benefit.

Controlling the board

Tax exemption

[216] 433 N.W.2d 8 (Wis. 1988).

[217] Wis. Stat. §§135.02(4)-135.03.

[218] 433 N.W.2d at 12.

[219] 432 A.2d 48 (N.J. 1981).

[220] The statute stated: "good cause for terminating, canceling, or failing to renew a franchise shall be limited to failure by the franchise to substantially comply with those requirements imposed upon him by the franchise." N.J. Stat. §56:10-5.

[221] James J. Fishman, Stephen Schwarz & Lloyd Mayer, *Non-profit Organizations: Cases and Materials* (6th ed. 2021); Bruce R. Hopkins, *The Second Legal Answer Book for Non-profit Organizations* (1999).

§8.8 Governmental Ownership

Public lands law

A vast amount of land in the United States is owned by governmental entities, from the federal and state governments, to municipalities and other subdivisions of the states, to independent authorities, such as the Port Authority of New York and New Jersey or the Massachusetts Turnpike Authority. Fully one-third of the land in the United States is owned by the federal government.[222] The law governing the management and disposition of federal public lands is complex. It includes specialized regulation of water, minerals, timber, range, wildlife, recreation, and preservation uses by various federal agencies.[223]

[222] Robert L. Glicksman & George Cameron Coggins, *Modern Public Land Law in a Nutshell* v, 1 (5th ed. 2019).

[223] *See* George Cameron et al., *Federal Public Land and Resources Law* (7th ed. 2014); Robert L. Glicksman & George Cameron Coggins, *Modern Public Land Law in a Nutshell* (5th ed. 2019); 7-55 *Thompson on Real Property, Third Thomas Edition* §§55.01 to 55.09.

CHAPTER 9

Family Property

§9.1 Introduction
§9.2 Historical Background
  §9.2.1 Dower and Curtesy
  §9.2.2 *Married Women's Property Acts*
§9.3 Marital Property
  §9.3.1 Separate Property
  §9.3.2 Community Property
  §9.3.3 Tenancy by the Entirety
§9.4 Same-Sex Marriage
§9.5 Unmarried Couples
§9.6 Parents and Children
§9.7 Inheritance
  §9.7.1 Wills and Will Substitutes
  §9.7.2 Intestate Succession
    §9.7.2.1 Surviving Spouse But No Surviving Children or Parents
    §9.7.2.2 Surviving Spouse and Surviving Parents But No Children
    §9.7.2.3 Surviving Spouse and Children

§9.1 Introduction

Family relationships

Spouses

Unmarried partners

Parents and children

Family relationships are of fundamental importance, both to individuals and to society. It is therefore not surprising that special rules have developed to regulate property rights among family members. The most obvious concern is relations between spouses, whose property rights have long been regulated by law. New law has developed to regulate relationships between unmarried partners, including those involving same-sex partners. Other rules regulate the obligations of parents to children, both during marriage and after divorce. Still other rules regulate obligations of children to parents. These rules are generally governed by the doctrines associated not only with property law, but family law and contract law. In addition, the law of trusts, wills, and inheritance substantially affects access to property within the family. Trusts can be created during the grantor's lifetime (*inter vivos* trusts) or at death (testamentary trusts). The law of wills and inheritance governs the disposition of both real and personal property at death. And, although beyond the scope of this treatise, tax law has a profound effect in all these areas in the form of income, gift, and inheritance taxes. Finally, another set of issues beyond the full scope of this treatise involves special issues involved in setting up and running family businesses, held either in the form of sole proprietorships, partnerships, or corporations.

Trusts

Wills and inheritance

Marriage

Central to the law of family property is the institution of marriage. The law has always treated married couples differently from unmarried couples or others with close relationships.[1] At one time, the legal incidents of marriage could be obtained only by marriage itself. Today, however, some, but definitely not all, of the incidents of marriage can be obtained by an explicit contract between the parties. There is a tension between the conception of marriage as a *status* (conferred and recognized by the state with privileges granted to married persons and denied to unmarried persons) and as a *contract* (which can be entered into by the parties of their own free will and then will be recognized by the state). If marriage were merely a contract, then anyone could enter the marriage relationship by agreement and obtain its benefits. This is not the law. In every state, marriage law regulates who can marry and denies certain incidents of marriage to unmarried persons. The status of being married affects not only the spouses but third parties as well, such as other family members and creditors.

Status or contract

Separate v. community property

Within the marriage relationship, different models exist to regulate the relationships between spouses regarding property. Under the *separate property* model, each of the spouses retains whatever property rights they possessed prior to marriage, and each retains individual ownership of the property acquired after marriage. Separate ownership is supplemented by mutual obligations of support, but legal enforcement of such obligations is

[1] 4-37 *Thompson on Real Property, Third Thomas Edition* §37.01 ("In all American jurisdictions, marriage affects property rights.").

rarely invoked short of separation or divorce. Under the *community property* model, the couple is viewed as a kind of partnership in which the parties share equally in the property earned by either party during the marriage while property earned prior to the marriage or obtained by gift or inheritance during the marriage is held separately.[2] A central issue in both marital property systems is the extent to which individuals can alter the default rules by contract, either through premarital (or *antenuptial*) agreements or by agreement during the marriage or at separation. Within each system, a set of rules has developed to regulate relations during marriage, at divorce, and at death. These rules affect not only the relations between the partners but the rights of creditors of the parties and other family members.

Parents and children

A separate set of rules has developed to regulate the property rights of children. Generally, children have only the property given to them by their parents or others. However, parents have obligations to support their children, obligations that usually only become legal questions when the parents separate or divorce. Questions obviously abound about the appropriate contours of the support owed to children. These issues become especially acute when large expenditures are concerned, such as college education. They are also painfully present when parents divorce and remarry. In such cases, the birth of new children may affect the ability of the parent to support prior children, and courts must choose between allowing the parent to reduce obligations to prior children or maintain those obligations, leaving less available for subsequent children. Whatever rules are adopted will obviously affect incentives to remarry and have more children as well as creating legal norms to govern relations between parents and children in separated or blended families.

Inheritance

An entire area of law has developed around the law of inheritance. This general category includes the law of wills (testamentary transfers of property) and the law of intestate succession applicable when a decedent dies without a valid will. Although every state grants some amount of protection for surviving spouses, they generally provide no protection for children, allowing parents to disinherit their children at-will. This practice differs from that prevalent in some European countries, which ensure that children, as well as surviving spouses, receive some portion of the estate.[3] This obviously raises a tension between the goal of protecting the power of the decedent to control her property after her death and providing for the needs of surviving family members who depended on the decedent for support or claim to be entitled to some or all of the decedent's property because of their family relationship.

[2] Of course, both models have many variations across the states.

[3] England, for example, has a statutory scheme known as *Testator's Family Maintenance* (TFM), which allows the chancery judge to "revise the dispositive provisions of a testator's will (including intestate shares, in an intestate estate) for the benefit of the decedent's relatives and other dependents." Lawrence W. Waggoner et al., *Family Property Law: Cases and Materials on Wills, Trusts, and Future Interests* 10-1 (4th ed. 2006) (*citing Inheritance (Provision for Family and Dependents) Act 1975*, ch. 63 (U.K.)).

§9.2 Historical Background

§9.2.1 Dower and Curtesy

Historical disabilities of married women

Until the middle of the nineteenth century, married women in the United States were deprived of the right to control property.[4] The states adopted the common law of England, which limited to single women the right to hold and manage property and to enter into binding contracts. Married women, in contrast, were required, by virtue of their married status, to give up powers over their property owned prior to marriage; they also lost the ability to purchase property without their husbands' consent during the marriage. Married women had no capacity to enter into binding contracts, and the law gave the husband the sole power to possess and control the profits of all land owned by himself and his wife. In addition, all personal property acquired by the wife before or during the marriage belonged to the husband absolutely as soon as the wife acquired it.[5] A married woman was called a *feme covert* (meaning "covered" or protected by marriage), and her status was described by the institution of *coverture.* The husband and wife were treated as one person in the eyes of the law and that person was the husband. He had the power to convey his wife's property without her consent and to control all the profits of the land. In addition, she could not sell her own land without his consent.[6]

Coverture

Dower

The common law did give the wife certain important property interests to take effect at the death of her husband. The common law gave surviving spouses a life estate in all or some of the land owned by the deceased spouse at the time of his death. The wife's *dower* interest consisted of a life estate in one-third of the freehold lands the husband owned at any time during the marriage and which could be inherited by the couple's children.[7] Some states limited the wife's dower interest to property owned by the husband at the time of his death.[8] The wife's dower interest could not be alienated by her husband without her consent, nor could it be used to satisfy the husband's debts. The husband's equivalent *curtesy* interest consisted of a life estate in *all* the lands in which his wife owned a present freehold estate during the marriage and which were inheritable by issue of the couple. However, the husband's curtesy interest sprang into being only if the couple had a child capable of inheriting the property.[9]

Curtesy

Equity courts

In contrast to the rigidity of the law courts, the equity courts created a variety of mechanisms by which some married women could exercise property rights during marriage.[10] First, equity courts began to enforce premarital agreements by which some husbands voluntarily gave control over

[4] Richard H. Chused, *Married Women's Property Law: 1800-1850,* 71 Geo. L.J. 1359, 1361 (1983); 4-37 *Thompson on Real Property, Third Thomas Edition* §37.06(a).
[5] 4-37 *Thompson on Real Property, Third Thomas Edition* §37.06(a).
[6] *Id.*
[7] *Id.* at §37.06(b).
[8] Richard H. Chused, *Married Women's Property Law: 1800-1850,* 71 Geo. L.J. 1359, 1393 (1983).
[9] *Id.*; Dale A. Whitman et al., *The Law of Property* §2.13, at 55-56 (4th ed. 2019).
[10] 4-37 *Thompson on Real Property, Third Thomas Edition* §37.06(a).

property to their wives.[11] Second, they would enforce trusts created for the benefit of the wife, and she could enforce the trust as the beneficiary without her husband's consent. Fathers often took this route to keep property in their daughters' control rather than allowing it to pass to their prospective sons-in-law.[12]

Tenancy by the entirety

Women were entitled to own property jointly with their husbands as tenants by the entirety, although, as with all other property belonging to the wife, such property was subject to control by the husband. Husbands were entitled to exclusive possession and control of property held in tenancy by the entirety.[13] However, husbands could not sever or partition during the joint lives of the couple. This meant that the husband could not unilaterally defeat the wife's right of survivorship by transferring the property to a third party. That third party's interest would be subject to the wife's survivorship rights and would terminate if the husband died before the wife, triggering her survivorship right.[14]

Dower and curtesy today

Some version of dower and curtesy remain in only a few states,[15] and the states that retain these institutions generally allow surviving spouses to choose between dower/curtesy and a statutorily defined elective share of marital assets owned by the decedent at the time of death.[16]

§9.2.2 Married Women's Property Acts

Removing disabilities of married women

In the second half of the nineteenth century (starting with Arkansas in 1835),[17] all common law states passed *Married Women's Property Acts.*[18] These statutes abolished coverture and removed the economic disabilities previously imposed on married women. After passage of the statutes, married women had the same rights as single women and married men to contract, to hold and manage property, and to sue and be sued. The wife's earnings were her separate property and could not be controlled or taken by her husband without her consent; nor could her separate property be seized by her husband's creditors.[19]

[11] Richard H. Chused, *Married Women's Property Law: 1800-1850*, 71 Geo. L.J. 1359, 1368-1372 (1983).

[12] Dale A. Whitman et al., *The Law of Property* §2.13, at 51-56 (4th ed. 2019).

[13] *King v. Greene*, 153 A.2d 49, 52 (N.J. 1959) ("in an estate by the entirety the husband had absolute dominion and control over the property during the joint lives"); 4-33 *Thompson on Real Property, Third Thomas Edition* §33.05.

[14] 4-37 *Thompson on Real Property, Third Thomas Edition* §37.06(a), (b).

[15] These include Arkansas, Kentucky, and Ohio. Ark. Code §§28-11-101 to 28-11-404; Ky. Rev. Stat. §§392.020, 392.080; Ohio Rev. Code §2103.02; 15-85A *Powell on Real Property* §85A.04. *See also* Conn. Gen. Stat. §45a-436 (giving the surviving spouse an interest for life in one-third of the decedent spouse's property).

[16] *See, e.g.*, Ark. Code §28-11-404.

[17] Act of Nov. 2, 1835, 1835 Ark. Terr. Laws 34-35. It is commonly asserted that the first *Married Women's Property Act* appeared in Mississippi in 1839, but Professor Richard Chused has shown that the first statute actually appeared in Arkansas in 1835. *See* Richard H. Chused, *Married Women's Property Law: 1800-1850*, 71 Geo. L.J. 1359, 1399 (1983). The Mississippi statute commonly cited appears as Act of Feb. 15, 1839, ch. 46, 1839 Miss. Laws 72. Chused, 71 Geo. L.J. at 1399 n.207.

[18] 4-37 *Thompson on Real Property, Third Thomas Edition* §37.07(b).

[19] *Id.*

Failure to achieve demands of women's rights advocates

At the same time, these acts failed to achieve the aims of nineteenth-century women's rights advocates who "sought to emancipate wives' labor in the household as well as in the market, and to do so, advocated 'joint property' laws that would recognize wives' claims to marital assets to which husbands otherwise had title."[20] The husband's income earned outside the home was still owned by the husband alone and wives who did not work outside the home therefore had no earnings of their own.[21] They argued that wives were "entitled to joint rights in marital property by reason of the labor they contributed to the family economy."[22] Many women worked inside the home for no wages; the *Married Women's Property Acts* failed to grant such women any rights in marital property, while family law doctrines preserved their duties to render services inside the home. Other women engaged in labor inside the home for which wages were earned, such as taking in laundry or sewing, keeping boarders, and gardening and dairying and selling the crops or milk products for cash. Although some states gave married women property rights in such earnings, most *Married Women's Property Acts* granted the husband control over such earnings or were interpreted by courts in this fashion on the ground that these acts were not intended to alter family law doctrines requiring women to provide services inside the home.[23] Because most men worked outside the home and most married women worked inside the home, gender equality in access to property was a long time in coming.

Abolition of dower and curtesy in most states

As a result of the *Married Women's Property Acts*, most states also abolished dower and curtesy; at the same time, they amended intestacy laws to make surviving spouses heirs, allowing them to inherit the real and personal property owned by their deceased spouse at the time of death, and passed "elective share" statutes, allowing surviving spouses to elect a share of the decedent's estate in preference to the provisions in the decedent's will.[24] Some states still retain dower and curtesy, but in those states the husband's and wife's interests have been equalized, and the surviving spouse is generally authorized to choose between the dower or curtesy interest in real estate owned during the marriage and the portion of the deceased spouse's property guaranteed to the surviving spouse by statutory "elective share" legislation. These statutes today guarantee the survivor a specified portion of the deceased spouse's real and personal property, thereby overriding a will that leaves the spouse less than this minimum amount.[25]

[20] Reva B. Siegel, *The Modernization of Marital Status Law: Adjudicating Wives' Rights to Earnings, 1860-1930*, 82 Geo. L.J. 2127 (1994).

[21] 4-37 *Thompson on Real Property, Third Thomas Edition* §37.07(a).

[22] Reva B. Siegel, *Home as Work: The First Woman's Rights Claims Concerning Wives' Household Labor, 1850-1880*, 103 Yale L.J. 1073, 1077 (1994).

[23] *Id.* at 1181-1188.

[24] Richard H. Chused, *Married Women's Property Law: 1800-1850*, 71 Geo. L.J. 1359, 1394-1395 (1983).

[25] Dale A. Whitman et al., *The Law of Property* §2.13, at 56-58 (4th ed. 2019).

§9.3 Marital Property

Separate v. community property

Two different marital property systems exist in the United States. The *separate property* system allows each spouse to retain his or her property earned both prior to, and during, marriage. In contrast, the *community property system* in force in nine states[26] gives each spouse joint ownership of property earned by either party during the marriage, while allowing each to retain separate ownership of property acquired before marriage and property acquired during marriage by gift or inheritance. Each system has effects on spousal property rights during marriage, at divorce, and at death. In addition, whichever system is adopted must confront the question of whether, or to what extent, the parties should be free to vary the default rules by agreement, either before marriage in a *premarital (antenuptial) agreement* or at separation or divorce. In general, the parties are free to vary the terms of the relationship, but many states will review such agreements for fairness. Although community property exists only in nine states, the separate property system has been altered by statutes in ways that make it closer to the community property system in significant respects.

§9.3.1 *Separate Property*

Separate ownership

Separate property states retain, for the most part, the ordinary rules about property acquisition and ownership. Each spouse is entitled to earn or receive property and owns the property she or he individually earns or receives by gift or inheritance. During marriage, each spouse continues to own property separately unless they take joint title to property such as purchasing a house as tenants by the entirety or establishing a joint bank account under a joint tenancy arrangement.[27] However, the marriage status does effect some changes in property, especially in the case of divorce or death.

During marriage

In separate property states, each spouse owns whatever property he or she possessed before the marriage and is individually liable for prior debts. Creditors cannot go after a spouse's property to satisfy a debt individually undertaken by the other spouse. Property earned after the marriage, including wages and dividends, also is owned separately. A husband and wife may of course choose to share property with each other either informally, by sharing the costs of the household or giving part of individual earnings to his or her spouse, or formally, by having a joint bank account to which either spouse has access as a joint tenant. The only major qualification to the principle of separate ownership is that spouses have a legal duty to support each other, and this duty may require a sharing of property earned during the marriage.[28] A spouse who fails to comply with this obligation

Separate ownership

Duty of mutual support

[26] The states are Arizona, California, Idaho, Louisiana, Nevada, New Mexico, Texas, Washington, and Wisconsin. 4-37 *Thompson on Real Property, Third Thomas Edition* §37.08(b).

[27] For the rules about joint tenancy and tenancy by the entirety, see §8.2.

[28] S.C. Code §20-7-40; *Sharpe Furniture, Inc. v. Buckstaff*, 299 N.W.2d 219, 221-222 (Wis. 1980).

may be forced to do so by a court order for maintenance, although this kind of lawsuit rarely happens outside of divorce or separation.

Divorce

On divorce, separate property states alter ownership interests dramatically. Almost all such states have statutes that provide for *equitable distribution* of property owned by each of the parties on divorce.[29] Property may well be redistributed from the title holder to the other spouse, on the assumption that the marriage formed a kind of partnership and that each spouse should benefit from their joint assets. This legal reform makes separate property states much more similar to community property states in the divorce context. Some states allow equitable distribution of all property owned by the parties, including property acquired prior to the marriage.[30] Most states, however, limit equitable distribution to property acquired during the marriage.[31] A few states that limit equitable distribution to property acquired during the marriage allow property acquired before the marriage to be distributed in restricted circumstances.[32]

Equitable distribution

Factors

The division is made on the basis of a wide range of factors such as need (support for necessities, including child support), status (maintaining the lifestyle shared during the marriage), rehabilitation (support sufficient to allow one spouse to attain marketable skills such that support will no longer be needed), and contribution (treating the marriage as a partnership and dividing the assets jointly earned from the enterprise).[33] A significant minority of the states allow marital fault to be considered, another significant minority explicitly exclude "marital misconduct" as a factor, and, today, even courts authorized to consider fault often minimize its role.[34] Specific factors that may be taken into account include age, health, occupation, income, vocational skills, contribution as a homemaker, dissipation of property during the marriage, income tax consequences, debts, obligations

[29] *E.g.*, Ala. Code §30-2-51; Conn. Gen. Stat. §46b-81; Haw. Rev. Stat. §580-47(a); Iowa Code Ann. §598.21; Kan. Stat. §23-2802; Mass. Gen. Laws ch. 208 §34; Mont. Code §40-4-202(1); Wyo. Stat. §20-2-114; 4-37 *Thompson on Real Property, Third Thomas Edition* §37.07(d).

[30] Ind. Code §31-15-7-4; Kan. Stat. §23-2802; Mass. Gen. Laws ch. 208 §34; Mont. Code §40-4-202(1); 4-37 *Thompson on Real Property, Third Thomas Edition* §37.07(d).

[31] Ark. Code §9-12-315; Del. Code tit. 13, §1513(b); D.C. Code §16-910(a); N.J. Stat. §2A:34-23.1; N.Y. Dom. Rel. §§236(B)(1)(d)(1) & 236(B)(5)(b); Va. Code §20-107.3(A); 4-37 *Thompson on Real Property, Third Thomas Edition* §37.07(d).

[32] Ala. Code §30-2-51 (if property is used regularly during the marriage for the benefit of the other spouse); Iowa Code §598.21(b) (if refusal to do so would be inequitable); Minn. Stat. §518.58 subd. 2 (up to one-half can be distributed if provision for one spouse is so inadequate that unfair hardship will result); 4-37 *Thompson on Real Property, Third Thomas Edition* §37.07(d).

[33] Judith Areen et al., *Family Law, Cases and Materials* 1157-1165 (7th ed. 2019). *See, e.g.*, Mont. Code §40-4-202 ("the court, without regard to marital misconduct, shall . . . equitably apportion between the parties the property and assets belonging to either or both, however and whenever acquired [taking into consideration] the duration of the marriage and prior marriage of either party, the age, health, station, occupation, amount and sources of income, vocational skills, employability, estate, liabilities, and needs of each of the parties, custodial provisions, whether the apportionment is in lieu of or in addition to maintenance [alimony], and the opportunity of each for future acquisition of capital assets and income").

[34] Leslie J. Harris, June Carbone & Rachel Rebouché, *Family Law* 249 (7th ed. 2023).

prior to marriage, and contribution of one spouse to the education of the other.[35]

How property is equitably distributed

In general, short-term marriages are likely to result in less property redistribution than in the case of long-term marriages (generally lasting for ten years or more). For long-term marriages, some states have adopted a presumption of equal distribution of marital assets on divorce, while others grant trial judges substantial discretion in this regard.[36]

Alimony or maintenance

Separate property states also have provision for court-ordered "alimony" or "maintenance."[37] These are periodic payments from one spouse to support the other. Before the 1960s, alimony was routinely awarded to women who were thought to be dependent on their ex-husbands for income. However, with the increase in women in the workforce, as well as the advent of no-fault divorce, alimony has become exceptional and, when awarded, is often temporary. Current policy in most states aims at eventual, if not immediate, financial independence for the parties (with the notable exception of child support).[38]

Death

Wills

Statutory or elective share

Intestacy

A spouse may dispose of her property by will, but almost every separate property state protects the rights of the surviving spouse by ensuring that he or she is entitled to a significant portion (usually one-third to one-half) of the property owned by the decedent at the time of death.[39] These state laws provide for a *statutory* (or "*elective*") share of the decedent's estate (the property owned by the decedent at the time of death), effectively allowing the widow or widower to override the will and elect to receive a stated portion of the estate.[40] The *Uniform Probate Code*, adopted in about 16 jurisdictions, provides for an increasing share of the estate for marriages of 1 to 15 years, while surviving spouses in marriages of 15 years or more are entitled to 50 percent of the estate.[41] When no will is written, a spouse's separate property is inherited according to the state intestacy statute. While some states grant the surviving spouse the decedent's entire property, other states divide the property between the surviving spouse and the children.[42]

Premarital (antenuptial) agreements

Spouses may attempt to vary their respective property rights during marriage or at divorce by signing a premarital (antenuptial) agreement.[43] Such agreements are generally enforceable. Although some courts hold that such agreements are enforceable whether or not they are reasonable,[44] most

[35] 4-37 *Thompson on Real Property, Third Thomas Edition* §37.07(d).

[36] Lee R. Russ, Annotation, *Divorce: Equitable Distribution Doctrine*, 41 A.L.R. 4th 481, § 10[a] (1985 & cumulative supplement).

[37] Leslie J. Harris, June Carbone & Rachel Rebouché, *Family Law* 272-295 (7th ed. 2023).

[38] *Id.* at 273.

[39] 4-37 *Thompson on Real Property, Third Thomas Edition* §37.07(b). *See, e.g.*, Mo. Stat. §474.160. Georgia does not have any legislative provision for a statutory share. Robert H. Sitkoff & Jesse Dukeminier, *Wills, Trusts, and Estates* 531 n.3 (11th ed. 2022).

[40] *See* N.J. Stat. §3B:8-1.

[41] *Unif. Probate Code* §2-203 (2008); 4-37 *Thompson on Real Property, Third Thomas Edition* §37.07(c).

[42] *See* §9.7.2.

[43] *Simeone v. Simeone*, 581 A.2d 162 (Pa. 1990).

[44] *Id.* at 166.

states review them to see if they were voluntary[45] and some review them for fairness.[46] Some states enforce such agreements unless they are "unconscionable"[47] while others review them more generally for fairness.[48] The states that review such agreements for voluntariness may require both spouses to disclose their assets to each other, prior to the marriage, to ensure that both parties are voluntarily agreeing to give up rights they otherwise would have had under equitable distribution laws.[49] Some states go further and review the substance of the agreement for fairness, to ensure that neither party is left with an inequitable share of the marital assets.[50] It is increasingly common, however, for states to review such agreements only to determine if they are procedurally fair, meaning that they were voluntarily made after appropriate disclosure, and to avoid consideration of the substantive fairness of the property division itself. The 1983 *Uniform Premarital Agreement Act* (*UPAA*), adopted in more than half the states,[51] provides that premarital agreements are not enforceable against a party (1) if that party "did not execute the agreement voluntarily" or (2) if the agreement is "unconscionable" and that party "was not provided a fair and reasonable disclosure of the property or financial obligations of the other party," did not voluntarily waive the right to disclosure in writing, and did not have (or reasonably could not have had) an adequate knowledge of the other party's financial assets.[52]

The *Uniform Premarital and Marital Agreement Act* (*UPMAA*) was adopted by the Uniform Law Commission in 2012.[53] It would alter the *UPAA* by requiring each party to have had reasonable time to decide whether to contact an attorney before signing the agreement, as well as time to locate such an attorney and obtain legal advice.[54] It also requires each party to provide a "reasonably accurate description and good faith estimate of value of the [other's] property, liabilities and income."[55] In addition, while it continues

[45] *In re Marriage of Bonds*, 83 Cal. Rptr. 2d 783, 785 (Ct. App. 1999), *judgment rev'd in part on other grounds by* 5 P.3d 815 (Cal. 2000). *See In re Estate of Hollett*, 834 A.2d 348 (N.H. 2003) (premarital agreement entered into the night before the wedding was invalid because signed under duress and thus not voluntary).

[46] Wis. Stat. §767.61(3)(L); *Greenwald v. Greenwald*, 454 N.W.2d 34 (Wis. Ct. App. 1990), *overruled on other grounds by Meyer v. Meyer*, 620 N.W.2d 382 (Wis. 2000).

[47] *In re Estate of Hollett*, 834 A.2d 348, 351 (N.H. 2003).

[48] *Compare In re Marriage of Bonds*, 5 P.3d 815, 831 (Cal. 2000) (unconscionable standard) *with DeMatteo v. DeMatteo*, 762 N.E.2d 797, 809 (Mass. 2002) ("Our test of 'fair and reasonable' is not the same as the test of 'unconscionability' that has been adopted in other jurisdictions.") *and Button v. Button*, 388 N.W.2d 546, 547 (Wis. 1986) (interpreting the requirement in Wis. Stat. §767.255(3)(L) that antenuptial agreements be reviewed to determine if they are "inequitable").

[49] *DeLorean v. DeLorean*, 511 A.2d 1257 (N.J. Super. Ct. 1986); *Simeone v. Simeone*, 581 A.2d 162 (Pa. 1990).

[50] N.J. Stat. §§37:2-32(c), 37:2-38(c); *Gentry v. Gentry*, 798 S.W.2d 928 (Ky. 1990) (reviewing an antenuptial agreement to examine whether the facts and circumstances have changed since the agreement was executed so as to make its enforcement unfair and unreasonable).

[51] Leslie J. Harris, June Carbone & Rachel Rebouché, *Family Law* 500 (7th ed. 2023).

[52] *Unif. Premarital Agreement Act* §6.

[53] *Unif. Premarital and Marital Agreement Act* (*UPMAA*) (2012).

[54] *UPMAA* §9(b).

[55] *Id.* at §9(d)(1).

to allow enforcement unless the agreement was unconscionable at the time of contracting,[56] an optional alternate section would deny enforcement of a contract term if it would result in substantial hardship due to a material change in the parties' circumstances during the marriage.[57]

Postmarital (postnuptial) agreements

Courts have generally been more reluctant to enforce postnuptial agreements than prenuptial agreements. The trend however is to enforce postnuptial agreements but to hold that to stricter fairness standards than premarital contracts on the grounds that before marriage the parties can freely choose whether to enter the agreement and the marriage, but that during the marriage there may be greater likelihood that the agreement does not reflect the genuine will of the parties. The Connecticut Supreme Court ruled, for example, in *Bedrick v. Bedrick*,[58] that postnuptial agreements are enforceable only if they are not unconscionable at the time of enforcement.

§9.3.2 *Community Property*

During marriage

Nine states have adopted the community property system.[59] Eight have had the system for a long time, and one, Wisconsin, more recently adopted the *Uniform Marital Property Act*, which adopted a version of the community property system.[60] Alaska passed a statute in 1998 allowing couples to choose to hold their property as community property.[61] In community property states, as in separate property states, property owned prior to the marriage, as well as property acquired after marriage by gift or inheritance, is separate property.[62] All other property acquired during the marriage, including earnings, is *community property* and is owned jointly and equally by both spouses. The community property system views marriage as "a partnership to which each spouse makes a different but equally important contribution."[63] In a few states (Idaho, Louisiana, Texas, and Wisconsin), earnings from separate property are community property, but in other states it remains separate.[64]

Management

Since the 1960s, most states have granted spouses equal rights to manage community property; each spouse individually may deal with the community property without the consent of the other spouse.[65] At the same

[56] *Id.* at §9(f).
[57] *Id.*
[58] 17 A.3d 17 (Conn. 2011).
[59] They are Arizona, California, Idaho, Louisiana, Nevada, New Mexico, Texas, Washington, and Wisconsin. Ariz. Rev. Stat. §§25-211 to 25-217; Cal. Fam. Code §§750 to 1620 (rights during marriage), §§2500 to 2660 (rights at divorce); Idaho Code §§32-903 to 32-912; La. Civ. Code arts. 2325 to 2376; Nev. Rev. Stat. §§123.010 to 123.310; N.M. Stat. §§40-3-6 to 40-3-13; Tex. Const. art. 16, §15; Tex. Fam. Code §§3.001 to 3.006; Wash. Rev. Code §§26.16.010 to 26.16.140; Wis. Stat. §§766.001 to 766.31.
[60] 4-37 *Thompson on Real Property, Third Thomas Edition* §37.07(b).
[61] Alaska Stat. §§34.77.010-34.77.160.
[62] 4-37 *Thompson on Real Property, Third Thomas Edition* §37.08(a).
[63] *Id.* at §37.07(d).
[64] Robert H. Sitkoff & Jesse Dukeminier, *Wills, Trusts, and Estates* 566 (11th ed. 2022).
[65] 4-37 *Thompson on Real Property, Third Thomas Edition* §37.12(d). *See, e.g.*, Wash. Rev. Code §26.16.030 (providing that, with some exceptions, "[e]ither spouse, acting alone, may manage and control community property").

time, managers of community property are fiduciaries; they have the duty to manage the property for the good of the community and to act in good faith to benefit the community.[66] Although each spouse can generally manage community property acting alone, community property statutes require *both* parties to agree to convey or mortgage community property interests in real estate and in assets in a business in which both spouses participate.[67] Texas has a unique system of management of community property. While each spouse is a joint and equal owner of community property, Texas allows separate management of community property earned by each spouse; at the same time, it subjects each spouse to fiduciary obligations toward the other spouse.[68]

Premarital debts

Reach by creditors

Community property states have widely divergent rules as to whether community property can be reached by creditors of individual spouses.[69] The states generally agree that debts incurred by one spouse before marriage can be satisfied by the separate property of that spouse and that the separate property of the non-debtor spouse cannot be reached to satisfy individual premarital debts of the other spouse.[70] Most states also provide that creditors may obtain payment for separate premarital debts by reaching the proportion of community property attributable to (earned by) the efforts of the debtor spouse.[71] California, however, provides that earnings of a married person during marriage cannot be used to satisfy premarital debts of the other spouse; therefore, no community property (including all earnings during marriage) can be used to satisfy premarital debts.[72]

Debts incurred during marriage

Separate property is reachable by the creditors of that spouse for debts incurred during marriage; it is not reachable by creditors of the other spouse as to debts for which both spouses are not jointly liable.[73] Some states allow some or all separate property to be reached, to satisfy community obligations (debts jointly incurred by both spouses during marriage).[74] Some states protect community property from being reached by creditors of individual spouses unless both spouses consented to the transaction.[75] Others, such as California or Louisiana, allow community

[66] 4-37 *Thompson on Real Property, Third Thomas Edition* §37.12(b). *See, e.g.*, Wis. Stat. §766.15.

[67] Wash. Rev. Code §26.16.030(3); 4-37 *Thompson on Real Property, Third Thomas Edition* §37.12(d).

[68] Tex. Fam. Code §3.102; *Ragan v. Commissioner of Internal Revenue*, 135 F.3d 329, 333 (5th Cir. 1998); 4-37 *Thompson on Real Property, Third Thomas Edition* §37.12(c).

[69] Dale A. Whitman et al., *The Law of Property* §§5.13 to 5.15, at 177-187 (4th ed. 2019).

[70] Cal. Fam. Code §913(b)(1); Idaho Code §§32-910 & 32-911; La. Civ. Code art. 2345; Wash. Rev. Code §26.16.200; 4-37 *Thompson on Real Property, Third Thomas Edition* §37.13(b)(4).

[71] Ariz. Rev. Stat. §25-215; Wis. Stat. §766.55(2)(c).

[72] Cal. Fam. Code §911.

[73] *Id.* at §913; La. Civ. Code art. 2345; N.M. Stat. §40-3-10(A); 4-37 *Thompson on Real Property, Third Thomas Edition* §37.13(b)(4).

[74] Ariz. Rev. Stat. §25-215(D); La. Civ. Code art. 2345; N.M. Stat. §40-3-11; Idaho Code §32-912; 4-37 *Thompson on Real Property, Third Thomas Edition* §37.13(b)(4).

[75] Ariz. Rev. Stat. §25-215(A); *Schilling v. Embree*, 575 P.2d 1262, 1265 (Ariz. Ct. App. 1977); Wash. Rev. Code §26.16.030(4); *Colorado National Bank v. Merlino*, 668 P.2d 1304, 1308 (Wash. 1983); 4-37 *Thompson on Real Property, Third Thomas Edition* §37.13(b)(5).

property to be used to satisfy separate debts incurred by only one spouse during marriage.[76] Still others limit the portion of the community property reachable by such creditors. New Mexico, for example, provides that the debtor spouse's one-half interest in community property is reachable to satisfy a separate debt of that spouse incurred during marriage, but only if the debtor spouse's separate property is insufficient to pay the debt.[77]

Divorce

At least two community property states allocate property on divorce relatively mechanically by giving each spouse his or her separate property and half of the community property.[78] Most community property states adopt the "equitable distribution" principle now existing in separate property states, authorizing the trial judge to exercise judgment in equitably apportioning property on divorce.[79] At the same time, such states may well start from the assumption that an "equitable" division of property would be to give each spouse his or her separate property and one-half the community property.[80]

Death

In community property states, a spouse may dispose of her separate property and one-half of the community property by will.[81] Statutory forced share statutes do not generally exist in community property states, given the spouse's vested ownership of one-half of the community property. Homestead laws may also protect the surviving spouse's ownership and occupancy rights in the family home.[82] If a spouse dies intestate (without a valid will), some community property states give the decedent's entire community property interest to the surviving spouse,[83] while others share the decedent's fifty percent interest in the community property between the surviving spouse and the children.[84]

Classification

In all community property states, a major issue is how to distinguish between separate and community property. There is a general presumption in favor of community property, placing the burden on the spouse who wishes property to be designated separate property to prove this.[85]

Earnings on separate property

The subject is complex and a great deal of law has developed on the subject. For example, in some community property states, earnings on separate

[76] Cal. Fam. Code §910; La. Civ. Code art. 2345; 4-37 *Thompson on Real Property, Third Thomas Edition* §37.13(b)(4) to (6).

[77] N.M. Stat. §40-3-10(A); 4-37 *Thompson on Real Property, Third Thomas Editions* §37.13(b)(5).

[78] Cal. Fam. Code §2550; La. Civ. Code art. 2365, 2369.2.

[79] Ariz. Rev. Stat. §25-318(A); Idaho Code §32-712; Nev. Rev. Stat. §125.150; Tex. Fam. Code §7.001; Wash. Rev. Code §26.09.080.

[80] 4-37 *Thompson on Real Property, Third Thomas Edition* §37.15.

[81] Cal. Prob. Code §100; Wis. Stat. §861.01; 4-37 *Thompson on Real Property, Third Thomas Edition* §37.14(c).

[82] Tex. Prob. Code §271.

[83] Cal. Prob. Code §6401(a); Idaho Code §15-2-102(b); N.M. Stat. §45-2-102; Wash. Rev. Code §11.04.015(1)(a).

[84] Tex. Prob. Code §45; La. Civ. Code art. 890 (children's interest subject to usufruct over the decedent's community property share terminable on death or remarriage).

[85] *Hebert v. Hebert*, 650 So. 2d 436, 439 (La. Ct. App. 1995); *Hunt v. Hunt*, 952 S.W.2d 564, 567 (Tex. Ct. App. 1997); *In re Marriage of Gillespie*, 948 P.2d 1338, 1343 (Wash. Ct. App. 1997).

property remain separate property.[86] In other states, however, earnings from separate property during marriage, including interest, rents, and profits, become community property.[87] A similar issue arises on the question of how to treat property acquired before marriage but paid for over time during the marriage, such as a home bought before marriage but paid for over many years. Most states adopt an *inception of title approach*, classifying the property as separate if initially acquired before marriage,[88] while others apply a *pro rata apportionment approach*, with the percentage paid off before marriage treated as separate property and the rest as community property.[89]

Tracing and commingling

Because property acquired before marriage is separate property, it is necessary to determine how to classify that property if it is exchanged for other property during the marriage. For example, if a car acquired before marriage is sold, are the proceeds separate property or community property? The courts treat the proceeds as separate property, *tracing* the source of funds to determine their current status. If those funds are used to buy a new car, that car also will be the separate property of the spouse that owned the original car. What happens, however, if the proceeds are not used to buy a new car but are *commingled* with other funds in a bank account or used, along with community property funds, to purchase a house? When funds become commingled, it may become extremely difficult to disentangle separate property from community property. Separate property commingled with community property retains its character as separate property if it can be traced, but, if it cannot be traced, then it will be treated as community property.[90]

Agreements to transmute community property into separate property and vice versa

Every community property state gives spouses substantial freedom to convert community property to separate property and vice versa. They may do so by a valid premarital agreement or by contract during marriage.[91] However, because community property is enshrined in the Texas Constitution, the Texas Supreme Court has limited the ability of spouses to convert community property to separate property.[92] In all community property states, the freedom to alter marital property rights is limited by the legal construction of the marital relationship as a "confidential" one governed by "duties of loyalty and trust."[93] As in separate property states, community property states may require mutual disclosure of assets before a premarital agreement will be enforced at divorce, and such agreements may even be subject to review for fairness, as well.[94]

[86] Ariz. Rev. Stat. §25-213; Cal. Fam. Code §770; Nev. Rev. Stat. §123.130; Wash. Rev. Code §§26.16.010 & 26.16.020.

[87] Idaho Code §32-906; La. Civ. Code. art. 2339; Tex. Const. art. 16, §15.

[88] *Cummings v. Anderson*, 614 P.2d 1283, 1286-1287 (Wash. 1980); *Hawkins v. Hawkins*, 612 S.W.2d 683 (Tex. Civ. App. 1981); *English v. Sanchez*, 796 P.2d 236, 238 (N.M. 1990).

[89] *In re Marriage of Marsden*, 181 Cal. Rptr. 910, 915 (Ct. App. 1982); *Malmquist v. Malmquist*, 792 P.2d 372, 376 (Nev. 1990).

[90] Wis. Stat. §766.63(1); 4-37 *Thompson on Real Property, Third Thomas Edition* §37.10(b).

[91] 4-3-7 *Thompson on Real Property, Third Thomas Edition* §37.09.

[92] Tex. Const. art. 16, §15.

[93] 4-37 *Thompson on Real Property, Third Thomas Edition* §37.09(d).

[94] Ariz. Rev. Stat. §§25-201 to 25-205; Cal. Fam. Code §§1610-1617; N.D. Cent. Code §§14-03.2-01 to 14-03.2-11.

▷ MIGRATORY COUPLE **HARD CASE** ◀

Movement from community property state to separate property state

When a couple from a community property state moves to a separate property state, they become subject to the law of equitable distribution on divorce and the statutory (elective) share on death. The court may apply the law of the place where the property was acquired, determining that some or all the marital property is "community property." However, in either a divorce proceeding or at death, the court is almost certain to apply its own law of equitable distribution or the statutory share, because those laws were intended to protect domiciliaries. Those statutes grant spouses a right to some share of the property owned by the other spouse, effectively ignoring the question of who has title to the property except to the extent this is relevant to determining a fair distribution on divorce. The only distinction most such states make is between property earned before or after the marriage.[95] The statutes creating equitable distribution and the statutory share apply, by their terms, to anyone who gets divorced or dies domiciled in those states. A joint move by a couple to a separate property state is generally counted as a voluntary submission to the legal regime of that jurisdiction. Thus, at either divorce or death, the interests of each spouse in obtaining some minimum share of the property acquired by the couple during the marriage is legally protected.

Movement from separate property state to community property state

However, when a couple from a separate property state moves to a community property state, things are not so simple. Because of the tracing rules, most community property states have traditionally classified property earned in separate property states as separate, rather than community property, on the theory that the law of the place where property is earned determines its character as separate or community property.[96] Because property ownership is determined in community property states as of the time of acquisition, the law of the place where it is earned applies, except with regard to real property. Many states apply the law of the *situs* (the place where the property is located) to adjudicate questions of ownership of real property.[97]

Quasi-community property

This creates a huge problem. Couples in separate property states are protected by equitable distribution and elective share statutes, while couples in community property states are protected by both community property laws and equitable distribution laws. However, community property states may define "equitable" distribution in a way that grants each

[95] A few separate property states allow equitable distribution of all property, whether acquired before or after the marriage. Ind. Code §31-15-7-4; Kan. Stat. §23-2802; Mass. Gen. Laws ch. 208, §34; Mont. Code §40-4-202(1); 4-37 *Thompson on Real Property, Third Thomas Edition* §37.07(d).

[96] 4-37 *Thompson on Real Property, Third Thomas Edition* §37.16(a).

[97] *Restatement (Second) of Conflict of Laws* §223 (1971); 4-37 *Thompson on Real Property, Third Thomas Edition* §37.16(a). Some courts apply the law of the marital domicile to determine ownership or distribution of real property rights on divorce. *See, e.g., Dority v. Dority*, 645 P.2d 56, 58 (Utah 1982) (applying the law of the plaintiff spouse's domicile to equitably distribute real property located elsewhere).

spouse their separate property and one-half the community property. In that case, a couple that moves from a separate property state to a community property state may be deprived of the protections granted under the law of either state. For example, assume a couple lives in New Jersey for 30 years, then moves to Texas and gets divorced. If Texas divides property on divorce by granting each spouse his or her separate property and one-half the community property, a spouse who had no earnings of her own during the marriage in New Jersey will be left with nothing because she will have little separate property and will have earned little or no community property in Texas. However, leaving her with nothing on the divorce is a result that neither state wants. Both states have adopted policies that would give her roughly 50 percent of the property accumulated during the marriage. To avoid this result, community property states have created the concept of "*quasi-community property*," which treats separate property earned in a separate property state as community property if it would have been community property had it been earned in the state where the divorce is taking place.[98] Some states treat such property as quasi-community property for the purpose of both death and divorce.[99] Others treat such property as quasi-community property for the purpose of divorce but not death.[100] Still others treat it as quasi-community property for the purpose of death but not for the purpose of divorce.[101]

Separate property inherently limited by equitable distribution laws

An alternative resolution of such cases is to find that equitable distribution statutes impose an inherent limitation on the property rights of spouses. Characterization of property earned in separate property states as "separate property" (as that term is used in community property states) is therefore a mischaracterization. "Separate property" earned in separate property states is subject to equitable division on divorce, while separate property earned in community property states is not. Thus, even if the equitable distribution statutes apply, by their terms, only to couples divorcing there or domiciled there at the time of the divorce, the principles contained in them constitute an inherent limitation on marital property rights. Thus, in *Berle v. Berle*,[102] Idaho, a community property state, held that property acquired in New Jersey, a separate property state, should be governed by the law of New Jersey on divorce in Idaho, including New Jersey's equitable distribution law. This made the property divisible on divorce under the standards used for equitable distribution in New Jersey rather than leaving the property in the hands of its formal owner, as would have

[98] *Addison v. Addison*, 399 P.2d 897 (Cal. 1965); *Cameron v. Cameron*, 641 S.W.2d 210, 221 (Tex. 1982); 4-37 *Thompson on Real Property, Third Thomas Edition* §37.16(a).

[99] Cal. Fam. Code §§125 & 2502 (divorce); Cal. Prob. Code §§66, 101, 6101, 6104 (death).

[100] Ariz. Rev. Stat. §25-318; Tex. Fam. Code §§3.001 & 3.002.

[101] Idaho Code §15-2-201; Wash. Rev. Code §§26.16.220 & 26.16.230.

[102] 546 P.2d 407, 409 (Idaho 1976). *Accord, Hughes v. Hughes*, 573 P.2d 1194, 1198 (N.M. 1978).

occurred had the property been designated "separate property" within the meaning of the Idaho community property statute. ◀

§9.3.3 *Tenancy by the Entirety*

Right of survivorship

Tenancy by the entirety is a form of marital ownership of real property. The spouses own the property jointly as tenants by the entirety, giving each a 50 percent interest; however, it is an *undivided* interest in the sense that each spouse has the right to possess the entire property. Tenancy by the entirety is similar to the joint tenancy because its key feature is the right of survivorship. When a spouse dies, the survivor succeeds to the decedent's 50 percent interest and becomes the sole owner of the property. Unlike the joint tenancy, however, the property cannot be partitioned except through divorce proceedings. In addition, in most states, the individual interests cannot be transferred or encumbered or reached by creditors of one spouse unless both spouses join in the transfer or were jointly liable for the debt. Abolished in the majority of states, the tenancy by the entirety is available in about 20 jurisdictions. The tenancy by the entirety is discussed in more detail in §8.2.3.

No encumbrances or transfers without consent of both parties

§9.4 Same-Sex Marriage

Due process clause protects the right to marry

In its momentous 2015 decision in *Obergefell v. Hodges*,[103] the Supreme Court held that both the due process clause and the equal protection clause of the Fourteenth Amendment to the U.S. Constitution protect the right of same-sex couples to marry and to enjoy the benefits of civil marriage on equal terms with opposite-sex couples. In so doing, the Court expressly overruled the 1972 one-line summary decision in *Baker v. Nelson*[104] that had held to the contrary. The Constitution prohibits deprivation of "liberty" without "due process of law."[105] That seemingly procedural clause has been interpreted to protect fundamental substantive liberties from interference by the state. Among those are "personal choices central to individual dignity and autonomy, including intimate choices that define personal identity and beliefs."[106] One liberty associated with individual identity is the right to marry, a right that had previously led the Court to invalidate state laws that prohibited interracial marriage.[107]

Equal protection clause protects rights of gays and lesbians

The Court interpreted the fundamental right to marry to extend to same-sex couples under the due process clause for four reasons. First, "the right to personal choice regarding marriage is inherent in the concept of individual autonomy."[108] Second, "the right to marry is

[103] 576 U.S. 644 (2015).
[104] 409 U.S. 810 (1972). *See Obergefell*, 576 U.S. at 672.
[105] U.S. Const. amends. V, IV.
[106] 576 U.S. at 662.
[107] *Loving v. Virginia*, 388 U.S. 1 (1967).
[108] 576 U.S. at 665.

fundamental because it supports a two-person union unlike any other in its importance to the committed individuals."[109] For that same reason, the Court had previously invalidated laws that made same-sex sexual intimacy a criminal act,[110] because "[s]ame-sex couples have the same right as opposite-sex couples to enjoy intimate association."[111] "A third basis for protecting the right to marry is that it safeguards children and families and thus draws meaning from related rights of childrearing, procreation, and education."[112] "Without the recognition, stability, and predictability marriage offers, their children suffer the stigma of knowing their families are somehow lesser. They also suffer the significant material costs of being raised by unmarried parents, relegated through no fault of their own to a more difficult and uncertain family life."[113] Fourth, marriage is "a keystone of our social order."[114] "Throughout our history [the states] made marriage the basis for an expanding list of governmental rights, benefits, and responsibilities."[115] Those aspects include: "taxation; inheritance and property rights; rules of intestate succession; spousal privilege in the law of evidence; hospital access; medical decision-making authority; adoption rights; the rights and benefits of survivors; birth and death certificates; professional ethics rules; campaign finance restrictions; workers' compensation benefits; health insurance; and child custody, support, and visitation rules."[116]

In addition, the Court held that the equal protection clause prohibits granting the benefits of civil marriage to opposite-sex couples while denying them to same-sex couples.[117] "[T]his denial to same-sex couples of the right to marry works a grave and continuing harm. The imposition of this disability on gays and lesbians serves to disrespect and subordinate them."[118] Just as "restricting the freedom to marry solely because of racial classifications violates the central meaning of the Equal Protection Clause,"[119] preventing same-sex couples from marrying denies equal rights to gays and lesbians. "[S]ame-sex couples are denied all the benefits afforded to opposite-sex couples and are barred from exercising a fundamental right,"[120] and no government interest justifies the discriminatory treatment.

Defense of Marriage Act (DOMA)

The *Obergefell* decision had been foreshadowed two years earlier in *United States v. Windsor*[121] when the Supreme Court struck down the provision of the 1996 *Defense of Marriage Act*[122] that had prohibited the federal

[109] *Id.*
[110] *Lawrence v. Texas*, 539 U.S. 588 (2003).
[111] 576 U.S. at 665.
[112] *Id.* at 666.
[113] *Id.*
[114] *Id.*
[115] *Id.* at 667.
[116] *Id.*
[117] *Id.* at 670.
[118] *Id.*
[119] *Id.* at 669.
[120] *Id.* at 670.
[121] 570 U.S. 744 (2013).
[122] 1 U.S.C. §7, Pub. L. No. 104-199, §3, 110 Stat. 2419 (held unconstitutional in *United States v. Windsor*, 570 U.S. 744 (2013)).

government from treating same-sex couples as married for federal purposes even if they were validly married under state law. While noting that states traditionally defined who could marry,[123] the *Windsor* opinion also emphasized that *DOMA* "seeks to injure the very class New York seeks to protect"[124] and interferes with the "equal dignity" of same-sex couples.[125] *Windsor* did not decide the validity of the part of *DOMA* that allowed states to refuse to recognize same-sex marriages valid under the laws of other states.[126] This meant that it was uncertain whether a couple married in Massachusetts could move to another state and be recognized as married under the law of their new domicile. For a while, couples were validly married in one state but treated as unmarried if they traveled to another state — a situation that not only interfered with the right to travel but was arguably inconsistent with *Windsor*'s "equal dignity" principle. This issue was resolved by the decision in *Obergefell.*

Civil unions and domestic partnerships

Protection for the legal liberties and rights of same-sex couples to marry began with recognition of a legal status that granted the rights of marriage without the name. In 1999, the Supreme Court of Vermont held, in *Baker v. State of Vermont,*[127] that the "common benefits" provision of the Vermont constitution required the state to grant same-sex couples the legal incidents of marriage, whether the state chose to call such relationships "marriages." Implementing this constitutional mandate, the Vermont legislature passed and the governor signed a bill allowing "civil unions" but not "marriages" between same-sex partners.[128] The New Jersey Supreme Court made a similar ruling in 2006 that was followed by "domestic partnership" legislation that conferred many but not all of the benefits of marriage on same-sex couples.[129] By contrast, legislatures passed civil union or domestic partnership legislation without court mandate in Connecticut[130] and California.[131] Eventually, such statuses were also recognized in Colorado, Hawai'i, Illinois, Nevada, Oregon, Rhode Island, and Wisconsin.

Recognition in Massachusetts

The first court to grant same-sex couples the right to marry was the Supreme Judicial Court of the Commonwealth of Massachusetts. On November 18, 2003, the decision in *Goodridge v. Department of Public Health*[132] held proscription on same-sex marriage violated the guarantees

[123] 570 U.S. at 770.
[124] *Id.*
[125] *Id.*
[126] 28 U.S.C. §1738C, Pub. L. No. 104-199, §2(a), Sept. 21, 1996, 110 Stat. 2419.
[127] 744 A.2d 864, 867 (Vt. 1999). The Vermont constitution states: That government is, or ought to be, instituted for the common benefit, protection, and security of the people, nation, or community, and not for the particular emolument or advantage of any single person, family, or set of persons, who are a part only of that community. Vt. Const. art. 7.
[128] 2000 Vt. Acts & Resolves 91 (H. 847). Vermont recognized same-sex marriages in 2009. 2009 Vt. Act 3; 2009 Vt. S. 115.
[129] *Lewis v. Harris*, 908 A.2d 196 (N.J. 2006); N.J. Stat. §§37:1-28 to 1-36.
[130] Conn. Pub. Act 05-10 (Jan. 2005), 2005 Ct. S.B. 963, 2005 Conn. Legis. Serv. P.A. 05-10 (S.S.B. 963).
[131] Cal. Fam. Code §§297-299.6.
[132] 798 N.E.2d 941 (Mass. 2003). *See also Opinion of the Justices to the Senate*, 802 N.E.2d 565 (Mass. 2004) (explaining the *Goodridge* decision).

of liberty and equality in the state constitution. Chief Justice Margaret Marshall wrote that the "Massachusetts Constitution affirms the dignity and equality of all individuals" and that "[i]t forbids the creation of second-class citizens."[133] Same-sex marriages began to be celebrated in Massachusetts on May 17, 2004.

Recognition in other states before *Obergefell*

State supreme court cases similar to *Goodridge* were decided in 2008 in California[134] and Connecticut,[135] and in 2009 in Iowa.[136] Legislation recognizing same-sex marriage followed between 2009 and 2011 in Vermont,[137] New Hampshire,[138] the District of Columbia,[139] and New York[140] while referenda were adopted allowing same-sex marriage in Maine, Maryland, and Washington in 2012.[141] The Rhode Island legislature joined the other New England states in 2013, as did Delaware[142] and Minnesota.[143]

Indian nations

In recent years, many Indian nations have recognized same-sex marriage, including the Coquille Indian Tribe,[144] the Confederated Tribes of the Colville Reservation,[145] the Little Traverse Bay Bands of Odawa Indians,[146] the Mashantucket Pequot Tribe,[147] the Pokagon Band of Potawatomi Indians,[148] the Puyallup Tribe,[149] the Suquamish Tribe,[150] and the Tlingit and Haida Indian Tribes of Alaska.[151] Some tribes have laws denying same-sex couples the right to marry under tribal law.[152] While *Obergefell* does not apply to Indian nations (because they are not governed by the Fifth or Fourteenth Amendments), the federal *Indian Civil Rights*

[133] 798 N.E.2d at 948.
[134] *In re Marriage Cases*, 183 P.2d 384 (Cal. 2008). The California ruling was overturned by Proposition 8, Cal. Const. art. I, §7.5 (added Nov. 4, 2008), which was later held unconstitutional by *Perry v. Schwarzenegger*, 704 F. Supp. 2d 921 (N.D. Cal. 2010), *aff'd, Perry v. Brown*, 671 F.3d 1052 (9th Cir. 2012), *cert. granted sub nom.* Hollingsworth v. Perry, 568 U.S. 1066 (2012), *vacated and remanded*, 570 U.S. 693 (2013).
[135] *Kerrigan v. Comm'r of Pub. Health*, 957 A.2d 407 (Conn. 2008).
[136] *Varnum v. Brien*, 763 N.W.2d 862 (Iowa 2009).
[137] 2009 Vt. Act 3; 2009 Vt. S. 115.
[138] 2009 N.H. Laws ch. 59.
[139] D.C. Code §46-401 (*Religious Freedom and Civil Marriage Equality Amendment Act of 2009*, D.C. Law 18-110, §2(b) (Mar. 3, 2010)).
[140] N.Y. Dom. Rel. §10-a, -b (*Marriage Equality Act*, 2011 N.Y. Laws ch. 95, §3 (June 24, 2011)).
[141] Me. Rev. Stat. tit. 19-A, §650-A; Md. Code, Fam. Law §2-201.
[142] Del. Code, tit. 13, §§101 to 122, *as amended by* 2013 Del. HB 75 (May 8, 2013); R.I. Gen. Laws §§15-1-1 to 15-1-5, *as amended by* 2013 R.I. Pub. Laws 4 (2013 R.I. HB 5015).
[143] Minn. Stat. §§517.01 to 517.09, *as amended by* 2013 Minn. Sess. Law Serv., ch. 74 (H.F. 1054) (May 14, 2013).
[144] Coquille Indian Tribal Code §§740.010, 740.100; Ann E. Tweedy, *Tribal Laws and Same-Sex Marriage: Theory, Process, and Content*, 46 Colum. Hum. Rts. L. Rev. 104, 107 (2015).
[145] Confederated Tribes of the Colville Reservation Tribal Code tit. 5, §§5-1-30, 5-1-32, 5-1-34.
[146] Little Traverse Bay Bands of Odawa Indians Tribal Code of Law §13.103.
[147] Mashantucket Pequot Tribal Laws tit. 6, ch. 3, §3.
[148] Pokagon Band of Potawatomi Indians Marriage Code ch. 1, §1.06(j)(2013).
[149] Puyallup Tribal Code tit. 7, §7.08.030 (2014).
[150] Suquamish Tribal Code tit. 9, §9.1.1 (2011).
[151] Central Council of the Tlingit and Haida Indian Tribes of Alaska Stat. Code, tit. 5, §05.01.004(C) (2015).
[152] Ann E. Tweedy, *Tribal Laws and Same-Sex Marriage: Theory, Process, and Content*, 46 Colum. Hum. Rts. L. Rev. 104, 108 (2015).

Act of 1968 (*ICRA*)[153] does protect the rights of tribal citizens to due process and equal protection of the laws as well as the free exercise of religion. However, *ICRA* does not prohibit the establishment of religion as the First Amendment does because some tribal governments are religious in nature. Any interpretation and enforcement of *ICRA* provisions must occur in tribal courts who will have to determine whether or not to adopt the reasoning of *Obergefell*.

International recognition

Same-sex marriage is now recognized, among other countries, in Argentina, Belgium, Brazil, Canada, Colombia, Denmark, Greenland, Finland, France, Iceland, Luxembourg, Mexico, the Netherlands, New Zealand, Norway, Portugal, South Africa, Spain, Sweden, the United Kingdom, and Uruguay.

§9.5 Unmarried Couples

Common law marriage

Couples who live together without benefit of a formal marriage ceremony can obtain some or all the legal incidents of a valid marriage in some states. Ten states and the District of Columbia recognize some form of "common law marriage," by which parties who agree to live as husband and wife, do in fact live together, and can show some public recognition of the existence of a marital relation, will be treated as married and entitled to the legal benefits of marriage.[154]

Agreements to share property

Most states, however, reject the institution of common law marriage. Until fairly recently, this meant that individuals could not, by agreement, obtain any of the benefits of marriage, such as property distribution if the partners break up. Such agreements were viewed as contrary to public policy because they involved sexual relationships outside of marriage, a practice that was illegal in most states until recently. Worse still, agreements to share resources in the context of a sexual relationship were viewed as exchanging value for sexual services, a practice otherwise known as prostitution that is illegal almost everywhere. Whether viewed as fornication or prostitution, such contracts were thought to implicate "meretricious" relationships, *i.e.*, illegal sexual relationships.

Palimony

This legal practice began to change, however, with the leading case of *Marvin v. Marvin*,[155] which recognized the ability of unmarried couples to agree to share property during their relationship and in the event of a dissolution of the relationship. That case popularized the term "palimony." The court found that whatever sexual component of the relationship was present could be separated from its non-sexual component. Viewing such agreements as an exchange of sex for money assumes that the woman is providing "sex" to the man and the man is providing money or resources. This conception of the woman as a sexual object fails to recognize that

[153] 25 U.S.C. §§1301-1304.

[154] 4-37 *Thompson on Real Property, Third Thomas Edition* §37.05(d). Those states include Colorado, Iowa, Kansas, Montana, Oklahoma, Rhode Island, Texas, and Utah. *Id.* at §37.05(d) n.43.

[155] 557 P.2d 106, 111 (Cal. 1976).

each partner is agreeing to have sexual relations with the other; one might as well view the contract as the provision of value by the woman (homemaking services) for sex provided by the man. Or one might view the sexual relationship as mutual and not in exchange for anything else.[156] With the repeal of many state fornication statutes, which had imposed criminal penalties for sex outside of marriage, and changing attitudes toward unmarried couples, the trend in the law has been to recognize agreements between unmarried partners to share property during and after their relationship.

Mutuality

Nonenforcement of contracts between unmarried partners in some states

Some states retain the older law, holding that such agreements between unmarried partners to provide support in return for services of various kinds violate public policy and are thus unenforceable. For example, in *Hewitt v. Hewitt*,[157] the Illinois Supreme Court held that enforcement of contracts between unmarried cohabitants was prohibited by virtue of the state statute outlawing common law marriage. The Michigan Court of Appeals found "contracts made in consideration of meretricious relationships" to be unenforceable in light of state laws criminalizing prostitution (payment for sexual services).[158]

Enforcing support agreements

Agreement v. relationship

Today, however, most states will enforce agreements of mutual support between unmarried partners, whether or not their relationship includes sexual relations.[159] Three different approaches have been adopted. Some states enforce explicit agreements between the parties, written or oral,[160] and some enforce only written contracts.[161] Others enforce *implicit* agreements based on the conduct of the parties.[162] Still others do not require an agreement at all, holding that the relationship gives rise to mutual obligations to share.[163] The Mississippi Supreme Court ruled, for example, in *Pickens v. Pickens*,[164] that "[w]here parties such as these live together in what must at least be acknowledged to be a partnership and where, through their joint efforts, real property or personal property, or both, are accumulated,

[156] These arguments come from Clare Dalton, *An Essay in the Deconstruction of Contract Doctrine*, 94 Yale L.J. 997 (1985).
[157] 394 N.E.2d 1204, 1210-1211 (Ill. 1979).
[158] *Carnes v. Sheldon*, 311 N.W.2d 747, 750-751 (Mich. Ct. App. 1981).
[159] At least 17 states have explicitly recognized such contracts. Albertina Antognini, *Nonmarital Contracts*, 73 Stan. L. Rev. 67, 95-97 (2021); Dominick Vetri, *Almost Everything You Always Wanted to Know About Lesbians and Gay Men, Their Families, and the Law*, 26 S.U. L. Rev. 1, 18, 18 n.54 (1998); *Carroll v. Lee*, 712 P.2d 923, 926-927 (Ariz. 1986); *Boland v. Catalano*, 521 A.2d 142, 145 (Conn. 1987); *Wilcox v. Trautz*, 693 N.E.2d 141, 146 (Mass. 1998); *Western States Construction, Inc. v. Michoff*, 840 P.2d 1220, 1224 (Nev. 1992) (unmarried partners may agree to hold their property in a manner analogous to community property); *Connell v. Francisco*, 898 P.2d 831, 836 (Wash. 1995), *aff'g in part, rev'g in part* 872 P.2d 1150 (Wash. Ct. App. 1994) (same); *Watts v. Watts*, 405 N.W.2d 303, 311 (Wis. 1987).
[160] *Morone v. Morone*, 413 N.E.2d 1154, 1156 (N.Y. 1980). *See Byrne v. Laura*, 60 Cal. Rptr. 2d 908, 913 (Ct. App. 1997).
[161] Minn. Stat. §513.075; Tex. Fam. Code §1.108; *Posik v. Layton*, 695 So. 2d 759, 762 (Fla. Dist. Ct. App. 1997); *Kohler v. Flynn*, 493 N.W.2d 647, 649 (N.D. 1992).
[162] *Marvin v. Marvin*, 557 P.2d 106, 110 (Cal. 1976); *Watts v. Watts*, 405 N.W.2d 303, 306 (Wis. 1987).
[163] *Pickens v. Pickens*, 490 So. 2d 872, 875 (Miss. 1986); *Connell v. Francisco*, 898 P.2d 831, 835-836 (Wash. 1995); *In re Marriage of Lindsey*, 678 P.2d 328, 331 (Wash. 1984).
[164] 490 So. 2d 872 (Miss. 1986).

an equitable division of such property will be ordered upon the permanent breakup and separation."[165] The underlying policy dispute is whether the plaintiff has to prove that an explicit agreement was reached whereby the parties promised to share property rights or whether the plaintiff need only show that the parties lived together in a close relationship in the same household in a manner that involved a mutual understanding that they would support each other and live as a couple. This latter approach bases the obligation on the fact that the parties entered a relationship akin to a partnership, while the former bases the obligation on the parties' mutual promises.

▷ REVIEW FOR FAIRNESS **HARD CASE ◀**

When married couples seek to enforce antenuptial agreements, most states will review those agreements to see whether they are fair.[166] Should the same review occur as to unmarried couples? The Massachusetts Supreme Judicial Court answered in the negative in the 1998 case of *Wilcox v. Trautz*,[167] explaining that "marriage gives each party substantial rights concerning the assets of the other which unmarried cohabitants do not have."[168] Agreements between unmarried partners are subject to ordinary contract law rather than the more searching inquiry into their "fairness and reasonableness" characteristic of antenuptial agreements.[169] This result can be criticized both for failing to respect the actual expectations of the parties to such a contract and for failing to protect adequately the parties to the agreement. A twenty-five year relationship, like that in *Wilcox*, generates expectations that may exceed those contained in an agreement entered into before the relationship began. Moreover, the mutual dependence of the parties and their long-standing relationship may make the terms of such an agreement fundamentally unfair. Reviewing such contracts for reasonableness does not equate the relationship with marriage; it merely recognizes that such contracts are not the same as arm's-length contracts between business parties and should be treated accordingly. ◀

▷ CONSTRUCTIVE TRUST **HARD CASE ◀**

When a couple lives together in a house owned by one of them, and the couple breaks up, does the non-owner acquire any rights in the family home? In *Sullivan v. Rooney*,[170] the Massachusetts Supreme Judicial Court

[165] *Id.* at 875-876. *Accord, Connell v. Francisco*, 898 P.2d 831 (Wash. 1995); *In re Marriage of Lindsey*, 678 P.2d 328 (Wash. 1984).
[166] *See* §9.3.1.
[167] *Wilcox v. Trautz*, 693 N.E.2d 141 (Mass. 1998).
[168] *Id.* at 147.
[169] *Id.*
[170] 533 N.E.2d 1372 (Mass. 1989).

imposed a constructive trust on a house in which an unmarried couple with a 13- or 14-year relationship had lived for several years. The court found that the defendant owner of the house held a one-half interest in the house in constructive trust for the benefit of his ex-partner and ordered him to convey the property to himself and his ex-partner as tenants in common. The trial judge found that the defendant had promised to convey joint title at the time of the purchase and later on, as well, and that, in reliance on those promises, defendant was induced to stay in the relationship, giving up employment opportunities and providing various homemaking services to the couple. The court ruled that the defendant would be unjustly enriched if he were not held to his promise, that the parties had a fiduciary relationship, and that the defendant had violated his fiduciary duties to the plaintiff.[171] However, in *Collins v. Guggenheim*,[172] decided several years later, the same court refused to impose a constructive trust on a farm jointly occupied and managed by an unmarried couple on the ground that there was no evidence of fraud or breach of fiduciary duty. In effect, the court ruled that it would enforce a promise to share title to real property if it was relied upon by the other party, but that it would not impose a constructive trust resulting in shared ownership of real property based solely on the relationship itself. A state such as Mississippi, however, might well have ruled that such property rights should be modified and interests in the real property shared to protect the interests of both parties in relying on their implicit partnership.[173] This approach would allow for equitable distribution of property acquired by "joint efforts" when the couple separates.[174] ◀

▶ HARD CASE ▷ SUCCESSION ON DEATH

In *Williams v. Mason*,[175] Roosevelt Adams promised Frances Mason in 1962 that if she would live in his home, take care of him, and "do his bidding," he would leave her all his property on his death. Mason lived with Adams for more than 20 years; when Adams died, he left a farm but, unfortunately, not a will or, indeed, any written memorandum of his promise to Mason. Adams never divorced his wife, who lived in Chicago, and he never promised to marry Mason. The court held that the promise to devise the property was unenforceable because it was not in writing, as required by the statute of frauds and the statute of wills. However, the court allowed a limited remedy of restitution for the value of services rendered. Although the New Jersey courts originally allowed such promises to be enforced whether

[171] *Compare Williams v. Mason*, 556 So. 2d 1045 (Miss. 1990) (ordering restitution for services rendered by a caretaker but refusing to enforce a promise by the decedent Roosevelt Adams to leave his property to Frances Mason on his death in exchange for her agreeing to live with him in his home and take care of him).

[172] 631 N.E.2d 1016 (Mass. 1994).

[173] *Pickens v. Pickens*, 490 So. 2d 872, 876 (Miss. 1986).

[174] *Id.* at 875-876. *Accord, Connell v. Francisco*, 898 P.2d 831, 835-836 (Wash. 1995); *In re Marriage of Lindsey*, 678 P.2d 328, 331-332 (Wash. 1984).

[175] 556 So. 2d 1045 (Miss. 1990).

they were explicit or implicit, the legislature overruled that decision and now requires all "palimony" agreements to be in writing.[176] ◀

Same-sex couple agreements

Same-sex couples may enter into agreements just as male-female couples may to share property both during their relationship and at separation.[177] Alternatively, courts may apply constructive trust or unjust enrichment doctrine to impose a remedy to protect the interests of one of the parties after dissolution of the relationship or death of one of the parties, as they may do in the case of male-female couples.[178] Until 1995, 22 states had "sodomy" statutes on the books, criminalizing certain types of private sexual conduct, some of which applied regardless of sex and some of which applied only to same-sex couples.[179] Some courts viewed same-sex relations as necessarily involving a violation of state sodomy laws and refused to enforce property agreements between same-sex partners on the ground that their relationship was "illegal and immoral."[180] Although the Supreme Court upheld the constitutionality of sodomy statutes in the 1986 case of *Bowers v. Hardwick*,[181] it overturned that ruling in 2003 in the case of *Lawrence v. Texas*,[182] on the ground that the due process clause protects the fundamental "liberty" interest in engaging in private sexual conduct in the home and that this interest extends to homosexual as well as heterosexual conduct.

"Illegal and immoral"

▷ INHERITANCE UNDER STATE INTESTACY LAWS **HARD CASE ◀**

In *Vasquez v. Hawthorne*,[183] a man involved in a "long term, stable, cohabiting relationship" with another man died without leaving a will. If the men had been married, the survivor would have inherited the decedent's property as a surviving spouse under the state intestacy statute. A literal reading of the statute would preclude a remedy for the survivor. This result might be justified as well on the ground that disputes over the estates of decedents are minimized by the use of wills and the formal relationship of

[176] *In re Estate of Roccamonte*, 1808 A.2d 838 (N.J. 2002), *superseded by* N.J. Stat. §25:1-5(h).
[177] See Frederick Hertz & Lina Guillen, *A Legal Guide for Lesbian and Gay Couples* 68-69, 208-216, 287-316 (20th ed. 2020).
[178] *See, e.g., Minieri v. Knittel*, 727 N.Y.S.2d 872 (June 1, 2001) (Sup. Ct. 2001) (separation); *Doe v. Burkland*, 808 A.2d 1090, 1092 (R.I. 2002) (unjust enrichment on separation); *Vasquez v. Hawthorne*, 33 P.3d 735 (Wash. 2001) (death). *Cf. Sullivan v. Rooney*, 533 N.E.2d 1372 (Mass. 1989) (using constructive trust doctrine in the case of a male-female couple).
[179] William B. Rubenstein, Carlos A. Ball & Jane S. Schacter, *Cases and Materials on Sexual Orientation and the Law* 113 (4th ed. 2011).
[180] *Crooke v. Gilden*, 414 S.E.2d 645, 646 (Ga. 1992) (reversing a lower court decision that an agreement was void because it was based on an "illegal and immoral" relationship). *See also Jones v. Daly*, 176 Cal. Rptr. 130, 133 (Ct. App. 1981) (denying enforcement to an agreement because it described the plaintiff as the "lover" of the decedent, making the contracts necessarily a meretricious one).
[181] 478 U.S. 186 (1986).
[182] 539 U.S. 558 (2003). *Cf. Gryczan v. State*, 942 P.2d 112 (Mont. 1997); *Campbell v. Sundquist*, 926 S.W.2d 250, 262 (Tenn. Ct. App. 1996), *abrogated on other grounds by Colonial Pipeline Co. v. Morgan*, 263 S.W.3d 827 (Tenn. 2008).
[183] 33 P.3d 735 (Wash. 2001).

marriage or consanguinity, which will grant property of the decedent to the decedent's surviving family members subject to the rights of decedent's creditors. Allowing unrelated parties to claim a share of the estate because of oral promises or relationships with the decedent will place ownership of the decedent's assets in doubt and open the way for fraudulent claims. Despite these dangers, the court in *Vasquez* allowed the decedent's partner to attempt to prove the existence of an implied partnership based on his relationship with the decedent and authorized the state courts to impose a constructive or equitable trust on the decedent's property that might allow the survivor to claim some or all of that property if such a partnership were found to exist. Although making the property rights less certain, this result arguably promotes the probable intent of the decedent as well as protecting the interests of the survivor who had established a relationship of trust and interdependence with the decedent and who might have married the decedent had that option been legally available. On the other hand, the parties could have entered a formal contract achieving this result and the decedent could have left a will ensuring that his property would go to his partner and his failure to do so might indicate an intent that his property not go to the decedent. ◀

▶ HARD CASE

▷ EQUITABLE DISTRIBUTION OF PROPERTY OF UNMARRIED SAME-SEX COUPLES

In *Gormley v. Robertson*,[184] the Washington Court of Appeals extended a doctrine applicable to male-female couples in a long-term relationship to a same-sex couple,[185] finding that the two women in the case had a stable, marriage-like relationship, which justified the court in ordering a just and equitable distribution of the property they jointly accumulated during their relationship when they decided to break up, to avoid unjust enrichment. In effect, this imposes a "constructive trust" on property held by each party for the benefit of the other to avoid unjust enrichment. Should such a remedy be available in a state that prohibits same-sex marriage? On one hand, this would seem to grant a remedy to a couple that is generally reserved for married couples, *i.e.*, equitable distribution of property, and thus be unavailable because of the statutory prohibition on the marriage. On the other hand, if the constructive trust doctrine is applied to the property of an unmarried couple, that does not give them the status of being married but simply recognizes the implicit contract between the parties to share their property during the relationship, giving them legitimate expectations of mutual division of the property upon separation of the parties. And if the state grants such a contract/property remedy to a male-female couple, it would arguably deny equal protection of the laws to refuse such a remedy to a same-sex couple. ◀

[184] 83 P.3d 1042 (Wash. Ct. App. 2004).

[185] *See Connell v. Francisco*, 898 P.2d 831, 836 (Wash. 1995).

§9.6 Parents and Children

Duty of support

Parents have a duty to support their minor children. This is true in both community property[186] and separate property states.[187] Child support payments are routinely ordered when couples divorce. Such awards are based on the needs of the child, as well as the ability of the parents to pay. They are also modifiable over time if circumstances (either of the child or the parent(s)) should change.

▷ COLLEGE EDUCATION **HARD CASE ◀**

The question often arises as to whether parents are obligated to pay for college education. Because most states emancipate children at the age of 18, and most individuals do not start college until they are 18, and not all people go to college, it was traditionally believed that parents had no duty to pay for a college education for their children. The states do not ordinarily require parents to pay for college for their children. The question arises whether they can be required to do so when the parents divorce. Many states do not require parents to pay for college, on the assumption that divorced parents do not have greater obligations than married parents.[188] Some states, however, have held that parents who stay together are likely to pay for college education for their children (or at least help pay for it) if they are able to do so, and the fact of divorce should not deprive the child of support that would otherwise have been provided.[189] ◀

▷ SECOND FAMILIES **HARD CASE ◀**

When a parent remarries and has additional children, the question arises whether child support obligations to his children from a prior marriage should be reduced to allow him to spread his support equally among all his children, including children of the second marriage.[190] On one hand, it seems unfair to the later-born children to relegate them to a lesser status than the earlier-born children, depriving them of property currently being earned by their parent. This suggests that all the parent's children should be equally supported by the parent. In addition, the parent has the

[186] Cal. Fam. Code §3900; Idaho Code §32-1003; La. Civ. Code art. 2372; Tex. Fam. Code §151.001; Wis. Stat. §766.55.

[187] Mich. Comp. Laws §722.3; 23 Pa. Cons. Stat. §4321.

[188] *Dowling v. Dowling*, 679 P.2d 480, 483 (Alaska 1984); *In re Marriage of Plummer*, 735 P.2d 165, 166 (Colo. 1987); *Grapin v. Grapin*, 450 So. 2d 853, 854 (Fla. 1984). *See also Curtis v. Kline*, 666 A.2d 265 (Pa. 1995) (holding unconstitutional as a violation of equal protection of law a statute that required divorced parents, but not married parents, to pay for college education for their children).

[189] *Childers v. Childers*, 575 P.2d 201 (Wash. 1978). Alabama initially followed this approach, *see Bayliss v. Bayliss*, 550 So. 2d 986 (Ala. 1989), but more recently joined the majority view, *see Ex parte Christopher*, 145 So. 3d 60 (Ala. 2013).

[190] Leslie J. Harris, June Carbone & Rachel Rebouché, *Family Law* 381-385 (7th ed. 2023).

right to remarry and have more children; limiting his ability to do so would infringe on fundamental constitutional liberties. On the other hand, if the parent had remained married to the first spouse, they would likely have made a joint decision whether to have more children, and might have not chosen to do so if the family could not afford to take care of them adequately. When the spouses divorce and the supporting parent makes a unilateral decision to remarry and have more children, the first spouse has no control over this decision. It is not clear that this decision should prejudice the rights of his pre-existing children.

Duty of stepparents to support stepchildren

The issue becomes even more complicated when one considers the earnings of stepparents. Traditionally, stepparents were not obligated to provide support for stepchildren, and most states continue to adhere to this common law rule.[191] However, statutes in a few states impose a support duty on stepparents living with stepchildren for the duration of the marriage.[192]

Duty of children to support parents

Traditionally, parents had a duty to support minor children, but adult children had no enforceable legal duty to support their parents. Many states have changed this in recent years and promulgated statutes requiring children to support their parents.[193] ◀

§9.7 Inheritance

§9.7.1 Wills and Will Substitutes

Testamentary transfers

The specifics of the law of inheritance are beyond the scope of this treatise. That subject is usually covered in upper-level courses in wills or trusts and estates.[194] It is important to know, however, that in every state, owners are entitled to write a will determining who will own their property when they die. The freedom to make testamentary transfers (transfers at death) is such a fundamental aspect of ownership, that the Supreme Court has ruled that a law that completely abolishes the ability to pass property on at death, constitutes an unconstitutional taking of property in violation of the Fifth or Fourteenth Amendment.[195] More limited intrusions on the right to pass on property have been upheld, such as the elective or statutory share and homestead laws, both of which protect the surviving spouse from being disinherited completely. Individuals may pass on property through use of a valid will (testate succession) or, if they do not write a will, by operation

[191] *Id.* at 384.

[192] Mo. Rev. Stat. §568.040; Mont. Code §40-6-217; N.D. Cent. Code §14-09-09; Or. Rev. Stat. §108.045; S.D. Codified Laws §25-7-8.

[193] Cal. Fam. Code §4400 ("Except as otherwise provided by law, an adult child shall, to the extent of his or her ability, support a parent who is in need and unable to self-maintain by work"); S.D. Codified Laws §25-7-27. *See* Leslie J. Harris, June Carbone & Rachel Rebouché, *Family Law* 384-385 (7th ed. 2023).

[194] For an overview, see Robert H. Sitkoff & Jesse Dukeminier, *Wills, Trusts, and Estates* (11th ed. 2022); 10-88/10-89 *Thompson on Real Property, Third Thomas Edition* §§88.01 to 89.09.

[195] *Babbitt v. Youpee*, 519 U.S. 234 (1997); *Hodel v. Irving*, 481 U.S. 704 (1987).

of the state intestacy statute (intestate succession), which determines who will inherit the property.

Every state regulates the formalities needed to create a valid will. Most states require the will to be in writing, signed by the testator, and attested by witnesses (usually two).[196] The 1990 version of the *Uniform Probate Code* (adopted in at least 18 states)[197] allows enforcement of a will even if it does not conform to these formalities, if the proponent can establish by "clear and convincing evidence" that the decedent intended the document to constitute a valid will.[198] The 2008 revision of the *Uniform Probate Code* allows a will to be enforced without witnesses if it is notarized, ensuring that there is at least one witness.[199]

Will formalities

Holographic wills

About half the states, primarily in the south and in the west, enforce so-called *holographic* or hand-written wills, while many do not.[200] The states that do enforce them generally require them to be in the testator's own handwriting and signed by the testator.[201] Early on, such wills were valid only if entirely in the testator's handwriting; recent revisions to the law have only required that "material portions" be in the testator's handwriting and may even allow extrinsic evidence to be used to establish testamentary intent.[202] Purely oral statements that property will be left to someone are usually not enforceable, although some courts have imposed constructive trusts in such cases to avoid injustice.[203]

Will substitutes

Many families utilize *will substitutes* to pass on property at death. These substitutes include joint bank and stock accounts, revocable *inter vivos* trusts (trusts created during the lifetime of the grantor), pension accounts, and life insurance contracts.[204] At least a dozen states have adopted laws that allow "transfer on death" deeds that enable people to transfer title automatically on the death of the grantor in a manner that avoids having the property be counted as part of the estate of the decedent.[205] These are will substitutes because they have the effect of passing on property at death while avoiding the formalities and attestation requirements for wills. Other arrangements also have the effect of passing on property at death, but are not perfect substitutes for wills. Examples include joint tenancies or tenancies by the entirety. These provide for the passing of title to property on death but are not full will substitutes because they involve granting another

[196] Robert H. Sitkoff & Jesse Dukeminier, *Wills, Trusts, and Estates* 142 (11th ed. 2022) (every state except Louisiana requires only two witnesses; Louisiana also requires notarization).

[197] Alaska, Arizona, Colorado, Florida, Hawai'i, Idaho, Maine, Massachusetts, Michigan, Minnesota, Montana, Nebraska, New Jersey, New Mexico, North Dakota, South Carolina, South Dakota, and Utah.

[198] *Unif. Probate Code* §2-503 (1990); Robert H. Sitkoff & Jesse Dukeminier, *Wills, Trusts, and Estates* 180-194 (11th ed. 2022).

[199] *Unif. Probate Code* §2-502 (2008); Robert H. Sitkoff & Jesse Dukeminier, *Wills, Trusts, and Estates* 145-146, 204-205 (11th ed. 2022).

[200] *In re Succession of Miller*, 479 So. 2d 1035 (La. Ct. App. 1985); Robert H. Sitkoff & Jesse Dukeminier, *Wills, Trusts, and Estates* 205-211 (11th ed. 2022).

[201] Robert H. Sitkoff & Jesse Dukeminier, *Wills, Trusts, and Estates* 205 (11th ed. 2022).

[202] *Id.* at 215-217.

[203] *Williams v. Mason*, 556 So. 2d 1045, 1048 (Miss. 1990).

[204] Robert H. Sitkoff & Jesse Dukeminier, *Wills, Trusts, and Estates* 449-507 (11th ed. 2022).

[205] *Id.* at 506-507.

person power over the property during the grantor's lifetime and therefore involve lifetime transfers as well as transfers at death. Some will substitutes are in common use because they make transfers of property on death seamless, removing the need to have the property be part of the estate that may be used to pay off the decedent's debts. Others are in use because they minimize estate taxes.

§9.7.2 *Intestate Succession*

Intestacy statutes

Every state has an *intestacy statute*, which determines who inherits property if someone dies without a valid will. Only those who survive the decedent are entitled to succeed to the decedent's property by testate or intestate succession.[206] The *Uniform Probate Code* (*UPC*), originally promulgated in 1969 and amended in 1990, 2008, 2010, and 2019, has been substantially or partially adopted in about 18 states.[207] The rest of the states have other systems with substantial variation among them. The general patterns are as follows.

UPC

Share of surviving spouse

§9.7.2.1 Surviving Spouse but no Surviving Children or Parents. If the decedent leaves a surviving spouse but no surviving children or parents, both the UPC and most states give the entire estate to the surviving spouse.[208]

§9.7.2.2 Surviving Spouse and Surviving Parents but no Children. If the decedent leaves no surviving children but leaves surviving parents, some states give the entire estate to the surviving spouse.[209] About half the states require the surviving spouse to share the estate with the decedent's surviving parents.[210] The 2008 version of the *UPC* gives the surviving spouse the first $300,000 of the estate (subject to an annual adjustment for inflation) plus three-fourths of any balance of the estate.[211]

§9.7.2.3 Surviving Spouse and Children. If the decedent leaves a surviving spouse and surviving children, some statutes give the entire

[206] *Id.* at 70.

[207] *See* Alaska Stat. §§13.06.005 to 13.36.100; Ariz. Rev. Stat. §§14-3101 to 14-3974; Colo. Rev. Stat. §§15-10-101 to 15-17-102; Fla. Stat. §§731.005 to 735.304; Haw. Rev. Stat. §§539-1 to 539-12, 560:1-101 to 560:8-101; Idaho Code §§15-1-101 to 15-6-404; Me. Rev. Stat. tit. 18-C, §§1-101 to 10-118; Mich. Comp. Laws §§700.1101 to 700.8102; Minn. Stat. §§524.1-101 to 524.8-103; Mont. Code §§72-1-101 to 72-6-418; Neb. Stat. §§30-2201 to 30-2902; N.M. Stat. §§45-1-101 to 45-7-522; N.D. Cent. Code §§30.1-01-01 to 30.1-30-01; S.C. Code §§62-1-100 to 62-7-604; S.D. Codified Laws §§29A-1-101 to 29A-8-101; Utah Code §§75-1-101 to 75-8-101.

[208] *Unif. Probate Code* §2-102 (2008); 10-89 *Thompson on Real Property, Third Thomas Edition* §89.05(b)(1), (2).

[209] Ariz. Rev. Stat. §14-2102; Colo. Rev. Stat. §15-11-102; Fla. Stat. §732.102; Ga. Code §53-2-1(c)(1); N.Y. Est. Powers & Trust §4-1.1. *See* 10-89 *Thompson on Real Property, Third Thomas Edition* §89.05(b)(3).

[210] N.C. Gen. Stat. §29-14; Wash. Rev. Code §11.04.015; Robert H. Sitkoff & Jesse Dukeminier, *Wills, Trusts, and Estates* 76 (11th ed. 2022).

[211] *Unif. Probate Code* §2-102(2) (2008); Robert H. Sitkoff & Jesse Dukeminier, *Wills, Trusts, and Estates* 72 (11th ed. 2022).

estate to the surviving spouse.[212] This is the approach taken by the *UPC*.[213] Other states require the surviving spouse to share the property with the surviving children. These states give a portion (often one-third) to the surviving spouse and the rest to the surviving children (or, if there are no surviving children, to the decedent's surviving parents).[214]

Stepchildren

Many states alter the intestacy rules in the case of stepchildren. The states that allow the surviving spouse to inherit the entire estate usually make an exception when the decedent had children who were not also the children of the surviving spouse. Because of a worry that the surviving spouse may not be as close to the children of her spouse as to the children they had together (or the survivor's own children with another father or mother), most states require the surviving spouse to share the estate with the surviving children (both the decedent's surviving children and the children of the surviving spouse).[215] If the decedent is survived by a child who is not the surviving spouse's child, the 1969 *UPC* split the entire estate 50/50 between the surviving spouse and the surviving children.[216] The 1990 *UPC* altered this division by again instituting the lump-sum-plus system. Under the 1990 *UPC*, when the decedent is survived by a child who is not also the surviving spouse's child, the surviving spouse is granted the first $100,000 ($143,000 plus probate exemptions and allowances) plus 50 percent of the balance, if any. However, if the decedent is survived by children of the surviving spouse who are not also children of the decedent, the 1990 *UPC* gives the surviving spouse the first $150,000 ($193,000 plus probate exemptions and allowances) plus 50 percent of any remainder.[217] The 2008 *UPC* gives the first $225,000 (subject to an annual adjustment for inflation) to the surviving spouse plus one-half of any balance if all the decedent's surviving children are also descendants of the surviving spouse and the surviving spouse has surviving children who are not descendants of the decedent; it gives the first $150,000 (subject to an annual adjustment for inflation) plus one-half of the balance if one or more of the decedent's surviving descendants are not descendants of the surviving spouse.[218]

Spouse v. children

Some states require the surviving spouse to share the estate with the surviving children. This system protects both the spouse and the children. At the same time, if the children are minors, they cannot control their own property, and the surviving spouse is likely to be appointed by the probate court to manage the property for the benefit of the children. Although this protects the children's interests, it imposes the expense of getting a court to appoint a "conservator" to manage the children's property. That conservator will usually be the surviving spouse. The *UPC* attempts to avoid the

[212] Ariz. Rev. Stat. §14-2102(1); Iowa Code §633.211; Or. Rev. Stat. §§112.025, 112.035.

[213] *Unif. Probate Code* §2-102 (2008); 10-89 *Thompson on Real Property, Third Thomas Edition* §89.05(b)(2).

[214] 10-89 *Thompson on Real Property, Third Thomas Edition* §89.05(b)(1), (2).

[215] Ariz. Rev. Stat. §14-2102(2); Iowa Code §633.212; Or. Rev. Stat. §112.025.

[216] *Unif. Probate Code* §2-102 (1969).

[217] *Unif. Probate Code* §2-102(4) (1990); 10-89 *Thompson on Real Property, Third Thomas Edition* §89.05(b)(1), (2).

[218] *Unif. Probate Code* §2-102(3) & (4) (2008); Robert H. Sitkoff & Jesse Dukeminier, *Wills, Trusts, and Estates* 72 (11th ed. 2022).

expense and cumbersome procedures of probate by giving all or the bulk of the property to the surviving spouse, on the assumption that she or he will best manage the property in the interest of the entire family, including the children. If, in contrast, the surviving children are adults, they are likely to have jobs of their own, and alternative sources of income, and the surviving spouse is likely to be more needy than the adult children. For this reason, also, the *UPC* gives the entire estate to the surviving spouse.[219] Some non-*UPC* states, however, require sharing of the estate between the surviving spouse and children, on the assumption that this represents what the decedent would have wanted or because it gives everyone in the immediate family a share of the estate.

Shares of surviving children

If there is no surviving spouse, the statutes generally give the estate to the decedent's surviving children in equal shares. Only those who survive a decedent can inherit property. If a child predeceases the parent, however, that child's share will generally pass to her children. For example, if *O* has three children, *A*, *B*, and *C*, when *O* dies, *A*, *B*, and *C* will each receive one-third of the estate. If, however, one of the children predeceases *O*, then that child's share will generally go to her children as "representatives" of their deceased parent. Assume *A* has three children, *B* has two children, and *C* has one child. If *A* predeceases *O*, then *A*'s three children will take *A*'s one-third share, while *B* and *C* will each receive one-third.[220]

Per stirpes* or *per capita

What happens if all three children predecease the decedent? There are a variety of possibilities. First, the estate could continue to be divided among the three children equally, with their shares passing "by representation" to their grandchildren. If this approach were adopted, *A*'s children would collectively receive one-third, *B*'s children would collectively receive one-third, and *C*'s children would collectively receive one-third; the result is that *A*'s three individual children would each receive one-ninth, *B*'s children would each receive one-sixth, and *C*'s child would receive one-third. This kind of inheritance system is called *per stirpes*, or by the line of descent or by representation.[221] An alternative possible system would be to count *A*'s three children equally with those of *B* and *C* and divide the estate *per capita* (or by head). In a *per capita* division, if we have no surviving children but six surviving grandchildren, each grandchild would receive one-sixth of the estate.[222]

[219] The only exception is the situation of stepchildren, where there may be a danger that the surviving spouse will favor her own children over those of the decedent. In such cases, the *UPC* mandates sharing the estate between the surviving spouse and the children, if the estate is large enough to ensure that the surviving spouse will be supported. *Unif. Probate Code* §2-102(3) & (4).

[220] Robert H. Sitkoff & Jesse Dukeminier, *Wills, Trusts, and Estates* 82 (11th ed. 2022).

[221] *See, e.g.*, Fla. Stat. §732.104; Ga. Code §53-2-1; W. Va. Code §42-1-3a.

[222] Many permutations on these systems are possible. One issue is how to divide the estate at the primary level. The states generally deny any share to a child of the decedent who died without leaving any children, dividing up the primary shares among the surviving children or the descendants of the children who predeceased the decedent. In addition, many states go to the first generation of descendants that contains a surviving member to determine the primary shares. In the above example, if *O*'s three children all predeceased him, the estate would be divided into six primary shares if there were six surviving grandchildren or if one or more of the grandchildren had died leaving surviving descendants.

Combined approaches

The traditional *per stirpes* system may have the effect of giving individuals in the same generation different portions of the estate depending on how many siblings they have. The *per capita* system gives each individual the same percentage of the estate as others in their generation. Many states combine these approaches.

If no children survive but there are surviving grandchildren, there are three different approaches. Assume *O* has three children, *A*, *B*, and *C*, all of whom predecease *O*; *A* has three children, *B* has two children, and *C* has one child, all of whom survive at *O*'s death. About one-third of the states follow the *English per stirpes* system that gives the grandchildren the share their parent would have gotten, so one-third goes to the children of *A*, one-third to the children of *B*, and one-third to the children of *C*.[223] Nearly half the states follow a *modern per stirpes* system. If any child survives the decedent, the *English per stirpes* system is followed. If no child survives, the grandchildren share equally *per capita*. Under the modern per stirpes system, "the decedent's estate is divided into shares at the generational level nearest to the decedent in which one or more descendants of the decedent are alive."[224] About a dozen states adopt a third approach embodied in the 1990 and 2008 versions of the *UPC*. The *per capita at each generation* approach rejects the *English per stirpes* entirely. It distributes property at the level where one or more descendants survive and then distributes the rest to the next generation *per capita*.[225] Thus, if *A* survives but *B* and *C* do not, *A* gets one-third and the remaining two-thirds is divided equally among the children of *B* and *C*.

Order of inheritance

Most state statutes grant the estate to descendants and, then, if there are none, give the estate to the parents, then to the descendants of the parents (other than the decedent). If none of those individuals is alive, then the property passes to the grandparents or their other surviving descendants. In every state, the ladder stops (usually at that point) and more distant relatives are not entitled to inherit, with the property *escheating* to the state.

Rigid ownership shares v. equity

In the divorce context, the default rule is that property acquired during marriage will be "equitably distributed" between the parties, and that antenuptial agreements will be enforced only if they are not fundamentally unfair. Property rights on divorce therefore give the judge substantial discretion to divide property rights in a "fair" manner. In contrast, intestacy statutes are written in a rigid manner, requiring property to be divided mechanically among the parties, with considerations of fairness, equity, and need removed entirely from the picture. Similarly, wills are enforced unless they disinherit the surviving spouse who has the right to take an elective share. Again, the courts are deprived of discretion to arrange property rights in an equitable manner. On one hand, it might be argued that inheritance law should be made as flexible as divorce law to ensure that property devolves to those who need or deserve it or who have maintained a relationship with the decedent, rather than to those

[223] Robert H. Sitkoff & Jesse Dukeminier, *Wills, Trusts, and Estates* 82-83 (11th ed. 2022).
[224] *Id.* at 83.
[225] *Unif. Probate Code* §§2-102, 2-106; Robert H. Sitkoff & Jesse Dukeminier, *Wills, Trusts, and Estates* 84-85 (11th ed. 2022).

who do not need or deserve it or who have had no contact with the decedent for many years. On the other hand, allowing such considerations into the picture would make inheritance law substantially more complicated, unpredictable, and expensive. At the same time, it is worth considering why the law treats divorce and inheritance so differently, having for the most part rejected the idea that division of property on divorce need be or should be mechanical.

PART IV

REGULATION OF THE MARKET FOR REAL ESTATE

CHAPTER 10

Leaseholds

§10.1 Introduction
§10.2 Distinguishing Leaseholds from Other Interests
§10.3 Types of Tenancies (Leasehold Estates)
- §10.3.1 Term of Years
- §10.3.2 Periodic Tenancy
- §10.3.3 Tenancy at Will
- §10.3.4 Tenancy at Sufferance

§10.4 Tenant's Obligations and Landlord's Remedies
- §10.4.1 Tenant's Duty to Pay Rent
- §10.4.2 Tenant's Duty to Operate
- §10.4.3 Illegality
- §10.4.4 Landlord's Remedies
  - §10.4.4.1 Forfeiture (Landlord's Recovery of Possession)
  - §10.4.4.2 Holding the Tenant to a New Tenancy
  - §10.4.4.3 Self-Help v. Summary Process
  - §10.4.4.4 Surrender, Reletting, Damages, and the Duty to Mitigate Damages

§10.5 Landlord's Obligations and Tenant's Remedies
- §10.5.1 Landlord's Duty to Deliver Possession
- §10.5.2 Security Deposits
- §10.5.3 Actual Eviction
- §10.5.4 Anti-eviction Laws
- §10.5.5 Rent Regulation

§10.6 Tenant's Right to Habitable Premises
- §10.6.1 Constructive Eviction
- §10.6.2 Housing Codes
- §10.6.3 Implied Warranty of Habitability
- §10.6.4 Retaliatory Eviction
- §10.6.5 Landlord's Tort Liability
- §10.6.6 Consumer Protection Laws
- §10.6.7 Lead Paint Laws

§10.7 Transfers by Landlord or Tenant
- §10.7.1 Landlord's Right to Transfer the Reversion
- §10.7.2 Tenant's Rights to Assign or Sublet

§10.1 Introduction

Historical origins

Many law students rent apartments and may therefore have personal experience with the set of issues encompassed by landlord/tenant relationships or the law of leaseholds. Yet this quintessentially modern practice has its origins in feudal tenures; we have even kept the old terminology of "lord" and "tenant." Under feudalism, individuals would obtain access to land by entering a hierarchical, personal relationship with a lord who had authority over that land. The word "tenant" used to refer to anyone who stood in a tenurial relationship with a "lord" with respect to land. The lord obtained control of the property from a higher lord or the king himself and, in turn, gave control of it to the tenant in return for services.[1] Over time, those services were reduced to money payments or "rents"; their current expression is the payment of rent by tenants to landlords for the right to occupy the landlord's property.

Transfer of possession by one with a larger estate

A leasehold is the *transfer of possession* of real property for either a determinate or an indefinite period.[2] When the leasehold ends, those possessory rights will revert to the original owner. "A tenant is one who holds a possessory estate in land for a determinate period or at-will by permission of another, the landlord, who holds an estate of larger duration in the same land."[3] The tenant owns a present possessory estate that is either for a determinate period (a *term of years*), or indeterminate but characterized by periodic rent payments (a *periodic tenancy*), or terminable at the will of either party (*tenancy-at-will*). While a leasehold is a temporary transfer of possession, it is also a "bilateral contract" comprising express and implied rights and obligations on both sides.[4] Almost all leaseholds, for example, require the tenant to pay rent to the landlord as a condition of the grant of possessory rights. Rent is not essential to the landlord/tenant relationship; a leasehold can exist without rental obligations as long as there is a temporary transfer of possessory rights in the land.[5] Nevertheless, owners ordinarily will not grant possession of their property unless they receive rent in return. Almost all leases, therefore, include express covenants to pay rent. Rent is such an expected part of the arrangement that one authority opines that "it is likely that a court would find an implied promise for rent unless the parties had overcome the implication."[6] The *Uniform Residential Landlord and Tenant Act* (adopted in about half the states) provides for reasonable rental payments in the absence of a rental agreement.[7]

Term of years

Periodic tenancy

Tenancy-at-will

[1] *See* §7.1.

[2] Robert S. Schoshinski, *American Law of Landlord and Tenant* §1:1, at 1 (1980).

[3] Dale A. Whitman et al., *The Law of Property* §6.1, at 193 (4th ed. 2019).

[4] Robert S. Schoshinski, *American Law of Landlord and Tenant* §1:1, at 2 (1980).

[5] *May v. May*, 300 S.E.2d 215 (Ga. Ct. App. 1983).

[6] Dale A. Whitman et al., *The Law of Property* §6.1, at 194 (4th ed. 2019).

[7] *Uniform Residential Landlord and Tenant Act* §1.401(b) ("fair rental value"); *see also Model Residential Landlord-Tenant Code* §2-301(1). In 2015, the Uniform Law Commission promulgated a *Revised Uniform Residential Landlord and Tenant Act* (RURLTA) with revisions to the coverage of the Act, landlord and tenant duties and remedies, and landlord access to rental units, among others, as well as new sections on security deposits, disposing of

Leaseholds were originally conceptualized as transfers of estates in land. They were governed by property law rather than contract law. This treatment traditionally had two major consequences. First, the covenants contained in the leasehold were independent rather than dependent.[8] When covenants are dependent, a breach of promise by one party to a contract relieves the other of the obligation to perform her obligations under the contract. When covenants are independent, breach by one party of her obligations does not relieve the other party of her contractual obligations. For example, breach of the tenant's covenant to pay rent would entitle the landlord to recover possession, if the landlord's promise to deliver possession of the premises to the tenant were *dependent* on the tenant's continued payment of rent. Conversely, if the promise to pay rent was *independent* of the landlord's promise to give the tenant possession, the landlord's only remedy would be to bring a lawsuit to enforce the rent obligations by asking for damages and an injunction ordering the tenant to pay the rent when due. Since the nineteenth century, summary process statutes have allowed landlords to evict tenants for nonpayment of rent. The doctrine of independence of covenants, including covenants other than the duty to pay rent, has now been substantially rejected in the United States as to residential leases; breach of material covenants in the lease by either party entitles the other to end the relationship.[9] For example, breach of a material obligation of the landlord may entitle the tenant to leave before the end of the lease term and stop paying rent. Breach of a material term in the contract by the tenant may entitle the landlord to recover unpaid past rent and to evict the tenant and recover possession of the premises. Although some courts continue to hold that covenants in commercial leases are independent,[10] others have held the opposite, allowing tenants to stop paying rent if the landlord breaches any material covenants in the lease.[11]

Property or contract

Independence or dependence of covenants

The second implication of treating leasehold estates through property law rather than contract was that, while implied warranties were increasingly found in the context of the sale of goods, they were not so implied in the case of real property.[12] Real property was governed by the doctrine of

Implied warranties

---

tenant property, and terminating leases in the context of domestic violence or sexual assault. *See generally* Sheldon F. Kurtz & Alice M. Noble-Allgire, *The Revised Uniform Residential Landlord and Tenant Act: A Perspective from the Reporters*, 52 Real Prop. Tr. & Est. L.J. 417 (2018). As of 2025, RURLTA has not yet been adopted by any state. However, versions of its provisions have been introduced in Virginia, Kentucky, Nebraska, and Georgia.

[8] Dale A. Whitman et al., *The Law of Property* §6.10, at 200 (4th ed. 2019).

[9] The *Uniform Residential Landlord and Tenant Act*, adopted in roughly half the states, provides that breach of a material term by either party entitles the other to terminate the arrangement. *Uniform Residential Landlord and Tenant Act* §§4.101, 4.102, 4.107, 4.201 & 4.202.

[10] *C & J Delivery, Inc. v. Vinyard & Lee & Partners, Inc.*, 647 S.W.2d 564, 568 (Mo. Ct. App. 1983); *Matte v. Shippee Auto, Inc.*, 876 A.2d 167 (N.H. 2005).

[11] *Wesson v. Leone Enterprises, Inc.*, 774 N.E.2d 611, 621 (Mass. 2002); *Davidow v. Inwood North Professional Group—Phase I*, 747 S.W.2d 373, 377 (Tex. 1988); *Richard Barton Enterprises, Inc. v. Tsern*, 928 P.2d 368, 376 (Utah 1996).

[12] Dale A. Whitman et al., *The Law of Property* §6.10, at 201-202 (4th ed. 2019).

Residential leases

caveat emptor ("let the buyer beware") and landlords had no obligations to repair or maintain the premises.[13] This traditional doctrine has also been substantially altered in the United States, at least in the case of residential property. When landlords rent residential housing, it is now assumed that they impliedly warrant that the premises will be habitable. This assumption is so strong that the obligation to provide habitable premises is generally held to be nondisclaimable.

Commercial leases

A few courts have extended this implied warranty to commercial tenancies as well, holding that commercial landlords impliedly warrant that the property is suitable for the intended purpose. Many courts, however, retain the traditional approach in the context of commercial tenancies, holding that no warranties of quality or fitness exist when property is leased for a commercial purpose. This residential/commercial distinction is a general one in landlord/tenant law. Legal rules designed to protect residential tenants may not apply to commercial tenants. Both the common law and statutes tend to extend greater protection to residential than commercial tenants, perhaps on the view that commercial tenants have greater information than residential tenants and sufficient bargaining power to protect themselves from unfair or unconscionable contract terms.

Historical changes

Until the 1960s, tenancies were equated with other estates in land, such as the fee simple, the life estate, and defeasible fees. Express covenants contained in leases were enforceable as real covenants or equitable servitudes, but covenants were generally not implied into the contractual relationship. The sole exception to this principle was that the courts generally assumed that the landlord had a duty not to disturb the tenant's quiet enjoyment of the property. This obligation seemed inherent in the transfer of possessory rights from landlord to tenant. This situation began to change with housing codes that required all housing to comply with certain minimum standards to protect the health and safety of residents. The courts began a revolution in landlord/tenant law after several leading cases held that landlords had a contractual obligation to provide habitable housing. This implied obligation was based partly on reconceptualizing leaseholds as contractual relations and not just conveyances of real property. Because the law had come to imply duties of good faith and fair dealing in all contracts, leaseholds were interpreted as containing such obligations as well.[14] In addition, courts interpreted state housing codes and consumer protection laws as placing affirmative obligations on landlords to maintain the premises and interpreted leasehold agreements as containing implied promises to comply with such statutory and regulatory enactments. Most states have also now passed at least some parts of the *Uniform Residential Landlord and Tenant Act*,

[13] Robert S. Schoshinski, *American Law of Landlord and Tenant* §1:1, at 2-3 (1980).

[14] *See Uno Restaurants, Inc. v. Boston Kenmore Realty Corp.*, 805 N.E.2d 957 (Mass. 2004) (covenant of good faith and fair dealing implied in all leasehold agreements) Dick Broad. Co. v. Oak Ridge FM, Inc., 395 S.W.3d 653, 665-66 (Tenn. 2013).

which codifies these affirmative landlord obligations,[15] while many other states have similar legislation.[16]

Tenant obligations and landlord remedies

Tenants generally have obligations (1) to pay *rent* when due; (2) to avoid damaging the premises (duty not to commit *waste*); and (3) to comply with other *covenants* in the lease agreement. The tenant has no duty to occupy the premises unless the contract provides otherwise. If the tenant breaches material terms in the lease, such as the duty to pay rent, the landlord may elect to terminate the contractual relationship by suing for back rent owed, damages for anticipatory breach,[17] and to recover possession of the premises (eviction).[18] Landlords are generally prohibited from using self-help to remove a tenant who has breached the contract; they are legally required to use court eviction proceedings to regain possession. Statutes regulating evictions may empower judges to give tenants extra time to stay to find a new place to live while paying rent to the landlord during the time of this continued occupation. Alternatively, if the tenant breaches the rental obligation and moves out, the landlord may seek to affirm and continue the tenancy relationship by finding a new tenant and renting the premises "on the tenant's account," thereby keeping the tenant liable if the new tenant does not pay rent when due.[19] Although the landlord used to be entitled to wait until the end of the lease and collect the rest of the rent when a tenant moved out early, most states today hold that the landlord has a duty to mitigate damages. This means that the landlord is expected to try to find a replacement tenant. If the landlord does find a replacement, the breaching tenant owes the landlord rent for the time the premises were vacant while the landlord was looking for a new tenant and any difference between the old rent and a lower new rent for the rest of the term. If the landlord does not look for a replacement, the tenant is only obligated to pay damages for what the landlord would have lost if the landlord had acted reasonably to mitigate damages by finding a replacement.

Landlord obligations and tenant remedies

The landlord is obligated (1) to deliver possession of the premises to the tenant;[20] (2) not to interfere with the tenant's quiet enjoyment of

[15] Alaska Stat. §§34.03.010 to 34.03.380; Ariz. Rev. Stat. §§33-1301 to 33-1381; Del. Code tit. 25, §§5101 *et seq.*; Fla. Stat. §§83.40 to 83.681; Haw. Rev. Stat. §§521-1 to 521-78; Iowa Code §§562A.1 to 562A.37; Kan. Stat. §§58-2540 to 58-2573; Ky. Rev. Stat. §§383.500 to 383.715; Mont. Code §§70-24-101 to 70-24-442; Neb. Rev. Stat. §§76-1401 to 76-1449; Nev. Rev. Stat. §§118A.010 to 118A.530; N.M. Stat. §§47-8-1 to 47-8-52; Ohio Rev. Code §§5321.01 to 5321.19; Okla. Stat. tit. 41, §§101 to 135; Or. Rev. Stat. §§90.100 to 90.940; R.I. Gen. Laws §§34-18-1 to 34-18-57; S.C. Code §§27-40-10 to 27-40-940; Tenn. Code §§66-28-101 to 66-28-516; Va. Code §§55.1–1200 to 55.1–1262; Wash. Rev. Code §§59.18.010 to 59.18.900.

[16] *See, e.g.*, N.J. Stat. §§2A:18-51 to 18-61.12.

[17] Such damages may be available if the tenant has announced an intention not to pay rent in the future. In that case, the landlord may well have a duty to mitigate damages by looking for another tenant, and the damages would be measured by the difference between the rental amount and the fair rental value of the property for the rest of the term of the tenancy, assuming a replacement tenant is found. *See* §10.4.4.4.

[18] The tenant may be able to avoid eviction if she can pay the rent that is due and it appears that she will pay her rent on time in the future.

[19] These remedies are further discussed in §§10.4 and 10.5.

[20] Some states retain the older rule requiring the landlord to give the tenant a right to possession, but not actual possession. In those states, if a holdover tenant remains and prevents

the premises by actually or constructively evicting the tenant; and (3) to maintain and repair the premises so that they comply with the housing code and are habitable. If the landlord violates these obligations, the tenant also has a range of remedies. If the breach is material, the tenant may be justified in terminating the contractual relationship, ceasing rent payments, and moving out. The tenant may also choose to stay and sue the landlord for injunctive relief ordering the landlord to comply with her obligations and/or to obtain damages resulting from the breach. State law may also give the tenant the right to stay in the premises while withholding rent until the violation is corrected. In a suit by the landlord for unpaid rent, the court may abate or reduce the rent owed for the period during which the contractual breach continued, and state law may even give the tenant the right to repair the premises and deduct the costs of the repair from the rent.

Issues

A variety of issues arise in disputes between landlords and tenants. Some issues involve interpretation of the lease agreement. Should the intent of the landlord prevail, or should the courts protect the expectations of tenants when they diverge from the formal terms of the contract or the landlord's probable intent? Should the courts create implied obligations in leasehold agreements or leave the parties to the formal terms of their contract? Other issues concern when it is appropriate to make specific terms in the agreement compulsory. Many rules governing leaseholds are regulatory or mandatory and render contrary terms unenforceable. Another set of issues concerns remedies for breach of contract. When are landlords and tenants entitled to use self-help to remedy breaches by the other side, and when must they go to court for assistance? When are tenants entitled to stop paying rent or get out of the lease, and when are landlords entitled to evict tenants?

Interpreting the leasehold arrangement

Landlord/tenant law has focused on a variety of specific topics. First, it is sometimes unclear whether the parties intended to create a leasehold or some other kind of property arrangement such as a license, an easement, or an employment contract. Rules of interpretation determine when a relationship will be deemed a landlord/tenant relationship rather than some other kind of property relationship. Interpretation issues also arise regarding the type of leasehold the parties intended to create. As with the estates system in general,[21] courts cram property rights into a small set of established packages. It therefore may be necessary to determine whether the parties intended the tenancy to be (1) for a definite period (*term of years*); (2) renewable (*periodic tenancy*); or (3) *at-will*. If it is not clear which form was created, the courts must interpret the arrangement to choose the estate that the parties probably intended to create.

Conflicts over possession

Second, conflicts arise between landlords and tenants over possessory rights. Does the landlord have an obligation to deliver actual

---

the new tenant from moving in, the new tenant's remedies are against the holdover tenant, not the landlord.

[21] *See* §7.7.2 (rule against creation of new estates).

possession of the premises to the tenant or merely the right to possession? What rights does the tenant have if a prior tenant holds over and prevents the new tenant from occupying the property? After the tenant moves in, what rights does the tenant have when the landlord bars the tenant from entering some or all the property (*actual eviction*)? Do those same rights attach if the landlord engages in activity that makes the premises unlivable (so-called *constructive eviction*)? When the leasehold terminates, does the tenant have a right to renew it? Is the landlord entitled to evict the tenant at the end of the leasehold and rent to someone else, or must the landlord have good cause to refuse to renew the lease?

Conflicts over rent

Third, conflicts often arise over the payment of rent. When the tenant breaches the obligation to pay rent, what remedies does the landlord have? Is the landlord limited to suing for back rent, or may the landlord also sue to recover possession? If the landlord is entitled to possession when the tenant reneges on the rent covenant, can the tenant defeat the landlord's claim if the landlord has breached the landlord's obligations under the lease, such as the duty to provide habitable premises? Conflicts also arise over rent regulation. Some local governments regulate rents and such regulations have been challenged as unconstitutional takings of property; although such challenges have generally failed, the wisdom of rent control as a mechanism for protecting low- and moderate-income tenants from displacement has been a topic of intense interest in many communities.

Condition of the premises

Fourth, disputes may arise over the condition of the premises. Common law and statutes now impose an obligation on all residential landlords to provide habitable housing. Some states extend warranties of fitness to commercial tenancies as well, although most still do not. What remedies do tenants have when the landlord breaches the duty to maintain the premises? If anyone is injured because of a defective condition in the premises, what standards determine when the landlord is liable in tort? What obligations do tenants have to landlords to maintain the premises in good condition?

Transfers by landlord and tenant

Fifth, disputes arise over transfers by both landlord and tenant. What are the tenant's rights when the landlord sells the property, effectively transferring the reversion to someone else? Does the tenant have the power to transfer the leasehold, in whole or in part, to someone else? Are terms in the contract that limit the tenant's ability to assign or sublet the apartment enforceable?

Illegality

Sixth, if a leasehold is for an illegal purpose, it is void. However, if the tenant uses the premises for an illegal purpose, the tenancy is generally held valid and the tenant must comply with her rental obligations. At the same time, the issue arises whether use of the premises for an illegal purpose violates an express or implied covenant not to do so, which would entitle the landlord to evict the tenant.

Legal ethics

A final set of issues concerns legal ethics. Is it a violation of the lawyer's ethical or moral obligations to include unenforceable terms in a lease agreement? What should an attorney do if a landlord asks her to draft such an agreement?

§10.2 Distinguishing Leaseholds from Other Interests

Grant of possession

A leasehold is a transfer of the right of possession of specific property either for a definite or an indefinite period.[22] Possession is the right to exert general control over the use of a specific piece of property and the right to exclude others from that area.[23] "A tenant's right to exclusive possession is the key characteristic which distinguishes a lease from other property interests such as a license or an easement."[24] Courts distinguish possessory rights from other permissive uses of property that (1) allow specific uses rather than general control; (2) do not include the right to exclude the owner; or (3) do not grant control over defined areas of land.[25] Permissive uses of land that do not comprise possessory rights include licenses, easements, and contractual grants of licenses. A licensee "receives only a revocable permission to engage in an act or series of acts on the property, the owner-licensor retaining control of and access to the property."[26] An easement confers a "specific right of use" rather than "complete possession."[27] Determining whether a leasehold has been established is important. It may determine whether the interest is revocable, whether the grantee has the power to exclude the owner, whether use rights are specific or general, whether the grantor has duties of repair and maintenance, and what remedies are available to the parties for breach of any express or implied contractual promises to each other, especially whether the grantor can use self-help to exclude the grantee or must use court eviction proceedings.

Difficulty of defining "possession"

Many cases concern the question of whether the parties have created a landlord/tenant relationship or some other kind of property arrangement. In most cases, the issue is whether the arrangement is a license or a leasehold. The courts generally answer this question by asking whether the owner has granted "possession" of specific property (or more accurately, the "right to possess" that property). Although this guideline provides a useful starting point, this traditional test is flawed. First, it is often difficult to determine what "possession" means and whether it has been conferred on the grantee. For example, to determine whether a "rental" of space on a billboard creates a landlord/tenant relationship, it is often not helpful to ask whether the owner has granted "possession" of the billboard. What evidence is sufficient to prove this? One might look to the language of the contract (if there is one), but such agreements are often ambiguous on this point. They might state that the owner grants a "license" but then provide for periodic "rent" payments. The courts could adopt presumptions to interpret such ambiguities. Alternatively, they could try to discern how much power over the space in question has been granted to the licensee

Rental of billboard example

[22] *Port of Coos Bay v. Department of Revenue*, 691 P.2d 100, 104 (Or. 1984) ("if the agreement grants sufficient control over the premises to fulfill the requirement of possession, a leasehold is created"); Robert S. Schoshinski, *American Law of Landlord and Tenant* §1:3, at 9 (1980).
[23] Robert S. Schoshinski, *American Law of Landlord and Tenant* §1:3, at 10 (1980).
[24] *Id.*
[25] *Publicker Chemical Corp. v. Belcher Oil Co.*, 792 F.2d 482, 487-488 (5th Cir. 1986) (contract for oil storage not a lease because it did not specify particular tanks to be used for storage).
[26] Robert S. Schoshinski, *American Law of Landlord and Tenant* §1:3, at 10 (1980).
[27] *Id.*

or tenant. But when an owner gives someone the right to put a sign on a billboard for three months, has the owner granted "possession" over the surface of the billboard? On the one hand, the grantee seems to have the right to exclude others from putting signs on the billboard and there is not much one can do with a billboard other than put a sign on it — so perhaps full control over the surface has been granted. On the other hand, it is not clear one can "possess" the surface of a wall; moreover, the permitted use seems so restricted (the right to place a sign) that it is hard to square with the notion of general control associated with possessory rights.

Formalistic v. functional approaches

The second difficulty with the "possession" test is that it bases results on a factual (or mixed factual/legal) distinction without consideration of whether the policies underlying the specific rule of leasehold law at issue should apply in the case at hand. A legal realist or functionalist approach would focus on the reason we are being asked to determine whether an arrangement is or is not a leasehold. For example, we might be concerned with the question of whether the owner of a billboard has the power to revoke permission to use the billboard (a result that might follow from classifying the interest as a license) or whether the grantee has the right to keep her sign on the billboard until the end of the term covered by the rental payment (as might follow from classifying the arrangement as a term of years). This issue involves regulation of commercial arrangements and might be resolved by reference to customs of the trade or common understandings of what it means to "rent" billboard space. In contrast, if we are concerned with the question of whether a college must use eviction proceedings rather than self-help to eject a student from a dormitory, we would be concerned with very different policy considerations, such as the school's ability to provide a good learning environment, the student's reliance on the availability of dormitory housing, the general practice of how universities control dormitory space, the student's potential due process rights to contest the eviction before removal to show that it is unlawful or unjustified, as well as her need to have time to find another place to live before being ejected. Although the policies underlying regulation of commercial rental of billboards overlap with those relating to residential housing, they also comprise different social worlds, types of relationships, and normative considerations. Rather than simply asking whether an arrangement involves a grant of possessory rights, the courts should ask whether the policies underlying the particular rule of law at issue, suggest that it is appropriate to extend the protections of landlord/tenant law to the parties in this kind of case.[28]

Language not determinative

The express language in an agreement is often helpful in determining whether an arrangement is intended to create a leasehold. However, such language is often not determinative.[29] Courts have interpreted "lease"

[28] This is not to say that classification of a relationship will be determinative. A court may well find the parties not to have created a landlord/tenant relationship but nonetheless extend some of the protections granted to tenants to the grantee of a license or an easement.

[29] *But see Jewelers Mutual Insurance Co. v. Firstar Bank Illinois*, 792 N.E.2d 1, 5-7 (Ill. App. Ct. 2003) (language of agreement conclusive as to whether agreement created leasehold or bailment).

arrangements as licenses[30] and "license" arrangements as leases.[31] Courts ignore the express language in a contractual arrangement when it is contradictory or when the substance of the relationship seems to diverge from the label given to the relationship by the parties in their contract. Ambiguities in language arise when conflicting terms are used. For example, a shopping center owner may grant a commercial tenant a "license" to use a particular space on a sign for a "term of three months" in exchange for "rent" payments, and reserve a right to "evict" the licensee if the rent is not paid on time. The agreement may even provide that it is "not intended to create a relationship of landlord and tenant." Such ambiguous arrangements (which use both license language and leasehold language) are common in the context of agreements to rent billboard space, concessions in shopping centers and department stores, student dormitory contracts, employment contracts that include a right to live on the premises (such as apartment supervisors and migrant farm workers), sharecroppers, rentals of hotel space for functions, and the provision of rooms in hotels to guests or lodgers.[32]

Form v. substance

In addition, ambiguities may arise because the language in the contract seems to diverge from its substance. For example, a landlord may rent an apartment for a year with a set monthly rent, but state in the contract that it is a "license," that parties are "licensor" and "licensee," and that, although the "licensee" is granted permission to stay for a year, that permission is revocable at any time without notice by the landlord, that no "landlord/tenant relationship is established," and that self-help is available to oust the licensee with no need to use court eviction proceedings. This arrangement uses all the language of license and it is clear the owner wished to create a license rather than a leasehold. At the same time, the *substance* of the arrangement looks like a term of years with the landlord attempting to evade all the statutory and common law obligations that now go along with a rental of property for a year. In other words, the contract appears to be a lease with the landlord attempting to disclaim the ordinary obligations of a landlord. But, if the jurisdiction makes these tenant protections nondisclaimable, to protect the interests of the tenant, the landlord should not be able to avoid those obligations by clever drafting.

▶ HARD CASE

▷ SIGNS AND BILLBOARDS

In *Keller v. Southwood North Medical Pavilion, Inc.*,[33] a chiropractor leased space in a shopping center pursuant to a written agreement that contained a clause giving him the right to place a sign on a large

[30] *Halley v. Harden Oil Co.*, 357 S.E.2d 138, 139 (Ga. Ct. App. 1987) (although contract stated that it was a "lease," owner retained possession, use, and responsibility for maintenance of property and thus was merely a license); *Macke Laundry Serv. Co. v. Overgaard*, 433 N.W.2d 813, 815 (Mich. Ct. App. 1989); *Loren v. Marry*, 600 N.Y.S.2d 369 (App. Div. 1993).

[31] *American Jewish Theatre, Inc. v. Roundabout Theatre Co., Inc.*, 610 N.Y.S.2d 256 (App. Div. 1994); *M & I First National Bank v. Episcopal Homes Mgmt., Inc.*, 536 N.W.2d 175, 186 (Wis. Ct. App. 1995).

[32] Dale A. Whitman et al., *The Law of Property* §§6.2 to 6.9 (4th ed. 2019).

[33] 959 P.2d 102 (Utah 1998).

monument located near the street. When the landlord sold the property, the new owner objected to the appearance of the tenant's sign and removed it. The tenant claimed that the landlord violated the state statute that required landlords to use court eviction proceedings rather than self-help to recover possession of property from tenants and that the tenant was entitled to the statutorily prescribed treble damages. The court held that the lease agreement gave the tenant a license to place a sign but did not constitute a "lease" of the space on the monument. Because the agreement did not identify any particular space on the sign that tenant had a right to occupy, it was a license and not a grant of "possessory" rights.[34]

Landlord's argument that it is a revocable license

The landlord might give functionalist arguments to defend this result. He might argue, for example, that shopping center owners have a strong interest in regulating the appearance of the signs to ensure that the shopping center attracts business for all his tenants. Moreover, only when an owner has granted a tenant the right to occupy a defined space, does the tenant have a justified expectation of a right to control the space in question, as well as a right to continue in possession. When the owner does not define a particular space within the grantee's control, then the grantor may be presumed to have intended to retain the power to revoke the permission.

Tenant's argument that it is a leasehold

The tenant could respond that courts often find a leasehold to exist when billboards are rented.[35] The fact that there was no agreement about which spot on the monument his sign would occupy should not be determinative of his rights. He would not have rented commercial space in the center, unless he could place a sign letting the public know that his business was located there; this obviously is essential to attract customers. The right to have his sign on the monument was thus, intimately connected with his rental of office space. Moreover, he has strong interests in determining the appearance of the sign because his choices about the sign will affect public views of his establishment and the clientele he wishes to attract. Because his interest was so fundamental to his business, he was forced to move out and relocate to another office when the sign was removed. The policies underlying the law prohibiting self-help apply here. A lawsuit would protect the tenant's reasonable expectations of continued occupancy while also protecting the landlord's legitimate economic interests. ◀

[34] *Accord, Devlin v. The Phoenix, Inc.*, 471 So. 2d 93, 95 (Fla. Dist. Ct. App. 1985). Note that this does not answer the question of whether the tenant was protected by remedies other than those provided in the "forcible entry" statute. Although the landlord was not required to use eviction proceedings to take down the tenant's sign, if the tenant has not already vacated the premises, the tenant might have asked for injunctive relief to enforce the agreement by which the landlord promised to give the tenant the right to place a sign on the monument.

[35] *Pieper v. American Sign/Outdoor Advertising, Inc.*, 564 So. 2d 49, 50 (Ala. 1990) (finding no significant distinction between the "right to use" and the "right of possession" in the lease of a billboard).

▶ HARD CASE ▷ CONCESSIONS

Landlord argument that it is a license

Disagreements sometimes arise between department store owners and concessions operating there over the question of whether the concession owner has merely a "license" to operate or a "lease." Department store owners sometimes enter into contracts with particular service providers, allowing them to operate in the store. For example, in *Layton v. A.I. Namm & Sons*,[36] a department store allowed an optometrist to operate an optical department in the store, but the contract did not identify a particular space he was entitled to occupy.[37] After he died, his widow kept up the business. When the store decided to end the arrangement, the issue arose whether the permission was a license revocable at-will (except perhaps with a right to damages for breach of contract) or whether it was a lease that entitled her to continued occupancy according to the terms of the agreement, as well as the protection of statutes that require landlords to use formal court eviction proceedings to recover possession from tenants.[38] The written agreement was ambiguous, stating that "the Licensor hereby leases unto the Licensee" a particular, defined space, while reserving the right to remove the optical department to another location in the store. The court held that the arrangement was a license, rather than a lease, partly based on the use of the terms "licensor" and "licensee," partly because the possession was not exclusive (the licensee could not exclude the owner from entering and inspecting the space at-will), and because the owner could relocate the department at-will.[39]

Tenant argument that it is a lease

The licensee/tenant could respond that retention of the power to move the licensee to another space in the store should not, by itself, make the arrangement a license rather than a lease. When a store grants the right to use a specific space, such as a kiosk, many courts will find a landlord/tenant relationship to have been established.[40] Although the owner could argue that it had intended to retain the power to end the arrangement, both the terms of the contract and the long-standing relationship suggest that the owner had induced the licensee to understand the relationship as a relatively permanent one. The reliance interests of the tenant in continued access to space in the store might suggest that the statutory policies that grant tenants the right to due process before they are evicted should apply here as well. ◀

[36] 89 N.Y.S.2d 72 (App. Div. 1949). *Accord, H.E.Y. Trust v. Popcorn Express Co., Inc.*, 35 S.W.3d 55 (Tex. Ct. App. 2000).

[37] 89 N.Y.S.2d at 73 (noting that the agreement identified a particular location but gave the owner the power unilaterally to change that location).

[38] *Id.* at 74-75.

[39] *Id.* at 75.

[40] *Friend v. Gem International, Inc.*, 476 S.W.2d 134, 139 (Mo. Ct. App. 1971) (operator of furniture department within department store held to be tenant despite language in contract calling the relationship a license); *Schloss v. Sachs*, 631 N.E.2d 212, 216 (Ohio Mun. Ct. 1993) (agreement to operate kiosk in shopping mall created lease rather than license because operator was granted exclusive possession of a defined space).

▷ EMPLOYMENT CONTRACTS **HARD CASE** ◀

Courts often must determine whether an employee is a tenant when the employer furnishes living space for the employee on the employer's premises. This question has arisen often in the context of building superintendents[41] and migrant farm workers.[42] Many courts hold that employees are licensees if their residence on the employer's property is in aid of their work responsibilities, unless the contract between the parties evinces an intent to create a leasehold arrangement that would last, even if the employee were fired or quit.[43] However, other courts have held that such arrangements create leaseholds[44] with tenants' rights to receive visitors[45] and to statutory thirty days' notice to quit before eviction.[46] Courts are likely to hold employees to be tenants if their residence on the premises preceded the employment,[47] or if the term extends beyond the period of employment.[48] In addition, if the employee pays rent, either in money or services, it is more likely that the courts will find the arrangement to constitute a lease rather than a license.[49] Conversely, if the employee pays no rent specifically set aside to pay for living accommodations, the courts are very likely to hold that the employee is merely a licensee.[50]

Superintendents

Most courts hold that building superintendents are licensees rather than tenants.[51] However, other courts disagree, holding that they are tenants.[52] The distinction matters because licensees can be excluded without notice and the owner may exercise self-help to change the locks rather than court eviction proceedings with their required notice and procedural protections for tenants.[53] This result might be justified on the ground that the employer needs an employee living on the premises and that once the employment terminates, the employer needs to remove the old employee to allow a new employee to move in. The counterargument is that employees,

[41] *Compare Chan v. Antepenko*, 250 Cal. Rptr. 851 (Ct. App. 1988) (building superintendent is not a tenant) *with Bigelow v. Bullard*, 901 P.2d 630 (Nev. 1995) (superintendent is a tenant).

[42] *Compare De Bruyn Produce Co. v. Romero*, 508 N.W.2d 150, 159 (Mich. Ct. App. 1993) (migrant farm workers are licensees, not tenants) *with State v. DeCoster*, 653 A.2d 891, 894 (Me. 1995) (migrant farm workers are "tenants").

[43] *Moreno v. Stahmann Farms, Inc.*, 693 F.2d 106 (10th Cir. 1982); *Chan v. Antepenko*, 250 Cal. Rptr. 851 (Ct. App. 1988); *De Bruyn Produce Co. v. Romero*, 508 N.W.2d 150 (Mich. Ct. App. 1993); Robert S. Schoshinski, *American Law of Landlord and Tenant* §1:6, at 17-18 (1980).

[44] *Turner v. White*, 579 P.2d 410 (Wash. Ct. App. 1978).

[45] *State v. DeCoster*, 653 A.2d 891, 893 (Me. 1995); *cf. Odumn v. United States*, 227 A.3d 1099 (D.C. 2020) (affirming the right to receive visitors).

[46] *Grant v. Detroit Ass'n of Women's Clubs*, 505 N.W.2d 254, 259 (Mich. 1993).

[47] *Bigelow v. Bullard*, 901 P.2d 630 (Nev. 1995).

[48] Robert S. Schoshinski, *American Law of Landlord and Tenant* §1:6, at 18 (1980).

[49] *Tatro v. Lehouiller*, 513 A.2d 610, 612 (Vt. 1986).

[50] *Mohr v. Gomez*, 662 N.Y.S.2d 979 (App. Term 1997).

[51] *De Villar v. New York*, 628 F. Supp. 80 (S.D.N.Y. 1986); *Chan v. Antepenko*, 250 Cal. Rptr. 851 (Ct. App. 1988); *Cruz v. Reatique*, 514 A.2d 549 (N.J. Super. Ct. Law Div. 1986).

[52] *Grant v. Detroit Ass'n of Women's Clubs*, 505 N.W.2d 254 (Mich. 1993).

[53] *Tantaro v. Common Ground Cmty. Hous. Dev. Fund, Inc.*, 147 A.D.3d 684 (N.Y. App. Div. 2017) (affirming that an owner may engage in peaceful self-help to remove a licensee).

like other tenants, should be entitled to the right to live in a habitable apartment and not to be evicted for complaining about pests or lack of heat. Moreover, employees, like other tenants, may need time to find a new place to live, if the owner has asked them to leave; this may especially be true if the employee has just lost her job.

Migrant farm workers

Most courts hold that migrant farm workers are licensees rather than tenants, either because their living accommodations are provided to assist them in their job responsibilities[54] or because they are not assigned specified premises and thus do not have "possession."[55] The *Uniform Residential Landlord and Tenant Act* also excludes from its coverage "occupancy by an employee of a landlord whose right to occupancy is conditional upon employment in and about the premises."[56] Several courts, however, have held that migrant farm workers are tenants, at least with respect to the tenant's right to receive visitors and possibly as to eviction protections as well.[57] Several courts have adopted a middle position, holding that farm workers are not tenants, but that they are both entitled to receive visitors[58] and entitled to notice and court proceedings before being ejected from their homes.[59] ◀

▶ HARD CASE ▷ DORMITORIES

Similar issues arise in the context of college dormitories. If a student signs a "license" agreement to get a dormitory room, pays a dorm fee that guarantees the room for an entire semester or school year, and the agreement provides that it is revocable within 48 hours by the college for any reason, is the student a mere "licensee" and the permission revocable at-will by the college, or is the student a "tenant" protected by the laws regulating eviction? Courts have gone both ways on this question, some holding that students are tenants[60] and others holding that they are not.[61] The Kansas Supreme Court ruled in 1998 that students were tenants even though the agreement did not use the words "lease," "rent," "landlord," or "tenant," and thus "was not technically a lease in the traditional sense."[62] The court concluded that

[54] *De Bruyn Produce Co. v. Romero*, 508 N.W.2d 150 (Mich. Ct. App. 1993).

[55] *Martinez v. Sonoma-Cutrer Vineyards*, 577 F. Supp. 451 (N.D. Cal. 1983).

[56] *Uniform Residential Landlord and Tenant Act* §1.202(5). *See* Iowa Code §562A.5; Ky. Rev. Stat. §383.535(5).

[57] *Franceschina v. Morgan*, 346 F. Supp. 833, 838-839 (S.D. Ind. 1972); *State v. DeCoster*, 653 A.2d 891 (Me. 1995).

[58] *State v. Shack*, 277 A.2d 369, 374 (N.J. 1971).

[59] *De Bruyn Produce Co. v. Romero*, 508 N.W.2d 150 (Mich. Ct. App. 1993); *Vásquez v. Glassboro Service Ass'n, Inc.*, 415 A.2d 1156 (N.J. 1980). *See also* S.C. Code §27-33-10 (including farm laborers in its definition of tenants).

[60] Ro v. Factory Mut. Insurance Co., 260 A.3d 811, 820 (N.H. 2021); *Burch v. University of Kansas*, 756 P.2d 431, 437-438 (Kan. 1988); *Green v. Dormitory Authority of the State of New York*, 577 N.Y.S.2d 675 (App. Div. 1991).

[61] *Houle v. Adams State College*, 547 P.2d 926 (Colo. 1976); *Cook v. University Plaza*, 427 N.E.2d 405 (Ill. App. Ct. 1981).

[62] *Burch v. University of Kansas*, 756 P.2d 431, 437-438 (Kan. 1988).

the "lessor/lessee relationship should be liberally construed to include factual situations where there is no traditional, common-law lease" but such a relationship has been "created by words or other conduct expressing consent by the lessor to the lessee's possession."[63] In contrast, the Colorado Supreme Court concluded that "[a] common sense assessment of the college-student concept militates against petitioner's contention that the relationship of the Trustees to the students is factually indistinguishable from that of landlord/tenant."[64] Among other things, students "had no choice except to live in the dormitory [and] [d]ormitory living involves more than providing a physical place to inhabit. Acclimation to college and attendant social and educational benefits are ingredients of dormitory living."[65] ◀

▷ ROOMMATES **HARD CASE ◀**

When a tenant invites her boyfriend to move in and he agrees to pay half the rent, is he a licensee or a subtenant? In *Kiehm v. Adams*,[66] the court held that the question should be decided by the intent of the parties, but that roommate arrangements should be presumed to be licenses if the roommate did not sign the original lease contract and does not have the "right to occupy a distinct and separate part of the premises," the right is not intended to be assignable, and is not for a particular term. However, a dissenting judge would have found a sublease because a state statute[67] defined a "rental agreement" to mean all agreements that concern the "use and occupancy of a dwelling unit and premises,"[68] and the policies furthered by those statutes would be promoted by recognizing a leasehold relationship because they would give the boyfriend notice and a right to a court hearing before being thrown out of his home. ◀

▷ HOTEL GUESTS AND LODGERS **HARD CASE ◀**

Guests in hotels are normally classified as licensees rather than tenants.[69] Hotels do not have to use eviction proceedings to eject troublesome guests. However, long-term guests (often called "lodgers") have sometimes been classified as tenants subject to the protections of landlord/tenant law.[70]

[63] *Id.* at 431, 437.
[64] *Houle v. Adams State College*, 547 P.2d 926, 927 (Colo. 1976).
[65] *Id.*
[66] 126 P.3d 339, 346 (Haw. 2006).
[67] Haw. Stat. §521-8.
[68] *Kiehm v. Adams*, 126 P.3d 339, 350 (Haw. 2006) (Acoba, J., dissenting).
[69] *See Robbins v. Reagan*, 616 F. Supp. 1259, 1270 (D.D.C. 1985) (residents of homeless shelter are licensees); *Bourque v. Morris*, 460 A.2d 1251, 1253 (Conn. 1983) (hotel guests are licensees); *In re Green Corp.*, 154 B.R. 819, 824 (Bankr. D. Me. 1993) (hotel guests are licensees). See generally Efficiency Lodge, Inc. v. Neason, 889 S.E.2d 789, 802 (Ga. 2023) (factors for distinguishing between landlord-tenant and innkeeper-guest relationships).
[70] *Thomas v. Lenhart*, 444 A.2d 246, 249 (Conn. 1982) ("lodgers" are tenants protected by state's laws regulating eviction); Robert S. Schoshinski, *American Law of Landlord and Tenant* §1:5, at 15-17 (1980).

A guest may be classified as a lodger with "possessory" rights if her occupancy is relatively permanent. On the other hand, retention of significant control by the owner, such as retention of keys, provision of room cleaning services, and provision of furniture and toiletries may indicate an intent to create a license rather than a lease. The *Uniform Residential Landlord and Tenant Act*, adopted in almost half the states, expressly extends the protections of landlord/tenant law to lodgers.[71] Distinguishing between licensees and tenants is beginning to arise in the context of short-term rentals through platforms such as Airbnb, VRBO, and HomeAway.[72] The 2015 *Revised Uniform Residential Landlord and Tenant Act* (*RURLTA*) excludes "vacation rentals," RURLTA §§103(a)(1), (c)(8), a provision drafted with the short-term rental market in mind.[73] ◀

§10.3 Types of Tenancies (Leasehold Estates)

Duration of tenancy

Tenancies are classified by reference to how long they last. The *term of years* is for a definite period; the *periodic tenancy* is indefinite in length and characterized by periodic rental payments; and the *tenancy-at-will* is terminable by either party at any time (unless state statutes require notice to end the tenancy). The *tenancy at sufferance* describes the relationship that exists between a landlord and a tenant who wrongfully holds over after the termination of the tenancy.

§10.3.1 Term of Years

Fixed term

A term of years is a leasehold for a specific term, such as one year. The term can be for any period, from one week to ninety-nine years.[74] One could even have a lease for a day or a few hours.[75] The tenancy ends automatically

[71] *Uniform Residential Landlord and Tenant Act* §1.202(4); Robert S. Schoshinski, *American Law of Landlord and Tenant* §1:5, at 17 (1980). At the same time, even if hotel guests are not tenants, they have a contractual relationship with the hotel and it is a separate question whether that contract places any limits on the ability of the hotel to eject the guest. One possibility is that the license is revocable-at-will, but that the hotel might be subject to damages for a removal without cause. This is the approach generally taken by the courts with respect to theater tickets. An alternative possibility is that hotels do not have the legal right to remove guests unless the guest has breached the agreement in some way.

[72] *See* Michelle Maese, Note, *Rethinking "Host" and "Guest" Relations in the Advent of Airbnb and the Sharing Economy*, 2 Tex. A&M J. Prop. L. 481 (2015) (noting a California case in which an Airbnb guest was considered a tenant after 30 days of occupancy).

[73] *See* Sheldon F. Kurtz & Alice M. Noble-Allgire, *The Revised Uniform Residential Landlord and Tenant Act: A Perspective from the Reporters*, 52 Real Prop. Tr. & Est. L.J. 417, 425-426 (2018).

[74] It may also be possible for the parties to create a lease intended to last for the lifetime of the lessee or tenant. This would create a lifetime lease. *Hartke v. Connecticut*, 429 N.E.2d 885, 891-892 (Ill. App. Ct. 1981).

[75] At the same time, such leases are rare and courts might well interpret them as other types of property rights such as licenses. Hotel guests, for example, are not generally classified as tenants but as licensees. The hotel enters into a contract to give a license, a property arrangement different from a leasehold because it is intended to give the hotel owner greater powers to use self-help to eject the guest if cause to do so arises.

when the term is up. However, state law may well not allow the landlord to remove a holdover tenant without going to court to obtain an eviction. This means that the tenant may be legally entitled to remain after the end of the lease term (as a so-called tenant at sufferance) until a court judgment grants the landlord possession and orders the tenant to vacate.[76] The landlord's future interest (the right to recover possession at the end of the term) is called a reversion.

Inheritable and alienable

Both the tenant's term of years and the landlord's reversion are alienable unless the lease agreement prohibits transfer of the tenant's leasehold.[77] If the landlord transfers her reversion, the new owner takes the property subject to the lease and has no power to terminate the lease unless the lease agreement provides otherwise.[78] Because the parties' interests are for a fixed duration, they also survive the death of either party.[79] If a tenant dies, her leasehold passes to her heirs or devisees; if the landlord dies, her reversion similarly passes to her heirs or devisees.

Limits on duration

There is no common law limitation on how long a term of years may be, although some states have statutes that prohibit leases of more than a prescribed number of years (such as 99).[80] Some statutes and state constitutions impose maximum terms for specific types of leases such as agricultural,[81] mining,[82] or oil and gas leases.[83]

Statute of frauds

Although short-term leases are enforceable if they are oral, the statute of frauds requires long-term leases to be in writing. Most states require a writing for leases of more than one year.[84] If a landlord and tenant sign a one-year lease to commence at some point in the future, a court might hold that the lease is for more than one year and thus must be in writing.[85] Most courts, however, now hold that a one-year oral lease is enforceable if it commences within a few weeks or months.[86] Because this is the usual way tenants arrange for term leases, oral year leases are generally enforceable.

[76] Robert S. Schoshinski, *American Law of Landlord and Tenant* §2:23, at 71-78 (1980).

[77] Rules about transferability of leaseholds are addressed in §10.7.

[78] The lease agreement may provide that the tenancy automatically terminates upon transfer of the landlord's reversion.

[79] *Mann v. Mann*, 671 N.E.2d 73, 76 (Ill. App. Ct. 1996); Robert S. Schoshinski, *American Law of Landlord and Tenant* §10:3, at 641 (1980).

[80] Nev. Rev. Stat. §111.200 (99 years).

[81] Cal. Civ. Code §717 (51 years); Minn. Const. art. I, §15 (21 years); Nev. Rev. Stat. §111.200 (25 years); S.D. Codified Laws §43-32-2 (20 years).

[82] Cal. Civ. Code §718f (99 years).

[83] *Id.*

[84] Originally, the statute of frauds in England requires a writing only if a lease was for more than three years. Most states have reduced that to one year.

[85] Note that the usual statute of frauds contains a "conveyancing" section that requires leases for more than a year to be in writing; under this provision, a lease for one year arguably is enforceable without a writing. *See* Cal. Civ. Code §1624(a)(3). However, the "contract" section of the statute of frauds requires a writing for "contracts" that cannot be performed within one year "from the making thereof"; under this provision, an agreement to rent for a year cannot be performed within a year if the leasehold is to begin in the future. *See* Cal. Civ. Code §1624(a)(1).

[86] 4-39 *Thompson on Real Property, Third Thomas Edition* §39.06(a)(4); *Restatement (Second) of Property (Landlord and Tenant)* §2.1 (1977).

Termination

A term of years ends automatically at the end of the term.[87] However, most states require landlords to use court eviction proceedings to remove holdover tenants.[88] Those statutes require notice to the tenant of the landlord's intent to recover possession.[89] State statutory law may therefore allow the tenant to stay on after the termination of the lease until eviction proceedings have resulted in a judgment. Even when a judgment is granted, the courts may be statutorily empowered to delay execution of the judgment to give the tenant some time to find a new place to live.[90] Thus, although the term of years ends at a fixed point, this does not necessarily mean that the landlord is entitled to recover possession at that same moment. California, Oregon, New Hampshire, New York, and New Jersey, as well as the District of Columbia, have laws requiring "just cause" or "good cause" before a landlord is entitled to evict a tenant.[91] In those jurisdictions, the landlord may be required to continue the tenancy after the end of the term, although the tenancy may be converted to a periodic tenancy.

§10.3.2 *Periodic Tenancy*

Indefinite term

Periodic rental payments

A *periodic tenancy* is for a period that is renewed automatically unless either party terminates the arrangement.[92] It may also be understood as a tenancy for an indefinite period with periodic rental payments. The tenancy continues until either party gives notice at the end of a period of an intent to terminate the arrangement. Many courts hold that each successive period is considered "a continuation of the original holding and not a new and separate tenancy."[93] However, other courts hold that each new period of a periodic tenancy is a "new contract."[94] The most common is

[87] However, the landlord may not be entitled to evict the tenant if the refusal to renew the lease is based on a retaliatory motive designed to punish the tenant for asserting rights protected by the implied warranty of habitability. *See* §10.6.4.

[88] Conn. Stat. §§47a-4(5) & 47a-23a.

[89] Conn. Stat. §47a-23; Robert S. Schoshinski, *American Law of Landlord and Tenant* §2:9, at 44 (1980).

[90] Mass. Gen. Laws ch. 239, §9 (judge may grant tenant up to six months to find a new place to live).

[91] Cal. Civ. Code §1946.2; D.C. Code §42-3505.01; N.H. Rev. Stat. Ann. §540:2 (2020); N.J. Stat. Ann. §§2A:18-53, 2A:18-61.1; N.Y. Real Prop. Law §§210-218; Or. Rev. Stat. Ann. §90.427 (2020). *See* §10.5.4.

[92] Various authorities emphasize that the periodic tenancy is for an indefinite period rather than for a set period that is renewed. Whitman and colleagues, for example, note that a month-to-month tenancy is not "a series of separate successive monthly terms" but, rather, "one indefinite term" characterized by monthly payment of rent. Dale A. Whitman et al., *The Law of Property* §6.16, at 208 (4th ed. 2019). Others view the periodic tenancy as a series of new and separate tenancies. The difference may not be merely formal; if the periodic tenancy is viewed as one indefinite tenancy, the landlord's rights would commence at the beginning of the tenancy and be prior in time to the rights of any subsequent creditor of the tenant.

[93] Robert S. Schoshinski, *American Law of Landlord and Tenant* §2:10, at 47 (1980). In some states, the periodic tenancy is called a tenancy-at-will. This is confusing because the "tenancy-at-will" is a separate leasehold estate in many states with characteristics different from the periodic tenancy. Some jurisdictions have effectively abolished the tenancy-at-will by interpreting all such tenancies as periodic tenancies.

[94] *City of Bridgeport v. Barbour-Daniel Electronics, Inc.*, 548 A.2d 744, 750 (Conn. App. Ct. 1988).

the "month-to-month" tenancy, under which the tenant agrees to pay a monthly rent and can remain in the premises indefinitely. The period of the tenancy may or may not be the same as the period of the rent payments. For example, the parties may agree to a year-to-year tenancy but agree that the yearly rent will be paid in monthly installments. In general, however, if the parties agree on monthly rental payments, the courts will infer an intent to create a month-to-month tenancy. Many states have statutes to this effect.[95] Other states have statutes that presumptively interpret leases as month-to-month tenancies, unless the rental agreement provides otherwise.[96]

Inheritable and alienable

Like the term of years, the periodic tenancy is both transferable and inheritable unless the lease agreement provides otherwise.[97] Oral periodic tenancies are enforceable as long as the period is less than that specified in the statute of frauds. Because a month-to-month tenancy can generally be terminated with a month's notice (or whatever notice is required by statute), it is viewed as a short-term lease even though it could last for many years.[98]

Statute of frauds

Many statutes require leases of more than a year to be in writing. Some states require leases to be in writing if the parties intend to create either a term of years or a periodic tenancy; failure for the lease to be in writing results in a tenancy-at-will.[99]

Terminating periodic tenancies

State statutes require notice to the tenant to terminate periodic tenancies. Unlike the term of years, which ends automatically when the term is over, the periodic tenancy continues until either party notifies the other of an intent to terminate.[100] Courts traditionally required six months' notice to terminate a year-to-year tenancy and notice equal to the period to terminate a periodic tenancy of less than a year (for example, one month's notice to terminate a month-to-month tenancy). However, most states now have statutes governing the amount of notice that must be given.[101]

Notice

Result when notice is defective

It is important to be careful about the requisite notice. If the landlord fails to give adequate notice, some courts have held that the notice is "a nullity and ineffective to terminate the tenancy at any date," while other courts hold that the notice is effective to terminate the tenancy at the end

[95] Fla. Stat. §83.02; Or. Rev. Stat. §§91.060 & 91.070; Haw. Rev. Stat. §666-2; Robert S. Schoshinski, *American Law of Landlord and Tenant* §2:12, at 52 (1980).
[96] Conn. Stat. §47a-3b; La. Civ. Code art. 2680.
[97] Robert S. Schoshinski, *American Law of Landlord and Tenant* §2:10, at 48 (1980).
[98] *Carter v. Schick*, 817 S.W.2d 238, 239 (Ky. Ct. App. 1991); *Estate of Saliba v. Dunning*, 682 A.2d 224, 227 (Me. 1996).
[99] Mass. Gen. Laws ch. 183, §3; N.H. Stat. §540:1; Vt. Stat. tit. 27, §302.
[100] Robert S. Schoshinski, *American Law of Landlord and Tenant* §2:13, at 53-58 (1980).
[101] D.C. Code §42-3202 (30 days' notice to terminate month-to-month tenancy or tenancy from quarter-to-quarter); Cal. Civ. Code §1946 (30 days' notice to terminate month-to-month tenancy or periodic tenancy of more than 30 days' base period); Fla. Stat. §83.03 (3 months' notice for year-to-year tenancy; 45 days' notice for quarter-to-quarter tenancy; 15 days' notice for month-to-month tenancy; 7 days' notice for week-to-week tenancy); N.J. Stat. §46:8-9 (3 months' notice required for all tenancies that require notice); *Uniform Residential Landlord and Tenant Act* §4.301(a) & (b) (60 days' notice for month-to-month tenancy; 10 days' notice for week-to-week tenancy). Agricultural tenancies are sometimes treated differently from residential or other types of commercial tenancies. Robert S. Schoshinski, *American Law of Landlord and Tenant* §2:13, at 54 n.36 (1980).

of the next period.[102] Similarly, some states require the notice to terminate both to provide the requisite number of days' notice and to terminate the tenancy on the last day of a period. This means that, even if one provides 30 days' notice, as required by statute, the notice may be held invalid if the 30 days end during the middle of a period rather than on the last day of a period.[103] For example, if a month-to-month tenancy runs from the first to the last day of the month, the landlord could not notify the tenant on March 15 that the tenancy would terminate on April 15. The older view was that such a notice would be fatally defective and would not count as notice at all.[104] Most courts today, however, will recognize that if a tenant is given more than the requisite notice, the tenant has no real cause for complaint and will count such notice as effective to terminate the tenancy at the end of the next period (April 30).[105]

Notice of rent increase

When the landlord wants to raise the rent and continue renting to an existing month-to-month tenant, the landlord must provide the required notice to terminate the existing tenancy, along with a separate offer to begin a new tenancy at the increased rent. When a landlord does this, two kinds of issues arise: first, whether the landlord has provided sufficient notice to terminate the old tenancy, and, second, whether the conduct of both parties indicates that the tenant has accepted the obligation to pay the higher rent.

Notice to quit accompanied by offer to continue leasehold at a higher rent

On the notice issue, a few states have held that a notice to terminate the tenancy combined with an offer of a new tenancy at a higher rent is not effective either to end the tenancy or to increase the rent.[106] The notice to terminate the tenancy is arguably defective because it does not definitely inform the tenant of the landlord's desire to terminate the relationship. One court reasoned that this kind of notice is "equivocal" because the tenant could construe the notice "to mean that they could remain at an increased rental."[107] If this notice is not effective to terminate the tenancy, then a new notice must be given to end the relationship. Most states today, however, will recognize a notice of a proposed rent increase that is accompanied by a separate notice to terminate the prior tenancy as sufficient to terminate the prior tenancy.[108]

[102] *Robert S. Schoshinski, American Law of Landlord and Tenant* §2:13, at 55-56 (1980). *See, e.g., Robinette v. French*, 724 S.W.2d 196 (Ark. Ct. App. 1987) (16 days' notice of rent increase was ineffective because 30 days' notice was required to terminate a month-to-month tenancy). *But see Alexander v. Steining*, 398 S.E.2d 390 (Ga. Ct. App. 1990) (where statute required 60 days' notice to terminate tenancy-at-will, a notice of increased rental would be effective only after the 60 days required by statute at which time a new tenancy-at-will would begin at the new rent).

[103] 4-39 *Thompson on Real Property, Third Thomas Edition* §39.05(c)(2).

[104] 2-16 *Powell on Real Property* §16.05.

[105] *See Steffen v. Paulus*, 465 N.E.2d 1021 (Ill. App. Ct. 1984) (if the date stated in the notice is not the end of a period, it will be effective to terminate the tenancy at the earliest possible date after the date stated); *Sage v. Rogers*, 848 P.2d 1034 (Mont. 1993) (same); *Harry's Village v. Egg Harbor Township*, 446 A.2d 862 (N.J. 1982) (same); *Dickens v. Hall*, 718 P.2d 683 (N.M. 1986) (same).

[106] *T.W.I.W., Inc. v. Rhudy*, 630 P.2d 753, 757 (N.M. 1981).

[107] *Id.*

[108] Robert S. Schoshinski, *American Law of Landlord and Tenant* §2:14, at 58 (1980).

Notice of rent increase without notice to quit

If the landlord notifies the tenant of a rent increase without notifying the tenant that the landlord intends to terminate the prior tenancy, some courts hold that there is no notice to terminate and thus the prior tenancy continues at the old rent.[109] Other states hold that a notice of rent increase (without a notice to quit) implicitly notifies the tenant of an intent to end the old tenancy and offer a new one at the new rental, and will enforce the new rental as long as the requisite amount of notice was given to the tenant to terminate the old tenancy and start a new one.[110]

Acceptance of increased rental obligation

When a landlord does effectively end the old tenancy and offer to begin a new periodic tenancy at a higher rental, what actions by the tenant are sufficient to constitute an acceptance of the higher rental obligation? Most courts interpret the tenant's decision to stay in the premises after a notice to quit and notice of an intended rent increase to be an implicit acceptance of the new, higher rental obligation. They hold that the "tenant's holdover after such notice results in a tenancy at the increased rental."[111] However, some courts limit the landlord to the old rent if the tenant notifies the landlord that she refuses to accept the higher rent.[112] If the tenant pays the higher rent, most courts will interpret that as an acceptance of the landlord's offer and hold the tenant to the new rent. Conversely, if the tenant continues to pay the older rent — and the landlord accepts those payments — the courts are likely to find that a new tenancy at the increased rental was not created.[113]

Death does not terminate

The death of either the landlord or the tenant usually does not terminate a periodic tenancy.[114]

§10.3.3 Tenancy at Will

At will

At common law, a *tenancy at will* is terminable at any time by either party.[115] It therefore resembles a license; the difference is that the tenant has been given the right to possess the property — a right that goes far beyond the usual license. However, the tenancy-at-will has been substantially modified in many states; at least half the states have statutes that require notice to terminate the tenancy-at-will.[116] Such notice requirements effectively convert the tenancy-at-will into a form of periodic tenancy.[117] Moreover, most states have outlawed self-help evictions, even in

Modified by statutes requiring notice to quit

[109] *Stewart v. Melnick*, 613 P.2d 1336 (Haw. Ct. App. 1980).

[110] *Rushing Construction Co. v. MCM Ventures, II, Inc.*, 395 S.E.2d 130 (N.C. Ct. App. 1990).

[111] Robert S. Schoshinski, *American Law of Landlord and Tenant* §2:14, at 58 (1980).

[112] *Id.* at §2:14, at 59.

[113] Dale A. Whitman et al., *The Law of Property* §6.53, at 285-286 (4th ed. 2019).

[114] *State v. Pierce*, 417 A.2d 1085, 1087 (N.J. Super. Ct. Law Div. 1980); Robert S. Schoshinski, *American Law of Landlord and Tenant* §10:3, at 641 (1980). *But see Miller & Desatnik Mgmt. Co. v. Bullock*, 270 Cal. Rptr. 600, 604 (App. Dep't Super. Ct. 1990) (interpreting a state statute to terminate the month-to-month tenancy on the tenant's death).

[115] *Day v. Kolar*, 341 N.W.2d 598 (Neb. 1983) (lease that permits cancellation with zero days' notice is a tenancy at will).

[116] Ala. Code §35-9-3 (10 days); Ga. Code §47-7-7 (60 days' notice from the landlord, 30 days' notice from the tenant); Me. Rev. Stat. tit. 14, §6002 (30 days); Wis. Stat. §704.19 (28 days).

[117] Dale A. Whitman et al., *The Law of Property* §6.74, at 311 (4th ed. 2019).

the case of tenancies-at-will, requiring landlords to use court proceedings to recover possession. In those states that do not require notice to terminate a tenancy-at-will, the landlord is still obligated to give the tenant "a reasonable time to vacate the premises."[118]

Periodic rent turns tenancy at will into periodic tenancy

The parties may agree to create a tenancy-at-will but it also arises by operation of law in the absence of agreement to the contrary. For example, if the landlord grants a tenant the right to move in and take possession of the premises but the parties have not agreed upon how long the tenant will be in possession or a periodic rental payment, the courts may infer an intent to create a tenancy-at-will.[119] A tenancy-at-will may also be found if a tenant holds on after the end of a prior tenancy with the consent of the landlord and the parties have not reached any agreement as to term or payment of rent.[120] If the parties agree to periodic payment of rent, the courts are very likely to interpret the arrangement as a periodic tenancy, rather than a tenancy-at-will; they may do so even if the parties call it a tenancy-at-will.[121]

Terminated at death of either party

Because the tenancy is at the will of the parties, the courts generally hold that, unlike the term of years or the periodic tenancy, the tenancy-at-will terminates at the death of either landlord or tenant.[122] In addition, because the tenancy is "at the will" of the parties, it has traditionally been held not to be transferable by the tenant.[123] A transfer of the landlord's title also terminates a tenancy-at-will.[124]

Not transferable

§10.3.4 Tenancy at Sufferance

Holdover tenant

A *tenancy at sufferance* arises when the tenant wrongfully holds over after the termination of a prior tenancy.[125] Such a tenant is liable to the owner for the fair rental value of the property during the period of occupation.[126] Notice is not generally required to terminate the tenancy, but state statutes may well outlaw self-help, instead requiring the owner to use court proceedings to dispossess the tenant; those statutes effectively require

[118] Robert S. Schoshinski, *American Law of Landlord and Tenant* §2:18, at 64 (1980).

[119] *Fraser v. Fraser*, 598 A.2d 751 (Me. 1991); *Womack v. Hyche*, 503 So. 2d 832 (Ala. 1987). *See also Kohnen v. Hameed*, 894 S.W.2d 196, 200 (Mo. Ct. App. 1995) ("Where a party occupies property under a lease with an option to buy, that party becomes a tenant-at-will upon the expiration of the option"); *BancTexas Westheimer v. Sumner*, 734 S.W.2d 57 (Tex. Ct. App. 1987) (persons occupying property by permission of mortgagor were tenants-at-will of purchaser of property at mortgage foreclosure sale).

[120] *Commonwealth Dep't of Transportation v. Di Furio*, 555 A.2d 1379, 1383-1384 (Pa. Commw. Ct. 1989). *See also Tage II Corp. v. Ducas (U.S.) Realty Corp.*, 461 N.E.2d 1222, 1224 (Mass. App. Ct. 1984) (assignment of tenancy in violation of lease agreement prohibiting assignment creates tenancy at will).

[121] *Melson v. Cook*, 545 So. 2d 796 (Ala. Ct. App. 1989); Dale A. Whitman et al., *The Law of Property* §6.19, at 211 (4th ed. 2019).

[122] Robert S. Schoshinski, *American Law of Landlord and Tenant* §2:16, at 61 (1980).

[123] 2-16 *Powell on Real Property* §16.05.

[124] *Hunt v. Happy Valley Ltd. Partnership*, 434 S.E.2d 285 (S.C. Ct. App. 1993).

[125] Robert S. Schoshinski, *American Law of Landlord and Tenant* §2:20, at 67-69 (1980).

[126] *Dale v. H.B. Smith Co., Inc.*, 136 F.3d 843, 850 (1st Cir. 1998) (Massachusetts law).

notice before the tenant can be dispossessed.[127] Some states, however, do have statutes that require notice to terminate a tenancy at sufferance, in addition to whatever notice is required through the eviction process.[128] The term "tenant at sufferance" is intended to distinguish the holdover tenant from a trespasser who never had lawfully occupied the premises. Although the holdover tenant is wrongfully occupying the property, she is legally entitled to do so until statutory procedures to evict the tenant have granted the landlord the right to have the tenant physically excluded from the premises.

Landlord's election to evict or begin a new tenancy

The landlord must elect whether to evict the holdover tenant or hold her to a new tenancy.[129] If the landlord chooses to evict the tenant, the landlord may recover possession from her, usually by summary eviction proceedings.[130] In such a lawsuit, the landlord would be entitled to recover the fair rental value of the premises during the wrongful occupation.[131] Some statutes provide for double damages for wrongful holdover.[132] If the landlord chooses to hold the tenant to a new tenancy, many states used to allow the landlord to hold the tenant under a term of years to a new term.[133] Some states may still adhere to this rule, although it now seems to be the minority approach.[134] The more modern approach is to treat the new tenancy as a periodic tenancy.[135] Some states presume the term of the period of the new tenancy is determined by the prior term of years,[136] while others measure the period on the basis of the manner in which rent was paid under the old lease arrangement.[137]

§10.4 Tenant's Obligations and Landlord's Remedies

§10.4.1 Tenant's Duty to Pay Rent

Promise by tenant to pay rent (privity of contract)

Rent is not a necessary feature of a leasehold, although most landlord-tenant relations include contractual arrangements obligating the tenant to pay an agreed-upon rent. When the tenant promises to pay rent, the rental

[127] *Hill v. Dobrowolski*, 484 A.2d 1123 (N.H. 1984) (holding over after two-day lease created tenancy at sufferance; state statute prohibits landlord from using self-help to recover possession). *But see* Donegal Assocs., LLC v. Christie-Scott, LLC, 241 A.3d 1011 (Md. Ct. Spec. App. 2020) (commercial landlord entitled to use self-help to repossess hair salon from holdover tenant).

[128] N.Y. Real Prop. §228 (30 days).

[129] *Bockelmann v. Marynick*, 788 S.W.2d 569 (Tex. 1990) (when only one co-tenant held over, only that tenant may be held to a new tenancy).

[130] Robert S. Schoshinski, *American Law of Landlord and Tenant* §2:24, at 78 (1980).

[131] *Booker v. Trizec Properties, Inc.*, 363 S.E.2d 13 (Ga. Ct. App. 1987).

[132] Miss. Code §89-7-25 (tenant is liable for double rent for the period of the holdover); Wis. Stat. §704.27 (double damages).

[133] Robert S. Schoshinski, *American Law of Landlord and Tenant* §2:23, at 71-72 (1980).

[134] *Mattas Motors, Inc. v. Heritage Homes of Nebraska, Inc.*, 749 P.2d 458 (Colo. App. 1987); Robert S. Schoshinski, *American Law of Landlord and Tenant* §2:23, at 73 (1980).

[135] *Karz v. Mecham*, 174 Cal. Rptr. 310 (Ct. App. 1981); Robert S. Schoshinski, *American Law of Landlord and Tenant* §2:23, at 73 (1980).

[136] *See Schartz v. Foster*, 805 P.2d 505 (Kan. Ct. App. 1991) (applying Kan. Stat. §58-2502).

[137] Cal. Civ. Code §1945; Mont. Code §70-26-204; Robert S. Schoshinski, *American Law of Landlord and Tenant* §2:23, at 75 (1980).

Leasehold conditioned on tenant duty to pay rent (privity of estate)

obligation is usually based on the tenant's express covenant to pay rent. When such a promise exists on the tenant's part, the liability will persist even if the tenant assigns her interest in the leasehold. Sometimes, however, the lease agreement does not contain an express covenant by which the tenant promises to pay rent; rather, the agreement may simply state that the landlord transfers possession "subject to" or "at" a stated rent.[138] In that case, the courts may conclude that the rental obligation rests not on an independent contractual promise or covenant, but is a condition of the transfer of possession. In that case, the tenant's obligation may be held to exist not because of "privity of contract," but because the rental obligation is a condition of the conveyance of an estate in land from landlord to tenant and thus rests on "privity of estate" rather than privity of contract. In this case, if the tenant assigns her interest in the leasehold, the courts may conclude that the rental obligation runs with the land and transfers to the assignee, leaving no contractual obligations on the original tenant at all. In addition, a lease that is based on a qualified estate rather than a separate contractual promise *may* be held to constitute a *defeasible leasehold*— meaning that if the tenant breaches the obligation to pay rent, the tenant's possessory interest is forfeited and the tenancy terminated automatically.

Back rent and eviction

If the tenant breaches the obligation to pay rent, the landlord may sue the tenant for unpaid back rent and/or to recover possession of the premises — otherwise known as *eviction*. If the written lease agreement provides that the leasehold is forfeited if the tenant does not pay rent, statutory law may nonetheless require eviction proceedings to remove the breaching tenant. The landlord may similarly choose to terminate the leasehold and sue to recover possession of the premises if the tenant breaches any other material terms of the lease agreement.

Covenants dependent rather than independent

Under modern law, the landlord's covenants in the residential rental context are dependent on the tenant's covenants and vice versa; this means that if the tenant breaches her contractual obligation to pay rent, for example, the landlord is relieved of his obligations under the lease, including the grant of possession of the property to the tenant. Statutes in all states empower landlords to recover possession upon default in rental obligations.[139] In effect, they provide that the tenant forfeits her possessory rights when she fails to pay the rent. This is also the approach taken by the *Restatement (Second) of Property (Landlord and Tenant).*[140] In addition, landlords ordinarily include contract terms giving them the right to recover possession if the tenant breaches any covenants in the lease, including the covenant to pay rent.[141] Normally, rental obligations exist during the term of the leasehold. However, those obligations may end early if the landlord violates the covenant of quiet enjoyment, constructively evicting the tenant. Conversely, the rental obligation may persist after the end of the lease if the tenant wrongfully holds over after the lease has terminated and the landlord exercises her right to hold the tenant to a new tenancy.

Rent obligations during the leasehold

[138] Robert S. Schoshinski, *American Law of Landlord and Tenant* §5:34, at 331 (1980).
[139] *Id.* at §6:1, at 377.
[140] *Restatement (Second) of Property (Landlord and Tenant)* §13.1 (1977).
[141] Robert S. Schoshinski, *American Law of Landlord and Tenant* §6:1, at 377-378 (1980).

Rent v. fair rental value

"Rent" normally refers to the agreed-upon rental obligation. However, a landlord may be entitled to the "fair rental value" of the property if the parties have not otherwise agreed on a particular rent or if the tenant wrongfully holds over after the end of the lease term. This latter obligation rests not on an express agreement, but on the notion that the landlord is entitled to compensation when another is possessing the landlord's property.[142]

Rental amount ordinarily essential term of the contract

When a lease agreement is ambiguous or indefinite about the amount of rent owed by the tenant to the landlord, the court may infer that the tenant agreed to pay "fair rental value."[143] However, the courts are more likely to find the entire agreement void for want of a material term.[144]

Acts of God

Does a tenant have a duty to keep paying rent if the property is destroyed or rendered unlivable because of a hurricane or other natural event (often called an act of God)? Traditionally, the answer was yes and some states will enforce a promise to pay rent even if the building is rendered uninhabitable, unless the lease contains a provision relieving the tenant of the duty to pay rent in such a case.[145] Most leases have a clause relieving the tenant of any duty to pay rent if the property is rendered uninhabitable through an act of God.[146] Many states protect tenants from rental obligations if the property is not habitable even if this were caused by nature rather than by the landlord.[147]

▷ PANDEMICS AND RENT OBLIGATIONS **HARD CASE ◀**

The Covid-19 pandemic brought government-mandated business closures, travel restrictions, social distancing, and stay-at-home orders, as well as a general public-health situation that greatly reduced demand for in-person retail, dining, and entertainment venues across the country. As a result, many commercial tenants faced difficulty paying rent for reasons entirely out of their own control. In the inevitable ensuing litigation, several related doctrines were tested. For example, many commercial leases contain "force majeure" clauses that excuse the performance of an obligation either on an open-ended standard such as "any event neither caused

142 *Id.* at §5:34, at 332. *See Parkmerced Co. v. San Francisco Rent Stabilization & Arbitration Board*, 263 Cal. Rptr. 617, 621 (Ct. App. 1989) ("liability for rent arises in one of two ways, either from a contractual agreement with the property owner or by actual occupancy of the premises with the owner's consent").

143 *Fuqua v. Fuqua*, 750 S.W.2d 238, 245 (Tex. Ct. App. 1988) (agreement to pay rent at a "reasonable rate" is sufficiently definite to be enforced; rent set at fair rental value).

144 *Mur-Mil Caterers, Inc. v. Werner*, 560 N.Y.S.2d 849 (App. Div. 1990) (agreement that rent was to be based on "normal increase" was too vague to be enforced, causing lease to fail); *Smith v. Smith*, 308 S.E.2d 504 (N.C. Ct. App. 1983) (amount of rent is essential term of the agreement and lease that leaves amount of rent open for future agreement is void for indefiniteness).

145 *Horne v. TGM Assocs., L.P.*, 56 So. 3d 615 (Ala. 2010); *Gardens at Maplewood v. Fowlin*, 2013 WL 1496552 (N.J. Super. Ct. Law Div. 2013) (duty to pay rent after Hurricane Sandy).

146 *Graci v. Gasper John Palazzo, Jr., LLC*, 119 So. 3d 741 (La. Ct. App. 2013); *Moody Nat'l Buffalo Speedway MT, L.P. v. Sirius Solutions, LLLP*, 2013 WL 315932 (Tex. Ct. App. 2013).

147 *See* §10.6.3. Miss. Code §89-7-3. *See Uniform Residential Landlord and Tenant Act* §4.106 (relieving the tenant of the duty to pay rent if the property is damaged or destroyed by fire or casualty "to the extent that enjoyment of the dwelling unit is substantially impaired").

nor reasonably foreseen by the parties," or on the occurrence of events specified in the lease.[148] When a tenant invokes a force majeure clause to excuse nonpayment of rent, courts look closely at the relevant lease language and tend to construe such clauses narrowly, on the theory that the parties should be able to capture the categories of risks that they would want to apply, even if an event like a global pandemic was not generally reflected in leases before 2020. During the pandemic, many courts continued to read force majeure clauses narrowly, even as some tenants were able to prevail.[149]

Tenants during the pandemic also invoked common law doctrines that can also excuse nonperformance. Frustration of purpose, for example, applies where performance is technically feasible but unforeseen changed circumstances frustrate the essential purpose of the contract. Impossibility and impracticality doctrines, as their name suggests, excuse nonperformance if an unforeseeable outside event makes performance impossible or excessively burdensome.[150] Decisions applying these doctrines during the pandemic took varying approaches, with many skeptical of excusing tenants if there was any basis to say that the lease could continue, while some courts were more sympathetic to tenants.[151] Courts rejecting claims for nonperformance tend to focus on the fact that the parties to commercial leases are sophisticated business entities; moreover, many courts noted, the disruptions posed by the pandemic and the governmental response were temporary and only indirectly caused the economic challenges

[148] George P. Bernhardt & Jack Fersko, *The Impacts of the Coronavirus Pandemic on Real Estate Contracts Force Majeure, Frustration of Purpose, and Impossibility*, 35 Prob. & Prop. 34, 34 (2021).

[149] *Compare, e.g., STORE SPE LA Fitness v. Fitness Int'l, LLC*, 2021 WL 3285036, at *7 (C.D. Cal. June 30, 2021) (rejecting force majeure claim because pandemic-related shutdown orders did not directly cause nonperformance) *with In re Hitz Rest. Grp.*, 616 B.R. 374 (Bankr. N.D. Ill. 2020) (clause specifying that where "performance of any of [the tenant's] obligations are prevented or delayed, retarded or hindered by . . . laws, governmental action or inaction, [or] orders of government" excused a bankrupt tenant's lease payments after a COVID-19 shutdown order); *see also West Pueblo Partners, LLC v. Stone Brewing Co., LLC*, 307 Cal. Rptr. 3d 626 (Cal. Ct. App. 2023) (force majeure clause applied, but tenant had resources to meet its obligations). Even without a force majeure clause, some states allow a party to forgo performance because of force majeure by statute. *See, e.g.*, Cal. Civ. Code §1511 (excusing performance if the parties face "an irresistible, superhuman cause . . . unless the parties have expressly agreed to the contrary"); Ga. Code Ann. §13-4-21 ("If performance of the terms of a contract becomes impossible as a result of an Act of God, such impossibility shall excuse nonperformance, except where, by proper prudence, such impossibility might have been avoided by the promisor.").

[150] George P. Bernhardt & Jack Fersko, *The Impacts of the Coronavirus Pandemic on Real Estate Contracts Force Majeure, Frustration of Purpose, and Impossibility*, 35 Prob. & Prop. 34, 35 (2021).

[151] *Compare, e.g., AGW Sono Partners, LLC v. Downtown Soho, LLC*, 273 A.3d 186 (Conn. 2022) (rejecting impossibility, impracticability, and frustration of purpose defenses by a restaurant initially closed and then allowed to operate on a limited basis given social distancing requirements) *and Gap Inc. v. 170 Broadway Retail Owner, LLC*, 195 A.D.3d 575 (N.Y. App. Div. 2021) (rejecting frustration of purpose defense where tenant was not completely deprived of the benefit of its bargain) *with, e.g., Bay City Realty LLC v. Mattress Firm Inc.*, 2021 WL 1295261 (E.D. Mich. 2021) (state shutdown order an unforeseen event that frustrated purpose of a retail lease).

..d. The argument in favor of excusing performance, however, ..ognizes just how unprecedented the governmental and public-health response to the Covid-19 pandemic was, and how even in the commercial context, landlords often have more power in drafting clauses that require tenants to bear unforeseen risks. ◀

§10.4.2 *Tenant's Duty to Operate*

Ordinarily no duty to operate

Ordinarily, courts will not imply a duty on the part of the tenant to occupy the premises or operate a business there.[152] The tenant does have a duty not to commit waste, and a complete failure to enter the premises may result in harm to the property. For example, a tenant who does not occupy may leave the property vulnerable to invasion by others, such as individuals looking for abandoned properties in which to commit drug deals. In such cases, it is conceivable that a court might find a tenant to have breached an obligation to care for the premises so as not to commit waste.

Express covenant to operate

Some courts will enforce express covenants to operate.[153] However, they will not force an unprofitable business to operate, and are very likely to deny injunctive relief ordering the tenant to continue operating in any case, relegating the landlord to damages on the ground that damages are an adequate remedy for the tenant's breach and because judges are not competent to manage the tenant's business operations to ensure compliance with the operating covenant.[154] Some courts have inferred a duty to operate from express covenants that limit the use of the land to a specific purpose, reasoning that not using the property at all violates that provision.[155] Most courts, however, will not imply such a covenant, reasoning that the use is permitted but not required.[156]

[152] *Serfecz v. Jewel Food Stores*, 67 F.3d 591, 603 (7th Cir. 1995) (applying Illinois common law) (holding that a lessee may close its store and move to a competing location across the street and leave the leased premises vacant, and that this does not violate a lease provision providing that "lessee shall use land only for operation of a grocery supermarket" because this clause prohibits operating a competing business but does not require the lessee to operate a supermarket); *Evans v. Grand Union Co.*, 759 F. Supp. 818 (M.D. Ga. 1990) (applying Georgia law). *Cf. Slater v. Pearle Vision Center, Inc.*, 546 A.2d 676 (Pa. Super. Ct. 1988) (sufficient language in the lease agreement to find an obligation to operate).

[153] 5-44 *Thompson on Real Property, Third Thomas Edition* §44.14(g)(1).

[154] *Summit Town Centre, Inc. v. Shoe Show of Rocky Mount, Inc.*, 828 A.2d 995 (Pa. 2003) (enforcing an express covenant to operate by a damages remedy and denying injunctive relief).

[155] *Simhawk Corp. v. Egler*, 202 N.E.2d 49 (Ill. App. Ct. 1964); *Ingannamorte v. Kings Super Markets, Inc.*, 260 A.2d 841 (N.J. 1970); *Columbia East Assocs. v. Bi-Lo, Inc.*, 386 S.E.2d 259 (S.C. Ct. App. 1989); *BVT Lebanon Shopping Center, Ltd. v. Wal-Mart Stores, Inc.*, 48 S.W.3d 132 (Tenn. 2001); *Ayres Jewelry Co. v. O & S Bldg.*, 419 P.2d 628 (Wyo. 1966).

[156] *Daniel G. Kamin Kilgore Enterprises v. Brookshire Grocery Co.*, 81 Fed. Appx. 827, 2003 U.S. App. LEXIS 24299 (5th Cir. 2003); *Casa D'Angelo, Inc. v. A & R Realty Co.*, 553 N.E.2d 515, 520 (Ind. Ct. App. 1990); *Rothe v. Revco D.S., Inc.*, 976 F. Supp. 784, 789 (S.D. Ind. 1997); *Oakwood Vill. LLC v. Albertsons, Inc.*, 104 P.3d 1226 (Utah 2004); *Sampson Investments v. Jondex Corp.*, 499 N.W.2d 177, 181 (Wis. 1993).

▶ **HARD CASE**

▷ TENANT'S GOOD FAITH DUTY TO OPERATE

In commercial leases to retail stores, landlords sometimes calculate rent as a percentage of profits generated by the business, usually measured as a percentage of "gross sales."[157] This "percentage rent" arrangement is often supplemented by a set minimum rent that is paid whether or not any profits are earned. Does a percentage rent arrangement mean that the tenant has an implied duty to operate to generate the sales from which the rent is to be paid? In *College Block v. Atlantic Richfield Co.*,[158] for example, a 20-year lease to a gas station provided for a $1,000-per-month rent payment supplemented by a percentage of the gasoline delivered. When the tenant ceased operations after 17 years, the landlord sued, arguing that, because the rent was partially calculated as a percentage of gasoline sold, the agreement implied a good faith obligation on the tenant actually to operate the gas station so that gas could be sold and the rent contemplated by the agreement could be generated.

Argument against an implied duty to operate

The tenant undoubtedly argued that the lease imposed no express covenant to operate and, that in the absence of an affirmative covenant to operate a gas station during the entire term of the lease, no such obligation should be implied. Affirmative covenants to keep operating a business are unusual, because the ability to operate a successful business depends on a host of factors—not the least of which is whether it is profitable. In the absence of clear language to that effect, the court might well be loath to conclude that a tenant promised to continue operating. Some courts adopt this approach, refusing to find a duty to operate in the absence of an express covenant to that effect.[159]

Argument for an implied duty to operate

On the other hand, the landlord in *College Block* undoubtedly argued in response that, because rents were calculated as a percent of sales, the parties must have contemplated that there would be sales. Otherwise, the landlord would not receive the agreed-upon rent. The court in *College Block* agreed with the landlord that covenants may sometimes be implied into lease agreements. "To effectuate the intent of the parties, implied covenants will be found if after examining the contract as a whole it is so obvious that the parties had no reason to state the covenant, the implication arises from the language of the agreement, and there is a legal necessity."[160] The court also held that a "covenant of continued operation can be implied into commercial leases containing percentage rental provisions in order for the lessor to receive that for which the lessor bargained."[161]

Exception to the duty to operate when the base rent is substantial or adequate

However, the court also held that it would *not* imply a covenant to operate if the base rent was "substantial or adequate."[162] Most courts agree

[157] Dale A. Whitman et al., *The Law of Property* §6.51, at 283 (4th ed. 2019).
[158] 254 Cal. Rptr. 179 (Ct. App. 1988).
[159] *Evans v. Grand Union Co.*, 759 F. Supp. 818 (M.D. Ga. 1990); *Walgreen Arizona Drug Co. v. Plaza Center Corp.*, 647 P.2d 643 (Ariz. Ct. App. 1982).
[160] 254 Cal. Rptr. at 182.
[161] *Id.*
[162] *Id.* at 184.

with this approach.[163] A "pure" percentage lease, in which the rent is calculated solely as a percent of sales, is very likely to be interpreted as including an implied duty to operate.[164] However, if there is a "fixed minimum" rental payment, in addition to the percentage rent, courts will not generally find an implied duty to operate if the base rent is "adequate compensation for the use of the property" with the percentage rent constituting a kind of bonus on top of the base payment.[165] On the other hand, if the base rent is not substantial, courts are likely to find an implied obligation to operate on the ground that the parties contemplated that, unless the business was unprofitable, rents would be generated.[166] If the percentage amount was intended to be the "basic compensation" rather than a "bonus" on top of an adequate base amount, then the courts are likely to find an implied duty to operate, although the cases are not unanimous.[167] ◀

§10.4.3 Illegality

Void if lease was for an illegal purpose

If both landlord and tenant contemplated that the tenant would use the property for an illegal purpose, the courts are likely to hold the contract to be void and unenforceable by either party.[168] Neither party can sue the other for relief; the law "leaves parties to an illegal contract where it finds them."[169] The landlord cannot sue for unpaid rent and the tenant has no defense to a claim for possession.[170] If, however, only the tenant intended to use the property for an illegal purpose, the lease is enforceable against the tenant.[171] The landlord may also obtain damages from the tenant for breach of an implied covenant not to use the property for illegal purposes. The landlord may also recover possession either under state statutes providing for forfeiture of the tenancy because of the illegal use or under common law doctrines entitling the landlord to recover possession if the tenant breaches material terms in the contract.[172] The federal 1988 *Anti-Drug Abuse Act*[173] similarly allows tenants of public housing to be evicted based on criminal

Enforceable if illegal use is tenant's choice

Supervening illegality

[163] Robert S. Schoshinski, *American Law of Landlord and Tenant* §5:3, at 231 (1980).
[164] *Pequot Spring Water Co. v. Brunelle*, 698 A.2d 920 (Conn. App. Ct. 1997); Robert S. Schoshinski, *American Law of Landlord and Tenant* §5:3, at 231 (1980).
[165] *Plaza Forty-Eight, Inc. v. Great Atlantic & Pacific Tea Co.*, 817 F. Supp. 774 (E.D. Wis. 1993) (applying Michigan law, court found that there was no implied duty to operate because the fixed base rent was "reasonable"); *Nalle v. Taco Bell Corp.*, 914 S.W.2d 685 (Tex. Ct. App. 1996) ("fixed rent in the lease was substantial and adequate"); Robert S. Schoshinski, *American Law of Landlord and Tenant* §5:3, at 231 (1980).
[166] *Hornwood v. Smith's Food King No. 1*, 807 P.2d 208 (Nev. 1991).
[167] Robert S. Schoshinski, *American Law of Landlord and Tenant* §5:3, at 231 (1980).
[168] *See Sippin v. Ellam*, 588 A.2d 660 (Conn. 1991); *Springlake Corp. v. Symmarron Ltd. Partnership*, 569 A.2d 715 (Md. Ct. App. 1990); Robert S. Schoshinski, *American Law of Landlord and Tenant* §5:12, at 257 (1980).
[169] Robert S. Schoshinski, American Law of Landlord and Tenant §5:12, at 258 (1980).
[170] *Id.*
[171] *Id.* at §5:12, at 259.
[172] *Id. See, e.g.*, Mass. Gen. Laws ch. 139, §19 (allowing eviction of tenants who commit or allow to be committed certain criminal offenses on the rented premises).
[173] 42 U.S.C. §1437d(l)(6); *Department of Housing & Urban Development v. Rucker*, 535 U.S. 125 (2002).

drug activity of any member of the household or a guest on the premises. A particular use of the premises may be illegal, because it contravenes a criminal statute or because it is inconsistent with a zoning law limiting use of the property.[174] A lease may also be held terminated if a change in the law makes a previously lawful use of the property unlawful.[175]

§10.4.4 *Landlord's Remedies*

Remedial issues

When the tenant breaches the lease agreement either by failing to pay rent or breaching other material terms in the agreement, the landlord has a variety of possible remedies. Similar remedies are available if the tenant wrongfully holds over after the lease ends.

Holding the tenant to a new tenancy

First, the landlord may seek to recover possession of the property from the breaching tenant. Alternatively, instead of removing the tenant, the landlord may instead seek to bind the tenant to a new leasehold, either on the same terms as the old one, or on different terms. The question here is whether the landlord should have the power to bind the tenant to a new lease without the tenant's express consent and, if so, what the terms of that lease would be.

Availability of self-help

Second, if the landlord seeks to recover possession, a primary issue is whether the landlord may engage in *self-help* by physically barring the tenant from the premises and removing her belongings or whether the landlord must instead use court proceedings to remove the holdover tenant.

Duty to mitigate damages

Third, the landlord is likely to be interested in obtaining back rent from a tenant who wrongfully failed to pay the rent owed. The landlord may also wish to obtain the fair rental value of the property during the time when a holdover tenant wrongfully occupies the premises. When the tenant stops paying rent, the landlord is entitled to sue immediately for damages. However, the issue arises whether the landlord may, instead, choose to wait until the end of the lease and sue the tenant for the remaining rent. The landlord may not be entitled to do this if the contract doctrine applies that obligates the promisee under the contract to mitigate damages by rerenting the premises rather than leaving them idle for the rest of the lease term.

Possession contingent on paying rent

§10.4.4.1 Forfeiture (Landlord's Recovery of Possession). Traditionally, breach of the tenant's obligation to pay rent did not result in a forfeiture of the tenancy unless the lease agreement expressly provided for forfeiture. Because the landlord's and tenant's covenants were independent, the landlord's remedy was to sue for damages. However, state statutes expressly make the continuation of the tenancy contingent on the tenant's payment of rent, thereby entitling

[174] Robert S. Schoshinski, *American Law of Landlord and Tenant* §5:12, at 261-262 (1980). *See, e.g., Howard Opera House Ass'n v. Urban Outfitters, Inc.*, 322 F.3d 125 (2d Cir. 2003) (retail store that violates local noise ordinance breaches lease term requiring tenant to comply with "all applicable laws"). *But see 12 Havemeyer Place Co., LLC v. Gordon*, 820 A.2d 299, 309 (Conn. App. Ct. 2003) ("[W]e hold that the violation of the zoning laws with regard to the parking required by the site plan was not sufficient to render the lease illegal as against public policy.").

[175] Dale A. Whitman et al., *The Law of Property* §6.28, at 223-224 (4th ed. 2019).

landlords to recover possession if the tenant fails to pay rent when due.[176] In addition, most written leases so provide.[177] Summary process statutes in every state allow the landlord to recover possession from the tenant if the tenant holds over after the end of the lease or fails to pay the rent when due. More broadly, under the modern doctrine of dependent covenants, courts are very likely to understand the landlord's obligation to grant possessory rights to the tenant to be dependent on the tenant's continued payment of rent; default on the tenant's part therefore entitles the landlord to recover possession.[178] Indeed, the *Uniform Residential Landlord and Tenant Act* provides that breach of a material term by either party entitles the other to terminate the arrangement.[179]

Relief from forfeiture

Many courts will provide equitable relief from forfeiture of the tenancy if the tenant pays the rent owed within a reasonable period.[180] The Connecticut Supreme Court held that the "equitable principle barring forfeitures may apply to summary process actions for nonpayment of rent if: (1) the tenant's breach was not willful or grossly negligent; (2) upon eviction the tenant will suffer a loss wholly disproportionate to the injury to the landlord; and (3) the landlord's injury is reparable."[181] Thus, even if the tenant has failed to pay the rent when due, the court may deny the landlord the right to recover possession if the tenant cures the default in a timely manner. In addition, it is crucial to note that statutes in most states prohibit the landlord from recovering possession by self-help even in the case of forfeiture, instead obligating the landlord to use court eviction proceedings.[182] Such statutes ordinarily require the landlord to notify the tenant of the default and allow eviction to proceed only if the tenant has not cured the default within a set period.[183] They may very well also protect the tenant from dispossession if the tenant pays the back rent owed (with interest) while the eviction proceedings are still pending.[184]

Waiver

The landlord may also be held to have *waived* her right to recover possession if she accepts rent checks from the tenant after the default.[185]

Recovery of possession from holdover tenant

§10.4.4.2 HOLDING THE TENANT TO A NEW TENANCY. When the tenant holds over after the termination of the tenancy, the landlord may be interested in recovering possession from the tenant. If the landlord chooses to evict the tenant, the landlord may recover possession from her, usually

[176] Robert S. Schoshinski, *American Law of Landlord and Tenant* §6:1, at 377 (1980).

[177] *Id.*

[178] *Id.* at §6:11, at 411-412. *See* §10.6.3.

[179] *Terry v. Gaslight Square Assocs.*, 897 P.2d 667, 671 (Ariz. Ct. App. 1994); *Cain Partnership, Ltd. v. Pioneer Investment Servs. Co.*, 914 S.W.2d 452, 456 (Tenn. 1996); *Restatement (Second) of Property (Landlord and Tenant)* §§7.1 & 13.1 (1977); Robert S. Schoshinski, *American Law of Landlord and Tenant* §6:1, at 229 (Cum. Supp. 1999).

[180] *Uniform Residential Landlord and Tenant Act* §§4.101, 4.102, 4.107, 4.201 & 4.202.

[181] Robert S. Schoshinski, *American Law of Landlord and Tenant* §6:2, at 392 (1980).

[182] *Cumberland Farms, Inc. v. Dairy Mart, Inc.*, 627 A.2d 386 (Conn. 1993).

[183] *See* §10.4.4.3.

[184] Robert S. Schoshinski, *American Law of Landlord and Tenant* §6:4, at 397 (1980).

[185] *Id.*

by summary eviction proceedings.[186] In such a lawsuit, the landlord would be entitled to recover the fair rental value of the premises during the wrongful occupation, usually measured by the rental amount under the prior agreement.[187] Some statutes provide for double damages for wrongful holdover.[188]

Holding the tenant to a new leasehold

The landlord may instead be interested in maintaining the leasehold relationship with the tenant and may attempt to treat the wrongful hold-over as an offer on the part of the tenant to enter a new leasehold with the landlord. The landlord may therefore wish to hold the holdover tenant to a new term or periodic tenancy, entitling the landlord to recover rent from the tenant on the same terms as before. The landlord must therefore elect whether to evict the holdover tenant or hold her to a new tenancy.[189] If the landlord chooses to hold the tenant to a new tenancy, many states used to allow the landlord to hold the tenant under a term of years to a new term.[190] Some states may still adhere to this rule, although it now seems to be the minority approach.[191] The more modern approach is to treat the new tenancy as a periodic tenancy.[192] Some states presume the term of the period of the new tenancy is determined by the prior term of years,[193] while others measure the period on the basis of the manner in which rent was paid under the old lease arrangement.[194]

Self-help generally outlawed

§10.4.4.3 Self-Help v. Summary Process. When the tenant holds over after the lease terminates or when the tenant breaches the agreement by failing to pay rent when due, the landlord may wish to recover possession of the property. In that case, the primary issue is *how* to recover possession. Under the older law, the landlord could engage in *self-help,* barring the tenant from the premises. Almost all states today outlaw self-help, instead obligating landlords to use court proceedings (eviction) to recover possession.[195] Every state has a statute, often called *forced entry and detainer* or *summary process* laws, that enable the landlord to recover possession in a court proceeding that allows the landlord to recover

[186] *Id.* at §6:2, at 387. *See Uniform Residential Landlord and Tenant Act* §4.204 (providing that acceptance of rent with knowledge of the tenant's breach waives the landlord's right to terminate the lease); Robert S. Schoshinski, *American Law of Landlord and Tenant* §2:24, at 78 (1980).

[187] *Booker v. Trizec Properties, Inc.*, 363 S.E.2d 13 (Ga. Ct. App. 1987).

[188] Miss. Code §89-7-25 (tenant is liable for double rent for the period of the holdover); Wis. Stat. §704.27 (double damages).

[189] Robert S. Schoshinski, *American Law of Landlord and Tenant* §2:23, at 71 (1980).

[190] *Id.* at §2:23, at 71-72.

[191] *Mattas Motors, Inc. v. Heritage Homes of Nebraska, Inc.*, 749 P.2d 458 (Colo. App. 1987); Robert S. Schoshinski, *American Law of Landlord and Tenant* §2:23, at 73 (1980).

[192] *Karz v. Mecham*, 174 Cal. Rptr. 310 (Ct. App. 1981); Robert S. Schoshinski, *American Law of Landlord and Tenant* §2:23, at 73 (1980).

[193] *See Schartz v. Foster*, 805 P.2d 505 (Kan. Ct. App. 1991) (applying Kan. Stat. §58-2502).

[194] Cal. Civ. Code §1945; Mont. Code §70-26-204; Robert S. Schoshinski, *American Law of Landlord and Tenant* §2:23, at 74-75 (1980).

[195] *Tantaro v. Common Ground Cmty. Hous. Dev. Fund, Inc.*, 147 A.D.3d 684 (N.Y. App. Div. 2017) (noting the requirement for court process for tenants, but noting that visitors are not similarly protected); *Berg v. Wiley*, 264 N.W.2d 145 (Minn. 1978) (outlawing self-help); Robert S. Schoshinski, *American Law of Landlord and Tenant* §6:5, at 400-401 (1980).

possession expeditiously.[196] In most states, the landlord is statutorily obligated to use these procedures and not to engage in self-help to regain possession when the tenant has breached material lease terms or has wrongfully held over after the termination of the tenancy. The landlord is not entitled to simply place the tenant's belongings on the street and change the locks on the door.

Trespass and recovery of possession

Note that two different issues are involved here. If the landlord enters the property without the tenant's permission, the landlord has committed a trespass, unless the lease agreement reserves the right to enter for specified purposes such as making an inspection and completing repairs. If the landlord is entitled to use self-help when the tenant breaches the lease, then the landlord's entry will not constitute a trespass but a privileged entry. If the landlord is not entitled to use self-help, then an entry by the landlord would constitute a trespass despite the tenant's breach of the agreement. The second issue is whether the landlord is entitled not only to enter the property, but also to exclude the tenant. As noted above, most states now outlaw self-help, relegating the landlord to court eviction proceedings to recover possession.

▷ CONVERSION OF PERSONAL ITEMS **HARD CASE ◀**

In *Chryar v. Wolf*,[197] a landlord sued to evict two tenants for failure to pay rent. Before the eviction proceeding, when the tenants were out of town, the landlord removed the tenants' personal property from the premises and placed it on the street with a sign saying "Free Take." When the tenants returned, they were evicted by the court and then brought a lawsuit against the landlord to recover damages for the value of the property he had taken. The court held that the landlord had wrongfully taken the property and awarded damages for the value of the property that was lost. The property was of a personal nature, including "photographs, journals, a family Bible, a copy of the Koran, a chessboard, a military album, a military jacket, a pair of military boots, various certificates documenting personal achievements, and personal journals and short novels one of the tenants was writing." The landlord argued that these items had little or no market value but the appellate court accepted the tenants' argument that they had sentimental value and upheld the trial court determination that they were reasonably valued at $3,850. When damages are awarded for "outrageous conduct, otherwise known as intentional or reckless infliction of emotional distress," damages can be granted for the emotional value imbued in the items taken.[198] The court rejected the landlord's argument that such claims were too hard to

---

[196] Robert S. Schoshinski, *American Law of Landlord and Tenant* §6:5, at 400 (1980).

[197] 21 P.3d 428 (Colo. App. 2000).

[198] *Accord, Campins v. Capels*, 461 N.E.2d 712, 720 (Ind. Ct. App. 1984); *Birchler v. Castello Land Co.*, 915 P.2d 564 (Wash. Ct. App. 1996), *aff'd*, 942 P.2d 968 (Wash. 1997). *But see Landers v. Municipality of Anchorage*, 915 P.2d 614, 617-618 (Alaska 1996) (no damages for sentimental value of lost personal items).

value, noting that a failure to increase damages in such cases would not adequately deter or compensate this kind of wrong. ◀

Is self-help ever allowed?

Some states allow self-help in the context of commercial leases but not residential leases.[199] Some courts have also held that the tenant may waive the right to the protection of the summary process laws and give the landlord the right to use self-help. In those states, lease terms that authorize the use of self-help are enforceable, making the tenant's right to be evicted only by court proceedings disclaimable.[200] The trend, however, is to hold such clauses void on the ground that they are inconsistent with the policy underlying the forcible entry and detainer statutes.[201] The courts that do enforce self-help lease provisions are likely to limit their availability to the commercial context, relegating residential landlords to court proceedings.[202] A few recent decisions that have authorized self-help have been overridden by statute.[203]

Self-help must be peaceable

Where self-help is allowed, it must be "peaceable" rather than "forcible."[204] In general, this has been held to mean voluntary transfer of possession back from the tenant to the landlord. Any force, or even threat of force, use of "ruse or stratagem," or "entry through an open window, by use of a passkey, by picking a lock, or by removing doors, and by padlocking or changing locks have been held to be forcible."[205]

Summary process

Summary process statutes were passed in the latter half of the nineteenth century to enable landlords to recover possession expeditiously of rented property from defaulting tenants.[206] These statutes replaced ejectment as the preferred method of recovering possession in the case of leaseholds. At the same time, by giving tenants notice and an opportunity to be heard, they provided tenants with due process and protected them from wrongful dispossession.[207] Today every state has a "summary process" statute (also called "summary proceeding" or "summary ejectment") allowing relatively quick judicial proceedings for landlords to evict tenants who have failed to pay rent or breached other material terms in the lease agreement.[208] The statute provides for trial dates with three to five days in some cases and

[199] *Watson v. Brown*, 686 P.2d 12 (Haw. 1984).

[200] *Rucker v. Wynn*, 441 S.E.2d 417 (Ga. Ct. App. 1994); *Jovana Spaghetti House, Inc. v. Heritage Co. of Massena*, 592 N.Y.S.2d 879 (App. Div. 1993).

[201] *See McCrory v. Johnson*, 755 S.W.2d 566, 572-573 (Ark. 1988); *Thomas v. Papadelis*, 476 N.E.2d 726, 728 (Ohio Ct. App. 1984); Robert S. Schoshinski, *American Law of Landlord and Tenant* §6:6, at 403 (1980).

[202] *See Watson v. Brown*, 686 P.2d 12 (Haw. 1984).

[203] *See Spinks v. Taylor*, 266 S.E.2d 857 (N.C. Ct. App.), *aff'd in part and mod. in part on other grounds, rev'd in part on other grounds*, 278 S.E.2d 501 (N.C. 1981), *overridden by statute as noted in Stanley v. Moore*, 454 S.E.2d 225 (N.C. 1995) (interpreting N.C. Gen. Stat. §42-25.6).

[204] *Klosterman v. Hickel Investment Co.*, 821 P.2d 118, 122 (Alaska 1991); Robert S. Schoshinski, *American Law of Landlord and Tenant* §6:7, at 404 (1980).

[205] Robert S. Schoshinski, *American Law of Landlord and Tenant* §6:7, at 404-405 (1980).

[206] *Id.* at §6:10, at 408.

[207] *Id.* at §6:10, at 409.

[208] *See, e.g.*, Cal. Code Civ. Proc. §§1159 to 1179a; Mass. Gen. Laws ch. 239, §§1-16; N.Y. Real Prop. Acts. §§701 to 768. Note that Massachusetts has amended its summary eviction statute to provide a process for tenants under certain circumstances to have their eviction records sealed. Mass. Gen. Laws ch. 239, §16.

seven to twelve days in others.[209] As noted above, in most states these methods of recovering possession are exclusive, self-help having been outlawed. In some states, the remedy is part of an older form of statute, the "forcible entry and detainer" or "unlawful detainer" statutes that were passed to prohibit "forcible" recovery of property while allowing "peaceable" self-help.[210]

Issues that can be litigated

Until recently, the issues that could be litigated in a summary proceeding were strictly limited to those related to the landlord's right to recover possession.[211] Most statutes also allow adjudication of the landlord's claim for unpaid back rent. Until recently, most courts did not allow adjudication of any claims by the tenant against the landlord based on the landlord's failure to comply with repair or maintenance obligations. Such defenses were not allowed either because landlords had no such affirmative obligations or the landlord's obligations were independent of the tenant's duty to pay rent; in that case, a breach by the landlord would not entitle the tenant to stop paying rent and the landlord would be entitled to possession regardless of any breach by the landlord. In recent years, however, most courts have held that the tenant's obligation to pay rent is contingent on the landlord's compliance with an implied warranty of habitability, so that the landlord will not be entitled to possession if the tenant's failure to pay rent is premised on the landlord's breach of the implied warranty.[212]

Due process issues in summary proceedings

The Supreme Court held in *Lindsey v. Normet*[213] that it was not a violation of due process for the legislature to deprive the tenant of the right to litigate issues related to breaches by the landlord in summary proceedings if the legislature wanted to exclude such claims. Thus, if the state wishes to relegate tenants to independent suits against the landlord for breach of the implied warranty of habitability, the Supreme Court has said it is constitutionally permissible to do so.

Stay of execution

Many summary process statutes authorize judges to stay the execution of the judgment for up to several months to give the tenant time to find a new place to live and to move.[214] Such stays are ordinarily contingent on the tenant's payment of rent in the interim.

Landlord's remedies when tenant stops paying rent and moves out early

§10.4.4.4 Surrender, Reletting, Damages, and the Duty to Mitigate Damages. When a tenant stops paying rent and moves out before the end of the lease term, the landlord has the right to sue to recover possession as well as back rent owed and the costs of finding a replacement tenant. The landlord has several other possible remedies as well, including (1) accepting the tenant's surrender of the lease; (2) reletting the premises

[209] Ariz. Rev. Stat. §12-1176 (five days); Cal. Code Civ. Proc. §1167 (five days); Wash. Rev. Code §§59.12.070 & 59.18.370 (seven to thirty days); Robert S. Schoshinski, *American Law of Landlord and Tenant* §6:14, at 416-417 (1980).

[210] *See* Ariz. Rev. Stat. §§12-1171 to 12-1183; Ky. Rev. Stat. §§383.200 to 383.285; Robert S. Schoshinski, *American Law of Landlord and Tenant* §6:10, at 409 (1980).

[211] Robert S. Schoshinski, *American Law of Landlord and Tenant* §6:17, at 421-425 (1980).

[212] *Id.* at §6:18, at 423. *See* §10.6.3.

[213] 405 U.S. 56 (1972).

[214] *See, e.g.*, Mass. Gen. Laws ch. 239, §9 (stay of up to six months); N.J. Stat. §2A:42-10.1 (execution of judgment may be stayed for up to six months if alternative housing is not available); Robert S. Schoshinski, *American Law of Landlord and Tenant* §6:19, at 427-428 (1980).

on the tenant's account; and (3) suing for damages. A fourth remedy might entitle the landlord to wait, allow the rent to accrue until the end of the lease term, and then sue the tenant for the entire rent at the end of the term. This remedy may be available in some states, but there is a strong trend to place a duty on the landlord to "mitigate damages" by rerenting the property rather than allowing the property to remain vacant for so long. The imposition of this duty would limit the landlord to the damages she would have suffered had she acted reasonably to find a replacement tenant.

Accepting the tenant's surrender

The first solution is for the landlord to treat the tenant's abandonment as an offer to terminate the tenancy. In effect, the tenant wants to renegotiate the contract and have both parties agree to release the other from the promises they had made. If the landlord "accepts the tenant's surrender," the leasehold will terminate, as will all obligations under it owed by either party to the other. The landlord is then free to lease the property to someone else.[215] However, the parties have legal rights and remedies for breaches that occurred prior to surrender; the landlord may sue the tenant for back rent, for example.[216]

Reletting on the tenant's account

Alternatively, the landlord may refuse to accept the tenant's surrender of the lease. Instead, the landlord might seek to find another person who could move in and pay the rent in the tenant's stead. Under this arrangement, the landlord will "relet the property on the tenant's account."[217] This means the landlord is treating the tenant's abandonment as an implied offer to end the relationship, but the landlord refuses to accept that offer, thereby maintaining the tenant's contractual obligation to pay the rent for the rest of the lease term. At the same time, the landlord treats the tenant's conduct as an implied representation that the tenant wishes to be relieved of rent liability and authorizing the landlord to reduce the tenant's potential rent obligation by finding a replacement tenant who will pay rent in place of the original tenant. Under this arrangement, the original tenant remains liable for the rent if the landlord cannot find a replacement or if the replacement defaults in the rental payments. The tenant also remains liable for the difference if the new rent is lower than the old rent.

Suing for damages

If the landlord accepts the tenant's surrender, the landlord may also sue immediately for *damages* based on the tenant's anticipatory breach of the rest of the lease agreement. The breach is "anticipatory" because the rent is not due all at once, so technically there has been no default or breach until the tenant fails to pay each rental installment as it comes due. When the tenant unequivocally demonstrates an intent not to pay rent ever again, the courts will allow the landlord to treat the breach as a breach of the whole agreement, including a breach of the obligation to pay rent in the future, and allow the landlord to sue immediately for damages for breach of the entire contract (not just back rent payments that were not paid when they came due). Such damages are measured by the difference between the reserved rent and the fair rental value of the premises — *i.e.*, the amount

[215] *Bargain Mart, Inc. v. Mordechai Lipkis*, 561 A.2d 1365 (Conn. 1989); *Vaswani v. Wohletz*, 396 S.E.2d 593 (Ga. Ct. App. 1990); Robert S. Schoshinski, *American Law of Landlord and Tenant* §10:2, at 638 (1980).

[216] Robert S. Schoshinski, *American Law of Landlord and Tenant* §10:2, at 638-639 (1980).

[217] *Id.* at §10:12, at 675.

the landlord would lose if the landlord rerented the premises at lower, prevailing rent rates. This measure of damages assumes that the landlord will attempt to relet the premises and that the only loss suffered by the landlord is the difference between the rent the landlord would have received and the rent the landlord does receive by reletting the premises.

Rent acceleration clauses

Some leases provide for "acceleration" of the rent, making all the remaining rent for the rest of the term due upon default. Courts generally treat such provisions as liquidated damages and refuse to enforce them if the amount far exceeds a reasonable estimate of the damages upon default.[218] Alternatively, courts give the tenant a credit for the rent the landlord actually receives by reletting the premises.[219]

Suing for rent as it accrues v. duty to mitigate damages

Traditionally, the landlord had a fourth alternative: waiting until the end of the lease and suing for the entire amount of rent owed under the lease agreement.[220] However, increasingly, this possibility has been foreclosed in almost every state by court cases and statutes that impose on the landlord a duty to mitigate damages by reletting the premises.[221] There is a strong modern trend to impose on the landlord a duty to mitigate damages either by common law decision or statute.[222] This duty requires the landlord to make reasonable efforts to find a new tenant.[223] Note that it is not a duty in the sense that the landlord *must* mitigate damages; it simply means

[218] *See HealthSouth Rehabilitation Corp. v. Falcon Mgmt. Co.*, 799 So. 2d 177, 183 (Ala. 2001); *NPS, LLC v. Minihane*, 886 N.E.2d 670 (Mass. 2008); *Cummings Properties, LLC v. Nat'l Communications Corp.*, 869 N.E.2d 617 (Mass. 2007). *Cf. Harbor Island Holdings, L.L.C. v. Kim*, 132 Cal. Rptr. 2d 406 (Ct. App. 2003) (lease provision for double rent in event of tenant breach void as an illegal penalty).

[219] *See Horizon Medical Group v. City Center of Charlotte County, Ltd.*, 779 So. 2d 545 (Fla. Dist. Ct. App. 2001).

[220] A small number of states may retain this rule. *See* Fla. Stat. §83.595; *Ex parte Kaschak*, 681 So. 2d 197, 200 (Ala. 1996) (holding that there is no duty to mitigate in residential leases); *Crestline Center v. Hinton*, 567 So. 2d 393, 396 (Ala. Civ. App. 1990) (commercial); *Weingarten/Arkansas, Inc. v. ABC Interstate Theatres, Inc.*, 811 S.W.2d 295 (Ark. 1991); *International Commission on English in the Liturgy v. Schwartz*, 573 A.2d 1303 (D.C. 1990); *Love v. McDevitt*, 152 S.E.2d 705, 706 (Ga. Ct. App. 1966) (residential); *Lamb v. Decatur Federal Savings & Loan Ass'n*, 411 S.E.2d 527, 530 (Ga. Ct. App. 1991) (commercial); *Fifty Assocs. v. Berger Dry Good Co., Inc.*, 176 N.E. 643 (Mass. 1931); *Markoe v. Naiditch & Sons*, 226 N.W.2d 289, 291 (Minn. 1975) (residential and commercial); *Alsup v. Banks*, 9 So. 895, 895 (Miss. 1891) (residential); *Holy Properties, Ltd. v. Kenneth Cole Products, Inc.*, 661 N.E.2d 694, 696 (N.Y. 1995) (commercial); *Stonehedge Square Ltd. Partnership v. Movie Merchants, Inc.*, 715 A.2d 1082 (Pa. 1998) (commercial); *Arbenz v. Exley, Watkins & Co.*, 44 S.E. 149, 151 (W. Va. 1903) (commercial).

[221] *Austin Hill Country Realty, Inc. v. Palisades Plaza, Inc.*, 948 S.W.2d 293, 296 (Tex. 1997) (noting that 42 states and the District of Columbia impose a duty to mitigate damages on landlords either in commercial or residential tenancies or both). New York has imposed the duty to mitigate on residential landlords by statute, N.Y. Real Prop. §227-e, settling the question of the duty to mitigate for residential leases, but courts there continue to note that the duty does not extend to commercial leases. *See, e.g., Mansion Realty LLC v. 656 6th Ave Gym LLC*, 190 N.Y.S.3d 259, 265 n.5 (Sup. Ct. N.Y. Cty. 2023).

[222] *Lennon v. United States Theatre Corp.*, 920 F.2d 996 (D.C. Cir. 1990); *D.R. Mobile Home Rentals v. Frost*, 545 N.W.2d 302 (Iowa 1996); *Properties Investment Group v. JBA, Inc.*, 495 N.W.2d 624 (Neb. 1993); *New Towne Ltd. Partnership v. Pier I Imports (U.S.), Inc.*, 680 N.E.2d 644 (Ohio Ct. App. 1996); *O'Brien v. Black*, 648 A.2d 1374, 1376 (Vt. 1994); Robert S. Schoshinski, *American Law of Landlord and Tenant* §10:12, at 677 (1980).

[223] *E.g., 14 E. 4th St. Unit 509 LLC v. Toporek*, 203 A.D.3d 17, 23-24 (N.Y. App. Div. 2022).

that, if the landlord does not mitigate damages, the amount of damages the landlord can recover from the tenant will be reduced by the amount of damages that would have been avoided had the landlord complied with the duty. Although the *Restatement (Second)* adheres to the traditional view that landlords have no duty to mitigate damages,[224] the *Uniform Residential Landlord and Tenant Act*, adopted in about half the states, does impose such a duty on the landlord in the case of residential tenancies.[225] In most states, the duty to mitigate damages is nondisclaimable, as well.[226] The cases conflict on the question of whether the burden of proving that the landlord did or did not mitigate damages is on the tenant or the landlord.[227]

▶ HARD CASE

▷ DUTY TO MITIGATE DAMAGES

Arguments for and against the duty to mitigate damages in residential leases illustrate interesting tensions within both contract and property law. In *Sommer v. Kridel*,[228] for example, a tenant backed out of a two-year lease about two weeks after signing the agreement when his impending marriage plans failed. Rather than accepting the tenant's surrender of the lease, the landlord failed to relet the premises, even when a third party indicated that she was ready, willing, and able to rent the apartment. Instead, the landlord held the tenant to the contract, left the apartment vacant, and sued more than a year later for 16 months' rent. The Supreme Court of New Jersey held that leases should be treated like ordinary contracts and that contract law generally imposes a duty on plaintiffs to mitigate damages by acting to minimize the damage caused by the breach, usually by "covering" or finding someone else who can fulfill the promisee's needs.

Landlord's argument against a duty to mitigate damages

The argument against a duty to mitigate damages is that the landlord has bargained for a particular arrangement that includes the right to receive a certain rental income from a particular tenant in exchange for relinquishing possession of the property. Contracts create expectations, and when the courts enforce contracts, they effectively create property rights in expectations. People are free to make contracts, but once they make them they are not free to break them. The institution of freedom of contract not only includes the liberty to make agreements but also guarantees security to the promisee that the promisor will do what she promised to do — or pay damages to make the promisee whole. Once the contract is

[224] *Restatement (Second) of Property (Landlord and Tenant)* §12.1(3) & cmt. i (1977).

[225] *Uniform Residential Landlord and Tenant Act* §4.203(c) (1972).

[226] *Drutman Realty Co. Ltd. Partnership v. Jindo Corp.*, 865 F. Supp. 1093, 1100 (S.D.N.Y. 1994) (applying N.J. law); Robert S. Schoshinski, *American Law of Landlord and Tenant* §10:12, at 461 (Cum. Supp. 1999). *But see Sylva Shops Ltd. P'ship v. Hibbard*, 623 S.E.2d 785 (N.C. Ct. App. 2006) (duty to mitigate damages can be waived).

[227] Robert S. Schoshinski, *American Law of Landlord and Tenant* §10:12, at 680 (1980). *Compare St. Louis North Venture v. P & L Enterprises, Inc.*, 116 F.3d 262, 265 (7th Cir. 1997) (burden is on the landlord) *with Del E. Webb Realty & Mgmt. Co. v. Wessbecker*, 628 P.2d 114, 116 (Colo. App. 1980) (burden is on tenant); *Middagh v. Stanal Sound Ltd.*, 452 N.W.2d 260 (Neb. 1990) (burden on tenant).

[228] 378 A.2d 767 (N.J. 1977).

made, the promisee has a right to performance by the promisor; this right of security means that the promisor is not free to break her promise without legal consequences. Landlords might have legitimate interests in looking to the original tenant rather than third parties to fulfill the obligation to pay rent. Having multiple tenants for one unit increases the vulnerability of the landlord to the possibility of nonpayment of rent. Moreover, landlords may legitimately not want to have to face the need to look for new tenants constantly. The tenant could attempt to induce the landlord to accept the tenant's proffered surrender of the tenancy, but if the landlord refuses to accept, we have evidence that the value of enforcing the contract to the landlord is greater than the value the tenant places on the right to get out of the contract. It would therefore both be inefficient and would violate the landlord's legitimate interests in enforcing the agreement to allow the tenant to escape his contractual obligations.

Tenant's argument for a duty to mitigate damages

The counterargument is that the tenant has a significant liberty inter est in being able to move out before the end of the lease term. As long as the landlord's financial interests are fully protected, the landlord should be indifferent as to whether the rent comes from the original tenant or an equally creditworthy substitute. If the tenant can move out and find a replacement, the landlord's financial interests can be fully protected while protecting the power of the tenant to move. This result might be considered an "efficient" breach of contract because it fully protects the landlord's property rights in the promise (the landlord's economic expectations based on the tenant's contractual undertakings), while also giving the tenant the freedom to get out of an arrangement that, although in the tenant's best interests at the time he signed, is no longer in the tenant's interest at this later time. In addition, a third party who wants to move into the apartment can be accommodated, promoting her welfare as well. ◀

▷ COMMERCIAL TENANCIES **HARD CASE ◀**

Some states have extended the duty to mitigate damages to commercial tenancies on the ground that they should be governed by ordinary contract principles that encourage parties to avoid damages by acting to protect their interests when a promisor breaches.[229] By lowering recoverable damages, such a rule also grants businesses the power to get out of existing contracts when it is in their interest to do so while protecting the landlord's reasonable financial expectations. However, other courts resist the trend, holding that a commercial landlord has no duty to mitigate damages when a tenant abandons the premises before the end of the lease term.[230] For example, the Pennsylvania Supreme Court found that the traditional

[229] *Frenchtown Square Partnership v. Lemstone, Inc.*, 791 N.E.2d 417 (Ohio 2003); *Austin Hill Country Realty, Inc. v. Palisades Plaza, Inc.*, 948 S.W.2d 293, 296 (Tex. 1997).

[230] *Stonehedge v. Square Limited Partnership v. Movie Merchants, Inc.*, 715 A.2d 1082 (Pa. 1998); *Holiday Furniture Factory Outlet Corp. v. State of Florida Dep't of Corrections*, 852 So. 2d 926 (Fla. Dist. Ct. App. 2003).

rule avoided the complexities involved in determining whether a landlord acted reasonably in attempting to mitigate damages. Moreover, "there is a fundamental unfairness in allowing the breaching tenant to require the nonbreaching landlord to mitigate the damages caused by the tenant. This unfairness takes the form of depriving the landlord of the benefit of his bargain, forcing the landlord to expend time, energy, and money to respond to the tenant's breach, and putting the landlord at risk of further expense of lawsuits and counterclaims in a matter that he justifiably assumed was closed."[231] ◀

▶ HARD CASE ▷ ACCELERATION CLAUSES

Some landlords attempt to contract around the duty to mitigate damages by including a term by which the tenant waives that right or through an "acceleration clause" making the rest of the rent due if the tenant abandons the premises or otherwise breaches the lease in a material way. Some courts enforce such provisions on the ground that the parties voluntarily agreed to them; however, they also police the term and will not enforce the clause if it constitutes a "penalty" or if the amount owed is "unconscionable."[232] Reviewing the clause to determine whether it is a reasonable assessment of damages effectively makes the right to mitigate nondisclaimable. ◀

§10.5 Landlord's Obligations and Tenant's Remedies

§10.5.1 Landlord's Duty to Deliver Possession

Duty to deliver right to possession

A lease is a transfer of possessory rights from landlord to tenant. What happens if a prior tenant fails to move out? Traditionally, the tenant had no remedy against the landlord.[233] The landlord, after all, gave the tenant the *right* to possess the property, and it is not the landlord's fault the old tenant has wrongfully held over. The tenant's only recourse was to sue to eject the holdover tenant. This remedy is not very useful, however. Ejectment proceedings can take quite some time. A more useful remedy would be summary process, but those statutes are often worded to give landlords the power to recover possession from breaching tenants and do not extend the same rights to new tenants seeking to evict prior tenants. In addition, a tenant who cannot move in because of a holdover tenant may need some place to live and may prefer to get out of the deal altogether and not be relegated to a lawsuit against the prior tenant.

Duty to deliver actual possession

For these reasons, the law has moved strongly in the direction of requiring the landlord not only to deliver to the new tenant the *right* to

[231] *Stonehedge Square Limited Partnership v. Movie Merchants, Inc.*, 715 A.2d 1082, 1085 (Pa. 1998).

[232] *Aurora Business Park Ass'n v. Albert, Inc.*, 548 N.W.2d 153 (Iowa 1996); *Restatement (Second) of Property (Landlord and Tenant)* §12.1 cmt. k (1977).

[233] Robert S. Schoshinski, *American Law of Landlord and Tenant* §3:1, at 87-89 (1980).

possess the property, but to deliver *actual* possession of the premises.[234] A majority of states now hold that the landlord has a duty to evict a holdover tenant or otherwise ensure that a new tenant can actually take possession. In effect, the landlord has an implied covenant to deliver actual possession of the premises to the tenant.[235] The landlord's failure to deliver actual possession will constitute a breach of the lease, entitling the new tenant to stop paying rent and to back out of the lease if she wishes to do so.[236]

§10.5.2 Security Deposits

Regulation of security deposits

Most landlords require tenants to pay an extra month or two of rent at the beginning of the lease to ensure that the landlord has a fund from which to make repairs on the premises caused by the tenant's conduct and to prevent the tenant from leaving without paying the last month's rent. Statutes in most states regulate the landlord's use of security deposits, often by limiting the amount of the security deposit the landlord can lawfully demand and by requiring landlords to deposit them in interest-bearing accounts.[237]

§10.5.3 Actual Eviction

Implied covenant of quiet enjoyment

Because leaseholds are transfers of possessory rights from landlords to tenants, landlords necessarily breach the lease agreement if they interfere with the tenant's possession by barring the tenant from the premises or otherwise physically excluding the tenant from the property. Every lease has an *implied covenant of quiet enjoyment* by which the landlord promises not to interfere with the tenant's possession, use, and enjoyment of the property.[238] If the landlord physically excludes the tenant from the property by changing the locks on the doors, blocking entry, removing the tenant's belongings, or otherwise preventing occupation of the property, the courts will hold that the landlord has "actually evicted" the tenant.[239] The tenant immediately is relieved of the obligation to pay rent and can choose to terminate the lease and move out.[240] Alternatively, the tenant can sue for damages and injunctive relief ordering the landlord to stop barring the tenant from possession.[241]

[234] *Moore v. Cameron Parish School Board*, 563 So. 2d 347 (La. Ct. App. 1990); *Restatement (Second) of Property (Landlord and Tenant)* §6.2 (1977).
[235] Dale A. Whitman et al., *The Law of Property* §6.21, at 214-215 (4th ed. 2019). *See also Uniform Residential Landlord and Tenant Act* §2.103; N.Y. Real Prop. §223-a.
[236] Robert S. Schoshinski, *American Law of Landlord and Tenant* §3:2, at 90 (1980).
[237] Dale A. Whitman et al., *The Law of Property* §6.58, at 293 (4th ed. 2019).
[238] *Versatile Metals, Inc. v. Union Corp.*, 693 F. Supp. 1563 (E.D. Pa. 1988) (enforcing Pennsylvania law); *Gardner v. Jones*, 464 So. 2d 1144 (Miss. 1985); Robert S. Schoshinski, *American Law of Landlord and Tenant* §3:3, at 94-95 (1980).
[239] *Turks Head Realty Trust v. Shearson Lehman Hutton, Inc.*, 736 F. Supp. 422, 428 (D.R.I. 1990) (changing locks is actual eviction under Rhode Island law); *In re Jewelcor Inc.*, 190 B.R. 532 (Bankr. M.D. Pa. 1995); *Olin v. Goehler*, 694 P.2d 1129, 1132 (Wash. Ct. App. 1985) (placing new locks on the doors constitutes actual eviction).
[240] Robert S. Schoshinski, *American Law of Landlord and Tenant* §3:4, at 96 (1980).
[241] Dale A. Whitman et al., *The Law of Property* §6.32, at 226 (4th ed. 2019).

Partial actual eviction

If the landlord bars the tenant from part of the premises, this constitutes a *partial actual eviction* and relieves the tenant of the rent obligation completely while the eviction occurs.[242] In addition, the tenant may remain in possession of the portion of the property from which the tenant has not been excluded.[243] However, the *Restatement (Second)* provides that the proper remedy is a rent reduction to reflect the partial eviction rather than a complete rent abatement, at least where the tenant chooses to continue occupying the property.[244]

§10.5.4 Anti-eviction Laws

Landlord's right to refuse to renew term of years and to terminate periodic and at-will tenancies

Landlords are generally entitled to terminate periodic tenancies and tenancies-at-will whenever they wish, as long as they comply with statutory notice requirements and use statutorily mandated court proceedings to recover possession. Similarly, landlords may choose not to renew tenancies under year-long leases or other leaseholds held as a term of years. The *Fair Housing Act*[245] prohibits landlords from evicting tenants or refusing to renew leaseholds for racially discriminatory reasons. Landlords may also be disempowered from recovering possession if they are violating the state housing code or otherwise violating the implied warranty of habitability.[246] With these exceptions, however, landlords are generally free to refuse to renew existing leaseholds.

Protections against eviction

California, New Jersey, New York, the District of Columbia, and other jurisdictions have general statutes prohibiting landlords from evicting covered tenants unless they can show one of an enumerated list of allowable reasons, such as failure to pay rent or that the landlord wishes to move into the property herself.[247] Connecticut provides such protections to elderly persons or persons with disabilities.[248] New Hampshire and Oregon similarly limit eviction in certain circumstances.[249] Most rent control statutes also prohibit eviction except for good cause.[250] Massachusetts passed a law prohibiting eviction of rent-paying tenants when the landlord loses the property to foreclosure, at least until title to the property passes to a third party other than the foreclosing bank itself.[251]

[242] *Washburn v. 166 East 96th Street Owners Corp.*, 564 N.Y.S.2d 115 (App. Div. 1990); Robert S. Schoshinski, *American Law of Landlord and Tenant* §3:4, at 96 (1980).

[243] Robert S. Schoshinski, *American Law of Landlord and Tenant* §3:4, at 96 (1980).

[244] *Restatement (Second) of Property (Landlord and Tenant)* §§6.1, 11.1 (1977).

[245] 42 U.S.C. §§3601 to 3631. *See* Chapter 12.

[246] *See* §§10.6.2 & 10.6.3.

[247] Cal. Civ. Code §1946.2; D.C. Code §42-3505.01; N.H. Rev. Stat. Ann. §540:2 (2020); N.J. Stat. Ann. §§2A:18-53, 2A:18-61.1; N.Y. Real Prop. Law §§210-218; Or. Rev. Stat. Ann. §90.427 (2020); Vicki Been, Ingrid Gould Ellen & Sophia House, *Laboratories of Regulation: Understanding the Diversity of Rent Regulation Laws*, 46 Fordham Urb. L.J. 1041, 1071-1073 (2019).

[248] Conn. Gen. Stat. §47a-23c. New Jersey also provides special protection for elderly persons and persons with disabilities by giving them the right to stay even if the landlord wants to recover possession to move into the property herself. N.J. Stat. §§2A:18-61.22 to 21:18-61.39.

[249] N.H. Rev. Stat. §§540:1-a, 540:2; Or. Rev. Stat. §90.427.

[250] Robert S. Schoshinski, *American Law of Landlord and Tenant* §1:1, at 5 (1980).

[251] Mass. Gen. Laws ch. 186A, §§1-6.

Because the COVID-19 pandemic brought major economic challenges to many tenants, and eviction is a recognized public-health risk, the federal government, most states, and many local governments temporarily halted evictions.[252] These provisions were designed to keep tenants housed even as they generally did not relieve tenants of the ultimate obligation to pay rent, which lead many tenants to accrue back rent. The Supreme Court held that the federal Centers for Disease Control and Prevention lacked the statutory authority to mandate a national eviction moratorium,[253] and that New York's moratorium unconstitutionally failed to provide for hearings for landlords to contest tenant assertions of the Act's application.[254] But most other state and local moratoria were upheld against claims that such limitations on the right to evict constituted a taking of the landlord's property, violated due process or the contracts clause, or otherwise.[255]

Eviction moratoria during the pandemic

§10.5.5 Rent Regulation

Many municipalities, at one time or another since the 1970s, have enacted ordinances or by-laws regulating rents.[256] Before that, rent regulation was common during the Second World War.[257] Rent regulation laws, sometimes called rent control and sometimes rent stabilization, are generally passed by municipalities pursuant to state statutes or municipal charters that authorize them to control rents. Usually, rents are set at a historical level and owners are allowed yearly increases. However, landlords in some jurisdictions are entitled to petition for higher increases to ensure that they receive a "fair return" on their investment and/or a "fair net operating income," to reflect increased costs of maintenance and to recoup the costs of major improvements.[258] Rent regulation has often been challenged as an unconstitutional taking of the landlord's property rights but, to date, has been upheld by the Supreme Court.[259]

Local ordinances controlling rents

§10.6 Tenant's Right to Habitable Premises

§10.6.1 Constructive Eviction

While an "actual eviction" is an act by the landlord that physically bars the tenant from the premises, "constructive eviction" refers to acts by the

Interference with implied covenant of quiet enjoyment

[252] *See* U.S. Gov't Accountability Office, *Covid-19 Housing Protections: Moratoriums Have Helped Limit Evictions, but Further Outreach Is Needed*, GAO-21-370 (2021).

[253] *Alabama Ass'n of Realtors v. Dep't of Health & Human Servs.*, 594 U.S. 758 (2021).

[254] *Chrysafis v. Marks*, 141 S. Ct. 2482 (2021) (provision allowing tenants to self-certify financial hardship and generally precluding landlords from contesting certification in a hearing violates due process).

[255] *See, e.g.*, *Elmsford Apartment Assocs. v. Cuomo*, 469 F. Supp. 3d 148 (S.D.N.Y. 2020); *Baptiste v. Kennealy*, 490 F. Supp. 3d 353 (D. Mass. 2020).

[256] Robert S. Schoshinski, *American Law of Landlord and Tenant* §7:1, at 501-506 (1980).

[257] *Id.* at §7:1, at 502.

[258] *Id.* at §7:8, at 518-527.

[259] *Yee v. City of Escondido*, 503 U.S. 519 (1992); *Pennell v. City of San Jose*, 485 U.S. 1 (1988); *Edgar A. Levy Leasing Co. v. Siegel*, 258 U.S. 242 (1922); *Block v. Hirsh*, 256 U.S. 135 (1921).

landlord (or a failure to act where the landlord has a duty to act) that so substantially interfere with the tenant's quiet enjoyment of the property as to justify the tenant's abandonment of the property.[260] Every lease, whether residential or commercial, has an implied covenant of quiet enjoyment.[261] This is almost a definitional aspect of every tenancy because leases represent transfers of possessory rights from landlord to tenant, and interference by the landlord with the tenant's possession would seem to contravene the initial grant. The covenant of quiet enjoyment protects tenants not only from trespass by the landlord but also from physical exclusion from the property. Landlord acts that "are so injurious to the tenant's enjoyment and use of the property as to justify abandonment by the tenant will be regarded as tantamount to an eviction."[262]

Remedies

When a tenant has been "constructively evicted" by landlord conduct that justifies abandonment, the tenant is entitled to leave the property and cease rent payments.[263] The constructive eviction doctrine therefore generally functions as a defense to landlord claims for unpaid rent. If the tenant can show that the landlord constructively evicted the tenant, the tenant is relieved of all obligations under the lease, including the duty to pay rent.[264] The tenant may also be entitled to damages, including the costs of relocating and the difference between the reserved rent and the fair rental value of the premises.[265] If these amounts are close, damages are small to nonexistent and the real remedy is the power to terminate the lease or to obtain injunctive relief ordering the landlord to remedy the problem.[266]

Landlord action or inaction

To take advantage of the doctrine, the tenant must show some intentional act on the landlord's part.[267] This does not mean the landlord must have intended to interfere with the tenant's quiet enjoyment, but that the landlord must have engaged in activity that caused the interference. The tenant may also show that the landlord caused the interference by not acting when the landlord had a duty to act.[268] Courts traditionally were reluctant to impose implied obligations on the landlord, so this latter theory had little currency until recently. With the adoption of the implied warranty of habitability, however,[269] the landlord's failure to repair or maintain the property may rise to the level of constructive eviction if conditions deteriorate such that the tenant would be justified in abandoning the property.

[260] *Harel Assocs. v. Cooper Healthcare Professional Servs.*, 638 A.2d 921 (N.J. Super. Ct. App. Div. 1994); *801 South Fulton Ave. Corp. v. Radin*, 526 N.Y.S.2d 143 (App. Div. 1988); Robert S. Schoshinski, *American Law of Landlord and Tenant* §3:5, at 97-98 (1980).

[261] *See Harel Assocs. v. Cooper Healthcare Professional Servs., Inc.*, 638 A.2d 921 (N.J. Super. Ct. App. Div. 1994) (commercial tenant protected by constructive eviction doctrine).

[262] Robert S. Schoshinski, *American Law of Landlord and Tenant* §3:5, at 97 (1980).

[263] *Barash v. Pennyslvania Terminal Real Estate Co.*, 256 N.E.2d 707, 710 (N.Y. 1970); Robert S. Schoshinski, *American Law of Landlord and Tenant* §3:5, at 98 (1980).

[264] Robert S. Schoshinski, *American Law of Landlord and Tenant* §3:8, at 105 (1980).

[265] *Id.* at §3:8, at 105-106.

[266] *Id.*

[267] *Id.* at §3:5, at 98.

[268] *Fidelity Mutual Life Insurance Co. v. Kaminsky*, 768 S.W.2d 818 (Tex. Ct. App. 1989) (landlord's failure to take action against antiabortion protesters at tenant's abortion clinic constituted constructive eviction, entitling tenant to move out).

[269] *See* §10.6.3.

▷ MUST THE TENANT MOVE OUT? **HARD CASE ◀**

Traditional rule: Tenant must move out

Traditionally, tenants could not take advantage of the constructive eviction doctrine unless they moved out within a reasonable time.[270] For the most part this rule has retained its force. Many courts still require tenants to move out to assert the defense.[271] This is partly because the theory of the doctrine is that the landlord's conduct so substantially impairs the livability of the property that it is equivalent to barring the door and physically evicting the tenant. If the tenant decides to stay, the decision maker may well conclude that the interference was not so substantial as to warrant relieving the tenant of the obligation to pay rent.

Argument that the tenant should not have to move out

However, recent cases have allowed tenants to stay and stop paying rent, although they have generally done so in the case of "partial constructive eviction" where part of the property is uninhabitable and the rest is habitable.[272] The *Restatement (Second) of Property* would apply the doctrine whether or not the tenant moves out.[273] Three reasons might justify allowing tenants to stay rather than forcing them to move out before they can take advantage of the constructive eviction doctrine. First, the tenant may not be able to tell whether a court would determine that the interference was so substantial that it justified abandonment. If the tenant moves out and stops paying rent and then fails to convince the court that she was constructively evicted, she may wind up liable for back rent. She should not have to move out and risk an adverse outcome before taking advantage of the doctrine.

Uncertainty about the application of the doctrine

Tenant's difficulty finding new housing

Second, tenants may have a hard time finding a suitable, affordable alternative place to live. Yet, they may nonetheless be entitled to a partial or total rent abatement if the landlord violates the implied covenant of quiet enjoyment.

Relation to implied warranty of habitability

Third, the implied warranty of habitability authorizes tenants to move out and repudiate the lease or to stay and stop paying rent if the landlord fails to maintain the premises in a habitable manner. If the tenant stays, she will be entitled to a reduction or complete abatement of rent during the time when the violation continues. It is arguably inconsistent to require the tenant to move out to take advantage of the constructive eviction doctrine

[270] *Stinson, Lyons, Gerlin & Bustamante, P.A. v. Brickell Bldg. 1 Holding Co.*, 923 F.2d 810 (11th Cir. 1991) (applying Florida law, court holds a tenant must abandon premises within a reasonable time after landlord's interference with tenant's quiet enjoyment); *West Broadway Glass Co. v. I.T.M. Bar, Inc.*, 666 N.Y.S.2d 629 (App. Div. 1997); *Cavalier Square Ltd. Partnership v. Virginia Alcoholic Beverage Control Board*, 435 S.E.2d 392 (Va. 1993); Robert S. Schoshinski, *American Law of Landlord and Tenant* §3:5, at 99 (1980).

[271] *Morrison v. Smith*, 757 S.W.2d 678 (Tenn. Ct. App. 1988) (tenant who fails to abandon premises within reasonable time after conditions constituting constructive eviction occur waives constructive eviction claim). *But see Zweighaft v. Remington*, 320 N.Y.S.2d 151 (Civ. Ct. 1971) (holding the contrary).

[272] *Stevan v. Brown*, 458 A.2d 466 (Md. Ct. Spec. App. 1983) (allowing tenant to remain on premises while court determines if constructive eviction occurred); *Dennison v. Marlowe*, 744 P.2d 906 (N.M. 1987); *Minjak v. Randolph*, 528 N.Y.S.2d 554 (App. Div. 1988); *East Haven Assocs. v. Gurian*, 313 N.Y.S.2d 927 (Civ. Ct. 1970); Robert S. Schoshinski, *American Law of Landlord and Tenant* §3:5, at 101 (1980). *See also Arbern Realty Co. v. Clay Craft Planters Co.*, 727 N.Y.S.2d 236 (App. Div. 2001) (applying the partial constructive eviction doctrine in the context of a commercial lease).

[273] *Restatement (Second) of Property (Landlord and Tenant)* §6.1 Reporter's Note 6 (1977).

when the implied warranty of habitability doctrine authorizes the tenant to stay. In either case, allowing the tenant to stay without paying rent may induce the landlord to fix the problem. ◀

▶ HARD CASE ▷ IS LANDLORD RESPONSIBLE FOR HARMS CAUSED BY OTHER TENANTS?

The doctrine applies only when the landlord has engaged in an intentional act that causes the interference or when the landlord has failed to act in accord with an express or implied duty in the lease agreement.[274] Courts disagree about whether the landlord is responsible for conduct of other tenants. In *Blackett v. Olanoff*,[275] for example, a landlord rented an apartment to several tenants and a neighboring premises to a noisy bar that had loud music late into the night. The court held that there was an inherent conflict between the two activities and that the bar had breached an express covenant in its lease not to disturb the quiet enjoyment of the neighbors. For the doctrine to apply more broadly, however, a court would have to imply three separate terms in the leases: (1) an implied covenant that the tenants will not disturb the quiet enjoyment of other tenants (breach of which duty would give the landlord the right to evict the offending tenant);[276] (2) an implied duty on the landlord to actually evict the offending tenant or otherwise control her behavior (a duty that might be viewed as part of the landlord's duty to act so as to avoid interfering with the tenant's quiet enjoyment); and (3) a power in the victimized tenant to abandon the lease early if the landlord fails to control the behavior of the other tenant or evict her. Although the *Restatement (Second)* adopts the *Blackett* doctrine,[277] as have some other courts,[278] many courts still refuse to hold the landlord responsible for conduct of other tenants.[279] ◀

▶ HARD CASE ▷ CAN A TENANT BE EVICTED BECAUSE SHE IS THE VICTIM OF DOMESTIC VIOLENCE?

Many municipalities have ordinances that prohibit landlords from causing a nuisance. If tenants on the property engage in domestic violence,

[274] Robert S. Schoshinski, *American Law of Landlord and Tenant* §3:5, at 98 (1980).

[275] 358 N.E.2d 817 (Mass. 1976). *See also McNamara v. Wilmington Mall Realty Corp.*, 466 S.E.2d 324 (N.C. Ct. App. 1996) (landlord constructively evicted tenant by renting adjoining space to aerobics studio and failing to control the noise emanating from the studio).

[276] *Cf. Howard Opera House Ass'n v. Urban Outfitters, Inc.*, 322 F.3d 125 (2d Cir. 2003) (retail store that violates local noise ordinance breaches lease term requiring tenant to comply with "all applicable laws").

[277] *Restatement (Second) of Property (Landlord and Tenant)* §6.1 cmt. d (1977).

[278] *Essen Development v. Marr*, 687 So. 2d 98, 100 (La. Ct. App. 1995) ("A lessor who allows one of his lessees to disturb the possession of his other lessees breaches his obligation to maintain the lessee in peaceable possession"); *Benitez v. Restifo*, 641 N.Y.S.2d 523 (N.Y. City Ct. Yonkers 1996).

[279] *International Comm'n on English in Liturgy v. Schwartz*, 573 A.2d 1303 (D.C. 1990).

necessitating police calls, landlords may face fines for keeping a public nuisance. In response, landlords may sue to evict tenants even if the victim has sought a domestic violence restraining order to keep the abuser from the premises. States have begun to pass legislation to protect such tenants from eviction in such cases. Colorado, for example, provides a defense against eviction for a victim of domestic violence that has been documented by the filing of a police report, the issuance of a restraining order, a self-attestation affidavit, or certain third-party letters.[280] ◀

§10.6.2 Housing Codes

Administrative enforcement

Many states and municipalities have housing codes that regulate construction and maintenance of residential structures.[281] These codes regulate

> (1) structural elements such as walls, roofs, ceilings, floors, window, and staircases; (2) facilities such as toilets, sinks, bathtubs, radiators or other heating fixtures, stoves, electrical outlets, window screens, and door and window locks; (3) services such as heat, hot and cold water, sanitary sewage disposal, electricity, elevator service, central air conditioning, and repair and maintenance services for each dwelling unit; and (4) occupancy standards setting limits on the number of occupants per dwelling or per bedroom.[282]

Such codes are generally enforced by public officials empowered to investigate the conditions of property and to order owners to fix problems. They are generally empowered to bring court actions for injunctive relief to order the owner to comply with the housing code or to impose civil or criminal fines for violation and even incarceration in certain cases.[283]

§10.6.3 Implied Warranty of Habitability

Traditional *caveat emptor* rule

Traditionally, leases were considered transfers of an estate in land and the landlord made no implied representations about the quality of the housing provided with the lease. Tenants had no right to habitable housing and courts found no implied duties on landlords to repair or maintain rental property.[284] Although housing codes were in effect in some states in the late nineteenth century, they did not become common until the 1960s.[285] Despite the existence of such statutes, courts did not consider compliance

[280] Colo. Rev. Stat. §§13-40-107.5(5)(c); 13-40-104(4).

[281] Dale A. Whitman et al., *The Law of Property* §6.37, at 236-239 (4th ed. 2019).

[282] *Id.* at §6.37, at 237.

[283] *Id.; see also* N.Y. Real Prop. Acts. Law §797 (Tenant Dignity and Safe Housing Act of 2022 simplifies procedures for tenants to bring actions against landlords for habitability and housing code violations).

[284] Many courts did hold that landlords had an obligation to reveal latent (nonobvious) defects of which the landlord was aware and about which the tenant could not have reasonably been aware. Violation of the duty meant that the tenant was privileged to vacate the premises and repudiate the lease. *Taylor v. Leedy & Co.*, 412 So. 2d 763 (Ala. 1982); Robert S. Schoshinski, *American Law of Landlord and Tenant* §3:12, at 109 (1980).

[285] Dale A. Whitman et al., *The Law of Property* §6.37, at 237 (4th ed. 2019).

with the housing code to be an implied contractual obligation of the landlord. Nor did they consider the lease agreement to contain any implied promises by the landlord to provide premises suitable for habitation. With few exceptions,[286] courts did not find implied contractual obligations to repair premises or make them "habitable" until the 1970s.

Implied warranty generally accepted today

Today, however, the overwhelming majority of courts have held that residential leases contain a implied warranty of habitability and most states codify that obligation in their statutes.[287] The Indiana Supreme Court has held that an implied warranty is implied in law when a housing code is in effect but not where no housing code regulates the landlord-tenant relationship.[288] In the absence of a housing code, an implied warranty will only be implied in fact; this means the tenant can show evidence that the landlord intended to warrant the habitability of the property. The tenant may prove this through "evidence of the parties' course of dealing or performance and by evidence of ordinary-practices in the trade."[289]

Rejection of *caveat emptor*

The adoption of the implied warranty required two changes in landlord-tenant law. First, the courts abandoned the doctrine of *caveat emptor* — let the buyer beware — that had long applied to residential leaseholds.[290] The doctrine had previously been abandoned in the sale of goods and in contracts generally,[291] but lingered on in property law. By adopting the implied warranty of habitability, the courts rejected the idea that a leasehold is merely a transfer of an estate in land governed only by the rules of property law. The courts began to hold that leases were contracts as well as conveyances of real property and that, as in other contracts for the sale of goods, residential landlords make implied representations that the property being rented is suitable for that purpose — that it is "habitable."[292]

Dependent covenants

Second, the courts began to treat landlord and tenant covenants as dependent rather than independent.[293] This is the usual result in contract law where each party's obligations are contingent on the other party complying with her obligations. Breach of a material term of a contract entitles

[286] *See, e.g., Delamater v. Foreman*, 239 N.W. 148 (Minn. 1931).

[287] Amy Pritchard, Lynn Foster & Jimmy Gazaway, *The Public Health Connection to the Implied Warranty of Habitability and HB1410*, 54-SUM Ark. Law. 24 (2019) (all states except Arkansas have a form of the implied warranty of habitability, either by statute or by judicial decision).

[288] *Johnson v. Scandia Assocs., Inc.*, 717 N.E.2d 24 (Ind. 1999).

[289] *Id.* at 24, 32 ("Indiana's common law of contract governing the landlord-tenant relationship has developed a warranty of habitability. The warranty is not universally imposed by law, but derives from the agreement between the tenant and the landlord and may be express or implied. The existence of an implied warranty may be proven through evidence of the parties' course of dealing or performance and by evidence of ordinary practices in the trade").

[290] Robert S. Schoshinski, *American Law of Landlord and Tenant* §3:10, at 109 (1980).

[291] *See Frantz v. Cantrell*, 711 N.E.2d 856, 858 (Ind. Ct. App. 1999) (Ind. version of UCC §2-314, Ind. Code §§26-1-1-101 to 26-1-10-104, imposes an implied warranty of merchantability as to goods sold by merchants).

[292] *Javins v. First National Realty Corp.*, 428 F.2d 1071 (D.C. Cir. 1970); Robert S. Schoshinski, *American Law of Landlord and Tenant* §3:16, at 124 (1980).

[293] "At common law the covenants of a lease are deemed to be independent so that a breach of the landlord's promise to perform services would not suspend the obligation of the tenant to pay the rent as agreed." *Greenwich Plaza, Inc. v. Whitman and Ransom*, 1996 WL 240458 (Conn. Super. Ct. 1996).

the other party to be relieved from her contractual obligations. Under the law of property, the traditional remedy for breach of an implied landlord covenant to maintain the premises would have been an action by the tenant for injunctive relief ordering the landlord to fix the place and/or damages for harm caused by the breach of the covenant. However, breach of the covenant would not result in forfeiture of the leasehold or the right to receive the agreed-upon rent.[294] The adoption of the contract doctrine of dependent covenants was interpreted to authorize the tenant to stop paying rent and to abandon the premises. More controversially, it entitles the tenant to stop paying rent and *stay* on the premises, with rent obligations suspended until the problem is fixed. Importantly, the landlord will not be allowed to evict the tenant for nonpayment of rent until the premises are brought up to compliance with the housing code.[295]

Bases for the warranty

The leading case of *Javins v. First National Realty Corp.*[296] involved a landlord claim for possession because of nonpayment of rent. The court denied the claim because the landlord had violated numerous provisions of the housing code and failed to provide the tenant with habitable premises. Judge J. Skelly Wright gave two independent bases for the ruling. The first was an implied warranty of habitability arising from the contractual relationship between the parties. He noted that "[m]odern contract law has recognized that the buyer of goods and services in an industrialized society must rely upon the skill and honesty of the supplier to assure that goods and services purchased are of adequate quality."[297] Tenants similarly legitimately expect to be furnished with premises suitable for habitation.[298] "Since a lease contract specifies a particular period of time during which the tenant has a right to use his apartment for shelter, he may legitimately expect that the apartment will be fit for habitation for the time period for which it is rented."[299] The second basis for the ruling was the housing code itself.[300] Because the housing code prohibited landlords from renting habitations that were not "clean, safe and sanitary," the act of renting residential property constituted an implied representation that the landlord would comply with the mandates of the housing code. In effect, the housing code not only imposed duties on landlords enforceable by administrative proceedings, but required landlords to agree to comply with the housing code as a condition of renting property, thereby making violation of the housing code a breach of contract as well.

[294] Under the usual rules of interpretation of estates, there is a presumption against forfeitures; if a clause can be interpreted either as a covenant or as a defeasible fee (such as a fee simple determinable or fee simple subject to condition subsequent), the courts would interpret it as a covenant, thereby avoiding forfeiture of the current estate. A leasehold includes a transfer of possession from landlord to tenant and a promise to pay rent at certain intervals to the landlord. The landlord's breach of the duty to maintain entitles the tenant to cease paying rent and abandon the premises.

[295] *Chazon v. Maugenest,* 971 N.E.2d 852 (N.Y. 2012).

[296] 428 F.2d 1071 (D.C. Cir. 1970).

[297] *Id.* at 1075.

[298] *Id.*

[299] *Id.* at 1079.

[300] *Id.* at 1080.

Standards of habitability

Some states measure the landlord's obligations by reference to state or local housing codes, holding that the warranty is breached when the landlord fails to comply with applicable building code provisions so as to materially impair health and safety.[301] Other courts, however, have measured the landlord's obligations independently of the applicable housing code, holding that landlords have an obligation to conform with "general community standards of suitability for occupancy."[302] Note that some violations of the housing code are not sufficiently serious to count as violations of the implied warranty; they must render the property "truly unsafe, unsanitary, or uninhabitable."[303] At the same time, some conditions that do not violate the code may well count as a breach of the implied warranty.[304] Examples of problems that are likely to violate the warranty include lack of heat or hot water, broken windows, pest infestation, and leaky roofs.[305]

Strict liability

Most courts hold that the obligation to provide a habitable dwelling imposes strict obligations on the landlord. The tenant need not show that the landlord did anything wrong, is at fault, or acted unreasonably to prove a violation of the warranty.[306] The tenant does have a duty to provide notice of the problem to the landlord.[307] Some courts find a violation the moment the condition occurs;[308] others when the landlord is notified;[309] and others after the landlord has had a reasonable time to fix the problem and has not done so.[310] Most courts appear to adopt the latter standard. The timing of the violation matters because one of the remedies for violation of the warranty is a right to rent reduction during the time the violation exists, and in states that find no violation until the landlord has a chance to remedy

Notice must be provided to landlord of the problem

301 *Smith v. David*, 176 Cal. Rptr. 112 (Ct. App. 1981); Robert S. Schoshinski, *American Law of Landlord and Tenant* §3:16, at 128 (1980).

302 Robert S. Schoshinski, *American Law of Landlord and Tenant* §3:17, at 128 (1980). *See Glasoe v. Trinkle*, 479 N.E.2d 915, 919 (Ill. 1985) (premises must be habitable and fit for living); *Detling v. Edelbrock*, 671 S.W.2d 265, 270 (Mo. 1984) (habitability to be judged by community standards, including but not limited to local housing codes).

303 Robert S. Schoshinski, *American Law of Landlord and Tenant* §3:17, at 130 (1980).

304 *Id.* at §3:17, at 128-129.

305 *Id.* at §3:17, at 130-131.

306 *Knight v. Hallsthammar*, 623 P.2d 268, 273 (Cal. 1981) (breach of warranty existed whether or not landlord had reasonable time to repair defects existing when he purchased the building); *Berman & Sons, Inc. v. Jefferson*, 396 N.E.2d 981, 985-986 (Mass. 1979) (breach occurred when landlord received notice of lack of heat and hot water even though he promptly fixed the problem); *Park West Mgmt. Corp. v. Mitchell*, 391 N.E.2d 1288, 1295 (N.Y. 1979) (lack of janitorial services breached covenant even though janitors were on strike); Robert S. Schoshinski, *American Law of Landlord and Tenant* §3:17, at 92 (Cum. Supp. 1999).

307 *Glasoe v. Trinkle*, 479 N.E.2d 915 (Ill. 1985); *Hilder v. St. Peter*, 478 A.2d 202 (Vt. 1984); Robert S. Schoshinski, *American Law of Landlord and Tenant* §3:24, at 140-141 (1980); *Uniform Residential Landlord and Tenant Act* §§1.304, 4.101(a).

308 *Knight v. Hallsthammar*, 623 P.2d 268, 273 (Cal. 1981) (breach of warranty existed whether or not landlord had reasonable time to repair defects existing when he purchased the building).

309 *Berman & Sons, Inc. v. Jefferson*, 396 N.E.2d 981, 985-986 (Mass. 1979) (breach occurred when landlord received notice of lack of heat and hot water even though he promptly fixed the problem).

310 *Chess v. Muhammad*, 430 A.2d 928, 929 (N.J. Super. Ct. 1981) (remedies for breach of implied warranty of habitability are limited to cases in which the landlord failed to make necessary repairs within a reasonable time).

the problem, no rent reduction would be available if the landlord fixes the problem promptly; conversely, in states that find a violation when the condition is present, such a reduction might well be available. Once the court finds that the condition violated the warranty, the tenant has the usual remedies, such as the power to repudiate the lease or to withhold rent.

Negligence standard for harms to the person or property

However, it is important to note that the courts do *not* impose strict tort liability on landlords for harm to the tenant (or guests of the tenant) arising out of violations of the implied warranty. Rather, the courts impose a *negligence* standard, requiring proof that the landlord acted unreasonably so as to create a foreseeable risk of harm to the tenant or the tenant's guests. Of course, violation of the implied warranty and failure to correct the problem once notified of it may constitute negligence on the part of the landlord.

Remedies

A variety of remedies are available for breach of the implied warranty of habitability.

Termination

(1) Termination of the Tenancy (Rescission of the Contract). Breach of the implied warranty of habitability gives the tenant the right to stop paying rent and abandon the premises, moving out before the end of the lease term and repudiating the lease agreement.[311] Most courts simply state that breach of the warranty gives the right to terminate; however, some courts emphasize that the breach must be "material" before it will justify rescinding the lease agreement.[312] The *Uniform Residential Landlord and Tenant Act* allows termination only if the breach "materially affect[s] health and safety."[313] It further requires the tenant to provide the landlord notice of the violation and give the landlord 14 days to fix the problem. The notice must also state that if the problem is not fixed within the 14-day window, the tenant will terminate the tenancy at a set date that shall be no less than 30 days after the notice was provided to the landlord.

Rent withholding

(2) Rent Withholding. The tenant is entitled to withhold rent until the landlord fixes the problem.[314] Some statutes authorize this remedy under procedures that may require the tenant to pay the rent into an escrow account managed by the court or other official designee.[315] This remedy

[311] *Heutel v. Walker*, 735 S.W.2d 196 (Mo. 1987); *Henry S. Miller Mgmt. Corp. v. Houston State Ass'n*, 792 S.W.2d 128 (Tex. Ct. App. 1990); Dale A. Whitman et al., *The Law of Property* §6.41, at 251-252 (4th ed. 2019); Robert S. Schoshinski, *American Law of Landlord and Tenant* §3:20, at 133 (1980).

[312] *Javins v. First National Realty Corp.*, 428 F.2d 1071, 1082-1083 (D.C. Cir. 1970) (violation of health code must be more than de minimis to constitute a violation of the implied warranty); *Lemle v. Breeden*, 462 P.2d 470, 476 (Haw. 1969) (breach must be material); *Mease v. Fox*, 200 N.W.2d 791, 796-797 (Iowa 1972) (breach must be material).

[313] *Uniform Residential Landlord and Tenant Act* §4.101(a).

[314] *Smith v. David*, 176 Cal. Rptr. 112 (Ct. App. 1981); *664 West 161 Street Tenants Ass'n v. Leal*, 545 N.Y.S.2d 925 (App. Div. 1989); *Napolski v. Champney*, 667 P.2d 1013 (Or. 1983); Dale A. Whitman et al., *The Law of Property* §6.41, at 256-260 (4th ed. 2019); Robert S. Schoshinski, *American Law of Landlord and Tenant* §3:22, at 136-140 (1980); *Uniform Residential Landlord and Tenant Act* §4.105.

[315] Or. Stat. §§90.370 & 105.140(2) (establishing procedures for paying rent into court); Robert S. Schoshinski, *American Law of Landlord and Tenant* §3:39, at 167 (1980).

substantially differs from the rules governing constructive eviction because the tenant is empowered to stay in the premises while the condition continues, even though its violation supposedly renders the property "uninhabitable." In general, the standard for violation of the warranty is not that the property is literally uninhabitable but that the condition impairs health, safety, or other minimum protections that a tenant is entitled to expect when she rents property. The effect of authorizing rent withholding is to give the tenant a defense to a landlord claim for possession and back rent based on the tenant's failure to pay rent. In other words, if the tenant fails to pay rent, and the landlord sues to evict the tenant and to recover possession and back rent, the landlord's violation of the implied warranty will constitute a defense both to the back rent claim and the claim for possession.[316]

Rent abatement

(3) Rent Abatement. If the landlord sues to evict the tenant for nonpayment of rent or sues for back rent, the court may reduce the rent owed during the period of the violation. The rent is likely to be reduced from the actual rent to the fair rental value of the premises subject to the unlawful condition. Alternatively, the rent could be reduced by some percentage amount designed to deter violations by the landlord and compensate the tenant for the loss.[317] If the court reduces but does not fully abate the rent, it will require the tenant to pay some of the rent withheld back to the landlord. This is because the court may find the rent to have been effectively reduced but not completely abated as a result of the violation. The tenant is well advised to save the money that would have gone to pay the rent because, if the landlord requires the tenant to repay some of the rent and the tenant cannot do so, the court may allow the landlord to evict the tenant on that account.

Damages

(4) Damages. The tenant may sue the landlord for breach of warranty and may request that some amount of past rent paid be forfeited by the landlord because of violations of the implied warranty during the time for which those rental payments applied.[318] In addition, if the tenant suffered any real damages to person or property arising out of the violation, the tenant may seek monetary damages for those injuries — damages that may exceed the amount of the rent. The tenant who repudiates the lease and moves out may also sue for damages for the amount the tenant lost because of the breach. If the tenant has to move out during the repairs, the tenant might sue for the cost of "substituted premises."[319] If the tenant

[316] Robert S. Schoshinski, *American Law of Landlord and Tenant* §3:22, at 136 (1980). Note that if state law rejects the defense, there is no violation of due process. *See Lindsey v. Normet*, 405 U.S. 56 (1972) (holding that a state may constitutionally treat the landlord's and tenant's claims as independent).

[317] Dale A. Whitman et al., *The Law of Property* §6.42, at 253 (4th ed. 2019); Robert S. Schoshinski, *American Law of Landlord and Tenant* §3:25, at 141-144 (1980).

[318] *Miller v. C.W. Meyers Trading Post, Inc.*, 355 S.E.2d 189 (N.C. Ct. App. 1987); *Hilder v. St. Peter*, 478 A.2d 202 (Vt. 1984); Dale A. Whitman et al., *The Law of Property* §6.42, at 252-256 (4th ed. 2019); Robert S. Schoshinski, *American Law of Landlord and Tenant* §3:21, at 134-136 (1980); *Uniform Residential Landlord and Tenant Act* §4.101(b), (c).

[319] *Restatement (Second) of Property (Landlord and Tenant)* §10.2(4) (allowing recovery of the cost of "substituted premises").

repudiates the lease and finds a comparable new place to live that has a higher rent than the old place, the tenant might sue for the difference between the two rents for the remainder of the lease on the ground that the tenant would not have had to move out if the landlord had not violated the lease. Alternatively, the tenant may have a right to the difference between the fair rental value of the premises and the reserved rent for the remainder of the term.[320] Courts have also allowed tenants to obtain damages for emotional distress when the conditions in the property were outrageously indecent.[321]

Injunctive relief

(5) **Injunction or Specific Performance.** The tenant may sue the landlord for a court order requiring the landlord to remedy the problem.[322]

Repair and deduct

(6) **Repair and Deduct.** By statute or common law, the tenant may be authorized to make minor repairs and deduct from the rent paid to the landlord the costs of making those repairs.

Administrative remedies

(7) **Housing Code Remedies.** If a housing code is in effect, the tenant may be empowered to call on a local housing inspector to inspect the premises and order the landlord to fix the problem. Such inspectors usually have the power to go to court for a court order to the landlord to remedy the problem and/or to pay civil or criminal fines for violation of the housing code. In egregious cases, criminal charges may be brought against the landlord.

Warranty is nondisclaimable

The implied warranty of habitability is nondisclaimable.[323] However, the *Restatement (Second)* would authorize the parties to "increase or decrease what would otherwise be the obligations of the landlord with respect to the condition of the lease property" as long as the agreement is not "unconscionable" or against public policy.[324] At the same time, the *Restatement (Second)* clearly provides that "the rule of this section does not allow waiver of housing code violations" or obligations whose breach would make the property unsafe or unhealthy.[325]

Unrepresented tenants

While most landlords are represented by lawyers, most tenants do not have lawyers in eviction proceedings.[326] If tenants do not know that

[320] *Id.* at §10.2 cmt. b.

[321] Guilford v. Weidner Inv. Servs., Inc., 522 P.3d 1085, 1102 (Alaska 2023); Garcia v. Myllyla, 254 Cal. Rptr. 3d 36, 44-45 (Ct. App. 2019); *Simon v. Solomon*, 431 N.E.2d 556 (Mass. 1982).

[322] *Uniform Residential Landlord and Tenant Act* §4.101(b); Robert S. Schoshinski, *American Law of Landlord and Tenant* §3:23, at 140 (1980).

[323] *George Washington University v. Weintraub*, 458 A.2d 43, 47 (D.C. 1983); *Berman and Sons, Inc. v. Jefferson*, 396 N.E.2d 981, 984 (Mass. 1979); *Fair v. Negley*, 390 A.2d 240, 242 (Pa. Super. Ct. 1978); *Nepveu v. Rau*, 583 A.2d 1273 (Vt. 1990); *Uniform Residential Landlord and Tenant Act* §1.403.

[324] *Restatement (Second) of Property (Landlord and Tenant)* §5.6 (1977).

[325] *Id.* at §5.3 cmt. c (1977). *See P.H. Investment v. Oliver*, 818 P.2d 1018 (Utah 1991) (adopting this approach).

[326] *See* Emily A. Benfer, et al., *Disrupting the Eviction System: Tenant Right to Counsel*, Eviction Lab Updates, Apr. 25, 2025 (noting that 96% of tenants facing eviction lack counsel); *see also* NPC Research, *Evaluation of the Sargent Shriver Civil Counsel Act (AB590) Housing Pilot Projects* 185-91 (2017) (tenant-representation pilot program reduced tenant

violation of the warranty of habitability can be a defense, they will not raise it to protect themselves from eviction. This reality substantially limits the effectiveness of the doctrine that makes the implied warranty nonwaivable.

▶ HARD CASE

▷ COMMERCIAL TENANCIES

Most courts have refused to extend the implied warranty to commercial leases.[327] However, the Texas Supreme Court did hold in 1988 that there is an implied warranty of suitability in a commercial lease that the premises will be suitable for their intended purpose and that the warranty and the tenant's obligation to pay rent are mutually dependent.[328] In 2002, the high court in Massachusetts agreed.[329] The argument for not extending the warranty is that commercial tenants are usually both sophisticated enough and have sufficient bargaining power to obtain fair terms in commercial leases. Moreover, commercial leases (especially if they are long term) often give tenants the power to make repairs and structural improvements to the property and therefore legitimately allocate obligations of maintenance and repair to the tenant. As a California court said,

> the parties in a commercial lease are more likely to have equal bargaining power, and, more importantly, a commercial tenant will presumably have sufficient interest in the demised premises to make needed repairs and the means to make the needed repairs himself or herself, if necessary, and then sue the lessor for damages.[330]

---

dispossession and eviction); Boston Bar Association Task Force on the Civil Right to Counsel, *The Importance of Representation in Eviction Cases and Homelessness Prevention* (2012) (pilot programs providing free representation to tenants significantly reduced the risk of eviction and improved financial outcomes); Barbara Bezdek, *Silence in the Court: Participation and Subordination of Poor Tenants' Voices in Legal Process*, 20 Hofstra L. Rev. 533 (1992) (arguing that most tenants facing eviction in Baltimore are both unrepresented by lawyers and living in substandard housing to which the implied warranty of habitability might apply, and that many would not be evicted if they had a lawyer).

[327] *Brendle's Stores, Inc. v. OTR*, 978 F.2d 150 (4th Cir. 1990); *Propst v. McNeill*, 932 S.W.2d 766 (Ark. 1996); *A.O. Smith Corp. v. Kaufman Grain Co.*, 596 N.E.2d 1156 (Ill. App. Ct. 1992); *Chausse v. Coz*, 540 N.E.2d 667 (Mass. 1989); *Russell-Stanley Corp. v. Plant Industries, Inc.*, 595 A.2d 534 (N.J. Super. Ct. 1991); *Manhattan Mansions v. Moe's Pizza*, 561 N.Y.S.2d 331 (Civ. Ct. 1990); Robert S. Schoshinski, *American Law of Landlord and Tenant* §3:29, at 148-150 (1980).

[328] *Davidow v. Inwood North Professional Group—Phase I*, 747 S.W.2d 373 (Tex. 1988). *Compare also 40 Assocs., Inc. v. Katz*, 446 N.Y.S.2d 844 (Civ. Ct. 1981) (implying a warranty of fitness for commercial purposes) *with Randall Co. v. Alan Cobel Photography*, 465 N.Y.S.2d 489 (Civ. Ct. 1983) (refusing to extend an implied warranty to commercial tenancies). *Compare also Golden v. Conway*, 128 Cal. Rptr. 69 (Ct. App. 1976) *and Four Seas Investment Corp. v. International Hotel Tenants' Ass'n*, 146 Cal. Rptr. 531 (Ct. App. 1978) (both adopting an implied warranty of fitness for commercial purposes) *with Schulman v. Vera*, 166 Cal. Rptr. 620 (Ct. App. 1980) *and Muro v. Superior Court*, 229 Cal. Rptr. 383 (Ct. App. 1986) (both rejecting the doctrine).

[329] *Wesson v. Leone Enterprises, Inc.*, 774 N.E.2d 611 (Mass. 2002) (landlord's failure to repair the roof did not amount to constructive eviction but was serious enough to be a breach of the implied warranty of suitability because it materially harmed the tenant's business, thereby allowing tenant to terminate the lease and recover relocation costs).

[330] *Schulman v. Vera*, 166 Cal. Rptr. 620, 625 (Ct. App. 1980).

The counterargument is that there is an implied duty of good faith in all contracts, and a landlord that places property on the market for rental for commercial purposes impliedly warrants that it is fit for that purpose and should not be heard to argue that it was not so suited. As the Texas Supreme Court noted in *Davidow*,

> commercial tenants [are] no more likely to be in a position to assure the suitability of the premises than the residential tenant. [M]any commercial tenants [have] short term leases and limited financial resources which decrease[] the likelihood that the tenant would make the necessary repairs. [T]here is no valid reason to imply a warranty of habitability in residential leases and not in commercial leases. Although minor distinctions can be drawn between residential and commercial tenants, those differences do not justify limiting the warranty to residential leaseholds.[331]

Unlike the implied warranty in the residential rental context, states that recognize the warranty for commercial tenancies make it disclaimable.[332] ◀

Commercial warranty disclaimable

§10.6.4 *Retaliatory Eviction*

Retaliatory eviction prohibited

Landlords may not bring eviction proceedings against tenants and recover possession, and may not otherwise retaliate against tenants (for example, by raising the rent) if their motive is to retaliate against the tenant for asserting legal rights protected by the implied warranty of habitability.[333] Many states have codified this rule.[334] In the leading case of *Edwards v. Habib*,[335] for example, the court refused to allow a landlord to evict a month-to-month tenant when the landlord's eviction notice followed the tenant's complaining to public authorities about housing code violations on the property. If the landlord were entitled to evict tenants who reported housing code violations, many tenants would be deterred from reporting such violations. Similarly, in *Robinson v. Diamond Housing Corp.*,[336] the landlord had pre-

[331] *Davidow v. Inwood North Professional Group—Phase I*, 747 S.W.2d 373, 376-377 (Tex. 1988).
[332] *Gym-N-I Playgrounds, Inc. v. Snider*, 220 S.W.3d 905 (Tex. 2007).
[333] *W.W.G. Corp. v. Hughes*, 960 P.2d 720 (Colo. App. 1998); *Edwards v. Habib*, 397 F.2d 687 (D.C. Cir. 1968); *Hillview Assocs. v. Bloomquist*, 440 N.W.2d 867 (Iowa 1989); Robert S. Schoshinski, *American Law of Landlord and Tenant* §§12.1 to 12.13 (1980). *But see W.W.G. Corp. v. Hughes*, 960 P.2d 720 (Colo. App. 1988) (limiting the doctrine to reprisals for tenant reporting of violations to public authorities and allowing a landlord to evict a tenant in retaliation for the tenant's reporting violation to the landlord but not to public authorities).
[334] Alaska Stat. §34.03.310; Ariz. Rev. Stat. §33-1381; Cal. Civ. Code §1942.5; Conn. Gen. Stat. §47a-20; Del. Code tit. 25, §5516; D.C. Code §42-3505.02; Fla. Stat. §83.64; Haw. Rev. Stat. §521-74; Iowa Code §562A.36; Kan. Stat. §58-2572; Ky. Rev. Stat. §383.705; Mass. Gen. Laws ch. 239, §2A; Mass. Gen. Laws ch. 186, §18; Md. Real Prop. Code §8-208.1; Minn. Stat. §504B.285; Mont. Code §70-24-431; Neb. Rev. Stat. §76-1439; Nev. Rev. Stat. §118A.510; N.H. Rev. Stat. §540:13-a; N.J. Stat. §2A:42-10.10; N.M. Stat. §47-8-39; N.Y. Real Prop. §223-b; N.C. Gen. Stat. §42-37.1; Ohio Rev. Code §5321.02; Or. Rev. Stat. §90.385; Pa. Stat. tit. 68, §250.205 (tenant association participation); R.I. Gen. Laws §34-18-46; S.C. Code §27-40-910; Tenn. Code §66-28-514; Tex. Prop. Code §92.331; Va. Code §55-248.39; Vt. Stat. tit. 9, §4465; Wash. Rev. Code §59.18.240; Wis. Stat. §704.45.
[335] 397 F.2d 687 (D.C. Cir. 1968).
[336] 463 F.2d 853 (D.C. Cir. 1972).

viously been prevented from evicting the tenant for nonpayment of rent because, at the time the tenant stopped paying rent, there were numerous housing code violations that breached the implied warranty of habitability. Rather than fix the place, the landlord sued to recover possession by ending the month-to-month tenancy. Rather than seeking possession on the ground that the tenant had stopped paying rent, the landlord simply gave the requisite notice to terminate the periodic tenancy and sought possession from a holdover tenant. The landlord further stated that the unit would be taken off the market and not rented to someone else. The court denied relief on the ground that the landlord's motive was to punish the tenant for withholding rent when the tenant had a legal right to withhold rent (because of the landlord's breach of the implied warranty of habitability). Allowing selective, retaliatory eviction would have a great chilling effect, preventing other tenants from feeling free to exercise their rights under the implied warranty. The landlord can evade the doctrine by going out of the residential rental business entirely, converting the property to other uses.

Burden of proof

Some courts have placed the burden of proof on the landlord, to show that an eviction is not retaliatory,[337] while some place the burden on the tenant to show that the eviction was made with the motive of retaliating against the tenant unlawfully.[338] The *Uniform Residential Landlord and Tenant Act* creates a presumption that an eviction is retaliatory, and therefore unlawful, if it comes within one year of the tenant taking a number of specified actions that were intended to protect or further the tenant's rights to habitable premises.[339] In effect, the landlord has the burden of production in showing a specific action within a certain time after the tenant's protected act was not retaliatory but legitimate and then the burden of persuasion shifts to the tenant to convince the factfinder that the landlord's motive was retaliatory.[340] The presumption can be rebutted by the landlord if she can show a legitimate business reason for evicting the tenant or can otherwise demonstrate that her motive was not retaliatory. The desire to have the tenant resume paying rent or to get rid of a tenant who complains about housing code violations is not a legitimate business purpose.

Uniform Residential Landlord and Tenant Act

Commercial leases

As with the implied warranty of habitability, the retaliatory eviction doctrine does not apply to commercial tenancies.[341]

▶ HARD CASE

▷ HOW LONG MAY THE TENANT STAY?

How long may the tenant stay in the premises if the landlord is denied the right to evict the tenant? Most courts hold that the landlord may not evict the tenant until the landlord can show a legitimate, nonretaliatory business

337 *Id.* at 865.

338 *Wright v. Brady*, 889 P.2d 105, 109 (Idaho Ct. App. 1995); *Building Monitoring Systems, Inc. v. Paxton*, 905 P.2d 1215, 1219 (Utah 1995).

339 *Uniform Residential Landlord and Tenant Act* §5.101(b).

340 Robert S. Schoshinski, *American Law of Landlord and Tenant* §12:11, at 742-743 (1980).

341 *Espenschied v. Mallick*, 633 A.2d 388 (D.C. 1993).

reason for the eviction.[342] They may not refuse to renew a lease (or grant a periodic tenancy in place of a term of years) for a retaliatory reason.[343] However, the Utah Supreme Court criticized this approach. Noting that "we cannot saddle the landlord with a perpetual tenant,"[344] and requiring the landlord to show that "his actions are not the result of retaliatory motives" will be a very difficult burden for a landlord to overcome, the court held that the tenant "should be permitted to remain until the landlord has made the repairs required by law."[345] The court held that the tenant may be evicted anytime after repairs have been made as long as the tenant is also given "sufficient time, without the pressure normally exerted in a holdover eviction proceeding, to find other suitable housing."[346]

Statutes determining when landlord can regain possession

A number of states have dealt with the issue by statute. Some states expressly apply the retaliatory eviction doctrine to the landlord's refusal to renew a tenancy, including a term of years.[347] Some states have interpreted their statutes to apply to nonrenewal of a tenancy.[348] In contrast, some states have held that their statutes prohibit retaliatory eviction of month-to-month tenants but allow landlords to refuse to renew term-of-years or fixed-term leases for retaliatory reasons.[349] Still other states adopt a middle position, prohibiting retaliatory eviction for a specified time. For example, California prohibits a landlord from retaliating against a tenant for exercising rights protected by the implied warranty for 180 days but allows landlords freedom not to renew a periodic tenancy or to increase the rent or otherwise change the terms of the leasehold after that time.[350] Connecticut has a similar statute.[351] New York has passed a statute that applies the retaliatory eviction doctrine to nonrenewal of a term of years but provides that "a landlord shall not be required ... to offer a new lease or a lease renewal for a term greater than one year."[352] ◀

▷ RETALIATION FOR NON-HOUSING-RELATED DISPUTES **HARD CASE ◀**

In *Imperial Colliery v. Fout*,[353] a coal miner living in rented property owned by a company related to his employer went on strike. When the landlord

[342] *Robinson v. Diamond Housing Corp.*, 463 F.2d 853, 865 (D.C. Cir. 1972); *Schweiger v. Superior Court*, 476 P.2d 97, 103 (Cal. 1970); *Dickhut v. Norton*, 173 N.W.2d 297, 302 (Wis. 1970); *Restatement (Second) of Property (Landlord and Tenant)* §§14.8 & 14.9 (1977).

[343] *Restatement (Second) of Property (Landlord and Tenant)* §§14.8 & 14.9 (1977).

[344] *Building Monitoring Systems, Inc. v. Paxton*, 905 P.2d 1215, 1219 (Utah 1995).

[345] *Id. (citing Markese v. Cooper*, 333 N.Y.S.2d 63, 75 (Monroe County Ct. 1972)).

[346] *Id.*

[347] D.C. Code §42-3505.02(a); N.J. Stat. §2A:42-10.10(d). Illinois recently expanded its statutory protections against landlord retaliation. See Ill. H.B. 4687 (signed into law Aug. 9, 2024) (creating a new Landlord Retaliation Act).

[348] *Van Buren Apartments v. Adams*, 701 P.2d 583 (Ariz. Ct. App. 1984) (interpreting Ariz. Rev. Stat. §33-1381); *Houle v. Quenneville*, 787 A.2d 1258, 1263 (Vt. 2001) (interpreting 9 Vt. Stat. §4465 to apply to nonrenewal of fixed term leases).

[349] *Frenchtown Villa v. Meadors*, 324 N.W.2d 133 (Mich. Ct. App. 1982) (interpreting Mich. Comp. Laws §600.5720).

[350] Cal. Civ. Code §1942.5.

[351] Conn. Gen. Stat. §47a-20 (prohibiting eviction for six months after a protected act by a tenant).

[352] N.Y. Real Prop. §223-b(2).

[353] 373 S.E.2d 489 (W. Va. 1988).

sued to evict him, the tenant claimed the landlord had no right to evict him in retaliation for his asserting the right to go on strike—a right protected by federal law. The West Virginia Supreme Court held that the retaliatory eviction doctrine protected tenants from retaliation by landlords only when the tenant's activity was related to the tenant's housing rights. Because the landlord was retaliating for a reason unrelated to the rented property, the doctrine did not apply. The California Supreme Court agreed in *S.P. Growers Association v. Rodriguez*[354] that a landlord could evict tenant-employees because they were on strike. However, the eviction had immediately followed a filing of a federal court lawsuit by the tenant-employees against the employer-landlord charging the landlord with a violation of the *Farm Labor Contractor Registration Act*, a statute requiring farm labor contractors to disclose relevant information to prospective employees.[355] The court held that the statutory policies would be eviscerated if farm workers were deterred from bringing lawsuits to enforce their rights under the Act. Similarly, the California Supreme Court held that a tenant could raise the retaliation doctrine as a defense to an eviction action brought against the tenant after the tenant had complained to the police that the landlord had committed a crime in sexually molesting the tenant's nine-year-old daughter.[356] The court interpreted a California statute that prohibits retaliating against a tenant "because he or she ... lawfully and peaceably exercised any rights under the law."[357] ◀

§10.6.5 *Landlord's Tort Liability*

Traditionally immune

Because landlords traditionally had no duty to repair or maintain rented property or warrant its habitability, they were also immune from tort liability for "injuries sustained because of a dangerous or defective condition of the premises."[358] Some states retain this rule.[359] With the advent of the implied warranty, courts began to hold that failure to maintain the premises in a habitable condition violated a duty owed by the landlord both to the tenant and to others who would foreseeably enter the property and that failure to comply with this obligation might constitute negligence, rendering the landlord liable for harms to person or property arising out of the

Today liable for negligence

[354] 552 P.2d 721 (Cal. 1976).

[355] 7 U.S.C. §§2041 *et seq.* (repealed by Pub. L. No. 97-470, Title V, §523, Jan. 14, 1983, 96 Stat. 2600).

[356] *Barela v. Superior Court*, 636 P.2d 582 (Cal. 1981) (interpreting Cal. Civ. Code §1942.5(c), which prohibits retaliation against tenants for exercising "any rights under the law"); *Custom Parking, Inc. v. Superior Court*, 187 Cal. Rptr. 674 (Ct. App. 1982) (holding that a commercial tenant could assert the defense of retaliatory eviction when the landlord terminated the tenancy because the tenant's officers and employees refused to perjure themselves in an unrelated action involving the landlord).

[357] Cal. Civ. Code §1942.5(c).

[358] *Bowles v. Mahoney*, 202 F.2d 320, 323–24 (D.C. Cir. 1952); Robert S. Schoshinski, *American Law of Landlord and Tenant* §4:1, at 186 (1980). This rule still exists in Wyoming, which has rejected the implied warranty doctrine, *Ortega v. Flaim*, 902 P.2d 199 (Wyo. 1995). *But see Taylor v. Schukei Family Trust*, 996 P.2d 13 (Wyo. 2000) (imposing a duty of care where the landlord contractually agreed to repair the premises).

[359] *Terry v. Pub. Serv. Co. of N.C., Inc.*, 898 S.E.2d 648 (N.C. 2024); *Isbell v. Commercial Inv. Assocs.*, 644 S.E.2d 72 (Va. 2007).

failure to act reasonably to keep the property safe.[360] It is now accepted that the "landlord has a duty to exercise reasonable care not to subject others to an unreasonable risk of harm."[361]

Argument for strict liability

For a while, it looked as if some states would begin to impose strict liability on landlords for injuries resulting from breach of the implied warranty of habitability.[362] The California Supreme Court adopted a strict liability standard in 1985 in *Becker v. IRM*,[363] but overruled *Becker* in 1995 in *Peterson v. Superior Court*.[364] In *Becker*, a tenant was injured when he slipped and fell against a shower door made of untempered glass that shattered. The court held that the landlord was strictly liable for damages arising out of a latent defect in the premises. The court noted that "the landlord in renting the premises makes an implied representation that the premises are fit for use as a dwelling" and the tenant "is in no position to inspect for latent defects in the increasingly complex modern apartment buildings or to bear the expense of repair whereas the landlord is in a much better position to inspect for and repair latent defects."[365] The court added:

> The tenant renting the dwelling is compelled to rely upon the implied assurance of safety made by the landlord. It is also apparent that the landlord by adjustment of price at the time he acquires the property, by rentals or by insurance is in a better position to bear the costs of injuries due to defects in the premises than the tenants.
>
> In these circumstances, strict liability in tort for latent defects existing at the time of renting must be applied to insure that the landlord who markets the product bears the costs of injuries resulting from the defects "rather than the injured persons who are powerless to protect themselves."
>
> The cost of protecting tenants is an appropriate cost of the enterprise. Within our marketplace economy, the cost of purchasing rental housing is obviously based on the anticipated risks and rewards of the purchase, and thus it may be expected that along with numerous other factors the price of used rental housing will depend in part on the quality of the building and reflect the anticipated costs of protecting tenants,

[360] *Newton v. Magill*, 872 P.2d 1213, 1216 (Alaska 1994); *Whetzel v. Jess Fisher Management Co.*, 282 F.2d 943 (D.C. Cir. 1960); *Johnson v. Scandia Assocs., Inc.*, 717 N.E.2d 24 (Ind. 1999); *Kunst v. Pass*, 957 P.2d 1 (Mont. 1998); *Crowell v. McCaffrey*, 386 N.E.2d 1256 (Mass. 1979); *Young v. Garwacki*, 402 N.E.2d 1045 (Mass. 1980); *Shroades v. Rental Homes, Inc.*, 427 N.E.2d 774 (Ohio 1981), *overruled in part on other grounds; Sikora v. Wenzel*, 727 N.E.2d 1277 (Ohio 2000); *Keck v. Doughman*, 572 A.2d 724 (Pa. Super. Ct. 1990); *Pagelsdorf v. Safeco Insurance Co.*, 284 N.W.2d 55 (Wis. 1979); Robert S. Schoshinski, *American Law of Landlord and Tenant* §4:9, at 203 (1980). *But see Humphrey v. Byron*, 850 N.E.2d 1044 (2006) (refusing this obligation to commercial landlords).

[361] *Tanguay v. Marston*, 503 A.2d 834 (N.H. 1986).

[362] Louisiana apparently imposes strict liability on landlords for injuries arising out of a landlord's failure to repair the property or a defect in the original condition of the property. La. Civ. Code art. 2317, 2322. *But see Jones v. Proctor*, 697 So. 2d 304 (La. Ct. App. 1997) (apportioning fault between landlord and tenant).

[363] 698 P.2d 116 (Cal. 1985).

[364] 899 P.2d 905 (Cal. 1995). *Accord, Stevens v. Fleming*, 777 P.2d 1196 (Idaho 1989); *Brady v. Rivella Developers, Inc.*, 424 So. 2d 1104 (La. Ct. App. 1982); *Collingwood v. General Electric Real Estate Equities, Inc.*, 376 S.E.2d 425 (N.C. 1989); *Bellikka v. Green*, 762 P.2d 997 (Or. 1988).

[365] 698 P.2d at 122.

including repairs, replacement of defects and insurance. Further, the landlord after purchase may be able to adjust rents to reflect such costs. The landlord will also often be able to seek equitable indemnity for losses.[366]

Argument against strict liability

However, in overruling *Becker*, the *Peterson* court explained:

> The effect of imposing upon landlords liability without fault is to compel them to insure the safety of their tenants in situations in which injury is caused by a defect of which the landlord neither knew nor should have known.
>
> A landlord or hotel owner, unlike a retailer, often cannot exert pressure upon the manufacturer to make the product safe and cannot share with the manufacturer the costs of insuring the safety of the tenant, because a landlord or hotel owner generally has no "continuing business relationship" with the manufacturer of the defective product. As one commentator has observed: "If the objective of the application of the stream of commerce approach is to distribute the risk of providing a product to society by allowing an injured plaintiff to find a remedy for injury along the chain of distribution, it will probably fail in the landlord/tenant situation. The cost of insuring risk will not be distributed along the chain of commerce but will probably be absorbed by tenants who will pay increased rents. One could argue that this was not the effect sought by the court in earlier cases which anticipated that the cost of risk would be distributed vertically in the stream of commerce." Alice L. Perlman, *Becker v. IRM Corporation*: Strict Liability in Tort for Residential Landlords, 16 Golden Gate L. Rev. 349, 360 (1986).[367]

The prevailing rule is that the landlord is liable for harms to tenants only if she has acted negligently.[368] This means that the landlord may be relieved of liability if the injury is caused by a latent defect of which the landlord could not reasonably have been aware.

▶ HARD CASE ▷ LIABILITY FOR CRIMINAL ACTS OF THIRD PARTIES

A number of cases have considered the question of whether landlords are liable for harm caused by the criminal acts of third parties. In *Kline v. 1500 Massachusetts Avenue. Apt. Corp.*,[369] for example, a tenant who was robbed and assaulted in her apartment building sued the landlord for

[366] *Id.* at 122-124.

[367] 899 P.2d at 912-913.

[368] *New Haverford Partnership v. Stroot*, 772 A.2d 792 (Del. 2001) (potential liability for injuries to tenant from toxic mold); Robert S. Schoshinski, *American Law of Landlord and Tenant* §4:9 at 203-206 (1980).

[369] 439 F.2d 477 (D.C. Cir. 1970). *Accord*, *Barber v. Chang*, 60 Cal. Rptr. 3d 760 (Ct. App. 2007); *Smith v. Lagow Construction & Developing Co.*, 642 N.W.2d 187 (S.D. 2002); *Trentacost v. Brussel*, 412 A.2d 436 (N.J. 1980); *Benser v. Johnson*, 763 S.W.2d 793 (Tex. Ct. App. 1988).

failing to adequately secure the building against such criminal conduct. The building had in the past had security guards or attendants but the landlord had discontinued this practice. The court held that the landlord had an obligation to act reasonably to protect the tenants from foreseeable risks of criminal activity and that the tenant had the legal right to try to prove that the landlord had acted negligently. More specifically, the court held that the intervening criminal act of a third party did not break the chain of causation and that the landlord's failure to reasonably secure the building might constitute a proximate cause of plaintiff's injuries.[370] ◀

§10.6.6 Consumer Protection Laws

Multiple damages

In recent years, many courts have held that tenants may bring claims against landlords under state consumer protection statutes.[371] Such laws prohibit unfair or deceptive practices in consumer transactions. Tenants bring claims under consumer protection acts[372] because some statutes provide for multiple damages or reimbursement for attorney's fees or both. Multiple damages are awarded both to punish the wrongdoer and to deter wrongful conduct. Legislatures fear that compensatory damages may not be enough to deter fraudulent conduct because defendants may simply factor possible liability into their cost-benefit calculations, thus treating it as a cost of doing business. If the benefits of such conduct outweigh the costs, businesses may simply continue the unlawful conduct, thereby defeating the purpose of the legislation, which aims to protect consumers from such activity in the first place.

Are landlords covered by consumer protection laws?

Various issues arise in these cases. First, courts must determine whether tenants are protected by general consumer protection statutes that prohibit "unfair" or "deceptive" trade practices in the sale of "goods" and "services" to consumers. Courts commonly hold that rental housing constitutes a "service" that is bought by tenants as consumers, thus enabling tenants to sue under these statutes.[373] Some courts, however, have held that

[370] See *Freyberg v. DCO 2400 14th Street, LLC*, 304 A.3d 971, 980 (D.C. 2023) (landlord liability for intervening criminal acts requires sufficient foreseeability); *cf. Saelzler v. Advanced Group 400*, 23 P.3d 1143 (Cal. 2001) (landlord not liable to Federal Express employee who was criminally assaulted while she was attempting to deliver a package to the building because landlord was not the cause of the harm and had no duty to hire security guards despite known dangers in the area).

[371] *Hernandez v. Stabach*, 193 Cal. Rptr. 350 (Ct. App. 1983); *Conaway v. Prestia*, 464 A.2d 847 (Conn. 1983); *Brown v. Veile*, 555 N.E.2d 1227 (Ill. App. Ct. 1990); Ndoro v. Torres, 249 N.E.3d 721 (Mass. Ct. App. 2024); *Love v. Amsler*, 441 N.W.2d 555 (Minn. Ct. App. 1989); *49 Prospect Street v. Sheva Gardens*, 547 A.2d 1134 (N.J. Super. Ct. App. Div. 1988); *Stanley v. Moore*, 454 S.E.2d 225 (N.C. 1995); *Commonwealth v. Monumental Properties, Inc.*, 329 A.2d 812 (Pa. 1974); *Woodhaven Apartments v. Washington*, 942 P.2d 918, 923 (Utah 1997).

[372] *See, e.g.*, Mass. Gen. Laws ch. 93A, §§1 to 11; N.C. Gen. Stat. §75-16.1.

[373] *Hernandez v. Stabach*, 193 Cal. Rptr. 350 (Ct. App. 1983); *Conaway v. Prestia*, 464 A.2d 847 (Conn. 1983); *Brown v. Veile*, 555 N.E.2d 1227 (Ill. App. Ct. 1990); *Love v. Amsler*, 441 N.W.2d 555 (Minn. Ct. App. 1989); *49 Prospect Street v. Sheva Gardens*, 547 A.2d 1134 (N.J. Super. Ct. App. Div. 1988); *Commonwealth v. Monumental Properties*, 329 A.2d 812 (Pa. 1974).

the presence of specific landlord-tenant legislation, such as the *Uniform Residential Landlord and Tenant Act*, demonstrates a legislative intent to exclude tenants from coverage under other statutes, and that tenants therefore cannot obtain additional remedies under general consumer protection legislation.[374]

What are unfair or deceptive consumer practices?

Second, courts must define what kinds of conduct constitute "unfair" or "deceptive" practices. For example, the Massachusetts Supreme Judicial Court has held that including illegal and unenforceable clauses in residential leases constitutes an unfair and deceptive practice that "injures" tenants, even if the landlord never attempts to enforce the clause and the tenant admits never having read the clause. In the absence of reliance, however, damages are nominal.[375] A lawyer who drafts a lease and deliberately includes in it a clause that is unenforceable, intending to mislead tenants into thinking they do not have rights that the law gives them, may be independently liable for violating consumer protection laws if they come within the ambit of those regulated by the law. Lawyers must take care not to violate ethical rules governing the conduct of attorneys; every state prohibits lawyers from engaging in conduct involving "dishonesty"; including clauses in leases that violate public policy in order to mislead tenants may implicate such concerns.[376] Other kinds of conduct held to constitute unfair or deceptive trade practices include retaliatory evictions,[377] and the failure to maintain rental housing in accordance with the housing code.[378]

▶ HARD CASE

▷ ARE SMALL LANDLORDS REGULATED BY CONSUMER PROTECTION LAWS?

Courts have addressed the question whether all landlords, or only some landlords, are involved in a "trade" or "business" that makes them subject to consumer protection acts. In *Billings v. Wilson*,[379] the Massachusetts Supreme Judicial Court held that a landlord of an owner-occupied two-unit building was not involved in a "trade or business."[380] The court held that "the relationship between the landlord and tenant here was of a private nature, and in no way concerned a trade or business."[381] The court could easily have found, however, that the act of renting property is inherently a business activity, especially because the landlord is subject to all the usual regulations of landlord-tenant relationships imposed by the

[374] *State v. Schwab*, 693 P.2d 108 (Wash. 1985).
[375] *Leardi v. Brown*, 474 N.E.2d 1094 (Mass. 1985).
[376] ABA Model Rules of Professional Conduct §8.4(c) ("It is professional misconduct for a lawyer to: (c) engage in conduct involving dishonesty, fraud, deceit or misrepresentation").
[377] *Hernandez v. Stabach*, 193 Cal. Rptr. 350 (Ct. App. 1983).
[378] *Dorgan v. Loukas*, 473 N.E.2d 1151 (Mass. App. Ct. 1985); *State v. Weller*, 327 N.W.2d 172 (Wis. 1982).
[379] 493 N.E.2d 187 (Mass. 1986).
[380] *Id. Accord, Young v. Patukonis*, 506 N.E.2d 1164 (Mass. App. Ct. 1987) (extending the ruling to owner-occupied three-unit dwelling).
[381] 493 N.E.2d at 188.

implied warranty of habitability, regulation of security deposits, eviction, and the like. ◀

Federal Debt Collections Practices Act

In *Romea v. Heiberger & Assocs.*,[382] Judge Calabresi held that the *Federal Debt Collections Practices Act*[383] applies to demand letters by landlords to tenants seeking back rent. The Act regulates "debt" collection and protects consumers from "abusive, deceptive, and unfair debt collection practices by debt collectors."[384] While the Second Circuit held that back rent constitutes "debt" within the meaning of the statute,[385] other courts have disagreed with the ruling.[386] In addition, the *Fair Credit Reporting Act*,[387] requiring agencies reporting consumer credit histories to adopt reasonable and fair procedures to protect consumers from false or misleading credit reports, has also been held to apply to agencies that collect information and report to landlords on rental payment histories of prospective tenants.[388]

Fair Credit Reporting Act

§10.6.7 Lead Paint Laws

Federal law

The problem of lead paint poisoning in children has resulted in substantial legislative activity. In 1992, Congress passed the *Residential Lead-Based Paint Hazard Reduction Act*,[389] which requires sellers and landlords to provide buyers or lessees of most property built before 1978 with a "lead hazard information pamphlet" and to disclose the presence of any known lead-based paint.[390]

State law

Many states also regulate lead paint in the home. Massachusetts, for example, banned lead from use in house paint in 1973.[391] The *Lead Paint Poisoning Prevention and Control Act* also requires that "every residence where a child under the age of six resides be made safe from lead by imposing a duty to abate on owners of residential property built before 1978."[392] Such statutes may result in liability imposed on landlords for harm to minor children caused by the presence of lead paint in the apartment.[393]

[382] 163 F.3d 111 (2d Cir. 1998).
[383] 15 U.S.C. §§1692 to 1692o.
[384] *Sarver v. Capital Recovery Assocs., Inc.*, 951 F. Supp. 550, 552 (E.D. Pa. 1996).
[385] The *FDCPA* defines the term "debt" as "any obligation or alleged obligation of a consumer to pay money arising out of a transaction in which the money, property, insurance, or services which are the subject of the transaction are primarily for personal, family, or household purposes, whether or not such obligation has been reduced to judgment." 15 U.S.C. §1692a(5).
[386] *Krevsky v. Equifax Check Servs., Inc.*, 85 F. Supp. 2d 479 (M.D. Pa. 2000).
[387] 15 U.S.C. §1681.
[388] *Cisneros v. U.D. Registry, Inc.*, 46 Cal. Rptr. 2d 233 (Ct. App. 1995).
[389] 42 U.S.C. §§4851 to 4856.
[390] *Id.* at §4852d. *See* 40 C.F.R. §§745.101 to 745.107.
[391] Mass. Gen. Laws ch. 111, §§190 to 199.
[392] Hon. Herman J. Smith, Jr., *Special Issues for Residential Leases*, in 2 *Lease Drafting in Massachusetts* ch. 13 (Mass. Continuing Leg. Educ., Inc., 1996).
[393] *Ankiewicz v. Kinder*, 563 N.E.2d 684 (Mass. 1990). *But see Chapman v. Silber*, 760 N.E.2d 329, 336 (N.Y. 2001) (no liability unless landlord was made aware of the lead paint condition, at least where there is no state statute requiring landlords to abate or test for lead paint).

§10.7 Transfers by Landlord or Tenant

§10.7.1 *Landlord's Right to Transfer the Reversion*

Landlord's interest transferable

The landlord has the legal power to sell property subject to existing leaseholds. The landlord's interest is a reversion, a nonpossessory interest ordinarily held in fee simple. Like other fee interests, it is alienable.[394] The transfer of the reversion carries with it the contractual rights of the landlord under the lease, including the right to receive the agreed-upon rent. This is because the benefit of the covenant to pay rent runs with the land and is enforceable by the new owner of the reversion.[395] If the lease is a periodic tenancy, the new owner is free to terminate the tenancy with the requisite notice. If the lease is a term of years, then the new owner holds the property subject to the leasehold and cannot terminate the lease before the fixed term runs out.

§10.7.2 *Tenant's Rights to Assign or Sublet*

Right to assign or sublease

In the absence of any covenants to the contrary, leaseholds held in the form of a term of years, or a periodic tenancy are transferable.[396] The sole exception to this principle is that most courts will treat a tenancy at will as nontransferable. Some states, however, have statutes that prohibit assignment or sublease unless the tenant gets the landlord's consent or the lease agreement provides for transfer without the landlord's consent.[397]

Assignment v. sublease

If a tenant assigns all her interests under the lease for the entire unexpired term of the lease, the transfer is called an *assignment*.[398] Traditionally, the courts hold assignment of the tenancy establishes vertical privity between the assignor (the original tenant) and assignee (the transferee). Thus, all the covenants in the original lease (including the covenant to pay rent) run with the land and are binding on the assignee. At the same time, the original landlord and tenant remain in privity of contract with each other. Thus, if an assignee fails to pay the rent, the landlord may sue either the original tenant (under the contract) or the assignee (because they are in privity of estate and the burden of the covenant to pay rent runs with the land to the assignee). When the tenant transfers the leasehold for a period less than the full remaining time, or reserves a right of entry, the arrangement is called a *sublease*.[399] Traditionally, vertical privity of estate is missing and covenants in the original lease may not run with the land. In that case, if the subtenant fails to pay rent, the landlord may have to sue the original

[394] Robert S. Schoshinski, *American Law of Landlord and Tenant* §8:3, at 539 (1980).
[395] *Id.* at §8:4, at 542.
[396] *Campagna v. Tenneco Oil Co.*, 522 So. 2d 159 (La. Ct. App. 1988); *Med Mac Realty Co. v. Lerner*, 547 N.Y.S.2d 65 (App. Div. 1989); Robert S. Schoshinski, *American Law of Landlord and Tenant* §8:10, at 552 (1980).
[397] N.Y. Real Prop. §226-b(1). The New York statute requires landlords in buildings with four or more units to allow subleases unless they have a good reason to withhold consent. *Id.* at §226-b(2).
[398] Robert S. Schoshinski, *American Law of Landlord and Tenant* §8:10, at 553 (1980).
[399] *Id.* at §8:11, at 556.

tenant, who would implead the subtenant to recover what the tenant owed the landlord. With the possible abolition of the strict privity requirements, courts in the future may make little or no distinction between sublease or assignment, allowing suits against sublessees in the same manner as suits against assignees.

No sublease or assignment clauses enforceable

Clauses that prohibit sublease or assignment are generally enforceable.[400] They are held to constitute reasonable (and thus enforceable) restraints on alienation. Because the landlord usually remains in control of the physical structure and is likely to get the property back at the end of the lease, the landlord has substantial interests in controlling the identity of tenants, both to ensure the physical security of the property and the landlord's financial interest in receiving the reserved rent.

▷ LANDLORD CONSENT CLAUSES **HARD CASE ◀**

Many leases contain a clause allowing sublease or assignment "with the landlord's consent." Conversely, they may prohibit sublease or assign "unless the landlord consents." Traditionally, such clauses were interpreted as giving the landlord absolute power to consent or not to consent to subleases. Many states still follow this interpretive rule.[401] After all, the clause does not limit the landlord's discretion or require consent to be granted reasonably. However, at least a dozen states have begun to infer an implied reasonableness requirement into these clauses, at least in the case of commercial leases, holding that the landlord *must* consent to a sublease or assignment unless the landlord has a commercially reasonable basis for refusing consent.[402] These courts suggest that the landlord has an implied duty of good faith and that, if the landlord had intended never to grant the tenant the right to assign or sublease, the lease should have simply prohibited transfer of the tenant's interest. Inclusion of a clause allowing sublease (subject to the landlord's consent) conveys the message that sublease or assignment *is* available. This, in turn, suggests that consent will be denied only if the landlord has a defensible reason for such denial, unless the landlord specifically bargained for the absolute right to withhold consent. This is the position taken by the *Restatement (Second)*.[403] New York has a statute

[400] *Id.* at §8:10, at 552. *See* Cal. Civ. Code §1995.230 ("A restriction on transfer of a tenant's interest in a lease may absolutely prohibit transfer.").

[401] Robert S. Schoshinski, *American Law of Landlord and Tenant* §8:10, at 552 (1980).

[402] *Vaswani v. Wohletz*, 396 S.E.2d 593 (Ga. Ct. App. 1990); *21 Merchants Row Corp. v. Merchants Row, Inc.*, 587 N.E.2d 788 (Mass. 1992) (commercial lease); *Slavin v. Rent Control Board of Brookline*, 548 N.E.2d 1226, 1228-1229 (Mass. 1990) (residential lease); *Caridi v. Markey*, 539 N.Y.S. 2d 404 (App. Div. 1989); *Pacific First Bank by Washington Mutual v. New Morgan Park Corp.*, 876 P.2d 761, 767 (Or. 1994); *Dobyns v. South Carolina Dep't of Parks, Recreation & Tourism*, 480 S.E.2d 81 (S.C. 1997); *Reynolds v. McCullough*, 739 S.W.2d 424, 429 (Tex. Ct. App. 1987).

[403] *Restatement (Second) of Property (Landlord and Tenant)* §15.2 (1977). *Accord, Hendrickson v. Fredericks*, 620 P.2d 205, 211 (Alaska 1980); *Campbell v. Westdahl*, 715 P.2d 288, 293 (Ariz. Ct. App. 1985); *Kendall v. Ernest Pestana, Inc.*, 709 P.2d 837, 842 (Cal. 1985); *Warner v. Konover*, 553 A.2d 1138 (Conn. 1989); *Julian v. Christopher*, 575 A.2d 735, 739 (Md. 1990); *Newman v. Hinky Dinky Omaha-Lincoln, Inc.*, 427 N.W.2d 50, 53 (Neb. 1988). *But see* Cal.

granting tenants in buildings with four or more units the right to sublet and share space without unreasonable interference by the landlord.[404] However, most courts appear to be applying the traditional rule giving the landlord unfettered discretion to refuse a sublet or assignment where residential tenancies are involved.[405] ◀

Civ. Code §§1995.020(b), 1995.240, 1995.260 & 1995.270 (adopting the implied reasonableness test but allowing parties to contract around it in certain instances). *Cf.* N.Y. Real Prop. §226-b (landlords may act unreasonably in withholding consent to a sublease unless the lease provides otherwise or their buildings contain four or more units).

[404] N.Y. Real Prop. §§226-b(2)(a), 235-f.

[405] *Slavin v. Rent Control Board of Brookline*, 548 N.E.2d 1226 (Mass. 1990); John G. Sprankling, *Understanding Property Law* §18.06, at 291-298 (4th ed. 2017). *See Dick Broad. Co., Inc. of Tennessee v. Oak Ridge FM, Inc.*, 395 S.W.3d 653, 665-666 (Tenn. 2013) ("Currently, some fourteen jurisdictions . . . continue to adhere to the older common law view that a landlord may arbitrarily or unreasonably refuse to consent under a silent consent clause in a lease's anti-assignment provision. Seventeen jurisdictions have adopted the 'modern' position discussed above, imposing an implied duty of good faith and fair dealing in interpreting a silent consent clause.").

CHAPTER 11

Real Estate Transactions

§11.1 Introduction
§11.2 Brokers
§11.3 Sales Contract (Purchase and Sale Agreement)
  §11.3.1 The Attorney's Role
  §11.3.2 Statute of Frauds
  §11.3.3 What Constitutes Breach
    §11.3.3.1 Fraud
    §11.3.3.2 Warranty of Habitability for New Homes
    §11.3.3.3 Marketable Title
    §11.3.3.4 Good Faith Effort to Obtain Financing
  §11.3.4 Remedies for Breach
    §11.3.4.1 Buyer's Remedies
    §11.3.4.2 Seller's Remedies
  §11.3.5 Risk of Loss During Executory Period
  §11.3.6 Death of a Contracting Party
  §11.3.7 Mistake
§11.4 Deeds and Title Protection
  §11.4.1 Formal Requirements
    §11.4.1.1 Writing
    §11.4.1.2 Delivery
  §11.4.2 Substantive Requirements
    §11.4.2.1 Forgery
    §11.4.2.2 Fraud
  §11.4.3 Title Covenants
  §11.4.4 Marketable Title Acts
  §11.4.5 Recording Acts
    §11.4.5.1 How the System Works
    §11.4.5.2 Types of Recording Acts
    §11.4.5.3 Chain-of-Title Problems
  §11.4.6 Title Insurance

§11.4.7 Title Registration
§11.5 Real Estate Finance
§11.5.1 Mortgages
§11.5.2 Installment Land Contracts, or Contracts for Deed
§11.5.3 Equitable Mortgages
§11.5.4 Subprime Mortgages
§11.5.5 Wrongful Foreclosure

§11.1 Introduction

Land transfers

The sale of land and buildings could be treated like any other contractual relationship, but it is not. For one thing, the performance required by the contract involves an exchange of money for a particular thing — property — and that thing involves complexities of definition that have taken us several hundred pages to define — with more to come. The specialized rules about the packages of rights in property that can be created and transferred differentiates the transfer of real property from the sale of a car, for example, or a contract for services, such as an employment contract. A second major difference between real estate transactions and other contracts is the need for an "executory period" between the initial deal and the final consummation. Although many service contracts have this feature (construction contracts, for example), particular problems arise in the real estate context that have led to the creation of a set of governing rules, practices, and procedures to facilitate those transactions and to protect consumers in the market for housing.

Consumer protection

Structure of the transaction

Land sales often begin when an owner who wishes to sell property hires a broker to find potential buyers. The seller sets an asking price and generally promises to pay the broker a percentage of the sales price if and when a buyer is found. A prospective buyer who wishes to purchase the property will make an offer to the seller, which may or may not be in writing and may be lower than the asking price. The parties may bargain about price and other terms of the agreement. The next step is to sign a written contract for the sale of the land (also called a *purchase and sale agreement*), almost always accompanied by a substantial down payment by the buyer. This contract ordinarily sets the date for the closing (when actual transfer of title will occur and the payment of the rest of the purchase price will be tendered) and will include various contingencies that would allow both parties to back out of the deal under specified circumstances. If everything goes well, we get to the *closing*, where the seller will give the buyer a *deed* to the property, transferring title, and the buyer will pay the rest of the purchase price to the seller. The deed will be recorded in the registry of deeds.

Brokers

While some land transfers happen without the aid of brokers or realtors, most sellers hire brokers to find potential purchasers and to show the property to them. A variety of legal disputes arise involving brokers, including questions of when the commission is due, issues surrounding rules prohibiting the unlicensed practice of law, and violations of duties to disclose hidden defects to potential buyers.

Contract

After negotiation about price, timing, and other factors, the seller may eventually accept the potential buyer's offer. This agreement is usually verbal (at least initially), and the parties then reduce it to writing by signing a contract or *purchase and sale agreement*. That contract contains a promise by the seller to transfer title to the property to the buyer in exchange for the purchase price at some future date. It also usually involves a substantial down payment, often deposited with the broker or the seller's attorney. The sale does not happen immediately because the buyer often needs to obtain financing (a loan from a bank), sell a prior home, inspect the premises, and check the seller's title to make sure there are no encumbrances on the property that might prevent the buyer from obtaining marketable title. The buyer usually wants the right to back out of the deal if it turns out that the seller does not have marketable title, if there are structural defects in the building, if the use fails to comply with applicable zoning and land use laws, and if the buyer cannot obtain financing to complete the transaction. The deal may also be contingent on the buyer being able to sell her previous house to raise the money necessary to buy the new house. The contract therefore usually makes the buyer's obligation conditional on satisfactory resolution of these issues. The seller may also include contingencies in the deal; she may need time to find another house or need to wait until that deal closes before she can move out of this house.

Contract problems

Many issues arise about how to interpret the obligations of buyer and seller under the contract and what constitutes a breach of the agreement. If there is a breach, and one of the parties wishes to back out of the arrangement, the courts must determine the appropriate remedy. If the buyer breaches, can the seller keep the deposit? If the seller changes her mind and refuses to sell, can the buyer force the seller to transfer title and complete the sale? What happens if the property suffers a fire in the executory period between the signing of the contract and the date set for the closing? Who bears the risk of loss?

Title problems

Additional problems concern the state of the title. The recording system encourages owners to record deeds at the registry of deeds to provide buyers with proof of who owns property and to put them on notice of any leases, mortgages, easements, covenants, or conflicting transfers made by the owner (or a prior owner) of the property they wish to purchase. What happens if a prior deed is unrecorded but the buyer knew about it when she signed the contract? What if some portion of the property is owned because of adverse possession? Does this render the title unmarketable and entitle the buyer to get out of the deal?

Financing

Finally, issues often arise in the context of real estate finance. To purchase the property, most buyers must borrow money from a bank or other lending institution. In return for the loan, the bank obtains a *lien* on the property, usually in the form of a *mortgage*, which will allow the bank to *foreclose* on the property and have it sold and the proceeds used to pay off the debt if the borrower defaults in repaying the loan. Both the initial lending process and the foreclosure process are regulated by state and federal law to protect buyers from losing their homes unnecessarily and to protect the ability of banks to recover their loans.

§11.2 Brokers

Licensed profession

Real estate brokers are in the business of helping owners sell real property by finding buyers for their property. They are generally hired by sellers and are compensated by a commission paid by the buyer, which may range from 5 to 6 percent of the purchase price of the property. The commission is generally taken out of the purchase price. Every state regulates brokers, like other professionals, such as doctors and lawyers, through licensing requirements.[1] Brokers are subject to a code of ethics established by the National Association of Realtors or a local real estate board and subject to oversight by the state licensing agency.[2] As with other licensed professionals, brokers who fail to take due care in the exercise of their business or who act unethically may lose their license to practice.

Types of listing contracts

Brokers are usually hired by sellers to find prospective buyers. Sometimes brokers are hired informally by oral agreements. However, written agreements called *listing contracts* are generally more common.[3] Several types of agreements between sellers and brokers are in wide use.

Open listing

First, an *open listing* allows the landowner to sell the property herself or use another broker.[4] The broker will receive a commission only if the broker finds a buyer ready, willing, and able to buy on the seller's terms before anyone else does.[5] When a broker finds such a buyer, she is called the "procuring cause" of the sale and is entitled to the commission. All informal oral listing arrangements are in this form.

Exclusive agency

Second, under an *exclusive agency* arrangement, the broker is entitled to a commission if she finds a buyer or if another broker finds a buyer, but not if the owner finds a buyer herself.[6]

Exclusive right to sell

Third, an *exclusive right to sell* promises the broker a commission if the property is sold no matter who finds the buyer. The named broker will receive a commission whether the buyer is found by her, another broker, the owner, or anyone else.[7]

Multiple listing services

A *multiple listing service* is an arrangement used by brokers in an area who pool their efforts by listing all properties for whom any of them has obtained a listing agreement. The original or *listing* broker ordinarily obtains an exclusive right to sell from the owner and then lists the property on the service. Other brokers who have subscribed to the service are then made aware that the property is for sale and all brokers with access to the service may show the property. If a broker other than the listing broker procures a buyer, the commission is shared between the listing broker, the selling broker, and perhaps the multiple listing service itself.[8]

Net listing

Several types of listing agreements have either been outlawed by statute in some states or are discouraged by state regulators. Under the *net listing*, the broker takes her commission out of the purchase price to the extent it exceeds the seller's price. Many states prohibit this arrangement by statute, and others discourage it through regulations issued by the licensing commissions.[9] This arrangement is problematic because it creates a conflict

[1] 11 *Thompson on Real Property, Third Thomas Edition* §95.03.

[2] Raymond J. Werner & Robert Kratovil, *Real Estate Law* §§10.04 to 10.05, at 80-81 (11th ed. 2002).

[3] 11 *Thompson on Real Property, Third Thomas Edition* §95.05.

[4] D. Barlow Burke, Jr., *Law of Real Estate Brokers* §2.02[A] (4th ed. 2025).

[5] *Id.*; 11 *Thompson on Real Property, Third Thomas Edition* §95.05(a); Raymond J. Werner & Robert Kratovil, *Real Estate Law* §10.08, at 84 (11th ed. 2002).

[6] D. Barlow Burke, Jr., *Law of Real Estate Brokers* §2.02[B] (4th ed. 2025); Raymond J. Werner & Robert Kratovil, *Real Estate Law* §10.09, at 84-85 (11th ed. 2002).

[7] D. Barlow Burke, Jr., *Law of Real Estate Brokers* §2.02[C] (4th ed. 2025); Raymond J. Werner & Robert Kratovil, *Real Estate Law* §10.10, at 85 (11th ed. 2002).

[8] Raymond J. Werner & Robert Kratovil, *Real Estate Law* §10.11, at 85-86 (11th ed. 2002).

[9] D. Barlow Burke, Jr., *Law of Real Estate Brokers* §2.02[D] (4th ed. 2025); 11 *Thompson on Real Property, Third Thomas Edition* §95.05(a).

of interest between the seller and the broker. Sellers often rely on the advice of brokers to help determine the price they should ask for their property. Under the net listing, the broker has an incentive to induce the seller to list the property for a price below its fair market value because the broker will pocket the excess.[10] Conversely, if the property is sold at fair market value and is listed at that amount, the broker recovers nothing and therefore may have an incentive not to tell the seller about an offer that will earn the broker nothing.[11]

Option listing

Another practice discouraged by state regulators is the *option listing*, whereby the broker promises to buy the property at a set price, revealing the commission only when the option is exercised. Under this arrangement, the broker has an incentive to suggest to the seller that the property is worth less than it really is because the broker can resell the property for its fair market value, pocketing the difference.[12]

When commission is due

Majority rule: Offer from ready, willing, and able buyer on seller's terms

The majority rule is that, unless the seller and the broker agree otherwise,[13] a broker is entitled to the commission when she "procures a purchaser who is ready, willing, and able to buy the listed property on the vendor's terms."[14] A buyer is procured when an offer is made by that buyer.[15] This traditional rule obligates the seller to pay the commission even if the buyer defaults and later backs out of the deal before the closing.[16] The commission is similarly payable if the seller changes her mind and wrongfully refuses to complete the transaction.[17] This rule also applies when the broker is employed to lease the property.[18] The buyer's execution of a binding contract of sale is taken by most courts as conclusive evidence that the buyer was ready, willing, and able to buy the property on the seller's terms.[19] The signing of a contract is evidence the seller agrees that the broker has procured a suitable buyer. However, a signed contract is not essential because

10 D. Barlow Burke, Jr., *Law of Real Estate Brokers* §2.02[D] (4th ed. 2025).

11 *Id.*

12 *Id.* at §2.02[E].

13 *Watson v. Fultz*, 782 P.2d 361 (Mont. 1989); D. Barlow Burke, Jr., *Law of Real Estate Brokers* §5.01 (4th ed. 2025).

14 D. Barlow Burke, Jr., *Law of Real Estate Brokers* §5.02 (4th ed. 2025). *See also* 11 *Thompson on Real Property, Third Thomas Edition* §95.05(b). *See Bennett Realty, Inc. v. Muller*, 396 S.E.2d 630, 632 (N.C. Ct. App. 1990); *Henri-Lynn Realty, Inc. v. Huang*, 552 N.Y.S.2d 357 (App. Div. 1990); *Key-Ventures, Inc. v. Rappleye*, 556 N.Y.S.2d 627 (App. Div. 1990); *Muirloch Realty, Inc. v. Periodical Charter & Leasing, Inc.*, 1996 WL 17579 (Ohio Ct. App. 1996); Raymond J. Werner & Robert Kratovil, *Real Estate Law* §10.16, at 96 (11th ed. 2002).

15 *William Raveis Real Estate, Inc. v. Stawski*, 626 A.2d 797, 798-799 (Conn. App. Ct. 1993).

16 *Cox v. Venters*, 887 S.W.2d 563, 566-567 (Ky. Ct. App. 1994); *Glassberg v. Warshawsky*, 638 N.E.2d 749, 755 (Ill. App. Ct. 1994); *Sayegusa v. Rogers*, 846 P.2d 1005 (Mont. 1993); *Blais v. Remillard*, 643 A.2d 967, 968 (N.H. 1994); *Key-Ventures, Inc. v. Rappleye*, 556 N.Y.S.2d 627 (App. Div. 1990); *French v. Ahlstrom*, 612 N.Y.S.2d 458 (App. Div. 1994); D. Barlow Burke, Jr., *Law of Real Estate Brokers* §5.02 (4th ed. 2025).

17 *Fourth Street Restaurant v. Venture Realty Group, Inc.*, 533 So. 2d 784 (Fla. Dist. Ct. App. 1988); 11 *Thompson on Real Property, Third Thomas Edition* §95.05(b).

18 *Vulcan Oil Co. v. Gorman*, 434 So. 2d 760 (Ala. 1983); *Kaplon-Belo Assocs. v. Farrelly*, 633 N.Y.S.2d 522 (App. Div. 1995); D. Barlow Burke, Jr., *Law of Real Estate Brokers* §5.02 (4th ed. 2025).

19 *May Partnership v. Barker*, 431 S.E.2d 331 (Va. 1993) (applying Maryland law); *Wertz Realty, Inc. v. Parden*, 607 N.E.2d 550 (Ohio Ct. App. 1992); *Cornelia and Broad Streets, Inc. v. Chase*, 587 N.Y.S.2d 809, 810 (App. Div. 1992).

the commission is earned when the offer is made by a suitable buyer on terms acceptable to the seller.[20]

Broker's rights upon default

Most listing agreements provide that the commission will be paid at the closing. This means that, although the commission may be *earned* at the time when the broker produces a suitable buyer, it is ordinarily not *due to be paid* under the contract terms until the date of the closing.[21] If the seller backs out of the deal, the seller owes the commission because the contract between the seller and the broker contains an implied obligation on the seller to go through with the deal once the broker finds a suitable buyer.[22] By hiring the broker, the seller commits to selling the property once a ready, willing, and able purchaser is found; that is why the broker is willing to spend the time looking for a buyer. Once the buyer makes an offer on the seller's terms, the seller cannot back out of the dealing without breaching her implied obligation to complete the deal once the broker finds a suitable buyer. The seller may choose to reject the offer; there is no enforceable duty to convey the property to the buyer until there is an offer and acceptance. However, the refusal to accept the offer is taken to be a breach of the seller's promise to the broker that the seller would go through with it if a suitable buyer were found. If a suitable offer is made by a ready, willing, and able buyer, the seller is obligated to pay the commission even if the seller refuses to agree to a contract of sale.[23] However, the seller may not be obligated to complete the deal (or to pay the broker's commission) if the seller acted in good faith and with the reasonable belief that he was able to convey good title but was not able to do so.[24]

Seller's default

Buyer's default

If the buyer backs out of the deal, the traditional rule still obligates the seller to pay the broker because the broker completed her duties when she found a buyer who was ready, willing, and able to purchase.[25] The argument is that the broker should not be harmed by the default of the buyer. The seller accepted the buyer as a suitable buyer and therefore demonstrated that the broker had performed the duties required of the broker under the listing agreement, *i.e.*, finding a buyer suitable to the seller. The buyer ordinarily makes a substantial down payment when the contract of sale is signed, and the contract normally allows the seller to keep the down payment as liquidated damages if the buyer defaults. The seller can use the

[20] *Johnson v. Nyhart*, 889 P.2d 1170, 1174 (Mont. 1995); *Muirloch Realty, Inc. v. Periodical Charter & Leasing, Inc.*, 1996 WL 17579 (Ohio Ct. App. 1996); D. Barlow Burke, Jr., *Law of Real Estate Brokers* §5.02 (4th ed. 2025).

[21] Depending on the wording of the contract, a provision requiring payment at the closing may be interpreted as providing that the commission is not owed unless the closing happens, thus releasing the owner from the duty to pay the commission if for any reason the deal falls through. *See, e.g., Greiner-Maltz Co. v. Kalex Chemical Products*, 530 N.Y.S.2d 220, 221 (App. Div. 1988) (making this argument).

[22] *Fourth Street Restaurant v. Venture Realty Group*, 533 So. 2d 784, 787 (Fla. Dist. Ct. App. 1988); D. Barlow Burke, Jr., *Law of Real Estate Brokers* §5.02 (4th ed. 2025).

[23] *Id.*

[24] *Van Winkle & Liggett v. G.B.R. Fabrics, Inc.*, 511 A.2d 124 (N.J. 1986).

[25] *Sayegusa v. Rogers*, 846 P.2d 1005 (Mont. 1993); D. Barlow Burke, Jr., *Law of Real Estate Brokers* §5.02 (4th ed. 2025).

down payment to pay off the broker. Or, instead, the seller and broker may split the deposit between them.[26]

▶ HARD CASE

▷ CONDITIONAL CONTRACTS

Traditional rule: Commission earned even if buyer defaults because of inability to secure financing

Most contracts impose conditions on the deal. Some condition the deal on completion of a satisfactory inspection. One could argue that such a buyer is not yet "ready and willing" to buy the property. Similarly, most purchase and sale agreements are contingent on the buyer obtaining financing for the deal. Again, such a buyer is arguably not "able" to buy until the financing comes through. The traditional rule requires the seller to pay the commission in such a case even if the buyer backed out of the deal because she could not obtain the financing.[27] Traditionally, the risk of the buyer not obtaining financing is on the seller once the contract of sale is signed. By signing the contract, the seller is thought to have accepted the buyer as "ready, willing, and able"; this places a burden on the seller to scrutinize the buyer's financial status *before* signing the contract. The signing of the contract is thought to provide evidence that the broker had produced a buyer acceptable to the seller, and because the broker's job was to produce such a buyer, the commission is owed even if the buyer backs out of the deal because she cannot obtain financing.

Developing rule: Commission is owed only if buyer obtains financing

An increasing number (but still a minority) of states have held that when a contract is conditional on the buyer obtaining financing, the buyer is not "able" to purchase unless she obtains financing, and thus the broker has not earned the commission until the financing is secured.[28] If the buyer makes a good faith effort to obtain financing but cannot do so, she is contractually entitled to get out of the arrangement and the commission would not be earned. A similar result should obtain if the inspection is unsatisfactory. A buyer who signs a contract that allows her to get out of the deal if an inspection is unsatisfactory is not yet "ready and willing." Conversely, once the financing is obtained and a satisfactory inspection has been completed, the buyer is "ready, willing, and able" to buy, and, at that point, the seller is obligated to pay the commission, although the listing agreement may well provide that the commission, although earned, is not payable until the date of the closing.[29]

[26] *Taylor Real Estate & Insurance Co. v. Greene*, 151 So. 2d 397 (Ala. 1963); 11 *Thompson on Real Property, Third Thomas Edition* §95.05(b). *See* Roger Bernhardt & Dale A. Whitman, *When Is a Commission Due? Problems with Broker Listing Agreements*, 27 Prob. & Prop. 30 (Jan./Feb. 2013).

[27] D. Barlow Burke, Jr., *Law of Real Estate Brokers* §5.02 (4th ed. 2025).

[28] *In re John Chezik Imports, Inc.*, 195 B.R. 417 (Bankr. E.D. Mo. 1996); *Century 21-Birdsell Realty, Inc. v. Hiebel*, 379 N.W.2d 201, 204 (Minn. Ct. App. 1985); *Goetz v. Anderson*, 274 N.W.2d 175 (N.D. 1978); *Woodland Realty, Inc. v. Winzenried*, 262 N.W.2d 106 (Wis. 1978); D. Barlow Burke, Jr., *Law of Real Estate Brokers* §5.03 (4th ed. 2025).

[29] *Rector-Phillips-Morse, Inc. v. Huntsman Farms, Inc.*, 590 S.W.2d 317 (Ark. 1979); *Timmerman v. Smith*, 413 So. 2d 627 (La. Ct. App. 1982); D. Barlow Burke, Jr., *Law of Real Estate Brokers* §5.03 (4th ed. 2025).

Minority rule: Commission due only at closing

A growing minority of states have gone even further than this, holding that the commission is not earned until the closing.[30] In the leading case of *Ellsworth Dobbs, Inc. v. Johnson*,[31] the court noted that sellers normally expect to pay the commission out of the sale proceeds obtained at the closing.[32] Under this approach, the seller owes the commission only if the seller wrongfully backs out of the deal before the closing. If, however, the buyer backs out of the deal, either because she could not obtain financing or because she changed her mind and decided to breach the contract, the commission has not been earned. This is because the "owner hires the broker with the expectation of becoming liable for a commission only in the event a sale of the property is consummated, unless the title does not pass because of the owner's improper or frustrating conduct."[33] Beyond that, the Supreme Court of New Jersey made this rule nondisclaimable, holding that allowing brokers to contract for the commission upon presentation of a suitable buyer would be unconscionable.[34] In contrast, although the Supreme Judicial Court in Massachusetts adopted the New Jersey rule, it held that the parties could contract around it.[35]

Policy arguments

The traditional rule is generally defended by arguing that the broker who produces a ready, willing, and able buyer has done what she promised to do in her listing agreement and thus is entitled to the agreed-upon compensation. It is not the broker's fault if the buyer defaults, and any loss to the seller can be made up by suing the defaulting buyer or by using the deposit retained by the seller when the purchase and sale agreement was signed. The counterargument is that this approach flies in the face of ordinary expectations of sellers, who uniformly expect to pay the commission out of the closing proceeds and thus do not intend to promise to pay a commission unless the sale actually happens. ◀

▷ OBLIGATIONS TO BUYERS

HARD CASE ◀

Brokers are generally hired by sellers and are their agents. However, buyers seeking homes contact brokers to show them various properties and often come to rely on the broker and trust her. Indeed, they often come to feel that the broker is working for them. Many states now require brokers to disclose to buyers that they are working for the seller rather than the

[30] *Harrin v. Brown Realty Co.*, 602 P.2d 79 (Kan. 1979); *Blumfield Agency v. Little Belt, Inc.*, 663 P.2d 1164 (Mont. 1983); *Dworak v. Michals*, 320 N.W.2d 485, 488 (Neb. 1982); *Brown v. Grimm*, 481 P.2d 63 (Or. 1971); *Sexton v. Neun*, 306 A.2d 113 (Vt. 1973); *Exotex Corp. v. Rinehart*, 3 P.3d 826 (Wyo. 2000).

[31] 236 A.2d 843 (N.J. 1967). *Accord, Tristram's Landing, Inc. v. Wait*, 327 N.E.2d 727 (Mass. 1975).

[32] 236 A.2d at 852.

[33] *Id.* at 853.

[34] *Id.* at 856. *See* D. Barlow Burke, Jr., *Law of Real Estate Brokers* §6.02 (4th ed. 2025) (criticizing this ruling and arguing that this rule should be nondisclaimable only in the case of standard form contracts and disclaimable if the parties are sophisticated and bargain for appropriate allocation of the risks of the deal falling through).

[35] *Cappezzuto v. John Hancock Mutual Life Insurance Co.*, 476 N.E.2d 188 (Mass. 1985); *Tristram's Landing v. Wait*, 327 N.E.2d 727 (Mass. 1975); *Currier v. Kosinski*, 506 N.E.2d 895 (Mass. App. Ct. 1987).

buyer.[36] Brokers may also be liable to buyers if they fail to disclose known latent defects in the property that might have led the buyer to decide not to buy.[37] Do buyers have obligations to brokers to pay the broker's commission if the buyer wrongfully reneges on the deal? The buyer has no contract with the broker who was hired by the seller. Some courts hold that

> when a prospective buyer solicits a broker to find or to show him property which he might be interested in buying, and the broker finds property satisfactory to him that the owner agrees to sell at the price offered, and the buyer knows the broker will earn a commission for the sale from the owner, the law will imply a promise on the part of the buyer to complete the transaction with the owner.[38]

Other courts hold the opposite.[39] ◀

Buyer's brokers

Some buyers, particularly in commercial real estate, but increasingly in residential real estate as well, hire their own brokers to obtain advice on the price and other features of property that is not biased toward the seller's views on these matters. In areas with multiple listing services, the buyer's broker will share the commission with the listing broker.[40] Conflicts of interest can arise if a single brokerage firm represents both buyers and sellers. A broker hired by a buyer might also have been hired to list the property by the seller. Such dual agents have conflicting interests, and many states now allow such arrangements but regulate them by requiring brokers to disclose to the buyer that they are acting as dual agents.[41] Concerns have also been raised about whether dual agents can adequately represent both sides.[42] Many states now also allow "designated agency" in which one broker in the agency represents the seller while another represents the buyer in the transaction.[43] Some states are now experimenting with allowing brokers to act as "transaction brokers" in which they do not represent either the seller or the buyer; instead, they act as professionals giving independent advice on the transaction.[44] While this form of practice mitigates the problems that occurred when brokers were working as agents for sellers while buyers were misled into thinking the brokers were working for them,

Conflicts of interest

[36] Ann Morales Olazábal, *Redefining Realtor Relationships and Responsibilities: The Failure of State Regulatory Responses*, 40 Harv. J. on Legis. 65, 67 (2003).

[37] Cal. Civ. Code §2079; N.J. Stat. §§46:3C-1 to -12; *Easton v. Strassburger*, 199 Cal. Rptr. 383, 387 (Ct. App. 1984); *Strawn v. Canuso*, 657 A.2d 420, 431 (N.J. 1995); *Nobrega v. Edison Glen Assocs.*, 743 A.2d 865 (N.J. Super. Ct. App. Div. 2000). *See also Lombardo v. Albu*, 14 P.3d 288 (Ariz. 2000) (buyer's broker liable to seller for failing to disclose buyer's financial problems that were likely to — and that did — lead to the deal falling through).

[38] *Ellsworth Dobbs, Inc. v. Johnson*, 236 A.2d 843, 859 (N.J. 1967). *Accord*, *Donnellan v. Rocks*, 99 Cal. Rptr. 692, 696 (Ct. App. 1972).

[39] *Rich v. Emerson-Dumont Distributing Corp.*, 222 N.W.2d 65 (Mich. Ct. App. 1974); *Professional Realty Corp. v. Bender*, 222 S.E.2d 810 (Va. 1976).

[40] 11 *Thompson on Real Property, Third Thomas Edition* §95.07(a)(2).

[41] Ga. Code §§10-6A-10 & 10-6A-12(a).

[42] *Horiike v. Coldwell Banker Residential Brokerage Co.*, 383 P.3d 1094 (Cal. 2016).

[43] Ann Morales Olazábal, *Redefining Realtor Relationships and Responsibilities: The Failure of State Regulatory Responses*, 40 Harv. J. on Legis. 65, 75-76 (2003).

[44] *Id.* at 87-91. *See* Ga. Code §10-6A-3(14).

it creates other problems. If the broker is not the agent of either the seller or the buyer, they cannot be liable for breach of fiduciary duty; while this may relieve the broker of worry about possible liability, it may also remove incentives to promote the interest of one or both parties to the transaction, and for this reason every state that has adopted this idea has imposed some statutory duties on such transaction brokers.[45]

Antitrust concerns with brokers

With home searching increasingly easily conducted online, regulators and consumer advocates are challenging residential broker's traditional fee structure. Past regulatory actions have lifted restrictions by the National Association of Realtors (NAR), the trade association for brokers, on brokers' ability to post listings online,[46] and prohibited NAR members from concealing fees and refusing to cooperate on listings with non-NAR members.[47] In 2024, facing antitrust claims from home sellers, NAR reached a national class-action settlement barring sellers from posting fees to be paid to buyer agents, mandating that buyer brokers detail their fees in writing, noting that compensation is negotiable, and bars brokers from choosing listings based on compensation.[48] The hope is that this new structure will foster negotiation over fees and lower costs.

▷ UNLICENSED PRACTICE OF LAW **HARD CASE ◀**

Changing role of the broker

Every state requires lawyers to be licensed to practice law, and brokers who provide legal advice or draft complex legal documents for their clients may be subject to penalties for the unauthorized practice of law.[49] Brokers often provide standard land sale contracts for sellers and buyers to use. If they do no more than fill in the blanks on such forms, these activities are thought be an "incident to the business" of providing brokerage services and courts are unlikely to find a violation of the laws prohibiting nonlawyers from "practicing law."[50] However, if they draft deeds, mortgages, or other documents that transfer interests in real property, express opinions on the status of titles or zoning law and the like, or conduct closings, they may be found to have engaged in the unauthorized practice of law.[51] These restrictions

[45] Ann Morales Olazábal, *Redefining Realtor Relationships and Responsibilities: The Failure of State Regulatory Responses*, 40 Harv. J. on Legis. at 90-91 (2003).

[46] *United States v. Nat'l Ass'n of Realtors*, Final J., Civil Action No. 05 C 5140 (N.D. Ill. Nov. 18, 2008) (approving settlement).

[47] *United States v. Nat'l Ass'n of Realtors*, No. 20-CV-3356 at V.F. (D.D.C. 2020) (approving settlement).

[48] *Burnett v. Nat'l Ass'n of Realtors*, No. 19-CV-00332-SRB (W.D. Mo. Nov. 27, 2024) (approving settlement).

[49] *State v. Buyers Service Co.*, 357 S.E.2d 15, 19 (S.C. 1987); D. Barlow Burke, Jr., *Law of Real Estate Brokers* §§12.01 to 12.02 (4th ed. 2025).

[50] *Pope County Bar Ass'n v. Suggs*, 624 S.W.2d 828 (Ark. 1981); *Sullivan as Tr. of Sylvester L. Sullivan Grantor Retained Income Tr. v. Max Spann Real Est. & Auction Co.*, 276 A.3d 92 (N.J. 2022); *Duncan & Hill Realty, Inc. v. Department of State*, 405 N.Y.S.2d 339 (App. Div. 1978); *Commonwealth v. Jones & Robbins*, 41 S.E.2d 720 (Va. 1947); *Cultum v. Heritage House Realtors, Inc.*, 694 P.2d 630 (Wash. 1985); D. Barlow Burke, Jr., *Law of Real Estate Brokers* §16.01 (4th ed. 2025).

[51] *Toledo Bar Ass'n v. Chelsea Title Agency of Dayton, Inc.*, 800 N.E.2d 29 (Ohio 2003); *Doe v. McMaster*, 585 S.E.2d 773 (S.C. 2003); *State v. Buyers Service Co.*, 357 S.E.2d 15 (S.C. 1987);

on the conduct of brokers are intended to "protect[] the public from the potentially severe economic and emotional consequences which may flow from erroneous advice given by persons untrained in the law."[52]

Some states have begun to loosen these regulations to allow brokers to perform functions that used to be performed by lawyers on the ground that this serves the public interest by lowering the costs of buying and selling real estate.[53] The Supreme Court of New Jersey, for example, authorized brokers and title companies to conduct closings in an area of the state where it was typical for neither seller nor buyer to be represented by a lawyer at the closing.[54] While holding that they were engaged in the practice of law, their activity was not "unauthorized" because it was in the public interest for them to help owners conduct real estate transactions and there was not sufficient warrant to force every owner and every buyer to hire a lawyer to buy or sell real estate.[55] ◀

§11.3 Sales Contract (Purchase and Sale Agreement)

Offer and acceptance

The seller sets an asking price that the broker communicates to potential buyers. A prospective buyer makes an offer that may match or be either below or above the asking price.[56] The seller may accept the offer or reduce the asking price somewhat. The parties may also bargain about other relevant terms of the sale, such as the date of the closing or whether the seller will leave fixtures in the property (such as light fixtures). In some states, the buyer makes a written offer and makes a deposit of a percentage of the purchase price, which may be as low as $1,000, to demonstrate the seriousness of the offer. In many states, this initial stage is done orally. The seller may accept the offer verbally or in writing.

§11.3.1 The Attorney's Role

Purchase and sale agreement

When the seller accepts the buyer's offer to purchase a contract is made, but it is usually contingent on their signing a written *purchase and sale*

Michael Braunstein, *Structural Change and Inter-Professional Competitive Advantage: An Example Drawn from Residential Real Estate Conveyancing*, 62 Mo. L. Rev. 241, 250-253 (1997); D. Barlow Burke, Jr., *Law of Real Estate Brokers* §16.01[B] (4th ed. 2025); 11 *Thompson on Real Property, Third Thomas Edition* §95.06(a). *See Ex parte Watson*, 589 S.E.2d 760 (S.C. 2003) (nonlawyer title abstractors who examine public records and issue an opinion in a title search performed in connection with tax foreclosure sale are engaged in the unauthorized practice of law).

52 *State v. Buyers Service Co.*, 357 S.E.2d 15, 18 (S.C. 1987).

53 *Countrywide Home Loans, Inc. v. Kentucky Bar Ass'n*, 113 S.W.3d 105 (Ky. 2003) (allowing laypersons to conduct real estate closings as long as they do not give legal advice); *Dressel v. Ameribank*, 664 N.W.2d 151 (Mich. 2003) (not unauthorized practice of law for title company to prepare leases, mortgages, and deeds).

54 *In re Opinion No. 26 of the Committee on Unauthorized Practice of Law*, 654 A.2d 1344, 1359 (N.J. 1995).

55 *Id.*

56 Although it would seem odd to offer more than the seller is asking, this sometimes happens in a tight housing market when a buyer really wants to ensure that she gets the house.

agreement or *land sale contract.* A written agreement is required by the statute of frauds. These contracts may be prepared by attorneys,[57] but, in most states, brokers help the parties fill in the blanks on form contracts.[58] Although many attorneys believe that they should be involved at this point in the transaction, in many areas of the country, most land sale contracts are signed without the aid of an attorney on either side.[59] One study showed that attorneys are involved in only about 40 percent of residential transactions in New Jersey.[60] In some cases, the contract will include an "attorney approval clause," giving the parties a specified time, such as three days, to consult with an attorney after signing the document and allowing the parties to withdraw if they wish.[61]

Decreasing role of attorneys

A survey of Ohio real estate attorneys found substantial variation in the percentage of residential real estate transactions that involved attorneys. Overall, in only one-third of the transactions did the parties consult an attorney before signing the purchase and sale agreement. Only one-eighth of all the attorneys consulted felt that more than 50 percent of land sales were made with the participation of a lawyer. One-third of the lawyers surveyed believed that attorneys were involved in less than 10 percent of the transactions in their area.[62] In most states, attorneys are often involved in neither the drafting of the purchase and sale agreement nor the preparation for the closing, let alone the closing itself.[63]

Efffect of these changes

Although the increasing marginalization of lawyers in residential land sales in many areas may reduce the cost of such transactions to home buyers and sellers, it may also leave the parties subject to legal vulnerabilities of which they were not aware when they signed the agreement. It may be the case that the actual understanding of the parties of the meaning and effect of their deal may diverge from the provisions contained in form contracts. If this is the case, the courts will more and more have to deal with the question of what to do when the parties' actual expectations diverge from the formal terms of their agreement. On the other hand, it has been argued that litigation about these issues has clarified the rights of the parties (or

[57] In only five states is it customary for lawyers to draw the contract of sale, and, even in those states, this practice is confined to large urban areas. Michael Braunstein, *Structural Change and Inter-Professional Competitive Advantage: An Example Drawn from Residential Real Estate Conveyancing*, 62 Mo. L. Rev. 241, 262 (1997) (Alabama, Connecticut, Illinois, Massachusetts, and New York).

[58] Michael Braunstein, *Structural Change and Inter-Professional Competitive Advantage: An Example Drawn from Residential Real Estate Conveyancing*, 62 Mo. L. Rev. 241, 261 (1997).

[59] Gary S. Moore, *Lawyers and the Residential Real Estate Transaction*, 26 Real Est. L.J. 351, 356-357 (1998).

[60] Michael Braunstein, *Structural Change and Inter-Professional Competitive Advantage: An Example Drawn from Residential Real Estate Conveyancing*, 62 Mo. L. Rev. 241, 276 (1997).

[61] Alice N. Noble-Allgire, *Attorney Approval Clauses in Residential Real Estate Contracts — Is Half a Loaf Better than None?*, 48 Kan. L. Rev. 339 (2000).

[62] Gary S. Moore, *Lawyers and the Residential Real Estate Transaction*, 26 Real Est. L.J. 351, 356-357 (1998).

[63] Michael Braunstein, *Structural Change and Inter-Professional Competitive Advantage: An Example Drawn from Residential Real Estate Conveyancing*, 62 Mo. L. Rev. 241, 265 (1997).

will do so in the future), and that ordinary home purchasers do not need the participation of an attorney in the transaction to protect their rights.[64]

▶ HARD CASE ▷ ATTORNEY LIABILITY TO THIRD PARTIES

When an attorney prepares documents for one party to a real estate transaction, is that attorney liable to the other party (typically the buyer) for failing to do so properly? Most courts hold no. For example, in *Fox v. Pollack*,[65] an attorney reduced the parties' agreement to writing and the plaintiffs later alleged that the writing failed to comply with the terms of the oral agreement. The court held that the attorney was not liable in negligence to the buyer because the buyer had not hired the attorney and thus the attorney had no duty to explain the transaction to the buyer or otherwise look out for the buyer's interests.[66] However, some courts disagree, holding instead that the attorney for the seller is liable in negligence to the buyer when the attorney knows the buyer would rely on the attorney's representations.[67] ◀

§11.3.2 Statute of Frauds

Writing containing essential terms

Every state has a *statute of frauds*, which requires contracts for the transfer of interests in real property to be in writing to be legally enforceable.[68] The requirement of a writing is to prevent fraud and to clarify the essential terms of the agreement. Those terms include the *parties*, the *price*, a description of the *property*, an expression of the *intent* to sell or buy, and a *signature* by the party to be charged. In the past, some courts have held that the price was not an essential term in the contract, but modern cases generally hold that it is.[69] When the parties sign a short contract called a *binder* that is intended to lead to negotiations for the terms of a longer sales contract, has the statute of frauds been satisfied? Some courts hold that the agreement is not enforceable because the parties intended further negotiation about its terms,[70] while other courts hold that the binder is enforceable

[64] *Id.* at 271-279.

[65] 226 Cal. Rptr. 532 (Ct. App. 1986).

[66] *Accord, Adams v. Chenowith*, 349 So. 2d 230 (Fla. Dist. Ct. App. 1977); *First National Bank of Moline v. Califf, Harper, Fox & Dailey*, 548 N.E.2d 1361 (Ill. App. Ct. 1989).

[67] *Petrillo v. Bachenberg*, 655 A.2d 1354, 1359-1360 (N.J. 1995); *Collins v. Binkley*, 750 S.W.2d 737 (Tenn. 1988); *Restatement (Second) of Torts* §552 (1977) ("One who, in the course of his business, profession or employment, or in any other transaction in which he has a pecuniary interest, supplies false information for the guidance of others in their business transactions, is subject to liability for pecuniary loss caused to them by their justifiable reliance upon the information, if he fails to exercise reasonable care or competence in obtaining or communicating the information.").

[68] Dale A. Whitman et al., *The Law of Property* §10.1, at 595-608 (4th ed. 2019); 14-81 *Powell on Real Property* §81.02[1].

[69] Dale A. Whitman et al., *The Law of Property* §10.1, at 603 (4th ed. 2019); 14-81 *Powell on Real Property* §81.02[2][d][i]. *See D'Agostino v. Bank of Ravenswood*, 563 N.E.2d 886 (Ill. App. Ct. 1990); *Cobble Hill Nursing Homes, Inc. v. Henry and Warren Corp.*, 548 N.E.2d 203 (N.Y. 1989); *Estate of Younge v. Huysmans*, 506 A.2d 282 (N.H. 1985) (all holding that the price is an essential term in the contract).

[70] *Behar v. Mawardi*, 702 N.Y.S.2d 326 (App. Div. 2000).

if the essential terms (such as the parties, the property, the price, and time for performance) are included.[71]

Conditions in the contract

The sales contract usually has a number of conditions in it. The buyer may seek to get out of the deal if inspections prove unsatisfactory, if the buyer cannot obtain adequate financing, or if it turns out that the title is encumbered by previously unknown servitudes or leases. The seller ordinarily will bargain to keep the *deposit* or *earnest money* as liquidated damages if the buyer wrongfully defaults and refuses to complete the transaction.

Exceptions to the statute of frauds: Part performance

Oral promises to convey real estate are sometimes enforced by courts, despite the statute of frauds, if the parties admit that a contract was made[72] or if the buyer relies on the promise to convey and substantially changes her position in reasonable reliance on the promise. Three doctrines have developed in this context: *part performance*, *estoppel*, and *constructive trust*.[73] The *part performance* doctrine allows an oral sales contract to be enforced if the buyer has taken substantial steps to complete the transaction.[74] Traditionally, some courts have held that the buyer must take steps that are "unequivocally referable" to a land sales contract.[75] Modern courts do not require this degree of certainty, instead relying on three factors that ordinarily will suggest that a contract has been made:[76] (1) payment of all or a substantial part of the *purchase price*; (2) taking *possession* of the property; and (3) making substantial *improvements* on the land.[77] The states differ on whether all three are required or only one or two of the three.[78] Payment of part of the purchase price is generally not enough to trigger the doctrine because the buyer can be made whole by having the money returned (with interest).[79] However, payment of the purchase price in combination with one or both of the other factors should be sufficient because they ordinarily would not occur without a promise to convey.

Evidentiary basis of the rule

The statute of frauds is intended to prevent fraudulent claims that a contract existed when it did not by ensuring that adequate evidence exists of an agreement to convey. Because possession and improvements

[71] *McCarthy v. Tobin*, 706 N.E.2d 629, 631 (Mass. 1999).

[72] *Isaac v. A & B Loan Co.*, 247 Cal. Rptr. 104, 106 (Ct. App. 1988); *Moloney v. Awad*, 550 N.Y.S.2d 91 (App. Div. 1989); 14-81 *Powell on Real Property* §81.02[2][a].

[73] *Heckman v. Nero*, 2000 WL 1041226 (Del. Ch. 2000) (holding that buyers could specifically enforce an oral promise to convey when seller made an oral promise to convey, the buyers had made a deposit in partial payment of the purchase price, and the buyers had relied on the promise by moving their house trailer onto the lot). *Cf. McBarron v. Kipling Woods, LLC*, 838 A.2d 490 (N.J. Super. Ct. App. Div. 2004) (enforcing an oral promise to convey real property under N.J. Statute of Frauds that provides that such a contract is enforceable if there is clear and convincing evidence, N.J. Stat. §25:1-13).

[74] *Sharp v. Sumner*, 528 S.E.2d 791 (Ga. 2000) (applying statutory part performance doctrine, Ga. Code §13-5-30(4)); *Gardner v. Gardner*, 454 N.W.2d 361 (Iowa 1990); *Spears v. Warr*, 44 P.3d 742, 751-752, 2002 UT 24 ¶¶22-25 (Utah 2002), *overruled on other grounds*, *Tangren Family Trust v. Tangren*, 182 P.3d 326, 2008 UT 20 (Utah 2008); 14-81 *Powell on Real Property* §81.02[2].

[75] *Burns v. McCormick*, 135 N.E. 273 (N.Y. 1922).

[76] 14-81 *Powell on Real Property* §81.02[2][c][i].

[77] Dale A. Whitman et al., *The Law of Property* §10.2, at 609 (4th ed. 2019).

[78] *Id.* §10.2, at 609-610; 14-81 *Powell on Real Property* §81.02[2][c].

[79] *Bouten v. Richard Miller Homes, Inc.*, 321 N.W.2d 895 (Minn. 1982); 14-81 *Powell on Real Property* §81.02[2].

would not ordinarily be made in the absence of a conveyance, they are viewed as adequate substitute evidence that an agreement was in fact reached.[80] If, in such a case, the contract were not enforceable, then the application of the statute of frauds might itself contribute to enabling one of the parties to commit a fraud on the other by denying a contract that in fact existed.[81] The payment of part of the purchase price may also be important to proving that a contract existed because sellers ordinarily do not give away real property for free. Many cases rely on a combination of payment of part of the purchase price plus the taking of possession as sufficient to take the case out of the statute of frauds and allow enforcement.[82]

Estoppel

An alternative basis for the part performance doctrine is *estoppel.*[83] When the seller makes a promise on which the buyer relies substantially, it is not fair to allow the seller to claim that she did not make a promise if this would cause detriment to the buyer who reasonably relied on the promise to convey.[84] The elements of promissory estoppel

> demand evidence that establishes (1) the existence of a clear and definite promise which the promisor should reasonably expect to induce action by the promise; (2) proof that the promise acted to its detriment in reasonable reliance on the promise; and (3) a finding that injustice can be avoided only if the court enforces the promise.[85]

The buyer who has taken substantial steps to complete the transaction by taking possession or making improvements will ordinarily suffer hardship if the contract is not enforced.[86] The seller may also seek specific enforcement of the contract if she has changed her position in reliance on the sale occurring, such as investing the proceeds in the purchase of another property.[87]

A third method of avoiding the statute of frauds is the *constructive trust* doctrine, which may be applied to prevent unjust enrichment when "property has been acquired in such circumstances that the holder of the legal title may not in good conscience retain the beneficial interest."[88] This

[80] 14-81 *Powell on Real Property* §81.02[2][b].
[81] *Id.* at §81.02[2][d][ii] & [iii].
[82] Dale A. Whitman et al., *The Law of Property* §10.2, at 609-610 (4th ed. 2019).
[83] 14-81 *Powell on Real Property* §81.020[2][b][ii].
[84] *Harvey v. Dow,* 11 A.3d 303 (Me. 2011); *Roussalis v. Wyoming Medical Center,* 4 P.3d 209 (Wyo. 2000); Dale A. Whitman et al., *The Law of Property* §10.1, at 607-608 (4th ed. 2019).
[85] *Roussalis v. Wyoming Medical Center,* 4 P.3d 209, 253 (Wyo. 2000). *But see Nix v. Wick,* 66 So. 3d 209 (Ala. 2010), and *DeFriece v. McCorquodale,* 998 So. 2d 465 (Ala. 2008) (oral promises to transfer property not enforceable even if there is reliance).
[86] 14-81 *Powell on Real Property* §81.02[2][a].
[87] *Id.*
[88] *Davis v. Barnfield,* 833 So. 2d 58, 64 (Ala. Ct. App. 2002). *But see Brown v. Branch,* 758 N.E.2d 48, 53 (Ind. 2001) (oral promise to convey title to a house not enforceable despite plaintiff's reliance in quitting her job, dropping out of college, and moving back to Indiana from Missouri when court finds that this reliance resulted in the "infliction of an unjust and unconscionable injury and loss").

doctrine may apply if the funds of one person are used to acquire property but title is held in the name of another.[89]

Oral modifications

Oral modifications to written land sales agreements violate the statute of frauds; like the original contract, they must be in writing to be enforceable. However, the same part performance and estoppel exceptions that apply to initial agreements apply to modifications.[90] Thus, if a party has acted in reliance on the oral modification, "the injured party can seek the equitable remedy of specific performance based on the doctrine of part performance."[91]

§11.3.3 What Constitutes Breach

Backing out of the deal

Refusal to complete the deal ordinarily will constitute a breach of the contract unless the contract contained a contingency that allows that party to back out of the arrangement. A number of typical conflicts arise when it is not so clear whether a breach has occurred. A number of these constitute breaches by the seller, including fraud, failure to provide marketable title, or a violation of an implied warranty of habitability in the sale of a new home. Others are typically breaches by the buyer. The most common is the failure to make good faith efforts to obtain adequate financing.

False representation and reasonable reliance

§11.3.3.1 Fraud. A seller who induces a buyer to sign a land sale contract by making false representations has committed the tort of fraud if the buyer reasonably relies on those representations to her detriment.[92] Fraud can be established if (1) the seller made a false representation of fact; (2) knew it was false at the time the statement was made; (3) intended to induce the buyer to rely on the statement; (4) the buyer did justifiably rely on the statement; and (5) suffered harm as a result of the reliance.[93] Some courts provide relief even if the misrepresentation was not knowingly made, as long as the one making the statement should have known, at the time the statement was made, that it was false.[94] Holding the seller who makes false statements to the standards of what a "reasonable person" should have known at the time the statement was made effectively imposes liability for a negligent misrepresentation.[95] "It is the duty of one who volunteers information to another not having equal knowledge, with the intention that he will act upon it, to exercise reasonable care to verify the truth of his statements before making them."[96] The seller will not be liable for fraud if the buyer should have discovered the truth through reasonable diligence; at

[89] *Davis*, 833 So. 2d at 64.

[90] 14-81 *Powell on Real Property* §81.02[2][d].

[91] *Id. See Heitz v. Circle Four Realty Co.*, 548 N.E.2d 11 (Ill. App. Ct. 1989).

[92] *Johnson v. Davis*, 480 So. 2d 625 (Fla. 1985); 14-81 *Powell on Real Property* §81.02[4][b].

[93] Dan B. Dobbs, Paul T. Hayden & Ellen M. Bublick, *Hornbook on Torts*, §43.1, at 1115 (2d ed. 2016). *See Cornelius v. Austin*, 542 So. 2d 1220 (Ala. 1989); *Kavarco v. T.J.E., Inc.*, 478 A.2d 257 (Conn. App. Ct. 1984), *overruled on other grounds by Kaczynski v. Kaczynski*, 981 A.2d 1068 (Conn. 2009).

[94] 14-81 *Powell on Real Property* §81.02[4][b].

[95] *Mertens v. Wolfeboro National Bank*, 402 A.2d 1335 (N.H. 1979).

[96] *Id.* at 1336-1337.

the same time, most courts do not place a duty on the buyer to investigate to determine whether what the seller said was true.[97] When a contract is induced by a material misrepresentation, the defrauded party generally may rescind the deal and recover damages.[98]

Rescission and damages

Opinions and puffery

A fraud claim requires a misrepresentation of a *fact*. If the seller voices an opinion on the desirability of the house or engages in puffery to extol its virtues, a disappointed buyer cannot claim fraud based on such statements of opinion.[99]

▶ HARD CASE

▷ FRAUDULENT NONDISCLOSURE

Courts are divided on the question of whether sellers have a duty to disclose to buyers defects in the property known to the seller and not obvious to the buyer. Traditionally, nondisclosure could never amount to fraud because one cannot make a misleading statement if one makes no statement at all. A rule of *caveat emptor*—let the buyer beware—still prevails in some states.[100] However, many states now require disclosure of latent defects, known to the seller, that substantially affect the value or habitability of the property and that are unknown and not reasonably discoverable by the buyer.[101] Moreover, some states have held that sellers have a duty to reveal material facts of which they are aware and that materially affect the value or desirability of the property.[102] More than half the states have passed statutes that impose some kind of disclosure obligation on sellers and/or

[97] 14-81 *Powell on Real Property* §81.02[4][b]; *Restatement (Second) of Torts* §540 (1977) (no duty to investigate).

[98] *Kavarco v. T.J.E., Inc.*, 478 A.2d 257, 261 (Conn. App. Ct. 1984), *overruled on other grounds by Kaczynski v. Kaczynski*, 981 A.2d 1068 (2009); Dan B. Dobbs, Paul T. Hayden & Ellen M. Bublick, *Hornbook on Torts*, §43.9, at 1138 (2d ed. 2016). *See also Riverisland Cold Storage, Inc. v. Fresno-Madera Prod. Credit Ass'n*, 291 P.3d 316 (Cal. 2013) (when oral pre-contract statements differed from the written real estate agreement, those oral statements may be admitted to show defendant committed fraud despite the parol evidence rule that ordinarily prevents use of oral statements to vary the terms of a written agreement).

[99] *Ray v. Montgomery*, 399 So. 2d 230, 232 (Ala. 1980); 14-81 *Powell on Real Property* §81.02[4][b].

[100] *Urman v. South Boston Savings Bank*, 674 N.E.2d 1078, 1081 (Mass. 1997); *Stambovsky v. Ackley*, 572 N.Y.S.2d 672 (App. Div. 1991) (adopting a narrow exception to this rule when the seller had fostered the public belief that her home was possessed by a ghost and the buyer did not know this when buying the property).

[101] *Blaylock v. Cary*, 709 So. 2d 1128, 1131 (Ala. 1997); *Hess v. Chase Manhattan Bank, USA*, 220 S.W.2d 758 (Mo. 2007); *Assilzadeh v. California Federal Bank*, 98 Cal. Rptr. 2d 176, 182 (Ct. App. 2000); *Shapiro v. Sutherland*, 76 Cal. Rptr. 2d 101, 107 (Ct. App. 1998); *Timm v. Clement*, 574 N.W.2d 368 (Iowa 1997); *Restatement (Second) of Torts* §353 (1977).

[102] *Reed v. King*, 193 Cal. Rptr. 130 (Ct. App. 1983); *Lingsch v. Savage*, 29 Cal. Rptr. 201, 204-205 (Ct. App. 1963); *Posner v. Davis*, 395 N.E.2d 133 (Ill. 1979); *Johnson v. Davis*, 480 So. 2d 625, 629 (Fla. 1985); *Conahan v. Fisher*, 463 N.W.2d 118 (Mich. Ct. App. 1990); *Kracl v. Loseke*, 461 N.W.2d 67, 72 (Neb. 1990); *Strawn v. Canuso*, 657 A.2d 420 (N.J. 1995) (superseded by N.J. Stat. §§46:3C-1 to -12); *Roberts v. Estate of Barbagallo*, 531 A.2d 1125, 1130-1131 (Pa. Super. Ct. 1988); *Chamberlaine & Flowers, Inc. v. McBee*, 356 S.E.2d 626 (W. Va. 1987); 14-81 *Powell on Real Property* §81.02[3][b].

brokers.[103] They have not, however, generally extended this obligation to commercial property.[104] ◀

Federal regulation

Federal law requires owners of residential property constructed before 1978 to disclose the presence of lead paint and provide the buyer with an information pamphlet issued by the federal government.[105] The Superfund law (*Comprehensive Environmental Response, Compensation, and Liability Act of 1980*, or *CERCLA*)[106] requires owners of property contaminated with hazardous substances to clean it up. An exemption exists for "innocent owners" who neither caused the pollution nor knew of it when they purchased. However, such innocent owners will lose the exemption and become responsible for cleanup costs if they do not reveal the contamination to the buyer when they sell the property.[107]

▷ BUYER'S DUTY TO DISCLOSE **HARD CASE ◀**

In *Zaschak v. Traverse Corp.*,[108] the seller did not know that the property was sitting atop substantial oil reserves, but the buyer (a petroleum engineer) did. After the buyer purchased the property at a price that reflected its use for agricultural purposes, the seller discovered that the buyer knew that the property was far more valuable than the seller thought it was. The court held that "a prospective purchaser is under no duty to disclose facts or possible opportunities within his knowledge which materially affect the value of the property."[109] This expresses the usual rule that "[a]lthough material facts are known to one party and not the other, failure to disclose them is ordinarily not actionable fraud unless there is some fiduciary relationship giving rise to a duty to disclose."[110] However, a California court noted that California had adopted the rule that required sellers and brokers of real property to divulge material facts to prospective buyers and held that buyers do have a duty to reveal material facts to sellers in "situations in which a fiduciary or confidential relationship exists, situations in which a partial or misleading disclosure is made, and situations in which the buyer knows that the seller would reasonably expect a disclosure to be made."[111] It could be argued that the buyer is attempting to pay less than a fair price for the property by taking advantage of the seller's ignorance and that the seller would never have sold at that

[103] Cal. Civ. Code §§1102 to 1102.17; N.J. Stat. §§46:3C-1 to -12 (interpreted by *Nobrega v. Edison Glen Assocs.*, 772 A.2d 368 (N.J. 2001)); Craig W. Dallon, *Theories of Real Estate Broker Liability and the Effect of the "As Is" Clause*, 54 Fla. L. Rev. 395, 428 (2002).
[104] *See, e.g., Futura Realty v. Lone Star Building Centers (Eastern) Inc.*, 578 So. 2d 363 (Fla. Dist. Ct. App. 1991).
[105] *Residential Lead-Based Paint Hazard Reduction Act*, 42 U.S.C. §§4851 to 4856.
[106] 42 U.S.C. §§9601 to 9675.
[107] John G. Sprankling, *Understanding Property Law* §21.02[C], at 358 (5th ed. 2023).
[108] 333 N.W.2d 191 (Mich. Ct. App. 1983).
[109] *Id.* at 192-193.
[110] *Nussbaum v. Weeks*, 263 Cal. Rptr. 360, 366 (Ct. App. 1989). *See also Easton v. Strassburger*, 199 Cal. Rptr. 383 (Ct. App. 1984) (duty on brokers to disclose off-site geologic conditions relevant to the nearby earth slides that might affect the house).
[111] 263 Cal. Rptr. at 367.

price had the seller known the information. Although small deviations in price should not ordinarily matter, a deviation of this magnitude may lead a decision maker to conclude that the buyer has been unjustly enriched at the expense of the seller. In addition, a mutuality argument could be made: If the seller has a duty to reveal facts the buyer would want to know, so should the buyer reveal facts the seller would want to know. ◀

▶ HARD CASE ▷ WAIVER

"As is" or "no reliance" clauses

Can a buyer sue for fraud if the contract states that the property is being taken "as is" or that the buyer "is not relying on any oral statements made by the seller"? Most courts hold that a fraud claim is still available[112] while some hold that no claim is available.[113] In the leading case of *Danann Realty Corp. v. Harris*,[114] for example, the seller falsely represented the operating expenses of the building and the profits that would likely be derived from the buyer's investment. However, the contract provided that the seller "has not made and does not make any representations as to *expenses*, *operation* or any other matter or thing affecting or related to the premises" other than those explicitly set forth in the contract. Moreover, the agreement went on to state that the buyer "*expressly acknowledges that no such representations have been made*" and that the buyer "*further acknowledges that it has inspected the premises and agrees to take the premises 'as is.'*"[115]

Argument against allowing a fraud claim

The court held that a general merger clause stating that the written agreement embodies the whole agreement does not protect the defendant from a claim of fraud. However, the plaintiff specifically stated that he was not relying on any representations as to the expenses or operation and thus could not have reasonably relied on any oral statements made by the seller. Judge Burke explained:

[112] *VSH Realty, Inc. v. Texaco, Inc.*, 757 F.2d 411 (1st Cir. 1985) (applying Massachusetts law) (despite "as is" clause, seller must disclose latent defects not known to tenant and not readily ascertainable); *Katz v. Department of Real Estate*, 158 Cal. Rptr. 766 (Ct. App. 1979) ("as is" clause invalid as to latent defects); *Ron Greenspan Volkswagen, Inc. v. Ford Motor Land Development Corp.*, 38 Cal. Rptr. 2d 783, 787 (Ct. App. 1995) ("It is settled beyond doubt, manifestly on sound grounds of justice, that a seller cannot escape liability for his own fraud or false representations by the insertion of provisions such as are embodied in the contract of sale herein"); *Danann Realty Corp. v. Harris*, 157 N.E.2d 597 (N.Y. 1959); *Bowman v. Presley*, 212 P.3d 1210 (Okla. 2009) (fraud claim available despite disclaimer of all warranties in the sales contract); *McNulty v. Chip*, 116 A.3d 173 (R.I. 2015) ("as is" clause does not protect seller from fraud claims); *Snyder v. Lovercheck*, 992 P.2d 1079 (Wyo. 1999).

[113] *Kidd v. Benson*, 321 So. 3d 676 (Ala. 2020); *Fla. Holding 4800, LLC v. Lauderhill Mall Inv., LLC*, 317 So. 3d 121, 124 (Fla. Dist. Ct. App. 2021) (for commercial property); *Mulkey v. Waggoner*, 338 S.E.2d 755 (Ga. Ct. App. 1985); *Alires v. McGhehee*, 85 P.3d 1191 (Kan. 2004); *Citibank, N.A. v. Plapinger*, 485 N.E.2d 974 (N.Y. 1985); *Forest Oil Corp. v. McAllen*, 268 S.W.3d 51 (Tex. 2008); *Richey v. Patrick*, 904 P.2d 798 (Wyo. 1995). *But see Italian Cowboy Partners, Ltd. v. Prudential Ins. Co. of America*, 341 S.W.3d 323 (Tex. 2011) (standard merger clause reciting that the written document is the entire agreement is not sufficient to protect contracting partner from claim for fraud).

[114] 157 N.E.2d 597 (N.Y. 1959).

[115] *Id.* at 598 (emphasis supplied by the court).

> [T]he plaintiff made a representation in the contract that it was not relying on specific representations not embodied in the contract, while, it now asserts, it was in fact relying on such oral representations. Plaintiff admits then that it is guilty of deliberately misrepresenting to the seller its true intention. To condone this fraud would place the purchaser in a favored position. This is particularly so, where, as here, the purchaser confirms the contract, but seeks damages. If the plaintiff has made a bad bargain he cannot avoid it in this manner.
>
> If the language here used is not sufficient to estop a party from claiming that he entered the contract because of fraudulent representations, then no language can accomplish that purpose. To hold otherwise would be to say that it is impossible for two businessmen dealing at arm's length to agree that the buyer is not buying in reliance on any representations of the seller as to a particular fact.[116]

Argument for allowing a fraud claim

Justice Stanley H. Fuld dissented, arguing that "[i]f a party has actually induced another to enter into a contract by means of fraud I conceive that language may not be devised to shield him from the consequences of such fraud."[117] That approach has been taken in some other cases.[118]

> The law does not temporize with trickery or duplicity, and this court, after having weighed the advantages of certainty in contractual relations against the harm and injustice which result from fraud, long ago unequivocally declared that "a party who has perpetrated a fraud upon his neighbor may [not] contract with him, in the very instrument by means of which it was perpetrated, for immunity against its consequences, close his mouth from complaining of it, and bind him never to seek redress. Public policy and morality are both ignored if such an agreement can be given effect in a court of justice. The maxim that fraud vitiates every transaction would no longer be the rule, but the exception." *Bridger v. Goldsmith*, 38 N.E. 458, 459 (N.Y. 1894). "In the realm of fact it is entirely possible for a party knowingly to agree that no representations have been made to him, while at the same time believing and relying upon representations which in fact have been made and in fact are false but for which he would not have made the agreement. To deny this possibility is to ignore the frequent instances in everyday experience where parties accept and act upon agreements containing exculpatory clauses in one form or another, but where they do so, nevertheless, in reliance upon the honesty of supposed friends, the plausible and disarming statements of salesmen, or the customary course of business. To refuse relief would result in opening the door to a multitude of frauds and in thwarting the general policy of the law." *Bates v. Southgate*, 31 N.E. 2d 551, 558 (Mass. 1941).
>
> The guiding rule [is] that fraud vitiates every agreement which it touches.

[116] *Id.* at 599-600. *Accord, Janian v. Barnes*, 742 N.Y.S.2d 445, 446 (App. Div. 2002).

[117] 157 N.E.2d at 600-602, 606.

[118] *McNulty v. Chip*, 116 A.3d 173 (R.I. 2015).

> Contrary to the intimation in the court's opinion, the nonreliance clause cannot possibly operate as an estoppel against the plaintiff. Essentially equitable in nature, the principle of estoppel is to be invoked to prevent fraud and injustice, not to further them. The statement that the representations in question were not made was, according to the complaint, false to the defendant's knowledge. Surely, the perpetrator of a fraud cannot close the lips of his victim and deny him the right to state the facts as they actually exist.[119] ◀

Real Estate Settlement and Procedures Act (RESPA)

A federal statute, the *Real Estate Settlement and Procedures Act* (*RESPA*),[120] imposes detailed procedural requirements on most residential real estate closings. These requirements are designed to force disclosure of all settlement costs. It also has some substantive regulations. For example, it protects real estate buyers from having to pay kickbacks or other unearned and/or undisclosed fees by prohibiting acceptance of fees for rendering of real estate settlement services in connection with federally related mortgage loans "other than for services actually performed."[121] A violation occurs, for example, when a lender gives or receives a portion of a charge with a third party for referral of real estate settlement business.[122]

Interstate Land Sales Full Disclosure Act

Another federal law, the *Interstate Land Sales Full Disclosure Act*,[123] regulates the sale or lease of most undeveloped, subdivided land if the developer uses any means of "transportation or communication in interstate commerce."[124] It requires developers to register with the Secretary of Housing and Urban Development (HUD), to disclose certain information to buyers prior to sale, and to refrain from false or misleading sales practices.[125]

***Caveat emptor* discarded**

§11.3.3.2 WARRANTY OF HABITABILITY FOR NEW HOMES. It is now well established that sellers of new homes impliedly warrant that they are habitable and fit for their intended purpose.[126] Some states make this warranty explicit by statute.[127] Almost all modern cases have also allowed a subsequent buyer of property to sue the builder/contractor for violation of the implied warranty of "workmanlike quality for latent defects which cause economic loss," despite the lack of privity of contract between the builder and the subsequent buyer.[128] A few cases still hold that such a claim

[119] 157 N.E.2d at 600, 601, 606.
[120] 12 U.S.C. §§2601 to 2617.
[121] *United States v. Gannon*, 684 F.2d 433 (7th Cir. 1982).
[122] *Mercado v. Calumet Federal Savings & Loan Ass'n*, 763 F.2d 269 (7th Cir. 1985).
[123] 15 U.S.C. §§1701 to 1720.
[124] *Id.* at §1703.
[125] Paul Barron, Michael Berenson & Dan Rosin, *Federal Regulation of Real Estate and Mortgage Lending* §§3.1 to 3.101 (4th ed. 2025 update).
[126] Zambrano v. M & RC II LLC, 517 P.3d 1168, 1179 (Ariz. 2022); *Blagg v. Fred Hunt Co., Inc.*, 612 S.W.2d 321 (Ark. 1981); *Albrecht v. Clifford*, 767 N.E.2d 42 (Mass. 2002) (home); *Berish v. Bornstein*, 770 N.E.2d 961, 972-973 (Mass. 2002) (condominium unit).
[127] *E.g.*, 2012 La. Acts 112 (for manufactured and modular homes).
[128] *Lempke v. Dagenais*, 547 A.2d 290, 291-292 (N.H. 1988). *Accord*, N.Y. Gen. Bus. §777-b; Va. Code §8.2-318; *Tusch Enterprises v. Coffin*, 740 P.2d 1022, 1034-1035 (Idaho 1987); *Real Estate Marketing, Inc. v. Franz*, 885 S.W.2d 921 (Ky. 1994); *Keyes v. Guy Baily Homes, Inc.*, 439 So. 2d 670 (Miss. 1983); *Aronsohn v. Mandara*, 484 A.2d 675, 679-680 (N.J. 1984). *See also*

is not available because of lack of a contractual relationship between the builder and the subsequent owner.[129]

State consumer protection statutes

All states and the District of Columbia have consumer protection statutes that prohibit unfair and deceptive practices by merchants who sell goods or provide services to consumers. Sales of homes may be covered by such statutes if the seller is the initial developer. They often provide for multiple damages when sellers of consumer goods make deceptive claims designed to mislead consumers.[130]

Implied right to convey marketable title

§11.3.3.3 Marketable Title. In the sales contract, the seller expressly or impliedly represents to the buyer that the seller is able to convey "marketable title."[131] "Title" means "[t]he union of all elements (as ownership, possession, and custody) constituting the legal right to control and dispose of property"; it is the "legal link between a person who owns property and the property itself."[132] A "marketable title" is one that "a reasonable buyer would accept because it appears to lack any defect and to cover the entire property that the seller has purported to sell."[133] Marketable title does not have to be perfect; it must only be reasonably free from doubt.[134]

Title as a relative proposition

Title is not an all-or-nothing proposition. "[I]t is an abstract concept which represents the legal system's conclusions as to how the interests in a parcel of realty are arranged and who owns them."[135] The title may be subject to doubt for a variety of reasons. Some relevant documents may be unrecorded; some recorded documents may be invalid; others may be facially valid but conflict with other facially valid documents; and still others may impair the ability of the prospective owner to use the property as she wishes. Title is relative partly because many people may have interests in the same parcel simultaneously; there may be covenants, easements, future interests, leases, mortgages, liens, marital rights, trusts, wills, and contractual rights. In addition, although some land is "registered," with ownership rights stated on the face of the registered title, most titles are documented through the recording system, which operates by authorizing individuals to file documents purporting to relate to the property. It is the legal rules concerning recording and chain of title that determine which transfers or documents prevail when they conflict and which take priority when they are valid but overlapping. Those rules do provide answers to such questions, but the rules are not mechanical ones; they often require judgment. And even when the rules are clear, uncertainty about the facts, such as the possibility that a right will be asserted before the statute of

Beachwalk Villas Condominium Ass'n, Inc. v. Martin, 406 S.E.2d 372 (S.C. 1991) (upholding a claim by a later buyer against the architect).

[129] *Sensenbrenner v. Rust, Orling & Neale*, 374 S.E.2d 55 (Va. 1988).

[130] *See, e.g.*, Mass. Gen. Laws ch. 93A, §§1 to 11.

[131] Dale A. Whitman et al., *The Law of Property* §10.12, at 664 (4th ed. 2019); 14-81 *Powell on Real Property* §81.03[6].

[132] *Black's Law Dictionary* (12th ed. 2024).

[133] *Id. See* 11 *Thompson on Real Property, Third Thomas Edition* §91.09(a)(1).

[134] Dale A. Whitman et al., *The Law of Property* §10.12, at 663-664 (4th ed. 2019).

[135] *Id.* at §10.12, at 663.

limitations passes, may well make the state of the title a matter of judgment rather than exact calculation.[136]

Title reasonably free from doubt

The concept of *marketable title* requires the buyer to accept some level of risk. At the same time, this level is held to a minimum. The seller is not obligated to convey a perfect title, but neither is the buyer required to accept a title that is likely to prove troublesome. "Whether a title is marketable — *i.e.*, a title that is free from reasonable doubt — must be tested from the prospective purchaser's standpoint, and not from the viewpoint either of the seller or of the court."[137] The buyer need not be able to prove that title is defective to back out of the deal — only that a reasonable buyer would hesitate to buy under the circumstances.[138] The test is whether a "reasonable person" would "accept the title without hesitation."[139] A marketable title "is one which can be readily sold or mortgaged to a person of reasonable prudence."[140] A buyer "may not be compelled to take a conveyance when there is a reasonable probability that it will be subjected to litigation."[141]

Circularity of the concept

In one sense, the definition of marketable title is circular.[142] A marketable title is one a reasonable buyer "would" accept — even though disputes about marketable title developed precisely because buyers did not accept such titles. Perhaps such refusals were "unreasonable," but perhaps not. After all, a buyer might be more risk averse than average without being unreasonable. In adopting a reasonable buyer standard, the courts are simply defining certain titles as marketable — and therefore acceptable to reasonable buyers — despite the presence of minor defects and despite the fact that particular buyers do not find them acceptable. In this way, the courts force some buyers to accept titles they do not wish to accept. In effect, marketable title is what the judges think buyers *should* accept rather than what they *do* accept.

Policy basis of the doctrine

Part of the reason for this is that buyers sometimes want to back out of land deals for reasons unrelated to the property in question. Perhaps the buyer found a less expensive house in a better location; she might be looking for an excuse to get out of the earlier deal. Finding a technical defect in the chain of title might just offer her that opportunity.[143] In so doing, the buyer might be able to breach the agreement without losing her deposit. However, if we believe the seller should be entitled to have the deal completed, and if we believe that the title defects are extremely unlikely ever to cause actual problems for the buyer, then allowing the buyer to get

[136] *Id.*

[137] *McClelland v. DeWulf*, 2000 WL 557929 (Minn. Ct. App. 2000) (quoting *Lucas v. Independent School District No. 284*, 433 N.W.2d 94, 97 (Minn. 1988)).

[138] 14-81 *Powell on Real Property* §81.03[6][a].

[139] *Id. See Seligman v. First National Investments, Inc.*, 540 N.E.2d 1057 (Ill. App. Ct. 1989); *Mucci v. Brockton Bocce Club, Inc.*, 472 N.E.2d 966 (Mass. App. Ct. 1985); *Shinn v. Thrust IV Inc.*, 786 P.2d 285 (Wash. Ct. App. 1990).

[140] *Regan v. Lanze*, 354 N.E.2d 818, 822 (N.Y. 1976).

[141] 14-81 *Powell on Real Property* §81.03[6][a].

[142] Dale A. Whitman et al., *The Law of Property* §10.12, at 663 (4th ed. 2019).

[143] *G/GM Real Estate Corp. v. Susse Chalet Motor Lodge of Ohio, Inc.*, 575 N.E.2d 141, 144 (Ohio 1991) ("The real cloud here was the one employed by the appellee in its attempt to divert attention from its failure to secure financing for the purchase").

out so easily may seem problematic. Many titles will have minor technical defects somewhere in the chain of title, and a rule that required a perfect title would deprive sellers of the security that is supposed to come from having the buyer sign the contract. At the same time, allowing the buyer to escape when defects in the title would be significant to the reasonable buyer protects the justified expectations of the buyer in the seller's ability to deliver what the seller promised to deliver, *i.e.*, good title to the property.

Title problems

Title problems may take a variety of forms.[144] The title itself may be contested or there may be encumbrances on the land. Title may be questionable for several reasons: (1) there may be defects in the chain of title such as a prior unrecorded conveyance, an unsigned deed, or a conveyance without the requisite consent of a spouse who was a co-owner of the property; (2) the seller's title may be based on adverse possession rather than record title; (3) the seller's title to some or all of the property may have been lost to another by adverse possession, foreclosure, or eminent domain; (4) the property may be subject to encumbrances belonging to third parties; or (5) the property may be landlocked and without any means of access to public roads.[145]

Chain-of-title problems

Problems may arise in the chain of title because of mistakes in prior deeds.[146] A deed may contain a faulty description of the land;[147] it may lack a required signature;[148] or a grantor's name may be spelled differently from the grantee's name in the prior deed.[149] These mistakes may be corrected by lawsuits to reform the relevant deeds brought against the parties who might claim that the transfer of title was not valid.[150] Claims may also arise that a prior deed was forged or a prior conveyance was induced by fraud.

▷ PRIOR UNRECORDED DEEDS **HARD CASE ◀**

One or more of the prior conveyances may be unrecorded. In such cases, the seller may be able to demonstrate that she has marketable title by producing affidavits or parol evidence sufficient to fill the gap in the record.[151] Most courts will accept such proof as sufficient to establish marketable title if the case comes to litigation.[152] However, some courts will hold that a title

[144] 14-81 *Powell on Real Property* §81.03[6][d]. *See Stewart Title Guaranty Co. v. Greenlands Realty*, 58 F. Supp. 2d 360, 366 (D.N.J. 1999).

[145] Dale A. Whitman et al., *The Law of Property* §10.12, at 667-672 (4th ed. 2019); 14-81 *Powell on Real Property* §81.03[6][d].

[146] 14-81 *Powell on Real Property* §81.03[6][d][i].

[147] *Christy Co., Inc. v. Ainbinder/Searcy Ltd.*, 621 S.W.2d 886 (Ark. Ct. App. 1981).

[148] *Boecher v. Borth*, 377 N.Y.S.2d 781 (App. Div. 1976).

[149] *Haye v. United States*, 461 F. Supp. 1168 (C.D. Cal. 1978).

[150] *See Flaherty v. Broadway Assocs. Ltd. Partnership by Sterling Development Corp.*, 566 N.Y.S.2d 982 (App. Div. 1991).

[151] *Barter v. Palmerton Area School District*, 581 A.2d 652 (Pa. Super. Ct. 1990); 14-81 *Powell on Real Property* §81.03[6][d][i].

[152] *Lucas v. Independent School District No. 284*, 433 N.W.2d 94 (Minn. 1988); 14-81 *Powell on Real Property* §81.03[6][d][i]; 11 *Thompson on Real Property, Third Thomas Edition* §91.09(a)(1).

is not marketable "where the record does not show the title to be good."[153] Oral testimony and affidavits are not equivalent to recorded documents; they can be contested, and until established to be valid and enforceable by a court judgment, place the owner at risk of competing claims. ◀

▶ HARD CASE

▷ TITLE BY ADVERSE POSSESSION

In *Conklin v. Davi*,[154] title to a portion of the property was based on adverse possession. The buyers argued that the title was not marketable and that they were entitled to back out of the deal unless the seller obtained "record title," by which the buyers meant a deed obtained from the owners of the disputed strip of land that conveyed title to the seller and that was then recorded in the registry of deeds. The court disagreed, holding that a "marketable title" was one "free from reasonable doubt, but not from every doubt."[155] Title based on adverse possession was sufficient, in the court's view, if it could be clearly established. Title based on adverse possession is marketable if the court concludes "(1) that the outstanding claimants could not succeed were they in fact to assert a claim, and (2) that there is no real likelihood that any claim will ever be asserted."[156] One might argue, nevertheless, that title based on adverse possession does subject the owner to a possible claim from the record owner and that, even if the adverse possessor would be likely to win the claim, she might have to undergo the expense of litigation to affirm her rights. ◀

Encumbrances

Buyer's knowledge may be relevant

Outstanding encumbrances on the land may make title unmarketable.[157] Examples include easements,[158] covenants,[159] mortgages,[160] liens,[161] contract rights, and options. Some courts hold that the "[p]urchaser's prior knowledge of an encumbrance" does not deprive purchaser "of a right to a marketable title."[162] However, other courts hold that title is not rendered unmarketable because of encumbrances of which the buyer was aware or

[153] 11 *Thompson on Real Property, Third Thomas Edition* §91.09(a)(1). *See Yamashita v. Guam*, 59 F.3d 114 (9th Cir. 1995) (title unmarketable because no documentary evidence of title in the earliest grantor in the chain of title).

[154] 388 A.2d 598 (N.J. 1978).

[155] *Id.* at 601 (quoting Justice Cardozo's opinion in *Norwegian Evangelical Free Church v. Milhauser*, 169 N.E. 134, 135 (N.Y. 1929)).

[156] *Id.* at 603. *Compare Barter v. Palmerton Area School District*, 581 A.2d 652 (Pa. Super. Ct. 1990) (adverse possession clearly established) *with Kipahulu Investment Co. v. Seltzer Partnership*, 675 P.2d 778 (Haw. Ct. App. 1983) (title is unmarketable because adverse possession was not provable).

[157] Dale A. Whitman et al., *The Law of Property* §10.12, at 669-670 (4th ed. 2019).

[158] *Ger v. Kammann*, 504 F. Supp. 446 (D. Del. 1980) (neither party aware of sewer easement running underneath house; title unmarketable); *Egeter v. West and North Properties*, 758 P.2d 361 (Or. Ct. App. 1988) (easement to drive cattle across land made title unmarketable).

[159] *Nelson v. Anderson*, 676 N.E.2d 735, 736-737 (Ill. App. Ct. 1997); *Staley v. Stephens*, 404 N.E.2d 633 (Ind. Ct. App. 1980); *Shinn v. Thrust IV, Inc.*, 786 P.2d 285 (Wash. Ct. App. 1990).

[160] *McClelland v. DeWulf*, 2000 WL 557929 (Minn. Ct. App. 2000).

[161] *Kessler v. Tortoise Development, Inc.*, 1 P.3d 292 (Idaho 2000).

[162] James C. Smith & Milton R. Friedman, *Contracts and Conveyances of Real Property* §14:9, at 4-59 (8th ed. 2017).

even of which a reasonable buyer would have been aware at the time the contract was signed because they were visible.[163]

Some courts distinguish between encumbrances affecting title, such as mortgages or other liens, which make title unmarketable, and those relating to the physical condition of the property, such as rights of way, which may be visible to the buyer and thus do not render title unmarketable.[164]

Visible easements

Some courts do hold buyers to be on notice of visible easements when they sign the contract of sale.[165] If this is so, the buyer may impliedly accept such easements and waive the right to have title free of them. Another common problem involves existing leases. Many cases hold that the existence of an unexpired lease on the closing date renders title unmarketable.[166] However, some cases hold buyers to be on inquiry notice of existing leases, and thus such leases do not render title unmarketable.[167] "Possession of property by a tenant at the time a contract of sale is executed, or at the time the premises are conveyed, puts the prospective purchaser or vendee on notice of the terms of the lease under which the tenant is holding; and this role applies notwithstanding the fact that the lease contract is not recorded."[168] Buyers are not expected to have agreed to leases of which they could not reasonably have been aware, such as mineral leases.[169] Moreover, such encumbrances do not render title unmarketable if the sale contract mentions their existence and provides for their continuation.[170]

Existing leases

Encroachments

Title is usually held to be unmarketable if a neighbor's structure encroaches on the property.[171] Courts sometimes remedy this problem by ordering an abatement of the purchase price. However, if the house being bought encroaches on neighboring land, the usual remedy is rescission of the contract, unless the seller can establish ownership of the disputed strip by adverse possession.[172]

Zoning violations

If the property is in compliance with the zoning law, the fact that the property is substantially restricted by the zoning law is not a reason for

[163] *Create 21 Chuo, Inc. v. Southwest Slopes, Inc.*, 918 P.2d 1168, 1183 (Haw. Ct. App. 1996); *Besse v. Blossman*, 521 So. 2d 570 (La. Ct. App. 1988); 14-81 *Powell on Real Property* §81.03[6][d][iii].

[164] *Memmert v. Mckeen*, 4 A. 542 (Pa. 1886); James C. Smith & Milton R. Friedman, *Contracts and Conveyances of Real Property* §15:2, at 15-5 (8th ed. 2017).

[165] *In re Oyster Bay Cove, Ltd.*, 161 B.R. 338 (Bankr. E.D.N.Y. 1993); *Wilfong v. W.A. Schickedanz Agency, Inc.*, 406 N.E.2d 828 (Ill. App. Ct. 1980); *Whitman v. Larson*, 568 N.Y.S.2d 485 (App. Div. 1991); 11 *Thompson on Real Property, Third Thomas Edition* §91.09(a)(3).

[166] *Schuler-Olsen Ranches, Inc. v. Garvin*, 250 N.W.2d 906 (Neb. 1977); James C. Smith & Milton R. Friedman, *Contracts and Conveyances of Real Property* §15:3, at 15-14 (8th ed. 2017).

[167] *Alumni Ass'n of the University of North Dakota v. Hart Agency, Inc.*, 283 N.W.2d 119 (N.D. 1979).

[168] *Lieb v. Roman Development Co.*, 716 S.W.2d 653, 655 (Tex. Ct. App. 1986).

[169] *Bailey v. First Mortgage Corp. of Boca Raton*, 478 So. 2d 502 (Fla. Dist. Ct. App. 1985).

[170] James C. Smith & Milton R. Friedman, *Contracts and Conveyances of Real Property* §15:3, at 15-54 (8th ed. 2017); 14-81 *Powell on Real Property* §81.03[6][d][iii].

[171] Dale A. Whitman et al., *The Law of Property* §10.12, at 670 (4th ed. 2019).

[172] *Bethurem v. Hammett*, 736 P.2d 1128, 1135 (Wyo. 1987); 14-81 *Powell on Real Property* §81.03[6][d][iii].

finding the title unmarketable.[173] Nor will a change in the zoning law make the title unmarketable even if it makes illegal the buyer's contemplated use; unless the contract provides otherwise, this risk is allocated to the buyer.[174] However, if the property is in violation of a zoning law courts generally hold title to be unmarketable.[175] In contrast, violation of an existing building or housing code does not render the title unmarketable.[176]

Building codes

Covenants

Title is unmarketable if the property violates existing covenants. A buyer was allowed to rescind the deal when it turned out that the house violated setback requirements contained in restrictive covenants by 0.1 to 1.6 feet.[177] Covenant violations make title unmarketable because they give covenant beneficiaries the right to sue to enforce the covenant. Both the covenant and the "accompanying risk of litigation undoubtedly affect the market value of the property."[178] However, one court has held that the existence of covenants restricting the use of the land will not render title unmarketable if the buyer's contemplated use will not violate those covenants.[179]

Contracts accepting "covenants and easements of record"

Many form contracts state that the property is subject to "covenants and easements of record."[180] This generally constitutes a waiver of objections to any existing covenants[181] and may surprise the buyer who was not aware of what existing covenants existed. But does such a clause protect the seller who is in fact violating existing covenants? The answer should be no.[182] However, some courts may interpret a contract stating that the property is "subject to covenants and restrictions of record" to render title marketable even if the covenants are being violated. It is thus preferable for the buyer to insist that the contract state that the purchase is subject to such covenants "provided that they are not violated by the existing improvements or use of the property."[183]

Time title must be marketable

Generally, courts hold that the seller's title must be marketable as of the date of the closing. Thus, curable defects existing at the time of the signing of the contract will not render title unmarketable if the seller is willing and

[173] *Decatur v. Barnett*, 398 S.E.2d 706 (Ga. Ct. App. 1990), *rev'd on other grounds*, 403 S.E.2d 46 (Ga. 1991). *But see Create 21 Chuo, Inc. v. Southwest Slopes, Inc.*, 918 P.2d 1168 (Haw. Ct. App. 1996) (finding title unmarketable when the property was an archeological site protected by state legislation regulating excavation of the site).

[174] 14-81 *Powell on Real Property* §81.03[6][e][ii][B].

[175] *Lohmeyer v. Bower*, 227 P.2d 102, 110 (Kan. 1951); *Wilcox v. Pioneer Homes, Inc.*, 254 S.E.2d 214 (N.C. Ct. App. 1979); James C. Smith & Milton R. Friedman, *Contracts and Conveyances of Real Property* §6:7, at 6-18 (8th ed. 2017); Dale A. Whitman et al., *The Law of Property* §10.12, at 671 (4th ed. 2019); 11 *Thompson on Real Property, Third Thomas Edition* §91.09(a)(3).

[176] James C. Smith & Milton R. Friedman, *Contracts and Conveyances of Real Property* §6:8, at 6-21 (8th ed. 2017).

[177] *Staley v. Stephens*, 404 N.E.2d 633, 636 (Ind. Ct. App. 1980).

[178] *Nelson v. Anderson*, 676 N.E.2d 735, 736-737 (Ill. App. Ct. 1997).

[179] *Caselli v. Messina*, 567 N.Y.S.2d 972 (Sup. Ct. 1990).

[180] 14-81 *Powell on Real Property* §81.03[6][d][iii].

[181] James C. Smith & Milton R. Friedman, *Contracts and Conveyances of Real Property* §14:4.1, at 14-20 (8th ed. 2017).

[182] *Id.* at §14:4.1.

[183] *Id.*

able to cure those defects prior to the conveyance of title.[184] However, some courts have allowed the buyer to terminate the contract before the closing if it is extremely unlikely the seller will be able to cure the defect in time.[185]

Contractual variations

The purchase and sale agreement ordinarily expressly authorizes the buyer to get out of the deal if the title is not marketable. Some contracts provide that title must be "*record title*"; this is more certain than "marketable title" because it is intended to exclude title based on adverse possession and to ensure that title has passed from hand to hand by recorded documents and that there are no gaps in the chain of title in which conveyances were unrecorded.

Record title

Insurable title

Other contracts provide for "*insurable title*," a term that refers to the ability to obtain title insurance for the property.[186] Some buyers may assume that this is a higher level of protection than mere "marketable title" because an insurance company is willing to wager that the title is good. However, many title insurance contracts exclude certain types of title defects from the scope of coverage; moreover, they may be willing to accept a greater level of risk that particular defects will not result in litigation or be asserted than would the average home buyer.[187] The insurability standard is likely to be a lower one than the marketability standard "because title insurers are often willing to insure title even though minor, technical defects exist that might prevent a title from being marketable."[188]

Remedies

If the title is unmarketable, the buyer has the right to rescind the deal and recover the deposit.[189] Almost all land sale contracts have an express provision to this effect. Alternatively, the buyer may bargain with the seller to take the property for a reduced price.[190]

Implied duty of good faith on buyer

§11.3.3.4 Good Faith Effort to Obtain Financing. When a sales contract is contingent on the buyer obtaining financing, the courts will imply an obligation into the contract to the effect that the buyer will make good faith efforts to obtain the requisite financing.[191]

§11.3.4 Remedies for Breach

Damages or specific performance

§11.3.4.1 Buyer's Remedies. If the seller breaches the contract and refuses to complete the transaction, the buyer may choose between

[184] *Rusch v. Kauker*, 479 N.W.2d 496 (S.D. 1991); *English v. Sanchez*, 796 P.2d 236 (N.M. 1990); 14-81 *Powell on Real Property* §81.03[6][d][iii]; Dale A. Whitman et al., *The Law of Property* §10.12, at 672-673 (4th ed. 2019).

[185] *Breuer-Harrison, Inc. v. Combe*, 799 P.2d 716 (Utah Ct. App. 1990).

[186] *See, e.g., Nelson v. Anderson*, 676 N.E.2d 735 (Ill. App. Ct. 1997); *Creative Living, Inc. v. Steinhauser*, 355 N.Y.S.2d 897 (Sup. Ct. 1974), *aff'd*, 365 N.Y.S.2d 987 (App. Div. 1975).

[187] Dale A. Whitman et al., *The Law of Property* §10.12, at 665-666 (4th ed. 2019).

[188] 14-81 *Powell on Real Property* §81.03 [6][a]. *Accord*, Dale A. Whitman et al., *The Law of Property* §10.12, at 665-666 (4th ed. 2019).

[189] Dale A. Whitman et al., *The Law of Property* §10.12, at 664-665 (4th ed. 2019). The buyer may be able to obtain expectation damages, as well. *Id.* at 665.

[190] 14-81 *Powell on Real Property* §81.03[6][a].

[191] *Bushmiller v. Schiller*, 368 A.2d 1044 (Md. Ct. Spec. App. 1977); *Lempke v. Dagenais*, 547 A.2d 290 (N.H. 1988).

damages and specific performance.[192] The buyer also has an equitable lien on the property to secure repayment of the deposit.[193]

Specific performance

Although damages are the usual remedy for breach of contract, specific performance is routinely awarded in land sale contracts because land is unique and money is not likely to be an adequate substitute for conveyance of title.[194] At the same time, as an equitable remedy, specific performance is discretionary and subject to judgments about justice, relative hardship, unclean hands (unfair acts by the one seeking injunctive relief), and the like.[195] Damages may also be awarded in addition to injunctive relief to compensate the buyer for the delay occasioned by the seller's breach. Alternatively, specific performance may be ordered with an abatement of the purchase price.[196]

Damages

Restitution damages

Expectation damages

The buyer may alternatively seek damages, including restitution damages, reliance damages, and/or expectation damages. Restitution damages return to the buyer payments made to the seller — most notably, the deposit.[197] Expectation damages or "benefit of the bargain" damages represent the lost profit from the transaction, measured by the difference between the market price and the contract price on the date of the breach.[198] If the contract price is the same as fair market value, then the buyer would get nothing under this measure of damages. If the seller breached because she received a higher offer, however, the courts are likely to take a subsequent sale as evidence of the market price and grant the initial buyer the difference between the resale price and the original contract price.[199]

▶ HARD CASE ▷ SELLER WHO ACTED IN GOOD FAITH

Courts traditionally would allow a buyer to obtain expectation damages from a breaching seller only if the seller acted in bad faith. If the seller acted in good faith, but for some reason could not convey good title, the buyer would be limited to restitution of the deposit and would not be able to recover the profit she would have made had the seller not breached.[200]

[192] James C. Smith & Milton R. Friedman, *Contracts and Conveyances of Real Property* §24:3, at 24-4 (8th ed. 2017).

[193] *Hurwitz v. Eagan Real Estate, Inc.*, 557 N.Y.S.2d 711 (App. Div. 1990).

[194] *Vincent v. Vits*, 566 N.E.2d 818 (Ill. App. Ct. 1991); *McCarthy v. Tobin*, 706 N.E.2d 629 (Mass. 1999) (an initial offer to purchase accepted and signed by the seller and buyer can be enforced by specific performance even if the parties contemplated later signing a full purchase and sale agreement); *Schumacher v. Ihrke*, 469 N.W.2d 329, 335 (Minn. Ct. App. 1991); Dale A. Whitman et al., *The Law of Property* §10.5, at 630 (4th ed. 2019).

[195] Dale A. Whitman et al., *The Law of Property* §10.5, at 633-634 (4th ed. 2019).

[196] James C. Smith & Milton R. Friedman, *Contracts and Conveyances of Real Property* §24:4, at 24-20 (8th ed. 2017).

[197] In the case of an installment sale contract, restitution would also include the value of any improvements made by the buyer on the property during the executory period.

[198] *BSL Development Corp. v. Broad Cove, Inc.*, 577 N.Y.S.2d 98 (App. Div. 1991); Dale A. Whitman et al., *The Law of Property* §10.3, at 615 (4th ed. 2019).

[199] *Middelthon v. Crowder*, 563 So. 2d 94 (Fla. Dist. Ct. App. 1990); Dale A. Whitman et al., *The Law of Property* §10.3, at 615-617 (4th ed. 2019).

[200] *Gomez v. Pagaduan*, 613 P.2d 658 (Haw. Ct. App. 1980); *Beard v. S/E Joint Venture*, 581 A.2d 1275 (Md. 1990).

Argument for denying expectation damages when the seller acted in good faith

This rule originated in an English case of 1776[201] and may have been based on the fact that titles were so uncertain and complicated in England that it was unreasonable for buyers to expect that sellers who promised to convey good title would be able to do so.[202] Many cases in the United States still adopt this approach, giving the buyer expectation damages only if the seller acted in bad faith through knowingly contracting to convey good title while knowing that the title was defective.[203] The rule might be justified because it saves administrative or litigation costs. Restitution is satisfied by return of the deposit to the buyer, while expectation damages are harder to measure and may require a lawsuit to determine or to induce the parties to settle. Adopting a restitution standard may deter buyers from bringing lawsuits against sellers and thus both lower transaction costs and encourage sellers to sell their land.

Argument for granting expectation damages to the buyer even if seller acted in good faith

However, courts are increasingly allowing buyers to obtain expectation damages whether or not the seller was acting in good faith or bad faith.[204] This rule has been adopted in half or more of the states.[205] They have concluded that the traditional rule is unjustified both because no comparable rule constrains the seller in seeking damages from a breaching buyer, because this rule does not apply in breach-of-contract cases that do not involve real estate transfers, and because, whether or not the seller acts in good faith, the seller has breached a promise to convey marketable title to the buyer. This promise is violated if the seller cannot convey good title, even if the seller did not know of the defect. Some burden should be placed on the seller to determine the state of the title before making such a promise. Moreover, sellers may breach for a variety of reasons — not the least of which is receiving a higher offer from another buyer. Limiting the buyer to restitution damages gives the seller an incentive to breach the contract if the seller receives a higher offer because all the seller need do is return the deposit and then take the higher bid. The buyer would not be able to recover the lost benefit of the bargain unless the buyer could argue that the seller was acting in bad faith at the time the contract was signed — a showing that will be very hard to prove. Expectation damages induce the seller to go through with the deal, protecting the buyer's expectations that the sale will be completed and giving buyers the security of knowing that

[201] *Flureau v. Thornhill*, 96 Eng. Rep. 635 (C.P. 1776); Dale A. Whitman et al., *The Law of Property* §10.3, at 618 (4th ed. 2019).

[202] 2 James C. Smith & Milton R. Friedman, *Contracts and Conveyances of Real Property* §24:3.3, at 24-11 (8th ed. 2017).

[203] *Id.* at §24:3.3; Dale A. Whitman et al., *The Law of Property* §10.3, at 619 (4th ed. 2019). *See, e.g.*, Okla. Stat. tit. 23, §27; *BGW Development Co. v. Mount Kisco Lodge No. 1552 of the Benevolent and Protective Order of Elks of the United States of America, Inc.*, 669 N.Y.S.2d 56, 60 (App. Div. 1998); *Mokar Properties Corp. v. Hall*, 179 N.Y.S.2d 814 (App. Div. 1958); *Carson v. Isabel Apartments, Inc.*, 579 P.2d 1027 (Wash. Ct. App. 1978).

[204] At least half the cases adopt this approach. Dale A. Whitman et al., *The Law of Property* §10.3, at 617-618 (4th ed. 2019).

[205] 2 James C. Smith & Milton R. Friedman, *Contracts and Conveyances of Real Property* §24:3.3, at 24-11 (8th ed. 2017). *See Miller v. Estate of Dawson*, 686 S.W.2d 443 (Ark. Ct. App. 1985); *Basiliko v. Pargo Corp.*, 532 A.2d 1346 (D.C. 1987); *Burgess v. Arita*, 704 P.2d 930 (Haw. Ct. App. 1985).

the signing of the contract is a meaningful event on which they can rely in planning their lives.

Expenditures and lost profits

In addition to restitution and expectation damages, the buyer may be able to recover expenditures made in reliance on the contract and lost profits from other transactions that would have been earned had the sale gone through. These consequential damages are generally recoverable under the ordinary rules of contract damages[206] only if they should have been foreseeable by the parties at the time the contract was signed.[207] It should be noted that a buyer who is awarded expectation damages may be denied the right to recover expenses because, if the deal had gone through, she would not have recovered such expenses from the seller; giving her only the benefit of the bargain (and not extra compensation for expenses) would put her in the position she would have been in had the contract been performed — which, after all, is the general understanding of the purpose of awarding expectation damages. If, on the other hand, the buyer is denied expectation damages, and is granted restitution only, the remedy is essentially a rescission of the contract, placing the buyer in the position she would have been in had the contract *not* been made, and thus recovery of expenses seems appropriate.[208] ◀

Remedies

§11.3.4.2 Seller's Remedies. When the buyer breaches, the seller is entitled to sue for damages or specific performance. These are similar remedies for the seller because they both involve the payment of money from the buyer to the seller. Specific performance does not only involve payment, however; it also transfers title from the seller to the buyer.

Damages

The seller is entitled to seek expectation damages or reliance damages. Restitution is usually not at issue here because the buyer usually makes payments to the seller, so there is usually nothing for the seller to recover from the buyer. The rule limiting the buyer to expectation damages unless the seller acted in bad faith does not apply to suits by sellers against buyers. The seller is entitled to the difference between the contract price and the market price at the time of the breach.[209] If the contract price was at the market price, the seller will recover nothing, because the law imposes on the seller a duty to mitigate damages.[210] If the seller resells the property for a price lower than the contract price, the courts will usually take that as the market price unless the sale was to a family member or friend for nominal value or an amount that clearly bore no relation to market value.

[206] This rule originates in the leading case of *Hadley v. Baxendale*, 156 Eng. Rep. 145 (Ex. 1854). *See* E. Allan Farnsworth, *Contracts* §12.14, at 821-834 (3d ed. 1999).

[207] *Lotito v. Mazzeo*, 518 N.Y.S.2d 22 (App. Div. 1987); *Danburg v. Keil*, 365 S.E.2d 754 (Va. 1988); Dale A. Whitman et al., *The Law of Property* §10.3, at 615 (4th ed. 2019).

[208] *Id.* at 621-622.

[209] *Iowa-Mo Enterprises, Inc. v. Avren*, 639 F.2d 443 (8th Cir. 1981) (applying Missouri law); 2 James C. Smith & Milton R. Friedman, *Contracts and Conveyances of Real Property* §23:3, at 23-6 to 23-14 (8th ed. 2017).

[210] 2 James C. Smith & Milton R. Friedman, *Contracts and Conveyances of Real Property* §23:3, at 23-6 to 23-14 (8th ed. 2017).

Liquidated damages (forfeiture of the deposit)

When a buyer refuses to complete the deal, the seller usually retains the deposit (sometimes called the "earnest money") as liquidated damages.[211] Liquidated damages are damages set by the parties as part of their contract. The contract ordinarily will expressly provide that the seller has the right to retain the deposit upon the buyer's breach.[212] The amount of the deposit varies according to local custom. It is often 10 percent of the purchase price but may be less than that, as well.[213] The issue that arises is whether the amount of the deposit would be held to be a valid estimate of the seller's damages (and thus enforceable as liquidated damages) or exceeds the seller's likely damages (and thus is an enforceable "penalty").[214] Many courts hold that retention of the deposit is appropriate without regard to actual damages suffered by the seller.[215] A New York court ruled, for example, that the seller could retain a deposit that amounted to 25 percent of the purchase price and exceeded $8 million when the buyer refused to go ahead with the deal.[216] The traditional approach determines whether the deposit is a reasonable estimate of damages at the time of the contract and, if so, allows the seller to keep the amount stipulated in the contract as liquidated damages.[217] However, if the seller is quickly able to find a new buyer, the seller suffers little or no damage from the breach. In such cases, courts are increasingly holding that retention of the deposit gives the seller an unreasonable windfall and are making the seller return all or some of the deposit to the buyer.[218] A very small number of courts hold that liquidated damages are inappropriate unless the damages would be difficult to calculate and that, because damages are not ordinarily difficult to determine in the context of land sales, sellers should ordinarily not be entitled to keep the deposit.[219]

Specific performance

Like buyers, sellers are generally given specific performance "as a matter of course," although, as an equitable remedy, it has also always been subject to the judge's discretion and thereby may be denied on fairness grounds.[220] Although buyers are virtually automatically granted the right to specific performance because land is unique (and damages are inadequate),

[211] *Id.* at §23:3, at 23-6 to 23-14.

[212] Dale A. Whitman et al., *The Law of Property* §10.4, at 625 (4th ed. 2019).

[213] *Id.*

[214] *Id. See Maxton Builders, Inc. v. Lo Galbo*, 502 N.E.2d 184 (N.Y. 1986) (seller may keep deposit if it is 10 percent of the purchase price or less but might not be allowed to keep all of it if it were greater than 10 percent).

[215] *Pima Savings & Loan Ass'n v. Rampello*, 812 P.2d 1115 (Ariz. Ct. App. 1991); *Shapiro v. Grinspoon*, 541 N.E.2d 359 (Mass. App. Ct. 1989); *Lynch v. Andrew*, 481 N.E.2d 1383 (Mass. App. Ct. 1985).

[216] *Uzan v. 845 UN Ltd. Partnership*, 778 N.Y.S.2d 171 (App. Div. 2004).

[217] *See, e.g., Kelly v. Marx*, 705 N.E.2d 1114, 1117 (Mass. 1999).

[218] *Stabenau v. Cairelli*, 577 A.2d 1130 (Conn. App. Ct. 1990); Dale A. Whitman et al., *The Law of Property* §10.4, at 626-628 (4th ed. 2019).

[219] *Walker v. Graham*, 706 P.2d 278 (Wyo. 1985); *DeLeon v. Aldrete*, 398 S.W.2d 160, 163 (Tex. Civ. App. 1965).

[220] 2 James C. Smith & Milton R. Friedman, *Contracts and Conveyances of Real Property* §23:4, at 23-14 (8th ed. 2017).

the same argument cannot be made about sellers. After all, what the seller wants is the money, and money is hardly unique.[221]

Argument for giving sellers specific performance

Some courts grant sellers specific performance partly on the ground that they believe remedies should be mutual.[222] If the buyer can obtain specific performance from the seller for breach, it may seem fair for the seller to be able to obtain a similar remedy from the buyer. But the notion that remedies should be the same for both parties is only justifiable if the parties are similarly situated. But because the buyer and seller are after different things (money versus land), it is not clear that they are similarly situated. An alternative reason for allowing the seller specific performance is the inadequacy of damages.[223] If the seller seeks damages, she is subject to the duty to mitigate damages; this means the seller must make efforts to sell the property to someone else and can only recover from the breaching buyer the difference between what the buyer would have paid and the amount the seller is likely to get from another buyer. This puts an obligation on the seller to make new efforts to sell the property — something that is not always easy or inexpensive in time or money. Moreover, as the *Restatement (Second) of Contracts* explains: "[B]ecause the value of land is to some extent speculative, it may be difficult for [the seller] to prove with reasonable certainty the difference between the contract price and the market price."[224] Allowing the seller to obtain specific performance will allow the seller to force the buyer to complete the transaction, pay the rest of the purchase price, and take title off the hands of the seller, making it the buyer's problem to find a new buyer if need be.

Argument against specific performance for sellers

The premises of the above argument may often be false. The fair market value of land is often easily discernable, and if the land is in demand, the seller may be able to find a new buyer quickly and recover any difference between the contract price and the market price from the defaulting buyer. It could be argued, therefore, that sellers should be granted specific performance only if the property is not readily marketable or if its value is hard to determine.[225] If the property is marketable and its value is discernable, then damages are an adequate remedy and there is no warrant for forcing the buyer to buy property she no longer wants. Forcing the buyer to buy will only force her to resell the property to someone else. Giving the seller damages will lower transaction costs by inducing the seller to find a new buyer and substituting one transaction for two. One court has refused specific performance to a seller who failed to mitigate damages by attempting to find another buyer.[226]

[221] Dale A. Whitman et al., *The Law of Property* §10.4, at 626 (4th ed. 2019). *See Walch v. Crandall*, 416 N.W.2d 375 (Mich. Ct. App. 1987).

[222] Dale A. Whitman et al., *The Law of Property* §10.5, at 630 (4th ed. 2019).

[223] *Id.* at §10.5, at 631.

[224] *Restatement (Second) of Contracts* §360 cmt. e (1981); Dale A. Whitman et al., *The Law of Property* §10.4, at 631 (4th ed. 2019).

[225] *Centex Homes Corp. v. Boag*, 320 A.2d 194, 198-199 (N.J. Ch. Div. 1974).

[226] *Kesler v. Marshall*, 792 N.E.2d 893, 897 (Ind. Ct. App. 2003).

§11.3.5 Risk of Loss During Executory Period

Equitable conversion

During the "executory period" between the signing of the contract and the closing, the property sometimes comes to harm. Who bears the risk of such harm? Traditionally, the courts have applied the doctrine of *equitable conversion* to hold that, once the contract is signed, the purchaser is treated as the equitable owner of the property and, as the owner, bears the risks associated with ownership.[227] Thus, the buyer must complete the deal even if the house burns down.

Criticism of the traditional rule

This traditional rule rarely accords with the parties' expectations. Generally, the seller retains possession of the property and maintains insurance on it. Thus, the seller has both the means to prevent harm to the property and the ability to collect existing insurance if harm does occur. The buyer, on the other hand, cannot control the seller's conduct on the property and ordinarily does not purchase insurance until the date of the closing, when title passes.[228] For these reasons, most contracts place the risk of loss on the seller and require the seller to maintain insurance through the executory period.[229] Moreover, some courts have abandoned the doctrine, placing the risk of loss on the buyer only if the buyer has taken possession of the property.[230]

§11.3.6 Death of a Contracting Party

Death of seller

The death of the buyer or seller during the executory period does not invalidate the agreement. The buyer's heirs or devisees have the right to enforce the contract against the seller (or the seller's heirs or devisees). The doctrine of equitable conversion transmutes the deceased seller's interest into *personal* property for purposes of inheritance laws, while the deceased buyer's interest is characterized as *real* property for those same purposes.[231] If the seller dies after the contract is signed but before the closing, the seller's legal title is "held in trust for the purchaser as equitable owner of the property."[232] The duty to complete the transaction descends to the seller's personal representative and (after probate) the seller's legatee, who inherits the seller's personal property.[233]

Death of buyer

If the buyer dies before the closing, the buyer's devisees (who inherit the buyer's real property) succeed to the buyer's interest in specifically enforcing the contract.[234] At the same time, the duty to pay the rest of the

[227] 14-81 *Powell on Real Property* §81.03[2].

[228] Dale A. Whitman et al., *The Law of Property* §10.13, at 681-682 (4th ed. 2019).

[229] *Id. See Bellucci v. Moore*, 585 So. 2d 490 (Fla. Dist. Ct. App. 1991) (clause allowing buyer to rescind if damage to the property exceeded 3 percent of the purchase price); *Winterchase Townhomes, Inc. v. Koether*, 387 S.E.2d 361 (Ga. Ct. App. 1989) (clause permitting buyer to rescind contract or purchase and receive insurance proceeds if the property were harmed during the executory period).

[230] *Anderson v. Yaworski*, 181 A. 205 (Conn. 1935); *Skelly Oil Co. v. Ashmore*, 365 S.W.2d 582, 588-589 (Mo. 1963); *Smith v. Warth*, 483 S.W.2d 834 (Tex. Civ. App. 1972).

[231] 14-81 *Powell on Real Property* §81.03[1].

[232] *Id.* at §81.03[1][a][i].

[233] *Id.*

[234] *Id.* at §81.03[1][a][ii].

purchase price is a personal obligation that traditionally was placed on the buyer's legatees (who inherit the decedent's personal property rights and obligations).[235] If the devisees and the legatees are different persons, the resulting allocation of the burdens and benefits of ownership may be strikingly unfair; the devisees get the property free and clear and the legatees' bequest may be completely eaten up by the payment due on the land sale contract. The *Uniform Probate Code* has changed this "rule of exoneration" by placing the duty on the devisees who inherit the land to pay the balance of the purchase price.[236]

§11.3.7 Mistake

Mutual (bilateral) mistake

If both parties to a land sales contract "base their agreement on a mistaken fact that was essential to the contract, either party may treat the contract as invalid and seek cancellation or rescission."[237] If the mutual (or *bilateral*) mistake is in the written deed and the closing has already occurred, the buyer may sue to *reform* the deed to correct the mistake.[238] When only one of the parties is mistaken as to a material fact (*unilateral mistake*), most courts will not allow rescission unless the other party committed fraud or engaged in other inequitable conduct.[239] However, some courts have allowed rescission in cases of unilateral mistake.[240]

Unilateral mistake

§11.4 Deeds and Title Protection

§11.4.1 Formal Requirements

Essential elements

§11.4.1.1 Writing. Like the land sale contract, the deed must (1) identify the parties; (2) describe the property being conveyed; (3) state the grantor's intent to convey the property interest in question; and (4) contain the grantor's signature.[241] The deed need not be recorded to transfer title; delivery of the deed to the grantee is sufficient.[242] Most deeds are — and should be — recorded to protect the grantee's rights. To be recorded, most states require the deed to be acknowledged by a public notary or other official and some require one or more witnesses to the transaction.[243] Thus,

[235] *Id.*

[236] U.P.C. §2-609; U.P.C. §3-814; 14-81 *Powell on Real Property* §81.03[1][a][ii].

[237] *Harding v. Willie*, 458 N.W.2d 612 (Iowa Ct. App. 1990); *Bonnco Petrol, Inc. v. Epstein*, 560 A.2d 655, 660 (N.J. 1989); *Williams v. Gash*, 789 S.W.2d 261, 264 (Tex. 1990); 14-81 *Powell on Real Property* §81.02[3][c].

[238] *St. Pius X House of Retreats, Salvatorian Fathers v. Diocese of Camden*, 443 A.2d 1052, 1065-1067 (N.J. 1982).

[239] *Broomall v. State*, 391 S.E.2d 918 (Ga. 1990); 14-81 *Powell on Real Property* §81.02[4][c].

[240] *Beatty v. Depue*, 103 N.W.2d 187 (S.D. 1960) (buyer mistakenly thought land included Forest Service land that was enclosed by the same fence).

[241] 23 Dale A. Whitman et al., The Law of Property §11.1, at 703 (4th ed. 2019); 14-81A Powell on Real Property §§81A.04 to 81A.05.

[242] 2 James C. Smith & Milton R. Friedman, *Contracts and Conveyances of Real Property* §27:2, at 27-3 (8th ed. 2017).

[243] Dale A. Whitman et al., *The Law of Property* §11.1, at 706 (4th ed. 2019); 2 James C. Smith & Milton R. Friedman, *Contracts and Conveyances of Real Property* §27:4.3, at 27-18 (8th ed. 2017).

although acknowledgments are not necessary to transfer title (except in a few states),[244] they usually accompany the transfer of the deed to enable the deed to be recorded.

Land description

The land being conveyed must be described in the deed. The description must be sufficiently precise to locate the boundaries of the property. Those boundaries may be defined by reference to official surveys, "plats," or by "metes and bounds." Most of the land in the United States has been surveyed under the Government Survey System devised by Thomas Jefferson and first adopted by the Continental Congress in 1785.[245] The system divides the land by a series of north-south and east-west lines and defines so-called townships, which are further subdivided into "sections."[246] These sections may be further divided into halves and quarters, or even smaller divisions.[247] Property can be located within these quarter sections by reference to these official land parcels.

Government Survey System

Plats or subdivision maps

Property may also be described by a "plat" or subdivision map.[248] A plat is a map produced by a private developer (not a government official) that describes the lots being created in a subdivision. These lots are generally the ones that actually will be bought and sold; their borders are often not straight. Often the subdivision is given a name and divided into "blocks," with each block being further subdivided into "lots." The plat is generally approved by a local agency before being filed in the recording office. Deeds may then describe the lot being sold by reference to the plat. So, for example, a lot being conveyed might be described as Block G, Lot 1 of Gerry's Landing Subdivision, recorded at Middletown County Registry of Deeds, Plat 46, in Plat Book 114, Page 75.

Metes and bounds

Property may also be described by "metes and bounds."[249] This system starts at a defined point (usually described by a natural or artificial "monument" such as a fence or a street edge) and identifies the direction and distance of the first border, then the second border, and so on, until returning to the original point. In effect, it describes how one would walk around the borders of the property. Direction is notated in degrees (and minutes and seconds) east or west of due north or south. The convention is to state north or south first and then describe the east or west deviation. So a border that runs in a northwesterly direction would be notated as "North

[244] *E.g.*, Ariz. Rev. Stat. §33-401(B); see 11 *Thompson on Real Property, Third Thomas Edition* §94.07(g).

[245] Dale A. Whitman et al., *The Law of Property* §11.2, at 716 (4th ed. 2019); 11 *Thompson on Real Property, Third Thomas Edition* §94.07(s).

[246] Dale A. Whitman et al., *The Law of Property* §11.2, at 716 (4th ed. 2019). The major north-south lines are called principal meridians and the major east-west lines are called base lines. Parallel to the principal meridians at six-mile intervals are north-south lines that divide the land into "ranges." Parallel to the base lines are east-west lines that divide the land into "townships." This system creates six-mile squares also referred to as "townships." Each township is divided into 36 "sections." *Id.*

[247] 11 *Thompson on Real Property, Third Thomas Edition* §94.07(s)(2).

[248] *Id.* at §94.07(s).

[249] *Southeast Bank, N.A. v. Sapp*, 554 So. 2d 1193, 1195 (Fla. Dist. Ct. App. 1989); *Lange v. Wyoming National Bank*, 706 P.2d 659 (Wyo. 1985), *appeal after remand*, 741 P.2d 109 (1987); 11 *Thompson on Real Property, Third Thomas Edition* §94.07(s)(1).

45 degrees West 30 feet." Subsequent borders take a similar form until one returns to the starting place.[250]

Approaches may be combined

These approaches to land descriptions may be combined with the general location stated as the southwest quarter of a Township on the Government Survey and the particular lot described by a plat and/or a metes and bounds description.

Mistakes and reformation

If a deed contains a mistaken description of the property, either party may sue to reform the deed.[251]

River borders

If a border is described by reference to a river or stream, disputes often arise when the location of the stream changes over time. A riparian owner may gain ground by *accretion* (a buildup of soil on the bank) or by *reliction* (a receding of the water from the land). Alternatively, she may lose ground through erosion. When these changes happen gradually, the borders shift with the shifting stream so that riparian owners next to the water remain adjacent to the water. However, if the stream changes suddenly (a process called *avulsion*), the courts will preserve the old borders.[252]

Transfer of deed necessary

§11.4.1.2 Delivery. To effectively transfer title, the grantor must *intend* to transfer title and a deed must be *delivered* to the grantee.[253] This usually does not create a problem when a transfer involves a sale. The buyer will generally not tender the rest of the purchase price at the closing unless the seller delivers the deed. Alternatively, the seller may give the deed to a third party, called an escrow, to hold until the buyer completes required payments or fulfills other contractual conditions. The escrow is obligated contractually to both the seller and the buyer, and, given the seller's promise to convey if the conditions are fulfilled, the seller has no power to take back the deed, as long as the conditions are in fact fulfilled.

Problems arise in the context of gifts

In the context of gifts, however, both intent and delivery are often at issue. The problem arises because grantors seek to avoid the formalities required to draft a will (and possibly the taxes associated with inheritance) by giving an *inter vivos* gift (a gift made during the grantor's life), which is intended to take effect at the donor's death. The donor may express an intent to give the property to the donee but retain the deed, or deposit it with another person (such as a friend or family member) or in a safety deposit box in a bank.[254] The donor may or may not tell the donee about the gift. When the donor dies, the donee may find out about the gift and claim the property. If the donor's heirs are different from the donee, they may well claim that the deed was never delivered during the donor's lifetime and that, consequently, title never passed and the real property became part

[250] Dale A. Whitman et al., *The Law of Property* §11.2, at 715 (4th ed. 2019).

[251] *Paradise Hills Church, Inc. v. International Church*, 467 F. Supp. 357, 363 (D. Ariz. 1979); Dale A. Whitman et al., *The Law of Property* §11.1, at 709-710 (4th ed. 2019).

[252] Dale A. Whitman et al., *The Law of Property* §11.2, at 721 (4th ed. 2019).

[253] *Sofsky v. Rosenberg*, 564 N.E.2d 662 (N.Y. 1990); *Jorgensen v. Crow*, 466 N.W.2d 120 (N.D. 1991); *Winegar v. Froerer Corp.*, 813 P.2d 104, 110 (Utah 1991).

[254] *See In re Estate of Hardy*, 910 So. 2d 1052 (Miss. 2005), 805 So. 2d 515 (Miss. 2002) (recording deed creates presumption of delivery, but no delivery exists when deed was not recorded and grantor retained deeds in her possession until her death and they were found in her purse, and there was no other indication that delivery was intended).

of the decedent's estate, which should pass to the devisees under the will, rather than the purported donee.[255]

Delivery must be immediate

For title to pass immediately, the grantor must *intend* immediate transfer of title and the deed must be *delivered* to the donee. Failure to deliver the deed may well suggest an intent to retain title until death. The rules applicable to wills require a writing that purports to be a will and witnesses. These rules are intended to avoid disputes about who the decedent intended to leave her property to when she died. They are also intended to protect creditors of the decedent by ensuring that property owned by the decedent at the time of death is available to pay the decedent's debts. The law requires the donor either actually to make the gift during her lifetime or to follow the procedures for devising the property through a valid will. Lifetime gifts are effectuated by the donor's expression of an intent to make an immediate transfer and delivery of the deed. Delivery is added evidence that the transfer actually occurred. Gifts are only complete when they are accepted. Delivery is taken to be evidence of acceptance by the donee. In the absence of delivery and acceptance, an immediate transfer has not occurred and when the donor dies, the title will not pass to the intended donee unless the gift is included in the will.

Acceptance by the donee

▷ CONDITIONAL GIFTS

HARD CASE ◀

Has a deed been "delivered" if the gift is conditional? If the condition is the death of the grantor, the courts will generally not find delivery to have occurred because the grantor is attempting to avoid the rules about wills.[256] However, if the condition is an event or occurrence other than the donor's death, the cases are divided. If the deed itself grants an interest only on the happening of a future event, it constitutes a present transfer of a future interest. However, if the deed is absolute on its face, but the donor expresses an intent to effectuate a gift only on the happening of a future event, the courts divide on whether delivery of the deed effectuates a transfer of title. Some courts find the condition inconsistent with delivery of the deed and hold that title passes when the gift is made and the deed delivered.[257] They hold that a grantee cannot serve as her own escrow; only if a third party is given the deed will the condition be enforced. Conditional delivery to a grantee therefore vests absolute title in that grantee.[258] This result might be justified on the ground that delivery of a deed that, on its face, purports to transfer title, should in fact transfer title, regardless of any verbal agreements that the transfer is conditional. This accords with the policy underlying the statute of frauds and prevents uncertainties that will arise when grantors claim that the delivery of the deed was not intended actually to transfer title. Other courts, however, find that the gift has not been made if it is conditional on some event happening before title will pass; title will

[255] Dale A. Whitman et al., *The Law of Property* §11.3, at 725 (4th ed. 2019).

[256] *Raim v. Stancel*, 339 N.W.2d 621, 624 (Iowa Ct. App. 1983).

[257] *State ex rel. Pai v. Thom*, 563 P.2d 982, 987 (Haw. 1977).

[258] *Sweeney, Administratrix v. Sweeney*, 11 A.2d 806 (Conn. 1940).

pass only when the event occurs.[259] This approach promotes the intent of the grantor.[260]

Argument that title passed despite the condition

In *State ex rel. Pai v. Thom*,[261] the state of Hawai'i sought to acquire 14 parcels of property from the owners in lieu of bringing eminent domain proceedings. The parties signed a contract providing for transfer of the property for an agreed price, with the proviso that the closing occur within 60 days. One month after the agreement, the owners delivered a deed to the state. However, the state made the requisite payment ten months later. The owners then sought to rescind the transfer on the ground that the payment was not made within 60 days. In effect, they argued that the deed was conditional on the purchase price being paid in accordance with the contract and that the delay triggered a right of entry in the grantors to revoke the transfer. The court noted that the legal issue was whether the grantors intended to transfer title immediately to the state and whether they reserved a power to change their minds. The court held that the transfer of a deed, absolute on its face, with an intent to transfer ownership, effectively transfers fee simple title. "[D]elivery of a deed complete on its face to the grantee, as here, is an absolute delivery."[262] The obligation to pay within 60 days was not included in the deed and was, thus, at most, a covenant and not a condition, and the grantors could sue for damages for breach of the covenant but could not undo the deal and take back title to the property. Looking to the face of the deed to determine whether an intent to make a present transfer was present is much more predictable than looking to other facts or circumstances to answer this question.

Argument that title does not pass until the condition is fulfilled

In contrast, in *Martinez v. Martinez*,[263] two parents sold land to the couple's son and his wife. They transferred the deed upon the buyers' assurance that they would assume the mortgage on the property and make the payments on it. The sellers instructed the buyers to bring the deed to the bank so that it could be held in escrow until the mortgage was paid off. When the buyers failed to make the mortgage payments, the sellers informed them that they were exercising their contractual right to retake the property. The buyers argued, under the authority of *State ex rel. Pai v. Thom*,[264] "that delivery of a deed is conditional only if the condition is expressed in the deed, and that there can be no delivery in escrow when the deed is given by the grantor to the grantee."[265] The New Mexico Supreme Court disagreed on the ground that "the intent to transfer title is an essential element of delivery and that the intent may be determined from the surrounding circumstances."[266] Delivery has not occurred if there is no evidence that the grantors intended to immediately divest themselves

259 *Martinez v. Martinez*, 678 P.2d 1163 (N.M. 1984).
260 *Chillemi v. Chillemi*, 78 A.2d 750, 753 (Md. 1951).
261 563 P.2d 982 (Haw. 1977).
262 *Id.* at 987.
263 678 P.2d 1163 (N.M. 1984).
264 563 P.2d 982 (Haw. 1977).
265 678 P.2d at 1165.
266 *Id.* at 1166.

of title.[267] The court concluded that delivery had not occurred and that the terms of the contract of sale remained in effect, allowing the grantors to retake possession and title to the property. The court's ruling was justified by reference to the desire to promote the intent of the parties and not to enforce formalistically the terms of the deed if this deviated from the parties' actual agreement. ◀

▷ JOINT BANK BOX **HARD CASE ◀**

When the donor places the deed in a jointly held security box, courts disagree about whether delivery has occurred. One might argue that it has because the donee is free to remove the deed from the box.[268] On the other hand, because the donor has the power to remove the deed as well, it may be unclear whether the donor actually intended to transfer title immediately.[269] ◀

Revocable trusts

A better way to achieve the result of making a conditional gift is to create a *revocable trust.* Although conditional or revocable deeds of land are not generally allowed, revocable trusts are valid everywhere. The grantor may declare a trust with herself as the grantor and identify herself as the beneficiary of the trust for her lifetime, with the remainder to go to another. The trust may be made revocable by the grantor. This arrangement in the trust form is enforced because the focus of trust law is to promote the intent of the grantor. A similar arrangement performed by the equivocal delivery of a deed will often not be enforced because the lack of clear evidence of delivery may seem to negate an intent actually to make a present gift rather than a testamentary gift to take effect on death. Of course, this technical distinction between the two approaches may well allow a grantor to evade the formalities required for wills and the protections created by the requirement that wills be witnessed.

§11.4.2 Substantive Requirements

Forged deed is void

§11.4.2.1 Forgery. A forged deed is void.[270] It does not transfer title to the grantee.[271] This is true even if the property has been subsequently conveyed to a bona fide purchaser who had no knowledge of the forgery. However, the courts may bar the owner from recovering possession

[267] *Id.*

[268] *Kresser v. Peterson*, 675 P.2d 1193 (Utah 1984) (finding that the donor did intend to give an immediate gift when deed was placed in jointly held safety deposit box).

[269] *Wiggill v. Cheney*, 597 P.2d 1351 (Utah 1979) (finding no intent to give an immediate gift when deed was placed in jointly held safety deposit box); *Lenhart v. Desmond*, 705 P.2d 338 (Wyo. 1985) (finding that donor did not intend to give an immediate gift when deed was deposited in jointly held safe deposit box).

[270] *Homeamerican Credit, Inc. v. Weiss*, 2000 WL 347785, at *3 (Conn. Super. Ct. 2000) ("As a general proposition, a forged document is a nullity"); *Zurstrassen v. Stonier*, 786 So. 2d 65, 68 (Fla. Dist. Ct. App. 2001); *Beasley v. Burns*, 7 S.W.3d 768, 769 (Tex. Ct. App. 1999).

[271] Dale A. Whitman et al., *The Law of Property* §11.1, at 711 (4th ed. 2019); 11 *Thompson on Real Property, Third Thomas Edition* §94.07(*l*). *See* §11.4.2.1.

from a subsequent bona fide purchaser on the basis of equitable factors such that the prior owner might be estopped to deny the validity of the conveyance.[272]

Fraud in the execution

§11.4.2.2 Fraud. If a grantor is tricked into signing a deed, the signature is treated like a forgery and the deed is void. Because the grantor had no intent to convey title, the deed is treated as a nullity.[273]

Fraud in the inducement

However, if the grantor is induced to transfer the property by fraudulent representations upon which the grantor relies, the deed is not void but voidable.[274] This means that the deed does pass title but that the grantor may choose to revoke the deed. However, if the grantee has subsequently transferred the property to a bona fide purchaser, the original grantor no longer has the power to choose to revoke the deed.

§11.4.3 Title Covenants

Warranty, special warranty, and quitclaim deeds

Most deeds contain some form of covenant promising that the grantor is able to, and does, convey good title. A deed expressing such a promise is generally called a *warranty* or a *general warranty* deed. Sometimes, however, the grantor makes no representation in the deed that the grantor has title to the property being conveyed or the right to convey title to the grantee. Such deeds are generally called *quitclaim* deeds. In the middle of these extremes are *special warranty* deeds, by which the grantor covenants against title defects arising from acts of the grantor herself but not of others.[275]

Relation to contractual duty to convey marketable title

Title covenants resemble the contractual duty to convey marketable title. However, they are not identical. The duty to convey marketable title may be breached if there is a significant risk that the grantee may be subject to litigation concerning the title. Title covenants in deeds are violated only if the title is in fact defective; they are not violated merely because the title is in doubt.[276]

Merger doctrine

Under the doctrine of merger, after the closing, the title covenants in the deed supersede any promises made in the initial contract of sale. The contract is "merged" into the deed and the sole basis of relief for the buyer is to sue on the title covenants in the deed. This matters because the remedies for breach of warranty in a deed differ from the remedies available for breach of contract. The merger doctrine does not apply to claims or

[272] *Zurstrassen v. Stonier*, 786 So. 2d 65, 68-70 (Fla. Dist. Ct. App. 2001) (acknowledging equitable estoppel might bar the true owner from recovering the property).

[273] *Schiavon v. Arnaudo Bros.*, 100 Cal. Rptr. 2d 801, 804 (Ct. App. 2001); *Upson v. Goodland State Bank & Trust Co.*, 823 P.2d 704 (Colo. 1992); Dale A. Whitman et al., *The Law of Property* §11.1, at 711 (4th ed. 2019); 11 *Thompson on Real Property, Third Thomas Edition* §94.07(*l*).

[274] Dale A. Whitman et al., *The Law of Property* §11.1, at 711 (4th ed. 2019); 11 *Thompson on Real Property, Third Thomas Edition* §94.07(*l*). *See* §11.4.2.2.

[275] *Rosado v. K & Y Mgt. Corp*, 212 A.D.3d 677, 678 (N.Y. App. Div. 2023); 11 *Thompson on Real Property, Third Thomas Edition* §94.07(b)(2).

[276] Dale A. Whitman et al., *The Law of Property* §11.13, at 802 (4th ed. 2019). *See* §11.3.3.3.

promises that would ordinarily not be part of a deed, such as a warranty that the property is in good condition.[277]

Remedies for breach of title covenants

If the seller breaches the duty to convey marketable title, the buyer is entitled to specific performance with an abatement of the price, rescission of the contract, and restitution of the deposit, or damages. About half the states allow recovery of expectation damages whether or not the seller acted in bad faith, while half limit the buyer to restitution if the seller acted in good faith.[278] Once title passes at the closing, and the buyer can sue only on the title covenants in the deed, the buyer's remedies are limited to damages, and most courts limit damages to the price the seller received for the land.[279]

General warranty deed

Courts traditionally have recognized six types of covenants. General warranty deeds contain them all, either explicitly or implicitly by reference to statutes that impose them on the grantor if certain words are used in the granting clause of the deed, or if the statutory covenants are referenced in the deed.[280] These six covenants include:

(1) **Seisin** The *covenant of seisin* is a promise that the grantor is in possession of the land and/or has the right to possess the land.
(2) **Right to convey** The *covenant of the right to convey* is a promise that the grantor has the right to transfer title to the property.
(3) **Against encumbrances** The *covenant against encumbrances* is a promise that there are no encumbrances on the land, such as easements, covenants, mortgages, or leases, other than those listed in the deed.
(4) **Warranty** The *covenant of warranty* is a promise to warrant and defend the grantee against any attack on the grantee's title.
(5) **Quiet enjoyment** The *covenant of quiet enjoyment* is a promise that the grantee's possession will not be disturbed and that, if it is, the grantor will compensate for the disturbance.
(6) **Further assurances** The *covenant of further assurances* is a promise to execute any documents needed to clear the grantee's title. This covenant, unlike the others, may be enforced by specific performance as well as damages.[281]

Time of breach

The "present" covenants (seisin, right to convey, and against encumbrances) are breached, if at all, at the moment the deed is delivered at the closing to the grantee.[282] The "future" covenants (warranty, quiet enjoyment, and further assurances) are breached, if at all, after the closing.[283] Traditionally, the

[277] *Mallin v. Good*, 417 N.E.2d 858, 861 (Ill. App. Ct. 1981); John G. Sprankling, *Understanding Property Law* §20.06[A], at 337 (5th ed. 2023).
[278] Dale A. Whitman et al., *The Law of Property* §11.13, at 802 (4th ed. 2019). *See* §11.3.3.3.
[279] *Woods v. Schmitt*, 439 N.W.2d 855, 866-867 (Iowa 1989); Dale A. Whitman et al., *The Law of Property* §11.13, at 808 (4th ed. 2019).
[280] *See* Cal. Civ. Code §1113; Or. Rev. Stat. §93.850.
[281] Dale A. Whitman et al., *The Law of Property* §11.13, at 802 (4th ed. 2019); 11 *Thompson on Real Property, Third Thomas Edition* §94.07(b)(1)(ii).
[282] Dale A. Whitman et al., *The Law of Property* §11.13, at 806-807 (4th ed. 2019).
[283] *Id.* at §11.13 at 807.

present covenants have not run with the land and future owners have no claim against the grantor who made them.[284] However, a few courts have held that present covenants run with the land and have allowed successors to sue on title covenants.[285] In contrast, the future covenants do run with the land.[286]

Special warranty deed

A special warranty deed warrants the title as to acts taken by the grantor herself. It is a promise that the grantor has not taken any actions that would give anyone superior title to the grantee.[287]

Quitclaim deed

A quitclaim deed makes no promises of any kind as to the title. It conveys to the grantee whatever rights the grantor had—which may be nothing.[288] Such deeds are usually used to release dormant or uncertain claims and to ensure that the grantee has whatever rights the grantor may be thought to retain.

Terminology

Local practice varies tremendously and in some states the names of the deeds vary from the usual practice. Massachusetts, for example, uses the term "quitclaim" deed to refer to what other states call a "warranty" deed.[289]

▶ HARD CASE ▷ REMEDIES

The three future covenants are usually breached when another claimant comes along. Because this could happen at any time, and the covenant is not breached until the grantee is actually disturbed, the grantee may lose possession and title to the property at a time when its value has substantially increased since the initial conveyance. If the grantee sues on the covenants of warranty and quiet enjoyment, however, the courts generally limit damages to the amount the grantor received from the grantee.[290] The grantee may lose property worth much more than this amount and not be made whole despite the grantor breach of covenant. On the other hand, the grantor/covenantor may be loath to sell the property if she will be liable for the lost fair market value of the property at any point in the future—no matter how remote—when the grantee's possession is disturbed. If both parties have acted in good faith and the market value of the property has increased, one or the other will suffer a substantial loss. The grantee can protect herself by purchasing title insurance—but, of course, the grantor could do so as well. ◀

[284] *Bridges v. Heimburger*, 360 So. 2d 929 (Miss. 1978). *See* 11 *Thompson on Real Property, Third Thomas Edition* §94.07(e).

[285] *Schofield v. Iowa Homestead Co.*, 32 Iowa 317 (1871); Dale A. Whitman et al., *The Law of Property* §11.13, at 810 (4th ed. 2019).

[286] Dale A. Whitman et al., *The Law of Property* §11.13, at 810-811 (4th ed. 2019).

[287] 11 *Thompson on Real Property, Third Thomas Edition* §94.07(b)(1)(i). *See* Cal. Civ. Code §§1092 & 1113.

[288] 11 *Thompson on Real Property, Third Thomas Edition* §94.07(b)(3)(i).

[289] Mass. Gen. Laws ch. 183, §2.

[290] Dale A. Whitman et al., *The Law of Property* §11.13, at 810-811 (4th ed. 2019); 11 *Thompson on Real Property, Third Thomas Edition* §94.07(c)(3).

§11.4.4 Marketable Title Acts

Root of title

Marketable title acts facilitate title searches and clear title by setting limits on how far back in the records the searcher must look when researching a title.[291] They exist in about a third of the states.[292] Marketable title acts void interests that are not re-recorded within a time period set by statute (typically 20 to 40 years before the present). The searcher must find a title that will count as the "root of title," which is the most recent recorded deed in an unbroken chain of title that is at least as many years long as the statutory period. If the period is 40 years and the search is being performed in the year 2025, a title from 1990 could not serve as the root of title but one from 1980 could.[293]

Curative acts

Some states have *curative acts* that validate recorded deeds that have some technical defects, such as lack of a seal or a defective acknowledgment.[294] Some states have more specific statutes that void certain types of interests, such as future interests or covenants, if they are not re-recorded every so often (21, 30, or 40 years are most common).[295] Others limit certain future interests, such as rights of entry and possibility of reverter, to a set period of 21, 30, or 40 years.[296] Still others limit enforceability of covenants and require a showing that they are of substantial benefit and/or do not impede reasonable land use.[297] Owners of these interests have challenged the laws as takings of property without just compensation because they cut off interests without notice to the owner. They have generally been upheld, at least where they give owners time to record before their interests are lost.[298]

Future interests and covenants

[291] 11 *Thompson on Real Property, Third Thomas Edition* §92.06(b)(1).

[292] Cal. Civ. Code §880.030 et seq.; Conn. Gen. Stat. §§47-33b to 47-33l; Fla. Stat. §§712.01 to 712.12; 735 Ill. Comp. Stat. 5/13-118 to -121; Ind. Code Ann. §§32-20-1-1 to 5-2; Iowa Code §§614.29 to 614.38; Kan. Stat. §§58-3401 to 58-3412; Mich. Stat. §§565.101 to 565.108; Minn. Stat. §541.023; Neb. Rev. Stat. §§76-288 to 76-298; N.C. Gen. Stat. §§47B-1 to 47B-9; N.D. Cent. Code §§47-19.1-01 to 47-19.1-11; Ohio Rev. Code §§5301.47 to 5301.55; Okla. Stat. tit. 16, §§71 to 80; S.D. Codified Laws §§43-30-1 to 43-30-17; R.I. Gen. Laws §§34-13.1-1 to -11; S.D. Codified Laws § 43-30-1 et seq.; Utah Code §§57-9-1 to 57-9-10; Vt. Stat. tit. 27, §§601 to 617; Wis. Stat. §893.33; Wyo. Stat. §§34-10-101 to 34-10-109; Dale A. Whitman et al., *The Law of Property* §11.12, at 796 n.645 (4th ed. 2019); 14-82 *Powell on Real Property* §82.04[3] n.35; 11 *Thompson on Real Property, Third Thomas Edition* §92.06(b).

[293] Dale A. Whitman et al., *The Law of Property* §11.12, at 794-800 (4th ed. 2019); 11 *Thompson on Real Property, Third Thomas Edition* §92.06(b)(3).

[294] 14-82 *Powell on Real Property* §82.04[1][a].

[295] Iowa Code §614.24 (21 years); Md. Real Prop. Code §6-102 (30 years); N.Y. Real Prop. §345 (30 years); Or. Rev. Stat. §105.772 (30 years); Dale A. Whitman et al., *The Law of Property* §11.12, at 797 (4th ed. 2019); 14-82 *Powell on Real Property* §82.04[1][a].

[296] Fla. Stat. §689.18 (21 years); 765 Ill. Comp. Stat. 330/4 (40 years); Md. Real Prop. Code §6-101 (30 years); Mass. Gen. Laws ch. 184A, §7 (30 years); Or. Rev. Stat. §105.770 (30 years).

[297] Mass. Gen. Laws ch. 184, §30; Minn. Stat. §500.20.

[298] *Trustees of Schools of Township No. 1 v. Batdorf*, 130 N.E.2d 111 (Ill. 1955); *Presbytery of Southeast Iowa v. Harris*, 226 N.W.2d 232 (Iowa 1975); *Cline v. Johnson County Board of Education*, 548 S.W.2d 507 (Ky. 1977); *Town of Brookline v. Carey*, 245 N.E.2d 446 (Mass. 1969); *Hiddleston v. Nebraska Jewish Education Society*, 186 N.W.2d 904 (Neb. 1971). *But see Board of Education v. Miles*, 207 N.E.2d 181 (N.Y. 1965) (holding unconstitutional the retrospective application of a statute that voided possibilities of reverter that were not re-recorded as applied to interests created before the effective date of the statute); *Biltmore Village v. Royal*, 71 So. 2d 727 (Fla. 1954) (holding unconstitutional a statute that retroactively voided

Adverse possession

Recall also that adverse possession functions to clear away old claims that have not been asserted for the statutory period.[299] The statute of limitations therefore functions on top of the marketable title acts to clear away old claims.

§11.4.5 *Recording Acts*

Recording of documents relating to title to land

§11.4.5.1 How the System Works. When property interests are created or transferred, the document that effectuates the transfer is "recorded" by the grantee in the recording office or registry of deeds. Although in almost all states recording is not required to validate the transfer of the property interest, it is essential both to provide an official record of the state of the title and to protect the buyer against any competing claims that may be created by the grantor in others. This system helps clarify the state of the title and provides buyers with assurances that the person purporting to sell them land actually owns it and that the land is not subject to any competing claims or encumbrances that might conflict with their ability to obtain title or use the property as they wish. Recording statutes put buyers on notice of prior claims or limits on land use rights. They identify the types of property interests that can be recorded. In general, deeds that convey title to land, long-term leases, mortgages, easements, and covenants may be recorded. Short-term leases (generally of one to three years' duration) are not recordable; this includes month-to-month tenancies.[300]

Recordable documents

Tract index

The simplest way to index and research the title would be to file information by *tract.* In a tract system, every document relating to a particular tract is filed together so that one can look at the records of that tract to determine all the possible claims that might exist on the property.[301] A tract system would probably constitute the most efficient method for collecting documents relating to a particular parcel. However, this is not how the recording system started, and converting to a tract system would be quite expensive. Most places do not have a tract index.

Acknowledgment

Most states require documents to be acknowledged by a notary public or other official before they can be recorded.[302] This is thought to decrease the likelihood of forged or fraudulently obtained deeds being recorded.[303]

▶ HARD CASE ▷ DEFECTIVELY ACKNOWLEDGED DOCUMENTS

If a deed is not acknowledged, or if the acknowledgment is technically defective (the notary forgot to sign it, for example), and the recorder accepts the deed for recording, most courts treat the deed as if it were unrecorded and

---

rights of entry and possibilities of reverter that had been in effect for more than 21 years without vesting).

[299] *See* Chapter 4.

[300] Dale A. Whitman et al., *The Law of Property* §11.9, at 770 (4th ed. 2019).

[301] *See* Okla. Stat. tit. 19, §291; 14-82 *Powell on Real Property* §82.03[2][c].

[302] 14-82 *Powell on Real Property* §82.03[1].

[303] *Id.*

insufficient to put a later buyer on constructive notice of the transaction it purports to manifest.[304] However, such a deed arguably puts the subsequent buyer on inquiry notice, and such a buyer can hardly be characterized as completely unaware of the earlier transaction. For this reason, some courts hold that a defectively acknowledged deed does put later buyers on constructive notice.[305] Indeed, if the subsequent buyer performs a title search and actually comes across the defectively acknowledged document, the buyer is on actual notice of its content and will not necessarily be seen as a bona fide purchaser without notice of the document.[306] ◀

Grantor-grantee index systems

The typical recording office uses a *grantor-grantee index*. Separate files are kept for grantors and grantees and, within each file, documents are indexed according to the year the document was filed. In the *grantor index*, all instruments are listed both alphabetically and chronologically by the grantor's last name. In the *grantee index*, all instruments are listed both alphabetically and chronologically by the grantee's last name. A deed from Johann Sebastian Bach to Wolfgang Mozart would be indexed under the name "Bach" in the grantor index and the name "Mozart" in the grantee index. The index describes the bare outlines of each transaction, including the grantor and grantee, a description of the land, the type of interest conveyed, the date recorded, and the book and page numbers where a copy of the document can be found. The title searcher must then look at each complete document.

How to conduct a title search

Start with the grantee index and go backward to the root of title

Suppose you are planning to buy a house from J. S. Bach. You want to find out if and how Bach obtained title to the property. You would therefore *start in the grantee index* to find who his grantor was. You start in the present in the grantee index and go backward until you find a deed to Bach conveying the property in question. You find a reference to a deed in 1983 from Ludwig van Beethoven. To find out how Beethoven obtained his title, you look backward in the grantee index from 1983 until you find a conveyance to Beethoven. You continue this process until you have gone back far enough to assure yourself that the title will be good. The practice in each locality differs on how far back to go. It may be to look backward for 50 or 60 years, or until the beginning of the twentieth century, or until a title can be traced to some sovereign. In most places, the practice is not to go all the way back to the beginning of the recording system but to some lesser number of years. Marketable title acts may describe a time period that is sufficient to identify a firm "root of title."[307] When you are done going back to the root of title in the grantee index, you have a list of grantors who are predecessors in interest of Bach.

Then come forward from the root of title in the grantor index

Suppose you have gone back to 1900 to find a deed from Elizabeth Cady Stanton. You now switch to the *grantor index* and go forward in time

[304] *Metropolitan National Bank v. United States*, 901 F.2d 1297 (5th Cir. 1990); 14-82 *Powell on Real Property* §82.03[1].

[305] *Leighton v. Leonard*, 589 P.2d 279 (Wash. Ct. App. 1978). *See also In re Barnacle*, 623 A.2d 445 (R.I. 1993) (holding that an unsigned, recorded mortgage did put subsequent buyers on constructive notice).

[306] 14-82 *Powell on Real Property* §§82.02[1][d][ii] & 82.03[1].

[307] *See* §11.4.4.

under the name of *each grantor* you have found, starting on the date that grantor acquired her interest and going forward until you find an instrument conveying that interest to a subsequent grantee. The period for each search starts when the grantor *acquired* her interest (the date of *execution* of the first deed giving title to the grantor) and stops on the date a new conveyance of that interest is *recorded*.[308] It is important to note that the search in the grantor index starts at the date of *execution* rather than at the date of *recording*. This is because the grantor may have mortgaged the property or encumbered it after acquiring it (after receiving the deed at the closing) but before recording her deed.

Chain-of-title doctrine

If one is entitled to look in the grantor index only between the moment when each prior grantor obtained title and the moment a deed out from that grantor was recorded, then each prior grantor's interest forms a link in the chain of prior grantors. Deeds filed outside each of these links will not be found by the searcher. The chain-of-title doctrine allows searchers to limit their search of the title records to the time period fashioned by each of the links in the chain.[309] This procedure limits the costs of searching and clears title of deeds outside the chain of title. However, it may sometimes happen that deeds fall outside this chain and the effect of the chain-of-title doctrine may be to dispossess innocent purchasers. For this reason, some states reject the chain-of-title doctrine and require searchers to perform a more extensive search in the grantor index, looking before a grantor was given title and/or after that grantor gave out a deed to the property.[310] This approach substantially increases the costs of searching but may better protect innocent buyers from fraudulent double-dealing grantors.

Other official records

The title searcher must also look for other official government records that may affect title. Such records may exist in court records (litigation concerning the land, divorce judgments, marriage records, tax and mortgage foreclosures), and probate court (probate proceedings regarding wills and inheritance).[311]

Common law: First in time, first in right

§11.4.5.2 Types of Recording Acts.

If an owner purports to make two conveyances of the same land, the earlier one will prevail unless a recording statute alters this result. Under the common law, if *O* conveys land to *A* and the next day conveys the same land to *B*, *A*'s title will prevail and *B*'s only remedy is to sue *O* for fraud. First in time, first in right.

Recording alters common law result to protect bona fide purchasers

However, under a recording system, *B* may prevail if *B* records her deed first. The purpose of the recording system is to place a buyer like *B* on notice of any earlier conveyances made by *O* to buyers such as *A*. If *A* does not record her deed and *B* was not aware of it at the time *B* purchased from *O*, *B* may be able to grab the title away from *A*. The purpose of recording

[308] *Friendship Manor, Inc. v. Greiman*, 581 A.2d 893, 896-897 (N.J. Super. Ct. 1990); 14-82 *Powell on Real Property* §82.03[2][a].

[309] 14-82 *Powell on Real Property* §82.03[2][b][i].

[310] *Id.*

[311] Dale A. Whitman et al., *The Law of Property* §11.9, at 771 (4th ed. 2019).

acts to protect *bona fide purchasers, i.e.*, those who pay value for the property and have no knowledge or notice of the prior claims. Recording acts assure buyers that the property will be free from any prior unrecorded claims. Note that they only protect *purchasers, i.e.*, those who pay value for the property. Donees — the recipients of gifts — and devisees — those who succeed to property under a valid will — are outside the scope of protection afforded by recording acts.[312]

Recording acts focus on protecting buyers who record first and/or purchase without notice of prior recorded claims. The major types of recording acts are: (1) race, (2) notice, and (3) race-notice. About half the states have notice statutes, and about half the states have race-notice statutes.

Notice and date of recording

Under a race statute, as between successive purchasers of Blackacre, the person who records first prevails — she has won the race to the registry. This is true even if the person who records first knows about an earlier conveyance to someone else. These statutes are the least typical. These statutes exist for all property in Louisiana,[313] for deeds in Delaware,[314] for deeds and mortgages in North Carolina,[315] and for certain interests, such as mortgages and mineral interests, in a handful more.[316] For example, *O* conveys Blackacre to *A*, who does not record. *O* subsequently conveys Blackacre a second time to *B*. *B* knows of the earlier conveyance to *A*. *B* records the deed from *O* to *B*. In a lawsuit between *A* and *B*, *B* prevails.[317]

Race statutes

Race statutes reward unscrupulous buyers like *B* who know of earlier, competing claims to land. On the other hand, it could easily be argued that *A* was negligent in not recording her deed as soon as she got it and that she has only herself to blame for losing her land. In addition, race statutes are easier to administer than notice or race-notice statutes because priorities are determined by a formal criterion — who recorded first — rather than by a criterion that may be hard to prove — whether the party who recorded first knew about the prior conveyance. Therefore, they arguably help clarify land titles.

[312] *Id.* at §11.10, at 774.
[313] La. Rev. Stat. §9:2721.
[314] Del. Code tit. 25, §153.
[315] N.C. Gen. Stat. §47-18.
[316] Arkansas and Pennsylvania have pure race rules for mortgages. *See* Ark. Code §18-40-102; Pa. Stat. tit. 42, §8141. Ohio has a pure race statute for mortgages and oil and gas leases. Ohio Rev. Code §5301.09, §5301.23. *See* 11 *Thompson on Real Property, Third Thomas Edition* §92.08(a).
[317] An example of a race statute is N.C. Gen. Stat. §47-18(a):

> No (i) conveyance of land, or (ii) contract to convey, or (iii) option to convey, or (iv) lease of land for more than three years shall be valid to pass any property interest as against lien creditors or purchasers for a valuable consideration from the donor, bargainor or lessor but from the time of registration thereof in the county where the land lies. . . . Unless otherwise stated either on the registered instrument or on a separate registered instrument duly executed by the party whose priority interest is adversely affected, (i) instruments registered in the office of the register of deeds shall have priority based on the order of registration as determined by the time of registration. . . .

Notice statutes

About half the states have *notice* statutes.[318] Under a notice statute, a subsequent purchaser prevails over an earlier purchaser only if the subsequent purchaser had no notice of the earlier conveyance at the time she purchased. Such a buyer is called a *bona fide purchaser* (a "BFP"). Further, the notice statute protects any bona fide purchaser even if she does not record first. For example, suppose *O* conveys to *A*, who does not record. *O* then conveys the same property to *B*. *B* has no knowledge of the earlier conveyance from *O* to *A*. *B* prevails over *A* even if *A* records the *O-A* deed before *B* records the *O-B* deed.[319] In contrast, if *O* conveys to *A* (who does not record) and then *O* conveys to *B*, a purchaser with notice of the earlier conveyance from *O* to *A*, then *A* will prevail in a contest with *B*, even if *B* records before *A* does.

Types of notice

Three types of notice are recognized by jurisdictions with notice statutes. First, a buyer may be on *actual* notice; this means that the buyer is aware, at the time she buys, of the earlier conveyance. Second, a buyer may be on *constructive* notice; this means that the second buyer would have found out about the earlier conveyance if she had performed a proper title search. Third, the buyer could be on *inquiry* notice; this would be present, for example, if the property were possessed by someone other than the grantor because the buyer should be induced to inquire who the possessor is and whether she claims from an earlier conveyance.

Advantages of notice statutes

The advantage of notice statutes over race statutes is that they correct the inequity in allowing later buyers to prevail over earlier buyers when they know about the earlier conveyance. They thereby prevent later buyers from fraudulently snatching property away from earlier buyers just because they record first. For example, if *O* conveys to *A* and then *O* conveys to *B*, a purchaser with notice of the earlier conveyance from *O* to *A*, and *B* records before *A*, then *B* will prevail over *A* under a race statute while *A* will prevail over *B* under a notice statute. At the same time, notice statutes arguably give buyers sufficient incentive to record because, if they do not record, a later buyer may not be on notice of the earlier conveyance and may purchase without notice and snatch the property away from them.

Disadvantages of notice statutes

The disadvantage of notice statutes is that they protect innocent buyers against unscrupulous ones at the cost of reducing the clarity of land titles. They reduce predictability because they depend on factual determinations about the parties' subjective knowledge—something that cannot be discerned from the face of the recorded documents. Moreover, notice statutes complicate title searches by later purchasers because they give priority to

[318] Ariz. Rev. Stat. §§33-411 & 33-412; Ark. Code §14-15-404; Conn. Gen. Stat. §47-10; Fla. Stat. §695.01; Iowa Code §558.41; Kan. Stat. §§58-2221 to 58-2223; Ky. Rev. Stat. §383.080; Me. Rev. Stat. tit. 33, §201; Mass. Gen. Laws ch. 183, §4; Mo. Rev. Stat. §§442.380, .390 & .400; N.H. Rev. Stat. §477:3-a; N.M. Stat. §§14-9-1 to 14-9-3; Ohio Rev. Code §5301.25; Okla. Stat. tit. 16, §§15 & 16; R.I. Gen. Laws §34-11-1; Tenn. Code §66-5-106; Tex. Prop. Code §§13.001 & 13.002; Vt. Stat. tit. 27, §342; Va. Code Ann. §55.1-407; W. Va. Code §§40-1-8 & 40-1-9; 11 *Thompson on Real Property, Third Thomas Edition* §92.08(b).

[319] An example of a notice statute is Iowa Code Ann. §558.41(1): "An instrument affecting real estate is of validity against subsequent purchasers for a valuable consideration, without notice, unless filed in the office of the recorder of the county in which the real estate is located, as provided in this chapter."

the first party who buys without notice even if she records second. They also decrease the incentives to record because it is possible for an earlier bona fide purchaser to prevail over a later buyer even if the later buyer records first if the later buyer is on notice of the earlier transaction. If the earlier buyer possesses the property before the later buyer purchases, the later buyer may be held to be on inquiry notice of the earlier claim and thus the earlier buyer will prevail even if she records second. Moreover, earlier buyers have an incentive to try to prove that later buyers knew of the earlier conveyance even if the later buyer did not know. This increases the possibility of litigation, undermines the security of titles, and impedes the alienability of land.

Race-notice statutes

Race-notice statutes protect bona fide purchasers only if they record first. Under a race-notice statute, a subsequent purchaser prevails over prior unrecorded interests only if she (1) had no notice of the prior conveyance at the time she acquired her interest and (2) records before the prior instrument is recorded. About half the states have such laws.[320] For example, *O* conveys to *A*, who does not record. *O* then conveys to *B*. *B* has no knowledge of the earlier conveyance from *O* to *A*. *A* records; then *B* records. Under a notice statute, *B* would prevail because *B* purchased without notice of the earlier conveyance from *O* to *A*. However, in a race-notice jurisdiction, *A* prevails over *B* because, even though *B* did not have notice of *A*'s deed at the time *B* purchased, *A* recorded before *B* did.[321] Race-notice laws represent a compromise between the predictability of race statutes and the fairness of protecting only those who buy without notice of the prior claim. They also attempt to mitigate the title search problems associated with notice statutes by requiring good faith purchasers to record their deeds before competing claimants to prevail. If buyers record diligently, they will not suffer from the race to the courthouse.

Policies of race-notice laws

Time of notice

Generally, the question of whether a buyer was on notice of an earlier conveyance is answered by looking at the moment the buyer obtains title to the property. Thus, a buyer who does not know of an earlier conveyance but finds out about it *after* having acquired title is protected as a bona fide purchaser.

[320] Ala. Code §35-4-90 (as interpreted by *Nelson v. Barnett Recovery Corp.*, 652 So. 2d 279 (Ala. Civ. App. 1994)); Alaska Stat. §40.17.080; Cal. Civ. Code §1107; Colo. Rev. Stat. §§38-35-108 & 38-35-105; D.C. Code §§45-801 & 45-802; Ga. Code §44-2-2; Haw. Rev. Stat. §502-83; Idaho Code §55-812; 765 Ill. Comp. Stat. 5/30; Ind. Code §§32-1-2-11 & 32-1-2-16; Md. Real Prop. Code §3-203; Mich. Comp. Laws §565.29; Minn. Stat. §507.34; Miss. Code §89-5-5; Mont. Code §§70-21-201, 70-21-302 & 70-21-304; Neb. Rev. Stat. §§76-237 & 76-238; Nev. Rev. Stat. §§111.320 & 111.325; N.J. Stat. §46:22-1; N.Y. Real Prop. §291; N.D. Cent. Code §47-19-41; Or. Rev. Stat. §93.640; Pa. Stat. tit. 21, §351; S.C. Code §30-7-10 (as interpreted by *Mi Co., Ltd. v. McLean*, 482 S.E.2d 597, 602 (S.C. Ct. App. 1997)); S.D. Codified Laws §43-28-17; Utah Code §57-3-103; Wash. Rev. Code §65.08.070; Wis. Stat. §706.08; Wyo. Stat. §34-1-121; 11 *Thompson on Real Property, Third Thomas Edition* §92.08(c).

[321] An example of a race-notice statute is Wash. Rev. Code §65.08.070(1):

> A conveyance of real property, when acknowledged by the person executing the same (the acknowledgment being certified as required by law), may be recorded in the office of the recording officer of the county where the property is situated. Every such conveyance not so recorded is void as against any subsequent purchaser or mortgagee in good faith and for a valuable consideration from the same vendor, his heirs or devisees, of the same real property or any portion thereof whose conveyance is first duly recorded.

▶ HARD CASE ▷ INSTALLMENT LAND CONTRACT

One exception to this principle may exist in the case of an installment land contract, by which the seller retains title to the land and the buyer pays the purchase prices over several (or many) years, with the expectation that the seller will deliver title when the entire purchase price is paid. What happens if the buyer discovers an earlier claim before paying off the entire purchaser price? In a contest between the earlier grantee and the buyer under the installment land contract, who should prevail now that the second buyer is on notice and has not yet completed paying the purchase price and not yet been granted the title? The courts split on this question. Most cases treat such a purchaser as a bona fide purchaser, as least to the extent of the payments already made, on the ground that the moment that matters was the moment the contract was signed when the seller agreed to transfer title to the buyer if all the payments were made on time.[322] In applying this rule, courts will (1) award the land to the holder of the earlier interest and grant the later buyer restitution of payments made; (2) award the later buyer a fractional interest in the land along with the earlier buyer; or (3) give title to the later buyer under the installment land contract but require payment of the remaining payments to the earlier purchaser.[323] ◀

Types of problems

§11.4.5.3 Chain-of-Title Problems. Problems can arise in determining the state of title from the recorded documents for a variety of reasons. First, the recorded documents may appear facially valid but be defective because of facts that cannot be determined from the face of the document. For example, a prior deed could be forged or the buyer may have been on notice of an earlier transaction and thus not protected in a notice or race-notice jurisdiction. Second, title could have been affected by events completely outside the recording system, such as adverse possession or divorce. Third, documents could be filed "outside the chain of title" so that a searcher would not find them.

Chain-of-title problems

Chain-of-title problems arise when someone does not record diligently or when an owner purports to convey property that she does not in fact own. Because the recording office contains huge numbers of documents, a search could not be performed unless the legal rules limited, to some extent, the scope of a prospective buyer's search. As described above, the courts have circumscribed the necessary search by limiting buyers to looking during the time period when a prior grantor had title to the property to determine whether that grantor gave out any interests in the property that might still be valid. Limiting the search in this way has a cost; deeds filed before or after this period may well be missed by the title searcher. Moreover, if some prior deeds are unrecorded, later deeds may be impossible to find.

[322] *Tomlinson v. Clarke*, 803 P.2d 828 (Wash. Ct. App. 1991), *aff'd*, 825 P.2d 706 (Wash. 1992); 14-82 *Powell on Real Property* §82.02[1][d].

[323] *Daniels v. Anderson*, 642 N.E.2d 128 (Ill. 1994); Dale A. Whitman et al., *The Law of Property* §11.10, at 785-786 (4th ed. 2019); 14-82 *Powell on Real Property* §82.02[1][d].

▷ WILD DEED **HARD CASE ◀**

"*Wild deeds*" are recorded deeds that a subsequent searcher could not be expected to find through normal searching procedures. For example, *O* conveys to *A*, who does not record. *A* then conveys to *B*, who does record. Before *B* takes possession,[324] *O* conveys to *X*, who records. When *X* was searching the title, *X* would have looked to see if *O* gave out any deeds during his time of ownership and will not find the *O-A* deed, which is unrecorded. Nor will *X* find the *A-B* deed, because the names of *A* and *B* are completely outside the chain of title and there is no way *X* would ever know about them. In a contest between *B* and *X*, courts uniformly treat the *A-B* deed as if it were not recorded.[325] Such a wild deed cannot put a subsequent buyer on constructive notice because she would never find it by searching the title records in the registry of deeds.[326] Perhaps this result can be justified on the ground that the courts want to protect the ability of *X* to rely on the record title and because *B* might have been negligent in not arranging for the recording of the *O-A* deed before accepting a deed from *A*.

Taming of the wild deed

Suppose, however, *B* obtains the *O-A* deed and records it before *X* records the *O-X* deed. In a notice jurisdiction, *X* should still prevail over *B* because, at the time *X* purchased, *X* was not on notice of the *O-A* transaction, nor the *A-B* transaction (because that deed, although recorded, was wild and unfindable). However, in a race-notice jurisdiction, the opposite result might well happen because the *O-A* deed was recorded before the *O-X* deed. Under a race-notice statute, *X* prevails over the prior purchaser *A* only if *X* records before *A*. Thus, because *X* did not record immediately, *A* won the race to the courthouse and takes title away from *X*. Because *A* already transferred whatever interests *A* had to *B*, *B* should prevail over *A* and *X*.

Estoppel by deed

After-acquired title

It may happen that a grantor, *O*, conveys property she does not own to *A* and the grantor *O* later acquires title to that property from the true owner, *OO*. For example, a mother may give her daughter a deed to property she is preparing to buy; when the mother later acquires the property, she has suffered a financial setback and desires to keep the property for herself. The doctrine of *estoppel by deed* or *after-acquired title* treats the grantor's newly acquired title (conveyed by the *OO-O* deed) as belonging, not to *O*, but to *O*'s prior grantee *A*, to whom *O* had previously purported

[324] This caveat may matter because, if *B* takes possession before *O* conveys to *X*, then *X* may be on inquiry notice of the prior transfers from *O* to *A* and from *A* to *B*. This means that *X* would be prompted to ask what *B* is doing there. *X* would be prompted further to ask who *B* is, look for the *A-B* deed, find the *O-A* deed, and then *X* would know about the earlier transactions and would not be a bona fide purchaser and so could not prevail over *B*.

[325] *Nile Valley Federal Saving & Loan Ass'n v. Security Title Guarantee Corp.*, 813 P.2d 849 (Colo. App. 1991); *Far West Savings & Loan Ass'n v. McLaughlin*, 246 Cal. Rptr. 872 (Ct. App. 1988); *Palmer v. Forrest, Mackey & Associates, Inc.*, 304 S.E.2d 704 (Ga. 1983); Dale A. Whitman et al., *The Law of Property* §11.11, at 789 (4th ed. 2019).

[326] A different result might well obtain in a notice jurisdiction if *X* actually knew of the earlier conveyance from *O* to *A* and from *A* to *B*. In that case, *X* would not be a bona fide purchaser without notice of the earlier transaction.

to convey the property.[327] Thus, in a dispute between *O* and *A* for title, *A* would prevail.◀

▶ HARD CASE

▷ DEED RECORDED TOO EARLY

The doctrine of *estoppel by deed* protects the initial buyer, *A*, by preventing the seller, *O*, from taking back title to property that *O* had purported to convey to *A*. What happens, however, if *O* conveys the same property to a second buyer? In this situation, the deed to the first buyer, *A*, may be recorded too early for the later buyer to find it. For example, *O* conveys property to *A* that *O* does not own. *A* records the deed. *OO*, the true owner, conveys the property to *O*. At this point, the property transfers automatically to *A* under the doctrine of estoppel by deed. However, unbeknownst to *A*, *O* then conveys title to *X*, a bona fide purchaser who has no knowledge of the conveyance from *O* to *A*. Although the first purchaser, *A*, would prevail in a contest between herself and the grantor, *O*, in most states, *A* will lose in a contest with the later purchaser *X*.[328] After all, *A* could protect herself by not buying property that her grantor does not actually own. Some states, however, reject the chain-of-title doctrine, and require the buyer *X* to look in the records for some period before the grantor appears to have acquired title (meaning outside the "chain of title") precisely to catch just such double-dealing.[329]

Argument that the second grantee should prevail

Most states adopt the chain-of-title doctrine and require *X* to search the records only so far back as the date when her grantor, *O*, acquired her interest; because *O* had purported to convey the interest to *A* *before* *O* obtained her title from *OO*, *X* would not be charged with notice of the conveyance to *A*.[330] This result, of course, protects the interests of the second bona fide purchaser, *X*, at the expense of the earlier bona fide purchaser, *A*, perhaps on the ground that *A* acted negligently in purchasing property from someone who did not in fact possess the right to convey it. It may also be justified because the expense of searching back before a grantor appears to have acquired the property is usually not worth it. To protect the ability of buyers to rely on the record title, confining the search to the period after it appears that a grantor acquired title is likely, most of the time, to be adequate, and the second purchaser should be able to rely on the records so construed. The first buyer has a remedy against the grantor for fraud.

[327] *Shedden v. Anadarko E. & P. Co., L.C., 136 A.3d 485* (Pa. 2016) (doctrine of estoppel by deed does not require detrimental reliance because it prevents the promisor from taking back a promise already made once the promisor becomes able to fulfill it); *Rendleman v. Heinley*, 149 P.3d 1009 (N.M. Ct. App. 2006); 11 *Thompson on Real Property, Third Thomas Edition* §92.09(c)(2)(B)(i).

[328] *Sabo v. Horvath*, 559 P.2d 1038 (Alaska 1976); *Far West Savings & Loan Ass'n v. McLaughlin*, 246 Cal. Rptr. 872 (Ct. App. 1988); *Glen Ellyn Savings & Loan Ass'n v. State Bank of Geneva*, 382 N.E.2d 1267 (Ill. App. Ct. 1978); *Palamarg Realty Co. v. Rehac*, 404 A.2d 21 (N.J. 1979). *See* 11 *Thompson on Real Property, Third Thomas Edition* §92.09(c)(2)(B)(i) (noting that the majority of courts follow this approach).

[329] 14-82 *Powell on Real Property* §82.03[2][b][i]; 11 *Thompson on Real Property, Third Thomas Edition* §92.09(c)(2)(B)(i).

[330] 14-82 *Powell on Real Property* §82.03[2][b][i].

One might respond that the first buyer did all she could to protect her interest by recording it and that extending the search backward is not that burdensome. Some states require a more extended search on the part of the subsequent grantee; in these states, the doctrine of estoppel by deed is extended to apply to disputes not only between the grantor and the first grantee but between the first grantee and subsequent grantees.[331] Under this theory, when the grantor gets the deed to the property already conveyed to the first grantee, title automatically passes to the first grantee, leaving the grantor nothing to convey to the subsequent purchaser. ◀

Argument that the first grantee should prevail

▷ DEED RECORDED TOO LATE **HARD CASE ◀**

The opposite problem may arise when a deed is recorded too late, rather than too early. For example, *O* conveys to *A*, who does not record. *O* then conveys to *B*, a purchaser with notice of the earlier conveyance from *O* to *A*. Under either a notice statute or a race-notice statute, *A* would prevail over *B* because *B* purchased with notice of the earlier conveyance (and thus *B* was not a "bona fide" purchaser). However, suppose *B* records before *A* does. Now *B* conveys to *X*. Who prevails as between *A* and *X* in a notice jurisdiction? The question is whether *X* should have been on constructive notice of the *O-A* deed. There are two problems here.

Argument that the deed was recorded too late

First, when *X* searches the title to find deeds given out by *O*, she will find a deed transferring all of *O*'s interests to *B* and would ordinarily feel entitled to stop searching rather than going forward in time to find any further conveyances of the property by *O*. If this is the case, *X* will not find the *O-A* deed because it was recorded after the *O-B* deed. It is outside the chain of title, recorded too late. So perhaps *X* should prevail over *A*. This is the result reached in many (perhaps half) of the cases.[332]

Argument that the deed was not recorded too late

However, the second problem is that the title searcher for *X* will not be able to tell, from the face of the records, whether or not *B* was a bona fide purchaser; it is possible that *B* knew of an earlier conveyance. *X* will arguably not be a bona fide purchaser if *X* should know that *B* is not the rightful title holder. Perhaps *X* should have a legal obligation to look outside the chain of title to protect innocent buyers who might be defrauded by unscrupulous parties like *O* and *B*. To protect the interests of that earlier bona fide purchaser, perhaps the law should place the burden on *X* to keep looking forward in the records to determine if a prior bona fide purchaser might have recorded later. This extra effort would protect the earlier buyer from losing the property and would avoid a possible lawsuit between that buyer and *X*. Under this approach, the searcher should search in the grantor index from the date each prior grantor acquired title until

[331] *Ayer v. Philadelphia & Boston Face Brick Co.*, 34 N.E. 177 (Mass. 1893) (opinion by Holmes, J.); *Tefft v. Munson*, 57 N.Y. 97 (1874); 14-82 *Powell on Real Property* §82.03[2][b][[i]; 11 *Thompson on Real Property, Third Thomas Edition* §92.09(c)(2)(B)(i).

[332] *Rolling "R" Construction, Inc. v. Dodd*, 477 So. 2d 330 (Ala. 1985); *Morse v. Curtis*, 2 N.E. 929 (Mass. 1885); Dale A. Whitman et al., *The Law of Property* §11.11, at 790 (4th ed. 2019); 11 *Thompson on Real Property, Third Thomas Edition* §92.09(c)(2)(B)(i).

the present to determine whether any other interests were given out by that grantor. Many cases (perhaps half) reach this result.[333]

The result in a race-notice jurisdiction

Note that in a race-notice jurisdiction, *A* would arguably prevail over *X* because *A* recorded before *X* recorded. *B* could not prevail over *A* because *B* was not a bona fide purchaser, being on notice of the earlier conveyance from *O* to *A*. And *X* will prevail only if *X* recorded first; but here, *A* recorded before *X* recorded.[334] However, one could argue in response that the chain-of-title doctrine should protect *X*. The fact that *A* recorded the *O-A* deed before *X* recorded the *B-X* deed does not change the fact that a bona fide purchaser like *X* should not be expected to find the *O-A* deed because it was recorded after the *O-B* deed, and a buyer from *B* would stop looking for conveyances out from *O* at that point. The deed from *O* to *A* was recorded too late and *X* is not on constructive notice of it.

Second example: Deed recorded too late

Here is a second example of a deed recorded too late. *O* conveys to *A*, who does not record. *O* then conveys to *X*, who has notice of the earlier conveyance to *A*. *X* records her deed; then *A* records her deed. At this point, as between *A* and *X*, *A* would prevail against *X* in either a notice jurisdiction or a race-notice jurisdiction because only buyers who purchase without notice of earlier claims are protected by those systems. However, now *X* conveys to *Z*, who has no notice of the earlier conveyance to *A*.

Argument that the deed was not recorded too late

In a contest between *A* and *Z*, *Z* might well prevail because the deed from *O* to *A* was recorded too late. This is true despite the fact that *X* was not a bona fide purchaser and the fact that *X* intended to steal property away from *A*, who should have been the rightful owner as against *X*. The result obtains because the recording system is attempting to protect *Z*, a bona fide purchaser who has no way to know that *X* was not a bona fide purchaser, and who would not be on notice of the *O-A* deed because it was recorded after the *O-X* deed and the searcher would not find the later-recorded *O-A* deed in a normal title search. This result is arguably fair to *A* because *A* should have recorded her deed right away, even in a notice jurisdiction, to prevent this dispute from arising in the first place. This result is reached in many states.[335]

Argument that the deed was recorded too late

However, many states will allow *A* to prevail.[336] They do so on the ground that *X* should not be able to dispossess *A* even if *A* does not record first and that, to protect *A*'s interests, a later purchaser like *Z* should look to see whether a prior grantor gave out an adverse title to someone other than *X*. To find this out, the searcher must look from the time a grantor in the chain of title acquired title to the present, rather than just looking up to the time a prior grantor handed out a deed to the property that was properly recorded. This approach increases the costs of the title search but is one way to test whether a prior buyer was or was not a bona fide purchaser and protects earlier buyers from being defrauded by two-timing grantors. ◀

[333] *Woods v. Garnett*, 16 So. 390 (Miss. 1894); Dale A. Whitman et al., *The Law of Property* §11.11 at 790 (4th ed. 2019); 11 *Thompson on Real Property, Third Thomas Edition* §92.09(c)(2)(B)(i).

[334] *See* 14-82 *Powell on Real Property* §82.03[2][b][i] (making this argument).

[335] Dale A. Whitman et al., *The Law of Property* §11.11, at 790 (4th ed. 2019).

[336] *Id.*

▷ SHELTER DOCTRINE **HARD CASE ◀**

Can a purchaser divest a prior grantee if the purchaser knows of the deed to that earlier grantee? Ordinarily, the answer is no, because recording acts generally protect only buyers who are not on notice of earlier, valid claims.[337] However, the shelter doctrine allows a bona fide purchaser to convey property to a third party even if the third party is on notice of an earlier conveyance.[338] For example, suppose *O* conveys to *A*, who does not record. *O* then conveys to *X*, a bona fide purchaser without notice of the conveyance to *A*; *X* records. Because *X* had no notice of the earlier conveyance to *A*, and because *X* recorded before *A*, *X* would prevail over *A* in either a notice jurisdiction or a race-notice jurisdiction. *X* then wants to convey to *C*, but *C* has notice of the earlier conveyance from *O* to *A*. The *shelter doctrine* allows *X* to convey the property to *C*, despite *C*'s knowledge of the earlier conveyance.[339] This doctrine allows bona fide purchasers to convey title even if they subsequently find out, after they buy the property, about the earlier conveyance. The bona fide purchaser who records first obtains full rights in the property over the earlier buyer who did not record. Any other rule would restrict the bona fide purchaser's ability to transfer the property and reward the earlier purchaser who should have, but did not, record first. ◀

Inquiry notice

To what extent should buyers be held to be on inquiry notice to find out facts that are not evident from the face of the recorded documents?[340] One typical problem is a recorded document that refers to another recorded document. Buyers are held to be on both inquiry and constructive notice of those other documents.[341] A prime example is a condominium declaration that will be referenced in the deeds to the individual units that are sold after the declaration is recorded.

▷ REFERENCE TO UNRECORDED DOCUMENT **HARD CASE ◀**

What happens if a recorded document mentions an unrecorded document? For example, commercial leases tend to be very long and the parties may not want some of the terms to be on the public record.

[337] The sole exceptions are the three states that have race statutes. Del. Code tit. 25, §153; La. Rev. Stat. §9:2721; N.C. Gen. Stat. §47-18(a).

[338] Dale A. Whitman et al., *The Law of Property* §11.10, at 784 (4th ed. 2019); 11 *Thompson on Real Property, Third Thomas Edition* §92.09(c)(2)(B)(i).

[339] The rule would not apply if *X* were conveying the property, not to *C* but to *O*. As between *O* and *A*, *A* should prevail if *X* reconveyed the property to *O*. *Chergosky v. Crosstown Bell, Inc.*, 463 N.W.2d 522 (Minn. 1990); *Walker v. Wilson*, 469 So. 2d 580 (Ala. 1985); Dale A. Whitman et al., *The Law of Property* §11.10, at 784 (4th ed. 2019).

[340] *Compare Guthrie v. National Advertising Co.*, 556 N.E.2d 337 (Ind. Ct. App. 1990) (holding that buyers who have information suggesting a prior claim have an obligation to find out about such claims) *with Mister Donut of America, Inc. v. Kemp*, 330 N.E.2d 810 (Mass. 1975) (rejecting the doctrine of inquiry notice).

[341] *Garneau v. City of Seattle*, 147 F.3d 802 (9th Cir. 1998); 11 *Thompson on Real Property, Third Thomas Edition* §92.09(c)(3).

They may therefore record a "memorandum of lease," but not record the entire lease itself. Some courts hold that a subsequent buyer is on inquiry notice of the contents of the unrecorded lease,[342] while other courts hold that subsequent buyers are not on inquiry notice of those contents.[343] ◀

▶ HARD CASE ▷ IMPROPERLY INDEXED DEED

If an attorney promptly records a document, problems may still arise if the clerk makes an error in indexing the deed, and courts are not in agreement about how to handle such cases. For example, the clerk may misspell the seller's name in the index. This may cause the courts to find subsequent purchasers not to be on record notice of the earlier conveyances or encumbrances, and may even subject the attorney who conducted the transaction to malpractice liability for failing to check to see that the document was properly recorded.[344] On the other hand, misspellings of names arguably place subsequent buyers on inquiry notice at least. Moreover, when a deed is improperly indexed, this is not the fault of the lawyer who handled the transaction, and it would seem to contravene the purpose of the recording statutes to allow negligence by a public official to deprive an owner of property rights. In addition, it has been held that a deed filed in a system that has electronic recording may place a subsequent buyer on notice if that buyer could or should have discovered the deed despite the indexing error.[345] Problems may also arise if a subsequent conveyance occurs after the deed is filed with the registry office but before it is indexed.[346] ◀

▶ HARD CASE ▷ POSSESSION AS INQUIRY NOTICE

One might think that a buyer should surely be on inquiry notice of a prior claim if someone other than the grantor is actually possessing the property. "It is settled law that actual possession is constructive notice to all the world, or anyone having knowledge of said possession of whatever right

[342] *Genovese Drug Stores, Inc. v. Connecticut Packing Co.*, 732 F.2d 286 (2d Cir. 1984); *Mister Donut of America, Inc. v. Kemp*, 330 N.E.2d 810 (Mass. 1975).
[343] *Howard D. Johnson Co. v. Parkside Development Corp.*, 348 N.E.2d 656, 661 (Ind. Ct. App. 1976).
[344] *See, e.g., Antonis v. Liberati*, 821 A.2d 666 (Pa. Commw. Ct. 2003).
[345] *First Citizens Nat'l Bank v. Sherwood*, 879 A.2d 178, 182 (2005) (electronic indices broaden search obligations so that a mortgage improperly recorded under the name of the beneficiary of a trust rather than the trustee was still found to provide constructive notice; buyers are on notice of properly recorded but improperly indexed conveyances). *Compare, e.g., Bindas v. Commonwealth of Pa., Dept. of Transp.*, 302 A.3d 644 (Pa. 2023) (proper indexing required for constructive notice).
[346] *Compare NYCTL 1998-1 Trust and The Bank of N.Y. v. Ibrahiem*, 15 Misc. 3d 294 (N.Y. Civ. Ct. 2007) (deed is considered recorded when delivered to registry office) *with Dyar v. Martinez*, 54 Cal. Rptr. 3d 907 (Ct. App. 2007) (unindexed *lis pendens* did not impart constructive notice).

the occupants have in the land."[347] However, such an obligation may prove burdensome. In *Waldorff Insurance and Bonding, Inc. v. Eglin National Bank*,[348] plaintiff company signed a purchase and sale agreement for a condominium unit with the developer of the condominium complex and took possession of the unit. Subsequently, before title to the condominium unit passed, the developer borrowed money from defendant bank and gave the bank a mortgage on the unit, as well as other units in the complex. The developer owed money to plaintiff company and agreed to give plaintiff a deed to the unit in return for writing off the debt. The deed was then recorded. When the developer later defaulted on the loan payments to the bank, the bank foreclosed on the condominium unit and the question was whether the bank should have been on notice of the earlier contract between the developer and the plaintiff.

Argument that possession does not provide inquiry notice

The bank argued that it should not have had to investigate the occupants of every unit to determine whether they had unrecorded purchase agreements with the plaintiff. The doctrine of inquiry notice substantially complicates the process of searching title, increases the costs of transactions, and impedes the alienability of land.

Argument that possession provides inquiry notice

However, the court held that, under the doctrine of equitable conversion, the buyer is ordinarily treated as the equitable owner after the purchase and sale agreement is signed. The court held that the bank should have been on inquiry notice of plaintiff's interest as equitable owner of the property because of plaintiff's possession of the unit. The fact that the mortgage was recorded before the deed did not change the fact that the bank should have been aware of the earlier claim at the time it took the mortgage on the unit. ◀

▷ SERVITUDES ON RETAINED LAND **HARD CASE ◀**

Sometimes a grantor will sell one lot while imposing a covenant or easement on the grantor's retained property. For example, *O* conveys Lot 1 to *A* by a deed, which states that *O* covenants not to use *O*'s retained land (Lot 2) to be used by a competing business. Then *O* conveys Lot 2 to *B* without informing *B* of the covenant. Is *B* bound by the covenant? Was *B* on constructive notice of it when *B* purchased Lot 2? The courts are split on this question.[349] Some hold that no covenant appears in the chain of title for Lot 2 and that *B* is not obligated to research deeds given by *O* to lots other than the one *B* is purchasing.[350] Other courts hold that *B* is on constructive notice of the covenant in the *O*-*A* deed,

[347] *Blackburn v. Venice Inlet Co.*, 38 So. 2d 43, 46 (Fla. 1948). *Accord, In re Probasco*, 839 F.2d 1352, 1354-1355 (9th Cir. 1988) (California law); *Willett v. Centerre Bank*, 792 S.W.2d 916 (Mo. Ct. App. 1990); *People's National Bank v. Birney's Enterprises, Inc.*, 775 P.2d 466 (Wis. Ct. App. 1989); Dale A. Whitman et al., *The Law of Property* §11.10, at 779 (4th ed. 2019); 11 *Thompson on Real Property, Third Thomas Edition* §92.09(c)(3)(A).

[348] 453 So. 2d 1383 (Fla. Dist. Ct. App. 1984).

[349] 11 *Thompson on Real Property, Third Thomas Edition* §92.09(c)(2)(B)(ii).

[350] *Witter v. Taggart*, 577 N.E.2d 338 (N.Y. 1991); *Spring Lakes, Ltd. v. O.F.M. Co.*, 467 N.E.2d 537 (Ohio 1984).

on the ground that it is not too great a burden to require buyers like *B* to look at deeds granted by their grantor within the chain of title, especially if those lots are contiguous or nearby.[351] Such a search is necessary to protect the reliance interests of the earlier buyer *A* and not unduly burdensome to *B*. ◀

The problem of fraud

Recording acts are intended to protect bona fide purchasers from fraud by assuring them that they will obtain good title to the property even if the seller has previously sold to someone else. To protect such buyers from fraud, however, these statutes authorize sellers to convey an interest they no longer own, thereby defrauding the first buyer. They therefore create a new property interest: a power in the grantor to transfer ownership from the first grantee, who did not record, to a second grantee. Recording acts fight fraud on the second buyer by affirmatively empowering the seller to commit a fraud on the first buyer, a power that was nonexistent before recording acts were in place. Note that, although a grantee who is defrauded by a double-dealing grantor may lose title to the property to someone else, he may be able to sue the grantor for damages for fraud.

▶ HARD CASE ▷ FORGED DEEDS

In *Martin v. Carter*,[352] one of two co-owners (Fletcher) signed his own name and forged the name of his co-owner (Martin) on a deed transferring their property to a buyer (Spicer). When the co-owner discovered the forgery, she notified the purchaser that she had not signed the deed. However, she waited almost two years to bring suit against the buyer, and by that time the buyer had reconveyed the property to defendants (the Carters) who had no knowledge that Martin's signature was forged. The Carters argued that they were bona fide purchasers with no knowledge of the forgery and that Martin had waited too long to assert her interests. If they were going to be divested of their title, no purchaser could rely on the recorded documents but would have to investigate to determine if any signatures in the chain of title were forged. The court disagreed, holding that a forged deed cannot convey title and that buyers can protect themselves from such risks by purchasing title insurance.[353] ◀

▶ HARD CASE ▷ FRAUD

In *McCoy v. Love*,[354] an owner agreed to sell part of her mineral interests to a buyer. The buyer drew up the deed and substituted a far greater

[351] *Guillette v. Daly Dry Wall, Inc.*, 325 N.E.2d 572 (Mass. 1975).

[352] 400 A.2d 326 (D.C. 1979).

[353] *Accord, Vanderwall v. Midkiff*, 421 N.W.2d 263, 270 (Mich. Ct. App. 1988); *Nickels v. Cohn*, 764 S.W.2d 124, 135 (Mo. Ct. App. 1989); *First National Bank in Albuquerque v. Enriquez*, 634 P.2d 1266, 1268 (N.M. 1981); 11 *Thompson on Real Property, Third Thomas Edition* §94.07(*l*).

[354] 382 So. 2d 647 (Fla. 1980).

portion of her property interests for the amount she had stated she was willing to sell, fraudulently executing the document. The buyer then reconveyed the property he had fraudulently taken from the seller to another buyer, who was unaware of the fraud. The original seller argued that the buyer had committed a form of theft and that he should not be able to get away with it. However, the court held that, although a forged deed does not pass title to a bona fide purchaser, a fraudulently obtained deed does pass title to a bona fide purchaser.[355] The court noted that she knew she was conveying some of her interests and it was incumbent on her to read and understand the deed she was signing. Unlike the owner defrauded by a forged deed, the defrauded seller is partially to blame for her predicament and, in that case, the policy of protecting bona fide purchasers comes to the fore.

Fraud in the inducement

Fraud in the execution

Some courts distinguish between *fraud in the inducement* and *fraud in the execution*.[356] *McCoy v. Love* involved fraud in the execution (also called *fraud in the factum*). The parties agreed to a deal, and one of the parties wrote the contract in a manner that diverged from the deal. If the seller is competent, the courts are likely to rule as the court did in *McCoy v. Love* and protect a later bona fide purchaser. However, some courts will treat fraud in the execution as akin to forgery because the documents purport to convey interests the grantor never intended to convey. Others distinguish such cases from forgery cases on the ground that the seller was negligent in not reading what she signed or in obtaining assistance in understanding it and that, as between a negligent grantor and an innocent bona fide purchaser, the purchaser should prevail. In contrast, courts are unanimous in protecting the bona fide purchaser when the case involves fraud in the inducement. Such cases concern misrepresentations made by buyers to induce sellers to part with their property. In such cases, the seller knows what she is selling and the interest in protecting the bona fide purchaser prevails over the seller's interests. The seller is relegated to a suit for damages against the tortfeasor.[357] ◀

§11.4.6 Title Insurance

Indemnification for losses associated with title

Because the recording system is less than perfect, and because even a diligent search may fail to reveal legally enforceable property rights, title insurance has arisen as a way to protect purchasers who want protection against the risks posed by undiscovered claims. Such contracts promise to indemnify the beneficiary for losses arising out of title problems.[358] The contract ordinarily lists known encumbrances and excepts those from its scope of

[355] *Accord, Fallon v. Triangle Management*, 215 Cal. Rptr. 748 (Ct. App. 1985); *Harding v. La Jaur*, 315 A.2d 132, 135 (Md. Ct. Spec. App. 1974).

[356] 11 *Thompson on Real Property, Third Thomas Edition* §94.07(*l*).

[357] *Id.*

[358] Dale A. Whitman et al., *The Law of Property* §11.14, at 813 (4th ed. 2019); 2 James C. Smith & Milton R. Friedman, *Contracts and Conveyances of Real Property* §31:3, at 31-8 to 31-36 (8th ed. 2017); 11 *Thompson on Real Property, Third Thomas Edition* §§93.01 to 93.09.

coverage.[359] They also ordinarily promise to cure title defects if possible and to defend the beneficiary of the contract in the event of litigation.[360]

§11.4.7 *Title Registration*

Response to the defects of the recording system

The defects of the recording system are evident. Documents may be out of the chain of title; technical defects in documents may deprive them of legal force; and conflicting claims may depend on facts outside the written record (such as whether a purchaser had notice of a prior claim). Moreover, one cannot determine the state of the title from the recording system without reviewing all the documents and making a legal judgment, based on the state recording act and judicial interpretations of it, as to the state of the title.

Certificate of title

Title registration is a system in which individual owners voluntarily "register" their land and a certificate of title is issued by an official of state or local government that represents the final word on the ownership of interests in a particular parcel of land.[361] Also called the "Torrens system" — after Richard Robert Torrens, the first premier of the state of South Australia in the 1850s who invented the system — the certificate of title is (with a few exceptions) taken to be conclusive as to the allocation of property rights in the parcel.

Torrens system

Due process

Because the certificate is regarded as conclusive as to almost all property rights in a particular parcel, it requires a judicial or quasi-judicial proceeding, with notice to all parties having possible interests in the land and to the public and a hearing to determine what the ownership interests and encumbrances are with respect to the parcel. The due process clause of the Constitution requires such notice and a hearing before divesting property rights, and the failure to follow such procedures might well constitute a taking of property rights without just compensation as to valid interests that would be cut off by the registration. An official title examiner or private attorney investigates the title and must report to the court. After notice to all interested parties, the hearing will result in an issuance of a *certificate of title* stating who owns the land, the estates in which it is held, and any encumbrances such as long-term leases, mortgages, easements, and covenants. The process takes a significant amount of time (from six to eight months) and may cost as much as $500 to $800 or more in attorney's fees and court costs.[362]

Changes noted on the certificate

The official certificate is held by the registrar in the recording office. If encumbrances are placed on the land, notations are made on the official certificate. When title changes hands, the grantee brings the deed to the registry of deeds and a new certificate is issued. A title searcher need only look at the certificate to determine the state of the title — at least in theory.

[359] 2 James C. Smith & Milton R. Friedman, *Contracts and Conveyances of Real Property* §31:3, at 31-8 to 31-36 (8th ed. 2017).
[360] Dale A. Whitman et al., *The Law of Property* §11.14, at 817 (4th ed. 2019).
[361] *Id.* at §11.15, at 819-825.
[362] *Id.* at §11.15, at 821.

The system is voluntary partly because of the cost in both time and money involved in undergoing an investigation and hearing for each parcel registered. Originally enacted into law in 21 states, the system is now available in only 9 states, the others having repealed their laws.[363] Registration does not appear worth it to most owners. In addition, the certificate is not completely determinative; certain types of claims are excluded from the system, such as short-term leases, property tax liens, mechanics liens, and public rights of way.[364] And the system poses the same problems with regard to forgery and fraud that are faced by the recording system. If the registrar does issue a new certificate and a bona fide purchaser relies on it, the system will generally protect that purchaser. At the same time, determining whether the purchaser should have been on inquiry notice of competing claims (or even actually knew of them) may be a complex process, reducing the certainty that is supposed to be associated with the system.[365] Some courts hold that possession puts the prospective purchaser on constructive notice of a prior claim while others refuse to find such notice.[366] Moreover, in the context of fraud and forgery, there is always pressure to protect the victim. When such cases present conflicts between the interests of owners victimized by forgery or fraud and the interests of bona fide purchasers who perhaps should have known something was amiss, the courts feel torn in opposite directions and may sometimes rule that the certificate is not the final word.

Rarely used

Limits to the system

§11.5 Real Estate Finance

§11.5.1 Mortgages

Most of the time buyers cannot afford to pay the full price of real property. They therefore borrow money from a bank or other lending institution to finance the purchase. The bank loans the money to the borrower through a loan contract (often called a *note*), which provides the repayment schedule and the amount of interest due over time. To secure repayment of the loan the bank will take a *security interest* in the property. In the context of real property, such interests are generally called *mortgages.* When the loan and mortgage facilitate the purchase of property, the arrangement is called a "purchase money mortgage" (although some locales use this term to refer

Security interest in real property

[363] *See, e.g.*, Ga. Code §§44-2-40 to 44-2-253; Haw. Rev. Stat. §§501-1 to 501-219; Mass. Gen. Laws ch. 185; Minn. Stat. §508.01 to §508.84; N.C. Gen. Stat. ch. 43; Ohio Rev. Code §§5309 & 5310; 14-83 *Powell on Real Property* §83.01[3]. See also Pa. Stat. tit. 21, §321 (registration for counties with populations over 500,000). Previously enacted title registration laws were most recently repealed in Illinois, New York, Virginia, and Washington. 765 Ill. Stat. 40/3 (repealed); N.Y. Real Prop. §436 (repealed); Va. Code §55-112 (repealed); Wash. Code §65.12 (repealed). In Colorado, registration was cut off as of January 1, 2018. Colo. Rev. Stat. §§38-36-101(2).

[364] Dale A. Whitman et al., *The Law of Property* §11.15, at 822 (4th ed. 2019).

[365] *Id.* at §11.15, at 824.

[366] *Compare Wells v. Lizama*, 396 F.2d 877 (9th Cir. 1968) (no constructive notice) *with Follette v. Pacific Light and Power Corp.*, 208 P. 295 (Cal. 1922) (constructive notice found).

to mortgages granted by the seller rather than by a third party).[367] The mortgage represents a grant of interests in the property from the owner to the bank. The buyer/homeowner/borrower is called the *mortgagor* (because she grants the security interest in the house to the bank), and the bank/lender is called the *mortgagee* (because it is the grantee of a security interest or "mortgage" in the property). By granting a security interest in the property, the mortgage contract authorizes the lender to arrange for the sale of the property if the borrower defaults on the loan (usually by failing to make the mortgage payments when due) to recover the unpaid debt.

Lien theory

In most states the purchaser/borrower obtains *title* to the property that the lender helps the purchaser to buy while the lender obtains a *lien* on the property. These states adopted the *lien theory* of mortgages. Lien is another word for security interest and refers to the lender's ability to use the collateral (the property securing repayment of the loan) to pay off the loan upon default. A few states, however, retain the older *title theory* of mortgages.[368] Under this approach the borrower hands over title to the property to the lender during the repayment period. Thus, the bank, rather than the homeowner, retains title to the property. The borrower's interest in the property is called an *equity of redemption* or *equity* because the borrower will have the right to obtain title upon repayment of the loan. A few states have an *intermediate theory*, under which the mortgagee's lien is converted into title upon the mortgagor's default.[369] There is little, if any, functional difference between the approaches today. One possible difference is that lenders in title theory or intermediate theory states may be entitled to "possession" immediately upon default (unless the mortgage agreement provides otherwise) and thus entitled to collect rents from leased property, while lenders in lien theory states may be required to go to court first to secure the right to receive rents from the property.[370] Whether this difference exists depends on state statutes regulating the rights of mortgagors. In addition, the agreement between the parties may alter the result created by the default rule.

Title theory

Historical background

Mortgages originated in the courts of equity in England.[371] The owner-borrower would convey title to the property to the lender with a

[367] Grant S. Nelson et al., *Real Estate Finance Law* §1.1 (6th ed. 2015).

[368] The title theory appears to exist in Alabama, Ala. Code §35-10-26; *Bailey Mortgage Co. v. Boggle-Fite Lumber*, 565 So. 2d 138, 143 (Ala. 1990); Arkansas, *Bank of Oak Grove v. Wilmot State Bank*, 648 S.W.2d 802 (Ark. 1983); *Harris v. Collins*, 150 S.W.2d 749 (Ark. 1941); Connecticut, *Barclays Bank of New York v. Ivler*, 565 A.2d 252 (Conn. App. Ct. 1989); Georgia, *Turner Advertising Co. v. Garcia*, 311 S.E.2d 466 (Ga. 1984); Maine, Me. Rev. Stat. tit. 33, §502; Massachusetts, *Negron v. Gordon*, 366 N.E.2d 241 (Mass. 1977); *Maglione v. BancBoston Mortgage Corp.*, 557 N.E.2d 756 (Mass. App. Ct. 1990); Mississippi, *Meyers v. American Oil Co.*, 5 So. 2d 218 (Miss. 1941); Rhode Island, *Houle v. Guilbeault*, 40 A.2d 438 (R.I. 1944); Tennessee, *In re Maryville Savings & Loan Corp.*, 31 B.R. 597 (Bankr. E.D. Tenn. 1983), *aff'd in part and rev'd in part on other grounds*, 743 F.2d 413 (6th Cir. 1984), *opinion supplemented by* 760 F.2d 119 (6th Cir. 1985); Vermont, *Rassman v. American Fidelity Co.*, 460 A.2d 461 (Vt. 1983).

[369] Grant S. Nelson et al., *Real Estate Finance Law* §4.3 (6th ed. 2015); 12 *Thompson on Real Property, Third Thomas Edition* §101.01(b)(4).

[370] Grant S. Nelson et al., *Real Estate Finance Law* §4.1 (6th ed. 2015).

[371] *See* A.W.B. Simpson, *A History of the Land Law* 242-247 (2d ed. 1986); 12 *Thompson on Real Property, Third Thomas Edition* §101.01(a).

condition subsequent, allowing the borrower to get the deed back when the borrower paid off the debt. Originally, the lender would actually take possession of the property and pay off the loan from the proceeds of the land. This arrangement evaded the rules against usury imposed by the Church's ban on interest. The transfer upon condition subsequent mutated into an unconditional transfer of a fee simple absolute with a covenant in the grantee to reconvey to the grantor upon payment of the debt. Over time, however, instead of the lender taking possession of the land, the borrower would keep possession of the land and pay the debt out of the proceeds of the land. This arrangement became common around the mid-sixteenth century.[372] The borrower came to be regarded as the equitable owner of the land and a "mortgage, whatever its outward form, was no more than a security for a debt. The result was that Chancery freely interfered with mortgage transactions with a complete indifference to the terms agreed to by the parties; in no branch of the law was the sanctity of agreement less regarded."[373]

Equity of redemption

If the borrower did not pay off the debt on the appointed day, she would lose the property forever. Because the land was usually worth more than the debt, the lender would often get a windfall. Borrowers began to ask the equity courts for relief from this result, and the chancellor responded by granting the borrower extra time to pay off the debt so that she could redeem the property (get it back). In so doing, the court effectively rewrote the contract, changing the terms of the condition. At first, this was subject to the equity court's discretion, but by the early seventeenth century it was a matter of right.[374] The borrower's interest came to be called the *equity of redemption*, while the mortgagee held title.

Strict foreclosure

Allowing the borrower some extra time to get the property back by paying off the debt protected the mortgagor's interest but left the mortgagee without any clear remedy. For this reason, the equity courts put a time limit on the mortgagor's right to redeem the property. The equity courts began a procedure called *foreclosure*, by which the lender could cut off forever the borrower's equity of redemption.[375] At first, the court used a procedure called *strict foreclosure*, by which the court would give the borrower extra time to pay off the debt but provide that if the debt remained unpaid by a particular date the mortgagor would automatically lose the property.[376] If the property was worth less than the debt, the lender could then go after the mortgagor for a *deficiency judgment*.[377] If the property was worth more than the debt, the mortgagee would have the right to keep the property without paying the excess value back to the mortgagor. This procedure has been substantially abolished in the United States[378] and is available in a modified

[372] 12 *Thompson on Real Property, Third Thomas Edition* §101.01(a).
[373] A.W.B. Simpson, *A History of the Land Law* 246 (2d ed. 1986).
[374] 12 *Thompson on Real Property, Third Thomas Edition* §101.01(a).
[375] *Id.*
[376] *Id.*
[377] *HawaiiUSA Federal Credit Union v. Monalim*, 464 P.3d 821 (Haw. 2020).
[378] Grant S. Nelson et al., *Real Estate Finance Law* §7.11 (6th ed. 2015).

form in only two states, Connecticut[379] and Vermont.[380] However, up to half the states may allow strict foreclosure in very limited circumstances.[381]

Modern foreclosure law

Because of the perceived unfairness of strict foreclosure, the courts began to order *foreclosure sales.* This is currently the practice in most states and is codified in legislation regulating the rights of mortgagors and mortgagees in foreclosure. This procedure is available in every state, and in about half the states such judicially supervised foreclosure sales are the only lawful method.[382] After default by the mortgagor, the mortgagee brings a lawsuit to foreclose on the property. The mortgagor may prevent loss of his property by paying off some or all of the debt before foreclosure. If the mortgagee proves the existence of the mortgage and that the mortgagor defaulted on the mortgage, the court will order a foreclosure decree. The decree provides for public sale of the property by a court officer, payment of the outstanding balance of the debt to the mortgagee, and transfer of any excess proceeds to the mortgagor. Upon the foreclosure sale, the mortgagor's equity of redemption is cut off. If the sale does not bring in enough to pay off the debt, in many states the lender may bring an action for a *deficiency judgment* personally against the mortgagor for the rest of the debt.[383] About half the states regulate or prohibit deficiency judgments.[384]

Statutory right of redemption

About half of the states add a *statutory right of redemption.*[385] This should not be confused with the *equity of redemption*, which is the mortgagor's right to pay off the rest of the debt *before foreclosure* and redeem the property. The statutory right of redemption allows the mortgagor to buy back the property for the price bid at the foreclosure sale for a designated period (often a year) *after foreclosure.* These statutes generally allow the mortgagor to remain in possession of the property in the meanwhile.

Problem of inadequate price at foreclosure sale

A common problem arises with the price bid for the property at the foreclosure sale. Anyone can bid on the property at the foreclosure sale, including the mortgagor and the mortgagee. Often the mortgagee is the only entity or person bidding at the foreclosure sale. There is a danger that the mortgagee will make a low bid; the mortgagee will not only get the property and be able to sell it, but may also be able to go after the mortgagor for a deficiency judgment. If the mortgagee buys the property for a low price (below its fair market value), the mortgagee may (1) decrease the excess proceeds that must be paid over to the mortgagor; (2) resell the property and retain the proceeds over the amount paid at the foreclosure

379 Conn. Gen. Stat. Ann. §§49-15 & 49-24; *Farmers & Mechanics Bank v. Arbucci*, 589 A.2d 14 (Conn. App. Ct. 1991); *Abacus Mortgage Insurance Co. v. Whitewood Hills Development Corp.*, 479 A.2d 1231 (Conn. App. Ct. 1984).

380 Vt. Stat. Ann. tit. 12, §4941; *Stowe Center, Inc. v. Burlington Savings Bank*, 451 A.2d 1114 (Vt. 1982).

381 4-37 *Powell on Real Property* §37.43.

382 12 *Thompson on Real Property, Third Thomas Edition* §101.04(b).

383 *See Capital Bank v. Needle*, 596 So. 2d 1134 (Fla. Dist. Ct. App. 1992); Grant S. Nelson et al., *Real Estate Finance Law* §8.1 (6th ed. 2015); 12 *Thompson on Real Property, Third Thomas Edition* §101.04(b)(1).

384 Alex M. Johnson, *Understanding Modern Real Estate Transactions* §12.07[A], at 258 (4th ed. 2018); *see also* Grant S. Nelson et al., *Real Estate Finance Law* §8.3 (6th ed. 2015).

385 Grant S. Nelson et al., *Real Estate Finance Law* §8.4 (6th ed. 2015); 4-37 *Powell on Real Property* §37.46.

sale; and (3) be able to file a deficiency judgment against the mortgagor who has other assets.

Regulation of foreclosure process

States have developed a wide variety of mechanisms to ensure that the price bid at the foreclosure sale is near the fair market value. This will protect the interests of both the mortgagor and the mortgagee: The mortgagor is less likely to be subject to a deficiency judgment, and the mortgagee can use the proceeds of the sale to pay off the debt.

Right to redeem

Equity of redemption

(1) *Right to redeem.* The most basic protection for the mortgagor is the right to redeem by paying the balance of the debt before foreclosure. This is called the *equity of redemption.*[386] The owner who can do this will be able to keep the property and have the title restored (or granted) free of the mortgage.[387]

Reinstatement

(2) *Reinstatement.* Some states allow the defaulting mortgagor to *reinstate* the mortgage prior to foreclosure by curing all defaults through paying any unpaid amounts due along with the mortgagee's costs due to the default.[388] This allows the mortgagor to keep the property by paying only the amounts then in default, not the entire remaining amount of the loan.

Public notice and mortgagor right to bid

(3) *Public notice and mortgagor right to bid.* The sale is publicized so that anyone may bid, including the mortgagor. This enables the mortgagor to go to another lender, who may be willing to lend the mortgagor the money so long as the property is worth more than the unpaid debt, and the property will constitute the security for *its* new loan. If the mortgagee bids too low, the mortgagor may be able to counter with a higher bid, forcing the mortgagee to bid more to get the property.

Unjust enrichment of deficiency judgments

(4) *Unjust enrichment.* If the price paid at the foreclosure sale is well below market value, the mortgagor may be able to sue the mortgagee for unjust enrichment if the mortgagee buys the property at a low price and resells it within a short period of time for a much higher price. The mortgagee may be forced to disgorge the profits and turn them over to the mortgagor.[389] This procedure protects the mortgagor's right to the excess proceeds and prevents the mortgagee from bidding low, reselling the property, and keeping those proceeds itself.

Prohibition or regulation

(5) *Prohibition of deficiency judgments.* Some states prohibit deficiency judgments, at least in the context of purchase money mortgages. Notably among them is California.[390] This decreases the mortgagee's incentive to bid below the fair market value of the property. Some states limit deficiency judgments to the difference between the unpaid loan balance and the fair market value of the property.[391]

Statutory right of redemption

(6) *Statutory right of redemption.* Some states include a statutory right of redemption as a means to encourage market prices to be bid at the foreclosure sale. If the mortgagee bids below the fair market price, the mortgagor could go to another lender to obtain the money to buy back the

[386] This is not to be confused with the statutory right of redemption, described below.
[387] Grant S. Nelson et al., *Real Estate Finance Law* §7.1 (6th ed. 2015).
[388] *See, e.g.*, 735 Ill. Comp. Stat. 5/15-1602.
[389] *Central Financial Services, Inc. v. Spears*, 425 So. 2d 403 (Miss. 1983).
[390] Cal. Civ. Proc. Code §§580b & 580d. *See also* Ariz. Rev. Stat. §33-729(A).
[391] Cal. Civ. Proc. Code §580(a); N.Y. Real Prop. Acts. §1371.

property for the price paid at the foreclosure sale. A second bank might be willing to do this because the fair market value of the property securing its loan will be greater than the loan itself, giving it a greater amount of security. Many states, however, do not have a statutory right of redemption on the ground that the ability of the mortgagor to redeem the property for one year after foreclosure will actually decrease the market value of the property *at the time of the foreclosure sale* because the buyer cannot possess the property immediately and, in fact, has no assurance it will ever be able to possess the property.

Judicial foreclosure

Some states require a *judicially supervised sale.*[392] This means that the mortgagee must bring a lawsuit to foreclose on the property, with the sale overseen by the court. The court may ensure that the price bid at the sale is adequate. Moreover, judicial proceedings allow the mortgagor to prove that she did not default on the mortgage. This is the "exclusive or generally used remedy" in about a third of the states and is available in every jurisdiction.[393]

Private or nonjudicial foreclosure

About two-thirds of the states allow the mortgagor to waive the protection of a judicial sale by granting the mortgagee a *power of sale.*[394] In this case, the mortgagee can conduct the public sale itself, after notice to all interested parties, without the need for judicial proceedings.[395] Many mortgage agreements allow the lender to change the locks on the door and take over the property when a mortgagor defaults or abandons the property; this is intended to prevent the property from becoming dilapidated or taken over by squatters. However, some banks have locked owners out of their homes after they default even if they are still living there and there is no evidence of abandonment or harm to the premises. The Washington Supreme Court outlawed this practice, interpreting a state statute that denies the "owner of the mortgage" the power to "recover possession of the real property, without a foreclosure and sale according to law."[396] The court emphasized that Washington is a lien theory state that leaves title with the homeowner and gives the lender a lien on the property, unlike title theory states that assign the property title to the lender and give the borrower an "equity of redemption." Under the lien theory and the terms of the statute, changing the locks without the consent of the homeowner constitutes a trespass. The court suggested that judicial remedies might nonetheless be available if the property were truly abandoned, and the value of the collateral was in jeopardy.

Deed of trust

Another arrangement that bypasses the judicially supervised sale is the *deed of trust*, which is prevalent in some states and lawful in about half the states.[397] Under this arrangement, the borrower or *trustor* conveys title to

[392] Grant S. Nelson et al., *Real Estate Finance Law* §7.12 (6th ed. 2015); 12 *Thompson on Real Property, Third Thomas Edition* §101.04(b).

[393] Grant S. Nelson et al., *Real Estate Finance Law* §7.12 (6th ed. 2015).

[394] *Id.* at §7.20.

[395] 12 *Thompson on Real Property, Third Thomas Edition* §101.04(c).

[396] *Jordan v. Nationstar Mortg., LLC*, 374 P.3d 1195, 1200 (Wash. 2016) (*citing* Wash. Rev. Code §7.28.230(1)).

[397] Grant S. Nelson et al., *Real Estate Finance Law* §1.6 (6th ed. 2015); 12 *Thompson on Real Property, Third Thomas Edition* §101.01(c)(3).

a third party (called the *trustee*) as security for the trustor's payment of its debt obligation to the lender (called the *beneficiary*). If the trustor defaults, the trustee can arrange a public nonjudicial sale of the property to satisfy the debt.

▷ REFINANCING AND MORTGAGE PRIORITIES **HARD CASE ◀**

Equitable subrogation

Property owners may take out more than one mortgage on their property. In such cases, the first mortgage has priority over later mortgages, at least if the first mortgage is recorded and the second mortgagee has notice of it. This means that if the borrower defaults on payments and the property is sold through a foreclosure process, the proceeds are paid to the first mortgagee and if there are assets left, they go to pay off the second mortgage and so on down the priority list. But what happens if a borrower refinances a particular loan? In *Countrywide Home Loans, Inc. v. First Nat'l Bank of Steamboat Springs*,[398] an owner took out a third mortgage for the purpose of paying off the first mortgage. When the borrower defaulted on the second mortgage, the court had to determine whether the second mortgagee or the third mortgagee had priority; who would get paid first if the foreclosure sale did not yield enough proceeds to pay off both mortgages? The court applied the recording act principle of "first in time, first in right." Because the third mortgage was not only given after the second mortgage, but recorded afterward (with notice of the second mortgage), the court held that the second mortgagee should be paid off first.

The opposite result was reached in *Bank of America v. Prestance Corp.*,[399] because the court applied the doctrine of *equitable subrogation*. Under that doctrine, someone who assumes the rights or obligations of another steps into their shoes and assumes whatever rights or obligations they had to the extent necessary to prevent unjust enrichment. Because the second mortgagee knew that its mortgage was subordinate to the first mortgage, it could not complain if the identity of the first mortgagee changed by assignment. If the refinancing of the loan and the assignment of the mortgagee's rights to a third party would mean that the second mortgage would move up and have priority over the first mortgagee, this would amount to a windfall neither earned nor deserved by the second mortgage and constitute unjust enrichment. The *Restatement (Third) of Mortgages* §7.6 (1997) adopts this position on the ground that it serves the interests of homeowners by making refinancing both cheaper and more available and does not hurt the interests of anyone else and found it not to conflict with the spirit (if not the letter) of the state recording statute. Note that the availability of the power to refinance a mortgage loan was one of the driving forces of the subprime mortgage crisis; many adjustable-rate mortgage loans were given to buyers who could not pay them back without refinancing once the higher interest rates kicked in. ◀

[398] *Countrywide Home Loans, Inc. v. First Nat'l Bank of Steamboat Springs*, 144 P.3d 1224 (Wyo. 2006).

[399] *Bank of America v. Prestance Corp.*, 160 P.3d 17 (Wash. 2007).

▶ **HARD CASE**

▷ JUDICIAL SUPERVISION OF PRICE PAID ON FORECLOSURE

If the buyer at the foreclosure sale bids too low, the mortgagor may be empowered to bring a lawsuit against the mortgagee for breach of fiduciary duty.[400] For example, in *Central Financial Services, Inc. v. Spears*,[401] the mortgagee made a low bid and bought the property at foreclosure sale for only $1,458.86 (the exact amount of the outstanding indebtedness then due plus costs of foreclosure), and then resold the property for $4,000 twelve days later. Four months after that, the property was resold again, this time for $6,500. The mortgagors sued the mortgagee, asking the court to set aside the foreclosure and/or require the mortgagee to disgorge its profits from the sale of the property. The court held that a foreclosure sale will not be set aside unless the price is "so inadequate as to shock the conscience of the court."[402] The discrepancy must be large:

> Mere inadequacy of price will not operate to set a sale aside, unless it is so gross as to furnish evidence of fraud, and there must be an inequality so strong, gross and manifest that it must be impossible to state it to a man of common sense without producing an exclamation at the inequality of it.[403]

The court held that the resale of the property within two weeks of foreclosure for two-and-a-half times the price paid at the foreclosure was sufficient to "shock the conscience" and ordered the mortgagee to hand over to the mortgagors the difference between the resale price ($4,000) and the amount it paid at the foreclosure sale ($1,458.86) with minor adjustments for costs.

Argument that the mortgagors should recover the fair market value minus the foreclosure price

The mortgagors had argued that the fair market value of the property was greater than $4,000, as evidenced by the resale four months later for $6,500, and that they should be entitled to the difference between the second resale price and the foreclosure price, or to the difference between the fair market value of the property and the foreclosure price. The court determined that the fair market value of the property was $6,000. If the lender had looked diligently for a buyer at that price it could have found one, and, in that case, the lender would have recovered its loan and the homeowners would have recovered the excess proceeds, *i.e.*, their equity built up in the house.

Argument for resale price minus foreclosure price

The court disagreed, holding that the mortgagee should not be required to suffer a loss from the foreclosure and should have to disgorge only the

[400] *See also Baskurt v. Beal*, 101 P.3d 1041 (Alaska 2004) (foreclosure can be rescinded when property worth $225,000 was sold at foreclosure for $26,780 — the amount of the outstanding debt); *In re Krohn*, 52 P.3d 774 (Ariz. 2002) (court may set aside trustee's sale for gross inadequacy of price); *Murphy v. Financial Development Corp.*, 495 A.2d 1245 (N.H. 1985) (mortgagee has duty to act reasonably so as to obtain a fair and reasonable price at the foreclosure sale).

[401] 425 So. 2d 403 (Miss. 1983).

[402] *Id.* at 404. *Accord, Shipp Corp., Inc. v. Charpilloz*, 414 So. 2d 1122 (Fla. Dist. Ct. App. 1982).

[403] 425 So. 2d at 405.

actual profits it made on the transaction (the difference between the first resale price of $4,000 and the foreclosure price) rather than punishing the mortgagee for not finding a buyer who would pay the fair market value (which the court determined was $6,000). The mortgagee had sufficient incentive to sell for fair market value and if it sold below fair market value, it should not be penalized for this. Moreover, a rule of law allowing the mortgagor to recover fair market value minus the foreclosure price is far less predictable a rule than one that allows recovery of the resale price minus the foreclosure price. ◀

Mortgage moratorium legislation

In times of economic depression, legislatures have sometimes passed emergency mortgage moratorium legislation. During the Great Depression, some states passed laws protecting homeowners from foreclosure under certain circumstances. In *Home Building & Loan Association v. Blaisdell*,[404] the Supreme Court upheld the constitutionality of the 1933 *Minnesota Mortgage Moratorium Act*, which temporarily authorized courts to extend periods of redemption — the time during which the homeowner-mortgagor could pay off the loan to the mortgagee — without being subject to a foreclosure sale.

Truth in Lending Act

The federal *Truth in Lending Act*[405] requires mortgagees to disclose to prospective residential borrowers the actual costs associated with the loan — the total cost of which often takes the borrower's breath away when she sees it at the closing.[406] The 1994 *Home Ownership and Equity Protection Act*[407] amended the *Truth in Lending Act* to require additional disclosure for certain high-rate loans and flatly prohibits certain abusive loan terms.

Home Ownership and Equity Protection Act

Transfers by mortgagor

The mortgagor's interest is transferable. If the property is sold "subject to" an existing mortgage, the original mortgagor remains liable on the debt and the new owner of the property is not personally liable on the debt. If the debt is not paid, the mortgagee can foreclose on the land. Generally, the new owner may pay off the old mortgage to obtain the property free of the debt. In contrast, if the new owner of the property "assumes" the mortgage, she is personally liable on the debt.[408] "Due-on-sale" clauses are often placed in mortgage contracts by lender/mortgages. They require the entire debt to be paid if the property is sold by the mortgagor. Although at one time held unenforceable as unreasonable restraints on alienations, federal law makes such clauses enforceable now, although exemptions apply to certain classes of loans.[409]

Priorities on foreclosure

Mortgaged property may be subject to a variety of encumbrances. For example, an owner who has granted a mortgage interest in her house may obtain a *second mortgage* on the same property. The second mortgage is subordinate to the first mortgage; if a foreclosure occurs, the proceeds are

[404] 290 U.S. 398 (1934).
[405] 15 U.S.C. §§1601 to 1693r.
[406] Paul Barron, Michael Berenson & Dan Rosin, *Federal Regulation of Real Estate and Mortgage Lending* §§10.01 to 10.91 (4th ed. 2025 update).
[407] 15 U.S.C. §1635.
[408] Grant S. Nelson et al., *Real Estate Finance Law* §§5.4 to 5.5 (6th ed. 2015).
[409] *Garn-St. Germain Depository Institutions Act of 1982*, 12 U.S.C. §1701j-03; *Fidelity Federal Savings & Loan Association v. De La Cuesta*, 458 U.S. 141 (1982).

used to pay off the first mortgagee and then if proceeds are left, the second mortgage, with the excess going to the mortgagor. Priorities among mortgages are generally established by the principle of "first in time, first in right" unless modified by recording laws. An unrecorded mortgage may not be given priority against a later mortgage if the second mortgagee was not on notice of the first mortgage.

Rights of lessees on foreclosure

If an owner leased the property prior to granting the mortgage, the lease will subsist after foreclosure. The property was already burdened by the lease at the time of the mortgage and the owner had no power to grant the property free of the lease. However, a prior lease may end with foreclosure if the lease agreement includes a subordination clause to that effect. Conversely, if the lease is granted after the mortgage, the lease will terminate upon foreclosure; the owner who has granted a mortgage cannot grant rights to the tenant that are superior to those of the mortgagee.[410]

§11.5.2 Installment Land Contracts, or Contracts for Deed

Long-term purchase from seller

Under an installment land contract, the seller keeps the title to the property while the buyer promises to pay the purchase price over time. In return, the buyer obtains the right to possess the property and is treated as the owner of the property. When the purchase price is paid off, the seller will deliver a deed to the property to the buyer.[411] The contract normally allows the seller to regain possession of the property on the buyer's default and to keep whatever payments the buyer has already made. This remedy for breach of the contract is called *forfeiture*.[412]

Forfeiture

Treatment as mortgage

This arrangement poses the same problems for the buyer as the mortgage does, but states often provide such buyer-borrowers fewer procedural protections than are granted to mortgagors. Some states implicitly or explicitly prohibit installment land contracts by making the protections of the mortgage foreclosure statute nonwaivable.[413] For example, in *Sebastian v. Floyd*,[414] a purchaser had paid $4,300 plus interest (40 percent of the purchase price) and defaulted on seven payments. The sellers sought to enforce a forfeiture clause in the installment land contract that would allow them to keep the payments made by the buyer rather than selling the property and giving any excess proceeds over to the buyer. The court noted that "[t]here is no practical distinction between the land sale contract and a purchase money mortgage,"[415] and held that the protections of the mortgage foreclosure laws should therefore be extended to all buyers under installment land contracts.

[410] Grant S. Nelson et al., *Real Estate Finance Law* §7.13 (6th ed. 2015).
[411] *Id.* at §3.26.
[412] *Id.*
[413] Ariz. Rev. Stat. §§33-741 & 33-742; N.D. Cent. Code §§32-18-01 to 32-18-06; Okla. Stat. tit. 16, §11a; *Mid-State Investment Corp. v. O'Steen*, 133 So. 2d 455 (Fla. 1961); *Morris v. Weigle*, 383 N.E.2d 341 (Ind. 1978); *Heritage Art Galleries v. Raia*, 570 N.Y.S.2d 67 (App. Div. 1991).
[414] 585 S.W.2d 381 (Ky. 1979).
[415] *Id.* at 383.

Grace periods

Some states enforce installment land contracts and do not find the mortgage foreclosure statutes to have outlawed these arrangements. Some impose an equitable redemption period, allowing the borrower to retain possession if she is able to pay off the remaining debt.[416] In effect, this remedy is one of specific performance (although allowing for tardy payment); it requires the seller to turn over title to the buyer upon payment of the rest of the purchase price.[417]

Prohibition of "penalties"

Others refuse to enforce forfeiture clauses if the amount of the payments already made by the buyer so exceeds the seller's damages as to constitute an unconscionable forfeiture or penalty. Liquidated damages are generally allowed in contract law if they constitute a reasonable measure of the anticipated damages. However, courts sometimes look at the time of the breach to determine whether the amount is significantly different from the actual damages. This approach appears to be followed in the context of installment land contracts. Some courts will require the seller to grant restitution to the buyer of payments made to the extent they exceed the seller's actual damages, where the court determines that the forfeiture would be "unconscionable."[418] For example, in *Stonebraker v. Zinn*,[419] the buyers under an installment land contract argued that their down payment plus the payments already made under the contract would together constitute an unreasonable penalty for breach of contract rather than a valid liquidated damages amount. The court determined that the monthly payment under the contract was close to the fair rental value of the premises and that the down payment was not so substantial as to render it an unconscionable penalty. It therefore allowed the sellers to retake possession of the property and keep all payments made by the buyers. Under this view, the buyer is not entitled to build up equity in the property; rather, buyers under installment land contracts are more like renters. They will obtain title (and the right to any increase in the fair market value of the property) only if they make all their payments and do not default. If they default and the down payment is not grossly disproportionate to the seller's damages, they will lose both the house and any equity they thought they were building up in it.[420]

Intermediate approach

Other states treat some installment land contracts like mortgages. They create a common law equivalent of the equity of redemption and make it available for installment land contract purchasers if the forfeiture shocks the conscience of the court.[421] Colorado, for example, has developed a test

[416] *MacFadden v. Walker*, 488 P.2d 1353 (Cal. 1971); *Jenkins v. Wise*, 574 P.2d 1337 (Haw. 1978); *Nigh v. Hickman*, 538 S.W.2d 936 (Mo. Ct. App. 1976); Grant S. Nelson & Dale A. Whitman, *Real Estate Finance Law* §3.29 (5th ed. 2007).

[417] *But see Kosloff v. Castle*, 171 Cal. Rptr. 308 (Ct. App. 1981) (refusing to grant the buyer specific performance).

[418] *Jacobson v. Swan*, 278 P.2d 294, 298-299 (Utah 1954).

[419] 286 S.E.2d 911 (W. Va. 1982).

[420] *Accord, Porter v. Smith*, 486 N.W.2d 846, 851 (Neb. 1992); *Murphy v. Murphy*, 466 N.W.2d 87 (Neb. 1991); *Post v. Schwall*, 460 N.W.2d 794, 797 (Wis. 1990).

[421] *Looney v. Farmers Home Administration*, 794 F.2d 310 (7th Cir. 1986); *MacFadden v. Walker*, 488 P.2d 1353 (Cal. 1971); *Jenkins v. Wise*, 574 P.2d 1337, 1341 (Haw. 1978); *Tidd v. Stauffer*, 308 N.E.2d 415 (Ind. Ct. App. 1974); *Bean v. Walker*, 464 N.Y.S.2d 895 (App. Div. 1983).

to distinguish installment land contracts that must be treated like mortgages from those that may be enforced according to their own terms. In *Grombone v. Krekel*,[422] the court held that trial courts have the discretion to make this determination based on a range of factors, including "the amount of the vendee's equity in the property, the length of the default period, the willfulness of the default, whether the vendee has made improvements, and whether the property has been adequately maintained."[423] If the buyer has made a large down payment, occupied the property for a long time, and paid a substantial portion of the purchase price, the court is likely to provide the buyer with all the protections accorded a mortgagor, including a right to redeem, a right to notice and a foreclosure sale, and a right to recover proceeds from the foreclosure sale exceeding the unpaid debt.[424] Texas has legislation that gives buyers foreclosure protection if they have paid more than 40 percent of the purchase price or made the equivalent of 48 monthly payments.[425]

Grace period legislation

Some states have passed legislation authorizing a "grace period" within which late payments must be accepted.[426] After this grace period, forfeiture is allowed in a manner similar to strict foreclosure.

§11.5.3 Equitable Mortgages

Treating arrangements as mortgages

An equitable mortgage is a transaction that is treated by the courts as a mortgage even though the contractual arrangements may appear to be something else.[427] For example, when an owner gives a lender a deed absolute on its face as security for a loan, the courts will treat the arrangement as a mortgage rather than a sale of the property if that was the intent of the parties.[428] In *Koenig v. Van Reken*,[429] an owner who was having trouble making her mortgage payments gave the deed to her house to an individual who paid off her debts and promised to return the deed when she repaid him. She also agreed to "lease" the property from him with the repayments geared to repaying the loan. When she defaulted on these payments, he evicted her from her home. She sued to have the deed and lease and loan arrangement declared to be an equitable mortgage. The court ruled in her favor. "The court of equity protects the necessitous by looking through

[422] 754 P.2d 777 (Colo. App. 1988).
[423] *Id.* at 779.
[424] *See also Petersen v. Hartell*, 707 P.2d 232 (Cal. 1985); *Skendzel v. Marshall*, 301 N.E.2d 641 (Ind. 1973); *Bean v. Walker*, 464 N.Y.S.2d 895 (App. Div. 1983).
[425] Tex. Prop. Code §5.066.
[426] Iowa Code §§656.1 to 656.9; Grant S. Nelson et al., *Real Estate Finance Law* §3.28 (6th ed. 2015); *see also* Ohio Rev. Code §§5313.05 to 5313.08 (allowing forfeiture after a 30-day grace period for "property improved by a dwelling" only if less than 20 percent of the principal has been repaid and the owner has had possession less than five years).
[427] *Bernstein v. New Beginnings Trustee, LLC*, 988 So. 2d 90 (Fla. Dist. Ct. App. 2008); *Hudson v. Vandiver*, 810 So. 2d 617, 622 (Miss. Ct. App. 2002); *Mathurin v. Lost & Found Recovery, LLC*, 9 Misc. 3d 756 (N.Y. Sup. Ct. 2008); 4-37 *Powell on Real Property* §37.18.
[428] Fla. Stat. §697.01; Idaho Code §§45-904 & 45-905; *Gilliland v. Port Authority of City of St. Paul*, 270 N.W.2d 743 (Minn. 1978); *Hanson v. Bonner*, 661 P.2d 421 (Mont. 1983); Grant S. Nelson et al., *Real Estate Finance Law* §3.8 (6th ed. 2015).
[429] 279 N.W.2d 590 (Mich. Ct. App. 1979).

form to the substance of the transaction."[430] A transfer of a deed will be treated as a mortgage if that is the intent of the parties. The court explained that "the adverse financial condition of the grantor, coupled with the inadequacy of the purchase price for the property, is sufficient to establish a deed absolute on its face to be a mortgage."[431]

§11.5.4 Subprime Mortgages

Changes in mortgage lending since 1980

Since 1980, the mortgage industry has changed dramatically. Legislation passed in the New Deal era sought to respond to the bank failures that had helped cause the Great Depression. Those statutes regulated how banks are run and created a federal insurance program for bank deposits. For many years, banking was a staid profession that was conservative in outlook. But beginning in the 1980s, things began to change. For one thing, *mortgage brokers* became prevalent. Instead of going to a bank to apply for a mortgage, a prospective home buyer may seek assistance from a broker who will help the buyer find a mortgage and compare rates and terms among various mortgages offered by different institutions. One cause of the subprime mortgage crisis was that these brokers had the incentive to induce buyers to obtain higher-cost loans because the brokers got higher fees that way. Also, mortgage brokers had an incentive to induce homeowners to refinance their mortgages even if there was no economic benefit to the homeowner because the broker gets a fee for every refinancing.

Mortgage brokers

New regulatory environment

More important, a new regulatory environment emerged with less government regulation and more competition among mortgage providers, and new forms of mortgages and mortgage markets were created. Although scholars will debate this question, these changes probably led to the subprime mortgage crisis. Here is an outline of what seems to have happened.

Federal preemption of state usury laws

First, a new passion for deregulation became prevalent. State usury laws had regulated the interest rates that could be charged for loans financing the purchase of a home, but they were preempted by federal law in 1980, allowing banks to charge whatever they wanted. *Depository Institutions Deregulation and Monetary Control Act (DIDMCA)*.[432] "DIDMCA was enacted by Congress early in 1980, when interest rates were at historic highs in the last year of the Carter Administration, in order to alleviate the mortgage credit crunch caused by state usury laws that were below the market rate of interest."[433]

Adjustable-rate mortgages

Second, with usury deregulation, lending institutions realized they could induce people to buy homes even if interest rates were high by offering *adjustable-rate mortgages* with initially low interest rate payments below the market rate of interest, which then increased over time. These loans

[430] *Id.* at 592. For a similar case, see *Johnson v. Cherry*, 726 S.W.2d 4 (Tex. 1987).

[431] 279 N.W.2d at 592; *see also Flack v. McClure*, 565 N.E.2d 131 (Ill. App. Ct. 1990).

[432] 12 U.S.C. §1735f-7a(a)(1).

[433] *Commonwealth of Massachusetts v. H & R Block, Inc.*, 2008 Mass. Super. LEXIS 427, at *24-*25 (Nov. 25, 2008) (noting that *DIDMCA* allowed states to pass laws opting out of the statute and continuing to enforce their usury laws applicable to home finance, 12 U.S.C. §1735f-7a(b)(2); *see, e.g.*, 1981 Mass. Acts ch. 231).

were thought to be secure because the value of real estate was continuing to rise and the lender could always recoup its investment by foreclosure. Over time, lenders began offering these loans to lower-income families as well based on the security that rising property values provided; to compensate for the added risk, the interest rates were very high. Some lenders decided that they could make money by loaning it to borrowers who could not pay back those loans when the higher interest rates kicked in. They even loaned money to people without any proof of their income or ability to pay. These "subprime" borrowers had a high credit risk and most could not qualify for normal "prime" loans (although some who could were steered to higher-priced subprime loans). They were charged a higher interest rate to borrow money because they presented a heightened risk of nonpayment; at the same time, many were assured that the loans were a good deal for them because they could either refinance when the higher interest rates kicked in or they could sell the property at a profit at that point. Some of these borrowers did not understand that rates would rise later while others were assured that they could refinance at that time to make monthly payments affordable. Everyone seemed to expect property values to keep rising indefinitely and borrowers were given mixed messages, *i.e.*, (a) that the loans were affordable (even though the rates would rise later to an unaffordable level); and (b) that their bad credit rating made the loan risky, justifying the higher payments while there was no risk to them or the bank because of the rising value of land.

Some lenders expected foreclosure on the increasingly valuable property to recover any unpaid loans, but most off-loaded the risk to another entity. Before 1980, a lender often kept the mortgage itself and the borrower paid off the loan to one institution for the entire 15- or 30-year period. But after 1980, most mortgage lenders sold those mortgages to others; home buyers would find themselves making mortgage payments to banks they had never heard of, often in other states.

Mortgage-backed securities

Third, lenders began to *securitize* the mortgage loans, taking a bunch of loans and packaging them together, placing them in the hands of "*special investment vehicles*" or trusts that would then sell shares or "securities" in these bundled loans to investors. These were called "mortgage-backed securities" (MBSs). Banks would even collect packages of MBSs and sell securities in these "collateralized debt obligations" (CDOs). These were investments like buying stock in a company and they were viewed as safe because of the constantly rising value of land. Because the subprime loans were receiving a high interest rate (because of the added risk of loaning to less creditworthy borrowers), investors would make a great deal of money as long as the borrowers kept making their payments and as long as the value of real property kept rising. As with the transactions with borrowers, investors were given mixed messages. On the one hand, the high interest rates earned on subprime loans were justified by the poor creditworthiness of subprime borrowers and the high risk of default. On the other hand, rating agencies would give the highest AAA rating to subprime mortgage securities because they "spread the risk" by packaging many loans together (assuming that defaults would not happen to all loans at once) and because the rising value of property gave security to the loans. In effect, investors were told that the loans were both risky and not risky. At the same time, it is hard to see how the rating agencies could reasonably classify packages of subprime mortgages sold uniformly to persons with low credit ratings and give securities based on those loans the highest rating possible (a rating usually reserved for the very safest of investments).

Leverage

Fourth, the risk posed by subprime mortgages was compounded by *leverage*. If you buy $100 million of assets with only $1 million of your own money and $99 million borrowed from someone else and the assets go up in value to $101 million, you have doubled your money. Of course, if you owe $100 million and you only have $1 or $2 million, and you cannot pay off the rest of the loan, then your lender will be in trouble if the asset securing the loan has decreased in value to under $99 million.

Credit default swaps

Fifth, banks bought (and sold) a complicated form of insurance for these mortgage-backed securities called "default credit swaps," which were unregulated and not backed by any security. Lenders like AIG sold this insurance because defaults on securities backed by real estate were thought to be unlikely even if particular borrowers defaulted on their loans because the rising value of land would recover the debts. But because many lending institutions were on both sides of these transactions (both insuring and being insured) and because many institutions held risky debt, any chink in the payment schedule, *combined with a decrease in the value of land*, had the possibility of making the whole system unravel.

Housing bubble bursts

And unravel it did, partly because borrowers were in over their heads and could not afford to make the higher payments when their adjustable-rate mortgages jumped to the new higher interest rates and partly because the housing bubble burst. These were partly independent and partly dependent events. The housing bubble would have burst at some point in any event but the inability of many subprime borrowers to make payments when adjustable-rate mortgages kicked into higher rates helped to precipitate foreclosures and to erode the value of mortgage-backed securities. For many years, the value of real estate had gone in only one direction — up. But when the value of real estate started to go down, the security for the subprime mortgages was eroded. It turned out that many unpaid loans were now higher than the value of the real estate securing those loans. As people began to stop making mortgage payments, foreclosures became frequent, and when the value of the property was not enough to pay off the loan, this started a chain reaction that made the entire system collapse. And because all of this was wrapped up in both banking institutions and lenders who were less regulated than banks, and because of the interrelated nature of all these institutions, we faced a worldwide credit crisis that could only be handled by some form of massive government bailout.[434]

Government intervention

The subprime mortgage crisis led to calls for government intervention to save the banks and to help the millions of homeowners facing foreclosure. These foreclosures affect not only the families who lose their

[434] *See* David Leonhardt, *Can't Grasp Credit Crisis? Join the Club*, N.Y. Times, Mar. 19, 2008, at A-1.

homes, but their neighbors as well. A neighborhood dotted with foreclosed homes rapidly affects the property values of those who remain, and in a recession, it is difficult to find buyers for those homes. Owners are also reluctant to sell at the low market values because they will have to suffer a big loss in their wealth. Pressure grew during the 2008 presidential election for Congress and the Federal Reserve Bank to do something. This raised the issue of whether changes were needed to the complicated federal laws regulating banking and the mortgage industry. From 2007 to 2009, a number of federal and state statutes were passed to shore up the banking industry and to help homeowners refinance their homes. And in 2010, Congress passed the *Mortgage Reform and Anti-Predatory Lending Act of 2010* (as part of the *Dodd-Frank Wall Street Reform and Consumer Protection Act*) to prevent banks from giving mortgages to people who cannot afford to pay them back.[435] Congress also created the Consumer Financial Protection Bureau to administer these reforms, and it has begun issuing regulations designed to prevent the sale of mortgages to people who cannot afford to pay them back, to mandate better disclosure of the terms of loans, and to better regulate the servicing of mortgage loans.[436]

▶ HARD CASE

▷ PROOF OF LOAN OWNERSHIP AND MERS (MORTGAGE ELECTRONIC REGISTRATION SYSTEMS)

Recording problems

The rush to securitize thousands of subprime mortgages led to sloppy record keeping, and it has become common for lenders seeking to foreclose to face difficulties when asked to prove they own the mortgage; they are sometimes unable to produce either the mortgage note to prove they have a right to foreclose or the chain of mortgage assignments from the original mortgagee that would be substitute proof that they are entitled to enforce the debt through foreclosure. In *U.S. Bank Nat'l Ass'n v. Ibañez,*[437] the Supreme Judicial Court of the Commonwealth of Massachusetts held that a nonjudicial foreclosure was invalid because the foreclosing bank did not prove through a chain of mortgage assignments that it was entitled to foreclose on the property. In a subsequent case called *Bevilacqua v. Rodriguez,*[438] the court held that a third party who obtains title from the bank that bought the property at foreclosure cannot obtain good title if the

[435] 15 U.S.C. §§1602, 1631 *et seq.*

[436] 12 C.F.R. §1026 (amending *Regulation Z,* implementing the *Truth in Lending Act* (*TILA*), 15 U.S.C. §1639c, which itself implements the *Mortgage Reform and Anti-Predatory Lending Act,* which comprised Title XIV of the *Dodd-Frank Wall Street Reform and Consumer Protection Act,* Pub. L. No. 111-203, H.R. 4173, July 21, 2010, at §§1411-1412). *See* www.consumerfinance.gov; Leonard J. Kennedy, Patricia A. McCoy & Ethan Bernstein, *The Consumer Financial Protection Bureau: Financial Regulation for the Twenty-First Century,* 97 Cornell L. Rev. 1141 (2012).

[437] 941 N.E.2d 40 (Mass. 2011). *Accord, Fed. Home Loan Mortgage Corp. v. Schwartzwald,* 979 N.E.2d 1214 (Ohio 2012); *Washington Mutual Bank v. Green,* 806 N.E.2d 604 (Ohio Ct. App. 2004).

[438] 955 N.E.2d 884 (Mass. 2011).

foreclosing bank did not prove, prior to the foreclosure, that it had the right to foreclose under the existing mortgage.[439]

Loan servicers

Many lenders hire *loan servicers* to collect mortgage payments on behalf of the mortgagee. This is especially true of mortgages that are securitized. These loan servicers may file foreclosure lawsuits on behalf of the mortgagee but are not the "owners" of the mortgage, and they may be required to present proof of ownership of the mortgage for the foreclosure to proceed. Some courts have refused to allow loan servicers to bring foreclosure lawsuits on behalf of the underlying mortgagee on the ground that the only party entitled to foreclose is the one that owns the mortgage or is the beneficiary of the note.[440]

MERS

Similar problems may arise with the *Mortgage Electronic Registration Systems, Inc.* (MERS). Mortgage lenders who engage in trades of mortgages established a private organization, referred to as MERS, to hold those mortgages for the benefit of the mortgagees. However, MERS does not actually "own" the mortgage; it has no right to the payments from the borrower; nor does it act as the loan servicer. Rather, it is the "nominee" or limited agent of the mortgagee.[441] According to the MERS website, it "eliminates the need to prepare and record assignments when trading residential and commercial mortgage loans."[442] Its goal is to "streamline the mortgage process by using electronic commerce to eliminate paper," and its "mission is to register every mortgage loan in the United States on the MERS System."[443] MERS is listed as the "nominee" owner of the mortgage in the recording office and is supposed to eliminate the need for new recordings when mortgages are transferred. If this system works, then mortgages can be traded more cheaply because mortgage assignments do not need to be recorded in public offices; MERS is listed as the "owner" of the mortgage in the documents in the recording office, and theoretically, MERS keeps track of who the mortgagee and the loan servicer are for each loan when the loans are transferred. In practice, banks that become MERS members choose when and whether to notify MERS of mortgage assignments; in many cases, they do not notify MERS when mortgages are transferred from one bank to another or from the original lender to the entity that collects mortgages for securitization and then transfers them to the trust that holds them for the benefits of investors who buy the securities.

Some states have allowed MERS to bring foreclosure proceedings in its own name.[444] They view the MERS system as beneficial to the real estate

[439] Massachusetts has tried to correct this problem by passing legislation giving victims of wrongful foreclosure three years to sue to recover their properties. Mass. Gen. Laws ch. 244, §15, *amended by* 2015 Mass. Acts ch. 141 (An Act Clearing Titles to Foreclosed Properties).

[440] *See Bayview Loan Servicing, L.L.C. v. Nelson*, 890 N.E.2d 940 (Ill. App. Ct. 2008) (denying a loan servicer the power to bring a foreclosure suit).

[441] *But see Culhane v. Aurora Loan Servs. of Neb.*, 708 F.3d 282 (1st Cir. 2013) (MERS possesses a legal interest in the mortgage enabling it to transfer the mortgage to the holder of the beneficial interest, *i.e.*, the bank that owns the right to foreclose to secure the underlying debt).

[442] http://www.mersinc.org.

[443] http://www.mersinc.org/about/index.asp.

[444] Minn. Stat. §507.413; *Gomes v. Countrywide Home Loans Inc.*, 121 Cal. Rptr. 3d 819, 826-827 (Ct. App. 2011); *Mortgage Electronic Registration Systems, Inc. v. Revoredo*, 955 So.

market and feel that the homeowner had agreed to let MERS act as an agent for the real mortgagee, whoever that was. So they shifted the burden of proof onto the homeowner to show that MERS was *not* acting on behalf of the real party in interest. Other courts, however, have refused to let MERS bring foreclosure proceedings on the ground that it had no title to the property or any interest whatsoever.[445] They argue that if you are going to eject someone from his home, you have to show you have a better right to his property than he does. But MERS has no property rights of any kind; it does not own the mortgage and it is not the one to whom the loan is owed. For that reason, some courts hold that it has no power to foreclose and no power to assign rights in the mortgage to the real owner of the mortgage to enable the mortgagee to foreclose.[446] Other courts have held the opposite on the ground that MERS has a "legal interest" in the mortgage that enables it to transfer the mortgage to another entity.[447]

One person or entity cannot serve both as the agent and the principal; yet the agreements that identify MERS as the nominee for the originator of the mortgage may have contradictory information on that score, calling MERS both the "mortgagee" and the "nominee" for the mortgagee. These conflicting roles have led courts to differing views about the powers and obligations that MERS has. Importantly, if MERS is an agent for the real mortgagee, it cannot serve in that capacity without knowing who its principal is.[448] If the mortgage has been transferred from the originator to another entity, MERS cannot fulfill its role without a clear record of that mortgage assignment. For the same reason, some courts refused to allow loan servicers to foreclose unless they can show a chain of mortgage assignments giving them the right to foreclose as agents for the mortgagee.[449] They also are agents for a principal, and unless they can show that the principal has rights in the mortgage, they are in no better a position than

---

2d 33, 34 (Fla. Dist. Ct. App. 2007); *Residential Funding Co., LLC v. Saurman*, 805 N.W.2d 183 (Mich. 2011); *Jackson v. Mortgage Electronic Registration Systems, Inc.*, 770 N.W.2d 487, 494-495, 501 (Minn. 2009).

[445] *Landmark Nat'l Bank v. Kessler*, 192 P.3d 177 (Kan. Ct. App. 2008) (MERS was not a necessary party to a foreclosure proceeding because it was not the mortgagee); *LaSalle Bank Nat'l Ass'n v. Lamy*, 824 N.Y.S.2d 769, 2006 WL 2251721, at *1 (Sup. Ct. 2006); *Bain v. Metropolitan Mortgage Group, Inc.*, 285 P.3d 34, 36-37 (Wash. 2012). *Cf. Fed. Home Loan Mortgage Corp. v. Schwartzwald*, 979 N.E.2d 1214 (Ohio 2012) (foreclosure action can be brought only by party that is the note beneficiary at the time the action is brought).

[446] *Bank of N.Y. v. Silverberg*, 926 N.Y.S.2d 532, 538-539 (App. Div. 2011); *LaSalle Bank Nat'l Ass'n v. Lamy*, 824 N.Y.S.2d 769 (Sup. Ct. 2006).

[447] *Culhane v. Aurora Loan Servs. of Neb.*, 708 F.3d 282 (1st Cir. 2013) (MERS possesses a legal interest in the mortgage enabling it to transfer the mortgage to the holder of the beneficial interest or the bank that owns the right to foreclose to secure the underlying debt); *In re Relka*, 2009 WL 5149262, at *3 (Bankr. D. Wyo. 2009) (MERS has power to assign the note and mortgage).

[448] *Bank of N.Y. v. Alderazi*, 900 N.Y.S.2d 821, 824 (Sup. Ct. 2010) (the "party who claims to be the agent of another bears the burden of proving the agency relationship"). On the difficulty of figuring out what to do when the identity of the principal is unclear, see *Bain v. Metropolitan Mortgage Group, Inc.*, 285 P.3d 34, 47-49 (Wash. 2012).

[449] *In re Maisel*, 378 B.R. 19, 22 (Bankr. D. Mass. 2007) (agent cannot foreclose without proof of its agency relationship and a showing of the chain of mortgage assignments giving its principal a right to foreclose).

MERS. Intended to simplify mortgage recordation, the MERS system, as it was implemented before and during the subprime crisis, has complicated rather than simplified property titles, leaving many of them clouded and uncertain. ◀

§11.5.5 Wrongful Foreclosure

It has long been the case that you cannot bring a claim to throw someone off land just by proving she has no right to own it. Plaintiff must prove she has a better title than a peaceable possessor. This is called the doctrine of relativity of title. The same principle applies in the context of foreclosure. A bank seeking to force property to be sold to pay a mortgage debt is only entitled to force a sale of the property if it has a right to foreclose. If it does not have the right to foreclose and does so anyway, it may have committed the tort of wrongful foreclosure.

The California Supreme Court held in *Yvanova v. New Century Mortgage Corp.*[450] that a borrower has standing to prove that a nonjudicial foreclosure was wrongful because an assignment by which the foreclosing entity purportedly took a beneficial interest was void, thereby depriving the foreclosing party of any authority to foreclose through a trustee's sale.

In a follow-up case, *Sciarratta v. U.S. Bank Nat'l Ass'n*,[451] the Court of Appeals held that foreclosure by an entity with no power to foreclose is, by itself, the tort of wrongful foreclosure. Even if the borrower is in default, and someone has the right to foreclose, that does not mean that any person with a claim can bring the foreclosure. Only a party with a better claim to title — someone with the legal authority to foreclose — can oust a peaceable possessor from his home.

"A homeowner who has been foreclosed on by one with no right to do so — by those facts alone — sustains prejudice or harm sufficient to constitute a cause of action for wrongful foreclosure. When a non-debtholder forecloses, a homeowner is harmed by losing her home to an entity with no legal right to take it."[452] Such a tort can be remedied either by damages or, in appropriate cases, by injunctive relief to undo the foreclosure sale. Damages, according to the court, include all consequential damages, including damages for emotional distress.

In a related ruling, the Massachusetts Supreme Judicial Court held that owners may make affirmative defenses to eviction claims by banks that acquired title to their property through a private or nonjudicial foreclosure.[453] Those defenses may challenge the way in which the bank acquired title to the property through the foreclosure process and the power of the bank to foreclose in the first place. They may also include any equitable defenses that would defeat the claim for a right to possession of the property (the right to evict).

[450] 365 P.3d 845 (Cal. 2016).
[451] 202 Cal. Rptr. 3d 219 (Ct. App. 2016).
[452] *Id.* at 221-222.
[453] *Bank of America v. Rosa*, 999 N.E.2d 1080 (Mass. 2013).

CHAPTER 12

Fair Housing Law

§12.1 Introduction
§12.2 Intentional Racial or National-Origin Discrimination
  §12.2.1 U.S. Constitution
  §12.2.2 *Fair Housing Act of 1968*
    §12.2.2.1 Prohibited Bases of Discrimination
    §12.2.2.2 Covered Dwellings
    §12.2.2.3 Exemptions
    §12.2.2.4 Prohibited Conduct
    §12.2.2.5 Standards of Proof
    §12.2.2.6 Standing
    §12.2.2.7 Advertising
    §12.2.2.8 Remedies
  §12.2.3 *Civil Rights Act of 1866*
§12.3 Sex Discrimination
§12.4 Sexual-Orientation and Gender Identity Discrimination
§12.5 Disability Discrimination
§12.6 Family Status Discrimination
  §12.6.1 Families with Children
  §12.6.2 Marital Status
§12.7 Religious Discrimination
§12.8 Disparate Impact Claims
  §12.8.1 Race
  §12.8.2 Sex
  §12.8.3 Sexual Orientation and Gender Identity
  §12.8.4 Disability
  §12.8.5 Familial Status
    §12.8.5.1 Families with Children
    §12.8.5.2 Group Homes and Nontraditional Families
  §12.8.6 Religion
  §12.8.7 National Origin
§12.9 Economic Discrimination
  §12.9.1 Intentional Wealth-Based Discrimination
  §12.9.2 Exclusionary Zoning
  §12.9.3 The Right to Be Somewhere: Homelessness and Public Loitering Laws

§12.1 Introduction

Laws regulating discriminatory practices

Discriminatory practices in the selling, financing, and renting of real property have long been a problem in the United States. Nor is this problem of merely historical interest: "Housing in the United States continues to be characterized by high levels of racial segregation and unlawful discrimination."[1] Most of the law that has developed in this area has concerned discrimination in the housing market, although discrimination has also been evident in commercial real estate.[2] Regulation of such practices began on the federal level with the *Civil Rights Act of 1866*,[3] a post–Civil War statute that provides, at 42 U.S.C. §1982, that "[a]ll citizens of the United States shall have the same right in every State and Territory, as is enjoyed by white citizens thereof to inherit, purchase, lease, sell, hold, and convey real and personal property."[4] Capacious as this statute seems to be, it had little effect on discriminatory practices for 100 years; it was interpreted as prohibiting state action mandating discrimination, but it was thought to permit private discrimination. This situation changed dramatically in 1968 for two reasons. First, the passage of the *Fair Housing Act*, Title VIII of the *Civil Rights Act of 1968*,[5] outlawed discrimination on the basis of race, color, religion, and national origin in housing transactions. Second, a major Supreme Court decision in *Jones v. Alfred H. Mayer Co.*[6] breathed life into the *Civil Rights Act of 1866*, reinterpreting it to regulate private discrimination as well as prohibiting public laws mandating racial discrimination.

Public and private discrimination

The *Fair Housing Act* (*FHA*) is the core of federal antidiscrimination law concerning real property. It outlaws private discrimination in housing transactions, including the selling, renting, advertising, and financing of housing. It outlaws racially discriminatory covenants, as well as discriminatory brokerage practices. In addition, the *FHA* prohibits discrimination by government entities, whether exercised through discriminatory zoning laws or public housing siting decisions.

Intentional discrimination and disparate impact claims

The *FHA* prohibits both *intentional discrimination* and facially neutral policies that have an unwarranted *disparate impact* on protected groups.[7] In 1974, Congress added sex as a prohibited form of discrimination[8] and, with the *Fair Housing Amendments Act of 1988*,[9] added discrimination on the basis of "handicap" along with discrimination against families with children. Thus, the *FHA* now prohibits discrimination based on race, color,

[1] Robert G. Schwemm, *Housing Discrimination: Law and Litigation* §2.1 (2025).

[2] Two excellent treatises are Robert G. Schwemm, *Housing Discrimination: Law and Litigation* (2025) and James A. Kushner, *Fair Housing: Discrimination in Real Estate, Community Development and Revitalization* (2d ed. 1995).

[3] Act of Apr. 9, 1866, ch. 31, §1, 14 Stat. 27 (codified at 42 U.S.C. §1982).

[4] 42 U.S.C. §1982.

[5] Pub. L. No. 90-284; 82 Stat. 73 (codified as amended at 42 U.S.C. §§3601 to 3619 & 3631).

[6] 392 U.S. 409 (1968).

[7] *See Raytheon Co. v. Hernandez*, 540 U.S. 44 (U.S. 2003) (explaining the difference between discriminatory treatment and disparate impact claims in the employment context).

[8] *Housing and Community Development Act of 1974*, Pub. L. No. 93-383, §808, 88 Stat. 633, 729.

[9] Pub. L. No. 100-430, 102 Stat. 1619.

religion, sex, national origin, disability, and familial status (families with children). States and many municipalities have also enacted fair housing laws, some of which address types of discrimination not covered by federal law, such as discrimination based on marital status, pregnancy, medical condition, ancestry, citizenship, military status, source of income, status as a victim of intimate partner violence, and other characteristics.[10]

Policies underlying fair housing laws

The policies underlying fair housing laws would seem to be self-explanatory. The United States has a long and shameful history of racial discrimination, ranging from slavery to segregation, in the areas of employment and housing segregation. The purpose of the fair housing laws is to prohibit public and private acts that have the intent or effect of denying access to housing because of race, religion, sex, familial status, or disability.[11] Such laws are based on notions of social justice and opposition to forms of social life based on racial hierarchy or forced separation.

Efficiency justifications

Antidiscrimination laws have sometimes been justified on the ground of efficiency.[12] One argument is that, if people had perfect information, they would not be prejudiced; such laws therefore give people what they would want if they had all the relevant information. A different argument is that racial and other forms of prejudice have harmful externalities on society as a whole, that the costs of deferring to such prejudices outweigh the benefits, that transaction costs prevent those who wish to prevent discrimination from contracting with those who seek to engage in it, and that regulatory

[10] *See, e.g.*, Ala. Code §24-8-4; Alaska Stat. §§18.80.210, 18.80.240; Ariz. Rev. Stat. §§41-1491 to 41-1491.37; Ark. Code Ann. §§16-123-201 to 16-123-210; Cal. Civ. Code §§51 to 53; Cal. Gov't Code §12955; Colo. Rev. Stat. §§23-34-501 to 23-34-509; Conn. Gen. Stat. §§46a-81a & 46a-81e; Del. Code tit. 6, §§4601 to 4620; D.C. Code §§2-1402.21 to 2-1402.24; Fla. Stat. §§760.20 to 760.37; Ga. Code §§8-3-200 to 8-3-223; Haw. Rev. Stat. §§368-1 to 368-17; Idaho Code §§67-5901 to 67-5912; 775 Ill. Comp. Stat. 5/1-102 to 5/1-103, 5/3-101 to 5/3-106; Ind. Code §§22-9.5-1-1 to 22-9.5-11-3; Iowa Code §§216.1 to 216.2, 216.8 to 216.8A, §§216.11 to 216.20; Kan. Stat. §§44-1015 to 44-1044; Ky. Rev. Stat. §§344.010, 344.360 to 344.450; La. Rev. Stat. §§51:2601 to 51:2614; Me. Rev. Stat. tit 5, §§4581-4583; Md. Code, State Gov't §§20-701 to 20-1203; Mass. Gen. Laws ch. 151B, §§1 to 10; Mich. Comp. Laws §§37.2501 to 37.2507; Minn. Stat. §§363A.01 to 363A.20; Miss. Code §43-33-723 (applies only to Mississippi Home Corp.); Mo. Rev. Stat. §§213.010 to 213.137; Mont. Code §§49-2-301 to 49-2-311; Neb. Rev. Stat. §§20-301 to 20-344; Nev. Rev. Stat. §§118.010 to 118.120; N.H. Rev. Stat. §§354-A:1 to 354-A:5, 354-A:8 to 354-A:15, 354-A:18 to 354-A:26; N.J. Stat. §§10:5-1 to 10:5-49; N.M. Stat. §§28-1-1 to 28-1-15; N.Y. Exec. §§291, 296 to 301; N.C. Gen. Stat. §§41A-1 to 41A-10; N.D. Cent. Code §§14-02.5-01 to 14-02.5-46; Ohio Rev. Code §§4112.01 to 4112.024; Okla. Stat. tit. 25, §§1451 to 1453; Or. Rev. Stat. §§659A.421 to 659A.425; Pa. Cons. Stat. tit. 43, §§951 to 963; R.I. Gen. Laws §§34-37-1 to 34-37-11; S.C. Code §§31-21-10 to 31-21-150; S.D. Codified Laws §§20-13-20 to 20-13-56; Tenn. Code §§4-21-601 to 4-21-607; Tex. Prop. §§301.021 to 301.027; Utah Code §§57-21-1 to 57-21-14; Vt. Stat. tit. 9, §§4500 to 4507; Va. Code §§36-96.1 to 36-96.23; Wash. Rev. Code §§49.60.010 to 49.60.401; W. Va. Code §§16B–18–1 to 16B–18–20; Wis. Stat. §§106.50 to 106.58.

[11] The *Civil Rights Act of 1866* prohibits racial discrimination in all contracts or transactions involving real or personal property, not just transactions involving residential housing. 42 U.S.C. §§1981 & 1982. *See* §12.2.3.

[12] *See, e.g.*, John J. Donohue III, *Is Title VII Efficient?*, 134 U. Pa. L. Rev. 1411 (1986); John J. Donohue III, *Further Thoughts on Employment Discrimination Legislation: A Reply to Judge Posner*, 136 U. Pa. L. Rev. 523 (1987); Edward M. Iacobucci, *Antidiscrimination and Affirmative Action Policies: Economic Efficiency and the Constitution*, 36 Osgoode Hall L.J. 293 (1998); Jennifer Bennett Shinall, *Less Is More: Procedural Efficacy in Vindicating Civil Rights*, 68 Ala. L. Rev. 49 (2016).

laws are thus needed to promote social welfare. Of course, some scholars have argued that antidiscrimination laws are inefficient because they prevent individuals from satisfying strong discriminatory preferences, because stereotypes are reasonable proxies for legitimate judgments about who is most qualified or eligible for housing or employment benefits, or because the market can be trusted to weed out inefficient discrimination over time and that the discrimination that is left promotes, rather than decreases, social welfare.[13]

Justice

These efficiency arguments seem out of place, however, geared as they are to satisfying human preferences. Antidiscrimination law seems to be one area where the law is not attempting to defer to individual preferences but to ignore or change them. The point of a fair housing law is to refuse to defer to discriminatory preferences on the grounds that such preferences are wrong and should not be indulged, at least in areas of social and economic life in which individuals interact in the marketplace. As Justice Potter Stewart wrote in *Jones v. Alfred Mayer Co.*,[14] "a dollar in the hands of a Negro [should] purchase the same thing as a dollar in the hands of a white man."[15]

§12.2 Intentional Racial or National-Origin Discrimination

§12.2.1 U.S. Constitution

Equal protection clause regulates state action

The Constitution prohibits both the federal and state governments from "denying equal protection of the laws."[16] The equal protection clause has been held to regulate "state action" but not private action.[17] This means that the equal protection clause prohibits discriminatory provisions in federal and state laws but does not require private individuals to abide by nondiscriminatory norms. Thus, state laws that mandate racial segregation are invalid under the equal protection clause of the Fourteenth Amendment, but a landlord who refuses to rent to a tenant because of that tenant's race has not violated the equal protection clause, although she may well have violated federal or state antidiscrimination statutes.

Prohibition of racial zoning

In the 1917 case of *Buchanan v. Warley*,[18] the Supreme Court struck down a Louisville, Kentucky, ordinance that prohibited Black people from buying a house on any block where a majority of owners were white. Conversely, the ordinance prohibited white people from purchasing homes on a block where the majority of owners were Black. The Court held that

[13] *See, e.g.*, Richard A. Posner, *The Economics of Justice* 351-363 (1981); Richard A. Posner, *The Efficiency and the Efficacy of Title VII*, 136 U. Pa. L. Rev. 513 (1987); Richard A. Epstein, *Forbidden Grounds: The Case Against Employment Discrimination Laws* (1992).

[14] 392 U.S. 409 (1968).

[15] *Id.* at 443.

[16] U.S. Const. amend. V (federal government) & amend. XIV (state governments); *Bolling v. Sharpe*, 347 U.S. 497 (1954).

[17] *The Civil Rights Cases*, 109 U.S. 3, 17 (1883).

[18] 245 U.S. 60 (1917).

both the equal protection clause of the Fourteenth Amendment and the *Civil Rights Act of 1866* granted individuals the right to purchase property free from state laws discriminating against them "solely because of [their] color."[19] In 1927, the Court struck down a similar ordinance in *Harmon v. Tyler*,[20] despite the fact that it allowed sales with the "written consent of a majority of the persons of the opposite race inhabiting such community."

No enforcement of racially restrictive covenants

In 1948, the Supreme Court held in *Shelley v. Kraemer*[21] that the equal protection clause barred enforcement of racially restrictive covenants. Because the equal protection clause has been interpreted to regulate state action, but not private action,[22] no violation occurs when owners enter into such covenants or when they refuse to sell or rent because of the buyer's or renter's race. Only when a party seeks aid of a court to enforce the covenant, does the equal protection clause come into play. Thus, the Court's decision in *Shelley* did not stop owners from entering such covenants, which remained common until they were themselves made unlawful by the *Fair Housing Act* in 1968. In 1953, the Supreme Court extended *Shelley v. Kraemer* by ruling in *Barrows v. Jackson*[23] that the equal protection clause barred a damages award against a property owner who violated a racially restrictive covenant.

▷ RACIALLY RESTRICTIVE TRUSTS — **HARD CASE ◀**

In *Evans v. Abney*,[24] a donor conveyed property in trust to the city of Macon, Georgia, mandating that the property be used as a park for white persons only. When the Supreme Court held that the equal protection clause prohibited the park from being limited to white persons,[25] the Georgia Supreme Court on remand held that the trust had failed and should revert to the heirs of the grantor. Black citizens of the city sued, claiming that closing a public park to prevent it from being desegregated violated the equal protection clause. The Supreme Court disagreed, holding that, under Georgia property law, the trust ended as soon as the wishes of the donor could not be fulfilled and ownership of the trust property reverted automatically to the grantor's heirs. Because the discriminatory intent was not the state's but the grantor's, because the interest in the heirs was already vested under state law, and because ownership shifted automatically to the retained interest of the grantor's heirs, the Court found that the termination of the city's property right did not constitute "state action."[26]

[19] *Id.* at 79.
[20] 273 U.S. 668 (1927). *See also City of Richmond v. Deans*, 281 U.S. 704 (1930).
[21] 334 U.S. 1 (1948).
[22] This principle was first established in *The Civil Rights Cases*, 109 U.S. 3 (1883), which struck down as unconstitutional the federal *Public Accommodations Law of 1875*.
[23] 346 U.S. 249 (1953).
[24] 396 U.S. 435 (1970).
[25] *Evans v. Newton*, 382 U.S. 296, 300 (1966).
[26] *Id.* at 317-318. *See Charlotte Park and Recreation Comm'n v. Barringer*, 88 S.E.2d 114 (N.C. 1955) (similar case involving possibility of reverter); *Hermitage Methodist Homes of Virginia, Inc. v. Dominion Trust Co.*, 387 S.E.2d 740 (Va. 1990) (approving an executory interest

In addition, the Court held that, even if state action were present, there was no denial of "equal protection" because both white and black citizens were equally deprived of the right to use the park.[27]

Critique of result in *Evans v. Abney*

In dissent, Justice Brennan argued that the decision to close the park was clearly state action. Moreover, deprivation of the right to use a public park that had been used by white citizens for many years treated the Black citizens of Macon unequally by denying them a right that they would have been granted had they been white.[28] In a similar case, the Colorado Supreme Court refused to enforce a racially restrictive condition that provided for an automatic executory interest in the neighbors if the property were ever sold or leased to a Black person.[29] Rejecting the contention that no state action was involved in divesting the present estate and transferring title to the future interest holders, the court commented: "No matter by what ariose terms the covenant under consideration may be classified by astute counsel, it is still a racial restriction in violation of the Fourteenth Amendment to the Federal Constitution."[30] The form of the restriction was less important than its substance. "High sounding phrases or outmoded common law terms cannot alter the effect of the agreement embraced in the instant case. While the hands may seem to be the hands of Esau to a blind Isaac, the voice is definitely Jacob's."[31] ◀

Prohibition of state constitutional rights to discriminate

In *Reitman v. Mulkey*,[32] the Supreme Court struck down an amendment to the California constitution, adopted by referendum, that repealed the state's fair housing law and any local fair housing ordinances. Because the effect of the referendum was to free owners to engage in discrimination, one might imagine that it would be viewed as a deregulatory law. The new law did not require anyone to discriminate, but merely enshrined in the state constitution the right to refuse to sell or lease one's property to "such person or persons as he, in his absolute discretion, chooses." Given the fact that the Court had interpreted the equal protection clause to prohibit discriminatory state action but not to prohibit discriminatory private action, one might have thought that the Court would approve the law. If it had, the only remedy would be a new amendment to the state constitution or a federal law overriding the state law.[33] However, the Supreme Court held the amendment to the California constitution to be unconstitutional because

---

divesting a school of the income from a private trust when it admitted nonwhite students because the executory interest vested automatically without "state action" and the holder of the executory interest was not required to discriminate so no continuing discrimination would exist).

[27] *But see Palmer v. Thompson*, 403 U.S. 217 (1971) (holding that it does not violate the equal protection clause to close a public swimming pool to prevent it from being integrated because there is no continuing discrimination; both white and Black residents are deprived of the right to swim).

[28] 396 U.S. at 450-459 (Brennan, J., dissenting).

[29] *Capitol Federal Savings & Loan Ass'n v. Smith*, 316 P.2d 252 (Colo. 1957).

[30] *Id.* at 255.

[31] *Id.*

[32] 387 U.S. 369 (1967).

[33] Federal laws that contradict state laws preempt those laws under the supremacy clause of the Constitution. U.S. Const. art. VI(2).

the right to discriminate was now enshrined in the state constitution. Not only were Californians free to engage in racial discrimination, their state constitution also deprived them of the power to lobby for legislation that would outlaw such discrimination. The constitution not only permitted but "authorized" discrimination, making the "right to discriminate one of the basic policies of the state."[34]

Intent required under equal protection clause

In *Village of Arlington Heights v. Metropolitan Housing Development Corp.*,[35] the Supreme Court held that a municipality's refusal to rezone a particular parcel to allow the construction of racially integrated low- and moderate-income housing would not constitute a violation of the equal protection clause unless it could be demonstrated that the municipality had acted with racially discriminatory intent.[36] No equal protection violation results solely because official actions have a racially disproportionate impact.[37] The result in *Village of Arlington Heights* is arguably inconsistent with the result in *Shelley v. Kraemer*,[38] which held that it was a violation of the equal protection clause to enforce a private racially discriminatory covenant even though there was no evidence that the court or the state had any discriminatory intent. Yet both *Shelley* and *Arlington Heights* remain the law. Perhaps they can be reconciled by noting that the state courts in *Shelley* would have refused to enforce certain types of covenants (such as general restraints on alienation), and thus the choice to enforce racially restrictive covenants but not other restraints on alienation demonstrated that the state approved of racial restrictions.

Criticism

▷ REMEDIES FOR DISCRIMINATION **HARD CASE ◀**

In *Walker v. City of Mesquite*,[39] the court found that both the Department of Housing and Urban Development (HUD) and the city of Dallas had intentionally discriminated on the basis of race by placing public housing so as to prevent Black people from moving into white areas of the city. As a partial remedy for this unlawful act, the court ordered new public housing to be built in white areas until there were as many units in white areas as

[34] 387 U.S. at 380-381. *But see City of Cuyahoga Falls v. Buckeye Community Hope Foundation*, 538 U.S. 188 (2003); *Eastlake v. Forest City Enterprises, Inc.*, 426 U.S. 668 (1976) (use of referendum to decide land use issues does not violate the equal protection clause).

[35] 429 U.S. 252 (1977).

[36] The requirement that intent be proved when a state action is challenged through a heightened standard of scrutiny under the equal protection clause was established in *Washington v. Davis*, 426 U.S. 229 (1976). *See also City of Cuyahoga Falls v. Buckeye Community Hope Foundation*, 538 U.S. 188 (2003). Outside of intentional discrimination, courts generally apply deferential rational-basis scrutiny to equal protection claims. *But see Bush v. Gore*, 531 U.S. 98 (2000) (finding an equal protection violation in the absence of intentional discrimination when a neutral standard could not be evenhandedly applied).

[37] Note that such a claim can be made under the *Fair Housing Act*, 42 U.S.C. §§3601 *et seq. See* §12.8.1.

[38] 334 U.S. 1 (1948). *See also Hurd v. Hodge*, 334 U.S. 24 (1948) (holding that the *Civil Rights Act of 1866*, 42 U.S.C. §1982, barred judicial enforcement of restrictive covenants in the District of Columbia).

[39] 169 F.3d 973 (5th Cir. 1999).

in areas dominated by minority inhabitants. This order was challenged by white owners who argued that the placement of low-income housing in their neighborhoods would lower their property values and that singling their neighborhoods out because of the race of the inhabitants violated the equal protection clause. The Fifth Circuit agreed with this challenge, striking down this remedy. Racial classifications are subject to strict scrutiny;[40] even though the remedy served the compelling state interest of redressing racial discrimination, the court found that it was not narrowly tailored to further that interest because a non-racial remedy was available, *i.e.*, granting Section 8 certificates that would enable poor families to afford housing in white areas of the city. The decision can be criticized on the ground that one cannot provide a remedy for intentional racial segregation perpetrated by public officials without taking race into account. The idea that Section 8 certificates may work to create desegregation is premised on acknowledging the racial composition of the poor. Professor Martha Mahoney argues that it was "bizarre" for the court to call "'race neutral' a plan to give certificates to Black people who were victims of discrimination, even when it approves sending these tenants to 'nonblack' neighborhoods, but it calls 'race-conscious' a plan to put two small apartment complexes into white neighborhoods."[41] Professor Michelle Adams adds that "[b]oth modes of remedial action sought exactly the same race-conscious end: the placement of minority tenants in white neighborhoods."[42] ◀

§12.2.2 Fair Housing Act of 1968

Protected individuals

§12.2.2.1 Prohibited Bases of Discrimination. The *FHA*[43] prohibits discrimination in the housing market on the basis of race, color, religion ("creed"), sex, familial status, national origin, or disability ("handicap").[44] The courts have treated race and color discrimination as comprising the same conduct. National-origin discrimination is distinct from racial discrimination but may overlap with it. Discrimination against Latinos, for example, is sometimes treated as race discrimination[45] and sometimes as national-origin discrimination.[46] The original Act in 1968 contained only race, color, creed, and national origin. Sex was added in 1974,[47] and both familial status and disability were added by the *Fair Housing Amendments*

[40] *Adarand Constructors, Inc. v. Pena*, 515 U.S. 200 (1995).

[41] Martha R. Mahoney, *Whiteness and Remedy: Under-Ruling Civil Rights in* Walker v. City of Mesquite, 85 Cornell L. Rev. 1309, 1351-1352 (2000).

[42] Michelle Adams, *Intergroup Rivalry, Anti-Competitive Conduct and Affirmative Action*, 82 B.U. L. Rev. 1089, 1148 (2002).

[43] 42 U.S.C. §§3601 to 3619 & 3631.

[44] *Id.* at §3604(a), (f).

[45] *Davis v. Boyle-Midway, Inc.*, 615 F. Supp. 560 (N.D. Ga. 1985) (interpreting *Civil Rights Act of 1866* and concluding that discrimination against Hispanics may be race-based).

[46] *United States v. Sea Winds of Marco, Inc.*, 893 F. Supp. 1051, 1053 (M.D. Fla. 1995) (national-origin discrimination).

[47] *Housing and Community Development Act of 1974*, Pub. L. No. 93-383, §808, 88 Stat. 633, 729.

Act (FHAA) in 1988.[48] Familial status refers to families with children, protecting such families from being denied housing because of the presence of children.[49]

§12.2.2.2 Covered Dwellings. The *FHA*[50] regulates the residential real estate market. Section 3601 declares that "it is the policy of the United States to provide, within constitutional limitations, for fair housing throughout the United States."[51] The operative sections prohibit various forms of discrimination in transactions involving "dwellings." "Dwelling" is defined as "any building, structure, or portion thereof which is occupied as, or designed or intended for occupancy as, a residence by one or more families, and any vacant land which is offered for sale or lease for the construction or location thereon of any such building, structure, or portion thereof."[52] It should be noted that the term "family" is defined to include "a single individual."[53]

Dwellings

▷ NURSING HOMES, COLLEGE DORMITORIES **HARD CASE ◀**

Does the *FHA* apply to facilities such as nursing homes or college dormitories or orphanages? One might argue that they are dwellings because they are places in which people live. On the other hand, one might argue that such facilities are commercial or institutional in nature, rather than "residential," and thus should not be considered dwellings. Or one might analogize them to hotels, which are not generally thought to constitute dwellings because patrons ordinarily stay in hotels for only brief periods of time.[54] Similarly, one could adopt the position that a dwelling is a place in which one "resides," and this means that one intends to stay there for a significant period of time. This standard is the one the courts seem to have adopted.[55] What constitutes a "significant period" is open to question; it might mean more than a few days, or that the residence is one's home for the time being. The statute has been held to cover nursing homes,[56] college dormitories,[57]

[48] Pub. L. No. 100-430, 102 Stat. 1619.

[49] 42 U.S.C. §3602(k).

[50] *Id.* at §§3601 to 3619 & 3631.

[51] *Id.* at §3601.

[52] *Id.* at §3602(b).

[53] *Id.* at §3602(c).

[54] *Schwarz v. City of Treasure Island*, 544 F.3d 1201, 1214 (11th Cir. 2008).

[55] *Lakeside Resort Enters., LP v. Board of Supervisors of Palmyra Township*, 455 F.3d 154 (2d Cir. 2006) (holding that a drug- and alcohol-treatment facility constituted a dwelling based on the length of the stay); *United States v. Columbus Country Club*, 915 F.2d 877, 881 (3d Cir. 1990); *United States v. Hughes Memorial Homes*, 396 F. Supp. 544, 549 (W.D. Va. 1975); Robert G. Schwemm, *Housing Discrimination: Law and Litigation* §9.2 (2025).

[56] *Montano v. Bonnie Brae Convalescent Hosp. Inc.*, 79 F. Supp. 3d 1120, 1125 (C.D. Cal. 2015); *Hovsons, Inc. v. Township of Brick*, 89 F.3d 1096 (3d Cir. 1996); *United States v. Lorantffy Care Center*, 999 F. Supp. 1037 (N.D. Ohio 1998); *United States v. Commonwealth of Puerto Rico*, 764 F. Supp. 220 (D.P.R. 1991).

[57] *United States v. University of Nebraska at Kearny*, 940 F. Supp. 2d 974 (D. Neb. 2013); *Hack v. President and Fellows of Yale College*, 16 F. Supp. 2d 183 (D. Conn. 1998).

and time-share condominiums.[58] Excluded are most hotels, which are regulated, not by the *FHA*, but by federal and state public accommodations laws and by §1981 of the *Civil Rights Act of 1866*.[59] ◀

▶ **HARD CASE**

▷ HOMELESS SHELTERS

Does the *FHA* cover homeless shelters? Under the definition given above, one might argue that the Act covers shelters in which families or individuals stay for extended periods of time,[60] but does not cover shelters in which individuals merely stay overnight. This resolution does not help much if some individuals stay for extended times and others stay only overnight. Perhaps the result should turn on the usual use of the facility. One might argue that defining "dwelling" on the basis of how long individuals stay is appropriate because it is intended to apply to one's home (even one's home for the time being), but not to public accommodations such as hotels. On the other hand, perhaps the *FHA* should be held to apply to all residential facilities regardless of the length of stay because determining a precise line between "hotels" and "dwellings" will be difficult and imprecise. Homeless shelters are places in which people without homes dwell, and on this basis some courts have applied the *FHA* to homeless shelters without regard to length of stay.[61] If the purpose of the *FHA* is to prevent discrimination in the housing market so that shelter may be found without regard to race, then this purpose would be served by applying the *FHA* to homeless shelters regardless of the length of stay. ◀

Overview

§12.2.2.3 EXEMPTIONS. The FHA has a number of important exemptions. One set, in §3603, concerns the type of dwelling involved. Another, in §3607(a), provides exemptions for religious organizations and private clubs. A final set, in §3607(b), contains an exemption to the familial status provisions when housing is reserved for older persons.

[58] *Louisiana Acorn Fair Housing v. Quarter House, Inc.*, 952 F. Supp. 352 (E.D. La. 1997).

[59] The federal public accommodations law, Title II of the *Civil Rights Act of 1964*, 42 U.S.C. §§2000a to 2000a-6, provides for injunctive relief but not damages. Damages, however, may be obtained under 42 U.S.C. §1981, the section of the *Civil Rights Act of 1866* guaranteeing the right to contract, which would allow damages if a hotel refuses to enter into a contract with a prospective guest because of race. *See* §§2.6.1 & 2.6.2.

[60] *See, e.g.*, *Boykin v. Gray*, F. Supp. 2d 199, 206-207 (D.D.C. 2012) (homeless shelter is covered by the Act based partly on residents' ability to stay habitually and regularly at shelter without imposition of time limits); *Defiore v. City Rescue Mission of New Castle*, 995 F. Supp. 2d 413, 418-419 (W.D. Pa. 2013) (emergency homeless shelter is "dwelling" under §3602(b) based on factors such as expected extended length of stay, fact that residents receive mail, residents receive medication from shelter staff, and residents have designated sleeping areas). *But see Jenkins v. N.Y. City Dep't of Homeless Services*, 643 F. Supp. 2d 507 (S.D.N.Y. 2009) (handicap provisions do not apply to homeless shelters because they only apply to a "renter or buyer"); *Intermountain Fair Housing Council v. Boise Rescue Mission Ministries*, 717 F. Supp. 2d 1101, 1101 (D. Idaho 2010) (homeless shelter not a "dwelling" under §3602(b) based on context-specific factors including limiting residents to 17 consecutive night stays and forbidding residents from staying in the shelter during the day).

[61] *Turning Point, Inc. v. City of Caldwell*, 74 F.3d 941 (9th Cir. 1996).

Single-family homes sold without a broker

Section 3603(b)(1) provides that the *FHA* does not apply to "any single family house sold or rented by an owner."[62] However, the exemption applies *only* (1) if the owner owns no more than three such dwellings *and* (2) does not use a broker *and* (3) has not posted a discriminatory advertisement, posting, mailing, or notice in violation of §3604(c).[63] Moreover, it applies only to single-family "houses" rented by "owners." It does not apply, for example, to a sublet by a tenant of an apartment.[64]

Owner-occupied four-family dwellings

Owners are also exempt under §3603(b)(2) if (1) they occupy one of the units in a multi-unit dwelling and (2) the dwelling contains no more than four units.[65] This provision applies only when the units are separate and contain families (or individuals) "living independently of each other."[66] In addition, the owner must "actually" maintain and occupy the unit "as his residence."[67]

No exemption from §3604(c)

It is crucial to note that the exemptions in §3603 for single-family homes and owner-occupied multi-unit dwellings do not apply to the provisions in §3604(c) prohibiting discriminatory advertisements.[68] Thus, although §3603 exempts some owners from the antidiscrimination requirements of §3604, they are not entitled to post an advertisement in the newspaper stating a racial preference.

No exemption from §1982

Moreover, even though, in some circumstances, owners of single-family homes and owner-occupied residences in multi-unit dwellings may be exempt from the antidiscrimination provisions of the *FHA*, they are not exempt from the *Civil Rights Act of 1866*, 42 U.S.C. §1982.[69] That provision has been interpreted to prohibit racial discrimination in *all* real estate transactions and thus applies to the properties otherwise exempt from the *FHA*.[70]

Religious organizations and private clubs

Section 3607(a) contains an exemption for religious organizations, who are entitled to limit the sale, rental, or occupancy of dwellings that they own or operate "for other than a commercial purpose to persons of the same religion, or from giving preference to such persons, unless membership in such religion is restricted on account of race, color, or national origin."[71] To take advantage of this section, an owner must really be a religious institution and not merely an owner attempting to avoid the *FHA* prohibitions against discrimination because of religion.[72] Section 3607(a) further provides that the *FHA* is inapplicable to "a private club not in fact

[62] 42 U.S.C. §3603(b)(1).

[63] *Id.*

[64] *Thurmond v. Bowman*, 211 F. Supp. 3d 554, 562 n.5 (W.D.N.Y. 2016).

[65] 42 U.S.C. §3603(b)(2).

[66] *Id.*

[67] *Id.*

[68] *Id.* at §3604(c).

[69] Robert G. Schwemm, *Housing Discrimination: Law and Litigation* §§9.3-9.5 (2025).

[70] Note, however, that §1982 prohibits only racial discrimination; it does not regulate sex discrimination, religious discrimination, or disability discrimination, or any other category otherwise covered by the *FHA*.

[71] 42 U.S.C. §3607(a).

[72] *See United States v. Columbus Country Club*, 915 F.2d 877, 882-883 (3d Cir. 1990) (holding the exemption inapplicable to a recreational club that restricted leasehold rights to Roman Catholics).

open to the public, which as an incident to its primary purpose or purposes provides lodgings which it owns or operates for other than a commercial purpose, from limiting the rental or occupancy of such lodgings to its members or from giving preference to its members."[73]

Housing for older persons

Although the *FHA* was amended in 1988 to prohibit discrimination against families with children, §3607(b) contains an exemption from this regulation, allowing owners to exclude children if their facilities constitute "housing for older persons." Housing qualifies for this exemption (1) if it is "intended for, and solely occupied by, persons 62 years of age or older";[74] or (2) if it is "intended and operated for occupancy by at least one person 55 years of age or older per unit"[75] and meets three criteria,[76] including (a) "at least 80 percent of the units are occupied by at least one person 55 years of age or older per unit";[77] (b) the owner publishes and adheres to "policies and procedures which demonstrate an intent by the owner or manager to provide housing for persons 55 years of age or older";[78] and (c) the owner complies with regulations designed to verify such occupancy by valid surveys.[79]

Exemption for reasonable occupancy limits

Section 3607(b)(1) exempts "any reasonable local, State, or Federal restrictions regarding the maximum number of occupants permitted to occupy a dwelling."[80] To qualify for this exemption a regulation must be neutrally applicable to similar dwellings, limiting the number of people who can occupy a certain space for safety reasons. If the regulations make distinctions based on the statutory categories, such as sex or race or disability, the regulation will not come within the exemption and will be unlawful if it otherwise violates the *FHA*.[81] In addition, the restriction must be reasonable; a local occupancy standard may not be adopted if the intent is to allow discrimination against families with children and the restriction is not reasonably related to safety concerns.[82]

No protection for convicted drug dealers

Another exemption added by the *FHAA of 1988*[83] permits owners to discriminate against individuals who have been convicted of the manufacture or distribution of illegal drugs.[84] The provision does not appear to preempt state law to the contrary because it merely provides that "nothing in [the *FHA*] prohibits conduct against a person" who has been so convicted. This wording does not affirmatively grant a right to discriminate that would prevail against a contrary state law that prohibited such discrimination.

[73] 42 U.S.C. §3607(a).
[74] *Id.* at §3607(b)(2)(B).
[75] *Id.* at §3607(b)(2)(C).
[76] As originally passed in 1988, the "55 or older" exemption required owners to show that they provided "significant facilities and services specifically designed to meet the physical or social needs of older persons." That provision was repealed by the *Housing for Older Persons Act of 1995*, Pub. L. No. 104-76, 109 Stat. 787.
[77] 42 U.S.C. §3607(b)(2)(C)(i).
[78] *Id.* at §3607(b)(2)(C)(ii).
[79] *Id.* at §3607(b)(2)(C)(iii).
[80] *Id.* at §3607(b)(1) (added to the *FHA* by the *FHAA of 1988*).
[81] *Edmonds v. Oxford House, Inc.*, 514 U.S. 725, 735 (1995).
[82] Robert G. Schwemm, *Housing Discrimination: Law and Litigation* §9.6 (2025).
[83] Pub. L. No. 100-430, 102 Stat. 1619.
[84] 42 U.S.C. §3607(b)(4).

§12.2.2.4 Prohibited Conduct. The core of the *FHA* is §3604,[85] which prohibits a variety of discriminatory acts in the residential real estate market. Other operative sections include §§3605, 3606, and 3617.[86] Section 3604(a) makes it unlawful to "refuse to sell or rent after the making of bona fide offer, or to refuse to negotiate for the sale or rental of, or otherwise make unavailable or deny, a dwelling to any person because of race, color, religion, sex, familial status, or national origin."[87] Note that the statute regulates the housing market, not the commercial real estate market; it prohibits an owner from refusing to sell or rent "a dwelling" because of the race, etc., of the buyer or renter.[88]

§3604(a): Prohibition of discriminatory refusals to sell or rent

In an open-ended phrase, §3604(a)[89] also makes it unlawful to "otherwise mak[e] [a dwelling] unavailable" because of a person's race, etc. This phrase outlaws almost any conceivable conduct that would discriminatorily deny access to housing. This "otherwise make unavailable" language has been interpreted to prohibit racial steering by brokers, the practice of showing buyers of different races houses in different neighborhoods.[90] It has also been held to prohibit discriminatory zoning laws, including those that have an unlawful disparate impact on a protected group.[91] The *FHA* also prohibits discrimination on the basis of disability (called "handicap") in §3604(f). The disability provisions are in a separate paragraph because of a unique series of requirements and exceptions.

§3604(a): "Otherwise make unavailable"

Section 3604(b) makes it unlawful "to discriminate against any person in the terms, conditions, or privileges of sale or rental of a dwelling, or in the provision of services or facilities in connection therewith, because of race, color, religion, sex, familial status, or national origin."[92] This makes it unlawful, for example, to charge a higher rent or provide fewer services to a tenant because of that tenant's race.

§3604(b): Terms and conditions; services

Section 3604(c) makes it unlawful to

§3604(c): Advertisements and statements

> make, print, or publish, or cause to be made, printed, or published any notice, statement, or advertisement, with respect to the sale or rental of

[85] *Id.* at §3604.

[86] While 42 U.S.C. §3604 provides core prohibitions against discriminatory treatment, as well as conduct that has a disparate impact on protected groups, §3605 prohibits discrimination in brokerage and mortgage services offered to potential buyers or renters; §3606 ensures nondiscriminatory access to brokerage services for professional brokers; and §3617 prohibits intimidation, threats, or coercion designed to inhibit anyone from exercising her fair housing rights.

[87] 42 U.S.C. §3604(a).

[88] "Dwelling" is defined at 42 U.S.C. §3602(b) as "any building, structure, or portion thereof which is occupied as, or designed or intended for occupancy as, a residence by one or more families, and any vacant land which is offered for sale or lease for the construction or location thereon of any such building, structure, or portion thereof."

[89] We will refer to sections in the *FHA* without reminding the reader that they appear in Title 42 of the United States Code.

[90] *See* Robert G. Schwemm, *Housing Discrimination: Law and Litigation* §§13.5-13.7 (2025). Such discrimination is also prohibited by 42 U.S.C. §3605.

[91] *LeBlanc-Sternberg v. Fletcher*, 67 F.3d 412, 424-425 (2d Cir. 1995); *see also* Richard Rothstein, *The Color of Law: A Forgotten History of How Our Government Segregated America* (2017).

[92] 42 U.S.C. §3604(b).

> a dwelling that indicates any preference, limitation, or discrimination based on race, color, religion, sex, handicap, familial status, or national origin, or an intention to make any such preference, limitation, or discrimination.[93]

Covenants

This provision makes it unlawful to post an advertisement that expresses a preference or an intent not to sell or rent property on the basis of race or the other protected categories.[94] It also constitutes a violation of §3604(c) to include a racially restrictive covenant in a deed or to record such a covenant. Thus, unlike *Shelley v. Kraemer*,[95] which held that merely entering into a restrictive covenant was not a violation of the equal protection clause, the act of putting such a covenant in writing *is* a direct violation of the *FHA*. The advertising prohibition applies not only to the person who writes the ad but also to the publisher as well. However, although a newspaper will be liable for posting a discriminatory advertisement,[96] a website or Internet service like Craigslist will not because the *Communications Decency Act of 1996*[97] immunizes Internet services providers from liability for third-party material they passively post.[98]

§3604(d): Misrepresentation

Section 3604(d) makes it unlawful "to represent to any person because of race, color, religion, sex, handicap, familial status, or national origin that any dwelling is not available for inspection, sale, or rental when such dwelling is in fact so available."[99]

§3604(e): Blockbusting

Section 3604(e) makes it unlawful "[f]or profit, to induce, or attempt to induce any person to sell or rent any dwelling by representations regarding the entry or prospective entry into the neighborhood of a person or persons of a particular race, color, religion, sex, handicap, familial status, or national origin."[100] This once common practice was called "blockbusting." It occurred when realtors urged white owners to sell their homes because Black people were moving into the neighborhood.

[93] *Id.* at §3604(c).

[94] *See generally* Robert G. Schwemm, *Discriminatory Housing Statements and Section 3604(c): A New Look at the Fair Housing Act's Most Intriguing Provision*, 29 Fordham Urb. L.J. 187 (2001).

[95] 334 U.S. 1 (1948).

[96] *See Ragin v. New York Times*, 923 F.2d 995 (2d Cir. 1991); *see also Inclusive Communities Project, Inc. v. Lincoln Prop. Co.*, 920 F.3d 890, 912 (5th Cir. 2019).

[97] 47 U.S.C. §230(c).

[98] *Chicago Lawyers' Committee for Civil Rights Under the Law, Inc. v. Craigslist, Inc.*, 519 F.3d 666 (7th Cir. 2008). *Compare Fair Housing Council of San Fernando Valley v. Roommate.com, LLC*, 521 F.3d 1157 (9th Cir. 2008) (*Communications Decency Act* immunity does not extend to websites that help create ads through questionnaires that shape roommate profiles by asking for information about sex and familial status and roommate preferences in those categories). A review of roughly 10,000 Craigslist postings in ten cities found that "a significant number of on-line housing ads—roughly several hundred on any given day—violate [§3604(c)]." Rigel C. Oliveri, *Discriminatory Housing Advertisements On-Line: Lessons from Craigslist*, 43 Ind. L. Rev. 1125, 1127-1128 (2010).

[99] 42 U.S.C. §3604(d).

[100] *Id.* at §3604(e).

Section 3605 prohibits discrimination in "real estate-related transactions," including brokerage[101] and appraisal services[102] and in residential real estate finance.[103] The brokerage provision in §3605 makes it unlawful for any real estate broker to "discriminate against any person in making available" a real estate transaction or to discriminate in the terms or conditions of brokerage services. This provision outlaws "steering," the practice of showing white customers homes in mostly white neighborhoods and Black customers homes in predominantly Black communities. In addition, §3606 makes it unlawful

§§3605, 3606: Brokers

> to deny any person access to or membership or participation in any multiple-listing service, real estate brokers' organization or other service, organization, or facility relating to the business of selling or renting dwellings, or to discriminate against him in the terms or conditions of such access, membership, or participation.[104]

This provision ensures that anyone can become a broker without regard to race and have access to the services available to others in the profession.

▷ CAN BROKERS ANSWER CLIENT QUESTIONS? **HARD CASE ◀**

In *Hannah v. Sibcy Cline Realtors*,[105] the court wrestled with the question of whether a real estate broker has a fiduciary duty to a buyer to answer questions about the racial make-up of a community when a mother wanted to live in a racially integrated community so that her children would not be the only Black children in the school. The court found no such obligation and noted that some courts have held that a broker who answers such a question may be liable for unlawful racial steering, while other courts have held that a broker has not engaged in steering when the racial information is provided in response to a buyer's question. ◀

§3605: Mortgages

The real estate finance provisions in §3605 prohibit discrimination in the granting of mortgages and other transactions providing financial assistance to purchase, construct, improve, repair, or maintain dwellings or any other loans secured by residential real estate.[106]

§3617: Coercion, intimidation, or interference with quiet enjoyment

A separate section of the *FHA*, §3617, makes it unlawful

> to coerce, intimidate, threaten, or interfere with any person in the exercise or enjoyment of, or on account of his having exercised or enjoyed, or on account of his having aided or encouraged any other person in the exercise or enjoyment of, any right granted or protected by section 3603, 3604, 3605, or 3606.

[101] *Id.* at §3605(b)(2).
[102] *Id.*
[103] *Id.* at §3605(b)(1).
[104] *Id.* at §3606.
[105] 769 N.E.2d 876 (Ohio Ct. App. 2001).
[106] 42 U.S.C. §3605.

This provision makes it unlawful, for example, to threaten someone or intimidate her to prevent her from moving into a neighborhood.

▶ HARD CASE

▷ LANDLORD'S DUTY TO PREVENT ONE TENANT FROM HARASSING ANOTHER

A landlord who treats one tenant differently from another because of race or sex or another protected category violates the *FHA* by denying equal housing rights. Does a landlord have a duty to prevent one tenant from harassing another on the basis of race, sex, or other covered forms of discrimination? On one hand, it can be argued the landlord is not the cause of the harm and has therefore in no way discriminated on a prohibited basis.[107] However, most leases have terms prohibiting tenants from causing a nuisance or otherwise disturbing the quiet enjoyment of neighbors; some courts may even imply such terms into residential leases. A breach of this obligation entitles the landlord to evict the defaulting tenant and a failure to exercise this power might constitute a wrongful omission that constitutes an act of discrimination.[108] It might even constitute an act of discrimination not to include in a lease a term requiring the tenant not to disturb other tenants, thereby giving the landlord the power to evict for such conduct.

In 2016, HUD promulgated regulations defining discriminatory housing harassment that make clear that a landlord's failure to "fulfill a duty to take prompt action to correct and end a discriminatory housing practice by a third party" may constitute discrimination where the landlord has a duty created by a lease or contract to take such action.[109] Courts, however, have split on when to hold landlords responsible for harassment by one tenant against another. *Wetzel v. Glen St. Andrew Living Community, LLC*[110] addressed a claim against the owner of a residential community for older adults for failing to intervene to protect a resident who "faced a torrent of physical and verbal abuse from other residents because she is openly lesbian" and had repeatedly sought help from the residential community's staff.[111] The court held that landlords may be liable if they knew of discriminatory harassment and evinced deliberate indifference to that harassment.[112] By contrast, *Francis v. Kings Park Manor, Inc.*[113] rejected landlord liability, even though a Black tenant asserted that a fellow tenant repeatedly used racially derogatory language against him and tried intimidation including a death threat. The tenant reported this harassment to the police,

[107] *Ohio Civ. Rights Comm'n v. Akron Metro Hous. Auth.*, 892 N.E.2d 415, 420 (Ohio 2008).
[108] *See Neudecker v. Boisclair Corp.*, 351 F.3d 361 (8th Cir. 2003) (tenant harassed because of disability by other tenants had an *FHA* claim against the landlord who revealed the disability to the other tenants).
[109] 24 C.F.R. §100.7(a)(iii); *Quid Pro Quo and Hostile Environment Harassment and Liability for Discriminatory Housing Practices Under the Fair Housing Act*, 81 Fed. Reg. 63,054 (Sept. 14, 2016).
[110] 901 F.3d 856 (7th Cir. 2018).
[111] *Id.* at 859.
[112] *Id.* at 864-865.
[113] 992 F.3d 67 (2d Cir. 2021).

who informed the landlord, who took no steps in response, but the court nonetheless held that the reason a landlord chose not to intervene had to be motivated by racial animus.[114] ◀

▷ POST-ACQUISITION INTERFERENCE WITH QUIET ENJOYMENT OF PROPERTY **HARD CASE** ◀

Because the *FHA* prohibits discrimination in the "provision of services," it would not allow a landlord to provide unequal services to tenants of different races. However, courts have disagreed about whether the statute applies to post-acquisition discrimination by parties other than landlords. The Fifth Circuit held in *Cox v. Dallas*[115] that Black residents of a neighborhood afflicted with an illegal dump had no remedy against the city that failed to clean it up. The court held that the dump merely made the housing less habitable but did not make it "unavailable" as required by 42 U.S.C. §3604(a), and that the prohibition against discriminatory terms in the sale or rental of a dwelling in §3604(b) did not apply when the city was not the seller or renter of the property. The court did not address §3617.

In contrast, the Seventh Circuit ruled in *Bloch v. Frischholz*[116] that post-acquisition discrimination by a condominium association and its president against Jewish unit owners might well have violated §3617 by "interfer[ing] in the exercise" of rights to nondiscriminatory access to and enjoyment of housing. Similarly, the Ninth Circuit held in *Committee Concerning Community Improvement v. Modesto*[117] that residents of primarily Latino neighborhoods did have *FHA* claims against the city for discriminatory provision of municipal services. The court found that the language in §3604(b) prohibiting discrimination "in the terms, conditions, or privileges of sale or rental of a dwelling, or in provision of services or facilities in connection therewith" did not only apply at the moment of renting or purchasing but "implicated continuing rights, such as the privilege of quiet enjoyment of the dwelling,"[118] and thus applied to post-acquisition enjoyment of property. ◀

Discriminatory treatment v. disparate impact

§12.2.2.5 STANDARDS OF PROOF. Two different types of claims may be brought under the *FHA*. Discriminatory treatment claims cover intentional discrimination, including the denial of the right to buy or rent or the granting of discriminatory terms "because of" the buyer's or renter's race, sex, etc. Disparate impact claims are allegations that a facially neutral policy has an unlawful disparate effect on members of a protected group. Disparate impact claims are covered below in §12.8.

[114] *Id.* at 73-74.
[115] 430 F.3d 734 (5th Cir. 2005).
[116] 587 F.3d 771 (7th Cir. 2009) (en banc).
[117] 583 F.3d 690 (9th Cir. 2009).
[118] *Id.* at 713.

Refusal to deal "because of" race

The prohibition against refusing to rent or sell because of the race, color, national origin, sex, religion, disability, or familial status[119] of the buyer or renter is the most basic protection in the statute. When an owner makes an explicit oral statement of her reason for refusing to rent or sell, a plaintiff may prove intent to discriminate by presenting evidence of the statement.[120] However, when the owner makes no overt admission of discriminatory intent, such proof is hard to come by because proof is in the mind of the defendant. The Supreme Court has never decided a case detailing the standards for proving intentional discrimination in the housing context from circumstantial evidence, but it has established detailed standards for such proof in the employment context, interpreting Title VII of the *Civil Rights Act of 1964* and the *Age Discrimination in Employment Act of 1967*,[121] and the lower federal courts have assumed that a similar approach applies in the case of the *FHA*.

***Prima facie* case**

To facilitate proof of discriminatory intent, the courts have held that a plaintiff may establish a *prima facie* case by showing (1) that she is a member of a racial minority or other protected class; (2) the plaintiff applied for and was qualified to rent or purchase the unit; (3) the plaintiff was denied the opportunity to rent or buy; and (4) the unit remained on the market.[122] Proof of the *prima facie* case establishes a rebuttable presumption of discrimination.[123] Note that these elements are relevant only in cases of a refusal to deal. In other cases, the plaintiff's case will include different elements.[124]

Defendant's rebuttal

Once the plaintiff has proffered evidence sufficient to state a *prima facie* case, the burden shifts to the defendant to produce evidence to show a legitimate, nondiscriminatory reason for the refusal to rent or sell.[125] The reason must be both legitimate and contemporaneous. It must be legiti-

Legitimate, nondiscriminatory reason

mate in the sense that it must provide a reasonable basis for denying the opportunity to rent. Fear that the tenant would not be able to pay the rent is a legitimate reason. In contrast, courts are skeptical of "subjective or

[119] In cases involving refusal to sell or rent, the standards are the same for other protected categories, such as sex or disability, as they are for race.

[120] *See, e.g.*, *Curto v. A Country Place Condominium Association, Inc.*, 921 F.3d 405, 410 (3d Cir. 2019). Of course, the defendant may deny having said what plaintiff alleges she said.

[121] Major cases include *Babb v. Wilkie*, 589 U.S. 399 (2020); *Gross v. FBL Fin. Servs., Inc.*, 557 U.S. 167, 177-178 (2009); *Reeves v. Sanderson Plumbing Products, Inc.*, 530 U.S. 133 (2000); *St. Mary's Honor Center v. Hicks*, 509 U.S. 502 (1993); *Texas Dep't of Community Affairs v. Burdine*, 450 U.S. 248 (1981); *McDonnell Douglas Corp. v. Green*, 411 U.S. 792 (1973).

[122] *Crain v. City of Selma*, 952 F.3d 634, 641 (5th Cir. 2020); *Gilligan v. Jamco Development Corp.*, 108 F.3d 246, 249 (9th Cir. 1997); Robert G. Schwemm, *Housing Discrimination: Law and Litigation* §10.2 (2025).

[123] It does not, however, automatically entitle the plaintiff to win. The evidence presented in the case must be sufficient to convince the factfinder that the actual reason for the refusal to deal was invidious discrimination. *See Reeves v. Sanderson Plumbing Products, Inc.*, 530 U.S. 133 (2000); *St. Mary's Honor Center v. Hicks*, 509 U.S. 502 (1993).

[124] *See, e.g.*, *Radecki v. Joura*, 114 F.3d 115, 116 (8th Cir. 1997) (eviction case); *Gamble v. City of Escondido*, 104 F.3d 300, 305 (9th Cir. 1997) (land use case); *Noland v. Commerce Mortgage Corp.*, 122 F.3d 551, 553 (8th Cir. 1997) (mortgage case); Robert G. Schwemm, *Housing Discrimination: Law and Litigation* §10.2 n.29 (2025).

[125] *Gilligan v. Jamco Development Corp.*, 108 F.3d 246, 249 (9th Cir. 1997); Robert G. Schwemm, *Housing Discrimination: Law and Litigation* §10.2 (2025).

arbitrary reasons," such as disapproval of a prospective tenant's hairstyle.[126] Courts often reject general evaluations of tenants that focus on their appearance or demeanor,[127] instead requiring owners to identify "objective criteria and facts to demonstrate an applicant's ineligibility."[128] On the other hand, some courts have approved such arbitrary reasons if they are applied in a nondiscriminatory manner and are not perceived to be mere covers for discriminatory intent.[129] In addition to being legitimate, the reason must have been the real reason for the refusal to rent or sell.[130] *Post hoc* rationalizations invented after the discriminatory act for the purpose of defense at trial are not sufficient to rebut a *prima facie* case.[131] Defendant's explanations are also suspect if they change several times and thus appear insincere or like covers for discriminatory intent.[132]

Plaintiff's rebuttal: Pretext

Once the defendant proffers evidence of a legitimate, nondiscriminatory reason, the plaintiff will try to show that the reason is pretextual and that the real reason for the refusal to deal was the defendant's intent to discriminate in an unlawful manner. Plaintiff may do this by showing that the reason was not offered at the time and that it is a mere *post hoc* rationalization. Or plaintiff may attempt to show that the reason, even if real and contemporaneous, was not applied in a nondiscriminatory manner.[133]

Burden of proof always remains on plaintiff

Although the *prima facie* case framework shifts the burden of producing evidence onto defendant, it does not shift the burden of proof or burden of persuasion onto the defendant. The plaintiff retains the burden of proving that the actual reason for the refusal to deal is a discriminatory one.[134]

Pretext plus

What happens if the plaintiff proves the *prima facie* case, defendant proffers a legitimate, nondiscriminatory reason, and plaintiff shows, to the factfinder's satisfaction, that the reason is pretextual? Is the plaintiff entitled

[126] Robert G. Schwemm, *Housing Discrimination: Law and Litigation* §10.2 (2025).

[127] *Jordan v. Dellway Villa of Tennessee, Ltd.*, 661 F.2d 588 (6th Cir. 1981); *Marable v. H. Walker & Assocs.*, 644 F.2d 390 (5th Cir. 1981) (court rejects as inadequate landlord's complaint that potential Black tenant "got a little smart"); *United States v. West Peachtree Tenth Corp.*, 437 F.2d 221, 223-224 (5th Cir. 1971).

[128] James A. Kushner, *Fair Housing: Discrimination in Real Estate, Community Development and Revitalization* §3.11, at 195 (2d ed. 1995).

[129] *Frazier v. Rominger*, 27 F.3d 828, 831-833 (2d Cir. 1994) (holding that defendant rental agent had proffered a legitimate, nondiscriminatory reason for refusing to rent when defendant expressed discomfort with plaintiffs because one of them had accused the rental agent of racial discrimination).

[130] James A. Kushner, *Fair Housing: Discrimination in Real Estate, Community Development and Revitalization* §3.12, at 199 (2d ed. 1995).

[131] *Id.* at §3.11; *cf. McKennon v. Nashville Banner Publishing Co.*, 513 U.S. 352, 360-361 (1995) (holding that defendant-employer cannot use after-acquired information to justify a prior discriminatory termination although such information might be relevant to determination of whether plaintiff should be entitled to reinstatement).

[132] James A. Kushner, *Fair Housing: Discrimination in Real Estate, Community Development and Revitalization* §3.12, at 201 (2d ed. 1995).

[133] *See Asbury v. Brougham*, 866 F.2d 1276 (10th Cir. 1989) (defendant did not consistently adhere to expressed "policies").

[134] *Reeves v. Sanderson Plumbing Products, Inc.*, 530 U.S. 133 (2000); *St. Mary's Honor Center v. Hicks*, 509 U.S. 502 (1993).

to win? In *St. Mary's Honor Center v. Hicks*,[135] the Supreme Court held, in an employment discrimination case, that the plaintiff is not necessarily entitled to win in such a case. As Justice O'Connor later explained in *Reeves v. Sanderson Plumbing Products, Inc.*,[136] "[t]he factfinder's rejection of the employer's legitimate, nondiscriminatory reason for its action does not compel judgment for the plaintiff."[137] The mere fact that the defendant's justification for the refusal to contract turns out to be a lie does not, without more, entitle the plaintiff to prevail on a discrimination claim, even if the *prima facie* case has been proved by a preponderance of the evidence. The jury in such a case may still conclude that the actual reason for the discrimination was a nondiscriminatory one. It was thought, after *St. Mary's*, that plaintiff had to present evidence other than the *prima facie* case plus a demonstration that the defendant's reason was pretextual to win — "pretext plus."

However, the Supreme Court ruled in *Reeves* that the jury may well be free to infer from the establishment of the *prima facie* case and the showing of pretext that the actual reason *was* a discriminatory one.[138] In *Reeves*, the Supreme Court clarified *St. Mary's Honor Center* by emphasizing that "the factfinder's disbelief of the reasons put forward by the defendant (particularly if disbelief is accompanied by a suspicion of mendacity), together with the elements of the *prima facie* case, may suffice to show intentional discrimination."[139] This is because

> [p]roof that the defendant's explanation is unworthy of credence is simply one form of circumstantial evidence that is probative of intentional discrimination, and it may be quite persuasive. In appropriate circumstances, the trier of fact can reasonably infer from the falsity of the explanation that the employer is dissembling to cover up a discriminatory purpose.[140]

Thus, a plaintiff's *prima facie* case, combined with sufficient evidence to find that the employer's asserted justification is false, may permit, but does not require, the trier of fact to conclude that the employer unlawfully discriminated.

Proving a municipality acted with discriminatory intent

How does one prove that a municipality engaged in intentional discrimination? If public officials give racist reasons for zoning decisions, the factfinder may be justified in attributing those reasons to the municipality itself. But what if racist statements are made by citizens at public hearings but not by public officials themselves? What if no racist statements are made by anyone? The Second Circuit held in *MHANY Management, Inc. v.*

135 509 U.S. 502 (1993).
136 530 U.S. 133 (2000).
137 *Id.* at 146 (citing *St. Mary's Honor Center v. Hicks*, 509 U.S. 502, 511 (1993)); *see also Gross v. FBL Fin. Servs., Inc.*, 557 U.S. 167, 177-178 (2009) (plaintiff retains the burden to show that discrimination was the but-for cause of an employer's adverse action).
138 530 U.S. 133 (2000).
139 *Id.* at 146 (quoting *St. Mary's Honor Center v. Hicks*, 509 U.S. 502, 511 (1993)).
140 *Id.* at 147.

Cnty. of Nassau[141] that discriminatory intent might be proven by showing that residents used "code words" for discrimination and that public officials deferred to the discriminatory wishes of voters.

▷ DESIRE TO PROMOTE INTEGRATION **HARD CASE ◀**

In a well-known case, the Second Circuit rejected the notion that a landlord may discriminate in access to rental housing when the landlord's goal is to promote integration. In *United States v. Starrett City Associates*,[142] an integrated housing complex established separate wait lists for white and Black tenants, believing that if too high a percentage of Black tenants moved in, the "tipping point" would be reached and there would be "white flight," converting the complex to a mostly Black composition. Dissenting Judge Jon Newman noted that promotion of integration was one of the major goals of the *FHA* and that a benign motive to promote integrated living was not a discriminatory purpose that Congress intended to regulate.[143] The majority opinion by Judge Roger Miner, noted, however, that the *FHA* was intended to combat discrimination as well as to promote integration. The defendant in this case was refusing to allow Black people to rent apartments because of the fear that if too many Black people moved in, whites would move out. In effect, the defendant landlord was denying housing opportunities to plaintiffs, based on their race, out of deference to the desire of white tenants to limit their numbers. The court found the *FHA* to be violated when the extent of housing opportunities for Black people was determined by the extent of prejudice existing in the neighborhood. The court thus held that, when the *FHA*'s nondiscrimination goal conflicts with its integration goal, the nondiscrimination goal prevails. Denial of a housing opportunity because of the prospective tenant's race violates the *FHA* even if the defendant's motive is a benign one of promoting integration. Because defendant would have rented to plaintiff if she were white, defendant has, in such a case, nonetheless refused to rent "because of" the plaintiff's race. ◀

▷ AFFIRMATIVE MARKETING TECHNIQUES **HARD CASE ◀**

In *South Suburban Housing Center v. Greater South Suburban Board of Realtors*,[144] a realtors' multiple listing service refused to list three properties owned by a private fair housing organization that engaged in affirmative efforts to attract white buyers to a historically Black neighborhood. Under the reasoning of *Starrett City*, one might argue that the benign goal of integration should not be achieved by engaging in discrimination. When sales

[141] 819 F.3d 581 (2d Cir. 2016).
[142] 840 F.2d 1096 (2d Cir. 1988).
[143] *Id.* at 1103-1108 (Newman, J., dissenting).
[144] 713 F. Supp. 1068 (N.D. Ill. 1988), *aff'd in part and rev'd in part*, 935 F.2d 868 (7th Cir. 1991).

efforts are directed especially at members of one race, the owner is arguably making the property less available to those who are not targeted. However, the District Court and the Seventh Circuit approved the practice of affirmative marketing designed to attract members of a less-represented group to promote integration. The trial court explained that "[s]ince affirmative marketing does not contemplate the lessening of normal marketing activities designed to reach the racial group most likely to be attracted to the property in question, there is little adverse impact on the availability of the housing in question."[145] The Seventh Circuit distinguished *Starrett City* by noting that the affirmative marketing plan here "does not exclude minorities from housing opportunities,"[146] nor does it deter minority home buyers from seeking to purchase the homes. ◀

Mixed motive cases

When a defendant has acted partly for discriminatory reasons and partly for legitimate reasons, courts have to determine whether the lawful or the unlawful aspect of a decision "caused" the decision or policy to have been made.[147] Reviewing a claim under 42 U.S.C. §1981 that a cable company had discriminated against a network owned by a Black entrepreneur, the U.S. Supreme Court in *Comcast Corp. v. National Ass'n of African American-Owned Media*[148] held that the plaintiff has the burden to prove that "but for" race, the defendant would not have taken the adverse action.[149] *Fair Housing Act* cases have generally applied a more lenient standard that asks instead whether an unlawful reason was "a motivating factor" or similar formulation.[150] This standard allows courts to hold a defendant liable if a prohibited reason contributed to the decision.[151]

Aggrieved person

§12.2.2.6 Standing. The *FHA* allows lawsuits by "aggrieved persons,"[152] which includes anyone who "claims to have been injured by a discriminatory housing practice."[153] In addition, plaintiffs who sue in federal court must have "standing" within the meaning of the Constitution's grant of jurisdiction to federal courts over "cases and controversies."[154] In *Bank of America Corp. v. City of Miami*,[155] the Supreme Court noted that in addition to standing, a party must also be within the Act's "zone of interests," or the type of parties Congress had in mind, to file suit. The city of Miami had

[145] *Id.* at 1087.
[146] 935 F.2d at 883.
[147] *See* Robert G. Schwemm, *Fair Housing and the Causation Standard After* Comcast, 66 Vill. L. Rev. 63, 66 (2021); Robert G. Schwemm, *Housing Discrimination: Law and Litigation* §10.3 (2025).
[148] 589 U.S. 327 (2020).
[149] *Id.* at 331-332; *see also Bostock v. Clayton County*, 590 U.S. 644, 656 (2020) ("but-for" causation asks whether a decision would have been different if the prohibited reason were not involved, even if a defendant can point to some other factor that motivated the decision).
[150] *E.g.*, Saint-Jean v. Emigrant Mortgage Company, 129 F.4th 124, 154 (2d Cir. 2025).
[151] *See* Robert G. Schwemm, *Fair Housing and the Causation Standard After* Comcast, 66 Vill. L. Rev. 63, 75 (2021); *see also* Andrew Verstein, *The Jurisprudence of Mixed Motives*, 127 Yale L.J. 1106, 1141 (2018).
[152] 42 U.S.C. §§3610(a)(1)(A)(i), 3613(a)(1)(A).
[153] *Id.* at §3602(i)(1).
[154] Erwin Chemerinsky, *Federal Jurisdiction* §2.3 (7th ed. 2016).
[155] 581 U.S. 189 (2017).

claimed that two banks discriminated against minority borrowers in the terms of their loans, concentrating defaults in minority communities that cost the city more in police, fire, and code enforcement services to respond to given the resulting neighborhood distress. The Court agreed that the city's alleged economic injuries — "specifically, lost tax revenue and extra municipal services" — brought the city within the *FHA*'s zone of interests, but required a showing that the discrimination "proximately cause[d]" the harm.[156]

Testers

Proving that a realtor has engaged in racial steering often involves the use of "testers."[157] Testers are "individuals who, without an intent to rent or purchase a home or apartment, pose as renters or purchasers for the purpose of collecting evidence of unlawful steering practices."[158] Testing is done, for example, by using one or more persons to pose as a potential buyer in seeking assistance from a realtor. Testers may approach a realtor who has told a Black customer that no housing is available in a certain area; if the realtor shows houses in that area to the white buyer that were not shown to the Black buyer, it may be possible to draw an inference that the realtor was discriminating against the initial buyer on account of her race. Similarly, a white tester may approach a seller to see whether the seller offers different terms than were offered to a prior potential Black purchaser. The Supreme Court held in *Havens Realty Corp. v. Coleman*[159] that testers have standing to bring claims in federal court under the *FHA* against realtors and sellers who have engaged in racial discrimination. Similarly, it held that an organization devoted to promoting equal access to housing could bring a lawsuit against a realtor who engaged in steering if it could demonstrate that the defendant's steering practices caused it to devote extra resources to identify available housing and counteract the defendant's steering practices.[160]

Associational claims

The *FHA* clearly protects white people who are denied housing because of their association with Black people. For example, a white plaintiff proved a violation in *Littlefield v. Mack*[161] when she showed that she was evicted from her apartment and harassed by defendant landlord because her boyfriend was Black. White persons are also entitled to bring an action against a realtor who engaged in racial steering on the ground that they have been denied the "right to the important social, professional, business and economic, political and aesthetic benefits of interracial associations that arise from living in integrated communities free from discriminatory housing

[156] *Id.* at 196-201.
[157] *See, e.g., Gilligan v. Jamco Development Corp.*, 108 F.3d 246 (9th Cir. 1997) (using testers to prove discrimination).
[158] *Havens Realty Corp. v. Coleman*, 455 U.S. 363, 373 (1982).
[159] *Id.*
[160] *Id.* at 363, 379. *Accord Smith v. Pacific Properties & Development Corp.*, 358 F.3d 1097 (9th Cir. 2004) (fair housing organizations that use testers may have standing to bring claims for disability discrimination under *FHA*). *But see Nationwide Mutual Ins. Co. v. Housing Opportunities Made Equal, Inc.*, 523 S.E.2d 217 (Va. 2000), *opinion withdrawn and rehearing granted* (holding that a fair housing organization had no standing to challenge defendant's alleged discriminatory mortgage practices because it was not itself applying for a mortgage).
[161] 750 F. Supp. 1395 (N.D. Ill. 1990).

practices."[162] The *FHA* clearly prohibits discrimination against white persons as well as persons of color, although the plaintiff's burden of proof might be heightened to show that race is actually the reason for the denial of the housing opportunity.[163]

§12.2.2.7 Advertising

▶ HARD CASE ▷ WHAT MESSAGE DOES THE RACE OF MODELS SEND?

Models

Advertisements that limit housing to whites clearly violate §3604(c) of the *FHA*.[164] In *Ragin v. The New York Times Co.*,[165] the court held that a newspaper's practice of publishing real estate advertisements almost always showing white models in a city with a significant minority population might violate the *FHA* by showing a discriminatory preference.[166] Judge Ralph Winter noted that §3604(c) makes it unlawful for an ad to "indicate[] any preference based on race." He concluded that the statute would be violated if the ad "suggests to an ordinary reader that a particular race is preferred or dispreferred for the housing in question."[167] This may mean that the *FHA* has been violated if a choice to include only white models indicates to an ordinary reader a racial preference. "In advertising, a conscious racial decision regarding models thus seems almost inevitable. All the statute requires is that in this make-up-your-own world the creator of an ad not make choices among models that create a suggestion of a racial preference."[168] ◀

Fair Housing Amendments Act of 1988

§12.2.2.8 Remedies. The remedies available under the *FHA* were substantially beefed up in 1988 with the passage of the *FHAA*. The *FHAA* extended the statute of limitations from six months to two years and eliminated a $1,000 limit on punitive damages. The *FHAA* also granted HUD the power to enforce the statute; under prior law, HUD was limited to attempting to resolve disputes by persuading housing providers to comply with the statute.

§3613: Federal court jurisdiction

Under the current Act, aggrieved persons may file a lawsuit in federal court for injunctive relief and for compensatory and punitive damages

[162] *Havens Realty Corp. v. Coleman*, 455 U.S. 363, 376 (1982).

[163] *Cf. Formella v. Brennan*, 817 F.3d 503 (7th Cir. 2016) (heightened scrutiny to prove discrimination against white persons in employment).

[164] *See* 24 C.F.R. §100.75; Robert G. Schwemm, *Housing Discrimination: Law and Litigation* §15.4 (2025).

[165] 923 F.2d 995 (2d Cir. 1991).

[166] *Accord Tyus v. Urban Search Management*, 102 F.3d 256 (7th Cir. 1996).

[167] 923 F.2d at 999.

[168] *Id.* at 1000. *Accord Spann v. Colonial Village, Inc.*, 899 F.2d 24 (D.C. Cir. 1990); *Saunders v. General Services Corp.*, 659 F. Supp. 1042 (E.D. Va. 1986) (holding that exclusive use of white models in advertising literature might operate as a steering method to indicate a racial preference). The *Spann* case was settled in 1995 for $841,000. Ann Mariano, *Mobil Land to Settle Bias Case; Firm's Condo Ads Failed Test on Racial Makeup*, Wash. Post, June 10, 1995, at E01.

from the person who committed the discriminatory act.[169] Since 1988, there is no limit on punitive damages. Employers are vicariously liable for the acts of their employees; thus, real estate brokerage firms may be liable if their brokers violate the Act.[170] However, officers of the corporation are not personally liable unless they acted as an employee or agent of the corporation to direct or approve those discriminatory practices.[171]

HUD mediation

Plaintiffs may choose instead to file a complaint with HUD, which has the power to investigate and mediate the dispute, as well as to hear and adjudicate the complaint. If HUD has certified a state agency as competent to adjudicate fair housing disputes, HUD will refer the complaint to that state agency rather than handle the complaint itself.[172]

State agency enforcement

§3610: HUD enforcement

If HUD itself investigates the complaint and finds reasonable cause to believe a violation of the law has been committed, it must issue a "charge" on behalf of the aggrieved person, explaining the "facts upon which the Secretary has found reasonable cause to believe that a discriminatory housing practice has occurred."[173] When a charge is filed, either the complainant or the respondent may elect to have the complaint heard in federal court rather than in an administrative proceeding held by HUD through an administrative law judge (ALJ).[174] If this option is chosen, HUD will authorize the U.S. Attorney General to file the lawsuit in federal district court, which is entitled to grant both compensatory and punitive damages, as well as injunctive relief.[175] If no party elects to go to federal court, an ALJ will conduct a hearing if the complainant so desires.[176] The ALJ is empowered to issue injunctive relief as well as assessing damages, which are limited to $10,000 for first offenses,[177] $25,000 if the defendant has been adjudged to have committed one other offense within five years before the filing of the charge,[178] and $50,000 if the defendant committed two or more offenses within seven years,[179] except that the penalties for second- and third-time offenses may be imposed without reference to the time limits if the same "natural person" committed them. Either plaintiff or defendant may appeal the ALJ's finding to federal court.[180]

Attorney General enforcement if "pattern or practice of resistance"

In addition to enforcement by HUD or a state agency under 42 U.S.C. §§3610 and 3612 and civil actions in federal court brought by the aggrieved party under 42 U.S.C. §3613, the Attorney General is empowered to bring lawsuits against persons who have engaged in a "pattern or practice of

[169] 42 U.S.C. §3613. *See United States v. Big D Enters.*, 184 F.3d 924 (8th Cir. 1999) ($100,000 punitive damages judgment).

[170] *Meyer v. Holley*, 537 U.S. 280, 286-287 (2003); *see also Rodriguez v. Village Green Realty, Inc.*, 788 F.3d 31, 38 n.7 (2d Cir. 2015); 24 C.F.R. §100.7(b).

[171] *Meyer*, 533 U.S. at 291.

[172] 42 U.S.C. §3610(f).

[173] *Id.* at §3610.

[174] *Id.* at §3612(a).

[175] *Id.* at §3612(o).

[176] *Id.* at §3612(b).

[177] *Id.* at §3612(g)(3)(A).

[178] *Id.* at §3612(g)(3)(B).

[179] *Id.* at §3612(g)(3)(C).

[180] *Id.* at §3610(i).

resistance to the full enjoyment of any rights" granted by the Act under 42 U.S.C. §3614.

§12.2.3 Civil Rights Act of 1866

42 U.S.C. §1982

The *Civil Rights Act of 1866*, codified at 42 U.S.C. §§1981 & 1982, protects the right to contract (§1981) and to purchase or rent real or personal property (§1982) without regard to race. In fair housing litigation today involving race discrimination, it is routine for plaintiffs to base their claims on both the *FHA* and the provisions of the *Civil Rights Act of 1866* (42 U.S.C. §1982) directly applicable to real property. Section 1982 provides that "[a]ll citizens of the United States shall have the same right in every State and Territory, as is enjoyed by white citizens thereof to inherit, purchase, lease, sell, hold, and convey real and personal property."[181] It has been interpreted to apply only to racial discrimination and not to other forms of discrimination, such as sex discrimination.[182]

Jones v. Alfred H. Mayer Co.

Prior to 1968, the courts interpreted §1982 as prohibiting state laws that mandated discrimination, such as zoning laws that mandated racial segregation. However, they had not interpreted the *Civil Rights Act of 1866* as reaching private discriminatory acts by landlords or sellers of real estate. This changed in 1968 with the decision in *Jones v. Alfred H. Mayer Co.*[183] Although controversial at the time, it is now settled law that §§1981 and 1982 reach private discriminatory conduct, particularly because §1981 was amended by the *Civil Rights Act of 1991* so as to enshrine this fact in the statutory language.[184]

Intent is probably required under §1982

Jones clearly holds that §1982 prohibits racially motivated refusals to deal.[185] What other acts are prohibited by the statute is not clear. The Act would certainly be violated if discriminatory terms and conditions were offered, especially because §1981 was amended by Congress in 1991 to include expressly a "terms and conditions" provision.[186] In *City of Memphis v. Greene*,[187] the Supreme Court rejected a claim that a city violated §1982 by blocking a street through which many Black residents had previously

[181] *Id.* at §1982.

[182] *Runyon v. McCrary*, 427 U.S. 160, 167-168 (1976); *Smith v. Woodhollow Apartments*, 463 F. Supp. 16, 20 (W.D. Okla. 1978) (sex discrimination not covered by §1982). *But see Anderson v. Conboy*, 156 F.3d 167 (2d Cir. 1998), *cert. granted sub nom. United Brotherhood of Carpenters and Joiners of America v. Anderson*, 526 U.S. 1086 (1999), *cert. dismissed*, 527 U.S. 1030 (1999) (holding that §1981 protects noncitizens from discrimination on the basis of alienage); *Duane v. Government Employees Insurance Co. (GEICO)*, 37 F.3d 1036 (4th Cir. 1994) (same). It has been held, however, that §1981 covers discrimination against Jewish and Arab people because they were viewed as separate races in 1866. *St. Francis College v. Al-Khazraji*, 481 U.S. 604 (1987); *Shaare Tefila Congregation v. Cobb*, 481 U.S. 615 (1987).

[183] 392 U.S. 409, 413 (1968).

[184] Paragraph (c) of §1981 now reads: "The rights protected by this section are protected against impairment by nongovernmental discrimination and impairment under color of State law." 42 U.S.C. §1981(c).

[185] *Jones v. Alfred H. Mayer Co.*, 392 U.S. 409, 413 (1968).

[186] 42 U.S.C. §1981(b), as amended by the *Civil Rights Act of 1991*, Act of Nov. 21, 1991, Pub. L. No. 102-166, Title I, §101, 105 Stat. 1071.

[187] 451 U.S. 100 (1981).

driven through a mostly white neighborhood to get downtown. The Court found insufficient evidence of an intent to deny rights to Black residents, but did hold that a claim might be made out if it could be proved that the city's action depreciated the value of property held by Black residents or severely restricted access to the homes of Black residents.[188] These latter claims suggest that a claim might be found even in the absence of discriminatory intent, yet the Court has also generally interpreted §1982 in a manner similar to §1981 and has held that discriminatory intent is essential to proving a claim under §1981.[189]

▷ APPLICABILITY TO PROPERTY EXEMPTED FROM THE *FHA* **HARD CASE ◀**

It is well settled now in the lower courts that §1982 applies to property exempted from the *FHA* under §3603.[190] For example, owner-occupied dwellings of four or fewer units are exempt from the *FHA*.[191] However, this exemption does not grant such owners an affirmative legal right to discriminate; rather §3603 merely states that "[n]othing in [42 U.S.C.] §3604 (other than [the advertisement provisions in] subsection [§3604(c)])" shall apply to such owners. This suggests that other federal and state statutes may well regulate such conduct. The counterargument, of course, is that the exemption loses its meaning if such owners are regulated by another statute; rather than being exempt from the antidiscrimination provisions of federal law, they are simply subjected to those same requirements under a different statutory section. The usual response is that the two statutes are not coextensive; while the *FHA* prohibits discrimination other than race discrimination (such as sex discrimination), §1982 is limited to race discrimination. In addition, the *FHA* has remedies absent from §1982, such as HUD enforcement. *Jones v. Alfred H. Mayer Co.* held that §1982 provides a remedy against private racial discrimination that is distinct from that provided by the *FHA*.[192] Although the Supreme Court has not ruled on the question of whether the exemptions in §3603 were intended to limit the applicability of §1982, it has accepted the idea that small employers exempt from Title VII of the 1968 *Civil Rights Act* are nonetheless prohibited from discriminating on the basis of race by §1981 of the *Civil Rights Act of 1866*.[193] By analogy, it is likely the Supreme Court would accept the settled view of lower courts that the exemptions in §3603 of the *FHA* do not immunize the affected parties from regulation by §1982 of the *Civil Rights Act of 1866*.[194] ◀

[188] *Id.* at 122-123.

[189] Robert G. Schwemm, *Housing Discrimination: Law and Litigation* §27.19 (2025).

[190] *Id.* at §27.2.

[191] 42 U.S.C. §3603(b)(2).

[192] *Jones v. Alfred H. Mayer Co.*, 392 U.S. 409, 416 (1968). *Accord*, *Tillman v. Wheaton-Haven Recreation Ass'n, Inc.*, 410 U.S. 431 (1973); *Sullivan v. Little Hunting Park, Inc.*, 396 U.S. 229 (1969).

[193] *See, e.g.*, *Lytle v. Household Manufacturing, Inc.*, 494 U.S. 545 (1990).

[194] *Bills v. Hodges*, 628 F.2d 844, 845 n.1 (4th Cir. 1980); *Morris v. Cizek*, 503 F.2d 1303 (7th Cir. 1974); *Lamb v. Sallee*, 417 F. Supp. 282 (E.D. Ky. 1976); *Johnson v. Zaremba*, 381 F. Supp.

§12.3 Sex Discrimination

Sex discrimination

The *FHA* was amended to prohibit sex discrimination in 1974.[195] Thus, landlords cannot refuse to rent to single women or single mothers if they are willing to rent to single men or single fathers.[196] Conversely, a refusal to rent to Black men while renting to Black women would constitute sex discrimination.[197]

▶ HARD CASE ▷ ROOMMATES

Does the *Fair Housing Act* apply to roommate choices? The Ninth Circuit held that it does not, but the statutory text is ambiguous. In *Fair Housing Council of San Fernando Valley v. Roommate, LLC*,[198] the court dismissed a claim against a Web site that allowed individuals to express preferences based on sex, sexual orientation, religion, and familial status in connection with roommate searches.

On one hand, the *FHA* defines a "dwelling" to include "any building, structure, *or portion thereof* which is occupied as, or designed or intended for occupancy as, a residence by one or more families."[199] An advertisement that limits potential roommates to those of a particular sex would seem to be a "refus[al] to negotiate for the sale or rental of, or otherwise make unavailable or deny, a dwelling . . . because of sex . . . ,"[200] as well as an "advertisement, with respect to the . . . rental of a dwelling that indicates [a] preference, limitation, or discrimination based on . . . sex. . . ."[201] And the exemption from the *FHA* in 42 U.S.C. §3603 for owner-occupied residences of four or fewer families or persons applies only when they are "living independently of each other" but does not apply at all to the prohibition on discriminatory advertisements in §3604(c).[202]

On the other hand, the Ninth Circuit noted that the First Amendment protects rights of intimate association and found that it would be unconstitutional to restrict roommate choices. For that reason, the court interpreted the statute to avoid the constitutional difficulty by interpreting the word "dwelling" to mean an independent living unit. If that is so, the *FHA*

---

165 (N.D. Ill. 1973); *Fred v. Kokinokos*, 347 F. Supp. 942 (E.D.N.Y. 1972); *Bush v. Kaim*, 297 F. Supp. 151, 161 (N.D. Ohio 1969); Robert G. Schwemm, *Housing Discrimination: Law and Litigation* §9.4 (2025).

[195] *Housing and Community Development Act*, Pub. L. No. 93-383, §808, 88 Stat. 633, 729.

[196] *See Walker v. Crigler*, 976 F.2d 900 (4th Cir. 1992) (holding rental property owner liable for sex discrimination for refusal to rent to single mother). *But see Wilson v. Glenwood Intermountain Properties, Inc.*, 876 F. Supp. 1231 (D. Utah 1995) (assuming that Title IX prevails over Title VIII (the *FHA*) allowing sex-segregated student housing at a university).

[197] *Cf. Marable v. H. Walker & Associates*, 644 F.2d 390 (5th Cir. 1981) (landlord discriminated on the basis of race against single Black male who had alleged discrimination on the basis of both race and sex).

[198] 666 F.3d 1216 (9th Cir. 2012).

[199] 42 U.S.C. §3602(b) (emphasis added).

[200] Id. at §3604(a).

[201] Id. at §3604(c).

[202] Id. at §§3603(b)(2), 3604(c).

only regulates the *transfer* of an independent living unit, rather than the decision to *share* the same unit. Note that the Department of Housing and Urban Development issued a memorandum opining that the *FHA* prohibits advertisements expressing preferences based on race, sex, and other listed categories but that it does not prohibit expressions of preference based on sex in roommate ads.[203] That policy would prohibit ads expressing a racial preference in roommate choices even if the Constitution protected the right to use racial criteria in choosing a roommate. The Ninth Circuit decision would, if extended, seem to allow expressions of racial preference in roommate ads as well as preferences based on sex. At the same time, the court did not address that question because the Web site neither sought nor published such preferences. ◀

Sexual harassment

An increasing number of cases have been brought alleging sexual harassment by landlords of tenants,[204] by building superintendents or managers of tenants,[205] or by brokers of customers.[206] "*Quid pro quo*" claims are, for example, demands that a tenant engage in sexual conduct with a landlord to avoid eviction.[207] "Hostile environment" claims, in contrast, involves sexual harassment that is "sufficiently severe or pervasive to alter the conditions of the housing arrangement."[208]

▷ PROVING SEXUAL HARASSMENT

HARD CASE ◀

What makes sexual harassment discrimination because of sex?

Future litigation is likely to further clarify what conduct is sufficient to constitute discriminatory sexual harassment. Most cases have denied recovery when a landlord has engaged in a single act, such as a sexual request or a sexual epithet or disparaging remark, even if these actions cause the tenant

[203] Roberta Achtenberg, Assistant Secretary for Fair Housing and Equal Opportunity, U.S. Department of Housing and Urban Development, *Guidance Regarding Advertisements Under §804(c) of the Fair Housing Act*, Jan. 9, 1995.

[204] *Fox v. Gaines*, 4 F.4th 1293 (11th Cir. 2021); *United States v. Hurt*, 676 F.3d 649, 654 (8th Cir. 2012); *Noah v. Assor*, 379 F. Supp. 3d 1284 (S.D. Fla. 2019); *Quigley v. Winter*, 598 F.3d 938 (8th Cir. 2010). *See also* Jennifer Preston, *$2 Million Penalty for Sexually Harassing West Side Tenants*, N.Y. Times, May 8, 2012, at A20.

[205] *Fox v. Gaines*, 4 F.4th 1293 (11th Cir. 2021); *Beliveau v. Caras*, 873 F. Supp. 1393 (C.D. Cal. 1995); *Williams v. Poretsky Management, Inc.*, 955 F. Supp. 490 (D. Md. 1996).

[206] *People of the State of New York v. Merlino*, 694 F. Supp. 1101 (S.D.N.Y. 1988); *Mass. Comm'n Against Discrimination v. Management Realty Co.*, 2003 Mass. Comm'n Discrim. LEXIS 11 (No. 98 BPR 1013) (2003) ($60,000 damages judgment against broker).

[207] *Quid Pro Quo and Hostile Environment Harassment and Liability for Discriminatory Housing Practices Under the Fair Housing Act*, 81 Fed. Reg. 63,054 (Sept. 14, 2016).

[208] *Honce v. Vigil*, 1 F.3d 1085, 1090 (10th Cir. 1993); *see also DiCenso v. Cisneros*, 96 F.3d 1004 (7th Cir. 1996); *People of the State of New York v. Merlino*, 694 F. Supp. 1101 (S.D.N.Y. 1988); *Gnerre v. Massachusetts Comm'n Against Discrimination*, 524 N.E.2d 84 (Mass. 1988); *Reeves v. Carrollsburg Condominium Unit Owners Ass'n*, 1997 U.S. Dist. LEXIS 21762 (D.D.C. 1997) (homeowners' association may be liable for sex discrimination when it failed to intervene to protect a homeowner from sexual harassment by another unit owner because, like landlords, such associations are responsible for maintaining common areas and enforcing regulations designed for the benefit of residents). *Quid Pro Quo and Hostile Environment Harassment and Liability for Discriminatory Housing Practices Under the Fair Housing Act*, 81 Fed. Reg. 63,054 (Sept. 14, 2016).

to choose to leave. In such cases, there may be no *quid pro quo* in the sense that the landlord conditioned continued rental on the tenant's agreeing to sexual relations with the landlord and the court may view the single incident as not sufficiently "severe or pervasive."[209] On the other hand, it has been argued that such incidents should be recognized as severe enough to alter the housing conditions in a discriminatory manner or alternatively that verbal statements violate 42 U.S.C. §3604(c) because they "indicate an intention to make [a] preference, limitation or discrimination" based on sex.[210]

Why is sexual harassment discrimination because of sex? The Supreme Court held in *Meritor Savings Bank, FSB v. Vinson*[211] that sexual harassment of female employees by a male supervisor constituted unlawful discrimination in employment on the basis of sex under Title VII. The Court appears to have assumed that the supervisor would not have subjected male employees to this conduct. If this is so, the plaintiff in a housing case can argue, for example, that the landlord who sexually harasses a woman tenant ordinarily would not be expected to sexually harass male tenants and that the landlord has discriminated against her in the terms and conditions of her rental because of her sex.[212]

Critique of the argument

This argument assumes that the landlord would not sexually harass men. There might be two reasons for this. First, the landlord might both be heterosexual and be motivated by sexual attraction to the tenant; in that case, it is unlikely he would have made similar overtures had the tenant been a man. Second, the landlord might be motivated by hostility to women and wishes to discourage them from renting his apartments; such a landlord might be either heterosexual or homosexual or even bisexual.[213] Defining sexual harassment of a man by a woman (or vice versa) as sex discrimination therefore assumes *either* that the landlord is not gay or bisexual *or* that the landlord is motivated by hostility to one sex but not the other. These are very different factual scenarios, however, and to date the courts have not asked for evidence one way or the other; they seem, instead, to assume that sexual harassment is usually based on attraction, that landlords are not gay or bisexual, and that the treatment accorded the plaintiff would not have occurred had she been a man. Consider that if the

[209] *Hall v. Meadowood Ltd. Partnership*, 7 Fed. Appx. 687, 2001 U.S. App. LEXIS 5718 (9th Cir. 2001); *DiCenso v. Cisneros*, 96 F.3d 1004 (7th Cir. 1996) (no sex discrimination claim based on single incident when landlord offered to forgo rent in exchange for tenant's sexual services); *Honce v. Vigil*, 1 F.3d 1085, 1089-1090 (10th Cir. 1993) (holding that evidence was insufficient to find sexual harassment); *United States v. Presidio Investments, Ltd.*, 4 F.3d 805 (9th Cir. 1993).

[210] Robert G. Schwemm & Rigel C. Oliveri, *A New Look at Sexual Harassment Under the Fair Housing Act: The Forgotten Role of §3604(c)*, 2002 Wis. L. Rev. 771, 796-816.

[211] 477 U.S. 57 (1986).

[212] 42 U.S.C. §3604(b).

[213] *See Oncale v. Sundowner Offshore Services, Inc.*, 523 U.S. 75, 80 (1998) ("[H]arassing conduct need not be motivated by sexual desire to support an inference of discrimination on the basis of sex. A trier of fact might reasonably find such discrimination, for example, if a female victim is harassed in such sex-specific and derogatory terms by another woman as to make it clear that the harasser is motivated by general hostility to the presence of women in the workplace.").

landlord were homosexual rather than heterosexual, the assumption that the landlord would not engage in the same conduct toward men seems less certain. Such a person might sexually harass male tenants because he is attracted to them and sexually harass female tenants because he is hostile to them. Assuming that sexual harassment of a female tenant by a male landlord is sex discrimination therefore makes several leaps in judgment about the motivations of the landlord.

Same-sex harassment

In the case of same-sex harassment, the Supreme Court has ruled in the employment context, in *Oncale v. Sundowner Offshore Services, Inc.*,[214] that same-sex harassment (of a male tenant by a male landlord, for example) may constitute sex discrimination if the harassment is "because of sex."[215] The Court did not clarify what "because of sex" means, but it clearly requires some kind of demonstration beyond the mere fact that the harassment was sexual in nature. "The critical issue is whether members of one sex are exposed to disadvantageous terms or conditions of employment to which members of the other sex are not exposed."[216] If the landlord were gay, the court might assume that such a person would likely not have harassed the tenant had he been a woman.[217] However, if the landlord were not gay, the court could not make the same assumption; the landlord might believe the tenant is gay and be hostile to him for that reason. In that case, the landlord might well engage in harassment of a male tenant (because of hostility to the tenant's sexual orientation) and engage in harassment of a female tenant (because of sexual attraction). In that case, a court might hold that the discrimination against the male tenant by the male landlord was not "because of sex" but "because of sexual orientation" — an unprotected class under federal law. It may seem unfair to find a landlord liable of sex discrimination in the same sex harassment case when the landlord is gay but not to find the landlord liable when he is not gay; the same conduct engaged in by two different landlords either will or will not be "sex discrimination" based on the happenstance of their sexual orientation. On the other hand, perhaps this is not so strange; harassment may be inappropriate and wrongful, but this does not necessarily make it an instance of

[214] 523 U.S. 75 (1998).

[215] *Id.* at 80-81.

[216] *Id.* at 80. Sexual orientation discrimination was not traditionally held to be a form of sex discrimination, *see, e.g.*, *Campbell v. Garden City Plumbing & Heating, Inc.*, 97 P.3d 546 (Mont. 2004) (male employee sexually harassed by supervisor cannot sue for sex discrimination unless he can prove that he was treated differently because of his sex, *i.e.*, that he was treated differently than he would have been treated had he been a woman), although that is now changing. *See* §§12.4, 12.8.3.

[217] *See Oncale*, 523 U.S. at 80 ("Courts and juries have found the inference of discrimination easy to draw in most male-female sexual harassment situations, because the challenged conduct typically involves explicit or implicit proposals of sexual activity; it is reasonable to assume those proposals would not have been made to someone of the same sex. The same chain of inference would be available to a plaintiff alleging same-sex harassment, if there were credible evidence that the harasser was homosexual."); *Tietgen v. Brown's Westminster Motors, Inc.*, 921 F. Supp. 1495, 1501 (E.D. Va. 1996) ("If a male employer touches a male employee in a sexual manner, or invites the male employee to engage in sexual conduct, the employer likely does so because the employee is male. In other words, the male employer in this circumstance is probably homosexual or bisexual.").

discrimination. Moreover, if the discrimination is really "because of sexual orientation" and Congress has intended *not* to protect gay and lesbian tenants from discrimination, then the inequity can be traced to Congress's refusal to prohibit sexual orientation discrimination. This does not explain, however, why there appears to be a presumption that opposite-sex harassment is sex discrimination while there is no such presumption in the same-sex context. ◀

Sex stereotyping

In *Price Waterhouse v. Hopkins,*[218] the Supreme Court found sex discrimination when a female was denied a partnership partly on the ground that she was too "masculine" and that she could improve her chances if she dressed and acted in a way that was more "feminine." The court characterized this as a form of sex stereotyping in that it was a demand that would not have been made of a man; the pressure to conform to a particular image of how women are to act involves sex discrimination if they are required to act in ways that men are not required to act. Similar arguments can be made in the context of same-sex harassment. Landlords engage in a discriminatory act when they harass a tenant because of that tenant's failure to conform to a sex stereotype.[219]

▶ HARD CASE ▷ SIMILAR HARASSMENT OF MEN AND WOMEN

Finally, consider a landlord who sexually harasses both male and female tenants; that landlord is arguably not treating men and women differently and is therefore arguably not "discriminating because of sex."[220] On the other hand, the harasser may harass men in different ways than he harasses women, or he may do so for different reasons; if this is so, then the harasser may be treating each sex differently than the other and engaging in wrongful discrimination.[221] For example, in *Chiapuzio v. BLT Operating Corp.,*[222] an employer sexually harassed both a husband and wife (among others) who worked for him; while the harassment of the wife (and other female employees) concerned the employer's professed desire to engage in sexual acts with them, his harassment of the men took the form of statements that he could make love to their wives better than they could. The court

[218] 490 U.S. 228 (1989).

[219] *See Nichols v. Azteca Restaurant Enterprises*, 256 F.3d 864, 874 (9th Cir. 2001); *Simonton v. Runyon*, 232 F.3d 33, 37-38 (2d Cir. 2000) (employer commits sex discrimination when harassment is based on employee's failure to act in accord with sex norms).

[220] *Holman v. Indiana*, 211 F.3d 399, 403 (7th Cir. 2000) (employer who sexually harassed both men and women not liable for sex discrimination because he did not harass "because of" sex).

[221] *See Kopp v. Samaritan Health System, Inc.*, 13 F.3d 264, 269 (8th Cir. 1993) (discrimination present when harassment of women was more severe than harassment of men); Kyle F. Mothershead (Note), *How the "Equal Opportunity" Sexual Harasser Discriminates on the Basis of Gender Under Title VII*, 55 Vand. L. Rev. 1205 (2002); Kenji Yoshino, *The Epistemic Contract of Bisexual Erasure*, 52 Stan. L. Rev. 353, 436-461 (2000).

[222] 826 F. Supp. 1334 (D. Wyo. 1993).

concluded that the male and female plaintiffs were being treated differently and that this different treatment was "because of their gender."[223]

In addition, if the courts are not going to question whether landlords are straight or gay in the case of sexual harassment by male landlords of female tenants (but simply assume that this is sex discrimination), it is not clear why such proof should become essential when the landlord harasses both men and women. Moreover, there is something quite bizarre about a rule of law that would turn unlawful, discriminatory sexual harassment into lawful, nondiscriminatory sexual harassment simply because the landlord has chosen to harass someone of the same sex as well as someone of the opposite sex. Such a rule might encourage landlords to act strategically to make sexual overtures both to male and female tenants to protect themselves from sex discrimination claims.[224] That would seem an odd result and one might adopt a prophylactic rule denying the equal opportunity harasser defense as a way to ensure that harassers are not free to engage in unlawful conduct merely by adding other victims of the opposite sex. ◀

§12.4 Sexual-Orientation and Gender Identity Discrimination

State laws

At least 24 states and the District of Columbia, as well as over 200 municipalities,[225] have laws that directly prohibit discrimination in the housing market on the basis of sexual orientation and/or gender identity.[226] Those jurisdictions include California, Colorado, Connecticut, Delaware, the District of Columbia, Hawai'i, Illinois, Iowa, Maine, Maryland, Massachusetts, Minnesota, Nevada, New Hampshire, New Jersey, New Mexico, New York, Oregon, Rhode Island, Utah, Vermont, Virginia, Washington, and Wisconsin.[227]

Federal law

Federal law does not facially prohibit sexual orientation or gender-identity discrimination although it does prohibit discrimination on

[223] *Id.* at 1337-1338.

[224] *See McDonnell v. Cisneros*, 84 F.3d 256, 260 (7th Cir. 1996) ("It would be exceedingly perverse if a male worker could buy his supervisors and his company immunity from Title VII liability [for employment discrimination] by taking care to harass sexually an occasional male worker, though his preferred targets were female"); *Steiner v. Showboat Operating Co.*, 25 F.3d 1459, 1464 (9th Cir. 1994) (consistent abuse of both men and women employees was not a defense to a sex discrimination claim).

[225] *See, e.g.*, Boston Code tit. 12, ch. 40; Chicago Mun. Code, ch. 199; Los Angeles Mun. Code, ch. IV; New York City, Admin. Code §8-102(20); Philadelphia Fair Prac. Ordinance, ch. 9-1100; and San Francisco Code, art. 33, §3301.

[226] Mack Kenner, et al., *Transgender and Nonbinary Persons' Rights and Issues*, 25 Geo. J. Gender & L. 1087, 1128-29 (2024).

[227] Cal. Civ. Code §51; Colo. Rev. Stat. §24-34-502; Conn. Gen. Stat. §46a-64c; Del. Code tit. 6, §4603; D.C. Code §2-1402.21; Haw. Stat. §515-3; 775 Ill. Comp. Stat. 5/3-101 to 5/3-106; Iowa Code §216.8; Me. Rev. Stat. tit. 5, §§4552, 4582; Md. Code Ann., State Gov't §20-304; Mass. Gen. Laws ch. 151B, §4; Minn. Stat. §363A.09; Nev. Rev Stat §118.100; N.H. Rev. Stat. §§354-A:1 to A:10; N.J. Stat. §10:5-4; N.M. Stat. §28-1-7; N.Y. Exec. §296; Or. Rev. Stat. §659A.030; R.I. Gen. Laws §§34-37-1 to 34-37-5.4; Utah Code §57-21-6; Vt. Stat. tit. 9, §§4502, 4503; Va. Stat. §2.2-3904 and §36-96.3; Wash. Rev. Code §49.60.222; Wis. Stat. §106.50.

the basis of sex.[228] In *Bostock v. Clayton County*,[229] a case involving employment discrimination claims under Title VII of the *Civil Rights Act*, the Supreme Court held that the statutory term "sex" includes sexual orientation and gender identity.[230] As the Court explained, if two employees, one male and one female, are both attracted to men, and the employer fires the male employee for no reason other than that attraction, "the employer discriminates against him for traits or actions it tolerates in his female colleague."[231] Likewise, if an employer takes an adverse action against a transgendered employee who was identified as a male at birth but who now identifies as a female, but takes no action against an employee identified as female at birth but otherwise identical, the employer has intentionally penalized the person identified as male at birth simply for that fact.[232] Courts generally apply Title VII precedent to the *FHA*, and there is no clear reason not to extend *Bostock* similarly, either in terms of textual analysis, congressional intent, or the underlying reason for interpreting sex to include sexual orientation and gender identity. At least one case before *Bostock* had found claims based on sexual orientation and gender identity covered by the *FHA* on the limited theory that making decisions based on sex stereotypes is sex discrimination,[233] but *Bostock* is likely to generate changes in the case law.[234]

§12.5 Disability Discrimination

City of Cleburne v. Cleburne Living Center

In *City of Cleburne v. Cleburne Living Center*,[235] the city zoning ordinance required operators of "hospitals for the feeble-minded" to obtain special use permits to operate. When the city denied a permit for a group home for intellectually disabled persons, the owner sued, claiming that the permit requirement violated the rights of mentally retarded citizens to equal protection of the laws under the Fourteenth Amendment. The Supreme Court agreed, noting that the city did not require a special use permit for other multiple-resident dwellings, including apartment buildings, dormitories, hotels, nursing homes, or fraternities. The Court concluded that the city could articulate no rational basis for differential treatment of persons with mental retardation and therefore violated the equal protection clause.[236]

[228] *See* §12.3.
[229] 590 U.S. 644 (2020).
[230] *Id.* at 659.
[231] *Id.*
[232] *Id.*
[233] *See, e.g., Smith v. Avanti*, 249 F. Supp. 3d 1194 (D. Colo. 2017) (married lesbian couple, one member of which was a trangender woman, successfully brought a claim under the *Fair Housing Act* against a landlord who refused to rent to them because of their purported "unique relationship").
[234] *See* Rigel C. Oliveri, *Sexual Orientation and Gender Identity Discrimination Claims Under the Fair Housing Act After* Bostock v. Clayton County, 69 U. Kan. L. Rev. 409, 431-437 (2021).
[235] 473 U.S. 432 (1985).
[236] *See also College Area Renters & Landlord Ass'n v. City of San Diego*, 50 Cal. Rptr. 2d 515 (Ct. App. 1996) (zoning ordinance violates equal protection clause by irrationally regulating

Handicap discrimination

Since the *FHAA of 1988*, the *FHA*, at §3604(f)(1), has made it unlawful to

> discriminate in the sale or rental, or to otherwise make unavailable or deny, a dwelling to any buyer or renter because of a handicap of (A) that buyer or renter; (B) a person residing in or intending to reside in that dwelling after it is so sold, rented, or made available; or (C) any person associated with that buyer or renter.[237]

A similar provision, at §3604(f)(2) makes it unlawful to discriminate

> against any person in the terms, conditions, or privileges of sale or rental of a dwelling, or in the provision of services or facilities in connection with such dwelling, because of a handicap of (A) that buyer or renter; (B) a person residing in or intending to reside in that dwelling after it is so sold, rented, or made available; or (C) any person associated with that buyer or renter.[238]

Definition of "handicap"

A "handicap" is defined at §3602(h) as "a physical or mental impairment which substantially limits one or more of [a] person's major life activities."[239] In addition, a handicap is "a record of having such an impairment" or "being regarded as having such an impairment."[240]

Reasonable modifications and accommodations

Section 3604(f)(3) requires owners (including, for example, landlords, condominium associations, and housing developers) to make reasonable accommodations for persons with disabilities.[241] Section 3604(f)(3)(A) makes it unlawful to "refuse to permit, at the expense of the handicapped person, *reasonable modifications of existing premises* occupied or to be occupied by such person if such modifications may be necessary to afford such person full enjoyment of the premises."[242] However, in the case of a rental, "the landlord may where it is reasonable to do so condition permission for a modification on the renter agreeing to restore the interior of the premises to the condition that existed before the modification, reasonable wear and tear excepted."[243] In addition, it is unlawful to refuse to "make *reasonable accommodations in rules, policies, practices, or services*, when such accommodations may be necessary to afford such person equal opportunity to use and enjoy a dwelling."[244] A landlord or condominium association, for example, might be required to give a tenant or owner a parking space near

---

the number of unrelated adults who could live in non-owner-occupied dwellings but not regulating the number of unrelated adults who could live in owner-occupied dwellings).

237 42 U.S.C. §3604(f)(1).

238 Prior to 1988, §504 of the *Rehabilitation Act of 1973*, 29 U.S.C. §794, prohibited discrimination on the basis of handicap in any program or activity that receives federal funds.

239 42 U.S.C. §3602(h).

240 *Id.*

241 *Id.* at §3604(f)(3).

242 *See Elliot v. Sherwood Manor Mobile Home Park*, 947 F. Supp. 1574 (M.D. Fla. 1996) (landlord violated *FHA* by removing a ramp that tenant had installed).

243 42 U.S.C. §3604(f)(3)(A).

244 *Id.* at §3604(f)(3)(B) (emphasis added).

the building rather than using the otherwise applicable procedure for allocating parking spaces.[245] It might also be required to allow a blind tenant to have a seeing-eye dog despite a no-pets policy,[246] or a deaf person to have a hearing dog.[247] The obligation to make reasonable accommodations means that the owner must assume a reasonable financial burden to accomplish the accommodation.[248]

Legitimate criteria for exclusion

The Act specifically provides, at §3604(f)(9), that the *FHA* does not require "that a dwelling be made available to an individual whose tenancy would constitute a direct threat to the health or safety of other individuals or whose tenancy would result in substantial physical damage to the property of others."[249] The Act also allows owners to refuse to deal with tenants with disabilities for legitimate reasons, such as excluding tenants who are noisy, although, as noted above, they are required to make "reasonable accommodations" and treat all tenants based on the same policies or criteria.[250]

New dwellings

New multifamily dwellings[251] consisting of four or more units if they have one or more elevators and ground floor units in buildings consisting of four or more units that do not have elevators must be designed so that

> [(i) the] public use and common use portions of such dwellings are readily accessible to and usable by handicapped persons; (ii) all the doors designed to allow passage into and within all premises within such dwellings are sufficiently wide to allow passage by handicapped persons in wheelchairs; and (iii) all premises within such dwellings contain (I) an accessible route into and through the dwelling; (II) light switches, electrical outlets, thermostats, and other environmental controls in accessible locations; (III) reinforcements in bathroom walls to allow later installation of grab bars; and (IV) usable kitchens and bathrooms such that an individual in a wheelchair can maneuver about the space.[252]

[245] *See* 24 C.F.R. §100.204(b), Example (2); *Jankowski Lee & Assocs. v. Dep't of Housing and Urban Development*, 91 F.3d 891, 895-896 (7th Cir. 1996); *Shapiro v. Cadman Towers, Inc.*, 51 F.3d 328, 335 (2d Cir. 1995); *Hubbard v. Samson Management Corp.*, 994 F. Supp. 187, 193 (S.D.N.Y. 1998); *Gittleman v. Woodhaven Condominium Ass'n, Inc.*, 972 F. Supp. 894, 899 (D.N.J. 1997).

[246] *See* 24 C.F.R. §100.204(b), Example (1).

[247] *Bronk v. Ineichen*, 54 F.3d 425, 429 (7th Cir. 1995); *Green v. Housing Authority of Clackamas County*, 994 F. Supp. 1253, 1256-1257 (D. Or. 1998).

[248] *United States v. California Mobile Home Park Management Co.*, 29 F.3d 1413, 1416-1417 (9th Cir. 1994); *see also Hollis v. Chestnut Bend Homeowners Ass'n*, 760 F.3d 531, 542 (6th Cir. 2014). *But see Rodriguez v. 551 West 157th Street Owners Corp.*, 992 F. Supp. 385 (S.D.N.Y. 1998) (reasonable accommodation provisions did not require landlord to construct a wheelchair ramp on existing building).

[249] 42 U.S.C. §3604(f)(9).

[250] *See* Robert G. Schwemm, *Housing Discrimination: Law and Litigation* §11D.3 (2025) (noting that landlord may only refuse to deal with people with disabilities as long as the same criteria is used to judge tenants without disabilities).

[251] New multifamily dwellings means those designed and constructed for first occupancy after March 13, 1991. 42 U.S.C. §3604(f)(3)(C).

[252] 42 U.S.C. §3604(f)(3)(C).

▷ TWO TENANTS WITH DISABILITIES AND COMPETING NEEDS **HARD CASE** ◀

In *Cohen v. Clark*,[253] the Iowa Supreme Court faced a landlord's dilemma, in a conflict between one tenant who needed an emotional support animal and another tenant who was allergic to dogs. Each tenant's lease had a no-pets clause, and the question was whether the landlord had a duty under the state's fair housing law to make an exception to that policy as a "reasonable accommodation" for the tenant with a disability. In this case, however, each tenant arguably had a disability and enabling one to enjoy the housing would have deprived the other of their housing. The court resolved the conflict by using the time-honored property law doctrine of "first in time, first in right." Since the tenant with pet allergies had moved into the building first, and did so in reliance on its no-pets policy, the court held that the landlord had no duty to waive the no-pets policy for a new tenant who needed an emotional support dog in these circumstances. ◀

§12.6 Family Status Discrimination

§12.6.1 Families with Children

Families with children

Since the *FHAA of 1988*, the *FHA* prohibits discrimination against families with children.[254] Section 3604(a) makes it unlawful to discriminate on the basis of "familial status," defined at §3602(k) as

> one or more individuals (who have not attained the age of 18 years) being domiciled with (1) a parent or another person having legal custody of such individual or individuals; or (2) the designee of such parent or other person having such custody, with the written permission of such parent or other person.[255]

Section 3602(k) also provides that the "protections against discrimination on the basis of familial status shall apply to any person who is pregnant or is in the process of securing legal custody of any individual who has not attained the age of 18 years."[256]

Housing for older persons

An exemption from the familial status regulations allows owners to exclude children if their facilities constitute "housing for older persons." Housing qualifies for this exemption (1) if it is "intended for, and solely occupied by, persons 62 years of age or older";[257] or (2) if it is "intended and operated for occupancy by at least one person 55 years of age or older

[253] 945 N.W.2d 792 (Iowa 2020).
[254] 42 U.S.C. §§3602(k) & 3604(a); *Kormoczy v. Secretary of Housing & Urban Development*, 53 F.3d 821, 824 (7th Cir. 1995); *Jancik v. Dep't of Housing and Urban Development*, 44 F.3d 553, 556-557 (7th Cir. 1995).
[255] 42 U.S.C. §3602(k).
[256] *Id.*
[257] *Id.* at §3607(b)(2)(B).

per unit"[258] and meets three criteria,[259] including (a) "at least 80 percent of the units are occupied by at least one person 55 years of age or older per unit";[260] (b) the owner publishes and adheres to "policies and procedures which demonstrate an intent by the owner or manager to provide housing for persons 55 years of age or older";[261] and (c) the owner complies with regulations designed to verify such occupancy by valid surveys.[262]

Reasonable occupancy limits

By analogy to §3607(b)(1), which exempts "any reasonable local, State, or Federal restrictions regarding the maximum number of occupants permitted to occupy a dwelling"[263] from the strictures of the *FHA*, private landlords have been held to be entitled to place reasonable occupancy limits on the number of residents who may live in a particular unit even if this has the effect of excluding families with children.[264] However, occupancy limits that are unreasonable or that are adopted for the sole purpose of excluding children will be held as unlawful discrimination because of familial status.[265]

§12.6.2 Marital Status

State laws

Many states have fair housing laws that prohibit discrimination because of "marital status."[266] Such laws protect tenants from being denied housing because they are not (or are) married.

▶ HARD CASE ▷ RELIGIOUSLY MOTIVATED REFUSALS TO RENT

A number of recent cases have wrestled with the question of whether a landlord may refuse to rent to a cohabiting unmarried couple when this

258 *Id.* at §3607(b)(2)(C).

259 As originally passed in 1988, the "55 or older" exemption required owners to show that they provided "significant facilities and services specifically designed to meet the physical or social needs of older persons." That provision was repealed by the *Housing for Older Persons Act of 1995*, Pub. L. No. 104-76, 109 Stat. 787.

260 42 U.S.C. §3607(b)(2)(C)(i).

261 *Id.* at §3607(b)(2)(C)(ii).

262 *Id.* at §3607(b)(2)(C)(iii).

263 *Id.* at §3607(b)(1) (added to the *FHA* by the *FHAA of 1988*).

264 *Pfaff v. Department of Housing and Urban Development*, 88 F.3d 739 (9th Cir. 1996) (no violation of *FHA* when landlord imposed numerical occupancy limitation in rental of small house).

265 *Fair Housing Council of Orange County, Inc. v. Ayers*, 855 F. Supp. 315, 318-319 (C.D. Cal. 1994).

266 Alaska Stat. § 18.80.240; Cal. Civ. Code § 51, Cal. Gov't Code § 12955; Colo. Rev. Stat. Ann. § 24-34-502; Conn. Gen. Stat. Ann. §§ 46a-63, 46a-64(b) to (c); Del. Code Ann. tit. 6, § 4603(b); Haw. Rev. Stat. Ann. § 515-3; 775 Ill. Comp. Stat. Ann. 5/3-102; Md. Code Ann., State Gov't § 20-705; Mass. Gen. Laws Ann. ch. 151B, § 4.7; Mich. Comp. Laws Ann. § 37.2502(1); Minn. Stat. Ann. § 363A.09; Mont. Code Ann. § 49-2-305; N.H. Rev. Stat. Ann. § 354-A:10; N.J. Stat. Ann. 10:5-4; N.Y. Exec. Law § 296.2-a; N.D. Cent. Code § 4-02.4-12; Or. Rev. Stat. Ann. § 659A.421(2); R.I. Gen. Laws § 34-37-4; Vt. Stat. Ann. tit. 9, § 4503(a); Wash. Rev. Code Ann. § 49.60.222; Wis. Stat. Ann. § 106.50; Robert G. Schwemm, *Housing Discrimination: Law and Litigation* §30.3 n.2 (2025). *But see Mister v. ARK Partnership*, 553 N.E.2d 1152 (Ill. App. Ct. 1990) (landlord may refuse to rent to unmarried cohabiting couple); Minn. Stat. §363.03(2)(a).

would violate the landlord's religious beliefs.[267] Such cases raise two issues. First, does the refusal to rent to an unmarried, cohabiting couple constitute discrimination "because of" marital status? Some courts hold that it does because the landlord would have rented to the couple had they been married.[268] Others hold that the refusal to rent is based, not on the tenants' *status* of being unmarried, but the tenants' *conduct* in engaging in cohabitation outside of marriage.[269]

Free exercise of religion

Second, do landlords have a constitutional right to refuse to rent in such cases? The First Amendment and all state constitutions protect the free exercise of religion and several courts have held, under either the federal or state constitutions, that landlords have constitutional rights to refuse to rent to unmarried cohabiting couples, effectively striking down as unconstitutional state antidiscrimination laws that require landlords to rent without regard to marital status.[270] Other courts have held that landlords have no constitutional right to refuse to rent because of religiously based objections to such conduct.[271]

Federal free exercise right weak

The claim that there is a federal constitutional right to an exemption from otherwise applicable antidiscrimination laws seems quite shaky since the Supreme Court's decisions in *Employment Division v. Smith*[272] and in *City of Boerne v. Flores*.[273] *Smith* held that, except in very unusual cases, neutral, generally applicable laws cannot be disregarded by individuals on the ground that compliance with them interferes with their free exercise of religion.[274] Congress tried to get around *Smith* by passing the *Religious Freedom Restoration Act (RFRA)*,[275] which prohibited the government from substantially burdening a person's exercise of religion unless the government could both demonstrate a compelling state interest and no

[267] *McCready v. Hoffius*, 586 N.W.2d 723 (Mich. 1998) (holding that a prohibition against marital status discrimination prohibited landlords from refusing to rent to an unmarried couple and that this prohibition did not interfere with the landlords' constitutionally protected rights to free exercise of religion), *opinion vacated in part and remanded in* 593 N.W.2d 545 (Mich. 1999) (to determine whether the statute violated the landlords' free exercise rights by requiring them to rent to a cohabiting unmarried couple).

[268] *Swanner v. Anchorage Equal Rights Comm'n*, 874 P.2d 274, 278 n.4 (Alaska 1994); *Smith v. Fair Employment & Housing Comm'n*, 913 P.2d 909, 915 (Cal. 1996); *Markham v. Colonial Mortgage Service Co.*, 605 F.2d 566 (D.C. Cir. 1979); *Attorney General v. Desilets*, 636 N.E.2d 233, 235 (Mass. 1994).

[269] *Mister v. A.R.K. Partnership*, 553 N.E.2d 1152, 1157 (Ill. 1990); *State by Cooper v. French*, 460 N.W.2d 2, 5-6 (Minn. 1990); *North Dakota Fair Housing Council, Inc. v. Peterson*, 625 N.W.2d 551, 562 (S.D. 2001); *McFadden v. Elma Country Club*, 613 P.2d 146, 150 (Wash. Ct. App. 1980); *County of Dane v. Norman*, 497 N.W.2d 714, 715-716 (Wis. 1993).

[270] *Thomas v. Anchorage Equal Rights Comm'n*, 165 F.3d 692 (9th Cir. 1999), *opinion withdrawn and remanded to dismiss the complaint on ground that the case was not ripe for decision*, 220 F.3d 1134 (9th Cir. 2000); *State by Cooper v. French*, 460 N.W.2d 2, 5-6 (Minn. 1990); *cf. Attorney General v. Desilets*, 636 N.E.2d 233, 235 (Mass. 1994) (holding that the state constitution protected a landlord's right not to rent to a cohabiting, unmarried couple unless they could demonstrate a compelling state interest in applying the marital status discrimination rules to such landlords).

[271] *Swanner v. Anchorage Equal Rights Comm'n*, 874 P.2d 274, 278 (Alaska 1994).

[272] 494 U.S. 872 (1990).

[273] 521 U.S. 507 (1997).

[274] 494 U.S. at 881-882.

[275] 42 U.S.C. §§2000bb *et seq.*

less-restrictive means of furthering that interest. However, the Supreme Court struck down *RFRA* in *City of Boerne v. Flores* because the Fourteenth Amendment gave Congress the power to protect "liberty" of religion, as defined by the First Amendment, but not to go beyond that.[276] Despite the decision in *Smith* and the invalidation of *RFRA*, some courts have held that the First Amendment's free exercise clause invalidates state marital status discrimination laws that obligate landlords to rent property to unmarried couples.[277]

State constitutional free exercise clauses

Some state courts have interpreted their state constitutions to grant further free exercise of religious rights than those granted by the federal constitution. Thus, some state courts have appealed to their state constitutions to limit the applicability of marital status discrimination provisions when they interfere with the landlord's religious views.[278] The argument against this conclusion is that tenants, as well as landlords, have rights to the free exercise of religion, may believe that divorce is wrong, and that cohabitation prior to marriage is a sensible precaution against the possibility of future divorce. On the other hand, if most landlords have no religious objections to renting to cohabiting unmarried couples, then such tenants might not be significantly hampered in their ability to find a place to live. At base, the question is whether a landlord's religious beliefs should entitle her to engage in what the state has determined is invidious discrimination. Had landlords been able to cite strong religious beliefs about segregation of the races, for example, the *FHA* would have lost most of its force. Even if landlords have strong religious objections to renting to unmarried couples, the state arguably has a compelling state interest in eradicating invidious discrimination in the housing market. ◀

§12.7 Religious Discrimination

▶ HARD CASE ▷ USE OF RELIGIOUS SYMBOLS BY BROKER

In *Lotz Realty Co. v. Department of Housing and Urban Development*,[279] the Anti-Defamation League, an organization dedicated to combating prejudice against Jews, challenged a realtor's use of Christian symbols and slogans in its housing ads. As in the *Ragin*[280] case, discussed above,[281] the issue

[276] Congress has since passed the *Religious Land Use and Institutionalized Persons Act of 2000 (RLUIPA)*, 42 U.S.C. §§2000cc to 2000cc-5 (Pub. L. No. 106-274, 114 Stat. 803, Sept. 22, 2000 (S. 2869)). This statute attempts to revive certain aspects of the *RFRA* struck down in *City of Boerne v. Flores*, 521 U.S. 507 (1997), by curing the constitutional impediments identified there; it would invalidate zoning laws that exclude or impose burdens on religious practice. *See* §12.8.6.

[277] *See Thomas v. Anchorage Equal Rights Comm'n*, 165 F.3d 692 (9th Cir. 1999), *opinion withdrawn and remanded to dismiss the complaint on ground that the case was not ripe for decision*, 220 F.3d 1134 (9th Cir. 2000).

[278] *See, e.g., Attorney General v. Desilets*, 636 N.E.2d 233, 235 (Mass. 1994).

[279] 717 F.2d 929 (4th Cir. 1983).

[280] *Ragin v. The New York Times Co.*, 923 F.2d 995 (2d Cir. 1991).

[281] *See* §12.2.2.7.

is whether the use of the symbols indicates a religious preference. It may not indicate such a preference; instead, it merely portrays the religious affiliation of the broker. On the other hand, it may both deter non-Christians from using the realtor's services and may express a preference for Christian customers, thereby violating §3604(c).[282] ◀

Landlords' religious objections to tenant conduct

As noted above at §12.5.2, courts have wrestled with landlords' religious objections to renting to unmarried couples or to other individuals protected by state or local antidiscrimination laws, such as gay and lesbian tenants.

§12.8 Disparate Impact Claims

§12.8.1 Race

While a discriminatory treatment claim proves that someone was treated differently because of race, a disparate impact claim is based on the fact that a practice that is uniformly applied has a disproportionate effect on a racial group. Discriminatory treatment claims are premised on an intent to discriminate based on race while disparate impact claims focus on the effects of a neutral policy or practice that either deny housing opportunities or promote racial segregation.[283]

Discriminatory effect

The courts have long held disparate impact claims to be available under the *FHA*.[284] Because there was some variation among federal Circuit Courts on how to prove a disparate impact claim, the Department of Housing and Urban Development (HUD) adopted regulations in 2013 to settle the substantive standard as well as burdens of proof. Under that regulation, facially neutral policies that have a discriminatory effect on protected groups will violate the *FHA* unless they are "necessary to achieve one or more substantial, legitimate, nondiscriminatory interests"

[282] *See also LeBlanc-Sternberg v. Fletcher*, 67 F.3d 412 (2d Cir. 1995) (finding that a town constructed its zoning laws to exclude Orthodox Jews from the community).

[283] *Tex. Dep't of Hous. & Cmty. Aff. v. Inclusive Communities Project, Inc.*, 576 U.S. 519 (2015); *MHANY Management, Inc. v. Cnty. of Nassau*, 819 F.3d 581 (2d Cir. 2016). State laws may also encompass disparate impact claims. *See Burbank Apartments Tenant Ass'n v. Kargman*, 48 N.E.3d 394 (Mass. 2016).

[284] *Tex. Dep't of Hous. & Cmty. Affairs v. Inclusive Communities Project, Inc.*, 576 U.S. 519 (2015). All federal Circuit Courts of Appeal that had considered the issue before *Inclusive Communities* had adopted an effects test. Robert G. Schwemm, *Housing Discrimination: Law and Litigation* §10.4 (2025); *see Langlois v. Abington Housing Authority*, 207 F.3d 43 (1st Cir. 2000); *Mountain Side Mobile Estates v. HUD*, 56 F.3d 1243, 1253 (10th Cir. 1995); *Village of Bellwood v. Dwivedi*, 895 F.2d 1521, 1533-1534 (7th Cir. 1990); *Huntington Branch, NAACP v. Town of Huntington*, 844 F.2d 926 (2d Cir.), *aff'd per curiam*, 488 U.S. 15 (1988); *Keith v. Volpe*, 858 F.2d 467 (9th Cir. 1988); *Arthur v. City of Toledo*, 782 F.2d 565 (6th Cir. 1986); *United States v. Parma*, 661 F.2d 562 (6th Cir. 1981); *Betsey v. Turtle Creek Assocs.*, 736 F.2d 983 (4th Cir. 1984); *Smith v. Town of Clarkton*, 682 F.2d 1055 (4th Cir. 1982); *Bonner v. City of Prichard*, 661 F.2d 1206 (11th Cir. 1981); *Robinson v. 12 Lofts Realty, Inc.*, 610 F.2d 1032 (2d Cir. 1979); *United States v. Mitchell*, 580 F.2d 789 (5th Cir. 1978); *Metropolitan Housing Development Corp. v. Village of Arlington Heights*, 558 F.2d 1283 (7th Cir. 1977); *Mount Holly Gardens Citizens in Action Inc. v. Mount Holly, N.J.*, 658 F.3d 375 (3d Cir. 2011); *United States v. Black Jack*, 508 F.2d 1179 (8th Cir. 1974).

and "those interests could not be served by another practice that has a less discriminatory effect."[285] Despite the long-standing agreement of the Circuit Courts on the availability of disparate impact claims under the *FHA* and HUD's regulation, the Supreme Court did not rule on the issue until its 2015 ruling in *Texas Department of Housing and Community Affairs v. Inclusive Communities Project Inc.*[286] That ruling laid to rest any doubts about the availability of disparate impact claims under the *FHA*. The Supreme Court noted that "antidiscrimination laws must be construed to encompass disparate-impact claims when their text refers to the consequences of actions and not just to the mindset of actors, and where that interpretation is consistent with the statutory purpose."[287] Because the *FHA* makes it unlawful not only to "refuse to sell or rent" but also to "otherwise make unavailable" housing because of race, the Court found that the *FHA* text referred to the consequences of actions and not just motivation.[288] The Court also found that this reading was consistent with the purpose of "providing for fair housing throughout the United States" and that some of the 1988 amendments to the *FHA* only made sense if disparate impact claims were available.[289]

Burdens of proof

Under the HUD regulation, the plaintiff can show that a practice of the defendant has a "discriminatory effect" on a protected group "where [the practice] actually or predictably results in a disparate impact on a group of persons or creates, increases, reinforces, or perpetuates segregated housing patterns because of race, color, religion, sex, handicap, familial status, or national origin."[290] In establishing a disparate impact, plaintiffs ordinarily rely on local statistics, but national statistics may be deemed relevant as well.[291] Those statistics focus on the relative percentages of people in each group affected by the policy rather than their absolute numbers.[292] If plaintiff produces sufficient evidence to enable the factfinder to determine that a disparate impact is present, the burden then shifts to the defendant to prove a "legally sufficient justification" for its practice.[293] To do that, defendant must demonstrate that the practice "is necessary to achieve one or more substantial, legitimate, nondiscriminatory interests" and that the justification is "supported by evidence" rather than being "hypothetical or

[285] 24 C.F.R. §100.500(a)-(b).

[286] 576 U.S. 519 (2015).

[287] *Id.* at 533.

[288] *Id.* at 534.

[289] *Id.* at 536-539.

[290] 24 C.F.R. §100.500(a). *See Simms v. First Gibraltar Bank*, 83 F.3d 1546, 1555 (5th Cir. 1996); *Huntington Branch, NAACP v. Town of Huntington*, 844 F.2d 926 (2d Cir.), *aff'd per curiam*, 488 U.S. 15 (1988); Robert G. Schwemm, *Housing Discrimination: Law and Litigation* §§10.6-10.7 (2025).

[291] Robert G. Schwemm, *Housing Discrimination: Law and Litigation* §10.6 (2025).

[292] *Graoch Assocs. #33, L.P. v. Louisville/Jefferson Cnty. Metro Human Relations Comm'n*, 508 F.3d 366, 378 (6th Cir. 2007); *Huntington Branch, NAACP v. Town of Huntington*, 844 F.2d 926, 938 (2d Cir.), *aff'd per curiam*, 488 U.S. 15 (1988).

[293] 24 C.F.R. §100.500(b); *Langlois v. Abington Housing Authority*, 207 F.3d 43, 49-50 (1st Cir. 2000); *see also* Robert G. Schwemm, *Housing Discrimination: Law and Litigation* §10.5 (2025).

speculative."[294] The evidentiary requirement is intended to ferret out justifications that are *post hoc* rationalizations designed to serve as a cover for intentional discrimination and to ensure that the interest is both substantial and legitimate. If defendant can produce evidence of a legally sufficient justification, the burden shifts back to the plaintiff to prove that those "interests could be served by another practice that has a less discriminatory effect."[295]

Zoning laws

Disparate impact claims are commonly brought against zoning laws that limit the construction of affordable housing.[296] A typical example is the ruling in *Huntington Branch, NAACP v. Town of Huntington*[297] that the town of Huntington violated the *FHA* by limiting the location of multifamily housing and refusing to rezone a particular parcel for multifamily housing affordable by low- and moderate-income families. The effect of the town's actions was to limit the ability of Black people to move into town because a greater percentage of Black families than white families needed access to affordable housing. The refusal to rezone the parcel to allow the housing to be built also had a segregative effect because the zoning law allowed multifamily housing in parts of town where many Black people lived and excluded such housing from areas where white residents lived. The Court found the town's justifications for its policies insubstantial either because they were unsupported by evidence, were *post hoc* rationalizations, or could have been achieved in a manner that did not have the effect of perpetuating racial segregation.

Discriminatory marketing practices

Disparate impact claims may also be brought against private defendants. For example, in *Adkins v. Morgan Stanley*,[298] the court agreed that plaintiffs had shown a *prima facie* disparate impact claim when defendant Morgan Stanley bought and securitized subprime loans from the mortgage lender that had issued the plaintiffs' predatory loans. The court found that those loans could plausibly be viewed as harmful to borrowers because they were structured to make default highly likely. It also found that Morgan Stanley promoted the creation of those loans by buying them from an independent mortgage lender; Morgan Stanley's support arguably made it economically profitable for the loans to be issued in the first place. Because the mortgage lender had aggressively marketed those loans to Black home purchasers and because Black people were more likely to be victims of predatory lending than others, the court found a *prima facie* case of disparate impact based on race in mortgage lending.

[294] 24 C.F.R. §100.500(b).

[295] 24 C.F.R. §100.500(c)(3); *Mount Holly Gardens Citizens in Action Inc. v. Mount Holly, N.J.*, 658 F.3d 375 (3d Cir. 2011) (displacement of low-income residents was justified by goal of removing blight but remanding to determine whether that goal could be achieved in a less discriminatory manner).

[296] *MHANY Management, Inc. v. Cnty. of Nassau*, 819 F.3d 581 (2d Cir. 2016) (challenge to exclusionary zoning law); *Dews v. Town of Sunnyvale*, 109 F. Supp. 2d 526, 532 (N.D. Tex. 2000) (city's one-acre minimum lot size and ban on apartments imposed a disparate impact on racial minorities, by excluding many minority families from the city, that was not justified by sufficiently strong governmental interests).

[297] 844 F.2d 926 (2d Cir.), *aff'd per curiam*, 488 U.S. 15 (1988).

[298] 2013 WL 3835198 (S.D.N.Y. 2013).

▶ HARD CASE ▷ ANTIWELFARE EXCLUSIONS

In *Bronson v. Crestwood Lake Section 1 Holding Corp.*,[299] the court held that a landlord's refusal to accept tenants with Section 8 (or Housing Choice Voucher) certificates[300] might violate the *FHA* by posing a disparate impact based on race because a greater percentage of Black and Latino people than white people applied for and needed Section 8 certificates.[301] Defendant claimed that it had valid business reasons for not wanting to participate in the Section 8 program because federal regulations imposed certain obligations on participating landlords. However, the court rejected defendant's justifications for refusing to accept tenants with Section 8 certificates as insubstantial because defendant had not shown the challenged policies were "reasonably necessary to insure payment of rent or that [defendant] has, in past experience, encountered losses or defaults as a result of accepting Section 8 tenants." Other courts have refused to apply the *FHA* to landlords who refuse to accept Section 8 tenants on the ground that the statute creating the Section 8 program makes it voluntary.[302] ◀

▶ HARD CASE ▷VOUCHER PREFERENCES FOR LOCAL RESIDENTS

In *Langlois v. Abington Housing Authority*,[303] a local public housing authority (PHA) gave a preference to local residents in issuing Section 8 housing vouchers or certificates. These federally funded vouchers are issued to low-income families (earning less than 80 percent of the median wage in the local area).[304] A family with a voucher is entitled to have the PHA pay to the family's landlord "the difference between the gross rent or a 'payment standard' adopted by the PHA, and a lesser amount paid by the family."[305] Because PHAs normally do not have enough funds to subsidize all of the families that meet the financial requirements for assistance, they maintain

[299] 724 F. Supp. 148 (S.D.N.Y. 1989).

[300] These certificates ensure federal payment of a portion of the rent for certain low-income families. *See* 42 U.S.C. §1437f. The Section 8 program was created by a 1974 amendment to the *Housing Act of 1937, Housing and Community Development Act of 1974*, Pub. L. No. 93-383, Title II, §201(a), 88 Stat. 633, 662-666, and has been revised, including in 1998 by the *Quality Housing and Work Responsibility Act of 1998*, Pub. L. No. 105-276, Title V, §545, 112 Stat. 2518, 2596-2604.

[301] *Graoch Assocs. #33, L.P. v. Louisville/Jefferson Cty. Metro. Hum. Relations Comm'n*, 508 F.3d 366, 377 (6th Cir. 2007); *Gilligan v. Jamco Development Corp.*, 108 F.3d 246 (9th Cir. 1997) (refusal to rent to AFDC recipients states a possible claim as discrimination because of familial status); *Ryan v. Ramsey*, 936 F. Supp. 417 (S.D. Tex. 1996) (refusal to rent to person with AIDS because he was dependent on Social Security benefits states a claim for disability discrimination under *FHA*).

[302] *Inclusive Cmtys. Project, Inc. v. Lincoln Prop. Co.*, 920 F.3d 890, 909 (5th Cir. 2019); *Salute v. Stratford Greens Garden Apartments*, 136 F.3d 293 (2d Cir. 1998); *see also Knapp v. Eagle Property Management Corp.*, 54 F.3d 1272 (7th Cir. 1995) (both holding that a landlord's refusal to accept Section 8 certificates cannot be the basis of a disparate impact claim under the *FHA* because the Section 8 statute makes participation voluntary).

[303] 207 F.3d 43 (1st Cir. 2000).

[304] 42 U.S.C. §1437a(b)(2).

[305] *See id.* at §1437f(o)(2); 24 C.F.R. §§982.503 & 982.505.

waiting lists. In this case, the PHAs in eight communities proposed to give preference to local residents, *i.e.*, those already residing in the community. Local preferences in the awarding of Section 8 vouchers are explicitly permitted by the governing statute, as amended in 1998.[306] Plaintiffs included the Massachusetts Coalition for the Homeless and four individuals who did not live in any of the eight communities. They claimed that the various communities were composed of mostly white residents, that this resulted from past societal discrimination, and that adopting a local preference would disproportionately exclude Black and Latino renters from the available pool of Section 8 certificate recipients in those communities and thus perpetuate racial segregation in violation of the *FHA*.

Competing arguments

The PHAs argued that a preference for local residents was a valid justification because it allowed local low-income families to remain in their own communities and such families have strong interests in remaining at home, not switching schools, and maintaining access to jobs. They further argued that, once a substantial justification is shown, the disparate impact cannot violate the *FHA*. Balancing legitimate government objectives against such disparate racial impacts is a job for the legislature, not individual judges deciding particular cases. And even if balancing must be done, these interests are sufficiently strong that they arguably outweigh the disparate racial impact. Plaintiffs responded that, although a preference for local residents might be legitimate as a general matter, it is arguably not sufficiently strong so as to outweigh a substantial disparate racial impact, particularly where the result is to perpetuate racial segregation and exclusion from a substantially white community. As noted above, the First Circuit found no *FHA* violation because defendant had a valid justification for its policy.[307] The Second Circuit, however, disagrees, requiring courts to determine whether the justification is sufficient to outweigh the segregative effect.[308] ◀

Affirmatively further fair housing regulations (AFFH)

The Fair Housing Act requires the Department of Housing and Urban Development (HUD) to administer its housing and urban development programs and activities in a manner that "affirmatively . . . further[s]" fair housing.[309] In 2015, HUD published final regulations giving guidance to municipalities that receive federal housing funds guidance on how to meet those obligations.[310] The summary of the regulations explains that HUD's program participants have an obligation "to take significant actions to overcome historic patterns of segregation, achieve truly balanced and integrated living patterns, promote fair housing choice, and foster inclusive communities that are free from discrimination." The revised rule changed the way that participants analyze "impediments to fair housing choice" as well the way they certify that they are meeting their obligation

[306] *See* 42 U.S.C. §1437f(o)(6).

[307] *Langlois v. Abington Housing Authority*, 207 F.3d 43 (1st Cir. 2000).

[308] *Huntington Branch, NAACP v. Town of Huntington*, 844 F.2d 926 (2d Cir.), *aff'd per curiam*, 488 U.S. 15 (1988).

[309] 42 U.S.C. 3608(e)(5).

[310] 24 C.F.R. Parts 5.150-5.168, 91.5, 91.105-91.505, 92.104-92.508, 570.3-570.094, 574.530, 576.500, 903.1-903.23, 80 Fed. Reg. 42,272 (July 16, 2015).

to "affirmatively further fair housing." HUD committed to provide participants with relevant data to enable them to assess fair housing issues such as segregation and conditions that restrict fair housing choice, and then enable participants to make changes over time. In 2025, HUD published a rule rescinding the 2015 regulations.[311]

§12.8.2 Sex

▶ HARD CASE ▷ SHELTER FOR BATTERED WOMEN

In *Doe v. City of Butler*,[312] a city policy required a special permit for "transitional dwellings" such as shelters for battered women and limited such dwellings to no more than six individuals. The low limit on the number of allowable occupants made it economically infeasible to operate a shelter anywhere within the city. Plaintiffs claimed that this violated the *FHA* because it imposed a disparate impact on women who are more likely than men to be victims of domestic violence and thus have a need for shelters to escape with their children from abusive relationships. The inability to set up a shelter anywhere in the city meant that women were less safe in their homes than men and therefore denied equal property rights. The Third Circuit rejected these arguments on the ground that men, as well as women, were denied the ability to set up transitional dwellings. Men might use halfway houses for parolees, alcohol treatment centers, and the like, and there was no showing that a greater percentage of women than men were adversely impacted by the law.[313] ◀

▶ HARD CASE ▷ "NO WELFARE" POLICY

In *Department of Housing and Urban Development v. Ross*,[314] a court held that a landlord's "no welfare policy" had a disparate impact on women because a greater percentage of women than men were recipients of government benefits. The effect of the no-welfare policy was to make it more difficult for such women to find places to live. The landlord might well have justified the policy by trying to prove that low-income tenants, including welfare recipients, were more likely than higher-income tenants to pay the rent inconsistently or to miss payments and that the landlord therefore had a legitimate justification for the refusal to rent. ◀

[311] *Affirmatively Furthering Fair Housing Revisions*, 90 Fed. Reg. 11,0020-02 (Mar. 3, 2025).
[312] 892 F.2d 315 (3d Cir. 1989).
[313] The court did remand for consideration on the question of whether the law created a disparate impact on the basis of familial status because, if such a shelter were created, the occupancy limit might prevent women from bringing their children to the shelter. *Cf.* Noah Kazis, *Fair Housing for a Non-Sexist City*, 134 Harv. L. Rev. 1683, 1686 (2021) (noting the role of sex stereotyping and sexual harassment in the market for housing).
[314] *Fair Housing—Fair Lending Rptr.* ¶25,075 (HUD ALJ 1994) (cited in Robert G. Schwemm, *Housing Discrimination: Law and Litigation* §11C:1 n.21 (2025)).

▷ RENTAL TO PERSONS WITH CRIMINAL RECORDS **HARD CASE ◀**

HUD has issued proposed guidelines advising that it may constitute unlawful racial discrimination to refuse to rent to persons with criminal records.[315] If exclusion has a discriminatory effect, a housing provider must have a legally sufficient justification for the refusal to rent. Such a justification might be absent if the person was only arrested but not convicted or if the conviction is for an offense that is insufficiently serious to justify the exclusion from housing. Similarly, a policy or practice that does not take into account the time that has passed may also not be sufficient to justify it. "Accordingly, a policy or practice that fails to consider the nature, severity, and recency of criminal conduct is unlikely to be proven necessary to serve a 'substantial, legitimate, nondiscriminatory interest' of the provider. The determination of whether any particular criminal history-based restriction on housing satisfies step two of the discriminatory effects standard must be made on a case-by-case basis."[316] ◀

§12.8.3 Sexual Orientation and Gender Identity

As we have discussed above,[317] the Supreme Court has held that the term "sex" in Title VII of the *Civil Rights Act* protects against discrimination on the basis of sexual orientation or gender identity.[318] Similar reasoning is likely to apply to the same statutory text in the *FHA*.[319]

▷ SAME-SEX COUPLES AND MARRIED STUDENTS HOUSING **HARD CASE ◀**

A university provides housing for married couples. A gay couple sues the university, claiming that the exclusion of gay couples violates a local law that prohibits discrimination because of sexual orientation. The plaintiffs claim that the university policy has a disparate impact on gay and lesbian couples because they, unlike heterosexual couples, cannot get married even if they want to do so. In *Levin v. Yeshiva University*,[320] the court held that such a policy imposed a disparate impact on gay and lesbian couples under the New York City law prohibiting sexual orientation discrimination and remanded to determine whether the disparate impact bore a "significant relationship to a significant business objective." ◀

[315] U.S. Dep't of Hous. & Urb. Dev., *Office of General Counsel Guidance on Application of Fair Housing Act Standards to the Use of Criminal Records by Providers of Housing and Real Estate-Related Transactions* (Apr. 4, 2016), https://www.fairhousingnc.org/wp-content/uploads/2022/08/06-10-2022-Implementation-of-OGC-Guidance-on-Application-of-FHA-Standards-to-the-Use-of-Criminal-Records-June-10-2022.pdf.

[316] *Id.*

[317] *See* §12.4.

[318] *Bostock v. Clayton County*, 590 U.S. 644 (2020).

[319] Rigel C. Oliveri, *Sexual Orientation and Gender Identity Discrimination Claims Under the Fair Housing Act After* Bostock v. Clayton County, 69 U. Kan. L. Rev. 409, 431-437 (2021).

[320] 754 N.E.2d 1099 (N.Y. 2001).

§12.8.4 Disability

Disparate impact and reasonable accommodation

Disparate impact claims based on disability have two separate doctrinal foundations. A plaintiff challenging a municipal zoning law, for example, might bring an ordinary disparate impact claim, arguing that the law has a disparate impact on people with disabilities. The plaintiff in *Ryan v. Ramsey*,[321] for example, argued that the landlord's refusal to rent to him because he was dependent on Social Security benefits imposed a disparate impact based on handicap because persons with AIDS, such as himself, were more likely than those without disabilities to need and receive public assistance. Alternatively, such a plaintiff might argue that §3604(f)(3)(B) of the *FHA* requires defendants to make "reasonable accommodations" in their "rules, policies, practices, or services, when such accommodations may be necessary to afford such person equal opportunity to use and enjoy a dwelling."[322] Often plaintiffs make both claims. In addition, a municipality's refusal to issue a permit for a group home for persons with disabilities, such as persons with AIDS, may violate not only the *FHA* by imposing a disparate impact on persons with disabilities, but may also violate the *Americans with Disabilities Act* by subjecting persons with disabilities to unequal permitting requirements or failing to administer their activities "in the most integrated setting appropriate to the needs of qualified individuals with disabilities."[323]

Group homes as single-family residences

Many cases address the question of local zoning requirements that limit the ability of owners to establish group homes for persons with disabilities, such as persons with mental retardation, persons with mental illness, or alcoholic treatment centers.[324] When a group home is established in a zone reserved for "single-family homes," the issue often arises whether

[321] *See Ryan v. Ramsey*, 936 F. Supp. 417 (S.D. Tex. 1996) (refusal to rent to person with AIDS because he was dependent on Social Security benefits states a claim for disability discrimination under *FHA*).

[322] *Smith & Lee Associates, Inc. v. City of Taylor, Michigan*, 13 F.3d 920, 932 (6th Cir. 1993) (remanding for findings on whether a city failed to make reasonable accommodation for an adult foster care facility by allowing it to locate in an area limited to "single-family homes" because "the handicapped may have little choice but to live in a commercial home if they desire to live in a residential neighborhood"); *Judy B. v. Borough of Tioga*, 889 F. Supp. 792 (M.D. Pa. 1995) (applying reasonable accommodation analysis to invalidate a borough decision denying a variance to turn a motel into a single-room-occupancy residence for homeless persons, many of whom were recovering alcoholics, drugs addicts, or who suffered from a mental or physical disability that hindered their ability to live independently); *Oxford House, Inc. v. Town of Babylon*, 819 F. Supp. 1179 (E.D.N.Y. 1993) (holding that a zoning law restricting occupancy to traditional families had a disparate impact on persons with disabilities because it excluded recovering alcoholics and drug addicts who were more likely than those without disabilities to live with unrelated individuals; and that the *FHA* required the town to make reasonable accommodations in its zoning code to prevent exclusion of the group home's residents from the community). *But see Oxford House-C v. City of St. Louis*, 77 F.3d 249 (8th Cir. 1996) (ordinance limiting group homes to eight residents did not violate the *FHA* because the city had legitimate interests in decreasing congestion, traffic, and noise in residential areas).

[323] *Pack v. Clayton County, Georgia*, 1993 WL 837007, at *8 (N.D. Ga. 1993), *aff'd*, 47 F.3d 430 (11th Cir. 1995). *See* §2.6.3.

[324] *See, e.g., Association for Advancement of the Mentally Handicapped, Inc. v. City of Elizabeth*, 876 F. Supp. 614 (D.N.J. 1994) (zoning ordinance limiting location of group homes for persons with developmental disabilities violated *FHA*).

the group home is a "residential" use, whether the "restriction to" refers to the structure (a "single-family home") or the occupants (who must be a "single family"), and, if the ordinance requires the occupants to be a "single family," whether a group home is a "single family."[325]

FHA challenges to restrictive zoning laws that exclude group homes

Challenges have been made to single-family zoning that is interpreted to exclude group homes[326] or other restrictive zoning requirements,[327] as well as special health and safety rules applicable only to group homes.[328] Many of these challenges have succeeded, on the ground that the zoning restrictions had a disproportionate impact on persons with disabilities that was not justified by a substantial government interest.[329] For example, the D.C. Circuit awarded damages in *Samaritan Inns, Inc. v. District of Columbia*[330] to the developer of a group home for former drug and alcohol abusers on the ground that the city's stop work order that prevented plaintiff from completing work on a residential care facility imposed a disparate impact on the basis of handicap in violation of the *FHA*. However, the Seventh Circuit held in *Hemisphere Building Co., Inc. v. Village of Richton Park*[331] that a village had no obligation to relax its zoning rules just to make housing more affordable to persons with disabilities.

▷ CO-SIGNER CASES **HARD CASE ◀**

Landlords sometimes seek to ensure that tenants have adequate income to pay the rent. Tenants who do not have an independent source of income and who thus cannot meet minimum income requirements may seek to have the lease co-signed by a parent or other person who is financially supporting them. Some landlords refuse to rent to such tenants because they do not want the expense or difficulty that might be involved in suing someone other than the tenant to recover unpaid rent. If a tenant is unable to work because of a disability and is dependent on family members for support, a landlord's refusal to waive such a policy against co-signers to the lease may have a disparate impact on persons with disabilities. Alternatively, the

[325] *See* §6.6.

[326] *City of Edmonds v. Oxford House, Inc.*, 514 U.S. 725 (1995); *Smith & Lee Assocs. v. City of Taylor*, 102 F.3d 781 (6th Cir. 1996); *Oxford House, Inc. v. Town of Babylon*, 819 F. Supp. 1179 (E.D.N.Y. 1993); *Samaritan Inns, Inc. v. District of Columbia*, 114 F.3d 1227 (D.C. Cir. 1997); *North Shore-Chicago Rehabilitation, Inc. v. Village of Skokie*, 827 F. Supp. 497 (N.D. Ill. 1993); *Potomac Group Homes v. Montgomery County*, 823 F. Supp. 1285 (D. Md. 1993); *Assisted Living Assocs. v. Moorestown Township*, 996 F. Supp. 409 (D.N.J. 1998).

[327] *Bryant Woods Inn, Inc. v. Howard County*, 124 F.3d 597 (4th Cir. 1997); *Gamble v. City of Escondido*, 104 F.3d 300 (9th Cir. 1997); *Hovsons, Inc. v. Township of Brick*, 89 F.3d 1096 (3d Cir. 1996); *Bryant Woods Inn, Inc. v. Howard County*, 124 F.3d 597 (4th Cir. 1997).

[328] *N.J. Rooming & Boarding House Owners v. Asbury Park*, 152 F.3d 217 (3d Cir. 1998); *Larkin v. State of Michigan Dep't of Social Servs.*, 89 F.3d 285 (6th Cir. 1996); *Bangerter v. City of Orem City*, 46 F.3d 1491 (10th Cir. 1995); *Marbrunak, Inc. v. City of Stow*, 974 F.2d 43 (6th Cir. 1992).

[329] *Tsombanidis v. City of West Haven*, 129 F. Supp. 2d 136 (D. Conn. 2001); Robert G. Schwemm, *Housing Discrimination: Law and Litigation* §11D.3 (2025).

[330] 114 F.3d 1227 (D.C. Cir. 1997).

[331] 171 F.3d 437 (7th Cir. 1999).

FHA may require the landlord to modify this policy to reasonably accommodate tenants with disabilities under 42 U.S.C. §3604(f)(3)(B). While the Ninth Circuit has held that the *FHA* mandates that a landlord alter a policy against co-signers that effectively prevented a tenant with AIDS from meeting minimum financial requirements to rent an apartment,[332] other courts have held that the *FHA* in no way prevents landlords from making business judgments about the financial qualifications needed to rent the apartment.[333] ◀

▶ **HARD CASE**

▷ SPACING REQUIREMENTS FOR GROUP HOMES

A number of cases have addressed the question of whether municipalities violate the *FHA* by imposing spacing requirements for group homes. Most of those cases have struck down the spacing requirements because they create an unjustified disparate impact on persons with disabilities.[334] An exception is *Familystyle of St. Paul, Inc. v. City of St. Paul*,[335] in which the state and city implemented a program of deinstitutionalization of the mentally ill, in part, by requiring new group homes for persons with mental illness to be located at least a quarter-mile away from an existing residential facility unless the local zoning board granted a special permit allowing the use.[336] Plaintiffs sought to establish such a group home and argued that the spacing requirement had a disparate impact on persons with disabilities in that it severely limited their choice of where to live or establish a home. Persons with mental illness were arguably more in need of such group homes than those without mental illness. The court found the spacing requirement justified and nondiscriminatory, accepting defendant city's argument that the spacing requirement was justified by the desire to integrate persons with mental illness into the community and that the clustering of group homes violated the state policy of promoting deinstitutionalization of persons with mental illness. Plaintiffs could have responded to this argument by citing *United States v. Starrett City*[337] to the effect that, when a city's integration goal conflicts with the *FHA*'s nondiscrimination goal, the nondiscrimination policy prevails. The city might respond by noting that the integration policy is based on a medical judgment rather than a policy judgment about segregation and that it should therefore be granted deference.

[332] *Giebeler v. M & B Assocs.*, 343 F.3d 1143 (9th Cir. 2003).

[333] *Salute v. Stratford Greens Garden Apartments*, 136 F.3d 293 (2d Cir. 1998) (landlord not required to accept Section 8 tenants); *cf. Hemisphere Bldg. Co., Inc. v. Village of Richton Park*, 171 F.3d 437 (7th Cir. 1999) (*FHA* does not require municipality to consider financial situation of individuals with disabilities in fashioning its zoning laws).

[334] *Larkin v. State of Michigan*, 89 F.3d 285 (6th Cir. 1996); *Horizon House Developmental Services, Inc. v. Town of Upper Southampton*, 804 F. Supp. 683 (E.D. Pa. 1992), *aff'd*, 995 F.2d 217 (3d Cir. 1993); *Association for Advancement of the Mentally Handicapped, Inc. v. City of Elizabeth*, 876 F. Supp. 614 (D.N.J. 1994).

[335] 923 F.2d 91 (8th Cir. 1991).

[336] Minn. Stat. §245A.11, subd. 4.

[337] 840 F.2d 1096 (2d Cir. 1988).

If the *FHA* protects the ability to establish a group home, it will override restrictive covenants to the contrary that purport to prohibit the use of property for group home purposes.[338] Moreover, the act of bringing a lawsuit to enforce such a covenant may constitute a separate, independent violation of the *FHA*.[339] ◀

Restrictive covenants overridden

§12.8.5 Familial Status

§12.8.5.1 Families with Children

▷ REFUSAL TO RENT TO WELFARE RECIPIENTS **HARD CASE ◀**

The landlord in *Gilligan v. Jamco Development Corp.*[340] refused to accept any welfare recipients of AFDC (Aid to Families with Dependent Children).[341] Plaintiffs claimed that this violated the *FHA* by discriminating because of familial status, noting that only families with children were recipients of AFDC. The Ninth Circuit refused to dismiss the complaint, finding that plaintiffs had stated a claim under the statute.[342] This does not mean that plaintiffs would necessarily win because defendant could present a valid business justification for refusing to rent to AFDC recipients. The landlord might argue, for example, that low-income tenants are more likely to face financial problems in meeting all their obligations and that, despite their right to a monthly government check, they are more likely than nonwelfare recipients to fail to pay rent on time. Plaintiffs would respond that the purpose of the *FHA* familial status provisions was to ensure that families would not be turned away from housing because they have children, that defendant's policy excludes those families with children who are in most desperate need of housing, and that stereotypical fears of welfare recipients are insufficient to justify this disparate impact. ◀

▷ SHELTERS FOR VICTIMS OF INTIMATE PARTNER VIOLENCE **HARD CASE ◀**

Doe v. City of Butler[343] presented the question of whether a zoning ordinance that limited the number of persons who could occupy a "transitional dwelling" and that therefore made either establishment of a shelter for women who had suffered intimate partner violence infeasible had

[338] *Board of Managers v. Rios*, 630 N.Y.S.2d 875 (Sup. Ct. 1995).
[339] *United States v. Wagner*, 940 F. Supp. 972, 978 (N.D. Tex. 1996); *Hill v. Community of Damien of Molokai*, 911 P.2d 861 (N.M. 1996).
[340] 108 F.3d 246 (9th Cir. 1997).
[341] This program was transformed by the *Personal Responsibility and Work Opportunity Act of 1996* into Temporary Assistance to Needy Families (TANF), 42 U.S.C. §§601 to 619.
[342] *See also United States v. Badgett*, 976 F.2d 1176 (8th Cir. 1992) (disparate impact shown when landlord refused to rent a one-bedroom apartment to more than one person, effectively excluding persons with children; landlord's justification — shortage of parking spaces — was unreasonable).
[343] 892 F.2d 315 (3d Cir. 1989).

a disparate impact on the basis of familial status because it limited the number of women with children who could be served by a shelter without regard to reasonable occupancy limits.[344] The Third Circuit refused to dismiss the complaint, holding that the ordinance might violate the *FHA* prohibition against familial status discrimination because the six-person limit might adversely affect "the ability of abused mothers to bring their children with them when seeking refuge" and thus have a "dampening effect on the ability of women with children to take advantage of transitional dwellings."[345] However, as the court noted with regard to plaintiffs' claim that the ordinance had a disparate impact based on sex, there was no showing that the limit on transitional dwellings had a statistically greater impact on families with children than families without children, given that the ordinance regulated all kinds of facilities, such as alcoholic treatment centers and group homes for persons with mental illness, that might well serve individuals without children. ◀

Zoning law limits on number of cohabiting unrelated adults

§12.8.5.2 Group Homes and Nontraditional Families. In addition to cases involving persons with disabilities seeking to establish group homes in the face of restrictive zoning laws, cases have been brought by a variety of plaintiffs seeking to avoid local restrictions on the number of unrelated adults who may live together. Such laws are often intended to prevent institutional uses, such as fraternities or religious orders, from locating in residential neighborhoods. Sometimes they are intended to exclude certain types of residents, such as students, who are likely to double up, from neighborhoods otherwise composed of traditional families. Such laws have often been challenged on the ground that they interfere with constitutionally protected rights of privacy and intimate association.

Village of Belle Terre v. Boraas

In *Village of Belle Terre v. Boraas*,[346] six students who wished to rent a single-family house challenged a town ordinance that prohibited more than two unrelated adults from living together. The Court upheld the ordinance even though it had the effect of excluding the students from living in the town, because they could not individually afford the rent charged for single-family houses in the town. The Court held that no fundamental rights were involved because unrelated adults do not constitute a "family." Moreover, Justice Douglas argued in his opinion, the town had legitimate interests in excluding students:

> A quiet place where yards are wide, people few, and motor vehicles restricted are legitimate guidelines in a land-use project addressed to family needs. This goal is a permissible one. The police power is not confined to elimination of filth, stench, and unhealthy places. It is ample to lay out zones where family values, youth values, and the blessings of quiet seclusion and clean air make the area a sanctuary for people.[347]

[344] This case is further discussed at §12.8.2 on the question of whether it discriminates on the basis of sex.
[345] 892 F.3d at 324.
[346] 416 U.S. 1 (1974).
[347] *Id.* at 9.

Justice Marshall dissented, arguing that the town could legitimately limit the number of individuals living together if the goal was to control density but that it could not distinguish between traditional and nontraditional families because the

> choice of household companions — of whether a person's intellectual and emotional needs are best met by living with family, friends, professional associates, or others — involves deeply personal considerations as to the kind and quality of intimate relationships within the home. That decision surely falls within the ambit of the right to privacy protected by the Constitution.[348]

Moore v. City of East Cleveland

In contrast, the Supreme Court struck down a local ordinance in *Moore v. City of East Cleveland*,[349] which effectively prohibited a grandmother from living with her two grandchildren because they were cousins rather than siblings. The Supreme Court limited the holding in *Belle Terre* to nontraditional families, finding that the Constitution protects the right of traditional family members to live together.

State constitutions

Most state courts accept the Supreme Court's reasoning in *Belle Terre*,[350] but some have interpreted their state constitutions to grant rights to unrelated adults to live together, adopting Justice Marshall's reasoning in his dissenting opinion in *Belle Terre*.[351] For example, the Michigan Supreme Court ruled in *Charter Township of Delta v. Dinolfo*[352] that a local zoning law unconstitutionally prohibited several owners from establishing households comprised of a married couple with children and six unrelated adults. These household members belonged to the Work of Christ Community, a nonprofit and federally tax-exempt organization chartered by the state of Michigan. Justice Brickley explained:

> Each of these households functions as a family in a single housekeeping unit and members intend to reside in their respective households permanently. All of the members of these "families" have adopted their lifestyle as a means of living out the Christian commitment that they stress is an important part of their lives.[353]

The limitations were not justified as reasonable occupancy limits designed to promote safety and there was no showing that groups of unrelated adults would be more noisy or less law-abiding than would members of traditional families.

---

[348] *Id.* at 16 (Marshall, J., dissenting).

[349] 431 U.S. 494 (1977).

[350] *City of Ladue v. Horn*, 720 S.W.2d 745, 749-750 (Mo. Ct. App. 1986).

[351] *City of Santa Barbara v. Adamson*, 610 P.2d 436 (Cal. 1980) (invalidating restrictive ordinance); *State v. Baker*, 405 A.2d 368 (N.J. 1979) (same); *McMinn v. Town of Oyster Bay*, 488 N.E.2d 1240 (N.Y. 1985) (invalidating an ordinance that limited occupancy to persons related by blood, marriage, or adoption, or two unrelated persons over the age of 62).

[352] 351 N.W.2d 831 (Mich. 1984).

[353] *Id.* at 834.

§12.8.6 Religion

▶ HARD CASE ▷ USE OF PRIVATE HOMES FOR RELIGIOUS SERVICES

In *LeBlanc-Sternberg v. Fletcher*,[354] the Second Circuit found that a town had violated the *FHA* by adopting a zoning law that was intended to exclude Orthodox Jews from the town by prohibiting them from using rabbis' homes for prayer services. Plaintiffs had also made a disparate impact claim because the zoning law required all religious institutions to have at least two acres of land and prohibited conducting services in lots zoned for residential purposes. The town might have justified such rules on the ground that they protected residential neighborhoods from the noise, traffic, and disruption of large gatherings of persons. The plaintiffs might have argued that Orthodox Jews do not drive on the Sabbath and that traffic concerns thus could not be substantial in their case. Moreover, because Orthodox Jews need to walk to service on the Sabbath, places of worship need to be located in or near residential neighborhoods and a zoning law that excludes them has a disparate impact on Jews that is not warranted by a sufficiently strong governmental interest as to justify prohibiting gatherings of persons for religious purposes in homes in the community. ◀

▶ HARD CASE ▷ LIVING ARRANGEMENTS IN DORMS

In *Hack v. President and Fellows of Yale College*,[355] a group of Orthodox Jewish students sued Yale University to challenge its policy of requiring all students (other than married students or students over 21) in their first and second years to live in co-educational residence halls. They claimed that their "religious beliefs and obligations regarding sexual modesty forbid them to reside in the co-educational housing provided and mandated by Yale." They sought and were denied exemptions from the policy. The courts rejected their claim that Yale had violated the *FHA*, noting that Yale had reserved rooms for each of the plaintiffs and had in no way denied them housing. Plaintiffs claimed that the housing offered was not of a type that they could accept because of their religious beliefs, that this policy had a disparate impact on them because of religion, and that the failure to accommodate their free exercise of religion was not justified by sufficiently powerful educational reasons. ◀

Religious Land Use and Institutionalized Persons Act of 2000

The *Religious Land Use and Institutionalized Persons Act of 2000 (RLUIPA)*[356] attempted to revive certain aspects of the *RFRA* struck

[354] 67 F.3d 412 (2d Cir. 1995).
[355] 16 F. Supp. 2d 183 (D. Conn. 1998), *aff'd*, 237 F.3d 81 (1st Cir. 2000).
[356] 42 U.S.C. §§2000cc to 2000cc-5; *see Midrash Sephardi, Inc. v. Town of Surfside*, 366 F.3d 1214 (11th Cir. 2004) (holding *RLUIPA* constitutional).

down in *City of Boerne v. Flores*,[357] by curing the constitutional impediments identified there. *RLUIPA* prohibits governments from "impos[ing] or implement[ing] a land use regulation in a manner that imposes a substantial burden on the religious exercise of a person, including a religious assembly or institution" unless the regulation furthers "a compelling governmental interest" and "is the least restrictive means of *furthering* that compelling governmental interest."[358] To attempt to meet the constitutional requirements set out in *City of Boerne*, the statute applies only (a) if the affected activity receives federal funds, or (b) if either the substantial burden or the removal of the burden would affect "interstate commerce," or (c) if the burden is imposed in the course of governmental procedures that involve "individualized assessments of the proposed uses for the property involved."[359] The statute further provides that no government "shall impose or implement a land use regulation that (A) totally excludes religious assemblies from a jurisdiction; or (B) unreasonably limits religious assemblies, institutions, or structures within a jurisdiction."[360] For more discussion of *RLUIPA*, see §13.7.4.3 below.

§12.8.7 National Origin

▷ LANGUAGE RESTRICTIONS **HARD CASE ◀**

In *Holmgren v. Little Village Community Reporter*,[361] a newspaper published an advertisement indicating a preference for buyers or tenants that spoke a particular language. Defendants argued that "[t]he ability to speak a given language is not related to national origin. The purpose of requiring contracting parties to speak the same language, they say, is to foster communication and understanding between the parties, a reasonable purpose which purportedly does not violate 42 U.S.C. §3604(c)."[362] Landlords have legitimate interests in being able to communicate with their tenants. Nor does the requirement that a particular language be spoken necessarily correspond to national origin; many people speak languages other than the language of their country of national origin. The court rejected this argument:

> [T]o say that the ability to speak a certain language is not related to the country of origin of that language is mere sophistry. An advertisement for a Polish-speaking tenant, for example, is tantamount to an advertisement

[357] 521 U.S. 507 (1997). The constitutionality of the law is in doubt.
[358] 42 U.S.C. §2000cc. *See Cottonwood Christian Center v. Cypress Redevelopment Agency*, 218 F. Supp. 2d 1203 (C.D. Cal. 2002); *Grace United Methodist Church v. City of Cheyenne*, 235 F. Supp. 2d 1186 (D. Wyo. 2002).
[359] 42 U.S.C. at §2000cc(2)(C).
[360] *Id.* at §2000cc(3). In addition, the *RLUIPA* amends *RFRA* to clarify that *RFRA* is intended only to apply to federal regulations. *Id.* at §§2000bb-2 & 2000bb-3.
[361] 342 F. Supp. 512 (N.D. Ill. 1971).
[362] *Id.* at 513.

> for an immigrant (or the offspring of an immigrant) of Poland itself. Thus, the ads which indicate a preference for a purchaser or a tenant who speaks a particular language are unlawful under §3604(c).[363]

Disparate impact analysis

Even if a court concluded that language discrimination is not the same as national origin discrimination, it might well conclude that discrimination because of language has a disparate impact on individuals based on national origin. Those born outside the United States are more likely than those born in the United States to speak a language other than English, for example, and choosing tenants based on language therefore will impose a disproportionate impact on those born in a particular place. The counterargument is that landlords have strong, legitimate interests in being able to communicate with tenants. ◀

§12.9 Economic Discrimination

§12.9.1 Intentional Wealth-Based Discrimination

Discrimination based on source of income

At least 24 states and more than 140 local governments address "source of income" discrimination in housing.[364] Such statutes prohibit discrimination against recipients of Section 8 certificates through which the federal government pays a portion of the rent to the landlord, as well as recipients of other forms of governmental assistance.[365]

▶ HARD CASE ▷ TENANT INCOME REQUIREMENTS

In *Harris v. Capital Growth Investors XIV*,[366] a landlord refused to rent to two women, Tamela Harris and Muriel Jordan, who were "female heads of low income families whose income consists solely of public assistance benefits" because the landlord had a policy of renting only to tenants who have gross monthly incomes of at least three times the rent to be charged. Plaintiffs could have attempted to sue under the *FHA*, arguing that the income policy had a disparate impact on women, Black people, and children, all of whom

[363] *Id.*

[364] *Appendix B: State, Local, and Federal Laws Barring Source-of-Income Discrimination*, Poverty & Race Rsch. Action Council, 2 (Jan. 2025), https://www.prrac.org/pdf/AppendixB.pdf; *see, e.g.*, *Burrello Group, LLC* v. Dist. *of Columbia*, 303 A.3d 618, 624 (D.C. 2023) (property "[n]ot approved for vouchers" advertisement); *Lopez* v. *William Raveis Real Estate*, Inc., 272 A.3d 150, 166 (Conn. 2022) (statements against potential renter's status as a housing voucher holder).

[365] Cal. Gov't Code §12955; Conn. Gen. Stat. §46a-64c; Del. Code Ann. Tit. 6, §4603(b); D.C. Code §2-1402.21; Me. Rev. Stat. tit. 5, §4581-A; Mass. Gen. Laws ch. 151B, §4(10); Minn. Stat. §363A.09; N.J. Stat. §§10:5-4, 10:5-12g; N.Y. Exec. §§296.2-a, 296.5(a); N.D. Cent. Code §§14-02.4-01 to 14-02.5-02; Okla. Stat. tit. 25, §1452.A.8; Or. Rev. Stat. §659A.421(2); Utah Code §57-21-5; Vt. Stat. tit. 9, §4503(a); Wash. Rev. Code §59.18; Wis. Stat. §106.50. *See DiLiddo v. Oxford St. Realty, Inc.*, 876 N.E.2d 421, 428 (2007); *Franklin Tower One, L.L.C. v. N.M.*, 725 A.2d 1104, 1112-1113 (N.J. 1999).

[366] 805 P.2d 884 (Cal. 1991).

are more likely to be poor and in need of welfare than adult white males. Instead, they sued under the *California Unruh Civil Rights Act*,[367] claiming that the income requirement constituted discriminatory treatment on the basis of income and was not necessary to protect the landlord's legitimate business interests.[368]

Argument that poverty should not be a protected class

The court rejected this claim, noting that "[b]usiness establishments have an obvious and important interest in obtaining full and timely payment for the goods and services they provide,"[369] and that the minimum-income policy merely pursues the "the objective of securing payment" in a reasonable manner.[370] In an earlier case, *In re Cox*,[371] the California Supreme Court had liberally interpreted the *Unruh Civil Rights Act*, holding that it prohibited all forms of invidious discrimination and that the list of protected groups in the statute was "illustrative rather than restrictive" of the kinds of discrimination prohibited by the Act. However, the court refused to recognize wealth or low income as a protected class, noting that "plaintiffs' view of the Act would involve the courts of this state in a multitude of microeconomic decisions we are ill equipped to make."[372]

Argument that poverty should be a protected class

In a dissenting opinion, Justice Allen Broussard argued that while "[i]t is obvious that a minimum income policy might be invoked legitimately by a business to ensure payments for goods sold on credit, it should be equally obvious that minimum income policies might be abused, motivated solely by a discriminatory animus."[373] ◀

§12.9.2 Exclusionary Zoning

Southern Burlington County, NAACP v. Township of Mount Laurel (Mount Laurel I)

In the 1975 case of *Southern Burlington County, NAACP v. Township of Mount Laurel* (*Mount Laurel I*),[374] the Supreme Court of New Jersey held that the state constitution prohibited municipalities from enacting zoning laws that effectively exclude poor people from living in the community. The Township of Mount Laurel had zoned most of its land for detached, single-family homes, which were unaffordable by low- and moderate-income families. None of the land was zoned for affordable multifamily housing. The court upheld the findings of the trial court that Mount Laurel had "exhibited economic discrimination in that the poor have been deprived of adequate housing."[375] The court held that a "developing municipality" like Mount Laurel may not use its land use regulation to make it "physically and economically impossible to provide low and moderate income housing in the municipality" because this effectively excludes such people from living within the community:[376]

[367] Cal. Civ. Code §§51 & 52.
[368] They also claimed that it imposed a disparate impact on women.
[369] 805 P.2d at 884.
[370] *Id.* at 885.
[371] 474 P.2d 992 (Cal. 1970).
[372] 805 P.2d at 887.
[373] *Id.* at 898.
[374] 336 A.2d 713 (N.J. 1975).
[375] *Id.* at 723.
[376] *Id.* at 724.

> We conclude that every such municipality must, by its land use regulations, presumptively make realistically possible an appropriate variety and choice of housing. More specifically, presumptively it cannot foreclose the opportunity of the classes of people mentioned for low and moderate income housing and in its regulations must affirmatively afford that opportunity, at least to the extent of the municipality's fair share of the present and prospective regional need therefor.[377]

The court noted that "a zoning regulation, like any police power enactment, must promote public health, safety, morals or the general welfare."[378] Because shelter is one of "the most basic human needs," the

> presumptive obligation arises for each [developing] municipality affirmatively to plan and provide, by its land use regulations, the reasonable opportunity for an appropriate variety and choice of housing, including, of course, low and moderate cost housing, to meet the needs, desires and resources of all categories of people who may desire to live within its boundaries. Negatively, it may not adopt regulations or policies which thwart or preclude that opportunity.[379]

The court held that Mount Laurel must permit multifamily housing, as well as small dwellings on very small lots, and other types of low-cost housing. Moreover, the "amount of land removed from residential use by allocation to industrial and commercial purposes must be reasonably related to the present and future potential for such purposes."[380]

Remedies for exclusionary zoning

In *Mount Laurel I*, the Supreme Court of New Jersey ordered the township of Mount Laurel to amend its zoning law to remove unconstitutional restrictions on the development of low- and moderate-income housing. When this remedy proved insufficient, the court issued a second ruling in

Mount Laurel II

Mount Laurel II[381] in 1983, using the state's development plan to distinguish growth communities, which had an obligation to provide for their fair share of the regional low-income housing need, from nondeveloping communities, which merely had the obligation to provide for their own resident poor families. In addition, the court created strong remedies, including requiring the use of available state or federal housing subsidies, providing incentives to private developers to set aside a portion of their developments for low- and moderate-income housing, for example, by relaxing various restrictions in a zoning ordinance (typically density limits) in exchange for the construction of certain numbers of low- and moderate-income housing units, and a builder's remedy (ordering a municipality to allow a developer

377 *Id.*

378 *Id.* at 725; *cf. C & M Developers, Inc. v. Bedminster Township Zoning Hearing Board*, 820 A.2d 143, 158 (Pa. 2002) ("In general, when a minimum lot size requirement is motivated solely by a concern that 'a small number of lovely old homes will have to start keeping company with a growing number of smaller, less expensive, more densely located houses,' it exudes an exclusionary purpose, which does not foster or promote the general welfare.").

379 336 A.2d at 728.

380 *Id.* at 732.

381 *Southern Burlington County NAACP v. Township of Mount Laurel*, 456 A.2d 390 (N.J. 1983) (*Mount Laurel II*).

to construct a particular project that includes a substantial amount of lower-income housing). The legislature then enacted the *New Jersey Fair Housing Act of 1985*,[382] which transferred authority over *Mount Laurel* cases to a state administrative agency called the Council on Affordable Housing. The Act also placed a moratorium on the builder's remedy and allowed municipalities to buy their way out of the *Mount Laurel* obligation by paying neighboring communities to absorb up to half of their fair-share obligation. The Act was upheld by the New Jersey Supreme Court in *Hills Development Co. v. Bernards Township* (often called *Mount Laurel III*).[383]

Reception in other states

California, Florida, Massachusetts, Oregon, and Rhode Island also have adopted legislation to limit exclusionary zoning.[384] California's statute, which resembles the *New Jersey Fair Housing Act*, mandates comprehensive planning by a state agency to ensure that local zoning laws take into account each municipality's fair share of the regional low-income housing need.[385] Both New Jersey and California employ inclusionary zoning techniques such as set-asides and density bonuses. In contrast, Massachusetts enacted a statute known as the "*Anti-Snob Zoning Act*," empowering developers to challenge local permit denials by appealing unfavorable local zoning board decisions to a state review board, which is authorized to overturn local board decisions that exclude low-income housing needed in the municipality.[386] Oregon, like Massachusetts, prevents local governments from excluding low-cost housing.[387] Florida requires municipalities to adopt plans for affordable housing.[388]

Efficiency concerns

Some scholars have argued that government-mandated inclusionary zoning likely will be inefficient. Professor Robert Ellickson has argued that such zoning effectively imposes a tax on new construction because some units that would not otherwise be profitable must be included in the development, thereby raising the costs of providing new housing. When the cost of new housing is artificially raised by government regulation, less will be provided, thereby exacerbating the already existing shortage of low-income housing and interfering with the filtering mechanism by which wealthy homeowners move to better housing and leave their prior residences for less wealthy consumers.[389] Other scholars, however, have contended that such techniques are likely to *restore* the efficient use of land by *removing*

[382] N.J. Stat. Ann. §§52:27D-301 to 52:27D-329.

[383] 510 A.2d 621 (N.J. 1986).

[384] Cal. Gov't Code §§65580 to 65589.8; Fla. Stat. §§163.3161 to 163.3215; Mass. Gen. Laws Ann. ch. 40B, §§20 to 23; Or. Rev. Stat. §§197.005 to 197.850; R.I. Gen. Laws §45-53-1 to -8; *see* Barbara Ehrlich Kautz, *In Defense of Inclusionary Zoning: Successfully Creating Affordable Housing*, 36 U.S.F. L. Rev. 971 (2002); Florence Wagman Roisman, *Opening the Suburbs to Racial Integration: Lessons for the 21st Century*, 23 W. New Eng. L. Rev. 65 (2001). *But see Town of Telluride v. Lot Thirty-Four Venture, L.L.C.*, 3 P.3d 30 (Colo. 2000) (ordinance requiring developers to build or pay for affordable housing for 40 percent of employees who would be needed by new development struck down on the ground that it conflicted with a state statute prohibiting rent control).

[385] Cal. Gov't Code §§65580 to 65589.8.

[386] Mass. Gen. Laws Ann. ch. 40B, §§20-23.

[387] Or. Rev. Stat. §§197.005 to 197.850.

[388] Fla. Stat. §163.3177(f).

[389] Robert C. Ellickson, *The Irony of "Inclusionary Zoning,"* 54 S. Cal. L. Rev. 1167 (1981).

inefficient restrictions on development contained in existing exclusionary zoning laws. Laws that exclude low-income housing from the community arguably decrease social welfare by attempting to create protected subdivisions without accounting for the externalities of limiting low-income housing to urban areas. They may also artificially increase the cost of low-income housing by excluding it from areas in which developers could otherwise profitably build it.[390]

FHA of 1968

Although most states have refused to adopt the *Mount Laurel* doctrine,[391] it should be noted that the Second Circuit held in *Huntington Branch, NAACP v. Town of Huntington*[392] that a town's refusal to alter its zoning law to allow for low-income, multifamily housing caused a disparate impact on Black families, who were more likely than white families to need such housing. The court also found the town's justifications for its policy to be insubstantial and ordered the town to grant a building permit for the project. Because it is possible to show that women and children are similarly more likely than men and adults to be poor, exclusionary zoning that limits opportunities for low-income families *may* be struck down in appropriate cases under the *FHA*'s disparate impact analysis.

§12.9.3 The Right to Be Somewhere: Homelessness and Public Loitering Laws

Homelessness and rights to use public property

Many states regulate uses of public streets, roads, and parks to ensure that they can be enjoyed safely by everyone. Issues arise when homeless persons sit or sleep on sidewalks or in public parks or next to public highways. In 2012, Rhode Island passed a "Homeless Bill of Rights"[393] that, among other things, ensures that homeless persons have "the right to use and move freely in public spaces, including, but not limited to, public sidewalks, public parks, public transportation and public buildings, in the same manner as any other person. . . . "[394]

▶ HARD CASE ▷ REGULATION OF PUBLIC ACTS OF HOMELESS PERSONS

Argument for protecting the rights of homeless persons

In *Martin v. City of Boise*,[395] the Ninth Circuit had confronted a challenge under the Eighth Amendment's prohibition against "cruel and unusual punishment" to city ordinances criminalizing "[o]ccupying, lodging, or sleeping in any building, structure or place, whether public or private" without permission,[396] as well as using "any of the streets, sidewalks, parks or public places as a camping place at any time."[397] The plaintiffs in the case had each

[390] Andrew Dietderich, *An Egalitarian's Market: The Economics of Inclusionary Zoning*, 24 Fordham Urb. L.J. 23 (1996).
[391] An exception is New Hampshire. *Britton v. Town of Chester*, 595 A.2d 492 (N.H. 1991).
[392] 844 F.2d 926 (2d Cir. 1988), *aff'd per curiam*, 488 U.S. 15 (1988).
[393] R.I. Gen. Laws §§34-37.1-1 to 34-37.1-5.
[394] R.I. Gen. Laws §34-37.1-3.
[395] 920 F.3d 584 (9th Cir. 2019).
[396] Boise City Code §6-01-05.
[397] Boise City Code §9-10-02.

been convicted under one or both of these statutes for being unhoused at a time when the city lacked sufficient shelter capacity. The court held that crimes that punish a status or a condition a person is powerless to change, as opposed to a voluntary act, violate the Eighth Amendment, which "prohibits the imposition of criminal penalties for sitting, sleeping, or lying outside on public property for homeless individuals who cannot obtain shelter."[398] As the court concluded, "resisting the need to eat, sleep or engage in other life-sustaining activities is impossible. Avoiding public places when engaging in this otherwise innocent conduct is also impossible. . . . As long as the homeless plaintiffs do not have a single place where they can lawfully be, the challenged ordinances . . . effectively punish them for . . . sleeping, eating and other innocent conduct."[399]

Argument that no such protections exist

However, in *City of Grants Pass v. Johnson*,[400] in a class-action suit on behalf of unhoused people challenging anti-public-camping ordinances in the city of Grants Pass, Oregon, the Supreme Court overruled *Martin*. In contrast to the Ninth Circuit, the Supreme Court viewed the criminalization of homelessness as involving not an involuntary status but rather actions such as "occupy[ing] a campsite" on public property "for the purpose of maintaining a temporary place to live,"[401] regardless of status.[402] Justice Sotomayor, joined by Justice Kagan and Justice Jackson, dissented, arguing that the Eighth Amendment has long been understood to impose "a substantive limit on what can be made criminal and punished as such."[403] Moreover, the Court had affirmed that inflicting "unnecessary suffering" that is "grossly disproportionate to the severity of the crime" or that serves no "penological purpose" violates the Amendment.[404] Accordingly, Justice Sotomayor concluded, the Amendment should bar statutes that criminalize the "status of being homeless (lacking available shelter)," as "defined by the very behavior singled out for punishment (sleeping outside)."[405] ◀

Right to housing

Although the constitutions of some countries, such as South Africa, contain a right to housing and basic welfare needs,[406] the U.S. Constitution

[398] 920 F.3d at 616.

[399] *Id.* at 617 (quoting *Pottinger v. City of Miami*, 810 F. Supp. 1551, 1565 (S.D. Fla. 1992); *see also Commonwealth v. Magadini*, 52 N.E.3d 1041 (Mass. 2016) (jury in criminal trespass case must be instructed that a homeless person is not committing trespass if he enters private property to save his life and has no alternative way to do so); *see* Jeremy Waldron, *Homelessness and the Issue of Freedom*, 39 UCLA L. Rev. 295 (1991) (arguing that everything must be done somewhere and criminalizing sleeping in public effectively prohibits a homeless person from sleeping).

[400] 603 U.S. 520 (2024).

[401] *Id.* at 546 (quoting Grants Pass Mun. Code §§ 5.61.030, 5.61.010).

[402] *Id.* at 546-547 ("Under the city's laws, it makes no difference whether the charged defendant is homeless, a backpacker on vacation passing through town, or a student who abandons his dorm room to camp out in protest on the lawn of a municipal building.").

[403] *Id.* at 574 (quoting *Rhodes v. Chapman*, 452 U.S. 337, 346, n.12 (1981)).

[404] *Id.* (quoting *Estelle v. Gamble*, 429 U.S. 97, 103 and n.7 (1976)).

[405] *Id.* at 575.

[406] *See, e.g.*, S. Afr. Const. ch. 2 §26 ("Everyone has the right to have access to adequate housing"); S. Afr. Const. ch. 2 §27(1) ("Everyone has the right to have access to — a. health care services, including reproductive health care; b. sufficient food and water; and c. social

does not. In 1996, the United States abolished its old welfare program, Aid to Families with Dependent Children (AFDC), and replaced it with Temporary Assistance to Needy Families (TANF),[407] a program that provides assistance to families but that emphasizes transition to work and places a five-year lifetime limit on the receipt of benefits. The New York Constitution requires provision of social welfare for the needy but its enforcement is subject to legislative discretion.[408] Some state courts, including the New York Supreme Court, have interpreted state statutes to impose obligations on the legislature to provide sufficient funding to allow families to live with their children and avoid placing their children in foster care, although those provisions are subject to revision by the legislature and legislative discretion in determining how to measure the applicable obligations.[409]

---

security, including, if they are unable to support themselves and their dependants, appropriate social assistance[.]").

[407] 42 U.S.C. §§601-619.

[408] N.Y. Const. art. XVII, §1 ("The aid, care and support of the needy are public concerns and shall be provided by the state and by such of its subdivisions, and in such manner and by such means, as the legislature may from time to tine determine"); *Tucker v. Toia*, 371 N.E.2d 449, 451 (N.Y. 1977) (although the legislature has the discretion to determine the means and amount of aid to the needy, it prohibits the legislature from refusing to aid those it has classified as needy).

[409] *Jiggetts v. Grinker*, 553 N.E.2d 570 (N.Y. 1990) (state statute imposed a duty to establish shelter allowances that bear a reasonable relation to the cost of housing in New York City and that would allow the parent to bring up the child properly); *Morillo v. City of New York*, 574 N.Y.S.2d 459, 467 (Sup. Ct. 1991) (N.Y. constitution does not require the government to provide subsidized housing or homeless shelters); *see also Callahan v. Carey*, N.Y.L.J., Dec. 11, 1979, at 10 (N.Y. Sup. Ct. Dec. 5, 1979), N.Y.L.J., Feb. 25, 2000, at 29 (N.Y. Sup. Ct. Feb. 22, 2000) (negotiated consent decree based on state statute that creates a right to shelter in New York City); Bradley R. Haywood, *The Right to Shelter as a Fundamental Interest Under the New York State Constitution*, 34 Colum. Hum. Rts. L. Rev. 157 (2002); *cf. McCain v. Koch*, 511 N.E.2d 62 (N.Y. 1987) (applying *Callahan* standards to homeless families).

PART V

PUBLIC LAND USE PLANNING

CHAPTER 13

Land Use Regulation

§13.1 Introduction
§13.2 Planning Process
- §13.2.1 Federal, State, and Local Regulation
- §13.2.2 Zoning Enabling Acts
- §13.2.3 Comprehensive Plan
- §13.2.4 Zoning Ordinances
- §13.2.5 Board of Adjustment or Board of Zoning Appeals

§13.3 Zoning Laws
- §13.3.1 Lot and Building Regulations
- §13.3.2 Use Regulations
- §13.3.3 Special Exceptions
- §13.3.4 Contract or Conditional Zoning
- §13.3.5 Floating Zones
- §13.3.6 Overlay Zones

§13.4 Protection of Pre-Existing Property Rights
- §13.4.1 Prior Nonconforming Uses
- §13.4.2 Vested Rights
- §13.4.3 Variances

§13.5 Rezoning: Limits on Preferential Zoning
- §13.5.1 Conformity with Comprehensive Plan
- §13.5.2 Spot Zoning

§13.6 Nonzoning Land Use Controls
- §13.6.1 Building and Housing Codes
- §13.6.2 Subdivision Regulations
  - §13.6.2.1 Subdivision Approval
  - §13.6.2.2 Planned Unit Developments
  - §13.6.2.3 Form-Based Codes
- §13.6.3 Growth Management and Regional Planning
- §13.6.4 Historic Landmarks
- §13.6.5 Environmental Protection
  - §13.6.5.1 Wetlands Regulations
  - §13.6.5.2 Endangered Species Laws
  - §13.6.5.3 Hazardous Waste Laws
- §13.6.6 Telecommunications Towers

§13.7 Constitutional Limits on Land Use Regulations
§13.7.1 Procedural Due Process
§13.7.2 Substantive Due Process
§13.7.2.1 Protection from Arbitrary Regulations
§13.7.2.2 Family Integrity and Freedom of Association
§13.7.3 Equal Protection
§13.7.4 First Amendment — Speech and Religion
§13.7.4.1 SLAPP Suits
§13.7.4.2 Free Speech
§13.7.4.3 Religious Uses

§13.1 Introduction

Nuisance law and servitudes

The basic tools of the common law land use system are nuisance law and the law of servitudes.[1] While useful, these tools have limits. Consider the question of imposing height limits on buildings — a goal that many owners desire. Nuisance law requires a showing both of substantial harm and unreasonable interference with use or enjoyment of property. An owner who builds a two-story addition on top of her one-story house in a neighborhood composed of other one-story dwellings would almost certainly not be held to have committed a nuisance. Nor would the law of public nuisance prove helpful. The construction of a building that is higher than the surrounding buildings is unlikely to be found to cause a level of harm to community interests sufficient to constitute a public nuisance.[2] Servitudes may be used to create mutually enforceable restrictions on the height of buildings in the neighborhood. However, it is almost never possible to create such a common plan in an existing neighborhood because it is extremely difficult to get every owner to agree to a uniform set of restrictions. For this reason, common plans created by servitudes are ordinarily created by developers before the properties are sold.

Zoning and other legislative controls

Yet, owners often want to preserve the character of a neighborhood by imposing height restrictions on buildings and separating residential, commercial, industrial, and agricultural uses. These goals have been accomplished by explicit governmental land use regulation passed by legislative bodies. The core of the system is the local zoning law. These laws are supplemented by subdivision regulations, regional planning processes and growth controls, state and federal protection of historic landmarks and the environment, and the prohibition of discriminatory regulations. The power to pass land use regulations is limited by basic constitutional protections for property owners and potential owners. The issue of regulatory takings is reserved for the next chapter, while other issues concerning free speech, religious freedom, equal protection, due process, and family integrity round out this chapter.

§13.2 Planning Process

§13.2.1 Federal, State, and Local Regulation

Primacy of local control

Most land use regulation is local. Municipal zoning ordinances form the core of the land use regulation system. Such regulations are supplemented by subdivision controls[3] and are also sometimes constrained by regional or state planning controls or growth management schemes.[4] State and federal

[1] *See* Chapter 3 for nuisance law and Chapters 5 and 6 for the law of servitudes. *See also* 1 Douglas W. Kmiec & Katherine Kmiec Turner, *Zoning and Planning Deskbook* §§2:2, 2:3 (2024-2025).

[2] *See* §3.3.

[3] Dale A. Whitman et al., *The Law of Property* §9.30, at 557-564 (4th ed. 2019).

[4] *Id.* at §9.31, at 564-572.

regulations further restrict land use to protect the environment[5] and historic landmarks.[6] Other laws, such as the *Fair Housing Act*,[7] prohibit invidious discrimination on the basis of race, sex, national origin, religion, familial status, or disability.

§13.2.2 Zoning Enabling Acts

State delegation of zoning powers to municipalities

State governments have basic powers to pass laws to promote public health, welfare, and safety. This general regulatory power is called the "police power."[8] Municipalities, such as counties, cities, and towns, are subdivisions of states and, under municipal law, have powers delegated to them by state law, which can be statutory or constitutional.[9] Every state has a *zoning enabling act* that delegates power to municipalities to pass land use regulations.[10] Such regulations are legitimate to the extent they fall within the scope of the delegated powers. Both the zoning law itself and particular decisions made by administrative bodies enforcing the zoning law, must comply with the procedural and substantive criteria set out in the zoning enabling act. Property owners sometimes challenge local regulations as *ultra vires* or beyond the powers of the municipality to regulate. Any regulation that exceeds the scope of the powers granted the municipality by the zoning enabling act may be challenged by an owner as unlawful.[11]

§13.2.3 Comprehensive Plan

Zoning law must be governed by a comprehensive plan

The first general municipal zoning ordinance was enacted in 1916 in New York City.[12] "By 1926, all but five of the then forty-eight states had adopted zoning enabling legislation and some 420 municipalities had enacted zoning ordinances."[13] Zoning enabling acts require zoning laws to be made "in accordance with" or "to be consistent with" a *comprehensive plan*.[14] When zoning laws were first enacted, municipalities would comply with this obligation by drafting and enacting a general zoning ordinance that creates a rational land use plan for the municipality.[15] Since then, it has become more customary for municipalities to engage in a planning process that results in a comprehensive plan that is a separate document from the zoning ordinance itself and that guides the drafting and amendment of the ordinance. Some jurisdictions require municipalities to create a plan that is

[5] 8 *Thompson on Real Property, Third Thomas Edition* §§75.01 to 75.12. *See* §13.6.5.

[6] Dale A. Whitman et al., *The Law of Property* §9.33, at 564-572 (4th ed. 2019).

[7] 42 U.S.C. §§3601-3631. *See* Chapter 12.

[8] *Village of Euclid v. Ambler Realty Co.*, 272 U.S. 365, 387 (1926).

[9] Gerald E. Frug, *The City as a Legal Concept*, 93 Harv. L. Rev. 1057, 1109-1115 (1980).

[10] 8 *Thompson on Real Property, Third Thomas Edition* §74.02(c)(2)(i). See *id.* at n.26 for citations to the zoning enabling acts in all the states.

[11] Dale A. Whitman et al., *The Law of Property* §9.12, at 496 n.225 (4th ed. 2019).

[12] *Id.* at §9.11, at 493.

[13] *Id.*

[14] *Id.* at §9.11, at 489, §9.12, at 496-499.

[15] *Kozesnik v. Township of Montgomery*, 131 A.2d 1, 7 (N.J. 1957); Dale A. Whitman et al., *The Law of Property* §9.12, at 496 (4th ed. 2019).

separate from the zoning ordinance itself.[16] Such plans include maps showing the general divisions of the municipality into residential, commercial, industrial, and agricultural districts and text, describing the objectives of the plan and the policies and standards that are to guide real estate development within the jurisdiction.[17] In some cities, the plan is adopted by the city council; in others, it forms the working document from which the zoning law will be drafted or amended. In either case, the plan does not itself directly regulate land use; only the zoning law itself does that. The plan sets the parameters for the zoning law.

Planning commission

Both the comprehensive plan and the zoning ordinance itself are generally prepared by a *planning commission* before adoption by the *city council* or other legislative body.[18] Planning commissions are composed of community members appointed by the local legislative body. The planning commission holds public hearings, investigates and obtains relevant information, develops the comprehensive plan and often the zoning law as well, and recommends changes over time in the local zoning law or in standards for applying or administering it.

Rezoning petitions

The planning commission also receives petitions from particular landowners who are seeking amendments to the zoning law as it applies to their particular parcels. Such petitions are called *rezoning petitions.*[19] Although the planning commission has no power to pass a zoning law itself, it does hold public hearings on such petitions and makes recommendations to the city council or other legislative body to accept or reject such petitions, and its recommendations are often accepted by the lawmaking body.[20]

Planning department

The commission is often aided by a *planning department* composed of professional city planners. If the municipality is too small to have a planning department, it may hire a private planning firm to aid it in drafting a comprehensive plan and/or the zoning law itself.

§13.2.4 Zoning Ordinances

Zoning ordinances or by-laws

Once the planning commission creates the comprehensive plan and drafts a proposed zoning law, the local legislative body (such as the city council) holds public hearings and enacts the zoning law, generally called an *ordinance* in the case of a city and a *by-law* in the case of a town.[21] In conjunction

[16] These include, for example, California, Cal. Gov't Code §§65300 *et seq.*; Florida, Fla. Stat. §§163.3161 to 163.3211; Oregon, Or. Rev. Stat. ch. 197; and, in certain instances, Washington, Wash. Rev. Code §§36.70.320 *et seq. See* Dale A. Whitman et al., *The Law of Property* §9.12, at 499 n.248 (4th ed. 2019) (collecting statutes from other states).

[17] Roger Bernhardt & Ann M. Burkhart, *Real Property in a Nutshell* 469-472 (7th ed. 2016).

[18] Dale A. Whitman et al., *The Law of Property* §9.15, at 501-504 (4th ed. 2019).

[19] *Id.* at §9.21, at 519.

[20] *Id.* at §9.15, at 502.

[21] Municipal governments are highly varied in their makeup. Cities are generally larger than towns and generally have an elected body that passes laws, often but not always supplemented by a mayor who functions as the executive branch. Towns are generally smaller than cities and may have a governing *board of selectmen* who draft local laws that are then voted on and passed at town meetings at which all (or a subset) of local voters are entitled to attend and vote. *See generally* Dale A. Whitman et al., *The Law of Property* §9.16, at 504-506 (4th ed. 2019).

with the zoning law, the municipality adopts one or more maps showing the various districts.[22] The ordinance and the maps will contain both area restrictions (lot size and shape requirements, setback requirements, frontage requirements), bulk restrictions (limits on building height, shape, and mass, often in the form of floor-area ratios (FARs)),[23] and use restrictions (limiting zones to industrial, commercial, agricultural, and/or residential uses). The zoning ordinance can become extremely complicated and may involve both basic rules and *overlays*, in which different types of districts overlap. For example, one map may explain districts that identify types of uses (commercial versus residential, for example), while another may identify historic districts subject to special controls and still another may describe districts that require special permits because of unique traffic problems and the like.

§13.2.5 Board of Adjustment or Board of Zoning Appeals

Administration of the zoning law

The zoning law is administered by a local agency often called the *zoning board of adjustment* or the *board of zoning appeals*. Unlike the planning commission, which serves the legislative function of helping to prepare and write the zoning law, the board of adjustment performs quasi-judicial functions. It will receive and act on applications for special exceptions and variances. Special exceptions are uses permitted by the zoning law once certain criteria are met. Variances are permissions to engage in otherwise-prohibited conduct either because the zoning law would result in undue hardship to the owner or deprive the owner of any economically viable use for the property. Both topics are covered later in this chapter.[24]

§13.3 Zoning Laws

§13.3.1 Lot and Building Regulations

Area, bulk, and use zoning

Zoning laws regulate development in at least three different ways. First, *area* or *lot zoning* regulates the size and shape of lots. Second, *building* or *bulk* regulations restrict the size, shape, and placement of buildings on the lot. Third, *use zoning* limits the kinds of activities that can be performed on the land.

Area or lot regulations

Area or *lot* zoning regulates the size and shape of lots. Typical techniques involve (1) minimum lot sizes and (2) minimum frontage requirements.[25]

[22] Roger Bernhardt & Ann M. Burkhart, *Real Property in a Nutshell* 472-473 (7th ed. 2016).

[23] A floor-area ratio relates the allowable square footage for buildings to the square footage of the land itself. For example, a 2:1 ratio permits the lot owner to erect a building containing two square feet of floor space for every one square foot of lot area. The owner can erect a two-story building covering the entire lot, a four-story building covering half the lot, an eight-story building covering a quarter of the lot, and so on. Roger Bernhardt & Ann M. Burkhart, *Real Property in a Nutshell* 464-465 (7th ed. 2016). Of course, setback requirements and height limitations will substantially limit the owner's options.

[24] *See* §§13.3.3 (special exceptions) & 13.4.3 (variances).

[25] Roger Bernhardt & Ann M. Burkhart, *Real Property in a Nutshell* 462 (7th ed. 2016).

Minimum lot sizes have often been challenged on the ground that they exclude low- or moderate-income families from the municipality.[26] They have also been challenged as unconstitutional takings of property rights.[27] Building regulations concern the placement, height, shape, and bulk of buildings. These regulations often include (1) *setback* requirements that mandate that structures be "set back" a certain distance from the front, side, and back boundaries of the lot; (2) *height* restrictions; (3) restrictions on the *percentage* of the lot that may be covered by structures; and (4) *floor-area ratios* that limit the allowable square footage of development by limiting construction to a multiple of the square footage of the lot. For example, a ratio of 2:1 would allow two square feet of development for every one square foot of the lot area. When combined with setback and height limitations, floor-area ratios have the effect of dictating the allowable shape of buildings. Bulk regulations also sometimes include (5) *minimum floor space* requirements, such as a mandate that a single-family home contain a minimum of 1,600 square feet. Minimum floor space requirements, like minimum lot requirements, have often been challenged on the ground that they exclude the poor, as well as moderate-income families, and have often been struck down.[28] Exclusionary zoning is covered in more depth above at §12.9.2.

Building or bulk regulations

§13.3.2 Use Regulations

Euclidean zoning

The most basic form of zoning separates residential, commercial, agricultural, and industrial uses. Often called *Euclidean zoning*, after the Supreme Court case that first upheld the constitutionality of zoning,[29] such zoning is relatively rigid, focusing on separation of different uses. Such zoning was originally *cumulative* in the sense that "less intense" uses (such as residential uses) were allowed in more intense zones (such as commercial or industrial zones), but more intense uses were excluded from less intense (residential) zones.[30] Under cumulative zoning, residential districts would be limited to residential uses, but commercial districts would allow both residential and commercial uses, and industrial districts allow all three types of use. Sometimes Euclidean zoning is *noncumulative* in the sense that residential uses are excluded from industrial and commercial districts.

Cumulative and noncumulative zoning

Zones

Within each type of use area, further distinctions are ordinarily made. For example, some residential zones may be restricted to large lots and large family homes, while other zones would allow smaller lots and smaller homes and still other zones would allow two- or three-family homes, and still others would allow apartment buildings of different sizes. Similar

[26] *See* §§12.9.2 & 13.7.3. *See Southern Burlington County, NAACP v. Township of Mt. Laurel*, 336 A.2d 713, 731-732 (N.J. 1975) (*Mt. Laurel I*).

[27] *See* Chapter 14. *See Eldridge v. City of Palo Alto*, 129 Cal. Rptr. 575 (Ct. App. 1976); *Aronson v. Town of Sharon*, 195 N.E.2d 341, 344-345 (Mass. 1964).

[28] *Builders Service Corp. v. Planning and Zoning Commission*, 545 A.2d 530, 537 (Conn. 1988); *Home Builders League of South Jersey, Inc. v. Township of Berlin*, 405 A.2d 381, 392 (N.J. 1979).

[29] *Village of Euclid v. Ambler Realty Co.*, 272 U.S. 365 (1926).

[30] Roger Bernhardt & Ann M. Burkhart, *Real Property in a Nutshell* 468 (7th ed. 2016).

distinctions may be made between light- and heavy-industrial areas and village business districts versus mall-type shopping centers.

Overly rigid

Euclidean zoning proved overly rigid over time and spawned both exceptions and more flexible devices to allow some case-by-case exceptions to be made or, alternatively, to regulate the mix of uses in particular zones or even on particular lots. These innovations included (1) special exceptions; (2) contract zoning; (3) floating zones; and (4) overlay zones, all explained next. Other innovations include (5) planned unit developments, (6) cluster zones, and (7) form-based codes, explained at §§13.6.2.2 and 13.6.2.3.

§13.3.3 Special Exceptions

Conditional use

A *special exception* or a *conditional use* is a use that is permitted by the zoning law in a particular district provided that certain specified conditions are met. This device is sometimes used to allow complementary uses to be placed in appropriate locations. For example, residential districts often allow the placement of schools, religious institutions, parks, or utility substations, as long as they are placed in ways that minimize negative impacts on homeowners. Rather than generally permitting these uses, the zoning law will authorize them as special uses, usually regulating their placement by defining criteria for where they can be placed and requiring the owner to apply for a special permit to obtain authorization for the use.[31] Such applications are generally made to the board of adjustment, which may add requirements, such as an increase in setback requirements or provisions for noise control.[32] Special exceptions are also used to relax lot and building restrictions under specified conditions.

Standard for granting a special exception

Special exceptions are generally granted "as of right" once the specified conditions are met. The theory is that the legislative body has already determined that the use is permitted in the district, as long as the special conditions are met.[33] Thus, the board of adjustment does not have the discretion to deny the permit once the conditions are met.[34] This rule is somewhat contradicted by the requirement contained in most zoning ordinances that the use not "be inimical to the public interest."[35] In theory, this requirement would authorize the board to make a considered judgment about the wisdom of allowing the proposed use at the proposed location. However, most courts consider the board not to have the discretion to make a wide-ranging inquiry and evaluation of the use; rather, its job in special-exceptions cases is more ministerial. Because the lawmaking body has already determined that the use is permitted (as long as the specified conditions are met), the

[31] Dale A. Whitman et al., *The Law of Property* §9.28, at 546-551 (4th ed. 2019).

[32] *Id.* at §9.28, at 547.

[33] *North Shore Steak House, Inc. v. Board of Appeals of the Incorporated Village of Thomaston*, 282 N.E.2d 606, 609 (N.Y. 1972); but see Monadnock Rod and Gun Club v. Town of Peterborough, 336 A.3d 909, 915 (N.H. 2024).

[34] *Harris v. Jefferson County Board of Zoning Adjustment*, 773 So. 2d 496, 499 (Ala. Civ. App. 2000).

[35] Dale A. Whitman et al., *The Law of Property* §9.28, at 547 (4th ed. 2019).

board's job is only to determine whether the conditions are satisfied and then to grant the permit automatically.

No delegation of unconstrained power to the zoning board

Because the theory is that the board is a law-enforcer rather than a law-maker, a zoning ordinance that delegates unconstrained power to the zoning board of adjustment may be struck down as inconsistent with the zoning enabling act.[36] For example, in *Wakelin v. Town of Yarmouth*,[37] the Maine Supreme Court struck down a provision in a zoning ordinance that gave the zoning board the discretion to deny special exception applications because the proposed use was not "compatible with the existing uses in the neighborhood, with respect to intensity of use and density of development."[38] The court concluded that the ordinance failed to "articulate the quantitative standards necessary to transform the unmeasured qualities 'intensity of use' and 'density of development' into specific criteria objectively useable by both the Board and the applicant."[39] Without such criteria, the board would be wrongfully making a legislative judgment that the zoning ordinance (and the zoning enabling act) allocated to the lawmaking body, not the board. A similar result was reached in a case that allowed a campground to be located in a "Limited Residential-Recreational District" as long as it "conserve[d] natural beauty."[40] The court held that the "conserve natural beauty" requirement was an unconstitutional delegation of legislative authority from the lawmaking body to the zoning board because it failed to "furnish a guide which will enable those to whom the law is to be applied to reasonably determine their rights."[41] Because the other conditions had been met, the court ordered the board to grant the conditional use permit.[42]

Nonetheless, the Colorado Supreme Court upheld a zoning law that provided that certain uses were "permitted" within an identified district but that retained in the planning commission the right to review each proposed use on the basis of "neighborhood compatibility."[43]

§13.3.4 *Contract or Conditional Zoning*

Negotiated rezoning

Developers who want to construct projects that are inconsistent with zoning requirements may approach the planning board or the city council with a proposal to *rezone* the parcel in a manner that will authorize the project. When this happens, the governing bodies often wish to affect the appearance or uses of the property to protect the neighborhood from negative externalities or to improve neighborhood amenities. They sometimes do so by negotiating with the owner over the zoning change and then allowing the rezoning subject to specified conditions designed to ensure that

[36] *Fordham v. Butera*, 876 N.E.2d 397, 399 (Mass. 2007).

[37] 523 A.2d 575 (Me. 1987).

[38] *Id.* at 576.

[39] *Id.* at 577.

[40] *Kosalka v. Town of Georgetown*, 2000 ME 106, ¶10, 752 A.2d 183, 186.

[41] *Id.* at 186 (quoting *Stucki v. Plavin*, 291 A.2d 508, 510 (Me. 1972)).

[42] *Id.* at 187.

[43] *City of Colorado Springs v. SecurCare Self Storage, Inc.*, 10 P.3d 1244 (Colo. 2000).

the development is not harmful to the neighbors or the community. These conditions may involve anything from special limitations on uses, to specially tailored height or bulk restrictions, to requiring dedication of land to the city to widen abutting public streets. This process is called *contract* or *conditional zoning*.[44]

Challenges to contract zoning

Contract zoning has often been challenged in court as (1) unauthorized by the zoning enabling act; (2) inconsistent with the comprehensive plan; or (3) illegal preferential "spot zoning."[45] It has also been challenged as an unconstitutional form of lawmaking on the ground that laws should not be negotiated with a private party but should be adopted through open procedures that can be monitored by the public. While some cases strike down contract zoning,[46] others approve it,[47] and some state statutes now expressly authorize it.[48] Some courts distinguish between so-called bilateral and unilateral arrangements. Bilateral agreements involve promises on both sides, by the owner and by the city. For example, the city may promise to rezone the lot in return for a promise by the owner to restrict the otherwise allowable development on her lot and perhaps to record the restrictions as covenants.[49] Such bilateral contracts are often struck down partly because they may bypass statutory procedures that require public hearings to amend the zoning law.[50] Unilateral promises are commitments by the owner to agree to certain conditions (again, often recorded) to induce the municipality to rezone the land.[51] Such arrangements protect the rights of the public to attend a public hearing on the rezoning proposal but still raise issues about whether such *ad hoc* decision making is desirable or promotes corruption and unfair deviations from the comprehensive plan. The Supreme Judicial Court of Massachusetts approved the rezoning of property for industrial use when the owner voluntarily donated $8 million to the town to be used to build a new school.[52]

[44] Julian Conrad Juergensmeyer et al., *Land Use Planning and Development Regulation Law* §5:11, at 163-168 (5th ed. 2023); Daniel R. Mandelker & Michael Allan Wolf, *Land Use Law* §6.62 (6th ed. 2020); Dale A. Whitman et al., *The Law of Property* §9.25, at 532-535 (4th ed. 2019).

[45] Daniel R. Mandelker & Michael Allan Wolf, *Land Use Law* §6.62 (6th ed. 2020). On spot zoning, see §13.5.2.

[46] *Hale v. Osborn Coal Enterprises, Inc.*, 729 So. 2d 853, 855 (Ala. Civ. App. 1997); *Hartman v. Buckson*, 467 A.2d 694, 699 (Del. Ch. 1983); *Rodriguez v. Prince George's City*, 558 A.2d 742, 750 (Md. Ct. Spec. App. 1989).

[47] *Giger v. City of Omaha*, 442 N.W.2d 182 (Neb. 1989).

[48] Daniel R. Mandelker & Michael Allan Wolf, *Land Use Law* §6.62 (6th ed. 2020). *See* Ariz. Rev. Stat. §§9-462.01(E), 11-832; Idaho Code §67-6511A; Md. Code, Land Use §4-103; R.I. Gen. Laws §45-24-53(h).

[49] Julian Conrad Juergensmeyer et al., *Land Use Planning and Development Regulation Law* §5:11, at 167-168 (5th ed. 2023).

[50] *Buckhorn Ventures, LLC v. Forsyth County*, 585 S.E.2d 229 (Ga. Ct. App. 2003) (agreement prohibiting zoning board from changing the zoning of a property at any time held to be void as contract zoning because it pre-commits the zoning board to ignore relevant legislative concerns at the relevant time); *Old Canton Hills Homeowners Ass'n v. City of Jackson*, 749 So. 2d 54 (Miss. 1999) (noting that contract zoning is unlawful because it binds the municipality before it has had the statutorily required public hearing and unlawfully circumvents the public decision making process).

[51] Daniel R. Mandelker & Michael Allan Wolf, *Land Use Law* §6.61 (6th ed. 2020).

[52] *Durand v. IDC Bellingham, LLC*, 793 N.E.2d 359 (Mass. 2003).

Reasons for contract or negotiated zoning

Municipalities began to engage in contract or conditional zoning because traditional Euclidean zoning laws proved to be too inflexible. Although the use of special exceptions provided some needed flexibility, this technique requires a pre-existing judgment about what criteria should apply to particular parcels. It does not, for example, allow for unanticipated possibilities or problems. It may be in the public interest to allow a small corner store to be set up on the end of a residential neighborhood to create a convenient place to buy milk and bread and other staples. It may not have been anticipated that an owner of that lot would want to use the property for that purpose. At the same time, if the lot were zoned for "commercial" use, the owner would be entitled to use the property as a clothing store. To limit the property for use as a 24-hour convenience store, the lawmaking body might want to condition the conversion to commercial use on the owner agreeing to limit use to this purpose and not other commercial purposes. This technique allows beneficial uses otherwise not allowed by the prior zoning law without opening the possibility of other uses that would not be compatible with the neighborhood.

Dangers of contract zoning

On the other hand, contract zoning poses some dangers, as well. It flies in the face of the requirement that the zoning law be consistent with a "comprehensive plan." Rather than rational planning that looks at the overall pattern of land use and development, parcel-by-parcel decisions may result in unanticipated consequences and slow erosion of governing principles over time. Moreover, this raises the possibility of special deals with politically connected citizens, resulting in zoning changes that are not in the public interest.

Bilateral contract zoning generally illegal

Contract zoning is likely to be struck down if it is bilateral. Bilateral zoning is especially problematic because the governing body is attempting either to bind itself contractually to pass a particular zoning law or to deprive a later governing body of the power to pass whatever law it wants, or to amend the existing zoning law.[53] In either case, the agreement illegally surrenders lawmaking power.[54] In addition, contractual commitments may bypass statutory procedures for public hearings that give citizens the chance to comment on proposed zoning changes.[55] For example, in *Dacy v. Village of Ruidoso*,[56] a town wanted to condemn land to build a highway but lacked funds to take the land by eminent domain. One owner who wanted a rezoning, donated some land to the town to build the road. In exchange, the town gave that owner some other land the town owned. As part of the deal, the town promised to rezone the land it would give the owner to allow multifamily use. When neighbors challenged the rezoning of that land, the New Mexico Supreme Court invalidated the contract, holding that a promise by a lawmaking body to pass a particular law is unenforceable as against public policy. Hence the promise to rezone the land was illegal.

[53] Dale A. Whitman et al., *The Law of Property* §9.25, at 533 (4th ed. 2019).

[54] *Hale v. Osborn Coal Enterprises, Inc.*, 729 So. 2d 853, 855 (Ala. Civ. App. 1997).

[55] *Old Canton Hills Homeowners Ass'n v. City of Jackson*, 749 So. 2d 54, 60 (Miss. 1999).

[56] 845 P.2d 793 (N.M. 1992).

Unilateral promises often upheld

Some courts hold unilateral conditional zoning to be just as illegal as bilateral conditional zoning.[57] However when the restrictions on the rezoned property are agreed to voluntarily — by the landowner as part of the rezoning process — courts are increasingly likely to uphold the arrangement.[58] These unilateral restrictions are often called conditional (rather than contract) zoning because no promise is made by the governing body that bargains away the police power.

Negotiated zoning as the new norm

The unilateral/bilateral distinction is not very helpful. It is hard to apply and does not really distinguish good from bad conditional zoning. Conditional zoning is problematic if exceptions to the zoning law are inconsistent with the comprehensive plan and violate important public interests. It either grants a particular owner an undeserved special benefit (violating equal protection norms) or actually harms the zoning scheme by amending it piecemeal rather than through a rational, overall change in the comprehensive plan.[59] On the other hand, flexibility is an essential aspect of modern zoning law and often serves the public interest. Owners may lament the need to negotiate with public officials to get permits to build, but the ability to negotiate also gives owners tools to achieve profitable development projects. Most courts today accept negotiated zoning unless it is manifestly contrary to the public interest.[60]

§13.3.5 Floating Zones

Unmapped conditional use districts

Another flexibility device is the *floating zone.* A floating zone is an "unmapped district with detailed and conditional use requirements."[61] In effect, the zone "floats" over the city until a developer seeks to locate it. Floating zones are used to regulate needed and desired developments that have significant community impact and whose appropriate location may vary depending on surrounding development. Examples include shopping centers and planned unit developments, and industrial parks.[62] The zoning law will authorize owners who meet specified conditions to have their property zoned by an alternative zoning ordinance that authorizes the new zoning limitations. When an owner wishes to take advantage of the floating

[57] *Bartsch v. Planning & Zoning Commission*, 506 A.2d 1093 (Conn. App. Ct. 1986); *Board of County Commissioners v. H. Manny Holtz, Inc.*, 501 A.2d 489 (Md. Ct. Spec. App. 1985); *Dacy v. Village of Ruidoso*, 845 P.2d 793 (N.M. 1992).

[58] *Sylvania Electric Products, Inc. v. City of Newton*, 183 N.E.2d 118, 122-123 (Mass. 1962); *Rando v. Town of North Attleboro*, 692 N.E.2d 544, 548 (Mass. App. Ct. 1998); *Collard v. Incorporated Village of Flower Hill*, 421 N.E.2d 818 (N.Y. 1981); Julian Conrad Juergensmeyer et al., *Land Use Planning and Development Regulation Law* §5:11, at 165 (5th ed. 2023); Daniel R. Mandelker & Michael Allan Wolf, *Land Use Law* §6.64 (6th ed. 2020); Dale A. Whitman et al., *The Law of Property* §9.25, at 533-534 (4th ed. 2019).

[59] Julian Conrad Juergensmeyer et al., *Land Use Planning and Development Regulation Law* §5:11, at 165 (5th ed. 2023).

[60] *Id.* at §5:11, at 161. *See* Daniel P. Selmi, *The Contract Transformation in Land Use Regulation*, 63 Stan. L. Rev. 591 (2011).

[61] Julian Conrad Juergensmeyer et al., *Land Use Planning and Development Regulation Law* §4:16, at 98-99 (5th ed. 2023).

[62] *Id.* at §4:16, at 98; *see also* Daniel R. Mandelker & Michael Allan Wolf, *Land Use Law* §6.58 (6th ed. 2020).

zone, she applies for permission to have her property zoned by the alternative ordinance and, if she can meet the stated conditions, is entitled to have the parcel included in the alternative zone. This procedure appears to rezone the parcel, although it is distinguished from a rezoning because the zone is already enacted into law; it was just not certain where this zone would be located.

Challenges to floating zones

As with contract zoning, floating zones may be challenged in application (1) as illegal preferential "spot zoning";[63] (2) as inconsistent with the comprehensive plan; (3) as invalid "contract zoning";[64] or (4) as an invalid delegation of legislative power to a private owner if the floating zone is not defined by specific criteria.[65] At the same time, many courts have approved floating zones.[66]

§13.3.6 Overlay Zones

Overlay districts

Overlay zoning places a parcel in two different zones. For example, a parcel might be in an educational-institutional district for its basic zoning and in an "overlay" historic preservation district. Overlay districts will cross over zone borders placing part or all of one zone in an overlay district with part or all in another zone.[67]

§13.4 Protection of Pre-Existing Property Rights

§13.4.1 Prior Nonconforming Uses

Nonconforming uses allowed to continue

Zoning laws have usually been enacted after many buildings and other structures are in place and homes and businesses established. The creation of zoning districts ordinarily leaves in place many uses that are inconsistent with the new zoning limitations. These are called *prior nonconforming uses.*[68] Because owners established their structures before the new restrictions were in place, it would often be unfair to apply the new limitations retroactively. For this reason, zoning enabling acts and zoning ordinances themselves authorize prior nonconforming uses to continue, despite their inconsistency with the zoning law; they are "grandfathered in." The nonconforming use doctrine is based on the sense that it would be unfair to

[63] *See* §13.5.2.

[64] *See* §13.3.4.

[65] Julian Conrad Juergensmeyer et al., *Land Use Planning and Development Regulation Law* §4:16, at 99 (5th ed. 2023).

[66] *Carron v. Board of County Commissioners*, 976 P.2d 359, 362 (Conn. App. Ct. 1998); *Rodgers v. Village of Tarrytown*, 96 N.E.2d 731 (N.Y. 1951); Daniel R. Mandelker & Michael Allan Wolf, *Land Use Law* §6.58 (6th ed. 2020).

[67] Julian Conrad Juergensmeyer et al., *Land Use Planning and Development Regulation Law* §4:22, at 106-107 (5th ed. 2023).

[68] *Town of Belleville v. Parrillo's, Inc.*, 416 A.2d 388, 391 (N.J. 1980); Julian Conrad Juergensmeyer et al., *Land Use Planning and Development Regulation Law* §4:32, at 115-116 (4th ed. 2018).

make a lawful use unlawful unless the use amounts to a nuisance[69] or otherwise is causing substantial harm. However, the doctrine is also a partial application of the constitutional takings clause, which prohibits the state from "taking" property without just compensation.[70] An order to tear down a five-story office building because it is now inconsistent with a single-family home zoning designation would almost certainly constitute an unconstitutional taking of property that cannot be accomplished without paying just compensation. Not all applications of the nonconforming use doctrine are mandated by the takings clause, however. Some protections may go beyond what the Constitution requires.

Lawful existence

For a nonconforming use to be entitled to continue, it must have been lawful and in existence at the time the zoning ordinance was passed.[71] Although the use is tolerated, it is inconsistent with the surrounding zoning. Thus, the municipality ordinarily wants to limit the inconsistency by prohibiting any intensification of the use or changes of the use. In addition, some zoning ordinances seek to reduce the nonconformity to consistency over time either by placing a time limit on the nonconforming use or strictly interpreting the rule against allowing extensions of the use.

Limits on intensification or change in use

The test: No substantial change

Nonconforming uses cannot be extended or intensified in a way that constitutes a substantial change.[72] Courts have also found that abandonment of a given use or the destruction of property may end the nonconforming use.[73] However, owners are entitled to make reasonable alterations to repair their facilities and render them practicable for their purposes.[74] Because nonconforming uses are inconsistent with the new zoning, any doubts are resolved against the change. When the neighborhood is adversely affected by the proposed change, this is fairly conclusive evidence that the change is substantial and not allowed. For example, in *Town of Belleville v. Parrillo's, Inc.*,[75] a restaurant and catering service converted into a discothèque (a dance club) that sold hamburgers to its patrons. The court had little difficulty finding the use had changed from a restaurant to a dance club and that the use had intensified in character in a way that harmed the public interest and was inconsistent with the surrounding zoning. Insubstantial changes are allowed, and much litigation occurs over whether changes in the use are prohibited or allowed. Prototypical "insubstantial" changes are

[69] Julian Conrad Juergensmeyer et al., *Land Use Planning and Development Regulation Law* §4:40, at 136-137 (5th ed. 2023).

[70] *See* Chapter 14.

[71] Julian Conrad Juergensmeyer et al., *Land Use Planning and Development Regulation Law* §4:33, at 129 (5th ed. 2023).

[72] *Baxter v. City of Preston*, 768 P.2d 1340, 1342-1343 (Idaho 1989); *Township of Chartiers v. William H. Martin, Inc.*, 542 A.2d 985 (Pa. 1988); Julian Conrad Juergensmeyer et al., *Land Use Planning and Development Regulation Law* §§4:34 to 4:35, at 130-131 (5th ed. 2023); Daniel R. Mandelker & Michael Allan Wolf, Land Use Law §5.75 (6th ed. 2020).

[73] See, e.g., Dakota Constructors, Inc. v. Hanson Cnty. Bd. of Adjustment, 994 N.W.2d 222 (S.D. 2023).

[74] *Budget Inn of Daphne, Inc. v. City of Daphne*, 789 So. 2d 154, 160 (Ala. 2000).

[75] 416 A.2d 388 (N.J. 1980).

repairs of the existing structure or increases in business volume that do not necessitate structural changes in the building.[76]

▷ NORMAL EXPANSION **HARD CASE** ◀

Argument against allowing the change in use

In *Cumberland Farms, Inc. v. Town of Groton*,[77] a gas station that was a prior nonconforming use needed to supplement its income to fix a leaking gas tank — a repair required by environmental laws. The owner applied for a right to open a small convenience store to supplement the owner's income so it could fix the facilities and continue its prior operation as a gas station. On one hand, this clearly constitutes a substantial change in use that would ordinarily be prohibited as an alteration in the nonconformity. It also represents an increase in the intensity of use because it will generate (or is intended to generate) more traffic. The goal of the nonconforming use doctrine is to protect prior investors, but not to allow them to change their uses. The use is inconsistent with the neighboring properties and therefore imposes negative externalities on the neighbors. The goal is to reduce the use to conformity as quickly as possible, and if the owner cannot afford to operate the gas station and pay its costs (including the costs of compliance with environmental laws), then the owner should sell and the property can be reduced to conformity consistent with the zoning plan.

Argument for allowing the change in use

On the other hand, the owner can argue that this change was necessitated by a legal obligation — to clean up a toxic waste site — that was clearly in the interest of the community. Refusing to allow the owner to change the use might have put the owner out of business and might have delayed the clean-up of the site because it might be hard to find a buyer willing to buy the property, pay the substantial costs of cleaning up the site, tear down the existing structures, and then convert to residential structures and sell them. Because gas stations often have small convenience stores attached to them, one might argue that it was a "normal expansion" of the prior use and that it should be authorized. The basis of the nonconforming use doctrine is to protect the investment-backed expectations of owners who established their uses in reliance on prior law. Such owners arguably assumed they would be able to make minor changes in the business to comply with changing regulatory requirements, especially when those requirements are intended to protect the public. ◀

▷ AMORTIZATION **HARD CASE** ◀

Some zoning ordinances seek to reduce the nonconformity to be consistent with the zoning planning by placing a time limit on its continuation. This procedure is called *amortization*, on the theory that the owner will recoup a

[76] *Redfearn v. Creppel*, 455 So. 2d 1356, 1360-1361 (La. 1984); *Powers v. Building Inspector*, 296 N.E.2d 491, 499 (Mass. 1973); Daniel R. Mandelker & Michael Allan Wolf, *Land Use Law* §5.75 (6th ed. 2020).

[77] 719 A.2d 465 (Conn. 1998).

reasonable return on the investment over time. Once that return is earned, it can be argued that the municipality may constitutionally prohibit the use. Creating a time cushion also allows the owner to plan for the change in use over time and thereby protects both the prior investment-backed expectations and the reliance on the prior zoning law. Most courts have upheld the amortization technique.[78] Some courts, however, view amortization provisions with distaste, and as fundamentally inconsistent with the notion that owners are entitled to rely on existing regulations when they invest substantially in developing land. In this view, any retroactive prohibition of the previously lawful nonconforming use is unfair and arguably unconstitutional as a taking of constitutionally vested rights.[79] A few courts have therefore struck down amortization provisions as takings of property in violation of the Constitution.[80] ◀

§13.4.2 Vested Rights

Substantial expenditures and/or efforts

An owner who begins construction in good faith reliance on a particular zoning designation will be protected from retroactive changes in the zoning law if the owner's efforts and expenditures were "so substantial as to create vested rights in the completion of the project."[81] In addition, the reliance on the existing law must be in good faith. Owners are not protected if they are aware that "an ordinance that would prohibit the use is pending and that adoption is imminent."[82] Because it would constitute a taking of property for a zoning law not to grandfather in a prior nonconforming use (unless that use caused a nuisance or was illegal under prior law), the courts must determine where to draw the line to determine when a use has begun. When an owner hires an architect, pays for plans, obtains a building permit, begins construction, and can demonstrate substantial expenditures, there is no question the vested rights doctrine will apply. When one or more of these is missing, results depend on the substantiality of the expenditures and, in some states, whether a building permit has been issued. Many states require the granting of a building permit before they will find a vested right while some do not.[83] On the other hand, the

[78] *South Lake Tahoe Property Owners Group v. City of South Lake Tahoe*, 310 Cal. Rptr.3d 9, 25-26 (Ct. App. 2023) (upholding a three-year amortization period); Julian Conrad Juergensmeyer et al., *Land Use Planning and Development Regulation Law* §4:39, at 136 (5th ed. 2023).

[79] Daniel R. Mandelker & Michael Allan Wolf, *Land Use Law* §5.81 (6th ed. 2020).

[80] *Lamar Advertising of South Georgia, Inc. v. City of Albany*, 389 S.E.2d 216 (Ga. 1990); *Board of Zoning Appeals v. Leisz*, 702 N.E.2d 1026, 1032 (Ind. 1998); *Sun Oil Co. v. City of Upper Arlington*, 379 N.E.2d 266, 271-272 (Ohio Ct. App. 1977); *PA Northwestern Distributors, Inc. v. Zoning Hearing Board*, 584 A.2d 1372, 1376 (Pa. 1991); Daniel R. Mandelker & Michael Allan Wolf, *Land Use Law* §5.81 (6th ed. 2020).

[81] *Stone v. City of Walton*, 331 N.W.2d 398, 404 (Iowa 1983); *Glacial Aggregates LLC v. Town of Yorkshire*, 924 N.E.2d 785 (N.Y. 2010). *See* Julian Conrad Juergensmeyer et al., *Land Use Planning and Development Regulation Law* §§5:27 to 5:31, at 192-205-189 (5th ed. 2023).

[82] Julian Conrad Juergensmeyer et al., *Land Use Planning and Development Regulation Law* §5:28, at 194 (5th ed. 2023).

[83] *Compare Prince George's County v. Sunrise Development Ltd. P'ship*, 623 A.2d 1296, 1304 (Md. 1993) (building permit required) *with* Va. Code §15.2-2307 (no building permit

granting of a building permit — without more — is generally not enough. The owner must make substantial expenditures in good faith reliance on existing law.[84] A minority of states grants developers vested rights if they have obtained site-specific approval for development, such as a preliminary subdivision plan; such protections mean that a vested right is created even before a building permit is issued; for example, Massachusetts and New Jersey provide such protection without any need to demonstrate substantial expenditures.[85] Some states even grant developers vested rights to use their land in accordance with the zoning law in place at the time they *apply* for a site-specific permit.[86]

Basis of the doctrine

The vested rights doctrine again rests on the need to prevent zoning regulations from effectuating unconstitutional takings of property. However, as with the nonconforming use doctrine and the standards for granting variances, the law of vested rights may go beyond preventing a taking, and protect owners in situations that would not constitute unconstitutional deprivations of property rights. Thus, the law of vested rights, variances, and nonconforming uses — although based on the norms underlying the takings clause — are not co-extensive with it.

§13.4.3 Variances

Unnecessary hardship

Not contrary to the public interest

Variances are permissions to deviate from the zoning law when application of the ordinance to a particular parcel would (1) impose an *unnecessary hardship* and (2) the proposed use would not be contrary to the public interest and would not substantially impair the purpose of the zoning plan and ordinance.[87] Unlike special exceptions, which are uses *permitted* by the zoning law as long as specified conditions are met, variances are uses *prohibited* by the zoning law but nonetheless allowed because the ordinance, as applied, would effectively constitute an unconstitutional taking of the owner's property rights.

Strict test for hardship

In most states, the formal test for showing "hardship" is quite strict.[88] A variance will not be granted where the hardship is self-imposed,[89] and some courts hold that the owner's refusal to sell the property for fair market value

required) *and* Julian Conrad Juergensmeyer et al., *Land Use Planning and Development Regulation Law* §5:27, at 192-193 (5th ed. 2023).

[84] Bracken v. City of Ketchum, 537 P.3d 44 (Idaho 2023); Julian Conrad Juergensmeyer et al., *Land Use Planning and Development Regulation Law* §5:28, at 193-195 (5th ed. 2023).

[85] *See, e.g.*, N.J. Stat. §§40:55D-49 to 40:55D-052. *Cf.* Va. Code §15.2-2307 (also requires substantial expenditures).

[86] Colo. Rev. Stat. §§24-68-101 to -106; Mass. Gen. Laws ch. 40A, §6; Tex. Loc. Gov't Code §245.002 to -006; Wash. Rev. Code §§19.27.095, 58.17.033.

[87] *Commons v. Westwood Zoning Board of Adjustment*, 410 A.2d 1138, 1143 (N.J. 1980); Julian Conrad Juergensmeyer et al., *Land Use Planning and Development Regulation Law* §§5:14 to 5:26, at 172-192 (5th ed. 2023); Daniel R. Mandelker & Michael Allan Wolf, *Land Use Law* §6.38 (6th ed. 2020).

[88] Julian Conrad Juergensmeyer et al., *Land Use Planning and Development Regulation Law* §5:16, at 177 (5th ed. 2023).

[89] *Ex parte Chapman*, 485 So. 2d 1161, 1163 (Ala. 1986); *Perez v. Board of Appeals of Norwood*, 765 N.E.2d 768, 769 n.5 (Mass. App. Ct. 2002); Daniel R. Mandelker & Michael Allan Wolf, *Land Use Law* §6.47 (6th ed. 2020).

No economically viable use or no reasonable return on investment

to a neighbor who is willing and able to buy, constitutes a self-imposed hardship. In addition, hardship will generally not be found unless there is no economically viable use of the property (or no reasonable return on the owner's investment) if the zoning law is enforced.[90] Many states add the requirement that the property must be different in some unique way from surrounding property, such as having an unduly narrow frontage or an odd shape or elevation, and that the hardship arises out of this unique condition of the land.[91]

Practical difficulties test

Some states allow variances to be granted on a lesser showing of *practical difficulties.*[92] To show practical difficulties, the owner must prove significant economic injury from enforcement of the zoning ordinance.[93] Some states interpret the "practical difficulties" test to mean the same thing as the unnecessary hardship test. The zoning enabling acts in some states require a showing *both* of unnecessary hardship and practical difficulties; others allow a variance if *either* of these tests is met.[94] Some states go further and allow variances to be issued if this will provide a significant public benefit and the variance can be granted "without substantial detriment to the public good and will not substantially impair the intent and purpose" of the zoning ordinance.[95]

Source of law

Ordinarily, the zoning enabling act will allow or require municipalities to make provisions for variances. The local zoning law will generally contain both the standard for obtaining variances and procedures for applying for a variance, generally from the board of adjustment. The case law interpreting the standard for variances is thus partly an interpretation of the local zoning ordinance, partly an interpretation of the zoning enabling act,

[90] *See Commons v. Westwood Zoning Board of Adjustment*, 410 A.2d 1138, 1142 (N.J. 1980) (holding that variance can be granted only where the owner can make "no effective use of the property"); *Matthew v. Smith*, 707 S.W.2d 411, 417-418 (Mo. 1986); *Carbonneau v. Town of Exeter*, 401 A.2d 675, 677 (N.H. 1979); Julian Conrad Juergensmeyer et al., *Land Use Planning and Development Regulation Law* §5:19, at 181-182 (5th ed. 2023); Daniel R. Mandelker & Michael Allan Wolf, *Land Use Law* §6.41 (6th ed. 2020). *But see Janssen v. Holland Charter Township Zoning Board of Appeals*, 651 N.W.2d 464, 468 (Mich. Ct. App. 2002) (granting a use variance when the income derived from the property was $19,000 per year while the property taxes were $7,900 on the ground that this did not give the owner a "reasonable economic return").

[91] *See, e.g.*, N.J. Stat. §40:55D-70(c)(1) (variance allowed "(a) by reason of exceptional narrowness, shallowness or shape of a specific piece of property, or (b) by reason of exceptional topographic conditions or physical features uniquely affecting a specific piece of property, or (c) by reason of an extraordinary and exceptional situation uniquely affecting a specific piece of property or the structures lawfully existing thereon"). *See Commons v. Westwood Zoning Board of Adjustment*, 410 A.2d 1138 (N.J. 1980) (applying an earlier version of this law).

[92] Ind. Code §36-7-4-918.5, *applied in Metropolitan Board of Zoning v. McDonald's Corp.*, 481 N.E.2d 141, 146 (Ind. Ct. App. 1985); *Kisil v. Sandusky*, 465 N.E.2d 848, 853 (Ohio 1984); Daniel P. Selmi & James A. Kushner, *Land Use Regulation: Cases and Materials* 83 (4th ed. 2012).

[93] *Metropolitan Board of Zoning v. McDonald's Corp.*, 481 N.E.2d 141, 146 (Ind. Ct. App. 1985).

[94] Julian Conrad Juergensmeyer et al., *Land Use Planning and Development Regulation Law* §5:23, at 185-186 (5th ed. 2023).

[95] N.J. Stat. §40:55D-70(d), *interpreted in Cell South of New Jersey, Inc. v. Zoning Board of Adjustment of West Windsor Township*, 796 A.2d 247 (N.J. 2002).

and, because it is intended to prevent unconstitutional takings of property, partly an interpretation of the takings clause.

Use variances generally prohibited

Variances are generally granted to relax lot and building restrictions, not use restrictions. Some states prohibit them from being granted by zoning boards on the ground that they are effectively rezonings that should be voted on by the city council (or other lawmaking body) and not granted by an administrative agency like the zoning board.[96] Some states allow use variances to be granted upon a showing of unnecessary hardship while allowing area variances to be granted on the lower standard of demonstration of practical difficulties.[97] Some states, however, are more open to granting use variances if there are "special reasons" to do so and this will not harm the "public good."[98]

Legal realism

It is important to note that, although the formal test for obtaining a variance should make it difficult to obtain one, in many locales, zoning boards routinely grant variances if the requested variance is not a dramatic change in the structure and if no one (especially abutting neighbors) objects to the granting of the variance. In effect, zoning boards often ignore the law and grant variances when there is no showing that the owner has been deprived of economically viable use.[99] In such cases, there is little chance the grant of the variance will be challenged in court because neither the owner who wants the variance, nor the zoning board that grants it, nor the neighbors who are not averse to the variance, have objections that would prompt any of them to bring an appeal. On the other hand, if a board grants a variance when hardship is absent, there is every likelihood that neighbors who are aggrieved by the variance will challenge the grant. If the statute or the zoning ordinance gives these neighbors standing to challenge the grant of the variance, and if the zoning board granted the variance when the standard was not met, the appellate court is likely to reverse the board's decision.

§13.5 Rezoning: Limits on Preferential Zoning

§13.5.1 Conformity with Comprehensive Plan

Planning and consistency with the public interest

Zoning enabling acts require zoning laws to conform to a *comprehensive plan.*[100] As explained earlier,[101] in many states, this now means that an

[96] *Cook v. Howard*, 215 S.E.2d 690 (Ga. Ct. App. 1975); Julian Conrad Juergensmeyer et al., *Land Use Planning and Development Regulation Law* §5:15, at 176 (5th ed. 2023).
[97] Daniel P. Selmi & James A. Kushner, *Land Use Regulation: Cases and Materials* 87 (1999).
[98] N.J. Stat. §40:55D-70(d). *See Price v. Himeji*, 2013 WL 3184784 (N.J. 2013) (use variance can be granted if land is particularly suitable to the proposed use and if the variance will not substantially harm the public good or impair the intent and the purpose of the zoning plan).
[99] John J. Infranca & Ronnie M. Farr, *Variances: A Canary in the Coal Mine for Zoning Reform?*, 50 Pepp. L. Rev. 443 (2023); Michael D. Donovan, Note, *Zoning Variation Administration in Vermont*, 8 Vt. L. Rev. 371 (1983); Jesse Dukeminier, Jr. & Clyde L. Stapleton, *The Zoning Board of Adjustment: A Case Study in Misrule*, 50 Ky. L.J. 273 (1962); Julian Conrad Juergensmeyer et al., *Land Use Planning and Development Regulation Law* §5:19, at 181-182 (5th ed. 2023).
[100] Dale A. Whitman et al., *The Law of Property* §9.10, at 489, §9.12, at 496-499 (4th ed. 2019).
[101] *See* §13.2.3.

actual plan is created by the planning commission. In some locales, the plan is contained in the zoning ordinance itself. In either case, when the lawmaking body rezones a particular parcel, neighbors may sue the municipality to invalidate the rezoning on the ground that it does not conform to the comprehensive plan.[102]

§13.5.2 Spot Zoning

No discriminatory benefits that do not promote public welfare

Spot zoning refers to selective rezoning by the municipal legislative body of a single parcel or small group of parcels of land.[103] Such zoning gives the owner a discriminatory benefit (relaxing zoning restrictions and allowing a more intensive use) in a manner that is inconsistent with the zoning of the surrounding area, is detrimental to the community, and is not justified as a police power measure designed to promote the public welfare. Spot zoning is a specific application of the doctrine that zoning ordinances should be consistent with a comprehensive plan. It is reminiscent of state constitutional proscriptions on "special legislation," that is, government grants or benefits given to individual citizens that are not justified as measures intended to promote the general welfare. It is also an application of the equal protection clause, which requires all classifications to be rationally related to a legitimate government interest. It is very difficult for an owner to win a spot zoning challenge.[104] Municipal governments generally do not rezone selective parcels unless they think it does serve some public purpose, such as creating jobs. As long as such a purpose is conceivably present, the courts are unlikely to strike down the rezoning, leaving such judgments to the legislative body. At the same time, municipal lawyers must be careful to advise municipal governments of the need to justify selective rezoning as both consistent with the zoning plan and justified as promoting the public welfare.

§13.6 Nonzoning Land Use Controls

§13.6.1 Building and Housing Codes

Regulation of construction and maintenance of housing

State and sometimes local laws regulate both building construction and maintenance to ensure that buildings are both safe and sanitary.[105] Such laws usually authorize the creation of state or local building code commissions or

[102] Julian Conrad Juergensmeyer et al., *Land Use Planning and Development Regulation Law* §2:12, at 33 (5th ed. 2023).
[103] *Id.* at §5:10, at 146-148.
[104] *See, e.g., Save Our Rural Environment v. Snohomish County*, 662 P.2d 816 (Wash. 1983) (denying a spot zoning challenge to a municipal decision changing the zoning law to allow construction of an industrial park near a residential neighborhood); *Egan Slough Community v. Flathead Cnty. Bd. Of Cnty. Comm'rs.*, 506 P.3d 996, 1012-14 (Mont. 2022) (rejecting a "reverse spot zoning" claim by the operator of a water bottling plan that a parcel was singled out for less favorable treatment).
[105] Julian Conrad Juergensmeyer et al., *Land Use Planning and Development Regulation Law* §§8:1 to 8:7, at 309-328 (5th ed. 2023).

agencies that have the power to promulgate the building code and enforce it. In general, local inspectors administer and enforce the law by approving construction plans, issuing building permits before construction can begin and occupancy permits once construction is completed. Other laws may also regulate housing quality and are often used to protect tenants from negligent landlords who fail to maintain habitable housing.[106] There may also be specific fire, safety, and health codes.[107]

Enforcement of building code

Building codes often require owners doing major renovations or new construction to submit their plans for approval to obtain a building permit. They may also be required to apply for a building permit that gives permission to perform the work. Building inspectors may enter and inspect the premises during construction to ensure that the work is proceeding in a safe manner and that the owner is complying with the submitted plans. Once construction is completed, owners must similarly request an inspection from the building inspector to obtain an occupancy permit.[108]

Housing codes

Housing codes regulate residential property and are usually intended to regulate rental property, protecting tenants from unsafe or unsanitary conditions. Tenants are often empowered to call local inspectors to determine if the property is in violation of the housing code, because of the presence of pests, lack of heat or hot water, broken windows or locks, or other major problems. The local inspector who finds a violation will order repairs to be made or will report to the building code enforcement agency and it will order those repairs to be made. The inspector is usually authorized to bring administrative or judicial proceedings to enforce the building code and fines or imprisonment may be imposed for serious violations.[109]

§13.6.2 Subdivision Regulations

Subdivision controls

§13.6.2.1 Subdivision Approval. State and local laws also govern the development of *subdivisions*. A "subdivision" is a large parcel of land that is subdivided to create an entire neighborhood composed of homes and/or businesses or other uses. Subdivision regulations are imposed by local ordinances. Applications must be made for review and approval of subdivision plans.[110]

Exactions

Municipal agencies may require the dedication of streets to the city and ensure that they are not too narrow and that their layout is acceptable. The developer will also be required to ensure that lots can or will be hooked up to municipal services, such as sewer and water lines, electricity, and cable

[106] *See* §10.6.
[107] Dale A. Whitman et al., *The Law of Property* §9.11, at 493 (4th ed. 2019).
[108] Julian Conrad Juergensmeyer et al., *Land Use Planning and Development Regulation Law* §8:7, at 327-328(5th ed. 2023).
[109] *Id.* at §8:6, at 301-302.
[110] *Id.* at §7:6, at 251-253; Daniel R. Mandelker & Michael Allan Wolf, *Land Use Law* §9.04 (6th ed. 2020).

television services.[111] The municipality may accomplish this by requiring developers of subdivisions to provide these public improvements at their own expense as a condition for granting the subdivision approval. These requirements are called *exactions*. Exactions have often been challenged as unconstitutional takings of property and the standards for their legality are addressed in Chapter 14.

Mix of uses that would otherwise be separated

§13.6.2.2 Planned Unit Developments. A *planned unit development* (PUD) is an area of land that is intended to be developed by a single developer and to include uses that are often separated into different zones such as a mix of single-family and multiple-family dwellings or a mix of residential, commercial, and even industrial uses.[112] Planned unit development regulations both authorize and guide the creation of PUD plans. The PUD allows approval of a plan for an entire neighborhood. It relaxes the rigidity of *Euclidean zoning* with its ideal of separation of different uses by allowing mixes that feel appropriate and that enhance, rather than detract, from the value and livability of different types of property. PUD plans provide for greater intensity of use in one portion of the property and compensation by less intense development elsewhere on another portion.

Relation to cluster zoning

This technique is also sometimes called *cluster zoning*, where several parcels are considered together and the total amount of development is kept the same but the distribution of development from site to site is changed. For example, under cluster zoning, an owner of two parcels might be able to put them together and build a larger building than would be allowed on either parcel (but not bigger than the two buildings combined) with open space concentrated on one of the parcels.

§13.6.2.3 Form-Based Codes. *Form-based codes* are increasingly popular, growing out of a movement known as New Urbanism that seeks to replicate older patterns of mixed-use, walkable development that were common before modern zoning. Such codes move away from the emphasis in Euclidean zoning on strictly regulating and separating the uses of land. Instead, form-based codes provide the general outlines of how much space on a plot an owner can develop and what that development has to look like, often through graphics and pictures, leaving a great deal of flexibility about allowable residential and commercial uses. The promise of such codes is that the resulting development will be environmentally sustainable and foster community, but the approach has raised concerns about the disenfranchisement of vulnerable communities.[113]

[111] Roger Bernhardt & Ann M. Burkhart, *Real Property in a Nutshell* 488-490 (7th ed. 2016).

[112] Julian Conrad Juergensmeyer et al., *Land Use Planning and Development Regulation Law* §7:17, at 293-294 (5th ed. 2023); Daniel R. Mandelker & Michael Allan Wolf, *Land Use Law* §9.25 (6th ed. 2020).

[113] Julian Daniela A. Tagtachian et al., *Building by Right: Social Equity Implications of Transitioning to Form-Based Code*, 28 J. Affordable Hous. & Cmty. Dev. L. 71 (2019).

§13.6.3 Growth Management and Regional Planning

Controlling pace and location of development

Some municipalities and state governments have enacted elaborate plans to curb or otherwise control both the pace and the location of development.[114] They generally identify the areas of the municipality where growth and development should occur and those where growth will be limited, at least for the time being, to their current uses or to less intense uses. They may set a limit on population growth.[115] They may also tie development of land to the construction and development of public services and plan for the sequence of such development.[116] In one such plan, the city of Petaluma limited the number of building permits that could be issued each year.[117] Other municipalities have imposed moratoria on growth.[118] State plans adopted in a few states identify growth areas and areas where growth will be curtailed or halted.[119]

Goals of growth management plans

The goals of such controls may be protection of the environment or the promotion of low-density development. Part of the motivation may be to curtail the cost of needed public facilities such as sewer and water lines and public schools.[120] In addition, the municipality may wish to control the character of development to preserve or improve the nature of the community and to obtain a desirable mix of uses.[121] In some cases, municipalities may have less noble motives, such as racial discrimination or an intent to exclude low- and moderate-income families from the suburbs. In recent years, complaints have surged about "suburban sprawl" with its attendant destruction of forest lands and increase in traffic.

Constitutional challenges

Growth management plans have been upheld against challenges that they take property rights without just compensation.[122] As long as they do not deprive property of economically viable use, they are likely to be upheld because no one is constitutionally entitled to the most profitable use of their property.[123] A growth moratorium is likely to be upheld if it is temporary in nature and responds to some perceived temporary difficulty in

[114] Julian Conrad Juergensmeyer et al., *Land Use Planning and Development Regulation Law* §§9:1 to 9:17, at 329-441(5th ed. 2023); Daniel R. Mandelker & Michael Allan Wolf, *Land Use Law* §10.01 (6th ed. 2020); Dale A. Whitman et al., *The Law of Property* §9.31, at 564-572 (4th ed. 2019).

[115] Julian Conrad Juergensmeyer et al., *Land Use Planning and Development Regulation Law* §9:2, at 338 (5th ed. 2023); Dale A. Whitman et al., *The Law of Property* §9.31, at 570-571 (4th ed. 2019).

[116] Julian Conrad Juergensmeyer et al., *Land Use Planning and Development Regulation Law* §9:7, at 348-350(5th ed. 2023); Dale A. Whitman et al., *The Law of Property* §9.31, at 571-572 (4th ed. 2019).

[117] *Construction Industry Ass'n v. City of Petaluma*, 522 F.2d 897 (9th Cir. 1975).

[118] Julian Conrad Juergensmeyer et al., *Land Use Planning and Development Regulation Law* §9:6, at 348 (5th ed. 2023); Dale A. Whitman et al., *The Law of Property* §9.31, at 565-566 (4th ed. 2019).

[119] Dale A. Whitman et al., *The Law of Property* §9.31, at 571 (4th ed. 2019).

[120] *Id.* at 566.

[121] Julian Conrad Juergensmeyer et al., *Land Use Planning and Development Regulation Law* §9:1, at 333-334 (5th ed. 2023).

[122] *See, e.g., Construction Industry Ass'n v. City of Petaluma*, 522 F.2d 897, 909 (9th Cir. 1975); *Golden v. Town of Ramapo*, 285 N.E.2d 291, 304 (N.Y. 1972).

[123] Dale A. Whitman et al., *The Law of Property* §9.31 at 567-570 (4th ed. 2019).

extending public services.[124] As a Colorado court explained, "a temporary limitation on property use, resulting from the otherwise good faith, reasonable institution of a moratorium in order to bring about effective governmental decision-making does not result in a categorical taking."[125]

§13.6.4 Historic Landmarks

Historic preservation

Both federal and state legislation protect historic landmarks by designating buildings or districts that are subject to special controls to prevent structures from being demolished, or from having their external (and in some cases internal) appearance altered.[126] In 1966, Congress passed the *National Historic Preservation Act (NHPA)*,[127] allowing for the designation of particular buildings and sites as historic landmarks and listing them on the National Register of Historic Places. Regulation of historic landmarks, however, takes place more directly on the state level. Every state has a historic preservation statute that authorizes a state agency to designate particular buildings or sites as historic landmarks or historic districts and to regulate or limit alteration of those sites or structures.[128] Local ordinances in some locales add locally designated historic sites.[129]

National Historic Preservation Act

State and local laws

Constitutional challenges

Historic landmark statutes have been challenged facially and as applied to particular sites as unconstitutional takings of property. Although upheld by the Supreme Court, as long as the property has an economically viable use, challenges have emerged in state courts and sometimes been successful.[130] This topic is treated in Chapter 14.

§13.6.5 Environmental Protection

Federal and state legislation

A vast array of federal and state legislation regulates property use to protect the environment.[131] The subject is complicated and intricate. The material

[124] *Williams v. City of Central*, 907 P.2d 701, 704-705 (Colo. App. 1995) (ten-month moratorium not a taking); *Sun Ridge Development, Inc. v. City of Cheyenne*, 787 P.2d 583, 590 (Wyo. 1990); *McCutchan Estates Corp. v. Evansville-Vanderburgh County Airport Authority District*, 580 N.E.2d 339, 342 (Ind. Ct. App. 1991) (nine-month delay not extraordinary as a matter of law); *Dufau v. United States*, 22 Cl. Ct. 156, 162-163 (1990), *aff'd without opinion*, 940 F.2d 677 (Fed. Cir. 1991) (16-month delay not extraordinary as a matter of law); *First English Evangelical Lutheran Church v. County of Los Angeles*, 258 Cal. Rptr. 893, 906 (Ct. App. 1989) (*First English II*) (delay of more than two years not unreasonable); *Guinnane v. City & County of San Francisco*, 241 Cal. Rptr. 787, 790 (Ct. App. 1987) (delay of more than one year not unreasonable as a matter of law); Dale A. Whitman et al., *The Law of Property* §9.31, at 565-566 (4th ed. 2019).

[125] *Williams v. City of Central*, 907 P.2d 701, 704 (Colo. App. 1995).

[126] Julian Conrad Juergensmeyer et al., *Land Use Planning and Development Regulation Law* §§12:4 to 12:8, at 609-622 (5th ed. 2023); Daniel R. Mandelker & Michael Allan Wolf, *Land Use Law* §11.27 (6th ed. 2020).

[127] 54 U.S.C. §§300101 *et seq.*

[128] Julian Conrad Juergensmeyer et al., *Land Use Planning and Development Regulation Law* §12:7, at 616-617 (5th ed. 2023).

[129] *Id.* at §12.8, at 559-562.

[130] *Penn Central Transportation Co. v. City of New York*, 438 U.S. 104 (1978) (historic preservation law constitutional as applied to Penn Central).

[131] William H. Rodgers, *Environmental Law* (2d ed. 1994).

here is intended to identify a few of the most important regulations that bear on property development.[132]

§13.6.5.1 Wetlands Regulations. Both federal and state law regulate so-called wetlands.[133] These lands (both saltwater and fresh water) have critical ecological importance both in terms of preserving fish and wildlife and in preserving the water supply, controlling floods, limiting pollution, and promoting soil conservation.[134]

Wetlands

Federal regulation

The federal government protects water quality and regulates development of wetlands under a number of important statutes, including the *Federal Water Pollution Control Act of 1972*,[135] the *Clean Water Act of 1977*,[136] and the *Water Quality Act of 1987*.[137] These Acts collectively are referred to as the "Clean Water Act." Section 404 of the *Clean Water Act* protects wetlands and gives the Army Corps of Engineers jurisdiction to regulate the discharge of certain dredged or fill materials and authorizes the Corps to grant or withhold permits for such activity.[138] Dredged material is anything that is excavated or dredged from "waters of the United States" (which includes most wetlands). Fill material is anything used to replace wetlands with dry land.[139] The national goal of this regulation is no net loss of wetlands.

State regulation

Many states have also passed statutes regulating both coastal areas and inland wetlands.[140] Those states typically authorize a state agency to map wetlands and regulate or limit their development, generally by requiring a special permit for development in a wetlands area or for dredging or filling the wetlands. Wetlands regulations have often been challenged as takings of property, especially when they prohibit construction.[141] This topic is considered in Chapter 14.

Protection of "critical habitats"

§13.6.5.2 Endangered Species Laws. The federal *Endangered Species Act (ESA)*[142] protects endangered species by halting development of sensitive areas where such species dwell.[143] The Act authorizes the Secretary of the Interior to designate certain areas as "critical habitats" for particular

[132] *See* Nicholas A. Robinson, *Environmental Regulation of Real Property* (Kevin Anthony Reilly ed., rev. ed. 1999); *Environmental Aspects of Real Estate Transactions* (James B. Witkin ed., 2d ed. 1999).
[133] Dale A. Whitman et al., *The Law of Property* §9.34, at 590-593 (4th ed. 2019).
[134] Julian Conrad Juergensmeyer et al., *Land Use Planning and Development Regulation Law* §11:2, at 555-556 (5th ed. 2023).
[135] 33 U.S.C. §§1251 to 1376.
[136] Pub. L. No. 95-217, 91 Stat. 1566 (1977).
[137] Pub. L. No. 100-4 (Feb. 4, 1987), 100th Cong., 1st Sess. 101 Stat. 7 (1987).
[138] 33 U.S.C. §1344. *See* Julian Conrad Juergensmeyer et al., *Land Use Planning and Development Regulation Law* §11:4, at 560-561 (5th ed. 2023).
[139] Julian Conrad Juergensmeyer et al., *Land Use Planning and Development Regulation Law* §11:4, at 563 (5th ed. 2023).
[140] Dale A. Whitman et al., *The Law of Property* §9.34, at 590 (4th ed. 2019).
[141] *See, e.g., Lucas v. South Carolina Coastal Council*, 505 U.S. 1003 (1992).
[142] 16 U.S.C. §§1531 to 1543.
[143] *Id.* at §§1533(a)(3)(A) & 1538(a)(1); Julian Conrad Juergensmeyer et al., *Land Use Planning and Development Regulation Law* §11:11, at 584 (5th ed. 2023).

endangered species and prohibits development that will harm the species.[144] The effect of this law may be to limit substantially the ability to develop certain lands. As with the wetlands laws, the *ESA* has been challenged as a taking of property without just compensation in a number of cases.[145]

RCRA and CERCLA

§13.6.5.3 Hazardous Waste Laws. Both federal and state laws regulate and mandate the cleanup of toxic wastes deposited or spilled into the ground on private property. The main federal laws are the *Resource Conservation and Recovery Act* (*RCRA*)[146] and the *Comprehensive Environmental Response, Compensation, and Liability Act of 1980* (*CERCLA* or the *Superfund Law*).[147] *RCRA* regulates the production, transportation, and disposal of hazardous wastes.[148] *CERCLA* imposes a tax on the production of toxic chemicals to provide a pool of money for cleanup of toxic wastes.[149] It also requires those who generated hazardous wastes to pay to clean up their polluted sites.[150] This obligation to pay for the cleanup extends to owners and operators of the site, and those who transported or disposed of the waste material.[151]

Liability on current owner

More far-reaching, however, was the imposition of strict liability on the current owner of the site, even if the contamination was caused by a prior owner.[152] *CERCLA* provides a defense for the current owner if she could show that the pollution was created by a third party (such as a prior owner) with whom the current owner had no contractual relationship.[153] This third-party defense was strengthened in 1986 with the passage of the *Superfund Amendments and Reauthorization Act* (*SARA*), which amended *CERCLA* to protect from liability a so-called innocent purchaser who bought the property after the disposal of the toxic waste and who did not know and did not have reason to know about it.[154] This effectively requires purchasers of such property to do an environmental audit prior to buying the land.[155]

Innocent purchaser defense

SARA

State laws

Some states regulate the transfer of property contaminated by toxic waste. Some require buyers to be notified of the presence of toxic waste on the property.[156] Other states impose strict liability on property owners

[144] Julian Conrad Juergensmeyer et al., *Land Use Planning and Development Regulation Law* §11:11, at 584-585 (5th ed. 2023).
[145] *See, e.g., United States v. Kepler*, 531 F.2d 796 (6th Cir. 1976).
[146] 42 U.S.C. §§6901 *et seq.*
[147] *Id.* at §§9601 *et seq.*
[148] *Id.* at §§6922 to 6925.
[149] *Id.* at §9611.
[150] *Id.* at §9607.
[151] *Id.*
[152] *Id.*
[153] *Id.* at §9607(b)(3).
[154] *Id.* at §§9601(35)(A), 9601(40). *See* Robert V. Percival et al., *Environmental Regulation: Law, Science, and Policy* 267-283 (2000).
[155] *See also Burlington N. & Santa Fe Ry. Co. v. United States*, 556 U.S. 599 (2009) (where possible, CERCLA requires cleanup costs to be apportioned among responsible parties; in such cases, parties cannot be held liable for more than their proportionate share of the harm).
[156] *Michigan Natural Resources and Environmental Protection Act*, Mich. Comp. Laws §§324.20116 to 324.20142; *Oregon Hazardous Waste Removal and Remedial Action Act*, Or. Rev. Stat. §§465.200 to 465.260 & 465.900.

to clean up their property or to reimburse the state for cleanup costs; to ensure payment for the cleanup, these states impose a "superlien" on the property, which takes priority over all or most other debts.[157] Still others require cleanup of the property before it can be transferred or sold.[158] New Jersey's *Industrial Site Recovery Act*, for example, prohibits certain owners from transferring their property until they either certify that no hazardous substances remain on the property or execute an approved cleanup plan.[159] The statute also triggers a review process when an industrial operation is shut down.[160] Failure to comply with the statute (such as a sale of the property before it is cleaned up) renders the sale voidable by the grantee, entitles the grantee to damages from the grantor, and renders the owner or operator of the site strictly liable for the cleanup. A similar statute has been passed in Connecticut.[161]

§13.6.6 Telecommunications Towers

Telecommunications Act of 1996

Many zoning disputes have erupted over the placement of telecommunications towers for cell phones and other uses. Such towers can exceed 250 feet in height and, when located in residential areas or in the midst of a scenic view, generate substantial opposition by local residents.[162] A portion of the *Telecommunications Act of 1996*[163] protected the power of municipalities to regulate the "placement, construction, and modification" of such towers[164] but prohibited them from regulating so as to "prohibit or have the effect of prohibiting the provision of personal wireless services."[165] The Act also prohibits discrimination among providers.[166] Courts have wrestled with the question of how much authority the statute gives municipalities, with most interpreting the statute in a functional manner, allowing regulations as long as they do not have the "effect of precluding a specific provider from providing wireless service."[167] At the same time, general esthetic concerns

[157] Ark. Stat. §8-7-516; Conn. Gen. Stat. §22a-452a; Mass. Gen. Laws ch. 21E, §13; *Acme Laundry Co., Inc. v. Secretary of Environmental Affairs*, 575 N.E.2d 1086, 1090 (Mass. 1991); Jeffrey T. Cox, *Industrial Property Transactions and Hazardous Waste Cleanup in America: An Analysis of State Innovations*, 15 U. Dayton L. Rev. 471 (1990).

[158] David B. Farer, *Transaction-Triggered Environmental Laws in Environmental Aspects of Real Estate Transactions* 70-88 (James B. Witkin ed., 2d ed. 1999).

[159] N.J. Stat. Ann. §§13:1k-6 *et seq.*

[160] *Id.* Ohio has a similar law, the *Ohio Cessation of Regulated Operations Program*, Ohio Rev. Code §§3752.01 to 3752.99.

[161] *Connecticut Transfer Act*, Conn. Gen. Stat. §§22a-134 to 22a-134e.

[162] *See, e.g., Omnipoint Corp. v. Zoning Hearing Board of Pine Grove Township*, 20 F. Supp. 2d 875, 880 (E.D. Pa. 1998).

[163] 47 U.S.C. §332.

[164] *Id.* at §332(c)(7)(A).

[165] *Id.* at §332(c)(7)(B)(i)(II).

[166] *Id.* at §332 (c)(7)(B)(i)(I).

[167] *See, e.g., APT Pittsburgh, L.P. v. Penn Township*, 196 F.3d 469, 478 (3d Cir. 1999). *See also Omnipoint Communications Enterprises, L.P. v. Zoning Hearing Bd. of Easttown Township*, 331 F.3d 386 (3d Cir. 2003); *Sprint Spectrum, L.P. v. Willoth*, 176 F.3d 630 (2d Cir. 1999); *Town of Amherst v. Omnipoint Communications Enterprises*, 173 F.3d 9, 13 (1st Cir. 1999); *AT&T Wireless PCS v. City Council of Virginia Beach*, 155 F.3d 423, 428 (4th Cir. 1998).

that such towers are ugly have generally been held not to be sufficient to allow municipalities to refuse permits for telecommunications towers.[168]

§13.7 Constitutional Limits on Land Use Regulations

Constitutional protections

A number of constitutional provisions protect property owners from unfair application of zoning laws or other land use regulations. Other than the law of regulatory takings, which is explored in Chapter 14, it is not possible to explore these issues fully here. It is important to know about possible claims and limitations on the enforceability of regulations that impinge on protected constitutional rights. The constitutional rights most often at issue in the land use context are the First Amendment (both free speech and free exercise of religion), the due process clause, and the equal protection clause.

§13.7.1 Procedural Due Process

Notice and opportunity to be heard

The due process clause of the Fourteenth Amendment prohibits a state from depriving owners of property without due process of law.[169] At a minimum, due process requires notice and an opportunity to be heard.[170] To show a constitutional violation, one must show that one has been deprived of a "property" right. Because no owner is entitled to a use that violates a zoning law (unless the limitation amounts to an unconstitutional taking of property without just compensation), it is hard for owners to demonstrate that they have been deprived of a property right by application of a zoning law. However, if a law gives a right to a certain use, as in the case of a special exception where the owner is entitled to a permit once listed conditions are shown, the owner probably can show a property right protected by the due process clause. If such an owner were denied a special permit without adequate opportunity to present the case or defend against challenges to the grant of the permit, it is possible a procedural due process claim could be made.

§13.7.2 Substantive Due Process

Substantive protection from deprivation

§13.7.2.1 Protection from Arbitrary Regulations. Substantive due process is an odd creature. Although the due process clause seems to allow the deprivation of life, liberty, and property, as long as proper

[168] *New Par v. City of Saginaw*, 301 F.3d 390, 398 (6th Cir. 2002); *Nextel Communications v. Manchester-by-the-Sea*, 115 F. Supp. 2d 65, 67 (D. Mass. 2000).
[169] Daniel R. Mandelker & Michael Allan Wolf, *Land Use Law* §2.41 (6th ed. 2020).
[170] *Hartland Sportsman's Club v. Town of Delafield*, 35 F.3d 1198, 1201 (7th Cir. 1994); *Harris v. County of Riverside*, 904 F.2d 497, 503 (9th Cir. 1990); Julian Conrad Juergensmeyer et al., *Land Use Planning and Development Regulation Law* §10:17, at 503 (5th ed. 2023); John E. Nowak & Ronald D. Rotunda, *Constitutional Law* §§13.7 to 13.8, at 547-557 (5th ed. 1995).

procedures (due process) are observed, courts have often interpreted the due process clause to place substantive limits on what governments can constitutionally do. In effect, the courts have held that, in some cases, deprivation of a particular interest is unconstitutional no matter what process is given.

At a minimum, the due process clause protects owners from deprivation of "property rights" by "arbitrary and capricious" government actions[171] or laws that advance no reasonable government interest.[172] The Supreme Court has specifically held that owners have a "right to be free from arbitrary or irrational zoning actions."[173] Of course, governments always act for reasons and generally do not do so "arbitrarily." This test actually means that the action must be rationally related to some legitimate government objective.[174] Easy as this test appears to be to meet, owners have been able to challenge government actions — including applications of zoning laws — under this standard.[175] For example, in *Marks v. City of Chesapeake*,[176] the court reversed the city's refusal to issue a special permit for a palmistry studio on the ground that the denial was based on irrational neighborhood objections.

In *Bonner v. City of Brighton*,[177] a city ordinance required demolition of an unsafe structure even though the owner was willing and able to repair it; the ordinance required demolition of unsafe structures whenever the cost of repairs exceeded the fair market value of the property. Because the purpose of the regulation was to promote safety, the owner argued that the demolition requirement was arbitrary and unreasonable; requiring demolition when the owner wanted to repair the home served no legitimate government interest. Although the owner won in the lower courts, the Michigan Supreme Court reversed, holding that it was rational for government to require unsafe structures to be demolished when the cost of repairs exceeded the market value of the property, and that there was no

[171] *Nectow v. City of Cambridge*, 277 U.S. 183, 187-188 (1928); Julian Conrad Juergensmeyer et al., *Land Use Planning and Development Regulation Law* §10:16, at 495 (5th ed. 2023); Paul D. Wilson, *When Sending Flowers Is Not Enough: Developments in Landowner Civil Rights Lawsuits Against Municipal Officials*, 34 Urb. Law. 981, 991 (2002).

[172] *Bonner v. City of Brighton*, 848 N.W.2d 380 (Mich. 2014), *rev'g* 828 N.W.2d 408 (Mich. Ct. App. 2012).

[173] *Village of Arlington Heights v. Metropolitan Housing Development Corp.*, 429 U.S. 252, 263 (1977). *See C & M Developers, Inc. v. Bedminster Township Zoning Hearing Bd.*, 820 A.2d 143, 154 (Pa. 2002) (zoning ordinance presumed valid unless "unreasonable, arbitrary, or not substantially related to . . . police power interests").

[174] Daniel R. Mandelker & Michael Allan Wolf, *Land Use Law* §2.47 (6th ed. 2020). *See Durand v. IDC Bellingham*, 793 N.E.2d 359 (Mass. 2003) (rezoning of land to allow previously prohibited development not arbitrary or unreasonable when done after developer offered to pay municipality $8 million to allow a new high school to be built).

[175] Dale A. Whitman et al., *The Law of Property* §9.6, at 471 (4th ed. 2019). *See, e.g., C & M Developers, Inc. v. Bedminster Township Zoning Hearing Bd.*, 820 A.2d 143, 158 (Pa. 2002) (large lot zoning was unrelated to town's interest in preserving agricultural land).

[176] 883 F.2d 308 (4th Cir. 1989).

[177] *Bonner v. City of Brighton*, 848 N.W.2d 380 (Mich. 2014), *rev'g* 828 N.W.2d 408 (Mich. Ct. App. 2012).

obligation to give owners a chance to fix their homes before such a demolition order.[178] Protection from unsafe structures is a legitimate government interest and the city was entitled to choose one method of correction (demolition) over another (repair).[179]

Requirement to show deprivation of "property"

Owners usually lose substantive due process claims because they must first show that they were deprived of "property." This is hard to do because the Constitution does not protect the right of owners to develop their land free of all land use regulations.[180] Once this hurdle is passed, owners sometimes succeed in showing that the municipal action is unrelated to a legitimate government interest.[181]

Relation to equal protection law

The protection against arbitrary government action under the due process clause blends into protection from deprivations of equal protection of the laws. This is because any deprivation distinguishes the victim from others and the minimum test for government action consistent with the equal protection clause is that the classification or differential treatment be rationally related to a legitimate government objective.[182]

Relation to the takings clause

Some courts have struck down applications of zoning laws as violations of substantive due process when the court deems the law to be "confiscatory."[183] Today this type of ruling is much more likely to be made under the takings clause. An act that is confiscatory is one that unconstitutionally takes a protected property right — something the Fifth and Fourteenth Amendments prohibit unless compensation is paid to the owner. This topic is covered in Chapter 14.

Shock the conscience

Because it is hard to prove a government act to be arbitrary or capricious, and because other constitutional clauses (such as equal protection and the takings clause) have taken over the role previously played by the due process clause, the doctrine of substantive due process is not of much utility to owners challenging zoning laws. At the same time, the Supreme Court has said that substantive due process requires that laws not be unduly oppressive to the affected class.[184] Moreover, courts will continue to strike down applications of zoning laws under the due process clause if they "shock the conscience."[185] This is especially so if the government conduct consists of delaying or deceptive conduct. Moreover, although hard to prove, the Court does still hold that regulatory laws are unconstitutional under the due process clause if they (or their application) are "arbitrary, discriminatory, or demonstrably irrelevant to the policy the

[178] 848 N.W.2d at 382-383.

[179] *Id.* at 393-394.

[180] *See, e.g.*, *Macone v. Town of Wakefield*, 277 F.3d 1, 10 (1st Cir. 2002); *Yalowizer v. Town of Rochester*, 2001 WL 1012206, 2001 U.S. App. LEXIS 19746 (10th Cir. 2001).

[181] *Simi Investment Co. v. Harris County*, 236 F.3d 240 (5th Cir. 2000); *Woodwind Estates, Ltd. v. Gretkowski*, 205 F.3d 118 (3d Cir. 2000).

[182] Julian Conrad Juergensmeyer et al., *Land Use Planning and Development Regulation Law* §10:16, at 497-498 (5th ed. 2023).

[183] *See, e.g.*, *Dooley v. Town of Fairfield*, 197 A.2d 770, 775 (Conn. 1964); Dale A. Whitman et al., *The Law of Property* §9.6, at 471 (4th ed. 2019).

[184] *Lawton v. Steele*, 152 U.S. 133, 137 (1894).

[185] *Harris v. City of Akron*, 20 F.3d 1396, 1401 (6th Cir. 1994); Julian Conrad Juergensmeyer et al., *Land Use Planning and Development Regulation Law* §10:16, at 500 (5th ed. 2023).

legislature is free to adopt."[186] This claim is easier to prove when a governmental authority denies a permit or zoning classification to an owner who is similarly situated to another owner who had previously been granted a similar permit.[187]

Sex offenders

The California Supreme Court struck down a local restriction on where sex offenders can live, finding it a violation of the due process clause because it was "unreasonable, arbitrary, and oppressive."[188] *In re Taylor* held that a law prohibiting sex offenders from living within 2,000 feet of any public or private school or any park where children regularly gather unconstitutionally deprived sex offenders of liberty without due process of law when the ordinance effectively excluded them from 97 percent of multifamily rental housing units in the county.[189] The law rendered many sex offenders homeless while failing to achieve its purpose to protect children. Depriving them of any place where they could live or receive medical treatment and services constituted a deprivation of constitutionally protected liberty interests. The law also made it difficult or impossible for the sex offenders to be monitored by parole officers, thereby defeating the purpose of the regulation and depriving it of any rational relationship to the legitimate government objective of protecting the public.

Family privacy

§13.7.2.2 Family Integrity and Freedom of Association. In *Moore v. City of East Cleveland*,[190] the Supreme Court struck down as unconstitutional a zoning law that prohibited a grandmother from living with two grandchildren who were cousins of each other. The ordinance would have allowed them to live together if they were siblings. The Court held that the zoning ordinance intruded into traditional family relationships that deserved constitutional protection. The Supreme Court distinguished an earlier case, *Village of Belle Terre v. Boraas*,[191] in which the Supreme Court upheld an ordinance that prohibited more than two unrelated persons from living with each other — a law clearly intended to prevent students from living in the town. Some state supreme courts have interpreted their state constitutions consistently with *Belle Terre* while others have found constitutional rights of intimate association that ensure the right to live with others of one's choice, subject to reasonable occupancy limits designed to promote safety.[192]

[186] *Pennell v. City of San Jose*, 485 U.S. 1, 12 (1988).

[187] *Board of Commissioners of Roane County v. Parker*, 88 S.W.3d 916 (Tenn. Ct. App. 2002).

[188] *In re Taylor*, 343 P.3d 867 (Cal. 2015).

[189] *Id.* at 869.

[190] 431 U.S. 494 (1977).

[191] 416 U.S. 1 (1974).

[192] *Compare City of Baton Rouge v. Myers*, 145 So. 3d 320 (La. 2014) (agreeing with *Belle Terre*) *with Charter Township of Delta v. Dinolfo*, 351 N.W.2d 831 (Mich. 1984) *and City of Santa Barbara v. Adamson*, 610 P.2d 436 (Cal. 1980) *and Borough of Glassboro v. Vallorosi*, 568 A.2d 888 (N.J. 1990) *and McMinn v. Town of Oyster Bay*, 488 N.E.2d 1240 (N.Y. 1985) (granting state constitutional rights to live with persons of one's choosing).

§13.7.3 Equal Protection

General

The equal protection clause requires, at a minimum, that government classifications be rationally related to a legitimate government interest.[193] Although difficult to violate this minimum level of scrutiny, the Supreme Court did invalidate an ordinance that required a special permit to locate a home for mentally impaired persons but did not require such a permit for other group homes, such as nursing homes or fraternity houses. The Court held that there was no conceivable reason from requiring the permit in one case but not the other, except irrational prejudice.[194] Moreover, the Supreme Court held in *Village of Willowbrook v. Olech*[195] that a landowner may claim a denial of equal protection of the laws even if she is a "class of one" if she is treated less advantageously than other similarly situated owners and there is no rational basis for the difference in treatment. The Connecticut Supreme Court upheld just such a claim in *Thomas v. City of West Haven*[196] when it ruled that it might constitute a violation of the equal protection clause if a zoning board denies a rezoning application for failure to submit a site plan when the zoning board does not generally require submission of site plans for such applications. In other words, adopting different requirements for similarly situated owners may constitute a denial of equal protection unless the city can show legitimate reasons for the differential treatment.

Village of Willowbrook v. Olech

Concern with constitutionalizing all zoning decisions

Justice Breyer concurred in *Olech* but voiced concern that the ruling might turn every zoning decision into a constitutional case because land use decisions often distinguish among parcels and reasonable people can differ about which parcels are "similarly situated." Breyer's agreement with the ruling was premised on the lower court's finding that the municipality had acted vindictively to punish this owner for having brought a prior lawsuit against the municipality.[197] Some lower courts have interpreted *Olech* to require a showing of personal animus against the landowner[198] while others have not.[199]

[193] *Pennell v. City of San Jose*, 485 U.S. 1 (1988) (holding that a rent control ordinance did not violate the equal protection clause because it was rationally related to a legitimate government objective); John E. Nowak & Ronald D. Rotunda, *Constitutional Law* §14.3, at 601 (5th ed. 1995).

[194] *City of Cleburne v. Cleburne Living Center*, 473 U.S. 432, 450 (1985). *See also Village of Willowbrook v. Olech*, 528 U.S. 562, 564-565 (2000) (protecting a "class of one" from a discriminatory, "irrational and wholly arbitrary" requirement); *Congregation Kol Ami v. Abington Township*, 161 F. Supp. 2d 432 (E.D. Pa. 2001), *judgment vacated and remanded by* 309 F.3d 120 (3d Cir. 2002) (striking down an ordinance that excludes places of worship from residential areas but allows arguably similarly situated municipal complexes, police barracks, train stations, and recreational facilities by special exception).

[195] 528 U.S. 562 (2000) (owner asked without adequate reason to grant a 33-foot easement to the municipality to connect the property to the municipal water supply when other owners were only required to grant a 15-foot easement).

[196] 734 A.2d 535 (Conn. 1999).

[197] 528 U.S. at 565-566 (Breyer, J., concurring).

[198] *Albiero v. City of Kankakee*, 246 F.3d 927, 932 (7th Cir. 2001). *See also Cruz v. Town of Cicero*, 275 F.3d 579, 587 (7th Cir. 2001) (finding an equal protection violation with evidence of personal animus against the landowner).

[199] *Harlen Assocs. v. Incorporated Village of Mineola*, 273 F.3d 494, 503 (2d Cir. 2001).

Race

Laws that make racial classifications are subject to the highest level of scrutiny. To be upheld under the equal protection clause, they must be necessary to achieve a compelling government interest.[200] In 1917, in the case of *Buchanan v. Warley*,[201] the Supreme Court early on held unconstitutional, a zoning law that segregated people through identifying zones where people were allowed to live based on their race. Facially neutral laws, however, will be struck down only if they were intended to discriminate on the basis of race. Thus, a law that may have had a disparate impact on Black families, because it restricted multifamily housing, was held not to violate the equal protection clause in *Village of Arlington Heights v. Metropolitan Housing Development Corporation*.[202] It is important to recall that zoning laws that have a disparate impact based on race may violate the *Fair Housing Act* or equivalent state laws.[203]

Much land use regulation has a negative effect on poor and moderate-income families by restricting or prohibiting affordable housing. Poverty has never been recognized as a suspect class under the equal protection clause, as have race, sex, and alienage. However, a few states have prohibited zoning laws that exclude low-income housing from the community. The foremost example is the *Mount Laurel* decision in New Jersey, covered fully in Chapter 12.[204]

§13.7.4 First Amendment — Speech and Religion

Strategic Lawsuits Against Public Participation (SLAPP)

§13.7.4.1 SLAPP Suits. SLAPP suits, or "Strategic Lawsuits Against Public Participation," are suits brought by property developers against opponents to a proposed development. The suits are designed either to retaliate against the opponents or to induce them to drop their opposition by making them suffer the expense of defending a lawsuit. Suits are often brought for defamation, tortious interference with business relationships, or similar theories.[205]

First Amendment rights of free speech and petition

Most SLAPP suits are dismissed before trial on the ground that the defendants were exercising their constitutionally protected right of free speech and/or the right to petition the government for redress of grievances.[206] For example, in *Protect Our Mountain Environment, Inc. v. District Court*

[200] John E. Nowak & Ronald D. Rotunda, *Constitutional Law* §14.3, at 601-602 (5th ed. 1995).

[201] 245 U.S. 60 (1917).

[202] 429 U.S. 252 (1977), *on remand*, 558 F.2d 1283 (7th Cir. 1977), *cert. denied*, 434 U.S. 1025, *on remand* 469 F. Supp. 836 (D. Ill. 1979), *aff'd*, 616 F.2d 1006 (7th Cir. 1980).

[203] *See* Chapter 12.

[204] *Southern Burlington County, NAACP v. Township of Mount Laurel*, 336 A.2d 713 (N.J. 1975).

[205] Julian Conrad Juergensmeyer et al., *Land Use Planning and Development Regulation Law* §5:2, at 141 (5th ed. 2-23); Daniel R. Mandelker & Michael Allan Wolf, *Land Use Law* §8.44 (6th ed. 2020); Penelope Canan & George W. Pring, *SLAPPs: Getting Sued for Speaking Out* (1996).

[206] *Gorman Towers, Inc. v. Bogoslavsky*, 626 F.2d 607, 614-615 (8th Cir. 1980); *Office One, Inc. v. Lopez*, 769 N.E.2d 749, 755 n.9 (Mass. 2002); Daniel R. Mandelker & Michael Allan Wolf, *Land Use Law* §8.44 (6th ed. 2020).

(*POME*),[207] after a developer obtained a rezoning of a 500-acre tract, several neighbors challenged the rezoning as both spot zoning and inconsistent with the comprehensive plan. While that challenge was pending, the developer sued the neighbors who had challenged the rezoning, claiming that they had abused the legal process by challenging the rezoning. The defendants in this lawsuit moved to dismiss the complaint on the ground that they were exercising their First Amendment free speech rights and rights to petition the government. The Colorado Supreme Court held that when defendants raise the First Amendment right to petition the government as a defense to their actions, the plaintiff has the burden of proving that their actions were not constitutionally protected.

Anti-SLAPP statutes

Several states have passed statutes limiting SLAPP suits.[208] They generally allow expedited procedures to dismiss frivolous complaints and, as in the *POME* case, place the burden on the plaintiff to show a factual and legal basis for finding that the defendants' speech is not constitutionally protected, as well as sanctions against the plaintiff for bringing unfounded claims.[209]

SLAPPbacks

Defendants in SLAPP suits have brought counterclaims against SLAPP suits called "*SLAPPbacks*."[210] These suits are based on claims of malicious prosecution or abuse of process.[211]

Regulation of signs

§13.7.4.2 Free Speech. Some land use regulations directly or indirectly regulate speech.[212] Several topics have generated substantial litigation. Signs have long been regulated both to promote traffic safety and for aesthetic reasons. Because signs involve speech, regulations that limit signs and billboards may run afoul of the First Amendment's protections for free speech.[213] The Supreme Court has distinguished between *commercial speech* and other types of speech such as political speech. Although at one time it was asserted that commercial speech was unprotected by the First

Commercial speech lesser level of protection

[207] 677 P.2d 1361 (Colo. 1984).

[208] Cal. Civ. Proc. Code §425.16; Del. Code tit. 10, §§8136 to 8138; Fla. Stat. §§57.105, 768.295; Ga. Code Ann. §9-11-11.1; Ind. Code §§34-7-7-1 *et seq*.; La Code Civ. Proc. Ann. art. 971; Mass. Gen. Laws ch. 231, §59H; Me. Rev. Stat. Ann. tit. 14, §731 et seq.; Minn. Stat. §§554.07 to 554.19; Neb. Rev. Stat. §§25-21,241 to 25-21,246; Nev. Rev. Stat. §§41.640 to 41.670; N.Y. Civ. Rights §§70-a & 76-a and N.Y. Civ. Prac. L. & R. §§3211(g) & 3212(h); R.I. Gen. Laws §9-33-1 to 9-33-4, *applied in Hometown Properties v. Fleming*, 680 A.2d 56 (R.I. 1996); Wash. Rev. Code §§4.24.500 to 4.24.520; Daniel R. Mandelker & Michael Allan Wolf, *Land Use Law* §8.45 (6th ed. 2020).

[209] Julian Conrad Juergensmeyer et al., *Land Use Planning and Development Regulation Law* §5:2, at 141-143 (5th ed. 2023); *see also* Naomi Harrow Franklin, *Pay Heed, All Who Enter: Why the Collateral Order Doctrine Does Not Encompass the Merits of Anti-SLAPP Motions*, 73 U. Kan. L. Rev. 177, 178 (2024).

[210] Daniel R. Mandelker & Michael Allan Wolf, *Land Use Law* §8.464 (6th ed. 2020).

[211] *Leonardini v. Shell Oil Co.*, 264 Cal. Rptr. 883 (Ct. App. 1989); Daniel R. Mandelker & Michael Allan Wolf, *Land Use Law* §8.44 (6th ed. 2020).

[212] *See, e.g.*, *Burns v. Town of Palm Beach*, 999 F.3d 1317 (11th Cir. 2021) (aesthetic review does not violate the First Amendment given "no great likelihood that some sort of message would be understood by those who viewed" the proposed development at issue).

[213] *Reed v. Town of Gilbert*, 576 U.S. 155 (2015); Julian Conrad Juergensmeyer et al., *Land Use Planning and Development Regulation Law* §10:21, at 514 (5th ed. 2023).

Amendment, such that it could be regulated or limited at will,[214] this is no longer the case.[215] At the same time, commercial speech is likely subject to a lower level of protection than political speech.[216]

Ban of off-site commercial billboards upheld

In *Metromedia, Inc. v. City of San Diego*,[217] the Supreme Court upheld a San Diego ordinance that banned most commercial billboards. The ordinance allowed only informational signs, such as government messages, historical plaques, religious symbols, time and temperature signs, temporary political campaign signs, and commercial signs that were "on-site." The Court held that municipalities could ban most off-site commercial billboards both to promote traffic safety and for aesthetic reasons.[218]

However, in the 2015 case of *Reed v. Town of Gilbert*,[219] the Court struck down a local ordinance that banned "ideological signs" that "communicat[e] a message or ideas." The ordinance also limited "political signs" to election season and limited the times when plaintiff church was allowed to post "directional signs" bearing the name of the church and the time and location of the next service. The Court noted that content-based restrictions on speech are presumptively unconstitutional and could only be justified if they serve a compelling government interest, a showing that could not be made by the town. Further, the town had ample alternative ways to regulate the placement and size of signs to satisfy public safety and aesthetic concerns. The Court more recently clarified in City of Austin v. Reagan Nat'l Advert. of Austin, LLC that distinguishing between on-premises and off-premises signs should be considered content neutral, hence not subject to strict scrutiny, even if the ordinance requires local government officials to review signs to draw such location-based distinctions.[220]

Yard signs

Owners of residential property sometimes place signs in their yards. Such signs include, for example, "for sale" signs, political campaign posters, religious symbols, and historic landmark status monuments. In *Linmark Associates, Inc. v. Township of Willingboro*,[221] the Supreme Court unanimously held that a town could not prohibit the posting of "for sale" or "sold" signs even though the town's motive was to stem the flight of white owners from a newly racially integrated community. In *City of Ladue v.*

[214] *See, e.g.*, *Valentine v. Chrestensen*, 316 U.S. 52, 54 (1942).

[215] *City of Cincinnati v. Discovery Network*, 507 U.S. 410 (1993) (invalidating a ban on commercial newsracks unless the city could show the ban was no more extensive than necessary to attain legitimate safety and aesthetic goals). *See also 44 Liquormart, Inc. v. Rhode Island*, 517 U.S. 484 (1996) (striking down a law that prohibited advertising the retail price of alcoholic beverages); *Virginia State Board of Pharmacy v. Virginia Citizens Consumer Council*, 425 U.S. 748 (1976) (striking down a law that prohibited the advertisement of prescription drug prices).

[216] John E. Nowak & Ronald D. Rotunda, *Constitutional Law* §16.31, at 1071 (5th ed. 1995).

[217] 453 U.S. 490 (1981).

[218] The Court did strike down the ban on on-site noncommercial signs because this constituted unconstitutional content discrimination between commercial and noncommercial speech and there was no showing that noncommercial signs were more distracting—and thus more problematic for traffic safety—than commercial signs. 453 U.S. at 512-513.

[219] 576 U.S. 155 (2015).

[220] 596 U.S. 61 (2022).

[221] 431 U.S. 85 (1977).

Gilleo,[222] the Court struck down an ordinance that prohibited all signs other than "for sale" signs (and a few other permitted categories of sign). In that case, the owner placed an 8.5-inch-by-11-inch poster in the window of her home stating "For Peace in the Gulf" — a comment on current military activities of the United States. Because her sign was prohibited by the ordinance, she sued the town and won a declaration that the ordinance was unconstitutional.

Sex-oriented businesses

Much litigation has ensued surrounding attempts by municipalities to ban or zone into certain areas sex-oriented businesses such as adult theaters, peep shows, adult bookstores, and nude dancing. The Supreme Court has upheld the power of the municipalities to limit where such businesses can be located, either by requiring them to be scattered[223] or confined to a single zone.[224] Although a 1981 case, *Schad v. Borough of Mount Ephraim*,[225] held that nude dancing was a protected form of expression that could not be entirely banned from the municipality, another case, *City of Erie v. Pap's A.M.*,[226] held the opposite, authorizing a total ban on such dancing when the ordinance was not designed to suppress expression but was part of a content-neutral prohibition on all public nudity in the city and was designed to protect the public from the negative "secondary effects" of nude dancing.[227]

Free exercise of religion

§13.7.4.3 Religious Uses. The First Amendment's protection of the free exercise of religion is at issue when zoning ordinances have the effect of limiting the ability of religious organizations to have places of worship or other activities where they like. Churches, synagogues, mosques, and other religious institutions are often located in residential neighborhoods. Most municipal zoning ordinances allow such uses as special exceptions under criteria that may effectively bar their placement in locations that the institution might prefer. Such regulations have often been upheld.[228] Although some states have allowed municipalities to exclude religious uses from residential zones,[229] it is unlikely a court would uphold an ordinance that banned places of worship entirely from a community.[230]

Neutral laws of general applicability

On the other hand, the Supreme Court has held in *Employment Division v. Smith*[231] that the free exercise clause of the First Amendment

[222] 512 U.S. 43 (1994).

[223] *Young v. American Mini Theatres*, 427 U.S. 50, 62 (1976).

[224] *City of Renton v. Playtime Theatres*, 475 U.S. 41, 52 (1986).

[225] *Schad v. Borough of Mount Ephraim*, 452 U.S. 61 (1981).

[226] 529 U.S. 277, 297 (2000).

[227] *See also Association of Club Executives of Dallas, Incorporated v. Dallas*, 83 F.4th 958, 961 (5th Cir. 2023).

[228] *Messiah Baptist Church v. County of Jefferson*, 859 F.2d 820, 823 (10th Cir. 1988); *Grosz v. City of Miami Beach*, 721 F.2d 729, 738-741 (11th Cir. 1983); *Jehovah's Witnesses v. City of Lakewood*, 699 F.2d 303, 307-308 (6th Cir. 1983); Julian Conrad Juergensmeyer et al., *Land Use Planning and Development Regulation Law* §10:23, at 525 (5th ed. 2023).

[229] *Mumaw v. Glendale*, 76 Cal. Rptr. 245 (Ct. App. 1969); Julian Conrad Juergensmeyer et al., *Land Use Planning and Development Regulation Law* §4:29, at 124-125 (5th ed. 2023).

[230] *Jehovah's Witnesses v. Woolwich Township*, 537 A.2d 1336 (N.J. Super. Ct. App. Div. 1988); Julian Conrad Juergensmeyer et al., *Land Use Planning and Development Regulation Law* §4:29, at 124-125 (5th ed. 2023).

[231] 494 U.S. 872 (1990).

does not protect individuals from burdens on religious practice if those burdens are not designed to interfere with religious freedoms[232] and if they are the byproduct of neutral laws of general application.[233] Congress tried to increase protection for religious interests in the *Religious Freedom Restoration Act of 1993* (*RFRA*),[234] by granting relief from regulations that "substantially burden a person's exercise of religion" unless those regulations both further a "compelling governmental interest" and are the "least restrictive means of furthering that compelling government interest." However, the Supreme Court held that Act unconstitutional, at least as applied to state regulations, in 1997 in the case of *City of Boerne v. Flores*,[235] on the ground that §5 of the Fourteenth Amendment grants Congress the power to pass laws protecting individuals from deprivations of constitutionally protected free exercise rights by the states, but that the Fourteenth Amendment does not give Congress the power to pass laws that grant greater rights than those encompassed by the First Amendment's free exercise clause. Courts have taken varying approaches to upheld local zoning laws that prohibit churches from operating homeless shelters, even if those activities are motivated by, or even arguably required by, religious conviction.[236]

State *RFRAs*

Several states reacted to *City of Boerne* by passing state versions of the *Religious Freedom Restoration Act*.[237] These laws may be subject to challenge on the ground that they unconstitutionally establish religion in violation of the First Amendment. If enforceable, they may limit the ability of municipalities to exclude or otherwise regulate land use by religious entities.

Religious Land Use and Institutionalized Persons Act of 2000

Congress returned to this issue in passing the *Religious Land Use and Institutionalized Persons Act of 2000* (*RLUIPA*).[238] This statute attempts to revive certain aspects of the *RFRA* struck down in *City of Boerne* by trying to cure the constitutional impediments identified there. The Supreme Court upheld its constitutionality in 2005.[239] *RLUIPA* prohibits governments from "impos[ing] or implement[ing] a land use regulation in a manner that imposes a substantial burden on the religious exercise of a person, including a religious assembly or institution" unless the regulation furthers "a compelling governmental interest" and "is the least restrictive means of furthering that compelling governmental interest."[240] To attempt

[232] *See, e.g.*, *Church of Lukumi Babalu Aye, Inc. v. City of Hialeah*, 508 U.S. 520 (1993) (ordinance struck down because it was targeted at one church's practice of ritual slaughter of animals and was not generally tailored).

[233] *Employment Division v. Smith*, 494 U.S. 872, 879 (1990).

[234] 42 U.S.C. §§2000bb *et seq.*

[235] 521 U.S. 507 (1997).

[236] Julian Conrad Juergensmeyer et al., *Land Use Planning and Development Regulation Law* §10:23, at 527-528 (5th ed. 2023) (noting that courts have split on this question).

[237] Ala. Const. of 1901, art. I, §3 (amended 1999); Fla. Stat. ch. 761.03; 775 Ill. Comp. Stat. 35/10; R.I. Gen. Laws §42-80.1-3(b)(1). *See also* Douglas Laycock, *State RFRAs and Land Use Regulation*, 32 U.C. Davis L. Rev. 755 (1999).

[238] 42 U.S.C. §§2000cc to 2000cc-5 (Pub. L. No. 106-274, 114 Stat. 803, Sept. 22, 2000, (S. 2869)).

[239] *Cutter v. Wilkinson*, 544 U.S. 709 (2005).

[240] 42 U.S.C. §2000cc. *See Cottonwood Christian Center v. Cypress Redevelopment Agency*, 218 F. Supp. 2d 1203 (C.D. Cal. 2002) (city's denial of conditional use permit and use of eminent

to meet the constitutional requirements set out in *City of Boerne*, the statute applies only (a) if the affected activity receives federal funds, or (b) if either the substantial burden or the removal of the burden would affect interstate commerce, or (c) if the burden is imposed in the course of government procedures that involve "individualized assessments of the proposed uses for the property involved."[241] The statute further provides that no government "shall impose or implement a land use regulation that (A) totally excludes religious assemblies from a jurisdiction; or (B) unreasonably limits religious assemblies, institutions, or structures within a jurisdiction."[242]

▶ HARD CASE ▷ IMPACT OF NEUTRAL ZONING LAWS ON RELIGIOUS USES

The neutral application of existing zoning laws may inhibit the ability of a religious organization to create a structure compatible with its beliefs and traditions. For example, in *Korean Buddhist Dae Won Sa Temple of Hawai'i v. Sullivan*,[243] the city of Honolulu denied a temple's application for a variance for its main temple hall that exceeded the allowable height limit under the zoning code. Although the architectural components of the structure had religious significance, the court held that the height restriction did not substantially burden the free exercise of religion because the church could have located its facility in a district of the city that would have allowed a building of that size. In contrast, the Ninth Circuit held in *International Church of the Foursquare Gospel v. City of San Leandro*[244] that *RLUIPA* prevented the city from denying a church the freedom to move to a larger building when that building was located in an area zoned for industrial use. The church had become bigger over time and was looking for a new facility and hoped to move into an abandoned industrial building. The city hoped to attract a business to the site that would employ city residents and argued that its interest in promoting jobs was a compelling government interest justifying refusal to rezone the property for church uses even if this refusal imposed a substantial burden on religious freedom. The Ninth Circuit held both that job creation was not a compelling government interest that justified such a burden on religious freedom and that even if it was, there were less burdensome ways to achieve that result. ◀

▶ HARD CASE ▷ CHURCHES AS HISTORIC LANDMARKS

Churches have sometimes been designated historic landmarks. When this prevents the church from renovating or changing its structure, it may

domain may violate the Act); *Grace United Methodist Church v. City of Cheyenne*, 235 F. Supp. 2d 1186, 1193-1194 (D. Wyo. 2002) (church denied daycare license must demonstrate that city's land use regulation imposes a substantial burden on its exercise of religion).

241 42 U.S.C. §2000cc(2)(C).

242 Id. at §2000cc(3). In addition, the *RLUIPA* amends *RFRA* to clarify that it is intended only to apply to federal regulations. Id. at §§2000bb-2 & 2000bb-3.

243 953 P.2d 1315 (Haw. 1998).

244 673 F.3d 1059 (9th Cir. 2011).

challenge the regulation as an interference with the free exercise of religion. Such claims are tenuous under the federal constitution under the theory of *Smith*. In a pre-*Smith* decision, the Second Circuit found no constitutional protection under the federal constitution from a landmark status for a church in New York.[245] However, in *Keeler v. Mayor & City Council of Cumberland*,[246] a federal district court held in 1996 that a city's refusal to grant permission to demolish a monastery and chapel in a historic district and replace them with other buildings that would better serve the needs of the church violated the church's freedom of religion under the federal and state constitutions. Several other courts have extended such protection under their state constitutions. A free exercise of religion claim was accepted and the historic landmark designation was struck down as unconstitutional under the federal constitution in *First Covenant Church v. City of Seattle*.[247] On appeal in that case, the Supreme Court reversed and remanded with instructions that clearly indicated the Court's view that the First Amendment did not render the historic landmark regulation unconstitutional. However, on remand the Washington Supreme Court reaffirmed its earlier ruling based on the state constitution, rather than the federal constitution.[248] A similar result was reached in Massachusetts under its state constitution.[249] ◀

▷ HOUSING THE HOMELESS **HARD CASE ◀**

Does a church have a First Amendment right to allow homeless persons to sleep on its landing and front steps? In *Fifth Avenue Presbyterian Church v. City of New York*,[250] the Second Circuit held that it did have such a right on the ground that the free exercise of religion encompasses the right to provide sanctuary for the poor and that the city could not point to a neutral law of general application that justified preventing the church from these practices. The counterargument is that the city was not singling out religious institutions by its policy of regulating homeless shelters to ensure minimum standards of care and of inducing homeless persons to sleep in shelters rather than in public areas. ◀

[245] *St. Bartholomew's Church v. City of New York*, 914 F.2d 348 (2d Cir. 1990).
[246] 940 F. Supp. 879 (D. Md. 1996).
[247] 787 P.2d 1352 (Wash. 1990).
[248] *First Covenant Church v. City of Seattle*, 840 P.2d 174 (Wash. 1992) (en banc). *Accord First United Methodist Church v. Hearing Examiner*, 916 P.2d 374 (Wash. 1996).
[249] *Society of Jesus of New England v. Boston Landmarks Commission*, 564 N.E.2d 571 (Mass. 1990).
[250] 293 F.3d 570 (2d Cir. 2002).

CHAPTER 14

Eminent Domain and Regulatory Takings

§14.1 Introduction
§14.2 Eminent Domain and the "Public Use" Requirement
  §14.2.1 U.S. Constitution
  §14.2.2 State Law
    §14.2.2.1 State Constitutions
    §14.2.2.2 State Statutes
§14.3 Just Compensation
§14.4 Regulatory Takings — Historical Background
  §14.4.1 Before 1922
  §14.4.2 1922 to 1978
  §14.4.3 After 1978
§14.5 General Balancing Test for Regulatory Takings
  §14.5.1 Character of Government Action
  §14.5.2 Economic Impact (Diminution in Value)
  §14.5.3 Interference with Reasonable Investment-Backed Expectations
  §14.5.4 Fairness and Justice
§14.6 "Categorical" Regulatory Takings
  §14.6.1 *Per Se* Takings
    §14.6.1.1 Physical Invasions
    §14.6.1.2 Deprivation of All Economically Viable Use
  §14.6.2 Established Property Rights
    §14.6.2.1 Core Property Rights
    §14.6.2.2 Vested Rights
§14.7 Judicial Takings
§14.8 Exactions
§14.9 Takings Legislation
§14.10 Remedies and Procedures for Regulatory Takings
  §14.10.1 Remedies for Regulatory Takings
  §14.10.2 Procedures
§14.11 Tribal Property

§14.1 Introduction

Takings clause

Property law determines who controls valued resources and what they can and cannot do with their property. Both common law and statutory law allocate and define the scope of property rights. This means that lawmakers exercise substantial power over property owners. By promulgating property law, the courts and legislatures determine what can be owned, who owns it, and what entitlements and obligations go along with ownership. Property cannot exist as a social institution without laws that define its scope and contours. Government power is therefore necessary to create property rights. However, government power is also threatening to owners. After all, what the government giveth, the government may taketh away. The power to define is the power is destroy. To protect owners from having their property rights wrongfully taken by government, the takings clause in the Constitution prohibits the government from taking private property for public use without just compensation.[1] The takings clause protects owners from uncompensated taking of their title or deprivation of their possessory rights. Outright expropriation of property clearly requires compensation except in extraordinary cases; thus, a government entity that takes property by eminent domain to construct a highway must compensate the owner.[2] But the takings clause goes beyond this. The Supreme Court has interpreted the takings clause to protect owners from fundamentally unjust alterations of their property rights by the state, including unjust limits on their ability to use their property as they wish.

Property law must both define and defend property

This creates a dilemma for property law. As Professor Jeremy Paul has written, property rights serve "twin roles — as protector of individual rights against other citizens and as safeguard against excessive government interference."[3] This dual role of property law poses potential conflicts for judges. As protector of property rights, a court might apply nuisance law to prohibit a company from releasing chemicals into the soil that harm neighboring property owners. A court might do this because those chemicals are now known to be toxic, even though when the company first started its operations 40 years ago, no one knew that the chemicals were dangerous. However, the company might object that it did not know the chemicals were dangerous until recent scientific discoveries revealed this, that it had received a government permit to operate, and that, in reliance on this permit, it had invested millions of dollars in building its factory and its business operations. Application of nuisance law here, by forcing the company to close, would arguably deprive it of pre-existing property rights created in reasonable reliance on prior law. This is the dilemma: The state must have the power to define the scope of property rights, and to redefine them over time by new legislation and common law rules as circumstances

[1] "[N]or shall private property be taken for public use without just compensation." U.S. Const. amend. V (1791).

[2] *See, e.g.*, *Glosemeyer v. United States*, 45 Fed. Cl. 771, 781 (2000) (federal Rails-to-Trails statute effectuates an unconstitutional taking of property by forcing a servient landowner to grant a public recreational easement when a railroad easement ends).

[3] Jeremy Paul, *The Hidden Structure of Takings Law*, 64 S. Cal. L. Rev. 1393, 1402 (1991).

and values change, but if this power to redefine property law is unlimited, the state would be able to unjustly deprive owners of pre-existing rights, infringing on their justified expectations based on prior law. Professor Paul concludes that to "reconcile American law's double-edge reliance on property concepts, [we] must successfully distinguish between the courts' role as definers and defenders of property rights."[4]

The role of the takings clause

The takings clause addresses this dilemma by defining certain core property rights as immune from alteration by the state without compensation. Lawmakers are free to alter property rights as long as they do not infringe on this protected core. And even then, it is important to understand that the takings clause does not prohibit the state from taking property rights; the state is free to impinge on these core rights as long as it does so for legitimate public purposes and as long as it compensates the owner.

Defining "takings"

Defining what constitutes an unconstitutional "taking" of property is difficult. The case law is conflicting, and the Supreme Court has adopted different tests over time. Three different elements are crucial to understanding the law. First, the Court has adopted a complex *doctrinal structure* to differentiate between a legitimate regulation and an unconstitutional "taking" of property. This doctrine includes a series of tests, some of which define types of deprivations that are *per se* takings of property, and some of which require consideration of a list of "factors" relevant to the takings determination and then application of a kind of balancing test. Those factors include (1) the economic impact of the regulation (the diminution in value of the property); (2) the extent to which it interferes with reasonable investment-backed expectations; and (3) the character of the government action.

Doctrinal framework

***Per se* tests**

Relevant factors

Precedent

Second, because the doctrine is not self-executing, lawyers pay a great deal of attention to *precedent*. It is crucial to understand the outcomes in the key Supreme Court cases because new cases will be adjudicated partly by application of the doctrine and partly by analogy to the decided cases. To predict how a case will be decided, or to write a good brief or draft opinion, one must be able to state how the case being considered is similar to or different from these key precedential rulings. This chapter will describe the holdings of all the key Supreme Court cases so you can attempt to argue how a case is similar to or different from these key precedents.

Fairness and justice

Third, the Court has stated over and over that the ultimate question is whether the regulation at issue wrongfully "forc[es] some people alone to bear public burdens which, in all fairness and justice, should be borne by the public as a whole."[5] Consideration of *fairness* and *justice* is therefore the ultimate criterion by which the Court distinguishes between constitutional regulations and unconstitutional takings. The takings clause protects property owners from being conscripted to pay for public programs whose cost should be spread among the taxpayers as a whole.[6] The key is whether the

[4] *Id.* at 1415.

[5] *Armstrong v. United States*, 364 U.S. 40, 49 (1960). *See also Agins v. Tiburon*, 447 U.S. 255, 260-261 (1980).

[6] The question under the takings clause is whether "the public at large, rather than a single owner, must bear the burden of an exercise of state power in the public interest." *Agins v. Tiburon*, 447 U.S. 255, 260 (1980).

obligation being imposed on the owner is one that she should fairly bear for the good of the community.

§14.2 Eminent Domain and the "Public Use" Requirement

§14.2.1 U.S. Constitution

Public purpose

The Fifth Amendment allows the government to take property as long as it pays "just compensation" to the owner. However, the government cannot take property unless it is for "public use." A taking that is for private rather than "public use" may be enjoined by a court upon petition of the affected owner. But what does "public use" mean? There is no question that "public use" is present when land is taken to build a highway. A highway is "used" by the "public." It is also generally agreed that public use is established even if the property is transferred to a private owner, if the property will be open to the public, as is the case for public accommodations like common carriers such as trains, which have legal duties to serve the public. But what if property is transferred from one private owner to another for economic development purposes? The Supreme Court has long held that the public use requirement is met if the taking serves a legitimate *public purpose*, even if the government achieves this purpose by taking property from one owner for the purpose of conveying it to another owner. In a highly controversial ruling, the Supreme Court upheld this traditional understanding by a 5-4 vote in the case of *Kelo v. City of New London*,[7] a case that built on two important precedents, the 1954 case of *Berman v. Parker*[8] and the 1980 ruling in *Hawai'i Housing Authority v. Midkiff*.[9]

***Berman v. Parker* (1954)**

Slum clearance and removal of "blight"

In *Berman v. Parker*,[10] the Supreme Court upheld the constitutionality of an urban renewal plan in Washington, D.C. that took property from multiple private owners in a "blighted area" and resold the property to developers who would develop it in a manner consistent with the plan. The owner of a department store in the area sued to enjoin the plan, arguing that it effectuated a "taking from one businessman for the benefit of another businessman"[11] — that the taking was for private, not public, use. He also argued that, although the area might be blighted, his grocery store was not. The Supreme Court rejected his claim, concluding that the taking was for "public use" if it effectuated a legitimate public purpose. A forced transfer of ownership from one owner to another might well promote public purposes of clearing dilapidated and unsafe buildings in a crowded neighborhood and replacing them with structures that were consistent with modern land use planning ideals to promote a safe

[7] 545 U.S. 469 (2005), *aff'g* 843 A.2d 500 (Conn. 2004).
[8] 348 U.S. 26 (1954).
[9] 467 U.S. 229 (1984).
[10] 348 U.S. 26 (1954).
[11] *Id.* at 33.

environment, as well as desirable economic development. If the taking would arguably promote the general welfare, it satisfied the public use test. To decide otherwise would force the government to retain ownership of the land rather than to decentralize control of the property by reselling the land to private owners. "We cannot say that public ownership is the sole method of promoting the public purposes of community redevelopment projects."[12] Nor did it matter that the grocery store was not itself dilapidated or in dangerous condition; the legislature had the discretion to choose to clear the whole area. Government is entitled to "attack the problem of the blighted parts of the community on an area rather than on a structure-by-structure basis."[13]

Deference to the legislature

Importantly, the Court held that

> [s]ubject to specific constitutional limitations, when the legislature has spoken, the public interest has been declared in terms well-nigh conclusive. In such cases the legislature, not the judiciary, is the main guardian of the public needs to be served by social legislation. . . . This principle admits of no exception merely because the power of eminent domain is involved. The role of the judiciary in determining whether that power is being exercised for a public purpose is an extremely narrow one.[14]

In other words, the courts should generally defer to the legislature in determining what is a public purpose.

***Hawai'i Housing Authority v. Midkiff* (1984)**

The Supreme Court extended this holding in a unanimous ruling in the 1984 case of *Hawai'i Housing Authority v. Midkiff*,[15] in an opinion written by Justice O'Connor. Because of its unique history, most of the land in Hawai'i was owned by a very small number of owners. The land was originally owned by Native Hawaiians through a system that granted control of the land to a high chief, the *ali'i nui*, who assigned parts of the land for development to certain subchiefs. "All land was held at the will of the *ali'i nui* and eventually had to be returned to his trust. There was no private ownership of land."[16] When Hawai'i was taken over by the United States, ownership of land remained concentrated. Although the state and federal governments owned almost 49 percent of the state's land in the mid-1960s,

> another 47 percent was in the hands of only 72 private landowners. The legislature further found that 18 landholders, with tracts of 21,000 acres or more, owned more than 40 percent of this land and that on Oahu, the most urbanized of the islands, 22 landowners owned 72.5 percent of the fee simple titles.[17]

[12] *Id.* at 34.
[13] *Id.*
[14] *Id.* at 32.
[15] 467 U.S. 229 (1984). *See Richardson v. City and County of Honolulu*, 124 F.3d 1150 (9th Cir. 1997) (refusing to reconsider the ruling in *Midkiff*).
[16] 467 U.S. at 232.
[17] *Id.*

One of the major landowners was the Bernice Pauahi Bishop Estate, a trust established by one of the last Hawaiian princesses descended from King Kamehameha I, whose income was dedicated to educational purposes for Native Hawaiians.[18]

Land reform

In 1967, the Hawai'i legislature passed a land reform act designed to deconcentrate land ownership and create a market for real estate rather than the existing market for rental property. It authorized existing tenants to purchase their property from their landlords by applying to a state agency that would take the property from the landlord by eminent domain and immediately transfer title to the tenant. Although formally the state would take the property and pay an eminent domain award to the owner and the tenant would reimburse the state for this cost, the statute effectively imposed a forced sale from landlord to tenant. The tenant would remain in possession of the property throughout the proceedings. The Supreme Court unanimously upheld the arrangement, rejecting the idea that the state must take possession of the property temporarily as it had in *Berman v. Parker.* Justice O'Connor noted that the statutory scheme was justified to create a vigorous real estate market and "to reduce the perceived social and economic evils of a land oligopoly," and that this constituted a legitimate public purpose.[19] Quoting an earlier case, she emphasized, as had the *Berman* Court, that "the Court has made clear that it will not substitute its judgment for a legislature's judgment as to what constitutes a public use unless the use be palpably without reasonable foundation."[20]

Effect on Native Hawaiians

Justice O'Connor's decision said nothing whatsoever about the effect of the land reform act on Native Hawaiians. The lease income earned by the Bishop Estate was the main source of funds for the Kamehameha Schools established to educate Native Hawaiian children. The Court justified the land reform act by noting that "[t]he people of Hawai'i have attempted, much as the settlers of the original 13 Colonies did, to reduce the perceived social and economic evils of a land oligopoly traceable to their monarchs."[21] Characterizing the act as an attack on feudalism, the Court failed to note that it also had the effect of continuing the process of taking land from Native Hawaiians and transferring it to non-Natives.[22] While the legislature might still be empowered under the public use clause to choose deconcentration of land ownership over protection of reserved Native property rights, it would have been harder for the Court to characterize the statute

[18] Judge Robert Mahealani M. Seto & Lynne Marie Kohm, *Of Princesses, Charities, Trustees, and Fairytales: A Lesson of the Simple Wishes of Princess Bernice Pauahi Bishop*, 21 U. Haw. L. Rev. 393 (1999).

[19] 467 U.S. at 241-242.

[20] *Id.* at 241. *See id.* at 242-243 ("When the legislature's purpose is legitimate and its means are not irrational, our cases make clear that empirical debates over the wisdom of takings — no less than debates over the wisdom of other kinds of socioeconomic legislation — are not to be carried out in the federal courts.").

[21] *Id.* at 241-242.

[22] Ezra Rosser, *Progress and the Taking of Indigenous Land*, 85 Ohio St. L.J 623 (2024) (reviewing ways in which the land reform at issue in Midkiff transferred Indigenous land to upper-class, relatively wealthy tenants).

as an unalloyed good, had it considered the act's place in continuing the historical expropriation of land from native peoples in the United States.[23]

***Kelo v. City of New London* (2005)**

In *Kelo v. City of New London*,[24] by a 5-4 vote, the Supreme Court reaffirmed its rulings in *Berman* and *Midkiff* that takings of property satisfy the public use test if they bear a rational relationship to a legitimate public purpose. *Kelo* involved an economically distressed municipality in Connecticut that sought to redevelop the waterfront area of the city to create a conference hotel in the center of a "small urban village" containing shops and restaurants, a pedestrian riverwalk, and other recreational areas, including a renovated marina, 80 new residences, and both office and commercial space. The development plan would not only revitalize the downtown area, but was also projected to increase municipal property tax revenues and to create more than 1,000 jobs. Suzette Kelo (along with nine other property owners in the affected area) challenged the taking of her house on the ground that the taking served a private, rather than a public use.

Justice Stevens, in an opinion joined by Justices Kennedy, Souter, Ginsburg, and Breyer, saw the case as following naturally from the Court's earlier rulings that the public use requirement was satisfied if the taking promoted a public purpose, that economic development and job creation are public purposes, and that the Court should defer to the legislative bodies in determining the best means to achieve those public purposes. He noted that "[t]hose who govern the City were not confronted with the need to remove blight in the Fort Trumbull area, but their determination that the area was sufficiently distressed to justify a program of economic rejuvenation is entitled to our deference."[25] He also emphasized that the city had "carefully formulated an economic development plan" and that "[g]iven the comprehensive character of the plan, the thorough deliberation that preceded its adoption, and the limited scope of our review, it is appropriate for us, as it was in *Berman*, to resolve the challenges of the individual owners, not on a piecemeal basis, but rather in light of the entire plan."[26]

Justice Kennedy's concurrence

Justice Kennedy concurred, emphasizing that the "taking occurred in the context of a comprehensive development plan meant to address a serious city wide depression, and the projected economic benefits of the project cannot be characterized as *de minimis*."[27] He also noted that the "identities of most of the private beneficiaries were unknown at the time the city formulated its plans,"[28] making it less likely that the takings were motivated by "impermissible favoritism."[29] He argued that the courts should strike down a taking for economic development purposes if it has "only incidental or pretextual public benefits."[30]

[23] Robert A. Williams, Jr., *The American Indian in Western Legal Thought: Discourses of Conquest* (1990); Robert A. Williams, Jr., *Jefferson, The Norman Yoke, and American Indian Lands*, 29 Ariz. L. Rev. 165 (1987).

[24] 545 U.S. 469 (2005), *aff'g* 843 A.2d 500 (Conn. 2004).

[25] *Id.* at 483.

[26] *Id.* at 484.

[27] *Id.* at 493 (Kennedy, J., concurring).

[28] *Id.* (Kennedy, J., concurring).

[29] *Id.* at 491 (Kennedy, J., concurring).

[30] *Id.* (Kennedy, J., concurring).

Justice O'Connor's dissent

Justice O'Connor dissented, along with Chief Justice Rehnquist, and Justices Scalia and Thomas. She argued that this case was unprecedented and wholly different from *Berman* and *Midkiff*, both which involved takings to respond to social harms caused by the use of the properties in question. "In both those cases, the extraordinary, precondemnation use of the targeted property inflicted affirmative harm on society — in *Berman* through blight resulting from extreme poverty and in *Midkiff* through oligopoly resulting from extreme wealth. And in both cases, the relevant legislative body had found that eliminating the existing property use was necessary to remedy the harm."[31] It did not matter that the grocery store in *Berman* was not blighted because the legislature is allowed to paint with a broad brush when solving a social problem. In contrast, there was no claim that Suzette Kelo's and Wilhelmina Dery's "well-maintained homes were a source of social harm."[32] She would have ruled that economic development takings do not satisfy the public use test, unless they respond to harm caused by the property being taken. This argument assumes that there is sharp constitutional distinction between eradicating slums and redeveloping economically depressed areas, perhaps based on the idea that slums are composed of "blighted property" that is dangerous or unhealthy. This distinction is particularly hard to draw if one wants to argue that the Hawai'i properties taken in *Midkiff* were "a source of social harm." Those properties were certainly not blighted and included many million-dollar homes. The social harm in *Midkiff* was caused, not by the properties themselves, but by the problem of concentration of ownership — a problem with the market for real property rather than the homes that were taken. If that is so, then underutilized properties in an economically depressed city might be similarly described as a source of harm because their current uses not only fail to provide as many jobs as possible but result in low property values, which not only discourage others from moving into the neighborhood but depress property taxes needed to fund local police, fire protection, and public schools.

Justice Thomas's dissent

In his dissent, Justice Thomas argued for the most radical position, arguing for a literal interpretation of the public use clause under which takings would be allowed for economic development purposes only if the property remained in public ownership or was open to the public, as in the case of public accommodations like trains with legal duties to serve the public.[33] One problem with a literal interpretation of the takings clause is that it appears only in the Fifth Amendment, which applies only to the United States. The takings clause has been applied to the states only through interpretation of the due process clause of the Fourteenth Amendment. If one wants to read the Fourteenth Amendment literally, then there is no takings clause at all applicable to the states. To read the prohibition against "deprivation of property without due process of law"

[31] *Id.* at 500 (O'Connor, J., dissenting).
[32] *Id.*
[33] *Id.* at 508 (Thomas, J., dissenting).

to mean "no taking of private property for public use without just compensation" requires deviation from a literal approach to constitutional interpretation.

§14.2.2 State Law

§14.2.2.1 State Constitutions. The *Kelo* decision unleashed a firestorm of protest across the nation, resulting in legislative and constitutional changes in most states to limit the power of states and municipalities to take property from one private person for transfer to another. Even before the Supreme Court's rulings, some state courts began to tread a different path. While many state supreme courts have continued to interpret their state constitutions in a manner consistent with the federal interpretation in *Kelo*,[34] an increasing number of state supreme courts have adopted a different path, interpreting their state constitutional "public use" requirements more stringently than has the U.S. Supreme Court.[35]

State public use law

Some state courts have adopted the highly restrictive interpretation of Justice Thomas and found that takings are for public use only if the public retains ownership or the property is open to the public, as is the case with common carriers. For example, in *Karesh v. City Council of Charleston*,[36] the city developed a complicated scheme to create a convention center-hotel in downtown Charleston. As part of the project, the city proposed to take some privately owned parcels and lease the land to a private corporation for the construction of a parking facility and convention center containing rental commercial space. The South Carolina Supreme Court ruled in favor of the owners who challenged the taking of their property, holding that the taking violated the "public use" requirement of the South Carolina constitution. Justice Ness noted that the taking would provide "benefit to the developer, with no assurance of more than negligible advantage to the general public."[37] The plan would take property from existing retail merchants and allow the new lessee-developer to sublet the new shops to "new merchants, not to the land-owner merchants whose property the city proposes to condemn. We cannot constitutionally condone the eviction of the

Karesh v. City Council of Charleston **(1978)**

[34] *See, e.g., City of Oakland v. Oakland Raiders*, 646 P.2d 835 (Cal. 1982); *Kelo v. City of New London*, 843 A.2d 500 (Conn. 2004), *aff'd*, 545 U.S. 469 (2005); *Township of West Orange v. 769 Assocs.*, 800 A.2d 86 (N.J. 2002).

[35] *See Bailey v. Myers*, 76 P.3d 898 (Ariz. Ct. App. 2003) (city could not take private property on which automobile service station was located for transfer to private developers to construct a retail shopping and office center when the intended use was not public and public benefits were incidental to the primarily private nature of the intended use); *Arvada Urban Renewal Authority v. Columbine Professional Plaza Ass'n*, 85 P.3d 1066 (Colo. 2004) (not a public purpose to take a private lake for a new Wal-Mart unless there was a recent finding that the property was blighted); *Southwestern Illinois Development Authority v. National City Envtl.*, 768 N.E.2d 1, 263 Ill. Dec. 241 (Ill. 2002) (not a public purpose to take a factory's property to expand a parking lot for a race track next door); *Tolksdorf v. Griffith*, 626 N.W.2d 163 (Mich. 2001) (holding unconstitutional a statute authorizing private owners to acquire easements over neighboring property to get access to a landlocked parcel).

[36] 247 S.E.2d 342 (S.C. 1978).

[37] *Id.* at 345.

present property owners by virtue of the power of eminent domain in favor other private shopkeepers."[38]

Other courts allow takings from one private party for transfer to another but adopt Justice O'Connor's view that such takings are for "public use" only if the property is blighted or causing social harm and the taking alleviates the burdens imposed by the property. For example, in a dramatic development, the Michigan Supreme Court unanimously overruled its famous 1981 decision in *Poletown Neighborhood Council v. City of Detroit*,[39] which had held that the public use requirement was met when a city took private homes and other properties in a residential area and transferred those lots to General Motors Corp. to construct an automobile manufacturing plant. *Poletown* had held that the goals of economic development and job promotion were sufficient public purposes to justify the use of the eminent domain power despite the transfer of the parcels to private ownership. However, in 2004 the Michigan Supreme Court overruled *Poletown*, holding in *Wayne County v. Hathcock*[40] that a taking of property of one owner for transfer to another private owner would satisfy the public use test only if the property being taken were blighted. The court held that use of the eminent domain power to transfer property from one private owner to another, satisfies the public use test only when (1) "public necessity of the extreme sort" requires collective action; (2) the property will be "subject to public oversight after transfer to a private entity"; and (3) the property is selected because of "facts of independent public significance" about the property being taken, rather than advantage to the private entity to whom the property is transferred, such as a conclusion that the area is blighted and in need of redevelopment that is unlikely to occur without public action of this sort.[41] A number of other state courts agree that the public use clause in their state constitutions is violated if property is taken for economic development purposes when the property being taken cannot be described as "blighted" and in inherent need of repair and upgrading.[42]

***Poletown Neighborhood Council v. City of Detroit* (1981)**

***Wayne County v. Hathcock* (2004)**

[38] *Id. See also HTA Ltd. Partnership v. Mass. Turnpike Auth.*, 747 N.E.2d 707 (Mass. App. Ct. 2001) (state turnpike authority can take property and retransfer it to private parties for highway purposes but cannot condemn property if the primary purpose is to benefit a private owner); *City of Bozeman v. Vaniman*, 898 P.2d 1208 (Mont. 1995) (not a public purpose to take property for space in visitor's center to be occupied by private Chamber of Commerce); *Casino Reinvestment Development Authority v. Banin*, 727 A.2d 102 (N.J. 1998) (a taking from a homeowner for transfer to a casino owned by Donald Trump did not serve a public taking when the purpose of the taking was to facilitate construction of a parking lot for the casino, but the conveyance did not limit use of the property for this purpose through an enforceable covenant or otherwise and thus the new private owner would be empowered to use the property for other, possibly private, purposes); In re Gen. Mun. Auth. of Nanticoke, 292 A.3d 1162, 1173 (Pa. Commw. Ct. 2023) (condemnation to build senior housing upheld, but noting that public use test in Pennsylvania requires that "the genuine purpose of the takings is for a public use, i.e., the public use is the true driving force").

[39] *Poletown Neighborhood Council v. City of Detroit*, 304 N.W.2d 455 (Mich. 1981), *overruled by Wayne County v. Hathcock*, 684 N.W.2d 765 (Mich. 2004).

[40] 684 N.W.2d 765 (Mich. 2004).

[41] *Id.*

[42] *See, e.g., Little Rock v. Raines*, 411 S.W.2d 486 (Ark. 1967); *Baycol, Inc. v. Downtown Development Authority*, 315 So. 2d 451, 456-458 (Fla. 1975); *Southwestern Illinois Dev. Auth. v. Nat'l City Envtl.*, 768 N.E.2d 1, 263 Ill. Dec. 241 (Ill. 2002); *Owensboro v. McCormick*, 581

§14.2.2.2 **STATE STATUTES.** In response to the *Kelo* decision, almost all states have passed legislation that limits the power of municipalities to take property for economic development purposes.[43] The legislation is varied. First, some states repudiated *Kelo* by prohibiting the use of eminent domain to take property from one person and transfer it to another if the taking is for economic development purposes, such as increased tax revenue or additional jobs.[44] Second, some states adopted Justice Thomas's literal approach by prohibiting all takings of property from one private owner for transfer to another — unless the property is open for public "use."[45] Third, a number of states passed laws prohibiting takings, unless the property being taken is "blighted," raising health or safety concerns.[46] Fourth, some states regulate takings by procedural measures designed to increase public participation in the process through more hearings, better notice, or requirements that the taking authority present evidence sufficient to justify the taking.[47] Fifth, some states require higher compensation than the usual "fair market value" if a person's home is taken.[48]

Post-*Kelo* state legislation

§14.3 Just Compensation

Fair market value

The Supreme Court has repeatedly defined the "just compensation" required by the takings clause to mean "fair market value" of the property at the time the taking occurs. This means the amount a willing buyer would pay a willing seller.[49] In addition, the property is valued not at its present use, but its "highest and best use" consistent with existing zoning and other land use restrictions.[50] This approach values the property by the amount it would be worth if it were sold on the open market. This way of valuing the property allows it to be valued in a relatively objective manner, through

S.W.2d 3, 5-8 (Ky. 1979); *Opinion of the Justices*, 152 Me. 440, 447, 131 A.2d 904 (Me. 1957); Malanga v. Twp. of W. Orange, 290 A.3d 1212, 1222 (N.J. 2023); *Karesh v. City Council*, 247 S.E.2d 342 (S.C. 1978); *In re Seattle*, 638 P.2d 549 (Wash. 1981).

43 Elisabeth Sperow, *The* Kelo *Legacy: Political Accountability, Not Legislation, Is the Cure*, 38 McGeorge L. Rev. 405, 418-422 (2007).

44 *See* Alaska Stat. §§09.55.240(d), 29.35.030; Idaho Code §7-701A(2); 735 Ill. Comp. Stat. 30/5-5-5(c); Ky. Rev. Stat. §416.675(3); Me. Rev. Stat. tit. 1, §816; Mo. Rev. Stat. §523.271; Neb. Rev. Stat. §76-710.04; N.H. Rev. Stat. §162-K:2(IX-a)(b); S.D. Codified Laws §11-7-22.1; Tenn. Code §29-17-102(2); Vt. Stat. tit. 12, §1040(a); W. Va. Code §54-1-2(a)(11).

45 *See* Fla. Stat. §73.013; Iowa Code §§6A.21 to 6A.22; Ky. Rev. Stat. §416.675(2); N.H. Rev. Stat. §162-K:2(IX-a)(a); Tenn. Code §29-17-102(2).

46 *See* Ala. Code §§24-2-2, 24-3-2 (housing and urban renewal); Iowa Code §6A.22; Me. Rev. Stat. tit. 1, §816; Mo. Rev. Stat. §523.271; Tenn. Code §29-17-102(2)(C); Wis. Stat. §32.03(6).

47 *See* 735 Ill. Comp. Stat. 30/5-5-5(d); W. Va. Code §16-18-6.

48 Ind. Code §32-24-4.5-8(2)(A) (owner of a residence entitled to 150 percent of fair market value; owner of a business entitled to "any loss incurred in a trade or business that is attributable to the exercise of eminent domain").

49 *Almota Farmers Elevator & Warehouse Co. v. United States*, 409 U.S. 470, 474 (1973).

50 *Housing Authority of the City of New Brunswick v. Suydam Investors, L.L.C.*, 826 A.2d 673, 684 (N.J. 2003) (owner of contaminated property has right to compensation for fair market value of property after remediation, but government has right under environmental protection laws to be reimbursed by the property owner for cleanup costs).

testimony from experts about the likely sales price, gleaned from sales of comparable property in the vicinity.

Fairness of the test

Payment of fair market value is arguably fair because it is based on an objective measure of value. It is where the supply and demand curves meet, or what the average buyer would pay the average seller. However, it is arguably unfair for the simple reason that most owners value their property at an amount higher than fair market value. This is because owners who value their property at or below fair market value would be indifferent between owning the property and putting it up for sale. If an owner has chosen *not* to put her property up for sale, this ordinarily means that she is not interested in selling at that time; she values owning the property more than the prospect of obtaining dollars in the amount of its fair market value. To induce such an owner to sell, one would have to offer *more* than "fair market value" to get her to agree to sell. And some owners have such strong sentimental attachment to their homes that they would not sell, no matter what price was offered. Taking property at fair market value fails to compensate owners for the full amount the property is worth *to them*. However, this unfairness is arguably something we need to live with because it is impossible, as a practical matter, to determine what an owner's asking price is. Owners whose property is taken, have an incentive to inflate their asking price, claiming that the property is worth more to them than it really is. Because values are subjective, there is no way to determine whether an award is really compensating an owner for what she lost or whether it is overcompensating an owner who is overstating the value of the property to her and is attempting to make money off the taxpayers. For this reason, although fair market value is arguably inevitably unfair to owners, it is nonetheless the established test.

Replacement cost

***United States v. 564.54 Acres of Land* (1979)**

The "fair market value" measure is also arguably unfair in two other situations. In *United States v. 564.54 Acres of Land*,[51] three church-owned summer camps were valued at $500,000 — the amount they would bring on the open market. However, if the owner were to attempt to *replace* the camps by building them elsewhere, they would have to spend almost $6 million because new regulatory requirements would then apply to the new construction. The old camps were exempt from these requirements because they had been built before the requirements went into effect and the requirements were not made retroactive to previously established uses. The Supreme Court held the proper measure of damages was fair market value, not the cost of replacing the facilities elsewhere. This is arguably unfair because it does not leave the owner in as good a position as it would have been had the taking never occurred, and thus the owner is not adequately compensated. On the other hand, the result may be justified because not all owners *will* want to re-establish the use elsewhere. If they do not, they will arguably receive a windfall, *i.e.*, the fair market value of the property (what they would have gotten if they had sold it) plus the extra premium needed to replace the facility, which they can just pocket if they wish.

[51] 441 U.S. 506 (1979).

A similar problem attends the issue of business goodwill. The state usually just takes the land and structures, not a business located on it. Thus, if property is used as a laundromat, the government will take the land and structures and not the business, and the owner is free to establish the business elsewhere. If the owner were compensated for loss of the business, and then reopened elsewhere, he would be overcompensated. For this reason, the courts will normally not allow compensation for any potential harm to the business. Calculating such harms is often speculative and will overcompensate the owner who chooses not to re-establish the business elsewhere. On the other hand, one of the major assets of a business is its location and the "goodwill" it has established with customers who know it and use it. If a business is unable to reopen in the vicinity, it must establish itself elsewhere and may thus lose its customers and have to work to attract new customers in the new location. This cost is not compensated and the business will lose substantially by the taking because of the need to re-establish goodwill elsewhere.

Business goodwill

In *Almota Farmers Elevator & Warehouse Co. v. United States*,[52] the government took a term of years in a grain elevator complex. The government argued that it need only compensate the owner of the leasehold for the market value of the remaining seven and a half years on the lease. However, the Supreme Court held that the leasehold would likely have been renewed and that, if the tenant had attempted to transfer the leasehold to an assignee, that possibility would have affected the price paid to take over the lease, and thus had to be considered in determining the fair market value of the leasehold.

***Almota Farmers Elevator & Warehouse Co. v. United States* (1973)**

Leaseholds

▷ PARTIAL TAKINGS **HARD CASE ◀**

If the state takes 40 acres from an owner of a 100-acre tract, it must compensate the owner not only for the fair market value of the 40 acres, but also for any reduction in value to the remaining 60 acres caused by the taking of the 40.[53] This reduction in the value of the remaining 60 acres is called *severance damages*.[54] However, if the taking *increases* the value of the remaining 60 acres by providing them a *special benefit* that will not accrue to the public at large (for example, by placing the land along a major road in a way that will increase its attractiveness to retail business), courts will generally offset the severance damages by the amount of the special

Severance damages

[52] 409 U.S. 470 (1973).

[53] *New Hampshire Department of Transportation v. Franchi*, 48 A.3d 849, 852 (N.H. 2012); *State v. Weiswasser*, 693 A.2d 864, 874-875 (N.J. 1997) (owner is entitled to compensation for diminution of value of remainder property that is specifically attributable to visibility lost as direct result of removal of portions of property through partial-taking condemnation); *State Dep't of Transportation & Development v. Regard*, 567 So. 2d 1174 (La. Ct. App. 1990).

[54] John G. Sprankling, *Understanding Property Law* §39.06[D], at 696 (5th ed. 2023). *See, e.g., Portland Natural Gas Transp. System v. 19.2 Acres of Land*, 318 F.3d 279 (1st Cir. 2003) (owner can recover damages for increased difficulty of developing land when government condemns property to take an easement to construct a natural gas pipeline).

benefit to the owner of the remaining 60 acres.[55] However, some courts allow an offset for both the special *and* the general benefits accruing to the remaining property.[56] Moreover, courts are divided on the question of whether the government may offset the special benefit accruing to the retained land against the amount owed the owner for the land that actually was taken. For example, assume the 40 acres taken by the government are worth $100,000, but that the taking increases the value of the remaining 60 acres by $50,000.

The Supreme Court *has* allowed the increase in value to the remaining 60 acres to be offset against the amount due the owner for the taking of the 40 acres (as long as it is a special benefit rather than a general benefit); thus, the owner would receive only $50,000.[57] A few states agree.[58] However, most states do not allow such an offset. For example, a court struck down a North Carolina statute that allowed the increased value of retained land due to special benefits to offset a just compensation award that would otherwise be paid to the owner to compensate for the value of the taken land.[59] This accords with the rule in most states that would award our owner the full $100,000 (the value of the taken land), not reduce that award by the increase in the value of the retained land that will result from the taking.[60]

The Supreme Court of New Jersey has taken a more modern approach and ruled in *Borough of Harvey Cedars v. Karan*[61] that *any* quantifiable benefits to the property from a partial taking must be counted against the losses in determining just compensation. In *Harvey Cedars*, the borough government took part of the beachfront owner's property to construct dunes to protect the property from erosion or loss during storms. The court held that just compensation for the partial taking

> must be based on a consideration of all relevant, reasonably calculable, and non-conjectural factors that either decrease or increase the value of the remaining property. In a partial-takings case, homeowners are entitled to the fair market value of their loss, not to a windfall, not to a pay out that disregards the home's enhanced value resulting from a public project. To calculate that loss, we must look to the difference between the fair market value of the property before the partial taking and after the taking.[62]

[55] *State of Oregon v. Fullerton*, 34 P.3d 1180 (Or. Ct. App. 2001); John G. Sprankling, *Understanding Property Law* §39.06[D], at 697 (5th ed. 2023).

[56] *Los Angeles County v. Continental Development Corp.*, 941 P.2d 809 (Cal. 1997); *Department of Transp. v. Rowe*, 549 S.E.2d 203 (N.C. 2001).

[57] *Bauman v. Ross*, 167 U.S. 548 (1897); *United States v. 930.65 Acres of Land*, 299 F. Supp. 673, 678 (D. Kan. 1968).

[58] *Acierno v. State of Delaware*, 643 A.2d 1328, 1332 (Del. 1994); *State v. Midkiff*, 516 P.2d 1250 (Haw. 1973); John G. Sprankling, *Understanding Property Law* §39.06[D], at 697 (5th ed. 2023).

[59] *Department of Transportation v. Rowe*, 531 S.E.2d 836 (N.C. Ct. App. 2000).

[60] *See Chiesa v. New York*, 351 N.Y.S.2d 735, 736 (App. Div. 1974); *Williams Natural Gas Co. v. Perkins*, 952 P.2d 483 (Okla. 1997).

[61] 70 A.3d 524 (N.J. 2013).

[62] *Id.* at 526.

That meant that, in determining just compensation for the partial taking, the court must take into account the increase in value of the property that remained because of the taking and construction of the dune. The holding overruled the traditional legal rule that distinguished between compensable benefits that were special to the homeowner and noncompensable ones that were general benefits to the whole community. Getting rid of that distinction, the court simply required any benefits to the owner to be reasonably quantifiable and to be measured against losses in market value caused by the partial taking. ◀

Some states have passed legislation providing for compensation for goodwill when a business is inextricably tied to a particular location and the loss cannot be avoided by relocation of the business after the land and structures are taken.[63] Some state courts have also allowed compensation for business losses in narrow instances if the business is not easily movable because of the unique character of the property.[64]

Legislation providing for relocation costs and lost goodwill

The federal government has passed legislation requiring compensation for moving costs, lost personal property occasioned by the move, and "actual reasonable expenses in searching for a replacement business" if property is taken by the federal government or by state governments with any federal funding.[65] The Act also provides extra compensation if a person's home is taken.[66]

Alternative source of compensation: "Damaging" clauses in state constitutional law

Twenty-seven state constitutions contain provisions barring "damaging" or "injuring" property for public use without just compensation.[67] These clauses, which began to appear in state constitutions after the Civil War, mandate compensation where the government reduces the value of property through some public project.[68] In an influential early case, *Rigney v. City of Chicago*,[69] a city's construction of a viaduct cut off an owner's primary street access, and the court highlighted "three important factors for a damagings action: (1) a 'direct physical disturbance' of (2) a valuable right enjoyed in connection with property; and (3) special harm, rather than harm suffered by the public at large."[70] Courts following *Rigney* have largely limited damagings claims to harms arising from loss of access from grading or public construction or periodic flooding, although some claimants have succeeded in cases involving police harming their property.[71]

[63] Cal. Civ. Proc. Code §1263.510; Wyo. Stat. §1-26-713.

[64] *See, e.g., State v. Hammer*, 550 P.2d 820 (Alaska 1976); *Housing Authority v. Southern Railway*, 264 S.E.2d 174 (Ga. 1980); *Housing & Redevelopment Authority v. Naegele Outdoor Advertising Co.*, 282 N.W.2d 537 (Minn. 1979); see also City of Baton Rouge v. Mucciacciaro, 342 So. 3d 955, 966-67 (La. Ct. App. 2022).

[65] *See Uniform Relocation Assistance and Real Property Acquisition Policies Act of 1970*, Pub. L. No. 91-646, 84 Stat. 1894 (*codified as amended at* 42 U.S.C. §§4601 to 4655).

[66] 42 U.S.C. §4623.

[67] *See generally* Maureen E. Brady, *The Damagings Clauses*, 104 Va. L. Rev. 341 (2018).

[68] *Id.* at 356-357.

[69] 102 Ill. 64 (1881).

[70] Brady, *supra*, at 383.

[71] *Id.* at 388, 393-395.

§14.4 Regulatory Takings — Historical Background

§14.4.1 *Before 1922*

Fifth Amendment

The Fifth Amendment limits the power of the federal government over property owners by providing: "nor shall private property be taken for public use without just compensation."[72] Although this "takings clause" does not apply to the state governments, the Fourteenth Amendment, adopted after the Civil War in 1868, prohibits the states from "depriv[ing]" any per son of "property" without "due process of law." In 1897, the U.S. Supreme Court held that the due process clause of the Fourteenth Amendment incorporated the takings clause, effectively protecting owners from state and local government, as well as federal, takings of property.[73] The Fourteenth Amendment says nothing about "taking" property without "just compensation"; it merely protects owners from being "deprived" of property "without due process." Protection against takings of property is thus an example of "substantive" due process, protecting persons from being deprived of certain rights, rather than merely requiring that adequate procedures be used when such rights are taken or impinged upon. Because of its incorporation into the Fourteenth Amendment, courts talk about the "takings clause" as if it applied to federal and state governments equally, developing the law under the Fifth and Fourteenth Amendments in tandem as if a single prohibition applied to both the state and federal governments.

Incorporation into Fourteenth Amendment

Prior to 1922, takings law interpreted literally

Before 1922, courts interpreted the takings clause fairly literally. A taking would be found when a state or local government, or the federal government, exercised its *eminent domain power* to take property for public uses. For example, a city might need an owner's property to use to build a public school, or a state might be building a highway. The city or state would either negotiate to purchase the property they need, or begin eminent domain proceedings to force a transfer of title from the owner upon payment of a court-determined eminent domain award based on the fair market value of the property. In such cases, the government not only takes title from the owner but also deprives her of all possessory rights. Similarly, if the state physically occupied the property and excluded the owner, the courts would find that the property had been taken even if the state did not formally begin eminent domain proceedings. For example, if the state allowed property to be flooded as part of a dam construction project, as in the 1872 case of *Pumpelly v. Green Bay Co.*,[74] the courts would find the property had been "taken" for public uses. However, if the state merely regulated what the owner could do on her own land, for example, by passing a zoning law, no taking would be found.[75]

[72] U.S. Const. amend. V (1791).

[73] *San Diego Gas & Electric Co. v. City of San Diego*, 450 U.S. 621, 623 n.1 (1981); *Chicago B. & Q. R. Co. v. Chicago*, 166 U.S. 226, 239 (1897).

[74] *Pumpelly v. Green Bay Co.*, 80 U.S. 166, 181 (1871). *Accord, United States v. Cress*, 243 U.S. 316, 328-330 (1917) (repeated floodings of land caused by water project is taking).

[75] *Lucas v. South Carolina Coastal Council*, 505 U.S. 1003, 1028 n.15 (1992) ("early constitutional theorists did not believe the Takings Clause embraced regulations of property at all"); John G. Sprankling, *Understanding Property Law* §40.02[A], at 702 (5th ed. 2023); William

Mugler v. Kansas (1887)

In the 1887 case of *Mugler v. Kansas*[76] the Supreme Court held that a state statute that prohibited the manufacture and sale of alcoholic beverages did not constitute a "taking" of plaintiff's property. It reached this result even though the brewery had been constructed solely for the purpose of manufacturing such beverages, the property had "little value" for any other purpose,[77] and that purpose had been lawful at the time plaintiff invested in building the factory and its business. The Court declared that "[a] prohibition simply upon the use of property for purposes that are declared, by valid legislation, to be injurious to the health, morals, or safety of the community, cannot, in any just sense, be deemed a taking or an appropriation of property."[78] A central component of the *police power* reserved to the states by the Constitution is the power to protect the public. The police power, noted the Court, "is not burdened with the condition that the State must compensate such individual owners for pecuniary losses they may sustain, by reason of their not being permitted, by a noxious use of their property, to inflict injury upon the community."[79] *Mugler v. Kansas* held that laws cannot constitute unconstitutional takings of property as long as they are intended, in good faith, to protect the public from harm of any kind, as long as they do not amount to an actual "taking" of title to the property or deprive the owner of possessory rights.

Deprivation of value was not a taking if it prohibited conduct injurious to the public

Powell v. Pennsylvania (1888)

The Supreme Court clarified *Mugler* a year later in the 1888 case of *Powell v. Pennsylvania.*[80] That case held that it was permissible to outlaw completely the manufacture of oleomargarine, as long as the legislature passed the law for the purpose of protecting public health and preventing fraud. The legislation would not be struck down merely because it was "unwise" or because the court disagreed with the legislature about its necessity,[81] even if "the value of [the owner's] property employed therein would be entirely lost and he be deprived of the means of livelihood."[82] And in the 1915 case of *Hadacheck v. Sebastian,*[83] the Court upheld an ordinance prohibiting operation of a brickyard, although the owner had made excavations on the land that prevented it from being utilized for any other purpose. The brickyard had been established outside the borders of Los Angeles and had been perfectly lawful at the time it was established. Subsequently, the area was incorporated into the city of Los Angeles, homes were built around it, and the operation of the brickyard constituted a common law nuisance despite the fact that the neighbors had come to the nuisance. Even though the owner had invested in reliance on existing law, which authorized operation of the facility, the legislation was upheld

Hadacheck v. Sebastian (1915)

M. Treanor, *The Original Understanding of the Takings Clause and the Political Process*, 95 Colum. L. Rev. 782 (1995).

[76] 123 U.S. 623 (1887).

[77] *Id.* at 657.

[78] *Id.* at 668-669.

[79] *Id.* at 669.

[80] 127 U.S. 678 (1888).

[81] *Id.* at 686.

[82] *Id.* at 682.

[83] 239 U.S. 394 (1915).

on the ground that no one could have a vested right to commit a nuisance and an operation that was not a nuisance initially might become so when circumstances changed. As long as the prohibition was designed to protect the community from a nuisance or a "noxious use," it would not constitute a taking of property.[84]

§14.4.2 1922 to 1978

***Pennsylvania Coal Co. v. Mahon* (1922)**

All this changed in 1922 in *Pennsylvania Coal Co. v. Mahon*.[85] Plaintiff homeowners sued to prevent the Pennsylvania Coal Company from mining under their property so as to remove subjacent support for the surface land and for their house. The property had been initially sold by the Pennsylvania Coal Co. to plaintiff's predecessor in interest with a reservation of the right to mine the subsurface for coal. Plaintiff Mahons bought the property knowing of the coal company's rights, which included, not only the right to remove all the coal under the surface, but also to do so even if this had the effect of removing support for the land surface, making habitation impossible. Presumably, the Mahons were aware of this reservation of rights when they purchased and adjusted their purchase price accordingly. However, the Pennsylvania legislature adopted a statute prohibiting the mining of coal under residential areas so as to remove subjacent support for any dwelling. The company was therefore required to keep sufficient pillars of coal in place as needed to support the land surface and any structures on it. When the company notified the Mahons that its future mining would cause their land and house to subside, they sued to stop the company from undermining subjacent support for their house, claiming the protection of the state statute. The Supreme Court, in an opinion by Justice Oliver Wendell Holmes whose meaning is contested to this day,[86] held that the statute effected an unconstitutional taking of property.

Justice Holmes's reasoning

Justice Holmes reasoned that regulations that deprive owners of the value of their property were as harmful to the legal rights and justified expectations of owners as outright seizure of their land. "What makes the right to mine coal valuable is that it can be exercised with profit. To make it commercially impracticable to mine certain coal has very nearly the same effect for constitutional purposes as appropriating or destroying it."[87]

Implied limitations on property rights

Justice Holmes acknowledged that lawmakers must be empowered to pass laws designed to promote the general welfare and, especially, to protect the public from harm. "Government hardly could go on if to some extent

[84] The Supreme Court reached a similar ruling in the 1962 case of *Goldblatt v. Hempstead*, 369 U.S. 590 (1962) (upholding a town regulation that barred continued operation of an existing sand and gravel operation to protect public safety).
[85] 260 U.S. 393 (1922).
[86] *Compare* Robert Brauneis, *"The Foundation of Our 'Regulatory Takings' Jurisprudence": The Myth and Meaning of Justice Holmes's Opinion in* Pennsylvania Coal Co. v. Mahon, 106 Yale L.J. 613 (1996) (arguing that *Pennsylvania Coal Co.* was based on substantive due process, not an application of the takings clause) *and* John G. Sprankling, *Understanding Property Law* §40.03[A], at 704 (5th ed. 2023) (arguing that *Pennsylvania Coal* is "generally recognized as the birthplace of the regulatory takings doctrine").
[87] 260 U.S. at 414.

values incident to property could not be diminished without paying for every such change in the general law. As long recognized some values are enjoyed under an implied limitation and must yield to the police power."[88] At the same time, this power is not without limits. "But obviously the implied limitation must have its limits or the contract and due process clauses are gone."[89] The property and contract clauses of the Constitution prohibit the state from taking property or impairing the obligations of contracts.[90] What are those limits? "The general rule at least is that while property may be regulated to a certain extent, if regulation goes too far it will be recognized as a taking."[91] And what is "too far"? "One fact for consideration in determining such limits is the extent of the diminution. When it reaches a certain magnitude, in most if not in all cases there must be an exercise of eminent domain and compensation to sustain the act."[92]

Extent of diminution in value: The "too far" test

This language suggests to some commentators that any regulation that deprives an owner of too great a percentage of the economic value of property would constitute an unconstitutional taking of property. However, according to Holmes's opinion, the extent of diminution in value is not the only relevant factor. The other major factor is the nature of the public interest served by the legislation. If the legislation is designed to protect the public, for example by prohibiting a "public nuisance," then it appears that Justice Holmes would have approved the legislation despite the diminution in value, on the ground that no one can have a vested right to commit a nuisance because the common law never gave owners the lawful power to commit public or private nuisances. The extent of diminution in value must be compared to the public interest; if the interference is great and the public interest is slight, then, according to Holmes, a taking should be found. "So the question depends upon the particular facts. The greatest weight is given to the judgment of the legislature but it always is open to interested parties to contend that the legislature has gone beyond its constitutional power."[93] In effect, the question was whether the statute went "too far" in infringing on the value of the plaintiff's private property without adequate justification.

Balancing the public interest underlying the regulation against the extent of diminution in value

Holmes's majority opinion on extent of diminution in value: Taking of an estate in land

How did Justice Holmes see the balance in this case? First, he understood the diminution in value as very great. He noted that Pennsylvania law recognizes a unique estate in land: the "support estate." This estate allows the owner to prevent another from undermining support for the surface or allows the owner to choose to remove support for the surface. Whoever owns the estate has the power to determine whether support should be provided or removed. If owned by the coal company, it would ordinarily be used to undermine support for the surface; if owned by the surface owner, it ordinarily would be exercised to prevent the owner of mineral rights

[88] *Id.* at 413.
[89] *Id.*
[90] U.S. Const. art. X cl. 1 ("No State shall pass any Law impairing the Obligation of Contracts").
[91] 260 U.S. at 415.
[92] *Id.* at 413.
[93] *Id.*

from undermining support for the surface. In this case, plaintiffs owned the surface rights, while the coal company owned both the mineral rights and the support estate. The statute effectively deprived the coal company of its support estate and transferred that support estate from the coal company to the surface owner, entitling plaintiffs to prevent subsidence of the surface. If the support estate is taken to be the relevant property right, then the legislation effectively deprived the owner of that estate of 100 percent of its interest. Thus, according to Justice Holmes, "the extent of the taking is great. It purports to abolish what is recognized in Pennsylvania as an estate in land — a very valuable estate — and what is declared by the Court below to be a contract hitherto binding the plaintiffs."[94]

Brandeis's dissent: Diminution in value must be determined with reference to the "whole property"

In contrast, Justice Brandeis argued in his dissenting opinion that the diminution in value was slight. He noted that "values are relative. If we are to consider the value of the coal kept in place by the restriction, we should compare it with the value of all other parts of the land. That is, with the value not of the coal alone, but with the value of the whole property."[95] In other words, the diminution in value should be calculated by looking at the property rights *as a whole*. "The rights of an owner as against the public are not increased by dividing the interests in his property into surface and subsoil. The sum of the rights in the parts can not be greater than the rights in the whole."[96] An owner could not sell the air rights over his house and thereby prevent the city from passing a zoning law limiting structures to two stories.[97] Similarly, the owner here could not, by separating the property rights into a mineral estate, a support estate, and a surface estate, prevent the legislature from passing a regulatory law designed to protect the public from subsidence of residences. Although this law may deprive the Pennsylvania Coal Company of the value of the "support estate," it still owns the entire mineral estate, and the right to withdraw those minerals is a valuable property right. Suppose the Act required the company to leave 2 percent of the coal in place to support the surface. While Holmes suggested that the statute effected a 100 percent taking of the support estate, Brandeis would argue that it merely effected a 2 percent taking of the mineral estate, and an even lesser percentage taking of the value of the combined mineral, surface, and support estates.

> For aught that appears the value of the coal kept in place by the restriction may be negligible as compared with the value of the whole property, or even as compared with that part of it which is represented by the coal remaining in place and which may be extracted despite the statute.[98]

Holmes's majority opinion on the nature of the public interest

In addition to finding a significant diminution in value, Holmes's majority opinion found the public interest furthered by the legislation to be slight to nonexistent. "This is the case of a single private house," Holmes noted.

[94] *Id.* at 414.
[95] *Id.* at 419 (Brandeis, J., dissenting).
[96] *Id.* at 420 (Brandeis, J., dissenting).
[97] *Id.* (Brandeis, J., dissenting).
[98] *Id.* at 419 (Brandeis, J., dissenting).

> No doubt there is a public interest even in this, as there is in every purchase and sale and in all that happens within the commonwealth. Some existing rights may be modified even in such a case. But usually in ordinary private affairs the public interest does not warrant much of this kind of interference. A source of damage to such a house is not a public nuisance even if similar damage is inflicted on others in different places. The damage is not common or public.[99]

Holmes found the public interest here to be weak because it was designed to protect dwellings rather than to preserve land surface generally. "The extent of the public interest is shown by the statute to be limited, because the statute ordinarily does not apply to land when the surface is owned by the owner of the coal."[100] More important, the regulation protected, not the public, but the owner of a single-family home. The public interest may sometimes justify regulation designed to protect the owner of a single home, especially if it was designed to protect "personal safety."[101] However, Holmes found that interest to be weak here because it could have been promoted by less-intrusive legislation, such as a rule requiring the company to give notice before undermining subjacent support.[102]

Justice Brandeis's dissent: Public interest justified the legislation

Justice Brandeis criticized this reasoning in a manner that the Supreme Court later accepted in the 1987 case of *Keystone Bituminous Coal Association v. DeBenedictis*,[103] a case very similar to *Pennsylvania Coal Co.* "Coal in place is land," Justice Brandeis argued, "and the right of the owner to use his land is not absolute. He may not so use it as to create a public nuisance, and uses, once harmless, may, owing to changed conditions, seriously threaten the public welfare. Whenever they do, the Legislature has power to prohibit such uses without paying compensation."[104] Arguing for an application of the *Mugler-Hadacheck* test, Brandeis asserted that any "restriction imposed to protect the public health, safety or morals from dangers threatened is not a taking."[105] This was not a case of a "single private house" but a general regulatory law designed to "protect the public" by preventing a "noxious use."[106] The preservation of existing dwellings promotes the public interest by preserving the availability of housing and the prevention of losses to existing property owners.

Reciprocity of advantage

Justice Holmes suggested that the statute would have been upheld if it had effectuated an average "reciprocity of advantage."[107] In other words, regulatory laws that limit an owner's use of land may be justified if those owners are benefited by the fact that similar restrictions are imposed on others. Without argument, he assumed that such reciprocity was absent here, presumably because coal companies would not benefit from the

99 *Id.* at 413.
100 *Id.* at 414.
101 *Id.*
102 *Id.*
103 480 U.S. 470 (1987).
104 260 U.S. at 417 (Brandeis, J., dissenting).
105 *Id.*
106 *Id.*
107 *Id.* at 415.

legislation. Justice Brandeis, however, argued that such considerations are relevant only when the legislation requires an owner to confer benefits on the community. When the legislation protects "the public from detriment and danger, there is in my opinion, no room for considering reciprocity of advantage," citing several cases, including *Mugler*, *Powell*, and *Hadacheck*.[108]

Fairness of the obligation

In 1987, the Supreme Court effectively repudiated the result in *Pennsylvania Coal Co.* in *Keystone Bituminous Coal Association v. DeBenedictis*,[109] a case involving similar facts that upheld the constitutionality of a similar law. In attempting (in our view unsuccessfully) to distinguish *Pennsylvania Coal Co.*, Justice Stevens noted numerous legitimate public interests served by the statute at issue in *Keystone*, including protection of public health, safety, the environment, and the local economy, that were arguably absent in *Pennsylvania Coal Co.* In addition, the *Keystone* court effectively adopted Brandeis's view that the relevant property interest to be considered was not the support estate but the "whole property." Despite these alterations in the *Pennsylvania Coal Co.* rule, *Keystone* retained the idea that regulations that "go too far" may still be deemed unconstitutional takings of property.

***Village of Euclid v. Ambler Realty Co.* (1926)**

Four years after *Pennsylvania Coal*, in the 1926 case of *Village of Euclid v. Ambler Realty Co.*,[110] the Supreme Court upheld the constitutionality of a local zoning law despite the fact that it diminished the value of the plaintiff's property by 75 percent. In that case, a developer who had purchased a 68-acre parcel for industrial purposes challenged a zoning law that prohibited industrial uses on most of the parcel and caused a 75 percent reduction in the market value of the land. The Supreme Court found that the ordinance served a legitimate public interest and thus did not unconstitutionally deprive the plaintiff of protected property rights under the Fourteenth Amendment, even though the decrease in market value of the land was very substantial. The Court analogized zoning law to nuisance law, which it found not controlling but helpful in determining the scope of the police power.[111] The Court further held that courts should defer to legislative judgments about what uses constitute either nuisances or harms to the community.[112] Laws limiting the height of buildings, setback requirements, or building codes, were all legitimate to "minimize the danger of fire or collapse, the evils of overcrowding and the like, and excluding from residential sections offensive trades, industries and structures likely to create nuisances."[113] This general purpose justified a general law that ensured that nuisances would not arise even if it were somewhat overinclusive in the sense that it prohibited uses that would not constitute nuisances at common law. A law "drawn in general terms [may] include individual cases that

[108] *Id.* at 422 (Brandeis, J., dissenting).
[109] 480 U.S. 470 (1987).
[110] 272 U.S. 365 (1926).
[111] *Id.* at 387-388 ("And the law of nuisances, likewise, may be consulted, not for the purpose of controlling, but for the helpful aid of its analogies in the process of ascertaining the scope of, the power.").
[112] *Id.* at 388 ("If the validity of the legislative classification for zoning purposes be fairly debatable, the legislative judgment must be allowed to control.").
[113] *Id.* at 388.

may turn out to be innocuous in themselves. The inclusion of a reasonable margin, to insure effective enforcement, will not put upon a law, otherwise valid, the stamp of invalidity."[114] Such laws are nonetheless valid even if "some industries of an innocent character might fall within the proscribed class"[115] because "in some fields, the bad fades into the good by such insensible degrees that the two are not capable of being readily distinguished and separated in terms of legislation."[116] Zoning laws were therefore constitutional because they were neither "clearly arbitrary" nor "unreasonable" in that they had "no substantial relation to the public health, safety, morals, or general welfare."[117] Because the ends of the legislation were legitimate and it was not obviously overinclusive, "[i]t cannot be said that the ordinance in this respect 'passes the bounds of reason and assumes the character of a merely arbitrary fiat.'"[118]

Nectow v. City of Cambridge (1928)

Two years later, in *Nectow v. City of Cambridge*,[119] a vacant lot was bisected by a newly enacted zoning ordinance. The bulk of the parcel was zoned for industrial uses, but one vacant part of the parcel was limited to residential use. Although the vacant part was 100 feet wide, the master who heard the case found that the city might widen the street in such a manner as to reduce the depth of that lot to 65 feet and that as a result, "no practical use can be made of the land in question for residential purposes, because there would not be adequate return on the amount of any investment for the development of the property."[120] The Supreme Court held that the statute, as applied to this portion of the land, impermissibly infringed on constitutionally protected property rights. The Court reaffirmed the *Euclid* ruling that a court should not set aside a zoning law unless it "has no foundation in reason and is a mere arbitrary or irrational exercise of power having no substantial relation to the public health, the public morals, the public safety or the public welfare in its proper sense."[121] In this case, the Court found this standard to have been violated both because "the invasion of the property was serious and highly injurious"[122] and because the public interest in bisecting the owner's property did not warrant this level of harm. The trial court had found that the portion of the property at issue could not be used for the purposes for which it had been zoned, depriving the owner of substantially all the benefits of ownership and that the purposes underlying the zoning code did not require that the line be drawn in this way. "The governmental power to interfere by zoning regulations with the general rights of the land owner by restricting the character of his use, is not unlimited, and, other questions aside, such restriction cannot be imposed if it does not bear a substantial relation to the public health, safety, morals, or

[114] *Id.* at 388-389.
[115] *Id.* at 389.
[116] *Id.*
[117] *Id.* at 395.
[118] *Id.* at 389.
[119] 277 U.S. 183 (1928).
[120] *Id.* at 187.
[121] *Id.* at 187-188 (quoting *Euclid v. Ambler Realty Co.*, 272 U.S. 365, 395 (1926)).
[122] *Id.* at 188.

general welfare."[123] That "substantial relation" appeared to be missing here in the sense that the extensive interference with the owner's property rights could not be justified by a sufficiently strong public purpose.[124]

Takings clause or substantive due process

The trio of opinions in *Pennsylvania Coal Co.*, *Euclid*, and *Nectow* has long baffled commentators. Although clearly based on a desire to protect property rights, their reasoning is more consistent with the legal doctrine associated with substantive due process than with the takings clause.[125] The base protection of both the equal protection clause and substantive due process is that the prohibition or classification created by the law has a reasonable relation to a legitimate government objective. A major difference between substantive due process and takings law is that takings are permissible as long as they are done for a public purpose and with just compensation. A violation of the due process clause, in contrast, can be enjoined; in other words, government action that violates the due process clause cannot be undertaken even if compensation is paid. At the same time, later cases cite these three cases as the foundation of modern takings law.

***Miller v. Schoene* (1928)**

The final crucial formative case is *Miller v. Schoene*,[126] a 1928 case involving a state statute that mandated the destruction of a large number of ornamental red cedar trees because they produced cedar rust fatal to apple trees cultivated nearby. A unanimous Supreme Court held that the state might properly make "a choice between the preservation of one class of property and that of the other" and concluded that the state had not exceeded "its constitutional powers by deciding upon the destruction of one class of property [without compensation] in order to save another which, in the judgment of the legislature, is of greater value to the public."[127]

§14.4.3 After 1978

***Penn Central Trans. Co. v. City of New York* (1978)**

After *Pennsylvania Coal Co.*, *Euclid*, *Nectow*, and *Miller*, the Supreme Court did not revisit the takings clause in a significant way until 1978 in the foundational case of *Penn Central Transportation Co. v. City of New York*.[128] In that case, the Penn Central Transportation Company challenged New York City's historic preservation ordinance that prevented it from building a tower on top of the Grand Central train station. Declared a historic monument, Penn Central had an obligation to maintain the outside appearance of the station and to seek approval from a city agency to effectuate any changes. Penn Central sought to place a 55-story skyscraper on top of its building, and when the city historic preservation commission

[123] *Id.*

[124] *Id.* at 188-189.

[125] *See* Robert Brauneis, *"The Foundation of Our 'Regulatory Takings' Jurisprudence": The Myth and Meaning of Justice Holmes's Opinion in* Pennsylvania Coal Co. v. Mahon, 106 Yale L.J. 613 (1996).

[126] 276 U.S. 272 (1928).

[127] *Id.* at 279.

[128] 438 U.S. 104 (1978). *But see National Board of Young Men's Christian Associations v. United States*, 395 U.S. 85 (1969); *Goldblatt v. Hempstead*, 369 U.S. 590 (1962); *Griggs v. Allegheny County*, 369 U.S. 84 (1962); *Armstrong v. United States*, 364 U.S. 40 (1960); *United States v. Causby*, 328 U.S. 256 (1946).

rejected two alternative plans, it sued, claiming that, as applied to its property, the historic preservation law effected a taking of property without just compensation because (1) it had been deprived of its air rights over the terminal, which it otherwise could have profitably developed; (2) the result was a substantial loss of economic value for its property; and (3) it had been wrongly singled out to pay for a program designed to benefit the public. The Supreme Court upheld the constitutionality of historic preservation legislation, both generally and as applied to Penn Central's property.

***Ad hoc* balancing test**

Justice Brennan's majority opinion created the doctrinal foundation for takings law to this day. Citing the 1960 case of *Armstrong v. United States*,[129] the Court held that the takings clause was "designed to bar Government from forcing some people alone to bear public burdens which, in all fairness and justice, should be borne by the public as a whole."[130] However, Justice Brennan acknowledged that the Court had been unable to identify a clear rule to determine what regulations constitute unconstitutional "takings" of "private property." Indeed, "[t]he question of what constitutes a 'taking' for purposes of the Fifth Amendment has proved to be a problem of considerable difficulty."[131] "[T]his Court, quite simply, has been unable to develop any 'set formula' for determining when 'justice and fairness' require that economic injuries caused by public action be compensated by the government, rather than remain disproportionately concentrated on a few persons."[132] Instead of a clear rule, the Court engages in "essentially ad hoc, factual inquiries" into the "particular circumstances" of the case,[133] involving three main factors. Those factors are (1) the "economic impact of the regulation on the claimant"; (2) the extent to which the regulation has "interfered with distinct investment-backed expectations"; and (3) the "character of the government action."[134] In a 6-3 vote, the Court found that the historic preservation law, as applied to Penn Central's property, was not an unconstitutional "taking" of property. Chief Justice Burger and Justices Rehnquist and Stevens dissented, not because they disagreed with the test applied by the Court but because they felt that applying that test should have resulted in a finding that an unconstitutional taking of property had occurred.

Economic impact

Economic Impact. The Court found the economic impact to be significant but not unfair. Quoting *Pennsylvania Coal Co. v. Mahon*,[135] the Court noted:

Argument that the economic impact was not unfair or unjust

> "Government hardly could go on if to some extent values incident to property could not be diminished without paying for every such change in the general law," and this Court has accordingly recognized, in a wide

[129] 364 U.S. 40 (1960).

[130] *Penn Central Transportation Co. v. City of New York*, 438 U.S. 123, 123 (1978) (*quoting Armstrong v. United States*, 364 U.S. 40, 49 (1960)).

[131] *Id.*

[132] *Id.* at 124.

[133] *Id.*

[134] *Id.*

[135] 260 U.S. 393, 413 (1922).

> variety of contexts, that government may execute laws or programs that adversely affect recognized economic values.[136]

Penn Central was already using its property as a train station and the use was a profitable one. The takings clause does not guarantee that owners will be able to use their property for its most profitable purpose.[137] Nor does "a diminution in property value, standing alone, . . . establish a 'taking.'"[138] Even a 75 percent reduction in value was upheld in Euclid where the Supreme Court approved of zoning laws. A regulation may constitute a taking if it prevents the owner from earning a "reasonable return on their investment,"[139] but the historic preservation act did not do this. The loss to Penn Central was a mere "opportunity loss," an inability to change the use of the property rather than a prohibition of a prior existing use. Although the law had a significant impact on the value of the property, that impact was not "unduly harsh"[140] and was substantially related to a legitimate public purpose of preserving the historic nature of important buildings in the city and thus preventing deterioration of the urban environment and attracting tourism and business.

The "parcel as a whole"

In addition, even though owners are generally free to sell "air rights" over their structures (the right to build on top of a building), the Court rejected the idea that a height limitation on a building would constitute a "taking" of those air rights.[141] Although the air rights above Penn Central were a distinct bundle of property rights that could be bought and sold, they were not a distinct bundle protected independently by the Constitution.

> "Taking" jurisprudence does not divide a single parcel into discrete segments and attempt to determine whether rights in a particular segment have been entirely abrogated. [Rather,] this Court focuses on the nature and extent of the interference with rights in the parcel as a whole — here, the city tax block designated as the "landmark site."[142]

Were the law to be otherwise, an ordinary zoning law that limits the height of buildings and imposes setback requirements would be unconstitutional in the absence of compensation. In addition, the historic preservation commission had rejected the two plans submitted by Penn Central but had not flatly refused to allow any construction on top of the train station. Moreover, even if this were the case, the ordinance granted Penn Central

136 438 U.S. at 126.

137 *Id.* at 127 (noting that owners are not entitled to the "most beneficial use of [their] property").

138 *Id.* at 131.

139 *Id.* at 129.

140 *Id.* at 127.

141 *Id.* at 130 (rejecting the owner's contention "that the Landmarks Law [had] deprived them of any gainful use of their 'air rights' above the Terminal and that, irrespective of the value of the remainder of their parcel, the city [had] 'taken' their right to this superadjacent airspace, thus entitling them to 'just compensation' measured by the fair market value of these air rights").

142 *Id.* at 130-131.

"transfer development rights" (TDRs), which would entitle it to transfer its air rights to at least eight parcels in the vicinity. These TDRs were valuable property rights whose value must be computed in determining the extent to which the ordinance had diminished the value of Penn Central's property.

Argument that the regulation took a valuable property right

In his dissenting opinion, Justice Rehnquist argued that the economic impact of the regulation was both substantial and unfair. The impact was substantial, first, because it both imposed substantial costs on the owner and diminished the fair market value of the property, and second, because it deprived the owner of its "air rights" over its building. The cost of the historic landmark designation to this particular owner was both very significant and out of proportion to that demanded of other owners in the city. Moreover, unlike zoning laws, there is no average reciprocity of advantage.

> Where a relatively few individual buildings, all separated from one another, are singled out and treated differently from surrounding buildings, no such reciprocity exists. The cost to the property owner which results from the imposition of restrictions applicable only to his property and not that of his neighbors may be substantial — in this case, several million dollars — with no comparable reciprocal benefits.[143]

Moreover, Justice Rehnquist noted, "[t]his Court has previously held that the 'air rights' over an area of land are 'property' for purposes of the Fifth Amendment."[144] A general zoning law does not constitute a taking of air rights because it creates an average reciprocity of advantage. However, Justice Rehnquist argued that historic preservation laws unfairly deprive only a few owners of the ability to develop their air rights.

> While neighboring landowners are free to use their land and "air rights" in any way consistent with the broad boundaries of New York zoning, Penn Central, absent the permission of appellees, must forever maintain its property in its present state. The property has been thus subjected to a nonconsensual servitude not borne by any neighboring or similar properties.[145]

Thus, in his view, the economic impact was severe and not shared by similarly situated owners.

Interference with reasonable investment-backed expectations

Interference with Reasonable Investment-Backed Expectations. Because Penn Central was entitled to continue its current, profitable use of the property, the Court determined that its primary investment-backed expectations had been protected by the regulation.[146] Owners are not

[143] *Id.* at 140 (Rehnquist, J., dissenting).

[144] *Id.* at 143 n.5 (Rehnquist, J., dissenting) (*citing United States v. Causby*, 328 U.S. 256 (1946) ("air rights" taken by low-flying airplanes) *and Griggs v. Allegheny County*, 369 U.S. 84 (1962) (same)).

[145] *Id.* at 143 (Rehnquist, J., dissenting).

[146] *Id.* at 136 ("Its designation as a landmark not only permits but contemplates that appellants may continue to use the property precisely as it has been used for the past 65 years: as a railroad terminal containing office space and concessions. So the law does not interfere

entitled to the "most beneficial use" of their property.[147] This is evident in the *Euclid* holding that zoning laws are not unconstitutional takings of property. The Court noted that the argument that a taking could be established "simply by showing that they have been denied the ability to exploit a property interest that they heretofore had believed was available for development is quite simply untenable."[148]

Majority opinion

Dissenting opinion

Justice Rehnquist argued, in dissent, that "the cost associated with landmark legislation is likely to be of a completely different order of magnitude than that which results from the imposition of normal zoning restrictions" and thus unfairly surprises owners who invested in property in reliance on laws that did not restrict the uses of their property to historical uses.

> Unlike the regime affected by the latter, the landowner is not simply prohibited from using his property for certain purposes, while allowed to use it for all other purposes. Under the historic-landmark preservation scheme adopted by New York, the property owner is under an affirmative duty to preserve his property as a landmark at his own expense. To suggest that because traditional zoning results in some limitation of use of the property zoned, the New York City landmark preservation scheme should likewise be upheld, represents the ultimate in treating as alike things which are different.[149]

Character of the government action

Character of the Government Action. The Court found the character of the government action to be the creation of a general regulatory regime to protect historic structures. This law applied to a large number of owners and thus did not wrongfully single out Penn Central. In addition, the law had a sufficient "average reciprocity of advantage" in that everyone in the city would benefit from the preservation of the city's historic heritage.

Dissenting opinion

Justice Rehnquist responded that unlike the prohibition of liquor manufacture upheld in *Mugler v. Kansas*[150] or the prohibition of brickmaking upheld in *Hadacheck v. Sebastian*,[151] the historic preservation law at issue in *Penn Central* did not prohibit a harmful activity or "noxious use."[152] Rather, the law prohibited "a legal and essential use, an attribute of its ownership."[153] Justice Rehnquist acknowledged that government may prevent "noninjurious use[s]" but that when it does so, there must be an "average reciprocity of advantage," which he found to be missing here.[154]

---

with what must be regarded as Penn Central's primary expectation concerning the use of the parcel."). *Penn Central* described this element as focusing on interference with "distinct" investment-backed expectations, *id.* at 124, but the Court now generally uses the phrase "reasonable" investment-backed expectations in recognition that not all expectations are necessarily reasonable given existing property law.

[147] *Id.* at 127.

[148] *Id.* at 130.

[149] *Id.* at 140 (Rehnquist, J., dissenting).

[150] 123 U.S. 623 (1887).

[151] 239 U.S. 394 (1915).

[152] 438 U.S. at 145.

[153] *Id.*

[154] *Id.* at 147. Two years after *Penn Central*, the Supreme Court rejected a facial challenge to a zoning law in *Agins v. Tiburon*, 447 U.S. 255 (1980), holding that a land use regulation would

§14.5 General Balancing Test for Regulatory Takings

Most cases are governed by the general *Penn Central* balancing test, with the Supreme Court identifying special rules applicable to narrow categories of physical invasions, deprivation of powers of devise and descent, deprivation of all economically viable use, and interference with vested rights.[155] As the Supreme Court held in *Kaiser Aetna v. United States*:[156]

> This Court has generally "been unable to develop any 'set formula' for determining when 'justice and fairness' require that economic injuries caused by public action be compensated by the government, rather than remain disproportionately concentrated on a few persons." Rather, it has examined the "taking" question by engaging in essentially ad hoc, factual inquiries that have identified several factors — such as the economic impact of the regulation, its interference with reasonable investment backed expectations, and the character of the government action — that have particular significance.[157]

Fairness and justice

Economic impact

Investment-backed expectations

This section summarizes how the Supreme Court has interpreted the various parts of the *Penn Central* test.

***Keystone Bituminous Coal Association v. DeBenedictis* (1987)**

To help illustrate the competing interpretations of the three central factors in the *Penn Central* test, we will use the opinion in *Keystone Bituminous Coal Association v. DeBenedictis*.[158] *Keystone* involved a Pennsylvania statute almost identical to that in *Pennsylvania Coal Co.* However, instead of striking down the Act, the Supreme Court upheld it in a 5-4 vote. The competing interpretations of the takings clause offered by the majority and dissenting opinions offer insights into the tensions and competing arguments that inform this area of law. To prevent subsidence of surface land, a Pennsylvania statute required coal mining companies to leave undisturbed 50 percent of the coal beneath the surface of land supporting public buildings, noncommercial buildings used by the public, dwellings, and cemeteries. In addition, Pennsylvania had a peculiar estate in land, called the *support estate*, consisting of either the right to support of the surface or the right to undermine the surface.[159] This right would ordinarily be owned by either the owner of the surface or the owner of the subsurface mineral rights. The Court held, in a 5-4 decision, that the statute did not constitute a

constitute a "taking" if it "does not substantially advance legitimate state interests or denies an owner economically viable use of his land." *Id.* at 260. This appeared to suggest that the Court would review zoning laws to determine whether they are not only "rationally related" to legitimate state interests but "substantially advance them," but in 2005, the Court reversed course and held that a regulation cannot be challenged as a taking on the basis of this test. *Lingle v. Chevron U.S.A. Inc.*, 544 U.S. 528 (2005).

[155] We will discuss these special rules in §14.6.

[156] 444 U.S. 164 (1979).

[157] *Id.* at 164, 175 (*cited in Hodel v. Virginia Surface Mining and Reclamation Ass'n, Inc.*, 452 U.S. 264, 295 (1981)).

[158] 480 U.S. 470 (1987).

[159] *See Machipongo Land & Coal Co. v. Commw. of Pennsylvania*, 799 A.2d 751 (Pa. 2002) (holding that the purpose of applying the takings clause, the division of estates under Pa. law into surface, mineral, and support is "without significance").

taking of property even though it required coal mining companies to leave about 27 million tons of coal in place and deprived them of all value of the support estate that they had previously purchased from the owners of the surface estates.

§14.5.1 Character of Government Action

The issue

Perhaps the most crucial factor in determining whether a regulation will amount to a taking is the "character of the government action." This factor concerns a central but hard-to-define quality about the government action. The question is whether the regulation is a legitimate regulation of conduct designed to protect individuals or the public or whether it is an illegitimate seizure or invasion of property rights that cannot be taken without compensation. Here is the dilemma: The state is, and must be, empowered by its *police power* to pass regulatory laws limiting conduct to protect the public and promote the general welfare. However, there must be some limit to the power when regulatory laws effectively destroy property rights, or the *takings clause* would be deprived of all force.

Core distinction

The Supreme Court has dealt with this dilemma by attempting to distinguish between regulations that unfairly strip owners of core property rights without adequate justification or that unfairly single them out to bear burdens that should be shared by the community at large and those that legitimately limit property use to prevent harm to other owners or to promote the general welfare and are sufficiently generalized so that they can be "properly treated as part of the burden of common citizenship."[160]

Government actions likely to be held to be takings

A government regulation is more likely to be held to be a taking if it can be characterized as:

(1) a forced *physical invasion* of private property;[161]
(2) a taking of a *core property right*;[162]
(3) an *extraction of a benefit* for the good of the community rather than prevention of harm by the property owner;[163] or
(4) a forced, *retroactive redistribution of vested property rights* based on executed contracts or actions taken in reliance on government permits rather than prospective general regulatory programs designed to respond to externalities caused by the property use.[164]

Regulations that are likely not to be takings

The regulation is more likely to be held a legitimate *exercise of the police power not requiring compensation* if the government action can be characterized as:

[160] *Kimball Laundry Co. v. United States*, 338 U.S. 1, 5 (1949).
[161] *Cedar Point Nursery v. Hassid*, 594 U.S. 139 (2021); *Loretto v. Teleprompter Manhattan CATV Corp.*, 458 U.S. 419, 441 (1982); *Kaiser Aetna v. United States*, 444 U.S. 164, 175 (1979).
[162] *Babbitt v. Youpee*, 519 U.S. 234 (1997); *Hodel v. Irving*, 481 U.S. 704 (1987).
[163] *Pennsylvania Coal Co. v. Mahon*, 260 U.S. 393 (1922).
[164] *Id.*

(1) a *regulation of property use* rather than a forced physical invasion;[165]
(2) a limitation on property use designed to *protect the community from harm*, or to respond to externalities caused by the property owner's use of the property rather than extraction of a benefit to the community for which the owner should receive compensation;[166]
(3) *prospective regulation* of the interests that can be owned as property (*estates in land*) or the *retroactive imposition* of *compulsory terms in ongoing contractual relationships* designed to protect the legitimate expectations of property owners or to set minimum standards for protection of consumers rather than retroactive redistribution of vested property rights;[167]
(4) designed to achieve an *average reciprocity of advantage*, meaning that those whose property interests are adversely affected by the regulation also benefit from it by the concomitant regulation of *other* people's property rights;[168] or
(5) a choice between *incompatible property interests.*[169]

Keystone **example**

In *Keystone*, the majority characterized coal mining that caused subsidence of surface land and the destruction of structures as a nuisance; the law therefore legitimately prevented some property owners from causing harm to other property owners and the public at large. The dissent, however, characterized the regulations as a physical taking of the 27 million tons of coal required to be left in place. The dissent further argued that the regulations constituted an expropriation of the support estate owned by the coal company; conversely, the majority argued that because the support estate was normally owned by either the surface owner or the owner of the mineral rights, it did not constitute a separate property interest for the purpose of the takings clause.

▷ TREE DESTRUCTION **HARD CASE ◀**

In *Miller v. Schoene*,[170] the Supreme Court held that the state of Virginia need not provide compensation to the owners of cedar trees ordered to be destroyed to protect apple trees owned by others. The state was compelled to choose "between the preservation of one class of property and that of the other" and thus had the power to insist on "the destruction of one class of property [without compensation] in order to save another which, in the judgment of the legislature, is of greater value to the public."[171] It would

[165] *Agins v. Tiburon*, 447 U.S. 255, 260-261 (1980); *Euclid v. Ambler Realty Co.*, 272 U.S. 365, 395 (1926).
[166] *Keystone Bituminous Coal Ass'n v. DeBenedictis*, 480 U.S. 470 (1987).
[167] *Yee v. City of Escondido*, 503 U.S. 519 (1992); *Pennell v. City of San Jose*, 485 U.S. 1 (1988).
[168] *Euclid v. Ambler Realty Co.*, 272 U.S. 365, 395 (1926).
[169] *Miller v. Schoene*, 276 U.S. 272 (1928).
[170] *Id.*
[171] *Id.* at 279.

concededly *not* have been a taking for the state to do nothing (and allow the disease in the cedar trees to destroy the apple trees) even though this "would have been none the less a choice" than ordering the destruction of the cedar trees to protect the apple trees.[172] However, in 1988, the Florida Supreme Court, in *Department of Agriculture and Consumer Services v. Mid-Florida Growers, Inc.*,[173] held that there was a difference. The court ordered the state to pay just compensation when it destroyed healthy orange trees to prevent the spread of citrus canker because "destruction of the healthy trees benefited the entire citrus industry and, in turn, Florida's economy, thereby conferring a public benefit rather than preventing a public harm."[174] ◀

▶ HARD CASE ▷ FORFEITURE LAWS

Various state and federal laws provide for forfeiture to the state of property used in the commission of a crime.[175] If the value of the property seized is substantially greater in value than the magnitude of the crime, the forfeiture may be held unconstitutional under the Constitution's excessive fines clause.[176] What happens if the property is used by someone other than the owner to commit a crime? Most laws have a defense for "innocent owners" who are not involved in the crime.[177] Does the forfeiture of property of an innocent owner violate the takings clause? The Supreme Court addressed

***Bennis v. Michigan* (1996)**

this question in *Bennis v. Michigan*.[178] A car that was jointly owned by a husband and wife was forfeited to the government pursuant to a Michigan statute without compensation when the husband used it to engage in sexual activity with a prostitute. The statute contained no defense for "innocent owners" and the wife claimed that because she did nothing wrong, the forfeiture of her 50 percent interest in the car was an unconstitutional taking

[172] *Id.*

[173] 521 So. 2d 101 (Fla. 1988).

[174] *Id.* at 103. *See also Rose Acre Farms, Inc. v. United States*, 373 F.3d 1177 (1st Cir. 2004) (egg producer entitled to compensation when more eggs were taken than necessary to respond to a salmonella outbreak).

[175] *See, e.g.*, 21 U.S.C. §881 (forfeiture of property used in connection with illegal drug transactions); *United States v. Leasehold Interest in 121 Nostrand Ave.*, 760 F. Supp. 1015 (E.D.N.Y. 1991). *Cf. Luis v. United States*, 578 U.S. 5 (2016) (Sixth Amendment right to counsel prohibits state from freezing legitimate assets of a criminal defendant needed to pay for counsel of choice).

[176] U.S. Const. amend. VIII; *United States v. Bajakajian*, 524 U.S. 321, 327-328 (1998); *Austin v. United States*, 509 U.S. 602, 609-610 (1993). *See also Ex parte Kelley*, 766 So. 2d 837 (Ala. 1999) (forfeiture of $30,000 car after conviction for drug possession was an "excessive fine" in violation of the Constitution when the highest penalty to which the owner otherwise would have been subject was a $5,000 fine); *One 1995 Toyota Pick-Up Truck v. District of Columbia*, 718 A.2d 558 (D.C. 1998) (unconstitutional excessive fine when $15,000 truck was forfeited for solicitation of a prostitute). *Cf. United States v. Jose*, 499 F.3d 105 (1st Cir. 2007) (2001 *USA Patriot Act* provided for forfeiture of all cash in bulk cash smuggling cases and thus redefined the gravity of the crime such that full forfeiture does not impose an excessive fine).

[177] The federal forfeiture statute contains an innocent owner defense. *See* 18 U.S.C. §983(d) (*added by* Pub. L. No. 106-185, §2(a), Apr. 25, 2000, 114 Stat. 202, *as amended by* Pub. L. No. 106-185, §9, Apr. 25, 2000, 114 Stat. 216) (replacing defenses formerly contained in 21 U.S.C. §§881(a)(6) & (7)).

[178] 516 U.S. 442 (1996).

of her property rights. In a 5-4 vote, the Supreme Court disagreed, noting that such forfeitures had traditionally been used in admiralty cases and that they served a deterrent function, inducing co-owners to take care that their property not be used in the commission of a crime.[179] Four Justices dissented, arguing that it violated due process to mandate forfeiture of property of an innocent owner. In 1998, the Ohio Supreme Court ruled that it violates the takings clause to seize property without compensation on the ground that it constitutes a public nuisance when the property owner was innocent in the creation of the nuisance.[180] ◀

▷ EVICTION OF INNOCENT PUBLIC HOUSING TENANTS **HARD CASE** ◀

In *Department of Housing & Urban Development v. Rucker*,[181] the Supreme Court interpreted a federal statute to allow eviction of innocent public housing tenants when members of their households have engaged in illegal drug use or sales on or off the housing site. The Court found no constitutional problem with forfeiture of property owned by an innocent party even if that tenant had done everything possible to prevent family members from using or selling drugs on the ground that the government was acting as an owner-landlord placing conditions in the lease with which the tenants voluntarily concurred and not as a sovereign regulating the lease terms or punishing an innocent party because of the criminal acts of another. This ruling can be criticized on the ground that it requires owners of leaseholds to forfeit their property rights because of the criminal actions of others even when those owners are using their best efforts to prevent the actions that cause the forfeiture. ◀

▷ DAMAGE CAUSED BY POLICE **HARD CASE** ◀

In *Sullivant v. Oklahoma City*,[182] police officers damaged three doors of an apartment unit in executing a valid search warrant, which uncovered evidence of drug selling and use by the tenants. The landlord sued the city, seeking to be reimbursed for the doors on the ground that the damage was a taking of the landlord's property under the state constitution. The Oklahoma Supreme Court rejected the claim, noting that, although the state constitution provided that "[p]rivate property shall not be taken *or damaged* for public use without just compensation,"[183] it was never intended to cover unintentional harms of this sort. Moreover, mandating compensation "might well deter law enforcement officers from acting swiftly and

[179] Justice Ruth Bader Ginsburg concurred on the ground that the car in question was worth only $600 and that, after deduction for court costs, nothing (or next to nothing) would have been left to distribute to her anyway, given that she only had a 50 percent interest in the car.
[180] *State ex rel. Pizza v. Rezcallah*, 702 N.E.2d 81 (Ohio 1998).
[181] 535 U.S. 125 (2002).
[182] 940 P.2d 220 (Okla. 1997).
[183] Okla. Const. art. 2, §24 (emphasis added).

effectively to protect public safety in emergency situations."[184] Although the California and Washington Supreme Courts agree with this analysis,[185] several others disagree on the ground that it is unfair to allocate the entire risk of loss in police raids to innocent homeowners who should not bear this burden for the public good.[186] The Federal Circuit has held that seizure and destruction of evidence to be used in a criminal investigation cannot constitute a taking of property.[187] It has also held that no taking occurred when an individual's computer was seized and examined at an airport immigration and customs station and returned with the hard drive damaged, resulting in the loss of irretrievable business records.[188] ◀

▶ HARD CASE ▷ REGULATORY PROPERTY

In Penn Central, one argument mitigating against finding a regulatory taking, was that New York City allowed the owners of Grand Central Terminal to sell their air rights to owners of nearby parcels. In 2006, investors purchased Grand Central Terminal, seeking to do just that. However, when a developer acquired property across the street from the station, planning to build an office tower with greater height than the parcel allowed, the developer reached an agreement with the city to rezone the plot in exchange for making infrastructure and transit improvements in the neighborhood — rather than purchase additional development rights from the owners of Grand Central Terminal. The Terminal's owners sued the city, arguing that the rezoning "took" their transferrable development rights, which the owners valued at $475 million.[189] The parties settled the case, but other cases have similarly raised the question whether the government is liable to holders of property rights created under regulatory regimes, such as New York City's transfer-of-development-rights program, when changes to public policy reduces the value of those rights. Owners of taxi medallions made a similar claim against Boston, arguing unsuccessfully that the failure to regulate ride-sharing companies such as Uber and Lyft took the property interest the taxi owners license to operate.[190] The arguments against takings liability, recognizes the contingent nature of property grounded in public licensing programs such as pollution credits, fishing quotas, telecommunications spectrum, and the like. Participants in such programs should recognize that policies change and it is unreasonable to assume that any

[184] 940 P.2d at 226-227.

[185] *Customer Co. v. Sacramento*, 895 P.2d 900, 906 (Cal. 1995); *Eggleston v. Pierce County*, 64 P.3d 618, 622-623 (Wash. 2003). *Accord, Simmons v. Loose*, 13 A.3d 366 (N.J. Super. Ct. App. Div. 2011).

[186] *See, e.g., Wegner v. Milwaukee Mutual Ins. Co.*, 479 N.W.2d 38, 42 (Minn. 1991); *Wallace v. Atlantic City*, 608 A.2d 480, 483 (N.J. Super. Ct. Law Div. 1992); *Steele v. Houston*, 603 S.W.2d 786, 789-790 (Tex. 1980).

[187] *Amerisource Corp. v. United States*, 525 F.3d 1149 (Fed. Cir. 2008).

[188] *Kam-Almaz v. United States*, 2012 U.S. App. LEXIS 12581 (Fed. Cir. 2012). See also Slaybaugh v. Rutherford Cnty., 114 F.4th 593 (6th Cir. 2024).

[189] *See* Christopher Serkin, Penn Central *Take Two*, 92 Notre Dame L. Rev. 913, 920-21 (2017).

[190] *See Boston Taxi Owners Ass'n, Inc. v. City of Boston*, 180 F. Supp. 3d 108 (D. Mass. 2016).

benefits the government provides will not be modified. On the other hand, part of what the government often seeks to do in these programs, is to encourage private parties to invest and make plans based on permission to act, or access to a limited market. Making it too easy to change the nature of such entitlements might make such programs less beneficial and be unfair to parties who invest in reliance. ◀

§14.5.2 Economic Impact (Diminution in Value)

The greater the diminution, the more important the public interest must be to justify the diminution

All laws affect the value of property, and many destroy the value of certain property rights completely. For example, a zoning law that limits the height of buildings to three stories "takes" air rights that could otherwise have been sold to build on top of three-story structures. The Supreme Court has long held that "a diminution in property value, standing alone [does not] establish a 'taking.'"[191] However, a diminution in value that goes "too far" may be equivalent to a government seizure of property and thus constitute a taking unless it is justified by a sufficiently strong public interest; in other words, the greater the diminution in value, the more important the public interest is needed to justify the diminution. For example, the Supreme Court has held that deprivation of all economically viable use is the functional equivalent of a physical ouster of an owner and thus constitutes a taking unless the restriction on use is justified by compelling state interests (such as the need to protect individuals from harm) or prohibits an action that an owner never would have been entitled to engage in at all, *i.e.*, was not part of the rights of an owner in the first place.

The denominator problem

The extent of the diminution in value depends on how the courts define property interests. A zoning law that prohibits construction above four stories may be characterized as a 100 percent taking of "air rights," or it may be characterized as a 50 percent reduction in the fair market value of the property as a whole if the value of the whole parcel would have been twice as great in the absence of the restriction. The dilemma arises because *every* regulation can be characterized as causing a large diminution in value if the property right at issue is characterized in a sufficiently narrow fashion. A zoning law that prohibits industrial uses takes 100 percent of the right to build a factory but a far lesser percentage of the right to build on one's land. If the courts look to particular strands in the bundle of property rights, then every government regulation potentially constitutes a taking of property and the state will not be able to regulate to protect the public welfare. If instead the courts look to the total bundle of property rights, then very few regulations will constitute takings because most regulations impinge only on particular uses of the property; thus, the government will be able to impinge on property interests at will and the takings clause will lose force. The majority in *Keystone* noted that the regulations required owners of the mineral estate to leave only 2 percent of the coal in place; further, the support estate was not considered a separate property interest for purposes of determining the extent of diminution in

[191] *Penn Central Transp. Co.*, 438 U.S. at 131.

value. The dissent, in contrast, noted that the 27 million tons of coal that the regulations required to be kept in place, as well as the support estate, constituted separate property interests whose value the regulations diminished by 100 percent.

Regulations that are more likely to be takings

The regulation is *more* likely to be held a taking:

(1) if the regulation destroys a *large percentage of the market value* of the property and cannot be justified by sufficiently strong public interests in protecting the public from harm; and
(2) if the regulation leaves the owner *without any economically viable use* of the land, it will be held to be a taking unless it prohibits property uses that were never part of the owner's right in the first place or if the regulation is necessary to protect human life or other compelling government interests (perhaps national defense).[192]

Regulations that are likely not to be takings

The regulation is *less* likely to be held a taking:

(1) if the diminution in value is *minimal*; or
(2) if the diminution in value is substantial but the regulation prohibits a property use that *never was part of the owner's rights in the first place* or is justified by a sufficiently strong public interest in preserving human life or in protecting the public from harm.[193]

Nuisance committed by government as a taking

When the government itself causes the nuisance to private property, the argument might be made that the government has engaged in state action that not only constitutes a common law nuisance, but also effectuates a taking of property under the Fifth or Fourteenth Amendment.[194] In

***United States v. Causby* (1946)**

United States v. Causby,[195] the Supreme Court held that regular military flights over plaintiff's land effectuated an unconstitutional taking of property rights when the noise of the planes made it impossible for the owner to use his property for normal living and farming purposes. In describing the effect of the flights, Justice Douglas noted that the noise of the planes was "startling," that the glare of the lights of the planes brightly lit up the place at night, and that the noise caused the owners to give up their chicken business because 150 chickens were killed as a result of flying into the wall from fright. Finding that the land was "uninhabitable," and that the government had engaged in a "definite exercise of complete dominion and control over the land,"[196] the Court ruled that the owner's property rights had been

[192] *Lucas v. South Carolina Coastal Council*, 505 U.S. 1003, 1028 n.15 (1992).
[193] *See First English Evangelical Lutheran Church v. County of Los Angeles*, 258 Cal. Rptr. 893 (Ct. App. 1989), *cert. denied*, 493 U.S. 1056 (1990) (holding that the state could prohibit an owner from rebuilding its property on a floodplain to prevent death and injury); *Gove v. Zoning Bd. of Appeals of Chatham*, 831 N.E.2d 865 (Mass. 2005) (no taking to prevent an owner from building a house on a floodplain when construction would exacerbate flooding of neighboring property).
[194] *United States v. Causby*, 328 U.S. 256 (1946); *Harris v. Town of Lincoln*, 668 A.2d 321, 326-327 (R.I. 1995).
[195] 328 U.S. 256 (1946).
[196] *Id.* at 261-262.

"taken" in violation of the Fifth Amendment. It is, however, extremely difficult to win on such a claim. The mere finding that the government has committed a nuisance is usually not sufficient to conclude that the plaintiff's property has been taken without just compensation.[197]

§14.5.3 *Interference with Reasonable Investment-Backed Expectations*

The issue

The dilemma here is that people must have some right to rely on existing law at the time they invest; otherwise, the state could pass a general law subjecting all property in the state to being taken for public use without just compensation, thereby rendering the constitutional protection meaningless. At the same time, the legislature must have the power to change the law; otherwise, it would not be able to pass legislation accounting for changing circumstances to protect the public welfare.

The solution

A regulation is more likely to be held a taking if a citizen has already invested substantially in reasonable reliance on an existing statutory or regulatory scheme; it is less likely to be ruled a taking if the regulation prevents the owner from realizing an expected benefit in the future.

Regulations that are more likely to be takings

The regulation is *more* likely to be held a taking if:

(1) it interferes with *vested rights*, such as revocation of a previously approved building permit after the developer has invested substantially in beginning construction; or
(2) it otherwise interferes with an existing *present use* of the property.

Regulations that are likely not to be takings

The regulation is *less* likely to be held a taking if:

(1) it imposes an *opportunity loss* preventing the owner from realizing the benefits of a future use that the owner intended to make but did not yet invest in, as long as the owner retains some economically viable use of the property; or
(2) the change in the law is one that could or should have been anticipated such that the owner's *reliance* on the continuation of prior law was *unreasonable.*

§14.5.4 *Fairness and Justice*

Ultimate question

The ultimate question in takings cases is whether a regulation wrongfully "forc[es] some people alone to bear public burdens that, in all fairness and justice, should be borne by the public as a whole."[198] Given the dilemmas involved in interpreting the takings clause and in applying the relevant factors to particular cases, what factors should affect or determine the

[197] *Harris v. Town of Lincoln*, 668 A.2d 321 (R.I. 1995) (noise from generator at sewer plant found to be a nuisance but not an unconstitutional taking).
[198] *Armstrong v. United States*, 364 U.S. 40, 49 (1960). *See also Agins v. Tiburon*, 447 U.S. 255, 260-261 (1980) (holding that the question under the takings clause is whether "the public at large, rather than a single owner, must bear the burden of an exercise of state power in the public interest").

outcome? The three most widely discussed possibilities are (1) tradition; (2) efficiency; and (3) distributive fairness.

Tradit

Perhaps the core principle of property law is to protect justified expectations. Those expectations are partly based on social norms about the meaning of property ownership and partly on existing legal rules that define the legitimate scope of property rights. Reliance on tradition is useful because it may give an objective baseline for determining what expectations of owners are, and are not, justified. However, there are three major problems with this approach. First, both social custom and law change over time and so it is not clear at what point one is to look to determine the justified expectations of property owners. The law of property changes over time, sometimes dramatically. Second, property law often recognizes and protects the *actual* expectations of individuals even when the formal rules in effect would not seem to have protected their interests. Ignorance of the law is not an excuse, but property law develops over time and does often protect expectations based on informal arrangements in the face of rules that attempt to fix property interests by reference to formal criteria. A third problem is that a part of our tradition is that legislatures have redefined property rights over time in response to public needs and changes in social norms. Is the basis of "tradition" the common law rules enacted by judges who are either unelected or partially insulated from the democratic process or legislative rules promulgated by the more democratic branches of government?

Efficiency

In an important article, Frank Michelman argued that compensation should be required when it will help to promote efficient (that is, wealth-maximizing) legislation.[199] Michelman explained that a utilitarian should be concerned about weighing the gains from public projects against three kinds of costs: (1) the harms to uncompensated victims resulting from the project; (2) the settlement or administrative costs of arranging for compensation for those victims; and (3) the demoralization costs that would accrue if the victims were not compensated and believed that this lack of compensation was unfair. He argued that from a utilitarian perspective, compensation should be awarded when the demoralization costs of failing to compensate are greater than the settlement costs of arranging for compensation, assuming the underlying legislation is welfare maximizing in the sense that its benefits outweigh its costs. Other scholars have similarly used efficiency analysis to argue for and against compensation for the effects of particular changes in regulatory laws.[200]

Conundrums of efficiency

Two problems attend the norm of efficiency as a solution to the takings dilemma. First, there are strong arguments both for and against the idea that compensation increases efficiency and social welfare. For example, it may be argued that legislation should be passed that improves the general

[199] Frank Michelman, *Property, Utility, and Fairness: Comments on the Ethical Foundations of "Just Compensation" Law*, 80 Harv. L. Rev. 1165, 1184 (1967).

[200] *See, e.g.*, Daniel Farber, *Economic Analysis and Just Compensation*, 12 Int'l Rev. L. & Econ. 125 (1992); William A. Fischel, *Introduction: Utilitarian Balancing and Formalism in Takings*, 88 Colum. L. Rev. 1581 (1988); Louis Kaplow, *An Economic Analysis of Legal Transitions*, 99 Harv. L. Rev. 509 (1986).

welfare, *i.e.*, its costs outweigh its benefits. Making the legislature compensate owners whose property is harmed by legislation will force the taxpayers to internalize the external costs of the regulation and test whether they believe the benefits of the legislation outweigh the costs associated with it.[201] However, it may be argued that precisely the reverse is true. If owners know that they will be compensated if any new regulatory laws affect their property rights, they will not take into account the negative external effects of their property uses and thus overinvest in socially harmful activities. Denying compensation when a regulatory law is passed will therefore force owners to anticipate the possibility of new regulation and induce them to invest accordingly.[202]

Efficiency may not be a legitimate goal of takings law

Second, nothing in the Constitution explicitly requires legislatures to adopt "efficient" legislation. Indeed, the core value of a "republican form of government" is the ability of the people to pass laws they view as in their interest or in the public interest as they conceive it. This may or may not cohere with efficiency, as it is defined by economists. There is no constitutional proscription on stupid legislation; under the due process clause, legislation will be upheld as long as it bears a rational relationship to a legitimate government objective, but the courts do not ordinarily substitute their judgment for that of the legislature in these matters. For example, many economists find rent control laws counterproductive (and some Supreme Court Justices obviously agree), but, because rational legislators believe them to be in the public interest, they are fully empowered to pass them.[203] Nor is it clear why a constitutional provision protecting owners from having their "property" taken by the state should be interpreted in light of efficiency. Constitutional protections are geared toward promoting individual rights or fundamental human interests while allowing for democratic rule. They are therefore arguably more appropriately understood in terms of justice and fairness than in terms of social welfare.

Distributive justice

Although tradition and efficiency play some role in interpreting the takings clause, the most fundamental principle underlying the takings clause is that of distributive justice. The takings clause does not enact a particular philosophy about distribution, but it does prohibit legislatures from imposing fundamentally unfair obligations on owners that they should not have to bear for the good of the community. It is fair to single out particular owners if their property uses harm the community and thus were never part of their vested rights in the first place. Regulations are also fair if they create an average reciprocity of advantage. However, regulations are unfair if they take core property rights and thus interfere with the fundamental, justified expectations of owners. Regulations are also unfair if they cause a loss that the community as a whole, rather than any individual property owners, should bear.

[201] Daniel Farber, *Economic Analysis and Just Compensation*, 12 Int'l Rev. L. & Econ. 125 (1992).
[202] Louis Kaplow, *An Economic Analysis of Legal Transitions*, 99 Harv. L. Rev. 509 (1986).
[203] *Lingle v. Chevron U.S.A, Inc.*, 544 U.S. 528 (2005); *Pennell v. City of San Jose*, 485 U.S. 1 (1988).

§14.6 "Categorical" Regulatory Takings

The *Penn Central* balancing test governs most regulatory takings cases, but the Supreme Court has identified several important exceptions. Since 1978, the Supreme Court has identified special situations that are governed by what the Court calls "*per se*" tests that find particular regulations of property to be takings without regard to the importance of the public interest served by the regulation or the extent of diminution in value of the property. Two situations represent categorical takings: (1) physical invasions of property[204] and (2) deprivation of all economically beneficial use.[205] However, although not formally classified as categorical takings, the Court treats two other types of takings in a fairly categorical manner. They are (3) deprivation of certain core property rights[206] and (4) interference with "vested rights."[207]

***Per se* tests**

When the Supreme Court affirms that some types of government regulation of property are categorical or *per se* takings of property, one has to approach these assertions with a grain of salt. First, each of the categorical rules applies only in very specific circumstances, and policy considerations are relevant to determining when they apply. Second, the categorical rules each have exceptions, and the scope and meaning of those exceptions render the *per se* tests more like standards than the bright-line rules they may first appear.

§14.6.1 Per Se *Takings*

Permanent physical invasions

§14.6.1.1 Physical Invasions. It is often stated that permanent physical invasions of property are *per se* unconstitutional takings of property regardless of the circumstances and regardless of the public interest served by the invasion. For example, in a 1992 case, Justice O'Connor wrote: "[T]he Takings Clause requires compensation if the government authorizes a compelled physical invasion of property."[208] Although oft-repeated, this proposition is only generally true. In fact, the Court has upheld permanent physical invasions of property in a number of instances. It is thus important to understand when the rule does and does not apply.

***Loretto v. Teleprompter Manhattan CATV Corp.* (1982)**

The physical invasion rule was first firmly articulated in the 1982 case of *Loretto v. Teleprompter Manhattan CATV Corp.*[209] New York City passed a law authorizing cable television companies to install cables and related equipment on residential rental property without the consent of the landlord upon payment of a "reasonable" fee, determined by a city agency to be $1.00. When the defendant installed a line designed to allow tenants to receive cable television signals, the landlord/owner sued the city claiming

[204] *See* §14.6.1.1.
[205] *See* §14.6.1.2.
[206] *See* §14.6.2.1.
[207] *See* §14.6.2.2.
[208] *Yee v. City of Escondido*, 503 U.S. 519, 527 (1992).
[209] 458 U.S. 419 (1982).

that the forced invasion was a "taking" of her property. The Supreme Court agreed, holding that any "permanent physical occupation authorized by government is a taking without regard to the public interests that it may serve," even if the invasion had no negative impact on the value of the property.[210] Justice Marshall explained that the "power to exclude has traditionally been considered one of the most treasured strands in an owner's bundle of property rights" and that "an owner suffers a special kind of injury when a *stranger* directly invades and occupies the owner's property."[211] Moreover, a rigid rule "avoids otherwise difficult line-drawing problems."[212]

Dissenting opinion

Justice Blackmun dissented, along with Justices Brennan and White, arguing that the majority's approach was formalistic and irrational. In particular, he argued that the ordinance in question was merely a kind of consumer protection law designed to regulate the landlord-tenant relationship to ensure that tenants had access to a vital service. The law "merely defines one of the many statutory responsibilities that a New Yorker accepts when she enters the rental business."[213] For example, New York landlords are required by law to provide and pay for mailboxes that occupy more than five times the volume that Teleprompter's cable occupied on the owner's building. "If the State constitutionally can insist that appellant make this sacrifice so that her tenants may receive mail, it is hard to understand why the state may not require her to surrender less space, filled at another's expense, so that those same tenants can receive television signals."[214] Justice Marshall's majority opinion answered the dissent's argument by admitting that if the ordinance required landlords to provide cable installation if a tenant so desires, the statute might be constitutional, because the landlord would own the installation. "Ownership would give the landlord rights to the placement, manner, use, and possibly the disposition of the installation."[215]

***Cedar Point Nursery v. Hassid* (2021)**

The Supreme Court revisited physical invasions in *Cedar Point Nursery v. Hassid*.[216] Responding to advocacy by Cesar Chavez, Dolores Huerta, and other organizers of what became the United Farm Workers, California had granted labor organizations the right to access the property of agricultural employers to solicit support for unionization, filling a gap left by an exception to the National Labor Relations Act. Union organizers had the right to organize on agricultural property three hours a day before and after work and during lunch breaks, up to 120 days a year. Growers challenged this limited access right as a violation of the takings clause, and the Supreme Court agreed. The Court distinguished between challenges to government regulation of the use of property, which would continue to be governed by the *Penn Central* test, and challenges to "physical appropriations," which would *per se* violate the takings clause. As the Court

[210] *Id.* at 426.
[211] *Id.* at 435-436.
[212] *Id.* at 436.
[213] *Id.* at 448 (Blackmun, J., dissenting).
[214] *Id.* at 453 (Blackmun, J., dissenting).
[215] *Id.* at 440 n.19.
[216] 594 U.S. 139 (2021).

framed it, the California law "appropriates a right to physically invade the growers' property—to literally 'take access,'"[217] and compensation must be granted to the owners. Where *Loretto* had distinguished between temporary physical occupations, governed by *Penn Central*, and permanent physical occupations, governed by a *per se* rule, *Cedar Point Nursery* held that all government-mandated physical invasions would violate the takings clause.

Exceptions to the *per se* physical invasion rule in *Cedar Point Nursery*

As with other nominally categorical takings, the Court in *Cedar Point Nursery* qualified the *per se* rule with a number of exceptions. First, the Court distinguished between "regulations granting a right to invade property closed to the public" and "[l]imitations on how a business generally open to the public may treat individuals on the premises," citing *PruneYard Shopping Center v. Robins*, 447 U.S. 74 (1980) and *Heart of Atlanta Motel, Inc. v. United States*, 379 U.S. 241, 261 (1964), a case in which the Court had rejected a takings challenge to Title II of the *Civil Rights Act of 1964*, 42 U.S.C. §2000a, the federal public accommodations antidiscrimination statute. Second, the Court held that "[i]solated physical invasions, not undertaken pursuant to a granted right of access," should be evaluated as "individual torts rather than appropriations of a property right."[218] Third, rights of access grounded in what the Court had described in *Lucas v. South Carolina Coastal Council* as inhering in the title to property[219] would mean that "traditional common law privileges to access private property," such as the necessity in trespass and the privilege officials have to enter property to enforce criminal law if consistent with the Fourth Amendment and state law, would not be a taking.[220] Finally, *per se* liability for physical invasions would not apply to access rights as conditions on the participation in public programs, which would be governed by the doctrine of exactions the Court developed in *Nollan v. California Coastal Commission*,[221] and *Dolan v. City of Tigard*,[222] requiring conditions to have an "essential nexus" to the relevant permission sought and "rough proportionality" for any mitigation (or benefit) sought in exchange for permission. *Cedar Point Nursery* suggested that this nexus and proportionality analysis should apply to all "permit, license, or registration" regimes that require "access for reasonable health and safety inspections."[223]

A prime example of the exceptions to *per se* liability that *Cedar Point Nursery* sought to preserve involves antidiscrimination laws that regulate public accommodations and the housing market. Those laws prohibit public accommodations from refusing to serve customers because of their race, religion, or national origin. In effect, they take away the owner's right to exclude strangers from their property on the basis of race, religion, or national origin, once they open their property for business or other public

[217] *Id.* at 152.
[218] *Id.* at 156-157.
[219] 505 U.S. 1003, 1029 (1992).
[220] 594 U.S. at 160-161.
[221] 483 U.S. 825 (1987).
[222] 512 U.S. 374 (1994).
[223] 594 U.S. at 161.

Heart of Atlanta Motel v. United States (1964)

purposes. In *Heart of Atlanta Motel, Inc. v. United States*,[224] for example, the Supreme Court upheld the constitutionality of the public accommodations provisions of the *Civil Rights Act of 1964*,[225] rejecting a motel's argument that the law took its property rights by requiring it to rent rooms to Black guests against its will. The Court found the takings argument to be so insubstantial that it was dismissed in a single sentence without explanation.[226] Similarly, various federal courts have upheld the constitutionality of the *Fair Housing Act*,[227] despite the fact that the law authorized courts to grant injunctive relief for racially motivated refusals to rent property, thereby effectively forcing landlords to rent property against their will if the landlord had refused to deal with a potential tenant merely because of the tenant's race.[228]

PruneYard Shopping Center v. Robins (1980)

As to places open to the public, the Supreme Court had given a fuller analysis of the physical invasion issue in 1980 in the case of *PruneYard Shopping Center v. Robins*.[229] Several state supreme courts, including that in California, have interpreted their state constitutional free speech clauses to grant this right.[230] A shopping center owner complained that the state constitutional provision took its property without just compensation when the California Supreme Court interpreted the state constitution to require it to allow individuals to enter its property to solicit signatures for a petition to protest the United Nations resolution against "Zionism." Although state law forced the owner to suffer a physical invasion by strangers beyond the scope of its general invitation to the public, the Court held that no taking had occurred.

Reasoning in *PruneYard*

In an opinion by then Justice Rehnquist, the Court acknowledged that "[i]t is true that one of the essential sticks in the bundle of property rights is the right to exclude others"[231] and that "here there has literally been a 'taking' of that right to the extent that the California Supreme Court has interpreted the State Constitution to entitle its citizens to exercise free expression and petition rights on shopping center property."[232] The Court found no taking here because there was no showing that the forced entry would "unreasonably impair the value or use of [the] property" or that "the 'right to exclude others' [was] so essential to the use or economic value of their property that the state-authorized limitation of it amounted to a 'taking.'"[233]

Kaiser Aetna v. United States (1979)

In holding that free speech rights in shopping centers did not constitute a taking, the *PruneYard* court had to distinguish the 1979 case of *Kaiser Aetna v. United States*.[234] In *Kaiser Aetna*, an owner of a private pond

[224] 379 U.S. 241 (1964).
[225] 42 U.S.C. §§2000a to 2000a-6.
[226] 379 U.S. at 261.
[227] 42 U.S.C. §§3601 to 3619 & 3631.
[228] *See, e.g., Meadows v. Edgewood Management Corp.*, 432 F. Supp. 334 (W.D. Va. 1977) (upholding constitutionality of the *Fair Housing Act* pursuant to the Thirteenth Amendment).
[229] 447 U.S. 74 (1980).
[230] *Robins v. PruneYard Shopping Center*, 592 P.2d 341 (Cal. 1979), *aff'd sub nom. PruneYard Shopping Center v. Robins*, 447 U.S. 74 (1980). *Accord, New Jersey Coalition Against the War in the Middle East v. J.M.B. Realty Corp.*, 650 A.2d 757 (N.J. 1994). *See* §2.7.2.
[231] 447 U.S. at 82 (*quoting Kaiser Aetna v. United States*, 444 U.S. 164, 179-180 (1979)).
[232] *Id.*
[233] *Id.* at 84.
[234] 444 U.S. 164 (1979).

in Hawai'i "invested substantial amounts of money in dredging the pond, developing it into an exclusive marina, and building a surrounding marina community."[235] The marina was a private club, open only to fee-paying members, which controlled access to the pond and excluded nonmembers from it, as it was allowed to do under Hawai'i property law. However, after the owner's improvements, the pond became connected to the ocean and the federal government sought to compel the owner to allow free public access to the pond on the ground that it was now connected to "navigable waters" and thus subject to the federal navigational servitude. The Court held that the marina could not be compelled to allow free public access to the pond without paying compensation. "In this case, we hold that the 'right to exclude,' so universally held to be a fundamental element of the property right, falls within [the] category of interests that the Government cannot take without compensation."[236] A taking was established because the property had not previously been subject to the navigational servitude and had only become connected to navigable waters because of the owner's investment in changing the land. Requiring public access would result in "an actual physical invasion of the privately owned marina,"[237] depriving the owner of "one of the most essential sticks in the bundle of rights that are commonly characterized as property—the right to exclude others."[238] The *PruneYard* court distinguished the result in *Kaiser Aetna* by noting that the regulation in *Kaiser Aetna* interfered with the owner's "reasonable investment backed expectations" and was a taking for that reason. The regulation in *PruneYard*, however, had not been shown to have any impact at all on the economic value of the property or to interfere with reasonable investment-backed expectations.[239]

Extent to which the property is open to the public

Justice Marshall also noted that the shopping center owner in *PruneYard* "had not exhibited an interest in excluding all persons from his property."[240] A shopping center invites the public to use the facility; it is open to the public in a way that a private residential rental building is not. Similarly, the Court in *Kaiser Aetna* focused on the fact that the government was trying to convert a fee-paying private club into a free public accommodation. Thus, one might distinguish *Cedar Point Nursery, Loretto,* and *Kaiser Aetna* from *PruneYard* by noting the differences in the extent to which the property has been made open to the public. The more open it is, the less the owner has legitimate privacy interests and the greater the public interest in equal access. This distinction is more convincing than the permanent/temporary distinction, but it is still problematic given the Supreme Court's ruling in *Lloyd Corp., Ltd. v. Tanner*,[241] holding that there is no free speech right to demonstrate at shopping centers. *Lloyd* was premised on the notion

[235] *See PruneYard Shopping Center v. Robins*, 447 U.S. 74, 84 (1980) (*quoting Kaiser Aetna v. United States*, 444 U.S. 164, 168 (1979)).
[236] 444 U.S. at 179-180.
[237] *Id.* at 180.
[238] *Id.* at 176.
[239] 447 U.S. at 84.
[240] 458 U.S. at 434.
[241] 407 U.S. 551 (1972). For more on *Lloyd, see* §2.7.1.

that "property [does not] lose its private character merely because the public is generally invited to use it for designated purposes."[242] Nonetheless, this ground of distinction appears to better reconcile the takings cases with each other. The shopping center in *PruneYard* was generally open to the public for browsing and shopping and other activities and, despite the language in *Lloyd Corp.* to the contrary, it does appear that "the more private property is devoted to public use, the more it must accommodate the rights which inhere in individual members of the general public who use that property."[243] The agricultural property in *Cedar Point Nursery* was open to workers, but not the general public. Similarly, the rental property in *Loretto* was open for tenants to rent and receive guests, but not the public. And the private marina in *Kaiser Aetna* was open only to fee-paying members. Thus, one way to distinguish *PruneYard* from the other major physical invasion cases is the extent to which the owner has opened the property to the public.

Antieviction cases

The *Loretto* court had also emphasized that the physical occupation was by a "stranger" rather than an invitee.[244] This observation was essential to distinguish the cases that had previously upheld the constitutionality of antieviction laws. In the 1921 case of *Block v. Hirsh*[245] and the 1922 case of *Edgar A. Levy Leasing Co. v. Siegel*,[246] the Supreme Court held that laws that prohibit the eviction of tenants are not, for that reason alone, unconstitutional takings of property. *Block v. Hirsh* involved a Washington, D.C., rent control law passed by Congress that prohibited landlords from evicting tenants at the end of the lease term as long as the tenant pays the mandated rent unless the landlord wants the premises for occupation by himself or herself or the landlord's spouse or children. The Supreme Court, in an opinion by Justice Holmes, upheld the law against a takings challenge, noting the control of rents was instituted to meet war conditions and to ensure that the owners of the limited supply of housing in the District of Columbia did not raise rent to such levels as to make the housing unaffordable by those who needed to work for the government. "The main point against the law," Holmes noted,

***Edgar A. Levy Leasing Co. v. Siegel* (1922)**

***Block v. Hirsh* (1921)**

> is that tenants are allowed to remain in possession at the same rent that they have been paying, unless modified by the Commission established by the act, and that thus the use of the land and the right of the owner to do what he will with his own and to make what contracts he pleases are cut down.[247]

However, protection against eviction was needed to ensure that the landlord would not demand higher rents in violation of the rent control law. "The preference given to the tenant in possession is an almost

[242] 407 U.S. at 569.
[243] *Uston v. Resorts International Hotel, Inc.*, 445 A.2d 370, 374 (N.J. 1982) (*quoting State v. Schmid*, 423 A.2d 615 (1980)).
[244] 458 U.S. at 436.
[245] 256 U.S. 135 (1921).
[246] 258 U.S. 242 (1922).
[247] 256 U.S. at 157.

necessary incident of the policy and is traditional in English law. If the tenant remained subject to the landlord's power to evict, the attempt to limit the landlord's demands would fail."[248] Despite the fact that the landlord appeared to want possession to occupy the property himself, the Court upheld the law although noting that Congress had "justified [it] only as a temporary measure"[249] to meet "emergencies growing out of the war."[250]

Yee v. City of Escondido (1992)

Requiring the landlord to suffer the continued occupation of the property by the tenant at the end of the lease term is a forced physical occupation of property. However, the occupation is not by a stranger, but by a tenant who was initially invited onto the premises. This distinction was crucial to the 1992 decision in *Yee v. City of Escondido*,[251] in which the Supreme Court upheld a rent control law that prohibited the eviction of mobile homeowners from rented spaces unless the landlord wished to convert the property to nonrental use. Justice O'Connor noted that "[w]here the government authorizes a physical occupation of property (or actually takes title), the Takings Clause *generally* requires compensation,"[252] but that this rule only applies to forced occupation by strangers. This antieviction law did not mandate the "unwanted"[253] or "compelled physical occupation" of land.[254] Citing *Heart of Atlanta Motel*[255] and *PruneYard*,[256] Justice O'Connor argued that landlords "voluntarily open their property to occupation by others," and that they therefore "cannot assert a per se right to compensation based on their inability to exclude particular individuals."[257] Rather than a forced physical occupation of property, the regulation was merely "a regulation of petitioners' *use* of their property, and thus does not amount to a *per se* taking."[258]

Critique

To say that one has not suffered a compelled physical occupation of land merely because there was an initial "invitation" strains credibility. If someone invites you to their house for dinner, and a court orders them to let you sleep in the back room for the next year, they would have suffered a forced physical occupation of property because the government mandate allows the invitee to exceed the scope of the initial invitation. A better defense of antieviction laws is the reasoning of *Miller v. Schoene*[259]

[248] *Id.* at 157-158.

[249] *Id.* at 157.

[250] *Id.* at 154. It was not at all clear the Court would have sustained the law if it were not intended as a temporary measure. However, both rent control in general and antieviction laws in particular have subsequently been upheld by the Supreme Court even in the absence of "emergency" conditions. *See Pennell v. City of San Jose*, 485 U.S. 1 (1988) (upholding the constitutionality of rent control laws against a takings challenge); *Yee v. City of Escondido*, 503 U.S. 519 (1992).

[251] 503 U.S. 519 (1992).

[252] *Id.* at 522.

[253] *Id.* at 531.

[254] *Id.* at 530.

[255] *Heart of Atlanta Motel, Inc. v. United States*, 379 U.S. 241, 261 (1964). *See also* 379 U.S. at 259 ("appellant has no 'right' to select its guests as it sees fit, free from governmental regulation").

[256] *PruneYard Shopping Center v. Robins*, 447 U.S. 74, 82-84 (1980).

[257] 503 U.S. at 531.

[258] *Id.* at 532.

[259] 276 U.S. 272 (1928).

to the effect that, when two property rights clash, the government must choose between them. Landlord-tenant relationships divide property rights between landlords and tenants, conferring possessory rights on tenants and reserving a reversion in the landlord, in conjunction with contractual and property-based rental rights. The termination point of the tenant's possessory rights is one term in the contractual relationship between the parties. Because regulation of landlord-tenant relationships is clearly constitutional, regulation of evictions must also be warranted. For example, to enforce the tenant's rights under the implied warranty of habitability, courts have denied landlords the right to evict tenants who withhold rent because the landlord is in violation of the warranty. A similar rule exists for retaliatory evictions. In addition, mortgage foreclosure laws require mortgagees to suffer the physical occupation of property before foreclosure, which, absent the regulation, might have shifted possessory rights to the mortgagee upon the homeowner's default. Antieviction laws do constitute compelled physical occupations of property but may be justified as regulations of the landlord-tenant relationship and as a decision to privilege the interests of tenants in continued access to their homes over the interests of landlords in recovering possession of the property.

***Horne v. Dep't of Agriculture* (2015)**

In *Horne v. Department of Agriculture*,[260] a federal statute sought to stabilize prices for agricultural commodities. One program did that by requiring raisin handlers to set aside a portion of their crop and transfer it to the government, which would dispose of it and turn any profits over to the growers. One set of raisin handlers refused to turn over any raisins to the government and defended an enforcement order by arguing that the obligation to give almost half their raisins to the government constituted a taking without just compensation. The Supreme Court agreed, holding (1) that the takings clause applies to personal property as well as real property and (2) that the requirement that raisins be given to the government was a *per se* "physical taking" of property. The Court noted that "the classic taking is one in which the government directly appropriates property for its own use."[261] Moreover, "[t]he Government has a categorical duty to pay just compensation when it takes your car, just as when it takes your home."[262]

The United States had argued that the reserve program was designed to regulate the raisin commodities market and to ensure stable and adequate prices for producers and that the manner by which that regulation occurred should not matter. For example, the law could have regulated raisin prices directly or limited the number that could be sold to ensure sufficient prices to allow the industry to make a profit, and such laws would very likely not constitute takings of property. The Court rejected this argument on the ground that "[a] physical taking of raisins and a regulatory limit on production may have the

[260] 576 U.S. 350 (2015).
[261] *Id.* at 356-357.
[262] *Id.* at 358-359.

same economic impact on a grower. The Constitution, however, is concerned with means as well as ends."[263] Nor could the government make raisin growers relinquish their property without just compensation as a condition of selling their raisins in interstate commerce. "The fact that the growers are entitled to the net proceeds of the raisin sales does not mean that there has been no taking at all," the Court explained. And if there is a taking, the owners were entitled to the market value of the property that was taken.

Regulation of agricultural commodities

Justices Breyer, Ginsburg, and Kagan dissented in part because the requirement that any proceeds of sales of the reserved raisins be turned over the handler might satisfy the constitutional obligation to pay compensation.[264] The program itself was intended to enhance the price of the raisins that the grower retained. That enhanced value, in conjunction with the proceeds of any sales of the reserved raisins, might be equivalent to the market value of reserved raisins. Justice Sotomayor dissented on the ground that the statute regulated the commodities market and did not constitute a *per se* taking of personal property. Here the regulatory program not only enhanced the value of the owner's property, but the owner retained a contingent right to any profits from the reserved raisins. She would have applied the *Penn Central ad hoc* test, especially since "the property at issue is a fungible commodity for sale, [and] the income that the property may yield is the property owner's most central interest."[265]

Seizure of personal property

▶ HARD CASE ▷ LANDLORD WANTS TO MOVE IN

In *Flynn v. City of Cambridge*,[266] the Massachusetts Supreme Judicial Court upheld against a takings challenge a rent control and condominium conversion ordinance requiring that certain apartments remain available as rental housing, thereby preventing an owner from occupying her own unit.[267] The landlord could argue that, despite the Supreme Court's approval of antieviction laws in *Block v. Hirsh* and *Yee*, it has never held that it is constitutional for the state to deny an owner the right to move into her own property. The antieviction law upheld in *Block* had an explicit exception that allowed eviction if the landlord sought possession for herself, her spouse, or her children. In *Cwynar v.*

263 *Id.* at 361-362.

264 *Id.* at 371-377 (Breyer, J., concurring).

265 *Id.* at 380-382 (Sotomayor, J., dissenting).

266 418 N.E.2d 335 (Mass. 1981).

267 For similar rulings, see *Puttrich v. Smith*, 407 A.2d 842, 843 (N.J. Super. Ct. App. Div. 1979); *Stamboulos v. McKee*, 342 A.2d 529 (N.J. Super. Ct. App. Div. 1975) (holding that the New Jersey antieviction statute was constitutional even though it prohibited an owner of a four-family apartment building from evicting a tenant to allow a member of the landlord's family to move in). *But see Sabato v. Sabato*, 342 A.2d 886 (N.J. Super. Ct. Law Div. 1975), *overruled by Puttrich v. Smith*, 407 A.2d 842, 843 (N.J. Super. Ct. App. Div. 1979) (holding that the state could not constitutionally prevent a landlord from evicting a tenant if the landlord wanted to move into the property).

City and County of San Francisco,[268] a California court held that an ordinance that prevents an owner from occupying her own property by evicting a tenant may well constitute an unconstitutional taking of property. Similarly, the law upheld in *Yee* allowed the owner to go out of the rental housing business altogether. On the other hand, the state can argue that established case law suggests that what matters is the initial invitation by the landlord, and that the state is allowed to choose to protect the tenant's possessory rights in an established home over the landlord's potential rights in establishing a future home. Antieviction laws are akin to rules of the estates system, which regulate the rights that go along with ownership of particular estates in land. Owners are free to choose not to create those estates in the first place, but their characteristics must be subject to regulation in the public interest. Some future interests are invalidated because of interests in promoting alienability. Protecting an owner's right to remain in her home is a legitimate public purpose, and the state may legitimately choose to treat tenants as owners of estates in land that include such rights.[269] Indeed, over a vigorous dissent by Justice Rehnquist, the Supreme Court dismissed the appeal in *Fresh Pond Shopping Center, Inc. v. Callahan*[270] when a corporate landlord complained that a local antieviction law prevented it from recovering possession for the purpose of changing the use of the property from residential rental use to another purpose. Justice Rehnquist noted that, although the law allowed owners to evict tenants if they wanted to move in themselves, this corporate tenant could not occupy the property for personal living purposes and, thus, unlike other landlords, had no ability to get out of the rental housing business. Without opinion, the majority rejected Justice Rehnquist's argument by refusing the appeal, presumably on the basis of precedents like *Block v. Hirsh*.

Following *Cedar Point Nursery*, some owners have begun challenging tenant-protection statutes such as public-health-related eviction moratoria and rent regulations as *per se* physical takings, but most courts have rejected such claims.[271] A few courts have found the argument, however, to have some merit.[272] ◀

[268] 109 Cal. Rptr. 2d 233 (Ct. App. 2001).

[269] *See, e.g., Nordlinger v. Hahn*, 505 U.S. 1 (1992) (holding that it was not a violation of the equal protection clause for California to impose lower property taxes on long-term residents than on new residents because "the State has a legitimate interest in local neighborhood preservation, continuity, and stability," and in protecting the "reliance interests" of older residents who "rationally may be thought to have vested expectations in [their] property or home that are more deserving of protection than the anticipatory expectations of a new owner at the point of purchase"); *Puttrich v. Smith*, 407 A.2d 842, 843 (N.J. Super. Ct. App. Div. 1979) ("the legislature could constitutionally decide that an owner's right to utilize his property must yield to a tenant's interest in keeping his home").

[270] 464 U.S. 875 (1983).

[271] *See, e.g., 74 Pinehurst LLC v. New York*, 59 F.4th 557, 563 (2d Cir. 2023); *Community Housing Improvement Program v. City of New York*, 59 F.4th 540, 551 (2d Cir. 2023); *Gonzales v. Inslee*, 535 P.3d 864, 872-73 (Wash. 2023).

[272] *See Heights Apartments, LLC v. Walz*, 30 F.4th 720, 733 (8th Cir. 2022) (physical takings claim under *Cedar Point Nursery* plausibly plead against Covid-era eviction limitations); *Darby Dev. Co. v. United States*, 112 F.4th 1017 (Fed. Cir. 2024) (same).

▶ **HARD CASE** ▷ ADVERSE POSSESSION

Does the government have to compensate an owner if it acquires title to private property by adverse possession? One federal court held that it did, citing *Loretto* and explaining that, although private owners do not have to compensate when they acquire property by adverse possession, the "government is not like another individual."[273] The state would have had to pay compensation if it had taken the property directly by eminent domain and should not be able to avoid that obligation simply by occupying the property for a long time. Most courts, however, have held that no compensation is due because the private property owner is always entitled to sue to eject the government if it is occupying her property and adverse possession occurs only when the statute of limitations runs out.[274] In that case, the claim for ejectment is time barred and arguably so is any regulatory taking claim. In addition, property has always been subject to loss through adverse possession, so an exercise of that power by the state takes no property rights to which the owner was ever entitled. The owner could have brought a claim in ejectment and obtained damages for the trespass before the running of the statutory period, and once that period runs out, there are no property rights left to protect from confiscation. ◀

▶ **HARD CASE** ▷ POST-FORECLOSURE EVICTION PROTECTION

The city council in Lynn, Massachusetts passed an ordinance that requires a showing of "just cause" to evict a homeowner after foreclosure. The effect of the law may be to give homeowners the right to rent from the new owner who purchased the property at foreclosure and stay on the property. If the law prohibits displacement of a foreclosed owner who can afford to pay market rents, does that constitute a taking of the property rights of the buyer at the foreclosure sale? Under the landlord-tenant cases, such as *Block v. Hirsh*,[275] one can argue that the answer is no because foreclosure regulations adjust rights to a contractual relationship; the purchaser at foreclosure is usually the bank that had the right to foreclose so a right to rent preserves a prior relationship. On the other hand, if the tenancy was created after the mortgage, under traditional property law it should end when the mortgagee exercises its right to seize the property through foreclosure. To force the buyer to allow the old homeowner to stay would constitute a forced, physical occupation of property and would discourage bidding at the foreclosure sale. ◀

***Lucas v. South Carolina Coastal Council* (1992)**

§14.6.1.2 Deprivation of All Economically Viable Use. The Supreme Court announced another "categorical rule" in 1992 in *Lucas v.*

[273] *Pascoag Reservoir & Dam, LLC v. State of Rhode Island*, 217 F. Supp. 2d 206, 226-227 (D.R.I. 2002), *aff'd on other grounds*, 337 F.3d 87 (1st Cir. 2003).
[274] *Weidner v. State of Alaska, Dep't of Transportation & Public Facilities*, 860 P.2d 1205, 1212 (Alaska 1993); *Stickney v. City of Saco*, 770 A.2d 592, 603, 2001 Me. 69 (Me. 2001).
[275] 256 U.S. 135 (1921).

South Carolina Coastal Council.[276] In 1986, David Lucas purchased two lots fronting on the ocean for $975,000, intending to build single-family homes on them. Although the state had previously placed limits on coastal development, there were no legal impediments to building the homes at the time he bought the land. Other houses had been built on property contiguous to his parcels. Two years after he bought the land, in 1988, but before he began construction, South Carolina passed a regulatory law[277] whose effect was to prohibit construction on Lucas's lots. Lucas brought suit, claiming that the prohibition on construction constituted a taking of his property. Lucas argued, and the state trial court accepted, the idea that "this prohibition rendered Lucas's parcels 'valueless.'"[278] Because the regulation "deprive[d] Lucas of any reasonable economic use of the lots [and] eliminated the unrestricted right of use," the court found that the regulation "rendered them valueless" and thus took his property without just compensation,[279] and ordered the state to pay Lucas just compensation of $1,232,387.50. The Supreme Court of South Carolina reversed, holding that, even if the regulation rendered the land "valueless," it did not effectuate a taking because the legislature had found that new construction on the beachfront threatened the coastline — a public resource — and that no compensation should be required when a regulation is designed "to prevent a serious public harm."[280] The U.S. Supreme Court reversed, holding that compensation is required when a "regulation denies all economically beneficial or productive use of land"[281] unless the prohibited action would have constituted a nuisance or been excluded from an owner's rights by other "background principles of the State's law of property."[282]

Deprivation of "all economically viable use"

Justice Scalia's majority opinion explained that a "total deprivation of beneficial use is, from the landowner's point of view, the equivalent of a physical appropriation"[283] and, thus, like permanent physical invasions, should constitute a categorical taking "without case-specific inquiry into the public interest advanced in support of the restraint."[284] In such cases, there is no average reciprocity of advantage,[285] and there is a "heightened risk that private property is being pressed into some form of public service

[276] 505 U.S. 1003, 1015 (1992). *Cf. Pumpelly v. Green Bay Co.*, 80 U.S. 166 (1871) (flooding property pursuant to dam project on neighboring land effects a taking of property); *Philip Morris, Inc. v. Reilly*, 312 F.3d 24 (1st Cir. 2002) (state law requirement of company disclosure of ingredients used in tobacco products is an unconstitutional taking of the company's property in its trade secrets).

[277] *Beachfront Management Act*, S.C. Code §§48-39-250 *et seq.*

[278] 505 U.S. at 1007.

[279] *Id.* at 1009.

[280] 404 S.E.2d 895, 899 (1991).

[281] 505 U.S. at 1015 (*citing Agins v. Tiburon*, 447 U.S. 255, 260 (1980)).

[282] *Id.* at 1029.

[283] *Id.* at 1017.

[284] *Id.* at 1015.

[285] *Id.* at 1017-1018 ("Surely, at least, in the extraordinary circumstance when no productive or economically beneficial use of land is permitted, it is less realistic to indulge our usual assumption that the legislature is simply 'adjusting the benefits and burdens of economic life,' *Penn Central Transportation Co.*, 438 U.S., at 124, in a manner that secures an 'average reciprocity of advantage' to everyone concerned, *Pennsylvania Coal Co. v. Mahon*, 260 U.S., at 415").

under the guise of mitigating serious public harm."[286] Thus, "when the owner of real property has been called upon to sacrifice all economically beneficial uses in the name of the common good, that is, to leave his property economically idle, he has suffered a taking."[287] The Supreme Court assumed that Lucas's land had been rendered "valueless" because the trial court found that this was so and the state had not appealed this ruling. Neither the South Carolina Supreme Court nor the U.S. Supreme Court addressed the question of whether the evidence adduced at trial was sufficient to support such a conclusion.

Distinguishing prior cases

Justice Scalia distinguished prior cases, such as *Mugler*, *Hadacheck*, *Miller v. Schoene*, and *Goldblatt*, by arguing that they had established that it was a public purpose to prevent "noxious uses,"[288] but that they had not answered the question of whether deprivation of all economically viable use constituted a "taking."[289] This interpretation of the earlier cases was surprising to most observers, many of whom view the decision in *Lucas* to elevate the *Agins* principle that owners cannot be deprived of economically viable use into a "categorical rule" to be a change from the prior law.[290]

The nuisance exception

However, *Lucas* also held that a taking will not be found, even if the owner is deprived of "all economically beneficial use," if the restriction prevents the owner from engaging in an action that he never had the legal right to do.[291] A regulation does not take property if it prohibits conduct that would have been unlawful under "background principles of the State's law of property and nuisance."[292] Justice Scalia rejected the idea that a taking would be found when a regulation requires the owner to grant a "benefit" to the community but not when it prevents the owner from committing "harm" to other owners or the community, noting that "the distinction between 'harm-preventing' and 'benefit-conferring' regulation is often in the eye of the beholder."[293] Instead, the Court based the exception to the rule that compensation is required when an owner is deprived of all economically beneficial use on the property law that pre-existed the regulation in question. "Where the State seeks to sustain regulation that deprives land of all economically beneficial use, we think it may resist compensation only if the logically antecedent inquiry into the nature of the owner's estate shows that the proscribed use interests were not part of his title to begin with."[294] For example, the common law of property never gave owners the

[286] 505 U.S. at 1018.

[287] *Id.* at 1019.

[288] *Id.* at 1024 ("'prevention of harmful use' was merely our early formulation of the police power justification necessary to sustain (without compensation) any regulatory diminution in value").

[289] *Id.* at 1023-1024 ("'Harmful or noxious use' analysis was, in other words, simply the progenitor of our more contemporary statements that 'land-use regulation does not effect a taking if it "substantially advance[s] legitimate state interests"'").

[290] *See, e.g.*, John G. Sprankling, *Understanding Property Law* §40.07[C], at 716 (5th ed. 2023) (describing the *Lucas* holding as a "new test").

[291] 505 U.S. at 1029.

[292] *Id.*

[293] *Id.* at 1024.

[294] *Id.* at 1027.

right to commit a nuisance, and thus a law prohibiting a nuisance cannot take a property right because no such property right ever existed.[295]

Dissenting opinion

Justice Blackmun's dissenting opinion criticized the result and reasoning of the majority. First,

Interpretation of prior law

> [w]hen the government regulation prevents the owner from any economically valuable use of his property, the private interest is unquestionably substantial, but we have never before held that no public interest can outweigh it. Instead the Court's prior decisions "uniformly reject the proposition that diminution in property value, standing alone, can establish a 'taking.'"[296]

Rejecting the majority's interpretation of the prior case law, and quoting from *Mugler v. Kansas*, Justice Blackmun explained that "[a] prohibition simply upon the use of property for purposes that are declared, by valid legislation, to be injurious to the health, morals, or safety of the community, cannot, in any just sense, be deemed a taking or an appropriation of property."[297]

Scope of the nuisance exception

Second, it has long been the case that property rights have been defined both by common law and legislation and that legislatures have redefined what constitutes a "nuisance" over time as knowledge and circumstances change. To hold that the legislature may not prohibit construction on sensitive coastline property merely because a court would not previously have held such development to constitute a nuisance is to take power away from the legislature to determine what is a harmful use and grant that power exclusively to the courts. It also falsely assumes that the definition of a nuisance has not changed over time.[298]

Third, the *Lucas* rule deprives the legislature of the power to prevent owners from committing serious public harms, and thus protecting the public, just because the prohibited action would not previously have been classified as a nuisance or otherwise been prohibited by common law.[299]

[295] *Cf. Esplanade Properties, LLC v. City of Seattle*, 307 F.3d 978 (9th Cir. 2002) (restriction on construction in tidelands area is not a taking because the public trust doctrine always prohibited such uses to preserve public access); *Gove v. Zoning Bd. of Appeals of Chatham*, 831 N.E.2d 865 (Mass. 2005) (no taking to prevent an owner from building a house on a floodplain when construction would exacerbate flooding to neighboring property).

[296] 505 U.S. at 1047 (Blackmun, J., dissenting) (*citing Penn Central Transp. Co. v. New York City*, 438 U.S. 104, 131 (1978)).

[297] *Id.* (Blackmun, J., dissenting) (*quoting Mugler v. Kansas*, 123 U.S. 623, 668-669 (1887)). *See also Keshbro, Inc. v. City of Miami*, 801 So. 2d 864 (Fla. 2001) (not a taking to order temporary closure of motel where prostitution and drug use was occurring when court determined the motel was a "public nuisance").

[298] 505 U.S. at 1052-1053 (Blackmun, J., dissenting) ("Until today, the Court explicitly had rejected the contention that the government's power to act without paying compensation turns on whether the prohibited activity is a common-law nuisance. The brewery closed in *Mugler* itself was not a common-law nuisance, and the Court specifically stated that it was the role of the legislature to determine what measures would be appropriate for the protection of public health and safety.").

[299] *Id.* at 1051 (Blackmun, J., dissenting) (*quoting Keystone Bituminous Coal Ass'n v. DeBenedictis*, 480 U.S. 470, 491, n.20 (1987)) ("since no individual has a right to use his

In effect, the *Lucas* decision requires the taxpayers to pay off owners to prevent them from harming the public as long as the type of harm being prevented is a newly recognized one.

Wetlands regulations

The *Lucas* rule is a narrow one because most regulations will not deprive owners of *all* economically viable use. The main types of regulations that might do this are restriction on development of wetlands and restrictions designed to protect endangered species. Both federal and state laws substantially restrict the ability of owners to build on property classified as "wetlands," and such restrictions may have the effect of depriving the owner of any ability to use the land for an economically viable purpose. The *Endangered Species Act*[300] may also have this effect in some cases. Application of the *Lucas* rule to such lands leaves a number of hard issues to resolve.

▶ HARD CASE ▷ THE DENOMINATOR PROBLEM

Argument for using the "whole property"

The *Lucas* case leaves several problems of interpretation. Perhaps the most significant is the so-called denominator problem. If an owner of 100 acres is prevented from developing 5 acres, is that a 100 percent taking of the 5 acres or it is a 5 percent taking of the 100 acres? What, in other words, is the denominator of the fraction? The Supreme Court has repeatedly emphasized that "we must focus on 'the parcel as a whole.'"[301] But what does that mean? In *Palm Beach Isles Associates v. United States*,[302] the Court of Federal Claims held that the refusal of the Army Corps of Engineers to issue a "dredge and fill permit" for 49.3 acres of submerged land out of 50.7 acres in their possession was not a categorical taking of property because the owners had originally purchased a 311.7-acre tract (and subsequently sold 261 acres) and were thus not denied economically viable use of their property. Because the owners had originally purchased a 311.7-acre tract, the relevant property interest for determining the owner's investment-backed expectations was the entire tract rather than any subset of it.[303] If this were not the case, then laws that restrict the height of buildings or impose setback requirements would constitute "total" takings of the area upon which construction is prohibited. Quoting *Penn Central*, the court held that the

---

property so as to create a nuisance or otherwise harm others, the State has not 'taken' anything when it asserts its power to enjoin the nuisance-like activity").

300 16 U.S.C. §§1531 to 1543.

301 *Tahoe-Sierra Preservation Council, Inc. v. Tahoe Regional Planning Agency*, 535 U.S. 302, 327 (2002).

302 42 Fed. Cl. 340 (1998), *overruled*, 208 F.3d 1374 (Fed. Cir. 2000).

303 *Accord, Forest Properties, Inc. v. United States*, 177 F.3d 1360, 1365 (Fed. Cir. 1999) ("[w]here the developer treats legally separate parcels as a single economic unit, together they may constitute the relevant parcel"); *Tabb Lakes, Ltd. v. United States*, 10 F.3d 796, 802 (Fed. Cir. 1993) ("Clearly the quantum of land to be considered is not [the] area of wetlands. If that were true, the [§404 program] would, *ipso facto*, constitute a taking in every case where it exercises its statutory authority"); *District Intown Properties L.P. v. District of Columbia*, 198 F.3d 874 (D.C. Cir. 1999) (relevant parcel was entire property, not individual subdivided lots).

relevant parcel to be considered was the original 311.7 acres rather than the 50.7 acres in dispute.[304] The owners

> still profited significantly from their investment as a result of the sale of the 261-acre piece of the property. The takings clause in the Constitution should not be construed to provide a windfall to claimants in light of the known regulatory permitting requirements or the selling off of valuable portions of a parcel by the plaintiffs and their retention of only those acres subject to regulation.[305]

Argument for using the individual lots

On appeal, the Federal Circuit reversed, holding that the relevant denominator was the 50.7-acre parcel in question, rather than entire 311.7-acre parcel of which it was originally part, and that the permit denial thus constituted a total taking of the 50.7 acres.[306] The court noted it had held in *Loveladies Harbor, Inc. v. United States*[307] that the courts must use a "flexible approach, designed to account for factual nuances"[308] to determine the appropriate "denominator" for calculating the economic impact of a regulation. In this case, the court found that the 50.7 acres were separated from the others by a road, and they were never intended to be developed as part of a single development.[309] Moreover, it can be argued that an owner of a large number of parcels should not have fewer rights than an owner of a small number. If a purchaser of five acres is deprived of the right to build, and this would deprive her of all economically viable use, she would be entitled to compensation unless the restriction prohibited a nuisance or was otherwise unlawful under prior property law. It is arguably unfair to deprive an owner of such protection just because she initially purchased ten acres and was allowed to develop the other five. If, under applicable zoning and other land use regulation laws, the owner would ordinarily have been entitled to develop the parcel, then it should arguably count as a separate property interest for takings purposes. But the Federal Circuit seems to have reversed course, holding in *Norman v. United States*[310] that the proper denominator was the entire 2,280 acres held for development purposes, not the individual parcels that could be developed.

Argument for using the developable tract

[304] 42 Fed. Cl. at 361 (*quoting Penn Central Transportation Co. v. New York City*, 438 U.S. 104, 130-131 (1978)) ("'Taking' jurisprudence does not divide a simple parcel into discrete segments and attempt to determine whether rights in a particular segment have been entirely abrogated. In deciding whether a particular governmental action has effected a taking, this Court focuses rather both on the character of the action and the nature and extent of the interference with rights in the parcel as a whole"). *Accord, Palazzolo v. State*, 2005 WL 1645974, at *3 (R.I. Super. Ct. 2005).

[305] 42 Fed. Cl. at 363.

[306] *Palm Beach Isles Assocs. v. United States, aff'd on reh'g*, 231 F.3d 1354 (Fed. Cir. 2000), *overruling* 42 Fed. Cl. 340 (1998). *Accord, Loveladies Harbor, Inc. v. United States*, 28 F.3d 1171 (Fed. Cir. 1994) (relevant parcel was a 12.5-acre tract out of an original 51-acre purchase).

[307] *Loveladies Harbor, Inc. v. United States*, 28 F.3d 1171 (Fed. Cir. 1994).

[308] *Palm Beach Isles Assocs. v. United States*, 208 F.3d 1374, 1381 (Fed. Cir. 2000) (*quoting Loveladies Harbor, Inc. v. United States*, 28 F.3d 1171, 1181 (Fed. Cir. 1994)).

[309] 208 F.3d at 1380-1381. *Accord*, City of Las Vegas v. 180 Land Co., LLC, 546 P.3d 1239, 1249-50, 1252-53 (Nev. 2024).

[310] *Norman v. United States*, 429 F.3d 1081, 1091 (Fed. Cir. 2005).

Circularity problem

The denominator problem is a hard one that has yet to be resolved by the Supreme Court. The problem is hard partly because the takings clause protects "investment-backed expectations" and those expectations are based on existing law. If the law prohibits a certain use of property, then an owner who expects to use property in that way may have expectations that are unreasonable because no one has a right to use land in a way that violates applicable regulations. However, if the regulations go "too far" in restricting property use, they are arguably invalid and may constitute unconstitutional takings of property, in which case the owner may have legitimately expected to be able to develop the property despite the existence of regulations. There is a problem of circularity in defining what investment-backed expectations are reasonable. If expectations are based on what the law will allow, then it is unreasonable to expect to develop land in violation of existing land use restrictions. However, if individuals have a right to develop property without regard to existing regulations if those regulations would deprive them of all economically viable use, then their investment-backed expectations are reasonable. Whether their expectations are reasonable, therefore, depends on a decision about whether the law could legitimately have restricted their property rights. This decision cannot be made by reference to expectations, but must be made independently. Whether their expectations are reasonable depends on a conclusion of law. It is circular to define a taking based on asking whether an owner had legitimate investment-backed expectations if the issue to be determined is whether it was legitimate for the owner to expect to be able to develop the land when the development would harm public interests. ◀

Test for determining the relevant parcel — *Murr v. Wisconsin* (2017)

The Supreme Court weighed in on the denominator problem in *Murr v. Wisconsin*.[311] In 1960, a couple had purchased land in Wisconsin for a vacation cabin and in 1963 bought an adjacent parcel, which they left undeveloped. The couple later transferred the parcels to their children, who then sought to sell the empty parcel, but a county ordinance would have prevented building on that lot because it was too small unless it was held in common ownership with an adjacent lot. The children challenged this requirement, asserting that the relevant parcel denominator was the empty lot, which would be worthless if separated from their other lot, and that the ordinance deprived them of "all, or practically all, of [its] use." The Supreme Court disagreed, holding that the "denominator" for regulatory takings purposes was the two lots together. To reach that conclusion, the Court articulated a multifactor test to determine whether "reasonable expectations about property ownership would lead a landowner to anticipate that his holdings would be treated as one parcel, or, instead, as separate tracts."[312] The inquiry is "objective," based on "a number of factors," "derive[d] from background customs and the whole of our legal tradition," including how land is treated under state and local law, the property's physical characteristics, and "the property's value under the challenged regulation."[313] This

[311] 582 U.S. 383 (2017).
[312] *Id.* at 397.
[313] *Id.* at 398.

approach recognizes that state law shapes owners' expectations about relevant parcels, although it reserves the ultimate determination to be resolved as a matter of federal law.

▷ CUMULATIVE HARMS **HARD CASE ◀**

Argument that wetlands development constitutes a public nuisance

The *Lucas* opinion suggests that a taking should be found when an owner has no economically viable use unless the development would have itself constituted a nuisance. What if the development of this one parcel would not constitute a nuisance, but the development of all similarly situated parcels would have cumulative, devastating environmental effects? On one hand, it would seem that the legislature should be able to prevent substantial harm to the environment caused by multiple property uses even if individual uses would not themselves cause appreciable harm. One might justify such regulations on that ground that development that contributes to destroying a scarce natural resource, such as water and wetlands, which is essential to community well-being, constitutes a *public* nuisance even if it does not constitute a private nuisance.[314] Numerous pre-*Lucas* cases upheld environmental regulations against takings challenges even if they deprived the owner of the ability to build on the land on the ground that such development harmed important community interests.[315]

Argument that wetlands development does not constitute a nuisance

On the other hand, if the effect of the prohibition is to deprive owners of all economically viable use, then it is arguably unfair to impose such a prohibition without compensation, particularly if similarly situated owners in the past were allowed to develop their land. On this ground, a number of recent cases in the Court of Federal Claims (formerly the Claims Court) have held that wetlands regulations constitute takings if they deprive owners of the ability to develop their land and thus destroy all economically viable use for it.[316] The law of private nuisance always required a balancing of interests of plaintiff and defendant with the goal of protecting property owners from harm while allowing them adequate freedom to develop their

[314] *Palazzolo v. Coastal Resources Management Council*, 1995 WL 941370 (R.I. Super. Ct. 1995), *aff'd on other grounds*, 746 A.2d 707 (R.I. 2000) (holding that filling 11.4 acres of salt marsh would constitute a public nuisance because it would reduce shellfish populations and harm filtering mechanisms, resulting in increased nitrate levels in a pond and a threat to the groundwater drinking supply).

[315] *See, e.g., Gardner v. New Jersey Pinelands Commission*, 593 A.2d 251 (N.J. 1991) (upholding legislation that protected pinelands by preventing residential development and allowing only agricultural uses despite the large decrease in the property's market value as a result; the legislation served the purposes of preventing harm to the public and conserving areas of ecological sensitivity, natural beauty, and cultural importance); *Presbytery of Seattle v. King County*, 787 P.2d 907 (Wash. 1990) (upholding wetlands protection regulations that prevented the owner from building a church on the property so long as the owner was not deprived of all economically viable use of the property); *Just v. Marinette County*, 201 N.W.2d 761 (Wis. 1972).

[316] *Florida Rock Indus., Inc. v. United States*, 45 Fed. Cl. 21, 27 (1999); *Bowles v. United States*, 31 Fed. Cl. 37 (1994); *Formanek v. United States*, 26 Cl. Ct. 332, 335 (1992); *Loveladies Harbor, Inc. v. United States*, 28 F.3d 1171, 1179 (Fed. Cir. 1994) (*Loveladies Harbor III*); *Loveladies Harbor, Inc. v. United States*, 21 Cl. Ct. 153 (1990) (*Loveladies Harbor II*); *Loveladies Harbor, Inc. v. United States*, 15 Cl. Ct. 381 (1988) (*Loveladies Harbor I*).

land. Similarly, the public nuisance doctrine has generally been used to prevent conduct that is criminal or, by itself, harmful to the community. In addition, public nuisance cases have always left the owner economically viable use of her own land. Although protection of wetlands is an important public purpose, the contributions of individual owners to their destruction are sufficiently small and the distribution of burdens from wetlands regulation sufficiently unequally distributed, that it is arguably unfair to require owners to suffer the loss of the ability to use their land without compensation. ◀

▶ **HARD CASE** ▷ TAKING OF MOST OF THE PROPERTY VALUE

Should the *Lucas* rule apply if a regulation protecting wetlands takes 95 percent of the economic value of property rather than 100 percent? A number of courts have held that no taking occurs unless an owner is denied all economically viable use.[317] This is probably a misreading of *Agins* and *Lucas*, which hold that deprivation of all economically beneficial use may well constitute a taking, but which do not hold that a taking will *only* be found in such cases. Neither *Agins* nor *Lucas* overruled *Penn Central* or other cases establishing the multifactor balancing test. However, the question remains whether the *Lucas* rule should extend to cases involving substantial deprivation of economic value but not deprivation of all conceivable uses.

Argument that compensation is required

In a number of cases involving wetlands, the Court of Federal Claims has held that denials of permits to fill in wetlands have constituted takings of property even though the property retained some market value. In *Formanek v. United States*,[318] for example, the Claims Court held that owners who were denied a permit to fill their wetlands by the Army Corps of Engineers under the *Clean Water Act* had suffered a taking of property when their property value was reduced from $933,921 to around $112,000. They had bought the property for industrial development and although it had value as a nature preserve, the court found that their legitimate investment-backed expectations were to develop it for industrial purposes and that they could not have known that their request for a permit would be denied. A similar result was reached in *Bowles v. United States*,[319] in which the court emphasized that "[n]othing in the language of the Fifth Amendment compels a court to find a taking only when the Government divests the total ownership of the property; the Fifth Amendment prohibits the uncompensated taking of private property without reference to the owner's remaining

[317] *Texas Manufactured Housing Ass'n v. Nederland*, 101 F.3d 1095, 1105 (5th Cir. 1996) (finding no taking where there was no showing of deprivation of all beneficial use); *Burnham v. Monroe County*, 738 So. 2d 471, 472 (Fla. Dist. Ct. App. 1999) ("To establish a taking by inverse condemnation, a plaintiff must show that the challenged regulation denies all economically beneficial or productive use of land"); *JWL Investments, Inc. v. Guilford County Bd. of Adjustment*, 515 S.E.2d 715, 719 (N.C. Ct. App. 1999) ("all economically beneficial or productive use" must be denied for there to be a taking).

[318] 26 Cl. Ct. 332 (1992).

[319] *Bowles v. United States*, 31 Fed. Cl. 37 (1994).

property interests."[320] And in the much-litigated case of *Florida Rock Industries, Inc. v. United States*,[321] the Court of Federal Claims found a taking when an owner was subjected to a severe, but not total, loss of economic value because the prohibited activity (mining for limestone) would not have constituted a nuisance prior to the enactment of wetlands regulations.

Argument that compensation is not required

Even severe deprivations of value are not takings if there is an average reciprocity of advantage (as in the zoning laws upheld in *Euclid*) or if the public interest is sufficiently important. Preventing owners from destroying wetlands is crucial to all owners and to the entire community because of the devastating consequences that loss of such wetlands would entail for the community. The Supreme Court has never required a parcel-by-parcel determination of the burdens and benefits of general regulatory laws, as evident by its approval of historic preservation laws in *Penn Central.* Owners are not entitled to develop their property in ways that destroy wetlands, and the federal and state governments should have the power to prevent such development without compensating owners who threaten to inflict harm on the community. ◀

▷ PURCHASE AFTER REGULATORY LAWS ARE IN EFFECT **HARD CASE ◀**

Argument that no compensation is owed

In *Good v. United States*,[322] an owner purchased lands for development knowing that he would have to obtain a permit to develop the lands and that, under current law, development might not be permitted on wetlands. The owner argued that the permit denial left him no economically viable use of the property and that, under *Lucas*, he was entitled to compensation. The Federal Circuit disagreed, holding that *Lucas* did not dispense with the requirement that an owner have "reasonable investment backed expectations." An owner who purchases after a specific regulatory law is put into effect cannot reasonably expect to develop in violation of the law.[323] Thus, any such expectations are unreasonable and the owner is not entitled to compensation, even if the land is left no economically viable use. When property is subject to regulation

[320] *Id.* at 45 (*quoting Florida Rock Industries, Inc. v. United States*, 18 F.3d 1560, 1568 (Fed. Cir. 1994)).

[321] *Florida Rock Indus., Inc. v. United States*, 45 Fed. Cl. 21 (1999). Here is the history of the case: *Florida Rock Indus., Inc. v. United States*, 8 Cl. Ct. 160 (1985) (*Florida Rock I*), *rev'd in part and remanded in Florida Rock Indus., Inc. v. United States*, 791 F.2d 893 (Fed. Cir. 1986), *cert. denied*, 479 U.S. 1053 (1987) (*Florida Rock II*), *on remand, Florida Rock Indus., Inc. v. United States*, 21 Cl. Ct. 161 (1990) (*Florida Rock III*), *rev'd in part, Florida Rock Indus., Inc. v. United States*, 18 F.3d 1560 (Fed. Cir. 1994), *on remand, Florida Rock Indus., Inc. v. United States*, 45 Fed. Cl. 21 (1999).

[322] 189 F.3d 1355 (Fed. Cir. 1999).

[323] *Accord, Creppel v. United States*, 41 F.3d 627, 632 (Fed. Cir. 1994) ("One who buys with knowledge of a restraint assumes the risk of economic loss"); *Loveladies Harbor, Inc. v. United States*, 28 F.3d 1171, 1179 (Fed. Cir. 1994) ("In legal terms, the owner who bought with knowledge of the restraint could be said to have no reliance interest, or to have assumed the risk of any economic loss. In economic terms, it could be said that the market had already discounted for the risk, so that a purchaser could not show a loss in his investment attributable to it"); *Palazzolo v. Coastal Resources Management Council*, 746 A.2d 707, 716 (R.I. 2000) (holding that regulations in effect when one purchases land limit the owner's rights and thus "the right to fill wetlands was not part of the title he acquired").

when an owner buys, that regulation becomes part of the background principles of property law applicable to that property; because no one has a right to violate existing regulations, such a right could never have been part of the owner's property rights in the first place. *Lucas* itself holds that deprivation of all economically viable use is permissible if the challenged conduct was never part of the owner's property rights in the first place. An owner who purchases property, knowing that an existing statute prohibits the use contemplated by the purchaser, never had the right to use the property in violation of established law. Thus, she has not been deprived of any property rights to which she was entitled under the law in existence at the time she bought. Such an owner should not be able to buy at a discounted price (because of the regulatory limits on development) and then double-dip by receiving compensation from the state for the regulation's effect on the market value of the property.[324] A similar argument was accepted by the Rhode Island Supreme Court in *Palazzolo v. State ex rel. Tavares.*[325]

Argument that compensation may be owed

The Supreme Court reversed the Rhode Island Supreme Court ruling in *Palazzolo*, on the ground that deprivation of all economically viable use should not be allowed even if an owner bought the property after enactment of the regulation, unless the regulation fits within the *Lucas* nuisance or "background rule" exception. A total deprivation of economic value is akin to a physical ouster and thus should arguably not be constitutional unless it prevents harm or prohibits the owner from engaging in other activities that were never within the owner's property rights in the first place. If this protection were not in place, the state could simply pass a law stating that all land is now subject to future land use restrictions that might destroy its economic viability. The state should not be able to evade the takings clause so easily. Retroactive regulatory laws may be imposed on existing land use, but if those laws go so far as to deprive the owner of economically viable use, the owner's rights have been taken as surely as if she were ousted from the land. Such a complete deprivation should not be countenanced unless it is justified as an inherent limit to the rights of owners.

The vote in *Palazzolo* was splintered, however, with the Justices disagreeing about whether and to what extent it should matter that a regulatory law was in place at the time an owner purchased or gained title to the land. While Justice O'Connor suggested that the timing of a regulatory enactment does matter because it affects the reasonableness of investment-backed expectations,[326] Justice Scalia argued that the investment-backed expectations "that the law will take into account do not include the assumed

[324] *See Palazzolo v. Coastal Resources Management Council*, 746 A.2d 707, 716 (R.I. 2000) (noting the possibility of "pernicious 'takings claims' based on speculative purchases in which an individual intentionally purchases land, the use of which is severely limited by environmental restrictions, and then seeks compensation from the state for that 'taking'").

[325] 746 A.2d 707 (R.I. 2000), *aff'd in part and rev'd in part sub nom. Palazzolo v. Rhode Island*, 533 U.S. 606 (2001), *on remand sub nom. Palazzolo v. State*, 785 A.2d 561 (R.I. 2001), *on remand, Palazzolo v. State*, 2005 WL 1645974 (R.I. Super. Ct. 2005). *Accord, MHC Financing Ltd. P'ship v. City of San Rafael*, 714 F.3d 1118 (9th Cir. 2013) (effect of rent control law to be determined by reference to the laws in effect at the time the owner purchased the land, not by reference to a completely unregulated property).

[326] 533 U.S. at 632-633.

validity of a restriction that in fact deprives property of so much of its value as to be unconstitutional."[327] ◀

▷ GRAVE PROTECTION LAWS **HARD CASE** ◀

In *Hunziker v. State*,[328] a lot owner was prevented from building a house on his lot when excavators discovered an American Indian burial mound made between 1,000 and 2,500 years ago in the middle of his property. A state statute in effect at the time the developer—and later the lot owner—purchased the land authorized the state archeologist to prohibit owners from disinterring human remains found on private land if they had historic significance. The archeologist so found and required a buffer zone around the mound to protect its continued existence.[329] The original developers of the subdivision refunded the purchase price and took back title and then sued the state, claiming that their inability to develop the lot deprived them of all economically viable use and that the statute, as applied to the lot, constituted a taking of property. The court held that the *Lucas* rule did not apply because the restriction on developing property where human beings are buried was part of the law of Iowa at the time the owner purchased the land and thus "inhered in the title." Because the law did not allow development in these circumstances, the owner could not have had a legitimate expectation of being able to so develop the property.

Counterargument

If the land has no economic value, this means that the owner who owned the property at the time the regulation was put into effect arguably would have a takings claim because such an owner would not be able to find a willing buyer. However, that owner *did* sell the property because it was not until excavation occurred that anyone could have known that an historically significant burial mound would be there. Thus, the current owner is deprived of all economically viable use and could not have known that it would not be able to develop the land. There is no average reciprocity of advantage. Moreover, if the state can pass a law stating that all property is subject to the possibility of being deprived of all economic value by new legislation, and thereby immunize itself from takings claims in the future, the takings clause would be deprived of all force. ◀

▷ INADVERTENT HARM **HARD CASE** ◀

Inadvertent flooding

Are governments liable for takings of property when they inadvertently or negligently cause damage to property? *Pumpelly v. Green Bay Co.*[330] held that a taking has occurred if the government constructs a dam it knows will

[327] *Id.* at 637.
[328] 519 N.W.2d 367 (Iowa 1994).
[329] Iowa Code §263B.9 (previously Iowa Code §305A.9). *See also* Vt. Stat. tit. 13, §3761 (making it a crime to intentionally remove or dig up human remains unless authorized by law to do so).
[330] 80 U.S. 166 (1872).

flood property. But is there a taking if the harm is neither intended nor an inevitable result of the project? *Pacific Bell v. City of San Diego*[331] held that a city had taken property when a pipe leading to a fire hydrant corroded and burst, flooding a house, because the "city's water delivery system was deliberately designed, constructed, and maintained without any method or program for monitoring the inevitable deterioration of cast iron pipes other than waiting for a pipe to break." Similarly, Hurricane Katrina led to the destruction of much of New Orleans, and it has been argued that the damage was partly caused by negligent construction of levees and the water drainage system, as well as design flaws in the canal system in the city that caused the erosion of wetlands and channeled water into particular areas of the city. If the homeowners in New Orleans could prove that the flooding that destroyed most of the property in the city would not have occurred if the flood control system had been designed, built, and maintained better, do they have a takings claim against the federal government, which designed the flood control system in the city? *Nicholson v. United States*[332] answered this question in the negative on the ground that a taking occurs only if the government intends to invade a property interest or the harm is the "direct, natural, or probable result of an authorized activity and not the incidental or consequential injury inflicted by the action. . . ."[333] On one hand, it would seem that government building projects that sacrifice the interests of some owners to benefit the community should ensure the fair distribution of the burdens and benefits of those projects. On the other hand, opening up the government to such takings claims creates a conceivably vast and unpredictable range of liability for ordinary government programs, depriving the government of the ability to use its police power in a sensible way.[334] ◀

▶ HARD CASE ▷ TEMPORARY BUILDING MORATORIUM

***Tahoe-Sierra Preservation Council, Inc. v. Tahoe Regional Planning Agency* (2002)**

In *Tahoe-Sierra Preservation Council, Inc. v. Tahoe Regional Planning Agency*,[335] real estate owners around Lake Tahoe challenged development moratoria totaling 32 months during which the planning agency sought to formulate a comprehensive land use plan for the area. The owners claimed that a total ban on development, even if temporary, constituted a *per se* taking of property. They relied on the *Lucas* decision, arguing that a ban

331 96 Cal. Rptr. 2d 897 (Ct. App. 2000).

332 77 Fed. Cl. 605 (2007).

333 *Id.* at 617. *See also Knutson v. City of Fargo*, 714 N.W.2d 44, 48-49 (N.D. 2006) (*quoting Pacific Bell v. City of San Diego*, 96 Cal. Rptr. 2d 897, 909 (Ct. App. 2000) (although a taking may occur when harm to private property is caused by a "*deliberate act* for the purpose of fulfilling one of the public objects of the project as a whole, [it is also true that] *negligent acts* committed during the *routine day-to-day operation* of the public improvement or *negligence in the routine operation* having no relation to the functioning of the project as conceived *does not create a claim in inverse condemnation*") (emphasis added by *Knutson*)).

334 *Cf. Alford v. United States*, 961 F.3d 1380 (Fed. Cir. 2020) (rejecting complaint by owners that the Army Corps of Engineers took their properties by temporarily flooding a nearby lake, knowing it would damage their property because the government was acting to forestall even greater damage from a breach of a levee, and thus was protecting, not taking, their property).

335 535 U.S. 302 (2002).

on development deprived them of all economically viable use of their land during the time when the ban was in place. The Supreme Court disagreed, refusing to find the temporary development moratorium to constitute a categorical taking of property rights. Noting that Lake Tahoe was known for its exceptional clarity and that if development continued to increase the impervious coverage of land in the area, this clarity would be lost and it "could take over 700 years for it to return to its prior state, if that were ever possible at all."[336] "Resisting 'the temptation to adopt what amount to *per se* rules in either direction,' we conclude that the circumstances in this case are best analyzed within the *Penn Central* framework."[337] This meant, of course, that on remand, the lower courts would have to apply the *Penn Central* three-factor test to determine the regulatory takings question. This test is "characterized by essentially ad hoc, factual inquiries, designed to allow careful examination and weighing of all the relevant circumstances."[338] While one can argue that preventing the loss of the incredible beauty of the lake is a legitimate government purpose, it can also be argued that any permanent ban on construction would effectuate a taking of the owners' property for the benefit of the public by depriving them of all economically viable use of their land. ◀

▷ TEMPORARY FLOODING **HARD CASE ◀**

Arkansas Game & Fish Comm'n v. United States **(2012)**

In *Arkansas Game & Fish Comm'n v. United States*,[339] the Supreme Court held that government-induced flooding may be a taking despite the fact that it is temporary. While it is clear under *Pumpelly v. Green Bay Co.*[340] that permanently flooding property or doing so in a repeated seasonal manner results in a taking, temporary flooding may or may not be a taking. The Federal Circuit had held that no taking occurs if the flooding is temporary because such an interference does not permanently deprive the owner of property rights. The Supreme Court reversed, holding that the temporary nature of the taking does not immunize the government from a compensation claim. Relevant factors include the amount of time the flooding endures, whether the invasion is intended or is the foreseeable result of government action, the character of the land, and the owner's reasonable investment-backed expectations. ◀

▷ MAP ACTS AND TAKINGS LIMBO **HARD CASE ◀**

Kirby v. N.C. Dep't of Transp. **(N.C. 2016)**

In *Kirby v. North Carolina Department of Transportation*,[341] the North Carolina Supreme Court held that the state took property without just

[336] *Id.* at 308 n.3.
[337] *Id.* at 321 (*quoting Palazzolo v. Rhode Island*, 533 U.S. 606, 636 (2001) (O'Connor, J., concurring)).
[338] *Id.* at 322 (citations omitted).
[339] 568 U.S. 23 (2012).
[340] 80 U.S. 166 (1872).
[341] 786 S.E.2d 919 (N.C. 2016).

compensation under the state constitution when it published maps showing where roads would be placed in the future and what properties would have to be taken to enable those roads to exist. The underlying statute imposes restrictions on properties identified on the official maps as likely to be taken for road purposes. No owner is allowed to obtain a building permit or a subdivision approval, although owners can apply for hardship exceptions to the building permit limitation. On the other hand, property tax relief is also provided to these owners. Publication of the map does not mean the property actually will be taken; the state Department of Transportation is not obligated to build or complete the highway project.

The Map Act could be justified as a legitimate regulation because it did not interfere with any existing use of the property but merely prohibited new construction. Nor did it impede sale or inheritance of the listed properties. Any future owner would be compensated with fair market value if the property were ever taken. There is always a period after a government entity begins considering taking property for public uses and before the actual taking, and owners are not generally entitled to extra compensation for lost property rights during this period when their existing uses continue unabated. However, the court held that the Map Act did effect a taking without just compensation under the state constitution because the published maps were part of projects designed to take property for public purposes and because an "indefinite restraint on fundamental property rights is squarely outside the scope of the police power."[342] Those restraints included limits on the owners' "rights to improve, develop, and subdivide their property for an indefinite period of time."[343] How do the limitations on these owners differ from a law that downzones an area of town to restrict development beyond what is allowed in the neighboring zone? Perhaps the area under consideration is more limited and the owners are singled out in a way that is not typical of zoning law, or it could be that the properties are under an imminent threat of being taken by the government rather than left in control of the owners. ◀

▶ HARD CASE ▷ COVID-19 BUSINESS RESTRICTIONS

Early in the COVID-19 pandemic that emerged in 2020, various states and local governments issued stay-at-home orders and mandatory business closures for non-essential businesses, to limit the spread of a highly contagious airborne disease. Business owners filed suit to challenge these closure orders to protect the public from COVID-19 as regulatory takings of property. Generally, the courts have rejected these challenges, finding that temporary limitations on the right to use property in the face of a public health emergency do not require compensation.[344] ◀

342 *Id.* at 925.

343 *Id.* at 926.

344 *See, e.g., Friends of Danny DeVito v. Wolf*, 227 A.3d 872, 895-896 (Pa.), *cert. denied*, 141 S. Ct. 239 (2020) (relying on *Tahoe-Sierra Pres. Council, Inc. v. Tahoe Regional Planning Agency*, 535 U.S. 302 (2002) and holding that the relevant order "results in only a temporary loss of

§14.6.2 Established Property Rights

§14.6.2.1 Core Property Rights. A majority of Justices on the Supreme Court affirmed in the 2010 case of *Stop the Beach Renourishment, Inc. v. Florida Department of Environmental Protection* that the Constitution provides protection for "established property rights."[345] While that case involved the contested question whether a common law ruling could ever constitute a taking of property,[346] it reflected the intuition that certain property rights are so central to an owner's justified expectations that deprivation of them may go beyond mere regulation of property and become an unconstitutional deprivation of a core property right. Four examples of such core property rights that cannot be taken without just compensation are (a) the right to pass on property at death;[347] (b) the right to earn interest on one's principal;[348] (c) the right to collect surplus home equity after tax foreclosure;[349] and (d) the right to recover land free of an easement at the natural termination of the easement.[350]

Right to pass on property at death

(a) The right to pass on property at death. The Supreme Court has effectively ruled that a state cannot transform an inheritable fee simple into a life estate. Because a fee simple (or the equivalent property right) gives the owner the power to leave the property at death by devise or inheritance, a law that takes that power away denies the owner a core property right. The 1987 case of *Hodel v. Irving*[351] held that this cannot be accomplished without just compensation for the lost property right. The issue arose in the context of property rights held by citizens of Indian nations. In the late nineteenth century and early twentieth century, Congress passed laws "allotting" tribally owned land to individual tribal members. These allotments created individual property rights but, like the tribal lands, were subject to an absolute restraint on alienation that could be waived only by the United States. Allotments were held in trust in an estate in land that applies to land held by Indian nations or their citizens. The lands could be inherited but not alienated without federal consent. Because many allottees did not write wills, many allotments were inherited by children and, over time, the number of owners of each allotment grew, sometimes into the hundreds or even thousands. Such fractionated ownership is problematic because it is difficult for the land to be used for anything other than leasing

***Hodel v. Irving* (1987)**

the use of the Petitioners' business premises," with the government's "reason for imposing said restrictions on the use of their property, namely to protect the lives and health of millions of Pennsylvania citizens, undoubtedly constitut[ing] a classic example of the use of the police power to protect the lives, health, morals, comfort, and general welfare of the people") (citation omitted).

345 *Stop the Beach Renourishment, Inc. v. Fla. Dep't of Envtl. Prot.*, 560 U.S. 702, 716 (2010); *id.* at 735 (Kennedy, J., concurring).

346 *See* §14.7. Four Justices would have applied the takings clause to judicial changes in certain core property rights while two would have applied the due process clause.

347 *Babbitt v. Youpee*, 519 U.S. 234 (1997); *Hodel v. Irving*, 481 U.S. 704 (1987).

348 *Phillips v. Washington Legal Foundation*, 524 U.S. 156 (1998); *Webb's Fabulous Pharmacies, Inc. v. Beckwith*, 449 U.S. 155, 162 (1980).

349 *Tyler v. Hennepin Cnty.*, 598 U.S. 631, 635 (2023).

350 *Marvin M. Brandt Revocable Trust v. United States*, 572 U.S. 93 (2014).

351 481 U.S. 704 (1987).

and because the rents earned by individuals were often so small that the cost of administering the allotments was greater than the earnings from the land. Congress sought to respond to this fractionation problem by passing a statute called the *Indian Land Consolidation Act of 1983*, which provided that any fractional interest in a restricted trust allotment would escheat to the tribe rather than be inherited by the owner's heirs if the interest were less than 2 percent of the total acreage of the tract and had earned the owner less than $100 in the preceding year.

Critique

The Supreme Court treated the property interests in *Hodel* as if they were fee simple interests rather than trust allotments. Restricted trust allotments are a unique form of title, one of the several forms of title recognized in Indian tribes or tribal members. Those property rights are subject to special rules, such as the restraint on alienation, and are held by tribes or tribal citizens subject to the ultimate fee interest held by the United States.[352] Indeed, when Congress passed the allotment acts, it took property from Indian nations and transferred it to tribal members without compensation on the ground that this was a "mere change in the form of investment of Indian tribal property" from communal to individual ownership.[353] It is quite clear that the Supreme Court would not approve a law that took the property of General Motors and transferred it to the shareholders, or that of the Catholic Church to its parishioners, or Harvard University to its alumni. Yet the transfer from tribes to tribal members was approved as constitutional, partly because the Supreme Court has interpreted the Constitution as granting Congress "plenary power" over Indian nations. It is possible that a forced transfer from a tribe to its members would today be held to be an unconstitutional taking of property rather than a "mere change in the form of investment." However, if the original allotment was a mere change in the form of investment, it is not clear why the *1983 Land Consolidation Act* is any different. The Constitution protects communal ownership as much as it protects individual ownership. Of course, it could be argued that, if the owners of fee simple interests have a right to pass on property at death, it would be discriminatory to deny tribal members the same rights. This argument has substantial force but fails to address the unique legal status of restricted trust allotment land, such as the fact that its use is often governed by tribal law, not state law, and that ownership rights are thus qualified in ways that do not exist in the context of fee simple property held by non-Indians.

Congress responded to the litigation in *Hodel v. Irving* by passing a new statute designed to respond to certain objections to the *1983 Indian Land Consolidation Act*. The Court had noted that some fractional interests might be very valuable even though they had not generated more than $100 in income in the previous year. The new version of the law provided for escheat to the tribe of interests that were less than 2 percent of the allotment only if they were not capable of producing $100 in income in any one

[352] *See* Chapter 15.

[353] *Lone Wolf v. Hitchcock*, 187 U.S. 553, 568 (1903). For an extended analysis and critique of the *Lone Wolf* case, see §15.4.2.

of the five years after the death of the decedent, and only if the owner had chosen not to devise the interest to another owner of a fractional interest in the same allotment or it were not inherited by such an owner through intestate succession. Further, tribal governments were empowered to pass their own laws governing the disposition of fractional interests. But the Supreme Court liked this law no better than the 1983 version, again striking it down as a taking of property in 1997 in *Babbitt v. Youpee.*[354] The land might be very valuable even if the income generated from it is *de minimis*. In *Babbitt*, the interest in question was valued at $1,239, an amount the Court found "not trivial."[355] More important, the Court held that restricting the class of possible devisees to other owners of fractional interests in the same allotment "shrinks drastically the universe of possible successors"[356] and may well prevent an owner from leaving her property to her children.[357]

***Babbitt v. Youpee* (1997)**

Taking found

The Supreme Court struck down the escheat provision on the ground that it effectively converted an inheritable interest (akin to a fee simple) into a life estate with a remainder in the tribe. Justice O'Connor's opinion noted that the government could regulate inheritance in significant ways — for example, by statutory share legislation, which guarantees a surviving spouse a significant portion of the estate (one-third to one-half) even if this is not the will of the decedent. What was unique about the statute here was that it completely abolished both descent (inheritance by heirs if no will was written) and devise (receipt of title by devisees under a valid will). The Court acknowledged that heirs had no legitimate investment-backed expectations and that most of the allottees had themselves inherited the property rather than investing in it. Moreover, the economic values involved here were minimal. But the character of the government action was deemed determinative: It abolished a "valuable right," *i.e.*, "the right to pass on valuable property to one's heirs."[358] Just as the regulation in *Kaiser Aetna* "destroyed 'one of the most essential sticks in the bundle of rights that are commonly characterized as property — the right to exclude others' [— the] regulation here amounts to virtually the abrogation of the right to pass on a certain type of property — the small undivided interest — to one's heirs."[359] Justice O'Connor distinguished *Andrus v. Allard*,[360] an earlier case that had sustained a federal prohibition on selling eagle feathers even though it completely abolished a traditional property right, *i.e.*, the power to transfer title by sale on the ground that the statute allowed the owner full use of the property they did own.

Interest earned on principal

(b) The right to earn interest on one's principal. *Webb's Fabulous Pharmacies, Inc. v. Beckwith*[361] involved a state statute that allowed a county to take as its own the interest earned on a fund deposited with the court

[354] 519 U.S. 234 (1997).
[355] *Id.* at 243.
[356] *Id.* at 244-245.
[357] *Id.* at 245.
[358] 481 U.S. at 715.
[359] *Id.* at 717.
[360] 444 U.S. 51 (1979).
[361] 449 U.S. 155 (1980).

Webb's Fabulous Pharmacies, Inc. v. Beckwith (1980)

during litigation. The purpose of the litigation was to determine to whom the funds should be paid and in what amounts. The state statute provided that the money deposited in the fund pending litigation remained the private property of the depositor until paid out; it belonged either to that litigant or those who prevailed in the lawsuit. The Court had no objection to charging the owner of the funds a fee for the court's services in managing the fund; nor was there any constitutional objection to imposing fines or civil penalties for violation of legal obligations. However, the Court found no justification for the statutory provision allowing the government to keep the interest earned on the account during the litigation. The Court held that interest earned on principal has historically always belonged to the owner of the principal and is necessarily attached to it. In effect, the Court defined interest as a core property right that cannot be taken from the owner of the principal without compensation. Of course, most required payments of money to the government will not constitute takings; these include, for example, taxes, fees for services, criminal or civil fines, or forfeiture of funds earned through criminal conduct. But no legitimate government interest justified seizing the interest earned on the principal when it was not intended to be a fee for service or other legitimate charge.[362] In what is now a famous quotation, Justice Blackmun explained: "[A] State, by *ipse dixit*, may not transform private property into public property without compensation, even for the limited duration of the deposit in court. This is the very kind of thing that the Taking Clause of the Fifth Amendment was meant to prevent."[363]

Interest on Lawyers Trust Accounts

Phillips v. Washington Legal Foundation **(1998)**

The "interest follows the principal" theory was applied in 1998 in the case of *Phillips v. Washington Legal Foundation*.[364] In that case, a public interest organization challenged a Texas practice, used by almost every state, of requiring lawyers to place client funds held by lawyers in a common pool to generate interest on those funds (so-called Interest on Lawyers Trust Accounts, or IOLTA) so that the interest could be used to help fund legal services for the poor. Texas had argued that the interest earned on the pooled account was not "property" because it was only earned because the state mandated pooling of funds and thus the client lost nothing that she would ever have earned. The Supreme Court held that interest earned on such accounts was "property" belonging to the client whose funds generated the interest even if the client account was so small and the account held by the lawyer for so short a time that it would not have generated any interest unless it were pooled with other such accounts. Justice Rehnquist noted that states generally hold that "interest follows the principal" and that whoever owns the principal also owns the interest.[365]

On remand, however, the trial court held that, even though the interest was *property*, the IOLTA program did not constitute a *taking* of property because the program applied only to client funds that would not have

[362] *Id.* at 163.
[363] *Id.* at 164.
[364] 524 U.S. 156 (1998).
[365] *Id.* at 165 (*citing Webb's Fabulous Pharmacies, Inc. v. Beckwith*, 449 U.S. 155, 162 (1980) for the proposition that "any interest follows the principal").

earned interest absent the program and that the clients therefore "lost nothing of economically realizable value."[366] On appeal when the Supreme Court heard the case for the second time, it held by a 5-4 vote in *Brown v. Legal Foundation of Washington*[367] that although the IOLTA program had "taken property" belonging to the clients, it had not done so "without just compensation." Justice Stevens explained that no compensation was due because the clients would not have earned any interest on their funds absent the IOLTA program; thus their loss of this interest caused them no economic loss and just compensation is measured "by the property owner's loss rather than the government's gain."[368] Further, no compensation is due for the "nonpecuniary consequences" of using the interest for purposes other than those that might have been chosen by the owner.[369] Justice Scalia argued in dissent that the "just compensation owed to former owners of confiscated property is the fair market value of the property taken."[370] Although owners of the interest would not have earned it but for the IOLTA program, the fact is that they earned it, that *Phillips* held that it is "property" within the meaning of the Fourteenth Amendment, and that it has value that can be measured by the amount actually earned and taken by the government.

Brown v. Legal Foundation of Washington **(2003)**

(c) The right to surplus home equity after tax foreclosure. A third example of a core property right is the right to retain any home equity remaining if a person fails to pay their taxes and the government forecloses. Geraldine Tyler, the 94-year-old owner of a one-bedroom condominium in Hennepin County, Minnesota, failed to pay her property taxes after she moved into a senior community, accumulating about $2,300 in unpaid taxes and $13,000 in interest and penalties. To collect these funds, the county invoked the Minnesota forfeiture process and had the condo sold for $40,000. In Minnesota, counties may obtain a judgment against a delinquent owner transferring a limited title to the state, with the taxpayer retaining a right to occupy and redeem the property within three years by paying all taxes and late fees. If the owner is not able to do so, the state obtains absolute title, and the tax debt is extinguished. Under this statute, Hennepin County could retain the $25,000 surplus value in Tyler's property above the amount she owed.[371]

Tyler v. Hennepin County **(2023)**

Tyler challenged this process as an unconstitutional taking of her property. Although the Minnesota law at issue had been in place since 1935, long before Tyler purchased her condo, the Supreme Court held that "state law cannot be the only source" to define property rights protected by the takings clause. Otherwise, "a State could 'sidestep the Takings Clause by disavowing traditional property interests' in assets it wishes to

[366] *Washington Legal Foundation v. Texas Equal Access to Justice*, 86 F. Supp. 2d 624, 643 (E.D. Tex. 2000). *But see Washington Legal Foundation v. Legal Foundation of Washington*, 236 F.3d 1097 (9th Cir. 2001) (striking down the Washington IOLTA program as an unconstitutional taking).

[367] *Brown v. Legal Foundation of Washington*, 538 U.S. 216 (2003).

[368] *Id.* at 235-236.

[369] *Id.* at 236-237.

[370] 538 U.S. at 243.

[371] *Tyler v. Hennepin Cnty.*, 598 U.S. 631, 635 (2023).

appropriate."[372] The Court noted that the "principle that a government may not take more from a taxpayer than she owes can trace its origins at least as far back as" the Magna Carta in 1215 and became rooted in English law,[373] with the federal government and thirty-six states recognizing the principle.[374] Accordingly, the Court unanimously concluded that when the government forecloses on property, the taxpayer is entitled to the surplus realized from a sale in excess of the debt owed.

Marvin M. Brandt Revocable Trust v. United States (2014)

(d) The right to recover land when an easement terminates. A fourth example of a core property right is the right to recover land free from an easement when the easement terminates. In *Marvin M. Brandt Revocable Trust v. United States*,[375] landowners objected when an easement that had been granted for railroad purposes was converted to a trail for public hiking. An easement is a permanent right to use land owned by another for a specific purpose. State law determines how to interpret the scope of the purpose. Some states interpret a general right of way as not only giving the easement owner the right to pass over the land by walking or driving but also a right to install utility lines; other states interpret the scope of the easement narrowly and would view utility lines as exceeding the scope of the easement.[376] In addition, state law determines when an easement ends because of abandonment. Most states find that mere nonuse does not constitute abandonment. However, once state law determines that a use exceeds the scope of the easement or that the easement has ended, the owner of the underlying land has a property right to be free from the intended use of the easement.

In the face of this legal structure, Congress passed a law in 1875 providing railroads rights of way through public lands. Over time, some of those lands were conveyed to private owners; the Brandt family acquired such property in 1976. When the railroad that owned one of those easements formally abandoned the easement, the question arose whether the Brandts owned the property free of the easement or whether title to the land transferred to the United States. The Supreme Court majority held that a prior case had definitively held that the 1875 Act granted the United States the power to convey easements to railroads and that the statute gave no rights in the United States to the underlying land.[377] Justice Sotomayor dissented because she interpreted the prior case as giving the United States more than a mere easement. Instead, she read the statute and the prior case as giving the railroads a fee simple determinable; once the use ended, title reverted to the United States. Determining whether something is an established property right depends on interpreting the legal documents and rules in force at the time the interest was created to determine the existence and scope of the property right.

[372] *Id.* at 638 (quoting Phillips v. Washington Legal Foundation, 524 U.S. 156, 167 (1998)).
[373] *Id.* at 639-40.
[374] *Id.* at 640-42.
[375] 572 U.S. 93 (2014).
[376] *See* §5.3.4.
[377] 572 U.S. at 102-103 (*citing Great Northern Railway Co. v. United States*, 315 U.S. 262 (1942)).

In contrast to *Brandt*, the Federal Circuit found no taking when an elevated railway in New York was converted to a linear park. The court in *Romanoff Equities, Inc. v. United States*[378] found that the language in the 1932 easement was broad enough to encompass various public uses. The easement gave the railroad the right to use the property "for railroad purposes and *for such other purposes* as the Railroad Company, its successors and assigns, *may from time to time or at any time or times desire to make use of the same.*" The court found the grant not to limit uses to railroad purposes and rejected the servient estate owner's claimed right to be free of the park.

▷ PUBLIC PREEMPTIVE RIGHT **HARD CASE ◀**

Massachusetts statutes give cities and towns a right of first refusal for agricultural land. This right allows the municipality to match a bona fide third-party offer for the land when the owner seeks to sell it or an option to purchase the land for its fair market value if the owner seeks to convert to a non-agricultural use. This statutorily conferred right deprives the owner of the power to determine to whom to sell the land by giving the municipality the power to take title upon payment of fair value. An owner might argue that the right to determine to whom to sell one's land is a core property right, and a regulation that completely abolishes that right by vesting the power in state officials to take title when the owner wishes to sell takes that core property right. The state may respond that many statutes limit the right to sell; prime examples are antidiscrimination laws. The owner may respond that *Babbitt v. Youpee*[379] found a taking when the statute completely destroyed the power to pass on property at death despite the fact that statutory share statutes partially limited these rights by protecting the right of a surviving spouse to a significant portion of the property owned by the decedent at the time of death. At the same time, the Massachusetts statute does ensure that the owner receives fair market value of the property at the point when the owner is attempting to sell or convert to another use and just compensation is after all what the Constitution ensures when property is taken. ◀

Protection of investment-backed expectations

Kaiser Aetna v. United States **(1979)**

§14.6.2.2 Vested Rights. *Kaiser Aetna v. United States*[380] held that an owner of a private marina that served fee-paying customers could not be forced to allow free public access to its pond when it connected its private pond to public, navigable waters (the Pacific Ocean). The decision rested partly on the conclusion that the "right to exclude others" was "one of the most essential sticks in the bundle of rights that are commonly characterized as property."[381] However, it was also essential to the decision that the pond had become part of the navigable waters of the United States

[378] *Romanoff Equities, Inc. v. United States*, 815 F.3d 809 (Fed. Cir. 2016).
[379] 519 U.S. 234 (1997).
[380] 444 U.S. 164 (1979).
[381] *Id.* at 176.

only because of a private owner's decision to "invest[] substantial amounts of money in making improvements," which connected the pond to such waters.[382] Forcing the owner to open the pond to the public would interfere with the owner's reasonable investment-backed expectations because the pond had become connected to navigable waters only after substantial investment by the owner that the owner hoped to recoup by fees from members of the marina.

Prior nonconforming uses

The protection of reasonable investment-backed expectations is the core norm behind the zoning cases that hold that prior nonconforming uses may continue after enactment of the law.[383] When a zoning law is first enacted, or when it is amended, it will often be the case that existing uses of many parcels are not in conformity with the new zoning restrictions. For example, an ordinance may restrict uses to residential purposes in a neighborhood that contains a gas station or some retail shops. Such prior nonconforming uses are allowed to continue under state zoning enabling acts partly because it would be an unconstitutional taking of property not to allow the continued existence of such uses.[384] Similarly, a downzoning amendment reducing the allowable height of buildings in an area from four stories to two stories cannot be retroactively applied to an existing three-story building without effecting a taking of property. In addition, once an owner has obtained a building permit and begun substantial expenditures toward construction, a city may not change the zoning classification and rescind the permit because the owner has what is called a *vested right*.[385] This doctrine is less firmly grounded in the Constitution than is the prior nonconforming-use doctrine, but is similarly premised on the idea that it is fundamentally unfair to apply new zoning restrictions laws retroactively on owners who have invested substantially in reasonable reliance on the laws in place at the time they acted.

▶ HARD CASE ▷ PUBLIC TRUST

The vested rights doctrine arguably should not apply in cases in which private property rights are inherently limited. For example, because state law grants the state of Hawai'i continuing authority over its water resources, the Hawai'i Supreme Court has held that the public trust doctrine limits private property rights in water and precludes any grant or assertion of vested rights to use water to the detriment of public trust purposes.[386] If private water rights never included the right to breach the public trust, then no property rights are taken when water rights are limited to protect public

[382] *Id.* at 177.

[383] *See* §13.4.1.

[384] *Testa v. Planning & Zoning Commission of the Town of Newtown*, 2000 WL 1056606 (Conn. Super. Ct. 2000); *O & G Industries, Inc. v. Planning & Zoning Commission*, 232 Conn. 419, 430 (1995); *Standard Materials, Inc. v. City of Slidell*, 700 So. 2d 975, 984 (La. Ct. App. 1997); *BP America, Inc. v. Council of City of University Heights*, 2000 WL 1177508 (Ohio Ct. App. 2000).

[385] *See Glacial Aggregates LLC v. Town of Yorkshire*, 924 N.E.2d 785 (N.Y. 2010). *See* §13.4.2.

[386] *In the Matter of the Water Use Permit Applications*, 9 P.3d 409 (Haw. 2000).

water resources. On the other hand, one can argue that investment in developing such resources creates expectations that constitute vested property rights within the meaning of the Fifth and Fourteenth Amendments, which cannot be divested without compensation, no matter how important the public interest. If the public trust doctrine limits property rights, then there is no limit to the ability of the state to rescind water rights because almost every change could be justified by the need to correctly manage the state's water resources. ◀

Economic legislation

Laws that adjust the burdens of economic life, such as consumer protection laws, workplace regulations, and changes in tort laws that require compensation when one causes harm to others, are hardly ever ruled unconstitutional takings of property. However, some such changes so alter established expectations that they have been challenged as unconstitutional takings of property.[387]

***Eastern Enterprises v. Apfel* (1998)**

In *Eastern Enterprises v. Apfel*,[388] the Supreme Court held in a split decision that a 1992 congressional statute (the *Coal Act*) effected an unconstitutional deprivation of property when it imposed retroactive liability on a coal company to pay health benefits for retired coal miners. That company had signed earlier labor agreements obligating it to contribute certain amounts to trust funds established for this purpose. The 1992 statute required Eastern Enterprises to contribute new funds for health benefits for retired coal miners who had worked for it before 1966 even though it left the coal business in 1966.

A four-Justice plurality would have held that economic regulation such as the 1992 *Coal Act* may effectuate a taking.[389] "Congress has considerable leeway to fashion economic legislation, including the power to affect contractual commitments between private parties."[390] It may even "impose retroactive liability to some degree, particularly where it is 'confined to short and limited periods required by the practicalities of producing national legislation.'"[391] However, such legislation will be unconstitutional "if it imposes severe retroactive liability on a limited class of parties that could not have anticipated the liability, and the extent of that liability is substantially disproportionate to the parties' experience."[392] In this case, the Court found this standard met because plaintiff's new liability of $50 to $100 million was not proportional to its experience with the plan and substantially interfered with Eastern's investment-backed expectations by imposing

[387] *See, e.g., Sienkiewicz v. PennDOT*, 2003 WL 22841693 (Pa. Ct. Com. Pl. 2003) (narrowing of access route to gas station that made it impossible for large trucks to continue to access the station and that put the gas station out of business ruled an unconstitutional taking of property).

[388] 524 U.S. 498 (1998).

[389] Previous cases considering whether economic regulations effect takings include: *Concrete Pipe & Products of Cal., Inc. v. Construction Laborers Pension Trust for Southern Cal.*, 508 U.S. 602 (1993); *Connolly v. Pension Benefit Guaranty Corp.*, 475 U.S. 211 (1986); *Usery v. Turner Elkhorn Mining Co.*, 428 U.S. 1 (1976).

[390] 524 U.S. at 528.

[391] *Id.* (*quoting Pension Benefit Guaranty Corp. v. R.A. Gray & Co.*, 467 U.S. 717, 731 (1986)).

[392] *Id.* at 528-529.

retroactive obligations based on events that happened 30 years earlier. In addition, no pattern of regulation would have placed Eastern on notice that such large, disproportionate, retroactive obligations might be forthcoming.

However, a five-Justice majority agreed that the takings clause was inapposite. Justice Kennedy voted with the four-Justice plurality to hold the *Coal Act* unconstitutional as applied to Eastern. However, he did not believe the takings clause applied to this kind of case. A majority of the Court appears to have agreed with his conclusion that the takings clause applies only to takings of specific property interests, such as interests in real property or interests in a particular identifiable fund of money; it does not apply to general obligations to pay money from whatever funds one possesses. Nonetheless, Justice Kennedy voted with the four-Justice plurality to strike down the law under the due process clause. The Supreme Court has interpreted the Constitution's prohibition on the "deprivation of property without due process of law" to contain a substantive dimension.[393] The due process clause not only requires that adequate procedures be implemented to deprive owners of property (*procedural due process*), such as notice and a hearing, but also prohibits certain types of deprivations from occurring at all (*substantive due process*). Among the substantive protections for property are prohibitions on retroactive legislation. Justice Kennedy argued that the problem with the law in *Eastern Enterprises* was not that it "took" property, but its unfair retroactive nature. "If retroactive laws [of great severity] change the legal consequences of transactions long closed, the change can destroy the reasonable certainty and security which are the very objects of property ownership."[394]

The four other dissenting Justices believed that the *Coal Act* was not unfair retroactive legislation. Justice Stevens noted that, at the time Eastern was in business, there "was an implicit understanding on both sides of the bargaining table that the operators would provide the miners with lifetime health benefits."[395] Subsequent legislation requiring an employer to honor this understanding would not result in any fundamental unfairness. Justice Breyer, joined by four Justices, argued that the *Coal Act* did not violate due process both because Eastern had led its employees to expect that it would take care of them and because it was not unfair to require Eastern to compensate its own workers for medical problems caused by their exposure to coal dust on the job. "Insofar as working conditions created a risk of future health problems for those miners, Eastern created those conditions."[396]

§14.7 Judicial Takings

Takings by changes in common law

Almost all claims that property has been unlawfully "taken" without compensation involve challenges to legislative or administrative actions. Can a judicial interpretation of the common law or a change in a common law

[393] U.S. Const. amend. XIV, §1.
[394] 524 U.S. at 548-549 (Kennedy, J., concurring in the judgment and dissenting in part).
[395] *Id.* at 551 (Stevens, J., dissenting).
[396] *Id.* at 560 (Breyer, J., dissenting).

rule constitute a taking of property?[397] Such a finding would be problematic. Courts define the rights that go along with property ownership through the common law process; if changes in common law rules represented takings of property, the courts could never modernize the law. They might even be disempowered from holding that a prior case was distinguishable. On the other hand, a state supreme court's interpretation of common law *could* unfairly divest owners of rights they had assumed belonged to them, thereby unjustly interfering with investment-backed expectations based on prior case law. If there were no limits to the ability of judges to reinterpret property law, then the takings clause would lose any force. In 2010, four Justices expressed a willingness to find a judge's decision to change the law to constitute a taking of property without just compensation, but the majority refused to adopt such a principle.[398] All agreed that a common law ruling will not constitute a taking if it constitutes a reasonable interpretation of what prior law required in any event.

▷ NATIVE WATER RIGHTS **HARD CASE ◀**

In the 1973 case of *McBryde Sugar Co. v. Robinson*,[399] the Hawai'i Supreme Court overruled a 1930 Territorial Court decision, *Territory v. Gay*,[400] which had held that two sugar plantation owners possessed certain water rights in their land to the exclusion of native Hawaiians who claimed rights of access to the water. The Hawai'i Supreme Court held in *McBryde* that this prestatehood court decision had unlawfully divested native Hawaiians of their traditional customary rights of access to water and that the state had the exclusive right to control the flow of the river in question. In effect, the court held that the 1930 decision had itself taken property rights unlawfully from Native Hawaiians. The property owners whose water rights were divested by the *McBryde* decision brought a federal civil rights suit against state officials, claiming that the court's 1973 decision in *McBryde* effectuated a taking of their property rights. The state defended on the grounds that the *McBryde* court overruled a prior decision in an effort to correct an error, that the overruled decision had itself effectuated a taking of native Hawaiians' property, and that the sugar companies never had rights to the land free of pre-existing water easements. The Ninth Circuit ruled, in *Robinson v. Ariyoshi*,[401] that the *McBryde* decision unconstitutionally took the "vested" property rights of the plantation owners without compensation.[402]

[397] *See* Barton H. Thompson, Jr., *Judicial Takings*, 76 Va. L. Rev. 1449 (1990) (arguing that property owners should be able to challenge common law rulings as takings of property).

[398] *Stop the Beach Renourishment, Inc. v. Fla. Dep't of Envtl. Prot.*, 560 U.S. 702 (2010).

[399] 504 P.2d 1330, 517 P.2d 26 (Haw. 1973).

[400] 31 Haw. 376, 387-388, *aff'd*, 52 F.2d 356 (9th Cir. 1930).

[401] 753 F.2d 1468 (9th Cir. 1984), *aff'g* 441 F. Supp. 559 (D. Haw. 1977), *overruled by Robinson v. Ariyoshi*, 887 F.2d 215 (9th Cir. 1989).

[402] *Robinson* was later overruled on the ground that the claim was not ripe, *i.e.*, that the Hawai'i Supreme Court had not rendered a "final judgment" adjudicating the property rights

Critique

Courts change the common law of property over time. Such changes ordinarily do not constitute takings of property because they are based on the protection of justified expectations and what expectations are justified changes over time, depending on changes in social custom and in social understandings of the meaning of property use and ownership. Common law decisions define the baseline from which owners' expectations arise. Although we do not want a court to unfairly overturn established expectations, we do want courts to modernize common law rules to define property rights in ways that accord with contemporary values. A change in the common law that requires entertainment facilities to serve the public without regard to race is not a taking of property, even though it limits the right to exclude and even though prior law allowed the owner to exclude whomever she wanted to exclude.[403] Here the original decision in *Territory v. Gay* wrongfully divested Native Hawaiians of property rights and the current court should be able to correct the mistake. The Hawai'i Supreme Court did not completely divest water rights from the plantation owners; they retained their right to use the water. It merely required the water to be shared with those from whom it had been unlawfully seized many years earlier. Moreover, the current owners had been wrongfully benefiting from the water for over 40 years to the exclusion of other rightful owners. The court simply made their rights nonexclusive. The court should have been allowed to choose a compromise that allowed all parties to obtain some benefit from the water rather than requiring the court to continue to deny native rights. It is true that two wrongs do not make a right, but it is also true that the refusal to right an historic wrong constitutes a continuing wrong. The court's ruling represented a legitimate compromise between the conflicting claims. ◀

▶ HARD CASE ▷ BEACH ACCESS

In *State ex rel. Thornton v. Hay*,[404] the Oregon Supreme Court applied the common law doctrine of custom in ruling that the public had a right of access to dry sand areas of beaches for recreational purposes. Although the court narrowed this ruling in *McDonald v. Halvorson*,[405] holding that the doctrine of custom applied only to beaches for which proof could be shown of actual public use, it reaffirmed that the ruling applied to beaches for which customary use could be shown. In *Stevens v. City of Cannon Beach*,[406] Oregon beachfront owners charged that the doctrine of custom had been newly announced in *Thornton* in 1969 and that it effectuated a taking of the property of beachfront owners without

---

at issue in the case. *Robinson v. Ariyoshi*, 887 F.2d 215 (9th Cir. 1989), *overruling Robinson v. Ariyoshi*, 753 F.2d 1468 (9th Cir. 1984).

[403] *See Uston v. Resorts International Hotel, Inc.*, 445 A.2d 370 (N.J. 1982).

[404] 462 P.2d 671 (Or. 1969).

[405] 780 P.2d 714 (Or. 1989).

[406] 854 P.2d 449 (Or. 1993).

compensation. The U.S. Supreme Court denied *certiorari*, in *Stevens v. City of Cannon Beach*,[407] but Justices Scalia and O'Connor dissented from that decision, Justice Scalia writing that, although "the Constitution leaves the law of real property to the States," a state may not "deny" property rights "by invoking nonexistent rules of state substantive law."[408] Justice Scalia argued that the Oregon Supreme Court had misapplied the English doctrine of custom. "It is by no means clear that the facts — either as to the entire Oregon coast, or as to the small segment at issue here — meet the requirements for the English doctrine of custom."[409] He explained:

***Stevens v. City of Cannon Beach* (1994)**

> Our opinion in *Lucas*, for example, would be a nullity if anything that a State court chooses to denominate "background law" — regardless of whether it is really such — could eliminate property rights. "[A] State cannot be permitted to defeat the constitutional prohibition against taking property without due process of law by the simple device of asserting retroactively that the property it has taken never existed at all." No more by judicial decree than by legislative fiat may a State transform private property into public property without compensation. Since opening private property to public use constitutes a taking, if it cannot fairly be said that an Oregon doctrine of custom deprived Cannon Beach property owners of their rights to exclude others from the dry sand, then the decision now before us has effected an uncompensated taking.[410]

Critique

It is quite odd to say that Oregon got the English doctrine of custom wrong. What the Oregon Supreme Court enforced was the Oregon doctrine of custom, not the English doctrine. It may be that *Thornton* was the first case to adopt the principle, but this does not mean that it was not part of Oregon law before it was announced in *Thornton*. If this were true, then any case of first impression regarding property that limited what owners can do on their land would constitute a taking of property. The common law includes not only the rules announced in decided opinions but also the principles that will be used to decide cases in the future. Courts must be allowed to rule in cases of first impression without subjecting the state to takings claims. Justice Scalia's view appears to be that owners are allowed to do whatever the law does not expressly prohibit them from doing; this reads property law as a series of discrete rules rather than principles that are interpreted and enforced in cases as they are decided over time.[411] Yet many states have evolved their common law of property over time and some of the most important of those evolutions have involved limitations on the right to exclude (such as public accommodations laws and fair housing laws). ◀

[407] 510 U.S. 1207 (1994).

[408] *Id.*

[409] *Id.*

[410] *Id.*

[411] Frank Michelman, *Property, Federalism, and Jurisprudence: A Comment on* Lucas *and Judicial Conservatism*, 35 Wm. & Mary L. Rev. 301 (1993).

▶ HARD CASE

▷BOUNDARIES OF BEACHFRONT PROPERTY AS THE COAST CHANGES

In general, when property borders change because of gradual accretion or erosion along rivers or oceans, owners gain or lose land because of those changes. If land is added to an owner's land by gradual build-up of sand or silt, then the owner's property increases to that extent; the reverse is also true. But if the land changes suddenly ("avulsion"), then the borders do not change.[412] The courts have generally applied these principles to beachfront property to determine the border between the private property rights of beachfront owners and the land owned by the public accessible by anyone.

***Stop the Beach Renourishment, Inc. v. Fla. Dep't of Envt'l Protection* (2010)**

Stop the Beach Renourishment, Inc. v. Florida Department of Environmental Protection[413] challenged a common law rule giving the public access to a new sand area on the beach created by government landfill. While refusing to decide whether a judicial common law ruling could be a taking, the Court unanimously agreed that Florida law did not change borders if a sudden event added more land between a riparian owner and public waters. While the public always had a right to use the wet sand area under the public trust doctrine, it gained a right to use the new dry sand area that was created by the beach renourishment program.

Conversely, the Texas Supreme Court issued a similar ruling in 2012 when beachfront property was suddenly reduced because of Hurricane Rita.[414] In Texas, the boundary between private property and public lands is the mean high tide line. Hurricane Rita moved an owner's house closer to the wet sand area owned by the public. Before the hurricane, her house was landward of the vegetation line; afterward it was on the seaward side but still on the dry sand area. The court held that the dry sand area is not open to the public unless a public easement has been established by express grant, prescription, or dedication. The court noted that a "person purchasing beachfront property along the Texas coast does so with the risk that her property may eventually, or suddenly, recede into the ocean."[415] If that happens gradually, then the property owner loses some or all of her property, and if a house gradually comes to be located on the wet sand area, the state can order its removal from public lands. The reverse is also true; gradual addition to the beach will add to the beachfront owner's property. However, if that line changes suddenly, as it did in this case, then borders remain the same as before.[416]

In this case, that meant that if a public easement has existed over the property in this case, it no longer existed. Because there had never been a public easement over the land where the house sat, that did not change when the hurricane reduced the size of the beach. The private property rights of the homeowner would be retained on her property, and a new

[412] *See* §4.7.6.
[413] 560 U.S. 702 (2010).
[414] *Severance v. Patterson*, 370 S.W.3d 705 (Tex. 2012).
[415] *Id.* at 718.
[416] *Id.* at 722-723.

public easement would have to be established. The Court rejected the idea that a public easement of access to the dry sand area would "roll" with changes in the line between the beach and the sea. Any imposition of such an easement would be a taking of property requiring just compensation. ◀

Effect of gradual and sudden changes in beachfront property

§14.8 Exactions

Conditions on building permits

Exactions are demands made by cities with which property owners must comply to obtain a government permit to build on their land. State courts have long regulated exactions to ensure owners are not forced to agree to unreasonable conditions as the price of being allowed to build or to obtain a special permit or a variance. In two cases, the Supreme Court has held that it may constitute a violation of the takings clause for a city to condition a building permit on an owner's refusal to agree to a condition that is unrelated to the original reason for the land use restriction.

***Nollan v. California Coastal Comm'n* (1987)**

In *Nollan v. California Coastal Comm'n*,[417] the owners of a beachfront lot in California, the Nollans, applied for a special coastal development permit to tear down their dilapidated bungalow and replace it with a three-bedroom house consistent with others in the area. The state coastal development commission granted their request for a permit on condition that they grant the public an easement to walk across their lot on the dry sand area between an eight-foot-high concrete seawall parallel to the ocean and the mean high tide line. They challenged the condition in court as a taking of property and the Supreme Court agreed in a 5-4 vote.

Majority opinion

Justice Scalia noted that it would clearly have constituted a taking for the state to grant a public right of passage over previously private beachfront property because this would constitute a permanent forced physical invasion of property.[418] Assuming this was so, the Court asked whether the state could achieve this result indirectly by refusing to grant a development permit unless the owner dedicated an easement to the public. The Court held that the permit condition would be valid only if there was an "essential nexus" between the permit condition and the reason for the development limitation in the first place. For example, a city agency may legitimately require a university to provide on-site parking in a new building if the city suffers from traffic congestion and a shortage of availability parking spaces in the vicinity and the amount of required parking is reasonably related to the increase likely to be generated by the users of the new structure. However, in this case, the Court found no relationship at all between the permit condition and the evil sought to be avoided by the land use restriction. The state argued that the owners were seeking to expand their structure, and this expansion would harm public interests by blocking the

"Essential nexus" required

[417] 483 U.S. 825 (1987).

[418] *Id.* at 831. We have earlier criticized this reasoning because the Supreme Court held in *Loretto* that a public easement of access was *not* a taking in *PruneYard* because the invasion was merely temporary. *See* §14.6.1.1. After *Cedar Point Nursery*, the Supreme Court has replaced temporary/permanent distinction with other tests for when a seemingly *per se* violation of the takings clause might nonetheless be upheld, including conditional permits.

public's ability to see the beach from the road. However, granting the public a right to walk along the beach helps not at all in enabling the public to see the beach from the road.[419] Here the "lack of nexus between the condition and the original purpose of the building restriction converts that purpose to something other than what it was. The purpose then becomes, quite simply, the obtaining of an easement to serve some valid governmental purpose, but without payment of compensation."[420]

Dissenting opinion

Justice Brennan's dissenting opinion emphasized that "[t]he Coastal Commission, if it had so chosen, could have denied the Nollans' request for a development permit, because the property would have remained economically viable without the requested new development."[421] Instead, it allowed them to intensify the use of coastal land in a manner that would prejudice public interests in preserving the coastline from such development in return for giving something back to the public to make up for the loss. Justice Brennan argued that the courts should generally defer to land use decisions made by state agencies if they are rationally related to legitimate state interests. Part of the problem here is to determine the appropriate level of generality. While the majority found no connection between the permit condition and the initial prohibition, such a connection could easily be found if the reason for the initial prohibition were stated at a higher level of generality. "The Commission is charged to preserve overall public access to the California coastline. It has sought to balance private and public interests and to accept tradeoffs: to permit development that reduces access in some ways as long as other means of access are enhanced."[422] If an intensified development causes loss to public interests in limiting coastal development, that public loss might be compensated by a related public gain in access to the coast.

Because the *Nollan* Court found no "essential nexus" at all between the permit condition and the initial prohibition, it did not address how tight the connection need be between the condition and the prohibition. The Supreme Court answered this question in *Dolan v. City of Tigard.*[423] In *Dolan*, an owner of a plumbing and electric supply store wished to double the size of the store, pave the gravel parking lot, and construct a new retail building on the property. The city granted the building permit on the condition that Dolan dedicate about 10 percent of her land

***Dolan v. City of Tigard* (1992)**

[419] *Id.* at 838 ("It is quite impossible to understand how a requirement that people already on the public beaches be able to walk across the Nollans' property reduces any obstacles to viewing the beach created by the new house.").

[420] *Id.* at 837. *Compare Sparks v. Douglas County*, 904 P.2d 738, 742 (Wash. 1995) (upholding a requirement that a developer dedicate some of its property to widen public streets as a condition of obtaining a development permit because "as a prerequisite for development permission, a regulation may require a landowner to dedicate property rights for public use if the regulatory exaction is reasonably calculated to prevent, or compensate for, adverse public impacts of the proposed development").

[421] 483 U.S. at 844-845 (Brennan, J., dissenting). *Cf. Ruckelshaus v. Monsanto*, 467 U.S. 986 (1984) (holding that it was not an unconstitutional taking to condition the grant of a government permit to use a pesticide on disclosing trade secrets about the composition of the pesticide).

[422] 483 U.S. at 847 (Brennan, J., dissenting).

[423] 512 U.S. 374 (1992).

to the city. The state courts had developed three different tests to judge the legitimacy of exactions. Some courts required that the exaction bear a very general relationship to the asserted state interest; others required a rational or reasonable relationship to the state interest; and still others strictly required states to impose exactions only if they alleviated harms that were "specifically and uniquely attributable" to the proposed development. In *Dolan*,[424] the Court adopted a test somewhat like the middle position: There must not only be some relationship between the permit condition and the projected impact of the development (an "essential nexus," as *Nollan* put it), but there must also be some "rough proportionality" between the permit condition and the projected impact of the proposed development to satisfy the takings clause. Although no precise mathematical calculation is required, the Court did require municipalities to make some sort of individualized determination that the required dedication was related both in nature and extent to the impact of the proposed development.

Majority opinion

In this case, the Court rejected the city's explanations for the permit conditions. Because the development would increase the amount of impervious surface on the land and thus exacerbate flooding problems, Dolan was required to dedicate some of her land to the city to remove it from development. However, the city could have achieved its aim simply by preventing her from building or paving over the part of her land that was situated on the floodplain; there was no need for the city to take title to that property. In addition, the city required her to dedicate an easement to the public for use as a bike or pedestrian path on the ground that her intensified development would increase traffic and that a public path would help to alleviate that problem. The Court found that the city had made no individualized determination sufficient to conclude that the bike path actually *would* alleviate the traffic problem associated with the development because the city had only concluded that it "could" help.

Monetary exactions

Some municipalities impose a tax or fee on certain classes of developers to mitigate negative externalities of their proposed development, such as environmental damage or reduction in the availability of low-income housing. It was unclear for some time whether the holdings in *Nollan* and *Dolan* apply to such fees at all; some courts had held that the *Nollan-Dolan* rule applies only to required dedications of land.[425] However, most courts applied the *Nollan-Dolan* test to monetary exactions,[426] and the Supreme Court approved that approach in the 2013 case of *Koontz v. St. Johns River Water Mgmt. Dist.*,[427] which involved a developer who sought to mitigate

***Koontz v. St. Johns River Water Mgmt. Dist.* (2013)**

[424] *Id.*

[425] *Garneau v. City of Seattle*, 147 F.3d 802 (9th Cir. 1998); *Blue Jeans Equities West v. City & County of San Francisco*, 4 Cal. Rptr. 2d 114 (Ct. App. 1992). This approach finds some basis in the decision in *City of Monterey v. Del Monte Dunes at Monterey, Ltd.*, 526 U.S. 687 (1999), in which the Court characterized its opinions in *Nollan* and *Dolan* as applying to exactions and defining exactions as "land-use decisions conditioning approval of development on the dedication of property to public use." Id. at 702-703.

[426] *Erlich v. Culver City*, 911 P.2d 429 (Cal. 1996), *on remand from* 512 U.S. 1231 (1994); *Benchmark Land Co. v. City of Battle Ground*, 14 P.3d 172 (Wash. Ct. App. 2000).

[427] 570 U.S. 595 (2013).

the environmental impact of his development by granting a water management district a conservation easement on nearly three-quarters of his property. The district refused to grant him a development permit unless he reduced the size of his development, gave the district a conservation easement on the rest of his property, and paid to improve wetlands located several miles away. Koontz claimed the district's demands were excessive in relation to the environmental damage his development would have caused. The Supreme Court held that the *Nollan-Dolan* test was an application of the more general unconstitutional conditions doctrine, which prohibits the government from "deny[ing] a benefit to a person because he exercises a constitutional right."[428] It further held that that doctrine applies to exactions that do not involve required dedications of property to the public but merely money payments. Even if it would not constitute a taking of property to deny an owner the right to develop at all (or in the way he wants to develop), it may violate the takings clause to demand a monetary exaction for a building permit in an amount that bears no reasonable relation to the damage caused by the development. The *Nollan-Dolan* test mandates a "nexus" between the government purpose and the exaction and a "rough proportionality" between the exaction and the social costs being avoided or mitigated.[429]

Unconstitutional conditions doctrine

Nollan, *Dolan*, and *Koontz* all involved government agencies making individualized determinations about particular owners in the permitting process. Some conditions on development, however, involve general conditions that all owners are required to take, such as paying fees to fund mitigation efforts related to traffic engendered by new development or similar linkage requirements. Some courts held that the *Nollan-Dolan* test does not apply to such generalized fees.[430] In *Sheetz v. County of El Dorado*,[431] the Supreme Court disagreed. The case involved schedule of traffic-mitigation impact fees adopted by rural El Dorado County, California, that required George Sheetz to pay $23,420 for permission to erect a prefabricated single-family home on land he owned. The Court held that *Nollan-Dolan* exactions analysis applies to legislative permit conditions, as much as it does to individualized administrative determinations.[432]

▶ HARD CASE ▷ INCLUSIONARY ZONING

Inclusionary zoning programs require developers to set aside a portion of the units they sell as affordable housing. Those units are normally sold subject to covenants that require them to be used only for low- or moderate-income families. Such regulations have been challenged as takings of property either because they amount to physical invasions by strangers

[428] *Koontz v. St. Johns River Water Mgmt. Dist.*, 570 U.S. 595, 603-605 (2013).
[429] *Id.* at 599.
[430] *See, e.g., San Remo Hotel L.P. v. City & Cnty. of S.F.*, 41 P.3d 87, 102-03 (Cal. 2002), *aff'd on other grounds*, 545 U.S. 323 (2005).
[431] 601 U.S. 267 (2024).
[432] *Id. at 279.*

or because developers are not responsible for poverty or the shortage of affordable housing and thus should not be singled out to provide it.

Inclusionary zoning requirements may be valid, despite the *Nollan-Dolan* rule on the ground that they represent legitimate general land use regulations and that the forced inclusion of poor residents is no more a taking than is a fair housing ordinance requiring those in the housing business to rent or sell without regard to race.[433]

In 2015, the California Supreme Court upheld an inclusionary zoning ordinance that required developers to set aside 15 percent of their on-site for-sale units for affordable housing prices. *Cal. Bldg. Indus. Ass'n v. City of San Jose*[434] held that this requirement was not a violation of the takings clause and that government had no obligation to prove that the restrictions on a particular owner were reasonably related to the impact of that particular development. The court held that inclusionary zoning is not an "exaction" that is subject to the unconstitutional conditions doctrine elaborated in *Koontz*. The inclusionary zoning obligation is not based solely on mitigating the development's impact on the availability of affordable housing, but on two other distinct government purposes: "(1) *increasing the number of affordable housing units in the city* in recognition of the insufficient number of existing affordable housing units in relation to the city's current and future needs, and (2) assuring that new affordable housing units that are constructed *are distributed throughout the city as part of mixed-income developments* in order to obtain the benefits that flow from economically diverse communities and avoid the problems that have historically been associated with isolated low income housing."

***Cal. Bldg. Indus. Ass'n v. City of San Jose* (Cal. 2015)**

The court held that neither the *Nollan-Dolan* principle nor the *Koontz* principle was relevant to inclusionary zoning. The court argued that inclusionary zoning is a regulation of land use and neither requires dedication of property to the public (as occurred in the easements in *Nollan* and *Dolan*) nor a monetary exaction. Inclusionary zoning is closer to a rent control ordinance that regulates the prices at which housing can be provided to the public or an antidiscrimination ordinance that requires offering property to particular persons, neither of which is an unconstitutional taking. The court also noted that cities are entitled to determine where particular uses of property are allowed, such as residential or commercial; such regulations are no different from an ordinance that limits property to affordable housing. Nor did it matter that a developer could avoid the 15 percent obligation by paying a fee because neither obligation was solely premised on mitigating the externalities of the development.[435] ◀

[433] *Home Builders Ass'n v. City of Napa*, 108 Cal. Rptr. 2d 60 (Ct. App. 2001) (*Nollan-Dolan* rule does not apply to legislative land use regulations); *Holmdel Builders Association v. Holmdel*, 583 A.2d 277 (N.J. 1990) (upholding inclusionary zoning requirements on the ground that "[w]e find a sound basis to support a legislative judgment that there is a reasonable relationship between unrestrained nonresidential development and the need for affordable residential development").

[434] 351 P.3d 974 (Cal. 2015).

[435] *Id.* at 1002.

§14.9 Takings Legislation

Assessment, relief, and compensation statutes

Four kinds of legislation have been passed relevant to takings law: (1) assessment; (2) conflict resolution; (3) injunctive relief; and (4) compensation.[436] Assessment statutes require government entities to consider the impact of regulations on private property owners before promulgating them to avoid unconstitutional takings of property. Statutes providing for injunctive relief allow owners to obtain court orders preventing enforcement of regulations in regard to their particular lots, and compensation statutes provide for damages for deprivation of economic value caused by a regulation. Some of these statutes limit their scope to regulatory takings as defined by the U.S. Supreme Court under the federal constitution.[437] Others define "regulatory takings" much more broadly and include laws that reduce the value of property, but that would not constitute takings under the Fifth or Fourteenth Amendments.[438]

Assessment laws

Federal law

State laws

In 1988, President Reagan issued an executive order that requires all federal agencies to conduct a "takings impact analysis" of all regulations that may affect the use of private property to avoid government actions that might result in an unconstitutional taking of property.[439] At least 15 states require administrative agencies to review regulatory rules if an owner challenges them as regulatory takings or if they reduce property value by a certain amount.[440] Some states now mandate a "formal process for dialogue between regulatory agencies and affected landowners," such as requiring a period in which the landowner and regulatory agency must negotiate before the owner can bring suit.[441]

State takings laws providing injunctive relief
Texas Private Real Property Rights Preservation Act

Texas has adopted a statute that allows owners relief from enforcement of statutes that lower the value of their property in certain cases, even if those deprivations do not constitute unconstitutional takings of property. Entitled the *Private Real Property Rights Preservation Act*,[442] it defines a "taking" of property as a government action that either constitutes a taking within the meaning of the Fifth or Fourteenth Amendments or "restricts or limits the owner's right to [his or her private] property that would otherwise exist in the absence of governmental action" and "is the producing cause of a reduction of at least 25 percent in the market value of the affected

[436] *See* Nestor M. Davidson & Timothy M. Mulvaney, *Takings Localism*, 121 Colum. L. Rev. 215, 236-238 (2021); Mark E. Sabath, *The Perils of the Property Rights Initiative: Taking Stock of Nevada County's Measure D*, 28 Harv. Envtl. L. Rev. 249, 254-261 (2004).

[437] *See* Idaho Code §§67-8001 to 67-8004.

[438] *See* Fla. Stat. §70.001.

[439] Exec. Order No. 12,630, 3 C.F.R. §554 (1988), *reprinted in* 5 U.S.C. §601 (1994).

[440] Del. Code tit. 29, §605; Fla. Stat. §70.001; Idaho Code §§67-8001 to 67-8004; Ind. Code §§4-22-2-31 to 4-22-2-32; Kan. Stat. §§77-701 to 77-711; La. Rev. Stat. §3:3622.1 (forest land); Miss. Code §§49-33-1 to 49-33-17 (agriculture and forestry land); Mo. Rev. Stat. §536.017; Mont. Code §§2-10-101 to 2-10-112; N.D. Cent. Code §28-32-09; Tenn. Code §§12-1-201 to 12-1-206; Tex. Gov't Code §§2007.041 to .045; Utah §§63l-3-101 to 63l-3-202; Wash. Rev. Code §36.70a.370; W. Va. Code §§22-1A-1 to 22-1A-3; Wyo. Stat. §§9-5-301 to 9-5-305.

[441] Mark E. Sabath, *The Perils of the Property Rights Initiative: Taking Stock of Nevada County's Measure D*, 28 Harv. Envtl. L. Rev. 249, 255 (2004). *See, e.g.*, Del. Code tit. 29, §605; Fla. Stat. §70.001(4)(a).

[442] Tex. Gov't Code §§2007.001 to 2007.045.

private real property."[443] The statute gives a right to obtain an injunction invalidating the law as it applies to an owner's property, as well as a right to obtain damages.[444] Regulations that reduce the value of property are exempt from the law (are not considered "takings") in a variety of circumstances. Most important, the law does not apply if a regulation prohibits a public or private nuisance "as defined by background principles of nuisance and property law of this state,"[445] if it is "taken out of a reasonable good faith belief that the action is necessary to prevent a grave and immediate threat to life or property,"[446] or if it "(A) is taken in response to a real and substantial threat to public health and safety; (B) is designed to significantly advance the health and safety purpose; and (C) does not impose a greater burden than is necessary to achieve the health and safety purpose."[447]

Florida *Bert J. Harris, Jr. Private Property Rights Protection Act*

In Florida, the *Bert J. Harris, Jr. Private Property Rights Protection Act of 1995*[448] provides a right to compensation when "a new law, rule, regulation, or ordinance of the state or a political entity in the state, as applied, unfairly affects real property" even though the regulation does not amount to an unconstitutional taking.[449] Compensation is mandated when a government entity has "inordinately burdened an existing use of real property or a vested right to a specific use of real property."[450] The statute defines an "inordinate burden" as permanently preventing an owner from attaining "the reasonable, investment-backed expectation for the existing use of the real property" or "that the property owner is left with existing or vested uses that are unreasonable such that the property owner bears permanently a disproportionate share of a burden imposed for the good of the public, which in fairness should be borne by the public at large,"[451] even if the restriction would not amount to an unconstitutional taking under the Fifth or Fourteenth Amendments, unless the restriction prohibits a public or private nuisance.

State compensation statutes

Two other states, Louisiana and Mississippi, have passed statutes providing for compensation for deprivations of economic value of agricultural lands even when those deprivations do not amount to unconstitutional takings.[452]

Oregon Measure 37

On November 2, 2004, Oregon voters adopted a state law known as *Measure 37* that required compensation when any regulation "restricts the

[443] *Id.* at §2007.002(5).
[444] *Id.* at §2007.023 (injunctive relief invalidating application of the regulation); id. at §2007.024 (damages).
[445] Id. at §2007.003(b)(6). The statute applies only to state laws; it does not apply to cities and counties and hence zoning laws are exempt from its coverage. *Id.* at §2007.003(b)(1).
[446] *Id.* at §2007.003(b)(7).
[447] *Id.* at §2007.003(b)(13).
[448] Fla. Stat. §70.001.
[449] *Id.* at §70.001(1).
[450] *Id.* at §70.001(2).
[451] *Id.* at §70.001(3)(e)(1).
[452] *See* La. Rev. Stat. §3:3602 (providing compensation when a regulation decreases the value of agricultural land by 20 percent or more); Miss. Code §49-33-7 (providing compensation when a regulation decreases the value of agricultural or forest land by more than 40 percent). *See also* Lynda J. Oswald, *Property Rights Legislation and the Police Power*, 37 Am. Bus. L.J. 527 (2000).

use of real property" and is enacted after an owner or a family member acquires title to land if the regulation "has the effect of reducing the fair market value of property" unless the regulation restricts activities "commonly and historically recognized as public nuisances under common law" or protects "public health and safety, such as fire and building codes, health and sanitation regulations, solid or hazardous waste regulations, and pollution control regulations."[453] The measure applied both to statutes and to zoning ordinances.[454] Because the law applies to any regulations passed after an owner (or a family member) acquired title, present owners may go back to the laws in effect at the time their family first acquired the land — for some families, this may go back to a time before any zoning or environmental laws were in effect. This "inheritance right" would mean that zoning in a particular area would be inconsistent if acquired by different families at different times, possibly making each parcel subject to different land use regulations. For this reason — and because it turned out that deregulating neighboring property might lead to a strip mall next to one's house and even have the effect of reducing the value of one's home — Measure 37 proved unpopular in various respects and was substantially modified when Oregon voters passed Measure 49 on November 6, 2007. Measure 49 eliminated the "inheritance right" and restricted Measure 37 claims to laws that restricted restrict residential, farm, or forest uses of property, while allowing, without compensation, laws that limit commercial or industrial uses like strip malls and mines. Measure 49 also limited the number of homes that may be built on property freed from regulation by Measure 37. Claimants may build up to three homes if home construction was allowed when they acquired their properties, whether or not the post-acquisition restriction on construction reduced the value of their land; they may build four to ten homes if a post-acquisition regulation reduced their property value; however, they may not build more than three homes on high-value farmlands, forestlands, and groundwater-restricted lands. And Measure 49 capped at 20 the number of homes sites any owner may build through Measure 37 waivers of land use laws regardless of the amount of property she owns. In 2006, Arizona passed an act similar to Measure 37, known as Proposition 207 or the *Private Property Rights Protection Act.*[455]

Measure 49

Arizona Proposition 207 *(Private Property Rights Protection Act)*

§14.10 Remedies and Procedures for Regulatory Takings

§14.10.1 Remedies for Regulatory Takings

Inverse condemnation

Regulatory takings claims are brought through inverse condemnation, a takings claim by an owner against a public body. In eminent domain cases, the government generally brings a "condemnation" proceeding

[453] Or. Rev. Stat. §195:305; Michael C. Blumm & Erik Grafe, *Enacting Libertarian Property: Oregon's Measure 37 and Its Implications*, 85 Denv. U. L. Rev. 279 (2007).
[454] *See* Or. Rev. Stat. §§195.305 to 195.314.
[455] Ariz. Stat. §12-1134.

against the property and courts set the amount of just compensation. Lawsuits by property owners for damages are the "inverse" of this. One way to remedy a regulatory taking, moreover, is to grant an owner injunctive relief invalidating the restriction. That was the historic practice in the courts for much of the twentieth century, until the Supreme Court's ruling in *First English Evangelical Lutheran Church v. Los Angeles County*[456] held that owners whose property is "taken" by an unconstitutional regulation have the right to be compensated for the lost value of their property during the time when they were illegitimately restricted in their use. The state can choose to rescind the regulation and pay damages for the lost value of the property during the time it was temporarily "taken," or it can choose to enforce the regulation and thus be forced to pay permanent damages.

***First English Evangelical Lutheran Church v. Los Angeles County* (1987)**

§14.10.2 Procedures

Owners may bring takings claims against the federal government in the Court of Federal Claims under a statute called the *Tucker Act*, 28 U.S.C. §1491(a)(1), and such claims are generally required to be brought in the Court of Federal Claims, unless Congress has specified otherwise.[457] Owners challenging state and local regulations may choose to bring suit in state court or in federal court under 42 U.S.C. §1983, a federal statute that authorizes a party who has been deprived of a federal right under the color of state law to seek relief.[458] However, courts have held that inverse condemnation cases against state — as opposed to local — governments are barred in federal court by Eleventh Amendment immunity, requiring such challenges to be brought in state court.[459]

Where owners file inverse condemnation cases

Owners may still assert takings claims, seeking prospective injunctive relief against state officials in federal court under an exception to the sovereign immunity bar that the Supreme Court set out in Ex Parte Young.[460] Under that exception, if a case presents an ongoing violation of federal law, including the Takings Clause, and the relief is prospective — as opposed to seeking damages for past harms — then courts are not barred from

[456] 482 U.S. 304 (1987).

[457] *See Horne v. Department of Agriculture*, 569 U.S. 513, 527 (2013).

[458] *Knick v. Township of Scott*, 588 U.S. 180 (2019); *City of Monterey v. Del Monte Dunes at Monterey, Ltd.*, 526 U.S. 687 (1999). Before *Knick*, the Supreme Court had required owners seeking to bring takings challenges in federal court to state regulations to bring suit in state court first to determine whether the state would provide just compensation. *Williamson County Regional Planning Commission v. Hamilton Bank of Johnson City*, 473 U.S. 172, 194-195 (1985). Because the federal full faith and credit statute, 28 U.S.C. §1738, requires federal courts to give preclusive effect to final state court judgments, *San Remo Hotel L.P. v. City & County of San Francisco*, 545 U.S. 323 (2005), being required to exhaust state-court proceedings meant that owners were generally precluded from proceeding in federal court. *Knick* overturned that requirement.

[459] *See* Gerlach v. Rokita, 95 F.4th 493, 498-500 (7th Cir. 2024); *Ladd v. Marchbanks*, 971 F.3d 574, 578 (6th Cir. 2020); *Bay Point Props., Inc. v. Miss.* Transp. *Comm'n*, 937 F.3d 454, 456-457 (5th Cir. 2019).

[460] 209 U.S. 123 (1908).

proceeding.[461] And challengers may bring federal takings claims against states and local governments under state causes of action.[462]

Ripeness

The Supreme Court has held that a claim in federal court that the government has unconstitutionally taken an owner's property without just compensation is premature (not "ripe") if the agency empowered to regulate the land use at issue has not made a final decision on the scope of the relevant property rights being challenged.[463] In general, this means that an owner must apply for a permit to develop the land and be denied that right in a manner that suggests that further applications will be fruitless. However, this finality requirement does not require claimants to exhaust all available administrative processes to challenge a position taken by a decision maker; just that the decision maker has adopted a definitive position on the scope of the rights at issue.[464]

§14.11 Tribal Property

Tribal property owned by American Indian nations is subject to special takings rules. These rules are best understood in light of the history of federal Indian law and knowledge of the specialized estates in land in which Indian title is held. This topic is thus treated in depth in Chapter 15.

[461] Pharmaceutical Research & Manufacturers of America v. Williams, 64 F.4th 932, 950 (8th Cir. 2023).

[462] DeVillier v. Texas, 601 U.S. 285 (2024).

[463] *MacDonald, Sommer & Frates v. Yolo County*, 477 U.S. 340 (1986).

[464] *Pakdel v. City and County of San Francisco*, 594 U.S. 474 (2021) (per curiam).

PART VI

TRIBAL PROPERTY

CHAPTER 15

American Indian Property

§15.1 Introduction
§15.2 Tribal Title
  §15.2.1 Original Indian Title (Aboriginal Title)
  §15.2.2 Recognized Title
  §15.2.3 Executive Order Title
§15.3 Individual Title
  §15.3.1 Restricted Trust Allotments
  §15.3.2 Assignments
§15.4 Compensability
  §15.4.1 Original Indian Title
  §15.4.2 Recognized Title
  §15.4.3 Executive Order Title
  §15.4.4 Restricted Trust Allotments
§15.5 Protection of Tribal Possession
  §15.5.1 Restraint on Alienation
  §15.5.2 Extinguishment
§15.6 Reparations
  §15.6.1 *Indian Claims Commission Act*
  §15.6.2 Eastern Land Claims
  §15.6.3 Land Claims Settlement Acts
  §15.6.4 Breach of Trust Claims
  §15.6.5 *Native American Graves Protection and Repatriation Act*
§15.7 Tribal Easements
  §15.7.1 Hunting and Fishing Rights
  §15.7.2 Water Rights

§15.1 Introduction

Tribal ownership

All the land in the continental United States was originally owned by American Indian nations.[1] Most of that land was wrested from the tribes by the United States or earlier colonial powers. However, the process by which this occurred is not well understood by most Americans.[2] Nor is the fact that the tribes were, and remain, sovereign powers whose sovereignty is recognized by federal law and is constitutionally protected. Nor is it well understood that most of the land that is still in tribal ownership is subject both to special rules and to special protections imposed by both federal and tribal law. These tribally and federally protected property rights are subject to rules that supersede state law. There were 574 federally recognized Indian nations within the borders of the United States as of 2024,[3] and scores of others that have not yet been recognized officially. The tribes not only own land but also exercise governmental powers over their land and, to some extent, over land owned by non-Indians located inside reservation borders, otherwise known as Indian country.

Treaties, statutes, and federal constitutional and common law

Tribal law

United States law relating to tribal property rights is based on the U.S. Constitution, treaties between the United States and American Indian nations, federal statutes, and on federal common law. Unlike almost all other property rights covered in this treatise, the rules governing tribal property rights are based on a combination of federal and tribal law — not state law. This means, for example, that most state laws — such as the law of adverse possession — do not apply to tribal property; they are preempted by federal law. It also means that the law relating to tribal property is created not by state legislatures and/or court development of the (state) common law, but by Congress (through treaties and federal statutes) and the federal courts applying federal constitutional principles and federal common law. In addition, each tribe controls its own property within its own jurisdiction and tribal governments develop tribal law to determine the use, allocation, and regulation of tribally owned land.

Why it is important to know about tribal property rights

Understanding the origins of property rights

Knowledge of the law governing tribal property is important for non-Indians as well as Indians for several reasons.[4] First, knowledge of the way in which property was transferred from American Indian nations to the United States is crucial to understanding the origins of property rights in the United States. It is sometimes supposed that property is based on the concept of first possession. This observation is historically true in the United States only if one focuses on the original possession of land by Indian nations. However, this is not how the observation is generally

[1] Most Indians prefer to be called by the name of their tribe, such as Cherokee or Yakima, rather than the generic term Indian, much the same as Europeans prefer to be called French or Italian rather than European. As between the term "Indian" and "Native American," there is a divergence of preferences. Probably the majority of Indians prefer the term Indian or American Indian to the term Native American; that accounts for the usage here. However, the preference is not unanimous and apologies are extended to anyone who prefers the term Native American.

[2] For a history of political and legal relationships between the United States and American Indian Nations, see Francis Paul Prucha, *The Great Father* (2 vols. 1984).

[3] *Indian Entities Recognized by and Eligible to Receive Services from the United States Bureau of Indian Affairs*, 89 Fed. Reg. 944-02 (Jan. 8, 2024).

[4] The subject is complex. For an excellent, quick overview, see William C. Canby, Jr., *American Indian Law in a Nutshell* (8th ed. 2025). For more in-depth coverage, see *Cohen's Handbook of Federal Indian Law* (Nell Jessup Newton & Kevin K. Washburn, eds., 2024).

used in texts on property. Some texts suggest that Indian nations did not recognize individual property rights and thus the land was "unpossessed" when America was invaded by European colonial powers and the land settled by European immigrants.[5] Others suggest that land rights began when those immigrants staked their claims in the wilderness on land that had not been occupied by Indian nations. As Richard Epstein argues, "As inheritors of the Lockean tradition, the basic theory [in the United States] was that property rights emerged from first possession, from first occupation, from homesteading, and not from state grant."[6]

Original Indian title transferred to the federal government

The truth of the matter is that the land in the United States was claimed and inhabited by hundreds of Indian nations who had fairly clearly delineated claims to territory. Although the tribal system of ownership differed substantially from that of the Europeans, it is not the case that lawful control of property was not recognized until the Europeans came. Moreover, property rights did not originate in settlement by non-Indians; rather, most of the property in the United States was formally transferred from tribal ownership to the United States through treaties. Once the United States obtained title from the relevant Indian nation, the federal government then granted patents (titles) to the land to individuals, corporations, and state governments. Non-Indian titles therefore generally derive not from first possession, but from "state grant" by the federal government.

Federal patents

Transfer from tribes to the United States

It is also crucial to recognize that, in most cases, land transfers were *from* the Indian nation *to* the United States. The lands retained by the tribes were *reserved* by them. This is the origin of the term "reservation" for Indian country. In some cases, lands were transferred by the United States to the affected tribes. For example, when the Cherokees, Choctaws, and Chickasaws were "removed" from their lands east of the Mississippi River in the 1830s, the United States granted them particular lands in Indian Territory (later the state of Oklahoma).

A second reason why knowledge of tribal property rights is important is that a huge amount of land is still owned by tribes. Approximately 56.2 million acres of land are now owned by tribes; this is roughly 2 percent of the land mass of the United States.[7] Not only is a great deal of land in tribal ownership, but the legal rules governing that land also differ in substantial

[5] *See* John Locke, *Second Treatise of Government* 29 (Oskar Piest ed. 1952) (original 1690) (arguing that in the beginning "all the world was America"—meaning that the land was unpossessed and free to be appropriated by Europeans); Robert A. Williams, Jr., *Documents of Barbarism: The Contemporary Legacy of European Racism and Colonialism in the Narrative Traditions of Federal Indian Law*, 31 Ariz. L. Rev. 237, 250-253 (1989). On the justifications given for conquest, see Robert A. Williams, Jr., *The American Indian in Western Legal Thought: Discourses of Conquest* (1990).

[6] Richard Epstein, *No New Property*, 56 Brook. L. Rev. 747, 749-750 (1990). *See also* Richard A. Epstein, *Possession as the Root of Title*, 13 Ga. L. Rev. 1221 (1979). *But cf.* Richard A. Epstein, *Property Rights Claims of Indigenous Populations: The View from the Common Law*, 31 U. Tol. L. Rev. 1 (1999) (recognizing the conflict between the principle of first possession and the reality of conquest).

[7] *Cohen's Handbook of Federal Indian Law* §18.01 (Nell Jessup Newton & Kevin K. Washburn, eds., 2024). Overall, tribes and Native Alaskan governments control more than 100 million acres, an area larger than the state of California and would make tribal territory, if contiguous, the fourth-largest state. *See* Nat'l Cong. of Am. Indians, *Tribal Nations and the United*

ways from the property interests that can lawfully exist outside Indian country. The fact that this retained ownership — and the special rules governing tribal property — is not well known to non-Indians has consequences for public debate about these topics. For example, many tribes retained hunting and fishing rights in lands otherwise ceded to the federal government in treaty negotiations. These retained property rights are akin to easements; they are full-fledged property rights owned by the tribes. Some non-Indians view such rights as discriminatory special rights that Indians have, to resources in federal parks and other federal lands. This view is misguided, both because those rights are not held by Indians in general but by specific identifiable tribes, and because such rights are not "special benefits" but retained property rights never given up to the federal government. Some private owners retain homes on land that has been converted into federal parks and such property rights are not considered special benefits or invidious racial discrimination. It is important to know the history and current status of retained tribal rights so that tribes are not discriminatorily denied protection for property rights recognized for non-Indians.

Retained property rights

Relevance of tribal law to non-Indians who do business with tribal governments

Third, as tribes develop economically, more tribal land is devoted to business ventures run by tribal corporations. These corporations often enter into agreements with non-Indian companies that come onto the reservation to do business. Legal issues that arise concerning the contracts that non-Indians enter into with tribes or that concern business on the reservation will, in many cases, involve both tribal law and tribal judicial jurisdiction. It is thus important, not only for tribal lawyers to know something about federal Indian law, but also for non-Indian clients and attorneys to learn about it to facilitate dealings with tribal governments. In some instances, even land owned in fee simple by non-Indians located within reservation borders may be subject to tribal law.

Types of tribal property rights

Trust status

Many American Indian nations and individual Indians own property in the fee simple form, just as non-Indians do. When the property is located outside reservation borders, such lands are usually subject to the same legal rules that apply to property held by non-Indians.[8] However, much property held by tribes, and a significant amount of property held by tribal members individually, is held in a special form called *trust status.* Such property is further subdivided into three major categories, including (1) *original Indian title* or *aboriginal title* (property originally possessed by a tribe or tribal member but that has not been recognized by either a treaty or a federal statute); (2) *recognized title* (tribal property that has been recognized by treaty or statute); and (3) *restricted trust allotments* (property held by individual tribal members, rather than by the tribe as a whole, which is under trust status and subject to the special rules relating to that status).

States: An Introduction 1 (2020); Elizabeth E. Reese, *The Other American Law*, 73 Stan. L. Rev. 555, 558 (2021).

[8] However, tribes are generally immune from suit unless they have waived the sovereign immunity accorded them because of their status as government entities. *Kiowa Tribe of Oklahoma v. Manufacturing Technologies, Inc.*, 523 U.S. 751 (1998); *Sac and Fox Nation v. Hanson*, 47 F.3d 1061 (10th Cir. 1995); *Carl E. Gungoll Exploration Joint Venture v. Kiowa Tribe of Oklahoma*, 975 P.2d 442 (Okla. 1998); *Breakthrough Mgmt. Grp., Inc. v. Chukchansi Gold Casino & Resort*, 629 F.3d 1173 (10th Cir. 2010).

§15.2 Tribal Title

§15.2.1 *Original Indian Title (Aboriginal Title)*

Original Indian title vs. recognized title

Original Indian title (or *aboriginal title*) refers to property that has long been possessed by a tribe or tribal member but that is not formally recognized by either a treaty with the federal government or a federal statute.[9] *Recognized title*, in contrast, is formally recognized by either treaty or federal statute. Both original Indian title and recognized title represent unique forms of property rights in the American legal system not exactly like any other estates recognized by law. These estates are shaped by several unique features.

U.S. fee title and tribal title of occupancy

First, title is shared between the United States and the relevant Indian nation; the United States possesses the "fee" while the tribe possesses the "title of occupancy." Second, the tribal title of occupancy is subject to a strict restraint on alienation; it can be transferred only to the United States.[10] Third, as the owner of the "fee," the United States has the power to convey the fee interest without the consent of the tribe.[11] When such a conveyance occurs, the grantee holds the fee subject to the tribal right of occupancy; the fee holder has no right to occupy or use the property until the United States extinguishes the tribal title. Fourth, under existing law, the United States has the power to extinguish the tribal title of occupancy without the consent of the tribe.[12] Existing precedent further holds that the United States may extinguish original Indian title without compensation.[13] Fifth, in addition to its power to convey the fee and to extinguish tribal title without tribal consent, the United States *may* have other management powers over the property. Some precedents suggest that the only power the United States possesses is the power to purchase the tribal title when the tribe wishes to sell.[14] Other precedents suggest that, in its role as trustee over tribal property, the United States has *plenary power* to "manage" tribal property as it sees fit and that such management is not subject to judicial review.[15] Still others hold that such management *is* subject to judicial review and that the exercise of such powers is constitutionally legitimate

[9] Reservations created by executive order represent a special case and are dealt with in §15.2.3.

[10] This does not mean that the tribe may not grant licenses to use its property subject to tribal law. *See* §15.3.2.

[11] *Johnson v. M'Intosh*, 21 U.S. (8 Wheat.) 543, 574 (1823).

[12] *United States ex rel. Hualpai Indians v. Santa Fe Pacific Railroad*, 314 U.S. 339, 347 (1941).

[13] *Tee-Hit-Ton Indians v. United States*, 348 U.S. 272, 279-280 (1955). This rule is described and criticized below, at §15.4.1.

[14] *Johnson v. M'Intosh*, 21 U.S. (8 Wheat.) 543, 587 (1823).

[15] In *Lone Wolf v. Hitchcock*, 187 U.S. 553 (1903), the Supreme Court held that "Congress possesse[s] a paramount power over the property of the Indians, by reason of its exercise of guardianship over their interests, and that such authority might be implied, even though opposed to the strict letter of a treaty with the Indians." 187 U.S. at 565. *See also United States v. Sioux Nation of Indians*, 448 U.S. 371, 408 (1980) (quoting this passage) and *United States v. Mitchell*, 445 U.S. 535 (1980) (*Mitchell I*) (holding that its role as trustee and owner of the fee places no enforceable legal obligations on the United States to act affirmatively to protect tribal interests).

only if done in the interest of the tribe.[16] Sixth, the United States is in a *trust* relationship with the tribe. This relationship is partly based on the government-to-government relationship that exists between tribal sovereigns and the United States and is partly based on the fact that the United States holds the fee title in trust for the tribe. In either case, it can be argued that the trust relationship places obligations on the United States to protect the tribe's possessory rights.[17]

Johnson v. M'Intosh

In the foundational 1823 case of *Johnson v. M'Intosh*,[18] Chief Justice John Marshall created the legal framework for Indian title, which forms a unique estate in land. That case involved a transfer of lands by the Illinois and Piankeshaw Indians to various non-Indian purchasers. After that purported transfer, the United States entered into treaties with both tribes and arranged for the transfer of those same lands from the tribes to the United States. Subsequently, the United States transferred those lands to William M'Intosh, who was promptly sued by the original grantees who traced their title from their direct purchase from the tribes. The Supreme Court held that the original conveyances to the plaintiffs from the tribes would not be recognized under U.S. law and that only the transfer to the United States and subsequently to M'Intosh was valid. In effect, the title to Indian lands was impressed with a restraint on alienation that rendered void any transfer of fee title other than a transfer to the United States.[19]

Restraint on alienation

Title split between United States and the tribe

In explaining the Court's decision, Justice Marshall constructed an estate in land that differs in significant ways from fee simple interests, leaseholds, or trusts. Title to tribal lands is split between the United States and the relevant Indian nation. The United States possesses the "fee" or the "ultimate fee" (not to be confused with a "fee simple"), while the tribe possesses a "title of occupancy," or a "right of occupancy," or "Indian title." This division of ownership rights is unlike any other in the U.S. legal system. The closest analogy — but still way off the mark — is the trust, with its division between legal title in the trustee and beneficial or equitable title in the beneficiary. The analogy to the trust is imperfect because the division of rights between the United States and the Indian nations is quite different from the division of rights and obligations in the trust form. A second possible analogy is the leasehold, which grants possessory rights to the lessee and a reversion to the landlord. Again, the analogy is quite imperfect because the

[16] *United States v. Mitchell*, 463 U.S. 206 (1983) (*Mitchell II*) (allowing a tribe to bring a claim against the United States for breach of trust). *See also Shoshone Tribe v. United States*, 299 U.S. 476 (1937), recognizing the "paramount power" of Congress over Indian property, but holding, nonetheless, that "[t]he power does not extend so far as to enable the Government 'to give the tribal lands to others, or to appropriate them to its own purposes, without rendering, or assuming an obligation to render, just compensation.'" 299 U.S. at 497 (*quoting United States v. Creek Nation*, 295 U.S. 103, 110 (1935)).

[17] *But compare United States v. Mitchell*, 445 U.S. 535 (1980) (*Mitchell I*) (no enforceable legal obligation based on the mere fact that the United States holds the fee interest) *with United States v. Mitchell*, 463 U.S. 206 (1983) (*Mitchell II*) (such obligations are implied by comprehensive statutory schemes giving the United States certain management powers and responsibilities over tribal resources).

[18] 21 U.S. (8 Wheat.) 543 (1823).

[19] *Cf. United States v. Percheman*, 32 U.S. 51 (1833) (validating titles to private citizens granted by Spain before the United States acquired Florida).

tribal title of occupancy is permanent rather than temporary; the United States possesses not a reversion, but a "right of preemption" — a right to purchase the land from the tribe. The U.S. interest is therefore more like an option to purchase, or a right of first refusal than a reversion. According to Justice Marshall's opinion in *Johnson v. M'Intosh*, only the United States could extinguish the Indian right of occupancy, "either by purchase or conquest."[20]

What rights the United States has under the fee

The "fee" interest retained by the United States over tribal lands grants the United States several powers regarding tribal property. First, the United States has the right to buy the tribal interest if, and when, the tribe wishes to sell to the United States. Second, the United States has the power to extinguish the tribal title with or without the consent of the tribe. If done with the consent of the tribe, the transfer of the interest would either be through a treaty or negotiations culminating in passage of a federal statute. This would effectively be an exercise of the eminent domain power; the United States has the power, as a sovereign, to take the tribal interest by eminent domain without tribal consent.[21] Although it was the practice of the United States to negotiate treaties for the purchase of tribal land in most of the nineteenth century, and thus to obtain at least the formal consent of the affected tribe, Congress passed a statute in 1871 ending the practice of entering treaties with Indian nations.[22] Since then, transfers of title have been effectuated through statute rather than treaty. In some cases, such statutory transfers have been effectuated without tribal consent and over the objections of the affected tribe. Federal law nevertheless recognizes that such statutes extinguish tribal title.

U.S. power to extinguish tribal title by purchase or eminent domain

U.S. power to convey the fee subject to tribal rights

Third, the United States has the power to convey the "fee" interest without the tribe's consent. A grantee of that fee interest would hold the property subject to the tribal title of occupancy.[23] The situation is somewhat like the effect of the sale of property subject to a one-year lease; the buyer of the property obtains the landlord's reversion and is assigned the right to receive rental payments under the lease agreement while the tenant maintains the leasehold with the right to possess the property until the term expires. A conveyance of the "fee" gives the recipient the right to possess the property if the United States ever extinguishes the tribal title of occupancy.

Trust status: U.S. obligation to protect tribal rights

Fourth, offsetting the powers of the United States over tribal lands are obligations on the United States toward the tribes in general and with respect to tribal lands in particular. The fee interest in the United States gives it obligations as well as rights. The United States has the obligation under the trust status to protect the tribe's ownership rights. Although the federal government has *plenary power* over Indian affairs (to the exclusion of the states), it has obligations to the tribes and is said to be in a "*trust relationship*" with the tribes.[24] Because of the trust responsibilities of the

[20] 21 U.S. at 587. *Accord, Oneida Indian Nation v. County of Oneida*, 414 U.S. 661, 668-670 (1974).

[21] The question of the obligation to pay compensation is discussed at §15.4.

[22] 25 U.S.C. §71 (Act of Mar. 3, 1871, ch. 120, §1, 16 Stat. 566 (1871)).

[23] *Catawba Indian Tribe v. South Carolina*, 865 F.2d 1444, 1448 (4th Cir. 1989).

[24] *Cohen's Handbook of Federal Indian Law* §6.04[3] (Nell Jessup Newton & Kevin K. Washburn, eds., 2024).

United States to the tribes, tribal title is said to be in "*trust status.*" These responsibilities include the duty to protect the tribes from dispossession by others and to manage responsibly tribal funds held by the United States. At the same time, the Supreme Court has held that Indian nations have no powers to sue the United States for violation of its trust obligations, even when the United States manages tribal lands unless Congress has passed a statute clearly recognizing such obligations and providing for compensation if they are mismanaged.[25]

What rights the tribe has under its title of occupancy

The tribal title includes most of the rights that go along with fee simple ownership, including the right to possess and use the property. Several important differences exist, however. Perhaps the most important is that

Restraint on alienation

tribal property is subject to an absolute restraint on alienation to every grantee other than the United States. This does not mean that the tribe cannot authorize its members to occupy particular lots of its property, or that Indian nations cannot create protected property rights as a matter of tribal law. It means that the tribe can neither convey fee simple title to the property nor lease it without the consent of the United States (generally exercised through the Bureau of Indian Affairs of the Department of the Interior (BIA)) unless a federal statute or regulation lifts the restraint on alienation. A corollary of the restraint on alienation of the land is a prohibition on the tribal government entering into a treaty with a government other than the United States.

Trade and Intercourse Acts

The restraint on alienation has its origins in the *Proclamation of 1763* (and a prior *Royal Instruction of 1761*), issued by the English Crown. The restraint on alienation was codified by the United States in the first *Trade and Intercourse Act* (often called the *Non-Intercourse Act*), passed in 1790, one year after adoption of the U.S. Constitution. That Act, as amended over time, provides that no sale or lease of Indian land "shall be of any validity in law or equity, unless the same be made by treaty or convention entered into pursuant to the Constitution."[26] Taken literally, this means (1) that no transfer of tribal land shall be valid to any person or state other than the United States, and (2) that no transfer shall be valid unless the tribe agrees to it (because treaties and conventions are agreements and not unilateral statutes passed by Congress). This second requirement has not always been adhered to by the United States; some later statutes have authorized the taking of tribal property against the will of the affected tribe. Such statutes have the force of law under the principle that later statutes may amend the terms of prior statutes.

Purpose of the restraint on alienation

Although the restraint on alienation may appear to be a significant limitation on tribal ownership rights, subjecting tribal owners to control by the United States, it was intended to protect tribes from loss of their property rights and to confirm tribal power to control the use of tribal land through tribal governance and tribal, rather than state or federal, law. It also ensures that any transfers that do take place are made by

[25] *Navajo Nation v. United States*, 556 U.S. 287 (2009).

[26] Act of July 22, 1790, ch. 33, §4, 1 Stat. 137 (1790) (current version codified at 25 U.S.C. §177). *See Cohen's Handbook of Federal Indian Law* §18.03 (Nell Jessup Newton & Kevin K. Washburn, eds., 2024).

relevant tribal officials, rather than by individuals purporting to act for the tribe but who do not have the lawful power to do so. The restraint does have some current disadvantages. For example, it makes it difficult for tribes to borrow money from banks, given the tribes' inability to grant a mortgage in tribal lands without the consent of the United States. Nevertheless, the restraint on alienation enjoys the support of most tribal governments, who often seek to have land purchased by the tribe in fee simple placed under trust status and thus subject to the restraint on alienation this entails.

§15.2.2 Recognized Title

Recognized by treaty or statute

Recognized title differs from original Indian title only in the sense that title is "recognized" by federal treaty or statute. Most tribal land today is held under recognized title. The difference between recognized title and original Indian title was first established in the 1955 case of *Tee-Hit-Ton Indians v. United States.*[27] The effect of recognition is (1) to settle disputes about the borders of tribal land and (2) to provide a constitutional right to compensation when and if the land is taken by eminent domain by the United States. The issue of compensability is further developed in §15.4 below.

Tribal easements

Many Indian nations have off-reservation easements recognized and protected by treaties with the United States. The most common are rights to hunt and fish at "usual and accustomed places," water rights, and rights to travel. In recent years, the Supreme Court has interpreted these easement broadly, in line with the Indian law canons of interpretation that require treaties to be "liberally construed in favor of the Indians," that "all ambiguities be resolved in their favor," that they be "construed as the Indians would have understood them," and that "tribal property rights ... are preserved unless Congress's intent to the contrary is clear and unambiguous."[28] For example, the Supreme Court held that a treaty right to hunt on "unoccupied lands of the United States" applied to a federal park,[29] and that a tribal right to travel on public roads "in common with US citizens" outside the reservation meant that it can do so free of a state fuel tax.[30] The Supreme Court also affirmed, by equally divided Court, a Ninth Circuit holding that off-reservation tribal fishing rights required the state to remove culverts that decreased water supply to rivers, harming the fish population, because the treaty required that fish would in fact be available.[31] On the other hand, the Supreme Court held that the United States had no duty to help the Navajo Nation quantify its water rights reserved by treaty, so that the Navajo Nation could claim those water rights and either use or sell them.[32]

27 348 U.S. 272 (1955).
28 *Cohen's Handbook of Federal Indian Law* §3.01[1], at 153-154 (Nell Jessup Newton & Kevin K. Washburn, eds., 2024).
29 *Herrera v. Wyo.*, 587 U.S. 329 (2019).
30 *Wash. State Dep't of Licensing v. Cougar Den, Inc.*, 586 U.S. 347 (2019).
31 *Washington v. United States*, 584 U.S. 837 (2018), *aff'g United States v. Washington*, 853 F.3d 946 (9th Cir. 2017).
32 *Arizona v. Navajo Nation*, 599 U.S. 555 (2023).

§15.2.3 Executive Order Title

Lands set aside by the President

Between 1855 and 1919, 23 million acres of land were set aside for tribal occupation by *executive order* issued by the President of the United States.[33] This problematic exercise of power has been sustained by the courts on the ground that Congress "acquiesced" in the practice over a long period of time.[34] Because executive order reservations were not established by treaty or statute, they may constitute unrecognized title and thus are not subject to the protections granted recognized title. However, in many instances, Congress has effectively ratified such executive orders, either by explicit subsequent legislation recognizing tribal title or by implicit action treating such reservation properties the same as those recognized by treaty or statute.

▶ HARD CASE

▷ CAN EXECUTIVE ORDER RESERVATIONS BE RESCINDED BY THE EXECUTIVE?

Executive order reservations were established by presidential order. Can they be rescinded by executive order without the involvement of Congress? Two older cases hold that they can. The 1942 case of *Sioux Tribe v. United States*[35] and the 1949 case of *Hynes v. Grimes Packing Co.*[36] both hold that executive orders are subject to termination at the will of either Congress or the President. After all, executive orders may be rescinded in the absence of express congressional ratification. However, the rulings in those cases involved reservations that had not been in existence for a long time and may have been intended to be temporary. Given the long-standing congressional acquiescence in the many executive order reservations, the reliance interests of the affected tribes, and subsequent statutory enactments that fail to distinguish between reservations created by treaty or statute and those created by executive order, it is likely that congressional ratification would be found in most instances today. Moreover, failure to treat executive order reservations as conferring recognized title on the affected tribes would have the effect of subjecting such tribes to the special rules relevant to original Indian title, including the rule that denies a constitutional right to compensation if the property is taken by the United States. Given the problematic moral character of that rule of law and the legitimate interests of executive order reservation tribes in relying on control of property granted by executive order, it would be unjust to allow such revocation without both consent of Congress and compensation.[37] ◀

[33] *Cohen's Handbook of Federal Indian Law* §18.02[1][a][iv] (Nell Jessup Newton & Kevin K. Washburn, eds., 2024). Congress ended this practice by statute in 1919. Act of June 30, 1919, ch. 4, §27, 41 Stat. 3, 34 (codified at 43 U.S.C. §150).

[34] *Arizona v. California*, 373 U.S. 546, 598 (1963), *overruled on other grounds by California v. United States*, 438 U.S. 645 (1978); *Mason v. United States*, 260 U.S. 545 (1923).

[35] 316 U.S. 317, 324-325 (1942).

[36] 337 U.S. 86, 103-104 (1949).

[37] On the compensation issue, see §15.4.3.

§15.3 Individual Title

§15.3.1 Restricted Trust Allotments

General Allotment Act of 1887 (Dawes Act)

In the late nineteenth century, the United States sought to convert tribal land ownership to individual ownership. To that end, in 1887 Congress passed the *General Allotment Act* (also known as the *Dawes Act*).[38] That Act provided for the subdivision and allotment of tribal lands to individual tribal members[39] and, once that occurred, the sale of so-called surplus lands to non-Indians. The allotted lands were to remain subject to the restraint on alienation for 25 years, after which it was to be removed. Both individual tribal member lands and surplus lands transferred to non-Indians were then to become alienable. Although many allotments did become alienable when their restraints on alienation were lifted, many others remained inalienable when statutes extended the time during which particular allotments would be subject to the restraint. When allotments did become alienable, many owners sold their land or lost it through tax foreclosures. Because of the *Dawes Act*, between 1887 and 1934 (when Congress repudiated the allotment policy), the tribes lost two-thirds of their lands (90 million acres) to non-Indian ownership. Total tribal land holdings were reduced from 138 million acres in 1887 to 48 million acres in 1934. The tribes were never compensated for the value of the allotted land.

Purpose of the Act

The allotment policy was implemented during a period when Congress sought to convert Indians to Christianity, to induce tribes and tribal members to adopt agriculture as the main source of livelihood, and to break up communal tribal ownership of land with its ethos of land as a common, shared asset with spiritual significance and adopt instead individual ownership and market participation as governing norms for economic and social life.[40] Although the Act succeeded in creating individual property rights, it did not succeed in most of its other goals. Many Indians did convert to Christianity under the influence of schools funded by the federal government and run by religious institutions and the Courts of Indian Offenses created by federal regulations, which prohibited many traditional tribal religious practices. However, the allotment policy failed to work to create vigorous tribal economies. The main effect of the statute was to facilitate the transfer of tribal property to non-Indians. In recognition of this reality, although the restraints on alienation were lifted for many parcels, they were extended for many others under subsequent legislation and regulations to stem the loss of tribal lands. In 1934, the allotment policy was repudiated

Consequences of the *Dawes Act*

[38] Acts of 1887, ch. 119, 24 Stat. 388 (*codified as amended* at 25 U.S.C. §§334-358).

[39] Initially, the Act granted 160 acres to each "family head," 80 acres to each single person over 18 and to each orphan under 18, and 40 acres to each other single person under 18. Acts of 1887, ch. 119, 24 Stat. 388.

[40] Rebecca Tsosie et al., *American Indian Law: Native Nations and the Federal System* 29-35 (8th ed. 2025); *see also* Kenneth H. Bobroff, *Retelling Allotment: Indian Property Rights and the Myth of Common Ownership*, 54 Vand. L. Rev. 1559 (2001) (surveying the variety of Native American property systems).

when Congress passed the *Indian Reorganization Act.*[41] That Act provided that no further lands were to be allotted[42] and extended indefinitely the restraint on alienation of existing allotments.[43]

Restricted trust allotments today

Today, many tribal members own *restricted trust allotments.* These properties are held by individual tribal members in a form of ownership similar to recognized title. The fee title is in the United States and the individual owner has a full beneficial interest. Under the *Dawes Act* and other relevant legislation, ownership is subject to a restraint on alienation, which prohibits sale, lease, or mortgage of the property without the consent of the United States; such consent is exercised by the BIA.[44] Decisions about the land use are made by allottees, with the concurrence of the United States. Although allotments cannot be sold or leased (without the consent of the BIA), federal legislation authorizes inheritance through application of state intestacy laws[45] and authorizes individual allotment owners to write wills (which must be approved by the Secretary of the Interior) determining who gets the allotment on the death of the allottee.[46] When wills are not written (a common occurrence), the land passes to the heirs.

Problems in managing allotments

This process has led to many allotments having dozens of owners, making management difficult. Such lands are generally leased with the rental payments divided among the allottees. In such cases, the costs of management may exceed the returns on the land. Congress has attempted to fix this problem, but its two most recent attempts have been declared unconstitutional by the Supreme Court.[47] Although the Supreme Court has held that the trust status by itself places no obligations on the United States to manage allotments in a responsible manner,[48] comprehensive statutes and regulations providing for such management do imply such an obligation.[49]

§15.3.2 Assignments

Tribal law

Communally held tribal land may be assigned to individual tribal members by the tribe pursuant to tribal law.[50] Although the tribe has no power to convey fee simple title to the land to an individual tribal member, it is free to allocate its property as it wishes by granting tribal members licenses to occupy tribal land. The rights encompassed by such licenses will be determined by tribal law.

41 25 U.S.C. §§461-479.
42 *Id.* at §461.
43 *Id.* at §462.
44 Rebecca Tsosie et al., *American Indian Law: Native Nations and the Federal System* 33 (8th ed. 2025).
45 25 U.S.C. §348.
46 *Id.* at §373.
47 *See* §15.4.4.
48 *United States v. Mitchell,* 445 U.S. 535 (1980) (*Mitchell I*).
49 *United States v. Mitchell,* 463 U.S. 206 (1983) (*Mitchell II*).
50 William C. Canby, Jr., *American Indian Law in a Nutshell* 494-495 (8th ed. 2025).

▷ CHECKERBOARD RESERVATIONS, PROPERTY, AND SOVEREIGNTY **HARD CASE ◀**

The ongoing legacy of allotment and the resulting checkerboard reservations, with some land owned by tribes and their members and some land owned by non-Indians or nonmembers, raises ongoing sovereignty and governance challenges. In *Brendale v. Confederated Tribes & Bands of the Yakima Indian Nation*,[51] the Supreme Court held that tribes can zone property owned by the tribe and allotments owned by tribal members, while cities and counties have the authority to zone property owned in fee simple by non-Indians or Indians who are not members of the relevant tribe. The result is that there is no coherent zoning system in checkerboarded towns or areas, and to make a coherent plan that does not change plot by plot, tribes and local governments must negotiate to reach an agreement — in practice, mini-treaties — on zoning rules.[52]

Allotment undermining rational land use planning

Checkerboard reservations also raise taxation challenges for tribes. The Supreme Court has held that tribes have authority to tax non-Indians who engage in business on tribal property within reservation borders,[53] but tribes cannot tax non-Indians who engage in activities on land they owned in fee even if the land is within reservation borders.[54] ◀

Uneven taxation authority

§15.4 Compensability

§15.4.1 *Original Indian Title*

Tee-Hit-Ton Indians v. United States

In *Tee-Hit-Ton Indians v. United States*,[55] the Supreme Court held that property held under original Indian title could be taken by the United States without compensation because aboriginal title did not constitute "property" within the meaning of the Fifth Amendment. Thus, the Fifth Amendment's guarantee against the taking of "property" without just compensation did not apply, and Congress could take tribal property without paying compensation. *Tee-Hit-Ton* involved the seizure and sale of timber on lands belonging to the Tee-Hit-Ton Indians, a clan of the Tlingit Tribe, in Alaska. The opinion is unsupportable and unjust and should be overruled.

Reasons for the *Tee-Hit-Ton* ruling and critique

The Court gave several reasons for its ruling. First, Justice Reed's majority opinion argued that "it is well settled" that original Indian title merely means "permission from the whites to occupy."[56] This permission grants "mere possession" that is not specifically recognized as ownership by Congress. This is not a property right but amounts to a right of occupancy which the sovereign grants and protects against intrusion by third parties

Precedent

[51] 492 U.S. 408 (1989).
[52] *Cf.* Rebecca M. Webster, *This Land Can Sustain Us: Cooperative Land Use Planning on the Oneida Reservation*, 17 Plan. Theory & Prac. 9 (2016).
[53] *Merrion v. Jicarilla Apache Tribe*, 455 U.S. 130 (1982).
[54] *Atkinson Trading Co. v. Shirley*, 532 U.S. 645 (2001).
[55] 348 U.S. 272 (1955).
[56] *Id.* at 279.

but which right of occupancy may be terminated and such lands fully disposed of by the sovereign itself without any legally enforceable obligation to compensate the Indians.[57]

Critique

The ruling in *Tee-Hit-Ton* misinterprets precedent, violates fundamental constitutional norms (both of equal protection and federal Indian law), and should be overruled. First, the legal basis for the ruling is extraordinarily weak. The main case that Justice Reed cites for the proposition that tribal possession is not "property" is *Johnson v. M'Intosh*,[58] a case that holds no such thing. *Johnson* held that the United States possessed the power to convey the fee without the consent of the tribe and gave the United States the power to extinguish the Indian title "by purchase or conquest," but was silent on the question of whether the United States would be obligated to pay compensation when it extinguished tribal title. Justice Reed cites only two other cases to support the Court's position. The first, *Beecher v. Wetherby*,[59] similarly held that the United States could convey the fee without tribal consent (and that the taker would hold the property subject to the tribal title of occupancy). The other case, *United States ex rel. Hualpai Indians v. Santa Fe Pacific Railroad Co.*,[60] held that Congress has the power to extinguish tribal title without tribal consent. Justice Reed quotes out of context a paragraph from *Santa Fe* to the effect that "[t]he power of Congress in regard [to extinguishment of Indian title based on aboriginal possession] is supreme. The manner, method and time of such extinguishment raise political, not justiciable issues."[61] This does not mean that there are no constitutional limits on extinguishment; indeed, in *Santa Fe*, the Court ruled that extinguishment will not be "lightly implied" but must be accomplished by an express act of Congress.[62] *Santa Fe* merely held that tribal consent was not required to extinguish tribal title; the case did not address the question of whether compensation was required when tribal title was extinguished. Indeed, both in *Santa Fe* and in *Beecher v. Wetherby*, Congress *had* arranged for compensation.[63] In fact, the first case to hold that tribal title may be extinguished without compensation is *Tee-Hit-Ton*. In stark contrast, an 1835 case called *Mitchel v. United States* emphasized that Indian title is "as sacred as the fee simple of the whites."[64]

Number of owners

Second, the Court noted that the tribe had been "greatly reduced in numbers" and now had only 65 members.[65] Why this is relevant to an ownership claim is uncertain; there is no rule that limits the amount of property one or two or sixty-five people may own. Such a rule would be surprising to individuals such as Bill Gates, whose wealth exceeds that of millions of Americans. Third, "ownership was not individual but tribal."[66]

Tribal ownership

[57] *Id.*
[58] 21 U.S. (8 Wheat.) 543 (1823).
[59] 95 U.S. 517, 525-526 (1877).
[60] 314 U.S. 339, 347 (1941).
[61] *Id.* at 347.
[62] *Id.* at 354.
[63] *Id.* at 353-354.
[64] 34 U.S. 711, 746 (1835).
[65] 348 U.S. at 285.
[66] *Id.* at 286.

Why this negates a claim of ownership is uncertain. There is no rule against communal ownership of property. Indeed, joint tenancy property is common, and many nonprofit organizations with many members own property in common. If communal ownership is not constitutionally protected, it would be a big surprise to the Catholic Church, Harvard University, or the Audubon Society. Fourth, Justice Reed argues that because the tribe's claim was "wholly tribal," it "was more a claim of sovereignty than of ownership."[67] Again, common ownership of land is not unusual; what is unusual is to fail to accord it constitutional protection. Fifth, Justice Reed notes that "the various tribes of the Tlingits allowed one another to use their lands."[68] This suggests hospitality rather than an absence of possession. One ordinarily does not lose title by inviting others to come onto one's land. Finally, Justice Reed argues that "the Tee-Hit-Tons were in a hunting and fishing stage of civilization, with shelters fitted to their environment, and claims to rights to use identified territory for these activities as well as the gathering of wild products of the earth."[69] Again, it is uncertain why use of an "identified territory" does not constitute possession merely because the use is nomadic. Rich people who commute between summer and winter homes are not deprived of their rights because they are peripatetic.

Hospitality

Nomadic use

Needs of the United States

Justice Reed's final argument is that "no other course would meet the problem of the growth of the United States except to make congressional contributions for Indian lands rather than to subject the Government to an obligation to pay the value when taken with interest to the date of payment."[70] This argument is hard to fathom. It is, for one thing, factually untrue. For the most part, contrary to popular belief, the United States *did* compensate Indian nations when it took their property pursuant to treaties. Moreover, *Tee-Hit-Ton* was decided in 1955, only a few years after Congress established the Indian Claims Commission (ICC) in 1946. The ICC was an administrative agency empowered to hear claims by tribes that their property—including original Indian title property—had been taken by the United States without compensation or with inadequate compensation. Thus, Congress had recently provided for compensation for wrongful takings of tribal land. Not only did the needs of the United States *not* require that the land be taken without compensation, but an existing agency was also at that moment hearing cases to determine how much compensation the United States owed dozens of tribes. By the end of 1947, 17 claims had been filed with the ICC seeking an aggregate amount of $253 million.[71] By 1951 (several years before the Supreme Court heard the *Tee-Hit-Ton* case), the ICC docket totaled some 600 claims that had been filed on behalf of various Indian nations.[72] Thus, even if not all these claims were vindicated, the Supreme Court must have known that Congress had

[67] *Id.* at 287.
[68] *Id.*
[69] *Id.*
[70] *Id.* at 290.
[71] *Irredeemable America: The Indians' Estate and Land Claims* 46 (Imre Sutton ed. 1985).
[72] *Id.*

statutorily accepted very substantial obligations to compensate for wrongful takings of Indian land in the past, including land held under original Indian title. There was therefore no excuse for the Supreme Court not to recognize tribal possession as sufficient to constitute "property" within the meaning of the Fifth Amendment as to present and future takings. The *Tee-Hit-Ton* case was wrongly decided and should be overruled because it continues to be cited to this day.[73]

§15.4.2 Recognized Title

Duty to compensate when recognized title land is taken by the United States

Although *Tee-Hit-Ton* held in 1955 that Congress may extinguish original Indian title without paying compensation, the Supreme Court has held that the United States must pay compensation when it takes recognized title.[74] As the criticism of the reasoning in the *Tee-Hit-Ton* case suggests,[75] U.S. law has consistently held to the principle that federal power over tribal lands is subject to constitutional limitations.

History of the compensation issue

Originally, the Supreme Court suggested in the 1823 case of *Johnson v. M'Intosh* that the United States had the power to extinguish tribal title "by purchase or conquest."[76] Justice Marshall's opinion in *Johnson* also famously stated that "discovery gave title to the government by whose subjects, or by whose authority, it was made, against all other European governments, which title might be consummated by possession."[77] Although one might have thought that the "conquest" language and the idea that "discovery gave title" meant that the tribe had no protected property rights, Justice Marshall was careful to state that the "discovery" doctrine was adopted to regulate disputes among colonial powers:

The Marshall Court cases

> [A]s they were all in pursuit of nearly the same object, it was necessary, in order to avoid conflicting settlements, and consequent war with each other, to establish a principle, which all should acknowledge as the law by which the right of acquisition, which they all asserted, should be regulated as between themselves.[78]

In other words, the discovery doctrine determined which colonial power had the fee; it did not mean that the tribes had no protected property rights. In fact, the discovery doctrine was irrelevant to that particular problem: "Those relations which were to exist between the discoverer and the natives, were to be regulated by themselves."[79]

[73] *See Karuk Tribe of California v. Ammon*, 209 F.3d 1366, 1374 (Fed. Cir. 2000), *aff'g Karuk Tribe of California v. United States*, 41 Fed. Cl. 468 (Fed. Cl. 1998), *State v. Elliott*, 616 A.2d 210, 213 (Vt. 1992), and *El Paso Nat. Gas Co. LLC v. United States*, 2017 WL 3492993, at *3 (D. Ariz. Aug. 15, 2017 (citing *Tee-Hit-Ton*).
[74] *United States v. Sioux Nation of Indians*, 448 U.S. 371, 415-416 (1980); *Tee-Hit-Ton Indians v. United States*, 348 U.S. 272, 277-278 (1955).
[75] *See* §15.4.1.
[76] *Johnson v. M'Intosh*, 21 U.S. (8 Wheat.) 543, 587 (1823).
[77] *Id.* at 573.
[78] *Id.*
[79] *Id.*

"As sacred as the fee simple of the whites"

Rather than holding that the tribal title could be extinguished without compensation, Marshall noted that in the establishment of the relations between colonizing powers and native nations, "the rights of the original inhabitants were, in no instance, entirely disregarded."[80] Indeed, "[t]hey were admitted to be the rightful occupants of the soil, with a legal as well as just claim to retain possession of it, and to use it according to their own discretion."[81] He further argued: "It has never been contended, that the Indian title amounted to nothing. Their right of possession has never been questioned. The claim of government extends to the complete ultimate title, charged with this right of possession, and to the exclusive power of acquiring that right."[82] Marshall further explained in the 1831 case of *Cherokee Nation v. Georgia*[83] that "the Indians are acknowledged to have an unquestionable, and heretofore unquestioned, right to the lands they occupy, until that right shall be extinguished by a *voluntary cession to our government.*"[84] And the Marshall Court ruled in the 1835 case of *Mitchel v. United States*[85] that "it [is] a settled principle, that their right of occupancy is considered as sacred as the fee simple of the whites."[86]

Plenary power doctrine: Repudiation of the right to compensate in *Lone Wolf v. Hitchcock*

The idea that tribal property could be taken by the United States only through a "voluntary cession"—*i.e.*, negotiation of a treaty—and compensation was accepted until the 1903 case of *Lone Wolf v. Hitchcock.*[87] That case concerned the forced allotment of property belonging to the Kiowa, Comanche, and Apache Nations without a two-thirds vote of the adult males, as required by a prior treaty. The Court held that the federal government had "plenary power" over Indian affairs and that there were no constitutional limits on congressional power over Indian nations. These were "political questions" that could not be submitted to the courts for judicial review. In explaining its ruling, Justice White said, "It is true that in decisions of this court, the Indian right of occupancy of tribal lands, whether declared in a treaty or otherwise created, has been stated to be sacred, or, as sometimes expressed, as sacred as the fee of the United States in the same lands."[88] However, he dismissed those prior cases because none of them involved a claim for compensation by a tribe against the United States; rather, they all involved controversies between tribes and states or between tribes and individual claimants.[89] As to relations between tribal owners and the United States, the Court held: "Plenary authority over the tribal relations of the Indians has been exercised by Congress from the beginning, and the power has always been deemed a political one, not subject to be controlled by the judicial department of the government."[90] Just as treaties

[80] *Id.* at 574.
[81] *Id.*
[82] *Id.* at 603.
[83] 30 U.S. (5 Pet.) 1 (1831).
[84] *Id.* at 17.
[85] 34 U.S. 711 (1835).
[86] *Id.* at 746.
[87] 187 U.S. 553 (1903).
[88] *Id.* at 564.
[89] *Id.* at 565.
[90] *Id.*

with foreign nations may be abrogated unilaterally by Congress through subsequent legislation, so may treaties with Indian nations be abrogated unilaterally without compensation.[91]

Mere change in the form of investment

In a famous passage, Justice White went on to hold that "full administrative power was possessed by Congress over Indian tribal property. In effect, the action of Congress now complained of was but an exercise of such power, a mere change in the form of investment of Indian tribal property."[92] The allotment act converted communally owned property to individually owned property. In this view, nothing was taken from the tribe; merely the "form of investment" changed. Moreover, "[w]e must presume that Congress acted in perfect good faith in the dealings with the Indians of which complaint is made, and that the legislative branch of the government exercised its best judgment in the premises."[93] "In any event," Justice White continued,

Presumption of good faith

> as Congress possessed full power in the matter, the judiciary cannot question or inquire into the motives which prompted the enactment of this legislation. If injury was occasioned, which we do not wish to be understood as implying, by the use made by Congress of its power, relief must be sought by an appeal to that body for redress, and not to the courts.[94]

Reaffirmation of the right to compensation in *United States v. Creek Nation*

The *Lone Wolf* case has been called the *Dred Scott* of federal Indian law for its callous disregard of tribal rights. The idea that there were no constitutional limits on congressional power over tribal lands was repudiated by the Supreme Court in 1935 in *United States v. Creek Nation*,[95] which held that the United States had a constitutional obligation to compensate the Creek Nation for the wrongful taking of its lands. The Court noted that the "tribe was a dependent Indian community under the guardianship of the United States, and therefore its property and affairs were subject to the control and management of that government." However, the Court noted, "this power to control and manage was not absolute."[96]

> While extending to all appropriate measures for protecting and advancing the tribe, it was subject to limitations inhering in such a guardianship and to pertinent constitutional restrictions. It did not enable the United States to give the tribal lands to others, or to appropriate them to its own purposes, without rendering, or assuming an obligation to render, just compensation for them; for that "would not be an exercise of guardianship, but an act of confiscation."[97]

Similarly, the *Tee-Hit-Ton* case ruled in 1955 that, although Congress had no constitutional obligation to compensate tribes for the taking of land

[91] *Id.* at 565-566.
[92] *Id.* at 568.
[93] *Id.*
[94] *Id.*
[95] 295 U.S. 103 (1935).
[96] *Id.* at 109-110.
[97] *Id.* at 110.

held under original Indian title, "[w]here the Congress by treaty or other agreement has declared that thereafter Indians were to hold the lands permanently, compensation must be paid for subsequent taking."[98]

Equivocal rights granted by *Sioux Nation*

The right to be compensated when recognized title lands are taken was reaffirmed by the Supreme Court in *United States v. Sioux Nation of Indians.*[99] That right, however, was qualified. The Court noted that the United States has certain powers over tribal land, partly because of its ownership of the fee (which it holds "in trust" for the benefit of the relevant Indian tribes) and partly because of its general trust relationship with the tribes. These powers enable the United States to act *as a trustee* for the benefit of the tribe. Quoting *Lone Wolf,*[100] the Court held in *Sioux Nation* that "Congress possesse[s] a paramount power over the property of the Indians, by reason of its exercise of guardianship over their interests, and that such authority might be implied, even though opposed to the strict letter of a treaty with the Indians."[101] However, a different set of powers enables the United States to take tribal property for its own use or the use of others — in other words, for public purposes that do not necessarily benefit the tribal owner. Quoting *Shoshone Tribe v. United States*[102] and *Creek Nation,*[103] the Court held that "Congressional power over tribal lands does not extend so far as to enable the Government 'to give the tribal lands to others, or to appropriate them to its own purposes, without rendering, or assuming an obligation to render, just compensation.'"[104] When the United States exercises the power of eminent domain, it has the obligation to compensate the tribe. To determine whether compensation is due, the court must determine whether the Congress was unconstitutionally taking tribal property without just compensation or constitutionally exercising its plenary power to manage tribal land for the benefit of the tribe. Adopting a test articulated by the Indian Claims Commission, the Court held: "Where Congress makes a good faith effort to give the Indians the full value of the land and thus merely transmutes the property from land to money, there is no taking."[105]

Critique of "good faith effort" test

What is troubling about this ruling is that it deprives Indian nations of a remedy if it can be shown that Congress made a "good faith effort" to provide full value for the land. This defense is not available in the non-Indian context; there, when Congress takes property, it must pay fair market value, not make a good faith effort to do so. Rather than a subjective test based on congressional intent or good faith, the takings clause in the non-Indian context applies an objective test based on the market value of the land. One might defend the *Sioux Nation* rule on the ground that exercise by the United States of its trust powers may help tribes rather than

[98] *Tee-Hit-Ton Indians v. United States*, 348 U.S. 272, 277-278 (1955).
[99] 448 U.S. 371 (1980).
[100] *Lone Wolf v. Hitchcock*, 187 U.S. 553 (1903).
[101] 448 U.S. at 408 (*quoting Lone Wolf*, 187 U.S. at 565).
[102] 299 U.S. 476 (1937).
[103] 295 U.S. 103 (1935).
[104] 299 U.S. at 497 (*quoting United States v. Creek Nation*, 295 U.S. 103, 110 (1935)).
[105] 448 U.S. at 409 (*quoting Fort Berthold Reservation v. United States*, 182 Ct. Cl. 543, 553, 390 F.2d 686, 691 (1968)).

hurt them because the placement of too stringent limits on congressional power might have the effect of depriving Congress of legitimate regulatory power that could be exercised to protect or promote tribal property rights. This argument is unconvincing because the *Sioux Nation* test purports to determine whether a taking occurred by reference to Congress's good faith rather than by reference to Congress's objective conduct in seizing tribal property. If Congress effectively deprives a tribe of control of its property, full compensation should be paid, not merely a "good faith effort" to provide "full value."

▶ HARD CASE

▷ ALLOTMENT

In both *Lone Wolf* and *Sioux Nation*, the Supreme Court held that allotment could not constitute a taking of tribal property because it was "a mere change in the form of investment."[106] After all, when tribal property was transferred to non-Indians, the United States did pay compensation. When tribal property was transferred to tribal members through the allotment program, nothing changed but the form of ownership; instead of communal ownership, title was held individually. This argument is not only hard to understand, but also contravenes accepted norms that would govern similar cases in the non-Indian context. Corporate enterprises are "persons" within the meaning of the Fifth Amendment.[107] If the United States were to take the real property of General Motors and "allot" it by dividing it up among the shareholders of General Motors, there is no doubt whatsoever that this would be held to be an unconstitutional taking of the property of General Motors Corporation. Similar rulings would clearly follow if the property of Harvard University were forcibly distributed among its alumni and students or if the property of the Catholic Church were forcibly distributed among its parishioners. The Indian nations lost millions of acres through allotment, taken from them without compensation. ◀

§15.4.3 Executive Order Title

▶ HARD CASE

▷ COMPENSABILITY OF EXECUTIVE ORDER RESERVATIONS

The distinction between original Indian title property and recognized property established by the 1955 *Tee-Hit-Ton* case created an issue with regard to 23 million acres of land on executive order reservations. By definition, they are not formally recognized by treaty nor statute. Although it might be argued that little land remains in the United States that continues to be held

[106] *United States v. Sioux Nation of Indians*, 448 U.S. 371, 413 (1980); *Lone Wolf v. Hitchcock*, 187 U.S. 553, 568 (1903).

[107] *Minneapolis & St. Louis Railroad v. Beckwith*, 129 U.S. 26, 28 (1889) (due process clause); *Santa Clara County v. Southern Pacific Railroad*, 118 U.S. 394 (1886) (equal protection clause).

under original Indian title,[108] a great deal of land is held by tribes established by executive order. It is therefore an important question whether the title to such lands constitutes "property" within the meaning of the Fifth Amendment. Are executive order reservations akin to original Indian title, which can be taken without compensation under *Tee-Hit-Ton*,[109] or are they sufficiently "recognized" by Congress to constitute "property," which cannot be taken without compensation under *Sioux Nation*?[110] Several Supreme Court cases from the 1940s appear to have decided that executive order reservations are not recognized by Congress and therefore do not constitute "property" within the meaning of the Fifth Amendment's prohibition on federal taking of property without compensation.[111] The current status of these holdings is unclear because territory originally created by executive order may be later recognized by federal statute.[112] Both Congress and the courts have not, in general, treated executive order reservations any differently from those created by treaty or statute.[113] Moreover, Congress in modern times has compensated tribes for the taking of property on executive order lands.[114]

Are executive order reservations "recognized" by Congress?

In *Karuk Tribe of California v. Ammon*,[115] the Federal Circuit affirmed a Court of Federal Claims ruling that reservations established by executive order are not "recognized" within the meaning of *Tee-Hit-Ton* and *Sioux Nation* and that tribal property rights in such reservations may be constitutionally taken without compensation. *Karuk* concerned the Hoopa Valley Reservation, established by executive order in 1876 and increased in size by an addition established by a second executive order in 1891. The Yurok and Hoopa Valley Tribes shared the reservation. A 1988 statute, the *Hoopa-Yurok Settlement Act*,[116] granted the addition to the Yuroks and reserved the original area for the Hoopa Valley Tribe. A member of the Yurok tribe claimed that the *Settlement Act* deprived the Yuroks of their property rights

[108] Many tribes would dispute that observation. *See, e.g., State v. Elliott*, 616 A.2d 210 (Vt. 1992).

[109] 348 U.S. 272 (1955).

[110] 448 U.S. 371 (1980).

[111] *Hynes v. Grimes Packing Co.*, 337 U.S. 86, 101 (1949); *Confederated Band of Ute Indians v. United States*, 330 U.S. 169, 179-180 (1947); *Sioux Tribe of Indians v. United States*, 316 U.S. 317, 325 (1942); William C. Canby, Jr., *American Indian Law in a Nutshell* 484-485 (8th ed. 2025).

[112] William C. Canby, Jr., *American Indian Law in a Nutshell* 485 (8th ed. 2025).

[113] *Cohen's Handbook of Federal Indian Law* §18.02[1][a][iv] (Nell Jessup Newton & Kevin K. Washburn, eds., 2024).

[114] *See, e.g.*, Act of Sept. 30, 1968, Pub. L. No. 90-537, §302, 82 Stat. 885, 888 (codified at 43 U.S.C. §1522) (taking lands of Salt River Pima-Maricopa Indian Community and Fort McDowell-Apache Indian Community for Orme Dam); Act of July 8, 1940, ch. 552, §2, 54 Stat. 744 (taking of lands of Fort Mohave and Chemehuevi Reservations for construction of Parker Dam); Act of June 29, 1940, ch. 460, §2, 54 Stat. 703 (codified at 16 U.S.C. §835d) (taking lands of Colville and Spokane Reservations for construction of Grand Coulee Dam); see also *Cohen's Handbook of Federal Indian Law* §18.02[1][a][iv] (Nell Jessup Newton & Kevin K. Washburn, eds., 2024).

[115] *Karuk Tribe of California v. Ammon*, 209 F.3d 1366, 1374 (Fed. Cir. 2000), *aff'g*, *Karuk Tribe of California v. United States*, 41 Fed. Cl. 468 (Fed. Cl. 1998), *cert. denied*, 532 U.S. 941 (2001).

[116] 25 U.S.C. §§1300i to 1300i-11.

in the area reserved for the Hoopa Valley Tribe and that Congress could not take Yurok property rights without compensation.

Argument that compensation is not required

The Court of Federal Claims noted that the "Constitution grants Congress, not the President, the power to 'dispose of and make all needful Rules and Regulations respecting the Territory or other Property belonging to the United States.'"[117] This arguably means that "only an Act of Congress can grant a right of permanent occupancy as opposed to permissive occupancy."[118] An executive order therefore grants only "permissive occupation" rather than "legal rights."[119] Any congressional enactment granting permanent rights must do so expressly and not implicitly.[120] Thus, an "Indian reservation created by Executive Order of the President conveys no right of use or occupancy 'beyond the pleasure of Congress or the President.'"[121]

Argument that compensation is required

Congress has authorized appropriations for tribes on executive order reservations and otherwise treated such reservations in a manner similar to reservations recognized by treaty or statute. One might argue that both congressional action and congressional acquiescence in tribal occupation for more than 100 years should suffice to fix vested property rights in tribes on executive order reservations. In addition, the same criticisms rehearsed above of the *Tee-Hit-Ton* decision apply here. It is not at all clear why formal recognition by Congress is necessary to find that original Indian title lands constitute "property" within the meaning of the Fifth Amendment. Such lands are "possessed" by tribes, and possession is sufficient to vest title in non-Indians under state adverse possession law. Executive order reservations not only have the benefit of long-standing tribal possession but also have an order by the President and long-standing acquiescence by Congress. Certainly, tribes on executive order reservations have substantial reliance interests in access to their lands, and often expectations based on original possession. If the tribal title of occupancy is "as sacred as the fee simple of the whites,"[122] it is fundamentally unjust to deprive tribal owners of property rights that would be granted to non-Indian owners. ◀

§15.4.4 Restricted Trust Allotments

Hodel v. Irving

As discussed above,[123] many allotments are severely fractionated with multiple owners. The cost of managing such properties may exceed the returns they earn. Moreover, the multiplicity of owners hinders management of those lands, effectively devolving power to the Bureau of Indian Affairs rather than in the hands of the allottees themselves. The problem of fractionation of allotments and the various attempts by Congress to repair the problem were discussed in Chapter 14.[124] The Supreme Court has twice

[117] U.S. Const., art. IV, §3.
[118] *Karuk Tribe of California v. Ammon*, 209 F.3d 1366, 1373 (Fed. Cir. 2000).
[119] *Id.* at 1374 (*citing Sioux Tribe of Indians v. United States*, 316 U.S. 317, 325 (1942), and *Hynes v. Grimes Packing Co.*, 337 U.S. 86, 101 (1949)).
[120] *Karuk Tribe*, 209 F.3d at 1374 (*citing Hynes*, 337 U.S. at 104).
[121] *Id.* (*quoting Hynes*, 337 U.S. at 103).
[122] *Mitchel v. United States*, 34 U.S. 711, 746 (1835).
[123] *See* §15.3.1.
[124] *See* §14.6.2.1.

struck down statutes intended to reconsolidate fractionated allotments by providing for transfer of such interests to the tribe when current owners die.[125] The general issues involved in determining whether such statutes constitute takings of property without just compensation are described in Chapter 14. In effect, the Court has held in *Hodel v. Irving*[126] or *Babbitt v. Youpee*[127] that the right to pass on property at death is a core property right and that a statute that converts a fee simple into a life estate by divesting the owner of the right to leave the property by inheritance or devise constitutes a *per se* taking of property.

Babbitt v. Youpee

What the Court does not adequately address in either *Hodel* or *Babbitt* is the fact the allotment property is not fee simple property. It is not only subject to a restraint on alienation, but is also held subject to the fee interest retained by the United States. The Supreme Court interpreted that retained fee interest to give the United States certain management powers because of its position as trustee, holding the fee for the benefit of the tribal interest.[128] It is this retained power of management that the Supreme Court believed justified allotment in the first place. If allotment — the transfer of tribal title to tribal members — was not a taking of property because it was "a mere change in the form of investment,"[129] it is not clear why a transfer the other way is not similarly "a mere change in the form of investment" and not a taking of property. If, on the other hand, deprivation of the right to pass on allotment property at death is a *per se* violation of the takings clause, then it is hard to conclude anything other than that the original allotment represented a taking of tribal property, to the tune of 90 million acres — a deprivation for most of which the tribes never did receive compensation.

Tribal interests v. restricted trust allotments

§15.5 Protection of Tribal Possession

§15.5.1 Restraint on Alienation

Tribal lands within Indian country (and sometimes outside Indian country), whether held under recognized or original Indian title, are subject to a restraint on alienation under both federal common law[130] and the *Non-Intercourse Act*.[131]

Federal common law and *Non-Intercourse Act*

[125] *Babbitt v. Youpee*, 519 U.S. 234 (1997); *Hodel v. Irving*, 481 U.S. 704 (1987).
[126] 481 U.S. 704 (1987).
[127] 519 U.S. 234 (1997).
[128] *See United States v. Sioux Nation of Indians*, 448 U.S. 371, 408 (1980) (quoting *Lone Wolf v. Hitchcock*, 187 U.S. 553, 565 (1903), to the effect that "Congress possesse[s] a paramount power over the property of the Indians, by reason of its exercise of guardianship over their interests, and that such authority might be implied, even though opposed to the strict letter of a treaty with the Indians."). *See also United States v. Mitchell*, 445 U.S. 535 (1980) (*Mitchell I*) (holding that its role as trustee and owner of the fee places no enforceable legal obligations on the United States to act affirmatively to protect tribal interests).
[129] *Lone Wolf v. Hitchcock*, 187 U.S. 553, 568 (1903).
[130] *Johnson v. M'Intosh*, 21 U.S. (8 Wheat.) 543 (1823).
[131] Act of July 22, 1790, ch. 33, §4, 1 Stat. 137 (1790) (current version codified at 25 U.S.C. §177).

§15.5.2 Extinguishment

Only Congress can extinguish tribal title

The tribal title can only be extinguished by Congress. Moreover, the Supreme Court has often held that extinguishment will not be implied. Rather, Indian title can only be extinguished by a "clear and plain" expression of intent to extinguish by Congress[132] and will not be "lightly implied."[133]

▶ HARD CASE ▷ INCREASING WEIGHT OF HISTORY

The 1992 case of *State v. Elliott* involved the arrest of 36 members of the Missisquoi Abenaki Tribe for fishing without a state license.[134] The trial judge, Joseph J. Wolchik, found that the federal government — the only entity with the lawful power to extinguish Indian title — had never extinguished Abenaki title to the tribe's traditional lands in the state of Vermont, including the land on which the defendants were fishing.[135] Because the defendants were fishing on tribally owned land, the state of Vermont had no jurisdiction over them and Judge Wolchik dismissed the charges against them. The ruling placed in doubt the title to every parcel of land in the entire state. It was overturned on appeal by the Vermont Supreme Court, which ruled, in an opinion by Justice James Morse, that the Abenakis had lost their original property rights to their lands in Vermont by the "increasing weight of history."[136]

The argument that Abenaki title had been extinguished

Justice Morse recognized that no act of Congress expressly extinguished Abenaki title. Nor did any prior act of either Great Britain or the state of Vermont when it was arguably independent from both Britain and the United States between 1777 and 1791. However, Justice Morse explained that Vermont lands had been in dispute between New York and New Hampshire, that the Royal Governor of New Hampshire had granted Vermont lands conditional on settlement, that the New Hampshire grantees had fought against New York claimants to secure their claims and to declare the independence of Vermont from New York (and from Great Britain), and that Congress was aware of, and intended to validate these claims (and the fact that they were conditional on settlement) when Vermont was admitted to the Union as the fourteenth state in 1791. Although no single act established that the tribal title had been extinguished, the court held that this series of events, coupled with the long-standing acquiescence of the United States in settlement of Abenaki lands by non-Indian Vermonters, meant that Abenaki title had clearly

[132] *United States ex rel. Hualpai Indians v. Santa Fe Pacific Railroad*, 314 U.S. 339, 353 (1941).

[133] *Id.* at 354.

[134] *State v. Elliott*, 616 A.2d 210 (Vt. 1992), *cert. denied*, 507 U.S. 911 (1993), *rev'g State v. St. Francis*, No. 1170-10-86Fcr, slip op. at 1 (Vt. Dist. Ct., Aug. 11, 1989).

[135] Whether recognition of original Indian title would give the Abenaki Nation the right to evict non-Indian residents from Abenaki land or to collect rent from them is a separate question not addressed by the court.

[136] 616 A.2d at 218; *see also id.* at 213-218 (describing the way in which Indian title was extinguished by historical events).

been extinguished. This argument might be further supported by the idea that non-Indians in Vermont had long relied on the titles they were granted by the state of Vermont, by the failure of the United States to intervene to protect Abenaki occupancy rights, and by the long-standing occupancy of those lands. Although no formal statute or treaty extinguished Abenaki title, informal acquiescence by the United States in non-Indian possession and state grants of title suggest an intent to extinguish tribal title.

The argument that Abenaki title was not extinguished is based on the formal rules of property law. Tribal title is a matter of federal, not state, law. Federal precedent clearly requires an explicit act of Congress to extinguish tribal title. No such act exists. A federal statute first passed in 1834 places the burden of persuasion squarely on the party challenging tribal title.[137]

Critique of *State v. Elliott*: The argument that Abenaki title had not been extinguished

That presumption can be overcome only by an express sovereign act by Congress.[138] Moreover, "an extinguishment cannot be lightly implied in view of the avowed solicitude of the United States for the welfare of its Indian wards."[139] The Supreme Court held in the 1985 case of *County of Oneida v. Oneida Indian Nation*[140] that "congressional intent to extinguish Indian title must be 'plain and unambiguous,' and will not be 'lightly implied.'"[141] It further noted that "[r]elying on the strong policy of the United States 'from the beginning to respect the Indian right of occupancy,' it '[c]ertainly' would require 'plain and unambiguous action to deprive the [Indians] of the benefits of that policy.'"[142]

Conflicting property rights

While it is true that recognition of Abenaki title would undermine the expectations of non-Indian possessors in Vermont, the recognition that Abenaki title had never been extinguished would not necessarily mean that the Abenakis would have the lawful power to eject those non-Indian possessors. In fact, precisely because Congress does, under federal Indian law, have plenary power to extinguish tribal title, Congress could have negotiated a land claims settlement act with the Missisquoi Abenakis, as it did with the natives in Alaska and the Penobscot and Passamaquoddy nations in Maine.[143] As it is, the Supreme Court of Vermont has sent a peculiar message to the Abenakis, who are now citizens of the state of Vermont, as well as the United States. It has held that Vermont was established, and its constitution adopted, to protect the property rights of all Vermonters except the Abenakis. ◀

137 25 U.S.C. §194 provides: In all trials about the right of property in which an Indian may be a party on one side, and a white person on the other, the burden of proof shall rest upon the white person, whenever the Indian shall make out a presumption of title in himself from the fact of previous possession or ownership.

138 *County of Oneida v. Oneida Indian Nation*, 470 U.S. 226, 247 (1985) (*Oneida II*).

139 *United States ex rel. Hualpai (Walapai) Indians v. Santa Fe Pacific Railroad*, 314 U.S. 339, 354 (1941).

140 470 U.S. 226 (1985).

141 *Id.* at 247-248.

142 *Id.* at 248.

143 *Alaska Native Claims Settlement Act of 1971 (ANCSA)*, Act of Dec. 18, 1971, Pub. L. No. 92-203 (codified at 43 U.S.C. §§1601 to 1628); *Maine Indian Claims Settlement Act*, 25 U.S.C. §§1721 *et seq.*

§15.6 Reparations

§15.6.1 Indian Claims Commission Act

Tribal claims prior to 1946

Before 1946, Indian nations needed to obtain a special jurisdictional act from Congress before they would be entitled to sue the United States in federal court seeking compensation for wrongful taking of tribal lands. Several barriers to suit existed. First, the United States had sovereign immunity and could not be sued without its consent.[144] The United States had created the Court of Claims in 1855 to hear cases against the United States; however, claims based on violation of Indian treaties were statutorily excluded from its jurisdiction in 1863.[145] Second, until 1966, it was not thought that Indian nations could bring suits in federal court on their own behalf unless a special act of Congress conferred that right. In 1966, Congress passed a jurisdictional act granting federal district courts jurisdiction over any claims based on federal law brought by federally recognized Indian tribes.[146] Before 1966, federal courts arguably did not have subject matter jurisdiction over claims brought by tribes — even if their claims were based on federal questions. This was a second reason why tribes needed special jurisdictional acts of Congress to bring claims in federal court to vindicate their rights against the United States.

Indian Claims Commission

Between 1863 and 1946, Congress passed 142 special jurisdictional statutes granting tribes the right to sue the United States for specific claims in federal court.[147] However, in 1946, Congress passed the *Indian Claims Commission Act*.[148] The Act established the ICC and granted it power to hear a wide variety of claims, including (1) claims in law or equity arising under the Constitution, laws, or treaties of the United States, and executive orders of the President; (2) all other claims in law or equity, including torts claims, against the United States; (3) claims that "would result if the treaties, contracts, and agreements between the claimant and the United States were revised on the ground of fraud, duress, unconscionable consideration, mutual or unilateral mistake"; (4) claims for takings of "lands owned or occupied by the claimant without the payment for such lands of compensation agreed to by the claimant"; and (5) "claims based on fair and honorable dealings that are not recognized by any existing rule of law or equity."[149]

Terms of the Act

The Act waived the sovereign immunity of the United States, allowed claims based on taking of tribal title without regard to whether it was recognized by treaty or statute, and waived the defense of *laches* and any

[144] William C. Canby, Jr., *American Indian Law in a Nutshell* 485 (8th ed. 2025).

[145] Act of March 3, 1863, ch. 92, §9, 12 Stat. 765, 767.

[146] Act of Oct. 10, 1966, Pub. L. No. 89-635, §1, 80 Stat. 880 (codified at 28 U.S.C. §1362).

[147] *Cohen's Handbook of Federal Indian Law* §6.03[2][e][ii] (Nell Jessup Newton & Kevin K. Washburn, eds., 2024).

[148] Act of Oct. 8, 1976, Pub. L. No. 94-465, 90 Stat. 1990 (formerly codified at 25 U.S.C. §70v); *Cohen's Handbook of Federal Indian Law* §6.03[2][e][iii] (Nell Jessup Newton & Kevin K. Washburn, eds., 2024).

[149] Act of Oct. 8, 1976, Pub. L. No. 94-465, 90 Stat. 1990 (formerly codified at 25 U.S.C. §70v).

applicable statutes of limitation.[150] It empowered the ICC to hear claims accruing before August 13, 1946, and filed before August 13, 1951.[151] Those accruing after that time could be brought in the Court of Federal Claims, and although they are not limited to claims by federally recognized tribes, their scope is much narrower; they are limited to claims arising under federal law or executive order or otherwise cognizable if brought by non-Indians.[152]

Implementation of the Act

The ICC was empowered to provide monetary relief and not injunctive relief to correct unlawful violations of federal law or breach of treaties.[153] The federal courts have also interpreted very narrowly the "fair and honorable dealings" provision, depriving it of almost any force.[154] In addition, it allowed interest only on claims that amounted to takings of property within the meaning of the Fifth Amendment. Thus, takings of aboriginal title, even if they had occurred 100 years earlier, were compensated at the nineteenth-century rate, without any interest to compensate the tribe for the lost value in the intervening years. In addition, it applied a rule later adopted by the Supreme Court in 1980 in *Sioux Nation* that distinguished between federal actions that "took" property (and thus entitled the tribe to interest) and those that constituted exercises of the federal trust responsibility and thus were merely "breach of trust" claims for which interest would not be payable.[155] The ICC expired in 1978, transferring roughly 80 uncompleted cases to the Court of Claims.[156] As of 1978, when it completed its work, the ICC had adjudicated approximately 670 cases and awarded $774,222,906.64.[157]

§15.6.2 Eastern Land Claims

Deprivations of property by the states

In the last quarter of the twentieth century, eastern tribes brought land claims based on takings of property by state governments. In some cases, the claims involved aboriginal title lands never formally taken by the United States.[158] In other cases, they involved violations of the *Non-Intercourse Act.*

[150] *Cohen's Handbook of Federal Indian Law* §6.03[2][e][iii] (Nell Jessup Newton & Kevin K. Washburn, eds., 2024).

[151] Act of Aug. 13, 1946, ch. 959, §12, 60 Stat. 1049 (formerly codified as 25 U.S.C. §70k).

[152] 28 U.S.C. §1505.

[153] *Cohen's Handbook of Federal Indian Law* §6.03[2][e][iii] (Nell Jessup Newton & Kevin K. Washburn, eds., 2024).

[154] *Fort Sill Apache Tribe v. United States*, 477 F.2d 1360 (Ct. Cl. 1973); *Gila River Pima-Maricopa Indian Community v. United States*, 427 F.2d 1194 (Ct. Cl. 1970).

[155] Howard M. Friedman, *Interest on Indian Claims: Judicial Protection of the Fisc*, 5 Val. U. L. Rev. 26 (1970).

[156] Wilcomb E. Washburn, *Land Claims in the Mainstream of Indian/White Land History in Irredeemable America: The Indians' Estate and Land Claims* 21, 24 (Imre Sutton ed. 1985).

[157] *Id.* at 24.

[158] *See, e.g., Golden Hill Paugussett Tribe v. Weicker*, 39 F.3d 51 (2d Cir. 1994); *Catawba Indian Tribe v. South Carolina*, 718 F.2d 1291 (4th Cir. 1983), *rev'd on other grounds*, 476 U.S. 498 (1986); *Mohegan Tribe v. Connecticut*, 483 F. Supp. 597 (D. Conn. 1980), *aff'd*, 638 F.2d 612 (2d Cir. 1981); *Mashpee Tribe v. New Seabury Corp.*, 592 F.2d 575 (1st Cir. 1979); *Narragansett Tribe v. Southern Rhode Island Land Development Corp.*, 418 F. Supp. 798 (D.R.I. 1976); *Schaghticoke Tribe v. Kent School Corp.*, 423 F. Supp. 780 (D. Conn. 1976); *Joint Tribal Council of Passamaquoddy Tribe v. Morton*, 528 F.2d 370 (1st Cir. 1975). *See also State v.*

For example, several Supreme Court cases have concerned claims by the Oneida Nation that Oneida lands were wrongfully taken by New York state in violation of the *Non-Intercourse Act.* The Supreme Court has ruled in favor of the Oneidas, holding that they have a federal common law right to sue for violation of the *Non-Intercourse Act,* that state statutes of limitation and adverse possession law are preempted by federal law (because the tribal land claims are based on federal, not state, law), and that no federal statute of limitations bars such claims.[159] Although not deciding whether *laches* was available as a defense to the tribe's property claim, for the majority, Justice Powell noted that "the application of *laches* would appear to be inconsistent with established federal policy."[160] Subsequent decisions by lower federal courts have similarly found that *laches* is not available as a defense to liability claims that tribes were wrongfully deprived of their lands by the state of New York in violation of the *Non-Intercourse Act* although *laches* might bar an ejectment remedy.[161]

Eleventh Amendment limitations on tribal claims against the states in federal court

However, the Supreme Court has ruled that the Eleventh Amendment bars suits in federal court brought by tribes against the states for damages.[162] It has also held that the Eleventh Amendment bars suits to quiet title to property held by the state.[163] Finally, it has ruled that Congress does not possess the power under the Indian commerce clause to abrogate state sovereign immunity by statutes authorizing suits against the states.[164] However, the Supreme Court has allowed tribal claims to be heard in federal court if they are brought by the United States as plaintiff; in such cases, tribes are entitled to intervene as interested parties to bring their claims.[165] The Oneida Indian Nation bought back some of its own land from the non-Indian possessor. The parcels had been sold by a tribal member to a non-Indian in 1807 in violation of the *Non-Intercourse Act* and were repurchased by the tribe in 1997 and 1998. The tribe began to operate a gas station,

---

Elliott, 616 A.2d 210 (Vt. 1992), *cert. denied*, 507 U.S. 911 (1993), *rev'g State v. St. Francis*, No. 1170-10-86Fcr, slip op. at 1 (Vt. Dist. Ct., Aug. 11, 1989).

159 *Oneida Indian Nation v. County of Oneida*, 414 U.S. 661 (1974) (*Oneida I*); *County of Oneida v. Oneida Indian Nation*, 470 U.S. 226 (1985) (*Oneida II*). *See also Cayuga Indian Nation of New York v. Cuomo*, 771 F. Supp. 19 (N.D.N.Y. 1991) (*laches* unavailable as a defense). *See* §15.2.1.

160 *County of Oneida v. Oneida Indian Nation*, 470 U.S. 226, 245 n.16 (1985) (*Oneida II*). This ruling is largely superseded by the case of *Sherrill v. Oneida Indian Nation of New York*, 544 U.S. 197 (2005), discussed below.

161 *Canadian St. Regis Band of Mohawk Indians v. State of New York*, 278 F. Supp. 2d 313 (N.D.N.Y. 2003); *Cayuga Indian Nation of New York v. Cuomo*, 771 F. Supp. 19 (N.D.N.Y. 1991), *later proceedings sub nom. Cayuga Indian Nation of New York v. Pataki*, 2000 U.S. Dist. LEXIS 7045 (N.D.N.Y. 2000), 165 F. Supp. 2d 266 (N.D.N.Y. 2001). *Compare Hohri v. United States* (*Hohri I*), 782 F.2d 227, 252 (D.C. Cir. 1986) (holding that takings claims by Japanese internees were timely and not barred by the statute of limitations because the government had fraudulently deceived the courts and the internees about that basis for internment) *with Hohri v. United States* (*Hohri II*), 847 F.2d 779 (Fed. Cir. 1988) (holding that such claims were barred by the statute of limitations).

162 *Blatchford v. Native Village of Noatak and Circle Village*, 501 U.S. 775 (1991).

163 *Idaho v. Coeur d'Alene Tribe*, 521 U.S. 261, 281-282 (1997). *See Ysleta Del Sur Pueblo v. Laney*, 199 F.3d 281, 287 (5th Cir. 2000).

164 *Seminole Tribe of Florida v. Florida*, 517 U.S. 44, 47 (1996).

165 *Blatchford v. Native Village of Noatak and Circle Village*, 501 U.S. 775, 783 (1991).

convenience store, and a textile facility on the disputed parcels. The tribe argued that, under the ruling in *Oneida II*, it had never lost title to the land and that Congress had never diminished the scope of the Oneida reservation; as tribal land it would therefore be classified as "Indian country" and exempt from state property taxation. The federal district court agreed with the tribe but the Supreme Court reversed in *Sherrill v. Oneida Indian Nation of New York*, on the ground that the long passage of time meant that it would be inequitable to grant the tribe the equitable remedy it sought.[166] The Court noted that the state had exercised sovereignty over the lost Oneida lands for almost 200 years and that the Oneidas had *acquiesced* in this state of affairs, unreasonably delaying in going to court to seek return of the land and protection of tribal sovereignty (*laches*). The Court also found that it would be disruptive and *impracticable* to alter the sovereignty arrangements by allowing the tribe to recover sovereignty over its land bit by bit as it bought back its own land; this would create checkerboard jurisdiction with some parcels governed by the tribe and others by the local municipal government. The Court therefore applied the doctrines of *laches*, acquiescence, and impracticability and barred the Oneida claim. However, on remand, at least one lower court has held that the counties in New York cannot foreclose on tribal land even if they fail to pay state property taxes both because the tribes have sovereign immunity that has not been abrogated by the federal government and because the federal *Non-Intercourse Act* prohibits transfer of tribal title without the consent of the United States.[167]

Sherrill v. Oneida Indian Nation of New York

Laches

▷ RELIEF **HARD CASE ◀**

The *Non-Intercourse Act* clearly provides that "[n]o purchase, grant, lease, or other conveyance of lands, or of any title or claim thereto, from any Indian nation or tribe of Indians shall be of any validity in law or equity, unless the same be made by treaty or convention entered into pursuant to the Constitution."[168] The Supreme Court has held that transfers by the Oneidas to New York state violated this statute, that no statute of limitations bars the claim even though the transfer occurred in the 1790s, that the Oneidas have a federal common law right of action, and that New York is not immune to suit by the United States on behalf of the Oneidas.[169] Similar suits have been brought by the Cayuga and Seneca-Cayuga Tribe against the governor of New York (in his official capacity), the state of New York,[170] and individual landowners in New York now living on land previously

[166] *Sherrill v. Oneida Indian Nation of New York*, 544 U.S. 197 (2005).

[167] *Oneida Indian Nation of New York v. Madison County*, 401 F. Supp. 2d 219 (N.D.N.Y. 2005).

[168] Act of July 22, 1790, ch. 33, §4, 1 Stat. 137 (1790) (current version codified at 25 U.S.C. §177). *See Cohen's Handbook of Federal Indian Law* §18.03[2][b] (Nell Jessup Newton & Kevin K. Washburn, eds., 2024).

[169] *Oneida Indian Nation v. County of Oneida*, 414 U.S. 661 (1974) (*Oneida I*); *County of Oneida v. Oneida Indian Nation*, 470 U.S. 226 (1985) (*Oneida II*).

[170] New York was added as a defendant in *Cayuga Indian Nation of New York v. Pataki*, 79 F. Supp. 2d 78 (N.D.N.Y. 1999).

owned by plaintiffs;[171] they have similarly prevailed on the underlying substantive claims adjudicated to date to the effect that their treaty-based property rights were wrongfully taken by New York state in 1795 and 1807 without the consent of the United States as required by the *Non-Intercourse Act.* In *Cayuga Indian Nation of New York v. Cuomo*,[172] the court considered the question of whether ejectment was available as a potential remedy against the non-Indian possessors of land claimed by the Cayuga and Seneca-Cayuga Tribes.

Argument that ejectment is not available

The court, in an opinion by Judge McCurn, held that ejectment is not available as a remedy against the non-Indian possessors of land belonging to the Cayuga and Seneca-Cayuga Tribes.[173] The court applied the *Restatement (Second) of Torts* §936(1)[174] to determine whether an injunction was an appropriate remedy for the conceded continuing trespass on Cayuga lands. The tribes had several factors in their favor; their interest was a strong one: "[T]he loss of their homeland has had an immeasurable impact upon the Cayuga culture and Cayuga society as a whole."[175] Moreover, because land is unique, damages are usually viewed as inadequate remedies for wrongful possession of land belonging to another.[176] And although one might think that the Cayugas delayed by waiting until 1980 to bring a claim based on conduct in 1795 and 1807, the court found that the delay was not unreasonable given the consistent efforts of the Cayugas over that time, other than court action, to recover their lands and the fact the governments that were supposed to protect their interests (especially the federal government) failed to do so; indeed, the "systems which theoretically should have assisted the Cayugas seemingly thwarted their efforts."[177] The *Indian Claims Commission Act*, for example, provided no remedy for takings of property by the states. On the other hand, the court concluded that the substantial delay had the effect of creating substantial reliance interests in the non-Indian owners who did develop the land and that the "public interest" would not be served by declaring the Cayugas the owners of huge amounts of property inhabited by nonmembers of the tribe, and that there was a significant likelihood that an order of ejectment would not be practicable in the sense that many defendants would refuse to comply, creating enormous enforcement problems.[178] Although "[i]ndisputably great hardships

[171] The suits against the individual landowners have now been dismissed, *Cayuga Indian Nation of New York v. Pataki*, 188 F. Supp. 2d 223 (N.D.N.Y. 2002).

[172] 1999 WL 509442, 1999 U.S. Dist. LEXIS 10579 (N.D.N.Y. 1999).

[173] *Cayuga Indian Nation of New York v. Cuomo*, 1999 WL 509442, 1999 U.S. Dist. LEXIS 10579 (N.D.N.Y. 1999).

[174] Section 936(1) of the *Restatement (Second) of Torts* lists seven factors to consider in determining whether to grant an injunction against a trespass: (1) The nature of the interest to be protected; (2) The relative adequacy of injunctive and other remedies available to the plaintiff; (3) Any unreasonable delay of the plaintiff in initiating the action; (4) Any related misconduct on the part of the plaintiff; (5) The relative hardship of the parties if the injunction is granted or denied; (6) The interests of third persons and the public; (7) The practicability of framing and enforcing the injunction.

[175] 1999 WL 509442, at *23.

[176] *Id.* at *24.

[177] *Id.* at *25.

[178] *Id.* at *27.

have befallen the Cayugas as a result of the 1795 and 1807 cessions, the court must balance those hardships against those which would result from ejectment." Ejectment would "potentially displace literally thousands of private landowners and several public landowners" and would "prove all too vividly the old axiom: 'Two wrongs don't make a right.'"[179] Finally, a damages remedy would allow the Cayuga Nation to purchase back property from willing sellers and thereby achieve its goals without displacement of innocent homeowners.[180]

Argument that ejectment should be available

The argument against considering ejectment as a possible remedy is understandable, given the substantial reliance interests built up by defendants. But the argument is also problematic for several reasons. First, it is not clear why the *Restatement of Torts* is the relevant legal source for determining the remedy for violation of the *Non-Intercourse Act.* Tribal rights are based on federal, not state, law, and existing canons of construction in federal Indian law require statutes enacted for the benefit of Indian tribes to be interpreted "liberally" in favor of establishing Indian rights.[181] These canons are not mere maxims to discern the intent of Congress, but are based on the basic trust responsibility of the United States toward Indian tribes and its trust obligation as owner of the fee interest in tribal lands; trust obligations are, in turn, based on the constitutional structure of relations among the tribes, the states, and the federal government, as well as federal treaties.[182]

Inadequacy of damages

Second, even if the criteria in the *Restatement* are relevant, the court failed to consider that the usual remedy in property cases is injunctive relief, not damages, precisely because damages are not adequate as a remedy. Consider the legal posture of the case. Title to the land is in the Cayugas, and the defendants are occupying the land illegally — they derive their titles from the state, and the transfer of title from the tribe to the state was completely "invalid." You can only convey what you own, and if the state had no rights, it could transfer none to its grantees; nor could they transfer rights to the current owners. Yet, of course, the current grantees have substantial interests in continued access to what the state and federal governments led them to believe was their land. This brings us to the third problem with the *Cayuga* ruling. The judge failed to consider that the actual outcome of a ruling in favor of the tribe would be a settlement. Either the state of New York would finally offer the Cayugas an attractive enough package to induce them to settle the lawsuit or Congress would exercise its plenary power and pass a land claims settlement act extinguishing tribal title, vesting title to the non-Indian–held lands in the current possessors, compensating the tribes for loss of their land, and granting them state and/or federal land for expansion of their reservations. The question is what the

179 *Id.*

180 *Id.* at *24.

181 *Cohen's Handbook of Federal Indian Law* §3.01[1] (Nell Jessup Newton & Kevin K. Washburn, eds., 2024).

182 *Id.* at §3.01[2]; Philip P. Frickey, *Marshalling Past and Present: Colonialism, Constitutionalism, and Interpretation in Federal Indian Law*, 107 Harv. L. Rev. 381 (1993). *See also* Philip P. Frickey, *Domesticating Federal Indian Law*, 81 Minn. L. Rev. 31 (1996).

bargaining power of the parties will be in such settlement negotiations. If the court takes ejectment off the table as a possible remedy, this gives the state of New York an incentive to continue to litigate the case for another 20 years and to continue to refuse to honor the Cayuga title to its lands or to offer the tribe enough to induce the tribe to settle the case. Because it is the tribe that is the actual legal owner of the lands in question, telling the state that ejectment is available as a remedy would have strengthened the Cayugas' hand in negotiations and helped induce a settlement that honored property rights on both sides.

Finally, making ejectment unavailable as a remedy relegates the Cayuga Indian Nation to damages for loss of their land.[183] However, this may have the effect of depriving the Cayuga Nation of their property in violation of the *Non-Intercourse Act*. Moreover, it has long been held that only Congress has the power to extinguish Indian title.[184] So after the *Cayuga* litigation, has the tribe's title been extinguished or not?

Effect of the *Sherrill* ruling on damages claims

On appeal from Judge McCurn's ruling in *Cayuga Indian Nation of New York v. Cuomo*,[185] the Second Circuit applied the equitable doctrines of *laches*, acquiescence, and impossibility that had been used in *Sherrill* to deny the Oneida Indian Nation protection from state property taxes to hold that even the claim for trespass damages brought by the United States on behalf of the Cayuga Indian Nation of New York and the Seneca-Cayuga Tribe of Oklahoma against the state of New York was barred.[186] Justice Cabranes explained that the United States had waited 200 years to bring the lawsuit on behalf of the tribes and that even though the court awarded a damages remedy, the claim had sought a declaration that the tribes had a legal right to possession of their land and hence a right to eject the non-Indian inhabitants. He noted that the trespass claim (with the associated remedy of damages) was also barred by *laches* because "we must recognize that the trespass claim, like all of plaintiffs' claims in this action, is predicated entirely upon plaintiffs' possessory claim, for the simple reason that there can be no trespass unless the Cayugas possessed the land in question."[187] However, in *Oneida Indian Nation of New York v. State of New York*,[188] the court allowed the Oneidas to bring a "nondisruptive" nonpossessory common law claim against the state of New York for damages caused by its dispossession of Oneida land in violation of the *Non-Intercourse Act* for less than fair market value—a claim the court said was

[183] *Cayuga Indian Nation of New York v. Pataki*, 165 F. Supp. 2d 266, 366 (N.D.N.Y. 2002), *rev'd, Cayuga Indian Nation of New York v. Pataki*, 413 F.3d 266 (2d Cir. 2005) (awarding $1,911,672.62 for the fair rental value of the claim area from July 27, 1795 to February 17, 2000, and $35,000,000.00 for the future loss of use and possession of the claim area, and $211,000,326.80 for prejudgment interest in connection with the reasonable rental award against the state, making a total award of $247,911,999.42).

[184] *United States ex rel. Hualpai Indians v. Santa Fe Pacific Railroad*, 314 U.S. 339, 353-354 (1941) (Indian title can only be extinguished by a "clear and plain" expression of congressional intent to extinguish tribal title).

[185] 1999 WL 509442, 1999 U.S. Dist. LEXIS 10579 (N.D.N.Y. 1999).

[186] *Cayuga Indian Nation of New York v. Pataki*, 413 F.3d 266 (2d Cir. 2005). *Accord, New York v. Shinnecock Indian Nation*, 628 Fed. Appx. 54 (2d Cir. 2015).

[187] *Cayuga Indian Nation of New York v. Pataki*, 413 F.3d 266, 278 (2d Cir. 2005).

[188] *Oneida Indian Nation of New York v. State of New York*, 500 F. Supp. 2d 128 (N.D.N.Y. 2007).

not the same as a claim for trespass damages based on lost use and possession of land, but is "best styled as a contract claim that seeks to reform or revise a contract that is void for unconscionability. This type of contract claim is not disruptive."[189] However, the New York Court of Appeals overturned that decision on the ground that New York's sovereign immunity bars the contract claim.[190] ◀

§15.6.3 Land Claims Settlement Acts

Negotiated, statutory settlements

Many eastern land claims have been settled by land claims settlement acts. These statutes were negotiated with the relevant tribes. They extinguish tribal title to lands not covered by the act and recognize and vest tribal title in particular lands described by the act. They also provide compensation for the deprivation of property. Such acts have been passed involving the Penobscot, Passamaquoddy, and Maliseet Tribes in Maine,[191] the Narragansetts in Rhode Island,[192] the Miccosukee Indian Tribe in Florida,[193] and the Mashantucket Pequots in Connecticut.[194]

Alaska Native Claims Settlement Act

A massive land claims settlement act was passed by Congress regarding natives in Alaska. The *Alaska Native Claims Settlement Act of 1971 (ANCSA)*[195] extinguished all Alaskan aboriginal titles,[196] granted Native Alaskans fee title to over 40 million acres of land, $462.5 million over an 11-year period, and a royalty of 2 percent up to a ceiling of $500 million on mineral development in Alaska.[197] "This settlement provide[d] far more money and [left] far more land in native ownership than any previous treaty, agreement, or statute for the extinguishment of aboriginal title in our nation's history."[198] At the same time, the Act compromised tribal sovereignty by vesting ownership, not in native governments, but in regional and village corporations in which enrolled natives would receive corporate stock.[199] Shares of stock in the native corporation were subject to a restraint on alienation for 20 years,[200] although the *ANCSA Amendments*

[189] *Id.* at 140. *See Shinnecock Indian Nation v. New York*, 2006 U.S. Dist. LEXIS 87516 (E.D.N.Y. 2006) (dismissing a claim based on unconscionable consideration for land taken by the state).

[190] *Oneida Indian Nation of New York v. Cnty. of Oneida*, 617 F.3d 114, 131 (2d Cir. 2010).

[191] *Maine Indian Claims Settlement Act*, 25 U.S.C. §§1721 *et seq.*

[192] *Rhode Island Indian Claims Settlement Act*, 25 U.S.C. §§1701 *et seq.*

[193] *Florida Indian Land Claims Settlement Act*, 25 U.S.C. §§1741 *et seq.*

[194] *Connecticut Indian Land Claims Settlement Act*, 25 U.S.C. §§1751 *et seq.*

[195] Act of Dec. 18, 1971, Pub. L. No. 92-203 (codified at 43 U.S.C. §§1601 to 1628).

[196] 43 U.S.C. §1603.

[197] William C. Canby, Jr., *American Indian Law in a Nutshell* 511 (8th ed. 2025).

[198] Arthur Lazarus & W. Richard West, *The Alaska Native Claims Settlement Act: A Flawed Victory*, 40 Law & Contemp. Probs. 132 (1976).

[199] William C. Canby, Jr., *American Indian Law in a Nutshell* 512-513 (8th ed. 2025); Marylin J. Ward Ford & Robert Rude, *ANCSA: Sovereignty and a Just Settlement of Land Claims or an Act of Deception*, 15 Touro L. Rev. 479 (1999); Marylin J. Ward Ford, *Twenty Five Years of the Alaska Native Claims Settlement Act: Self-Determination or Destruction of the Heritage, Culture, and Way of Life of Alaska's Native Americans*, 12 J. Envtl. L. & Litig. 305 (1997); Monroe Price, *A Moment in History: The Alaska Native Claims Settlement Act*, 8 U.C.L.A.-Alaska L. Rev. 89 (1979).

[200] William C. Canby, Jr., *American Indian Law in a Nutshell* 447 (7th ed. 2020).

Act of 1987 permitted the corporations to extend the restraints on alienation beyond that term.[201] *ANCSA* also substantially limited native sovereignty by revoking all reserves previously established in Alaska, effectively destroying some previously recognized sovereign governing powers.[202]

§15.6.4 Breach of Trust Claims

Trust relationship

The Supreme Court has often characterized the United States as in a "trust" relationship with the Indian nations.[203] The United States' role as "trustee" places obligations on it. Those obligations arise partly because the United States is in a government-to-government relationship with the tribes and partly because the United States holds the fee to tribal lands in trust for the tribes. The trust relationship gives the United States powers over the tribes and tribal lands and imposes correlative vulnerabilities on the tribes. At the same time, the trust relationship imposes obligations, both moral and legal, on the United States toward the tribes. Some of these obligations are negative; they limit the power of the United States.[204] Others are affirmative; they obligate the United States to take certain actions for the benefit of the tribes.[205]

Domestic dependent nations

As Chief Justice Marshall noted in *Cherokee Nation v. Georgia*[206] in 1831, the United States–Indian relationship is "perhaps unlike that of any two people in existence" and "marked by peculiar and cardinal distinctions which exist nowhere else."[207] Indian tribes are nations because they are "distinct political societ[ies] separated from others, capable of managing [their] own affairs and governing [themselves]."[208] Moreover, they have "an unquestionable, and, heretofore, unquestioned, right to the lands they occupy, until that right shall be extinguished by a voluntary cession to our government."[209] On the other hand, the tribes are nations that "reside within the acknowledged boundaries of the United States."[210] Rather than

[201] Pub. L. No. 100-241, 101 Stat. 1788.

[202] *See Alaska v. Native Village of Venetie*, 522 U.S. 520 (1998).

[203] *Seminole Nation v. United States*, 316 U.S. 286, 297 (1942) (noting that the federal government had assumed "moral obligations of the highest responsibility and trust" with respect to Indian nations and therefore should be "judged by the most exacting fiduciary standards"). *See also Menominee Tribe of Indians v. United States*, 101 Ct. Cl. 10, 19 (1944) (finding it to be settled doctrine that the United States acts as trustee for Indian property).

[204] *See, e.g., Lane v. Pueblo of Santa Rosa*, 249 U.S. 110, 113 (1919) (holding that the Secretary of the Interior could not dispose of lands claimed by an Indian Pueblo in the same manner as he could dispose of other public lands because "[t]hat would not be an exercise of guardianship, but an act of confiscation").

[205] *See, e.g., Joint Tribal Council of Passamaquoddy Tribe v. Morton*, 528 F.2d 370 (1st Cir. 1975) (invoking the trust responsibility to compel the government to bring litigation to protect tribal lands or resources). *But see Cherokee Nation v. United States*, 21 Cl. Ct. 565 (1990) (holding that the federal government had no duty to bring suit to eject trespassers from Cherokee lands).

[206] 30 U.S. (5 Pet.) 1 (1831).

[207] *Id.* at 16.

[208] *Id.*

[209] *Id.* at 17.

[210] *Id.*

"foreign nations," they are "domestic dependent nations."[211] In an unfortunate turn of phrase, Marshall added, "they are in a state of pupilage; their relation to the United States resembles that of a ward to his guardian."[212] This "guardian/ward" language was one source of the idea that there is a trust relationship between the tribes and the United States. It has sometimes been used to justify expansive federal regulation of the tribes.[213] It has even been used to justify granting the United States "plenary power" over the tribes, which was unlimited by any constitutional limits whatsoever.[214] This expansive reading of the plenary power doctrine has since been repudiated.[215] At the same, it has been very hard for tribes to convince the courts to limit the power of the United States over them.

Property

Two exceptions to this generalization exist. First, the tribes have been able, sometimes, to limit congressional power when Congress has acted so as to deprive the tribes of recognized property rights.[216] Second, the tribes have had some limited success in challenging executive action that has deprived the tribes of statutorily based entitlements. In *United States v. Mitchell* (*Mitchell I*),[217] the Supreme Court held that, despite the fact that the *General Allotment Act* provided that the United States would hold allotted land "in trust" for Indian allottees, it did not create enforceable fiduciary obligations on the United States to manage that property.[218] Thus, even though the United States was actually managing allotment property, the allottees had no claim for breach of trust if that property was mismanaged.

Breach of trust

However, the Court subsequently held in *United States v. Mitchell* (*Mitchell II*)[219] that more specific statutes authorizing federal management of Indian property (in this case, timber) might well create enforceable obligations on the United States if those statutes either expressly refer to trust obligations or authorize the United States actually to manage tribal lands.[220] Moreover, the Court held that the *Tucker Act*[221] and the *Indian Tucker Act*[222] waive the sovereign immunity of the United States for such claims. Nonetheless, the Supreme Court has recently affirmed in *Navajo Nation v. United States*,[223] that no compensation for mismanagement of tribal lands can be obtained unless a federal statute affirmatively recognizes a trust obligation and explicitly provides for such compensatory rights.

211 *Id.*

212 *Id.*

213 *United States v. Kagama*, 118 U.S. 375, 383-384 (1886); *see also United States v. Sandoval*, 231 U.S. 28 (1913).

214 *Lone Wolf v. Hitchcock*, 187 U.S. 553, 565 (1903).

215 *United States v. Sioux Nation of Indians*, 448 U.S. 371, 413-415 (1980).

216 *United States v. Creek Nation*, 295 U.S. 103 (1935).

217 445 U.S. 535 (1980).

218 *Accord, Navajo Nation v. United States*, 556 U.S. 287 (2009).

219 463 U.S. 206 (1983).

220 *Id.* at 224 (when statutes give the United States "full responsibility to manage Indian resources and land for the benefit of the Indians[, they] thereby establish a fiduciary relationship and define the contours of the United States' fiduciary responsibilities"); Nell Jessup Newton, *Indian Claims in the Courts of the Conqueror*, 41 Am. U. L. Rev. 753, 787 (1992).

221 28 U.S.C. §1491.

222 *Id.* at §1505.

223 *Navajo Nation v. United States*, 556 U.S. 287 (2009).

Nonetheless, the Supreme Court found the United States liable to the White Mountain Apache Tribe for allowing the buildings at Fort Apache to become dilapidated. That property had been granted to the tribe in a 1960 statute that allowed the United States to use the property for school and administrative purposes as long as needed for those purposes. When the United States decided to end those uses and deliver possession of the property to the tribe, the property was in a sorry state. On the ground that a tenant is liable to the landlord for waste of the property that occurs while in the tenant's possession, the Court held that the fact that the United States had control of the property obligated it to ensure that the property was maintained.[224]

Individual Indian Money Trust

Because of the problem of fractionation of allotments, Congress provided for the management of income from restricted trust allotments by the BIA. In *Cobell v. Babbitt*,[225] Judge Royce Lamberth found that the BIA had severely mismanaged the Individual Indian Money Trust (IIM), the repository of trust funds earned by allotment property.

> It would be difficult to find a more historically mismanaged federal program than the Individual Indian Money (IIM) trust. The United States, the trustee of the IIM trust, cannot say how much money is or should be in the trust. As the trustee admitted on the eve of trial, it cannot render an accurate accounting to the beneficiaries, contrary to a specific statutory mandate and the century-old obligation to do so. More specifically, as Secretary Babbitt testified, an accounting cannot be rendered for most of the 300,000-plus beneficiaries, who are now plaintiffs in this lawsuit. Generations of IIM trust beneficiaries have been born and raised with the assurance that their trustee, the United States, was acting properly with their money. Just as many generations have been denied any such proof, however. "If courts were permitted to indulge their sympathies, a case better calculated to excite them could scarcely be imagined."[226]

The plaintiff class, composed of more than 300,000 American Indians, argued that the BIA had breached its fiduciary duty as trustee and demanded a right to an accounting.[227] The court held that the United States "is currently in breach of certain trust duties owed to plaintiffs."[228] The court held because federal power over Indian lands is so different in nature and origin from that of a private trustee, plaintiffs could not bring a breach of fiduciary duty claim. They were, however, statutorily entitled to an accounting of IIM

[224] *United States v. White Mountain Apache Tribe*, 537 U.S. 465, 474-475 (2003). *Cf. United States v. Navajo Nation*, 537 U.S. 488, 506-507 (2003) (United States not liable to Navajo Nation for approving a royalty rate that was below fair market value when the decision to approve the rate had been made by the tribe).

[225] 91 F. Supp. 2d 1 (D.D.C. 1999), *aff'd in part and remanded in part sub nom. Cobell v. Norton*, 240 F.3d 1081 (D.C. Cir. 2001), *later proceeding at* 2003 U.S. Dist. LEXIS 16875 (D.D.C. Sept. 25, 2003).

[226] 91 F. Supp. 2d at 6 (*quoting Cherokee Nation v. Georgia*, 30 U.S. (5 Pet.) 1, 15 (1831) (Marshall, C.J.)).

[227] *See* 25 U.S.C. §162a(d)(1)-(7).

[228] 91 F. Supp. 2d at 7.

funds.[229] After years of litigation, the parties settled and Congress appropriated $3.4 billion, $1.9 billion of which would be used for a program to buy back and consolidate fractionated tribal interests. The federal courts approved the settlement.[230]

§15.6.5 Native American Graves Protection and Repatriation Act

Native American Graves Protection and Repatriation Act

The *Native American Graves Protection and Repatriation Act* of 1990[231] affirms tribal ownership of American Indian and Native Hawaiian human remains and funerary and cultural objects found on tribal or federal lands after the effective date of the statute. Such remains and objects belong to the lineal descendants of the person buried with the items or, if such descendants cannot be found, to the tribe on whose tribal land the object was found, or to the tribe having the closest cultural affiliation with the items.[232]

Human remains in museums

The Act further requires federal agencies and museums receiving federal funds to turn over human remains and associated funerary objects to lineal descendants or to the appropriate American Indian tribe or Native Hawaiian organization.[233] The only exception to this rule occurs when "the items are indispensable for completion of a specific scientific study, the outcome of which would be of major benefit to the United States."[234]

▷ KENNEWICK MAN **HARD CASE ◀**

The so-called Kennewick Man is a human skeleton over 9,000 years old found in Washington state. The remains were found on land in the control of the Army Corps of Engineers, which intended to return the

229 *See* 25 U.S.C. §162a(d)(1)-(7).

230 *Cobell v. Salazar*, 2011 WL 7719672 (D.D.C. 2011); *Judge Approves $3.4 Billion in Indian Royalties Settlement*, N.Y. Times, June 21, 2011, at A18; Rosalie Murphy, *Trapped in Outdated System, Cobell Settlement Offers Opportunity for Indian Land*, Desert Sun, Sept. 22, 2016 (describing progress but significant ongoing challenges in the implementation of the *Cobell* settlement).

231 25 U.S.C. §§3001 to 3013, 18 U.S.C. §1170.

232 25 U.S.C. §3002(a).

233 *Id.* at §3005(a). Museums are not required to turn over the objects and remains if this forced transfer would constitute a taking of property without just compensation in violation of the Fifth Amendment. 25 U.S.C. §3001(13). The meaning of this provision is unclear, as are the circumstances under which a museum acquired title to the remains or objects that would be sufficient to cause a forced transfer to violate the takings clause. *See* Daniel J. Hurtado, *Native American Graves Protection and Repatriation Act: Does It Subject Museums to an Unconstitutional "Taking"?*, 1 Hofstra Prop. L.J. 1 (1993).

234 25 U.S.C. §3005(b). Although the Smithsonian Institution is expressly excluded from coverage by the statute, 25 U.S.C. §3001(4) and (8), it is required to return those remains by the *National Museum of the American Indian Act*, 20 U.S.C. §§80q to 80q-15, passed November 28, 1989. This statute requires the Smithsonian to return "any Indian human remains identified by a preponderance of the evidence as those of a particular individual or as those of an individual culturally affiliated with a particular Indian tribe, upon the request of the descendants of such individual or of the Indian tribe." 20 U.S.C. §80q-9(c). It therefore allows the museum to retain any human remains for study that cannot be proven to have a connection to an identifiable tribe.

remains to a group of Columbia River tribes.[235] This plan was challenged by some scientists and a pre-Christian European church who claimed that the physiological features of the Kennewick man meant that he was Caucasian rather than Indian, that this meant that he could not be a lineal ancestor of the tribes in the area, and that examination of the remains was essential for scientific purposes. The tribes contended that his genetic make-up was irrelevant and that if he had died in that spot 9,000 years ago, then he was on tribal land and within the jurisdiction of the tribe. They also claimed a right to rebury him and a strong religious claim to prevent him from being prodded by scientists. The case presents a conflict of world views and a possible clash between religion and science. The court sided with the scientists, holding that the Kennewick man was not a Native American and that the tribes could not prove they were related to him.[236] ◀

State restrictions on removing human remains

A number of states have statutes prohibiting the removal of human remains found on private land or requiring their reburial elsewhere.[237] For example, in response to a court opinion that allowed a private owner to do whatever he wanted with Native American human remains found on his land,[238] California passed statutes requiring owners who discover American Indian human remains on their property to notify public officials and to negotiate with representatives of the affected tribe for reburial of the remains and associated objects.[239]

§15.7 Tribal Easements

§15.7.1 Hunting and Fishing Rights

Reserved rights

While many treaties provided for the transfer of huge amounts of land from the tribe in question to the United States, many treaties expressly reserved the right to hunt and fish on lands ceded to the United States.[240]

[235] William C. Canby, Jr., *American Indian Law in a Nutshell* 448 (8th ed. 2025).

[236] *Bonnichsen v. United States Department of Army*, 217 F. Supp. 2d 1116 (D. Or. 2002), *aff'd and remanded*, 367 F.3d 864 (9th Cir. 2004). *See* Rebecca Tsosie, *Privileging Claims to the Past: Ancient Human Remains and Contemporary Cultural Values*, 31 Ariz. St. L.J. 583 (1999).

[237] Vt. Stat. tit. 13, §3761.

[238] *Wana the Bear v. Community Construction, Inc.*, 180 Cal. Rptr. 423 (Ct. App. 1982).

[239] Cal. Gov't Code §7927.000; Cal. Health & Safety Code §7050.5(c); Cal. Pub. Res. Code §§5097.94, 5097.98, 5097.99; *People v. Van Horn*, 267 Cal. Rptr. 804 (Ct. App. 1990) (upholding the constitutionality of the statute and requiring an archaeologist to return two objects found in a site he excavated on private land while making a survey for the city of Vista, California, which was in the process of determining whether to buy the land); H. Marcus Price III, *Disputing the Dead: U.S. Law on Aboriginal Remains and Grave Goods* (1991); Thomas Boyd, *Disputes Regarding the Possession of Native American Religious and Cultural Objects and Human Remains: A Discussion of the Applicable Law and Proposed Legislation*, 55 Mo. L. Rev. 883 (1990). *But see Castro Romero v. Becken*, 256 F.3d 349 (5th Cir. 2001) (human remains found on municipal land turned over to city for reburial rather than to the tribe related to the remains).

[240] *Minnesota v. Mille Lacs Band of Chippewa Indians*, 526 U.S. 172, 175 (1999); *Tulee v. Washington*, 315 U.S. 681, 683 (1942); *United States v. Winans*, 198 U.S. 371, 378 (1905).

Such reserved rights are easements that remain enforceable until extinguished by the United States.

Interpretation of reserved fishing rights

Many issues of interpretation arise. For example, one treaty reserved the right to fish at "all usual and accustomed places."[241] Such language requires a choice about where such places were and are.[242] It also has often been interpreted to immunize tribal members from state fishing regulations, including licensing requirements.[243] In *United States v. Washington*, the Ninth Circuit interpreted a treaty right to fish off-reservation to include a right to sufficient water amount and quality to sustain fish so that culverts that disrupt river patterns must be altered to sustain an environment in which fish can flourish.[244] However, courts have sometimes subjected tribes to state conservation regulations. Similarly, where a tribe is given the right to fish "in common" with others,[245] several courts have ruled that such "in common" language grants the tribe a right to one-half the fish.[246]

§15.7.2 Water Rights

Winters **doctrine**

As with reserved hunting and fishing rights, many tribes expressly reserved the right to use water in streams flowing through Indian country. Such rights are established by the *Winters* doctrine, so called because they were first recognized in *Winters v. United States.*[247] The definition and allocation of tribal water rights is extremely complicated. Ignored for many years, the tribes' rights to water were reaffirmed by the Supreme Court in 1963 in *Arizona v. California.*[248] That case established the principle that the tribes were entitled to water sufficient to irrigate the *practicably irrigable acreage* on the reservation even if that land was not all being used for agricultural purposes. In effect, the ruling held that the tribes would have intended to reserve water sufficient for current *and possible future* needs and defined their rights with that in mind.

[241] *Tulee v. Washington*, 315 U.S. 681, 683 (1942).
[242] *See Herrera v. Wyoming*, 139 S. Ct. 1686 (2019) (treaty right to hunt on "unoccupied lands of the US" applies to hunting in national parks).
[243] William C. Canby, Jr., *American Indian Law in a Nutshell* 566 (8th ed. 2025); *see also Washington State Dep't of Licensing v. Cougar Den, Inc.*, 139 S. Ct. 1000 (2019) (treaty-based tribal right to travel on public highways means freedom from taxation on use of those roads).
[244] 853 F.3d 946 (9th Cir. 2017), *aff'd by an equally divided court sub. nom Washington v. United States*, 138 S. Ct. 1832 (2018).
[245] *Antoine v. Washington*, 420 U.S. 194, 196 (1975).
[246] *Washington v. Fishing Vessel Ass'n*, 443 U.S. 658, 690 (1979).
[247] 207 U.S. 564 (1908).
[248] 373 U.S. 546, 600 (1963).

PART VII

PERSONAL AND INTELLECTUAL PROPERTY

CHAPTER 16

Personal Property

§16.1 Introduction
§16.2 Animals
§16.3 Finders
§16.4 Gifts
§16.5 Bailments
§16.6 Good Faith Purchasers
§16.7 Adverse Possession
§16.8 Accession and Fixtures
§16.9 Human Bodies

§16.1 Introduction

Real and personal property

Most of this book has focused on real property. Real property is land and permanent, immovable structures built on land. Personal property is everything else, including both tangible property such as cars, and intangible property such as stocks and bonds. A somewhat old-fashioned legal term for tangible personal property is *chattel*. Real property is the core of the traditional property law course generally taught to first-year students in law schools. However, some aspects of personal property are often covered, particularly in introducing students to the field. This chapter will focus on tangible personal property while the next chapter will address the fascinating subject of intellectual property.[1]

Tangible personal property

This chapter will focus on issues that arise with ownership of wild animals, the law of finders (lost, mislaid, and abandoned property), gifts, bailments, good faith purchasers, adverse possession, and accession and fixtures (personal property that is altered or mixed with real property). In the next chapter, we will review the outline of the basic law of intellectual property regarding copyright, patents, trademarks, unfair competition law, publicity rights, and moral rights of artists.

Origins of property

Before we begin, a cautionary note is in order. Personal property is often the starting place for property law courses because it illustrates the rule of first possession. Wild animals are owned by the one who captures them or reduces them to possession. Lost property is owned by the finder, as long as the true owner has abandoned her claims to it. In each case, first possession of the previously unowned object fixes title in the possessor. This rule has intuitive appeal. It is the basis on which people form lines to go into the theater, stake out seats in a classroom where seats are not assigned, or establish the right to purchase a particular product in a store by taking it off the shelf.

Cautionary note

At the same time, starting a course on property in this way suggests that all (or at least most) property rights originate in this way. In reality, this is not so. The very unimportance of the topics of wild animals and abandoned personal property to the overall property system demonstrates how far afield we have to go to find completely unowned objects whose ownership is first established by possession.[2] Most ownership rights in personal property today, for example, are created or established, not by mere possession, but by entering into relationships with others. They obtain their value or are initially created by contract (including employment contracts, partnerships, corporations, stocks, bonds, bank accounts, sales of goods or services, insurance contracts), gift (gifts during life and at death through inheritance), marriage, or authorship or invention (copyright or patent). All these examples involve transfers or relations with others, rather than individual possession. Even authorship and invention depend on using

[1] For further information on the law governing personal property, see Barlow Burke, *Personal Property in a Nutshell* (4th ed. 2018).

[2] 2-13 *Thompson on Real Property, Third Thomas Edition* §13.03(b) ("In the modern world only relatively rarely does one have opportunity to acquire personal property by establishing original possession.").

prior knowledge — the work of others — and then converting new ideas to wealth through transactions with others.

Individual effort crucial

This is not to say that individual effort and desert are not crucial to the process by which property is created and property rights acknowledged; they are. At the same time, we must understand that property rights entail recognition of claims by others. Even the notion of first possession depends on the ability of those excluded from that which is possessed to recognize the legitimacy of that possession. This, in turn, depends on the ability of the property system to afford sufficient real opportunities for others to obtain similar rights.

§16.2 Animals

Capture

Many property law courses begin with the topic of wild animals. This is not because of the intrinsic importance of the subject, but because the topic affords an occasion for discussing the original acquisition of property. The textbook standard is *Pierson v. Post*,[3] an 1805 case in which one hunter (Post) was pursuing a fox on uninhabited lands when he was intercepted by another hunter (Pierson) who, knowing that Post was in pursuit of the fox, killed the animal first and took possession of it. Post sued Pierson on the ground that he had interfered with Post's pursuit of the fox and taken possession of an animal that should rightly have belonged to the hunter who was in active pursuit. The court held that ownership of wild animals is established not by mere pursuit, but only by actual capture.

▷ ACTIVE PURSUIT **HARD CASE ◀**

Argument for a capture rule

The rule of capture is well established and amply supported. The case of *Pierson v. Post* is thought to be hard, however, because the plaintiff, Post, was in active pursuit of the fox at the time defendant Pierson stepped in and snatched the animal away from him. Moreover, it appears that Pierson was well aware of this. One argument for a rule of capture is that it is certain in application. We are likely to agree in most cases about whether or not someone has actually captured an animal — either by wounding or killing it, or by trapping it and taking possession of it. A rule that assigns ownership on the basis of attempts to capture will be hard to apply because more than one person may be attempting to capture the animal at the same time. Moreover, before anyone has actually seized the animal, it is hard to say that it is under anyone's control; the first person to capture the animal is the first legitimately entitled to claim to possess it, and possession, after all, is crucial to ownership. Thus, before capture, anyone should be free to pursue the animal. Finally, a rule of capture may encourage competition. Before an animal is seized, it is open to anyone to make the attempt to capture it. This should induce individuals to attempt

[3] 3 Cai. R. 175, 2 Am. Dec. 264 (N.Y. Sup. Ct. 1805).

to capture animals because they have an equal chance of winning the race. A rule of pursuit, on the other hand, might well discourage competition because it allows only one person to pursue an animal at a time. One might make genuine efforts to hunt, only to be surprised at the last minute by a competing claim by someone who will turn out to have begun the chase earlier.

Argument for an active pursuit rule

The argument against the capture rule is that it authorizes interference by one person with the activity of another. Freedom to pursue an object is a good thing, but so is the right to be secure in one's ability to engage in that pursuit without undue interference. When one person sees that another is in active pursuit of an object, a rule of capture would arguably promote not competition, but meddlesome interference. Moreover, such meddling can result in violent confrontation. Consider the case of drivers in a packed parking lot. When a space appears about to open, many drivers approach it and put on their turn signals to indicate that they intend to occupy the space. If another car zips into the space before you, knowing you were waiting to occupy it, harsh words might be exchanged. Peaceful coexistence seems to suggest a rule that encourages noninterference with one who is in active pursuit. Although less certain a rule than the capture rule, it arguably better represents social custom and norms of civil interaction. Indeed, it has generally been the custom of hunters *not* to interfere with others engaged in active pursuit of an animal. Custom, rather than capture, might be an alternative basis for assigning property rights in this kind of case. Moreover, one can pursue an activity only if others have obligations to leave you alone to do it; if they are free to put roadblocks in your path, you will be discouraged from the activity in the first place. Runners race against each other, but they are not free to trip each other. Businesses are free to compete with pre-existing businesses, but they are not entitled to block each other's mail or make false representations about each other's products. Competition is a good thing, but unfair competition is not. Unfair methods of competition will discourage, rather than encourage, the creation of wealth.

Constructive possession

Mortal wounding or trapping

The rule of capture grants property rights to the first person to possess the animal. What constitutes possession? Is wounding an animal enough? The law has generally held that *mortally wounding* an animal (so that it is certain to die) is enough to constitute capture.[4] This amounts to a rule of *constructive possession.* Although a mortally wounded animal that is running away is not literally within the hunter's control, the law treats the animal *as if* it were within the hunter's control because the animal will eventually stop running and the hunter able to actually possess it. If Post had shot the fox and Pierson swooped in to take it away, it would be literally true that Pierson would have captured it and physically possessed it first. However, both social custom and norms of conduct suggest that such a seizure would be understood as wrongful conduct and Pierson's ownership would seem undeserved — reaping where he had not sowed. It would also

[4] *Id.*; *Liesner v. Wanie*, 145 N.W. 374 (Wis. 1914); Barlow Burke, *Personal Property in a Nutshell* 11 (4th ed. 2018).

arguably discourage hunting in the first place if one's efforts can come to naught by others seizing one's prey at the last moment.

Whales

Similar customary rules developed in the whaling industry. A whale was owned by the first whaler to harpoon it, as long as the harpoon had marks sufficient to identify the whaler so that a later finder would be able to turn the whale over to him.[5] Similar rules apply to animals caught in traps or fish caught in nets.[6] In *Ghen v. Rich*,[7] it was held that a harpooned whale that washed up on a beach was owned by the whaler that harpooned it and that the one who found it had an obligation to tell that whaler about it, receiving only a salvage award and not ownership of the whale itself. Any alternative rule would remove the incentives to engage in whaling in the first place, because whales could not necessarily be captured on the spot immediately after being harpooned in the ocean. In addition, it also appeared that the finder did not deserve ownership and that the one who had hunted the whale successfully did.

Trespass

Pierson v. Post would have come out differently if Post had been trespassing on Pierson's land. "[O]ne who takes possession of wild animals while trespassing on the private land of another must surrender title to the landowner."[8] ◀

▷ CONSTRUCTIVE POSSESSION ON ONE'S LAND **HARD CASE** ◀

Because landowners have the right to exclude non-owners, they are deemed to have a form of constructive possession of wild animals on their land, at least to the extent of having the exclusive right to hunt on their own lands with the intent of capturing those animals. An owner on neighboring property who fired a gun across the border onto your land, hitting a wild animal there, would be committing a trespass (because of the physical entry of the bullet onto your land), would not be entitled to enter your land without your consent to recover the animal, and would have no claim to own it. In the textbook case of *Keeble v. Hickeringill*,[9] plaintiff owner had a decoy pond designed to capture ducks on his land. Defendant fired a gun on defendant's own land next door to scare the ducks away and prevent plaintiff from capturing them. Although ownership of wild animals is obtained by capture and not mere pursuit, the court held for the plaintiff, on the ground that defendant had maliciously and wrongfully interfered with plaintiff's operation of a lawful business on his own land. Thus, although *Pierson v. Post* authorized interference with another's active pursuit of an animal, *Keeble* prohibited malicious interference with an individual's pursuit of wild animals, at least where the intermeddler was not attempting to capture the animals herself. In addition, *Pierson* involved no trespass on lands of another, so no presumption could arise that a landowner might

[5] *Ghen v. Rich*, 8 F. 159 (D.C. Mass. 1881).
[6] Barlow Burke, *Personal Property in a Nutshell* 12 (4th ed. 2018).
[7] 8 F. 159 (D.C. Mass. 1881).
[8] 2-13 *Thompson on Real Property, Third Thomas Edition* §13.03(c).
[9] 103 Eng. Rep. 1127 (K.B. 1707).

have special rights to animals found on her own land. *Keeble* would probably have been decided differently if no malice had been involved and defendant had simply been hunting on his own land, rather than firing a weapon for the sole purpose of preventing his neighbor from capturing the ducks. In such a case, each owner could legitimately claim a right to hunt on his own land. ◀

Pets

Pets belong to their owners, and that relationship does not end if they escape. Capture of a domesticated animal does not create new property rights because the animal has a previous owner. A "pet is not just a thing but occupies a special place somewhere in between a person and a piece of personal property."[10] However, "where the finder of a lost pet makes a reasonable effort to locate its owner, and responsibly cares for the animal over a reasonably extensive period of time, the finder may acquire possession of the animal."[11] In contrast to the law governing pets, wild animals are free for capture if they escape unless they have developed an *animus revertendi* — a habit of returning — in which case they are treated as domestic animals would be.[12] If someone negligently kills someone else's pet, courts generally limit damages to the market value of the animal and do not allow damages to be assessed for loss of companionship even though this amount does not adequately account for the emotional loss.[13]

§16.3 Finders

Lost and abandoned property

"Finders keepers, losers weepers" is a well-known children's rhyme, but it is not the law.[14] Owners who lose their personal property retain their ownership rights unless they intentionally relinquish them. Finders do have substantial rights, however. Finders generally have the right to possess lost objects in preference to everyone but the true owner, but they must hand them over if the true owner demands their return.[15] In contrast, when property is intentionally abandoned by the original owner rather than lost, then it *is* the case that one who finds it becomes the owner.[16] Thus, the law has made a significant difference between *lost* and *abandoned* property. Personal property is abandoned only when the owner intends to relinquish

[10] *Morgan v. Kroupa*, 702 A.2d 630, 633 (Vt. 1997).
[11] *Id.*
[12] 1 Ray Andrews Brown, *The Law of Personal Property* §2.5, at 18 (Walter B. Raushenbush ed., 3d ed. 1975).
[13] *Barking Hound Vill., LLC v. Monyak*, 787 S.E.2d 191 (Ga. 2016); *Strickland v. Medlen*, 397 S.W.3d 184 (Tex. 2013).
[14] Barlow Burke, *Personal Property in a Nutshell* 143 (4th ed. 2018). Moreover, failure to undertake reasonable efforts to discover the true owner may constitute larceny. *State v. Evans*, 807 P.2d 62, 64 (Idaho 1991).
[15] 2-13 *Thompson on Real Property, Third Thomas Edition* §13.04(e)(1).
[16] *Campbell v. Cochran*, 416 A.2d 211, 222 (Del. Super. Ct. 1980); Barlow Burke, *Personal Property in a Nutshell* 53 (4th ed. 2018). *See Long v. Dilling Mechanical Contractors, Inc.*, 705 N.E.2d 1022 (Ind. Ct. App. 1999) (trash placed in dumpster by employer was abandoned property that could be removed by union organizers to find names and addresses of employees).

ownership of it and engages in some type of action to demonstrate that intent, such as leaving a newspaper on the table in a restaurant when one leaves. The finder of abandoned property becomes its owner, while the finder of lost property merely acquires a right to possess it, which must be relinquished to the true owner should she appear.

Finders v. third parties

A finder of a lost object has superior rights to it as against everyone but the true owner.[17] Thus, in the case of *Armory v. Delamirie*,[18] a chimney sweep found a jewel in a setting and was held to have superior rights to it as against a jeweler to whom he had entrusted the jewel for appraisal. However, if the true owner had come forward to claim the jewel from the chimney sweep, the owner would have prevailed unless that owner could be shown to have abandoned the jewel. The finder of personal property has the right to possess it against all but the true owner. Title is *relative* rather than absolute. In a lawsuit between *A* and *B*, the question is who has the better title; the jeweler could not defeat the chimney sweep's claim by showing that the chimney sweep was not the true owner. The jeweler is not entitled to prevail by asserting the rights of the true owner; the rights of a third party (*jus tertii*) are not a defense to a claim of wrongful retention of property that had been possessed by a prior peaceable possessor. A prior possessor prevails over a later possessor even if that prior possessor would lose a contest with the true owner.

Relativity of title

▷ TRESPASSING FINDER **HARD CASE ◀**

What if the finder acquired the property illegally, for example, in the course of trespassing? Although the landowner would certainly prevail against the trespasser,[19] the cases appear to be split when the dispute is between a trespassing finder and a subsequent possessor of the object; older cases grant the finder rights against subsequent possessors, while some modern cases deny possessory rights to those who obtained possession illegally.[20] ◀

▷ FINDERS v. LANDOWNERS **HARD CASE ◀**

Argument for granting title to the landowner

Of course, the jewel in *Armory* could also have been claimed by the owner of the house where it was found. If the chimney sweep had been

[17] *State v. Repp*, 73 N.W. 829 (Iowa 1898); 2-13 *Thompson on Real Property, Third Thomas Edition* §13.04(e)(1); *see also* 1 Ray Andrews Brown, *The Law of Personal Property* §3.1, at 24 (Walter B. Raushenbush ed., 3d ed. 1975). *But see In re Funds in the Possession of Conemaugh Township Supervisors*, 753 A.2d 788 (Pa. 2000), *and Commonwealth v. $7,000.00 in US Currency*, 742 A.2d 711 (Pa. Commw. Ct. 1999) (both holding that police officers do not become owners of property found in the course of exercising their official duties because this would undermine public confidence).

[18] 93 Eng. Rep. 664 (K.B. 1722).

[19] *Favorite v. Miller*, 407 A.2d 974, 978 (Conn. 1978); *Bishop v. Ellsworth*, 234 N.E.2d 49, 52 (Ill. App. Ct. 1968).

[20] Barlow Burke, *Personal Property in a Nutshell* 104-110 (4th ed. 2018); Richard H. Helmholz, *Wrongful Possession of Chattels: Hornbook Law and Case Law*, 80 Nw. U. L. Rev. 1221, 1225-1226 (1986).

trespassing, the jewel would belong to the landowner.[21] But if one is not trespassing, the courts are divided on the question of whether a found object belongs to the finder or to the landowner. One might conclude that an owner of a building has constructive possession of all personal property located within it. An owner of a private home might well consider herself the owner of a jewel found under a radiator, even if it had belonged to the previous owner of the house, and even if she only knew about it because a guest had located it.[22] A chattel found in a private place (one not generally open to the public) may thus be granted to the owner of the land rather than the finder.[23]

Argument for granting title to the finder

However, not all courts agree with this resolution of the issue. After all, constructive possession is a fiction; the landowner did not know about the object and may never have come to find out about it but for the efforts of the finder. Thus, the court in *Hannah v. Peel*[24] awarded a brooch to the finder rather than the landowner when the landowner was not physically occupying the property and the finder turned the brooch over to the police to make it available for recovery by the true owner. It did so partly because his conduct was "commendable and meritorious" and partly because the landowner had never been in physical possession of the premises. And in *Hendle v. Stevens*,[25] the court interpreted a state statute to give title to the finders to achieve the statute's purposes of "encouraging and facilitating the return of property to the true owner and of then rewarding the finder for his honesty if the property remains unclaimed."[26] *Hendle* involved children who were playing in the wooded area of property belonging to a neighbor. They were there with the owner's permission and were thus not trespassing. The court awarded them, rather than the landowner, ownership of money found on the land after they reported and turned over the money to the police and the true owner did not come forward.[27] ◀

Embedded in the soil

If personal property is found *embedded* in the soil, courts ordinarily award it to the landowner rather than the finder, in the absence of agreement or statute to the contrary, on the ground that it is, in effect, part of the real property.[28] A possible exception to this principle applies to so-called

[21] *Hendle v. Stevens*, 586 N.E.2d 826 (Ill. App. Ct. 1992); 1 Ray Andrews Brown, *The Law of Personal Property* §3.1, at 24 (Walter B. Raushenbush ed., 3d ed. 1975); 2-13 *Thompson on Real Property, Third Thomas Edition* §13.04(e)(1).

[22] *Bishop v. Ellsworth*, 234 N.E.2d 49, 52 (Ill. App. Ct. 1968) (any property found on private land "is and always has been in the constructive possession of the owner of said premises and in a legal sense the property can neither be mislaid nor lost").

[23] 1 Ray Andrews Brown, *The Law of Personal Property* §3.2, at 26 (Walter B. Raushenbush ed., 3d ed. 1975).

[24] 1 K.B. 509 (1945).

[25] 586 N.E.2d 826 (Ill. App. Ct. 1992).

[26] *Id.* at 832.

[27] *See also Grande v. Jennings*, 278 P.3d 1287 (Ariz. Ct. App. 2012) (contractor who found $500,000 hidden in a home was not entitled to the funds because prior owner of the home did not abandon the money; the funds were simply mislaid).

[28] *Goddard v. Winchell*, 52 N.W. 1124 (Iowa 1892) (meteorite found in the soil); *Morgan v. Wiser*, 711 S.W.2d 220 (Tenn. Ct. App. 1985); 1 Ray Andrews Brown, *The Law of Personal Property* §3.2, at 26 (Walter B. Raushenbush ed., 3d ed. 1975).

treasure troves, or gold, silver, or money intentionally buried in the earth for recovery later.[29] In England, ownership of a treasure trove was historically given to the Crown, while in the United States ownership was given to the finder rather than the owner of the land, as long as the finder was not trespassing at the time it was found.[30]

Treasure trove

In contrast to chattels found in private places, a chattel found in a public place, such as a store or restaurant, has traditionally been awarded to the finder rather than the landowner on the ground that landowners of property open to the public should not be deemed to have constructive possession of all property lost or abandoned by customers.[31]

Finder wins if on property open to the public

A third category, in addition to lost and abandoned property, is *mislaid* property. Such property is intentionally placed in a particular place and mistakenly left there. One who leaves a pocketbook or cell phone on the table in a restaurant, for example, has almost certainly not intended to abandon it. She is likely to remember where she might have placed the object and retrace her steps to retrieve it. To increase the chances that such an owner would be able to recover her property, the law has generally granted the owner of the land superior rights to the finder. So, the law grants possessory rights to the restaurant owner, as opposed to the waiter or the customer who finds the mislaid object.[32] This result differs from that applicable to lost or abandoned property, which tends to grant ownership to the finder when the property is found in a public place. Of course, determining whether an object was mislaid or abandoned or lost may be a tricky proposition, and for this reason statutes have begun to dissolve these categories.

Mislaid property

Many states now have statutes governing lost personal property.[33] Those statutes often dispense with the confusing distinctions among lost, mislaid, and abandoned property and grant ownership to the finder of property found in a public place, as long as the finder reports the find and the true owner fails to claim the object within a specified period of time.

Finders statutes

[29] *Morgan v. Wiser*, 711 S.W.2d 220 (Tenn. Ct. App. 1985); Barlow Burke, *Personal Property in a Nutshell* 157-159 (4th ed. 2018).

[30] Barlow Burke, *Personal Property in a Nutshell* 159 (4th ed. 2018).

[31] *Terry v. Lock Hospitality, Inc.*, 37 S.W.3d 202 (Ark. 2001); *Paset v. Old Orchard Bank & Trust Co.*, 378 N.E.2d 1264 (Ill. App. Ct. 1978); 1 Ray Andrews Brown, *The Law of Personal Property* §3.2, at 26 (Walter B. Raushenbush ed., 3d ed. 1975); Barlow Burke, *Personal Property in a Nutshell* 158-159 (4th ed. 2018). However, employers are generally deemed owners of property found by their employees. *Hurley v. City of Niagara Falls*, 289 N.Y.S.2d 889 (App. Div. 1968).

[32] *Terry v. Lock Hospitality, Inc.*, 37 S.W.3d 202 (Ark. 2001); *Hendle v. Stevens*, 586 N.E.2d 826, 833 (Ill. App. Ct. 1992); *Ray v. Flower Hospital*, 439 N.E.2d 942 (Ohio Ct. App. 1981); 2 Ray Andrews Brown, *The Law of Personal Property* §3.2, at 26 (Walter B. Raushenbush ed., 3d ed. 1975); Barlow Burke, *Personal Property in a Nutshell* 154 (4th ed. 2018); 2-13 *Thompson on Real Property, Third Thomas Edition* §13.04(e)(2).

[33] Del. Code tit. 11, §8307(c); Fla. Stat. §§705.102 to 705.104; Haw. Rev. Stat. §§52D-10, 52D-14; 765 Ill. Comp. Stat. 1020/27 to 1020/35; Iowa Code §§556F.6 to 556F.18; Mich. Comp. Laws §§434.21 to 434.29; Mont. Code §§70-5-101 to 70-5-107, 70-5-201 to 70-5-209; N.H. Stat. §§471-C:1 to 471-C:14; N.Y. Gen. Mun. §250; Okla. Stat. tit. 15, §§511 to 518; Or. Rev. Stat. §§98.005 to 98.025; Vt. Stat. tit. 27, §§1101 to 1108; Wash. Rev. Code §§63.21.010 to 63.21.050; Barlow Burke, *Personal Property in a Nutshell* 157-160 (4th ed. 2018); 2-13 *Thompson on Real Property, Third Thomas Edition* §13.04(e)(3).

Some statutes require the finder to turn the object over to the authorities in the interim. They may also make provision for the finder to receive an award from the true owner.[34] Most states also have statutes governing the disposition of unclaimed intangible personal property, such as corporate dividend checks, deeming such property abandoned after a period of time and providing that the property *escheats* to the state.[35]

▶ HARD CASE ▷ GOODS IN UNMARKED GRAVES

In *Charrier v. Bell*,[36] an amateur archeologist found funeral objects embedded in the ground that had been placed there long ago by members of the local Indian tribe at the time of burial. He alleged that he had the landowner's permission to survey the property for possible burial locations; it turned out he had the permission of the caretaker of the property, but not the owner. The state of Louisiana intervened in the lawsuit and eventually purchased the land. Ownership of the objects was contested between the finder, the landowner (now the state), and the Tunica and Biloxi Tribe (the descendants of those who had inhabited the region). The court held that such goods had not been abandoned, but had been intentionally placed in the earth with the intent that they remain there. Ownership of the funeral objects was given, however, not to the landowner, but to the descendants of the tribe whose members had been buried there, entitling them to retake possession of the objects. ◀

Shipwrecks

Shipwrecks abandoned at sea were traditionally owned by those who found them, although much controversy ensued over whether the owner (or the insurance company that had paid off the owner) had intended to abandon its rights in the sunken ship and its contents.[37] If a ship has not been abandoned by its owner (or the insurance company that succeeds to the owner's interests), a finder is entitled to possession of recovered goods but not title; however, the finder is entitled to a reward for saving the goods under the *law of salvage*.[38] There appears to be a strong presumption against abandonment.[39] Abandoned shipwrecks are now governed

Law of salvage

34 *See* N.Y. Pers. Prop. §§251 to 258.

35 *Uniform Unclaimed Property Act and Uniform Disposition of Unclaimed Property Act*; Barlow Burke, *Personal Property in a Nutshell* 173-178 (4th ed. 2018); 2-13 *Thompson on Real Property, Third Thomas Edition* §13.04(e)(3).

36 380 So. 2d 155 (La. Ct. App. 1979).

37 Barlow Burke, *Personal Property in a Nutshell* 159-161 (4th ed. 2018).

38 *Adams v. Unione Mediterranea di Sicurta*, 220 F.3d 659, 670-671 (5th Cir. 2000); *International Aircraft Recovery, L.L.C. v. Unidentified, Wrecked, and Abandoned Aircraft*, 218 F.3d 1255 (11th Cir. 2000); *Platoro, Ltd., Inc. v. Unidentified Remains of a Vessel, Her Cargo, Apparel, Tackle, and Furniture, in a Cause of Salvage, Civil and Maritime*, 695 F.2d 893 (5th Cir. 1983); Barlow Burke, *Personal Property in a Nutshell* 162-165 (4th ed. 2018); 2-13 *Thompson on Real Property, Third Thomas Edition* §13.12(b).

39 *Adams v. Unione Mediterranea di Sicurta*, 220 F.3d 659, 671 (5th Cir. 2000) (law of salvage applies rather than law of finds unless finder demonstrates by clear and convincing evidence that true owner abandoned the property).

by a federal statute, the *Abandoned Shipwreck Act of 1987*,[40] which asserts federal ownership by the United States of any abandoned shipwrecks that are embedded in state lands and then transfers such ownership to the state. Wrecks found on federal lands are owned by the U.S. government, and those found on Indian lands by the relevant Indian nation. Shipwrecks that are not "embedded" are governed by the law of salvage (if they have not been abandoned) or by the law of finds (if they have been abandoned).

▷ GOVERNMENTAL PAPERS **HARD CASE ◀**

Thomas Law Willcox found 444 documents from the administrations of two governors of South Carolina during the Civil War in a shopping bag in a closet at his late stepmother's home. They had an appraised value of $2.4 million. When he filed for bankruptcy, the question was whether he owned the documents or whether they were owned by the state of South Carolina. The court held, in *Wilcox v. Stroup*,[41] that "possession is nine-tenths of the law" and that, in the absence of evidence that the papers belonged to anyone else, they would belong to Willcox. The state had argued that the papers had enormous historical importance and that they should be owned by the state and preserved for posterity. The court concluded, however, that in the absence of a statute to the contrary, the papers of state governors are the private property of the particular governor. The papers of U.S. Presidents were their private property until Congress passed a law granting the United States "complete ownership, possession, and control" of official presidential records.[42] ◀

§16.4 Gifts

Inter vivos **gifts**

A gift is a transfer of property from one person to another without payment. *Inter vivos* gifts are transfers from one living person to another. They are distinguished from *testamentary transfers*, by which individuals transfer their property when they die through a valid will or inheritance.

Elements

Delivery

Traditionally, the law of gifts requires (1) *intent* to transfer ownership; (2) *delivery* of the property; and (3) *acceptance* by the donee.[43] Delivery requires physical transfer of the object itself. However, constructive or symbolic delivery might be sufficient. For example, constructive delivery would be recognized if the owner of a locked box gave the only key to the donee.[44]

[40] 43 U.S.C. §§2101 to 2106.

[41] *Wilcox v. Stroup*, 467 F.3d 409 (4th Cir. 2006).

[42] *See Presidential Records Act of 1978*, 44 U.S.C. §§2201 *et seq.* (implementing process for archiving records and making them publicly available as soon as possible, subject to exceptions for confidential and privileged materials).

[43] In re Marriage of McCulloch and Parker, 546 P.3d 109 (Ariz. Ct. App. 2024); *Westleigh v. Conger*, 755 A.2d 518, 520, 2000 ME 134, ¶7 (Me. 2000); 2-13 *Thompson on Real Property, Third Thomas Edition* §13.04(a)(2)(i).

[44] Barlow Burke, *Personal Property in a Nutshell* 284 (4th ed. 2018).

Some courts, however, recognize constructive delivery only if physical delivery is inconvenient or impossible.[45] Today, the delivery requirement may be accomplished by a writing rather than physical delivery. Many

Deed of gift

states allow a gift to be made through a formal deed or even a more informal writing that indicates a present intent to relinquish possession and to transfer title to the donee.[46]

▶ HARD CASE ▷ JOINT BANK ACCOUNTS AND JOINT SAFETY BOXES

When property is held in a way that affords joint control by the donor and the donee, has a gift been made? For example, what happens if, instead of giving the donee the sole key to a lock box, the donor gives a duplicate key, retaining one for herself? Has the gift been delivered? The cases are split with some holding that delivery has not occurred and others finding it to have occurred if the intent to make the gift is sufficiently clear.[47] A similar problem arises where the parties share possession, as when they live in the same house and a piano is given by one member of the household to another. ◀

▶ HARD CASE ▷ JOINT BANK ACCOUNTS

When two parties open a joint bank account, are they each entitled to use all the money in the account? Some courts hold that the owners are joint tenants having the right to possess all the money in the account. Some courts, however, look to the circumstances under which the account was formed to determine that the owners own the portion of money they deposited. Alternatively, they hold that each owner is not entitled to withdraw excessive amounts of the money.[48] When one owner of a joint bank account dies, the remaining money is owned by the surviving parties.[49] ◀

Present intent

To make a gift, the donor must have a *present intent* to transfer ownership rights in the object. However, this does not mean that actual possession of the gift must be transferred to the donee. For example, a mother could give her daughter a piano but retain the right to keep it in her house until her death. In effect, the mother has retained a life estate in the piano and presently transferred a vested remainder to the daughter.[50]

[45] 2-13 *Thompson on Real Property, Third Thomas Edition* §13.04(a)(2)(i).

[46] Barlow Burke, *Personal Property in a Nutshell* 279-281 (4th ed. 2018); 2-13 *Thompson on Real Property, Third Thomas Edition* §13.04(a)(2)(i).

[47] 2-13 *Thompson on Real Property, Third Thomas Edition* §13.04(a)(2)(i).

[48] Uniform Probate Code §6-103; Barlow Burke, *Personal Property in a Nutshell* 324 (4th ed. 2018); John G. Sprankling, *Understanding Property Law* §10.02[B][5], at 136-144 (4th ed. 2017).

[49] Uniform Probate Code §6-104.

[50] 2-13 *Thompson on Real Property, Third Thomas Edition* §13.04(a)(2)(ii).

▷ CONDITIONAL GIFTS **HARD CASE ◀**

Gifts through third parties

Traditionally, conditional gifts were not allowed.[51] If a gift is given to a donee but is subject to a condition precedent (a condition that must be fulfilled before title will transfer to the donee), the courts may hold that a gift has not occurred, even if the condition is later fulfilled. Alternatively, if the gift is delivered but is subject to a written or oral condition, the courts may hold the condition to be unenforceable and find that the gift was made despite the donee's failure to fulfill the condition.[52] However, if the future condition is a certain event (such as the death of the donor), courts are likely to find a present intent to convey a future interest in the object and validate the gift.[53] In contrast, if the gift is subject to a condition subsequent (such that the donee will lose the gift upon the happening of an event), the condition will usually be enforceable. Thus, if a mother gave her daughter a car but provided that the mother would retake title if the daughter got into an accident, the condition may well be enforced; the daughter has a fee simple subject to a condition subsequent. ◀

Gifts *causa mortis*

An example of a conditional gift that has been traditionally allowed is the gift *causa mortis*. Such a gift is given when the donor believes she is on the verge of dying and intends to transfer the object if she dies but to retain possession if she does not die. If the donor survives the illness or the situation that made her think she was near death, the courts traditionally would find that the donor did not intend to give the gift in that case.[54]

▷ ENGAGEMENT PRESENTS **HARD CASE ◀**

Two people get engaged and exchange rings; they break up the engagement. Must they return the rings? Traditionally, conditional gifts were not allowed, so the delivery of the rings with intent to transfer title was held to be irrevocable. However, such gifts were clearly given under the understanding that the parties would be married and the rings were symbolic of that understanding. Because of this fundamental understanding, courts have held that such gifts are contingent on the parties marrying and have required the gifts to be returned if the engagement is called off.[55] Some courts continue to adhere to the view that engagement rings may be kept even if the marriage does not occur because they are given and accepted, title has passed, and the giver retains no reversionary interests in the ring.[56] Some courts have

[51] *Id.*

[52] Barlow Burke, *Personal Property in a Nutshell* 287-288 (4th ed. 2018).

[53] 2-13 *Thompson on Real Property, Third Thomas Edition* §13.04(a)(2)(ii).

[54] Barlow Burke, *Personal Property in a Nutshell* 307-308 (4th ed. 2018); 2-13 *Thompson on Real Property, Third Thomas Edition* §13.04(a)(3).

[55] *Cooper v. Smith*, 800 N.E.2d 372 (Ohio Ct. App. 2003); *Lindh v. Surman*, 742 A.2d 643 (Pa. 1999); McGrath v. Dockendorf, 793 S.E.2d 336 (Va. 2016); Barlow Burke, *Personal Property in a Nutshell* 298-300 (4th ed. 2018).

[56] *Albinger v. Harris*, 48 P.3d 711, 719, 2002 MT 118 ¶¶32-34 (Mont. 2002).

taken a different approach, focusing instead on fault. Such courts may not allow the donor to recover the gift if the donor breaks off the engagement without justification. Conversely, the donee who breaks off the engagement may be allowed to keep the gift if she had good reason to break the engagement.[57] Most courts today, however, avoid looking into fault, finding the gift conditional on marriage occurring and ordering return of the ring if the engagement falls through regardless of fault.[58] They note that statutes have abolished a claim for breach of promise to marry and that it is better for courts not to be involved in determining fault in such cases. ◀

§16.5 Bailments

Delivery of possession but not title

A *bailment* is a delivery of possession of personal property to another without conveyance of title.[59] Examples include cars parked in parking lots, coats checked in a restaurant, VCRs and wristwatches submitted to repair shops for repair, and suitcases checked for transport in airplanes. Obviously, the bailee has a duty to return the property to the bailor who deposited it with the bailee.[60] The bailor-bailee relationship is a contractual one, and either contract or tort law (or both) will determine the standard of care that must be exercised by the bailee and the liability, if any, if the property is lost, stolen, or damaged while in the bailee's possession. Traditionally, the law made public accommodations (such as hotels and common carriers) strictly liable if such property was lost or stolen.[61] On the other hand, gratuitous bailees who were taking care of another's goods for free were held to a very low standard. For example, finders of lost goods are arguably bailees in relation to the true owner and are liable for loss or damage to the property only if they are grossly negligent.[62] In the nineteenth century, courts tended to divide bailments into categories depending on whether the bailment benefited only the bailor (as in the case of the finder of a lost object), only the bailee (as in the case of a neighbor borrowing a lawn mower), or both (as in the case of a barber shop that stores a customer's goods while he gets his hair cut).[63] Given the difficulty of distinguishing between the categories, the tendency today is to adopt a general requirement of reasonableness.[64]

[57] *See Curtis v. Anderson*, 106 S.W.3d 251, 256 (Tex. Ct. App. 2003) (fault-based approach to conditional gift doctrine so that "absent a written agreement a donor is not entitled to the return of an engagement ring if he terminates the engagement"); 2-13 *Thompson on Real Property, Third Thomas Edition* §13.04(a)(2)(ii).

[58] Johnson v. Settino, 245 N.E.3d 196 (Mass. 2024); *Lindh v. Surman*, 742 A.2d 643 (Pa. 1999); Barlow Burke, *Personal Property in a Nutshell* 298-300 (4th ed. 2018).

[59] Barlow Burke, *Personal Property in a Nutshell* 181-234 (4th ed. 2018).

[60] *Id.* at 204-205.

[61] *Id.* at 220, 233-234.

[62] *Id.* at 208-209.

[63] *Id.*; 2-13 *Thompson on Real Property, Third Thomas Edition* §13.07(b).

[64] *See* U.C.C. §7-204(1) (providing that a "warehouseman is liable for damages for loss of or injury to the goods caused by his failure to exercise such care in regard to them as a reasonably careful man would exercise under like circumstances"); *Coster v. Piekarski*, 3 P.3d 333 (Alaska 2000) ("bailee has the duty to exercise the degree of care of a reasonably careful owner"); *Wasland v. Porter Auto & Marine, Inc.*, 600 N.W.2d 904, 907 (S.D. 1999).

Today, statutes in every state limit the liability of innkeepers by requiring guests to notify them if they have extraordinarily valuable goods. Such statutes may limit the dollar amount of potential liability or require guests to store valuable items in the hotel safe.[65] They may also require the dollar limitations on the hotel's liability to be conspicuously posted.[66]

Statutory limitations on innkeeper liability

Personal property may also be *entrusted* to the care of another. In *Congregation Jeshuat Israel v. Congregation Shearith Israel*,[67] a synagogue in Rhode Island entrusted rimonim (objects that decorate the scrolls of the Torah) to a sister congregation in New York. After many years, the congregations contested over ownership of the rimonim, with the New York congregation claiming that the transfer of possession was a gift rather than a trust. The New York congregation sought to prevent the Rhode Island congregation from selling the objects to the Boston Museum of Fine Arts for $7 million. Judge John McConnell, Jr. focused on the language in the original documents creating the synagogue in Rhode Island as well as in the instruments transferring possession of the rimonim to the New York congregation. Applying Rhode Island law, he also determined that the court "must rely on the totality of the circumstances which appear in evidence to determine whether property was intended to be devoted to a charitable project."[68] Long-standing possession of the objects was also relevant to determining who had the right to control them.

Trusts of personal property

▷ DATA PROPERTY AND CLOUD COMPUTING AS BAILMENTS **HARD CASE ◀**

Cloud computing involves people and firms storing their data — everything from personal photographs to proprietary documents to customer records — on servers maintained by third parties, such as Dropbox and Amazon Web Services. Cloud storage companies generally disclaim liability for lost data by contract, but one scholar has argued that such relationships are akin to the storage of other property, which is to say a bailment.[69] Although no court has applied the law of bailments to the contractual relationships that govern cloud computing, doing so would arguably impose a duty of care and an obligation to return digital property that can be modified by contract, but not disclaimed entirely.[70] ◀

§16.6 Good Faith Purchasers

Ordinarily, an owner does not lose title to her property when it is stolen, even if it is subsequently purchased by a buyer who was not aware of the

Stolen goods

[65] Barlow Burke, *Personal Property in a Nutshell* 232-234 (4th ed. 2018).

[66] *Terry v. Lincscott Hotel Corp.*, 617 P.2d 56 (Ariz. 1980).

[67] *Congregation Jeshuat Israel v. Congregation Shearith Israel*, 186 F. Supp. 3d 158 (D.R.I. 2016), *rev'd*, 866 F.3d 53 (1st Cir. 2017).

[68] *Id.* at 188.

[69] Danielle D'Onfro, *The New Bailments*, 96 Wash. L. Rev. 97 (2022).

[70] *Id.*

theft.[71] The thief's title is void; a transfer of such title transfers nothing. As between the innocent purchaser and the original victim of the theft, the courts have traditionally sought to protect the initial owner's rights in such cases.[72] This may induce buyers to investigate or to act reasonably to discern whether the seller really owns the good she purports to be entitled to sell. On the other hand, the buyer may have no way of finding this out. One or the other party may well be left with a loss that cannot be compensated, especially if the thief is nowhere to be found or is judgment-proof.

U.C.C. §2-403

An exception to the rule that a thief cannot convey good title appears in the *Uniform Commercial Code* §2-403. If an owner entrusts an item to a "merchant who deals in goods of that kind," the merchant has the power to "transfer all rights of the entruster to a buyer in the ordinary course of business."[73]

Fraud

In contrast to the rules governing wrongful sale and dispossession by a merchant, when an owner is induced to sell personal property by fraud, title is *voidable* rather than *void*. This means that the seller may sue to regain title from the buyer who defrauded her. However, if that buyer has resold the property to a good faith purchaser who was not aware of the fraud, then U.C.C. §2-403(1)[74] provides that title cannot be reclaimed by the original owner and the seller is relegated to damages.[75]

§16.7 Adverse Possession

Adverse possession

Personal property, like real property, can be adversely possessed. This topic is covered in §4.8.

§16.8 Accession and Fixtures

Accession

When one takes personal property belonging to another and either "adds significant value to it or incorporates it into the taker's own valuable property, so that it would be unjust to require the taker to return the improperly taken item to its owner," the law of *accession* transfers title to the property from the original owner to the owner of the property with which it has been mixed.[76] The original owner is entitled to damages for loss of her property, however.[77] On the other hand, accession is usually denied if the taking was originally wrongful or if the original property's identity

[71] Barlow Burke, *Personal Property in a Nutshell* 228-289 (4th ed. 2018); 2-13 *Thompson on Real Property, Third Thomas Edition* §13.11.

[72] 2-13 *Thompson on Real Property, Third Thomas Edition* §13.04(c).

[73] U.C.C. §2-403(2). *See* Santana Equestrian Priv. Fin., LLC v. Richtmyer, 349 So.3d 441 (Fla. Dist. Ct. App. 2022); *Candela v. Port Motors, Inc.*, 617 N.Y.S.2d 49 (App. Div. 1994).

[74] U.C.C. §2-403(1).

[75] Barlow Burke, *Personal Property in a Nutshell* 250-251 (4th ed. 2018); 2-13 *Thompson on Real Property, Third Thomas Edition* §13.04(c).

[76] 2-13 *Thompson on Real Property, Third Thomas Edition* §13.04(g)(1).

[77] *Id.*

has not been lost.[78] The term *confusion* is generally used to describe the situation in which the goods of one person become so mixed with those of another that ownership of the individual items can no longer be separated.[79] **Confusion**

Fixtures are personal property that has become fixed to real property and is treated as part of the real property.[80] For example, when one purchases a house, the usual understanding is that the existing light fixtures will stay. A seller who wants to remove the fixtures and not include them in the sale of the house generally must make her intent clear in the land sale contract.[81] **Fixtures**

Crops are normally treated as part of the land unless the owner has contracted to treat them otherwise.[82] However, once they are severed from the land, they become personal property.[83] **Crops**

§16.9 Human Bodies

Courts and commentators have often said that there can be no property rights in human bodies.[84] The use of property language to describe human beings may seem inappropriate. For one thing, it is too reminiscent of slavery to be palatable. It appears to convert something sacred into a commodity.[85] For like reasons, courts have been reluctant to say that family members have "property rights" in a corpse.[86] Property language for human body parts would appear to sanction a market in body parts, inducing individuals to sell organs, for example. Such sales are prohibited by the *National Organ Transplant Act*.[87] **No property in human bodies**

However, in some sense this delicacy is hard to fathom. Control rights over human bodies must be assigned to someone and such assignments are what we mean by property.[88] Moreover, courts have said that the next of kin "have a 'quasi-property' right in a decedent's body for purposes of burial or other lawful disposition."[89] This right, for example, entitles the family to obtain damages where an autopsy is performed without consent.[90] **Quasi-property**

[78] *Id.* at §§13.04(g)(2), 13.04(g)(3).

[79] *Id.* at §13.04(h).

[80] *Id.* at §13.05(a).

[81] 5-46 *Thompson on Real Property, Third Thomas Edition* §46.02.

[82] 2-13 *Thompson on Real Property, Third Thomas Edition* §13.02(c).

[83] Barlow Burke, *Personal Property in a Nutshell* 68-69 (4th ed. 2018).

[84] *Janicki v. Hospital of St. Raphael*, 744 A.2d 963, 967-968 (Conn. Super. Ct. 1999).

[85] *See* Margaret Jane Radin, *Contested Commodities: The Trouble with Trade in Sex, Children, Body Parts, and Other Things* (1996).

[86] 744 A.2d at 967-968.

[87] 42 U.S.C. §274e(a); *see, e.g., Flynn v. Holder*, 684 F.3d 852 (9th Cir. 2012) (upholding a challenge to the *National Organ Transplant Act* under the equal protection clause).

[88] For explorations of these issues, see Margaret Jane Radin, *Contested Commodities: The Trouble with Trade in Sex, Children, Body Parts, and Other Things* (1996); Radhika Rao, *Property, Privacy, and the Human Body*, 80 B.U. L. Rev. 359 (2000).

[89] 744 A.2d at 968. *See* Ela A. Leshem, *Dead Bodies as Quasi-Persons*, 77 Vand. 999 (2024); *see also* M. Bourianoff Bray, *Personalizing Personality: Toward a Property Right in Human Bodies*, 69 Tex. L. Rev. 209 (1990).

[90] 744 A.2d at 968.

In *Brotherton v. Cleveland*,[91] plaintiff Deborah Brotherton alleged that defendants, in the course of performing an autopsy, removed her deceased husband's corneas for use as anatomical gifts without her consent. The court noted that Ohio Rev. Code §2108.02(B), as part of the *Uniform Anatomical Gift Act*,[92] governing gifts of organs and tissues for research or transplants, granted her the right to control the disposal of Steven Brotherton's body. The court held that "the aggregate of rights granted by the state of Ohio to Deborah Brotherton rises to the level of a 'legitimate claim of entitlement' in Steven Brotherton's body, including his corneas," and that this was sufficient to establish a property interest protected by the Fourteenth Amendment's prohibition on deprivations of property without due process of law.[93]

▶ HARD CASE

▷ MOORE v. REGENTS OF THE UNIVERSITY OF CALIFORNIA

In the famous case of *Moore v. Regents of the University of California*,[94] doctors treating a patient used some of his spleen cells removed during an operation to develop a "cell line" that had substantial commercial value. Moore's cancerous cells in his blood had the unique ability to produce a protein that regulates the immune system. The cell line developed from his cells was capable of reproduction indefinitely and could thus produce proteins of great value. Moore claimed that the doctors had "converted" his personal property in his cells by unlawfully taking them for this purpose without his consent and that he was thus entitled to a share of the profits from the cell line developed from his cells. The court held that Moore had no property claim in his cells but that the doctors had breached their fiduciary duty to him by not disclosing what they intended to do with his cells.

Competing arguments

On one hand, one can argue that it is undignified and inappropriate to treat body parts as property. Moreover, Moore arguably abandoned his cells when they were removed during an operation. In addition, it was the labor and ingenuity of the doctors who created economic value out of Moore's cells and they, rather than he, therefore deserve the fruits of their invention. Finally, granting cell donors property rights in their cells may halt research because it is often hard to determine the origin of such cells used in research. On the other hand, it is contradictory to say that body parts cannot be property and then to allow the doctors to treat them as property and earn profits from selling them. The court actually did not hold that cells could not be property, but simply awarded control over those cells to the doctors rather than the patient. Moreover, property is not awarded only to those who labor; landlords who rent their property and stockholders who loan their capital to a corporation earn profits based on their ownership of property rather than their labor. ◀

[91] 923 F.2d 477 (6th Cir. 1991).
[92] 8A U.L.A. 63 (1993).
[93] *See also Newman v. Sathyavaglswaran*, 287 F.3d 786 (9th Cir. 2002); *Whaley v. County of Tuscola*, 58 F.3d 1111 (6th Cir. 1991).
[94] 793 P.2d 479 (Cal. 1990).

▷ SPERM **HARD CASE ◀**

In *Hecht v. Superior Court*,[95] a man committed suicide after writing a will leaving 15 vials of semen he had earlier deposited at a sperm bank to his girlfriend, who argued that they belonged to her as property bequeathed to her in his will. The decedent's adult children argued that the sperm belonged to them under an earlier settlement agreement between them and the girlfriend. Although initially ruling that the sperm were "property,"[96] the court later reversed itself, holding that sperm cannot be property.[97] Instead, the court treated the issue as one of "privacy" and granted the sperm to the girlfriend on the ground that the decedent's wishes as to whether he should procreate should be honored. ◀

▷ HUMAN EMBRYOS **HARD CASE ◀**

In *Davis v. Davis*,[98] a married couple, Mary Sue Davis and Junior Davis, jointly decided to attempt to have a child by in vitro fertilization. As part of that process, nine of Mary Sue's ova were successfully fertilized. Two were implanted and the rest were preserved by a freezing process for future use. The couple then divorced and Mary Sue sought to have the other frozen embryos implanted so that she could have a child, but Junior objected. The trial judge held that Mary Sue could go ahead over her husband's objections because "life begins at conception" and "human embryos are not property" but children. He ruled that it was in the best interests of those children to be available for implantation, and that "custody" of the children should be awarded to Mary Sue.[99] A similar result was reached by a trial court in New York in the case of *Kass v. Kass*.[100] However, that court held that fertilized eggs (frozen embryos) *were* property. The court gave control of those embryos to the wife in a divorce proceeding despite the husband's objection, on the ground that once the eggs were fertilized, the husband had no right to force the wife to stop the pregnancy.

> Just as an in vivo husband's "right to avoid procreation" is waived and ceases to exist after intercourse in a coital reproduction, such right should be deemed waived and non-existent after his participation in an in vitro program. Upon entering he knows, or should have known, that technology is such that the possibility and probability of a delayed implantation are very real. Absent some indication of a contrary intent, the agreement to participate, if it does not expressly provide for such an eventuality, must be deemed an agreement to permit a delayed implantation.[101]

95 20 Cal. Rptr. 2d 275 (Ct. App. 1993).
96 *Id.* at 283.
97 *Hecht v. Superior Court*, 59 Cal. Rptr. 2d 222, 226 (Ct. App. 1996), *as modified* (Nov. 19, 1996), *rev. denied and ordered not to be officially published* (Jan. 15, 1997).
98 842 S.W.2d 588 (Tenn. 1992).
99 *Id.* at 594.
100 1995 WL 110368 (N.Y. Sup. Ct. 1995).
101 *Id.* at *3.

Argument that the right to procreate should prevail

Some courts have held that pre-embryos should be given to one of the parties if it is the person's "last chance" to have a biological child because in such cases, that person's rights should prevail over those of the person who wishes not to become a parent.[102] A Pennsylvania court explained that while "ordinarily the party wishing to avoid procreation should prevail, in our balancing of the facts unique to this case, we find that Wife's inability to achieve biological parenthood without the use of the pre-embryos is an interest which outweighs Husband's desire to avoid procreation."[103] The Colorado Supreme Court has characterized pre-embryos as "marital property of a special character" because while pre-embryos are not "'persons' as a legal matter" they "contain the potential for human life."[104]

Argument that right not to procreate should prevail

However, the results in both the *Davis* and the *Kass* cases were reversed on appeal. In *Davis*, the court of appeals reversed on the ground that individuals have constitutionally protected rights to procreate, including the right not to be forced to procreate. "It would be repugnant and offensive to constitutional principles to order Mary Sue to implant these fertilized ova against her will. It would be equally repugnant to order Junior to bear the psychological, if not the legal, consequences of paternity against his will."[105] The court argued that fetuses are not "persons" for a variety of purposes under Tennessee law, that the parties "share an interest in the seven fertilized ova," and that they had the right to joint control with equal voice over their disposition. By the time the Tennessee Supreme Court heard the case, Mary Sue Davis (now Mary Sue Stowe) had remarried and no longer wanted to use the frozen embryos for herself, but sought authority to donate them to a childless couple. Her ex-husband vehemently opposed such a donation and preferred to see the embryos destroyed. The Tennessee Supreme Court agreed with the court of appeals that frozen embryos were not "persons" under Tennessee law. The court also concluded, however, that frozen embryos deserved greater respect than accorded other human tissue because of their potential to become persons. The court held that "pre-embryos are not, strictly speaking, either 'persons' or 'property,' but occupy an interim category that entitles them to special respect because of their potential for human life."[106] The interest that the parties had in the pre-embryos "is not a true property interest. However, they do have an interest in the nature of ownership, to the extent that they have decision-making authority concerning disposition of the pre-embryos, within the scope of policy set by law."[107] The court held that "[o]rdinarily, the party wishing to avoid procreation should prevail, assuming that the other party has a reasonable possibility of achieving parenthood by means other than

[102] *Reber v. Reiss*, 42 A.3d 1131 (Pa. Super. Ct. 2012).

[103] *Id.* at 1134.

[104] *In re Marriage of Rooks*, 429 P.3d 579 (Colo. 2018). Other courts have described embryos as marital property. *See, e.g.*, *Terrell v. Torres*, 456 P.3d 13, 15 (Ariz. 2020).

[105] *Davis v. Davis*, 1990 WL 130807, at *3 (Tenn. Ct. App. 1990).

[106] 842 S.W.2d at 597.

[107] *Id.*

use of the pre-embryos in question."[108] However, if "no other reasonable alternatives exist, then the argument in favor of using the pre-embryos to achieve pregnancy should be considered."[109] In this case, because "the party seeking control of the pre-embryos intends merely to donate them to another couple, the objecting party obviously has the greater interest and should prevail."[110] ◀

▷ ENFORCEABILITY OF CONTRACT TO RELINQUISH CONTROL OF FROZEN EMBRYOS **HARD CASE ◀**

In the *Kass* case, in contrast, the New York Court of Appeals reversed the trial court on appeal and held the parties to their contractual agreement with the fertility clinic, which provided that the remaining pre-embryos would be donated to the fertility clinic for research purposes. The plaintiff had changed her mind when the parties began divorce proceedings and wanted to be implanted with the remaining pre-embryos. The Court of Appeals ruled against her, not allowing her to change her mind once she had signed the agreement to give up control over the pre-embryos.[111] In contrast, in *J.B. v. M.B.*,[112] a New Jersey appellate court refused to enforce such an agreement. In that case, the husband wanted to preserve the frozen embryos for future use either with a woman with whom he would develop a relationship or for donation to an infertile couple. Relying on a similar court ruling in Massachusetts,[113] the court held that agreements to procreate violate public policy because their enforcement effectively forces one person to become a parent against his or her will. ◀

▷ AMERICAN INDIAN HUMAN REMAINS IN UNMARKED BURIAL GROUNDS **HARD CASE ◀**

In *Wana the Bear v. Community Construction, Inc.*,[114] a private subdivision developer uncovered human remains of over 200 persons when it began

[108] *Id.* at 604.
[109] *Id.*
[110] *Id.*; *see also E.B. v. R.N.*, 242 N.E.3d 791, 796 (Ohio App. 2024) (ex-wife allowed to bring frozen embryos to term over ex-husband's request that they be donated to another couple).
[111] 696 N.E.2d 174 (N.Y. 1998). *Accord, Jocelyn P. v. Joshua P.*, 302 A.3d 1111 (Md. App. 2023) (endorsing the enforcement of contracts regarding frozen embryos, noting that a subsequent oral agreement to allow the implantation of embryos superseded their prior written contract); *In re Marriage of Litowitz*, 48 P.3d 261 (Wash. 2002) (enforcing contract between husband and wife that fertilized embryos would be thawed out and destroyed if they were not implanted within five years). *Cf. Szafranski v. Dunston*, 34 N.E.3d 1132 (Ill. App. Ct. 2015) (enforcing an agreement that a woman would be entitled to use pre-embryos to have a child in conformity with both a written and an oral agreement when she had lymphoma and this was her last chance to have a biological child).
[112] 751 A.2d 613 (N.J. Super. Ct. App. Div. 2000).
[113] *A.Z. v. B.Z.*, 725 N.E.2d 1051 (Mass. 2000).
[114] 180 Cal. Rptr. 423 (Ct. App. 1982).

excavation of its property to develop a residential tract. The property had been used as a burial ground by the Miwok Indians until they were driven out of the area between 1850 and 1870. Plaintiff, a descendant of the Bear People Lodge of the Miwok Indians and related to some or all of the persons whose remains lie there, brought suit to enjoin further excavation and other "desecration." The court held the property had not achieved the status of a "cemetery" under state statutory law because the property had neither been dedicated to the public nor been established as a cemetery by prescriptive use. The legal rule announced in the case was partly overturned by California legislation expressly protecting American Indian burial sites.[115] The legislation requires property owners who discover American Indian human remains on their property to notify public officials and to negotiate with representatives of the affected tribe for reburial of the remains and associated objects.[116] At least 13 states have passed legislation to protect all unmarked graves, including American Indian burial sites on private land owned by non-Indians.[117] ◀

Native American Graves Protection and Repatriation Act

In 1990, Congress passed the *Native American Graves Protection and Repatriation Act*[118] (discussed at §15.6.5). The act provides that American Indian and Native Hawaiian human remains and funerary objects placed with the body upon burial that are found on tribal or federal lands after the effective date of the statute belong to the lineal descendants of the person buried with the items. If such descendants cannot be found, the items belong to the tribe on whose tribal land the object was found or to the tribe having the closest cultural affiliation with the items.[119] Sacred objects "needed by traditional Native American religious leaders for the practice of traditional Native American religions by their present day adherents"[120] and "objects of cultural patrimony" that have "ongoing historical, traditional or cultural importance central to the Native American group or culture" similarly belong to the tribe on whose land they are found or to the tribe having the closest affiliation with the objects.[121]

Human remains in museums

The Smithsonian Institution and other institutions in the United States have returned approximately 40,000 human remains of American

[115] Cal. Gov't Code §6254(r); Cal. Health & Safety Code §7050.5; Cal. Pub. Res. Code §§5097.94, 5097.98 & 5097.99.

[116] *See People v. Van Horn*, 267 Cal. Rptr. 804 (Ct. App. 1990) (upholding the constitutionality of the statute and requiring an archaeologist to return two objects found in a site he excavated on private land while making a survey for the city of Vista, California, which was in the process of determining whether to buy the land); Thomas Boyd, *Disputes Regarding the Possession of Native American Religious and Cultural Objects and Human Remains: A Discussion of the Applicable Law and Proposed Legislation*, 55 Mo. L. Rev. 883 (1990); Walter Echo-Hawk, *Museum Rights vs. Indian Rights: Guidelines for Assessing Competing Legal Interests in Native Cultural Resources*, 14 N.Y.U. Rev. L. & Soc. Change 437 (1986).

[117] *See, e.g.*, Ala. Code §§41-3-1 to 41-3-6; Del. Code Ann. tit. 7, §§5301 to 5306; Idaho Code §§27-501 to 27-504; 20 Ill. Ann. Stat. 3440/0 to 3440/16; Neb. Stat. §§12-1202 to 12-1212; Okla. Stat. Ann. tit. 21, §§1168 to 1168.6, tit. 53, §361.

[118] 25 U.S.C. §§3001 to 3013; 18 U.S.C. §1170.

[119] 25 U.S.C. §3002(a).

[120] *Id.* at §3001(3)(C).

[121] *Id.* at §3002(a).

Indians.[122] The *Native American Graves Protection and Repatriation Act* provides that human remains and cultural items held by federal agencies and museums receiving federal funds shall be turned over to lineal descendants or to the appropriate American Indian tribe or Native Hawaiian organization.[123] The only exception to this rule occurs when "the items are indispensable for completion of a specific scientific study, the outcome of which would be of major benefit to the United States."[124] Such items shall be returned within 90 days of the completion of the scientific study. Although the Smithsonian Institution is expressly excluded from coverage by the statute,[125] it is required to return those remains by the *National Museum of the Indian Act*,[126] passed November 28, 1989. This statute requires the Smithsonian to return "any Indian human remains identified by a preponderance of the evidence as those of a particular individual or as those of an individual culturally affiliated with a particular Indian tribe, upon the request of the descendants of such individual or of the Indian tribe."[127] It therefore allows the museum to retain any human remains for study that cannot be proven to have a connection to an identifiable tribe.

[122] U.S. Dep't of Interior, National Park Service, *National NAGPA*, http://www.nps.gov/history/nagpra/FAQ/#How_many; see also GAO, Native American Priorities: Protection and Repatriation of Human Remains and Other Cultural Items, GAO-24-106870, Oct. 10, 2023 (noting that as of 2023, only half of more than 200,000 Native American human remains held by museums had been evaluated under NAGPRA).

[123] 25 U.S.C. §3005(a).

[124] *Id.* at §3005(b). The statute also provides, somewhat cryptically, that it does not apply if a forced transfer of property rights from the museum to the relevant Indian tribe would constitute an unconstitutional taking of property. *Id.* at §3001(13).

[125] *Id.* at §§3001(4) & (8).

[126] 20 U.S.C. §§80q to 80q-15.

[127] *Id.* at §80q-9(c).

CHAPTER 17

Intellectual Property

§17.1 Introduction
§17.2 Copyright
§17.3 Patents
§17.4 Trademarks
§17.5 Unfair Competition
§17.6 Publicity Rights
§17.7 Moral Rights of Artists
§17.8 Cultural Property
§17.9 Digital Property

§17.1 Introduction

Ownership of original ideas or information

Intellectual property includes the various laws governing ownership of information or ideas.[1] The topic is quite complex, and much of it is based on intricate federal statutes. Upper-level courses specialize in the subject. It will be useful to introduce the subject here because some general courses on property law are beginning to cover some basic aspects of intellectual property law.

Constitutional source

The Constitution gives Congress the power to pass laws to "promote the progress of science and useful arts, by securing for limited times to authors and inventors the exclusive right to their respective writings and discoveries."[2] This constitutional provision is the source of the federal copyright and patent laws. Copyright law protects authors, while patent law protects inventors. Conspicuously missing from this provision is trademark law, which, as noted below, is grounded in the congressional power to regulate interstate commerce rather than in the patent and copyright clause.

§17.2 Copyright

The Copyright Acts

Original works of authorship

The first copyright act was enacted by Congress in 1790 and substantially revised in 1831, 1870, 1909, 1976, with a myriad of more limited amendments.[3] Copyright law protects "original works of authorship fixed in any tangible medium of expression," including literary, musical, dramatic, graphic, pictorial, choreographic, architectural, or sculptural works.[4] Up until 1976, protection lasted for 50 years after the death of the author; however, a 1998 revision increased that period to 70 years.[5] A work is copyrighted as soon as it is produced; no registration or special designation need be made to obtain copyright protection. The author has the exclusive right to reproduce the work, to prepare derivative works based on it, to distribute copies by sale or other transfer of ownership to others, and to publicly perform or display the work.[6] The copyright owner may also sue for injunctive relief and damages.[7] Criminal penalties may also be assessed in certain types of cases, generally when one willfully copies and distributes a copyrighted work for commercial gain.[8]

What can be copyrighted: Original expressions, not ideas

It is important to note that *ideas* and *facts* cannot be copyrighted. Ideas are in the *public domain* and are free for all to use. For example, the Supreme Court held in *Feist Publications, Inc. v. Rural Telephone Service*[9]

[1] Donald A. Chisum et al., *Understanding Intellectual Property Law* §1A (3d ed. 2015); Michael A. Epstein, *Epstein on Intellectual Property* (5th ed. 2006 & Supp. 2020).
[2] U.S. Const., art. I, §8, cl. 8.
[3] 17 U.S.C. §§101 to 1316, §1401; Arthur R. Miller, Michael H. Davis, and Dana Neacsu, *Intellectual Property: Patents, Trademarks, and Copyright in a Nutshell* 326 (7th ed. 2023).
[4] 17 U.S.C. §102(a).
[5] *Id.* at §302(a).
[6] *Id.* at §106.
[7] *Id.* at §502, 504.
[8] *Id.* at §506.
[9] 499 U.S. 340 (1991).

that the data contained in the white pages of a phonebook did not constitute copyrightable material. Ideas cannot be copyrighted, but *original expressions* of ideas can be.[10] Moreover, a violation occurs only if one copies an original expression of another; no violation occurs if the idea originated with the author.[11]

Originality

Fair use

The *Copyright Act* allows uses of copyrighted works without the copyright owner's consent under the "*fair use*" exception.[12] Use of copyrighted works is privileged "for purposes such as criticism, comment, news reporting, teaching (including multiple copies for classroom use), scholarship, or research."[13] However, use is not automatically "fair use" if it is used for one of these purposes; the use must also satisfy a series of statutory criteria. Section 107 of the *Copyright Act* requires consideration of a variety of factors, including

> (1) the purpose and character of the use, including whether such use is of a commercial nature or is for nonprofit educational purposes; (2) the nature of the copyrighted work; (3) the amount and substantiality of the portion used in relation to the copyrighted work as a whole; and (4) the effect of the use upon the potential market for or value of the copyrighted work.[14]

In determining whether a use constitutes "fair use," a noncommercial, educational use is much more likely to be allowed than a commercial one;[15] use of an entire work or a substantial portion of it is quite likely to be held not to be a fair use;[16] and a use that has an impact on the potential market for the work is quite likely to be held not to constitute a fair use.[17]

▷ FAIR USE, "TRANSFORMATIVE USE," AND PARODY — **HARD CASE ◀**

The standard for determining what is a fair use is less than crystal clear. Sometimes even substantial copying may be allowed, such as when the

[10] Arthur R. Miller, Michael H. Davis, and Dana Neacsu, *Intellectual Property: Patents, Trademarks, and Copyright in a Nutshell* 332 (7th ed. 2023).
[11] *Id.* at 333.
[12] 17 U.S.C. §107; Andy Warhol Foundation for the Visual Arts, Inc. v. Goldsmith, 598 U.S. 508 (2023); *Dr. Seuss Enterprises, L.P. v. ComicMix LLC,* 983 F.3d 443 (9th Cir. 2020) (rejecting a fair use claim for using Dr. Seuss's *Oh, the Places You'll Go!* in a Star-Trek-themed book); *Sony Computer Entertainment America, Inc. v. Bleem, LLC,* 214 F.3d 1022 (9th Cir. 2000) (finding the unauthorized use of a "screen shot"—a frozen image from a personal video game—in advertisement is likely to be a fair use). *See* Marshall A. Leaffer, *Understanding Copyright Law* 487-530 (7th ed. 2019).
[13] 17 U.S.C. §107.
[14] *Id.*
[15] *Id.* at §107(1).
[16] *Id.* at §107(3).
[17] *Id.* at §107(4). *See Harper & Row, Publishers, Inc. v. Nation Enterprises,* 471 U.S. 539 (1985) (publication by *The Nation* magazine of 300 to 400 words from President Gerald Ford's account of his pardon of President Nixon was not a fair use when the material was obtained without consent and was intended to "scoop" *Time* magazine by publishing the information first).

purpose is to create a parody.[18] However, even small amounts of copying may be held not to be a fair use if the material is distributed in a manner that has a substantial impact on the market for the copyrighted material. The classic movie *Gone with the Wind* is based on a novel of that name by Margaret Mitchell. The copyright persists and is owned by the Mitchell Trusts, which have authorized a number of derivative works from the novel, as well as the use of certain elements in commercial contexts. The Trusts authorized a sequel to the novel, to be entitled *Scarlett: The Sequel.* Without the Trusts' permission, Alice Randall wrote for publication a novel entitled *The Wind Done Gone*, retelling the story of *Gone with the Wind* from the perspective of Cynara, who is a slave and the illegitimate daughter of Planter, a plantation owner, and Mammy, a slave who cares for his children. The Trusts sued the prospective publisher of *The Wind Done Gone* to enjoin publication on the ground that publication would infringe the copyright by unauthorized copying and by publishing a derivative work (an unauthorized sequel) without permission.[19] Defendant noted that the Supreme Court had held that "parodies" of prior works were a fair use of them, and that Randall's novel was intended to bring attention to the unconscious racism in *Gone With the Wind.* "The new work reverses the stereotypes of the earlier novel and thereby 'endows the stereotypical black characters in *Gone with the Wind* with agency, cunning, and effectiveness.'"[20] However, Judge Charles A. Pannell, Jr. granted a preliminary injunction halting publication of the book, noting that parodies are generally intended for comic effect and that Randall's work is better seen as a sequel than a parody. On appeal, the Eleventh Circuit reversed, dissolving the injunction and allowing the book to be published, on the grounds that parodies may be intended to comment on the original work and need not be limited to variations intended for comic effect. On this ground, the court found that Randall was using fiction to criticize the earlier work "to rebut and destroy the perspective, judgments, and mythology of *Gone with the Wind*" and to "explode the romantic, idealized portrait of the antebellum South during and after the Civil War."[21]

The Supreme Court has clarified that to qualify for the fair use defense to copyright, one important factor is whether the use of the copied source is "transformative,"[22] — the new use should be for a different purpose than the original. A parody of an original meets this criterion, but merely altering an image or song for general commercial use likely does not. In *Andy Warhol Foundation for the Visual Arts, Inc. v. Goldsmith*, the artist Andy Warhol used a copyrighted photograph of the musician Prince, taken by the professional photographer Lynn Goldsmith as the basis for a silkscreen portrait.[23] Even though Warhol had significantly

[18] *Campbell v. Acuff-Rose Music, Inc.*, 510 U.S. 569 (1994).
[19] *Suntrust Bank v. Houghton Mifflin Co.*, 136 F. Supp. 2d 1357 (N.D. Ga. 2001), *rev'd*, 268 F.3d 1257 (11th Cir. 2001).
[20] *Id.* at 1373.
[21] *268 F.3d* at 1269.
[22] *Andy Warhol Foundation for the Visual Arts, Inc. v. Goldsmith*, 598 U.S. 508, 529 (2023).
[23] *Id.* at 518.

altered the image, as he had famously done with other celebrity images and everyday objects like Cambell's soup cans, the fact that this particular image was used for the cover of a special edition magazine, which was substantially similar to the purpose of the original photograph, undermined the fair use defense.[24] ◀

Contributory infringement

One can violate the copyright laws by helping others to infringe a copyright. For example, in *Sony Corp. v. Universal City Studios*,[25] the producers of television shows claimed that the producers of videocassette recorders (VCRs) were engaged in "contributory infringement" by allowing home viewers to copy copyrighted movies rather than buying or renting those movies. To determine whether the VCR manufacturers had engaged in contributory infringement, the Supreme Court asked two questions. First, were VCRs capable of being used for substantial non-infringing uses?[26] A major purpose of VCRs is to allow viewers to "time-shift," *i.e.*, to view a movie later rather than when it is shown on television. Because the movie could have been viewed for free at the time it was aired, the Court concluded that time-shifting was a non-infringing use. Moreover, many copyright owners of television shows and movies believed that VCRs would increase their audience, and welcomed this prospect. Because VCRs were capable of substantial non-infringing uses, the VCR manufacturers were not liable for contributory infringement. Second, the Court asked whether there was proof that the use in question would affect the market for the copyrighted works. In determining whether a use is fair, the Supreme Court has explained that

> [t]he purpose of copyright is to create incentives for creative effort. [A] use that has no demonstrable effect upon the potential market for, or the value of, the copyrighted work need not be prohibited in order to protect the author's incentive to create. The prohibition of such noncommercial uses would merely inhibit access to ideas without any countervailing benefit.[27]

In this case, the Court found that plaintiffs had failed to prove that VCR use would result in a decrease of audiences for shows aired on television or even in a decrease in theater attendance or video rentals.[28] Indeed, VCR use might, on balance, increase the profitability of film and television show production.[29] The Supreme Court thus concluded that home time-shifting is fair use and thus, a manufacturer of VCRs that enabled this time-shifting to occur could not be liable for contributory infringement.[30]

[24] *Id.* at 537.
[25] 464 U.S. 417 (1984).
[26] *Id.* at 442 ("The sale of copying equipment, like the sale of other articles of commerce, does not constitute contributory infringement if the product is widely used for legitimate, unobjectionable purposes, or, indeed, is merely capable of substantial non-infringing uses.").
[27] *Sony Corp. v. Universal City Studios*, 464 U.S. 417, 450-451 (1984).
[28] *Id.* at 454.
[29] *Id.*
[30] *Id.* at 454-455.

▶ HARD CASE ▷ GROKSTER AND STREAMCAST

Internet sites that allow people to share copyrighted materials have raised controversies. Grokster, Inc. and StreamCast Networks, Inc., distributed software products that allowed people to share files (including copyrighted content) through peer-to-peer computer networks that communicated directly with one another. A group of copyright holders sued the companies for contributory infringement.

Argument that Grokster and StreamCast were not engaged in contributory infringement

Grokster and StreamCast argued that they did not monitor the file sharing and that even copyrighted works may be authorized by the right holders to be copied for free. They also argued that there were significant potential non-infringing uses of their software, such as musical performers who gain new audiences by distributing copyrighted works for free across peer-to-peer networks. Because *Sony Corp.* held that there can be no contributory infringement if a product is capable of substantial non-infringing use, Grokster and StreamCast argued that they should not be liable for contributory infringement, even if the evidence showed that the majority of the uses on the software infringed on copyright.

Argument that Grokster and StreamCast engaged in contributory infringement

The court rejected this argument, holding that it made a big difference that the companies were enabling users to obtain copies of copyrighted content without paying for them. The essence of copyright is the right to control reproduction of the work—to prevent others from copying the work without the owner's consent. The possible effect on the market for a work of allowing it to be duplicated without limit over the Internet is obvious. Because every copy of a copyrighted work constitutes an infringement, and most of the works available through Grokster and StreamCast were copyrighted, the companies were liable for contributory infringement, notwithstanding *Sony*.[31] ◀

▶ HARD CASE ▷ HARRY POTTER LEXICON

Reference works to literature

In 2000, a fan of the Harry Potter series, Steven Vander Ark, created an on-line encyclopedia about the Harry Potter books, called The Harry Potter Lexicon (http://www.hp-lexicon.org). Although J.K. Rowling was a fan of the Web site, when Vander Ark made plans to publish the encyclopedia in book form as an A-to-Z guide to the creatures, characters, objects, events, and places that exist in the world of *Harry Potter*, she sued to enjoin the publication because she was planning to publish her own encyclopedia about the series. The court found the encyclopedia to violate Rowling's copyright because it copied so much of the original works.

> Most of the Lexicon's 2,437 entries contain direct quotations or paraphrases, plot details, or summaries of scenes from one or more of the *Harry Potter* novels. Although hundreds of pages or thousands of

[31] *See Metro-Goldwyn-Mayer Studios v. Grokster, Inc.*, 545 U.S. 913 (2005); *see also UMG Recordings, Inc. v. MP3.com, Inc.*, 92 F. Supp. 2d 349 (S.D.N.Y. 2000) (no fair use to make digital music available to those who had previously bought those works).

> fictional facts may amount to only a fraction of the seven-book series, this quantum of copying is sufficient to support a finding of substantial similarity where the copied expression is entirely the product of the original author's imagination and creation.[32]

The court found the encyclopedia not to be a derivative work because it does not "retell the story of *Harry Potter*, but instead gives the copyrighted material another purpose," and thus does not "represent the original works of authorship."[33] However, the court found the encyclopedia not to constitute a fair use. Although the "purpose and character" of the encyclopedia were "transformative," the "commercial nature" of the intended publication counted heavily against finding a fair use and it often copied more than necessary for its informative purposes and thus "appropriates too much of Rowling's creative work for its purposes as a reference guide."[34] At the same, the court seemed ambivalent about its ruling. Determining the precise amount of copying that goes over the line is a tricky business, especially if it is correct that reference works are not "derivative works." ◀

§17.3 Patents

New, useful, nonobvious inventions or discoveries

Patent law protects new, useful, and nonobvious inventions or discoveries, including processes, machines, methods of manufacture, or composition of matter, or any improvements in any of these inventions or discoveries.[35] The *Patent Act*[36] was first passed in 1790, pursuant to the patent and copyright clause[37] and was revised in 1793, 1836, 1870, 1897, and 1952.[38] Unlike copyright protection, which occurs automatically once one authors a work, patents must be granted by the United States Patent and Trademark Office established by the *Patent Act.*[39] Upon application, the Patent and Trademark Office undertakes an examination process to determine whether the invention is patentable. The *Patent Act* gives priority to the "first to invent" the product or process.[40] Once a patent is granted, the owner has the exclusive right to use or sell the invention to others for 17 years, or up to 22 years for certain devices if their approval process was delayed.[41]

[32] *Warner Bros. Entertainment, Inc. & J.K. Rowling v. RDR Books*, 575 F. Supp. 2d 513, 535 (S.D.N.Y. 2008).

[33] *Id.* at 539.

[34] *Id.* at 553.

[35] 35 U.S.C. §101. *See* Donald A. Chisum et al., *Understanding Intellectual Property Law* §2C (3d ed. 2015).

[36] 35 U.S.C. §§101 to 212.

[37] U.S. Const., art. I, §8, cl. 8.

[38] Donald A. Chisum et al., *Understanding Intellectual Property Law* §2B (3d ed. 2015); Arthur R. Miller, Michael H. Davis, and Dana Neacsu, *Intellectual Property: Patents, Trademarks, and Copyright in a Nutshell* 11 (7th ed. 2023).

[39] Note that state common law may protect trade secrets and prohibit unfair competition. *See* §§17.4 & 17.5.

[40] Donald A. Chisum et al., *Understanding Intellectual Property Law* §2B[3] (3d ed. 2015).

[41] 35 U.S.C. §§154 & 156. *See Bowman v. Monsanto Co.*, 569 U.S. 278 (2013) (farmer must buy patented seeds from patent owner rather than use the seeds produced by the plants grown from those seeds).

Ideas v. applications

Ideas can be neither copyrighted nor patented.[42] Just as copyright protects *expression* (but not ideas), patent law protects *products* or *processes* — *applications* of ideas rather than ideas themselves.[43] For example, natural processes, laws of nature, and naturally occurring products or organisms cannot be patented.[44] The line between a nonpatentable natural law or process and a patentable process for manipulating nature may be hard to draw. The Supreme Court did allow a patent to be issued in 1980 in *Diamond v. Chakrabarty*[45] for new life forms, in that case bacteria genetically altered to digest petroleum waste. Although the bacteria was a life form, it did not exist in nature but was created by scientists. However, in the 1972 case of *Gottschalk v. Benson*,[46] the Court held that a process for converting binary-coded decimal numbers into pure binary numbers could not be patented; the process was a kind of algorithm and, if patentable, would give the applicant a monopoly on a scientific truth.[47]

▶ HARD CASE ▷ NONOBVIOUS

Competing arguments

To obtain a patent, the invention must be "nonobvious."[48] A determination of obviousness is based on four factors: "(1) the scope and content of the prior art; (2) the differences between the claims and the prior art; (3) the level of ordinary skill in the pertinent art; and (4) secondary considerations, if any, of nonobviousness."[49] In *McGinley v. Franklin Sports, Inc.*,[50] an owner of a baseball used to teach pitching students brought an infringement action to enforce its patent. The patent was issued for a "baseball with specific finger placement indicia used to teach students how to grasp a baseball in order to throw different types of pitches."[51] It was marketed as the Roger Clemens Instructional Baseball. One prior patent (the Pratt patent) had been issued for a ball that placed round dots (as opposed to egg-shaped dots) where the tips of one's fingers should go and then placed "phantom lines" to show how one's fingers should be placed; a second prior patent (the Morgan patent) drew the outlines showing where fingers

[42] *Gottschalk v. Benson*, 409 U.S. 63, 71 (1972) ("one may not patent an idea").

[43] *Parker v. Flook*, 437 U.S. 584 (1978) (ideas not patentable).

[44] *Ass'n for Molecular Pathology v. Myriad Genetics, Inc.*, 569 U.S. 576 (2013) (while human genes cannot be patented because they are naturally occurring products, both methods of extracting or manipulating them and constructed non-naturally occurring variations on them can be patented); Donald A. Chisum et al., *Understanding Intellectual Property Law* §2C[1][d] (3d ed. 2015).

[45] 447 U.S. 303 (1980).

[46] 409 U.S. 63 (1972).

[47] Id. at 67. *See also* Donald A. Chisum et al., *Understanding Intellectual Property Law* §2C[1][f] (3d ed. 2015).

[48] 35 U.S.C. §101; *Amazon.com, Inc. v. Barnesandnoble.com, Inc.*, 73 F. Supp. 2d 1228 (W.D. Wash. 1999), *rev'd*, 239 F.3d 1343 (Fed. Cir. 2001); Donald A. Chisum et al., *Understanding Intellectual Property Law* §2C[4][a] (3d ed. 2015).

[49] *Graham v. John Deere Co.*, 383 U.S. 1, 17-18 (1966); *McGinley v. Franklin Sports, Inc.*, 92 F. Supp. 2d 1216 (D. Kan. 2000).

[50] *McGinley v. Franklin Sports, Inc.*, 92 F. Supp. 2d 1216 (D. Kan. 2000), *rev'd*, 262 F.3d 1339 (Fed. Cir. 2001).

[51] *Id.* at 1218.

should be placed on a sphere, but not on a baseball, to show how to hold the ball to throw a curve ball. The patent in *McGinley* filled in the outlines and placed them on an actual baseball; it also showed how to hold the baseball for a variety of pitches rather than just curve balls. In effect, the McGinley patent arguably combined the insights of the two earlier patents with some modifications. The question was whether those modifications were "nonobvious."

The jury found that the McGinley patent was nonobvious because neither of the prior patents had actually drawn the placement of fingers on a baseball itself; they had either used only dots or not used a baseball. Their finding was overruled by the trial judge, who issued a judgment notwithstanding the verdict for the defendant on the ground that the two prior patents were sufficiently similar to the McGinley patent to render it "obvious to one of ordinary skill in the art" as a matter of law.[52] The judge was also unpersuaded by so-called secondary considerations, including the fact that no baseball prior to the Roger Clemens Instructional Baseball had ever been marketed, despite plaintiff's argument that the grant of legal protection for its patent is what induced it to market the product and that consumers, at least, thought that the product was a significant advance over the current state of the art. However, the judge's rule was overturned on appeal when the Federal Circuit found that the jury could have reasonably concluded that the McGinley patent was not obvious.[53] ◀

▷ "ONE-CLICK" METHOD **HARD CASE ◀**

In *Amazon.com v. Barnesandnoble.com*,[54] the trial court held that the "one-click" method of on-line shopping invented by Amazon.com was nonobvious and thus enjoined competitor Barnesandnoble.com from using it on its Web site.[55] The court noted that the method was a substantial improvement over prior methods by making such purchases easier and more profitable for on-line companies because many "shopping carts" of items collected by consumers on-line are abandoned before the purchase is completed. The long-standing problems solved by the one-click method and the immediate imitation of it by competitors demonstrated that the method was not obvious. However, this ruling was reversed on appeal. It can be argued that the method simply reduces the steps needed to make an on-line purchase, and that this does not constitute the type of "invention" that the patent laws were meant to protect. No need exists to protect the "inventor" to generate incentives to create improvements of this kind, nor is the one-click procedure such a drastic change from prior art that its inventor should be given a statutory monopoly. ◀

[52] 92 F. Supp. 2d at 1223.

[53] 262 F.3d at 1351-1356.

[54] 73 F. Supp. 2d 1228 (W.D. Wash. 1999), *rev'd in part and aff'd in part and remanded*, 239 F.3d 1343 (9th Cir. 2001).

[55] *See Bilski v. Kappos*, 561 U.S. 593 (2010) (reaffirming that patents can be granted for non-obvious business methods).

▶ HARD CASE ▷ INVENTIONS BY GENERATIVE ARTIFICIAL INTELLIGENCE

Generative artificial intelligence (AI) can help create new, useful, nonobvious innovations, including an airline cabin design, a race-car chassis, and the potential for a range of scientific advancements.[56] Google has also created AutoML, "an automated approach to the making of machine learning models," allowing "AI to create more sophisticated AIs."[57] The rapid pace of change in AI capabilities raises fundamental questions about the patentability of their inventions. If machine-generated inventions can be patented, who should control that patent, if not the owner of the AI itself?[58] Arguments in favor of patentability include the encouragement of broader commercial acceptance of the products of AI invention and transparency, in the nature of any technology created, because patenting allows — indeed requires — disclosure.[59] On the other hand, the argument that incentives are needed through the patent system for creation do not seem to pertain to automated inventors.[60] ◀

§17.4 Trademarks

Trademarks

Trademarks are names or images that mark a particular company or product line. Unlike copyright and patent law, trademark law is primarily based on state common law, not federal statute. This is to a large extent because the Constitution specifically protects authors (copyright) and inventors (patent), but not trademarks.[61] For this reason, the first trademark laws, passed by Congress in 1870 and 1876, were struck down as unconstitutional in 1879 by the Supreme Court.[62] Because the Court held that trademarks could not be the subject of either copyright or patent, the only source of constitutional power by which Congress could regulate trademarks was the interstate commerce clause. In 1879, the Court considered trademarks to be a form of property within the purview of state property law. Congress responded by passing statutes in 1881 and 1905 that addressed the interstate use of trademarks. Those statutes, rather than providing for the recognition of trademarks, merely provide for the registration of trademarks created by state law.

Character of trademarks

A trademark identifies the producer of a good or service and/or a particular product or product line.[63] Trademark law gives the owner of the

[56] Todd Bishop, *Can AI Cure Cancer?*, Geekwire, Oct. 2, 2024.

[57] Michael McLaughlin, *Computer-Generated Inventions*, 101 J. Patent and Trademark Office Soc'y 224, 238 (2019).

[58] *See* Gaétan de Rassen-fosse et al., *AI-Generated Inventions: Implications for the Patent System*, 96 S. Cal. L. Rev. 1453 (2024).

[59] *Id.*

[60] *Id.*

[61] *See* U.S. Const. art. I, §8, cl. 8 ("The Congress shall have power to promote the progress of science and useful arts, by securing for limited times to authors and inventors the exclusive right to their respective writings and discoveries.").

[62] *In re Trade-Mark Cases*, 100 U.S. 82 (1879).

[63] Arthur R. Miller, Michael H. Davis, and Dana Neacsu, *Intellectual Property: Patents, Trademarks, and Copyright in a Nutshell* 179 (7th ed. 2023).

mark the exclusive right to use it in connection with the sale of a particular good or service in a particular area.[64] The first to use the mark in connection with a business prevails over a later user. The trademark owner may even enjoin use of a similar name if it is likely to cause confusion or mistake.[65] The trademark's value, of course, is much more than just ease of identification. Once customers develop loyalty to a brand name, the trademark itself has substantial value; that value is the goodwill associated with it. A name can become associated with quality and this goodwill is a substantial property right. Unlike copyrights and patents, trademarks generally must be used to garner legal protection. One must *use* a name or mark in connection with a business to create the mark that identifies the good or service and can capture the goodwill associated with the mark. The mark is *appurtenant* to the business.[66] Copyright and patent law, in contrast, do not require the copyrighted or patented items to be used or sold.

Must be used in connection with a business

Geographic limits

A corollary of the rule that trademarks must be used is that they are recognized only within the geographic region where the product is sold or marketed.[67] Thus, a store in Los Angeles might have the same name as a store in Boston without infringing the Boston trademark, as long as the use is not confusing. In some cases, a store name may be so well known that the public might believe a store of that name opening locally was a part of a national chain. In such a case, the use of the name might well infringe on the trademark.

Intent

Trademark law developed as part of the law of unfair competition.[68] For this reason, it was traditionally believed that a use of another's mark was wrongful only if the user intended to confuse the public by "palming off" one's own products as those of another. If one used another's trademark without knowing that the mark was previously used, the courts might well hold that there was no trademark violation.[69]

Registration

The federal trademark law, called the *Lanham Act*,[70] changes this situation by allowing trademarks to be *registered*.[71] Registration functions in a manner similar to the recording system for deeds. Registration places the whole world on constructive notice of the registered trademark so later users of a mark cannot claim to have used it in good faith or without knowledge of its prior use.[72] This may have the effect of creating property rights in the mark even if it is not fully exploited by the registrant. A trademark may not be registered if it was in prior use by another (unless that use has

[64] Donald A. Chisum et al., *Understanding Intellectual Property Law* §5A (3d ed. 2015).

[65] *Frank's Restaurant, Inc. v. Lauramar Enterprises, Inc.*, 711 N.Y.S.2d 433 (App. Div. 2000) (applying state law to hold that a defendant's use of a name to plaintiff's trademark may be enjoined where it is likely to cause confusion, mistake, or deception).

[66] Arthur R. Miller, Michael H. Davis, and Dana Neacsu, *Intellectual Property: Patents, Trademarks, and Copyright in a Nutshell* 182 (7th ed. 2023).

[67] *Id.* at 171-172.

[68] *Id.* at 171.

[69] *Id.* at 172.

[70] 15 U.S.C. §1114.

[71] *Id.* at §1072.

[72] *Id.*; Arthur R. Miller, Michael H. Davis, and Dana Neacsu, *Intellectual Property: Patents, Trademarks, and Copyright in a Nutshell* 186 (7th ed. 2023).

been abandoned) or if there is a likelihood of confusion.[73] Registration also gives the trademark owner the benefits of *incontestability*, protecting the registrant against loss of registration except on very specifically stated statutory grounds.[74] A mark may lose incontestability if it becomes the generic name for the product, such as Xerox (make me a Xerox), Kleenex (get me a Kleenex), or Scotch tape. One case held that the term "Lite" as applied to beer had become a generic term for a reduced-calorie food product.[75]

What cannot be trademarked

The *Lanham Act* prohibits registration of geographic names, marks that are primarily surnames (and have not become synonymous with products), or immoral marks.[76] A mark that is a surname, such as Ford, can come to be so closely connected with a particular company that it functions more as the name of that company in the marketplace than an identifier of a particular family name.[77]

▶ HARD CASE ▷ DISPARAGING NAMES

After two decades of litigation, a federal court upheld a federal agency's cancellation of the registration for the Redskins trademark. *Pro-Football, Inc. v. Blackhorse*[78] enforced the provision of the *Lanham Act* that prohibits registration of any mark that is "immoral, deceptive, or scandalous" or that "consists of or comprises matter which may disparage persons, living or dead, institutions, beliefs, or national symbols, or bring them into contempt or disrepute."[79] The court found the term "redskin" to be a racial epithet that denigrates American Indians. The trademark owner argued that many Indians do not find the name offensive and that the name is intended to honor them. The court considered but rejected the argument that the team owner has a free speech right under the First Amendment to use the name even if it was offensive. Denying the benefits of registration did not prevent the owner from continuing to use the name and thus did not limit speech.

By contrast, in *Matal v. Tam*,[80] the Supreme Court held that conditioning a federal benefit on the content of speech was a regulation of speech. As such it violated the First Amendment because it regulated the expressive content of speech. *Matal* involved a band called The Slants. The Patent and Trademark Office had determined that the name represented a racial slur that was disparaging to people of Asian descent and thus could not be registered as a trademark under the *Lanham Act*, and its ruling was upheld by the federal district court. Band leader Simon Shiao Tam had argued

[73] 15 U.S.C. §1052(d).
[74] *Id.* at §1115(b); Arthur R. Miller, Michael H. Davis, and Dana Neacsu, *Intellectual Property: Patents, Trademarks, and Copyright in a Nutshell* 186 (7th ed. 2023).
[75] *Miller Brewing Co. v. Falstaff Brewing Co.*, 655 F.2d 5 (1st Cir. 1980).
[76] Arthur R. Miller, Michael H. Davis, and Dana Neacsu, *Intellectual Property: Patents, Trademarks, and Copyright in a Nutshell* 205-213 (7th ed. 2023).
[77] *Singer Manufacturing Co. v. Briley*, 207 F.2d 519 (5th Cir. 1953).
[78] *Pro-Football, Inc. v. Blackhorse*, 112 F. Supp. 3d 439 (E.D. Va. 2015).
[79] 15 U.S.C. §§1052(a), 1064.
[80] 582 U.S. 218 (2017).

that he was trying to reclaim the word just as the previously derogatory word "queer" had been reclaimed by LGBTQ persons. The Supreme Court affirmed the Federal Circuit's reversal of the trial court's ruling, finding Tam's expressive speech to be protected by the First Amendment even if the name was disparaging and its use a violation of the *Lanham Act*. The Court did not address the question of how to deal with regulation of discriminatory speech by employers or public accommodations that has long been regulated under antidiscrimination laws to ensure equal access to the market and has never been held to violate free speech rights. In *Iancu v. Brunetti*,[81] the Supreme Court extended its decision in *Tam* to hold that 15 U.S.C. §1052(a)'s prohibition on registering trademarks that are "immoral" or "scandalous" likewise violates the First Amendment. ◀

Dilution and unfair competition

Trademark law protects the mark owner not only against confusion, but also against *dilution* of the value of the mark by unfair competition.[82] For example, if a business starts selling Singer vacuum cleaners, and they are of inferior quality, the Singer name might come to be associated with shoddy products and the value of the Singer name associated with sewing machines might decrease.[83] Some courts allow trademark owners to enjoin other uses of the mark even if no confusion will result to protect against dilution, even if there is no showing that the goods being sold by the competitor are inferior.[84] This view is based on the notion that the owner of a mark should not have to determine whether it is being harmed or helped by the sale of the products.[85] Trademarks may be protected against dilution either to allow the trademark owner to enter a related field (using its mark to sell goods it had not previously sold), to protect it from association with inferior products, or to protect the public from confusion.[86]

§17.5 Unfair Competition

Unfair methods of competition

Palming off

Although competition is generally viewed favorably by the law, the common law early developed protections against unfair methods of competition. The law focused on (1) prohibiting the deception of customers as to the origin of products (so-called *palming off* one's products as those of

[81] 588 U.S. 388 (2019).
[82] *Allied Maintenance Corp. v. Allied Mechanical Trades, Inc.*, 369 N.E.2d 1162 (N.Y. 1977); Arthur R. Miller, Michael H. Davis, and Dana Neacsu, *Intellectual Property: Patents, Trademarks, and Copyright in a Nutshell* 217-218 (7th ed. 2023).
[83] In case anyone is wondering, Professor Singer, one of the authors of this treatise, is not related to the original owners of the Singer Sewing Machine Company.
[84] Moreover, unlike with the fair use defense to copyright infringement, an image or the like that constitutes a parody of trademark may nonetheless be a violation. *Jack Daniels Properties, Inc. v. VIP Products LLC*, 599 U.S. 140 (2023) (dog toy seller's "Bad Spaniels Silly Squeaker" toy had the potential to cause confusion with and dilute the value of whiskey manufacturer's "Jack Daniel's" trademark).
[85] *Mobil Oil Corp. v. Pegasus Petroleum Corp.*, 818 F.2d 254 (2d Cir. 1987).
[86] *Scarves by Vera, Inc. v. Todo Imports, Ltd., Inc.*, 544 F.2d 1167 (2d Cir. 1976); Arthur R. Miller, Michael H. Davis, and Dana Neacsu, *Intellectual Property: Patents, Trademarks, and Copyright in a Nutshell* 224-225 (7th ed. 2023).

Trade secrets

another), and (2) prohibiting improper means of obtaining information about a competitor's business (the origin of modern *trade secrets* law).[87] The prohibition against "palming off" widened to include a prohibition against false advertising, *i.e.*, making false statements about a competitor's products.[88]

▶ HARD CASE ▷ MISAPPROPRIATION

In the 1918 textbook case of *International News Service v. Associated Press* (*INS v. AP*),[89] the Supreme Court addressed the question of whether unfair competition law should be expanded to prohibit "misappropriation" or the "unauthorized taking of publicly disclosed information that a first competitor invests time and effort to create when the taking diminishes or eliminates the first competitor's incentive to continue to create the information."[90] The topic of misappropriation is now the subject of state common law (and not federal common law), and the states have demonstrated reluctance either to embrace the doctrine or to completely reject it. In *INS v. AP*, one news service, Associated Press (AP), collected news and wrote stories and sold them to newspapers who contracted with AP for this service. INS, a competing news service, copied news from bulletin boards and other early editions of stories collected and written by AP and sold them to its own (competing) member newspapers.

The debate

AP argued that this constituted a wrongful misappropriation of AP's property rights in its stories; it had invested in collecting the news and deserved to be rewarded with the material benefits of having produced it. By its work and investment, it produced something of value and should be entitled to legal protection from misappropriation of its product. Moreover, if it could not have a monopoly on the sale of news it collected, its incentive to gather news would be either substantially reduced or eliminated entirely. The majority of the Supreme Court agreed with AP. INS argued, in contrast, that the news, once made public, could no longer be considered the private property of AP. If individuals could repeat to others the news they read in the papers, so should INS be able to do so. INS argued that it was anomalous for INS to be the only entity not entitled to repeat the information it read on AP's bulletin boards, which was now in the public domain. Justice Holmes dissented, agreeing with INS that there could be no property interest in publicly disclosed facts and that AP's only ground of complaint would be that INS suggested that it, rather than AP, had collected the news — a form of palming off. Justice Brandeis also dissented, agreeing with INS on the ground that no positive law granted protection for AP's property claims. He also argued that it was circular to argue that AP had produced something of value that the law should protect because

87 Donald A. Chisum et al., *Understanding Intellectual Property Law* §6F (3d ed. 2015).
88 *Id.*
89 248 U.S. 215 (1918). For a similar modern case, see *Barclays Capital Inc. v. Theflyonthewall.com*, 650 F.3d 876 (2d Cir. 2011).
90 Donald A. Chisum et al., *Understanding Intellectual Property Law* §6F (3d ed. 2015).

the existence of market value for the news would be affected by the legal decision whether or not to grant AP a monopoly on the right to sell its information. Justice Brandeis thought that the question of whether to grant a monopoly was a policy question that should be left to the legislature. ◀

▷ FABRIC PATTERNS **HARD CASE** ◀

Another textbook case, *Cheney Brothers v. Doris Silk Corp.*,[91] involved the copying of fabric designs imprinted on silk scarves. The Second Circuit found it perfectly permissible to copy such designs and distinguished *INS v. AP* on the ground that recognition of an unfair competition claim in the context of news-gathering would not create a monopoly in the production of news, but that a law prohibiting any imitation of a good would set up an impermissible monopoly.[92] ◀

Preemption

Two 1964 Supreme Court cases held that federal patent and copyright law policy preempt state unfair competition law "insofar as it would bar copying of publicly distributed products not covered by a valid patent or copyright."[93] However, §301 of the *Copyright Act of 1976* explicitly preempts state misappropriation law only where copyrightable material is involved (expression in a tangible medium) or where the state right or remedy is not equivalent to any of the exclusive rights granted by copyright law.[94]

Trade dress: *Lanham Act* §43(a)

Section 43(a) of the *Lanham Act*[95] prohibits "any false designation of origin, false or misleading description of fact, or false or misleading representation of fact" that is likely to cause confusion or mistake as to the origin of goods. This provision has been held to protect "trade dress," or the packaging and appearance of a product that identifies it with a particular producer.[96] This statutory provision supplements state common law principles that similarly protect companies against competitors who copy the form of another's product or packaging to mislead consumers about its origin.[97]

§17.6 Publicity Rights

Control over commercial use of one's identity

Publicity rights give individuals control over the commercial use of their names or images.[98] An individual might want to exploit her own name commercially

[91] 35 F.2d 279 (2d Cir. 1929).
[92] *Id.* at 280.
[93] Donald A. Chisum et al., *Understanding Intellectual Property Law* §6F[4] (3d ed. 2015). *See Sears, Roebuck & Co. v. Stiffel Co.*, 376 U.S. 225 (1964); *Compco Corp. v. Day-Brite Lighting, Inc.*, 376 U.S. 234 (1964).
[94] 17 U.S.C. §301(b)(3).
[95] 15 U.S.C. §1125.
[96] *Truck Equip. Serv. Co. v. Fruehauf Corp.*, 536 F.2d 1210 (8th Cir. 1976).
[97] *Time Mechanisms, Inc. v. Qonaar*, 422 F. Supp. 905 (D.N.J. 1976); Donald A. Chisum et al., *Understanding Intellectual Property Law* §5C[2][c][iv] (3d ed. 2015).
[98] Cal. Civ. Code §3344; *Zacchini v. Scripps-Howard Broadcasting Co.*, 433 U.S. 562 (1977); *Rosa and Raymond Parks Institute for Self-Development v. Target Corp.*, 812 F.3d 824 (11th Cir. 2016); *ETW Corp. v. Jireh Publishing, Inc.*, 332 F.3d 915 (6th Cir. 2003); *Lugosi v. Universal Pictures*, 603

by licensing its use in connection with a product. Conversely, an individual might be interested in *preventing* her name or image from being used commercially by anyone; this is sometimes called the *right of privacy*.[99] Like some aspects of unfair competition and most trade secret law, publicity rights arise under state common law or statute, not federal law.[100] However, §43(a) of the federal *Lanham Act*[101] may support a publicity rights claim because it creates a civil claim against any person who identifies his product so to deceive consumers as to the association of the producer of the product with another person, or to cause consumers to falsely believe that other person has sponsored or approved of the product.[102] In contrast, to show infringement of the common law right of publicity, the claimant need not show a possibility of confusion; all that is required is unauthorized use. Publicity rights both protect individual dignity and give an incentive to engage in commercially exploitable name recognition.[103] One court has explained that "[r]ecognition of the right of publicity rewards and thereby encourages effort and creativity."[104] Although publicity rights originated in the common law, many states have statutes recognizing them and setting limits to them.[105]

Free speech

The right of publicity is not absolute; it is limited by the free speech rights of authors.[106] For example, one court held that a fictional novel and movie concerning an unexplained 11-day disappearance by Agatha Christie, author of numerous mystery novels, was protected by the First Amendment.[107] Similarly, when Janis Joplin's family protested the production of a play about the life of Janis Joplin (after Joplin's death), a court held the play to be a protected form of expression under the First Amendment and found that Joplin's family could not control artistic expressions based on her life.[108]

P.2d 425 (Cal. 1979); *KNB Enterprises v. Matthews*, 92 Cal. Rptr. 2d 713 (Ct. App. 2000); *Martin Luther King, Jr. Center for Social Change v. American Heritage Products*, 296 S.E.2d 697 (Ga. 1982); *Carson v. Here's Johnny Portable Toilets, Inc.*, 698 F.2d 831 (6th Cir. 1983) (applying Missouri law); Donald A. Chisum et al., *Understanding Intellectual Property Law* §6G (3d ed. 2015).

99 *KNB Enterprises v. Matthews*, 92 Cal. Rptr. 2d 713, 717 (Ct. App. 2000); *cf.* Jennifer E. Rothman, *The Right of Publicity: Privacy Reimagined for a Public World* 11 (2018) (discussing the roots of the right of publicity in common law privacy rights).

100 Donald A. Chisum et al., *Understanding Intellectual Property Law* §6G (3d ed. 2015).

101 15 U.S.C. §1125.

102 *See Parks v. La Face Records*, 329 F.3d 437 (6th Cir. 2003).

103 Donald A. Chisum et al., *Understanding Intellectual Property Law* §6 (3d ed. 2015).

104 *Martin Luther King, Jr. Center for Social Change v. American Heritage Products*, 296 S.E.2d 697, 705 (Ga. 1982).

105 Cal. Civ. Code §3344; Fla. Stat. §540.08; Ky. Rev. Stat. §391.170; Mass. Gen. Laws ch. 214, §3A; Neb. Rev. Stat. §20-202; Nev. Rev. Stat. §§597.770 to 597.810; N.Y. Civ. Rights §51; Okla. Stat. tit. 21, §§839.1 to 839.3; R.I. Gen. Laws §9-1-28; Tenn. Code §§47-25-1101 to 47-25-1108; Tex. Prop. Code §26.001 et seq.; Va. Code §§8.01-40 & 18.2-216.1; Wis. Stat. §995.50.

106 *ETW Corp. v. Jireh Publishing, Inc.*, 332 F.3d 915 (6th Cir. 2003) (First Amendment prevents assertion of publicity right when an artist painted Tiger Woods's victory at 1997 Masters Tournament); *Haskell v. Stauffer Communications, Inc.*, 990 P.2d 163 (Kan. Ct. App. 1999). *See also Parks v. La Face Records*, 329 F.3d 437 (6th Cir. 2003) (discussing how courts have balanced *Lanham Act* claims against First Amendment freedoms).

107 *Hicks v. Casablanca Records*, 464 F. Supp. 426 (S.D.N.Y. 1978).

108 Timothy Egan, *Estate Loses Suit to Control Play on Janis Joplin*, N.Y. Times, Dec. 18, 1991, at C-23, col. 1. *See also Groucho Marx Productions, Inc. v. Day and Night Co., Inc.*, 689 F.2d 317 (2d Cir. 1982) (holding that the right of publicity does not survive the death of the owner and that producers of a play mimicking the Marx Brothers could not be held liable to his heirs).

▷ IMITATORS **HARD CASE ◀**

A version of the right of publicity has been used to challenge advertisements that *imitate* artists as a way to appropriate their image. The singer and actress Bette Midler brought a lawsuit against Young & Rubicam, an advertising agency that had hired one of her former backup singers to imitate Midler's rendition of her 1973 hit "Do You Want to Dance?" to promote Ford Motor Co.'s Mercury Sable car. Midler claimed that the agency had stolen her voice. The Ninth Circuit agreed, holding that "when a distinctive voice of a professional singer is widely known and deliberately imitated in order to sell a product, the sellers have appropriated what is not theirs and have committed a tort in California."[109] ◀

▷ PUBLICITY RIGHTS AFTER DEATH **HARD CASE ◀**

In *Martin Luther King, Jr. Center for Social Change v. American Heritage Products*,[110] plaintiffs Coretta Scott King, administrator of Dr. King's estate and Martin Luther King, Jr. Center for Social Change, and Motown Records, an assignee of the rights to several of Dr. King's recorded speeches, sued defendants to stop them from manufacturing and selling plastic busts of Dr. Martin Luther King, Jr. They argued that Dr. King's estate possessed a right of publicity under Georgia law and that this was a personal property right that had been inherited by his wife.

Argument for inheritability

In addition, the Georgia Supreme Court in the *King* case held that the right of publicity was devisable and inheritable. The right is assignable during one's lifetime, and if it did not survive the death of the owner of the right, "full commercial exploitation of one's name and likeness [would be] practically impossible."[111]

> [I]f publicity dies with the celebrity, the economic value of the right of publicity during life would be diminished because the celebrity's untimely death would seriously impair, if not destroy, the value of the right of continued commercial use. Conversely, those who would profit from the fame of a celebrity after his or her death for their own benefit and without authorization have failed to establish their claim that they should be the beneficiaries of the celebrity's death.[112]

Argument against inheritability

Although some states refuse to extend the right of publicity after death,[113] most states, like Georgia, do recognize such rights and sometimes

[109] *Midler v. Ford Motor Co.*, 849 F.2d 460, 463 (9th Cir. 1988). *See Waits v. Frito-Lay, Inc.*, 978 F.2d 1093 (9th Cir. 1992) (singer Tom Waits obtains $375,000 in compensatory damages and $2 million in punitive damages against company that imitated his distinctive voice and singing style in a radio commercial).
[110] 296 S.E.2d 697 (Ga. 1982).
[111] *Id.* at 704.
[112] *Id.*
[113] *See* N.Y. Civ. Rights §50.

provide statutory time limits.[114] If the publicity right survives death and no statute limits its duration, how long does it last? Consider that the great-grandson of Tasunke Witko, also known as Crazy Horse, brought suit in Rosebud Sioux Tribal Court to enjoin the use of Crazy Horse's name in connection with the sale of beer.[115] The suit was brought more than 100 years after the death of Tasunke Witko. The family had strong reasons for objecting to the name. Crazy Horse (Tasunke Witko) was a spiritual leader of the Sioux and a teetotaler who viewed liquor as an evil spirit that caused devastating harm to the Sioux people. In response, defendant brewing company argued that it intended to honor Crazy Horse and the Sioux people and that, in any event, it should be able to use the name of an historical figure without accounting to that person's descendants. ◀

▶ HARD CASE ▷ PUBLICITY RIGHTS AND FREE SPEECH

In *Martin Luther King, Jr. Center for Social Change v. American Heritage Products*,[116] the Georgia Supreme Court rejected the contention that the First Amendment protected the right to manufacture and sell busts of public figures and it overrode publicity rights. The dissenting judge in the *Martin Luther King* case, Justice Weltner, argued that a prohibition against selling busts of Martin Luther King without the family's consent violated the free speech rights of the defendants. The right of publicity "fully extended, would eliminate scholarly research, historical analysis, and public comment" because they are often associated with employment and the sale of books and therefore financial gain. "Were it otherwise, no newspaper might identify any person or any incident of his life without accounting to him for violation of his right to publicity [and] no author might refer to any event in history wherein his reference is identifiable to any individual (or his heirs!) without accounting for his royalties."[117]

In contrast, the Sixth Circuit held in *ETW Corp. v. Jireh Publishing, Inc.*[118] that the First Amendment protects an artist's right to sell prints of his painting that depicted Tiger Woods's victory at the 1997 Masters Tournament. In a similar ruling, the Eleventh Circuit ruled in *Rosa and Raymond Parks Institute for Self-Development v. Target Corp.*[119] that Michigan publicity rights law could not stop a store from selling books, movies, and plaques

[114] *See* Cal. Civ. Code §3344.1 (70 years after death); Tenn. Code §47-25-1104 (10 years after death if not exploited; if commercially exploited, the rights end 2 years after the use ceases).

[115] *In the Matter of the Estate of Tasunke Witko v. G. Heileman Brewing Co.* (Civ. No. 93-204) (Rosebud Sioux Tr. Ct., Oct. 25, 1994), *rev'd* (Rosebud Sioux Sup. Ct. May 1, 1996). *See also Hornell Brewing Co. v. Rosebud Sioux Tribal Court*, 133 F.3d 1087 (8th Cir. 1998) (overturning the holding of the Rosebud Sioux Supreme Court on the ground that it did not have personal jurisdiction over defendant because defendant did not sell the beer on the reservation).

[116] 296 S.E.2d 697 (Ga. 1982).

[117] *Id.* at 708-709.

[118] 332 F.3d 915 (6th Cir. 2003).

[119] *Rosa and Raymond Parks Institute for Self-Development v. Target Corp.*, 812 F.3d 824 (11th Cir. 2016).

honoring civil rights leader Rosa Parks because those activities were protected by the First Amendment's guarantee of freedom of speech. ◀

§17.7 Moral Rights of Artists

Rights of artists to integrity of their works

In many European countries, artists have the right to prevent the mutilation or alteration of their artworks after the works have been sold.[120] This legally protected interest is called "moral right," or *droit moral.*[121] Artworks protected by moral rights are effectively encumbered by a covenant, which runs with the artwork when it is sold, containing an implied promise not to mutilate the artwork so as to destroy the artist's vision. Such rights are generally inalienable; the interest in preserving the artist's vision is seen as a collective good that benefits the community and thus cannot be traded away.

Recognition in the United States

Until recently, moral rights were not recognized in the United States.[122] However, in 1976, the Second Circuit held that an author's right to control the preparation of derivative works might be exercised so as to prevent the mutilation of a work.[123] In *Gilliam v. ABC, Inc.*,[124] Monty Python sued to prevent an American television network from editing Monty Python episodes to accommodate them to commercial advertising and to omit "offensive or obscene matter." The court held that the owner of the copyright was entitled to prevent such alterations of the work. In 1979, California passed the *California Art Preservation Act*,[125] which permits injunctive relief, damages, and attorney's fees for intentional or threatened mutilation or alteration of an artist's work. A more limited bill was passed in New York in 1983 prohibiting alterations that would harm the artist's reputation,[126] but has been found preempted by federal law.[127] Moral rights legislation has been passed in at least 11 jurisdictions in the United States.[128]

The *Visual Artists Rights Act*

In 1990, Congress passed the *Visual Artists Rights Act*,[129] granting living artists rights to protect "works of visual art" unless the works are "made for hire,"[130] or are "applied art," meaning "ornamentation or decoration that

[120] Donald A. Chisum et al., *Understanding Intellectual Property Law* §4E[6] (3d ed. 2015).

[121] Joseph L. Sax, *Playing Darts with a Rembrandt: Public and Private Rights in Cultural Treasures* 21 (1999).

[122] *See, e.g., Vargas v. Esquire*, 164 F.2d 522 (7th Cir. 1947); *Crimi v. Rutger's Presbyterian Church*, 89 N.Y.S.2d 813 (Sup. Ct. 1949).

[123] *Gilliam v. American Broadcasting Co., Inc.*, 538 F.2d 14 (2d Cir. 1976).

[124] *Id.*

[125] Cal. Civ. Code §987.

[126] *New York Artists' Authorship Rights Act*, N.Y. Arts & Cult. Aff. §14.03(1).

[127] Board of Managers of Soho International Arts Condominium v. City of New York, 2003 WL 21403333 (S.D. N.Y. 2003) (AARA rights "equivalent" to, and therefore preempted by, the federal *Visual Artists Rights Act*).

[128] Cal. Civ. Code §987; Conn. Gen. Stat. §§42-116s to 42-116t; La. Rev. Stat. §§51:2151 to 51:2156; Me. Rev. Stat. tit. 27, §303; Mass. Gen. Laws ch. 231, §85S; N.J. Stat. §§2A:24A-1 to 2A:24-8; N.M. Stat. §§56-11-1 to 56-11-3; N.Y. Arts & Cult. Aff. §§11.01 to 16.01; Pa. Stat. tit. 73, §§2101 to 2110; R.I. Gen. Laws §§5-62-2 to 5-62-6. Donald A. Chisum et al., *Understanding Intellectual Property Law* §4E[6], n.119 (3d ed. 2015).

[129] 17 U.S.C. §§101, 106a & 113.

[130] *Id.* at §101(B).

is affixed to otherwise utilitarian objects."[131] The statute partially preempts the state laws on the subject.[132] The statute grants the artist the right to prevent "any intentional distortion, mutilation, or other modification of [the] work which would be prejudicial to his or her honor or reputation,"[133] and to prevent any intentional or grossly negligent destruction of a work of "recognized stature."[134] Owners of buildings can remove works of art, such as murals, floor mosaics, or architectural components, if they can do so without destroying or mutilating them, so long as they make a good faith effort to notify the artist.[135] The artist's right to prevent mutilation of the work that is part of a building is lost if the artist fails to remove the work or pay for its removal. If the artwork cannot be removed without destroying it, the artist who has not waived her right to do so may have the power to prevent destruction of the work and therefore may have the extraordinary power to control whether the building is renovated, destroyed, or redeveloped. The Act allows the artist to waive this right,[136] and the owner who wishes to change the building may have to purchase the right from the artist. Building developers ordinarily require artists to waive their rights to prevent destruction of the work when they are embedded in a building such that they cannot be removed without destroying them.

▶ HARD CASE ▷ SITE-SPECIFIC WORKS

In *Phillips v. Pembroke Real Estate, Inc.*,[137] the court held that the *Visual Artists Rights Act of 1990* generally preserves artworks from destruction but does not require they be kept in place. However, it held that a state statute, the *Massachusetts Art Preservation Act*,[138] may prevent a site-specific work from being moved without the artist's consent when the "location of a piece is a constituent element of the art."[139] The artist, David Phillips, objected to alteration of a park that he helped design when those alterations would modify or remove his sculptures that were specifically created for that public park. Enforcement of such a right to prevent alteration would mean that the artist could prevent any change in the park to protect the artwork, even if this would interfere with public interests in modifying or improving the park. ◀

▶ HARD CASE ▷ TEMPORARY WORKS

In *Castillo v. G&M Realty L.P.*,[140] the owner of rundown warehouses in Long Island City, New York, invited prominent aerosol artist Jonathan

[131] *Carter v. Helmsley-Spear, Inc.*, 71 F.3d 77, 84-85 (2d Cir. 1995).
[132] 17 U.S.C. §301(f)(1).
[133] *Id.* at §106A(a)(3)(A).
[134] *Id.* at §106A(a)(3)(B).
[135] *Id.* at §113(d)(2).
[136] *Id.* at §106A(e).
[137] 288 F. Supp. 2d 89 (D. Mass. 2003).
[138] Mass. Gen. Laws ch. 231, §85S(a).
[139] 288 F. Supp. 2d at 89, 102.
[140] 950 F.3d 155 (2d Cir. 2020).

Cohen and others to fill the walls with aerosol art. Under Cohen's curatorship, the site, known as 5Pointz, became a major global center for aerosol art, attracting "thousands of daily visitors, numerous celebrities, and extensive media coverage."[141] When the owner sought approval to tear down the warehouses for luxury condominiums, the artists sought an injunction under the *Visual Rights Act of 1990* (*VARA*) to prevent the destruction of their art, even though that would have prevented the conversion of the warehouses.[142] Because not all of the art on the warehouse walls had achieved the requisite stature, the district court denied a preliminary injunction, and the developer rushed in to destroy the art by whitewashing the warehouse walls. The district court, offended by this behavior, determined that 45 of the destroyed works were protected under *VARA*, and imposed maximum statutory damages for willful violations of $150,000 per work, for damages totaling $6.75 million.[143] On appeal, the Second Circuit affirmed, holding that nothing in *VARA* "excludes temporary artwork from attaining recognized stature."[144] ◀

§17.8 Cultural Property

Preservation of cultural treasures

In recent years, claims have been made for national ownership or preservation of works of art or of historic or cultural heritage, particularly antiquities.[145] Such claims are recognized in many countries around the world.[146] For example, the idea that antiquities (especially those buried in the soil) should be legally protected is widely accepted throughout the world.[147] Mexico, for example, asserts national ownership of all pre-Columbian artifacts.[148] Other countries regulate excavations and regulate what private owners may do with such objects, such as preventing their destruction.[149] Such protection, however, has little recognition in the United States,[150] with the notable exception of architectural historic preservation statutes[151] and

[141] *Id.* at 162.
[142] 17 U.S.C. §106A.
[143] 950 F.3d at 163-164.
[144] *Id.* at 173.
[145] *See, e.g., Republic of Turkey v. Christie's Inc.*, 425 F. Supp. 3d 204 (S.D.N.Y. 2019).
[146] *See* Josep Ballart, *El patrimonio historico y arqueológico* (1997); Marie Cornu, *Le droit culturel des biens: l'interet culturel juridiquement protégé* (1996); Jeanette Greenfield, *The Return of Cultural Treasures* (3d ed. 2007); Joseph L. Sax, *Playing Darts with a Rembrandt: Public and Private Rights in Cultural Treasures* (1999); Bruce Ziff & Pratima V. Rao eds., *Borrowed Power: Essays on Cultural Appropriation* (1997).
[147] Joseph L. Sax, *Playing Darts with a Rembrandt: Public and Private Rights in Cultural Treasures* 184 (1999).
[148] *Id.* at 185.
[149] *Id.*
[150] *Id.* at 184-185.
[151] *See* §13.6.4. *See Historic Sites, Buildings, and Antiquities Act of 1935*, 16 U.S.C. §§461 to 467 (authorizing the Secretary of the Interior to restore and maintain historic sites owned by the United States); *National Trust for Historical Preservation Act*, 16 U.S.C. §468 (establishing the National Trust for Historic Preservation as a private institution to receive donations of sites, buildings, and objects, and to administer them in the public interest); *Archaeological and Historic Data Preservation Act of 1974*, 16 U.S.C. §§469 to 469c (requiring data to be preserved from sites affected by federally related construction projects and permitting the

regulation of excavation on federal and state lands.[152] It has been argued that such protection should be expanded.[153] For example, there is little to no regulation of the disposition of archeological resources discovered on private land.[154] In addition, under current law, private owners of artistic masterpieces, such as paintings, sculptures, or musical instruments, have the power to hide them from public view and even to destroy or mutilate them. The only limitation on their power to do this is the governmental power to take the objects by eminent domain. Professor Joseph Sax and others have argued that private owners of such "cultural treasures" should be regulated to preserve those treasures for the public.[155]

§17.9 Digital Property

Inheritance of access to digital music, books, movies, bank accounts, and social media accounts

A rapidly emerging issue is ownership of digital property. When someone dies, do relatives have access to her social media accounts, digital books, music, and movies? These issues have generally been governed by the

---

federal authorizing agency to require such projects to budget funds for the salvage of sites and materials found at those sites); *National Historic Preservation Act of 1966*, 54 U.S.C. §300101 *et seq.* (providing for the listing of specific federally owned structures and historic districts and encouraging the states to preserve comparable areas through the provision of federal funds).

[152] Federal legislation includes: *Antiquities Act of 1906*, 16 U.S.C. §§431 to 431m (declared unconstitutional as a violation of due process in *United States v. Diaz*, 499 F.2d 113 (9th Cir. 1974), because terms of the law were too vague to justify imposition of criminal penalties) (giving the President the power to set aside as national monuments, historic landmarks, and other objects of historic or scientific interest located on lands owned or controlled by the federal government); *Archaeological Resources Protection Act of 1979*, 16 U.S.C. §§470ee to 470mm (declared constitutional in *United States v. Austin*, 902 F.2d 743 (9th Cir. 1990)) (criminalizing the excavation, destruction, or unauthorized removal of archaeological resources from federally owned or controlled land); *Abandoned Shipwreck Act of 1987*, 43 U.S.C. §§2101 to 2106 (transferring title to abandoned and embedded shipwrecks to the relevant state government and abrogating the law of finds and salvage); *Native American Graves Protection and Repatriation Act of 1990*, 25 U.S.C. §§3001 to 3013 (requiring federal museums and agencies to inventory Native American human remains and associated grave artifacts and return them to the relevant tribe, as well as requiring notification of appropriate tribal groups when graves are found on federal or Indian tribal lands and vesting ownership in those tribes). Examples of state legislation include La. Rev. Stat. §41:1605(b) (stating that no person may "take, alter, damage, destroy, or excavate on state owned lands" without a permit and that permits may be issued only for "purely scientific and educational" purposes); R.I. Gen. Laws §42-45.1-4(a) (reserving to the state the "exclusive right and privilege of field investigation on sites owned or controlled by the state, in order to protect and preserve archaeological and scientific information, matter, and objects"); S.D. Codified Laws §1-20-25 (stating that archaeological information and objects derived from state lands are the property of the state and shall be used for scientific or educational purposes). *See also* Alaska Stat. §41.35.020 (subjecting the state's right to title of historic, prehistoric, and archaeological resources to the rights of persons of aboriginal descent).

[153] Patty Gerstenblith, *Identity and Cultural Property: The Protection of Cultural Property in the United States*, 73 B.U. L. Rev. 559 (1995); Joseph L. Sax, *Playing Darts with a Rembrandt: Public and Private Rights in Cultural Treasures* (1999).

[154] Patty Gerstenblith, *Identity and Cultural Property: The Protection of Cultural Property in the United States*, 73 B.U. L. Rev. 559, 600 (1995).

[155] Joseph L. Sax, *Playing Darts with a Rembrandt: Public and Private Rights in Cultural Treasures* (1999).

agreements between users of digital media and the companies that distribute the media. These agreements, however, may not correspond to the expectations of consumers. Moreover, some digital assets constitute inheritable property but they cannot be accessed without the necessary information. In 2014, Delaware passed a statute governing heirs' rights to digital and social media accounts. It requires digital media companies to provide heirs with the user name and password to log in to the digital accounts of the decedent.[156] The statute is based on a uniform act proposed by the Uniform Law Commission that is designed to enable heirs to manage digital property while protecting, as much as possible, the privacy interests of the decedent.[157]

[156] Del. Code tit. 12, §§5001 to 5007 (*Fiduciary Access to Digital Assets and Digital Accounts*).
[157] *Uniform Fiduciary Access to Digital Assets Act, Revised* §§1-21 (2015).

TABLE OF CASES

Alphabetization is letter-by-letter (e.g., "Littlefield" precedes "Little Rock").

A

Abacus Mortg. Ins. Co. v. Whitewood Hills Dev. Corp., 479 A.2d 1231 (Conn. App. Ct. 1984), 558
Abington Ltd. P'ship v. Heublein, 717 A.2d 1232 (Conn. 1998), 195
Abo Petroleum Corp. v. Amstutz, 600 P.2d 278 (N.M. 1979), 313
A.C. v. Metropolitan Sch. Dist., 75 F.4th 760 (7th Cir. 2023), 75
Acadian Heritage Realty, Inc. v. City of Lafayette, 394 So. 2d 855 (La. Ct. App. 1981), 119
Acierno v. Delaware, 643 A.2d 1328 (Del. 1994), 692
Ackaa v. Tommy Hilfiger Co., 1998 WL 136522 (E.D. Pa. 1998), 55, 59
Ackerman v. Food-4-Less, 1998 WL 316084 (E.D. Pa. 1998), 34, 58
Acme Laundry Co. v. Secretary of Envtl. Affairs, 575 N.E.2d 1085 (Mass. 1991), 665
Adams v. Chenowith, 349 So. 2d 230 (Fla. Dist. Ct. App. 1977), 506
Adams v. Cleveland-Cliffs Iron Co., 602 N.W.2d 215 (Mich. Ct. App. 1999), 44
Adams v. Kimberley One Townhouse Owner's Ass'n, 352 P.3d 492 (Idaho 2015), 378
Adams v. School Bd. of St. Johns Cnty., 57 F.4th 791 (11th Cir. 2022), 75
Adams v. Star Enter., 51 F.3d 417 (4th Cir. 1995), 119
Adams v. Unione Mediterranea Di Sicurta, 220 F.3d 659 (5th Cir. 2000), 820
Adarand Constructors, Inc. v. Pena, 515 U.S. 200 (1995), 582
Addison v. Addison, 399 P.2d 897 (Cal. 1965), 406
Addison v. Signet Jewelers, Ltd., No. 1:23-cv-22956, 2025 WL 1766119 (D.N.J. June 26, 2025), 48
Adkins v. Morgan Stanley, 2013 WL 3835198 (S.D.N.Y. 2013), 617
Agins v. Tiburon, 447 U.S. 255 (1980), 20, 681, 706, 709, 715, 729, 730, 736
Agua Fria Save the Open Space Ass'n v. Rowe, 255 P.3d 390 (N.M. Ct. App. 2011), 239, 270
AGW Sono Partners, LLC v. Downtown Soho, LLC, 273 A.3d 186 (Conn. 2022), 452
Aizpitarte v. Minear, 508 P.3d 1260 (Idaho 2022), 209
Akau v. Olohana Corp., 652 P.2d 1130 (Haw. 1982), 87
Akin v. Castleberry, 286 P.3d 638 (Okla. 2012), 147
Alabama Ass'n of Realtors v. Department of Health & Human Servs., 594 U.S. 758 (2021), 469
Alaska v. Native Vill. of Venetie, 522 U.S. 520 (1998), 802
Albanese v. Condit, 450 A.2d 1141 (Vt. 1982), 366
Albert v. Fort Worth & W. R.R. Co., 690 S.W.3d 92 (Tex. 2024), 214
Albiero v. City of Kankakee, 246 F.3d 927 (7th Cir. 2001), 670
Albinger v. Harris, 48 P.3d 711, 2002 MT 118 (Mont. 2002), 823
Albrecht v. Clifford, 767 N.E.2d 42 (Mass. 2002), 514
Albro v. Allen, 454 N.W.2d 85 (Mich. 1990), 351
Alburger v. Philadelphia Elec. Co., 535 A.2d 729 (Pa. Commw. Ct. 1988), 130
Alderwood Assocs. v. Washington Envtl. Council, 635 P.2d 108 (Wash. 1981), 81
Alexander v. Boyer, 253 A.2d 359 (Md. 1969), 354
Alexander v. Steining, 398 S.E.2d 390 (Ga. Ct. App. 1990), 446
Alexis v. McDonald's Rests. of Mass., Inc., 67 F.3d 341 (1st Cir. 1995), 35, 53, 56, 182
Alexy v. Salvador, 630 N.Y.S.2d 133 (App. Div. 1995), 218
Alford v. Alford, 372 S.E.2d 389 (Va. 1988), 151
Alford v. United States, 961 F.3d 1380 (Fed. Cir. 2020), 740
Alires v. McGhehee, 85 P.3d 1191 (Kan. 2004), 512
Allemong v. Frendzel, 363 S.E.2d 487 (W. Va. 1987), 250–251, 292
Allen v. Dickerson, 385 So. 3d 1209 (Miss. 2024), 117
Allen v. Moran, 760 N.E.2d 198 (Ind. Ct. App. 2001), 144
Allied Maint. Corp. v. Allied Mech. Trades, Inc., 369 N.E.2d 1162 (N.Y. 1977), 847
Almota Farmers Elevator & Warehouse Co. v. United States, 409 U.S. 470 (1973), 689, 691
Alsup v. Banks, 9 So. 895 (Miss. 1891), 463
Alumni Ass'n of the Univ. of N.D. v. Hart Agency, Inc., 283 N.W.2d 119 (N.D. 1979), 519
Amalgamated Food Emps. Union Local 590 v. Logan Valley Plaza, Inc., 391 U.S. 308 (1968), 77–78, 84
Amazon.com, Inc. v. Barnesandnoble.com, Inc., 73 F. Supp. 2d 1228 (W.D. Wash. 1999), *vacated and remanded*, 239 F.3d 1343 (Fed. Cir. 2001), 842
AMC Entm't, Inc.; United States v., 232 F. Supp. 2d 1092 (C.D. Cal. 2002), 70
American Civil Liberties Union of Nev. v. City of Las Vegas, 333 F.3d 1092 (9th Cir. 2003), 76

American Elec. Power Co. v. Connecticut, 564 U.S. 410 (2011), 125
American Jewish Theatre, Inc. v. Roundabout Theatre Co., 610 N.Y.S.2d 256 (App. Div. 1994), 436
American Trading Real Estate Props., Inc. v. Town of Trumbull, 574 A.2d 796 (Conn. 1990), 168
American Transmission, Inc. v. Channel 7 of Detroit, Inc., 609 N.W.2d 607 (Mich. Ct. App. 2000), 37
Amerisource Corp. v. United States, 525 F.3d 1149 (Fed. Cir. 2008), 712
Amherst, Town of v. Omnipoint Commnc'ns Enters., 173 F.3d 9 (1st Cir. 1999), 665
Anchors v. Manter, 714 A.2d 134 (Me. 1998), 191
Anderson v. Conboy, 156 F.3d 167 (2d Cir. 1998), *cert. granted sub nom.* United Bhd. of Carpenters & Joiners of Am. v. Anderson, 526 U.S. 1086, *cert. dismissed*, 527 U.S. 1030 (1999), 55, 600
Anderson v. Jackson, 338 So. 3d 629 (Miss. Ct. App. 2022), 163
Anderson v. Yaworski, 181 A. 205 (Conn. 1935), 527
Andrews v. United States, 108 Fed. Cl. 150 (2012), 43
Androkites v. White, 10 A.3d 677 (Me. 2010), 150, 217
Andrus v. Allard, 444 U.S. 51 (1979), 745
Andy Warhol Found. for the Visual Arts, Inc. v. Goldsmith, 598 U.S. 508 (2023), 837–839
Anglado v. Leaf River Forest Prods., Inc., 716 So. 2d 543 (Miss. 1998), 119
Ankiewicz v. Kinder, 563 N.E.2d 684 (Mass. 1990), 489
Antoine v. Washington, 420 U.S. 194 (1975), 807
Antonis v. Liberati, 821 A.2d 666 (Pa. Commw. Ct. 2003), 550
A.O. Smith Corp. v. Kaufman Grain Co., 596 N.E.2d 1156 (Ill. App. Ct. 1992), 480
Appel v. Presley Cos., 806 P.2d 1054 (N.M. 1991), 380
Apple, Inc. Device Performance Litig., In re, 347 F. Supp. 3d 434 (N.D. Cal. 2018), 92
Application of. *See name of party*
APT Pittsburgh, LP v. Penn Twp., 196 F.3d 469 (3d Cir. 1999), 665
Aquarian Found., Inc. v. Sholom House, Inc., 448 So. 2d 1166 (Fla. Dist. Ct. App. 1984), 283, 374
A.R. v. Kogan, 964 F. Supp. 269 (N.D. Ill. 1997), 62
Arbenz v. Exley, Watkins & Co., 44 S.E. 149 (W. Va. 1903), 463
Arbern Realty Co. v. Clay Craft Planters Co., 727 N.Y.S.2d 236 (App. Div. 2001), 471
Arguello v. Conoco, Inc., 330 F.3d 355 (5th Cir. 2003), 57, 59
Argyelan v. Haviland, 435 N.E.2d 973 (Ind. 1982), 128
Arizona v. California, 373 U.S. 546 (1963), 778, 807
Arizona v. Navajo Nation, 599 U.S. 555 (2023), 777
Arizona v. San Carlos Apache Tribe of Ariz., 463 U.S. 545 (1983), 131
Arkansas Game & Fish Comm'n v. United States, 568 U.S. 23 (2012), 741
Arlene's Flowers, Inc.; State v., 441 P.3d 1203 (Wash. 2019), 73
Arlington Heights, Vill. of v. Metropolitan Hous. Dev. Corp., 429 U.S. 252, *on remand*, 558 F.2d 1283 (7th Cir. 1977), *cert. denied*, 434 U.S. 1025, *on remand*, 469 F. Supp. 836 (D. Ill. 1979), *aff'd*, 616 F.2d 1006 (7th Cir. 1980), 581, 667, 671
Armory v. Delamirie, 93 Eng. Rep. 664 (K.B. 1722), 817
Armstrong v. Francis Corp., 120 A.2d 4 (N.J. 1956), 129
Armstrong v. Roberts, 325 S.E.2d 769 (Ga. 1985), 260
Armstrong v. United States, 364 U.S. 40 (1960), 20, 681, 702–703, 715
Arnold v. Chandler, 428 A.2d 1235 (N.H. 1981), 236
Aronsohn v. Mandara, 484 A.2d 675 (N.J. 1984), 514
Aronson v. Town of Sharon, 195 N.E.2d 341 (Mass. 1964), 645
Arthur v. City of Toledo, Ohio, 782 F.2d 565 (6th Cir. 1986), 615
Arthur v. Lake Tansi Vill., Inc., 590 S.W.2d 923 (Tenn. 1979), 238
Arvada Urban Renewal Auth. v. Columbine Prof'l Plaza Ass'n, 85 P.3d 1066 (Colo. 2004), 687
Asbury v. Brougham, 866 F.2d 1276 (10th Cir. 1989), 57, 593
Ashford, Application of, 440 P.2d 76 (Haw. 1968), 89
Ashley v. Baker, 867 P.2d 792 (Alaska 1994), 361
Assilzadeh v. California Fed. Bank, 98 Cal. Rptr. 2d 176 (Ct. App. 2000), 510
Assisted Living Assocs. v. Moorestown Twp., 996 F. Supp. 409 (D.N.J. 1998), 623
Association for Advancement of the Mentally Handicapped, Inc. v. City of Elizabeth, 876 F. Supp. 614 (D.N.J. 1994), 622, 624
Association for Molecular Pathology v. Myriad Genetics, Inc., 569 U.S. 576 (2013), 842
Association of Club Execs. of Dallas, Inc. v. Dallas, 83 F.4th 958 (5th Cir. 2023), 674
Astemborski v. Manetta, 988 N.W.2d 857 (Mich. Ct. App. 2022), 182
AT&T Wireless PCS v. City Council of Va. Beach, 155 F.3d 423 (4th Cir. 1998), 665
Atkinson Trading Co. v. Shirley, 532 U.S. 645 (2001), 781
Atlantic Richfield Co. v. Whiting Oil & Gas Corp., 320 P.3d 1179 (Colo. 2014), 331
Attorney Gen. v. Desilets, 636 N.E.2d 233 (Mass. 1994), 613–614
Atwood v. Walter, 714 N.E.2d 365 (Mass. App. Ct. 1999), 298
Aurora Bus. Park Ass'n v. Albert, Inc., 548 N.W.2d 153 (Iowa 1996), 466
Austin v. United States, 509 U.S. 602 (1993), 710
Austin, City of v. Reagan Nat'l Advert. of Austin, LLC, 596 U.S. 61 (2022), 673
Austin; United States v., 902 F.2d 743 (9th Cir. 1990), 856
Austin Hill Country Realty, Inc. v. Palisades Plaza, Inc., 948 S.W.2d 293 (Tex. 1997), 463, 465
Auther v. Furst, 2008 WL 4965347 (Ariz. Ct. App. 2008), 250
Autocephalous Greek-Orthodox Church of Cyprus v. Goldberg & Feldman Fine Arts, Inc., 717 F. Supp. 1374 (S.D. Ind. 1989), 172
Ayer v. Philadelphia & Bos. Face Brick Co., 34 N.E. 177 (Mass. 1893), 547
Ayres Jewelry Co. v. O & S Bldg., 419 P.2d 628 (Wyo. 1966), 453
A.Z. v. B.Z., 725 N.E.2d 1051 (Mass. 2000), 831

B

Babb v. Lee Cnty. Landfill SC, LLC, 747 S.E.2d 468 (S.C. 2013), 44, 97
Babb v. Wilkie, 589 U.S. 399 (2020), 592
Babbitt v. Youpee, 519 U.S. 234 (1997), 328, 418, 708, 743, 745, 749, 791
Babcock & Wilcox Co.; NLRB v., 351 U.S. 105 (1956), 84
Badgett; United States v., 976 F.2d 1176 (8th Cir. 1992), 625
Bailey v. First Mortg. Corp. of Boca Raton, 478 So. 2d 502 (Fla. Dist. Ct. App. 1985), 519
Bailey v. Myers, 76 P.3d 898 (Ariz. Ct. App. 2003), 687
Bailey Mortg. Co. v. Boggle-Fite Lumber, 565 So. 2d 138 (Ala. 1990), 556
Bain v. Bain, 360 S.E.2d 849 (Va. 1987), 237
Bain v. Metropolitan Mortg. Grp., Inc., 285 P.3d 34 (Wash. 2012), 572
Bajakajian; United States v., 524 U.S. 321 (1998), 710
Baker v. Nelson, 409 U.S. 810 (1972), 407
Baker; State v., 405 A.2d 368 (N.J. 1979), 627
Baker v. Vermont, 744 A.2d 864 (Vt. 1999), 409
Baldwin v. McClendon, 288 So. 2d 761 (Ala. 1974), 112
Ballard v. Ace Wrecking Co., 289 A.2d 888 (D.C. 1971), 128
Ballard v. Harman, 737 N.E.2d 411 (Ind. Ct. App. 2000), 144
BancTexas Westheimer v. Summer, 734 S.W.2d 57 (Tex. App. 1987), 448
Bangerter v. City of Orem, Utah, 46 F.3d 1491 (10th Cir. 1995), 623
Bank of Am. v. Prestance Corp., 160 P.3d 17 (Wash. 2007), 561
Bank of Am. Corp. v. City of Miami, 581 U.S. 189 (2017), 596
Bank of Am. v. Rosa, 999 N.E.2d 1080 (Mass. 2013), 573
Bank of N.Y. v. Alderazi, 900 N.Y.S.2d 821 (Sup. Ct. 2010), 572
Bank of N.Y. v. Ibrahiem, 15 Misc. 3d 294 (N.Y. Civ. Ct. 2007), 550
Bank of N.Y. v. Silverberg, 926 N.Y.S.2d 532 (App. Div. 2011), 572
Bank of Oak Grove v. Wilmot State Bank, 648 S.W.2d 802 (Ark. 1983), 556
Banner v. United States, 238 F.3d 1348 (Fed. Cir. 2001), 42
Banning, In re, 832 P.2d 724 (Haw. 1992), 87
Baptiste v. Kennealy, 490 F. Supp. 3d 353 (D. Mass. 2020), 469
Baptist Youth Camp v. Robinson, 714 A.2d 809 (Me. 1998), 219
Baran v. Juskulski, 689 A.2d 1283 (Md. Ct. Spec. App. 1997), 364
Barash v. Pennsylvania Terminal Real Estate Co., 256 N.E.2d 707 (N.Y. 1970), 470
Barber v. Chang, 60 Cal. Rptr. 3d 760 (Ct. App. 2007), 486
Barchowsky v. Silver Farms, Inc., 659 A.2d 347 (Md. Ct. Spec. App. 1995), 216
Barclay v. DeVeau, 429 N.E.2d 323 (Mass. 1981), 373
Barclays Bank of N.Y. v. Ivler, 565 A.2d 252 (Conn. App. Ct. 1989), 556
Barclays Capital Inc. v. Theflyonthewall.com, 650 F.3d 876 (2d Cir. 2011), 848
Barela v. Superior Court, 636 P.2d 582 (Cal. 1981), 484
Bargain Mart, Inc. v. Mordechai Lipkis, 561 A.2d 1365 (Conn. 1989), 462
Bargmann v. Soll Oil Co., 574 N.W.2d 478 (Neb. 1998), 105–106, 117
Barking Hound Vill., LLC v. Monyak, 2016 WL 3144352 (Ga. 2016), 816
Barnacle, In re, 623 A.2d 445 (R.I. 1993), 539
Barrow v. Barrow, 527 So. 2d 1373 (Fla. 1988), 364, 368
Barrows v. Jackson, 346 U.S. 249 (1953), 281, 579
Barstow, City of v. Mojave Water Agency, 99 Cal. Rptr. 2d 294 (Cal. 2000), 132
Barter v. Palmerton Area Sch. Dist., 581 A.2d 652 (Pa. Super. Ct. 1990), 517–518
Bartkowski v. Ramondo, 219 A.3d 1083 (Pa. 2019), 210
Bartsch v. Planning & Zoning Comm'n, 506 A.2d 1093 (Conn. App. Ct. 1986), 650
Basiliko v. Pargo Corp., 532 A.2d 1346 (D.C. 1987), 523
Baskurt v. Beal, 101 P.3d 1041 (Alaska 2004), 562
Batchelder v. Allied Stores Int'l, Inc., 445 N.E.2d 590 (Mass. 1983), 81
Bateman v. Board of Appeals of Georgetown, 775 N.E.2d 1276 (Mass. App. Ct. 2002), 195
Bates v. Southgate, 31 N.E.2d 551 (Mass. 1941), 513
Baton Rouge, City of v. Mucciacciaro, 342 So. 3d 955 (La. Ct. App. 2022), 693
Baton Rouge, City of v. Myers, 145 So. 3d 320 (La. 2014), 669
Bauer v. Migliaccio, 561 A.2d 674 (N.J. Super. Ct. Ch. Div. 1989), 362
Bauman v. Ross, 167 U.S. 548 (1897), 692
Baxter v. City of Preston, 768 P.2d 1340 (Idaho 1989), 652
Bayberry Cove Childrens' Land Tr. v. Town of Steuben, 65 A.3d 1188 (Me. 2013), 220
Bay City Realty LLC v. Mattress Firm Inc., 2021 WL 1295261 (E.D. Mich. 2021), 452
Baycol, Inc. v. Downtown Dev. Auth., 315 So. 2d 451 (Fla. 1975), 688
Bayliss v. Bayliss, 550 So. 2d 986 (Ala. 1989), 417
Bay Point Props., Inc. v. Mississippi Transp. Comm'n, 937 F.3d 454 (5th Cir. 2019), 765
Bayview Loan Servicing, L.L.C. v. Nelson, 890 N.E.2d 940 (Ill. App. Ct. 2008), 571
Baywood Estates Prop. Owners Ass'n, Inc. v. Caolo, 392 S.W.3d 776 (Tex. App. 2012), 234
B.C.E. Dev., Inc. v. Smith, 264 Cal. Rptr. 55 (Ct. App. 1989), 236, 260, 276
Beachside Bungalow Pres. Ass'n of Far Rockaway, Inc. v. Oceanview Assocs., 753 N.Y.S.2d 133 (App. Div. 2003), 184
Beachwalk Villas Condo. Ass'n, Inc. v. Martin, 406 S.E.2d 372 (S.C. 1991), 515
Bean v. Walker, 464 N.Y.S.2d 895 (App. Div. 1983), 565–566
Beard v. S/E Joint Venture, 581 A.2d 1275 (Md. 1990), 522
Beasley v. Burns, 7 S.W.2d 768 (Tex. App. 1999), 533

Beatty v. Depue, 103 N.W.2d 187 (S.D. 1960), 528
Becker v. IRM, 698 P.2d 116 (Cal. 1985), 485–486
Bedford, Town of v. Cerasuolo, 814 N.E.2d 1162 (Mass. App. Ct. 2004), 195, 212
Bednar v. Bednar, 688 A.2d 1200 (Pa. Super. Ct. 1997), 364
Bedrick v. Bedrick, 17 A.3d 17 (Conn. 2011), 401
Beecher v. Wetherby, 95 U.S. 517 (1877), 782
Beechler v. Beechler, 641 N.E.2d 1189 (Ohio Ct. App. 1994), 342
Beeren & Barry Invs., L.L.C. v. AHC, Inc., 671 S.E.2d 147 (Va. 2009), 244
Behar v. Mawardi, 702 N.Y.S.2d 326 (App. Div. 2000), 506
Bel-Aire, Inc. v. RB Trexlertown, LLC, 2005 WL 2335372 (Va. Cir. Ct. 2005), 338
Beliveau v. Caras, 873 F. Supp. 1393 (C.D. Cal. 1995), 603
Bell v. Town of Wells, 557 A.2d 168 (Me. 1989), 87
Belle Terre, Vill. of v. Boraas, 416 U.S. 1 (1974), 626–627, 669
Belleville, Town of v. Parrillo's, Inc., 416 A.2d 388 (N.J. 1980), 651–652
Bellikka v. Green, 762 P.2d 997 (Or. 1988), 485
Bellucci v. Moore, 585 So. 2d 490 (Fla. Dist. Ct. App. 1991), 527
Bellwood, Vill. of v. Dwivedi, 895 F.2d 1521 (7th Cir. 1990), 615
Benchmark Land Co. v. City of Battle Ground, 14 P.3d 172 (Wash. Ct. App. 2000), 759
Benitez v. Restifo, 641 N.Y.S.2d 523 (N.Y. City Ct. Yonker 1996), 472
Bennett v. Charles Corp., 226 S.E.2d 559 (W. Va. 1976), 238, 295–296
Bennett Realty, Inc. v. Muller, 396 S.E.2d 630 (N.C. Ct. App. 1990), 498
Bennis v. Michigan, 516 U.S. 442 (1996), 710
Benser v. Johnson, 763 S.W.2d 793 (Tex. App. 1988), 486
Berg v. Wiley, 264 N.W.2d 145 (Minn. 1978), 458
Berger v. Sellers, 996 N.W.2d 329 (N.D. 2023), 136
Berger v. State, 364 A.2d 993 (N.J. 1976), 272, 276
Bergh & Mission Farms, Inc. v. Great Lakes Transmission Co., 565 N.W.2d 23 (Minn. 1997), 191
Berish v. Bornstein, 770 N.E.2d 961 (Mass. 2002), 514
Berle v. Berle, 546 P.2d 407 (Idaho 1976), 406
Berman v. Parker, 348 U.S. 26 (1954), 682–686
Berman & Sons, Inc. v. Jefferson, 396 N.E.2d 981 (Mass. 1979), 476, 479
Bermudez Zenon v. Restaurant Compostela, Inc., 790 F. Supp. 41 (D.P.R. 1992), 48, 55–56
Bernstein v. New Beginnings Tr., LLC, 988 So. 2d 90 (Fla. Dist. Ct. App. 2008), 566
Berry v. Armstrong Rubber Co., 989 F.2d 822 (5th Cir. 1993), 119
Berryhill v. Moore, 881 P.2d 1182 (Ariz. Ct. App. 1994), 167
Besnilian v. Wilkinson, 25 P.3d 187 (Nev. 2001), 352
Besse v. Blossman, 521 So. 2d 570 (La. Ct. App. 1988), 519
Bethurem v. Hammett, 736 P.2d 1128 (Wyo. 1987), 519
Betsey v. Turtle Creek Assocs., 736 F.2d 983 (4th Cir. 1984), 615
Bevilacqua v. Rodriguez, 955 N.E.2d 884 (Mass. 2011), 570
BGW Dev. Co. v. Mount Kisco Lodge No. 1552 of the Benevolent & Protective Order of Elks of the U.S.A., Inc., 669 N.Y.S.2d 56 (App. Div. 1998), 523
Big D Enters.; United States v., 184 F.3d 924 (8th Cir. 1999), 599
Bigelow v. Bullard, 901 P.2d 630 (Nev. 1995), 184, 439
Biggers v. Crook, 656 S.E.2d 835 (Ga. 2008), 353
Billings v. Wilson, 493 N.E.2d 187 (Mass. 1986), 488
Bills v. Hodges, 628 F.2d 844 (4th Cir. 1980), 601
Bilski v. Kappos, 561 U.S. 593 (2010), 843
Biltmore Vill. v. Royal, 71 So. 2d 727 (Fla. 1954), 537
Bindas v. Commonwealth, Dep't of Transp., 302 A.3d 644 (Pa. 2023), 550
Birchler v. Castello Land Co., 915 P.2d 564 (Wash. Ct. App. 1996), *aff'd*, 942 P.2d 968 (Wash. 1997), 459
Bishop v. Ellsworth, 234 N.E.2d 49 (Ill. App. Ct. 1968), 817–818
Bishop v. Reinhold, 311 S.E.2d 298 (N.C. Ct. App. 1984), 42
Blackburn v. Venice Inlet Co., 38 So. 2d 43 (Fla. 1948), 551
Blackett v. Olanoff, 358 N.E.2d 817 (Mass. 1976), 472
Black Jack; United States v., 508 F.2d 1179 (8th Cir. 1974), 615
Blagg v. Fred Hunt Co., 612 S.W.2d 321 (Ark. 1981), 514
Blair; State v., 827 P.2d 356 (Wash. Ct. App. 1992), 30
Blais v. Remillard, 643 A.2d 967 (N.H. 1994), 498
Blakely v. Chicago, K. & N. R. Co., 64 N.W. 972 (Neb. 1895), 319
Blakely v. Gorin, 313 N.E.2d 903 (Mass. 1974), 298
Blankinship v. Payton, 605 So. 2d 817 (Miss. 1992), 166
Blaszkowski v. Schmitt, 597 N.W.2d 773 (Wis. Ct. App. 1999), 143–144
Blatchford v. Native Vill. of Noatak & Circle Vill., 501 U.S. 775 (1991), 796
Blaylock v. Cary, 709 So. 2d 1128 (Ala. 1997), 510
Bleecker St. Tenants Corp. v. Bleeker Jones LLC, 945 N.E.2d 484 (N.Y. 2001), 337
Blevins v. Barry-Lawrence Cnty. Ass'n for Retarded Citizens, 707 S.W.2d 407 (Mo. 1986), 271–272
Blevins v. Mullan Contracting Co., 201 A.2d 348 (Md. 1964), 29
Blevins v. Shelton, 383 S.E.2d 509 (W. Va. 1989), 366
Bloch v. Frischholz, 587 F.3d 771 (7th Cir. 2009), 591
Block v. DEA Props.-2 LLC, 501 P.3d 545 (Or. Ct. App. 2021), 188, 197
Block v. Hirsh, 256 U.S. 135 (1921), 469, 723–724, 726–727
Blue Jeans Equities W. v. City & Cnty. of San Francisco, 4 Cal. Rptr. 2d 114 (Ct. App. 1992), 759
Blumfield Agency v. Little Belt, Inc., 663 P.2d 1164 (Mont. 1983), 501
BM-Clarence Cardwell, Inc. v. Cocca Dev., Ltd., 65 N.E.3d 829 (Ohio Ct. App. 2016), 244, 252
Board of Cnty. Comm'rs v. H. Manny Holtz, Inc., 501 A.2d 489 (Md. Ct. Spec. App. 1985), 650
Board of Cnty. Comm'rs of Boulder Cnty. v. Suncor Energy (U.S.A.), Inc., 965 F.3d 792 (10th Cir. 2020), 126
Board of Comm'rs of Roane Cnty. v. Parker, 88 S.W.2d 916 (Tenn. Ct. App. 2002), 669

Board of Educ. v. Miles, 207 N.E.2d 181 (N.Y. 1965), 338, 537
Board of Managers v. Rios, 630 N.Y.S.2d 875 (Sup. Ct. 1995), 625
Board of Managers of Soho Int'l Arts Condo. v. City of New York, 2003 WL 403333 (S.D.N.Y. 2003), 853
Board of Trs. of Columbia Rd. Methodist Episcopal Church of Bogalusa v. Richardson, 44 So. 2d 321 (La. 1949), 319
Board of Zoning Appeals v. Leisz, 702 N.E.2d 1026 (Ind. 1998), 654
Bobbitt v. Rage Inc., 19 F. Supp. 2d 512 (W.D.N.C. 1998), 57
Bockelmann v. Marynick, 788 S.W.2d 569 (Tex. 1990), 449
Boecher v. Borth, 377 N.Y.S.2d 781 (App. Div. 1976), 517
Boerne, City of v. Flores, 521 U.S. 507 (1997), 613–614, 629, 675–676
Bogner v. Villiger, 796 N.E.2d 679 (Ill. App. Ct. 2003), 210
Boissy v. Chevron, 33 A.3d 1109 (N.H. 2011), 223
Boland v. Catalano, 521 A.2d 142 (Conn. 1987), 412
Bolling v. Sharpe, 347 U.S. 497 (1954), 578
Bonds, In re Marriage of, 83 Cal. Rptr. 2d 783 (Ct. App. 1999), *judgment rev'd in part*, 5 P.3d 815 (Cal. 2000), 400
Bonnco Petrol, Inc. v. Epstein, 560 A.2d 655 (N.J. 1989), 528
Bonner v. City of Brighton, 828 N.W.2d 408 (Mich. Ct. App. 2012), *rev'd*, 848 N.W.2d 380 (Mich. 2014), 667–668
Bonner v. City of Prichard, Ala., 661 F.2d 1206 (11th Cir. 1981), 615
Bonnichsen v. United States Dep't of Army, 217 F. Supp. 2d 1116 (D. Or. 2002), *aff'd and remanded*, 367 F.3d 864 (9th Cir. 2004), 806
Booker v. Trizec Props., Inc., 363 S.E.2d 13 (Ga. Ct. App. 1987), 449, 458
Boomer v. Atlantic Cement Co., 257 N.E.2d 870 (N.Y. 1970), 107–108, 109, 110–112, 114–115
Boot Ranch, LLC v. Wagonhound Land & Livestock Co., 560 P.3d 887 (Wyo. 2024), 144
Borenkind v. Consolidated Edison Co. of N.Y., Inc., 626 N.Y.S.2d 414 (Sup. Ct. 1995), 117
Boring v. Google Inc., 362 Fed. Appx. 273 (3d Cir. 2010), 28
Bormann v. Board of Supervisors in & for Kossuth Cnty., 584 N.W.2d 309 (Iowa 1998), 100–101
Born v. Exxon Corp., 388 So. 2d 933 (Ala. 1980), 44
Borough of. *See name of borough*
Bortolotti v. Hayden, 866 N.E.2d 882 (Mass. 2007), 338
Bosarge v. State ex rel. Price, 666 So. 2d 485 (Miss. 1995), 122
Bostock v. Clayton Cnty., 590 U.S. 644 (2020), 74, 596, 608, 621
Boston Taxi Owners Ass'n, Inc. v. City of Boston, 180 F. Supp. 3d 108 (D. Mass. 2016), 712
Boudreau v. Coleman, 564 N.E.2d 1 (Mass. App. Ct. 1990), 194
Bourque v. Morris, 460 A.2d 1251 (Conn. 1983), 441
Bouten v. Richard Miller Homes, Inc., 321 N.W.2d 895 (Minn. 1982), 507
Bowers v. Andrews, 557 A.2d 606 (Me. 1989), 207
Bowers v. Hardwick, 478 U.S. 186 (1986), 415
Bowers v. Westvaco Corp., 419 S.E.2d 661 (Va. 1992), 117
Bowers, State ex rel. v. Elida Rd. Video & Books, Inc., 696 N.E.2d 668 (Ohio Ct. App. 1997), 123
Bowie, City of v. MIE Props., Inc., 922 A.2d 509 (Md. 2007), 271, 291
Bowles v. Mahoney, 202 F.2d 320 (D.C. Cir. 1952), 484
Bowles v. United States, 31 Fed. Cl. 37 (1994), 735–736
Bowman v. Monsanto Co., 569 U.S. 278 (2013), 841
Bowman v. Presley, 212 P.3d 1210 (Okla. 2009), 512
Boykin v. Gray, F. Supp. 2d 199 (D.D.C. 2012), 584
Boyle v. City of Portsmouth, 235 A.3d 985 (N.H. 2020), 217
Boy Scouts of Am. v. Dale. *See* Dale v. Boy Scouts of Am.; Fraser v. Robin Dee Day Camp
Bozeman, City of v. Vaniman, 898 P.2d 1208 (Mont. 1995), 688
BP Am., Inc. v. Council of City of Univ. Heights, 2000 WL 1177508 (Ohio Ct. App. 2000), 750
BP Prods. N. Am., Inc. v. Stanley, 669 F.3d 184 (4th Cir. 2012), 286
Bracken v. City of Ketchum, 537 P.3d 44 (Idaho 2023), 655
Bradley v. American Smelting & Ref. Co., 635 F. Supp. 1154 (W.D. Wash. 1986), 44–45
Bradley v. American Smelting & Ref. Co., 709 P.2d 782 (Wash. 1985), 45
Bradley v. McLeod, 984 S.W.2d 929 (Tenn. Ct. App. 1998), 219
Brady v. Rivella Developers, Inc., 424 So. 2d 1104 (La. Ct. App. 1982), 485
Brander v. Stoddard, 164 A.3d 889 (Conn. App. Ct. 2017), 150
Brant v. Hargrove, 632 P.2d 978 (Ariz. Ct. App. 1981), 353–354
Breakthrough Mgmt. Grp., Inc. v. Chukchansi Gold Casino & Resort, 629 F.3d 1173 (10th Cir. 2010), 772
Breene v. Plaza Towers Ass'n, 310 N.W.2d 730 (N.D. 1981), 374, 378
Breiner v. Holt Cnty., 581 N.W.2d 89 (Neb. 1998), 220
Brendale v. Confederated Tribes & Bands of the Yakima Indian Nation, 492 U.S. 408 (1989), 781
Brendle's Stores, Inc. v. OTR, 978 F.2d 150 (4th Cir. 1990), 480
Breuer-Harrison, Inc. v. Combe, 799 P.2d 716 (Utah Ct. App. 1990), 521
Brewton v. Young, 596 So. 2d 577 (Ala. 1991), 117
Bridgeport, City of v. Barbour-Daniel Elecs., Inc., 548 A.2d 744 (Conn. App. Ct. 1988), 444
Bridger v. Goldsmith, 38 N.E. 458 (N.Y. 1894), 513
Bridges v. Heimburger, 360 So. 2d 929 (Miss. 1978), 536
Bridgeton Hosp. Ass'n, Inc.; Doe v., 366 A.2d 641 (N.J. 1976), 31
Bright v. Lake Linganore Ass'n, Inc., 656 A.2d 377 (Md. Ct. Spec. App. 1995), 242–243
Britton v. Town of Chester, 595 A.2d 492 (N.H. 1991), 634

Broach v. City of Hampton, 677 S.W.2d 851 (Ark. 1984), 337
Bronk v. Ineichen, 54 F.3d 425 (7th Cir. 1995), 610
Bronson v. Crestwood Lake Section 1 Holding Corp., 724 F. Supp. 148 (S.D.N.Y. 1989), 618
Brookline, Town of v. Carey, 245 N.E.2d 446 (Mass. 1969), 537
Brooks v. Chicago Downs Ass'n, Inc., 791 F.2d 512 (7th Cir. 1986), 30, 32
Brooks, Gill & Co. v. Landmark Props., 503 N.E.2d 983 (Mass. App. Ct. 1987), 216
Broomall v. State, 391 S.E.2d 918 (Ga. 1990), 528
Brotherton v. Cleveland, 923 F.2d 477 (6th Cir. 1991), 828
Brown v. Branch, 758 N.E.2d 48 (Ind. 2001), 508
Brown v. Clemens, 338 S.E.2d 338 (S.C. 1985), 153
Brown v. Fuller, 347 A.2d 127 (Me. 1975), 250
Brown v. Gobble, 474 S.E.2d 489 (W. Va. 1996), 146, 166
Brown v. Grimm, 481 P.2d 63 (Or. 1971), 501
Brown v. Legal Found. of Wash., 538 U.S. 216 (2003), 747
Brown v. Veile, 555 N.E.2d 1227 (Ill. App. Ct. 1990), 487
Brown v. Voss, 715 P.2d 514 (Wash. 1986), 195
Brown Jug, Inc. v. International Bhd. of Teamsters, Chauffeurs, Warehousemen & Helpers of Am., Local 959, 688 P.2d 932 (Alaska 1984), 28
Brush & Nib Studio, L.C. v. City of Phoenix, 448 P.3d 890 (Ariz. 2019), 74
Bryant Woods Inn, Inc. v. Howard Cnty., Md., 124 F.3d 597 (4th Cir. 1997), 623
BSL Dev. Corp. v. Broad Cove, Inc., 577 N.Y.S.2d 98 (App. Div. 1991), 522
Bubis v. Kassin, 733 A.2d 1232 (N.J. Super. Ct. App. Div. 1999), 201, 207–209
Buchanan v. Simplot Feeders, Ltd. P'ship, 952 P.2d 610 (Wash. 1998), 116
Buchanan v. Warley, 245 U.S. 60 (1917), 578, 671
Buck v. Banks, 668 N.E.2d 1259 (Ind. Ct. App. 1996), 338
Buck, Estate of, No. 23259 (Cal. Super. Ct. 1986), 321
Buckhorn Ventures, LLC v. Forsyth Cnty., 585 S.E.2d 229 (Ga. Ct. App. 2003), 648
Budget Inn of Daphne, Inc. v. City of Daphne, 789 So. 2d 154 (Ala. 2000), 652
Buffalo Sewer Auth. v. Town of Cheektowaga, 228 N.E.2d 386 (N.Y. 1967), 128
Buhl v. U.S. Sprint Commc'ns Co., 840 S.W.2d 904 (Tenn. 1992), 193
Builders Serv. Corp. v. Planning & Zoning Comm'n, 545 A.2d 530 (Conn. 1988), 645
Building Monitoring Sys., Inc. v. Paxton, 905 P.2d 1215 (Utah 1995), 482–483
Bunjer v. Edwards, 985 F. Supp. 165 (D.D.C. 1997), 65
Bunker v. Peyton, 312 F.3d 145 (4th Cir. 2002), 359
Burbank Apartments Tenant Ass'n v. Kargman, 48 N.E.3d 394 (Mass. 2016), 615
Burch v. University of Kan., 756 P.2d 431 (Kan. 1988), 184, 440
Burgess v. Arita, 704 P.2d 930 (Haw. Ct. App. 1985), 523
Burgess v. Pelkey, 738 A.2d 783 (D.C. 1999), 378
Burke-Tarr Co. v. Ferland Corp., 724 A.2d 1014 (R.I. 1999), 213, 216
Burkland; Doe v., 808 A.2d 1090 (R.I. 2002), 415
Burley Brick & Sand Co. v. Cofer, 629 P.2d 1166 (Idaho 1981), 211
Burlington N. & Santa Fe Ry. Co. v. United States, 556 U.S. 599 (2009), 664
Burnett v. National Ass'n of Realtors, No. 19-CV-00332-SRB (W.D. Mo. Nov. 27, 2024), 503
Burnham v. Monroe Cnty., 738 So. 2d 471 (Fla. Dist. Ct. App. 1999), 736
Burns v. McCormick, 135 N.E. 273 (N.Y. 1922), 507
Burns v. Town of Palm Beach, 999 F.3d 1317 (11th Cir. 2021), 672
Burrello Grp., LLC v. District of Columbia, 303 A.3d 618 (D.C. 2023), 630
Burt v. Beautiful Savior Lutheran Church of Broomfield, 809 P.2d 1064 (Colo. Ct. App. 1990), 45
Bush v. Gore, 531 U.S. 98 (2000), 581
Bush v. Kaim, 297 F. Supp. 151 (N.D. Ohio 1969), 602
Bushmiller v. Schiller, 368 A.2d 1044 (Md. Ct. Spec. App. 1977), 521
Butler v. Lindsey, 361 S.E.2d 621 (S.C. 1987), 141
Butler, City of; Doe v., 892 F.2d 315 (3d Cir. 1989), 620, 625–626
Button v. Button, 388 N.W.2d 546 (Wis. 1986), 400
Buyers Serv. Co.; State v., 357 S.E.2d 15 (S.C. 1987), 504
BVT Lebanon Shopping Ctr., Ltd. v. Wal-Mart Stores, Inc., 48 S.W.3d 132 (Tenn. 2001), 453
Byrne v. Laura, 60 Cal. Rptr. 2d 908 (Ct. App. 1997), 412
Byse v. Lewis, 400 S.E.2d 618 (Ga. 1990), 366

C

Cain v. Finnie, 785 N.E.2d 1039 (Ill. App. Ct. 2003), 317
Cain P'ship, Ltd. v. Pioneer Inv. Servs. Co., 914 S.W.2d 452 (Tenn. 1996), 457
California v. United States, 438 U.S. 645 (1978), 778
California Bldg. Indus. Ass'n v. City of San Jose, 351 P.3d 974 (Cal. 2015), 761
California Mobile Home Park Mgmt. Co.; United States v., 29 F.3d 1413 (9th Cir. 1994), 610
California Tahoe Reg'l Planning Agency v. Jenkins, 594 F.2d 181 (9th Cir. 1979), 121
Calkins; NLRB v., 187 F.3d 1080 (9th Cir. 1999), 85
Callahan v. Carey, N.Y.L.J., Dec. 11, 1979 (N.Y. Sup. Ct. Dec. 5, 1979), 636
Cambridge Co. v. East Slope Inv. Co., 700 P.2d 537 (Colo. 1985), 338, 340, 374
Cameron v. Cameron, 641 S.W.2d 210 (Tex. 1982), 406
Campagna v. Tenneco Oil Co., 522 So. 2d 159 (La. Ct. App. 1988), 490
Campbell, In re Estate of, 942 P.2d 1008 (Wash. Ct. App. 1997), 318
Campbell v. Acuff-Rose Music, Inc., 510 U.S. 569 (1994), 838
Campbell v. Cochran, 416 A.2d 211 (Del. Super. Ct. 1980), 816
Campbell v. Garden City Plumbing & Heating, Inc., 97 P.3d 546 (Mont. 2004), 605
Campbell v. Sundquist, 926 S.W.2d 250 (Tenn. Ct. App. 1996), 415
Campbell v. Westdahl, 715 P.2d 288 (Ariz. Ct. App. 1985), 491

Campins v. Capels, 461 N.E.2d 712 (Ind. Ct. App. 1984), 459
Canada v. City of Shawnee, 64 P.2d 694 (Okla. 1936), 132
Canadian St. Regis Band of Mohawk Indians v. State of N.Y., 2003 U.S. Dist. LEXIS 13557 (N.D.N.Y. 2003), 796
Candela v. Port Motors, Inc., 617 N.Y.S.2d 49 (App. Div. 1994), 826
C & J Delivery, Inc. v. Vinyard & Lee & Partners, Inc., 647 S.W.2d 564 (Mo. Ct. App. 1983), 429
C & M Developers, Inc. v. Bedminster Twp. Zoning Hearing Bd., 820 A.2d 143 (Pa. 2002), 632, 667
Canova Land & Inv. Co. v. Lynn, 856 S.E.2d 581 (Va. 2021), 307, 329
Capital Bank v. Needle, 596 So. 2d 1134 (Fla. Dist. Ct. App. 1992), 558
Capitol Fed. Sav. & Loan Ass'n v. Smith, 316 P.2d 252 (Colo. 1957), 341, 580
Cappezzuto v. John Hancock Mut. Life Ins. Co., 476 N.E.2d 188 (Mass. 1985), 501
Carbonneau v. Town of Exeter, 401 A.2d 675 (N.H. 1979), 656
Caridi v. Markey, 539 N.Y.S.2d 404 (App. Div. 1989), 491
Carl E. Gungoll Exploration Joint Venture v. Kiowa Tribe of Okla., 975 P.2d 442 (Okla. 1998), 772
Carnes v. Sheldon, 311 N.W.2d 747 (Mich. Ct. App. 1981), 412
Carparts Distrib. Ctr., Inc. v. Automotive Wholesalers Ass'n of New England, 37 F.3d 12 (1st Cir. 1994), 64
Carpenter v. Double R Cattle Co., 669 P.2d 643 (Idaho Ct. App. 1983), 111
Carpenter v. Ruperto, 315 N.W.2d 782 (Iowa 1982), 143, 154
Carr v. Deking, 765 P.2d 40 (Wash. Ct. App. 1988), 369
Carrillo v. My Way Holdings, LLC, 389 P.3d 1087 (N.M. Ct. App. 2016), 30
Carroll v. Lee, 712 P.2d 923 (Ariz. 1986), 412
Carrollsburg v. Anderson, 791 A.2d 54 (D.C. 2002), 196
Carron v. Board of Cnty. Comm'rs, 976 P.2d 359 (Conn. App. Ct. 1998), 651
Carson v. Elliott, 728 P.2d 778 (Idaho Ct. App. 1986), 191
Carson v. Here's Johnny Portable Toilets, Inc., 698 F.2d 831 (6th Cir. 1983), 850
Carson v. Isabel Apartments, Inc., 579 P.2d 1027 (Wash. Ct. App. 1978), 523
Carter v. Carter, 516 A.2d 917 (D.C. 1986), 361
Carter v. Helmsley-Spear, Inc., 71 F.3d 77 (2d Cir. 1995), 854
Carter v. Schick, 817 S.W.2d 238 (Ky. Ct. App. 1991), 445
Carter v. Voncannon, 327 A.3d 9 (Me. 2024), 146
Carthage, City of v. United Mo. Bank of Kan. City, N.A., 873 S.W.2d 610 (Mo. Ct. App. 1994), 307
Caruso v. Blockbuster-SONY Music Entm't Centre at the Waterfront, 193 F.3d 730 (3d Cir. 1999), 69
Caruso v. Young, 582 S.W.3d 634 (Tex. App. 2019), 337
Casa D'Angelo, Inc. v. A & R Realty Co., 553 N.E.2d 515 (Ind. Ct. App. 1990), 453
Caselli v. Messina, 567 N.Y.S.2d 972 (App. Term 1990), 520
Casey v. Casey, 700 S.W.2d 46 (Ark. 1985), 282, 329
Casino Reinvestment Dev. Auth. v. Banin, 727 A.2d 102 (N.J. 1998), 688
Cassirer v. Thyssen-Bornemisza Collection Found., 862 F.3d 951 (9th Cir. 2017), 175
Castillo v. G&M Realty L.P., 950 F.3d 155 (2d Cir. 2020), 854–855
Castlebrook, Ltd. v. Dayton Props. Ltd. P'ship, 604 N.E.2d 808 (Ohio Ct. App. 1992), 257
Castro Romero v. Becken, 256 F.3d 349 (5th Cir. 2001), 806
Catalano v. Woodward, 617 A.2d 1363 (R.I. 1992), 133
Catawba Indian Tribe v. South Carolina, 718 F.2d 1291 (4th Cir. 1983), *rev'd*, 476 U.S. 498 (1986), 795
Catawba Indian Tribe v. South Carolina, 865 F.2d 1444 (4th Cir. 1989), 775
Cater v. Bednarek, 969 N.E.2d 705 (Mass. 2012), 194, 223
Cathedral of the Incarnation in the Diocese of Long Island, Inc. v. Garden City Co., 697 N.Y.S.2d 56 (App. Div. 1999), 319
Caullett v. Stanley Stilwell & Sons, Inc., 170 A.2d 52 (N.J. Super. Ct. App. Div. 1961), 258
Causby; United States v., 328 U.S. 256 (1946), 43, 702, 705, 714
Causey v. Sewell Cadillac-Chevrolet, Inc., 394 F.3d 295 (5th Cir. 2004), 57
Cavalier Square Ltd. P'ship v. Virginia Alcoholic Beverage Control Bd., 435 S.E.2d 392 (Va. 1993), 471
Cawiezell, Estate of v. Coronelli, 958 N.W.2d 842 (Iowa 2021), 281, 329
Cayuga Indian Nation of N.Y. v. Cuomo, 1999 WL 509442, 1999 U.S. Dist. LEXIS 10579 (N.D.N.Y. 1999), 798–799, 800
Cayuga Indian Nation of N.Y. v. Cuomo, 771 F. Supp. 19 (1991), *later proceedings sub nom.* Cayuga Indian Nation of N.Y. v. Pataki, 2000 U.S. Dist. LEXIS 7045 (2000), *amended*, 165 F. Supp. 2d 266 (N.D.N.Y. 2001), *rev'd*, 413 F.3d 266 (2d Cir. 2005), 796, 800
Cayuga Indian Nation of N.Y. v. Pataki, 165 F. Supp. 2d 266 (N.D.N.Y. 2002), *rev'd*, 413 F.3d 266 (2d Cir. 2005), 796, 800
Cayuga Indian Nation of N.Y. v. Pataki, 188 F. Supp. 2d 223 (N.D.N.Y. 2002), 798
Cayuga Indian Nation of N.Y. v. Pataki, 79 F. Supp. 2d 78 (N.D.N.Y. 1999), 797
Cedar Point Nursery v. Hassid, 594 U.S. 139 (2021), 24–25, 85, 100, 708, 719–720, 722–723, 727, 757
Cell S. of N.J., Inc. v. Zoning Bd. of Adjustment of W. Windsor Twp., 796 A.2d 247 (N.J. 2002), 656
Centel Cable Television Co. of Ohio v. Cook, 567 N.E.2d 1010 (Ohio 1991), 198
Centex Homes Corp. v. Boag, 320 A.2d 194 (N.J. Ch. Div. 1974), 526
Central Del. Cnty. Auth. v. Greyhound Corp., 588 A.2d 485 (Pa. 1991), 319, 331
Central Fin. Servs., Inc. v. Spears, 425 So. 2d 403 (Miss. 1983), 559, 562–563
Century 21-Birdsell Realty, Inc. v. Hiebel, 379 N.W.2d 201 (Minn. Ct. App. 1985), 500
Certain Land in Cape Girardeau; United States v., 79 F. Supp. 558 (E.D. Mo. 1947), 319
Certain Scholarship Funds, In re, 575 A.2d 1325 (N.H. 1990), 279, 322

Chalas v. Pork King Good, 673 F. Supp. 3d 339 (S.D.N.Y. 2023), 64
Chamberlaine & Flowers, Inc. v. McBee, 356 S.E.2d 626 (W. Va. 1987), 510
Chan v. Antepenko, 250 Cal. Rptr. 851 (Ct. App. 1988), 184, 439
Chance v. BP Chems., Inc., 670 N.E.2d 985 (Ohio 1996), 44–45
Chaplin v. Sanders, 676 P.2d 431 (Wash. 1984), 147–148, 151, 154
Chapman, Ex parte, 485 So. 2d 1161 (Ala. 1986), 655
Chapman v. Higbee, 319 F.3d 825 (6th Cir. 2003), 57
Chapman v. Silber, 760 N.E.2d 329 (N.Y. 2001), 489
Charash v. Oberlin Coll., 14 F.3d 291 (6th Cir. 1994), 172
Charleston Joint Venture v. McPherson, 417 S.E.2d 544 (S.C. 1992), 80
Charlotte Park & Recreation Comm'n v. Barringer, 88 S.E.2d 114 (N.C. 1955), 341, 579
Charping v. J.P. Scurry & Co., 372 S.E.2d 120 (S.C. Ct. App. 1988), 243
Charrier v. Bell, 380 So. 2d 155 (La. Ct. App. 1979), 820
Charter Twp. of Delta v. Dinolfo, 351 N.W.2d 831 (Mich. 1984), 627, 669
Chartiers, Twp. of v. William H. Martin, Inc., 542 A.2d 985 (Pa. 1988), 652
Chase v. Eastman, 563 A.2d 1099 (Me. 1989), 192
Chausse v. Coz, 540 N.E.2d 667 (Mass. 1989), 480
Chazon v. Maugenest, 971 N.E.2d 852 (N.Y. 2012), 475
Cheek v. Wainwright, 269 S.E.2d 443 (Ga. 1980), 147
Chen v. Conway, 829 P.2d 1355 (Idaho Ct. App. 1991), 217
Cheney v. Mueller, 485 P.2d 1218 (Or. 1971), 207
Cheney Bros. v. Doris Silk Corp., 35 F.2d 279 (2d Cir. 1929), 849
Chergosky v. Crosstown Bell, Inc., 463 N.W.2d 522 (Minn. 1990), 549
Cherokee Nation v. Georgia, 30 U.S. (5 Pet.) 1 (1831), 785, 802, 804
Cherokee Nation v. United States, 21 Cl. Ct. 565 (1990), 802
Chesapeake Ranch Club, Inc. v. C.R.C. United Members, Inc., 483 A.2d 1334 (Md. Ct. Spec. App. 1984), 257
Chess v. Muhammad, 430 A.2d 928 (N.J. Super. Ct. App. Div. 1981), 476
Chesus v. Watts, 967 S.W.2d 97 (Mo. Ct. App. 1998), 237
Chiapuzio v. BLT Operating Corp., 826 F. Supp. 1334 (D. Wyo. 1993), 606
Chicago, City of v. Morales, 527 U.S. 41 (1999), 124–125
Chicago B. & Q. R. Co. v. Chicago, 166 U.S. 226 (1897), 694
Chicago Flood Litig., In re, 680 N.E.2d 265 (Ill. 1997), 97, 102, 106
Chicago Lawyers' Comm. for Civil Rights Under the Law, Inc. v. Craigslist, Inc., 519 F.3d 666 (7th Cir. 2008), 588
Chiesa v. New York, 351 N.Y.S.2d 735 (App. Div. 1974), 692
Childers v. Childers, 575 P.2d 201 (Wash. 1978), 417
Chillemi v. Chillemi, 78 A.2d 750 (Md. 1951), 532
Choman v. Epperley, 592 P.2d 714 (Wyo. 1979), 360
Christian v. Wal-Mart Stores, Inc., 252 F.3d 862 (6th Cir. 2001), 56, 57
Christiansen v. Casey, 613 S.W.2d 906 (Mo. Ct. App. 1981), 260, 276
Christopher, Ex parte, 145 So. 3d 60 (Ala. 2013), 417
Christy Co. v. Ainbinder/Searcy Ltd., 621 S.W.2d 886 (Ark. Ct. App. 1981), 517
Chryar v. Wolf, 21 P.3d 428 (Colo. Ct. App. 2000), 459
Chrysafis v. Marks, 141 S. Ct. 2482 (2021), 469
Church of Lukumi Babalu Aye, Inc. v. City of Hialeah, 508 U.S. 520 (1993), 675
Cincinnati, City of v. Discovery Network, 507 U.S. 410 (1993), 673
Cincotta v. Jerome, 717 A.2d 639 (R.I. 1998), 214
Cinemark USA, Inc.; United States v., 348 F.3d 569 (6th Cir. 2003), 70
Cisneros v. U.D. Registry, Inc., 46 Cal. Rptr. 2d 233 (Ct. App. 1995), 489
Citibank, N.A. v. Plapinger, 485 N.E.2d 974 (N.Y. 1985), 512
CitiMortgage, Inc. v. Brown, 45 N.E.3d 258 (Ohio Ct. App. 2015), 353
Citizens for Covenant Compliance v. Anderson, 906 P.2d 1314 (Cal. 1995), 226, 228, 236
Citizens for Ethical Gov't, Inc. v. Gwinnett Place Assocs., 392 S.E.2d 8 (Ga. 1990), 80
City of. *See name of city*
The Civil Rights Cases, 109 U.S. 3 (1883), 47, 49, 56, 578–579
Clallam Cnty. for Foreclosure of Liens, In re Proceedings for, 922 P.2d 73 (Wash. 1996), 365
Clark v. Asheville Contracting Co., 323 S.E.2d 765 (N.C. Ct. App. 1984), *aff'd as modified*, 342 S.E.2d 832 (N.C. 1986), 266
Clark v. Carter, 70 Cal. Rptr. 923 (Ct. App. 1968), 351
Clark v. Galaxy Apartments, 427 N.W.2d 723 (Minn. Ct. App. 1988), 209
Clark v. Safeway, Inc., 478 F. Supp. 3d 1080 (D. Or. 2020), 57
Clark v. Williamsburg, City of, 541 P.3d 764 (Kan. Ct. App. 2024), 319
Cleburne, City of v. Cleburne Living Ctr., 473 U.S. 432 (1985), 274, 608, 670
Clegg v. Cult Awareness Network, 18 F.3d 752 (9th Cir. 1994), 48, 51
Cline v. Johnson Cnty. Bd. of Educ., 548 S.W.2d 507 (Ky. 1977), 537
Cline v. Richardson, 526 N.W.2d 166 (Iowa Ct. App. 1994), 192
Coalite, Inc. v. Aldridge, 229 So. 2d 539 (Ala. 1969), 45
Cobb v. Western Union Tel. Co., 98 A. 758 (Vt. 1916), 222
Cobble Hill Nursing Homes, Inc. v. Henry & Warren Corp., 548 N.E.2d 203 (N.Y. 1989), 506
Cobell v. Babbitt, 91 F. Supp. 2d 1 (D.D.C. 1999), *aff'd in part and remanded in part sub nom.* Cobell v. Norton, 240 F.3d 1081 (D.C. Cir. 2001), *later proceeding at* 2003 U.S. Dist. LEXIS 16875 (D.D.C. Sept. 25, 2003), 804
Cobell v. Salazar, 2011 WL 7719672 (D.D.C. 2011), 805
Coble v. Patterson, 442 S.E.2d 119 (N.C. Ct. App. 1994), 317

Coe Coll., In re, 935 N.W.2d 581 (Iowa 2019), 284, 329
Coffee v. William Marsh Rice Univ., 408 S.W.2d 269 (Tex. Civ. App. 1966), 279, 322
Cohen v. Clark, 945 N.W.2d 792 (Iowa 2020), 611
Cohen v. Cohen, 746 N.Y.S.2d 22 (App. Div. 2002), 366, 368
Cole v. Colorado Springs Co., 381 P.2d 13 (Colo. 1963), 323
Cole v. Steinlauf, 136 A.2d 744 (Conn. 1957), 306
Coleman v. Zatechka, 824 F. Supp. 1360 (D. Neb. 1993), 65
Collard v. Incorporated Vill. of Flower Hill, 421 N.E.2d 818 (N.Y. 1981), 650
College Area Renters & Landlord Ass'n v. City of San Diego, 50 Cal. Rptr. 2d 515 (Ct. App. 1996), 608
College Art Theatres, Inc. v. State, 476 So. 2d 40 (Ala. 1985), 123
College Block v. Atlantic Richfield Co., 254 Cal. Rptr. 179 (Ct. App. 1988), 454–455
Collett v. Cordovana, 772 S.E.2d 584 (Va. 2015), 128
Collingwood v. General Elec. Real Estate Equities, Inc., 376 S.E.2d 425 (N.C. 1989), 485
Collins v. Binkley, 750 S.W.2d 737 (Tenn. 1988), 506
Collins v. Church of God Prophecy, 800 S.W.2d 418 (Ark. 1990), 331
Collins v. City of El Campo, 684 S.W.2d 756 (Tex. App. 1984), 243, 270
Collins v. Guggenheim, 631 N.E.2d 1016 (Mass. 1994), 206, 414
Cologne v. Westfarms Assocs., 469 A.2d 1201 (Conn. 1984), 80
Colonial Pipeline Co. v. Morgan, 263 S.W.3d 827 (Tenn. 2008), 415
Colorado Nat'l Bank v. Merlino, 668 P.2d 1304 (Wash. 1983), 402
Colorado River Water Conservation Dist. v. United States, 424 U.S. 800 (1976), 131
Colorado Springs, City of v. SecurCare Self Storage, Inc., 10 P.3d 1244 (Colo. 2000), 647
Columbia E. Assocs. v. Bi-Lo, Inc., 386 S.E.2d 259 (S.C. Ct. App. 1989), 453
Columbia Gas Transmission Corp. v. Bishop, 809 F. Supp. 220 (W.D.N.Y. 1992), 191
Columbus Country Club; United States v., 915 F.2d 877 (3d Cir. 1990), 583, 585
Comcast Corp. v. National Ass'n of African-Am.-Owned Media, 589 U.S. 327 (2020), 596
Comcast of Fla. v. L'Ambiance Beach Condo. Ass'n, Inc., 17 So. 3d 839 (Fla. Dist. Ct. App. 2009), 373
Comer v. Murphy Oil USA, Inc., 839 F. Supp. 2d 849 (S.D. Miss. 2012), 125
Commercial Wharf E. Condo. Ass'n v. Waterfront Parking Corp., 552 N.E.2d 66 (Mass. 1990), 192
Committee Concerning Cmty. Improvement v. Modesto, Cal., 583 F.3d 690 (9th Cir. 2009), 591
Committee for a Better Twin Rivers v. Twin Rivers Homeowners Ass'n, 929 A.2d 1060 (N.J. 2007), 289–290
Commons v. Westwood Zoning Bd. of Adjustment, 410 A.2d 1138 (N.J. 1980), 655
Commonwealth v. *See name of opposing party*
Commonwealth Dep't of Transp. v. Di Furio, 555 A.2d 1379 (Pa. Commw. Ct. 1989), 448
Community Feed Store, Inc. v. Northeastern Culvert Corp., 559 A.2d 1068 (Vt. 1989), 217–218
Community Hous. Improvement Program v. City of New York, 59 F.4th 540 (2d Cir. 2023), 727
Compco Corp. v. Day-Brite Lighting, Inc., 376 U.S. 234 (1964), 849
CompuServe v. Cyber Promotions, Inc., 962 F. Supp. 1015 (S.D. Ohio 1997), 91
Conahan v. Fisher, 463 N.W.2d 118 (Mich. Ct. App. 1990), 510
Conaway v. Prestia, 464 A.2d 847 (Conn. 1983), 487
Concerned Citizens of Brunswick Cnty. Taxpayers Ass'n v. Rhodes, 404 S.E.2d 677 (N.C. 1991), 88, 220
Concord & Bay Point Land Co. v. City of Concord, 280 Cal. Rptr. 623 (Ct. App. 1991), 309
Concord Oil Co. v. Pennzoil Exploration & Prod. Co., 966 S.W.2d 451 (Tex. 1998), 307
Concrete Pipe & Prods. of Cal., Inc. v. Construction Laborers Pension Tr. for S. Cal., 508 U.S. 602 736 (1993), 751
Confederated Band of Ute Indians v. United States, 330 U.S. 169 (1947), 789
Congregation Jeshuat Israel v. Congregation Shearith Israel, 186 F. Supp. 3d 158 (D.R.I. 2016), *rev'd*, 866 F.3d 53 (1st Cir. 2017), 825
Congregation Kol Ami v. Abington Twp., 161 F. Supp. 2d 432 (E.D. Pa. 2001), *vacated and remanded*, 309 F.3d 120 (3d Cir. 2002), 670
Conklin v. Davi, 388 A.2d 598 (N.J. 1978), 518
Connell v. Francisco, 872 P.2d 1150 (Wash. Ct. App. 1994), *aff'd in part and rev'd in part*, 898 P.2d 831 (Wash. 1995), 412–414, 416
Connolly v. Pension Benefit Guar. Corp., 475 U.S. 211 (1986), 750
Consolidated Rail Corp. v. MASP Equip. Corp., 490 N.E.2d 514 (N.Y. 1986), 223
Construction Indus. Ass'n v. City of Petaluma, 522 F.2d 897 (9th Cir. 1975), 661
Cook v. Hoover, 428 So. 2d 836 (La. Ct. App. 1983), 297
Cook v. Howard, 215 S.E.2d 690 (Ga. Ct. App. 1975), 657
Cook v. Nissimov, 580 S.W.3d 745 (Tex. App. 2019), 197
Cook v. University Plaza, 427 N.E.2d 405 (Ill. App. Ct. 1981), 184, 440
Cooper v. Smith, 800 N.E.2d 372 (Ohio Ct. App. 2003), 823
Cooper, State by v. French, 460 N.W.2d 2 (Minn. 1990), 613
Cornelia & Broad Sts., Inc. v. Chase, 587 N.Y.S.2d 809 (App. Div. 1992), 498
Cornelius v. Austin, 542 So. 2d 1220 (Ala. 1989), 509
Cornelius v. Benevolent Protective Order of the Elks, 382 F. Supp. 1182 (D. Conn. 1974), 61
Cornell Glasgow, LLC v. LaGrange Props., LLC, 2012 WL 3157124 (Del. Super. Ct. 2012), 339
Corpus Christi, City of v. City of Pleasanton, 276 S.W.2d 798 (Tex. 1955), 132
Coster v. Piekarski, 3 P.3d 333 (Alaska 2000), 824

Cottonwood Christian Ctr. v. Cypress Redevelopment Agency, 218 F. Supp. 2d 1203 (C.D. Cal. 2002), 629, 675
Country Club Dist. Homes Ass'n v. Country Club Christian Church, 118 S.W.3d 185 (Mo. Ct. App. 2003), 270–271
Countrywide Funding Corp. v. Palmer, 589 So. 2d 994 (Fla. Dist. Ct. App. 1991), 352
Countrywide Home Loans, Inc. v. First Nat'l Bank of Steamboat Springs, 144 P.3d 1224 (Wyo. 2006), 561
Countrywide Home Loans, Inc. v. Kentucky Bar Ass'n, 113 S.W.2d 105 (Ky. 2003), 504
County of. *See name of county*
Cox, In re, 474 P.2d 992 (Cal. 1970), 631
Cox v. Dallas, 430 F.3d 734 (5th Cir. 2005), 591
Cox v. Glenbrook Co., 371 P.2d 647 (Nev. 1962), 193–194
Cox v. Venters, 887 S.W.2d 563 (Ky. Ct. App. 1994), 498
Craig v. Bossenbery, 351 N.W.2d 596 (Mich. Ct. App. 1984), 274
Crain v. City of Selma, 952 F.3d 634 (5th Cir. 2020), 592
Cram; State v., 600 A.2d 733 (Vt. 1991), 39
Crane Neck Ass'n, Inc. v. New York City/Long Island Cnty. Servs. Grp., 460 N.E.2d 1336 (N.Y. 1984), 272–274
Create 21 Chuo, Inc. v. Southwest Slopes, Inc., 918 P.2d 1168 (Haw. Ct. App. 1996), 519–520
Creative Living, Inc. v. Steinhauser, 355 N.Y.S.2d 897 (Sup. Ct. 1974), *aff'd*, 365 N.Y.S.2d 987 (App. Div. 1975), 521
Creegan v. State, 391 P.3d 36 (Kan. 2017), 226
Creek Nation; United States v., 295 U.S. 103 (1935), 774, 786–787, 803
Creola v. Ruley, 12 S.W.3d 848 (Tex. App. 2000), 133
Creppel v. United States, 41 F.3d 627 (Fed. Cir. 1994), 737
Cress; United States v., 243 U.S. 316 (1917), 694
Crestline Ctr. v. Hinton, 567 So. 2d 393 (Ala. Civ. App. 1990), 463
Crichfield Tr., In re, 426 A.2d 88 (N.J. Super. Ct. Ch. Div. 1980), 279, 321, 341
Crimi v. Rutger's Presbyterian Church, 89 N.Y.S.2d 813 (Sup. Ct. 1949), 853
Crooke v. Gilden, 414 S.E.2d 645 (Ga. 1992), 415
Crosstex N. Tex. Pipeline, L.P. v. Gardiner, 505 S.W.3d 580 (Tex. 2016), 105
Crowell v. McCaffrey, 386 N.E.2d 1256 (Mass. 1979), 485
Cruz v. Reatique, 514 A.2d 549 (N.J. Super. Ct. Law Div. 1986), 439
Cruz v. Town of Cicero, 275 F.3d 579 (7th Cir. 2001), 670
Culhane v. Aurora Loan Servs. of Neb., 708 F.3d 282 (1st Cir. 2013), 571–572
Cullin v. Netflix, Inc., 880 F. Supp. 2d 1017 (N.D. Cal. 2012), 64
Cultum v. Heritage House Realtors, Inc., 694 P.2d 630 (Wash. 1985), 503
Cumberland Farms, Inc. v. Dairy Mart, Inc., 627 A.2d 386 (Conn. 1993), 457
Cumberland Farms, Inc. v. Town of Groton, 719 A.2d 465 (Conn. 1998), 653
Cummings v. Anderson, 614 P.2d 1283 (Wash. 1980), 368, 404
Cummings Props., LLC v. National Commc'ns Corp., 869 N.E.2d 617 (Mass. 2007), 463
Cunningham v. City of Greensboro, 711 S.E.2d 477 (N.C. Ct. App. 2011), 244
Curran v. Mount Diablo Council of the Boy Scouts of Am., 952 P.2d 218 (Cal. 1998), 51
Currier v. Kosinski, 506 N.E.2d 895 (Mass. App. Ct. 1987), 501
Curtis v. Anderson, 106 S.W.3d 251 (Tex. App. 2003), 824
Curtis v. Dorn, 234 P.3d 682 (Haw. 2010), 368
Curtis v. Kline, 666 A.2d 265 (Pa. 1995), 417
Curto v. A Country Place Condo. Ass'n, Inc., 921 F.3d 405 (3d Cir. 2019), 592
Cushman v. Davis, 145 Cal. Rptr. 791 (Ct. App. 1978), 213
Customer Co. v. Sacramento, 895 P.2d 900 (Cal. 1995), 712
Custom Parking, Inc. v. Superior Court, 187 Cal. Rptr. 674 (Ct. App. 1982), 484
Cutter v. Wilkinson, 544 U.S. 709 (2005), 675
Cuyahoga Falls, City of v. Buckeye Cmty. Hope Found., 538 U.S. 188 (2003), 581
Cwynar v. City & Cnty. of San Francisco, 109 Cal. Rptr. 2d 233 (Ct. App. 2001), 726–727

D

Dacy v. Village of Ruidoso, 845 P.2d 793 (N.M. 1992), 649
D'Agostino v. Bank of Ravenswood, 563 N.E.2d 886 (Ill. App. Ct. 1990), 506
Dakota Constructors, Inc. v. Hanson Cnty. Bd. of Adjustment, 994 N.W.2d 222 (S.D. 2023), 652
Dale v. Boy Scouts of Am., 734 A.2d 1196 (N.J. 1999), *rev'd*, 530 U.S. 40 (2000), 49, 51–53, 64
Dale v. H.B. Smith Co., 136 F.3d 843 (1st Cir. 1998), 448
Dalliance Real Est., Inc. v. Covert, 1 N.E.3d 850 (Ohio Ct. App. 2013), 183
Dalton v. Eller, 284 S.W. 68 (Tenn. 1926), 185
Danaan Realty Corp. v. Harris, 157 N.E.2d 597 (N.Y. 1959), 512
Danburg v. Keil, 365 S.E.2d 754 (Va. 1988), 524
Dane, Cnty. of v. Norman, 497 N.W.2d 714 (Wis. 1993), 613
Daniel G. Kamin Kilgore Enters. v. Brookshire Grocery Co., 81 Fed. Appx. 827, 2003 U.S. App. LEXIS 24299 (5th Cir. 2003), 453
Daniell v. Sherrill, 48 So. 2d 736 (Fla. 1950), 169
Daniello v. Wagner, 200 N.Y.S.3d 423 (App. Div. 2d Dep't 2023), 214, 219
Daniels v. Anderson, 642 N.E.2d 128 (Ill. 1994), 544
Darby Dev. Co. v. United States, 112 F.4th 1017 (Fed. Cir. 2024), 727
D.A. Realestate Inv., LLC v. City of Norfolk, 126 F.4th 309 (4th Cir. 2024), 123
Davidow v. Inwood N. Prof'l Grp. — Phase I, 747 S.W.2d 373 (Tex. 1988), 429, 480–481
Davidson Bros., Inc. v. D. Katz & Sons, Inc., 579 A.2d 288 (N.J. 1990), *remanded*, 643 A.2d 642 (N.J. Super. Ct. App. Div. 1994), 235, 254, 269, 287

Davis v. Barnfield, 833 So. 2d 58 (Ala. Ct. App. 2002), 508
Davis v. Boyle-Midway, Inc., 615 F. Supp. 560 (N.D. Ga. 1985), 582
Davis v. Bruk, 411 A.2d 660 (Me. 1980), 196
Davis v. Davis, 1990 WL 130807 (Tenn. Ct. App. 1990), 830
Davis v. Davis, 842 S.W.2d 588 (Tenn. 1992), 829–831
Davis v. Konjicija, 620 N.E.2d 1010 (Ohio 1993), 166
Davis v. St. Joe Sch. Dist., 284 S.W.2d 635 (Ark. 1955), 319
Day v. Kolar, 341 N.W.2d 598 (Neb. 1983), 447
Daytona Beach, City of v. Tona-Rama, Inc., 294 So. 2d 73 (Fla. 1974), 88, 220
De Bruyn Produce Co. v. Romero, 508 N.W.2d 150 (Mich. Ct. App. 1993), 184, 439–440
Decatur v. Barnett, 398 S.E.2d 706 (Ga. Ct. App. 1990), *rev'd*, 403 S.E.2d 46 (Ga. 1991), 520
DeCecco v. Beach, 381 A.2d 543 (Conn. 1977), 136
DeCoster; State v., 653 A.2d 891 (Me. 1995), 30, 184, 439, 440
Deep E. Tex. Reg'l Mental Health & Mental Retardation Servs. v. Kinnear, 877 S.W.2d 550 (Tex. App. 1994), 272, 274
De Freitas v. Coke, 380 P.2d 762 (Haw. 1963), 306
Defiore v. City Rescue Mission of New Castle, 995 F. Supp. 2d 413 (W.D. Pa. 2013), 584
DeFriece v. McCorquodale, 998 So. 2d 465 (Ala. 2008), 508
Delamater v. Foreman, 239 N.W. 148 (Minn. 1931), 474
DeLeon v. Aldrete, 398 S.W.2d 160 (Tex. Civ. App. 1965), 525
Del E. Webb Realty & Mgmt. Co. v. Wessbecker, 628 P.2d 114 (Colo. Ct. App. 1980), 464
Delfino v. Vealencis, 436 A.2d 27 (Conn. 1980), 361
DeLorean v. DeLorean, 511 A.2d 1257 (N.J. Super. Ct. 1986), 400
DeMatteo v. DeMatteo, 762 N.E.2d 797 (Mass. 2002), 400
Dennis v. Bird, 941 S.W.2d 486 (Ky. Ct. App. 1997), 320
Dennison v. Marlowe, 744 P.2d 906 (N.M. 1987), 471
Denny v. Elizabeth Arden Salons, Inc., 456 F.3d 427 (4th Cir. 2006), 49, 56
Denver & San Francisco Ry. v. School Dist. No. 22, 23 P. 978 (Colo. 1890), 307
Department of Agric. & Consumer Servs. v. Mid-Fla. Growers, Inc., 521 So. 2d 101 (Fla. 1988), 710
Department of Highways, State by & through v. Feenan, 752 P.2d 182 (Mont. 1988), 128
Department of Hous. & Urban Dev. v. Ross, Fair Hous.—Fair Lending Rptr. ¶25,075 (HUD ALJ 1994), 620
Department of Hous. & Urban Dev. v. Rucker, 535 U.S. 125 (2002), 455, 711
Department of Nat. Res. v. Mayor & Council of Ocean City, 332 A.2d 630 (Md. 1975), 87
Department of Transp. v. Rowe, 531 S.E.2d 836 (N.C. Ct. App. 2000), 692
Department of Transp. v. Rowe, 549 S.E.2d 203 (N.C. 2001), 692
DePeyster v. Michael, 6 N.Y. 467 (1852), 284
DeRosa v. Quang Loi Jewelry Co., No. 95-BPA-0068 (Mass. Comm'n Against Discrimination, June 17, 1998), 50
DeSario v. Industrial Excess Land Fill Inc., No. 89570 (Ohio Ct. Com. Pl. 1994), 119
Desnick v. ABC, Inc., 44 F.3d 1345 (7th Cir. 1995), 36–37, 40, 178
Detling v. Edelbrock, 671 S.W.2d 265 (Mo. 1984), 476
De Villar v. New York, 628 F. Supp. 80 (S.D.N.Y. 1986), 439
DeVillier v. Texas, 601 U.S. 285 (2024), 766
Deviney v. Nationsbank, 993 S.W.2d 443 (Tex. App. 1999), 282
Devins v. Borough of Bogota, 592 A.2d 199 (N.J. 1991), 169
Devlin v. The Phoenix, Inc., 471 So. 2d 93 (Fla. Dist. Ct. App. 1985), 437
Dewire v. Haveles, 534 N.E.2d 782 (Mass. 1989), 360
Dews v. Town of Sunnyvale, 109 F. Supp. 2d 526 (N.D. Tex. 2000), 617
Diamond v. Chakrabarty, 447 U.S. 303 (1980), 842
Diamond v. State Bd. of Land & Nat. Res., 145 P.3d 704 (Haw. 2006), 89
Diaz; United States v., 499 F.2d 113 (9th Cir. 1974), 856
DiBlasi v. City of Seattle, 969 P.2d 10 (Wash. 1998), 128
DiCenso v. Cisneros, 96 F.3d 1004 (7th Cir. 1996), 603–604
Dick Broad. Co. of Tenn. v. Oak Ridge FM, Inc., 395 S.W.3d 653 (Tenn. 2013), 430, 492
Dickens v. Hall, 718 P.2d 683 (N.M. 1986), 446
Dickhut v. Norton, 173 N.W.2d 297 (Wis. 1970), 483
Dierberg v. Wills, 700 S.W.2d 461 (Mo. Ct. App. 1985), 239–240, 291, 296–297
DiLiddo v. Oxford St. Realty, Inc., 876 N.E.2d 421 (Mass. 2007), 630
District Intown Props. LP v. District of Columbia, 198 F.3d 874 (D.C. Cir. 1999), 732
Dittmer v. Jacwin Farms, Inc., 637 N.Y.S.2d 785 (App. Div. 1996), 166
Dobie v. Morrison, 575 N.W. 817 (Mich. Ct. App. 1998), 192
Dobrinsky v. Waddell, 599 N.E.2d 188 (Ill. App. Ct. 1992), 171
Dobyns v. South Carolina Dep't of Parks, Recreation & Tourism, 480 S.E.2d 81 (S.C. 1997), 491
Doe v. *See name of opposing party*
Dolan v. City of Tigard, 512 U.S. 374 (1994), 720, 758–761
Donaldson v. Farrakhan, 762 N.E.2d 835 (Mass. 2002), 50
Donegal Assocs., LLC v. Christie-Scott, LLC, 241 A.3d 1011 (Md. Ct. Spec. App. 2020), 449
Donnellan v. Rocks, 99 Cal. Rptr. 692 (Ct. App. 1972), 502
Donner, Matter of Estate of, 623 A.2d 307 (N.J. Super. Ct. App. Div., 1993), 344
Donovan v. Grand Victoria Casino & Resort, LP, 934 N.E.2d 1111 (Ind. 2010), 31
Dooley v. Town of Fairfield, 197 A.2d 770 (Conn. 1964), 668
Dorey v. Estate of Spicer, 715 A.2d 182 (Me. 1998), 197
Dorgan v. Loukas, 473 N.E.2d 1151 (Mass. App. Ct. 1985), 488
Dority v. Dority, 645 P.2d 56 (Utah 1982), 405
Dougan v. Rossville Drainage Dist., 757 P.2d 272 (Kan. 1988), 127

Dowling v. Dowling, 679 P.2d 480 (Alaska 1984), 417
Downey v. Jackson, 65 So. 2d 825 (Ala. 1953), 117
Dred Scott v. Sandford, 60 U.S. 393 (1857), 786
Dressel v. Ameribank, 664 N.W.2d 151 (Mich. 2003), 504
D.R. Mobile Home Rentals v. Frost, 545 N.W.2d 302 (Iowa 1996), 463
Dr. Seuss Enters., L.P. v. ComicMix LLC, 983 F.3d 443 (9th Cir. 2020), 837
Drummond Co. v. Boshell, 641 So. 2d 1240 (Ala. 1994), 117
Drutman Realty Co. v. Jindo Corp., 865 F. Supp. 1093 (S.D.N.Y. 1994), 464
Duane v. Government Emps. Ins. Co. (GEICO), 37 F.3d 1036 (4th Cir. 1994), 600
Dubin v. Chesebrough Tr., 116 Cal. Rptr. 2d 872 (Ct. App. 2002), 207
Dublirer v. 2000 Linwood Ave. Owners, Inc., 103 A.3d 249 (N.J. 2014), 289
Dufau v. United States, 22 Cl. Ct. 156 (1990), *aff'd without opinion*, 940 F.2d 677 (Fed. Cir. 1991), 662
Dugan v. Jensen, 510 N.W.2d 313 (Neb. 1994), 166
Dulaney Towers Maint. Corp. v. O'Brey, 418 A.2d 1233 (Md. Ct. Spec. App. 1980), 379
Dumont Oaks Cmty. Ass'n, Inc. v. Montgomery Cnty., 634 A.2d 459 (Md. 1993), 371
Dunafon v. Delaware McDonald's Corp., 691 F. Supp. 1232 (W.D. Mo. 1988), 285–286
Dunbar v. Board of Trs. of Clayton Coll., 461 P.2d 28 (Colo. 1969), 279
Duncan v. Vassaur, 550 P.2d 929 (Okla. 1976), 350, 357
Duncan & Hill Realty, Inc. v. Department of State, 405 N.Y.S.2d 339 (App. Div. 1978), 503
Dunning v. Larsen, 2015 WL 5920263 (Mass. Land Ct. 2015), 214
Durand v. IDC Bellingham, LLC, 793 N.E.2d 359 (Mass. 2003), 648, 667
Duvall v. Ford Leasing Dev. Corp., 255 S.E.2d 470 (Va. 1979), 266
Dworak v. Michals, 320 N.W.2d 485 (Neb. 1982), 501
Dyar v. Martinez, 54 Cal. Rptr. 3d 907 (Ct. App. 2007), 550

E

Eagle Enters. v. Gross, 349 N.E.2d 816 (N.Y. 1976), 255–256
Eastern Enters. v. Apfel, 524 U.S. 498 (1998), 751–752
East Haven Assocs. v. Gurian, 313 N.Y.S.2d 927 (Civ. Ct. 1970), 471
Eastlake v. Forest City Enters., Inc., 426 U.S. 668 (1976), 581
Easton v. Strassburger, 199 Cal. Rptr. 383 (Ct. App. 1984), 502, 511
Eastwood, In re, 192 B.R. 96 (Bankr. D.N.J. 1996), 305
Eastwood Mall, Inc. v. Slanco, 626 N.E.2d 59 (Ohio 1994), 80
E.B. v. R.N., 242 N.E.3d 791 (Ohio Ct. App. 2024), 831
eBay, Inc. v. Bidder's Edge, Inc., 100 F. Supp. 2d 1058 (N.D. Cal. 2000), 92
Ebbe v. Senior Estates Golf & Country Club, 657 P.2d 696 (Or. Ct. App. 1983), 257
Edgar A. Levy Leasing Co. v. Siegel, 258 U.S. 242 (1922), 469, 723
Edgell v. Canning, 976 P.2d 1193 (Utah 1999), 213
Edmonds v. Oxford House, Inc., 514 U.S. 725 (1995), 586, 623
Edwards v. Habib, 397 F.2d 687 (D.C. Cir. 1968), 481
Efficiency Lodge, Inc. v. Neason, 889 S.E.2d 789 (Ga. 2023), 441
Egan Slough Cmty. v. Flathead Cnty. Bd. of Cnty. Comm'rs, 506 P.3d 996 (Mont. 2022), 658
Egeter v. West & N. Props., 758 P.2d 361 (Or. Ct. App. 1988), 518
Eggleston v. Pierce Cnty., 64 P.3d 618 (Wash. 2003), 712
Ehlerbracht v. Crowned Ridge Wind II, LLC, 972 N.W.2d 477 (S.D. 2022), 101
801 S. Fulton Ave. Corp. v. Radin, 526 N.Y.S.2d 143 (App. Div. 1988), 470
El Di, Inc. v. Town of Bethany Beach, 477 A.2d 1066 (Del. 1984), 291, 323
Eldridge v. City of Palo Alto, 129 Cal. Rptr. 575 (Ct. App. 1976), 645
Eli v. Eli, 557 N.W.2d 405 (S.D. 1997), 361
Eller Media Co. v. Bruckner Outdoor Signs, Inc., 753 N.Y.S.2d 28 (App. Div. 2002), 169
Ellettsville, Town of v. DeSpirito, 111 N.E.3d 987 (Ind. 2018), 196
Elliot v. Sherwood Manor Mobile Home Park, 947 F. Supp. 1574 (M.D. Fla. 1996), 609
Elliott; State v., 616 A.2d 210 (Vt. 1992), *cert. denied*, 507 U.S. 911 (1993), 784, 789, 792–793, 795–796
Ellis v. Jansing, 620 S.W.2d 569 (Tex. 1981), 152–153
Ellsworth Dobbs, Inc. v. Johnson, 236 A.2d 843 (N.J. 1967), 501–502
Elmsford Apartment Assocs. v. Cuomo, 469 F. Supp. 3d 148 (S.D.N.Y. 2020), 469
El Paso Nat. Gas Co. LLC v. United States, 2017 WL 3492993 (D. Ariz. Aug. 15, 2017), 784
Emery v. Caravan of Dreams, Inc., 879 F. Supp. 640 (N.D. Tex. 1995), 68
Employment Div. v. Smith, 494 U.S. 872 (1990), 613–614, 674–677
Enderson v. Kelehan, 32 N.W.2d 286 (Minn. 1948), 129
Englebrecht, In re, 79 Cal. Rptr. 2d 89 (Ct. App. 1998), 124
English v. Sanchez, 796 P.2d 236 (N.M. 1990), 404, 521
Enid, City of v. Crow, 316 P.2d 834 (Okla. 1957), 132
Equestrian Ridge Homeowners Ass'n v. Equestrian Ridge Estates II Homeowners Ass'n, 953 N.W.2d 16 (Neb. 2021), 249, 254
Erie, City of v. Pap's A.M., 529 U.S. 277 (2000), 674
Erlich v. Culver City, 512 U.S. 1231 (1994), *on remand*, 911 P.2d 429 (Cal. 1996), 759
Espenschied v. Mallick, 633 A.2d 388 (D.C. 1993), 482
Esplanade Props., LLC v. City of Seattle, 307 F.3d 978 (9th Cir. 2002), 731
Essen Dev. v. Marr, 687 So. 2d 98 (La. Ct. App. 1995), 472
Estate of. *See name of estate*
Estelle v. Gamble, 429 U.S. 97 (1976), 635
Esteves v. Esteves, 775 A.2d 163 (N.J. Super. Ct. App. Div. 2001), 364

ETW Corp. v. Jireh Publ'g, Inc., 332 F.3d 915 (6th Cir. 2003), 849–850, 852
Euclid, Vill. of v. Ambler Realty Co., 272 U.S. 365 (1926), 97, 120, 642, 645, 700–702, 704, 706, 709, 737
Evans v. Abney, 396 U.S. 435 (1970), 278, 322, 341–342, 579
Evans v. Evans, 772 S.E.2d 576 (Va. 2015), 359
Evans v. Grand Union Co., 759 F. Supp. 818 (M.D. Ga. 1990), 453, 454
Evans v. Merriweather, 4 Ill. 492 (1842), 130
Evans v. Newton, 382 U.S. 296 (1966), 278, 323, 579
Evans v. Newton, 148 S.E.2d 329 (Ga. 1966), 322
Evans v. Pollock, 796 S.W.2d 465 (Tex. 1990), 263
Evergreen Highlands Ass'n v. West, 73 P.3d 1 (Colo. 2003), 376
EWB-I, LLC v. PlazAmericas Mall Tex., LLC, 527 S.W.3d 447 (Tex. App. 2017), 291
Exotex Corp. v. Rinehart, 3 P.3d 826 (Wyo. 2000), 501
Ex parte. *See name of party*
Exxon Mobil Corp. v. Albright, 71 A.3d 30 (Md. 2013), 27, 102, 119

F

Fair v. Negley, 390 A.2d 240 (Pa. Super. Ct. 1978), 479
Fair Hous. Council of Orange Cnty., Inc. v. Ayers, 855 F. Supp. 315 (C.D. Cal. 1994), 612
Fair Hous. Council of San Fernando Valley v. Roommate.com, LLC, 521 F.3d 1157 (9th Cir. 2008), 588, 602
Fallon v. Triangle Mgmt., 215 Cal. Rptr. 748 (Ct. App. 1985), 553
Familystyle of St. Paul, Inc. v. City of St. Paul, 923 F.2d 91 (8th Cir. 1991), 624
Farkas v. Calamia, 373 S.W.2d 1 (Mo. 1963), 318
Farmers & Mechs. Bank v. Arbucci, 589 A.2d 14 (Conn. App. Ct. 1991), 558
Farmer's Inv. Co. v. Bettwy, 558 P.2d 14 (Ariz. 1976), 132
Far W. Sav. & Loan Ass'n v. McLaughlin, 246 Cal. Rptr. 872 (Ct. App. 1988), 545, 546
Fast v. DeRaeve, 714 P.2d 1077 (Or. Ct. App. 1986), 200
Favart v. Ouellette, 239 A.3d 994 (N.H. 2020), 208
Favorite v. Miller, 407 A.2d 974 (Conn. 1978), 817
Federal Beef Processors, Inc. v. CBS Inc., 1994 WL 408366 (D.S.D. 1994), 36
Federal Home Loan Mortg. Corp. v. Schwartzwald, 979 N.E.2d 1214 (Ohio 2012), 570, 572
Federated Retail Holdings, Inc. v. County of Ramsey, 820 N.W.2d 553 (Minn. 2012), 246
Feinberg, In re Estate of, 919 N.E.2d 888 (Ill. 2009), 343–344
Feist Publ'ns, Inc. v. Rural Tel. Serv., 499 U.S. 340 (1991), 836
Felker, In re, 211 B.R. 165 (Bankr. M.D. Pa. 1997), 320
Felmet; State v., 273 S.E.2d 708 (N.C. 1981), 80
Fidelity Fed. Sav. & Loan Ass'n v. De La Cuesta, 458 U.S. 141 (1982), 563
Fidelity Mut. Life Ins. Co. v. Kaminsky, 768 S.W.2d 818 (Tex. App. 1989), 470
Fields v. Griffen, 1999 WL 349872 (Ark. Ct. App. 1999), 143
1515-1519 Lakeview Blvd. Condo. Ass'n v. Apartment Sales Corp., 43 P.3d 1233 (Wash. 2002), 253
Fifth Ave. Presbyterian Church v. City of New York, 293 F.3d 570 (2d Cir. 2002), 677
Fifty Assocs. v. Berger Dry Good Co., 176 N.E. 643 (Mass. 1931), 463
Fike v. Shelton, 860 So. 2d 1227 (Miss. Ct. App. 2003), 210
Fine Line, Inc. v. Blake, 677 A.2d 1061 (Me. 1996), 193
Fink v. Miller, 896 P.2d 649 (Utah Ct. App. 1995), 291, 297
Finley v. Glenn, 154 A. 299 (Pa. 1931), 242
Finn v. Williams, 33 N.E.2d 226 (Ill. 1941), 210
First Citizens Nat'l Bank v. Sherwood, 817 A.2d 501 (Pa. Super. Ct. 2003), 550
First Covenant Church v. City of Seattle, 787 P.2d 1352 (Wash. 1990), 677
First English Evangelical Lutheran Church v. County of Los Angeles, 258 Cal. Rptr. 893 (Ct. App. 1989), *cert. denied*, 493 U.S. 1056 (1990), 662, 714
First English Evangelical Lutheran Church v. Los Angeles Cnty., 482 U.S. 304 (1987), 765
First Nat'l Bank in Albuquerque v. Enriquez, 634 P.2d 1266 (N.M. 1981), 552
First Nat'l Bank of Moline v. Califf, Harper, Fox & Dailey, 548 N.E.2d 1361 (Ill. App. Ct. 1989), 506
First Unitarian Church of Salt Lake City v. Salt Lake City Corp., 308 F.3d 1114 (10th Cir. 2002), 76
First United Methodist Church v. Hearing Exam'r, 916 P.2d 374 (Wash. 1996), 677
Fisel v. Wynns, 667 So. 2d 761 (Fla. 1996), 46
Fisher, Matter of Estate of, 645 N.Y.S.2d 1020 (Sup. Ct. 1996), 320
Fisher v. Space of Pensacola, Inc., 483 So. 2d 392 (Ala. 1986), 127
Fitzgarrald v. City of Iowa City, 492 N.W.2d 659 (Iowa 1992), 103
564.54 Acres of Land; United States v., 441 U.S. 506 (1979), 690
Flack v. McClure, 565 N.E.2d 131 (Ill. App. Ct. 1990), 567
Flaherty v. Broadway Assocs. Ltd. P'ship by Sterling Dev. Corp., 566 N.Y.S.2d 982 (App. Div. 1991), 517
Flaig v. Gramm, 983 P.2d 396 (Mont. 1999), 203, 207
Fleetwood Chateau Owners Corp. v. Fleetwood Garage Corp., 61 N.Y.S.3d 287 (App. Div. 2017), 270
Fleming v. Napili Kai, Ltd., 430 P.2d 316 (Haw. 1967), 192
Fleming v. Watson, 416 So. 2d 706 (Ala. 1982), 167
Florida Holding 4800, LLC v. Lauderhill Mall Inv., LLC, 317 So. 3d 121 (Fla. Dist. Ct. App. 2021), 512
Florida Rock Indus., Inc. v. United States, 18 F.3d 1560 (Fed. Cir. 1994), 737
Florida Rock Indus., Inc. v. United States, 8 Cl. Ct. 160 (1985), *rev'd in part and remanded*, 791 F.2d 893 (Fed. Cir. 1986), *cert. denied*, 479 U.S. 1053 (1987), *on remand*, 21 Cl. Ct. 161 (1990), *rev'd in part*, 18 F.3d 1560 (Fed. Cir. 1994), *on remand*, 45 Fed. Cl. 21 (1999), 735, 737
Florida Rock Indus., Inc. v. United States, 45 Fed. Cl. 21 (1999), 735, 737
Flowers v. TJX Cos., 1994 WL 382515 (N.D.N.Y. 1994), 58, 59
Flureau v. Thornhill, 96 Eng. Rep. 635 (C.P. 1776), 523

Flynn v. City of Cambridge, 418 N.E.2d 335 (Mass. 1981), 726
Flynn v. Holder, 684 F.3d 852 (9th Cir. 2012), 827
Fogerty v. State, 231 Cal. Rptr. 810 (Ct. App. 1986), 170
Follette v. Pacific Light & Power Corp., 208 P. 295 (Cal. 1922), 555
Fontainebleau Hotel Corp. v. Forty-Five Twenty-Five, Inc., 114 So. 2d 357 (Fla. Dist. Ct. App. 1959), 136–137, 221
Food Lion v. Capital Cities/ABC, Inc., 887 F. Supp. 811 (M.D.N.C. 1995), *aff'd in part and rev'd in part*, 194 F.3d 505 (4th Cir. 1999), 35–36, 41, 178
Foods First, Inc. v. Gables Assocs., 418 S.E.2d 888 (Va. 1992), 243, 270
Ford v. Long, 713 S.W.2d 798 (Tex. App. 1986), 357
Ford v. Schering-Plough Corp., 145 F.3d 601 (3d Cir. 1998), 64
Fordham v. Butera, 876 N.E.2d 397 (Mass. 2007), 647
Forest Hills Gardens Corp. v. Baroth, 555 N.Y.S.2d 1000 (Sup. Ct. 1990), 220
Forest Oil Corp. v. McAllen, 268 S.W.3d 51 (Tex. 2008), 512
Forest Props., Inc. v. United States, 177 F.3d 1360 (Fed. Cir. 1999), 732
Formanek v. United States, 26 Cl. Ct. 332 (1992), 735–736
Formella v. Brennan, 817 F.3d 503 (7th Cir. 2016), 598
Forster v. Hall, 576 S.E.2d 746 (Va. 2003), 261, 270
Fort Berthold Reservation v. United States, 182 Ct. Cl. 543, 390 F.2d 686 (1968), 787
Fort Sill Apache Tribe v. United States, 477 F.2d 1360 (Ct. Cl. 1973), 795
40 Assocs., Inc. v. Katz, 446 N.Y.S.2d 844 (Civ. Ct. 1981), 480
44 Liquormart, Inc. v. Rhode Island, 517 U.S. 484 (1996), 673
49 Prospect St. v. Sheva Gardens, 547 A.2d 1134 (N.J. Super. Ct. App. Div. 1988), 487
Fortyune v. American Multi-Cinema, Inc., 364 F.3d 1075 (9th Cir. 2004), 70
Foster v. Back Bay Spas, Inc., d/b/a Healthworks Fitness Ctr., 7 Mass. L. Rptr. 462, 1997 WL 634354 (Mass. Super. Ct. 1997), 72
Foster v. Wasson, 483 S.W.3d 301 (Ark. Ct. App. 2016), 146
Four Seas Inv. Corp. v. International Hotel Tenants' Ass'n, 146 Cal. Rptr. 531 (Ct. App. 1978), 480
14 E. 4th St. Unit 509 LLC v. Toporek, 203 A.D.3d 17 (N.Y. App. Div. 2022), 463
Fourth St. Rest. v. Venture Realty Grp., Inc., 533 So. 2d 784 (Fla. Dist. Ct. App. 1988), 498–499
Fox v. Gaines, 4 F.4th 1293 (11th Cir. 2021), 603
Fox v. Pollack, 226 Cal. Rptr. 532 (Ct. App. 1986), 506
Fox v. Snow, 76 A.2d 877 (N.J. 1950), 317
Fraley v. Minger. *See* Williams v. Rogier
Franceschi v. Hyatt Corp., 782 F. Supp. 712 (D.P.R. 1992), 56
Franceschina v. Morgan, 346 F. Supp. 833 (S.D. Ind. 1972), 440
Francini v. Goodspeed Airport, LLC, 174 A.3d 779 (Conn. 2018), 210
Francis v. Kings Park Manor, Inc., 992 F.3d 67 (2d Cir. 2021), 590
Franklin v. Spadafora, 447 N.E.2d 1244 (Mass. 1983), 378
Franklin Tower One, L.L.C. v. N.M., 725 A.2d 1104 (N.J. 1999), 630
Frank's Rest., Inc. v. Lauramar Enters., Inc., 711 N.Y.S.2d 433 (App. Div. 2000), 845
Frantz v. Cantrell, 711 N.E.2d 856 (Ind. Ct. App. 1999), 474
Fraser v. Fraser, 598 A.2d 751 (Me. 1991), 448
Fraser v. Robin Dee Day Camp, 210 A.2d 208 (N.J. 1965), *rev'd sub nom.* Boy Scouts of Am. v. Dale, 530 U.S. 640 (2000), 49
Frazier v. Rominger, 27 F.3d 828 (2d Cir. 1994), 593
Fred v. Kokinokos, 347 F. Supp. 942 (E.D.N.Y. 1972), 602
Freda v. Commercial Tr. Co., 570 A.2d 409 (N.J. 2000), 358
Frederick v. Consolidated Waste Servs., Inc., 573 A.2d 387 (Me. 1990), 211
Freetown Holdings Co.; People v., 320 Cal. Rptr. 3d 20 (Ct. App. 2024), 117
French v. Ahlstrom, 612 N.Y.S.2d 458 (App. Div. 1994), 498
French v. Estate of Gutzan, 128 A.3d 657 (Me. 2015), 188
French v. Estate of Selectmen of Amherst, 646 N.E.2d 418 (Mass. App. Ct. 1995), 188
Frenchtown Square P'ship v. Lemstone, Inc., 791 N.E.2d 417 (Ohio 2003), 465
Frenchtown Villa v. Meadors, 324 N.W.2d 133 (Mich. Ct. App. 1982), 483
Fresh Pond Shopping Ctr., Inc. v. Callahan, 464 U.S. 875 (1983), 727
Freyberg v. DCO 2400 14th St. LLC, 304 A.3d 971 (D.C. 2023), 487
Friend v. Gem Int'l, Inc., 476 S.W.2d 134 (Mo. Ct. App. 1971), 438
Friendship Manor, Inc. v. Greiman, 581 A.2d 893 (N.J. Super. Ct. 1990), 540
Friends of Danny DeVito v. Wolf, 227 A.3d 872 (Pa.), *cert. denied*, 141 S. Ct. 239 (2020), 742
Friendswood Dev. Co. v. Smith-Southwest Indus., Inc., 576 S.W.2d 21 (Tex. 1978), 97, 135–136
Frisk v. Thomas, 553 P.3d 350 (Mont. 2024), 41
FTR Farms, Inc. v. Rist Farms, Inc., 942 N.W.2d 204 (Neb. 2020), 361
Funds in the Possession of Conemaugh Twp. Supervisors, In re, 753 A.2d 788 (Pa. 2000), 817
Fuqua v. Fuqua, 750 S.W.2d 238 (Tex. App. 1988), 451
Furnas v. Cirone, 221 N.E.3d 772 (Mass. 2023), 350
Futura Realty v. Lone Star Bldg. Ctrs. (E.) Inc., 578 So. 2d 363 (Fla. Dist. Ct. App. 1991), 511

G

G&D Enters. v. Liebelt, 949 N.W.2d 853 (N.D. 2020), 28
Gallimore v. Washington, 666 A.2d 1200 (D.C. 1995), 357
Gallo, People ex rel. v. Acuna, 929 P.2d 596 (Cal. 1997), 122–124
Gamble v. City of Escondido, 104 F.3d 300 (9th Cir. 1997), 592, 623

Gamer v. Town of Milton, 195 N.E.2d 65 (Mass. 1964), 132, 136
Gannon; United States v., 684 F.2d 433 (7th Cir. 1982), 514
Gap Inc. v. 170 Broadway Retail Owner, LLC, 195 A.D.3d 575 (N.Y. App. Div. 2021), 452
Garcia v. Myllyla, 254 Cal. Rptr. 3d 36 (Ct. App. 2019), 479
Gardens at Maplewood v. Fowlin, 2013 WL 1496552 (N.J. Super. Ct. Law Div. 2013), 451
Gardner v. Gardner, 454 N.W.2d 361 (Iowa 1990), 507
Gardner v. Jones, 464 So. 2d 1144 (Miss. 1985), 467
Gardner v. New Jersey Pinelands Comm'n, 593 A.2d 251 (N.J. 1991), 735
Gardner; United States v., 903 F. Supp. 1394 (D. Nev. 1995), 38
Garland v. Rosenshein, 649 N.E.2d 756 (Mass. 1995), 236, 259–260
Garneau v. City of Seattle, 147 F.3d 802 (9th Cir. 1998), 549, 759
Garrett v. Tandy Corp., 295 F.3d 94 (1st Cir. 2002), 58
Gay; Territory v., 31 Haw. 376, *aff'd*, 52 F.2d 356 (9th Cir. 1930), 753–754
Geib v. McKinney, 617 A.2d 1377 (Conn. 1992), 358
Gelinas LLC v. Hayes, 221 N.Y.S.3d 877 (Sup. Ct. 2024), 363
Gemmell v. Lee, 757 A.2d 1171 (Conn. App. Ct. 2000), 209
GENC Realty LLC v. Nezaj, 860 N.Y.S.2d 106 (App. Div. 2008), 184
General Auto Serv. Station v. Maniatis, 765 N.E.2d 1176 (Ill. App. Ct. 2002), 170
General Credit Co. v. Cleck, 609 A.2d 553 (Pa. 1992), 350, 352, 353
General Mun. Auth. of Nanticoke, 292 A.3d 1162 (Pa. Commw. Ct. 2023), 688
Genovese Drug Stores, Inc. v. Connecticut Packing Co., 732 F.2d 286 (2d Cir. 1984), 550
Gentry v. Gentry, 798 S.W.2d 928 (Ky. 1990), 400
George S. May Int'l Co. v. International Profit Ass'n, 628 N.E.2d 647 (Ill. App. Ct. 1993), 285
George Washington Univ. v. Weintraub, 458 A.2d 43 (D.C. 1983), 479
Ger v. Kammann, 504 F. Supp. 446 (D. Del. 1980), 518
Geragosian v. Union Realty Co., 193 N.E. 726 (Mass. 1935), 42
Gerlach v. Rokita, 95 F.4th 493 (7th Cir. 2024), 765
Gertz v. Estes, 879 N.E.2d 617 (Ind. Ct. App. 2008), 136
G/GM Real Estate Corp. v. Susse Chalet Motor Lodge of Ohio, Inc., 575 N.E.2d 141 (Ohio 1991), 516
Ghen v. Rich, 8 F. 159 (D.C. Mass. 1881), 815
Giebeler v. M & B Assocs., 343 F.3d 1143 (9th Cir. 2003), 624
Gifford v. McCarthy, 23 N.Y.S.3d 422 (App. Div. 2016), 73
Giger v. City of Omaha, 442 N.W.2d 182 (Neb. 1989), 648
Gil v. Winn-Dixie Stores, Inc., 993 F.3d 1266 (11th Cir. 2021), 64
Gila River Pima-Maricopa Indian Cmty. v. United States, 427 F.2d 1194 (Ct. Cl. 1970), 795
Gilbert v. Beaver Dam Ass'n of Stratford, Inc., 2002 Conn. Super. LEXIS 2765 (2002), *rev'd*, 858 A.2d 860 (Conn. App. Ct. 2004), 285
Gilder v. Mitchell, 668 A.2d 879 (Me. 1995), 198
Gill v. LDI, 19 F. Supp. 2d 1188 (W.D. Wash. 1998), 45
Gillespie, In re Marriage of, 948 P.2d 1338 (Wash. Ct. App. 1997), 403
Gillespie Land & Irrigation Co. v. Gonzalez, 379 P.2d 135 (Ariz. 1963), 128
Gilliam v. American Broad. Co., 538 F.2d 14 (2d Cir. 1976), 853
Gilligan v. Jamco Dev. Corp., 108 F.3d 246 (9th Cir. 1997), 592, 597, 618, 625
Gilliland v. Port Auth. of City of St. Paul, 270 N.W.2d 743 (Minn. 1978), 566
Gilman v. Pebble Cove Home Owners Ass'n, Inc., 546 N.Y.S.2d 134 (App. Div. 1989), 379
Gilmore v. Driscoll, 122 Mass. 199 (1877), 133
Gilpin v. Jacob Ellis Realties, Inc., 135 A.2d 204 (N.J. Super. Ct. App. Div. 1957), 270, 295
Gion v. City of Santa Cruz, 465 P.2d 50 (Cal. 1970), 86–87, 170
Girani v. Lovorn, 270 So. 3d 1070 (Miss. Ct. App. 2018), 203
Girard Coll. Trusteeship, In re, 138 A.2d 844 (Pa. 1958), 278
Gitlow v. New York, 268 U.S. 652 (1921), 75
Gittleman v. Woodhaven Condo. Ass'n, Inc., 972 F. Supp. 894 (D.N.J. 1997), 274, 610
Glacial Aggregates LLC v. Town of Yorkshire, 924 N.E.2d 785 (N.Y. 2010), 654, 750
Glasoe v. Trinkle, 479 N.E.2d 915 (Ill. 1985), 476
Glassberg v. Warshawsky, 638 N.E.2d 749 (Ill. App. Ct. 1994), 498
Glassboro, Borough of v. Vallorosi, 568 A.2d 888 (N.J. 1990), 669
Glavin v. Eckman, 881 N.E.2d 820 (Mass. 2008), 28
Glen Ellyn Sav. & Loan Ass'n v. State Bank of Geneva, 382 N.E.2d 1267 (Ill. App. Ct. 1978), 546
Glenn v. Shuey, 595 A.2d 606 (Pa. Super. Ct. 1991), 146, 148
Glosemeyer v. United States, 45 Fed. Cl. 771 (2000), 680
Gnerre v. Massachusetts Comm'n Against Discrimination, 524 N.E.2d 84 (Mass. 1988), 603
Goddard v. Winchell, 52 N.W. 1124 (Iowa 1892), 818
Goeke v. National Farms, Inc., 512 N.W.2d 626 (Neb. 1994), 112, 116
Goetz v. Anderson, 274 N.W.2d 175 (N.D. 1978), 500
Goldblatt v. Hempstead, 369 U.S. 590 (1962), 696, 702, 730
Golden v. Conway, 128 Cal. Rptr. 69 (Ct. App. 1976), 480
Golden v. Town of Ramapo, 285 N.E.2d 291 (N.Y. 1972), 661
Golden Gateway Ctr. v. Golden Gateway Tenants Ass'n, 29 P.3d 797 (Cal. 2001), 81
Golden Hill Paugussett Tribe v. Weicker, 39 F.3d 51 (2d Cir. 1994), 795
Gomes v. Countrywide Home Loans Inc., 121 Cal. Rptr. 3d 819 (Ct. App. 2011), 571
Gomez v. Pagaduan, 613 P.2d 658 (Haw. Ct. App. 1980), 522
Gonzales v. Inslee, 535 P.3d 864 (Wash. 2023), 727
Good v. United States, 189 F.3d 1355 (Fed. Cir. 1999), 737

Goodridge v. Department of Pub. Health, 798 N.E.2d 941 (Mass. 2003), 409–410
Gordon v. Gordon, 124 N.E.2d 228 (Mass. 1955), 344
Gordon v. Whittle, 57 S.E.2d 169 (Ga. 1950), 319
Gore v. Beren, 867 P.2d 330 (Kan. 1994), 361
Gorman Towers, Inc. v. Bogoslavaky, 626 F.2d 607 (8th Cir. 1980), 671
Gormley v. Robertson, 83 P.3d 1042 (Wash. Ct. App. 2004), 416
Gottschalk v. Benson, 409 U.S. 63 (1972), 842
Goulding v. Cook, 661 N.E.2d 1322 (Mass. 1996), 41–42
Gove v. Zoning Bd. of Appeals of Chatham, 831 N.E.2d 865 (Mass. 2005), 714, 731
Grace United Methodist Church v. City of Cheyenne, 235 F. Supp. 2d 1186 (D. Wyo. 2002), 629, 676
Graci v. Gasper John Palazzo, Jr., LLC, 119 So. 3d 741 (La. Ct. App. 2013), 451
Graham v. John Deere Co., 383 U.S. 1 (1966), 842
Graham v. Mack, 699 P.2d 590 (Mont. 1984), 207
Grande v. Jennings, 278 P.3d 1287 (Ariz. Ct. App. 2012), 818
Granite Props. Ltd. P'ship v. Manns, 512 N.E.2d 1230 (Ill. 1987), 207–209
Grant v. Detroit Ass'n of Women's Clubs, 505 N.W.2d 254 (Mich. 1993), 439
Grants Pass, City of v. Johnson, 603 U.S. 520 (2024), 39, 635
Graoch Assocs. #33, L.P. v. Louisville/Jefferson Cnty. Metro Hum. Relations Comm'n, 508 F.3d 366 (6th Cir. 2007), 616, 618
Grapin v. Grapin, 450 So. 2d 853 (Fla. 1984), 417
Grappo v. Blanks, 400 S.E.2d 168 (Va. 1991), 152
Grasso v. Thimons, 559 A.2d 925 (Pa. Super. Ct. 1989), 226
Gray v. Vandver, 623 S.W.2d 172 (Tex. App. 1981), 285, 340
Greater Providence Chamber of Commerce v. State of Rhode Island, 657 A.2d 1038 (R.I. 1995), 86
Great N. Ry. Co. v. United States, 315 U.S. 262 (1942), 748
Green v. Dormitory Auth. of the State of N.Y., 577 N.Y.S.2d 675 (App. Div. 1991), 184, 440
Green v. Housing Auth. of Clackamas Cnty., 994 F. Supp. 1253 (D. Or. 1998), 610
Green v. Lupo, 647 P.2d 51 (Wash. Ct. App. 1982), 188–190
Green v. Mann, 655 N.Y.S.2d 627 (App. Div. 1997), 194
Green Corp., In re, 154 B.R. 819 (Bankr. Me. 1993), 441
Green Party of N.J. v. Hartz Mountain Indus., Inc., 752 A.2d 315 (N.J. 2000), 81, 83
Greenwald v. Greenwald, 454 N.W.2d 34 (Wis. Ct. App. 1990), 400
Greenwalt Family Tr. v. Kehler, 885 P.2d 421 (Mont. 1994), 150
Greenwich Plaza, Inc. v. Whitman & Ransom, 1996 WL 240458 (Conn. Super. Ct. 1996), 474
Greeson v. Ace Pipe Cleaning, Inc., 830 S.W.2d 444 (Mo. 1992), 360
Gregory v. Dillard's Inc., 565 F.3d 464 (8th Cir. 2009), 34, 58
Greiner-Maltz Co. v. Kalex Chem. Prods., 530 N.Y.S.2d 220 (App. Div. 1988), 499
Griggs v. Allegheny Cnty., 369 U.S. 84 (1962), 43, 702, 705
Grombone v. Krekel, 754 P.2d 777 (Colo. Ct. App. 1988), 566
Gross v. FBL Fin. Servs., Inc., 557 U.S. 167 (2009), 592, 594
Grosz v. City of Miami Beach, 721 F.2d 303 (6th Cir. 1983), 674
Groucho Marx Prods., Inc. v. Day & Night Co., 689 F.2d 317 (2d Cir. 1982), 850
Grulke, In re Estate of, 546 N.W.2d 626 (Iowa Ct. App. 1996), 313
Gryczan v. State, 942 P.2d 112 (Mont. 1997), 415
Guild v. Hinman, 695 A.2d 1190 (Me. 1997), 193
Guilford v. Weidner Inv. Servs., Inc., 522 P.3d 1085 (Alaska 2023), 479
Guillette v. Daly Dry Wall, Inc., 325 N.E.2d 572 (Mass. 1975), 242, 552
Guillot v. Town of Lutcher, 373 So. 2d 1385 (La. Ct. App. 1979), 104
Guinnane v. City & Cnty. of San Francisco, 241 Cal. Rptr. 787 (Ct. App. 1987), 662
Gulledge, Estate of, 673 A.2d 1278 (D.C. 1996), 354
Gunpowder Horse Stables, Inc. v. State Farm Auto. Ins. Co., 673 A.2d 721 (Md. 1996), 46
Gustin v. Scheele, 549 N.W.2d 135 (Neb. 1996), 166–167
Guthrie v. National Adver. Co., 556 N.E.2d 337 (Ind. Ct. App. 1990), 549
Gym-N-I Playgrounds, Inc. v. Snider, 220 S.W.2d 905 (Tex. 2007), 481

H

H&R Block, Inc. v. Lovelace, 493 P.2d 211 (Kan. 1972), 387
H & Y Realty Co. v. Baron, 554 N.Y.S.2d 111 (App. Div. 1990), 366
Hack v. President & Fellows of Yale Coll., 16 F. Supp. 2d 183 (D. Conn. 1998), 583, 628
Hadacheck v. Sebastian, 239 U.S. 394 (1915), 695, 699–700, 706, 730
Hadley v. Baxendale, 156 Eng. Rep. 145 (Ex. 1854), 524
Hagemann v. Worth, 782 P.2d 1072 (Wash. Ct. App. 1989), 272, 274
Hahn v. J.C. Land, Inc., 1999 WL 378766 (Va. Cir. Ct. 1999), 218–219
Haines v. Minnock Constr. Co., 433 A.2d 30 (Pa. Super. Ct. 1981), 238
Haith v. Atchison Cnty., 793 S.W.2d 151 (Mo. Ct. App. 1990), 128
Hale v. Osborn Coal Enters., Inc., 729 So. 2d 853 (Ala. Civ. App. 1997), 648–649
Hall v. Meadowood Ltd. P'ship, 7 Fed. Appx. 687, 2001 U.S. App. LEXIS 5718 (9th Cir. 2001), 604
Hall v. Pennsylvania State Police, 570 F.2d 86 (3d Cir. 1978), 34, 59
Hall v. Phillips, 436 N.W.2d 139 (Neb. 1989), 104–105
Hall v. Wood, 443 So. 2d 834 (Miss. 1983), 129
Halley v. Harden Oil Co., 357 S.E.2d 138 (Ga. Ct. App. 1987), 436
Halpern v. Lacy Inv. Corp., 379 S.E.2d 519 (Ga. 1989), 143, 154

Halverson v. Skagit Cnty., 983 P.2d 643 (Wash. 1999), 128
Hammer; State v., 550 P.2d 820 (Alaska 1976), 693
Hammonds v. Hammonds, 522 So. 2d 305 (Ala. Civ. App. 1988), 366
Hampton v. Dillard Dep't Stores, Inc., 247 F.3d 1091 (10th Cir. 2001), 34, 56, 58
Hanapi; State v., 970 P.2d 485 (Haw. 1998), 40
Hankins v. Mathews, 425 S.W.2d 608 (Tenn. 1968), 329
Hannah v. Peel, 1 K.B. 509 (1945), 818
Hannah v. Sibcy Cline Realtors, 769 N.E.2d 876, 2001 Ohio 3912 (Ohio Ct. App. 2001), 589
Hanson v. Bonner, 661 P.2d 421 (Mont. 1983), 566
Hanson v. Summers, unpublished (Mich. Ct. App. Sept. 22, 2000), 148
Harbor Island Holdings, L.L.C. v. Kim, 132 Cal. Rptr. 2d 406 (Ct. App. 2003), 463
Harding v. La Jaur, 315 A.2d 132 (Md. Ct. Spec. App. 1974), 553
Harding v. Willie, 458 N.W.2d 612 (Iowa Ct. App. 1990), 528
Hardy, In re Estate of, 805 So. 2d 515 (Miss. 2002), 910 So. 2d 1052 (Miss. 2005), 530
Hare v. McClellan, 662 A.2d 1242 (Conn. 1995), 285
Harel Assocs. v. Cooper Healthcare Prof'l Servs., 638 A.2d 921 (N.J. Super. Ct. App. Div. 1994), 470
Harkins v. Fuller, 652 A.2d 90 (Me. 1995), 166
Harkness v. Butterworth Hunting Club, Inc., 58 So. 3d 703 (Miss. Ct. App. 2011), 209
Harlen Assocs. v. Incorporated Vill. of Mineola, 273 F.3d 494 (2d Cir. 2001), 670
Harmon v. Tyler, 273 U.S. 668 (1927), 579
Harms v. Sprague, 456 N.E.2d 976 (Ill. App. Ct. 1983), 354
Harper & Row Publishers, Inc. v. Nation Enters., 471 U.S. 539 (1985), 837
Harrin v. Brown Realty Co., 602 P.2d 79 (Kan. 1979), 501
Harrington v. Building Sys., Inc., 656 A.2d 624 (R.I. 1995), 192
Harrington v. Lamarque, 677 N.E.2d 258 (Mass. App. Ct. 1997), 207
Harris v. Capital Growth Inv'rs XIV, 805 P.2d 884 (Cal. 1991), 630–631
Harris v. City of Akron, 20 F.3d 1396 (6th Cir. 1994), 668
Harris v. Collins, 150 S.W.2d 740 (Ark. 1941), 556
Harris v. County of Riverside, 904 F.2d 497 (9th Cir. 1990), 666
Harris v. Jefferson Cnty. Bd. of Zoning Adjustment, 773 So. 2d 496 (Ala. Civ. App. 2000), 646
Harris v. Lynch, 940 S.W.2d 42 (Mo. Ct. App. 1997), 144
Harris v. Town of Lincoln, 668 A.2d 321 (R.I. 1995), 112, 116–117, 714–715
Harrison v. Denny's Rest., Inc., 1997 WL 227963 (N.D. Cal. Apr. 24, 1997), 56
Harry's Vill. v. Egg Harbor Twp., 446 A.2d 862 (N.J. 1982), 446
Hartke v. Connecticut, 429 N.E.2d 885 (Ill. App. Ct. 1981), 442
Hartland Sportsman's Club v. Town of Delafield, 35 F.3d 1198 (7th Cir. 1994), 666
Hartman v. Buckson, 467 A.2d 694 (Del. Ch. 1983), 648
Harvey Cedars, Borough of v. Karan, 70 A.3d 524 (N.J. 2013), 692
Harvey v. Dow, 11 A.3d 303 (Me. 2011), 508
Hasgo Power Equip. Sales, Inc. v. Lewis, 624 N.Y.S.2d 713 (App. Div. 1995), 218
Haskell v. Stauffer Commc'ns, Inc., 990 P.2d 163 (Kan. Ct. App. 1999), 850
Havens Realty Corp. v. Coleman, 455 U.S. 363 (1982), 41, 597–598
Hawai'i Hous. Auth. v. Midkiff, 467 U.S. 229 (1984), 213, 682–686
HawaiiUSA Fed. Credit Union v. Monalim, 464 P.3d 821 (Haw. 2020), 557
Hawkins v. Hawkins, 612 S.W.2d 683 (Tex. Civ. App. 1981), 404
Hay v. Bruno, 344 F. Supp. 286 (D. Or. 1972), 89
Haye v. United States, 461 F. Supp. 1168 (C.D. Cal. 1978), 517
Hayes v. Aquia Marina, Inc., 414 S.E.2d 820 (Va. 1992), 194
Haygood v. State, 483 S.E.2d 302 (Ga. Ct. App. 1997), 43
HealthSouth Rehabilitation Corp. v. Falcon Mgmt. Co., 799 So. 2d 177 (Ala. 2001), 463
Heart of Atlanta Motel, Inc. v. United States, 379 U.S. 241 (1964), 47, 720–721, 724
Hebert v. Hebert, 650 So. 2d 436 (La. Ct. App. 1995), 403
Hecht v. Superior Court, 20 Cal. Rptr. 2d 275 (Ct. App. 1993), 829
Hecht v. Superior Court, 59 Cal. Rptr. 2d 222 (Ct. App. 1996), *as modified* (Nov. 19, 1996), *review denied and ordered not to be officially published* (Jan. 15, 1997), 829
Heckman v. Nero, 2000 WL 1041226 (Del. Ch. 2000), 507
Heights Apartments, LLC v. Walz, 30 F.4th 720 (8th Cir. 2022), 727
Heim v. Conroy, 621 N.Y.S.2d 210 (App. Div. 1995), 208
Heins Implement Co. v. Missouri Highway & Transp. Comm'n, 859 S.W.2d 681 (Mo. 1993), 127–128, 129–130
Heitz v. Circle Four Realty Co., 548 N.E.2d 11 (Ill. App. Ct. 1989), 509
Hemisphere Bldg. Co. v. Village of Richton Park, 171 F.3d 437 (7th Cir. 1999), 623–624
Henderson v. Jewel Food Stores, Inc., 1996 WL 617165 (N.D. Ill. Oct. 23, 1996), 34, 58
Hendle v. Stevens, 586 N.E.2d 826 (Ill. App. Ct. 1992), 818–819
Hendrickson v. Fredericks, 620 P.2d 205 (Alaska 1980), 491
Hendrickson v. Minneapolis Fed. Sav. & Loan Ass'n, 161 N.W.2d 688 (Minn. 1968), 352
Hendricks v. Stalnaker, 380 S.E.2d 198 (W. Va. 1989), 105
Henley v. Continental Cablevision of St. Louis Cnty., Inc., 692 S.W.2d 825 (Mo. Ct. App. 1985), 198
Henrickson v. Wagners, 598 N.W.2d 507 (S.D. 1999), 127
Henri-Lynn Realty, Inc. v. Huang, 552 N.Y.S.2d 357 (App. Div. 1990), 498
Henry v. Dalton, 151 A.2d 362 (R.I. 1959), 203
Henry S. Miller Mgmt. Corp. v. Houston State Ass'n, 792 S.W.2d 128 (Tex. App. 1990), 477
Henson v. Boal, 2009 WL 279336 (Mich. Ct. App. 2009), 153

Heritage Art Galleries v. Raia, 570 N.Y.S.2d 67 (App. Div. 1991), 564
Heritage Homes of De La Warr, Inc. v. Alexander, Inc., 2005 WL 2173992 (Del. Ch. Sept. 1, 2005), *aff'd*, 900 A.2d 100 (Del. 2006), 337
Hermitage Methodist Homes of Va., Inc. v. Dominion Tr. Co., 387 S.E.2d 740 (Va. 1990), 322–323, 342, 579
Hernandez v. Hernandez, 645 So. 2d 171 (Fla. Dist. Ct. App. 1994), 364
Hernandez v. Stabach, 193 Cal. Rptr. 350 (Ct. App. 1983), 487–488
Herren v. Pettengill, 538 S.E.2d 735 (Ga. 2000), 196
Herrera v. Wyoming, 587 U.S. 329 (2019), 777
Hertz v. Hertz, 657 P.2d 1169 (N.M. 1983), 368
Hess v. Chase Manhattan Bank, USA, 220 S.W.2d 758 (Mo. 2007), 510
Heutel v. Walker, 735 S.W.2d 196 (Mo. 1987), 477
Hewitt v. Hewitt, 394 N.E.2d 1204 (Ill. 1979), 412
Hewitt v. Meaney, 226 Cal. Rptr. 349 (Ct. App. 1986), 210–211
H.E.Y. Tr. v. Popcorn Express Co., 35 S.W.3d 55 (Tex. App. 2000), 438
Hicks v. Casablanca Records, 464 F. Supp. 426 (S.D.N.Y. 1978), 850
Hidden Harbour Estates v. Basso, 393 So. 2d 637 (Fla. Dist. Ct. App. 1981), 287
Hiddleston v. Nebraska Jewish Educ. Soc'y, 186 N.W.2d 904 (Neb. 1971), 537
Higday v. Nickolaus, 469 S.W.2d 859 (Mo. Ct. App. 1971), 132
Hilder v. St. Peter, 478 A.2d 202 (Vt. 1984), 476, 478
Hill v. Community of Damien of Molokai, 911 P.2d 861 (N.M. 1996), 272–274, 625
Hill v. Dobrowolski, 484 A.2d 1123 (N.H. 1984), 449
Hill v. Fontaine Condo. Ass'n, Inc., 334 S.E.2d 690 (Ga. 1985), 378
Hill v. State, 688 So. 2d 901 (Fla. 1996), 39
Hillary Corp. v. United States Cold Storage, Inc., 550 N.W.2d 889 (Neb. 1996), 223
Hills Dev. Co. v. Bernards Twp., 510 A.2d 621 (N.J. 1986), 633
Hillview Assocs. v. Bloomquist, 440 N.W.2d 867 (Iowa 1989), 481
Himsel v. Himsel, 122 N.E.3d 935 (Ind. Ct. App. 2019), 101
Hinman v. Cornett, 900 S.E.2d 872 (N.C. 2024), 149
Hitz Rest. Grp., In re, 616 B.R. 374 (Bankr. N.D. Ill. 2020), 452
Hixon v. Public Serv. Comm'n, 146 N.W.2d 577 (Wis. 1966), 86
Hodel v. Irving, 481 U.S. 704 (1987), 328, 418, 708, 743–744, 790–791
Hodel v. Virginia Surface Mining & Reclamation Ass'n, Inc., 452 U.S. 264 (1981), 707
Hoery v. United States, 64 P.3d 214 (Colo. 2003), 44–45
Hoffman v. Bob Law, Inc., 888 N.W.2d 569 (S.D. 2016), 169
Hoffman v. Capitol Cablevision Sys., Inc., 383 N.Y.S.2d 674 (App. Div. 1976), 198
Hoffman v. United Iron & Metal Co., 671 A.2d 55 (Md. Ct. Spec. App. 1996), 213, 222
Hohri v. United States, 782 F.2d 227 (D.C. Cir. 1986), 796
Hohri v. United States, 847 F.2d 779 (Fed. Cir. 1988), 796
Holbrook v. Taylor, 532 S.W.2d 763 (Ky. 1976), 200, 202
Holden v. Weidenfeller, 929 S.W.2d 124 (Tex. App. 1996), 204, 207
Holiday Furniture Factory Outlet Corp v. Florida Dep't of Corr., 852 So. 2d 926 (Fla. Dist. Ct. App. 2003), 465
Hollett, In re Estate of, 834 A.2d 348 (N.H. 2003), 400
Hollingsworth v. Perry, 568 U.S. 1066 (2012), 410
Hollis v. Chestnut Bend Homeowners Ass'n, 760 F.3d 531 (6th Cir. 2014), 610
Holman v. Indiana, 211 F.3d 399 (7th Cir. 2000), 606
Holmdel Builders Ass'n v. Holmdel, 583 A.2d 277 (N.J. 1990), 761
Holmes v. Sprint United Tel. of Kan., 35 P.3d 928 (Kan. Ct. App. 2001), 197
Holmgren v. Little Vill. Cmty. Reporter, 342 F. Supp. 512 (N.D. Ill. 1971), 629
Holy Props., Ltd. v. Kenneth Cole Prods., Inc., 661 N.E.2d 694 (N.Y. 1995), 463
Homeamerican Credit, Inc. v. Weiss, 2000 WL 347785 (Conn. Super. Ct. 2000), 533
Home Bldg. & Loan Ass'n v. Blaisdell, 290 U.S. 398 (1934), 563
Home Builders Ass'n v. City of Napa, 108 Cal. Rptr. 2d 60 (Ct. App. 2001), 761
Home Builders League of S. Jersey, Inc. v. Township of Berlin, 405 A.2d 381 (N.J. 1979), 645
Home for Incurables of Balt. City v. University of Md. Med. Sys. Corp., 797 A.2d 746 (Md. 2002), 322
Hometown Props. v. Fleming, 680 A.2d 56 (R.I. 1996), 672
Homsey v. University Gardens Racquet Club, 730 S.W.2d 763 (Tex. App. 1987), 256
Honce v. Vigil, 1 F.3d 1085 (10th Cir. 1993), 603–604
Hood; Commonwealth v., 452 N.E.2d 188 (Mass. 1983), 81
Horiike v. Coldwell Banker Residential Brokerage Co., 383 P.3d 1094 (Cal. 2016), 502
Horizon House Developmental Servs., Inc. v. Town of Upper Southampton, 804 F. Supp. 683 (E.D. Pa. 1992), *aff'd*, 995 F.2d 217 (3d Cir. 1993), 624
Horizon Med. Grp. v. City Ctr. of Charlotte Cnty., Ltd., 779 So. 2d 545 (Fla. Dist. Ct. App. 2001), 463
Horne v. Department of Agric., 576 U.S. 350 (2015), 725–726, 765
Hornell Brewing Co. v. Rosebud Sioux Tribal Court, 133 F.3d 1087 (8th Cir. 1998), 852
Horne v. TGM Assocs., LP, 56 So. 3d 615 (Ala. 2010), 451
Hornwood v. Smith's Food King No. 1, 807 P.2d 208 (Nev. 1991), 455
Horse Pond Fish & Game Club, Inc. v. Cormier, 581 A.2d 478 (N.H. 1990), 284, 329
Houle v. Adams State Coll., 547 P.2d 926 (Colo. 1976), 184, 440–441
Houle v. Guilbeault, 40 A.2d 438 (R.I. 1944), 556
Houle v. Quenneville, 787 A.3d 1258 (Vt. 2001), 483
Household Realty Corp. v. Pelzar, 1995 WL 371189 (Conn. Super. Ct. 1995), 357
Housing & Redevelopment Auth. v. Naegele Outdoor Adver. Co., 282 N.W.2d 537 (Minn. 1979), 693

Housing Auth. v. Southern Ry., 264 S.E.2d 174 (Ga. 1980), 693
Housing Auth. of New Brunswick v. Suydam Inv'rs, L.L.C., 826 A.2d 673 (N.J. 2003), 689
Houston Bellaire, Ltd. v. TCP LB Portfolio I, 981 S.W.2d 916 (Tex. App. 1998), 207
Hovendick v. Ruby, 10 P.3d 1119 (Wyo. 2000), 144
Hovsons, Inc. v. Township of Brick, N.J., 89 F.3d 1096 (3d Cir. 1996), 583, 623
Howard v. Kunto, 477 P.2d 210 (Wash. Ct. App. 1970), 148
Howard D. Johnson Co. v. Parkside Dev. Corp., 348 N.E.2d 656 (Ind. Ct. App. 1976), 550
Howard Opera House Ass'n v. Urban Outfitters, Inc., 322 F.3d 125 (2d Cir. 2003), 117, 456, 472
Howson v. Crombie St. Congregational Church, 590 N.E.2d 687 (Mass. 1992), 316
Hoyts Cinemas Corp.; United States v., 380 F.3d 558 (1st Cir. 2004), 69
HTA Ltd. P'ship v. Massachusetts Turnpike Auth., 747 N.E.2d 707 (Mass. App. Ct. 2001), 688
Hualpai Indians, United States ex rel. v. Santa Fe Pac. R.R., 314 U.S. 339 (1941), 773, 782, 792, 800
Hubbard; People v., 320 N.W.2d 294 (Mich. Ct. App. 1982), 39
Hubbard v. Samson Mgmt. Corp., 994 F. Supp. 187 (S.D.N.Y. 1998), 610
Hubert v. Williams, 184 Cal. Rptr. 161 (App. Dep't Super. Ct. 1982), 71
Hudgens v. National Labor Relations Bd., 424 U.S. 507 (1976), 80, 84
Hudson v. Vandiver, 810 So. 2d 617 (Miss. Ct. App. 2002), 566
Hudson Valley Cablevision Corp. v. 202 Developers, Inc., 587 N.Y.S.2d 385 (App. Div. 1992), 192
Huggins v. Wright, 774 So. 2d 408 (Miss. 2000), 196
Hughes v. Hughes, 573 P.2d 1194 (N.M. 1978), 406
Hughes v. Krueger, 67 So. 2d 279 (Fla. 2011), 368
Hughes Mem'l Homes; United States v., 396 F. Supp. 544 (W.D. Va. 1975), 279, 322, 583
Humphrey v. Byron, 850 N.E.2d 1044 (Mass. 2006), 483
Hunt v. Happy Valley Ltd. P'ship, 434 S.E.2d 285 (S.C. Ct. App. 1993), 448
Hunt v. Hunt, 952 S.W.2d 564 (Tex. App. 1997), 403
Hunt v. Pole Bridge Hunting Club, Inc., 631 N.Y.S.2d 711 (App. Div. 1995), 195
Hunter; United States v., 459 F.2d 205 (4th Cir. 1972), 54
Huntington v. Riggs, 862 N.E.2d 1263 (Ind. Ct. App. 2007), 171
Huntington Branch, NAACP v. Town of Huntington, 844 F.2d 926 (2d Cir.), *aff'd per curiam*, 488 U.S. 15 (1988), 615–617, 619, 634
Hunziker v. State, 519 N.W.2d 367 (Iowa 1994), 739
Hurd v. Henley, 478 P.3d 208 (Alaska 2020), 153
Hurd v. Hodge, 334 U.S. 24 (1948), 581
Hurley v. City of Niagara Falls, 289 N.Y.S.2d 889 (App. Div. 1968), 819
Hurley v. Irish-American Gay, Lesbian, & Bisexual Grp. of Bos., 515 U.S. 557 (1995), 52
Hurwitz v. Eagan Real Est., Inc., 557 N.Y.S.2d 711 (App. Div. 1990), 522
Hurt; United States v., 676 F.3d 649 (8th Cir. 2012), 603
Huynh v. Blanchard, 694 S.W.3d 648 (Tex. 2024), 112
Hynes v. Grimes Packing Co., 337 U.S. 86 (1949), 778, 789–790

I

Iancu v. Brunetti, 588 U.S. 388 (2019), 847
Idaho v. Coeur d'Alene Tribe, 521 U.S. 261 (1997), 796
Idaho v. Evans, 807 P.2d 62 (Idaho 1991), 816
Il Giardino v. Belle Haven Land Co., 1999 WL 436368 (Conn. Super. Ct. 1999), *rev'd*, 757 A.2d 1103 (Conn. 2000), 209
Illinois Cent. R.R. Co. v. Illinois, 146 U.S. 387 (1892), 85
Imperial Colliery v. Fout, 373 S.E.2d 489 (W. Va. 1988), 483–484
Inclusive Cmtys. Project, Inc. v. Lincoln Prop. Co. 920 F.3d 890 (5th Cir. 2019), 588, 618
Ingannamorte v. Kings Super Mkts., Inc., 260 A.2d 841 (N.J. 1970), 453
Inhabitants of Middlefield v. Church Mills Knitting Co., 35 N.E. 780 (Mass. 1894), 259
In re. *See name of party*
Intel Corp. v. Hamidi, 71 P.3d 296 (Cal. 2003), 91
Intermountain Fair Hous. Council v. Boise Rescue Mission Ministries, 717 F. Supp. 2d 1101 (D. Idaho 2010), 584
International Aircraft Recovery, L.L.C. v. Unidentified, Wrecked, & Abandoned Aircraft, 218 F.3d 1255 (11th Cir. 2000), 820
International Church of the Foursquare Gospel v. City of San Leandro, 673 F.3d 1059 (9th Cir. 2011), 676
International Comm'n on English in the Liturgy v. Schwartz, 573 A.2d 1303 (D.C. 1990), 463, 472
International News Serv. v. Associated Press (INS v. AP), 248 U.S. 215 (1918), 848–849
Inwood N. Homeowners' Ass'n v. Harris, 736 S.W.2d 632 (Tex. 1987), 240
Iowa-Mo Enters., Inc. v. Avren, 639 F.2d 443 (8th Cir. 1981), 524
Iraheta v. Superior Court, 83 Cal. Rptr. 2d 471 (Ct. App. 1999), 124
I.R.T. Prop. Co. v. Sheehan, 581 So. 2d 591 (Fla. Dist. Ct. App. 1991), 203
Isaac v. A & B Loan Co., 247 Cal. Rptr. 104 (Ct. App. 1988), 507
Isbell v. Commercial Inv. Assocs., 644 S.E.2d 72 (Va. 2007), 484
Italian Cowboy Partners, Ltd. v. Prudential Ins. Co. of Am., 341 S.W.3d 323 (Tex. 2011), 512

J

Jack Daniels Props., Inc. v. VIP Prods. LLC, 599 U.S. 140 (2023), 847
Jackson v. Mortgage Elec. Registration Sys., Inc., 770 N.W.2d 487 (Minn. 2009), 572
Jackson v. Tyler's Dad's Place, Inc., 850 F. Supp. 53 (D.D.C. 1994), *aff'd by unpublished order*, 107 F.3d 923 (D.C. Cir. 1996), 56
Jacobs v. Major, 407 N.W.2d 832 (Wis. 1987), 80

Jacobson v. Swan, 278 P.2d 294 (Utah 1954), 565
Jacque v. Steenberg Homes, Inc., 563 N.W.2d 154 (Wis. 1997), 28
James v. Griffin, 626 N.W.2d 704 (N.D. 2001), 171
James Vault & Precast Co. v. B&B Hot Oil Serv., Inc., 927 N.W.2d 452 (N.D. 2019), 369
Jancik v. Department of Hous. & Urban Dev., 44 F.3d 553 (7th Cir. 1995), 611
Janian v. Barnes, 742 N.Y.S.2d 445 (App. Div. 2002), 513
Janicki v. Hospital of St. Raphael, 744 A.2d 963 (Conn. Super. Ct. 1999), 827
Jankowski Lee & Assocs. v. Department of Hous. & Urban Dev., 91 F.3d 891 (7th Cir. 1996), 610
Janssen v. Holland Charter Twp. Zoning Bd. of Appeals, 651 N.W.2d 464 (Mich. Ct. App. 2002), 656
Jarvis v. Gillespie, 587 A.2d 981 (Vt. 1991), 147, 169
Javins v. First Nat'l Realty Corp., 428 F.2d 1071 (D.C. Cir. 1970), 474–475, 477
J.B. v. M.B., 751 A.2d 613 (N.J. Super. Ct. App. Div. 2000), 831
Jedlicka v. Clemmer, 677 A.2d 1232 (Pa. Super. Ct. 1996), 171
Jehovah's Witnesses v. City of Lakewood, 699 F.2d 303 (6th Cir. 1983), 674
Jehovah's Witnesses v. Woolwich Twp., 537 A.2d 1336 (N.J. Super. Ct. App. Div. 1988), 674
Jenkins v. CSX Transp., Inc., 906 S.W.2d 460 (Tenn. Ct. App. 1995), 103
Jenkins v. Johnson, 2006 WL 2506778 (Mass. Land Ct. 2006), 184
Jenkins v. New York City Dep't of Homeless Servs., 643 F. Supp. 2d 507 (S.D.N.Y. 2009), 584
Jenkins v. Wise, 574 P.2d 1337 (Haw. 1978), 565
Jesurum v. WBTSCC Ltd. P'ship, 151 A.3d 949 (N.H. 2016), 217
Jewelcor Inc., In re, 190 B.R. 532 (Bankr. M.D. Pa. 1995), 467
Jewelers Mut. Ins. Co. v. Firstar Bank Ill., 792 N.E.2d 1 (Ill. App. Ct. 2003), 435
J.H. Borland v. Sanders Lead Co., 369 So. 2d 523 (Ala. 1979), 44–45
Jiggetts v. Grinker, 553 N.E.2d 570 (N.Y. 1990), 636
Jocelyn P. v. Joshua P., 302 A.3d 1111 (Md. Ct. App. 2023), 831
John Chezik Imps., Inc., In re, 195 B.R. 417 (Bankr. E.D. Mo. 1996), 500
John Price Assocs. v. Utah State Conf., Bricklayers Locals, 615 P.2d 1210 (Utah 1980), 27
Johnson v. Becker, 903 P.2d 901 (Or. Ct. App. 1995), 220
Johnson v. Cherry, 726 S.W.2d 4 (Tex. 1987), 567
Johnson v. City of Wheat Ridge, 532 P.2d 985 (Colo. 1975), 309
Johnson v. Davis, 480 So. 2d 625 (Fla. 1985), 509–510
Johnson v. M'Intosh, 21 U.S. (8 Wheat.) 543 (1823), 773–775, 782, 784, 791
Johnson v. Nyhart, 889 P.2d 1170 (Mont. 1995), 499
Johnson v. Paynesville Farmers Union Co-op. Oil Co., 817 N.W.2d 693 (Minn. 2012), 28, 97
Johnson v. Railway Express Agency, 421 U.S. 454 (1975), 60
Johnson v. Scandia Assocs., Inc., 717 N.E.2d 24 (Ind. 1999), 474, 485
Johnson v. Settino, 245 N.E.3d 196 (Mass. 2024), 824
Johnson v. Stanley, 384 S.E.2d 577 (N.C. Ct. App. 1989), 216
Johnson v. Whiton, 34 N.E. 542 (Mass. 1893), 327
Johnson v. Zaremba, 381 F. Supp. 165 (N.D. Ill. 1973), 60, 601
Johnson-White v. Houston, 229 N.E.3d 1259 (Ohio Ct. App. 2023), 223
Joint Tribal Council of Passamaquoddy Tribe v. Morton, 528 F.2d 370 (1st Cir. 1975), 795, 802
Jolliff v. Hardin Cable Television Co., 269 N.E.2d 588 (Ohio 1971), 198
Jolly v. Eli Lilly & Co., 751 P.2d 923 (Cal. 1988), 173
Jones v. Alfred H. Mayer Co., 392 U.S. 409 (1968), 27, 47–48, 54, 61, 576, 578, 600–601
Jones v. Beavers, 269 S.E.2d 775 (Va. 1980), 200
Jones v. Cullen, 1998 WL 811558 (Minn. Ct. App. 1998), 189, 216
Jones v. Daly, 176 Cal. Rptr. 130 (Ct. App. 1981), 415
Jones v. Hart, 261 A.3d 1126 (Vt. 2021), 102
Jones v. Proctor, 697 So. 2d 304 (La. Ct. App. 1997), 485
Jones v. Rives, 680 So. 2d 450 (Fla. Dist. Ct. App. 1996), 170
Jones v. R.R. Donnelley & Sons Co., 541 U.S. 369 (2004), 55
Jones v. Wagner, 624 A.2d 166 (Pa. Super. Ct. 1993), 43, 222
Jones v. Winckelmann, 516 S.E.2d 876 (N.C. Ct. App. 1999), 213
Jones & Robbins; Commonwealth v., 41 S.E.2d 720 (Va. 1947), 503
Jordan v. Dellway Villa of Tenn., Ltd., 661 F.2d 588 (6th Cir. 1981), 593
Jordan v. Nationstar Mortg., LLC, 374 P.3d 1195 (Wash. 2016), 560
Jordan v. Rash, 745 S.W.2d 549 (Tex. App. 1988), 203
Jorgensen v. Crow, 466 N.W.2d 120 (N.D. 1991), 530
Jose; United States v., 499 F.3d 105 (1st Cir. 2007), 710
Jovana Spaghetti House, Inc. v. Heritage Co. of Massena, 592 N.Y.S.2d 879 (App. Div. 1993), 460
Judy B. v. Borough of Tioga, 889 F. Supp. 792 (M.D. Pa. 1995), 622
Julian v. Christopher, 575 A.2d 735 (Md. 1990), 491
Just v. Marinette Cnty., 201 N.W.2d 761 (Wis. 1972), 735
Jutting v. Hendrix, 606 N.W.2d 140 (S.D. 2000), 144
JWL Invs., Inc. v. Guilford Cnty. Bd. of Adjustment, 515 S.E.2d 715 (N.C. Ct. App. 1999), 736

K

Kaczynski v. Kaczynski. *See* Kavarco v. T.J.E., Inc.
Kagama; United States v., 118 U.S. 375 (1886), 803
Kahnovsky v. Kahnovsky, 21 A.2d 569 (R.I. 1941), 368
Kaiser Aetna v. United States, 444 U.S. 164 (1979), 25, 707, 708, 721–723, 745, 749
Kalenka v. Taylor, 896 P.2d 222 (Alaska 1995), 297
Kalipi v. Hawaiian Tr. Co., 656 P.2d 745 (Haw. 1982), 90
Kam-Almaz v. United States, 2012 U.S. App. LEXIS 12581 (Fed. Cir. 2012), 712

Ka Pa'akai O Ka'aina v. Land Use Comm'n, State of Haw., 7 P.3d 1068 (Haw. 2000), 89, 90
Kaplon-Belo Assocs. v. Farrelly, 633 N.Y.S.2d 522 (App. Div. 1995), 498
Karesh v. City Council of Charleston, 247 S.E.2d 342 (S.C. 1978), 687–689
Karuk Tribe of Cal. v. United States, 41 Fed. Cl. 468 (1998), *aff'd sub nom.* Karuk Tribe of Cal. v. Ammon, 209 F.3d 1366 (Fed. Cir. 2000), *cert. denied*, 532 U.S. 941 (2001), 784, 789–790
Karz v. Mecham, 174 Cal. Rptr. 310 (Ct. App. 1981), 449, 458
Kaschak, Ex parte, 681 So. 2d 197 (Ala. 1996), 463
Kass v. Kass, 1995 WL 110368 (N.Y. Sup. Ct. 1995), *rev'd*, 663 N.Y.S.2d 581 (App. Div. 1997), *aff'd*, 696 N.E.2d 174 (N.Y. 1998), 829–830, 831
Katz v. Department of Real Estate, 158 Cal. Rptr. 766 (Ct. App. 1979), 512
Katzenbach v. McClung, 379 U.S. 294 (1964), 47
Kavarco v. T.J.E., Inc., 478 A.2d 257 (Conn. App. Ct. 1984), *overruled by* Kaczynski v. Kaczynski, 981 A.2d 1068 (Conn. 2009), 510
Keck v. Doughman, 572 A.2d 724 (Pa. Super. Ct. 1990), 485
Keeble v. Hickeringill, 103 Eng. Rep. 1127 (K.B. 1707), 815
Keeler v. Mayor & City Council of Cumberland, 940 F. Supp. 879 (D. Md. 1996), 677
Keith v. Volpe, 858 F.2d 467 (9th Cir. 1988), 615
Keller v. Southwood N. Med. Pavilion, Inc., 959 P.2d 102 (Utah 1998), 184, 436–437
Kelley, Ex parte, 766 So. 2d 837 (Ala. 1999), 710
Kellner v. Cappellini, 516 N.Y.S.2d 827 (Civ. Ct. 1986), 98, 118, 123
Kelly v. Marx, 705 N.E.2d 1114 (Mass. 1999), 525
Kelly v. Schmelz, 439 S.W.2d 211 (Mo. Ct. App. 1969), 192, 197
Kelo v. City of New London, 843 A.2d 500 (Conn. 2004), *aff'd*, 545 U.S. 469 (2005), 682, 685–687, 689
Kendall v. Ernest Pestana, Inc., 709 P.2d 837 (Cal. 1985), 491
Kendall v. Lowther, 356 N.W.2d 181 (Iowa 1984), 170
Kephart v. Portmann, 855 P.2d 120 (Mont. 1993), 200
Kepler; United States v., 531 F.2d 796 (6th Cir. 1976), 664
Kerrigan v. Commissioner of Pub. Health, 957 A.2d 407 (Conn. 2008), 410
Keshbro, Inc. v. City of Miami, 801 So. 2d 864 (Fla. 2001), 123, 731
Kesler v. Marshall, 792 N.E.2d 893 (Ind. Ct. App. 2003), 526
Kessler v. Tortoise Dev., Inc., 1 P.3d 292 (Idaho 2000), 518
Keyes v. Guy Baily Homes, Inc., 439 So. 2d 670 (Miss. 1983), 514
Keys v. Romley, 412 P.2d 529 (Cal. 1966), 129
Keystone Bituminous Coal Ass'n v. DeBenedictis, 480 U.S. 470 (1987), 699–700, 707, 709, 713, 731
Key-Ventures, Inc. v. Rappleye, 556 N.Y.S.2d 627 (App. Div. 1990), 498
Kidd v. Benson, 321 So. 3d 676 (Ala. 2020), 512
Kiehm v. Adams, 126 P.3d 339 (Haw. 2006), 441
Kimball Laundry Co. v. United States, 338 U.S. 1 (1949), 708
Kimlow, Inc. v. Seminole Landing Ass'n, 586 So. 2d 1290 (Fla. Dist. Ct. App. 1991), 192
Kincheloe v. Milatzo, 678 P.2d 855 (Wyo. 1984), 238, 296
King v. Greene, 153 A.2d 49 (N.J. 1959), 358–359, 395
King v. Town of Lyme, 490 A.2d 1369 (N.H. 1985), 192
Kinghorn v. Hughes, 761 S.W.2d 930 (Ark. 1988), 360
Kinslow v. State, 860 S.E.2d 444 (Ga. 2021), 91
Kiowa Creek Land & Cattle Co. v. Nazarian, 554 N.W.2d 175 (Neb. Ct. App. 1996), 220
Kiowa Tribe of Okla. v. Manufacturing Techs., Inc., 523 U.S. 751 (1998), 772
Kipahulu Inv. Co. v. Seltzer P'ship, 675 P.2d 778 (Haw. Ct. App. 1983), 518
Kipp v. Chips Estate, 732 A.2d 127 (Vt. 1999), 360
Kirby v. North Carolina Dep't of Transp., 786 S.E.2d 919 (N.C. 2016), 741–742
Kirchberg v. Feenstra, 450 U.S. 455 (1981), 359
Kiser v. Morris, 274 S.E.2d 610 (Ga. Ct. App. 1980), 46
Kisil v. Sandusky, 465 N.E.2d 848 (Ohio 1984), 656
Kitchen v. Kitchen, 641 N.W.2d 245 (Mich. 2002), 203
Kitras v. Town of Aquinnah, 49 N.E.3d 198 (Mass. 2016), 211
Kitsap Cnty. v. Allstate Ins. Co., 964 P.2d 1173 (Wash. 1998), 45
Kiwanis Int'l v. Ridgewood Kiwanis Club, 806 F.2d 468 (3d Cir. 1986), 52
Klebs v. Yim, 772 P.2d 523 (Wash. Ct. App. 1989), 133, 134
Kline v. Bernardsville Assocs., 631 A.2d 1263 (N.J. Super. Ct. App. Div. 1993), 196
Kline v. 1500 Mass. View Apt. Corp., 439 F.2d 477 (D.C. Cir. 1970), 486–487
Klobucar v. Stancik, 485 N.E.2d 1334 (Neb. Ct. App. 1985), 200
Klosterman v. Hickel Inv. Co., 821 P.2d 118 (Alaska 1991), 460
Klutey v. Commonwealth, Dep't of Highways, 428 S.W.2d 766 (Ky. 1967), 129
Knapp v. Eagle Prop. Mgmt. Corp., 54 F.3d 1272 (7th Cir. 1995), 618
KNB Enters. v. Matthews, 92 Cal. Rptr. 2d 713 (Ct. App. 2000), 850
Knick v. Township of Scott, 588 U.S. 180 (2019), 765
Knickerbocker v. Cannon (In re Estate of Knickerbocker), 912 P.2d 969 (Utah 1996), 352
Knight v. Hallsthammar, 623 P.2d 268 (Cal. 1981), 476
Knudtson v. Trainor, 345 N.W.2d 4 (Neb. 1984), 272
Knutson v. City of Fargo, 714 N.W.2d 44 (N.D. 2006), 740
Kobrine, L.L.C. v. Metzger, 824 A.2d 1031 (Md. Ct. Spec. App. 2003), 285
Koch v. Wick, 87 So. 2d 47 (Fla. 1956), 132
Koenig v. Van Reken, 279 N.W.2d 590 (Mich. Ct. App. 1979), 566
Koeppen v. Bolich, 79 P.3d 1100 (Mont. 2003), 196
Kohler v. Flynn, 493 N.W.2d 647 (N.D. 1992), 412
Kohnen v. Hameed, 894 S.W.2d 196 (Mo. Ct. App. 1995), 448
Koontz v. St. Johns River Water Mgmt. Dist., 570 U.S. 595 (2013), 759–760, 761

Kopp v. Samaritan Health Sys., Inc., 13 F.3d 264 (8th Cir. 1993), 606
Korean Buddhist Dae Won Sa Temple of Haw. v. Sullivan, 953 P.2d 1315 (Haw. 1998), 676
Koresko v. Farley, 844 A.2d 607 (Pa. Commw. Ct. 2004), 43, 222
Kormoczy v. Secretary of Hous. & Urban Dev., 53 F.3d 821 (7th Cir. 1995), 611
Kosalka v. Town of Georgetown, 752 A.2d 183, 2000 ME 106 (Me. 2000), 647
Kosloff v. Castle, 171 Cal. Rptr. 308 (Ct. App. 1981), 565
Kozesnik v. Township of Montgomery, 131 A.2d 1 (N.J. 1957), 642
Kracl v. Loseke, 461 N.W.2d 67 (Neb. 1990), 510
Krause v. Taylor, 343 A.2d 767 (N.J. Super. Ct. App. Div. 1975), 194
Kresha v. Kresha, 371 N.W.2d 280 (Neb. 1985), 369
Kresser v. Peterson, 675 P.2d 1193 (Utah 1984), 533
Krevsky v. Equifax Check Servs., Inc., 85 F. Supp. 2d 479 (M.D. Pa. 2000), 489
Krohn, In re, 52 P.3d 774 (Ariz. 2002), 562
Krosmico v. Pettit, 968 P.2d 345 (Okla. 1998), 144
Kruger v. Shramek, 565 N.W.2d 742 (Neb. Ct. App. 1997), 221
Kruvant v. 12-22 Woodland Ave. Corp., 350 A.2d 102 (N.J. Super. Ct. 1975), *aff'd*, 376 A.2d 188 (App. Div. 1997), 217
Kucera v. Lizza, 69 Cal. Rptr. 2d 582 (Ct. App. 1997), 221
Kunst v. Pass, 957 P.2d 1 (Mont. 1998), 485
Kuntz v. Leiss, 952 N.W.2d 35 (N.D. 2020), 27

L

LaBorde, In re, 231 B.R. 162 (Bankr. W.D.N.Y. 1999), 358
Lacer v. Navajo Cnty., 687 P.2d 404 (Ariz. Ct. App. 1983), 259, 295
Ladd v. Marchbanks, 971 F.3d 574 (6th Cir. 2020), 765
Ladue, City of v. Gilleo, 512 U.S. 43 (1994), 673–674
Ladue, City of v. Horn, 720 S.W.2d 745 (Mo. Ct. App. 1986), 627
LaFond v. Rumler, 574 N.W.2d 40 (Mich. Ct. App. 1998), 284
Lakatos v. Estate of Billotti, 509 S.E.2d 594 (W. Va. 1998), 350
Lake Anne Homeowners Ass'n v. Lake Anne Realty Corp., 640 N.Y.S.2d 200 (App. Div. 1996), 193
Lake Arrowhead Cmty. Club, Inc. v. Looney, 770 P.2d 1046 (Wash. 1989), 244
Lakeside Resort Enters., LP v. Board of Supervisors of Palmyra Twp., 455 F.3d 143 (2d Cir. 2006), 583
Lakewood Racquet Club, Inc. v. Jensen, 232 P.3d 1147 (Wash. Ct. App. 2010), 259
Lamar Adver. v. Larry & Vicki Nicholls, LLC, 213 P.3d 641 (Wyo. 2009), 329
Lamar Adver. of S. Ga., Inc. v. City of Albany, 389 S.E.2d 216 (Ga. 1990), 654
Lamb v. Decatur Fed'l Sav. & Loan Ass'n, 411 S.E.2d 527 (Ga. Ct. App. 1991), 463
Lamb v. Sallee, 417 F. Supp. 282 (E.D. Ky. 1976), 601
Landers v. Municipality of Anchorage, 915 P.2d 614 (Alaska 1996), 459
Landgray Assocs. v. 450 Lexington Venture, LP, 788 F. Supp. 776 (S.D.N.Y. 1992), 297
Landmark Nat'l Bank v. Kessler, 192 P.3d 177 (Kan. Ct. App. 2008), 572
Lane v. Pueblo of Santa Rosa, 249 U.S. 110 (1919), 802
Lane v. W.J. Curry & Sons, 92 S.W.3d 355 (Tenn. 2002), 43, 102, 117
Lange v. Scofield, 567 So. 2d 1299 (Ala. 1990), 295
Lange v. Wyoming Nat'l Bank, 706 P.2d 659 (Wyo. 1985), *appeal after remand*, 741 P.2d 109 (1987), 529
Langlois v. Abington Hous. Auth., 207 F.3d 43 (1st Cir. 2000), 615–616, 618
Lapon; Commonwealth v., 554 N.E.2d 1225 (Mass. App. Ct. 1990), 35, 182
Lara v. Cinemark USA, Inc., 207 F.3d 783 (5th Cir. 2000), 69
Larkin v. State of Mich. Dep't of Soc. Servs., 89 F.3d 285 (6th Cir. 1996), 623–624
LaSalle Bank Nat'l Ass'n v. Lamy, 824 N.Y.S.2d 769, 2006 WL 2251721 (Sup. Ct. 2006), 572
Las Vegas, City of v. 180 Land Co., LLC, 546 P.3d 1239 (Nev. 2024), 733
Lathem v. Hestley, 514 S.E.2d 440 (Ga. 1999), 205–206
Lawrence v. National Fruit Co., 1997 WL 1070444 (Va. Cir. Ct. 1997), 200–201
Lawrence v. Texas, 539 U.S. 558 (2003), 408, 415
Lawrence v. Town of Concord, 788 N.E.2d 546 (Mass. 2003), 146
Lawton v. Steele, 152 U.S. 133 (1894), 668
Lay v. Inhabitants of Town of Merrimac, 24 Mass. Lawyers Weekly 2460 (Aug. 8, 1996), 88
Layton v. A.I. Namm & Sons, 89 N.Y.S.2d 72 (App. Div. 1949), *aff'd*, 98 N.E.2d 590 (N.Y. 1951), 184, 428
Leardi v. Brown, 474 N.E.2d 1094 (Mass. 1985), 488
Leasehold Interest in 121 Nostrand Ave.; United States v., 760 F. Supp. 1015 (E.D.N.Y. 1991), 710
LeBlanc-Sternberg v. Fletcher, 67 F.3d 412 (2d Cir. 1995), 587, 615, 628
Lechmere v. National Labor Relations Bd., 502 U.S. 527 (1992), 84
Lee v. Schultz, 425 N.W.2d 380 (S.D. 1988), 127
Lee v. Snell, 25 Mass. Lawyers Weekly 1210 (Mass. Probate Ct., Feb. 10, 1997), 357
Leffingwell v. Glendenning, 238 S.W.2d 942 (Ark. 1951), 42
LEG Invs. v. Boxler, 107 Cal. Rptr. 3d 519 (2010), 362
Leighton v. Leonard, 589 P.2d 279 (Wash. Ct. App. 1978), 539
LeMay v. Anderson, 397 A.2d 984 (Me. 1979), 208
Lemle v. Breeden, 462 P.2d 470 (Haw. 1969), 477
Lemon v. Curington, 306 P.2d 1091 (Idaho 1957), 43
Lemont Land Corp. v. Rogers, 887 P.2d 724 (Mont. 1994), 218
Lempke v. Dagenais, 547 A.2d 290 (N.H. 1988), 514, 521
Lenhart v. Desmond, 705 P.2d 338 (Wyo. 1985), 533
Lennon v. United States Theatre Corp., 920 F.2d 996 (D.C. Cir. 1990), 463
Leonard v. Pugh, 356 S.E.2d 812 (N.C. Ct. App. 1987), 191
Leonardini v. Shell Oil Co., 264 Cal. Rptr. 883 (Ct. App. 1989), 672

Lerman v. Levine, 541 A.2d 523 (Conn. App. Ct.), *appeal denied*, 546 A.2d 281 (Conn. 1988), 366
Levandusky v. One Fifth Ave. Apartment Corp., 553 N.E.2d 1317 (N.Y. 1990), 379
Levin v. Yeshiva Univ., 754 N.E.2d 1099 (N.Y. 2001), 621
Lew v. Superior Court, 25 Cal. Rptr. 2d 42 (Ct. App. 1993), 98, 118, 123
Lewis v. Harris, 908 A.2d 196 (N.J. 2006), 409
Lewis v. JC Penney Co., 948 F. Supp. 367 (D. Del. 1996), 55, 58–59
Lewis v. Searles, 452 S.W.2d 153 (Mo. 1970), 343
Lewis v. Young, 705 N.E.2d 649 (N.Y. 1998), 196
Lewis-Levett v. Day, 875 N.E.2d 293 (Ind. Ct. App. 2008), 276
Leydon v. Town of Greenwich, 750 A.2d 1122 (Conn. App. Ct. 2000), *aff'd*, 777 A.2d 552 (Conn. 2001), 86
Lieb v. Roman Dev. Co., 716 S.W.2d 653 (Tex. App. 1986), 519
Liesner v. Wanie, 145 N.W. 374 (Wis. 1914), 814
Lincoln v. Burbank, 147 A.3d 1165 (Me. 2016), 217
Lindh v. Surman, 742 A.2d 643 (Pa. 1999), 823–824
Lindsey, In re Marriage of, 678 P.2d 328 (Wash. 1984), 412–414
Lindsey v. Normet, 405 U.S. 56 (1972), 461, 478
Lingle v. Chevron U.S.A. Inc., 544 U.S. 528 (2005), 707, 717
Lingsch v. Savage, 29 Cal. Rptr. 201 (Ct. App. 1963), 510
Lingvall v. Bartmess, 982 P.2d 690 (Wash. Ct. App. 1999), 215
Linmark Assocs., Inc. v. Township of Willingboro, 431 U.S. 85 (1977), 673
Litowitz, In re Marriage of, 48 P.3d 261 (Wash. 2002), 831
Littlefield v. Mack, 750 F. Supp. 1395 (N.D. Ill. 1990), 597
Little Rock v. Raines, 411 S.W.2d 486 (Ark. 1967), 688
LivingWell (N.) Inc. v. Pennsylvania Human Relations Comm'n, 606 A.2d 1287 (Pa. Commw. Ct. 1992), 72
Lloyd Corp. v. Tanner, 407 U.S. 551 (1972), 78–80, 722–723
Lloyd Corp. v. Whiffen, 773 P.2d 1294 (Or. 1989), 82
Lloyd Corp. v. Whiffen, 813 P.2d 573 (Or. 1991), 82
LoBianco v. Clark, 596 N.E.2d 56 (Ill. App. Ct. 1992), 291
Locke v. O'Brien, 610 A.2d 552 (R.I. 1992), 166
Locklin v. City of Lafayette, 867 P.2d 724 (Cal. 1994), 129
Lockwood v. Killian, 375 A.2d 998 (Conn. 1977), 279
Logan v. McGee, 320 So. 2d 792 (Miss. 1975), 213
Lohmeyer v. Bower, 227 P.2d 102 (Kan. 1951), 520
Lombardo v. Albu, 14 P.3d 288 (Ariz. 2000), 502
Lone Wolf v. Hitchcock, 187 U.S. 553 (1903), 744, 773, 785–788, 791, 803
Long v. Dilling Mech. Contractors, Inc., 705 N.E.2d 1022 (Ind. Ct. App. 1999), 816
Long's Estate, In re, 5 Pa. D. & C.3d 602 (1978), 279, 322
Looney v. Famers Home Admin., 794 F.2d 310 (7th Cir. 1986), 565
Lopardo v. Flemming Cos., 97 F.3d 921 (7th Cir. 1996), 130
Lopez v. William Raveis Real Est., Inc., 272 A.3d 150 (Conn. 2022), 630
Lorantffy Care Ctr.; United States v., 999 F. Supp. 1037 (N.D. Ohio 1998), 583
Lord v. Society for Preservation of New England Antiquities, Inc., 639 A.2d 623 (Me. 1994), 319
Loren v. Marry, 600 N.Y.S.2d 369 (App. Div. 1993), 436
Loretto v. Teleprompter Manhattan CATV Corp., 458 U.S. 419 (1982), 24–25, 708, 718–719, 710, 722–723, 728, 757
Los Angeles Cnty. v. Continental Dev. Corp., 941 P.2d 809 (Cal. 1997), 692
Lotito v. Mazzeo, 518 N.Y.S.2d 22 (App. Div. 1987), 524
Lotz Realty Co. v. Department of Hous. & Urban Dev., 717 F.2d 929 (4th Cir. 1983), 614
Loughhead v. 1717 Bissonnet, LLC, 2014 WL 8774060 (Tex. Dist. Ct.), *final judgment*, 2014 WL 8774079 (Tex. Dist. Ct. May 1, 2014), *aff'd in part and rev'd in part*, 500 S.W.3d 488 (Tex. App. 2016), 111, 120
Louisiana Acorn Fair Hous. v. Quarter House, Inc., 952 F. Supp. 352 (E.D. La. 1997), 584
Love v. Amsler, 441 N.W.2d 555 (Minn. Ct. App. 1989), 487
Love v. Klosky, 413 P.3d 1267 (Colo. 2018), 43
Love v. McDevitt, 152 S.E.2d 705 (Ga. Ct. App. 1991), 463
Loveladies Harbor, Inc. v. United States, 15 Cl. Ct. 381 (1988), 735
Loveladies Harbor, Inc. v. United States, 21 Cl. Ct. 153 (1990), 735
Loveladies Harbor, Inc. v. United States, 28 F.3d 1171 (Fed. Cir. 1994), 733, 735, 737
Loveridge v. United States, 148 Fed. Cl. 279 (2020), 192
Loving v. Virginia, 388 U.S. 1 (1967), 344, 407
Lowenburg v. City of Saraland, 489 So. 2d 562 (Ala. 1986), 255
Lucas v. Hamm, 364 P.2d 685 (Cal. 1961), 330
Lucas v. Independent Sch. Dist. No. 284, 433 N.W.2d 94 (Minn. 1988), 516, 517
Lucas v. Rawl Family Ltd. P'ship, 598 S.E.2d 712 (S.C. 2004), 128
Lucas v. South Carolina Coastal Council, 404 S.E.2d 895 (S.C. 1991), *rev'd and remanded*, 505 U.S. 1003 (1992), 663, 694, 714, 720, 728–732, 735–740, 755
Lugosi v. Universal Pictures, 603 P.2d 425 (Cal. 1979), 849
Luis v. United States, 578 U.S. 5 (2016), 710
Lusk v. Broyles, 694 So. 2d 4 (Ala. Civ. App. 1997), 314
Lynch v. Andrew, 481 N.E.2d 1383 (Mass. App. Ct. 1985), 525
Lytle v. Harden, 275 P. 45 (Or. 1929), 325
Lytle v. Household Mfg., Inc., 494 U.S. 545 (1990), 57, 601

M

Mabee v. Nordic Aquafarms Inc., 290 A.3d 79 (Me. 2023), 243
MacDonald, Sommer & Frates v. Yolo Cnty., 477 U.S. 340 (1986), 766
MacFadden v. Walker, 488 P.2d 1353 (Cal. 1971), 565
Machado v. Ryan, 280 P.3d 715 (Idaho 2012), 210
Machipongo Land & Coal Co. v. Commonwealth, 799 A.2d 751 (Pa. 2002), 707
Macke Laundry Serv. Co. v. Overgaard, 433 N.W.2d 813 (Mich. Ct. App. 1989), 436
MacMeekin v. Low Income Hous. Inst., Inc., 45 P.3d 570 (Wash. Ct. App. 2002), 196

MacMillan v. City of Jackson, 701 So. 2d 1105 (Miss. 1997), 39
MacMillan Bloedell, Inc. v. Ezell, 475 So. 2d 493 (Alaska 1985), 29
MacNeil v. Time Ins. Co., 205 F.3d 179 (5th Cir. 2000), 64
Macone v. Town of Wakefield, 277 F.3d 1 (1st Cir. 2002), 668
Maddocks v. Giles, 728 A.2d 150 (Me. 1999), 132
Maddy v. Vulcan Materials Co., 737 F. Supp. 1528 (D. Kan. 1990), 45
Magadini; Commonwealth v., 52 N.E.3d 1041 (Mass. 2016), 39, 635
Maglione v. BancBoston Mortg. Corp., 557 N.E.2d 756 (Mass. App. Ct. 1990), 556
Mains Farm Homeowners Ass'n v. Worthington, 824 P.2d 495 (Wash. Ct. App. 1992), *aff'd on reh'g*, 854 P.2d 1072 (Wash. 1993), 272–274
Maioriello v. Arlotta, 73 A.2d 374 (Pa. 1950), 136
Maisel, In re, 378 B.R. 19 (Bankr. D. Mass. 2007), 572
Malanga v. Township of W. Orange, 290 A.3d 1212 (N.J. 2023), 689
Malcolm v. Shamie, 290 N.W.2d 101 (Mich. Ct. App. 1980), 272–273
Mallin v. Good, 417 N.E.2d 858 (Ill. App. Ct. 1981), 535
Mallock v. Southern Mem'l Park, Inc., 561 So. 2d 330 (Fla. Dist. Ct. App. 1990), 210
Malmquist v. Malmquist, 792 P.2d 372 (Nev. 1990), 404
M & I First Nat'l Bank v. Episcopal Homes Mgmt., Inc., 536 N.W.2d 175 (Wis. Ct. App. 1995), 436
Manhattan Mansions v. Moe's Pizza, 561 N.Y.S.2d 331 (Civ. Ct. 1990), 480
Mann v. Mann, 671 N.E.2d 73 (Ill. App. Ct. 1996), 443
Mannillo v. Gorski, 241 A.2d 276 (N.J. Super. Ct. 1968), *rev'd*, 255 A.2d 258 (N.J. 1969), 146, 152–153, 169
Mansion Realty LLC v. 656 6th Ave Gym LLC, 190 N.Y.S.3d 259 (Sup. Ct. N.Y. Cnty. 2023), 463
Marable v. H. Walker & Assocs., 644 F.2d 390 (5th Cir. 1981), 593, 602
Marbrunak, Inc. v. City of Stow, Ohio, 974 F.2d 43 (6th Cir. 1992), 623
Marchetti v. Karpowich, 667 A.2d 724 (Pa. Super. Ct. 1995), 361
Marcus Cable Assocs. v. Krohn, 90 S.W.3d 697 (Tex. 2002), 192
Marder v. Realty Constr. Co., 202 A.2d 175 (N.J. Super. Ct. App. Div. 1964), 29
Mardis v. Brantley, 717 So. 2d 702 (La. Ct. App. 1998), 281, 329
Mark v. State Dep't of Fish & Wildlife, 84 P.3d (Ot. Ct. App. 2004), 117
Markese v. Cooper, 333 N.Y.S.2d 63 (Monroe Cnty. Ct. 1972), 483
Markham v. Colonial Mortg. Serv. Co., 605 F.2d 566 (D.C. Cir. 1979), 613
Markoe v. Naiditch & Sons, 226 N.W.2d 289 (Minn. 1975), 463
Marks v. City of Chesapeake, 883 F.2d 308 (4th Cir. 1989), 667
Markstein v. Countryside I, L.L.C., 77 P.3d 389 (Wyo. 2003), 183
Marriage Cases, In re, 183 P.2d 384 (Cal. 2008), 410
Marriage of. *See name of party*
Marsden, In re Marriage of, 181 Cal. Rptr. 910 (Ct. App. 1982), 404
Marsh v. Alabama, 326 U.S. 501 (1946), 76–80
Martin v. Boise, City of, 920 F.3d 584 (9th Cir. 2019), 39, 634–635
Martin v. Carter, 400 A.2d 326 (D.C. 1979), 552
Martin v. Linden, City of, 667 So. 2d 732 (Ala. 1995), 132
Martin v. PGA Tour, Inc., 984 F. Supp. 1320 and 994 F. Supp. 1242 (D. Or. 1998), *aff'd*, 204 F.3d 994 (9th Cir.), *aff'd*, 532 U.S. 661 (2001), 67–68
Martin v. Reynolds Metals Co., 342 P.2d 790 (Or. 1959), 44–45
Martin v. Seattle, City of, 765 P.2d 257 (Wash. 1988), 308
Martin v. Seeley, 142 N.Y.S.3d 252 (App. Div. 2021), 340
Martin v. Simmons Props., LLC, 2 N.E.3d 886 (Mass. 2014), 196
Martin v. Struthers, 319 U.S. 141 (1943), 76
Martinez v. Martinez, 678 P.2d 1163 (N.M. 1984), 532–533
Martinez v. Sonoma-Cutrer Vineyards, 577 F. Supp. 451 (N.D. Cal. 1983), 440
Martinez-Noda v. Pascual, 305 So. 3d 321 (Fla. Dist. Ct. App. 2020), 365
Martin Luther King, Jr. Ctr. for Soc. Change v. American Heritage Prods., 296 S.E.2d 697 (Ga. 1982), 850–852
Martino v. Fleenor, 365 P.2d 247 (Colo. 1961), 211
Marvin v. Marvin, 557 P.2d 106 (Cal. 1976), 411–412
Marvin M. Brandt Revocable Tr. v. United States, 572 U.S. 93 (2014), 743, 747–748
Maryville Sav. & Loan Corp., In re, 31 B.R. 597 (Bankr. E.D. Tenn. 1983), *aff'd in part and rev'd in part*, 743 F.2d 413 (6th Cir. 1984), *opinion supplemented by* 760 F.2d 119 (6th Cir. 1985), 556
Mashpee Tribe v. New Seabury Corp., 592 F.2d 575 (1st Cir. 1979), 795
Mason v. Garrison, 998 P.2d 531 (Mont. 2000), 193
Mason v. Loveless, 24 P.3d 997 (Utah Ct. App. 2001), 171
Mason v. United States, 260 U.S. 545 (1923), 778
Masonic Bldg. Ass'n of Houston v. McWhorter, 177 S.W.3d 465 (Tex. App. 2005), 153
Massachusetts v. Exxon Mobil Corp., 462 F. Supp. 3d 31 (D. Mass. 2020), 126
Massachusetts v. H & R Block, Inc., 2008 Mass. Super. LEXIS 427 (Nov. 25, 2008), 567
Massachusetts Comm'n Against Discrimination v. Management Realty Co., No. 98 BPR 1013, 2003 Mass. Comm. Discrim. LEXIS 11 (2003), 603
Masterpiece Cakeshop, Inc. v. Colorado Civil Rights Comm'n, 584 U.S. 617 (2018), 73–74
Matal v. Tam, 582 U.S. 218 (2017), 53, 846
Matcha v. Mattox, 711 S.W.2d 95 (Tex. App. 1986), 88
Mathurin v. Lost & Found Recovery, LLC, 9 Misc. 3d 756 (N.Y. Sup. Ct. 2008), 566
Mattas Motors, Inc. v. Heritage Homes of Neb., Inc., 749 P.2d 458 (Colo. Ct. App. 1987), 449, 458
Matte v. Shippee Auto, Inc., 876 A.2d 167 (N.H. 2005), 429
Matter of. *See name of party*
Matthew v. Smith, 707 S.W.2d 411 (Mo. 1986), 656
Matthews v. Bay Head Improvement Ass'n, 471 A.2d 355 (N.J. 1984), 86–87

Matthews v. Pernell, 582 N.E.2d 1075 (Ohio Ct. App. 1990), 123
Mavromoustakos v. Padussis, 684 A.2d 51 (Md. Ct. Spec. App. 1996), 218
Maxton Builders, Inc. v. Lo Galbo, 502 N.E.2d 184 (N.Y. 1986), 525
May v. May, 300 S.E.2d 215 (Ga. Ct. App. 1983), 428
Mayor & City Council of Balt. v. BP plc, 952 F.3d 452 (4th Cir. 2020), 126
May P'ship v. Barker, 431 S.E.2d 331 (Va. 1993), 498
Mays v. Hogue, 260 S.E.2d 291 (W. Va. 1979), 190
Mazdabrook Commons Homeowners' Ass'n v. Khan, 46 A.3d 507 (N.J. 2012), 290
McBarron v. Kipling Woods, LLC, 838 A.2d 490 (N.J. Super. Ct. App. Div. 2004), 507
McBryde Sugar Co. v. Robinson, 504 P.2d 1330 (Haw.), 517 P.2d 26 (Haw. 1973), 90, 753
McCain v. Koch, 511 N.E.2d 62 (N.Y. 1987), 636
McCaleb v. Pizza Hut of Am., Inc., 28 F. Supp. 2d 1043 (N.D. Ill. 1998), 56, 57, 59
McCarthy v. Tobin, 706 N.E.2d 629 (Mass. 1999), 507, 522
McClelland v. DeWulf, 2000 WL 557929 (Minn. Ct. App. 2000), 516, 518
McClure Mgmt., LLC v. Taylor, 849 S.E.2d 604 (W. Va. 2020), 71
McCoy v. Love, 382 So. 2d 647 (Fla. 1980), 552–553
McCrea v. Marsh, 78 Mass. (12 Gray) 211 (1858), 31
McCready v. Hoffius, 586 N.W.2d 723 (Mich. 1998), *vacated in part and remanded*, 593 N.W.2d 545 (Mich. 1999), 613
McCrory v. Johnson, 755 S.W.2d 566 (Ark. 1988), 460
McCulloch & Parker, In re Marriage of, 546 P.3d 109 (Ariz. Ct. App. 2024), 821
McCutchan Estates Corp. v. Evansville-Vanderburgh Cnty. Airport Auth. Dist., 580 N.E.2d 339 (Ind. Ct. App. 1991), 662
McDaniel v. Calvert, 875 S.W.2d 482 (Tex. App. 1994), 198
McDonald v. Halvorson, 780 P.2d 714 (Or. 1989), 88, 89, 754
McDonald v. Harris, 978 P.2d 81 (Alaska 1999), 213–215, 217, 219
McDonnell v. Cisneros, 84 F.3d 256 (7th Cir. 1996), 607
McDonnell Douglas Corp. v. Green, 411 U.S. 792 (1973), 592
McElveen-Hunter v. Fountain Manor Ass'n, Inc., 386 S.E.2d 435 (N.C. Ct. App. 1989), 374, 378
McFadden v. Elma Country Club, 613 P.2d 146 (Wash. Ct. App. 1980), 613
McGinley v. Franklin Sports, Inc., 92 F. Supp. 2d 1216 (D. Kan. 2000), *rev'd*, 262 F.3d 1339 (Fed. Cir. 2001), 842–843
McGrath v. Dockendorf, 793 S.E.2d 336 (Va. 2016), 823
McIntyre v. Scarbrough, 471 S.E.2d 199 (Ga. 1996), 320
McKennon v. Nashville Banner Publ'g Co., 513 U.S. 352 (1995), 593
McLaurin v. McLaurin, 217 S.E.2d 41 (S.C. 1975), 306
McMaster; Doe v., 585 S.E.2d 773 (S.C. 2003), 503
McMinn v. Town of Oyster Bay, 488 N.E.2d 1240 (N.Y. 1985), 627, 669
McNamara v. Wilmington Mall Realty Corp., 466 S.E.2d 324 (N.C. Ct. App. 1996), 472
McNulty v. Chip, 116 A.3d 173 (R.I. 2015), 512–513
McPherson v. Michigan High Sch. Athletic Ass'n, Inc., 90 F.3d 129 (6th Cir. 1996), 67
McQueen v. Black, 425 N.W.2d 203 (Mich. Ct. App. 1988), 153
Meadows v. Edgewood Mgmt. Corp., 432 F. Supp. 334 (W.D. Va. 1977), 721
Meadows Country Club, Inc. v. Unnever, 702 So. 2d 586 (Fla. Dist. Ct. App. 1997), 193
Mease v. Fox, 200 N.W.2d 791 (Iowa 1972), 477
Mecimore v. Cothren, 428 S.E.2d 470 (N.C. Ct. App. 1993), 217
Medical Lab. Mgmt. Consultants v. ABC, Inc., 30 F. Supp. 2d 1182 (D. Ariz. 1998), 35–36, 41
Medical Soc'y of S.C.; United States v., 298 F. Supp. 145 (D.S.C. 1969), 48
Med Mac Realty Co. v. Lerner, 547 N.Y.S.2d 65 (App. Div. 1989), 490
Meinhard v. Salmon, 164 N.E. 545 (N.Y. 1928), 384
Melms v. Pabst Brewing Co., 79 N.W. 738 (Wis. 1899), 321
Melnick v. C.S.X. Corp., 540 A.2d 1133 (Md. 1988), 43
Melson v. Cook, 545 So. 2d 796 (Ala. Ct. App. 1989), 448
Memmert v. Mckeen, 4 A. 542 (Pa. 1886), 519
Memphis, City of v. Greene, 451 U.S. 100 (1981), 600–601
Menominee Tribe of Indians v. United States, 101 Ct. Cl. 10 (1944), 802
Mercado v. Calumet Fed. Sav. & Loan Ass'n, 763 F.2d 269 (7th Cir. 1985), 514
Mercantile-Safe Deposit & Tr. Co. v. Mayor & City Council of Balt., 521 A.2d 734 (Md. 1987), 253
Mercer v. Rockwell Int'l Corp., 24 F. Supp. 2d 735 (W.D. Ky. 1998), 45
Meritor Sav. Bank, FSB v. Vinson, 477 U.S. 57 (1986), 604
Merrion v. Jicarilla Apache Tribe, 455 U.S. 130 (1982), 781
Mertens v. Wolfeboro Nat'l Bank, 402 A.2d 1335 (N.H. 1979), 509
Messiah Baptist Church v. County of Jefferson, 859 F.2d 820 (10th Cir. 1988), 674
Metro-Goldwyn-Mayer Studios v. Grokster, Inc., 545 U.S. 913 (2005), 840
Metromedia, Inc. v. City of San Diego, 453 U.S. 490 (1981), 673
Metropolitan Bd. of Zoning v. McDonald's Corp., 481 N.E.2d 141 (Ind. Ct. App. 1985), 656
Metropolitan Hous. Dev. Corp. v. Village of Arlington Heights, 558 F.2d 1283 (7th Cir. 1977), 615
Metropolitan Nat'l Bank v. United States, 901 F.2d 1297 (5th Cir. 1990), 539
Metzner v. Wojdyla, 886 P.2d 154 (Wash. 1994), 276
Meyer v. Holley, 537 U.S. 280 (2003), 599
Meyer v. Meyer, 620 N.W.2d 382 (Wis. 2000), 400
Meyers v. American Oil Co., 5 So. 2d 218 (Miss. 1941), 556
MHANY Mgmt., Inc. v. County of Nassau, 819 F.3d 581 (2d Cir. 2016), 595, 615, 617
MHC Fin. Ltd. P'ship v. City of San Rafael, 714 F.3d 1118 (9th Cir. 2013), 738
Miami, City of v. Keshbro, Inc., 717 So. 2d 601 (Fla. Dist. Ct. App. 1998), *partially aff'd and partially rev'd*, 801 So. 2d 864 (Fla. 2001), 123

Michigan v. Dizzy Duck, 535 N.W.2d 178 (Mich. 1995), 123
Mi Co. v. McLean, 482 S.E.2d 597 (S.C. Ct. App. 1997), 543
Middagh v. Stanal Sound Ltd., 452 N.W.2d 260 (Neb. 1990), 464
Middelthon v. Crowder, 563 So. 2d 94 (Fla. Dist. Ct. App. 1990), 522
Midkiff; State v., 516 P.2d 1250 (Haw. 1973), 692
Midlake on Big Boulder Lake Condo. Ass'n v. Cappuccio, 673 A.2d 340 (Pa. Super. Ct. 1996), 289
Midler v. Ford Motor Co., 849 F.2d 460 (9th Cir. 1988), 851
Midrash Sephardi, Inc. v. Town of Surfside, 366 F.3d 1214 (11th Cir. 2004), 628
Mid-State Inv. Corp. v. O'Steen, 133 So. 2d 455 (Fla. 1961), 564
Mid-Valley Res., Inc. v. Engelson, 13 P.3d 118 (Or. Ct. App. 2000), 152–153
Mihalczo v. Borough of Woodmont, 400 A.2d 270 (Conn. 1978), 220
Miller v. California Speedway Corp., 536 F.3d 1020 (9th Cir. 2008), 69
Miller v. C.W. Meyers Trading Post, Inc., 355 S.E.2d 189 (N.C. Ct. App. 1987), 478
Miller v. Estate of Dawson, 686 S.W.2d 443 (Ark. Ct. App. 1985), 523
Miller v. Schoene, 276 U.S. 272 (1928), 702, 709, 724, 730
Miller, In re Succession of, 479 So. 2d 1035 (La. Ct. App. 1985), 419
Miller & Desatnik Mgmt. Co. v. Bullock, 270 Cal. Rptr. 600 (App. Dep't Super Ct. 1990), 447
Miller Brewing Co. v. Falstaff Brewing Co., 655 F.2d 5 (1st Cir. 1980), 846
Minieri v. Knittel, 727 N.Y.S.2d 872 (Sup. Ct. 2001), 415
Minjak v. Randolph, 528 N.Y.S.2d 554 (App. Div. 1988), 471
Minneapolis & St. Louis R.R. v. Beckwith, 129 U.S. 26 (1889), 788
Minnesota v. Mille Lacs Band of Chippewa Indians, 526 U.S. 172 (1999), 806
Mississippi Power Co. v. Fairchild, 791 So. 2d 262 (Miss. Ct. App. 2001), 210
Mister v. A.R.K. P'ship, 553 N.E.2d 1152 (Ill. App. Ct. 1990), 612–613
Mister Donut of Am., Inc. v. Kemp, 330 N.E.2d 810 (Mass. 1975), 549–550
Mitchel v. United States, 34 U.S. 711 (1835), 782, 785, 790
Mitchell v. United States, 313 U.S. 80 (1941), 47
Mitchell; United States v., 445 U.S. 535 (1980), 773–774, 780, 791, 803
Mitchell; United States v., 463 U.S. 206 (1983), 774, 780, 803
Mitchell; United States v., 580 F.2d 789 (5th Cir. 1978), 615
Mobil Oil Corp. v. Pegasus Petroleum Corp., 818 F.2d 254 (2d Cir. 1987), 847
Mohegan Tribe v. Connecticut, 483 F. Supp. 597 (D. Conn. 1980), *aff'd*, 638 F.2d 612 (2d Cir. 1981), 795
Mohr v. Gomez, 662 N.Y.S.2d 979 (App. Term 1997), 439
Mohr v. Midas Realty Corp., 431 N.W.2d 380 (Iowa 1988), 221
Mokar Props. Corp. v. Hall, 179 N.Y.S.2d 814 (App. Div. 1958), 523
Moloney v. Awad, 550 N.Y.S.2d 91 (App. Div. 1989), 507
Monadnock Rod & Gun Club v. Town of Peterborough, 336 A.3d 909 (N.H. 2024), 646
Monfee v. Seymore, 392 So. 2d 1198 (Ala. Civ. App. 1980), 46
Montano v. Bonnie Brae Convalescent Hosp. Inc., 79 F. Supp. 3d 1120 (C.D. Cal. 2015), 583
Monterey, City of v. Del Monte Dunes at Monterey, Ltd., 526 U.S. 687 (1999), 759, 765
Monumental Props., Inc.; Commonwealth v., 329 A.2d 812 (Pa. 1974), 487
Moody Nat'l Buffalo Speedway MT, LP v. Sirius Sols., LLLP, 2013 WL 315932 (Tex. App. 2013), 451
Moore v. Cameron Parish Sch. Bd., 563 So. 2d 347 (La. Ct. App. 1990), 467
Moore v. City of E. Cleveland, 431 U.S. 494 (1977), 627, 669
Moore v. Dudley, 904 S.W.2d 496 (E.D. Mo. 1995), 166
Moore v. Leveris, 495 S.E.2d 153 (N.C. Ct. App. 1998), 193
Moore v. Regents of the Univ. of Cal., 793 P.2d 479 (Cal. 1990), 828
Morehouse v. Dux N. LLC, 226 N.E.3d 758 (Ind. 2024), 210
Moreno v. Stahmann Farms, Inc., 693 F.2d 106 (10th Cir. 1982), 439
Morgan v. Kroupa, 702 A.2d 630 (Vt. 1997), 816
Morgan v. Wiser, 711 S.W.2d 220 (Tenn. Ct. App. 1985), 818–819
Morillo v. City of N.Y., 574 N.Y.S.2d 459 (Sup. Ct. 1991), 636
Morone v. Morone, 413 N.E.2d 1154 (N.Y. 1980), 412
Morris v. Cizek, 503 F.2d 1303 (7th Cir. 1974), 60, 601
Morris v. Nease, 238 S.E.2d 844 (W. Va. 1977), 296
Morris v. Office Max, Inc., 89 F.3d 411 (7th Cir. 1996), 58
Morris v. Solesbee, 892 S.W.2d 281 (Ark. Ct. App. 1995), 358
Morris v. Weigle, 383 N.E.2d 341 (Ind. 1978), 564
Morris Assocs., Inc. v. Priddy, 383 S.E.2d 770 (W. Va. 1989), 129
Morrison v. Piper, 566 N.E.2d 643 (N.Y. 1990), *appeal after remand*, 567 N.Y.S.2d 903 (App. Div. 1991), 331
Morrison v. Potter, 764 A.2d 234 (D.C. 2000), 358
Morrison v. Smith, 757 S.W.2d 678 (Tenn. Ct. App. 1988), 471
Morrissey v. Haley, 865 P.2d 961 (Idaho 1993), 170
Morse v. Curtis, 2 N.E. 929 (Mass. 1885), 547
Mortgage Elec. Registration Sys., Inc. v. Revoredo, 955 So. 2d 33 (Fla. Dist. Ct. App. 2007), 571–572
Moseley v. Bishop, 470 N.E.2d 773 (Ind. Ct. App. 1984), 247
Mountain Side Mobile Estates v. HUD, 56 F.3d 1243 (10th Cir. 1995), 615
Mount Holly Gardens Citizens in Action Inc. v. Mount Holly, N.J., 658 F.3d 375 (3d Cir. 2011), 615, 617
M.P.M. Builders v. Dwyer, 809 N.E.2d 1053 (Mass. 2004), 196

Mucci v. Brockton Bocce Club, Inc., 472 N.E.2d 966 (Mass. App. Ct. 1985), 516
Mueller v. Hoblyn, 887 P.2d 500 (Wyo. 1994), 223
Mugler v. Kansas, 123 U.S. 623 (1887), 695, 699–700, 706, 730–731
Muhr v. Willenborg, 6 N.W.3d 752 (Iowa Ct. App. 2024), 363
Muirloch Realty, Inc. v. Periodical Charter & Leasing, Inc., 1996 WL 17579 (Ohio Ct. App. 1996), 498–499
Muldawer v. Stribling, 256 S.E.2d 357 (Ga. 1979), 250–251
Mulkey v. Waggoner, 338 S.E.2d 755 (Ga. Ct. App. 1985), 512
Mullendore Theatres, Inc. v. Growth Realty Inv'rs Co., 691 P.2d 970 (Wash. Ct. App. 1984), 257
Mulligan v. Panther Valley Prop. Owners Ass'n, 766 A.2d 1186 (N.J. Super. Ct. App. Div. 2001), 287
Mumaw v. Glendale, 76 Cal. Rptr. 245 (Ct. App. 1969), 674
Mur-Mil Caterers, Inc. v. Werner, 560 N.Y.S.2d 849 (App. Div. 1990), 451
Muro v. Superior Court, 229 Cal. Rptr. 383 (Ct. App. 1986), 480
Murphy v. Burch, 2009 WL 1109758 (Cal. 2009), 211
Murphy v. Financial Dev. Corp., 495 A.2d 1245 (N.H. 1985), 562
Murphy v. Murphy, 466 N.W.2d 87 (Neb. 1991), 565
Murphy v. Westberg, 1998 WL 341965 (Wash. Ct. App. 1999), 219
Murphy Exploration & Prod. Co. v. Sun Operating Ltd. P'ship, 747 So. 2d 260 (Miss. 1999), 337
Murr v. Wisconsin, 582 U.S. 383 (2017), 734
Myrick v. Peck Elec. Co., 164 A.3d 658 (Va. 2017), 117

N

Naab v. Nolan, 327 S.E.2d 151 (W. Va. 1985), 146–147
Nahrstedt v. Lakeside Vill. Condo. Ass'n, 878 P.2d 1275 (Cal. 1994), 287, 288
Nalle v. Taco Bell Corp., 914 S.W.2d 685 (Tex. App. 1996), 455
Napolski v. Champney, 667 P.2d 1013 (Or. 1983), 477
Narragansett Tribe v. Southern R.I. Land Dev. Corp., 418 F. Supp. 798 (D.R.I. 1976), 795
Nathanson v. Spring Lake Park Panther Youth Football Ass'n, 129 F. Supp. 3d 743 (D. Minn. 2015), 63
Nation v. Apache Greyhound Park, Inc., 579 P.2d 580 (Ariz. Ct. App. 1978), 30
National Ass'n of Realtors; United States v., No. 20-CV-3356 at V.F. (D.D.C. 2020), 503
National Ass'n of Realtors; United States v., No. 05 C 5140 (N.D. Ill. Nov. 18, 2008), 503
National Ass'n of the Deaf v. Netflix, Inc., 869 F. Supp. 2d 196 (D. Mass. 2012), 64
National Bd. of Young Men's Christian Ass'ns v. United States, 395 U.S. 85 (1969), 702
National Fed'n of the Blind v. America Online, Inc., No. 99CV12303EFH (D. Mass., filed Nov. 4, 1999), 64
National Fed'n of the Blind v. Target Corp., 452 F. Supp. 2d 946 (N.D. Cal. 2006), 64
National Org. for Women v. Little League Baseball, 318 A.2d 33 (N.J. Super. Ct. App. Div.), *aff'd mem.*, 338 A.2d 198 (N.J. 1974), 51
Nationwide Mut. Ins. Co. v. Housing Opportunities Made Equal, Inc., 523 S.E.2d 217 (Va. 2000), 597
Nature Conservancy v. Congel, 689 N.Y.S.2d 317 (App. Div. 999), 250
Navajo Nation; United States v., 537 U.S. 488 (2003), 804
Navajo Nation v. United States, 556 U.S. 287 (2009), 776, 803
Ndoro v. Torres, 249 N.E.3d 721 (Mass. App. Ct. 2024), 487
Nectow v. City of Cambridge, 277 U.S. 183 (1928), 667, 701–702
Negron v. Gordon, 366 N.E.2d 241 (Mass. 1977), 556
Nelson v. American Tel. & Tel. Co., 170 N.E. 416 (Mass. 1930), 203
Nelson v. Anderson, 676 N.E.2d 735 (Ill. App. Ct. 1997), 518, 520
Nelson v. Barnett Recovery Corp., 652 So. 2d 279 (Ala. Civ. App. 1994), 543
Nelson v. Nelson, 917 N.W.2d 479 (N.D. 2018), 367
Neponsit Prop. Owners' Ass'n v. Emigrant Indus. Sav. Bank, 15 N.E.2d 793 (N.Y. 1938), 253, 256
Neptune City, Borough of v. Borough of Avon-By-The-Sea, 294 A.2d 47 (N.J. 1972), 85–86
Nepveu v. Rau, 583 A.2d 1273 (Vt. 1990), 479
Neudecker v. Boisclair Corp., 351 F.3d 361 (8th Cir. 2003), 590
New Bedford Hous. Auth.; Doe v., 630 N.E.2d 248 (Mass. 1994), 105
New Hampshire Dep't of Transp. v. Franchi, 48 A.3d 849 (N.H. 2012), 691
New Haverford P'ship v. Stroot, 722 A.2d 792 (Del. 2001), 486
New Jersey Coal. Against the War in the Middle E. v. J.M.B. Realty Corp., 650 A.2d 757 (N.J. 1994), 81–82, 721
New Jersey Dep't of Envtl. Prot. v. Alden Leeds, Inc., 708 A.2d 1161 (N.J. 1998), 106
New Jersey Rooming & Boarding House Owners v. Asbury Park, 152 F.3d 217 (3d Cir. 1998), 623
New Jersey State Bar Ass'n v. New Jersey Ass'n of Realtor Bds., 452 A.2d 1323 (N.J. Super. Ct. 1982), 503
Newman v. Chase, 359 A.2d 474 (N.J. 1976), 362, 368
Newman v. Hinky Dinky Omaha-Lincoln, Inc., 427 N.W.2d 50 (Neb. 1988), 491
Newman v. Sathyavaglswaran, 287 F.3d 786 (9th Cir. 2002), 828
Newmark v. Vogelgesang, 915 S.W.2d 337 (Mo. Ct. App. 1996), 41
New Par v. City of Saginaw, 301 F.3d 390 (6th Cir. 2002), 666
Newton v. Magill, 872 P.2d 1213 (Alaska 1994), 485
New Towne Ltd. P'ship v. Pier I Imps. (U.S.), Inc., 680 N.E.2d 644 (Ohio Ct. App. 1996), 463
New York v. Shinnecock Indian Nation, 628 Fed. Appx. 54 (2d Cir. 2015), 800–801
New York, City of v. Utsey, 714 N.Y.S.2d 410 (App. Div. 2000), 165

New York State v. Fermenta ASC Corp., 630 N.Y.S.2d 884 (Sup. Ct. 1995), 45
New York State, People of v. Merlino, 694 F. Supp. 1101 (S.D.N.Y. 1988), 603
Nextel Commc'ns v. Manchester-by-the-Sea, 115 F. Supp. 2d 65 (D. Mass. 2000), 666
Neyland v. Hunter, 668 S.W.2d 530 (Ark. 1984), 219
Nichols v. Azteca Rest. Enters., 256 F.3d 864 (9th Cir. 2001), 606
Nichols v. Haehn, 187 N.Y.S.2d 773 (App. Div. 1959), 307
Nichols v. Mid-Continent Pipe Line Co., 933 P.2d 272 (Okla. 1996), 102, 117
Nicholson v. 300 Broadway Realty Corp., 164 N.E.2d 832 (N.Y. 1959), 255
Nicholson v. United States, 77 Fed. Cl. 605 (2007), 740
Nickels v. Cohn, 764 S.W.2d 124 (Mo. Ct. App. 1989), 552
Nigh v. Hickman, 538 S.W.2d 936 (Mo. Ct. App. 1976), 565
Nile Valley Fed. Sav. & Loan Ass'n v. Security Title Guarantee Corp., 813 P.2d 849 (Colo. Ct. App. 1991), 545
930.65 Acres of Land; United States v., 299 F. Supp. 673 (D. Kan. 1968), 692
Nix v. Wick, 66 So. 3d 209 (Ala. 2010), 508
Nixon v. Harris, 238 N.E.2d 785 (Ohio 1968), 46
NLRB v. *See name of opposing party*
Noah v. AOL Time Warner Inc., 261 F. Supp. 2d 532 (E.D. Va. 2003), 51, 64
Noah v. Assor, 379 F. Supp. 3d 1284 (S.D. Fla. 2019), 603
Noble v. Murphy, 612 N.E.2d 266 (Mass. App. Ct. 1993), 378–379
Nobrega v. Edison Glen Assocs., 772 A.2d 368 (N.J. 2001), 502, 511
Noland v. Commerce Mortg. Corp., 122 F.3d 551 (8th Cir. 1997), 592
Nollan v. California Coastal Comm'n, 483 U.S. 825 (1987), 720, 757–761
Nome 2000 v. Fagerstrom, 799 P.2d 304 (Alaska 1990), 143–144, 147–148, 164
Noone v. Price, 298 S.E.2d 218 (W. Va. 1982), 133–134
Nordlinger v. Hahn, 505 U.S. 1 (1992), 727
Norman v. United States, 429 F.3d 1081 (Fed. Cir. 2005), 733
North Country Villas Homeowners Ass'n v. Kokenge, 163 P.3d 1247 (Kan. Ct. App. 2007), 276
North Dakota Fair Hous. Council, Inc. v. Peterson, 625 N.W.2d 551 (S.D. 2001), 613
North Shore-Chi. Rehab., Inc. v. Village of Skokie, 827 F. Supp. 497 (N.D. Ill. 1993), 623
North Shore Steak House, Inc. v. Board of Appeals of the Inc. Vill. of Thomaston, 282 N.E.2d 606 (N.Y. 1972), 646
Northwest Real Estate Co. v. Serio, 144 A. 245 (Md. 1929), 284
Norwegian Evangelical Free Church v. Milhauser, 169 N.E. 134 (N.Y. 1929), 518
Nott v. Gundick, 180 N.W. 376 (Mich. 1920), 367
N.O.W. v. Operation Rescue, 747 F. Supp. 760 (D.D.C. 1990), *aff'd in part and remanded in part*, 37 F.3d 646 (D.C. Cir. 1997), 38
NPS, LLC v. Minihane, 886 N.E.2d 670 (Mass. 2008), 463
Nu-Dwarf Farms, Inc. v. Stratbucker Farms, Ltd., 470 N.W.2d 772 (Neb. 1991), 128
Nulman v. Four Twenty Corp. *See* Rose Nulman Park Found.
Nussbaum v. Weeks, 263 Cal. Rptr. 360 (Ct. App. 1989), 511
Nwakpuda v. Falley's, Inc., 14 F. Supp. 2d 1213 (D. Kan. 1998), 57, 59

O

Oakbrook Civic Ass'n, Inc. v. Sonnier, 481 So. 2d 1008 (La. 1986), 275
Oakland, City of v. BP plc, 960 F.3d 570 (9th Cir. 2020), 126
Oakland, City of v. Oakland Raiders, 646 P.2d 835 (Cal. 1982), 687
Oakwood Vill. LLC v. Albertsons, Inc., 104 P.3d 1226 (Utah 2004), 453
O & G Indus., Inc. v. Planning & Zoning Comm'n, 232 Conn. 419 (1995), 750
Obergefell v. Hodges, 576 U.S. 644 (2015), 407–411
O'Brien v. Black, 648 A.2d 1374 (Vt. 1994), 463
O'Buck v. Cottonwood Vill. Condo. Ass'n, Inc., 750 P.2d 813 (Alaska 1988), 288
O'Cain v. O'Cain, 473 S.E.2d 460 (S.C. 1996), 103, 116
Oceanside, City of v. McKenna, 264 Cal. Rptr. 275 (Ct. App. 1989), 285
Oceanside Cmty. Assocs. v. Oceanside Land Co., 195 Cal. Rptr. 14 (Ct. App. 1983), 255
Odumn v. United States, 227 A.3d 1099 (D.C. 2020), 30, 439
Oechsner v. Courcier, 155 S.W.2d 963 (Tex. App. 1941), 367
Office One, Inc. v. Lopez, 769 N.E.2d 749 (Mass. 2002), 671
O'Hagan v. United States, 86 F.3d 776 (8th Cir. 1996), 353
Ohio Civil Rights Comm'n v. Akron Metro Hous. Auth., 892 N.E.2d 415 (Ohio 2008), 590
O'Keeffe v. Snyder, 416 A.2d 862 (N.J. 1980), 172
Old Canton Hills Homeowners Ass'n v. City of Jackson, 749 So. 2d 54 (Miss. 1999), 648–649
Oldfield v. Stoeco Homes, Inc., 139 A.2d 291 (N.J. 1958), 315
Old Port Cove Condo. Ass'n One, Inc. v. Old Port Cove Holdings, Inc., 954 So. 2d 742 (Fla. Dist. Ct. App. 2007), 285
Olin v. Goehler, 694 P.2d 11219 (Wash. Ct. App. 1985), 467
Olinger v. United States Golf Ass'n, 205 F.3d 1001 (7th Cir. 2000), 68
Olivas v. Olivas, 780 P.2d 640 (N.M. Ct. App. 1989), 367–368
Ollinger v. Bennett, 562 N.W.2d 167 (Iowa 1997), 171
Omega Chem. Co. v. United Seeds, Inc., 560 N.W.2d 820 (Neb. 1997), 112
Omega Corp. of Chesterfield v. Malloy, 319 S.E.2d 728 (Va. 1984), 273
Omnipoint Commc'ns Enters., L.P. v. Zoning Hearing Bd. of Easttown Twp., 331 F.3d 386 (3d Cir. 2003), 665

Omnipoint Corp. v. Zoning Hearing Bd. of Pine Grove Twp., 20 F. Supp. 2d 875 (E.D. Pa. 1998), 665
Oncale v. Sundowner Offshore Servs., Inc., 523 U.S. 75 (1998), 604–605
143-145 Nahant Rd, LLC v. Mastoras, 2014 WL 2548094 (Mass. Land Ct. 2014), 214
170 W. 85 St. HDFC v. Jones, 673 N.Y.S.2d 830 (Civ. Ct. 1998), 381
One 1995 Toyota Pick-Up Truck v. District of Columbia, 718 A.2d 558 (D.C. 1998), 710
Oneida, Cnty. of v. Oneida Indian Nation, 470 U.S. 226 (1985), 162, 793, 796–797
Oneida Indian Nation of N.Y. v. Madison Cnty., 401 F. Supp. 2d 219 (N.D.N.Y. 2005), 797
Oneida Indian Nation of N.Y. v. New York State, 500 F. Supp. 2d 128 (N.D.N.Y. 2007), 800
Oneida Indian Nation of N.Y. v. Oneida, Cnty. of, 414 U.S. 661 (1974), 775, 796, 797
Oneida Indian Nation of N.Y. v. Oneida, Cnty. of, 617 F.3d 114 (2d Cir. 2010), 801
O'Neil's Mkts. v. United Food & Commercial Workers' Union, Meatcutters Local 88, 95 F.3d 733 (8th Cir. 1996), 84
1000 Brickell, Ltd. v. City of Miami, 339 So. 3d 1091 (Fla. Dist. Ct. App. 2022), 308
Opening Private Rd. ex rel. O'Reilly, In re, 5 A.3d 246 (Pa. 2010), 213
Opinion No. 26 of the Comm. on Unauthorized Practice of Law, In re, 654 A.2d 1344 (N.J. 1995), 504
Opinion of the Justices, 152 Me. 440, 131 A.2d 904 (1957), 689
Opinion of the Justices, 313 N.E.2d 561 (Mass. 1974), 87
Opinion of the Justices, 649 A.2d 604 (N.H. 1994), 220
Opinion of the Justices to the Senate, 802 N.E.2d 565 (Mass. 2004), 409
Optivision, Inc. v. Syracuse Shopping Ctr. Assocs., 472 F. Supp. 665 (N.D.N.Y. 1979), 286
Oregon v. Fullerton, 34 P.3d 1180 (Or. Ct. App. 2001), 692
Oregon Account Sys. v. Greer, 996 P.2d 1025 (Or. Ct. App. 2000), 358
Oregon Paralyzed Veterans of Am. v. Regal Cinemas, Inc., 339 F.3d 1126 (9th Cir. 2003), 70
O'Reilly, In re. *See* Opening Private Rd.
Ortega v. Flaim, 902 P.2d 199 (Wyo. 1995), 484
Osborne v. Power, 890 S.W.2d 570 (Ark. 1994), 117
Osborne v. Power, 908 S.W.2d 340 (Ark. 1995), 117
Owen, In re Estate of, 855 N.E.2d 603 (Ind. 2006), 345
Owensboro v. McCormick, 581 S.W.2d 3 (Ky. 1979), 688
Oxford House, Inc. v. Town of Babylon, 819 F. Supp. 1179 (E.D.N.Y. 1993), 622
Oxford House-C v. City of St. Louis, 77 F.3d 249 (8th Cir. 1996), 622
Oyster Bay Cove, Ltd., In re, 161 B.R. 338 (Bankr. E.D.N.Y. 1993), 519

P

Pacific Bell v. City of San Diego, 96 Cal. Rptr. 2d 897 (Ct. App. 2000), 740
Pacific First Bank v. New Morgan Park Corp., 857 P.2d 895 (Or. Ct. App. 1993), *aff'd and remanded*, 876 P.2d 761 (Or. 1994), 283, 491
Pack v. Clayton Cnty., Ga., 1993 WL 837007 (N.D. Ga. 1993), *aff'd*, 47 F.3d 430 (11th Cir. 1995), 622
Packett v. Herbert, 377 S.E.2d 438 (Va. 1989), 104
Page Cnty. Appliance Ctr., Inc. v. Honeywell, Inc., 347 N.W.2d 171 (Iowa 1984), 103–104
Pagelsdorf v. Safeco Ins. Co., 284 N.W.2d 55 (Wis. 1979), 485
Page Motor Co. v. Baker, 438 A.2d 739 (Conn. 1980), 129
Pai, State ex rel. v. Thom, 563 P.2d 982 (Haw. 1977), 531–532
Pakdel v. City & Cnty. of San Francisco, 594 U.S. 474 (2021), 766
Palamarg Realty Co. v. Rehac, 404 A.2d 21 (N.J. 1979), 546
Palazzolo v. Coastal Res. Mgmt. Council, 1995 WL 941370 (R.I. Super. Ct. 1995), *aff'd*, 746 A.2d 707 (R.I. 2000), 735, 737–738
Palazzolo v. Malba Estates, Inc., 500 N.Y.S.2d 327 (App. Div. 1986), 215
Palazzolo v. State ex rel. Tavares, 746 A.2d 707 (R.I. 2000), *aff'd in part and rev'd in part sub nom.* Palazzolo v. Rhode Island, 533 U.S. 606 (2001), *on remand sub nom.* Palazzolo v. State, 785 A.2d 561 (R.I. 2001), *on remand*, 2005 WL 1645974 (R.I. Super. Ct. 2005), 733, 737, 738, 741
Palm Beach Isles Assocs. v. United States, 42 Fed. Cl. 340 (1998), *overruled*, 208 F.3d 1374 (Fed. Cir.), *aff'd on reh'g*, 231 F.3d 1354 (Fed. Cir. 2000), 732–733
Palmer v. Amazon.com, Inc., 51 F.4th 491 (2d Cir. 2022), 122
Palmer v. Forrest, Mackey & Assocs., Inc., 304 S.E.2d 704 (Ga. 1983), 545
Palmer v. Protrka, 476 P.2d 185 (Or. 1970), 368
Palmer v. Thompson, 403 U.S. 217 (1971), 342, 580
PA Nw. Distribs., Inc. v. Zoning Hearing Bd., 584 A.2d 1372 (Pa. 1991), 654
Paradise Hills Church, Inc. v. International Church, 467 F. Supp. 357 (D. Ariz. 1979), 530
Paralyzed Veterans of Am. v. D.C. Arena L.P., 117 F.3d 579 (D.C. Cir. 1997), 69
Parker v. Ashford, 661 So. 2d 213 (Ala. 1995), 112, 117
Parker v. Flook, 437 U.S. 584 (1978), 842
Parker v. Metropolitan Life Co., 121 F.3d 1006 (6th Cir. 1997), 64
Parker v. Shecut, 562 S.E.2d 620 (S.C. 2002), 370
Parkmerced Co. v. San Francisco Rent Stabilization & Arbitration Bd., 263 Cal. Rptr. 617 (Ct. App. 1989), 451
Parks v. La Face Records, 329 F.3d 437 (6th Cir. 2003), 850
Park W. Mgmt. Corp. v. Mitchell, 391 N.E.2d 1288 (N.Y. 1979), 476
Parma; United States v., 661 F.2d 562 (6th Cir. 1981), 615
Pascoag Reservoir & Dam, LLC v. Rhode Island, 217 F. Supp. 2d 206 (D.R.I. 2002), *aff'd*, 337 F.3d 87 (1st Cir. 2003), 728
Paset v. Old Orchard Bank & Tr. Co., 378 N.E.2d 1264 (Ill. App. Ct. 1978), 819

Patterson v. McLean Credit Union, 491 U.S. 164 (1989), 54, 55, 59
Patterson v. Oye, 333 N.W.2d 389 (Neb. 1983), 43
Pave v. Mills, No. 97-5210B (Mass. Super. Ct. 1999), 207
Payne v. Skaar, 900 P.2d 1352 (Idaho 1995), 112, 116
Pele Def. Fund v. Puna Geothermal Venture, 881 P.2d 1210 (Haw. 1994), 90
Pendergrast v. Aiken, 236 S.E.2d 787 (N.C. 1977), 129
Penn Cent. Transp. Co. v. City of New York, 438 U.S. 104 (1978), 662, 702–707, 712–713, 718–720, 726, 729, 731–733, 736–737, 741
Penn Cent. Transp. Co. v. Wilson, 292 N.E.2d 827 (Ind. Ct. App. 1973), 117
Pennell v. City of San Jose, 485 U.S. 1 (1988), 469, 670, 709, 717, 724
Pennsylvania v. Board of Dirs. of City Trs. of Phila., 353 U.S. 230 (1957), 278, 341
Pennsylvania v. Brown, 392 F.2d 120 (3d Cir. 1968), 278
Pennsylvania Coal Co. v. Mahon, 260 U.S. 393 (1922), 696–699, 700, 702–703, 708, 729
Pension Benefit Guar. Corp. v. R.A. Gray & Co., 467 U.S. 717 (1986), 751
People v. *See name of opposing party*
People for the Ethical Treatment of Animals, Inc. v. North, 60 F.4th 815 (4th Cir. 2023), 37
People's Nat'l Bank v. Birney's Enters., Inc., 775 P.2d 466 (Wis. Ct. App. 1989), 551
Pequot Spring Water Co. v. Brunelle, 698 A.2d 920 (Conn. App. Ct. 1997), 455
Percheman; United States v., 32 U.S. 51 (1833), 774
Perez v. Board of Appeals of Norwood, 765 N.E.2d 768 (Mass. App. Ct. 2002), 655
Permian Basin Ctrs. for Mental Health & Mental Retardation v. Alsobrook, 723 S.W.2d 774 (Tex. App. 1986), 272
Perry v. Brown. *See* Perry v. Schwarzenegger
Perry v. Burger King Corp., 924 F. Supp. 548 (S.D.N.Y. 1996), 56
Perry v. Command Performance, 913 F.2d 99 (3d Cir. 1990), 34, 56
Perry v. Heirs at Law & Distributees of Gadsden, 449 S.E.2d 250 (S.C. 1994), 153
Perry v. Schwarzenegger, 704 F. Supp. 2d 921 (N.D. Cal. 2010), *aff'd sub nom.* Perry v. Brown, 671 F.3d 1052 (9th Cir.), *reh'g en banc denied*, 681 F.3d 1065 (9th Cir. 2012), *cert. granted sub nom.* Hollingsworth v. Perry, 568 U.S. 1066 (2012), *vacated and remanded*, 570 U.S. 693 (2013), 410
Peter H. & Barbara J. Steuck Living Tr. v. Easley, 325 Wis. 2d 455 (Ct. App. 2010), 143, 147
Peters v. O'Leary, 30 A.3d 825 (Me. 2011), 136
Petersen v. Beekmere, Inc., 283 A.2d 911 (N.J. Super. Ct. Ch. Div. 1971), 264
Petersen v. Hartell, 707 P.2d 232 (Cal. 1985), 566
Peterson v. Superior Court, 899 P.2d 905 (Cal. 1995), 485–486
Petrillo v. Bachenberg, 655 A.2d 1354 (N.J. 1995), 506
Petsch v. Widger, 335 N.W.2d 254 (Neb. 1983), 150–152
Pfaff v. Department of Hous. & Urban Dev., 88 F.3d 739 (9th Cir. 1996), 612
PGA Tour, Inc. v. Martin, 532 U.S. 661 (2001), 67–68
Pharmaceutical Rsch. & Mfrs. of Am. v. Williams, 64 F.4th 932 (8th Cir. 2023), 766
Phelps v. Wichita Eagle-Beacon, 886 F.2d 1262 (10th Cir. 1989), 58
Philadelphia, City of v. Galdo, 217 A.3d 811 (Pa. 2019), 169
Philip Morris, Inc. v. Reilly, 312 F.3d 24 (1st Cir. 2002), 729
Phillip v. University of Rochester, 316 F.3d 291 (2d Cir. 2003), 57
Phillips v. Pembroke Real Estate, Inc., 2003 U.S. Dist. LEXIS 19051 (D. Mass. 2003), 854
Phillips v. Washington Legal Found., 524 U.S. 156 (1998), 743, 746
P.H. Inv. v. Oliver, 818 P.2d 1018 (Utah 1991), 479
Pickens v. Pickens, 490 So. 2d 872 (Miss. 1986), 412–414
Pieper v. American Sign/Outdoor Adver., Inc., 564 So. 2d 49 (Ala. 1990), 437
Pierce v. Casady, 711 P.2d 766 (Kan. Ct. App. 1985), 222
Pierce; State v., 417 A.2d 1085 (N.J. Super. Ct. Law Div. 1980), 447
Pierson v. Post, 3 Cai. R. 175, 2 Am. Dec. 264 (N.Y. Sup. Ct. 1805), 813–815
Pilip v. United States, 186 F. Supp. 397 (D. Alaska 1960), 358
Pima Sav. & Loan Ass'n v. Rampello, 812 P.2d 1115 (Ariz. Ct. App. 1991), 525
Pines of Boca Barwood Condo. Ass'n, Inc. v. Cavouti, 605 So. 2d 984 (Fla. Dist. Ct. App. 1992), 378
Pinkston v. Hartley, 511 So. 2d 168 (Ala. 1987), 200
Pitman v. Sweeney, 661 P.2d 153 (Wash. Ct. App. 1983), 184–185
Pitson v. Sellers, 613 N.Y.S.2d 1005 (App. Div. 1994), 370
Pitts v. Foster, 743 So. 2d 1066 (Miss. Ct. App. 1999), 210
Pittsburgh Press Co. v. Human Relations Comm'n, 413 U.S. 376 (1973), 53
Pizza, State ex rel. v. Rezcallah, 702 N.E.2d 81 (Ohio 1998), 711
Platoro, Ltd., Inc. v. Unidentified Remains of a Vessel, Her Cargo, Apparel, Tackle, & Furniture, in a Cause of Salvage, Civil & Maritime, 695 F.2d 893 (5th Cir. 1983), 820
Plaza Forty-Eight, Inc. v. Great Atl. & Pac. Tea Co., 817 F. Supp. 774 (E.D. Wis. 1993), 455
Plummer, In re Marriage of, 735 P.2d 165 (Colo. 1987), 417
PMZ Oil Co. v. Lucroy, 449 So. 2d 201 (Miss. 1984), 237–238
0.08246 Acres of Land; United States v., 888 F. Supp. 693 (E.D. Pa. 1995), 221
Poletown Neighborhood Council v. City of Detroit, 304 N.W.2d 455 (Mich. 1981), 688
Ponke v. Ponke, 564 N.W.2d 101 (Mich. Ct. App. 1997), 357
Pope Cnty. Bar Ass'n v. Suggs, 624 S.W.2d 828 (Ark. 1981), 503
Popov v. Hayashi, 2002 WL 31833731 (Cal. Super. Ct. 2002), 24
Poppleton v. Village Realty Co., 535 N.W.2d 400 (Neb. 1995), 329

Porter v. Smith, 486 N.W.2d 846 (Neb. 1992), 565
Portland Nat. Gas Transp. Sys. v. 19.2 Acres of Land, 318 F.3d 279 (1st Cir. 2003), 691
Port of Coos Bay v. Department of Revenue, 691 P.2d 100 (Or. 1984), 434
Portola Hills Cmty. Ass'n v. James, 5 Cal. Rptr. 2d 580 (Ct. App. 1992), 253, 275
Posik v. Layton, 695 So. 2d 759 (Fla. Dist. Ct. App. 1997), 412
Posner v. Davis, 395 N.E.2d 133 (Ill. 1979), 510
Post v. Schwall, 460 N.W.2d 794 (Wis. 1990), 565
Potlatch Corp. v. Hannegan, 586 S.W.2d 256 (Ark. 1979), 166
Potomac Grp. Homes v. Montgomery Cnty., 823 F. Supp. 1285 (D. Md. 1993), 623
Pottgen v. Missouri High Sch. Activities Ass'n, 40 F.3d 926 (8th Cir. 1994), 67
Pottinger v. City of Miami, 810 F. Supp. 1551 (S.D. Fla. 1992), 635
Poullos v. Pine Crest Homes, LLC, 876 N.W.2d 356 (Neb. 2016), 147
Powell v. Pennsylvania, 127 U.S. 678 (1888), 695, 700
Powers v. Building Inspector, 296 N.E.2d 491 (Mass. 1973), 653
Powers v. Judd, 553 A.2d 139 (Vt. 1988), 127
Powers v. Olsen, 742 A.2d 799 (Conn. 2000), 133
Prah v. Maretti, 321 N.W.2d 182 (Wis. 1982), 137, 221
Pratt v. Langston, 669 So. 2d 967 (Ala. 1995), 352
Presbytery of Seattle v. King Cnty., 787 P.2d 907 (Wash. 1990), 735
Presbytery of Se. Iowa v. Harris, 226 N.W.2d 232 (Iowa 1975), 338, 537
Prescott v. Philadelphia Hous. Auth., 555 A.2d 305 (Pa. Commw. Ct. 1989), 24
Presidio Invs., Ltd.; United States v., 4 F.3d 805 (9th Cir. 1993), 604
Price v. Himeji, 2013 WL 3184784 (N.J. 2013), 657
Price ex rel. Estate of Price v. City of Seattle, 24 P.3d 1098 (Wash. Ct. App. 2001), 118
Price Waterhouse v. Hopkins, 490 U.S. 228 (1989), 606
Prichard v. Department of Revenue, 164 N.W.2d 113 (Iowa 1969), 325
Priddy v. Shopko Corp., 918 F. Supp. 358 (D. Utah 1995), 48
Prieskorn v. Maloof, 991 P.2d 511 (N.M. Ct. App. 1999), 318, 323
Prince; State v., 595 N.E.2d 376 (Ohio Ct. App. 1991), 39
Prince George's Cnty. v. Sunrise Dev. Ltd. P'ship, 623 A.2d 1296 (Md. 1993), 654
Pritchett v. Turner, 437 So. 2d 104 (Ala. 1983), 282
Probasco, In re, 839 F.2d 1352 (9th Cir. 1988), 551
Proctor v. Huntington, 238 P.3d 1117 (Wash. 2010), 42, 169
Professional Realty Corp. v. Bender, 222 S.E.2d 810 (Va. 1976), 502
Pro-Football, Inc. v. Blackhorse, 112 F. Supp. 3d 439 (E.D. Va. 2015), *vacated*, 709 Fed. Appx. 182 (4th Cir. 2018), 54, 846
Properties Inv. Grp. v. JBA, Inc., 495 N.W.2d 624 (Neb. 1993), 463
Propst v. McNeill, 932 S.W.2d 766 (Ark. 1996), 480
Prospect Dev. Co. v. Bershader, 515 S.E.2d 291 (Va. 1999), 200
Protect Our Mountain Env't, Inc. v. District Court (POME), 677 P.2d 1361 (Colo. 1984), 671–672
PruneYard Shopping Ctr. v. Robins, 447 U.S. 74 (1980), 81–83, 720–724, 757
Public Access Shoreline Haw. (PASH) v. Hawaii Cnty. Planning Comm'n, 903 P.2d 1246 (Haw. 1995), 89–91
Publicker Chem. Corp. v. Belcher Oil Co., 792 F.2d 482 (5th Cir. 1986), 434
Public Land/Water Access Ass'n v. Robbins, 483 P.3d 1102 (Mont. 2021), 220
Public Serv. Co. of Colo. v. Van Wyck, 27 P.3d 377 (Colo. 2001), 45, 117
Puchalski v. Wedemeyer, 586 N.Y.S.2d 387 (App. Div. 1992), 242
Puckett v. St. Andrews Place Ret. Cmty., Inc., 2012 WL 1072418 (Ky. Ct. App. 2012), 285
Puerto Rico, Commonwealth of; United States v., 764 F. Supp. 220 (D.P.R. 1991), 583
Pumpelly v. Green Bay Co., 80 U.S. 166 (1871), 694, 729, 739, 741
Puttrich v. Smith, 407 A.2d 842 (N.J. Super. Ct. App. Div. 1979), 726–727

Q

Q-2 LLC v. Hughes, 368 P.3d 86 (Utah 2016), 171
Quigley v. Winter, 598 F.3d 938 (8th Cir. 2010), 603
Quinnipiac Council, Boy Scouts of Am., Inc. v. Commission on Human Rights & Opportunities, 528 A.2d 352 (Conn. 1987), 51

R

Radecki v. Joura, 114 F.3d 115 (8th Cir. 1997), 592
Rae v. Flynn, 690 So. 2d 1341 (Fla. Dist. Ct. App. 1997), 117
Ragan v. Commissioner of Internal Revenue, 135 F.3d 329 (5th Cir. 1998), 402
Ragin v. New York Times Co., 923 F.2d 995 (2d Cir. 1991), 53, 588, 598, 614
Raim v. Stancel, 339 N.W.2d 621 (Iowa Ct. App. 1983), 531
Raleigh Ave. Beach Ass'n v. Atlantis Beach Club, Inc., 851 A.2d 19 (N.J. Ct. App. 2004), 87
Ramirez v. Akzo Nobel Coatings, Inc., 791 N.E.2d 1031 (Ohio Ct. App. 2003), 119
Rancho Santa Paula Mobilehome Park, Ltd. v. Evans, 32 Cal. Rptr. 2d 464 (Ct. App. 1994), 378
Randall v. Orange Cnty. Council, Boy Scouts of Am., 952 P.2d 261 (Cal. 1998), 51
Randall Co. v. Alan Cobel Photography, 465 N.Y.S.2d 489 (Civ. Ct. 1983), 480
Rando v. Town of N. Attleboro, 692 N.E.2d 544 (Mass. App. Ct. 1998), 650
Rase v. Castle Mountain Ranch, 631 P.2d 680 (Mont. 1981), 205–207
Rassman v. American Fid. Co., 460 A.2d 461 (Vt. 1983), 556

Ratinska v. Estate of Denesuk, 447 So. 2d 241 (Fla. Dist. Ct. App. 1983), 351
Ray v. Flower Hosp., 439 N.E.2d 942 (Ohio Ct. App. 1981), 819
Ray v. Miller, 916 S.W.2d 117 (Ark. 1996), 236
Ray v. Montgomery, 399 So. 2d 230 (Ala. 1980), 510
Raytheon Co. v. Hernandez, 540 U.S. 44 (2003), 576
Reagan v. Brissey, 844 N.E.2d 672 (Mass. 2006), 239
Real Estate Mktg., Inc. v. Franz, 885 S.W.2d 921 (Ky. 1994), 514
Rear Door Bookstore, State ex rel. v. Tenth Dist. Court of Appeals, 588 N.E.2d 116 (Ohio 1992), 123
Reber v. Reiss, 42 A.3d 1131 (Pa. Super. Ct. 2012), 830
Rector-Phillips-Morse, Inc. v. Huntsman Farms, Inc., 590 S.W.2d 317 (Ark. 1979), 500
Redfearn v. Creppel, 455 So. 2d 1356 (La. 1984), 653
Reed v. King, 193 Cal. Rptr. 130 (Ct. App. 1983), 510
Reed v. Town of Gilbert, 576 U.S. 155 (2015), 672–673
Reeves v. Carrollsburg Condo. Unit Owners Ass'n, 1997 U.S. Dist. LEXIS 21762 (D.D.C. 1997), 603
Reeves v. Sanderson Plumbing Prods., Inc., 530 U.S. 133 (2000), 592–594
Regan v. Lanze, 354 N.E.2d 818 (N.Y. 1976), 516
Regency Homes Ass'n v. Egermayer, 498 N.W.2d 783 (Neb. 1993), 254, 257
Reitman v. Mulkey, 387 U.S. 369 (1967), 580
Relka, In re, 2009 WL 5149262 (Bankr. D. Wyo. 2009), 572
Rendleman v. Heinley, 149 P.3d 1009 (N.M. Ct. App. 2006), 546
Renton, City of v. Playtime Theatres, 475 U.S. 41 (1986), 674
Repp; State v., 73 N.W. 829 (Iowa 1898), 817
Republican Party v. Dietz, 940 S.W.2d 86 (Tex. 1997), 80
Republic of. *See name of republic*
Residential Funding Co., LLC v. Saurman, 805 N.W.2d 183 (Mich. 2011), 572
Reynolds v. Gagen, 739 N.Y.S.2d 704 (App. Div. 2002), 337
Reynolds v. McCullough, 739 S.W.2d 424 (Tex. App. 1987), 491
Rhaney v. University of Md., E. Shores, 880 A.2d 357 (Md. 2005), 184
RHN Corp. v. Veibell, 96 P.3d 935 (Utah 2004), 171
Rhode Island v. Shell Oil Prods. Co., 979 F.3d 50 (1st Cir. 2020), 126
Rhodes v. Cahill, 802 S.W.2d 643 (Tex. 1990), 147
Rhodes v. Chapman, 452 U.S. 337 (1981), 635
Rich v. Emerson-Dumont Distrib. Corp., 222 N.W.2d 65 (Mich. Ct. App. 1974), 502
Richard Barton Enters., Inc. v. Tsern, 928 P.2d 368 (Utah 1996), 429
Richards v. Washington Terminal Co., 233 U.S. 546 (1914), 101
Richardson v. City & Cnty. of Honolulu, 124 F.3d 1150 (9th Cir. 1997), 683
Richey v. Patrick, 904 P.2d 798 (Wyo. 1995), 512
Richmond, City of v. Deans, 281 U.S. 704 (1930), 579
Riddle v. Harmon, 162 Cal. Rptr. 530 (Ct. App. 1980), 352
Riddle v. Lanser, 421 P.3d 35 (Alaska 2018), 116
Ridgely Condo. Ass'n v. Smyrnioudis, 660 A.2d 942 (Md. Ct. Spec. App. 1995), 288, 377
Rigney v. City of Chicago, 102 Ill. 64 (1881), 693
Riley v. Bear Creek Planning Comm., 551 P.2d 1213 (Cal. 1976), 242, 264
Riley v. Boles, 394 So. 3d 543 (Ala. 2024), 216
Riss v. Angel, 934 P.2d 669 (Wash. 1997), 270, 275, 379
Riste v. Eastern Wash. Bible Camp, Inc., 605 P.2d 1294 (Wash. Ct. App. 1980), 284
Ritchey v. Villa Nueva Condo. Ass'n, Inc., 146 Cal. Rptr. 695 (Ct. App. 1978), 378
Riverisland Cold Storage, Inc. v. Fresno-Madera Prod. Credit Ass'n, 291 P.3d 316 (Cal. 2013), 510
Rivers v. Roadway Express, Inc., 511 U.S. 298 (1994), 60
R.M.A. ex rel. Appleberry v. Blue Springs R-IV Sch. Dist., 568 S.W.3d 420 (Mo. 2019), 74
Ro v. Factory Mut. Ins. Co., 260 A.3d 811 (N.H. 2021), 440
Roaring Fork Club L.P. v. St. Jude's Co., 36 P.3d 1229 (Colo. 2001), 196
Robarge v. Willett, 636 N.Y.S.2d 938 (App. Div. 1996), 149
Robbins v. HNG Oil Co., 878 S.W.2d 351 (Tex. App. 1994), 281
Robbins v. Reagan, 616 F. Supp. 1259 (D.D.C. 1985), 441
Roberts v. Estate of Barbagallo, 531 A.2d 1125 (Pa. Super. Ct. 1988), 510
Roberts v. Rhodes, 643 P.2d 116 (Kan. 1982), 315, 319
Roberts v. United States Jaycees. *See* United States Jaycees v. McClure
Robert T. Keeler Maint. Fund for Hanover Country Club, In re, 306 A.3d 795 (N.H. 2023), 322
Robinette v. French, 724 S.W.2d 196 (Ark. Ct. App. 1987), 446
Robins v. PruneYard Shopping Ctr., 592 P.2d 341 (Cal. 1979), *aff'd*, 447 U.S. 74 (1980), 81–82, 721
Robinson v. Ariyoshi, 441 F. Supp. 559 (D. Haw. 1977), *aff'd*, 753 F.2d 1468 (9th Cir. 1985), *vacated*, 477 U.S. 902 (1986), *on remand*, 887 F.2d 215 (9th Cir. 1989), 90, 753–754
Robinson v. California, 370 U.S. 660 (1962), 640
Robinson v. Diamond Hous. Corp., 463 F.2d 853 (D.C. Cir. 1972), 481–4823
Robinson v. 12 Lofts Realty, Inc., 610 F.2d 1032 (2d Cir. 1979), 615
Robles v. Domino's Pizza, LLC, 913 F.3d 898 (9th Cir. 2019), 64
Roccamonte, In re Estate of, 1808 A.2d 838 (N.J. 2002), 415
Rodenberg-Roberts v. Kindercare Learning Ctrs., Inc., 86 F.3d 844 (8th Cir. 1996), 66
Rodgers v. Village of Tarrytown, 96 N.E.2d 731 (N.Y. 1951), 651
Rodrigue v. Copeland, 475 So. 2d 1071 (La. 1985), 117
Rodriguez v. 551 W. 157th St. Owners Corp., 992 F. Supp. 385 (S.D.N.Y. 1998), 610
Rodriguez v. Prince George's County, 558 A.2d 742 (Md. Ct. Spec. App. 1989), 648
Rodriguez v. Village Green Realty, Inc., 788 F.3d 31 (2d Cir. 2015), 599
Roeder; State v., 336 P.3d 831 (Kan. 2014), 39
Roehrs v. Lees, 429 A.2d 388 (N.J. Super. Ct. App. Div. 1981), 250–251

Rogers v. Marlin, 754 So. 2d 1267 (Miss. Ct. App. 1999), 214
Rogers v. Roach, 2012 WL 2337616 (Tenn. Ct. App. 2012), 207
Rolling "R" Constr., Inc. v. Dodd, 477 So. 2d 330 (Ala. 1985), 547
Romanoff Equities, Inc. v. United States, 815 F.3d 809 (Fed. Cir. 2016), 749
Romea v. Heiberger & Assocs., 163 F.3d 111 (2d Cir. 1998), 489
Romero, Matter of Estate of, 847 P.2d 319 (N.M. Ct. App. 1993), 345
Romshek v. Osantowski, 466 N.W.2d 482 (Neb. 1991), 128
Ron Greenspan Volkswagen, Inc. v. Ford Motor Land Dev. Corp., 38 Cal. Rptr. 2d 783 (Ct. App. 1995), 512
Rooks, In re Marriage of, 429 P.3d 579 (Colo. 2018), 830
Rosa & Raymond Parks Inst. for Self Dev. v. Target Corp., 812 F.3d 824 (11th Cir. 2016), 849, 852
Rosado v. K & Y Mgmt. Corp., 212 A.D.3d 677 (N.Y. App. Div. 2023), 534
Rose Acre Farms, Inc. v. United States, 373 F.3d 1177 (1st Cir. 2004), 710
Rosen v. Keeler, 986 A.2d 731 (N.J. Super. Ct. App. Div. 2010), 197
Rose Nulman Park Found. ex rel. Nulman v. Four Twenty Corp., 93 A.3d 25 (R.I. 2014), 42, 169
Rothe v. Revco D.S., Inc., 976 F. Supp. 784 (S.D. Ind. 1997), 453
Rothrauff v. Sinking Spring Water Co., 14 A.2d 87 (Pa. 1940), 132
Roussalis v. Wyoming Med. Ctr., 4 P.3d 209 (Wyo. 2000), 508
Rowley v. American Tr. Co., 132 S.E. 347 (Va. 1926), 282
Roy v. Woodstock Cmty. Tr., Inc., 94 A.3d 530 (Vt. 2014), 196
Rubin v. Moys, 97 Wash. App. 1020 (1999), 281
Ruckelshaus v. Monsanto, 467 U.S. 986 (1984), 758
Rucker v. Wynn, 441 S.E.2d 417 (Ga. Ct. App. 1994), 460
Rudow v. Fogel, 426 N.E.2d 155 (Mass. App. Ct. 1981), 206
Runyon v. McCrary, 427 U.S. 160 (1976), 54–55, 56–57, 61, 600
Runyon v. Paley, 416 S.E.2d 177 (N.C. 1992), 249–251, 253–254
Rusch v. Kauker, 479 N.W.2d 496 (S.D. 1991), 521
Rushing Constr. Co. v. MCM Ventures, II, Inc., 395 S.E.2d 130 (N.C. Ct. App. 1990), 447
Russell-Stanley Corp. v. Plant Indus., Inc., 595 A.2d 534 (N.J. Super. Ct. 1991), 480
Ryan v. Ramsey, 936 F. Supp. 417 (S.D. Tex. 1996), 618, 622

S

Sabato v. Sabato, 342 A.2d 886 (N.J. Super. Ct. Law Div. 1975), 726
Sabo v. Horvath, 559 P.2d 1038 (Alaska 1976), 546
Sac & Fox Nation v. Hanson, 47 F.3d 1061 (10th Cir. 1995), 772
Sack v. Tomlin, 871 P.2d 298 (Nev. 1994), 361
Saelzler v. Advanced Grp. 400, 23 P.3d 1143 (Cal. 2001), 487
Sage v. Rogers, 848 P.2d 1034 (Mont. 1993), 446
St. Bartholomew's Church v. City of New York, 914 F.2d 348 (2d Cir. 1990), 677
St. Francis; State v., No. 1170-10-86Fcr (Vt. Dist. Ct., Aug. 11, 1989), 792, 796
St. Francis Coll. v. Al-Khazraji, 481 U.S. 604 (1987), 55, 600
Saint-Jean v. Emigrant Mortg. Co., 129 F.4th 124 (2d Cir. 2025), 596
St. Louis North Venture v. P & L Enters., Inc., 116 F.3d 262 (7th Cir. 1997), 464
St. Mary's Honor Ctr. v. Hicks, 509 U.S. 502 (1993), 592–594
St. Petersburg, City of v. Bowen, 675 So. 2d 626 (Fla. Dist. Ct. App. 1996), 123
St. Pius X House of Retreats, Salvatorian Fathers v. Diocese of Camden, 443 A.2d 1052 (N.J. 1982), 528
Saliba, Estate of v. Dunning, 682 A.2d 224 (Me. 1996), 445
Salisbury Livestock Co. v. Colorado Century Credit Union, 793 P.2d 470 (Wyo. 1990), 34
Salmon v. Peterson, 311 N.W.2d 205 (S.D. 1981), 134
Salute v. Stratford Greens Garden Apartments, 136 F.3d 293 (2d Cir. 1998), 618, 624
Salvaty v. Falcon Cable Television, 212 Cal. Rptr. 31 (Ct. App. 1985), 198
Samaritan Inns, Inc. v. District of Columbia, 114 F.3d 1227 (D.C. Cir. 1997), 623
Sambo's Rests., Inc. v. City of Ann Arbor, 663 F.2d 686 (6th Cir. 1981), 54
Sampson Invs. v. Jondex Corp., 499 N.W.2d 177 (Wis. 1993), 453
Sanborn v. McLean, 206 N.W. 496 (Mich. 1925), 241, 242
San Carlos Apache Tribe v. Superior Court, 972 P.2d 179 (Ariz. 1999), 130–131
Sander v. Ball, 781 So. 2d 527 (Fla. Dist. Ct. App. 2001), 285
Sanders v. Dobbs Houses, Inc., 431 F.2d 1097 (5th Cir. 1970), 48, 55
San Diego Gas & Elec. Co. v. City of San Diego, 450 U.S. 621 (1981), 694
San Diego Gas & Elec. Co. v. Superior Court, 920 P.2d 669 (Cal. 1996), 45, 96, 102, 117
Sandoval; United States v., 231 U.S. 28 (1913), 803
Sanford v. Vinal, 552 N.E.2d 579 (Mass. App. Ct. 1990), 210
San Remo Hotel L.P. v. City & Cnty. of San Francisco, 41 P.3d 87 (Cal. 2002), 760, 765
Santa Barbara, City of v. Adamson, 610 P.2d 436 (Cal. 1980), 627, 669
Santa Clara Cnty. v. Southern Pac. R.R., 118 U.S. 394 (1886), 788
Santana Equestrian Priv. Fin., LLC v. Richtmyer, 349 So. 3d 441 (Fla. Dist. Ct. App. 2022), 826
Sarver v. Capital Recovery Assocs., Inc., 951 F. Supp. 550 (E.D. Pa. 1996), 489
Sathoff v. Sutterer, 869 N.E.2d 354 (Ill. App. Ct. 2007), 352
Satterfield v. J.M. Huber Corp., 888 F. Supp. 1567 (N.D. Ga. 1995), 45

Saunders v. General Servs. Corp., 659 F. Supp. 1042 (E.D. Va. 1986), 598
Save Our Rural Env't v. Snohomish Cnty., 662 P.2d 816 (Wash. 1983), 658
Sawada v. Endo, 561 P.2d 1291 (Haw. 1977), 359
Sayegusa v. Rogers, 846 P.2d 1005 (Mont. 1993), 498–499
Scarborough v. Scarborough, 142 S.E.2d 706 (S.C. 1965), 325
Scarves by Vera, Inc. v. Todo Imps., Ltd., 544 F.2d 1167 (2d Cir. 1976), 847
Schad v. Borough of Mount Ephraim, 452 U.S. 61 (1981), 674
Schaefer v. Peoples Heritage Sav. Bank, 669 A.2d 185 (Me. 1996), 353
Schaghticoke Tribe v. Kent Sch. Corp., 423 F. Supp. 780 (D. Conn. 1976), 795
Schartz v. Foster, 805 P.2d 505 (Kan. Ct. App. 1991), 449, 458
Scheg v. Agway, Inc., 645 N.Y.S.2d 687 (App. Div. 1996), 119
Scheufler v. General Host Corp., 126 F.3d 1261 (10th Cir. 1997), 117
Schiavon v. Arnaudo Bros., 100 Cal. Rptr. 2d 801 (Ct. App. 2001), 534
Schilling v. Embree, 575 P.2d 1262 (Ariz. Ct. App. 1977), 402
Schloss v. Sachs, 631 N.E.2d 212 (Ohio Mun. Ct. 1993), 438
Schmid; State v., 423 A.2d 615 (N.J. 1980), 81–82, 723
Schofield v. Iowa Homestead Co., 32 Iowa 317 (1871), 536
Schoon; United States v., 971 F.2d 193 (9th Cir. 1991), 38
Schovee v. Mikolasko, 737 A.2d 578 (Md. 1999), 261
Schuchardt; Commonwealth v., 557 N.E.2d 1380 (Mass. 1990), 39
Schuler-Olsen Ranches, Inc. v. Garvin, 250 N.W.2d 906 (Neb. 1977), 519
Schulman v. Vera, 166 Cal. Rptr. 620 (Ct. App. 1980), 480
Schultz v. Hemet Youth Pony League, Inc., 943 F. Supp. 1222 (C.D. Cal. 1996), 63, 66
Schumacher v. Ihrke, 469 N.W.2d 329 (Minn. Ct. App. 1991), 522
Schwab; State v., 693 P.2d 108 (Wash. 1985), 488
Schwartzman v. Schoening, 669 N.E.2d 228 (Mass. App. Ct. 1996), 197
Schwarz v. City of Treasure Island, 544 F.3d 1201 (11th Cir. 2008), 583
Schweiger v. Superior Court, 476 P.2d 97 (Cal. 1970), 483
Schwenk v. Boy Scouts of Am., 551 P.2d 465 (Or. 1976), 51
Sciarratta v. U.S. Bank Nat'l Ass'n, 202 Cal. Rptr. 3d 219 (Ct. App. 2016), 573
Sciotto v. Sciotto, 288 A.2d 822 (Pa. 1972), 366
Scott v. West, 594 S.W.3d 397 (Tex. 2019), 135
Scott v. Yarbro, 2008 WL 4613979 (Tenn. Ct. App. 2008), 370
Scruby v. Vintage Grapevine, Inc., 43 Cal. Rptr. 2d 810 (Ct. App. 1995), 193
Seabourn v. Coronado Area Council, Boy Scouts of Am., 891 P.2d 385 (Kan. 1995), 51, 64
Seabrook Vill. v. Murphy, 853 A.2d 280 (N.J. Super. Ct. App. Div. 2004), 382
Sears, Roebuck & Co. v. Stiffel Co., 376 U.S. 225 (1964), 849
Seattle, In re, 638 P.2d 549 (Wash. 1981), 689
Sea Winds of Marco, Inc.; United States v., 893 F. Supp. 1051 (M.D. Fla. 1995), 582
Sebastian v. Floyd, 585 S.W.2d 381 (Ky. 1979), 564
Seifert v. Sanders, 358 S.E.2d 775 (W. Va. 1987), 306
Selected Lands Corp. v. Speich, 702 S.W.2d 197 (Tex. App. 1985), 234, 262
Seligman v. First Nat'l Invs., Inc., 540 N.E.2d 1057 (Ill. App. Ct. 1989), 516
Seminole Nation v. United States, 316 U.S. 286 (1942), 802
Seminole Tribe of Fla. v. Florida, 517 U.S. 44 (1996), 796
Sensenbrenner v. Rust, Orling & Neale, 374 S.E.2d 55 (Va. 1988), 515
Serfecz v. Jewel Food Stores, 67 F.3d 591 (7th Cir. 1995), 453
74 Pinehurst LLC v. New York, 59 F.4th 557 (2d Cir. 2023), 727
$7,000.00 in U.S. Currency; Commonwealth v., 742 A.2d 711 (Pa. Commw. Ct. 1999), 817
Severa v. Solvay Specialty Polymers USA, LLC, 524 F. Supp. 3d 381 (D.N.J. 2021), 122
Severance v. Patterson, 370 S.W.3d 705 (Tex. 2012), 86, 88, 172, 756
Severns v. Union Pac. R.R. Co., 125 Cal. Rptr. 2d 100 (Ct. App. 2002), 338
Sexton v. Neun, 306 A.2d 113 (Vt. 1973), 501
Shaare Tefila Congregation v. Cobb, 481 U.S. 615 (1987), 55, 600
Shack; State v., 277 A.2d 369 (N.J. 1971), 29–30, 40, 440
Shad Alliance v. Smith Haven Mall, 488 N.E.2d 1211 (N.Y. 1985), 80
Shaff v. Leyland, 914 A.2d 1240 (N.H. 2006), 258
Shaffer v. Bellows, 260 P.3d 1064 (Alaska 2011), 285
Shalimar Ass'n v. D.O.C. Enters., Inc., 688 P.2d 682 (Ariz. Ct. App. 1984), 255, 295
Shapira v. Union Nat'l Bank, 315 N.E.2d 825 (Ohio Ct. Com. Pl. 1974), 344
Shapiro v. Cadman Towers, Inc., 51 F.3d 328 (2d Cir. 1995), 610
Shapiro v. Grinspoon, 541 N.E.2d 359 (Mass. App. Ct. 1989), 525
Shapiro v. Sutherland, 76 Cal. Rptr. 2d 101 (Ct. App. 1998), 510
Sharp v. Sumner, 528 S.E.2d 791 (Ga. 2000), 507
Sharpe Furniture, Inc. v. Buckstaff, 299 N.W.2d 219 (Wis. 1980), 397
Sharper v. Harlem Teams for Self-Help, Inc., 696 N.Y.S.2d 109 (App. Div. 1999), 205–206
Shaver v. Hunter, 626 S.W.2d 574 (Tex. App. 1981), 272–274
Shearer v. Hodnette, 674 So. 2d 548 (Ala. Civ. App. 1995), 200
Shedden v. Anadarko E. & P. Co., L.C., 136 A.3d 485 (Pa. 2016), 546
Sheetz v. County of El Dorado, 601 U.S. 267 (2024), 760
Shelley v. Kraemer, 334 U.S. 1 (1948), 277–278, 341, 579, 581, 588

Shelton v. Strickland, 21 P.3d 1179 (Wash. Ct. App. 2001), 149
Shen v. A&P Food Stores, 1995 WL 728416 (E.D.N.Y. 1995), 34
Shepard v. Purvine, 248 P.2d 352 (Or. 1952), 200
Sherrill v. Oneida Indian Nation of N.Y., 544 U.S. 197 (2005), 796–797, 800
Shiffman v. Empire Blue Cross & Blue Shield, 681 N.Y.S.2d 511 (App. Div. 1998), 28, 35–36, 41
Shinn v. Thrust IV, Inc., 786 P.2d 285 (Wash. Ct. App. 1990), 516, 518
Shinnecock Indian Nation v. New York, 2006 U.S. Dist. LEXIS 87516 (E.D.N.Y. 2006), 801
Shipp v. Stoker, 923 S.W.2d 100 (Tex. App. 1996), 193
Shipp Corp. v. Charpilloz, 414 So. 2d 1122 (Fla. Dist. Ct. App. 1982), 562
Shirley v. Shirley, 525 S.E.2d 274 (Va. 2000), 184
Shorewood W. Condo. Ass'n v. Sadri, 992 P.2d 1008 (Wash. 2000), 378
Shoshone Tribe v. United States, 299 U.S. 476 (1937), 774, 787
Shpak v. Oletsky, 373 A.2d 1234 (Md. 1977), 211
Shroades v. Rental Homes, Inc., 427 N.E.2d 774 (Ohio 1981), 485
Shultz v. Johnson, 654 So. 2d 567 (Fla. Dist. Ct. App. 1995), 170
Shumway v. Tom Sanford, Inc., 637 P.2d 666 (Wyo. 1981), 216
Siejack v. City of Baltimore, 313 A.2d 843 (N.J. 1974), 169
Sienkiewicz v. PennDOT, 2003 WL 22841693 (Pa. Ct. Com. Pl. 2003), 751
Sikora v. Wenzel, 727 N.E.2d 1277 (Ohio 2000), 485
Simeone v. Simeone, 581 A.2d 162 (Pa. 1990), 399–400
Simhawk Corp. v. Egler, 202 N.E.2d 49 (Ill. App. Ct. 1964), 453
Simi Inv. Co. v. Harris Cnty., 236 F.3d 240 (5th Cir. 2000), 668
Simmons v. Loose, 13 A.3d 366 (N.J. Super. Ct. App. Div. 2011), 712
Simms v. First Gibraltar Bank, 83 F.3d 1546 (5th Cir. 1996), 616
Simms v. Lakewood Vill. Prop. Owners Ass'n, Inc., 895 S.W.2d 779 (Tex. App. 1995), 297
Simon v. Solomon, 431 N.E.2d 556 (Mass. 1982), 479
Simons v. Simons, 978 N.W.2d 121 (Neb. 2022), 205
Simonton v. Runyon, 232 F.3d 33 (2d Cir. 2000), 606
Simpkins v. Speck, 443 P.3d 428 (Mont. 2019), 116
Sims v. Daker, 2013 WL 2249396 (Idaho 2013), 171
Singer Mfg. Co. v. Briley, 207 F.2d 519 (5th Cir. 1953), 846
Sioux Nation of Indians; United States v., 448 U.S. 371 (1980), 773, 784, 787–789, 791, 795, 803
Sioux Tribe of Indians v. United States, 316 U.S. 317 (1942), 778, 789–790
Sippin v. Ellam, 588 A.2d 660 (Conn. 1991), 455
Sipriano v. Great Spring Waters of Am., Inc., 1 S.W.3d 75 (Tex. 1999), 132
664 W. 161 St. Tenants Ass'n v. Leal, 545 N.Y.S.2d 925 (App. Div. 1989), 477
Skelly Oil Co. v. Ashmore, 365 S.W.2d 582 (Mo. 1963), 527
Skendzel v. Marshall, 301 N.E.2d 641 (Ind. 1973), 566
Slade v. Caesars Entm't Corp., 373 P.3d 74 (Nev. 2016), 30
Slater v. Pearle Vision Ctr., Inc., 546 A.2d 676 (Pa. Super. Ct. 1988), 453
Slavin v. Rent Control Bd. of Brookline, 548 N.E.2d 1226 (Mass. 1990), 491–492
Slaybaugh v. Rutherford Cnty., 114 F.4th 593 (6th Cir. 2024), 712
Sligh v. Plair, 569 S.W.2d 58 (Ark. 1978), 308
Sloan v. Johnson, 491 S.E.2d 725 (Va. 1997), 239, 266
Smith v. Avanti, 249 F. Supp. 3d 1194 (D. Colo. 2017), 608
Smith v. Bank of Am., 957 N.Y.S.2d 705 (App. Div. 2012), 353
Smith v. Butler Mountain Estates Prop. Owners' Ass'n, Inc., 367 S.E.2d 401 (N.C. Ct. App. 1988), 275
Smith v. Carbide & Chems. Corp., 226 S.W.3d 52 (Ky. 2007), 28
Smith v. David, 176 Cal. Rptr. 112 (Ct. App. 1981), 476–477
Smith v. Fair Emp't & Hous. Comm'n, 913 P.2d 909 (Cal. 1996), 613
Smith v. First Sav. of La., 575 So. 2d 1033 (Ala. 1991), 260, 276
Smith v. Hayden, 772 P.2d 47 (Colo. 1989), 144, 146–148
Smith v. Kansas Gas Serv. Co., 169 P.3d 1052 (Kan. 2007), 119
Smith v. Lagow Constr. & Dev. Co., 642 N.W.2d 187 (S.D. 2002), 486
Smith v. McCullough Dredging Co., 152 So. 2d 194 (Fla. Dist. Ct. App. 1963), 45
Smith v. Pacific Props. & Dev. Corp., 358 F.3d 1097 (9th Cir. 2004), 597
Smith v. Renne, 46 N.E.2d 587 (Ill. 1943), 337
Smith v. Smith, 308 S.E.2d 504 (N.C. Ct. App. 1983), 451
Smith v. Tippett, 569 A.2d 1186 (D.C. 1990), 146, 148, 151, 153
Smith v. Town of Clarkton, N.C., 682 F.2d 1055 (4th Cir. 1982), 615
Smith v. Warth, 483 S.W.2d 834 (Tex. Civ. App. 1972), 527
Smith v. Woodhollow Apartments, 463 F. Supp. 16 (W.D. Okla. 1978), 600
Smith & Lee Assocs., Inc. v. City of Taylor, Mich., 13 F.3d 920 (6th Cir. 1993), 622
Smithson v. Lindzey, 479 P.3d 759 (Wyo. 2021), 188
Snider v. Arnold, 289 P.3d 43 (Idaho 2012), 205
Snook v. Bowers, 12 P.3d 771 (Alaska 2000), 143, 156
Snow v. Van Dam, 197 N.E. 224 (Mass. 1935), 266
Snyder v. Lovercheck, 992 P.2d 1079 (Wyo. 1999), 512
Society of Jesus of New England v. Boston Landmarks Comm'n, 564 N.E.2d 571 (Mass. 1990), 677
Sofsky v. Rosenberg, 564 N.E.2d 662 (N.Y. 1990), 530
Solomon R. Guggenheim Found. v. Lubell, 569 N.E.2d 426 (N.Y. 1991), 173
Somerville v. Jacobs, 170 S.E.2d 805 (W. Va. 1969), 42, 169
Sommer v. Kridel, 378 A.2d 767 (N.J. 1977), 464–465
Songbyrd, Inc. v. Estate of Albert B. Grossman, 23 F. Supp. 2d 219 (N.D.N.Y. 1998), 172
Sonoma Dev., Inc. v. Miller, 515 S.E.2d 577 (Va. 1999), 239–240, 247
Sony Computer Entm't Am., Inc. v. Bleem, LLC, 214 F.3d 1022 (9th Cir. 2000), 837

Sony Corp. v. Universal City Studios, 464 U.S. 417 (1984), 839
Sotomura v. County of Hawai'i, 460 F. Supp. 473 (D. Haw. 1978), 90
Southcenter Joint Venture v. National Democratic Policy Comm., 780 P.2d 1282 (Wash. 1989), 80–81
South Covington & Cincinnati St. Ry. Co.; Commonwealth v., 205 S.W. 581 (Ky. 1918), 121
Southeast Ark. Landfill, Inc. v. State, 858 S.W.2d 665 (Ark. 1993), 117
Southeast Bank, N.A. v. Sapp, 554 So. 2d 1193 (Fla. Dist. Ct. App. 1989), 529
Southern Burlington Cnty., NAACP v. Township of Mount Laurel, 336 A.2d 713 (N.J. 1975), 631–632, 634, 671
Southern Burlington Cnty., NAACP v. Township of Mount Laurel, 456 A.2d 390 (N.J. 1983), 632–633
South Lake Tahoe Prop. Owners Grp. v. City of S. Lake Tahoe, 310 Cal. Rptr. 3d 9 (Ct. App. 2023), 654
South Suburban Hous. Ctr. v. Greater S. Suburban Bd. of Realtors, 713 F. Supp. 1068 (N.D. Ill. 1988), *aff'd in part and rev'd in part*, 935 F.2d 868 (7th Cir. 1991), 595–596
Southwestern Ill. Dev. Auth. v. National City Envtl., 768 N.E.2d 1, 263 Ill. Dec. 241 (Ill. 2002), 687
Spall v. Janota, 406 N.E.2d 378 (Ind. Ct. App. 1980), 133–134
Spann v. Colonial Vill., Inc., 899 F.2d 24 (D.C. Cir. 1990), 598
Sparks v. Douglas Cnty., 904 P.2d 738 (Wash. 1995), 758
Sparling v. Fon Du Lac Twp., 745 N.E.2d 660 (Ill. App. Ct. 2001), 219
Spears v. Warr, 44 P.3d 742, 2002 UT 24 (Utah 2002), 507
Special Force Ministries v. WCCO Television, 584 N.W.2d 789 (Minn. Ct. App. 1998), 36
Spencer's Case, 77 Eng. Rep. 72 (1583), 245
S.P. Growers Ass'n v. Rodriguez, 552 P.2d 721 (Cal. 1976), 484
Spinks v. Taylor, 266 S.E.2d 857 (N.C. Ct. App.), *aff'd in part and modified in part, rev'd in part*, 278 S.E.2d 501 (N.C. 1981), 460
Spokane Cnty. Dist. Ct.; State v., 491 P.3d 119 (Wash. 2021), 38
Sprankle v. Burns, 675 A.2d 1287 (Pa. Super. Ct. 1996), 217
Spratt v. Spratt, 456 N.W.2d 181 (Iowa 1990), 362
Sprecher v. Adamson, 636 P.2d 1121 (Cal. 1981), 118
Springlake Corp. v. Symmarron Ltd. P'ship, 569 A.2d 715 (Md. Ct. App. 1990), 455
Spring Lakes, Ltd. v. O.F.M. Co., 467 N.E.2d 537 (Ohio 1984), 242, 551
Sprint Spectrum, L.P. v. Willoth, 176 F.3d 630 (2d Cir. 1999), 665
Sprunk v. Creekwood Condo. Unit Owners' Ass'n, 573 N.E.2d 197 (Ohio Ct. App. 1989), 380
Spur Indus. v. Webb, 494 P.2d 700 (Ariz. 1972), 112
Sramek v. Korth, 559 N.W.2d 924 (Wis. Ct. App. 1996), 117
Stabenau v. Cairelli, 577 A.2d 1130 (Conn. App. Ct. 1990), 525
Staley v. Stephens, 404 N.E.2d 633 (Ind. Ct. App. 1980), 518, 520
Stamboulos v. McKee, 342 A.2d 529 (N.J. Super. Ct. App. Div. 1975), 726
Stambovsky v. Ackley, 572 N.Y.S.2d 672 (App. Div. 1991), 510
Standard Materials, Inc. v. City of Slidell, 700 So. 2d 975 (La. Ct. App. 1997), 750
Stanley v. Moore, 454 S.E.2d 225 (N.C. 1995), 460, 487
Staron v. McDonald's Corp., 51 F.3d 353 (2d Cir. 1995), 69
Starrett City Assocs.; United States v., 840 F.2d 1096 (2d Cir. 1988), 595–596, 624
State v. *See name of opposing party*
State ex rel. v. *See name of related party*
State Dep't of Transp. & Dev. v. Regard, 567 So. 2d 1174 (La. Ct. App. 1990), 691
State Highway Comm'n v. Batts, 144 S.E.2d 126 (N.C. 1965), 213
Stat-O-Matic Ret. Fund v. Assistance League of Yuma, 941 P.2d 233 (Ariz. Ct. App. 1997), 166
Steagall v. Robinson, 344 S.E.2d 803 (N.C. Ct. App. 1986), 242
Steel Creek Dev. Co. v. Smith, 268 S.E.2d 205 (N.C. 1980), 38
Steele v. Houston, 603 S.W.2d 786 (Tex. 1980), 712
Steffen v. Paulus, 465 N.E.2d 1021 (Ill. App. Ct. 1984), 446
Steil v. Smith, 901 P.2d 395 (Wyo. 1995), 192
Steiner v. Showboat Operating Co., 25 F.3d 1459 (9th Cir. 1994), 607
Sterling v. Kazmierczak, 983 F. Supp. 1186 (N.D. Ill. 1997), 58–59
Stern v. Metropolitan Water Dist. of Salt Lake & Sandy, 274 P.3d 935 (Utah 2012), 243
Stevan v. Brown, 458 A.2d 466 (Md. Ct. Spec. App. 1983), 471
Stevens v. City of Cannon Beach, 835 P.2d 940 (Or. Ct. App. 1992), *aff'd*, 854 P.2d 449 (Or. 1993), *cert. denied*, 510 U.S. 1207 (1994), 89, 754–755
Stevens v. Fleming, 777 P.2d 1196 (Idaho 1989), 485
Stevenson v. E.I. Dupont de Nemours, 327 F.3d 400 (5th Cir. 2003), 44
Stevenson v. Goodson, 924 P.2d 339 (Utah 1996), 102
Stewart v. AmSouth Mortg. Co., 679 So. 2d 247 (Ala. Ct. App.), *rev'd*, 679 So. 2d 251 (Ala. 1996), 352, 353
Stewart v. Melnick, 613 P.2d 1336 (Haw. Ct. App. 1980), 447
Stewart Title Guar. Co. v. Greenlands Realty, 58 F. Supp. 2d 360 (D.N.J. 1999), 517
Stickney v. City of Saco, 770 A.2d 592, 2001 ME 69 (Me. 2001), 728
Stiefel v. Lindemann, 638 A.2d 642 (Conn. App. Ct. 1994), 188–191, 214, 216
Stiglianese v. Vallone, 637 N.Y.S.2d 284 (Civ. Ct. 1995), 117
Stimson Lumber Co. v. United States, 82 F.4th 1346 (Fed. Cir. 2023), 223
Stinson, Lyons, Gerlin & Bustamante, P.A. v. Brickell Bldg. 1 Holding Co., 923 F.2d 810 (11th Cir. 1991), 471
Stone v. City of Walton, 331 N.W.2d 398 (Iowa 1983), 654
Stonebraker v. Zinn, 286 S.E.2d 911 (W. Va. 1982), 565
Stonehedge Square Ltd. P'ship v. Movie Merchs., Inc., 715 A.2d 1082 (Pa. 1998), 463, 465–466

Stoner v. Zucker, 83 P. 808 (Cal. 1906), 200
Stop the Beach Renourishment, Inc. v. Florida Dep't of Envtl. Prot., 560 U.S. 702 (2010), 172, 743, 753, 756
Storck v. Storck, 1999 WL 326160 (Minn. Ct. App. 1999), 207
STORE SPE LA Fitness v. Fitness Int'l, LLC, 2021 WL 3285036 (C.D. Cal. June 30, 2021), 452
Storey v. Patterson, 437 So. 2d 491 (Ala. 1983), 42
Stowe Ctr., Inc. v. Burlington Sav. Bank, 451 A.2d 1114 (Vt. 1982), 558
Strahin v. Lantz, 456 S.E.2d 12 (W. Va. 1995), 223
Stranahan v. Fred Meyer, Inc., 11 P.3d 228 (Or. 2000), 82
Strawn v. Canuso, 657 A.2d 420 (N.J. 1995), 502, 510
Streams Sports Club, Ltd. v. Richmond, 457 N.E.2d 1226 (Ill. 1983), 256–257
Strickland v. Medlen, 397 S.W.3d 184 (Tex. 2013), 816
Strollo v. Iannantuoni, 734 A.2d 144 (Conn. App. Ct. 1999), 210, 212
Stucki v. Plavin, 291 A.2d 508 (Me. 1972), 647
Stump v. Whibco, 715 A.2d 1006 (N.J. Super. Ct. App. Div. 1998), 147–148, 156, 166
Stylianopoulos v. Stylianopoulos, 455 N.E.2d 477 (Mass. App. Ct. 1983), 368
Succession of. *See name of party*
Suggs v. Carroll, 333 S.E.2d 510 (N.C. Ct. App. 1985), 28
Sullivan v. Little Hunting Park, Inc., 396 U.S. 229 (1969), 601
Sullivan v. Rooney, 533 N.E.2d 1372 (Mass. 1989), 206, 413, 415
Sullivan as Tr. of Sylvester L. Sullivan Grantor Retained Income Tr. v. Max Spann Real Est. & Auction Co., 276 A.3d 92 (N.J. 2022), 503
Sullivant v. Oklahoma City, 940 P.2d 220 (Okla. 1997), 711
Summit Town Centre, Inc. v. Shoe Show of Rocky Mount, Inc., 828 A.2d 995 (Pa. 2003), 453
Sunday Canyon Prop. Owners Ass'n v. Annett, 978 S.W.2d 654 (Tex. App. 1998), 376
Sunnyside Feed Co. v. City of Portage, 588 N.W.2d 278 (Wis. Ct. App. 1998), 112
Sun Oil Co. v. City of Upper Arlington, 379 N.E.2d 266 (Ohio Ct. App. 1977), 654
Sun Ridge Dev., Inc. v. City of Cheyenne, 787 P.2d 583 (Wyo. 1990), 662
Suntrust Bank v. Houghton Mifflin Co., 136 F. Supp. 2d 1357 (N.D. Ga.), *rev'd*, 268 F.3d 1257 (11th Cir. 2001), 838
Sutherlin Sch. Dist. #130 v. Herrera, 851 P.2d 1171 (Or. Ct. App. 1993), 214–215
Swanner v. Anchorage Equal Rights Comm'n, 874 P.2d 274 (Alaska 1994), 613
Swartzbaugh v. Sampson, 54 P.2d 73 (Cal. 1936), 355
Sweeney v. Landings Ass'n, Inc., 595 S.E.2d 74 (Ga. 2004), 297
Sweeney, Adm'x v. Sweeney, 11 A.2d 806 (Conn. 1940), 531
Swenson v. Erickson, 998 P.2d 807 (Utah 2000), 297
Switzer v. Pratt, 23 N.W.2d 837 (Iowa 1946), 351
Sylvania Elec. Prods., Inc. v. City of Newton, 183 N.E.2d 118 (Mass. 1962), 650
Sylva Shops Ltd. P'ship v. Hibbard, 623 S.E.2d 785 (N.C. Ct. App. 2006), 464
Symphony Space, Inc. v. Pergola Props., Inc., 646 N.Y.S.2d 641 (App. Div. 1996), 337
Szafranski v. Dunston, 34 N.E.3d 1132 (Ill. App. Ct. 2015), 831

T

Tabb Lakes, Ltd. v. United States, 10 F.3d 796 (Fed. Cir. 1993), 732
Tage II Corp. v. Ducas (U.S.) Realty Corp., 461 N.E.2d 1222 (Mass. App. Ct. 1984), 448
Tahoe-Sierra Pres. Council, Inc. v. Tahoe Reg'l Planning Agency, 535 U.S. 302 (2002), 732, 740–741, 742
Tamalunis v. City of Georgetown, 542 N.E.2d 402 (Ill. App. Ct. 1989), 111–112
Tangren Family Tr. v. Tangren, 182 P.3d 326, 2008 UT 20 (Utah 2008), 507
Tanguay v. Marston, 503 A.2d 834 (N.H. 1986), 485
Tantaro v. Common Ground Cmty. Hous. Dev. Fund, Inc., 147 A.D.3d 684 (N.Y. App. Div. 2017), 439, 458
Tate; Commonwealth v., 432 A.2d 1382 (Pa. 1981), 81
Tatro v. Lehouiller, 513 A.2d 610 (Vt. 1986), 439
Taylor, In re, 343 P.3d 867 (Cal. 2015), 669
Taylor v. Canterbury, 92 P.3d 961 (Colo. 2004), 352
Taylor v. Hays, 551 So. 2d 906 (Miss. 1989), 210
Taylor v. Leedy & Co., 412 So. 2d 763 (Ala. 1982), 473
Taylor v. Martha's Vineyard Land Bank Comm'n, 60 N.E.3d 319 (Mass. 2016), 196
Taylor v. Northam, 862 S.E.2d 458 (2021), 290
Taylor v. Schukei Family Tr., 996 P.2d 13 (Wyo. 2000), 484
Taylor v. Tellez, 610 A.2d 252 (D.C. 1992), 117
Taylor Real Estate & Ins. Co. v. Greene, 151 So. 2d 397 (Ala. 1963), 500
Tee-Hit-Ton Indians v. United States, 348 U.S. 272 (1955), 18, 773, 777, 781–784, 786–787, 788–790
Tefft v. Munson, 57 N.Y. 97 (1874), 547
Telluride, Town of v. Lot Thirty-Four Venture, L.L.C., 3 P.3d 30 (Colo. 2000), 633
Tenhet v. Boswell, 554 P.2d 330 (Cal. 1976), 354, 356
Tenn v. 889 Assocs., Ltd., 500 A.2d 366 (N.H. 1985), 137, 221
Tennessee v. Lane, 541 U.S. 509 (2004), 66
Terrell v. Torres, 456 P.3d 13 (Ariz. 2020), 830
Terrien v. Zwit, 648 N.W.2d 602 (Mich. 2002), 271, 287
Territory v. *See name of party*
Terry v. Gaslight Square Assocs., 897 P.2d 667 (Ariz. Ct. App. 1994), 457
Terry v. Lincscott Hotel Corp., 617 P.2d 56 (Ariz. 1980), 825
Terry v. Lock Hospitality, Inc., 37 S.W.3d 202 (Ark. 2001), 819
Terry v. Public Serv. Co. of N.C., Inc., 898 S.E.2d 648 (N.C. 2024), 484
Testa v. Planning & Zoning Comm'n of the Town of Newtown, 2000 WL 1056606 (Conn. Super. Ct. 2000), 750
Texaco Ref. & Mktg., Inc. v. Samowitz, 570 A.2d 170 (Conn. 1990), 337
Texas Dep't of Cmty. Affairs v. Burdine, 450 U.S. 248 (1981), 592

Texas Dep't of Hous. & Cmty. Affairs v. Inclusive Cmtys. Project, Inc., 576 U.S. 519 (2015), 615–616
Texas Manufactured Hous. Ass'n v. Nederland, 101 F.3d 1095 (5th Cir. 1996), 736
Thayer v. Thompson, 677 P.2d 787 (Wash. Ct. App. 1984), 288
Thomas v. Anchorage Equal Rights Comm'n, 165 F.3d 692 (9th Cir. 1999), *withdrawn and remanded to dismiss*, 220 F.3d 1134 (9th Cir. 2000), 613–614
Thomas v. City of West Haven, 734 A.2d 535 (Conn. 1999), 670
Thomas v. Lenhart, 444 A.2d 246 (Conn. 1982), 441
Thomas v. Papadelis, 476 N.E.2d 726 (Ohio Ct. App. 1984), 460
Thompson v. Pendleton, 697 A.2d 56 (Me. 1997), 193
Thomsen v. Greve, 550 N.W.2d 49 (Neb. Ct. App. 1996), 105, 116
Thomson, Estate of v. Wade, 509 N.E.2d 309 (N.Y. 1987), 184, 198
Thornton v. Driscoll, 2022 WL 4102263 (Mass. Land Ct. Sept. 8, 2022), 166
Thornton, State ex rel. v. Hay, 462 P.2d 671 (Or. 1969), 86, 88–89, 754
303 Creative L.L.C. v. Elenis, 600 U.S. 570 (2023), 74
Thurmond v. Bowman, 211 F. Supp. 3d 554 (W.D.N.Y. 2016), 585
Thurston v. Hancock, 12 Mass. 220 (1815), 133
Tidd v. Stauffer, 308 N.E.2d 415 (Ind. Ct. App. 1974), 565
Tiegs v. Watts, 954 P.2d 877 (Wash. 1998), 102, 117
Tietgen v. Brown's Westminster Motors, Inc., 921 F. Supp. 1495 (E.D. Va. 1996), 605
Tillman v. Wheaton-Haven Recreation Ass'n, Inc., 410 U.S. 431 (1973), 601
Timberstone Homeowner's Ass'n, Inc. v. Summerlin, 467 S.E.2d 330 (Ga. 1996), 227–228
Time Mechanisms, Inc. v. Qonaar, 422 F. Supp. 905 (D.N.J. 1976), 849
Timm v. Clement, 574 N.W.2d 368 (Iowa 1997), 510
Timmerman v. Smith, 413 So. 2d 627 (La. Ct. App. 1982), 500
Tinnin v. First United Bank of Miss., 502 So. 2d 659 (Miss. 1987), *after remand*, 570 So. 2d 1193 (Miss. 1990), 279–280, 322
Tioga Coal Co. v. Supermarkets Gen. Corp., 546 A.2d 1 (Pa. 1988), 158
T.K. Stanley, Inc. v. Cason, 614 So. 2d 942 (Miss. 1992), 117
Tobin v. Stevens, 251 Cal. Rptr. 587 (Ct. App. 1988), 171
Toledo Bar Ass'n v. Chelsea Title Agency of Dayton, Inc., 800 N.E.2d 29 (Ohio 2003), 503
Tolksdorf v. Griffith, 626 N.W.2d 163 (Mich. 2001), 213, 687
Tomasso Bros., Inc. v. October Twenty-Four, Inc., 646 A.2d 133 (Conn. 1994), 117
Tomlinson v. Clarke, 803 P.2d 828 (Wash. Ct. App. 1991), *aff'd*, 825 P.2d 706 (Wash. 1992), 544
Totman v. Malloy, 725 N.E.2d 1045 (Mass. 2000), 150
Town of. *See name of town*
Townsend v. Cable, 378 S.W.2d 806 (Ky. 1964), 185
Trade-Mark Cases, In re, 100 U.S. 82 (1879), 844
Traders, Inc. v. Bartholomew, 459 A.2d 974 (Vt. 1983), 211
Trammell v. Elliott, 199 S.E.2d 194 (Ga. 1973), 322
Tranfield v. Arcuni-English, 215 A.3d 222 (Me. 2019), 105
Trapasso v. Lewis, 239 A.3d 703 (Md. 2020), 358
Trentacost v. Brussel, 412 A.2d 436 (N.J. 1980), 486
Tresemer v. Albuquerque Pub. Sch. Dist., 619 P.2d 819 (N.M. 1980), 171
Tripp v. Huff, 606 A.2d 792 (Me. 1992), 184
Tristram's Landing, Inc. v. Wait, 327 N.E.2d 727 (Mass. 1975), 501
Truck Equip. Serv. Co. v. Fruehauf Corp., 536 F.2d 1210 (8th Cir. 1976), 849
Trustees of Schs. of Twp. No. 1 v. Batdorf, 130 N.E.2d 111 (Ill. 1955), 338, 537
Tsombanidis v. City of W. Haven, 129 F. Supp. 2d 136 (D. Conn. 2001), 623
Tubwell v. FV-1, Inc., So. 3d 987 (Miss. 2024), 29
Tucker v. Badoian, 384 N.E.2d 1195 (Mass. 1978), 129
Tucker v. Toia, 371 N.E.2d 449 (N.Y. 1977), 636
Tudor City Place Ass'n v. 2 Tudor City Tenants Corp., 924 F.2d 1247 (2d Cir. 1991), 373
Tulee v. Washington, 315 U.S. 681 (1942), 806
Tulk v. Moxhay, 41 Eng. Rep. 1143 (1848), 246
Tupper v. Dorchester Cnty., 487 S.E.2d 187 (S.C. 1997), 189, 198
Turkey, Republic of v. Christie's Inc., 425 F. Supp. 3d 204 (S.D.N.Y. 2019), 855
Turks Head Realty Tr. v. Shearson Lehman Hutton, Inc., 736 F. Supp. 422 (D.R.I. 1990), 467
Turner v. Baisley, 602 N.Y.S.2d 907 (App. Div. 1993), 217
Turner v. White, 579 P.2d 410 (Wash. Ct. App. 1978), 439
Turner Adver. Co. v. Garcia, 311 S.E.2d 466 (Ga. 1984), 556
Turning Point, Inc. v. City of Caldwell, 74 F.3d 941 (9th Cir. 1996), 584
Tuscarora MarketPlace Partners, LLC v. First Nat'l Bank, 906 S.E.2d 171 (Va. Ct. App. 2024), 253–254
Tusch Enters. v. Coffin, 740 P.2d 1022 (Idaho 1987), 514
12 Havemeyer Place Co., LLC v. Gordon, 820 A.2d 299 (Conn. App. Ct. 2003), 456
21 Merchants Row Corp v. Merchants Row, Inc., 587 N.E.2d 788 (Mass. 1992), 491
T.W.I.W., Inc. v. Rhudy, 630 P.2d 753 (N.M. 1981), 446
Tyler v. Hennepin Cnty., 598 U.S. 631 (2023), 743, 747–748
Tyler, City of v. Likes, 962 S.W.2d 489 (Tex. 1997), 102
Tyus v. Urban Search Mgmt., 102 F.3d 256 (7th Cir. 1996), 598

U

U & ME Homes, LLC v. County of Suffolk, 148 N.Y.S.3d 682 (Sup. Ct. 2021), 243
Uliasz v. Gillette, 256 N.E.2d 290 (Mass. 1970), 201
UMG Recordings, Inc. v. MP3.com, Inc., 92 F. Supp. 2d 349 (S.D.N.Y. 2000), 840
Umphres v. J.R. Mayer Enters., 889 S.W.2d 86 (Mo. Ct. App. 1994), 196
Underwood v. Bunger, 70 N.E.3d 338 (Ind. 2017), 360

Union Pac. Res. Co. v. Cooper, 109 S.W.3d 557 (Tex. App. 2003), 119
United Bhd. of Carpenters & Joiners of Am. v. Anderson. *See* Anderson v. Conboy
United States v. *See name of opposing party*
United States ex rel. v. *See name of related party*
United States Jaycees v. Bloomfield, 434 A.2d 1379 (D.C. Ct. App. 1981), 50
United States Jaycees v. Iowa Civil Rights Comm'n, 427 N.W.2d 450 (Iowa 1988), 50–51
United States Jaycees v. Massachusetts Comm'n Against Discrimination, 463 N.E.2d 1151 (Mass. 1984), 51, 64
United States Jaycees v. McClure, 305 N.W.2d 764 (Minn. 1981), *aff'd sub nom.* Roberts v. United States Jaycees, 468 U.S. 609 (1984), 51–52
United States Jaycees v. Richardet, 666 P.2d 1008 (Alaska 1983), 50–51, 64
United States Power Squadrons v. State Human Rights Appeal Bd., 452 N.E.2d 1199 (N.Y. 1983), 51
University of Neb. at Kearny; United States v., 940 F. Supp. 2d 974 (D. Neb. 2013), 583
University Place-Lincoln Assocs. LP v. Nelson, 530 N.W.2d 241 (Neb. 1995), 192
Uno Rests., Inc. v. Boston Kenmore Realty Corp., 805 N.E.2d 957 (Mass. 2004), 430
Upson v. Goodland State Bank & Tr. Co., 823 P.2d 704 (Colo. 1992), 534
Urban League of R.I. v. Sambo's of R.I., Inc., File Nos. 79 PRA 074-06/06, 79 ERA 073-06/06, EEOC No. 011790461 (R.I. Comm'n for Human Rights 1981), 54
Urban Site Venture II Ltd. P'ship v. Levering Assocs. Ltd. P'ship, 665 A.2d 1062 (Md. 1995), 42
Urman v. South Bos. Sav. Bank, 674 N.E.2d 1078 (Mass. 1997), 510
U.S. Bank Nat'l Ass'n v. Ibañez, 941 N.E.2d 40 (Mass. 2011), 570
U.S. Coast Guard, United States on Behalf of v. Cerio, 831 F. Supp. 530 (E.D. Va. 1993), 337
Usery v. Turner Elkhorn Mining Co., 428 U.S. 1 (1976), 751
Uston v. Airport Casino, Inc., 564 F.2d 1216 (9th Cir. 1977), 30, 32
Uston v. Resorts Int'l Hotel, Inc., 445 A.2d 370 (N.J. 1982), 31–32, 33, 723, 754
Uthus v. Valley Mill Camp, Inc., 246 A.3d 1225 (Md. 2021), 27, 184
Uzan v. 845 UN Ltd. P'ship, 778 N.Y.S.2d 171 (2004), 525

V

Vadney, In re Estate of, 634 N.E.2d 976 (N.Y. 1994), 360
Vagts v. Northern Nat. Gas Co., 8 N.W.3d 501 (Iowa 2024), 106
Valenti v. Hopkins, 926 P.2d 813 (Or. 1996), 275
Valentine v. Chrestensen, 315 U.S. 52 (1942), 673
Van Buren Apartments v. Adams, 701 P.2d 583 (Ariz. Ct. App. 1984), 483
Vanderwall v. Midkiff, 421 N.W.2d 263 (Mich. Ct. App. 1988), 552
Van Horn; People v., 267 Cal. Rptr. 804 (Ct. App. 1990), 806, 832
Van Schaack v. Torsoe, 555 N.Y.S.2d 836 (App. Div. 1990), 204
Van Winkle & Liggett v. G.B.R. Fabrics, Inc., 511 A.2d 124 (N.J. 1986), 499
Vargas v. Esquire, 164 F.2d 522 (7th Cir. 1947), 853
Varnum v. Brien, 763 N.W.2d 862 (Iowa 2009), 410
Vásquez v. Glassboro Serv. Ass'n, Inc., 415 A.2d 1156 (N.J. 1980), 440
Vasquez v. Hawthorne, 33 P.3d 735 (Wash. 2001), 415–416
Vaswani v. Wohletz, 396 S.E.2d 593 (Ga. Ct. App. 1990), 462, 491
Versatile Metals, Inc. v. Union Corp., 693 F. Supp. 1563 (E.D. Pa. 1988), 467
Victorville W. Ltd. P'ship v. Inverrary Ass'n, Inc., 226 So. 3d 888 (Fla. Dist. Ct. App. 2017), 284
Vigeant v. Donel Realty Tr., 540 A.2d 1243 (N.H. 1988), 211, 214
Vigilant Ins. Co. of Am. v. Housing Auth. of El Paso, 660 N.E.2d 1121 (N.Y. 1995), 172
Villa de las Palmas Homeowners Ass'n v. Terifaj, 90 P.3d 1223 (Cal. 2004), 287, 380
Village of. *See name of village*
Villa Nova Resort, Inc. v. State, 711 S.W.2d 120 (Tex. App. 1986), 220
Vincent v. Lake Erie Transp. Co., 124 N.W. 221 (Minn. 1910), 38
Vincent v. Vits, 566 N.E.2d 818 (Ill. App. Ct. 1991), 522
Virginia State Bd. of Pharmacy v. Virginia Citizens Consumer Council, 425 U.S. 484 (1976), 673
Vogel v. Grant-Lafayette Elec. Coop., 548 N.W.2d 829 (Wis. 1996), 102, 105–106
Volkmann v. City of Crosby, 120 N.W.2d 18 (N.D. 1963), 132
Vrazel v. Skrabanek, 725 S.W.2d 709 (Tex. 1987), 220
VSH Realty, Inc. v. Texaco, Inc., 757 F.2d 411 (1st Cir. 1985), 512
Vulcan Materials Co. v. Miller, 691 So. 2d 908 (Miss. 1997), 259
Vulcan Oil Co. v. Gorman, 434 So. 2d 760 (Ala. 1983), 498

W

Wagner; United States v., 940 F. Supp. 972 (N.D. Tex. 1996), 625
Waits v. Frito-Lay, Inc., 978 F.2d 1093 (9th Cir. 1992), 851
Wakelin v. Town of Yarmouth, 523 A.2d 575 (Me. 1987), 647
Walch v. Crandall, 416 N.W.2d 375 (Mich. Ct. App. 1987), 526
Waldorff Ins. & Bonding, Inc. v. Eglin Nat'l Bank, 453 So. 2d 1383 (Fla. Dist. Ct. App. 1984), 551
Walgreen Ariz. Drug Co. v. Plaza Ctr. Corp., 647 P.2d 643 (Ariz. Ct. App. 1982), 454
Walgreen Co. v. Sara Creek Prop. Co., 966 F.2d 273 (7th Cir. 1992), 268
Walker v. City of Mesquite, 169 F.3d 973 (5th Cir. 1999), 581
Walker v. Crigler, 976 F.2d 900 (4th Cir. 1992), 602
Walker v. Graham, 706 P.2d 278 (Wyo. 1985), 525
Walker v. Wilson, 469 So. 2d 580 (Ala. 1985), 549

Walker Drug Co. v. La Sal Oil Co., 972 P.2d 1238 (Utah 1998), 27, 119
Wallace v. Atlantic City, 608 A.2d 480 (N.J. Super. Ct. Law Div. 1992), 712
Walters v. Servidio, 320 A.3d 1008 (Conn. App. Ct. 2024), 224
Walters v. Smith, 41 S.E.2d 617 (Va. 1947), 201
Wana the Bear v. Community Constr., Inc., 180 Cal. Rptr. 423 (Ct. App. 1982), 806, 831–832
Wanha v. Long, 587 N.W.2d 531 (Neb. 1998), 166
Ward v. McGlory, 265 N.E.2d 78 (Mass. 1970), 193, 197
Ward v. Ward, 783 S.E.2d 873 (W. Va. 2016), 169
Ward; People v., 805 N.E.2d 645 (Ill. App. Ct. 2004), 24
Wareing v. Schreckendgust, 930 P.2d 37 (Mont. 1996), 214
Waremart v. Progressive Campaigns, 989 P.2d 524 (Wash. 1999), 80
Warnack v. Coneen Family Tr., 879 P.2d 715 (Mont. 1994), 150
Warner v. Konover, 553 A.2d 1138 (Conn. 1989), 491
Warner Bros. Entm't, Inc. & J.K. Rowling v. RDR Books, 575 F. Supp. 2d 513 (S.D.N.Y. 2008), 841
Warren v. Detlefsen, 663 S.W.2d 710 (Ark. 1984), 238
Warsaw v. Chicago Metallic Ceilings, Inc., 676 P.2d 584 (Cal. 1984), 42, 221
Warshow; State v., 410 A.2d 1000 (Vt. 1979), 39
Washburn v. 166 E. 96th St. Owners Corp., 564 N.Y.S.2d 115 (App. Div. 1990), 468
Washington v. Davis, 426 U.S. 229 (1976), 581
Washington v. Fishing Vessel Ass'n, 443 U.S. 658 (1979), 807
Washington v. United States, 584 U.S. 837 (2018), 777
Washington; United States v., 135 F.3d 618 (9th Cir. 1998), 90
Washington; United States v., 853 F.3d 946 (9th Cir. 2017), *aff'd by an equally divided Court,* 584 U.S. 837 (2018), 777, 807
Washington Legal Found. v. Legal Found. of Wash., 236 F.3d 1097 (9th Cir. 2001), 747
Washington Legal Found. v. Texas Equal Access to Justice, 86 F. Supp. 2d 624 (E.D. Tex. 2000), 747
Washington Mut. Bank v. Green, 806 N.E.2d 604 (Ohio Ct. App. 2004), 570
Washington State Dep't of Licensing v. Cougar Den, Inc., 586 U.S. 347 (2019), 777, 807
Washington Suburban Sanitary Comm'n v. CAE-Link Corp., 622 A.2d 745 (Md. 1993), 117
Wasland v. Porter Auto & Marine, Inc., 600 N.W.2d 904 (S.D. 1999), 824
Waters v. Biesecker, 305 S.E.2d 539 (N.C. 1983), 134
Water Use Permit Applications, Matter of, 9 P.3d 409 (Haw. 2000), 750
Watrous v. Steel, 4 Vt. 629 (Vt. 1829), 31
Watson, Ex parte, 589 S.E.2d 760 (S.C. 2003), 503
Watson v. Brown, 686 P.2d 12 (Haw. 1984), 460
Watson v. Fraternal Order of Eagles, 915 F.2d 235 (6th Cir. 1990), 56, 60
Watson v. Fultz, 782 P.2d 361 (Mont. 1989), 498
Watts, In re Marriage of, 217 Cal. Rptr. 301 (Ct. App. 1985), 368
Watts v. Watts, 405 N.W.2d 303 (Wis. 1987), 206, 412
Wayne Cnty. v. Hathcock, 684 N.W.2d 765 (Mich. 2004), 688
Waynesboro Vill. v. BMC Props., 496 S.E.2d 64 (Va. 1998), 244, 249
Weatherby Lake Improvement Co. v. Sherman, 611 S.W.2d 326 (Mo. Ct. App. 1980), 376
Webb's Fabulous Pharmacies, Inc. v. Beckwith, 449 U.S. 155 (1980), 743, 745–746
Weeks v. Krysa, 955 A.2d 234 (Me. 2008), 148
Wegner v. Milwaukee Mut. Ins. Co., 479 N.W.2d 38 (Minn. 1991), 712
Weidner v. Alaska Dep't of Transp. & Pub. Facilities, 860 P.2d 1205 (Alaska 1993), 728
Weighaft v. Remington, 320 N.Y.S.2d 151 (Civ. Ct. 1971), 471
Weingarten/Ark., Inc. v. ABC Interstate Theatres, Inc., 811 S.W.2d 295 (Ark. 1991), 463
Weinhold v. Wolff, 555 N.W.2d 454 (Iowa 1996), 112, 116
Weiswasser; State v., 693 A.2d 864 (N.J. 1997), 691
Weller; State v., 327 N.W.2d 172 (Wis. 1982), 488
Wells v. Lizama, 396 F.2d 877 (9th Cir. 1968), 555
Welsh v. Boy Scouts of Am., 993 F.2d 1267 (7th Cir. 1993), 49, 51, 52, 63
Wendover Rd. Prop. Owners Ass'n v. Kornicks, 502 N.E.2d 226 (Ohio Ct. App. 1985), 376
Wendy's of Fort Wayne, Inc. v. Fagan, 644 N.E.2d 159 (Ind. Ct. App. 1994), 193
Wertz Realty, Inc. v. Parden, 607 N.E.2d 550 (Ohio Ct. App. 1992), 498
Wesley v. Don Stein Buick, Inc., 42 F. Supp. 2d 1192 (D. Kan. 1999), 57–59
Wesson v. Leone Enters., Inc., 774 N.E.2d 611 (Mass. 2002), 429, 480
West v. Louisville Gas & Elec. Co., 951 F.3d 827 (7th Cir. 2020), 192
West Broadway Glass Co. v. I.T.M. Bar, Inc., 666 N.Y.S.2d 629 (App. Div. 1997), 471
West Des Moines, City of v. Engler, 641 N.W.2d 803 (Iowa 2002), 80
Western Pa. Socialist Workers 1982 Campaign v. Connecticut Gen. Life Ins. Co., 515 A.2d 1331 (Pa. 1986), 80, 82
Western States Constr., Inc. v. Michoff, 840 P.2d 1220 (Nev. 1992), 412
Westfield Centre Serv., Inc. v. Cities Serv. Oil Co., 432 A.2d 48 (N.J. 1981), 388
Westfield Homes, Inc. v. Herrick, 593 N.E.2d 97 (Ill. App. Ct. 1992), 275
Westland Skating Ctr. v. Gus Machado Buick, 542 So. 2d 959 (Fla. 1989), 129
Westleigh v. Conger, 755 A.2d 518, 2000 ME 134 (Me. 2000), 821
West Orange, Twp. of v. 769 Assocs., 800 A.2d 86 (N.J. 2002), 687
West Peachtree Tenth Corp.; United States v., 437 F.2d 221 (5th Cir. 1971), 593
West Pueblo Partners, LLC v. Stone Brewing Co., LLC, 307 Cal. Rptr. 3d 626 (Ct. App. 2023), 452
Westwood Homeowners Ass'n v. Tenhoff, 745 P.2d 976 (Ariz. Ct. App. 1987), 274

Wetlands Am. Tr., Inc. v. White Cloud Nine Ventures, L.P., 782 S.E.2d 131 (Va. 2016), 259, 270
Wetzel v. Glen St. Andrew Living Cmty., LLC, 901 F.3d 856 (7th Cir. 2018), 590
Whaley v. County of Tuscola, 58 F.3d 1111 (6th Cir. 1991), 828
Whetzel v. Jess Fisher Mgmt. Co., 282 F.2d 943 (D.C. Cir. 1960), 485
White v. Emmons, 2012 WL 1595084 (Ohio Ct. App. 2012), 200
White v. Hartigan, 982 N.E.2d 1115 (Mass. 2013), 213
White v. Hughes, 190 So. 446 (Fla. 1939), 86
White Mountain Apache Tribe; United States v., 537 U.S. 465 (2003), 804
White River Chair Co. v. Connecticut River Power Co. of N.H., 162 A. 859 (Vt. 1932), 132
Whitinsville Plaza, Inc. v. Kotseas, 390 N.E.2d 243 (Mass. 1979), 241, 246, 286
Whitman v. Larson, 568 N.Y.S.2d 485 (App. Div. 1991), 519
Whittlesey v. Fuller, 11 Conn. 337 (1836), 357
Whole Foods Mkt. Grp., Inc. v. Sarasota Coal. for a Living Wage, 2010 WL 2380390 (Fla. Cir. Ct. 2010), 82
Whorton v. Malone, 549 S.E.2d 57 (W. Va. 2001), 129
Wichita, City of v. Tilson, 855 P.2d 911 (Kan. 1993), 39
Wiggill v. Cheney, 597 P.2d 1351 (Utah 1979), 533
Wiggins v. Brazil Coal & Clay Corp., 452 N.E.2d 958 (Ind. 1983), 132
Wilcox v. Estate of Hines, 849 N.W.2d 280 (Wis. 2014), 153
Wilcox v. Pioneer Homes, Inc., 254 S.E.2d 214 (N.C. Ct. App. 1979), 520
Wilcox v. Stroup, 467 F.3d 409 (4th Cir. 2006), 821
Wilcox v. Timberon Protective Ass'n, 806 P.2d 1068 (N.M. 1990), 291
Wilcox v. Trautz, 693 N.E.2d 141 (Mass. 1998), 412–413
Wilfong v. W.A. Schickedanz Agency, Inc., 406 N.E.2d 828 (Ill. App. Ct. 1980), 519
Wilkinson v. Chiwawa Cmtys. Ass'n, 327 P.3d 614 (Wash. 2014), 378
Willard v. First Church of Christ, Scientist, 498 P.2d 987 (Cal. 1972), 185
Willett v. Centerre Bank, 792 S.W.2d 916 (Mo. Ct. App. 1990), 551
William Raveis Real Estate, Inc. v. Stawski, 626 A.2d 797 (Conn. App. Ct. 1993), 498
Williams v. City of Central, 907 P.2d 701 (Colo. Ct. App. 1995), 662
Williams v. Gash, 789 S.W.2d 261 (Tex. 1990), 528
Williams v. Lubbering, 63 A. 90 (N.J. 1906), 30
Williams v. Mason, 556 So. 2d 1045 (Miss. 1990), 414, 419
Williams v. Monsanto Co., 856 S.W.2d 338 (Mo. Ct. App. 1993), 45
Williams v. Poretsky Mgmt., Inc., 955 F. Supp. 490 (D. Md. 1996), 603
Williams v. Rogier, 611 N.E.2d 189 (Ind. 1993), *disapproved of by* Fraley v. Minger, 829 N.E.2d 476 (Ind. 2005), 151
Williams v. South & S. Rentals, Inc., 346 S.E.2d 665 (N.C. Ct. App. 1986), 42
Williams Nat. Gas Co. v. Perkins, 952 P.2d 483 (Okla. 1997), 692
Williamson v. Grizzard, 387 S.W.2d 807 (Tenn. 1965), 323
Williamson Cnty. Reg'l Planning Comm'n v. Hamilton Bank of Johnson City, 473 U.S. 172 (1985), 765
Willis v. Magette, 491 S.E.2d 735 (Va. 1997), 218
Willmschen v. Trinity Lakes Improvement Ass'n, 840 N.E.2d 1275 (Ill. App. Ct. 2005), 98
Willowbrook, Vill. of v. Olech, 528 U.S. 562 (2000), 670
Willson v. Strattan, 2006 WL 287591 (Mich. Ct. App. 2006), 285
Wilshire Westwood Assocs. v. Atlantic Richfield Co., 24 Cal. Rptr. 2d 562 (Ct. App. 1993), 104
Wilson, Matter of Estate of, 452 N.E.2d 1228 (N.Y. 1983), 279
Wilson v. Diche, 13 Cal. Rptr. 243 (Dist. Ct. App. 1961), 29
Wilson v. Glenwood Intermountain Props., Inc., 876 F. Supp. 1231 (D. Utah 1995), 602
Wilson v. Handley, 119 Cal. Rptr. 263 (Ct. App. 2002), 136
Wilson v. Interlake Steel Co., 649 P.2d 922 (Cal. 1982), 97
Wilson v. Owen, 261 S.W.2d 19 (Mo. 1953), 183
Winans; United States v., 198 U.S. 371 (1905), 806
Windemere Homeowner's Ass'n v. McCue, 990 P.2d 769 (Mont. 1999), 376
Windsor; United States v., 570 U.S. 12 (2013), 408
Winegar v. Froerer Corp., 813 P.2d 104 (Utah 1991), 530
Winn-Dixie Stores, Inc. v. Dolgencorp, LLC, 746 F.3d 1008 (11th Cir. 2014), 250, 286, 291
Winterchase Townhomes, Inc. v. Koether, 387 S.E.2d 361 (Ga. Ct. App. 1989), 527
Winters v. United States, 207 U.S. 564 (1908), 131, 807
Wise v. Poston, 316 S.E.2d 412 (S.C. 1984), 329
Wisniewski v. Kelly, 437 N.W.2d 25 (Mich. Ct. App. 1989), 376
Withers v. Dick's Sporting Goods, Inc., 636 F.3d 958 (8th Cir. 2011), 57
Witko, Estate of v. G. Heileman Brewing Co., No. Civ. 93-204 (Rosebud Sioux Tribal Ct., Oct. 25, 1994), *rev'd* (Rosebud Sioux Sup. Ct. May 1, 1996), 852
Witter v. Taggart, 577 N.E.2d 338 (N.Y. 1991), 551
Wolfe v. Estate of Wolfe, 756 So. 2d 788 (Miss. Ct. App. 1999), 320
Wolinsky v. Kadison, 449 N.E.2d 151 (Ill. App. Ct. 1983), 283, 374–375, 379
Womack v. Hyche, 503 So. 2d 832 (Ala. 1987), 448
Wood v. Board of Cnty. Comm'rs of Fremont Cnty., 759 P.2d 1250 (Wyo. 1988), 318
Wood v. Hoglund, 963 P.2d 383 (Idaho 1998), 213–214
Wood v. State, 2003 WL 1955433 (Fla. Cir. Ct. 2003), 82
Woodhaven Apartments v. Washington, 942 P.2d 918 (Utah 1997), 487
Woodland v. Michigan Citizens Lobby, 378 N.W.2d 337 (Mich. 1985), 80
Woodland Realty, Inc. v. Winzenried, 262 N.W.2d 106 (Wis. 1978), 500
Woods v. Garnett, 16 So. 390 (Miss. 1894), 548
Woods v. Schmitt, 439 N.W.2d 855 (Iowa 1989), 535
Woodstone Townhouses, LLC v. Southern Fiber Worx, LLC, 855 S.E.2d 719 (Ga. Ct. App. 2021), 28
Woodwind Estates, Ltd. v. Gretkowski, 205 F.3d 118 (3d Cir. 2000), 668

Worthinglen Condo. Unit Owners' Ass'n v. Brown, 566 N.E.2d 1275 (Ohio Ct. App. 1989), 374
Wright v. Brady, 889 P.2d 105 (Idaho Ct. App. 1995), 482
W.W.G. Corp. v. Hughes, 960 P.2d 720 (Colo. Ct. App. 1998), 481

Y

Yalowizer v. Town of Rochester, 2001 WL 1012206, 2001 U.S. App. LEXIS 19746 (10th Cir. 2001), 668
Yamashita v. Guam, 59 F.3d 114 (9th Cir. 1995), 518
Yee v. City of Escondido, 503 U.S. 519 (1992), 469, 709, 718, 724
Yogman v. Parrott, 937 P.2d 1019 (Or. 1997), 243, 270–271
Young, Ex parte, 209 U.S. 123 (1908), 765
Young v. American Mini Theatres, 427 U.S. 50 (1976), 674
Young v. Garwacki, 402 N.E.2d 1045 (Mass. 1980), 485
Young v. Ledford, 37 So. 3d 832 (Ala. Civ. App. 2009), 43
Young v. Patukonis, 506 N.E.2d 1164 (Mass. App. Ct. 1987), 488
Younge, Estate of v. Huysmans, 506 A.2d 282 (N.H. 1985), 506
Younggren v. Younggren, 556 N.W.2d 228 (Minn. Ct. App. 1996), 320
Ysleta Del Sur Pueblo v. Laney, 199 F.3d 281 (5th Cir. 2000), 796
Yvanova v. New Century Mortg. Corp., 365 P.3d 845 (Cal. 2016), 573

Z

Zacchini v. Scripps-Howard Broad. Co., 433 U.S. 562 (1977), 849
Zambrano v. M & RC II LLC, 517 P.3d 1169 (Ariz. 2022), 514
Zaschak v. Traverse Corp., 333 N.W.2d 191 (Mich. Ct. App. 1983), 511
Ziegler Co. v. Rexnord, Inc., 433 N.W.2d 8 (Wis. 1988), 388
Zissler v. Saville, 240 Cal. Rptr. 3d 590 (Ct. App. 2018), 192
Zuni Tribe of N.M., United States ex rel. v. Platt, 730 F. Supp. 318 (D. Ariz. 1990), 216
Zurstrassen v. Stonier, 786 So. 2d 65 (Fla. Dist. Ct. App. 2001), 533–534
Zweighaft v. Remington, 320 N.Y.S.2d 151 (Civ. Ct. 1971), 471

TABLE OF STATUTES AND REGULATIONS

United States Constitution

U.S. Const. art. I, §8, cl. 8 836, 841, 844
U.S. Const. art. IV, §3 790
U.S. Const. art. VI, cl. 2 580
U.S. Const. art. X, cl. 1 697
U.S. Const. amend. I 36–37, 51–54, 73–74, 75–80, 82–83, 123, 411, 602, 613, 614, 671–675, 677, 846–847, 850, 852–853
U.S. Const. amend. IV 37, 407, 720
U.S. Const. amend. V 25, 407, 578, 668, 680, 682, 686, 694, 703, 705, 714–715, 736, 746, 751, 762–763, 781, 784, 788–790, 795, 805
U.S. Const. amend. VI 710
U.S. Const. amend. VIII 39, 635, 710
U.S. Const. amend. XI 765, 796
U.S. Const. amend. XIII 47–48, 61, 721
U.S. Const. amend. XIV 25, 47, 56, 75–77, 83, 125, 280, 341, 407, 410, 418, 578–579, 580, 608, 614, 666, 668, 675, 686, 694, 700, 714, 747, 751, 762–763, 828
U.S. Const. amend. XIV §1 752
U.S. Const. amend. XIV §5 675

United States Code

Title 1

1 U.S.C. §7 (*Defense of Marriage Act*) 408–409

Title 4

4 U.S.C. §5 (*Freedom to Display the American Flag Act*) 289

Title 5

5 U.S.C. §601 (1994) 762

Title 7

7 U.S.C. §§2041 *et seq.* (*Farm Labor Contractor Registration Act*) 484

Title 12

12 U.S.C. §1701j-03 (*Garn-St. Germain Depository Institutions Act*) 563
12 U.S.C. §1735f-7a(a)(1) (*Depository Institutions Deregulation and Monetary Control Act (DIDMCA)*) 567
12 U.S.C. §1735f-7a(b)(2) 567
12 U.S.C. §§2601 to 2617 (*Real Estate Settlement Procedures Act (RESPA)*) 514

Title 15

15 U.S.C. §1 (*Sherman Act*) 286
15 U.S.C. §1052(a) (*Lanham Act*) 53, 846
15 U.S.C. §1052(d) 846
15 U.S.C. §1064 846
15 U.S.C. §1072 845
15 U.S.C. §1114 845
15 U.S.C. §1115(b) 846
15 U.S.C. §1125(a) (*Lanham Act*) 845
15 U.S.C. §§1601 to 1693r (*Truth in Lending Act*) 563
15 U.S.C. §1602 570
15 U.S.C. §§1631 *et seq.* 570
15 U.S.C. §1635 (*Home Ownership and Equity Protection Act*) 563
15 U.S.C. §1639c (*Truth in Lending Act*) 570
15 U.S.C. §1681 (*Fair Credit Reporting Act*) 489
15 U.S.C. §§1692 to 1692o (*Federal Debt Collections Practices Act*) 489
15 U.S.C. §1692a(5) 489
15 U.S.C. §§1701 to 1720 (*Interstate Land Sales Full Disclosure Act*) 514
15 U.S.C. §1703 514
15 U.S.C. §§2801 to 2806 (*Petroleum Marketing Practices Act*) 387
15 U.S.C. §§3601 to 3616 (*Condominium and Cooperative Conversion Protection and Abuse Relief Act*) 373
15 U.S.C. §3607(a) 373
15 U.S.C. §3607(b) 373
15 U.S.C. §§7901-7903 (*Protection of Lawful Commerce in Arms Act of 2005*) 123

Title 16

16 U.S.C. §§431 to 431m (*Antiquities Act of 1906*) 856

16 U.S.C. §§461 to 467 (*Historic Sites, Buildings, and Antiquities Act*) 855
16 U.S.C. §468 (*National Trust for Historical Preservation Act*) 855
16 U.S.C. §§469 to 469c (*Archaeological and Historic Data Preservation Act of 1974*) 855
16 U.S.C. §§470ee to 470mm (*Archaeological Resources Protection Act of 1979*) 856
16 U.S.C. §835d 789
16 U.S.C. §§1531 to 1543 (*Endangered Species Act* (*ESA*)) 663, 732
16 U.S.C. §1533(a)(3)(A) 663
16 U.S.C. §1538(a)(1) 663

Title 17

17 U.S.C. §§101 to 1316 836
17 U.S.C. §101 (*Visual Artists Rights Act*) 853
17 U.S.C. §101(B) 853
17 U.S.C. §102(a) 836
17 U.S.C. §106 836
17 U.S.C. §106A 853–855
17 U.S.C. §106A(a)(3)(A) 854
17 U.S.C. §106A(a)(3)(B) 854
17 U.S.C. §106A(e) 854
17 U.S.C. §107 (*Copyright Act*) 837
17 U.S.C. §107(1) 837
17 U.S.C. §107(3) 837
17 U.S.C. §107(4) 837
17 U.S.C. §113 853
17 U.S.C. §113(d)(2) 854
17 U.S.C. §301(b)(3) (*Copyright Act of 1976*) 849
17 U.S.C. §301(f)(1) 854
17 U.S.C. §302(a) 836
17 U.S.C. §502 836
17 U.S.C. §504 836
17 U.S.C. §506 836
17 U.S.C. §1401 836

Title 18

18 U.S.C. §983(d) 710
18 U.S.C. §1170 805, 832

Title 20

20 U.S.C. §§80q to 80q-15 (*National Museum of the American Indian Act of 1989*) 805, 833
20 U.S.C. §80q-9(c) 805, 833
20 U.S.C. §§1681 *et seq.* (*Title IX of Education Amendments of 1972*) 74

Title 21

21 U.S.C. §881 710
21 U.S.C. §881(a)(6) 710
21 U.S.C. §881(a)(7) 710

Title 22

22 U.S.C. §1621 Note (*Holocaust Expropriated Art Recovery Act of 2016*) (*HEAR Act*) 174–175

Title 25

25 U.S.C. §70k 795
25 U.S.C. §70v 794
25 U.S.C. §71 775
25 U.S.C. §162a(d)(1)-(7) 804–805
25 U.S.C. §177 (*Non-Intercourse Act of 1790*) 776, 791, 797–800
25 U.S.C. §194 793
25 U.S.C. §§334 to 358 779
25 U.S.C. §348 780
25 U.S.C. §373 780
25 U.S.C. §§461 to 479 780
25 U.S.C. §461 780
25 U.S.C. §462 780
25 U.S.C. §§1300i to 1300i-11 (*Hoopa-Yurok Settlement Act*) 789
25 U.S.C. §§1301 to 1304 (*Indian Civil Rights Act of 1968 (ICRA)*) 411
25 U.S.C. §§1701 *et seq.* (*Rhode Island Indian Claims Settlement Act*) 801
25 U.S.C. §§1721 *et seq.* (*Maine Indian Claims Settlement Act*) 793, 801
25 U.S.C. §§1741 *et seq.* (*Florida Indian Land Claims Settlement Act*) 801
25 U.S.C. §§1751 *et seq.* (*Connecticut Indian Land Claims Settlement Act*) 801
25 U.S.C. §§3001 to 3013 (*Native American Graves Protection and Repatriation Act*) 805, 832, 856
25 U.S.C. §3001(3)(C) 832
25 U.S.C. §3001(4) 805, 833
25 U.S.C. §3001(8) 805, 833
25 U.S.C. §3001(13) 805, 833
25 U.S.C. §3002(a) 805, 832
25 U.S.C. §3005(a) 805, 833
25 U.S.C. §3005(b) 805, 833

Title 28

28 U.S.C. §1362 794
28 U.S.C. §1491 (*Tucker Act*) 803
28 U.S.C. §1491(a)(1) 765
28 U.S.C. §1505 (*Indian Tucker Act*) 795, 803
28 U.S.C. §1658(a) 55
28 U.S.C. §1738 765
28 U.S.C. §1738C (*Defense of Marriage Act*) 409

Title 29

29 U.S.C. §157 (*National Labor Relations Act, §§7 & 8*) 84
29 U.S.C. §158 84
29 U.S.C. §794 (*Rehabilitation Act of 1973*) 609

Title 33

33 U.S.C. §§1251 to 1376 (*Federal Water Pollution Control Act of 1972*) 663
33 U.S.C. §1344 (*Clean Water Act*) 127, 663

Title 35

35 U.S.C. §101 to 212 (*Patent Act*) 841
35 U.S.C. §101 841–842
35 U.S.C. §154 841
35 U.S.C. §156 841

Title 42

42 U.S.C. §274e(a) (*National Organ Transplant Act*) 827
42 U.S.C. §§601 to 619 (*Temporary Assistance to Needy Families (TANF)*) 625, 636
42 U.S.C. §1437a(b)(2) 618
42 U.S.C. §1437d(*l*)(6) (*Anti-Drug Abuse Act*) 455
42 U.S.C. §1437f 618
42 U.S.C. §1437f(o)(2) 618
42 U.S.C. §1437f(o)(6) 619
42 U.S.C. §1981 (*Civil Rights Act of 1866*) 33–34, 47–48, 54–61, 277, 280, 577, 584, 596, 600–601
42 U.S.C. §1981(a) 54–55
42 U.S.C. §1981(b) 55, 59, 600
42 U.S.C. §1981(c) 55, 600
42 U.S.C. §1982 33–34, 47, 54, 57–58, 59–62, 277, 576–577, 581, 585, 600–601
42 U.S.C. §1983 765
42 U.S.C. §2000a to 2000a-6 (*Title II, Civil Rights Act of 1964, Public Accommodations Law*) 31, 46, 51, 584, 721
42 U.S.C. §2000a 61, 720
42 U.S.C. §2000a(a) 46, 49, 60
42 U.S.C. §2000a(b) 47–48, 49–50
42 U.S.C. §2000a(e) 50, 52, 61, 63
42 U.S.C. §2000a-3 (*Civil Rights Act of 1964*) 48, 55
42 U.S.C. §2000a-6(b) 60–61
42 U.S.C. §§2000bb *et seq.* (*Religious Freedom Restoration Act (RFRA)*) 613, 675
42 U.S.C. §2000bb-2 629, 676
42 U.S.C. §2000bb-3 629, 676
42 U.S.C. §§2000cc to 2000cc-5 (*Religious Land Use and Institutionalized Persons Act (RLUIPA)*) 614, 628, 675
42 U.S.C. §2000cc 629, 675
42 U.S.C. §2000cc(2)(C) 629, 676
42 U.S.C. §2000cc(3) 629, 676
42 U.S.C. §2000e 57
42 U.S.C. §2000e(b) 60
42 U.S.C. §2000e-2 74
42 U.S.C. §§3601 *et seq.* (*Fair Housing Act*) 279, 581
42 U.S.C. §§3601 to 3631 468, 642
42 U.S.C. §§3601 to 3619 57, 62, 277, 576, 582–583, 721
42 U.S.C. §3601 583
42 U.S.C. §3602(b) 583, 584, 587, 602
42 U.S.C. §3602(c) 583
42 U.S.C. §3602(h) 609
42 U.S.C. §3602(i)(1) 596
42 U.S.C. §3602(k) (*Fair Housing Amendments Act*) 583, 611
42 U.S.C. §3603 60, 584, 589, 601–602
42 U.S.C. §3603(b)(1) 585
42 U.S.C. §3603(b)(2) 585, 601, 602
42 U.S.C. §§3604 to 3606 74
42 U.S.C. §3604 585, 587, 589, 601
42 U.S.C. §3604(a) (*Fair Housing Act*) 582, 587, 591, 602, 611
42 U.S.C. §3604(b) (*Fair Housing Act*) 587, 591, 604
42 U.S.C. §3604(c) 585, 587–588, 598, 601–602, 604, 615, 629
42 U.S.C. §3604(d) 588
42 U.S.C. §3604(e) 588
42 U.S.C. §3604(f) 62, 582, 587
42 U.S.C. §3604(f)(1) 609
42 U.S.C. §3604(f)(2) 609
42 U.S.C. §3604(f)(3) 609
42 U.S.C. §3604(f)(3)(A) 609
42 U.S.C. §3604(f)(3)(B) 609, 622, 624
42 U.S.C. §3604(f)(3)(C) 610
42 U.S.C. §3604(f)(9) 610
42 U.S.C. §3604(k) 103
42 U.S.C. §3605 587, 589
42 U.S.C. §3605(b)(1) 589
42 U.S.C. §3605(b)(2) 589
42 U.S.C. §3606 587, 589
42 U.S.C. §3607(a) 584–586
42 U.S.C. §3607(b) 584, 586
42 U.S.C. §3607(b)(1) 586, 612
42 U.S.C. §3607(b)(2)(B) 586, 612
42 U.S.C. §3607(b)(2)(C) 586, 612
42 U.S.C. §3607(b)(2)(C)(i) 586, 612
42 U.S.C. §3607(b)(2)(C)(ii) 586, 612
42 U.S.C. §3607(b)(2)(C)(iii) 586, 612
42 U.S.C. §3607(b)(4) 586
42 U.S.C. §3608(e)(5) 619
42 U.S.C. §3610 599
42 U.S.C. §3610(a)(1)(A)(i) 596
42 U.S.C. §3610(f) 599
42 U.S.C. §3610(i) 599
42 U.S.C. §3612 599
42 U.S.C. §3612(a) 599
42 U.S.C. §3612(b) 599
42 U.S.C. §3612(g)(3)(A) 599
42 U.S.C. §3612(g)(3)(B) 599
42 U.S.C. §3612(g)(3)(C) 599
42 U.S.C. §3612(o) 599
42 U.S.C. §3613 599
42 U.S.C. §3613(a)(1)(A) 596
42 U.S.C. §3614 600
42 U.S.C. §3617 587, 589, 591
42 U.S.C. §§3631 *et seq.* 581
42 U.S.C. §3631 57, 62, 277, 576, 582–583, 721

42 U.S.C. §§4601 to 4655 (*Uniform Relocation Assistance and Real Property Acquisition Policies Act of 1970*) 693
42 U.S.C. §4623 693
42 U.S.C. §§4851 to 4856 (*Residential Lead-Based Paint Hazard Reduction Act*) 489, 511
42 U.S.C. §§4852d 489
42 U.S.C. §§6901 *et seq.* (*Resource Conservation and Recovery Act* (*RCRA*)) 664
42 U.S.C. §§6922 to 6925 664
42 U.S.C. §§9601 *et seq.* (*Superfund Amendments and Reauthorization Act* (*SARA*)) 664
42 U.S.C. §§9601 to 9675 (*Comprehensive Environmental Response, Compensation, and Liability Act of 1980*) 511
42 U.S.C. §9601(35)(A) (*Superfund Amendments and Reauthorization Act* (*SARA*)) 664
42 U.S.C. §9601(40) 664
42 U.S.C. §9607 664
42 U.S.C. §9607(b)(3) 664
42 U.S.C. §9611 664
42 U.S.C. §§12101 to 12213 (*Americans with Disabilities Act of 1990*) 31, 32–33, 62, 274
42 U.S.C. §12102(1) 62
42 U.S.C. §12181 63
42 U.S.C. §12181(7) 32, 63
42 U.S.C. §12181(9) 66
42 U.S.C. §12182 62–63
42 U.S.C. §12182(a) 65
42 U.S.C. §12182(b)(1) 65
42 U.S.C. §12182(b)(2)(A)(i) 65
42 U.S.C. §12182(b)(2)(A)(ii) 66–67
42 U.S.C. §12182(b)(2)(A)(iii) 65
42 U.S.C. §12182(b)(2)(A)(iv) 66
42 U.S.C. §12182(b)(2)(A)(v) 66
42 U.S.C. §12183 69
42 U.S.C. §12183(a)(1) 62, 69–70
42 U.S.C. §12183(a)(2) 62, 70
42 U.S.C. §12187 63
42 U.S.C. §12188(a)(1) 62
42 U.S.C. §12188(b) 62
42 U.S.C. §12188(b)(2) 62
42 U.S.C. §12201(b) 68
42 U.S.C. §12204 70
42 U.S.C. §12204(c)(2) 70
42 U.S.C. §12204(c)(3) 70
42 U.S.C. §12210 63
42 U.S.C. §12211 63

Title 43

43 U.S.C. §150 778
43 U.S.C. §1068 169
43 U.S.C. §1522 789
43 U.S.C. §§1601 to 1628 (*Alaska Native Claims Settlement Act* (*ANCSA*)) 793, 801
43 U.S.C. §1603 801
43 U.S.C. §§2101 to 2106 (*Abandoned Shipwreck Act*) 821, 856

Title 44

44 U.S.C. §§2201 *et seq.* (*Presidential Records Act*) 821

Title 47

47 U.S.C. §230(c) (*Communications Decency Act*) 588
47 U.S.C. §332 (*Telecommunications Act*) 665
47 U.S.C. §332(c)(7)(A) 665
47 U.S.C. §332(c)(7)(B)(i)(I) 665
47 U.S.C. §332(c)(7)(B)(i)(II) 665

Title 49

49 U.S.C. §3 (predecessor to 49 U.S.C. §10741) 47
49 U.S.C. §10741 (*Interstate Commerce Act*) 47
49 U.S.C. §10741(a)(1) 47
49 U.S.C. §10741(b) 32
49 U.S.C. §11101(a) 47

Title 54

54 U.S.C. §§300101 *et seq.* (*National Historic Preservation Act*) 70, 662, 856

United States Public Laws

Pub. L. No. 89-635, §1, 80 Stat. 880, Act of Oct. 10, 1966 (codified at 28 U.S.C. §1362) 794
Pub. L. No. 90-284, 82 Stat. 73 (*Fair Housing Act*) 576
Pub. L. No. 90-537, §302, 82 Stat. 885, 888, Act of Sept. 30, 1968 (codified at 43 U.S.C. §1522) 789
Pub. L. No. 91-646, 84 Stat. 1894 (*Uniform Relocation Assistance and Real Property Acquisition Policies Act of 1970*) 693
Pub. L. No. 92-203, Act of Dec. 18, 1971 (codified at 43 U.S.C. §§1601-1628) (*Alaska Native Claims Settlement Act of 1971*) (*ANCSA*) 793, 801
Pub. L. No. 93-383, Title II, §201(a), 88 Stat. 633 (*Housing and Community Development Act of 1974*) 576, 582, 602, 618
Pub. L. No. 94-465, 90 Stat. 1990, Act of Oct. 8, 1976 (formerly codified at 25 U.S.C. §70v) (*Indian Claims Commission Act*) 794–795, 798
Pub. L. No. 95-217, 91 Stat. 1566 (1977) (*Clean Water Act of 1977*) 663
Pub. L. No. 97-470, Title V, §523, Jan. 14, 1983, 96 Stat. 2600 484
Pub. L. No. 100-4 (Feb. 4, 1987), 100th Cong., 1st Sess. 101 Stat. 7 (1987) (*Water Quality Act of 1987*) 663
Pub. L. No. 100-241, 101 Stat. 1788 802
Pub. L. No. 100-430, 102 Stat. 1619 (*Fair Housing Amendments Act of 1988*) 576, 582–583, 586, 598

Pub. L. No. 101-336, July 26, 1990, 104 Stat. 327 (*Americans with Disabilities Act of 1990*) 62
Pub. L. No. 102-166, Title I, §101, Nov. 21, 1991, 105 Stat. 1071, Act of Nov. 21, 1991 (partially codified at 42 U.S.C. §1981(c)) (*Civil Rights Act of 1991*) 55, 600
Pub. L. No. 104-76, 109 Stat. 787 (*Housing for Older Persons Act of 1995*) 586, 612
Pub. L. No. 104-199, 110 Stat. 2419 408–409
Pub. L. No. 105-276, Title V, §545, 112 Stat. 2518 (*Quality Housing and Work Responsibility Act of 1998*) 618
Pub. L. No. 106-185, §2(a), Apr. 25, 2000, 114 Stat. 202 710
Pub. L. No. 106-185, §9, Apr. 25, 2000, 114 Stat. 216 710
Pub. L. No. 106-274, 114 Stat. 803, Sept. 22, 2000 (S. 2869) (*Religious Land Use and Institutionalized Persons Act of 2000 (RLUIPA)*) 614, 628–629, 675
Pub. L. No. 109-243, 120 Stat. 572 (July 24, 2006) (*Freedom to Display the American Flag Act*) 289
Pub. L. No. 111-203, H.R. 4173, July 21, 2010 (*Dodd-Frank Wall Street Reform and Consumer Protection Act*) 570
Pub. L. No. 114-308, §5(a), 130 Stat. 1524 (codified at 22 U.S.C. §1621 Note) (*Holocaust Expropriated Art Recovery Act of 2016 (HEAR Act)*) 174–175

Federal Regulations

3 C.F.R. §554 762
12 C.F.R. §1026 570
14 C.F.R. pt. 107 44
24 C.F.R. §§5.150 to 5.168 619
24 C.F.R. §91.5 619
24 C.F.R. §§91.105 to 91.505 619
24 C.F.R. §§92.104 to 92.508 619
24 C.F.R. §100.7(a)(iii) 590
24 C.F.R. §100.7(b) 599
24 C.F.R. §100.75 598
24 C.F.R. §100.204(b), Example (1) 610
24 C.F.R. §100.204(b), Example (2) 610
24 C.F.R. §100.500(a) to (b) 616
24 C.F.R. §100.500(a) 616
24 C.F.R. §100.500(b) 617
24 C.F.R. §100.500(c)(3) 617
24 C.F.R. §§570.3 to 570.094 619
24 C.F.R. §§574.530 619
24 C.F.R. §576.500 619
24 C.F.R. §§903.1 to 903.23 619
24 C.F.R. §982.503 618
24 C.F.R. §982.505 618
28 C.F.R. §§36.101 to 36.608 62
28 C.F.R. §36.301 65
28 C.F.R. §§36.301 to 36.406 69
28 C.F.R. §36.302 66
28 C.F.R. §36.303 65
28 C.F.R. §36.304 66
28 C.F.R. §36.305 66
28 C.F.R. §36.308 69
28 C.F.R. §36.405 70
28 C.F.R. Part 36, App. A, §4.1.7 (*ADA Accessibility Guidelines for Buildings & Facilities*) 70
28 C.F.R. Part 36, App. A, §4.33.3 69
28 C.F.R. §§106.1 *et seq.* 74
40 C.F.R. §§745.101 to 745.107 489

Proposed Legislation

H.R. 4173, July 21, 2010 570

State Laws

Alabama

Constitution

art. I, §3 675

Code

§3-4-6 46
§3-5-2 46
§3-5-2(a) 46
§6-2-33 155
§6-7-40 365
§§13A-7-2 to 13A-7-4 29
§18-3-1 213
§24-2-2 689
§24-3-2 689
§24-8-4 577
§30-2-51 398
§35-4-90 543
§35-9-3 447
§35-10-26 556
§§41-3-1 to 41-3-6 832

Alaska

Statutes

§05.01.004(C) 410
§09.01.030 155
§09.45.052 155
§09.45.052(a) 153
§09.55.240(d) 689
§§13.06.005 to 13.36.100 420
§18.80.210 577
§18.80.240 577, 612
§29.35.030 689
§§34.03.010 to 34.03.380 431
§34.03.310 481
§34.15.130 357
§§34.17.010 to 34.17.060 (*Uniform Conservation Easement Act*) 186

§34.27.100(a) 339
§§34.77.010-34.77.160 401
§40.17.080 543
§41.35.020 856

Arizona

Revised Statutes

§9-462.01(E) 648
§11-832 648
§12-526 155
§12-1134 (*Private Property Rights Protection Act*) 764
§§12-1171 to 12-1183 461
§12-1176 461
§14-2102 420
§14-2102(1) 421
§14-2102(2) 421
§14-2901(A)(3) 339
§§14-3101 to 14-3974 420
§§25-201 to 25-205 404
§§25-211 to 25-217 401
§25-213 404
§25-215 402
§25-215(A) 402
§25-215(D) 402
§25-318 406
§25-318(A) 403
§33-401(B) 529
§33-411 542
§33-412 542
§33-729(A) 559
§33-741 564
§33-742 564
§§33-1301 to 33-1381 431
§33-1381 481, 483
§§41-1491 to 41-1491.37 577

Arkansas

Code

§8-7-516 665
§9-12-315 398
§14-15-404 542
§§16-123-201 to 16-123-210 577
§18-40-102 541
§18-61-101 155
§27-66-401 213
§§28-11-101 to 28-11-404 395
§28-11-404 395

Session Laws

Act of Nov. 2, 1835, 1835 Ark. Terr. Laws 34-35 395

California

Constitution

art. I, §7.5 410

Civil Code

§§51 to 53 (*California Unruh Civil Rights Act*) 51, 577
§51 71, 607, 612, 631
§51(b) 280
§52 631
§53(a) 280
§683.2(c) 352
§683(a) 351
§717 443
§718f 443
§763 325
§769 307
§813 170
§841.4 136
§§880.020 to 887.090 338
§880.030 et seq. 537
§885.020 307
§885.070 309
§987 (*California Art Preservation*) 853
§1009 86, 87, 170
§1092 536
§§1102 to 1102.17 511
§1107 543
§1113 535, 536
§1352.5 277
§1353.6(a) 288
§1460 259
§1462 259
§1511 452
§1624(a)(1) 443
§1624(a)(3) 443
§1942.5 481, 483
§1942.5(c) 484
§1945 449, 458
§1946 445
§1946.2 444, 468
§1995.020(b) 492
§1995.230 491
§1995.240 492
§1995.260 492
§1995.270 492
§2079 502
§3344 849, 850
§3344.1 852
§3480 121
§4715 287, 380
§5975 286
§12596.1 277

Civil Procedure Code

§§317–321 155
§323 143
§338(c) 173
§425.16 672

§580(a) 559
§580b 559
§580d 559
§872.820 361
§§1159 to 1179a 460
§1167 461
§1263.510 693

Family Code

§125 406
§§297–299.6 409
§§750 to 1620 401
§770 404
§910 403
§911 402
§913 402
§913(b)(1) 402
§§1610–1617 404
§§2500 to 2660 401
§2502 406
§2550 504
§3900 417
§4400 418

Government Code

§6254(r) 832
§7927.000 806
§12955 277, 577, 612, 630
§§65300 *et seq.* 643
§§65580 to 65589.8 633

Health & Safety Code

§7050.5 832
§7050.5(c) 806

Probate Code

§66 406
§100 403
§101 406
§6101 406
§6104 406
§6401(a) 403

Public Resources Code

§5097.94 806, 832
§5097.98 806, 832
§5097.99 806, 832

Colorado

Revised Statutes

§13-40-104(4) 473
§13-40-107.5(5)(c) 473
§§15-10-101 to 15-17-102 420
§15-11-102 420
§15-11-1102.5 339
§§23-34-501 to 23-34-509 577
§24-34-502 607, 612
§24-34-601 71
§§24-68-101 to -106 655
§38-30-106 325
§38-31-101(5)(a) 352
§38-35-105 543
§38-35-108 543
§38-36-101(2) 555
§38-41-101 155
§38-41-101(3)(b)(II) 143, 153, 155

Connecticut

General Statutes

§§22a-134 to 22a-134e (*Connecticut Transfer Act*) 665
§22a-452a 665
§33-756 386
§§42-116s to 42-116t 853
§45a-436 395
§46a-63 612
§46a-64(b) to (c) 612
§46a-64c 607, 630
§46a-81a 577
§46a-81d 71
§46a-81e 577
§46b-81 398
§47-10 542
§47-14a 350, 357
§§47-33b to 47-33*l* 537
§47a-3b 445
§47a-4(5) 444
§47a-20 481, 483
§47a-23 444
§47a-23a 444
§47a-23c 468
§49-15 558
§49-24 558
§52-570 136
§52-575 155

Public Acts

05-10 (Jan. 2005), 2005 Ct. S.B. 963, 2005 Conn. Legis. Serv. P.A. 05-10 (S.S.B. 963) 409

Delaware

Code

tit. 6, §4503 71
tit. 6, §§4601 to 4620 577
tit. 6, §4603 607
tit. 6, §4603(b) 612, 630
tit. 7, §§5301 to 5306 832
tit. 10, §7901 155
tit. 10, §7902 155
tit. 10, §§8136 to 8138 672

tit. 11, §8307(c) 819
tit. 12, §§5001 to 5007 (*Fiduciary Access to Digital Assets and Digital Accounts*) 857
tit. 13, §§101 to 122 410
tit. 13, §1513(b) 398
tit. 25, §153 541, 549
tit. 25, §302 325
tit. 25, §309 358
tit. 25, §503 339
tit. 25, §503(b) 340
tit. 25, §§5101 *et seq.* 431
tit. 25, §5516 481
tit. 29, §605 762

Session Laws

2013 Del. HB 75 410

District of Columbia

Code

§2-1042.31 71
§§2-1402.21 to -1402.24 577
§2-1402.21 607, 630
§16-101 365
§16-910(a) 398
§42-3202 445
§42-3505.01 444, 468
§42-3505.02 481
§42-3505.02(a) 483
§45-801 543
§45-802 543
§46-401 (*Religious Freedom and Civil Marriage Equality Amendment Act of 2009*) 410

Florida

Statutes

§57.105 672
§70.001 (*Bert J. Harris, Jr. Private Property Rights Protection Act*) 762–763
§70.001(1) 763
§70.001(2) 763
§70.001(3)(e)(1) 763
§70.001(4)(a) 762
§73.013 689
§83.02 445
§83.03 445
§§83.40 to 83.681 431
§83.64 481
§83.595 463
§95.12 155
§95.14 155
§95.16 143
§95.18 143, 153, 155
§§163.3161 to 163.3211 643
§§163.3161 to 163.3215 633
§163.3177(f) 633
§540.08 850
§689.18 537
§695.01 542
§697.01 566
§704.08 210
§§705.102 to 705.104 819
§§712.01 to 712.12 537
§718.110(13) 378
§§731.005 to 735.304 420
§732.102 420
§732.104 422
§§760.20 to 760.37 577
§761.03 675
§768.295 672

Georgia

Code

§§8-3-200 to 8-3-223 577
§9-11-11.1 672
§10-6A-3(14) 502
§10-6A-10 502
§10-6A-12(a) 502
§13-4-21 452
§13-5-30(4) 507
§19-3-6 342
§44-2-2 543
§§44-2-40 to 44-2-253 555
§44-5-60(b) 297
§§44-5-161 to 44-5-162 143
§44-5-161 153
§44-5-163 155
§44-6-121(a) 367
§44-6-121(b)(3) 367
§44-6-121(b)(4) 367
§44-6-121(b)(5) 367
§§44-6-200 to 44-6-206 338
§47-7-7 447
§53-2-1 422
§53-2-1(c)(1) 420

Hawaii

Constitution

art. XII, §7 90

Revised Statutes

§1-1 90
§7-1 90
§52D-10 819
§52D-14 819
§§368-1 to 368-17 577
§489-3 71
§§501-1 to 501-219 555
§502-83 543

§509-2 351
§515-3 607, 612
§§521-1 to 521-78 431
§521-8 441
§521-74 481
§§539-1 to 539-12 420
§§560:1-101 to 560:8-101 420
§580-47(a) 398
§666-2 445
§675-31 155
§675-31.5 155
§708-814 29

Idaho

Code

§5-203 155
§7-701A(2) 689
§§15-1-101 to 15-6-404 420
§15-2-102(b) 403
§15-2-201 406
§§27-501 to 27-504 832
§32-712 403
§§32-903 to 32-912 401
§32-906 404
§32-910 402
§32-911 402
§32-912 402
§32-1003 417
§40-202 220
§45-904 566
§45-905 566
§55-111 339
§55-812 543
§§55-2101 to 55-2109 186
§§67-5901 to 67-5912 577
§67-6511A 648
§§67-8001 to 67-8004 762

Illinois

Compiled Statutes

20 3440/0 to 3440/16 832
735 5/13-101 155
735 5/13-109 155
735 5/13-118 to -121 537
735 5/15-1602 559
735 30/5-5-5(c) 689
735 30/5-5-5(d) 689
765 5/30 543
765 40/3 (repealed) 555
765 305/4(a)(7) 339
765 330/4 338, 537
765 605/18.6 288
765 1005/1b 352
765 1020/27 to 1020/35 819
775 5/1-101 to 5/1-103 71
775 5/1-102 to -103 577
775 5/3-101 to 5/3-106 577, 607
775 5/3-102 612
775 35/10 675
805 105/103.30 288
H.B. 4687 (*Landlord Retaliation Act*) 483

Indiana

Code

§§4-22-2-31 to 4-22-2-32 762
§§22-9.5-1-1 to 22-9.5-11-3 577
§§26-1-1-101 to 26-1-10-104 474
§31-15-7-4 398, 405
§32-1-2-11 543
§32-1-2-16 543
§§32-20-1-1 to 32-20-5-2 537
§32-23-2-2 198
§32-24-4.5-8(2)(A) 689
§32-26-10-1 136
§32-26-10-2 136
§§34-7-7-1 *et seq.* 672
§34-11-2-11 155
§§34-13-9-1 to 34-13-9-11 *(Indiana Religious Freedom Restoration Act)* 73
§34-13-9.0.7 73
§36-7-4-918.5 656

Iowa

Code

§§6A.21 to 6A.22 689
§6A.22 689
§§216.1 to 216.2 577
§216.7 71
§§216.8 to 216.8A 577
§216.8 607
§§216.11 to 216.20 577
§263B.9 (previously §305A.9) 739
§§556F.6 to 556F.18 819
§558.41 542
§558.41(1) 542
§558.68 336
§§562A.1 to 562A.37 431
§562A.5 440
§562A.36 481
§598.21 398
§598.21(b) 398
§614.24 338, 537
§§614.29 to 614.38 537
§614.31 155
§633.211 421
§633.212 421
§§656.1 to 656.9 566

Kansas

Statutes

§23-2802 398, 405
§§44-1015 to 44-1044 577
§§58-2221 to 58-2223 542
§58-2502 449, 458
§§58-2540 to 58-2573 431
§58-2572 481
§§58-3401 to 58-3412 537
§60-503 155
§§77-701 to 77-711 762
§82a-707(c) 131

Kentucky

Revised Statutes

§344.010 577
§§344.360 to 344.450 577
§383.080 542
§§383.200 to 383.285 461
§§383.500 to 383.715 431
§383.535(5) 440
§383.705 481
§391.170 850
§392.020 395
§392.080 395
§413.010 155
§413.150 168
§416.675(2) 689
§416.675(3) 689

Louisiana

Civil Code

art. 890 403
art. 2317 485
art. 2322 485
arts. 2325 to 2376 401
art. 2339 404
art. 2345 402, 403
art. 2365 403
art. 2369.2 403
art. 2372 417
art. 2680 445
art. 3473 154, 155
art. 3475 154, 155
art. 3486 154
art. 3499 155

Code of Civil Procedure

art. 971 672

Revised Statutes

§3:3602 763
§3:3622.1 762
§9:2721 541, 549
§41:1605(b) 856
§§51:2151 to 51:2156 853
§§51:2601 to 51:2614 577

Session Laws

2012 La. Acts 112 514

Maine

Revised Statutes

tit. 1, §816 689
tit. 5, §4552 607
tit. 5, §§4581 to 4583 577
tit. 5, §4581-A 630
tit. 5, §4582 607
tit. 5, §4592 71
tit. 14, §§731 et seq. 672
tit. 14, §801 155
tit. 14, §6002 447
tit. 17, §2801 136
tit. 18-C, §§1-101 to 10-118 420
tit. 19-A, §650-A 410
tit. 27, §303 853
tit. 33, §156 325
tit. 33, §159 351
tit. 33, §201 542
tit. 33, §502 556

Maryland

Code Annotated

Courts & Judicial Practice

§5-103 155

Estates & Trusts

§11-102(b)(5) 339

Family Law

§2-201 410

Land Use

§4-103 648

Real Property

§3-203 543
§6-101 537
§6-102 537
§6-103 309
§8-208.1 481

State Government

§20-101 71
§20-304 71, 607
§§20-701 to 20-1203 577
§20-705 612

Massachusetts

General Laws

ch. 9, §§26 to 27 (*Massachusetts Historical Commission*) 70
ch. 21E, §13 665
ch. 21G, §§1 to 19 127
ch. 22, §13A (*Massachusetts Architectural Access Board*) 70
ch. 40A, §6 655
ch. 40B, §§20 to 23 633
ch. 82, §24 213
ch. 93A, §§1 to 11 487, 515
ch. 111, §§190 to 199 489
ch. 139, §19 455
ch. 151B, §§1 to 10 577
ch. 151B, §4 607
ch. 151B, §4(10) 630
ch. 151B, §4.7 612
ch. 160, §205 71
ch. 183, §3 445
ch. 183, §4 542
ch. 183, §§45 to 47 325
ch. 183A, §§1 to 22 372
ch. 184, §8 351, 358
ch. 184, §27 297
ch. 184, §30 292, 298, 537
ch. 184, §31 259
ch. 184, §32 259
ch. 184A, §5 331, 339
ch. 184A, §7 338, 537
ch. 185 555
ch. 186, §18 481
ch. 186A, §§1 to 6 468
ch. 190B, §2-710 314
ch. 190B, §§2-901 to 2-906 338
ch. 208, §34 398, 405
ch. 209, §1 359
ch. 214, §3A 850
ch. 231, §59H 672
ch. 231, §85S 853
ch. 231, §85S(a) (*Massachusetts Art Preservation Act*) 854
ch. 239, §§1 to 16 460
ch. 239, §2A 481
ch. 239, §9 444, 461
ch. 239, §16 460
ch. 244, §15 571
ch. 260, §21 155
ch. 266, §120 29
ch. 272, §92A 71, 72
ch. 272, §98 71
ch. 272, §98A 70

Code of Regulations

780 §3307.1 (*Massachusetts State Building Code*) 134

Session Laws

1981 Mass. Acts ch. 231 567
1983 Mass. Acts ch. 527, §§1-5D, 7 371
1998 Mass. Acts ch. 19, §1 72
2015 Mass. Acts ch. 141 (*An Act Clearing Titles to Foreclosed Properties*) 571

Michigan

Compiled Laws

§§37.2501 to 37.2507 577
§37.2502(1) 612
§§324.20116 to 324.20142 (*Michigan Natural Resources and Environmental Protection Act*) 664
§§434.21 to 434.29 819
§§554.71 to 554.78 338
§565.29 543
§600.5720 483
§§700.1101 to 700.8102 420
§722.3 417

Statutes

§§565.101 to 565.108 537
§600.5801(4) 155

Minnesota

Constitution

art. I, §15 443

Session Laws

2013 ch. 74 (H.F. 1054) 410

Statutes

§245A.11, subd. 4 624
§363.03(2)(a) 612
§§363A.01 to 363A.20 577
§363A.03(34) 31, 71
§363A.09 607, 612, 630
§363A.11 71
§500.19(3) 351
§500.20 297, 537
§504B.285 481
§507.34 543
§507.413 571
§§508.01 to 508.84 555
§513.075 412
§§517.01 to 517.09 410
§518.58 subd. 2 398
§§524.1-101 to 524.8-103 420
§541.02 155
§541.023 537
§§554.07 to 554.19 672

Mississippi

Code

§15-1-7 155
§15-1-13 168
§43-33-723 577
§§49-33-1 to 49-33-17 762
§49-33-7 763
§65-7-201 213
§89-5-5 543
§89-7-3 451
§89-7-25 449, 458
§97-23-17 56

Public Laws

1839 Miss. Laws 72 395

Missouri

Revised Statutes

§§213.010 to 213.137 577
§442.380 542
§442.390 542
§442.400 542
§442.555 336
§474.160 399
§516.010 155
§523.271 689
§536.017 762
§568.040 418

Montana

Code

§§2-10-101 to 2-10-112 762
§40-4-202 398
§40-4-202(1) 398, 405
§40-6-217 418
§§49-2-301 to 49-2-311 577
§49-2-305 612
§§70-5-101 to 70-5-107 819
§§70-5-201 to 70-5-209 819
§70-17-203 259
§§70-19-401 to 70-19-411 155
§70-19-413 156
§70-21-201 543
§70-21-302 543
§70-21-304 543
§§70-24-101 to 70-24-442 431
§70-24-431 481
§70-26-204 449, 458
§§72-1-101 to 72-6-418 420

Nebraska

Revised Statutes

§§12-1202 to 12-1212 832
§20-202 850
§§20-301 to 20-344 577
§25-202 155
§§25-21,241 to 25-21,246 672
§§30-2201 to 30-2902 420
§76-107 338
§76-237 543
§76-238 543
§§76-288 to 76-298 537
§76-710.04 689
§§76-1401 to 76-1449 431
§76-1439 481

Nevada

Revised Statutes

§§41.640 to 41.670 672
§111.200 443
§111.320 543
§111.325 543
§§118.010 to 118.120 577
§118.100 607
§§118A.010 to 118A.530 431
§118A.510 481
§§123.010 to 123.310 401
§123.130 404
§125.150 403
§233.010 71
§§597.770 to 597.810 850

New Hampshire

Revised Statutes

§162-K:2(IX-a)(a) 689
§162-K:2(IX-a)(b) 689
§§354-A:1 to 354-A:5 577
§§354-A:1 to 354-A:10 607
§§354-A:8 to 354-A:15 577
§354-A:10 612
§354-A:17 71
§§354-A:18 to 354-A:26 577
§§471-C:1 to 471-C:14 819
§477:3-a 542
§498:4-a 321
ch. 508 §2 155
§540:1 445
§540:1-a 468
§540:2 444, 468
§540:13-a 481

Session Laws

2009 N.H. Laws ch. 59 410

New Jersey

Statutes

§2A:14-30 155
§§2A:18-51 to 2A:18-61.12 431
§2A:18-53 444, 468

§2A:18-61.1 444, 468
§§2A:18-61.22 to 2A:21:18-61.39 468
§§2A:24A-1 to 2A:24-8 853
§2A:34-23.1 398
§2A:42-10.1 461
§2A:42-10.10 481
§2A:42-10.10(d) 483
§2C:18-3 29
§3B:8-1 399
§§10:5-1 to 10:5-49 577
§10:5-4 71, 607, 612, 630
§10:5-5 71
§10:5-12 71
§10:5-12g 630
§§13:1k-6 *et seq.* (*New Jersey Industrial Site Recovery Act*) 665
§14A:6-1(2) 386
§25:1-5(h) 415
§25:1-13 507
§§37:1-28 to 37:1-36 409
§37:2-32(c) 400
§37:2-38(c) 400
§§40:55D-49 to 40:55D-052 655
§40:55D-70(c)(1) 656
§40:55D-70(d) 656–657
§46:2F-9 339
§46:2F-10 339
§46:3-17.1 351
§46:3-17.4 359
§46:3-23 280
§§46:3-28 to 46:3-33 284
§§46:3C-1 to 46:3C-12 502, 510, 511
§46:8-9 445
§46:22-1 543
§§52:27D-301 to 52:27D-329 (*New Jersey Fair Housing Act of 1985*) 633
§§52:27D-330 to 52:27D-360 (*Continuing Care Retirement Community Regulation and Financial Disclosure Act*) 382
§52:27D-344(d) 382
§56:10-5 388

New Mexico

Statutes

§§14-9-1 to 14-9-3 542
§§28-1-1 to 28-1-15 577
§28-1-2 71
§28-1-7 71, 607
§37-1-22 143, 153, 155
§§40-3-6 to 40-3-13 401
§40-3-10(A) 402–403
§40-3-11 402
§§45-1-101 to 45-7-522 420
§45-2-102 403
§§47-8-1 to 47-8-52 431
§47-8-39 481
§§56-11-1 to 56-11-3 853

New York

Constitution

art. XVII, §1 636

Arts & Cultural Affairs

§§11.01 to 16.01 853
§14.03(1) (*New York Artists' Authorship Rights Act*) 853

Business Corporation

§717(b) 386

Civil Practice Law and Rules

§3211(g) 672
§3212(h) 672

Civil Rights

§50 851
§51 850
§70-a 672
§76-a 672

Domestic Relations

§§10-a to 10-b (*Marriage Equality Act*) 410
§263(B)(1)(d)(1) 398
§263(B)(5)(b) 398

Estates, Powers & Trusts

§4-1.1 420
§6-2.2(b) 360
§6-3.2 307

Executive

§291 577
§296 71, 607
§§296 to 301 577
§296.2-a 612, 630
§296.5(a) 630

General Business

§777-b 514

General Municipal

§250 819

Personal Property

§§251 to 258 820

Real Property

§§210 to 218 444, 468
§223-a 467
§223-b 481
§223-b(2) 483

§226-b 492
§226-b(1) 490
§226-b(2) 490
§226-b(2)(a) 492
§227-e 463
§228 449
§235-f 492
§291 543
§345 537
§436 (repealed) 555

Real Property Actions & Proceedings

§§501 to 551 155
§501 153
§522 143
§543 144, 149, 150
§§701 to 768 460
§797 (*Tenant Dignity and Safe Housing Act of 2022*) 473
§1201 365
§1371 559
§1951 292

North Carolina

Constitution

art. 10, §2 352
art. 10, §2(1) 352
art. 10, §2(3) 353
art. 10, §2(4) 358

General Statutes

§1-35 168
§1-40 155
§29-14 420
§41-29 331, 339
§41-32 338
§41-56(b) 358
§§41A-1 to 41A-10 577
§42-25.6 460
§42-37.1 481
ch. 43 555
§47-18 541
§47-18(a) 541, 549
§§47B-1 to 47B-9 537
§47B-2 297
§47B-4 297
§75-16.1 487
§§121-34 to 121-42 186
§143-422.11(a) 75
Property Protection Act 37

Session Laws

2016-3 (H.B. 2) 75
2017-4 (H.B. 142) 75

North Dakota

Century Code

§4-02.4-12 612
§§14-02.4-01 to 14-02.5-02 630
§§14-02.5-01 to 14-02.5-46 577
§§14-03.2-01 to 14-03.2-11 404
§14-09-09 418
§28-01-01 168
§28-01-08 155–156, 168
§28-01-14 156
§28-32-09 762
§§30.1-01-01 to 30.1-30-01 420
§§32-18-01 to 32-18-06 564
§47-06-03 168
§47-19-41 543
§§47-19.1-01 to 47-19.1-11 537

Ohio

Revised Code

§2103.02 395
§2108.02(B) (*Uniform Anatomical Gift Act*) 828
§2131.08 336
§2131.09(B) 339
§2305.04 155
§§3752.01 to 3752.99 (*Ohio Cessation of Regulated Operations Program*) 665
§§4112.01 to 4112.024 577
§5301.09 541
§5301.23 541
§5301.25 542
§§5301.47 to 5301.55 537
§5309 555
§5310 555
§§5313.05 to 5313.08 566
§§5321.01 to 5321.19 431
§5321.02 481

Oklahoma

Constitution

art. 2, §24 711

Statutes

tit. 12, §93 155
tit. 15, §§511 to 518 819
tit. 16, §11a 564
tit. 16, §15 542
tit. 16, §16 542
tit. 16, §§71 to 80 537
tit. 19, §291 538
tit. 21, §§839.1 to 839.3 850
tit. 21, §§1168 to 1168.6 832
tit. 23, §27 523
tit. 25, §§1451 to 1453 577

tit. 25, §1452.A.8 630
tit. 41, §§101 to 135 431
tit. 53, §361 832

Oregon

Revised Statutes

§12.050 155
§12.160 156
§§90.100 to 90.940 431
§90.370 477
§90.385 481
§90.427 444, 468
§91.060 445
§91.070 445
§93.180 357, 358
§93.640 543
§93.850 535
§§98.005 to 98.025 819
§105.140(2) 477
§105.620(1)(b) 153
§105.770 537
§105.772 537
§§105.950 to 105.975 338
§108.045 418
§108.090 358
§112.025 421
§112.035 421
§§195.305 to 195.314 764
§195.305 764
ch. 197 643
§§197.005 to 197.850 633
§§376.150 to 376.200 213
§390.610 89
§§465.200 to 465.260 (*Oregon Hazardous Waste Removal and Remedial Action Act*) 664
§465.900 664
§659A.001 577
§659A.030 607
§659A.403 71
§§659A.421 to 659A.425 577
§659A.421(2) 612, 630

Pennsylvania

Consolidated Statutes

tit. 23, §4321 417
tit. 42, §5530 155
tit. 43, §§951 to 963 71, 577
tit. 68, §§8101 to 8107 284

Statutes

tit. 21, §321 555
tit. 21, §351 543
tit. 42, §8141 541
tit. 68, §250.205 481
tit. 68, §411 217
tit. 73, §§2101 to 2110 853

Rhode Island

General Laws

§§5-62-2 to 5-62-6 853
§9-1-28 850
§§9-33-1 to 9-33-4 672
§11-24-2 71
§11-24-2.2 71
§§15-1-1 to 15-1-5 410
§§34-4-15 to 34-4-17 325
§34-7-1 155
§34-11-1 542
§34-11-38 339
§§34-13.1-1 to 34-13.1-11 537
§§34-18-1 to 34-18-57 431
§34-18-46 481
§§34-37-1 to 34-37-5.4 607
§§34-37-1 to 34-37-11 577
§34-37-4 612
§§34-37.1-1 to 34-37.1-5 634
§34-37.1-3 634
§42-45.1-4(a) 856
§42.80.1-3(b)(1) 675
§45-24-53(h) 648
§§45-53-1 to 45-53-8 633

Session Laws

2013 R.I. Pub. Laws 4 410

South Carolina

Code

§15-67-210 155
§15-67-220 155
§15-67-260 155
§20-7-40 397
§27-33-10 440
§§27-40-10 to 27-40-940 431
§27-40-910 481
§30-7-10 543
§§31-21-10 to 31-21-150 577
§45-9-10(B)(4) 56
§§48-39-250 *et seq.* (*Beachfront Management Act*) 729
§§62-1-100 to 62-7-604 420

South Dakota

Codified Laws

§1-20-25 856
§11-7-22.1 689
§15-3-1 155
§§15-3-1 to 15-3-10 155, 168
§15-3-4 168
§15-3-15 155

§§20-13-20 to 20-13-56 577
§25-7-8 418
§25-7-27 418
§§29A-1-101 to 29A-8-101 420
§§43-4-47 to 43-4-57 284
§43-5-1 339
§43-5-2 339
§43-5-8 339
§43-28-17 543
§§43-30-1 et seq. 537
§§43-30-1 to 43-30-17 537
§43-32-2 443

Tennessee

Code

§§4-21-601 to 4-21-607 577
§§12-1-201 to 12-1-206 762
§28-20-102 155
§29-17-102(2) 689
§29-17-102(2)(C) 689
§§47-25-1101 to 47-25-1108 850
§47-25-1104 852
§§66-28-101 to 66-28-516 431
§66-28-514 481
§66-51-106 542

Texas

Constitution

art. 16, §15 401, 404

Code

§16.024 156
§16.025 156
§16.026 155, 156

Family Code

§1.108 412
§§3.001 to 3.002 406
§§3.001 to 3.006 401
§3.102 402
§7.001 403
§151.001 417

Government Code

§§2007.001 to 2007.045 (*Private Real Property Rights Preservation Act*) 762
§2007.002(5) 763
§2007.003(b)(1) 763
§2007.003(b)(6) 763
§2007.003(b)(7) 763
§2007.003(b)(13) 763
§2007.023 763
§2007.024 763
§§2007.041 to 2007.045 762

Local Government Code

§§245.002 to 245.006 655

Probate Code

§45 403
§271 403

Property Code

§5.066 566
§13.001 542
§13.002 542
§§26.001 et seq. 850
§92.331 481
§209-00591(c) 373
§§301.021 to 301.027 577

Utah

Code

§57-3-103 543
§§57-9-1 to 57-9-10 537
§§57-21-1 to 57-21-14 577
§57-21-5 630
§57-21-6 607
§§63*l*-3-101 to 63*l*-3-202 762
§§75-1-101 to 75-8-101 420
§78B-2-201 168
§78B-2-214 155

Vermont

Constitution

art. 7 409

Statutes

tit. 9, §4465 481, 483
tit. 9, §§4500 to 4507 577
tit. 9, §4502 71, 607
tit. 9, §4503 71, 607
tit. 9, §4503(a) 612, 630
tit. 12, §501 155
tit. 12, §1040(a) 689
tit. 12, §4941 558
tit. 13, §3761 739, 806
tit. 27, §302 445
tit. 27, §342 542
tit. 27, §§601 to 617 537
tit. 27, §§1101 to 1108 819

Acts & Resolves

2000 Vt. Acts & Resolves 91 (H. 847) 409
2009 Vt. Act 3 409, 410
2009 Vt. S. 115 409, 410

Virginia

Code

§1-10 184
§2.2-3904 71, 607
§8.01-40 850
§8.01-236 155
§8.2-318 514
§15.2-2307 654–655
§18.2-216.1 850
§20-107.3(A) 398
§§36-96.1 to 36-96.23 577
§36-96.3 71, 607
§55-70.2 284
§55-112 (repealed) 555
§55-248.39 481
§55.1-105 198
§55.1-407 542
§§55.1-1200 to 55.1-1262 431

Washington

Constitution

art. 2, §1(a) (amend. 72) 81

Revised Code

§4.16.020 155
§§4.24.500 to 4.24.520 672
§7.28.230(1) 560
§7.43.010 117
§8.24.010 213
§11.04.015 420
§11.04.015(1)(a) 403
§11.98.130 339
§19.27.095 655
§26.09.080 403
§26.16.010 404
§§26.16.010 to 26.16.140 401
§26.16.020 404
§26.16.030 401
§26.16.030(3) 402
§26.16.030(4) 402
§26.16.200 402
§26.16.220 406
§26.16.230 406
§§29A.72.010 to 29A.72.070 81
§§36.70.320 *et seq.* 643
§36.70a.370 762
§39.60.22 577
§§49.60.010 to 49.60.401 577
§49.60.215 71
§49.60.222 607, 612
§58.17.033 655
§59.12.070 461
§59.18 630
§§59.18.010 to 59.18.900 431
§59.18.240 481
§59.18.370 461
§§63.21.010 to 63.21.050 819
§§64.60.005 to 64.60.901 284
§65.08.070 543
§65.08.070(1) 543
§65.12 (repealed) 555

West Virginia

Code

§§5-11A-1 to 5-11A-20 577
§16-18-6 689
§§16B-18-1 to 16B-18-20 577
§§22-1A-1 to 22-1A-3 762
§40-1-8 542
§40-1-9 542
§42-1-3a 422
§54-1-2(a)(11) 689
§55-2-1 155

Wisconsin

Statutes

§32.03(6) 689
§106.50 607, 612, 630
§§106.50 to 106.58 577
§106.52 71
§§135.02(4) to 135.03 388
§700.16(5) 340
§700.24 354
§704.19 447
§704.27 449, 458
§704.45 481
§706.08 543
§§766.001 to 766.31 401
§766.15 402
§766.55 417
§766.55(2)(c) 402
§766.63(1) 404
§767.61(3)(L) 400
§767.255(3)(L) 400
§861.01 403
§893.25 155
§893.29 168
§893.33 537
§893.33(6) 297
§995.50 850

Wyoming

Statutes

§1-3-103 155
§1-26-713 693
§§9-5-301 to 9-5-305 762

§20-2-114 398
§34-1-121 543
§§34-10-101 to 34-10-109 537

American Indian Nation Tribal Codes

Confederated Tribes of the Colville Reservation

Tribal Code

tit. 5, §5-1-30 410
tit. 5, §5-1-32 410
tit. 5, §5-1-34 410

Coquille Indian Tribe

Tribal Code

§740.010 410
§740.100 410

Little Traverse Bay Bands of Odawa Indians

Code of Law

§13.103 410

Mashantucket Pequot Tribe

Tribal Laws

tit. 6, ch. 3, §3 410

Pokagon Band of Potawatomi Indians Marriage Code

Code of Law

ch. 1, §1.06(j) 410

Puyallup Tribe

Tribal Code

tit. 7, §7.08.030 410

Suquamish Tribe

Tribal Code

tit. 9, §9.1.1 410

Tlingit and Haida Indian Tribes of Alaska, Central Council of

Statutory Code

tit. 5, §05.01.004(C) 410

Uniform Laws

Uniform Anatomical Gift Act

8A U.L.A. 63 (1993) 828

Uniform Commercial Code

U.C.C. §2-314 474
U.C.C. §2-403 826
U.C.C. §2-403(1) 826
U.C.C. §2-403(2) 173, 826
U.C.C. §7-204(1) 824

Uniform Conservation Easement Act (1981)

§§1 to 6, 12 U.L.A. 170 186

Uniform Easement Relocation Act (2020)

generally 196

Uniform Fiduciary Access to Digital Assets Act, Revised (2015)

§§1 to 21 857

Uniform Limited Partnership Act (2001)

U.P.A. §303 384

Uniform Marital Property Act

generally 401

Uniform Partition of Heirs Property Act (UPHPA)

§6 363
§7 363
§8 363
§9 363
§10 363

Uniform Partnership Act (1916)

U.P.A. §8(3) 383
U.P.A. §24 383
U.P.A. §25 383
U.P.A. §26 383

Uniform Partnership Act (1977)

U.P.A. §101(6) 383
U.P.A. §103(b) 384
U.P.A. §203 384
U.P.A. §301 384
U.P.A. §306 384

Revised Uniform Partnership Act of 1994 (RUPA)

generally 383–384

Uniform Premarital Agreement Act (UPAA)

generally 400
§6 400

Uniform Premarital and Marital Agreement Act (UPMAA)

generally 400
§9(b) 400
§9(d)(1) 400
§9(f) 401

Uniform Probate Code

generally 399, 419, 420
§2-102 420–421, 423
§2-102(2) 420
§2-102(3) 421–422
§2-102(4) 421–422

§2-106 423
§2-203 399
§2-502 419
§2-503 419
§2-609 528
§2-803(c) 350
§2-904 338
§2-904(5) 339
§3-814 528
§6-103 822
§6-104 822

Uniform Residential Landlord and Tenant Act

generally 428, 488
§1.202(4) 442
§1.202(5) 440
§1.304 476
§1.401(b) 428
§1.403 479
§2.103 467
§4.101 429, 457
§4.101(a) 476–477
§4.101(b) 478–479
§4.101(c) 478
§4.102 429, 457
§4.105 477
§4.106 451
§4.107 429, 457
§4.201 429, 457
§4.202 429, 457
§4.203(c) 464
§4.204 458
§4.301(a) 445
§4.301(b) 445
§5.101(b) 482

Revised Uniform Residential Landlord and Tenant Act (RURLTA)

generally 429
§103(a)(1) 442
§103(c)(8) 442

Uniform Simultaneous Death Act

§4 350

Uniform Statutory Rule Against Perpetuities (USRAP)

generally 338–339
§4(5) 339

Uniform Unclaimed Property Act

generally 820

Uniform Disposition of Unclaimed Property Act

generally 820

Municipal Ordinances

Boise City Code §6-01-05 634
Boise City Code §9-10-02 634
Boston Code §12-9.7 71
Boston Code tit. 12, ch. 40 607
Chicago Mun. Code, §2-160-070 71
Chicago Mun. Code, ch. 199 607
Grants Pass Mun. Code §5.61.010 635
Grants Pass Mun. Code §5.61.030 635
Los Angeles Mun. Code, ch. IV 71, 607
New York City, Admin. Code §8-102(20) 607
New York City, Admin. Code §8-107(4) 71
Philadelphia Fair Prac. Ordinance, ch. 9-1100 607
Philadelphia Fair Prac. Ordinance, ch. 9-1106 71
San Francisco Code, art. 33, §3301 607
San Francisco Code, art. 33, §3305 71

Republic of South Africa Constitution

ch. 2 §26 635
ch. 2 §27(1) 635

TABLE OF RESTATEMENTS

Restatement (Second) of Conflict of Laws (1971)

§223 405

Restatement (Second) of Contracts (1981)

§360 cmt. e 526

Restatement (Third) of Mortgages (1997)

§7.6 561

Restatement of Property (1936–1944)

generally 2
§§1–4 5
§160 309
§524 237
§534 247
§535 249, 251
§537 254
§542 250, 251
§547 251
§548 234, 244, 249
§563 295
§564 291

Restatement (Second) of Property (Donative Transfers) (1983)

§4.1 281
§§4.1 to 4.2 282
§4.2 cmt. t 279
§6.1 342
§6.1(2) 343
§6.2 344
§6.3 345
§7.1 345

Restatement (Second) of Property (Landlord and Tenant) (1977)

§2.1 443
§5.3 cmt. c 479
§5.6 479
§6.1 468
§6.1 cmt. d 472
§6.1 Reporter's Note 6 471
§6.2 467
§7.1 457
§10.2 cmt. b 479
§10.2(4) 478
§11.1 468
§12.1 cmt. i 464
§12.1 cmt. k 466
§12.1(3) 464
§13.1 450, 457
§14.8 483
§14.9 483
§15.2 491

Restatement (Third) of Property (Servitudes) (2000)

generally 220
§1.1 179, 227
§1.2 228
§1.2 cmt. h 228
§1.5(1) 254
§2.4 235, 248, 249
§2.6 251, 252
§2.6 cmt. d 249, 258, 259, 260, 276
§2.6(1) 259, 260
§2.6(b) 185
§2.6(d) 187
§2.9 237
§2.10 200, 237
§2.12 207
§2.13 208
§2.14 262, 263
§2.14 cmt. b 264
§2.14 cmt. g 266
§2.15 211
§2.16 213
§2.17 213
§2.18 220
§3.1 254, 258, 277, 287, 288
§§3.1 to 3.2 235
§§3.1 to 3.7 187, 233
§3.1 cmt. a 287
§3.1 cmt. d 277–278
§3.1 cmt. e 232
§3.1 cmt. f 288
§3.1 cmt. i 277, 287, 289
§3.1 cmt. j 287
§3.1 Reporter's Note 278
§3.1(2) 289
§3.2 235
§3.2 cmt. e 255, 256

§3.3 338
§3.4 281
§3.4 cmt. d 284
§3.4 cmt. e 285, 340
§3.4 cmt. f 285, 340
§3.5(2) 284
§3.6 285
§3.7 289
§4.1 270
§4.1 cmt. a 271
§4.5 190
§4.5(1)(a) 255
§4.6 198
§4.8(3) 196
§4.10 cmt. b 194
§4.11 195
§5.1 cmt. b 237
§5.2 228, 252, 254
§5.2 cmt. b 235, 252
§5.3 228
§5.3(1) 252
§5.3(2) 252
§5.4 252
§5.6 197
§5.7 193
§5.8 198
§5.9 198
§6.1 372
§6.2 227, 371, 372
§6.2 cmt. e 375
§6.3 376, 377
§6.3 cmt. a 377
§6.4 361
§6.7 378
§6.7 cmt. b 378, 379
§6.7 cmt. e 378
§6.7(2) 378
§6.9 cmt. d 380
§6.10 377
§6.10 cmt. g 378
§6.10(2) 378
§6.11 253
§6.13 379
§6.14 379
§6.19 373
§6.19(1) 373
§6.19(2) 373
§6.21 276
§7.3 296
§7.4 296
§7.4 cmt. b 296–297
§7.4 cmt. c 297
§7.5 296
§7.6 297
§7.7 297
§7.10 187, 224, 292
§7.10 cmt. a 292
§7.10 cmt. c 291
§7.10 cmt. d 292
§7.10 Reporter's Note 224
§7.11 cmt. a 292
§7.12 cmt. a 294
§7.12(1) 294
§7.12(2) 294
§7.13 294
§7.14 240, 252, 263
§7.14 cmt. b 240
§8.1 260, 294
§8.2 266
§8.3 295
§8.3 cmt. a 295
§8.3 cmt. h 295
§8.3(1) 229

Restatement (Third) of Property (Servitudes) (2000) (Tentative Draft No. 1, Apr. 5, 1989)

xxii 239

Restatement of Restitution (1937)

§188 357
§188 cmt. b 357

Restatement of Torts (1939)

§818 135

Restatement (Second) of Torts (1965–1977)

§157 24, 214
§158 28
§§167–215 26
§197 38
§202 40
§§204–211 40
§217 91
§218 91
§353 510
§540 510
§552 506
§818 136
§818 illus. 2 136
§821B 121
§822 106
§822 cmt. d 111
§822 cmt. g 96
§825 105, 106
§826 cmt. f 111
§826(a) 103
§826(b) 104, 108
§827 104
§828 104
§846 126
§892B(2) 35
§936(1) 798

Restatement (Third) of Trusts (2003)

§29(c) cmt. j, illus. 3 345

Restatement (Third) of Trusts (2012)

§67 321

INDEX

A

Abandoned Shipwreck Act of 1987, 821
Abandonment
  adverse possession, 158, 161, 164, 165
  covenants, 296-297
  finders, 816-817
  licenses and easements, 223-224
  nonconforming use, 652
Aboriginal title, 773-777, 781-784
Accession and fixtures, 826-827
Access rights vs. exclusion rights, 6-7
Accretion, 172, 530
Acquiescence, 170, 171, 219, 296
Acquisition power vs. loss immunity, 8
Acts of God, 451
Actual notice
  express easements, 190
  recording acts, 542
Actual possession, 24, 143-146
ADA. See Americans with Disabilities Act of 1990
Adjustable rate mortgages, 567-568
Adjustment boards, 644
Adverse possession, 139-175
  abandonment, 158, 161, 164, 165
  boundary disputes, 145-146, 163-164
  burden of proof, 166
  co-tenants, 165-166
  efficient use of property, 159-160
  elements, 143-156
    actual possession, 143-146
    adverse or hostile possession, 143, 149-155
    claim of right, 143, 151-152
    color of title, 143, 145, 151, 156, 162-163
    continuous possession, 143, 148-149
    defective title, 156, 162-163
    exclusivity, 143, 147-148
    objective test, 151
    open and notorious, 143, 146-147
    permissiveness, 149-151
    privity, 148
    state of mind, 149, 151
    statutory period, 143, 155-156
    tacking, 148-149
    taxes paid, 143, 156
  federal lands, 169
  fee simple determinable, 307
  fee simple subject to condition subsequent, 308
  fences, 144
  fungible property, 158-159
  future interests, 168
  good faith possession, 143, 151, 154-155, 161
  government, claims against, 168-169
  hostile possession, 143, 149-155
  intentional dispossession, 152-153
  joint tenancy, 165-166
  justifications for, 156-162
  mortgages, 167
  mutual mistake, 164
  ouster, 165-166
  overview, 140-143
  personal property, 172-175, 826
    conversion rule, 172
    demand and refusal rule, 173-174
    demand rule, 172
    discovery rule, 172-173
    due diligence, 173
    laches, 174
    statute of limitations, 172-173
  prescriptive easements vs., 145-146
  prior encumbrances, effect on, 166-167
  procedures, 166-168
  reliance, 158
  repose, 161-162
  rights and obligations of co-tenants, 370
  rural land, 147
  shrubs, 144
  squatters, 161, 164-165
  statute of frauds, 163
  statutes of limitations
    legal basis of, 140-141
    ouster by co-tenant, 370
    personal property, 172-173
    repose, 161-162
    statutory period, 143, 155-156

Adverse possession (*continued*)
  stolen artworks, 172-175
  title clarification, 156-157
  title transfers, informal, 169-172
    acquiescence, 170, 171
    boundary disputes, 169-172
    dedication, 170
    estoppel, 151, 171
    improving trespasser, 169
    informal understanding, 170-171
    oral agreement, 170-171
    riparian owners, 172
  trees, 144
  trespass and public accommodations, 41, 168-169
  tribal lands, 161-162
Advertising, 587-588, 595-596, 598
AFDC (Aid to Families with Dependent Children), 625, 636
Affirmative covenants. *See* Covenants
Affirmative easements, 178
Affirmatively further fair housing (AFFH) regulations, 619-620
Affordable housing arrangements, 381-382
Age Discrimination in Employment Act of 1967, 592
Aggregate theory, 383
Aggrieved persons, 596-597
Agricultural commodities, 725-726
Aid to Families with Dependent Children (AFDC), 625, 636
Air
  easements, 136, 185
  Fontainebleau doctrine, 136-137
  nuisance, 98, 136
  pollution, 116-117
  space, public navigable, 43-44
  takings of rights, 704-705
Airbnb, 121, 442
Alaska, *Native Claims Settlement Act of 1971* (*ANCSA*), 801-802
Alexander, Gregory, 26
Alienability dilemma, 11
Alienation. *See also* Transfers
  concurrent ownership, 349-350
  licenses and easements, 181-182
  periodic tenancy, 445
  present estates and future interests, 302-304
    defeasible fees, 310
    fee simple, 306
    life estates, 311
    partial restraints on alienation, 329-330
    promotion of, 324, 327-328
    regulatory rules, 324, 328-330
    restraints on, 328-330
  restraints on
    American Indian property, 774, 776-777, 791
    antitrust, 285-286
    charities, 284, 329-330
    common law rule against, 340
    condominiums, 282-283, 373
    consent clauses, 283-284
    cooperatives, 282-283
    covenants, 230, 280-285
    disabling, 280-282
    first refusal rights, 284-285
    forfeiture, 280-282
    grantor fees on future sales, 284
    indirect, 284
    leaseholds, 283
    life estates, 282, 311
    low-income housing cooperatives, 283
    partial, 281-282
    present estates and future interests, 328-330
    promissory, 280-282
    public policy limitations, 280-285
    purchase options, 284-285
    total, 280-281
    transfer fee on future sales, 284
    unreasonable, 281-285, 328-330
  tenancy in common, 349-350
  term of years, 442-443
Alimony, 399
Allodialism, 302
Allotment, 788
Amazon Web Services, 825
Ambiguity
  concurrent ownership, 360
  covenants, 270-276
    generally, 233
    architectural review committees, 275
    group homes, 271-274
    home day care, 276
    intent vs. free use, 270-271
    privity requirement, 244
    public policy, 274
    reasonableness review, 275
    residential vs. commercial use, 271-272
    structure vs. occupants, 272
  deed references, 200-201, 208-209
  easements by estoppel, 200-201, 205
  leaseholds, 436
  nuisance, 107-108
  present estates and future interests, 315-324
    changed conditions, 323-324
    conflicts between granting clause and deed language, 317-318
    cy pres doctrine, 321-322
    discriminatory trusts, 322-323
    forfeitures, presumption against, 315-320
    grantor's intent, 315, 317
    in kind vs. market value, 321
    magic words, 316-317, 318
    market value vs. in kind, 321

precatory language, 315, 318-319
presumption against forfeitures, 315-320
public policy, 323
purpose, 318-319
repurchase rights, 319-320
reverter as remedy, 324
waste, 320-321
American Indian property, 769-807
aboriginal title, 773-777, 781-784
adverse possession, 161-162
alienation, 774, 776-777, 791
allotment, 788
beach access, 90-91
burial mounds, 739
checkerboard reservations, 781
compensability, 781-791
good faith, presumption of, 786-788
conflicting property rights, 793
discovery doctrine, 784
easements, tribal, 777, 806-807
Eleventh Amendment, 796
equivocal rights, 787
executive order title, 778, 788-790
extinguishment, 792-793
federal common law, 791
federal patents, 771
Fifth Amendment, 781, 788-790
fishing rights, 40, 90-91, 806-807
history of, 784-785, 792-793
hospitality, 783
hunting rights, 40, 91-92, 806-807
nomadic use, 783
number of owners, 782-783
original Indian title, 773-777, 781-784
origins of property rights, 770-771
overview, 770-772
plenary power doctrine, 785-786
protection of, 791-793
recognized title, 777, 784-788
regulatory takings, 766, 775
reparations, 794-806
breach of trust claims, 802-805
damages, inadequacy of, 799
domestic dependent nation status, 802-803
eastern land claims, 795-801
ejectment, 798-799
human remains, 805-806, 831-833
IIM, 804-805
Indian Claims Commission, 794-795, 798
Kennewick Man, 805-806
laches, 794, 796, 797, 800
land claims settlement acts, 801-802
relief, 797-801
sovereign immunity waiver, 794-795
restricted trust allotments, 744-745, 779-781, 790-791
right of occupancy, 785, 790
same-sex marriage, 410-411
takings, 766, 775
title, individual, 779-781
assignments, 780-781
checkerboard reservations, 781
restricted trust allotments, 779-781
tribal law, 780
title, tribal, 773-777
aboriginal title, 773-777, 781-784
executive order title, 778, 788-790
title of occupancy, 773-776
U.S. fee title, 773-775
transfers of, 797-801
tribal law, 770, 780
trust status, 771-772, 775-776, 802-805
U.S. needs, 783-784
water rights, 131, 753-754, 777, 807
Winters doctrine, 807
Americans with Disabilities Act of 1990 (*ADA*)
architectural barriers, 66
construction after January 26, 1993, 69
disparate impact, 622
exemptions, 63, 70-71
historic landmarks, 70-71
historic preservation laws, 70-71
movie theaters, 69-70
private clubs, 60-61, 63
public accommodations, 31-32, 62-71
readily achievable actions, 66
reasonable modifications, 66-67
renovations, 70
restrictive covenants, 274
smoking, 68-69
Web sites, 64
Ancient lights doctrine, 186, 221
Animals. *See also* Wild animals
animus revertendi, 816
fencing laws, 46
personal property, 813-816
pets, 46, 816
strict liability, 46
trespass and public accommodations law, 46
Animus revertendi, 816
Antenuptial agreements, 393, 397, 399-401
Anti-Drug Abuse Act of 1988, 455-456
Anti-eviction laws, 468-469, 723-724
Anti-Snob Zoning Act (Massachusetts), 633
Antitrust law, 285-286, 503
Apartment buildings, 120-121
Apportionment, 198-199, 404. *See also* Partition
Appurtenant easements. *See* Express easements; Licenses and easements
Architectural barriers, 66
Architectural controls, 380
Architectural review committees, 275
Arizona, *Private Property Rights Protection Act*, 764

Artificial intelligence. *See* Generative artificial intelligence
Artists' moral rights, 853-854
  applied art, 853-854
  integrity of work, 853
  made for hire works, 853
  site-specific works, 854
  temporary works, 854-855
  visual art works, 853-854
Art Preservation Act (California), 853
Art Preservation Act (Massachusetts), 854
"As is" clauses, 512
Assignment of American Indian property, 780-781
Association, freedom of
  public nuisance, 123
  roommates, 602-603
Associational interests, 52-53, 597, 669
Aviation, 43-44
Avulsion, 172, 530
Ayres, Ian, 112-113

B

Bailments
  cloud computing, 825
  data property, 825
  personal property, 824-825
  possession, 824-825
Bank accounts, 822
Bank boxes, 533, 822
Bathrooms and gender identity, 75
Battered women's shelters, 620, 625-626
Beach access, 86-91, 754-755
Beachfront property, 756-757
Bentham, Jeremy, 14, 20
Bert J. Harris, Jr. Private Property Rights Protection Act of 1995 (Florida), 763
BIA (Bureau of Indian Affairs), 776, 790, 804
Bilateral conditional zoning, 650
Bilateral contract, 428, 648-649
Bilateral mistake, 528
Billboards, 434-435, 436-437, 672-674
Blasting, 45
Blight, 682-683
Blockbusting, 588
Boundary disputes, 145-146, 163-164
Boy Scouts of America, 51-53
Brokers, 496-504
  answers to client questions, 589
  antitrust concerns, 503
  commissions, 498-499
  conditional contracts, 500-501
  conflicts of interest, 502-503
  default, rights on, 499-500
  exclusive agency, 497
  fee structures, 503
  licenses, 496-497
  listing contracts, 497
  multiple listing services, 497
  net listing, 497-498
  obligations to buyers, 501-502
  online home searching, 503
  open listings, 497
  option listings, 498
  racial or national origin discrimination, 589
  religious symbols, use of, 614-615
  subprime mortgages, 567
  unlicensed practice of law, 503-504
Building and housing codes
  generally, 658-659
  excavation regulation, 134-135
  leaseholds, 473
  lot and bulk regulations, 644-645
  remedies, 479-480
  sales contracts, 520
Burden of proof
  adverse possession, 166
  clear and convincing evidence, 166
  FHA claims, 591-592
  preponderance of evidence, 166
  retaliatory eviction, 482
Bureau of Indian Affairs (BIA), 776, 780, 790, 804
Burial grounds
  American Indian remains in unmarked, 805-806, 831-833
  mounds, 739
Business judgment rule, 378-379, 386
Business property
  concurrent ownership, 382-389
  conflicts, 385-386
  corporations, 382, 385-387
  duty of care, 386
  duty of loyalty, 386
  franchises, 387-388
  non-profit entities, 348, 382-383, 388
  ownership vs. management, 385-387
  partnerships, 383-385
    aggregate theory, 383
    common law, 383
    definition of, 383
    entity theory, 383
    fiduciary obligations, 384-385
    tenancy in partnership, 383
  shareholders, 385-387
  sole proprietorships, 348
  stakeholder laws, 386-387

C

Calabresi, Guido, 108-109
California
  Art Preservation Act, 853

doctrine for water rights, 131
inclusionary zoning ordinance for affordable housing, 761
labor relations, 85, 719-720
Unruh Civil Rights Act, 631
Caveat emptor, 429-430, 473, 474, 510, 514
CCRCs (Continuing care retirement communities), 382
Cemetery rights, 210
Centers for Disease Control and Prevention, 469
CERCLA (Comprehensive Environmental Response, Compensation, and Liability Act of 1980), 511, 664
Certificate of title, 554
Chain-of-title doctrine, 517, 540, 544
Changed conditions
covenants, 233, 291-294, 298, 323-324
licenses and easements, 223-224
present estates and future interests, 323-324
Charitable trusts, 278-279
Charities, 259, 284, 329-330
Chattels and trespass, 91-92
Checkerboard reservations, 781
Children
AFDC, 636
college education, 417
discrimination, 611-612
fair housing law, 625-626
family property, 392, 393, 417-418
inheritance, 420-424
stepparents and stepchildren, 418, 421
Choice of law, 291
Chused, Richard, 395
Civil Rights Act of 1866
contract, right to, 62
discriminatory practices, 576, 600-601
hotels, 584
prima facie case, 55
public accommodations, 33, 54-62
racial restrictions in deeds, 277
racial zoning, 578-579
remedies, 48
Section 1981 claims, 54-62
Section 1982 claims, 57, 62
Section 2000a, 60-61
slavery, 47-48
Thirteenth Amendment, 47-48, 61
Civil Rights Act of 1964
constitutionality, 721
employment discrimination, 608
exemptions, 49-50
full and equal enjoyment, 46, 49
gender identity discrimination, 608
injunctive relief, 48
locked stores, 50
membership organizations, 51-52
private clubs, 49-50, 52
public accommodations, 31-32, 46-54, 56, 63
race or national origin discrimination, 46
refusal to deal, 592
remedies, 48
sex discrimination, 608
sexual harassment, 604
sexual orientation discrimination, 608
Civil Rights Act of 1991
contract rights, 59
private discriminatory conduct, 55, 600
public accommodations, 55, 61
Civil Rights Cases (1883), 47, 49, 56
Civil unions, 409
Claeys, Eric, 17
Claim of right, 2, 143, 149, 151-152, 152-154, 214, 216
Claims against government entities
adverse possession, 168-169
prescriptive easements, 220
Clark, Elias, 279-280
Clean Water Act of 1977, 127, 663, 736
Clear and convincing evidence, 166
Climate change and public nuisance, 125-126
Cloud computing as bailment, 825
Clubs. *See* Private clubs
Coal Act of 1992, 751-752
Coercion, 589-590
Collective bargaining, 84-85
College dormitories, 440-441, 583-584, 628
College education, 417
Colorado doctrine for water rights, 131
Color of title, 143, 145, 151, 156, 162-163
Commerce Clause, 61, 844
Commercial leases. *See* Leaseholds
Commercial speech, 672-673
Common enemy rule, 127, 128
Common interest communities
affordable housing arrangements, 381-382
community land trusts, 381
condominiums
alienation restraints, 282-283, 374
architectural controls, 380
business judgment rule, 378-379
common ownership form, 348
concurrent ownership, 370-380
conversion, 371
covenants, 287, 289, 296-297
declaration, establishment by filing, 371, 375
developer duty to relinquish control, 372-373
fiduciary obligations, 379
first refusal rights, 374-375
free contract vs. protection from onerous provisions, 375
homeowners' associations, 371-372
as new estates, 372
partition, 361
pets, 379-380

Common interest communities (*continued*)
public policy, 375
rulemaking, reasonableness of, 378
statutes, 372
continuing care retirement communities, 382
cooperatives
alienation restraints, 282-283
common ownership form, 348
concurrent ownership, 380-381
discrimination or arbitrary treatment, 380-381
non-profit corporation ownership, 380
veto power over new members, 380
definition of, 372
homeowners' associations
condominium associations, 371-372
covenants, 227, 252-253
dues, obligation to pay, 256
in gross enforcement, 259
modification or termination of covenants, 296-297
private entity regulation, 232
privity, 252-253
implied right to create with assessment or taxing powers, 376-377
leasing, retroactive limits on, 377-378
limited equity cooperatives, 381
low-income housing cooperatives, 283
resale price limitations, 381-382
Common law
alienation of tribal land, 791
American Indian property, 791
competition, unreasonable restraints on, 286
deeds and title protection, 540
exclusion rights, limits on, 34-41
marriage, 411
negative easements, 186-187
nuisance, 98
partnerships, 383
public accommodations, 30-34
recording acts, 540
retail stores and duty to serve public, 32-34
takings, 752-757
trademarks, 844
trespass and public accommodations law, 34-41
consent, 34-38
estoppel, 38
necessity, 38-39
prescription, 41, 88
public policy, 40-41
social need, 40
unreasonable restraint on alienation, 340
water rights, 127-128, 753-754
Common nuisance. *See* Nuisance
Communications Decency Act of 1996, 588
Community land trusts, 381
Community property. *See* Family property
Company towns, 76-77, 78-79
Compelled government speech, 290-291
Compelled speech of business owner, 74
Competing arguments, 9
Competition
restraints on, 285-286
unfair competition, 847-849
Comprehensive Environmental Response, Compensation, and Liability Act of 1980 (*CERCLA*), 511, 664
Computer systems, trespass to, 91-92
Concurrent ownership, 347-389. *See also* Business property; Common interest communities; Leaseholds; Tenancies
ambiguities, interpretation of, 360
condominiums, 371-380
cooperatives, 380-381
equity of redemption, 353
four unities, 350-351
governmental ownership, 389
non-profit organizations, 388
overview, 348-349
ownership in common, 349-360
alienability, 349-350
death of joint tenant, 355-356
equity of redemption, 353
four unities, 350-351
homestead laws, 352-353
joint tenancy, 348, 350-358
leases, 354-356
mortgages, 353-354
murder of joint tenant, 356-357
secret conveyances, 352
self-conveyance, 351-352
severance, 351
survivorship rights, 350, 357
tenancy by the entirety, 348, 358-360
tenancy in common, 348-350
title theory, 353
undivided fractional interests, 349, 350
rights and obligations of co-tenants, 360-370. *See also* Co-tenants
Condemnation. *See* Regulatory takings
Conditional use, 646, 650-651
Condition subsequent, 307-309
Condominium and Cooperative Conversion Protection and Abuse Relief Act of 1980, 373
Condominiums. *See* Common interest communities
Consent, 34-37, 283-284, 491-492
Consequentialist approaches, 14-15
Conservation easements, 186
Consolidation, 181-182, 231, 303-304, 320
Constitution, U.S. *See also* Free speech rights; *specific amendments and clauses*
Commerce Clause, 61
land use regulation, 666-677
arbitrary regulations, protection from, 666-669
associational interests, 669

due process, 666-669
equal protection, 670-671
family integrity, 669
First Amendment, 671-677
free speech, 672-674
poverty, 671
privacy, 669
procedural due process, 666
racial classifications, 671
religious uses, 674-677
SLAPP suits, 671-672
substantive due process, 666-669
racial or national origin discrimination. *See* Racial or national origin discrimination
regulatory takings. *See* Regulatory takings
Constitutions, state. *See* State constitutions
Construction regulation, 4-5, 69, 658-659. *See also* Building and housing codes
Constructive eviction, 433, 469-473. *See also* Eviction
implied warranty of habitability, 471-472
landlord action or inaction, 470
quiet enjoyment, interference with, 469-470
remedies, 470
tenant's obligation to move out, 471-472
Constructive notice
covenants, 240-242
express easements, 190
grantors' covenants, 240-242
recording acts, 542
Constructive ouster, 367-368
Constructive possession, 24
Constructive trust, 204-207, 413-414
Consumer Financial Protection Bureau, 570
Consumer protection laws, 487-489, 495, 515
Contingent remainders
definition of, 333-335
destructibility of, 312-313
life estates, 311
rule against perpetuities, 333-335
Continuing care retirement communities (CCRCs), 382
Continuing Care Retirement Community Regulation and Financial Disclosure Act (New Jersey), 382
Continuous possession for adverse possession, 143, 148-149
Contract or conditional zoning, 647-650
Contracts Clause, 469
Contractual freedom, 11-12, 54-55, 57-59, 62
Contribution, 364-365
Contributory infringement, 839
Conversion
condominiums, 371-372
equitable conversion, 527
landlord's conversion of tenant's personal items, 459-460
rule, 172
Cooperatives
alienation restraints, 282-283
common ownership form, 348
concurrent ownership, 380-381
discrimination or arbitrary treatment, 380-381
non-profit corporation ownership, 380-381
veto power over new members, 381
Cooter, Robert, 159
Copyright, 836-841
acts, 836-837, 849
contributory infringement, 839
derivative works, 840-841
fair use, 837-839
Grokster, 840
Harry Potter Lexicon, 840-841
originality, 837
original works of authorship, 836
public domain, 836-837
reference works to literature, 840-841
sharing of copyrighted materials, 840
StreamCast, 840
transformative use, 837, 838-839
Copyright Acts, 836-837, 849
Core tensions, 6-8
access right vs. exclusion right, 6-8
acquisition power vs. loss immunity, 8
disaggregation limits vs. transfer power, 7-8
exclusion right vs. access right, 6-7
loss immunity vs. power to acquire, 8
security from harm vs. use privilege, 7
transfer power vs. disaggregation limits, 7-8
use privilege vs. security from harm, 7
Corporations. *See* Business property
Correlative rights test, 132
Co-tenants. *See also* Leaseholds; Tenancies
adverse possession, 165-166
in common, 165-166. *See also* Tenancies
alienation, 349-350
definition of, 349
inheritance, 349-350
ownership in common, 348-350
joint tenants. *See* Joint tenancy
ouster, 165-166, 366-368, 370
rights and obligations, 360-370
adverse possession, 370
constructive ouster, 367-368
contribution, 364-365
divorce, 368
emotional ouster, 368
forced division or sale, 361
heirs' property, 362-363
joint management, 363
leasing, 369-370
maintenance, 363-365
major improvements, 364
ouster, 165-166, 366-368, 370

Co-tenants (*continued*)
partition, 360-363, 369-370
physical impracticability, 367-368
rent, no duty to pay, 366
rental benefits and obligations, 365-368
repairs, 363-365
statute of limitations, 370
tenant out of possession, 364-365
Covenants, 225-298
abandonment, 296-297
acquiescence, 296
affirmative
economic frustration, 295-296
landowners' obligations to neighbors, 227-228
modification or termination, 294
to pay money, 294
right of way, 145
running with land, 252
touch and concern, 255-256
affirmative covenants, 294
alienability, 230, 280-285
ambiguity, 270-276
generally, 233
architectural review committees, 275
group homes, 271-274
home day care, 276
intent vs. free use, 270-271
privity requirement, 244
public policy, 274
reasonableness review, 275
residential vs. commercial use, 271-272
structure vs. occupants, 272
changed conditions, 233, 291-294, 298, 323-324
charities, 259
choice of law, 291
community associations, 227
competition, unreasonable restraints on, 285-286
compulsory terms, 232-233
condominium associations, 296
consolidation, 231
creation of, 228
formality vs. informality, 232-233
damages, 266-270
declarations of restrictions, 228
deeds, 228
disaggregation, 230-231
easements vs., 228
enforcement, equitable limitations on, 296
enforcement in gross, 258-260
estoppel, 234, 237-238, 297
facilitative and protective roles of, 230
fringe lots, 292
gated communities, 231-232
government entities, 259
grantee covenants on neighboring property, 241, 242
grantor covenants, constructive notice of, 241-242
in gross, 294
historical origins, 228-229
homeowners' associations. *See* Common interest communities
implied reciprocal negative servitudes, 261-266
early vs. later buyers, 261
general plan, 261-264
grantor's neighboring land, 265-266
privity of estate issues, 261-262
subdivisions, 261
third-party beneficiary doctrine, 262
injunctions, 266-270
interpretation of, 233, 270-276
laches, 296
land use, contractual regulation of, 226
marketable title acts, 297
merger, 296
modification or termination, 291-298
negative, 227-228, 252
notice, 239-242
generally, 234
actual notice, 240
constructive notice, 240
inquiry notice, 240-241
overview, 226-233
parties' conduct, 296-297
to pay money, 256
prescription, 297
privity of estate. *See* Privity
public policy limitations, 277-291
generally, 293
alienation, unreasonable restraints on, 280-285
ambiguity, 274
charitable trusts, 278-279
compelled government speech, 290-291
competition, unreasonable restraints on, 285-286
condominium rules, 287-289
cy pres doctrine, 279
discrimination, 233, 278-279
equal protection, 277
freedom of contract, 287
free speech, 289-291
modification or termination, 293
political signs, 289-290
public policy, 279-280, 286-291
racial restrictions, 277-280
reasonableness review, 286-289
unconscionability, 288-289
use restrictions, 288
racial discrimination, 277-280
recreational facilities, 256-257
relative hardship, 269-270, 294-296
release, 296
remedies, 266-270
requirements, formal, 234-253
actual notice, 240

constructive notice, 240-242
equitable servitudes, 234
estoppel, 234, 237-238
inquiry notice, 240-241
intent to run, 234, 242-244
maps, 237, 239
notice, 234, 239-242
oral representations, 237-238
privity of estate, 234, 235, 244-253
real covenants, 234
running with land, 234, 239
sales literature, 237-238
touch and concern, 234, 235-236
writing, 234, 237-238
requirements, substantive, 253-260
generally, 236
developer's attempted enforcement, 259-260, 276
enforcement in gross, 258-260
reasonableness, 254
touch and concern, 253-258
residential associations, 227, 231-232
restrictive and negative easements, 186-187
running with land, 226-227, 232, 234
Shelley doctrine, 277-278
statute of frauds, 236
statutory regulation, 297-298
tenant's security deposit, 257-258
termination, 233, 291-298
third-party beneficiaries, 250-251, 262
unclean hands, 296
undue hardship, 294-296
unrestricted lots and notice issues, 264-265
waiver, 296
Coverture, 394
COVID-19 pandemic
business restrictions as takings, rejection of challenges, 742
eviction moratoria, 468-469
rent obligations, 451-453
Creditors' rights, 359-360, 402-403
Criminal records, rental to persons with, 621
Criminal trespass, 29, 38-39. *See also* Trespass and public accommodations law
Critical habitats, 663-664
Crops, 29, 90, 147, 396, 725, 827
Cultural property, 855-856
Cunningham, Roger, 154
Curtesy, 394-395
Custom, doctrine of, 88, 89, 91, 754-755
Cy pres doctrine, 279, 321-322, 336-337

D

Damages
American Indian property, 799
covenants, 266-270
habitable premises, right to, 478-479
leaseholds, 461-466
nuisance, 108, 110-111
private nuisance, 118-119
real estate transactions, 521-524, 524-525
trespass and public accommodations law, 28
Data property and cloud computing as bailment, 825
Dawes Act of 1887, 779-780
Day care, 276
Death
gifts *causa mortis*, 823
joint tenant, 355-356
marital property, 399
periodic tenancies, termination of, 447
publicity rights after, 851-852
sales contracts, 527-528
spouse and community property, 403
takings, 743-745
tenancies at will, 448
unmarried couples and succession on death, 414-415
Declarations, 371, 375, 377-378
Dedication
adverse possession, 170
elements, 170
public trust doctrine, 87-88
Deeds and title protection, 528-555
acceptance, 531
ambiguity, 200-201, 208-209
certificate of title, 554
conditional gifts, 531-533
covenants, creation of, 228, 537
curative acts, 537
delivery, 530-533
due process, 554
forgery, 533-534
fraud, 534
gifts, 530-531
joint bank boxes, 533
marketable title acts, 224, 537-538
racial restrictions in deeds, 277
recording acts, 538-553. *See also* Recording acts
requirements, formal, 528-534
accretion, 530
avulsion, 530
land description, 529
metes and bounds, 529-530
mistakes, 530
plats or subdivision maps, 529
reformation, 530
river borders, 530
surveys, 529
requirements, substantive, 533-534
revocable trusts, 533
root of title, 537
statute of limitations, 538
title covenants, 534-536

Deeds and title protection (*continued*)
breach, 535
encumbrances, 535
further assurances, 535
general warranty deeds, 535
merger doctrine, 534-535
quiet enjoyment, 535
quitclaim deeds, 534, 536
remedies, 535, 536
right to convey, 535
seisin, 535
special warranty, 534, 536
terminology, 536
warranty, 534, 536
title insurance, 553-554
title registration, 554-555
title searches, 539-540
Torrens system, 554
wild deeds, 545-546
writing, 528-530
Defamation, 36, 671
Defeasible fees, 306-314
alienability, 310
condition subsequent, 307-309
executory interest, 306, 309-310
executory limitation, 309-310
fee simple determinable, 307
fee simple subject to condition subsequent, 304-305, 306, 307-309
fee simple subject to executory limitation, 305, 306, 309-310
first refusal rights, 310
laches, 308
perpetuities, rule against, 310
preemptive rights, 310
purchase options, 310
reverter, 306, 307
right of entry, 306-309
right of first refusal, 310
statute of limitations, 308-309
third-party interests, 309
transferability, 309
waiver, 308
Defective title, 156, 162-163
Defense of Marriage Act of 1996 (DOMA), 408-409
Definitions
actual possession, 143-144
appurtenant easements, 188
common interest communities, 372
contingent remainders, 333-335
disability, 62-63
dwellings, 583-584
easements in gross, 188
endless will contest, 336
executory interests, 332-333
fertile octogenarians, 335-336
future interest, creation of, 331
grantor interests, 332
handicap, 609
immunities, 6
liberties, 5
licenses, 27
lives in being, 332
marketable title, 515-516
nuisance, 102, 121-122
partnerships, 383
perpetuities period, 332
possession, 24, 434
powers, 5
privileges, 5
property, 2-6
public accommodations, 30-32, 46-47, 63
public nuisance, 121-122
public use, 682
rental agreement, 441
rights, 5
takings, 681
tenancy in common, 349
trespass, 27
unborn widow, 335
vesting, 331-332
Delivery
deeds and title protection, 530-533
gifts, 821-822
of possession, 431, 466-467, 824
Demand and refusal rule, 173-174
Demand rule, 172
Derivative works, 840-841
Destruction of evidence, 712
Destruction of property, 652, 661, 702-703, 709-710, 740, 854-855
Developers, 259-260, 276, 372-373
Diffuse surface water, 99, 126-130
Digital property, 856-857
Disability discrimination
competing needs of disabled tenants, 611
definition, 62-63
disparate impact, 622-625
exclusion, legitimate criteria for, 610
fair housing law, 608-611
"first in time, first in right," 611
modifications and accommodations, 609-610
two tenants with disabilities and competing needs, 611
Disaggregation
consolidation vs., 181-182, 303-304, 320
covenants, 230
regulatory rules, 328
transfer power vs., 7-8
Discovery doctrine for land ownership, 784
Discovery rule for personal property, 172-173

Discrimination. *See also Civil Rights Acts*; Fair housing law
antiwelfare exclusions, 618
associational interests, 52-33
Boy Scouts of America, 50-53
cooperatives, 380-381
covenants, 233, 278-279
disability
competing needs of disabled tenants, 611
definition, 62-63
disparate impact, 622-625
exclusion, legitimate criteria for, 610
fair housing law, 608-610
"first in time, first in right," 611
modifications and accommodations, 609-610
two tenants with disabilities and competing needs, 611
economic, 577, 630-636
exclusionary zoning, 631-634
homelessness, 634-635
loitering laws, 634-635
remedies, 632-633
right to housing, 635-636
tenant income requirements, 630-631
wealth-based, 630-631
efficiency justifications, 577-578
family status, 611-614
children, 611-612
housing for older persons, 611-612
marital status, 612-614
reasonable occupancy limits, 612
gender identity, 607-608, 621
intentional, 576-577
landlord's duty to end discriminatory housing harassment by third party, 590-591
membership organizations, 50-53
private clubs, 49-50, 52-53, 60-62, 585-586
private discriminatory conduct, 600
race or national origin. *See* Racial or national origin discrimination
religion, 46, 52, 55, 614-615
remedies for, 581-582
sex. *See* Sex discrimination
sexual orientation. *See also* Same-sex marriage
generally, 621
associational and religious interests, 52-53
fair housing law, 607-608, 621
harassment, 605-606
membership organizations, 52-53
religious liberty, 73-77
as sex discrimination, 74-75
state law, 607
"source of income," 577, 630
state laws, 71-72
trusts, 322-323
zoning, 631-634
Discriminatory trusts, 278-279, 322-323
Disparaging names, 53-54, 846-847
Disparate impact claims
ADA, 622
fair housing law, 615-630
antiwelfare exclusions, 618
children, families with, 625-626
co-signer cases, 623-624
criminal records, rental to persons with, 621
defendant's justification, 616-617
disability, 622-625
disproportionate effect, 615-616
familial status, 625-627
FHA, 576-577, 591, 615-616, 621
gender identity, 607-608, 621
group homes, 622-623, 624-625, 626-627
HUD, 615-616, 619-620
language restrictions, 629-630
national origin, 629-630
nontraditional families, 626-627
prima facie case, 617
private defendants, 617
race, 615-620
reasonable accommodation, 622
religion, 628
sex, 620-621
sexual orientation, 607-608, 621
voucher preferences for local residents, 618-619
welfare recipients, 625
zoning, 617
Distributive justice, 20
Divorce
community property, 403
co-tenants, 368
encouragement of, 345
inheritance, 423-424
marital property, 398-399, 403
Dodd-Frank Wall Street Reform and Consumer Protection Act, 570
DOMA (Defense of Marriage Act of 1996), 408-409
Domestic dependent nations, 802-803
Domestic partnerships, 409
Domestic violence, eviction of victims, 472-473
Dominant estates, 179, 180
Dormitories, 440-441, 583-584, 628
Dower and curtesy, 394-395
Drones, 44
Dropbox, 825
Drug dealers, 117-118, 123-124
Dual agents, 502
Due diligence, 173
Due process
deeds and title protection, 554
eviction moratoria, 469
Fourteenth Amendment, 666, 686
landlord's remedies, 461

Due process (*continued*)
land use regulation, 666-669
procedural
land use regulation, 666
takings, 752
same-sex marriage, 407
substantive
arbitrary or capricious government action, 666-669
associational interests, 669
equal protection, relation to, 668
family integrity, 669
land use regulation, 666-669
privacy, 669
sex offenders, 669
"shock the conscience" test, 668-669
standard of review, 668-669
takings, 668, 702, 752
Duties
condominium developer duty to relinquish control, 372-373
disclosure duty and sales contracts, 511-512
mutual support and marital property, 397-398
retail stores and common law duty to serve public, 32-34
sales contracts and disclosure duty, 511-512
tenant's obligations
operate, duty to, 453-455
rent, duty to pay, 431, 449-453, 454-455
rent, no duty to pay, 366
waste, duty not to commit, 431
Duty of care, 386
Duty of loyalty, 386
Dwellings, 583-584, 610-611. *See also* Building and housing codes
Dynasty trusts, 339-340

E

Easements. *See* Licenses and easements
Eastern land claims of Indian tribes, 795-801
Economic discrimination
fair housing law, 630-636
exclusionary zoning, 631-634
homelessness, 634-635
loitering laws, 634-635
remedies, 632-633
right to housing, 635-636
tenant income requirements, 630-631
wealth-based, 630-631
FHA, 634
homelessness, 634-635
remedies, 632-633
Efficiency
adverse possession, 159-160
fair housing law, 577-578
justificatory norms, 18
system, property as, 3-4
takings, 716-717
Ejectment, 29, 141-142, 798-799
Electric power lines, 117
Eleventh Amendment, 796
Ellickson, Robert, 633
Email as trespass, 91-92
Embryos, human, 829-831
Eminent domain, 679-766. *See also* Regulatory takings
"public use" requirement, 682-689
Emotional ouster, 368
Employment contracts, 439-440
Encroaching structures, 215, 519
Encroaching vegetation and trees, 42-43
Encumbrances
adverse possession, effects on, 166-167
sales contracts, 518-520
tenancies by the entirety, 407
title covenants, 535
Endangered species laws, 663-664, 732
Endless will contest, 336
Entitlements, 3-4, 113-116
Entity theory, 383
Environmental protection, 662-665
Epstein, Richard, 18
Equal protection
covenants, 277
fair housing law, 578, 580, 581
Fourteenth Amendment, 47, 578, 608
land use regulation, 670-671
racial or national origin discrimination, 578, 581
same-sex marriage, 407-408
substantive due process, relation to, 668
Equitable distribution, 398-399, 406-407, 416
Equitable mortgages, 566-567
Equitable servitudes. *See* Servitudes
Equity of redemption, 353
Estates. *See* Present estates and future interests
Estoppel
adverse possession, 151, 171
ambiguity, 200-201, 208-209
common law, 38
covenants, 234, 237-238, 297
easements by estoppel, 200-204, 205
express easements, 185
implied easements, 200-204
sales contracts, 508
trespass and public accommodations, 38
Euclidean zoning, 645, 649
Eviction. *See also* Leaseholds
actual, 433, 467-468, 469
anti-eviction laws, 468-469, 723-724
constructive eviction, 433, 469-473. *See also* Constructive eviction
domestic violence victims, 472-473
implied warranty of habitability, 471-472

landlord's remedies, 431, 432, 450, 470
leaseholds, 431, 432, 467-468
moratoria during pandemic, 469
partial actual eviction, 468
post-foreclosure protection, 728
protections against, 468-469, 727, 728
public-health-related eviction moratoria, 727
quiet enjoyment, interference with, 469-470
remedies, 470
retaliatory eviction, 481-484. *See also* Retaliatory eviction
takings, 711, 723-724, 727-728
tenancies at sufferance, 449
tenant's obligation to move out, 471-472
Exactions, 757-761
building permit conditions, 757, 760
essential nexus requirement, 757-758
generalized fees, 760
inclusionary zoning, 760-761
individualized administrative determinations, 760
monetary exactions, 759
rough proportionality, 759, 760-761
Excavation regulation, 134-135
Exclusion rights, 27-41. *See also* Trespass and public accommodations law
access rights vs., 6-7
actual possession, 24
common law limits on, 34-41
consent, 34-35
estoppel, 38
necessity, 38-39
prescription, 41, 88
public policy, 40-41
social need, 40
constructive possession, 24
exceptions, 24, 26
externalities, 26
human values, 25
investigative journalism, 35-37, 40-41
possession, 24, 25
private property, 27-29
public accommodations, 30-34
quiet enjoyment, 25
record title holder, 24
shared use or possession, 29-30
Exclusive possession, 143, 147-148
Executive order title, 778, 788-790
Executory interests
defeasible fees, 306, 309-310
definitions, 332-333
fee simple subject to executory limitation, 306
rule against perpetuities, 332-333
Expectations as justificatory norms, 20
Express easements, 184-199. *See also* Licenses and easements
generally, 180
actual notice, 190
air, 185
ancient lights doctrine, 186, 221
apportionment, 198-199
appurtenant, 180, 188, 195, 255
commercial utility, 189-190
conservation easements, 186
constructive notice, 190
creation of, 184-185
divisibility, 194
economic significance, 199
estoppel, 185
exceptions, 184
extension of appurtenant, 191, 195
grantor's intent, 191
in gross, 180, 188-190, 197-199, 255
historic preservation easements, 186
implied vs., 199
inquiry notice, 190
interpretation, 188-190
language, 189
light, 185
limitations, substantive, 185-187
location of appurtenant easements, 191-197
negative easements, 185-187
notice
actual notice, 190
constructive notice, 190
inquiry notice, 190
overburdening of, 193-194
personal character, 190
preference for easements in gross, 189
prescription, 194
presumption in favor of appurtenant easements, 188-189
public policy, 196-197
relocation, 195-197
requirements, formal, 184-185
Restatement (Third) of Property (Servitudes), 187
restrictive covenants, 186-187
rights of way, 192-193
running with land, 187-190
scope, 191-199
solar easements, 186
statute of frauds, 184
third parties, 184-185
transferability, 198
use, kind, quantity, or intensity of, 191-192
width, 194-195
writing, 184, 190
Externalities, 26
Extinguishment and American Indian property, 792-793

F

Fabric patterns, 849
Fair Credit Reporting Act of 1970, 489

Fair Housing Act of 1968 (*FHA*), 582-604
  advertisements, racially preferential, 53, 587-588, 598
  aggrieved persons, 596-597
  amendment of, 62
  associational claims, 597
  bases of discrimination, 582-583
  blockbusting, 588
  brokers, 589
  burden of proof, 591-592
  client questions, 589
  coercion, 589-590
  college dormitories, 583-584
  constitutionality, 721
  convicted drug dealers, 586
  discrimination claims, basis for, 57, 576
  disparate impact claims, 576-577, 591, 615-616
  dwellings, 583-584
  economic discrimination, 634
  exclusion, legitimate criteria for, 610
  exemptions, 584-586, 601
  families with children, 611-612, 625-626
  federal jurisdiction, 598-599
  gender-identity discrimination, 607-608, 621
  handicap discrimination, 609
  homeless shelters, 584
  housing for older persons, 586, 611-612
  integration, promotion of, 595
  intentional discrimination, 576-577
  intimidation, 589-590
  marketing techniques, affirmative, 595-596
  misrepresentation, 588
  mixed motives, 596
  models' race, 598
  mortgages, 589
  new dwellings, 610-611
  nursing homes, 583-584
  pretext, 593-594
  prima facie case, 592-594
  private clubs, 585-586
  prohibited conduct, 587-591
  racial discrimination, 468, 582-601
  racial restrictions, 277, 579, 601, 671
  reasonable accommodation, 622
  reasonable occupancy limits, 612
  rebuttal, 592-593
  refusal to deal, 592
  religious organizations, 585
  remedies, 598-600
  restrictive covenants and disabilities discrimination, 274
  sexual-orientation discrimination, 607-608, 621
  shelters for battered women, 620, 625-626
  single-family homes sold without broker, 585
  standards of proof, 591-596
  standing, 596-598
  tenant harassment of another tenant, 590-591
  testers, 597
Fair Housing Act of 1985 (New Jersey), 633
Fair Housing Amendments Act of 1988 (*FHAA*), 576, 582-583, 586, 598
Fair housing law, 575-636. *See also Fair Housing Act of 1968*
  affirmatively further fair housing (AFFH) regulations, 619-620
  disability discrimination, 608-611
  discriminatory practices, 576
  disparate impact claims, 615-630. *See also* Disparate impact claims
  economic discrimination, 630-636. *See also* Economic discrimination
  efficiency justifications, 577-578
  family status discrimination, 611-614
  gender-identity discrimination, 607-608, 621
  justice, 578
  "no welfare" policy, 620
  older persons, 586, 611-612
  overview, 576-578
  policies underlying, 577
  racial or national origin discrimination, 578-601. *See also* Racial or national origin discrimination
  religious discrimination, 614-615
  remedies for discrimination, 581-582
  sex discrimination, 602-607
  sexual orientation discrimination, 607-608, 621
Fair market value, 115, 689
Fair rental value, 451
Fair use and parody, 837-839
Family property, 391-424
  antenuptial agreements, 393, 397, 399-401
  children and parents, 392, 393, 417-418
  civil unions, 409
  college education, 417
  common law marriage, 411
  community property, 401-407
    classification of, 403-404
    creditors' reach, 402-403
    death of spouse, 403
    divorce, 403
    marital debts, 402-403
    marital property, 392-393, 397, 401-407
    migratory couple, 405-407
    premarital debts, 402-403
    quasi-community property, 405-406
    separate vs., 392-393, 397-407
    tracing and commingling, 404
    transmuting community property into separate property and vice versa, 404
  coverture, 394
  divorce. *See* Divorce
  domestic partnerships, 409
  dower and curtesy, 394-395

elective share, 399
equitable distribution, 398-399, 406-407
equity courts, 394-395
feme covert, 394
historical background, 394-396
inception of title approach, 404
inheritance, 418-424. *See also* Inheritance
intestacy, 399
intestate succession, 393, 420-424
life estates in, 394
maintenance, 399
marital property. *See* Marital property
mutual support, duty of, 397-398
overview, 392-393
palimony, 411-412
parents and children, 417-418
generally, 392, 393
stepchildren, 421
surviving spouse, no surviving children or parents, 420
surviving spouse and children, 420-424
surviving spouse and parents, no surviving children, 420
premarital agreements, 393, 397, 399-401
pro rata apportionment approach, 404
remarriage, 417-418
same-sex marriage, 407-411, 415, 416
second families, 417-418
separate property, 392-393, 397-401, 404, 407
separate vs. community, 392-393, 397-407
spouses, 392
statutory share, 399
stepparents and stepchildren, 418
succession on death, 414-415
survivorship rights, 407
tenancy by the entirety, 358-360, 395, 407
testamentary transfers, 418-419
trusts, 392
unmarried couples, 392, 411-416
wills and will substitutes, 392, 393, 418-420
Family status discrimination, 611-614
children, 611-612
housing for older persons, 611-612
marital status, 612-614
reasonable occupancy limits, 612
Farnsworth, Ward, 269
Federal Aviation Agency (FAA), 44
Federal Debt Collections Practices Act of 1977, 489
Federal lands and adverse possession, 169
Federal patents, 771
Federal Water Pollution Control Act of 1972, 663
Fee simple, 304, 305-306
absolute, 305-306
conditional, 325-326
determinable, 304, 306-307
life estates vs., 329
subject to condition subsequent, 304-305, 306, 307-309
subject to executory limitation, 305, 306
Fee simple determinable, 304, 306-307
Fee simple subject to condition subsequent, 304-305, 306, 307-309
Fee simple subject to executory limitation, 305, 306
Fee tail, abolition of, 325-327
Feme covert, 394
Fences
adverse possession, 144
animals, 46
nuisance, 136
spite, 136
Fertile octogenarians, 335-336
Feudalism, 302
FHA. See Fair Housing Act of 1968
FHAA. See Fair Housing Amendments Act of 1988
Fiduciary obligations
condominiums, 379
licenses and easements, 206-207
partnerships, 384-385
trusts, 315
Fifth Amendment
American Indian property, 781, 788-790
takings, 25, 682, 694, 703, 714, 763. *See also* Regulatory takings
Financing of real estate transactions, 555-573
equitable mortgages, 566-567
foreclosure, 496
installment land contracts, 564-566
liens, 496
mortgages, 496, 555-564
subprime mortgages, 567-573
Finders
goods in unmarked graves, 820
governmental papers, 821
landowners vs., 817-820
lost or abandoned property, 816-817
mislaid property, 819
personal property, 816-821
personal property embedded in soil, 818-819
public property, 819
relativity of title, 817
salvage, 820-821
shipwrecks, 820-821
state statutes, 819-820
third parties vs., 817
treasure trove, 819
trespassers as, 817
First Amendment. *See also* Free speech rights
handbills, 76, 77, 78, 82, 84
land use regulation, 671-677
offensive names, 53-54, 846-847
public accommodations laws, 53-54, 76
public nuisance, 123

First Amendment (*continued*)
religious freedom, 73-74, 613-614
roommates, 602-603
shopping centers, 77-80, 721
"First in time, first in right," 611
First refusal rights
alienation, 284-285
condominiums, 374-375
defeasible fees, 310
rule against perpetuities, 340
Fishing rights
American Indian property, 40, 90-91, 806-807
public trust doctrine, 85, 86-87, 90-91
Fixtures and accessions, 826-827
Floating zones, 650-651
Flooding, 99, 126-130
Florida, *Bert J. Harris, Jr. Private Property Rights Protection Act of 1995*, 763
Forced division, 360-361
Forced entry and detainer, 458-459
Forced purchases, 42, 112-113, 169
Forced sales, 42, 112-113, 169, 360-361, 362-363
Forced share statutes, 343
Force majeure clauses, 451-452
Foreclosure
eviction protection after, 728
home equity surplus after tax foreclosure, 743, 747-748
wrongful, 573
Forfeiture
alienation, 280-282
automatic, 307, 341
discriminatory forfeitures and racial restrictions, 341-342
installment land contracts, 564
leaseholds, 456-457
presumption against, 315-320
restraints, 329
takings, 710-711
Forgery, 533-534, 552
Formal sources of rights, 10-11, 163
Fontainebleau doctrine, 136-137
Fourteenth Amendment
discriminatory state action abolished by, 56-57, 77
due process, 666, 686
equal protection, 47, 578, 608
free speech, 76-77
racial restrictions, 578
religious liberty, 614
same-sex marriage, 407
state action, 77
takings, 25, 83, 694, 714, 763
Four unities, 350-351
Franchises
business property, 387-388
concurrent ownership, 387-388
franchisee protections, 387
termination, good cause for, 388
trademarks, 387
uniformity, promotion of, 387
Fraud
deeds and title protection, 533-534
good faith purchasers, 825-826
nondisclosure and sales contracts, 510-511
real estate transactions, 552-553
recording acts, 552
sales contracts, 509-514
Frauds, statute of, 506-509. *See also* Statute of frauds
Freedom of association and public nuisance, 123
Freedom to Display the American Flag Act of 2006, 289
Free speech rights
access to private property, 75-85
company towns, 76-77, 78
labor laws, 84-85
shopping centers, 77-80, 721-723
state constitutions, 80-83, 83-84
U.S. Constitution, 75-80
compelled government speech, 290-291
compelled speech of business owner, 74
covenants, 289-290
Fourteenth Amendment, 75
handbills, 76, 77, 78, 82, 84
intellectual property, 850, 852-853
labor, 84-85
land use regulation, 671-677
commercial speech, 672-673
sex-oriented business, 674
signs, 672-674
leaflets, 76-82
political messages on t-shirts, 83-84
public accommodations laws, 52-53, 73-74
publicity rights, 850, 852-853
public nuisance, 123
signs and billboards, 434-435, 436-437, 672-674
state action doctrine, 76-77
state constitutions, 80-83, 83-84
trespass and access to private property, 75-85
labor laws, 84-85
state constitutions, 80-83, 83-84
U.S. Constitution, 75-80
universities, access to, 81-82
Fringe lots, 292
Fuld, Stanley H., 513-514
Full and equal enjoyment, 46, 49
Fungible property vs. personal property, 158-159
Future interests. *See* Present estates and future interests

G

Gangs, 124-125
Gas stations, 47
Gas tank leaks, 117

Gated communities, 231-232
Gender identity
  disparate impact claims, 621
  housing discrimination, 607-608, 621
  public bathrooms, 75
General Allotment Act of 1887, 779-780, 803
General plans, 261-264
General warranty deeds, 535
Generative artificial intelligence, 844
Gifts, 821-824
  acceptance, 821
  causa mortis, 823
  class gifts, 312
  conditional, 531-533, 823
  deed of, 822
  delivery, 821-822
  elements, 821-822
  engagement presents, 823-824
  inter vivos, 821
  joint bank accounts, 822
  joint safety boxes, 822
  personal property, 821-824
  testamentary transfers, 821
  third parties, 823
  transfer intent, 821, 822
Gilman, Charlotte Perkins, 19
Good faith
  adverse possession, 154-155
  compensability, presumption of, 786-788
  fraud, 826
  possession, 143, 151, 154-155, 161
  purchasers, 825-826
  seller's good faith and sales contracts, 522-524
  stolen goods, 825-826
  tenant's duty to operate, 453-455
  UCC, 826
Goods in unmarked graves, 820
Goodwill, 691, 693
Government entities
  claims against
    adverse possession, 168-169
    prescriptive easements, 220
  concurrent ownership, 389
  covenants, 259
  public lands law, 389
Government speech, 290-291
Government Survey System, 529
Grantors and grantees
  ambiguous conveyances, interpretation of grantor's intent, 315, 317
  covenants, constructive notice of, 240-242
  covenants and grantor's intent, 265-266
  express easements and grantor's intent, 191
  fees on future sales, 284
  grantor-grantee index systems, 539-540
  grantor interests, definition of, 332
  implied easements and grantor's intent, 202, 210-211
  neighboring land, 265-266
  rule against perpetuities, 332
Groundwater, 99, 131-132, 135-136
Group homes, 271-274, 622-623, 624-625
Growth management, 661-662

H

Habitability, implied warranty of, 473-481
  commercial warranty, 480-481
  constructive eviction, 471-472
  leaseholds, 473-481
  new homes, 514-515
Habitable premises. *See* Leaseholds
Handbills, 79, 82, 84
Handicap, 609
Harassment, 590-591, 603-607
Hard cases, 9-10
Hardship, 42, 269-270, 294-296, 655-656
Harry Potter Lexicon, 840-841
Hawaii
  native rights, 90-91
  public trust doctrine, 89
  takings, 683-684
Hazardous waste laws, 664-665
HEAR Act (Holocaust Expropriated Art Recovery Act), 174-175
Hearsay, 204
Hegel, Georg Wilhelm Friedrich, 19
Height-limit zoning, 121
Heirs' property, 362-363
Helmholz, Richard, 154
Historic landmarks
  ADA accommodations, 70
  churches as, 676-677
  land use regulation, 662
  state laws, 662
Historic preservation easements, 186
Historic preservation laws, 70-71, 662, 703-706
Hohfeld, Wesley, 5, 140
Holocaust Expropriated Art Recovery Act (HEAR Act), 174-175
HomeAway, 442
Home day care, 276
Home equity after tax foreclosure, right to surplus, 743, 747-748
Homeless Bill of Rights (Rhode Island), 634
Homelessness
  anti-public-camping ordinances, 635
  church housing, 677
  criminalization of status of being homeless, 635
  economic discrimination, 634-636
  regulation of public acts of, 634-635
  shelters, 584

Homeowners' associations
  condominium associations, 371-372
  covenants, 227, 252-253
  dues, obligation to pay, 256
  in gross enforcement, 259
  modification or termination of covenants, 296-297
  private entity regulation, 232
  privity, 252-253
Home Ownership and Equity Protection Act of 1994, 563
Home searching online, 503
Homestead laws, 343, 352-353
Hoopa-Yurok Settlement Act of 1988, 789
Hotels, 46-48, 441-442, 584
Housing and Urban Development Department (HUD), 514, 590, 599, 601, 603, 615-616, 619-620
Housing codes. *See* Building and housing codes
Human bodies
  American Indian remains in unmarked burial grounds, 805-806, 831-833
  embryos, 829-831
  organ transplants, 827-828
  personal property, 827-833
  remains in museums, 832-833
  sperm, 829
Human embryos, 829-831
Human flourishing as justificatory norm, 19
Human sperm, 829
Hunting rights, 40, 90-91, 806-807

I

Ideological signs, 673
IIM (Individual Indian Money) trust, 804-805
Implied easements, 199-213. *See also* Licenses and easements
  generally, 180
  ambiguous deed references, 200-201, 208-209
  breach of trust, 203, 204-205
  cemetery rights, 210
  constructive trust, 199, 204-207
  default rule, 210-211
  by estoppel, 200-204
  express vs., 199
  by grant, 208
  grantee's reliance, 202-203
  grantor's intent, 202, 210-211
  irrevocable licenses, 202
  landlocked parcels, 210-213
  mandatory rule, 210, 211-212
  maps, 208-209
  necessity, 200, 210-213
  oral, 201
  prior use, 200, 207-210
  public policy, 211-212
  remedies, statutory, 212-213
  by reservation, 208
  types, 207-208
Implied reciprocal negative servitudes, 261-266
  early vs. later buyers, 261
  general plan, 261-264
  grantor's neighboring land, 265-266
  privity of estate issues, 261-262
  subdivisions, 261
  third-party beneficiary doctrine, 262
Implied warranty of habitability, 473-481
  commercial warranty, 480-481
  constructive eviction, 471-472
  leaseholds, 473-481
  new homes, 514-515
Impossibility doctrine, 452
Impracticality doctrine, 452
Improving trespasser, 169
Inception of title approach to marital property, 404
Inclusionary zoning, 760-761
Indian Affairs Bureau (BIA), 776, 780, 804
Indiana, *Religious Freedom Restoration Act*, 73
Indian Claims Commission, 794-795
Indian Claims Commission Act of 1946, 794-795, 798
Indian Commerce Clause, 796
Indian Land Consolidation Act of 1983, 744-745
Indian Reorganization Act of 1934, 780
Indian Tucker Act of 1887, 803
Individual entitlement vs. property as system, 3-4
Individual Indian Money Trust (IIM), 804-805
Industrial Site Recovery Act (New Jersey), 665
Informal sources of rights, 10, 163
Infringement, 839-839
In gross easements. *See* Licenses and easements
Inheritance. *See also* Intestate succession; Trusts; Wills and will substitutes
  divorce, 423-424
  family property, 418-424
  order of inheritance, 423-424
  per capita division, 422-423
  per stirpes division, 422-423
  stepchildren, 421
  surviving spouse, no surviving children or parents, 420
  surviving spouse and children, 420-424
  surviving spouse and parents, no surviving children, 420
  tenancy in common, 349-350
  testamentary transfers, 418-419
Injunctive relief
  Civil Rights Act of 1964, 48
  covenants, 266-270
  habitable premises, right to, 479
  landlord's obligations and tenant's remedies, 431-432
  nuisance, 109, 111-112
  purchased injunctions, 112
  takings, 762, 765-766
  trespass and public accommodations law, 28, 48

Innkeeper liability, 825
Inquiry notice
  covenants, 240-241
  express easements, 190
  possession as, 551
  recording acts, 542, 550-551
Installment land contracts
  financing, 564-566
  recording acts, 544
Insurance, 553-554
Integrated housing, promotion of, 595
Intellectual property, 835-857
  artists' moral rights, 853-855
    applied art, 853-854
    integrity of work, 853
    made for hire works, 853
    site-specific works, 854
    temporary works, 854-855
    visual art works, 853-854
  constitutional source, 836
  contributory infringement, 839
  copyright, 836-841
    acts, 836-837, 849
    contributory infringement, 839
    derivative works, 840-841
    fair use, 837-839
    Grokster, 840
    Harry Potter Lexicon, 840-841
    originality, 837
    original works of authorship, 836
    public domain, 836-837
    reference works to literature, 840-841
    StreamCast, 840
  cultural property, 855-856
  digital property, 856-857
  disparaging names, 54, 846-847
  fair use, 837-839
  infringement, 839
  overview, 836
  ownership of original ideas or information, 836
  patents, 841-844
    generative AI, inventions by, 844
    ideas vs. applications, 842
    new inventions, 841, 844
    nonobviousness, 842-844
    one-click method, 843
    usefulness, 841
  publicity rights, 849-853
    death, 851-852
    free speech, 850, 852-853
    identity, commercial use of, 849-850
    imitators, 851
    inheritability, 851-852
    privacy rights, 850
  trademarks, 844-847
    appurtenant to business, 845
    character of, 844
    dilution, 847
    disparaging names, 54, 846-847
    immoral marks, 846
    intent, 845
    parody of, 847
    registration, 845-846
    state common law based, 844
    subjects of, 846
    unfair competition, 847
  unfair competition, 847-849
    dilution of trademark by, 847
    fabric patterns, 849
    misappropriation, 848-849
    palming off, 847-848
    preemption, 849
    trade dress, 849
    trademarks, 847
    trade secrets, 848
Intentional dispossession, 152-153
Interstate Commerce Act of 1887, 47
Interstate Land Sales Full Disclosure Act of 1968, 514
Inter vivos gifts, 821
Inter vivos trusts, 392, 419
Intestate succession, 393, 399, 415-416, 420-424
Intimate partner violence
  discrimination based on status as victim of, 577
  fair housing laws, 577
  shelters for victims, 620, 625-626
Intimidation, 589-590
Inventions, 841-842, 844
Investigative journalism, 35-37, 40-41

J

Joint bank boxes, 533, 822
Joint tenancy
  abolition of, 357-358
  adverse possession, 165-166
  concurrent ownership, 348, 350-358
  death of joint tenant, 354, 355-356
  leaseholds, 354-356
  mortgages, 353-354
  murder of joint tenant, 356-357
Judicial sale and future interests, 346
Judicial takings, 752-757
Jurisdiction, 598-600
Just compensation, 689-693. *See also* Regulatory takings
  business goodwill, 691
  "damaging" property for public use without just compensation, 693
  fair market value, 689
  leaseholds, 691
  partial takings, 691-693
  relocation costs, 693

Just compensation (*continued*)
- replacement cost, 690
- severance damages, 691-693

Justice
- justificatory norms, 20
- normative approaches, 13-14
- regulatory takings, 707, 715-717

Justice Department, 62, 69
Justificatory norms, 17-20
- distributive justice, 20
- efficiency, 19
- expectations, 20
- human flourishing, 19
- justice, 20
- justified expectations, 20
- labor, 18-19
- personality, 19
- possession, 17-18

K

Kennewick Man, 805-806

L

Labor rights, 19, 84-85, 719-720
Laches
- adverse possession, 174
- American Indian property, 794, 796, 797, 800
- covenants, 296
- defeasible fees, 308

Lakes, 130-131
Land claims settlement acts, 801-802
Landfills, 117
Landlords. *See* Leaseholds
Landslides, 118
Land use regulation, 639-677
- air, 136
- commercial speech, 672-673
- conflicts, 96, 98
- constitutional rights, 671-677
    - arbitrary regulations, protection from, 666-669
    - associational interests, 669
    - due process, 666-669
    - equal protection, 670-671
    - family integrity, 669
    - First Amendment, 671-677
    - free speech, 672-674
    - poverty, 671
    - privacy, 669
    - procedural due process, 666
    - racial classifications, 671
    - religious uses, 674-677
    - SLAPP suits, 671-672
    - substantive due process, 666-669
- contractual regulation of land use, 226
- free speech rights, 671-677
    - commercial speech, 672-673
    - sex-oriented business, 674
    - signs, 672-674
- inclusionary zoning ordinance for affordable housing, 761
- light, 136-137
- nonzoning land use controls, 658-666
    - building and housing codes, 658-659
    - construction regulation, 658-659
    - endangered species laws, 663-664
    - environmental protection, 662-665
    - growth management, 661-662
    - hazardous waste laws, 664-665
    - historic landmarks, 662, 676-677
    - maintenance regulation, 658-659
    - planned unit developments, 660
    - regional planning, 661-662
    - subdivision approval, 659-660
    - telecommunications towers, 665-666
    - wetlands regulation, 663
- nuisance. *See* Nuisance
- overview, 641
- planning process, 641-644
    - adjustment, 644
    - board of adjustment, 644
    - board of zoning appeals, 644
    - comprehensive plan, 642-643
    - federal regulation, 641-642
    - local regulation, 641-642
    - state regulation, 641-642
- preexisting property rights, protection of, 651-657
    - amortization, 653-654
    - economic viability, 656
    - hardship test, 655-656
    - normal expansion, 653
    - no substantial change test, 652-653
    - practical difficulties test, 656
    - prior nonconforming use, 651-654
    - public interest, 655
    - substantial expenditures or efforts, 654
    - takings, 652
    - unnecessary hardship, 655-656
    - variances, 655-657
    - vested rights, 654-655
- preferential zoning, 657-658
- rezoning
    - comprehensive plan, conformity with, 657-658
    - negotiated, 648, 649
    - petitions for, 643
    - public interest, 657-658
    - spot zoning, 651, 658
- signs, 672-674
- types of, 98

zoning laws, 645-651
- *ad hoc* decision making, 648
- adjustment boards, 644
- administration of, 644
- appeals boards, 644
- area regulations, 644-645
- "as of right" standard, 646
- bilateral conditional zoning, 650
- bilateral contract zoning, 648-649
- building or bulk regulations, 645
- challenges to, 648
- comprehensive plan requirement, 642-643, 649
- conditional use, 646, 650
- contract or conditional zoning, 647-650
- cumulative and noncumulative zoning, 645
- delegation of authority, 647
- disparate impact claims, 617
- enabling acts, 642
- Euclidean zoning, 645, 649
- floating zones, 650-651
- inclusionary zoning, 760-761
- local control, primacy of, 641-642
- lot and building regulations, 644-645
- ordinances or by-laws, 643-644
- overlay zones, 651
- planning commissions, 643
- planning departments, 643
- rezoning, 658
- special exceptions, 646-647
- unilateral promises, 648, 650
- unmapped conditional use districts, 650
- use regulations, 645-646

Lanham Act of 1946, 846-847, 849
Lateral support, 99, 133-135
Lead paint laws, 489
Leaflets, 76-77, 78-79, 80-83, 85
Leaseholds, 427-492. *See also* Eviction; Tenancies
- Acts of God, 451
- alienability, 283
- ambiguity, 436
- *caveat emptor*, 429-430, 473, 474
- commercial leases, 430, 451-452, 465-466, 480-481, 482
- concessions, 438
- co-tenants, rights and obligations of, 369-370
- covenants, independence or dependence of, 429, 450
- distinguished from other interests, 434-442
- dormitories, 440-441
- employment contracts, 439-440
- estates. *See* Tenancies
- fair rental value, 451
- force majeure clauses, 451-452
- formalistic vs. functional, 435
- form vs. substance, 436
- grant of possession, 434
- habitable premises, right to, 469-489
  - administrative enforcement, 473
  - commercial warranty, 480-481
  - constructive eviction, 469-473
  - consumer protection laws, 487-489
  - covenants, dependent vs. independent, 474-475
  - criminal acts of third parties, landlords' liability for, 486-487
  - damages, multiple, 487
  - deceptive consumer practices, 488
  - housing codes, 473
  - implied warranty of habitability, 473-481
  - landlord's responsibility for other tenants' harms, 472
  - lead paint laws, 489
  - negligence standard, 477
  - non-housing-related disputes, 483-484
  - notice to landlord, 476-477
  - quiet enjoyment, interference with, 469-470
  - remedies, 477-480
  - retaliatory eviction, 481-484
  - standards of habitability, 476
  - strict liability, 476, 485-486
  - tort liability of landlord, 484-487
  - unfair consumer practices, 487-489
- historical origins, 428, 430
- hotel guests and lodgers, 441-442
- illegal purpose, 433, 455-456
- implied warranties, 429
- interpretation, 432
- joint tenancy, 354-356
- landlord's obligations and tenant's remedies, 466-469
  - anti-eviction laws, 468-469
  - delivery of possession, 431, 466-467
  - equity, 457
  - eviction, 431, 432, 467-468
  - implied covenant of quiet enjoyment, 467
  - injunctive relief, 431
  - maintenance and repair, 432
  - nuisance, 104-105
  - partial actual eviction, 468
  - quiet enjoyment, 430, 431, 467, 469-470
  - rent abatement, 432, 478
  - rent control, 469
  - rent withholding, 432
  - security deposits, 467
  - termination of lease, 431
- landlord's remedies, 455-466
  - back rent, 450
  - conversion of personal items, 459-460
  - damages, 461-466
  - due process issues, 461
  - eviction, 431, 432, 450
  - forced entry and detainer, 458-459
  - forfeiture, 456-457
  - mitigation duty, 456, 461-466
  - new tenancy, 457-458

Leaseholds (*continued*)
recovery of possession, 456-457
reletting, 461-466
remedial issues, 455-456
rent acceleration, 463, 466
self-help vs. summary process, 456, 458-461
stay of execution, 461
surrender, 461-466
trespass and recovery of possession, 459
waiver, 457
language not determinative, 435-436
legal ethics, 433
licenses and easements, 178, 183-184
limits, retroactive, 377-378
migrant farm workers, 440
overview, 428-433
partition, 361, 369-370
periodic tenancy, 428, 432, 444-447
possession
conflicts over, 432-433
definition of, 434
premises, condition of, 433
present estates and future interests, 304
rent, conflicts over, 433
rental benefits and obligations, 365-368
rent and rental agreements, 428, 441, 450, 451
roommates, 441
short-term rentals, 442
signs and billboards, 434-435, 436-437
small landlords, 488-489
superintendents, 439-440
takings, antieviction as, 723-724
tenant's obligations, 449-466
illegality, 455-456
moving out, 471-472
operate, duty to, 453-455
privity of contract, 449-450
privity of estate, 450
remedies, 455-466
rent, duty to pay, 431, 449-453, 454-455
waste, duty not to commit, 431
termination of rental agreement, 457
term of years, 305, 428, 432, 442-444
transfers
generally, 433
assignment, tenant's right of, 490-492
landlord consent clauses, 491-492
reversion, landlord's right to transfer, 490
subletting, tenant's right of, 490-492
vacation rental exclusion from RURLTA, 442
Leasing. *See* Leaseholds
Legal relations, 2, 5-6
Legislation and regulatory takings, 762-764
Liability. *See also* Strict liability; Tort liability
animals, 46
landlord's tort liability, 484-487
nuisance, 98, 104-105, 109
property rules vs., 108-109, 113
Libertarian approaches, 17
Liberty as normative approach, 13-14
Licenses and easements, 177-224
abandonment, 223-224
adverse possession vs., 145-146, 223
affirmative easements, 178
air, 136
alienability, 181-182
ambiguity, 200-201, 208-209
changed conditions, 223-224
comparison of, 178, 183
conservation easements, 186
consolidation vs. disaggregation, 181-182
covenants vs., 228
creation, 180, 182, 234
dominant estates, 179, 180
easements by estoppel, 200, 205
equitable servitudes, 179, 228-229, 234, 246
express easements, 184-199. *See also* Express easements
fiduciary relationship, 206-207
formality, 180, 182, 206
frustration of purpose, 223
grantor's intent, 202, 210-212
hearsay, 204
historic preservation easements, 186
implied easements. *See* Implied easements
interpretation, 181
leases and, 178, 183-184
licenses, 182-184
creation, 182
formality, 182
lease vs., 183-184
revocability, 182, 202
light, 136-137
location of appurtenant easements, 191-197
marketable title acts, 224
merger, 223
negative easements, 179, 186-187, 204, 220-221
oral easements, 201
overview, 178-182
positive easements, 178
prescriptive easements, 213-223. *See also* Prescriptive easements
public policy, 211-212
real covenants, 179
regulation of, 181
release, 223
relocation, 180, 195-197
restrictive covenants, 179
restrictive easements, 186-187
revocability, 178, 180, 182
right to recover land upon termination of easement, 748-749

scope of, 180, 212-213
servient estates, 179-180
servitudes, 179-180
solar easements, 186
statute of frauds, 200-201
support rights, 133-134
termination, 180-181, 223-224, 748-749
transferability, 180
tribal easements, 777, 806-807
Liens
co-tenants, 362
mortgages as, 353-354
partition, 362
Life estates, 310-314. *See also* Present estates and future interests
generally, 304
alienability, 282, 311
class gifts, 312
condition precedent, 311
contingent remainders, 311-313
convenience, rule of, 312
destructibility of contingent remainders, 312-313
dower and curtesy, 394
fee simple vs., 329
marital property, 394
perpetuities, rule against, 310
pur autre vie, 311
remainders, 305, 311-313
reversions, 305, 310
Shelley's Case rule, 314
unascertained persons, 311
vested remainders, 311-313
waste, 320-321
worthier title doctrine, 313-314
Light
ancient lights doctrine, 186, 221
express easements, 185
Fontainebleau doctrine, 136-137
land use regulation, 136-137
licenses and easements, 136
nuisance, 98, 117, 136-137
solar easements, 186
Limited equity cooperatives, 381
Limited liability partnerships, 384
Lives in being, 332
Locke, John, 18
Locked stores, 50
Loss immunity vs. power to acquire, 8
Lost or abandoned property, 816-817
Lot and building regulations, 644-645
Low-income housing cooperatives, 283

M

Machine learning, 844
Made for hire works, 853
Magna Carta, 748
Magnetic fields, 117
Maintenance
building and housing codes, 658-659
co-tenants' rights and obligations, 363-365
landlord's obligations and tenant's remedies, 432
marital property, 399
Map Act (North Carolina), 741-742
Map acts, 741-742
Maps, 208-209, 237, 238, 239, 263, 529, 643-644, 663, 742
Marital property, 397-407
alimony, 399
community property, 392-393, 397, 401-407
death of spouse, 399
divorce, 398-399, 403, 423-424
earnings on separate property, 403-404
elective share, 399
equitable distribution, 398-399, 406-407
inception of title approach, 404
intestacy, 399
life estates in, 394
maintenance, 399
Married Women's Property Acts, 395-396
mutual support, duty of, 397-398
pro rata apportionment approach, 404
separate property, 392-393, 397-401, 403-404, 407
statutory share, 399
survivorship rights, 407
tenancy by the entirety, 358-360, 395, 407
Marketable title
acts
adverse possession, 538
covenants, 297
curative acts, 537
deeds and title protection, 224, 537-538
future interests and covenants, 537
root of title, 537
rule against perpetuities, 338
statute of limitations, 538
definition of, 515-516
remedies for unmarketable title, 521
sales contracts, 515-521
Marketing techniques, affirmative, 595-596
Marriage. *See also* Marital property
common law, 411
divorce. *See* Divorce
dower and curtesy, 394-395
remarriage, 417-418
restraints on, 342-346
same-sex, 407-411
trusts, 345
Married Women's Property Acts, 395-396
Marx, Karl, 19

Massachusetts
  Anti-Snob Zoning Act, 633
  Art Preservation Act, 854
  test for mutual privity, 247
Measure 37 (Oregon), 763-764
Measure 49 (Oregon), 764
Melamed, Douglas, 108-109
Membership organizations
  Civil Rights Act of 1964, 50
  discrimination, 50-53
  religion, 52
Merger, 223, 296, 534-535
MERS (Mortgage Electronic Registration Systems), 570-573
Metes and bounds, 529-530
Michelman, Frank, 20, 716
Migrant farm workers, 440
Mill, John Stuart, 12, 14-15
Minnesota, *Mortgage Moratorium Act*, 563
Misappropriation, 848-849
Misrepresentation, 588. *See also* Fraud
Mistake
  bilateral, 528
  deeds and title protection, 530
  defense of, 27-28
  mutual, 164, 528
  trespass defense, 27-28
  unilateral, 528
Mitigation duties
  acceleration clauses, 466
  commercial leases, 465-466
  landlord's remedies, 456, 461-466
  residential leases, 463-464, 464-465
Moral rights of artists, 853-855
  applied art, 853-854
  integrity of work, 853
  made for hire works, 853
  site-specific works, 854
  temporary works, 854-855
  visual art works, 853-854
Mortgage Electronic Registration Systems (MERS), 570-573
Mortgage Moratorium Act (Minnesota), 563
Mortgage Reform and Anti-Predatory Lending Act of 2010, 570
Mortgages, 555-564
  adjustable rate mortgages, 567-568
  adverse possession, 167
  brokers, 567
  concurrent ownership, 353-354
  deeds of trust, 560-561
  deficiency judgments, 557, 558-559
  equitable mortgages, 566-567
  equitable subrogation, 561
  equity of redemption, 353, 556, 557
  financing, 496, 555-564
  foreclosure, 557-558, 562-564
  historical background, 556-557
  installment land contracts, treatment as, 564-566
  intermediate theory, 556
  joint tenancy, 353-354
  judicial sale, 560
  as liens, 353-354, 556
  moratorium legislation, 563
  private sales, 560
  refinancing, 561
  reinstatement, 559
  right of redemption, 558
  security interests in real property, 555-556
  statutory right of redemption, 558
  strict foreclosure, 557
  subprime, 567-573. *See also* Subprime mortgages
  title theory, 353, 556
  unjust enrichment, 559
  wrongful foreclosure, 573
Movie theaters, 69-70
Murder of joint tenant, 356-357
Museums, 832-833
Mutual mistake, 149, 164, 528

N

NAGPRA (*Native American Graves Protection and Repatriation Act of 1990*), 805-806, 832-833
Names, 53-54
National Association of Realtors (NAR), 503
National Historic Preservation Act of 1966 (*NHPA*), 70, 662
National Labor Relations Act of 1935 (*NLRA*), 84-85, 719
National Museum of the Indian Act of 1989, 833
National Organ Transplant Act of 1984, 827
National origin discrimination. *See* Racial or national origin discrimination
National Register of Historic Places, 70, 662
Native American Graves Protection and Repatriation Act of 1990 (*NAGPRA*), 805-806, 832-833
Native American property. *See* American Indian property
Native Claims Settlement Act of 1971 (Alaska), 801
Necessity
  implied easements, 199, 210-213
  trespass and public accommodations, 38-39
Negative covenants, 227-228, 252
Negative easements, 179, 186-187, 204, 220-221
Negative servitudes, 261-266. *See also* Covenants
Negligence vs. nuisance, 105-106, 137
New estates, 327-328, 372
New Jersey
  Continuing Care Retirement Community Regulation and Financial Disclosure Act, 382
  Fair Housing Act of 1985, 633
  Industrial Site Recovery Act, 665

NHPA (*National Historic Preservation Act of 1966*), 70, 662
NLRA (*National Labor Relations Act of 1935*), 84-85
Noise, 25, 117
Nonconforming use, 651-654
Non-Intercourse Act of 1809, 776, 791, 795-801
Nonobviousness, 841, 842-844
Non-profit organizations, 348, 380, 382-383, 388
Nontrespassory interferences with property rights, 97
Nonzoning land use controls. *See* Land use regulation
Normative approaches, 13-17
  consequentialist, 14-15
  conservative, 17
  democracy, 15-17
  efficiency, 14-15
  justice, 13-14
  libertarian, 17
  liberty, 13-14
  progressive, 17
  rights-based, 13-14
  social relations, 15-17
  utilitarian, 14-15
  virtue, 15-17
Norms, systemic, 12
North Carolina
  HB2 (2015) on transgender persons' restroom use, 75
  Map Act, 741-742
Notice
  actual notice
    express easements, 190
    recording acts, 542
  constructive notice
    covenants, 240-242
    express easements, 190
    grantors' covenants, 240-242
    recording acts, 542
  covenants, 239-242
    generally, 234
    actual notice, 240
    constructive notice, 240
    inquiry notice, 240-241
  express easements
    actual notice, 190
    constructive notice, 190
    inquiry notice, 190
  grantors' covenants, constructive notice of, 240-242
  inquiry notice
    covenants, 240-241
    express easements, 190
    possession as, 551
    recording acts, 542, 550-551
  to landlord, 476-477
  periodic tenancies, 445
  to quit, 446
  recording acts
    actual notice, 542
    constructive notice, 542
    inquiry notice, 542, 550-551
    notice statutes, 542-543
    race-notice statutes, 543
    tenancies at will, 447
    unrestricted lots and notice issues, 264-265
Nuisance, 95-137
  abnormally dangerous activity, 106
  air, 99, 116, 136
  Airbnb, 121
  ambiguity, 107-108
  apartment buildings, 120-121
  auction, 115
  bargaining, 99
  chemical pollution, 117
  coming to, 119-120
  common law, 98
  definition of, 102, 121-122
  electric power lines, 117
  elements, 641
  entitlements, 113-116
  fair market value, 115
  fences, 136
  flexibility vs. stability, 99
  freedom of association, 123
  free speech rights, 123
  free use vs. security, 96
  gas tank leaks, 117
  high-rise buildings, 120-121
  ideological plaintiffs, 114-115
  intentional nuisance, 105
  landfills, 117
  landslides, 118
  land use conflicts, 96
  liability, 98, 104-105, 109
  light, 99, 117, 136-137
  magnetic fields, 117
  negligence vs., 105-106
  noise, 25, 117
  nontrespassory interferences with property rights, 97
  nude beach, recreational use of, 117
  odors, 116
  overview, 96-101
  per se, 107, 110
  pollution, 25, 44-45, 97
  prescriptive easements, 222-223
  private, 102-121
    drug dealers, 117-118
    remedies, 108-116
    stigma damages, 118-119
    test, 102-108
    types, 116-121
  public, 121-126
    climate change, 125-126
    community interests, 122
    constitutional issues, 123

Nuisance (*continued*)
definition of, 121-122
drug dealers, 123-124
gangs, 124-125
reasonableness, 99, 103-104, 108
redistribution, 115
remedies
contractual renegotiation, 109
damages, 108, 110-112
forced purchases, 112-113
forced sales, 112-113
injunctions, 109, 111-112
no relief, 108
privileges, 109
purchased injunctions, 112
veto rights, 109
reverse auction, 115-116
sewage treatment facilities, 117
social welfare, 116
spite fences, 136
stability vs. flexibility, 99
status quo, 115
strict liability, 106
substantial harm, 97, 98, 102-103, 106-107
support rights, 133-135
generally, 99
lateral support, 99, 133-135
retaining walls, 134-135
subjacent support, 99, 135-136
taking, immunity as, 100-101
trees, 117
trespass vs., 97-98
types, 116-121
ultrahazardous activity, 106
unintentional nuisance, 106
unreasonable interference, 98, 101, 103-104, 107, 108
unusually sensitive plaintiffs, 103
water pollution, 117
water rights, 126-132. *See also* Water rights
wetlands regulation, 126-127, 735-736
Nursing homes, 583-584

O

Obergefell decision. *See* Same-sex marriage
Objects, 41-45
aviation, 43-44
blasting, 45
encroaching structures, 41-42, 215
forced purchase, 42, 169
forced sale, 42, 169
indirect harms, 44
invisible particles, 44
pollution, 25, 44-45, 97
relative hardship, 42
remedies, 42
removal, 42, 169
trees, 42-43
unjust enrichment, 42
vegetation, 42-43
Odors, 116
Offensive names, 53-54
Off-reservation easements, 777, 806-807. *See also* American Indian property
Older persons, housing for, 586, 611-612
Online home searching, 503
Open and notorious possession, 143, 146-147
Oral agreements
adverse possession, 170-171
covenants and oral representations, 237-238
easements, 201
implied easements, 201
promises to convey, 506-509
transfers, informal, 170-171
wills and will substitutes, 418-420
Oral easements, 201
Oregon
Measure 37, 763-764
Measure 49, 764
Organ transplants, 827-828
Original Indian title, 773-777, 781-784
Originality, 837
Original works of authorship, 836
Ouster, 165-166, 366-368, 370
Overlay zones, 651
Ownership, 2-3. *See also* Concurrent ownership; Tenancies

P

Palimony, 411-412
Palming off, 847-848
Pandemics
business restrictions as takings, rejection of challenges, 742
eviction moratoria, 469
rent obligations, 451-453
Parents and family property, 417-418
generally, 392, 393
stepchildren, 421
surviving spouse, no surviving children or parents, 420
surviving spouse and children, 420-424
surviving spouse and parents, no surviving children, 420
Parody and fair use, 837-839, 847
Partial actual eviction, 468
Partial takings, 691-693
Partition
condominiums, 361-362
credit for substantial improvements, 364

heirs' property, 362-363
involuntary, 361
judicial, 361
leases, 361, 369-370
liens, 362
physical, 361
remedies, 360-361
restraints on, 362
rights and obligations of co-tenants, 360-363, 370
by sale, 361, 362-363
voluntary, 361
Partnerships
business property, 382-385
aggregate theory, 383
common law, 383
entity theory, 383
fiduciary obligations, 384-385
tenancy in partnership, 383
common law, 383
concurrent ownership, 383-385
definition of, 383
limited liability partnerships, 384
Patent Acts, 841
Patent and Trademark Office, 846
Patents, 841-844
generative AI, inventions by, 844
ideas vs. applications, 842
machine-generated inventions, patentability of, 844
new inventions, 841-842, 844
nonobviousness, 841, 842-843
one-click method, 843
usefulness, 841
Paul, Jeremy, 680-681
Per capita division, 422-423
Percolating water, 99, 131-132
Periodic tenancies. *See* Tenancies
Permissiveness, 149-151
Perpetuities, rule against. *See* Rule against perpetuities
Per se nuisance, 107, 110
Per se regulatory takings, 718-742
economically viable use, deprivation of, 728-742
exceptions to per se physical invasion rule, 719-720
nuisance, 100-101
physical invasions, 718-728
tests, 681, 718
Personality and justificatory norms, 19
Personal property, 811-833
accession and fixtures, 826-827
adverse possession, 172-175, 826
conversion rule, 172
demand and refusal rule, 173-174
demand rule, 172
discovery rule, 172-173
due diligence, 173
laches, 174
statute of limitations, 172-173
animals, 813-816
bailments, 824-825
chattel, 91-92, 812
computer systems, trespass to, 91-92
confusion, 827
conversion of tenant's personal items, 459-460
crops, 827
finders, 816-821. *See also* Finders
fungible property vs., 158-159
gifts, 821-824. *See also* Gifts
good faith purchasers, 825-826
human bodies, 827-833
individual effort, 813
organ transplants, 827-828
overview, 812-813
tangible, 812
trespass to chattels, 91-92
wild animals, 813-816
Per stirpes division, 422-423
Petroleum Marketing Practices Act of 1978 (PMPA), 387
Pets, 46, 379-380, 816
Planes, trespassing by, 43-44
Planned unit developments, 660
Planning commissions, 643
Plats, 529
Plenary power doctrine, 785-786
Police searches, 40
Political messages, 83-84, 289-290
Political signs, 673
Pollution
air, 116
chemical, 117
nuisance, 25, 44-45, 97
toxic waste, 664-665
water pollution, 117
Positive easements, 178
Posner, Richard, 159, 268-269
Possession
actual possession, 24, 143-146
adverse possession, 139-175. *See also* Adverse possession
bailments, 824-825
constructive possession, 24
continuous possession, 143, 148-149
delivery of, 431, 466-467, 824
exclusive, 143, 147-148
good faith possession, 143, 151, 154-155, 161
hostile possession, 143, 149-155
justificatory norms, 17-18
open and notorious, 143, 146-147
Practical difficulties test, 656
Preemption, 567, 849, 853-854
Preferential zoning, 657-658
Premarital agreements, 393, 397, 399-401
Preponderance of evidence, 166

Prescriptive easements, 213-223. *See also* Licenses and easements
acquiescence, 219
adverse possession vs., 145-146
adverse use, 216
ancient lights doctrine, 186, 221
bad faith, 221-222
claim of right, 216
common law, 41
continuity requirement, 215-216
covenants, 297
custom, doctrine of, 89
driveways, 215
elements, 214
encroaching structures, 215
exclusivity, 219-220
express easements, 194
family members, 217
government, claims against, 220
knowledge of use, 219
lost grant, 213-214
negative easements, 220-221
negligence, 221-222
neighbors, 217-218
nuisance, right to commit, 222-223
open and notorious use, 218
permission, presumption of, 216
private roads, 217
public acquisition of, 220
public trust doctrine, 89
scope of express easement exceeded, 194
termination, 223-224
trees, 222
trespass and public accommodations law, 41, 89
use of another's property, 214-215
visibility requirement, 218
wild, unimproved land, 216-217
Present estates and future interests, 301-346
adverse possession, 168
alienation, 303-304
defeasible fees, 310
fee simple, 306
life estates, 311
partial restraints on, 329-330
promotion of, 324, 327-328
regulatory rules, 324, 328-330
restraints on, 328-330
allodialism, 302
ambiguous conveyances, interpretation of, 315-324. *See also* Ambiguity
changed conditions, 323-324
charity exception, 329-330
common recovery, 326-327
conflicts between granting clause and deed language, 317-318
consolidation vs. disaggregation, 303-304, 320
cy pres doctrine, 321-322
defeasible fees. *See* Defeasible fees
disaggregation, 328
consolidation vs., 303-304, 320
discriminatory forfeitures and racial restrictions, 341-342
discriminatory trusts, 322-323
divorce, encouragement of, 345
fee simple, 305-306
absolute, 305-306
conditional, 325-326
determinable, 306-307
life estates vs., 329
subject to condition subsequent, 304-305, 306, 307-309
subject to executory limitation, 305, 306
fee tail, abolition of, 325-327
feudalism, 302
forced share statutes, 343
forfeiture
automatic, 307
presumption against, 315-320
restraints, 328-329
freehold estates, 304-305
future interest, creation of, 331, 346
grantor's intent, 315, 317
historical background, 302-303
homestead laws, 343
judicial sale and future interests, 346
in kind vs. market value, 321
leaseholds, 304
life estates, 310-314. *See also* Life estates
livery of seisin, 304
magic words, 316-317, 318
market value vs. in kind, 321
marriage, restraints on, 342-346
new estates, restrictions on, 327-328
nonfreehold estates, 304, 305
overview, 302-305
periodic tenancy, 305
perpetuities, rule against, 330-340
precatory language, 315, 318-319
presumption against forfeitures, 315-320
public policy, 323, 345-346
purpose, 318-319
racial restrictions, 341-342
regulatory rules, 324
alienation, unreasonable restraints on, 328-330
repurchase rights, 319-320
reverter as remedy, 324
separation, encouragement of, 345
statutes of limitations
fee simple determinable, 307, 308
fee simple subject to condition subsequent, 307-309
tenancy at will, 305
trusts, 305, 314-315

vested remainders, 311-313
absolutely vested, 311
life estates, 311-313
subject to divestment, 312
subject to open, 311-312
waste, 320-321
Pretext, 593-594
Prior nonconforming use, 651-654
Prior use
implied easements, 199, 207-210
nonconforming, 651-654
Privacy
land use regulation, 669
publicity rights, 850
substantive due process, 669
Private clubs
ADA, 63
Civil Rights Act of 1964, 49-50, 52, 63
discrimination, 52, 60-62
FHA, 585-586
Private nuisance, 102-121
drug dealers, 117-118
remedies, 108-116
stigma damages, 118-119
test, 102-108
types, 116-121
Private property
clubs, 49-50, 60-61, 63
company towns, 76-77, 78
exclusion rights, 24-25, 27-29
free speech rights, 75-84
company towns, 76-77, 78
labor laws, 84-85
shopping centers, 77-80, 721-723
state constitutions, 80-83, 85
U.S. Constitution, 75-80
licenses, 27
physical invasion of, 708
shopping centers, 77-80, 721-723
standard of care, 27-28
takings, 708
trespass, 27-29
criminal, 29, 38-39
mistake, defense of, 27-28
remedies, 28-29
Private Property Rights Protection Act (Arizona), 764
Private Real Property Rights Preservation Act (Texas), 762-763
Privity
adverse possession, 148
ambiguity, 244
covenants, 228-229, 234, 235, 244-253
earlier buyers, obligations to, 248-249
estates of lesser duration, 249-250
historical origins, 244-246
homeowners' associations, 252-253
horizontal, 247-250
implied reciprocal negative servitudes, 261-262
instantaneous, 247
Massachusetts test, 247
mutual, 247
Spencer's Case, 245
tenant's duty to pay rent, 449-450
third-party beneficiaries, 250-251
vertical, 250-253
Procedural due process
land use regulation, 666
takings, 752
Proclamation of 1763, 776
Progressive approaches, 17
Public accommodations law. *See* Trespass and public accommodations law
Public bathrooms and gender identity, 75
Public domain, 836-837
Public interest, 655, 657-658
Publicity rights, 849-853
death, 851-852
free speech, 850, 852-853
identity, commercial use of, 849-850
imitators, 851
inheritability, 851-852
privacy rights, 850
Public navigable air space, 43-44
Public nuisance, 121-126
climate change and, 125-126
community interests, 122
constitutional issues, 123
definition of, 121-122
drug dealers, 123-124
gangs, 124-125
Public policy
condominium declarations, 375
covenants, 277-291
generally, 293
alienation, unreasonable restraints on, 280-285
ambiguity, 274
charitable trusts, 278-279
competition, unreasonable restraints on, 285-286
condominium rules, 288, 289
cy pres doctrine, 279
discrimination, 233, 278-279
equal protection, 277
freedom of contract, 287
free speech, 289-291
modification or termination, 293
political signs, 289-290
public policy, 274, 279-280, 286-291
racial restrictions, 277-280
reasonableness review, 286-289
unconscionability, 288-289
use restrictions, 288

Public policy (*continued*)
  easements by necessity, 211-212
  exclusion rights, 40
  express easements, 196-197
  implied easements, 211-212
  present estates and future interests, 323, 346
  trespass and public accommodations law, 40-41
Public trust doctrine, 85-91
  beach access, 86-91
  custom, doctrine of, 88
  dedication, 87
  fishing rights, 87, 90-91
  Hawaii, 89
  navigable waters, 85
  prescriptive easements, 88
  takings, 750-751
  tidelands, 85-89
  trespass and public accommodations law, 85-91
Public use requirement, 682-689. *See also* Regulatory takings
Purchased injunctions, 112
Purchase options
  alienation, 284-285
  rule against perpetuities, 337, 339
  time limits, 337, 339

Q

Quasi-categorical takings
  death, right to pass on property at, 743-745
  vested rights, 749-752
Quiet enjoyment
  constructive eviction and interference with, 469-470
  exclusion rights, 25
  implied covenant of, 467
  leaseholds, 430, 431-432, 467
  post-acquisition interference, 591
  title covenants, 536
Quitclaim deeds, 534, 536

R

Racial or national origin discrimination. *See also Civil Rights Acts*
  associational claims, 597
  blockbusting, 588
  brokers, 589
  coercion, 589-590
  college dormitories, 583-584
  covenants, 231, 277-280
  deeds, restrictions in, 277
  discriminatory forfeitures, 341-342
  dwellings, 583-584
  equal protection, 578, 580-582
  fair housing law, 578-601
    advertising, 587-588, 598
    Civil Rights Act of 1866, 576, 600-601
    covered dwellings, 583-584
    equal protection, 578, 580-582
    exemptions, 584-586
    FHA, 582-600
    national origin, 629-630
    prohibited bases of discrimination, 582-583
    prohibited conduct, 587-591
    race, 615-620
    remedies, 598-600
    standards of proof, 591-596
    standing, 596-598
    state constitutional rights to discriminate, 580-581
    trusts, 279-280, 579-580
  forfeitures and racial restrictions, 341-342
  Fourteenth Amendment, 579
  homeless shelters, 584
  hotels, 584
  integration, promotion of, 595
  intimidation, 589-590
  land use regulation, 671
  marketing techniques, affirmative, 595-596
  models' race, 598
  present estates and future interests, 341-342
  pretext, 593-594
  private clubs, 585-586
  public accommodations, 31-32, 34, 46-48, 48-49
  racial restrictions in deeds, 277
  refusal to deal, 592
  U.S. Constitution, 278-279, 578-582
  zoning, 578-579
Radin, Margaret Jane, 19, 158-159
Rails-to-Trails statute, 680
"Raisins" case (*Horne v. Department of Agriculture*, 2015), 725-726
RCRA (*Resource Conservation and Recovery Act of 1976*), 664
Real covenants. *See* Covenants
Real Estate Settlement Procedures Act of 1974 (*RESPA*), 514
Real estate transactions, 493-573. *See also* Alienation; Transfers
  adverse possession, 518
  brokers, 496-504. *See also* Brokers
  chain-of-title, 517
  consumer protection, 495
  deeds and title protection, 528-555. *See also* Deeds and title protection
  financing, 555-573
    equitable mortgages, 566-567
    foreclosure, 496
    installment land contracts, 564-566
    liens, 496
    mortgages, 496, 555-564
    subprime mortgages, 567-573

land sale contracts, 504-528
overview, 495-496
purchase and sale agreements, 504-528
recording acts, 538-553. *See also* Recording acts
sales contracts. *See* Sales contracts
structure of, 495
title problems, 496, 517
Reasonable accommodation, 622
Reasonableness
covenants, 254, 275, 286-289
nuisance, 98, 103-104, 108
review, 275, 286-289
rulemaking, 378
Reciprocal negative servitudes, 261-266
Recognized title, 777, 784-788
Recording acts, 538-553
acknowledgment, 538-539
actual notice, 542
after-acquired title, 545-546
chain-of-title doctrine, 540, 544
chain-of-title problems, 544
common law, 540
constructive notice, 542
date of recording, 541
deed recorded too early, 546-547
deed recorded too late, 547-548
estoppel by deed, 545-546
forged deeds, 552
fraud, 552-553
grantor-grantee index systems, 539-540
improperly indexed deeds, 550
inquiry notice, 542, 550-551
installment land contracts, 544
notice
actual notice, 542
constructive notice, 542
inquiry notice, 542, 550-551
race-notice statutes, 543
notice statutes, 542-543
possession as inquiry notice, 551
race-notice statutes, 543
race statutes, 541
recordable documents, 538
reference to unrecorded document, 549-550
servitudes on retained land, 551-552
shelter doctrine, 549
statutes, 540-544
system, how it works, 538-540
title searches, 539-540
tract index, 538
types, 540-544
wild deeds, 545-546
Recording issues
date of recording, 541
deed recorded too early, 546-547
deed recorded too late, 547-548
documents, 538, 549-550
subprime mortgages, 570-571
unrecorded documents, 549-550
Recovery of possession, 456-457
Recreational facilities, 256-257
Reference works to literature, 840-841
Reformation, 336-337, 530, 684
Refusal to deal, 592
Regional planning, 661-662
Regulation, construction of property system vs., 4-5
Regulatory property, 712-713
Regulatory takings, 679-766
ad hoc balancing test, 703
adverse possession, 728
agricultural commodities, 725-726
air rights, 704-705
American Indian property, 739, 766, 775
antieviction laws, 711, 723-724
beach access, 89-91
beachfront property, 756-757
business restrictions, 742
categorical takings, 718-752
common law takings, 752-757
COVID-19 business restrictions, 742
cumulative harms, 735-736
"damaging" property for public use without just compensation, 693
definition of, 681
denominator problem, 713-714, 732-735
deprivation of all economically beneficial use, 718, 728-742, 751
deprivation of certain core property rights, 718
diminution of value, 697-698, 713-715
doctrinal structure, 681, 703
due process vs., 702
easements, right to recover land upon termination of, 748-749
economic impact, 713-715
generally, 703-706
denominator problem, 713-714
economically viable use destroyed, 714
market value, large percentage destroyed, 714
minimal diminution, 714
nuisance, 714-715
use prohibited never part of owner's rights, 714
eviction, 711, 723-724, 728
exactions, 757-761
building permit conditions, 757
essential nexus requirement, 757-758
inclusionary zoning, 760-761
low-income housing linkage, 759, 760
monetary exactions, 759
rough proportionality, 759, 760-761
factors, 681
fairness and justice, 681-682, 700, 703-704, 715-717
Fifth Amendment, 682, 694, 703, 714, 763

Regulatory takings (*continued*)
- Fourteenth Amendment, 25, 83, 694, 714, 763
- general balancing test, 707-717
  - diminution in value, 713-715
  - distributive justice, 717
  - economic impact, 707, 713-715
  - efficiency, 716-717
  - fairness and justice, 707, 715-717
  - government action, character of, 708-713
  - opportunity loss, 715
  - police power, 708
  - reasonable investment-backed expectations, interference with, 707, 715
  - vested rights, 715
- government action, character of, 708-713
  - generally, 706
  - average reciprocity of advantage, 709
  - compulsory contract terms, retroactive imposition of, 709
  - core property rights, taking of, 708
  - damage caused by police, 711-712
  - eviction of innocent public housing tenants, 711
  - forfeiture laws, 710-711
  - good of community vs. prevention of harm by property owner, 708
  - harm, protecting community from, 709
  - incompatible property interests, choice between, 709
  - physical invasion of private property, 709
  - property use, regulation of, 709
  - prospective regulation, 709
  - tree destruction, 709-710
  - vested property rights, retroactive redistribution of, 709
- grave protection laws, 739
- historical background, 694-706
  - before 1922, 694-696
  - 1922-1978, 696-702
  - after 1978, 702-706
- home equity after tax foreclosure, 747-748
- inadvertent harm, 739-740
- injunctive relief, 762, 765-766
- interference with reasonable investment-backed expectations, 705-706, 715
- interference with vested rights, 718, 749-752
- inverse condemnation, 764-765
- investment-backed expectations, interference with, 749-750
- judicial takings, 752-757
  - beach access, 754-755
  - native water rights, 753-754
- just compensation, 689-693
  - business goodwill, 691
  - "damaging" property for public use without just compensation, 693
  - fair market value, 689
  - leaseholds, 691
  - partial takings, 691-693
  - relocation costs, 693
  - replacement cost, 690
  - severance damages, 691-693
- landlord occupation of own unit, 726-727
- lawyers' trust accounts, interest on, 746-747
- legislation, 762-764
  - assessment, 762
  - compensation, 762
  - conflict resolution, 762
  - injunctive relief, 762
  - state laws, 687-689, 762-764
- map acts, 741-742
- nuisance immunity as, 100-101
- nuisance exception, 730-732, 735-736
- overview, 680-682
- "parcel as a whole," 704-705
- permanent physical invasions, 718-719, 720
- *per se* takings, 718-742
  - economically viable use, deprivation of, 728-742
  - nuisance, 100-101
  - physical invasions, 718-728
  - public-health-related eviction moratoria, 727
  - tenant-protection statutes, 727
  - tests, 681, 718
- personal property, 725-726
- police power, 695, 697, 700, 708
- post-foreclosure eviction protection, 728
- precedent, 681
- prior nonconforming uses, 750
- procedures, 765-766
- property rights, implied limitations on, 696-697
- property value, 736-737
- public interest, 698-699
- public nuisance, 123
- public preemptive rights, 749
- public trust, 750-751
- public use requirement, 682-689
  - blight, 682-683
  - definition of, 682
  - Hawaii, 683-684
  - land reform, 684
  - state constitutions, 687-688
  - state law, 687-689
  - U.S. Constitution, 682-687
- purchase after regulatory laws in effect, 737-739
- quasi-categorical takings
  - death, right to pass on property at, 743-745
  - vested rights, 749-752
- reciprocity of advantage, 699-700
- regulatory property, 712-713
- relevant parcel, test for determining, 734-735
- remedies, 764-765
- right to pass on property at death, 743-745
- ripeness, 766

role of, 681
state laws, 687-689
generally, 762-764
public use, 687-689
state constitutions, 687-688
statutes, 689
substantive due process vs., 702
temporary building moratorium, 740-741
temporary flooding, 741
temporary limitations on right to use property, 742
transfer development rights, 705
tribal property, 766
union organizing, access for, 84-85, 719-720
vested rights, 718, 749-752
wetlands regulation, 732, 736-737
whole property, 732-735
Relations among people, 2, 5-6
Relative hardship, 42, 269-270
Release, 223, 296
Reletting, 461-466
Reliance and adverse possession, 158
Religion
broker's use of symbols, 614-615
churches as historic landmarks, 676-677
discrimination, 47, 52, 614-615
disparate impact claims, 628
dormitories, 628
fair housing law, 628
FHA, 585-586
First Amendment, 613-614
Fourteenth Amendment, 614
free exercise, 613-614, 674
homeless housing by churches, 677
land use regulation, 674-677
membership organizations, 52
neutral zoning laws, impact of, 676
public accommodations laws, 47
religious liberty, 73-74, 614, 628-629, 675
services in private homes, 628
sexual orientation discrimination, 52, 74-75
state constitutions on free exercise, 614
state laws, 675
Religious Freedom Restoration Act (Indiana), 73
Religious Freedom Restoration Act of 1993 (*RFRA*), 614, 628-629, 675
Religious Land Use and Institutionalized Persons Act of 2000 (*RLUIPA*), 628-629, 675
Remainders
contingent remainders
definition of, 334-335
destructibility of, 312-313
life estates, 311
rule against perpetuities, 334-335
life estates, 305, 311-313
vested remainders, 311-313. *See also* Vested remainders
Remedies
building and housing codes, 479-480
Civil Rights Act of 1866, 48
Civil Rights Act of 1964, 48
compensatory damages, 28
constructive eviction, 470
contractual renegotiation, 109
damages
American Indian property, 799
covenants, 266-270
habitable premises, right to, 478-479
leaseholds, 461-466
nuisance, 108, 110-112
private nuisance, 118-119
real estate transactions, 521-522, 524-525
trespass and public accommodations law, 28-29
discrimination, 581-582
easements by necessity, 212-213
economic discrimination, 632-633
ejectment, 29, 141-142
encroaching structures, 41-42
encroaching vegetation and trees, 42-43
exclusionary zoning, 632-633
expectation damages, 522
fair housing law, 598-600, 632-633
FHA, 598-600
forced purchases, 42, 112-113, 169
forced sales, 42, 112-113, 169
habitable premises, right to, 477-480
housing code, 479-480
implied easements, 212-213
injunctive relief
Civil Rights Act of 1964, 48
covenants, 266-270
habitable premises, right to, 479
landlord's obligations and tenant's remedies, 431-432
nuisance, 109, 111-112
purchased injunctions, 112
takings, 762
trespass and public accommodations law, 28, 48
landlocked parcels, 212-213
leaseholds, 456-466. *See also* Leaseholds
liquidated damages, 525
new tenancy, 457-458
nominal damages, 28
nuisance, 108-116
objects, 42-43
partition, 360-363
permanent damages, 28
punitive damages, 28
real estate transactions, 521-526
regulatory takings, 764-766
inverse condemnation, 764-765
procedures, 765-766
relative hardship, 42

Remedies (*continued*)
removal, 42, 169
rent abatement, 432, 478
rent withholding, 477-478
repair and deduct, 479
rescission of contract, 477
restitution damages, 522
reverter, 324
specific performance, 522, 525-526
takings, 689-766
takings, partial, 691-693
termination of tenancy, 477
title covenants, 535, 536
trespass and public accommodations law
compensatory damages, 28
ejectment, 29
injunctive relief, 28, 48
nominal damages, 28
permanent damages, 28
punitive damages, 28
removal of improvements, 169
statute of limitations, 140-141
unmarketable title, 521
Renovations, 62, 70, 76, 255, 659, 676, 685
Rent
abatement, 432, 478
acceleration, 463, 466
duty to pay, 449-453
pandemics and rent obligations, 451-453
withholding, 477-478
Rental issues. *See* Leaseholds
Rent control in leaseholds, 469
Repairs
rights and obligations of co-tenants, 363-365
tenants, repair and deduct, 479
Reparations. *See* American Indian property
Repose, adverse possession, 161-162
Resale price limitations, 381-382
Residential associations, 227, 231-232. *See also* Common interest communities
Residential Lead-Based Paint Hazard Reduction Act of 1992, 489
Resource Conservation and Recovery Act of 1976 (RCRA), 664
RESPA (*Real Estate Settlement Procedures Act of 1974*), 514
Restatement (Third) of Property (Servitudes)
affirmative covenants, 252
common interest communities, 376-378
covenants, 229
declaration amendments, 377-378
easements
express, 187
intent, 210-211
enforcement in gross, 259
implied reciprocal negative servitudes, 263
negative covenants, 252
touch and concern, 254-255
Restricted trust allotments, 744-745, 779-780, 790-791
Restrictive covenants. *See* Covenants
Restrooms and transgender persons, 75
Retained land, 551-552
Retaining walls, 134-135, 215
Retaliatory eviction, 481-484. *See also* Eviction
burden of proof, 482
commercial leases, 482
non-housing-related disputes, 483-484
prohibition of, 481-482
tenant's stay, length of, 482-483
Reverse auction, 115-116
Reversions, 305, 310, 490
Reverter
present estates and future interests, 306-307
as remedy, 324
rule against perpetuities, 338
Review
architectural, 275
of covenants for reasonableness, 286-289
of divorce agreements for fairness, 413
of zoning and regulatory takings, 668-669
Revised Uniform Partnership Act (RUPA), 383
Revised Uniform Residential Landlord and Tenant Act (RURLTA), 442
Revocable trusts, 533
Rezoning
comprehensive plan, conformity with, 658
negotiated, 648, 649
petitions for, 643
public interest, 657-658
spot zoning, 651, 658
RFRA. See Religious Freedom Restoration Act of 1993
Rhode Island, *Homeless Bill of Rights*, 634
Ride-sharing companies, regulation of, 712
Right of entry, 307-309
Right of occupancy, 785, 790
Rights-based approaches, 13-14
Rights of way, 192-193
Riparian owners. *See also* Water rights
accretion, 172
adverse possession, 172
avulsion, 172
erosion, 172
nuisance, 99, 130
reasonable use doctrine, 130
Ripeness of regulatory takings claims, 766
River borders, 530
River use by riparian owners and others, 99
Roommates, 441, 602-603
Rose, Carol, 18, 162
Royal Instruction of 1761, 776
Rule against perpetuities, 330-340
abolition/repeal of, 339-340

contingent remainders, 334-335
creation of interest, 331
cy pres doctrine, 336-337
defeasible fees, 310
drafting around the rule, 336
endless will contest, 336
equitable reformation, 336-337
exceptions to, 337-338
executory interests, 310, 332-333
fertile octogenarians, 335-336
first refusal rights, 340
grantor interests, 332
immunity from, 331
lives in being, 332
marketable title acts, 338
nonvested interests, 330-331
perpetuities period, 332
preemptive rights, 339-340
purchase option time limits, 337, 339
regulatory rules, 330-340
reverter, 338
rights of entry, 338
state laws, 330
terms defined, 331-336
trusts, 339-340
unborn widow, 335
Uniform Statutory Rule Against Perpetuities (*USRAP*), 330, 338, 339
vesting, 331-332
wait-and-see approach, 336

Rule choices, 8-10
Rule of reason, 286
Running with land, 187-190, 226-227, 232, 235, 239
Rural land, 147

S

Sales contracts, 504-528
generally, 495-496
adverse possession, 518
"as is" clauses, 512
attorney's role, 504-506
bilateral mistake, 528
binders, 506
breach, 509-521
building codes, 520
buyer's default, 499-500
buyer's remedies, 521-524
caveat emptor, 510
conditional, 500-501
conditions, 507
constructive trust, 508-509
covenants, 520
death of party, 527-528
description of property, 506
disclosure duty, 511-512
easements, 519, 520
encroachments, 519
encumbrances, 518-520
equitable conversion, 527
estoppel, 508
false representation, 509
federal regulation, 511
financing, 521
fraud, 509-514
fraudulent nondisclosure, 510-511
insurable title, 521
intent to sell or buy, 506
leases, 519
lost profits, 524
marketable title, 515-521
mistake, 528
mutual mistake, 528
"no reliance" clauses, 512
opinions, 510
oral promises to convey, 506-509
parties, 506
part performance, 507
price, 506
prior unrecorded deeds, 517-518
problems, 496
puffery, 510
reasonable reliance, 509
record title, 521
remedies for breach, 521-526
resale price limitations, 381-382
rescission and damages, 509
risk of loss during executory period, 527
seller's default, 499
seller's good faith, 522-524
seller's remedies, 524-526
signatures, 506
statute of frauds, 506-509
third parties, attorney's liability to, 506
title, 515-521
unilateral mistake, 528
unmarketable title remedies, 521
waiver, 512-514
warranty of habitability for new homes, 514-515
zoning violations, 519-520

Salvage, 820-821
Same-sex harassment, 605-606
Same-sex marriage, 407-411
American Indian nations, 410-411
due process, 407
equal protection, 407-408
equitable distribution of property of unmarried same-sex couples, 416
family property, 415-416
Fourteenth Amendment, 407
international recognition, 411

Same-sex marriage (*continued*)
  marriage, 407-411
  state laws, 410
  student housing, 621
Sax, Joseph, 856
Secret conveyances, 352
Security deposits, 257-258, 467
Security from harm vs. use privilege, 7
Seisin, 304, 535
Self-help vs. summary process, 456, 458-461
Separate property, 392-393, 397-401, 403-404, 407
Servient estates, 179-180
Servitudes. *See also* Covenants; Licenses and easements
  equitable, 179, 228-229, 234, 246
  implied reciprocal negative servitudes, 261-266
    early vs. later buyers, 261
    general plan, 261-264
    grantor's neighboring land, 265-266
    privity of estate issues, 261-262
    subdivisions, 261
    third-party beneficiary doctrine, 262
  licenses and easements, 179-180
  unification of law of, 229, 234
Severance, 351
Sewage treatment facilities, 117
Sex discrimination
  disparate impact claims, 620-621
  fair housing law, 602-607
  gender identity discrimination as, 74, 608
  harassment, 603-607
  health clubs and segregation, 72
  hostile environment claims, 603
  "no welfare" policy, 620
  public accommodations law, 52
  quid pro quo claims, 603
  roommates, 602-603
  same-sex harassment, 605-606
  sexual harassment, 603-607
  sexual orientation discrimination as, 74-75, 608
  shelters for victims of intimate partner violence, 620, 625-626
  similar harassment of men and women, 606-607
  stereotyping, 606
Sex offenders, 669
Sexual harassment, 603-607
Sexual orientation discrimination. *See also* Same-sex marriage
  generally, 621
  associational and religious interests, 52
  fair housing law, 607-608
  federal law, 608
  membership organizations, 52
  public accommodations, 73-74, 75
  public bathrooms and transgender persons, 75
  religious liberty, 73-74
  as sex discrimination, 74
  state law, 73-74, 607
Shared use or possession, 29-30
Sharing economy, 121, 442, 712
Shelley's Case rule, 314
Shelter doctrine, 549
Shelters for battered women, 620, 625-626
Sherman Act of 1890, 286
Shipwrecks, 820-821
"Shock the conscience" test, 668-669
Shopping centers, 77-80, 721-723
Shrubs, 42-43, 144
Signs and billboards, 289-290, 434-435, 436-437, 672-674
  location-based distinctions, 673
  on-premises vs. off-premises signs, 673
Single-family homes sold without broker, 585
SLAPP (Strategic Lawsuits Against Public Participation) Suits, 671-672
Slavery, 47-48
Smoking and public accommodations, 68-69
Social context, 10
Social need and exclusion rights, 40
Solar easements, 186
Sole proprietorships, 348
"Source of income" discrimination, 577, 630
Sovereign immunity bar, exception to, 765-766
Sovereign immunity waiver, 794-795
Speech. *See* Free speech rights
Spencer's Case, 245
Sperm, human, 829
Spite fences, 136
Sports teams, 53-54
Spot zoning, 648, 651, 658, 672
Squatters, 161, 164-165
Standing, 573, 596-598
State action doctrine, 56, 76-77, 341, 578, 579-580
State constitutions
  access to private property, 80-83, 85
  "damaging" property for public use without just compensation, 693
  discrimination rights, 580-581
  fair housing law, 627
  free speech rights, 80-83, 85
  handbills and leaflets, 80-82
  labor law, 85
  nontraditional families, 627
  regulatory takings, 687-688
  religion, free exercise of, 614
  takings, 687-688
  universities, access to and free speech, 82
State laws
  consumer protection, 515
  continuing care retirement communities, 382
  covenants, 297-298
  discrimination, 71-75
  environmental protection, 662-665

fair housing, 612
finders statutes, 819-820
historic landmarks, 662
human remains, removal of, 806
intestacy, 415-416, 420
land use regulation, 641-642
lead paint, 489
negative easements, 186
perpetuities, rule against, 330
preemption, 567, 849, 853-854
public accommodations laws, 34, 71-75
public use, 687-689
regulatory takings, 687-689
generally, 762-764
public use, 687-689
state constitutions, 687-688
statutes, 689
religious freedom, 675
retail stores, 71
same-sex marriage, 410
sexual orientation discrimination, 607
sodomy, 415
takings, 687-689, 762-764
usury laws, 567
worthier title doctrine, 314
State of mind, 149, 151
Statute of frauds, 506-509
adverse possession, 163
covenants, 236
express easements, 184
licenses and easements, 200-201
periodic tenancies, 445
sales contracts, 506-509
term of years, 443
Statutes of limitations
adverse possession
legal basis of, 140-141
ouster by co-tenant, 370
personal property, 172-173
repose, 161-162
statutory period, 143, 155-156
co-tenants' rights and obligations, 370
defeasible fees, 308-309
ejectment remedies, 141-142
fee simple determinable, 307-308
fee simple subject to condition subsequent, 308-309
marketable title acts, 538
tacking, 148-149
trespass and public accommodations law remedies, 140-141
Sterk, Stewart, 159-160
Stigma damages, 118-119
Stolen artworks, 172-175
Stolen goods, 825-826
Strategic Lawsuits Against Public Participation (SLAPP Suits), 671-672
Streams, 99, 130-131
Strict liability
animals, 46
habitable premises, right to, 476, 485-486
nuisance, 106
Subdivisions
approval, 659-660
cluster zoning, 660
exactions, 660
implied reciprocal negative servitudes, 261
land use regulation, 659-661
mixed uses, 660
planned unit development, 660
plats or maps, 528
Subjacent support, 99, 135-136
Subprime mortgages, 567-573
adjustable rate mortgages, 567-568
collateralized debt obligations, 568
credit default swaps, 569
federal preemption of state usury laws, 567
government intervention, 569-570
housing bubble burst, 569
leverage, 569
loan servicers, 571
MERS, 570-573
mortgage-backed securities, 568-569
mortgage brokers, 567
proof of loan ownership, 570-573
recording problems, 570-571
special investment vehicles, 568
state usury laws, 567
Substantive due process, 666-669
arbitrary or capricious government action, 666-669
associational interests, 669
equal protection, relation to, 668
family integrity, 669
land use regulation, 666-669
privacy, 669
sex offenders, 669
"shock the conscience" test, 668-669
standard of review, 668-669
takings, relation to, 668, 702, 752
Summary process vs. self-help, 456, 458-461
Superfund Amendments and Reauthorization Act of 1986 (SARA), 665
Superfund law (*CERCLA*), 511, 664
Superintendents, building, 439-440
Support rights
easements, 133
nuisance, 133-135
generally, 99
lateral support, 99, 133-135
retaining walls, 134-135
subjacent support, 99, 135-136
structures, 134-135
Surface water, 99, 126-130

Surrender of leaseholds, 461-466
Surveys, 529
Survivorship rights, 350, 357, 407
System, property as
community norms, 4
efficiency, 4
individual entitlement vs., 3-4
minimum standards, 4
regulation vs., 4-5
systemic norms, 3

T

Takings. *See* Regulatory takings
TANF (Temporary Assistance to Needy Families), 636
Taxes and taxation, 143, 156, 376-377, 747-748
Telecommunications Act of 1996, 665
Telecommunications towers, 665-666
Temporary art, 854-855
Temporary Assistance to Needy Families (TANF), 636
Temporary flooding, 741
Tenancies, 442-449. *See also* Concurrent ownership; Leaseholds
commercial, 430, 480-481
in common, 165-166
alienation, 349-350
definition of, 349
inheritance, 349-350
ownership in common, 348-350
co-tenants. *See* Co-tenants
by the entirety
concurrent ownership, 348, 358-360
creditors' rights, 359-360
encumbrances, 407
family property, 395, 407
married couples, 358-360, 395, 407
transfers, 407
joint. *See* Joint tenancy
ouster, 165-166, 366-368, 370
in partnership, 383
periodic
alienability, 445
death does not terminate, 447
inheritability, 445
leaseholds, 428, 432, 444-447
notice, 445
notice to quit, 446
periodic rental payments, 444
rent increase, 446
statute of frauds, 445
termination, 445
at sufferance, 448-449
generally, 442
eviction, 449
holdover tenants, 448-449
new tenancy, 449
term of years
alienability, 443
definite period, 432
duration, limits on, 443
fixed term, 442-443
inheritability, 443
leasehold, 428, 432, 442-444
nonfreehold estates, 305
statute of frauds, 443
termination, 444
at will, 447-448
generally, 432, 442
death of party, 448
notice to quit, 447
periodic rent, 448
termination, 448
transferability, 448
Testers, 597
Texas, *Private Real Property Rights Preservation Act*, 762-763
Theories of property, 13-20
justificatory norms, 17-20
normative approaches, 13-17
Third parties
attorney's liability to, 506
covenants, 250-251, 262
criminal acts of, landlords' liability for, 486-487
defeasible fees, 309
express easements, 184-185
finders vs., 817
gifts, 823
implied reciprocal negative servitudes, 262
privity, 250-251
third-party beneficiaries, 250-251, 262
Thirteenth Amendment, 47-48, 61, 721
Title. *See also* Deeds and title protection
aboriginal title, 773-777, 781-784
adverse possession, 518
after-acquired title, 545-546
American Indian property. *See* American Indian property
certificate of title, 554
chain-of-title doctrine, 517, 540, 544
clarification, 156-157
color of title, 143, 151, 156, 162-163
covenants, 534-536. *See also* Deeds and title protection
defective title, 156, 162-163
equitable title, 314
executive order title, 778, 788-790
insurance, 553-554
legal title, 314
marketable title. *See* Marketable title
mortgages and title theory, 353, 556
original Indian title, 773-777, 781-784

problems, 496, 517
recognized title, 777, 784-788
record title holder, 24
registration, 554-555
relativity of title, 817
root of title, 537
searches, 539-540
title of occupancy, 773-776
title theory, 353
transfers, informal, 169-172
acquiescence, 170, 171
dedication, 170
estoppel, 151, 171
improving trespasser, 169
informal understanding, 170-171
oral agreement, 170-171
riparian owners, 172
worthier title doctrine, 313-314
Torrens system, 554
Tort liability
defamation, 36
landlords, 484-487
leaseholds, 484-487
negligence vs. nuisance, 105-106, 110
trespass and public accommodations, 36
trespass to chattels, 91-92
Touch and concern, 235-236, 253-258
Toxic waste, 664-665
Tract index, 538
Trade and Intercourse Act of 1790, 776, 791, 795-801
Trade dress, 849
Trademarks, 844-847
appurtenant to business, 845
character of, 844
dilution, 847
disparaging names, 53-54, 846-847
immoral marks, 846
intent, 845
parody of, 847
registration, 845-846
state common law based, 844
subjects of, 846
unfair competition, 847
Trade secrets, 848
Transferable development rights, 712
Transfer power vs. disaggregation limits, 7-8
Transfers. *See also* Alienation; Sales contracts
adverse possession, 169-172
acquiescence, 170, 171
boundary disputes, 169-172
dedication, 170
estoppel, 151, 171
improving trespasser, 169
informal understanding, 170-171
oral agreement, 170-171
riparian owners, 172
defeasible fees, 309
easements in gross, 198
express easements, 198
fee simple determinable, 307
gifts, 508, 821-823
leaseholds, 490-492
generally, 433
assignment, tenant's right of, 490-492
landlord consent clauses, 491-492
reversion, landlord's right to transfer, 490
subletting, tenant's right of, 490-492
licenses and easements, 180
present estates and future interests, 307, 309
rights, 140
takings, 705
tenancies at will, 448
tenancies by the entirety, 407
testamentary, 418-419, 821
title. *See* Title
Transformative use, 837, 838-839. *See also* Copyright; Fair use
Transgender persons and public bathrooms, 75
Treasure trove, 819
Trees
adverse possession, 144
encroaching trees, 42-43
nuisance, 117
prescriptive easements, 222
trespass and accommodations law, 42-43
Trespass and public accommodations law, 23-92
adverse possession, 41, 168-169
animals, 46
aviation, 43-44
blasting, 45
chattels, 91-92
common law limits, 34-41
consent, 34-37
estoppel, 38
necessity, 38-39
prescription, 41, 88
public policy, 30-41
social need, 30
computer systems, 91-92
criminal trespass, 29, 38-39
defamation, 36
definition of trespass, 27
email, 91
encroaching structures, 41-42
excluding or admitting people, 27-34. *See also* Exclusion rights
fraudulent entrance, 37
free speech rights of access to private property, 75-85
labor laws, 84-85
state constitutions, 80-84
U.S. Constitution, 75-80
hospitals, 31

Trespass and public accommodations law (*continued*)
  improvements, 169
  indirect harms, 44
  investigative journalism, 35-37, 40-41
  mistake, defense of, 27-28
  noise, 25, 117
  nuisance vs., 97-98
  objects, 41-45
  overview, 24-27
  police searches, 40
  pollution, 25, 44-45, 97
  private property, 27-29
    criminal trespass, 29, 38-39
    mistake, defense of, 27-28
    remedies, 28-29
  public accommodations laws, 46-75
    ADA, 32, 62-71
    architectural barriers, 66
    auxiliary aids and services, 65-66
    Civil Rights Act of 1866, 34, 54-62
    Civil Rights Act of 1964, 31, 46-54, 56, 63
    Civil Rights Act of 1991, 54, 55, 59
    common carriers, 30-31
    common law, 30-34
    compelled speech, 74
    definitions, 31-32, 47, 62-64
    eligibility criteria, 65
    entertainment, places of, 30, 31, 47
    exclusion rights, 27-35
    First Amendment, 53-54, 74, 75-76
    free speech rights, 53-54, 73-74, 75-76
    fundamentally altering nature of accommodation, 67-68
    gas stations, 47
    gender identity and public bathrooms, 75
    hospitals, 31
    hotels, 30, 47
    innkeepers, 30-32
    locked stores, 50
    membership organizations, 50-53
    movie theaters, 64-70
    offensive names, 53-54
    religious liberty, 73-74
    restaurants, 47
    sexual orientation discrimination, 73-74
    sports teams, 53-54
    state laws, 72-75
  public trust doctrine, 85-91
  remedies
    compensatory damages, 28
    ejectment, 29, 140
    injunctive relief, 28, 48
    nominal damages, 28
    permanent damages, 28
    punitive damages, 28
    removal of improvements, 169
    statute of limitations, 140-141, 141-142
  retail stores, 32-34
  shared use or possession, 29-30
  standard of care, 27-28
  state action doctrine, 76-77
  statutes of limitation, 140-141, 141-142
  trespass, definition of, 27
  trespass to chattels, 91-92
  visitors, right to receive, 29-30
Tribal easements, 777, 806-807
Tribal property. *See* American Indian property
Trusts. *See also* Inheritance
  charitable trusts, 278-279, 314-315
  community land trusts, 381
  constructive trust, 204-207, 413-414
  discriminatory charitable trusts, 278-279, 322-323
  discriminatory trusts, 322-323
  dynasty trusts, 339-340
  equitable title, 314
  family property, 392
  fiduciary obligations, 315
  inter vivos, 392, 419
  legal title, 314
  marriage, restraints on, 344
  nonfreehold estates, 305
  perpetuities, rule against, 339-340
  present estates and future interests, 314-315
  public trust doctrine. *See* Public trust doctrine
  racially restrictive trusts, 279-280, 579-580
  restricted trust allotments, 790-791
  revocable trusts, 533
  testamentary, 392
Truth in Lending Act of 1968, 563
Tucker Act of 1887, 803

U

UCC (*Uniform Commercial Code*), 826
Ulen, Thomas, 159
Ultrahazardous activity, 106
Unborn widows, 335
Unclean hands, 296
Unconscionability, 288-289
Undivided fractional interests, 349, 350
Undue hardship, 294-296
Unfair competition, 847-849
  fabric patterns, 849
  misappropriation, 848-849
  palming off, 847-848
  preemption, 849
  trade dress, 849
  trademarks, 847
  trade secrets, 848
Uniform Anatomical Gift Act, 828
Uniform Commercial Code (*UCC*), 826

Uniform Easement Relocation Act, 196
Uniform Fiduciary Access to Digital Assets Act, Revised, 857
Uniform Marital Property Act, 401
Uniform Partition of Heirs Property Act (UPHPA), 362-363
Uniform Partnership Act (UPA), 383
Uniform Premarital Agreement Act (UPAA), 400
Uniform Premarital and Marital Agreement Act (UPMAA), 400
Uniform Probate Code (UPC)
  death of buyer, 527-528
  inheritance, 423
  intestate succession, 420
  marital property, 399
  will formalities, 419
Uniform Residential Landlord and Tenant Act
  consumer protection laws, 487-489
  employees as tenants, 440
  habitable premises, right to, 477
  landlord's duty to mitigate damages, 464
  landlord's obligations, 430
  lodgers, 442
  rent and rental agreements, 428
  retaliatory eviction, 482
  termination of rental agreement, 457
Uniform Statutory Rule Against Perpetuities (USRAP), 330, 338, 339
Unilateral mistake, 528
Union organizing
  handbill distribution, 84
  takings law as constraint on access for, 84-85, 719-720
United Farm Workers, 719
Universities
  dormitories, racial discrimination, 583-584
  free speech rights, 81
Unmarked graves, 820
Unmarried couples, 392, 411-416
Unruh Civil Rights Act (California), 631
Use privilege vs. security from harm, 7
Use regulations. *See* Land use regulation
Utilitarian approaches, 14-15

V

Vacation rentals, 121, 442
Valued resources, 2
Variances, 655-657
Vegetation, 42-43
Vested remainders, 311-313
  absolutely vested, 311
  life estates, 311-313
  subject to divestment, 311-312
  subject to open, 311-312
Vested rights, 654-655
Visual Artists Rights Act of 1990, 853-854
VRBO, 442

W

Waivers
  covenants, 296
  defeasible fees, 308
  landlord's remedies, 457
  sales contracts, 512-514
  sovereign immunity, 794-795
Waldron, Jeremy, 13, 18
Warranty of habitability, 473-481
  commercial warranty, 480-481
  constructive eviction, 471-472
  leaseholds, 473-481
  new homes, 514-515
Waste
  ambiguous conveyances, interpretation of, 320-321
  life estates, 320-321
  present estates and future interests, 320-321
  tenant's duty not to commit, 431
Water Quality Act of 1987, 663
Water rights. *See also* Riparian owners
  American Indian property, 131, 753-754, 777, 807
  common law rules, 127-128, 753-757
  nuisance, 126-132
    generally, 98-99
    absolute ownership doctrine, 132
    California doctrine, 131
    Colorado doctrine, 131
    common enemy, 127, 128
    correlative rights test, 130
    diffuse surface water, 99, 126-130
    flooding, 99, 126-130
    free use doctrine, 96, 132, 135-136
    groundwater, 99, 131-132, 135-136
    lakes, 130-131
    natural flow, 127-128
    percolating water, 99, 131-132
    prior appropriation, 130-131
    reasonable use, 127, 128-130, 132
    rivers, 99
    streams, 99, 130-131
  river borders, 530
  treaty-reserved rights, 777
  wetlands. *See* Wetlands regulation
Web sites as places of public accommodation, 64
Welfare, 618, 620, 625
Wetlands regulation
  land use regulation, 663
  nuisance, 126-127, 735-736
  takings, 732, 735-736, 736-737

Wild animals. *See also* Animals
  generally, 815
  active pursuit, 813-815
  capture, 813
  constructive possession, 814-816
  mortal wounding or trapping, 814-815
  personal property, 813-816
  trespass and public accommodations law, 46, 815
  whales, 815
Wild deeds, 545-546
Wills and will substitutes, 418-420. *See also* Inheritance; Intestate succession; Trusts
  clear and convincing evidence of validity, 419
  endless will contest, 336
  family property, 392-393, 418-420
  formalities, 419
  handwritten, 419
  holographic, 419
  oral statements, 419
Winter, Ralph, 598
Winters doctrine, 807
Women's shelters, 620, 625-626
Worthier title doctrine, 313-314
Writing requirement
  covenants, 234, 236-239
  deeds and title protection, 528-530
  express easements, 184, 190
Wrongful foreclosure, 573

Y

Yard signs, 673-674

Z

Zoning. *See* Land use regulation

www.ingramcontent.com/pod-product-compliance
Lightning Source LLC
LaVergne TN
LVHW081957200926
848481LV00010B/2756